FR

ENGLAND
&
SCOTLAND

DARWIN PORTER

assisted by **Danforth Prince**
and **Margaret Foresman**

1990

Published by Prentice Hall Trade Division
A Division of Simon & Schuster Inc.
15 Columbus Circle
New York, NY 10023

ISBN 0-13-217373-5

ISSN 1044-2359

Manufactured in the United States of America

*Although every effort was made to ensure the accuracy
of price information appearing in this book,
it should be kept in mind that prices
can and do fluctuate in the course of time.*

CONTENTS

PART TWO

SCOTLAND

MAPS

A Disclaimer

Although every effort was made to ensure the accuracy of the prices and travel information appearing in this book, it should be kept in mind that prices do fluctuate in the course of time, and that information does change under the impact of the varied and volatile factors that affect the travel industry.

Inflation Alert

It is hardly a secret that inflation has affected the countries of northern Europe, and Britain also has been hit. The author of this book has spent laborious hours researching to try and ensure the accuracy of prices appearing in this guide. As we go to press, I believe we have obtained the most reliable data possible. However, I cannot offer guarantees for the tariffs quoted.

Britain's VAT

Great Britain has a standard Value Added Tax (called VAT for short) of 15%. Most European Community countries already have a tax similar to VAT (France, for example, has a paralyzing one of 23%). This extra VAT charge will show up on your bill unless otherwise stated. It is in addition to the service charge. Should the service charge in a restaurant be 15%, you will, in effect, be paying 30% higher than the prices quoted. The service charges, if included as part of the bill, are also taxable.

As part of an energy-saving scheme, the British government has also added a special 25% tax on gasoline (petrol).

For more information on taxes, see "The ABCs of Britain" in Chapter II.

ENGLAND AND SCOTLAND

1. THE REASON WHY

2. FROMMER'S DOLLARWISE TRAVEL CLUB—HOW TO SAVE MONEY ON ALL YOUR TRAVELS

England, and Scotland too, sent her children across the waves to settle North America, Australia, New Zealand, and a host of other lands. Today the offspring of those children are returning to visit their mother lands at a rate that is practically an invasion.

What's the big attraction?

1. The Reason Why

England, as in Restoration days, has thrown out the Puritan and is experimenting in all sorts of imaginative, creative ways. Vigorous and exciting changes are taking place, and England today is, in a word, fun. The island may be small, but, like Mighty Mouse, it packs a powerful punch.

On the other hand, Scotland fulfills romantic myths—a land of shimmering lochs, pepper-pot towers and moated castles, clans with bagpipes, and balladeers. Scotland is very different from England. When English people go to Scotland, they are, in effect, "going abroad."

Connecting you with the life forces of both countries is one of the aims of this book.

I have set for myself the formidable task of seeking out the best of England and Scotland and condensing it between the covers of a guide. The best includes not only descriptions of hotels, restaurants, pubs, and nightspots, but descriptions of cities, towns, and sightseeing attractions. Part of the philosophy of this book is based on the fact that the best need not be the most expensive. Hence, my ultimate aim—beyond that of familiarizing you with the offerings of merrie old England and romantic Scotland—is to stretch your dollar power, to show you that you need not always pay scalper's prices for charm, top-grade comfort, and food.

In this guide, I'll devote a great deal of attention to the tourist meccas of London, Edinburgh, Stratford-upon-Avon, and Oxford. But these ancient cities and towns are not the full "reason why" of the book. Important as they are, they simply do not fully reflect the complexity and diversity of both countries. Unlike most nations of Europe, England and Scotland defy a clear, logical, coherent plan of sightseeing. Both lands are a patchwork quilt of treasures, with many of the most scenic items tucked away in remote corners—an Elizabethan country estate in Devon, a half-timbered thatched cottage by the sea in Cornwall, a Regency manor in the Lake District, an old whitewashed coaching inn at Loch Ness.

Meeting the English and the Scots is perhaps the most important reason for making the trip. If possible, try to arrive with few preconceived ideas. For example, generalizing about the character of the English in a land filled with "soopah" dukes, Cockney porters, Rudyard Kipling adventurers, and Miss Marple–type ladies is fraught with hazards. Suffice it to say, they'll surprise you—particularly if you think of the English as a cold, snobbish, withdrawn people. A few visits to the haunts of Soho, or to a local pub for a "lager and lime," or even a look at the racy London tabloids, will cure you of stereotypes.

A TRAVELER'S ADVISORY

You should take the figures quoted in this guide only as an indication of the regular charges of a hotel or other establishment. Almost all hotels have special offers at various times of year, and some, such as the Priory in Bath, may offer as much as a 40% discount for a two-night stay. Management has improved, and staffs, especially in lovely little country places, have become more English and friendly.

The standard of **cooking,** the use of high-quality products, and the current wave of chefs born, bred, and trained in England and Scotland has led to the appearance, during the last few years, of a number of pleasant small hotels where the main attraction for guests is the cooking and the comfort. These hotels are generally in attractive buildings on the outskirts of interesting towns. "Very Professional Amateurs" is how one food writer described the chef-proprietors of these new-wave restaurants and inns, dozens of which I have included in this edition. *A word of warning,* however: Don't be misled by prominently displayed plaques denoting awards for the culinary arts. If you wish to use such an award as a quick guide, ask if the chef who won it is still in charge of the kitchens. I have found on occasion that the hotel/restaurant claims the award, while the chef who actually earned it has already moved on. Also, many of these places do not permit smoking in the dining room or anywhere near it, so check this out before you light up.

The historic buildings for which the country is famous are well worth a visit, although many top places, such as Woburn Abbey, find it uneconomical to remain open during the winter, except on Saturday and Sunday. Security staffing costs are astronomical, I am told. Also, many of the fine houses looked after by the National Trust close at the end of October and do not reopen until the following Easter. However, there are still many places to see for the winter visitor who seeks history and a taste of the real Britain.

Traveling in Britain is becoming easier, as many destinations are now served by economical express buses, which are equipped with aircraft-type reclining seats, toilets, TV, and a hostess who serves light refreshments. Train service continues to improve, and although porters are often hard to find, the railways are becoming highly competitive with airlines for internal travel. Some services even have telephones now. Improved night sleeper accommodations enable you to enjoy dinner and a theater in London, catch the train, and be awakened for coffee and cookies some 500 miles away, before you arrive for breakfast in Scotland. Airlines offer all sorts of special tickets.

If you are writing for information to one of the organizations or individuals mentioned in this book, it is important that you include an **International Reply Coupon,** obtainable from your local post office. It won't cover the full cost of reply postage, but it helps. Remember that yours is probably only one of many inquiries.

Many visitors wonder what **VAT (Value Added Tax)** is. This is a Common Market tax, set in 1979 at 15% for Britain, which is lower than in some other Common Market countries. Basically, the tax is added to your hotel or restaurant bill, unless otherwise stated. Restaurants must include the tax in menu prices displayed outside their premises. In most stores and shops, it is included in the price of the item you purchase. If in doubt, ask if VAT is included or must be added to the cost of accommodation, food, or goods. If you wish to export an item on which the tax is charged, you can avoid paying it, provided certain requirements are fulfilled, but you must arrange this at the time of purchase and complete the appropriate forms.

Happy traveling!

WHAT IS A FROMMER GUIDE?

This guidebook gives specific, practical details (including prices) about the hotels, restaurants, pubs, sightseeing attractions, and nightlife of England and Scotland. First-class to budget establishments have been documented and described, from the elegant Park Lane Hotel in London to a bed-and-breakfast house in an old fishing village in Scotland. Each establishment has been judged by the strict yardstick of value.

The major focus of the book is on the average voyager who'd like to patronize the almost wholly undocumented establishments of England and Scotland—that is, the second-class hotels and some of the better, although less-heralded, restaurants where you can often get a superb dinner.

The sights of England and Scotland have been set forth in what I believe is a human, personal, and practical style. In both England and Scotland, the bewildered visitor is faced with a staggering number of attractions from the most catholic collection of art and artifacts in the world (the British Museum), to George Washington's ancestral home (Sulgrave Manor), to Anne Hathaway's Cottage at Stratford-upon-Avon, to some of the Scottish castles where Mary Queen of Scots lived during her brief, tragic reign.

What Frommer guides attempt is to lead the reader through the maze of important sights, such as the Tower of London and Edinburgh Castle, then introduce him or her to a number of lesser-known locales, such as the little hamlets, flint churches, and historic houses of East Anglia, perhaps the mellow old towns of the Scottish "Borders." The hours and VAT of admission to these attractions have been detailed.

SOME DISCLAIMERS

No restaurant, inn, hotel, guesthouse, or shop paid to be mentioned in this book. What you read are personal recommendations—in many cases, proprietors never knew their establishments were being investigated.

A word of warning: Unfortunately, prices change, and they rarely go downward, at least not in Britain. The government does not control hotel prices, as is customary in Spain and Italy. Nearly all British hotels are fond of quoting a rate of "from so many pence up," and many establishments simply refuse to quote anything else. The hotelier, anxious about inflation or a sudden tax imposed by the government, doesn't want to commit himself or herself too far in advance to a specific price. However, the "from" rate often—but not always—means the average price you're likely to be charged.

Always, when checking into a hotel, inquire about the price—and agree on it. This policy can save much embarrassment and disappointment when it comes time to settle the tab. In no circumstances can you invariably demand to be charged the price quoted in this book, although every effort has been made to state the accurate tariff as much as it was foreseeable when this guide was published.

This guide is revised every year, yet even in a book that appears fresh annually it may happen that that cozy little family dining room changes colors, blossoming out with cut-velvet walls and dining tabs that include the decorator's fee and the owner's new Bentley. It may be that some of the people, animals, and settings I've described are no longer there or have been changed beyond recognition.

THE ORGANIZATION OF THIS BOOK

Here's how Frommer's *England & Scotland* sets forth its information:

Chapter I, directly ahead, deals with getting to England and Scotland—mainly by air—and then with the various modes of transportation within these countries. The chapter also includes some vital data on the ABCs of life in Britain that will help ease your adjustment into these countries.

Chapter II tries to answer the question "Why go to England?" and discusses where you can go in this country for the most interesting visit, as well as giving a condensed look at the history, culture, and food and drink of the country.

Chapters III through V turn the spotlight on London, documenting the hotels, then the restaurants, pubs, and wine bars, concluding with data on the major sights (my personal list of the Top Ten), shopping bargains, nightlife, and one-day trips within Greater London.

Chapter VI explores some of the most history-rich sights within easy reach of London in the Home Counties: Windsor Castle, Woburn Abbey, and the university city of Oxford.

Chapters VII through XI move away from London to the south of England: Kent, Surrey, Sussex, then Hampshire and Dorset (Thomas Hardy country), followed by "The West"—Cornwall, Devon, Wiltshire, Somerset, and Avon. Here you'll find my descriptions of thatch-roofed cottages, hillside farms, and Elizabethan manor houses, which you may choose to use as bases for exploring this varied English countryside.

Chapters XII and XIII do the same with respect to the most tourist-trodden district of England, the Shakespeare Country and the sleepy hamlets of the Cotswolds.

Chapter XIV focuses on some less-visited but magnificent points for exploration—East Anglia (Cambridge, of course, but also Ely, Norwich, and the fen and broads country) and the pink villages of Suffolk.

Chapter XV cuts through little-known England, ferreting out the attractions of the East Midlands, including the cathedral city of Lincoln.

Chapters XVI and XVII travel across the entire northern sweep of England, from the wilds of Northumbria to the cathedral city of York, to Liverpool and Cheshire, all the way to the beautiful Lake District, immortalized by the poets.

Chapters XVIII through XXII journey to Britain's upper reaches, Scotland, visiting the gentle Lowlands, the rugged Highlands, and such historic islands as Skye, Mull, and Iona of the Inner Hebrides. You'll find accommodations described and also tips on sightseeing and some of the best pubs to visit from Edinburgh to Inverness and Aviemore to Glasgow.

AN INVITATION TO READERS

Like all the Frommer books, Frommer's *England & Scotland* hopes to maintain a continuing dialogue between its author and its readers. All of us share a common aim—to travel as widely and as well as possible, at the best value for our money. And in achieving that goal, your comments and suggestions can be of tremendous help. Therefore, if you come across a particularly appealing hotel, restaurant, store, even sightseeing attraction, please don't keep it to yourself. The solicitation for letters applies not only to new establishments, but to hotels or restaurants already recommended in this guide. The fact that a listing appears in this edition doesn't give it squatter's rights in future publications. If its services have deteriorated, its chef grown stale, its prices risen unfairly, whatever, these failings should be known. Even if you enjoyed every place and found every description accurate—that, too, can cheer many a gray day. Send your comments to Darwin Porter, c/o Prentice Hall Press, 15 Columbus Circle, New York, NY 10023.

TIME OUT FOR A COMMERCIAL

Even a book as fat as this one does not pretend to have covered fully the budget accommodations of Great Britain. Frommer's *England & Scotland* is a wide-ranging survey of accommodations, mainly hotels, as well as restaurants and other attractions. However, if you'd like to economize seriously but still maintain a good standard of living, you may want to go what is known as the "B&B route." B&B, of course, means "bed-and-breakfast," and the British invented the term.

A companion guide to this one, Frommer's *England on $50 a Day*, documents hundreds of budget accommodations, most often guesthouses, as well as low-cost restaurants serving good food at very reasonable prices, and dozens and dozens of pubs throughout the land.

Many budget travelers will want to venture beyond the borders of England and discover Scotland to the north and Wales to the west. With those people in mind, we now offer a separate guide, Frommer's *Scotland and Wales on $50 a Day*, which covers the two countries sharing the same island with England. How close they are geographically, but how different they are once you get there.

Like its older sister guide to England, the book on Scotland and Wales is written in the same theme, describing hundreds of budget hotels and inns, B&B houses, restaurants, tea rooms, and pubs—often offbeat favorites that offer the most authentic and enriching travel experience. In addition, budget-conscious travelers will find the information they need on low-cost transportation, shopping bargains, and inexpensive nightlife. Because of space limitations, this guide contains only the highlights of Scotland, whereas the book devoted to Scotland presents a full survey, including chapters on the more remote provinces and all the famous Hebridean islands, as well as the Shetlands and Orkneys. Even the Isle of Man, perched lonely and isolated in the Irish Sea, is included.

---

2. Frommer's Dollarwise Travel Club—How To Save Money On All Your Travels

In this book we'll be looking at how to get your money's worth in England and Scotland, but there is a "device" for saving money and determining value on *all* your trips. It's the popular, international Frommer's Dollarwise Travel Club, now in its 29th successful year of operation. The club was formed at the urging of numerous readers of the $-A-Day and Frommer Guides, who felt that such an organization could provide continuing travel information and a sense of community to value-minded travelers in all parts of the world. And so it does!

In keeping with the budget concept, the annual membership fee is low and is immediately exceeded by the value of your benefits. Upon receipt of $18 (U.S. residents), or $20 U.S. by check drawn on a U.S. bank or via international postal money order in U.S. funds (Canadian, Mexican, and other foreign residents) to cover one year's membership, we will send all new members the following items.

(1) Any *two* of the following books

Please designate in your letter which two you wish to receive:

Frommer $-A-Day Guides
Europe on $40 a Day
Australia on $30 a Day
Eastern Europe on $25 a Day
England on $50 a Day
Greece on $30 a Day
Hawaii on $60 a Day

India on $25 a Day
Ireland on $35 a Day
Israel on $40 a Day
Mexico (plus Belize and Guatemala) on $35 a Day
New York on $60 a Day
New Zealand on $40 a Day
Scandinavia on $60 a Day
Scotland and Wales on $40 a Day
South America on $35 a Day
Spain and Morocco (plus the Canary Is.) on $40 a Day
Turkey on $30 a Day
Washington, D.C., & Historic Virginia on $40 a Day

($-A-Day Guides document hundreds of budget accommodations and facilities, helping you get the most for your travel dollars.)

Frommer Guides

Australia
Austria & Hungary
Belgium, Holland & Luxembourg
Bermuda & The Bahamas
Brazil
Canada
Caribbean
Egypt
England & Scotland
France
Germany
Italy
Japan & Hong Kong
Portugal, Madeira & the Azores
Southeast Asia
South Pacific
Switzerland & Liechtenstein
Alaska
California & Las Vegas
Florida
Mid-Atlantic States
New England
New York State
Northwest
Skiing USA—East
Skiing USA—West
Southern Atlantic States
Southwest
Texas
USA

(Frommer Guides discuss accommodations and facilities in all price ranges, with emphasis on the medium-priced.)

Frommer Touring Guides

Australia
Egypt
Florence
London
Paris
Scotland

Thailand
Venice
(These new, color illustrated guides include walking tours, cultural and historic sites, and other vital travel information.)

Gault Millau
Chicago
France
Hong Kong
Italy
London
Los Angeles
New England
New York
San Francisco
Washington, D.C.
(Irreverent, savvy, and comprehensive, each of these renowned guides candidly reviews over 1,000 restaurants, hotels, shops, nightspots, museums, and sights.)

Serious Shopper's Guides
Italy
London
Los Angeles
Paris
(Practical and comprehensive, each of these handsomely illustrated guides lists hundreds of stores, selling everything from antiques to wine, conveniently organized alphabetically by category.)

A Shopper's Guide to the Caribbean
(Two experienced Caribbean hands guide you through this shopper's paradise, offering witty insights and helpful tips on the wares and emporia of more than 25 islands.)

Beat the High Cost of Travel
(This practical guide details how to save money on absolutely all travel items—accommodations, transportation, dining, sightseeing, shopping, taxes, and more. Includes special budget information for seniors, students, singles, and families.)

Bed & Breakfast—North America
(This guide contains a directory of over 150 organizations that offer bed & breakfast referrals and reservations throughout North America. The scenic attractions, and major schools and universities near the homes of each are also listed.)

California with Kids
(A must for parents traveling in California, providing key information on selecting the best accommodations, restaurants, and sightseeing attractions for the particular needs of the family, whether the kids are toddlers, school-age, preteens, or teens.)

Frommer's Belgium
(Arthur Frommer unlocks the treasures of a country overlooked by most travelers to Europe. Discover the medieval charm, modern sophistication, and natural beauty of this quintessentially European country.)

Frommer's Cruises
(This complete guide covers all the basics of cruising—ports of call, costs, fly-cruise package bargains, cabin selection booking, embarkation and debarkation and de-

scribes in detail over 60 or so ships cruising the waters of Alaska, the Caribbean, Mexico, Hawaii, Panama, Canada, and the United States.)

Frommer's Skiing Europe
(Describes top ski resorts in Austria, France, Italy, and Switzerland. Illustrated with maps of each resort area. Includes supplement on Argentinian resorts.)

Guide to Honeymoon Destinations
(A special guide for that most romantic trip of your life, with full details on planning and choosing the destination that will be just right in the U.S. [California, New England, Hawaii, Florida, New York, South Carolina, etc.], Canada, Mexico, and the Caribbean.)

Marilyn Wood's Wonderful Weekends
(This very selective guide covers the best mini-vacation destinations within a 200-mile radius of New York City. It describes special country inns and other accommodations, restaurants, picnic spots, sights, and activities—all the information needed for a two- or three-day stay.)

Manhattan's Outdoor Sculpture
(A total guide, fully illustrated with black and white photos, to more than 300 sculptures and monuments that grace Manhattan's plazas, parks, and other public spaces.)

Motorist's Phrase Book
(A practical phrase book in French, German, and Spanish designed specifically for the English-speaking motorist touring abroad.)

Paris Rendez-Vous
(An amusing and *au courant* guide to the best meeting places in Paris, organized for hour-to-hour use: from power breakfasts and fun brunches, through tea at four or cocktails at five, to romantic dinners and dancing 'til dawn.)

Swap and Go—Home Exchanging Made Easy
(Two veteran home exchangers explain in detail all the money-saving benefits of a home exchange, and then describe precisely how to do it. Also includes information on home rentals and many tips on low-cost travel.)

The Candy Apple: New York for Kids
(A spirited guide to the wonders of the Big Apple by a savvy New York grandmother with a kid's-eye view to fun. Indispensable for visitors and residents alike.)

The New World of Travel
(From America's #1 travel expert, Arthur Frommer, an annual sourcebook with the hottest news and latest trends that's guaranteed to change the way you travel—and save you hundreds of dollars. Jam-packed with alternative new modes of travel that will lead you to vacations that cater to the mind, the spirit, and a sense of thrift.)

Travel Diary and Record Book
(A 96-page diary for personal travel notes plus a section for such vital data as passport and traveler's check numbers, itinerary, postcard list, special people and places to visit, and a reference section with temperature and conversion charts, and world maps with distance zones.)

Where to Stay USA
(By the Council on International Educational Exchange, this extraordinary guide is the first to list accommodations in all 50 states that cost anywhere from $3 to $30 per night.)

(2) Any *one* of the Frommer City Guides

Amsterdam and Holland
Athens
Atlantic City and Cape May
Boston
Cancún, Cozumel, and the Yucatán
Chicago
Dublin and Ireland
Hawaii
Las Vegas
Lisbon, Madrid, and Costa del Sol
London
Los Angeles
Mexico City and Acapulco
Minneapolis and St. Paul
Montréal and Québec City
New Orleans
New York
Orlando, Disney World, and EPCOT
Paris
Philadelphia
Rio
Rome
San Francisco
Santa Fe, Taos, and Albuquerque
Sydney
Washington, D.C.

(Pocket-size guides to hotels, restaurants, nightspots, and sightseeing attractions covering all price ranges.)

(3) A one-year subscription to *The Dollarwise Traveler*

This quarterly eight-page tabloid newspaper keeps you up to date on fastbreaking developments in low-cost travel in all parts of the world bringing you the latest money-saving information—the kind of information you'd have to pay $35 a year to obtain elsewhere. This consumer-conscious publication also features columns of special interest to readers: **Hospitality Exchange** (members all over the world who are willing to provide hospitality to other members as they pass through their home cities); **Share-a-Trip** (offers and requests from members for travel companions who can share costs and help avoid the burdensome single supplement); and **Readers Ask . . . Readers Reply** (travel questions from members to which other members reply with authentic firsthand information).

(4) Your personal membership card

Membership entitles you to purchase through the club all Frommer publications for a third to a half off their regular retail prices during the term of your membership.

So why not join this hardy band of international budgeteers and participate in its exchange of travel information and hospitality? Simply send your name and address, together with your annual membership fee of $18 (U.S. residents) or $20 U.S. (Canadian, Mexican, and other foreign residents), by check drawn on a U.S. bank or via international postal money order in U.S. funds to: Frommer's

Dollarwise Travel Club, Inc., 15 Columbus Circle, New York, NY 10023. And please remember to specify which *two* of the books in section (1) and which *one* in section (2) you wish to receive in your initial package of members' benefits. Or, if you prefer, use the order form at the end of the book and enclose $18 or $20 in U.S. currency.

Once you are a member, there is no obligation to buy additional books. No books will be mailed to you without your specific order.

GETTING THERE, GETTING AROUND

The deregulation of the airline industry made world headlines in 1979, and since that time any vestiges of uniformity in price structures for transatlantic flights have disappeared. Airlines compete fiercely with one another, offering a confusing barrage of pricing systems and package deals, each straining the capacities of anyone trying to sort the system into a coherent whole. Travel agents refer to the masses of documentation they receive daily as "chaos." However, that can mean beneficial chaos to the alert traveler willing to study and consider all the options available.

1. Plane Economics

The best strategy for securing the least expensive airfare is to shop around and, above all, remain as flexible as possible. Keep calling the airlines or your travel agent. Sometimes you can purchase a ticket that is lower in price at the last minute. If the flight is not fully booked, an airline might discount ticket prices in an attempt to achieve a full passenger load.

Many passengers, however, find themselves locked into already defined vacation dates and rigid itineraries that require a prearranged departure and return date.

Most airlines charge different fares according to the season. For the pricing of flights to Europe, midsummer months are the peak travel times when fares are the most expensive. Basic season, which falls (with just a few exceptions) in the winter months, offers the least expensive fares. Travel during Christmas and Easter weeks is usually more expensive than in the weeks just before or after those holidays. The periods between basic and peak seasons are termed "shoulder."

Even within the various seasons, airlines offer a variety of seating arrangements, ranging from first class through business and economy classes. Most airlines also offer heavily discounted promotional fares available erratically according to last-minute market plans. But, be warned: the less expensive your ticket is, the more stringent the restrictions. These restrictions will most often include advance purchase, a minimum stay abroad, and cancellation or alteration penalties. The most common and frequently used such fare is the APEX or advance purchase excursion.

Also note that prices tend to be higher in many classes on weekends, which, depending on the airline, is usually defined as Friday, Saturday, and Sunday.

THE AIRLINES

Several airlines fly the enormously popular routes from North America to Great Britain. In fact, you have a greater choice of flights than you do for any other country in Europe. These include British Airways, American Airlines, Delta, Pan Am, TWA, and such smaller airlines as Virgin Atlantic.

Many passengers prefer to fly the national carrier of the nation they intend to visit as an advance preview of their trip abroad. **British Airways** is the premier airline of the United Kingdom. It offers the most frequent flights from North America to Great Britain. Today, BA flies to London (usually nonstop) from at least 18 different U.S. cities. That fact makes transfers through New York unnecessary for many visitors coming from such cities as Boston, Washington, D.C., Atlanta, Dallas, Houston, Miami, Chicago, Detroit, Philadelphia, Seattle, Los Angeles, San Francisco, Anchorage, Orlando, Tampa, and Pittsburgh. However, at New York's JFK Airport, British Airways is the only non-U.S. based carrier to have its own terminal.

From Canada, BA services Toronto, Montréal, and Vancouver. The airline is unique in offering service useful for business travelers, a daily nonstop flight from New York to Manchester. However, for the tourist, this flight can often serve as an efficient launching pad for tours of the Midlands and Shakespeare Country.

TWA offers connections out of New York from each of the more than 60 cities it services in the United States. **American Airlines** offers daily service to Gatwick Airport (on the periphery of London) from Dallas. It also features daily service from Chicago's O'Hare Airport to Manchester.

Pan Am makes nonstop runs from New York to London three times a day, landing at Heathrow Airport. Pan Am also offers daily nonstop service from Detroit, Miami, Los Angeles, San Francisco, and Washington, D.C., as well as five-times-a-week nonstop service from Seattle to London.

Delta Airlines, depending on the season, makes either one or two nonstop flights every day between its headquarters in Atlanta and London's Gatwick Airport. Seasonal discounts often apply, so residents of America's Southeast are well advised to research carefully current schedules of this particular carrier.

Northwest Airlines flies nonstop from both Minneapolis and Boston to London's Gatwick Airport, which is connected directly to the heart of London by train.

Canadians, for the most part, prefer **Air Canada,** whose aircraft depart for London on nonstop flights from Vancouver, Toronto, and Montréal, after connecting with dozens of Canadian cities.

Long considered a no-frills alternative to Western Europe's larger airlines, **Virgin Atlantic Airways** now offers services and amenities comparable to those offered by major carriers. Owned by the same people (Virgin Atlantic Records) who gave the world Boy George and the Culture Club, the airline offers competitive prices for its daily flights between New Jersey's Newark Airport and London's Gatwick Airport. The airline also offers five-times-a-week nonstop flights between Miami and Gatwick and audio entertainment that is arguably better (according to electronic music buffs) than the competition's.

TYPES OF FARES

Generally your cheapest option on a regular airline is to book a **Super APEX** fare. This is now the most frequently used fare to London from North America. Basically, Super APEX fares require a 20 to 30 day advance purchase for a minimum stay of 7 days with no stop-overs. These tickets all have some penalties for changes or cancellations, and some are totally non-refundable. So always check with the airlines or your travel agent to see what is available for the dates on which you wish to travel.

To give you a rough idea of prices, BA's APEX fares from New York to London in high season cost $776 midweek and $832 weekends. The same fare from Chicago to London goes for only $12 more per category, a small difference considering the greater air miles. High season APEX tickets from Los Angeles to London are $899 midweek and $953 weekends. Low season APEX fares are reduced. Round-trip, low season, midweek passage from New York to London is $511 and between Chicago and London $533. British Airways also matches its competitors by offering "giveaway" fares. For example, in 1989 for a short time it featured a $300 round-trip ticket from New York to London. But these fares come and go and you must always check with the airline or a reputable travel agent. On certain flights and in certain seasons, BA also offers a 10% senior citizen discount and youth fares to passengers under 25.

Predictably, the other airlines follow suit. Also, in 1989 for a period, Pan Am offered a "giveaway ticket" of $298.50 round trip between JFK and Heathrow. The ticket, of course, carried many restrictions.

In high season, with stringent qualifiers on the conditions of flight, TWA offers a round-trip APEX fare of $608 from New York to London, with favorable terms for add-on flights from other cities served by that carrier.

From Dallas, American Airlines offers a high-season round-trip fare of $776 to London if travel in both directions occurs on a weekday. On weekends, the price of a ticket goes up by $50.

On Virgin Atlantic Airways, fares can range from as low as $99 one way in low season to $669 (plus tax) for a round-trip midsummer crossing. Delta also comes through with discounts. In May (1989) it featured a $421 round-trip, nonrefundable, fare from Atlanta to London with a 30-day advance booking. Otherwise, its round-trip passage goes up to $744 with a 21-day advance purchase and a stay abroad of between 7 and 180 days.

These fares are only cited to give you an idea of what is available. They will surely change in the lifetime of this edition but others will come to take their places.

CHARTER FLIGHTS

Strictly for reasons of economy, some travelers may wish to accept the numerous restrictions and possible uncertainties of a charter flight to England. Charters require that passengers strictly specify departure and return dates, and full payment is required in advance. Any changes in flight dates are possible (if at all) upon payment of a stiff penalty. Any reputable travel agent can advise you about fares, cities of departure, and, most important, the reputation of the charter company.

Buyer Beware: With careful advance research, the much-vaunted discounts of the charter carriers can frequently be matched with an APEX ticket from one of the major carriers. A bit of advance telephone work and allegiance to the better-established carriers can often save you time, hassle, money, and heartbreak.

There are many charter specialists but three of the more reputable ones include **Council Travel,** a division of the Council on International Educational Exchange (CIEE), 205 East 42nd St., 16th floor, New York, NY 10017 (tel. 212/661-1450); **LTU,** 10 East 40th St., Suite 3705, New York, NY 10016 (tel. 212/532-0207 or 800/888-0200), and **Access International,** 250 West 57th St., Suite 511, New York, NY 10107 (tel. 212/333-7280 or 800/825-3633). For additional assistance, check with a travel agent.

2. By Ship

Traveling by air sometimes brings cultures jarringly close to one another, allowing only a few hours to elapse before total immersion in a different lifestyle. Because of that, you might find sea travel in either direction a distinctive and restful way to collect your thoughts and feelings before or after the onslaught of your British experience.

This means of travel is for those who crave a sea experience, either on a luxury liner with resort-level facilities or else on a more relaxed, time-consuming freighter.

Here is a description of the major service offered from the Atlantic seaboard to various ports in England (most often Southampton, where you'll pay a small debarkation fee):

THE PREMIER CRUISE LINE

Cunard Line, 555 Fifth Ave., New York, NY 10017 (tel. 212/880-7500), boasts the *Queen Elizabeth 2* as its flagship—self-styled, quite accurately, as "the most advanced ship of the age." It is the only ocean liner providing regular transatlantic service—20 sailings a year from June to November—between New York, Boston, Baltimore, or Charleston, and Cherbourg, France; Cork, Ireland; and Southampton, England. Built along the Clyde River near Glasgow in the late 1960s, the *QE2* was radically modernized in 1987, at a cost of $152 million. Designed for extended cruises, the *QE2* is reaching the younger market once leery of the traditional liner-type crossing. Hence, you'll find four swimming pools, a sauna, nightclubs, a balconied theater, cinema, chic boutiques (including the world's first seagoing branch of Harrods), as well as four restaurants, paddle tennis courts, and a children's playroom staffed with English nannies.

The tempting lifestyle on the ship also includes access to an on-board branch of California's Golden Door Health Spa, a computer learning center with 12 IBM personal computers, seminars by trained professionals on astrology, cooking, art, fitness, and medicine, and a Festival of Life series that introduces you to such personalities as Larry Hagman or Meryl Streep.

Fares are extremely complicated, based on the desirability of the cabin and the season of sailing. I suggest that you call your travel agent or a Cunard representative at their toll-free number (tel. 800/221-4770). In New York City, call 212/661-7777.

One of the most popular packages offered is the air/sea trip. On it, you cross in one direction by air and sail the other direction. The round-trip fares for this air/sea passage depend on the time of year and the size and opulence of your cabin. British Airways serves some 60 gateways in North America through which you can start or end your trip. However, conditions strictly state that the amount of time spent abroad cannot exceed 20 days for transatlantic-class passengers and 40 days for first-class passengers—and this includes the time spent on board.

A series of maneuvers as to scheduling is possible, but in thrift season—roughly defined as early spring and late autumn—sailings usually cost a minimum of $1,350 in transatlantic class and around $2,500 in first class. Prices go up from there and can reach a maximum of $8,415 per person. For a supplement of less than $1,000, you can fly the Concorde on one of the legs of your trip. All passengers pay a $90 port tax for each direction of sailing regardless of the options chosen.

The Cunard Line divides its sailing year into superthrift, thrift, value, and regular season. The prices quoted by Cunard are per person, based on double occupancy.

THE FREIGHTERS

For an offbeat alternative, if you have time and an adventurous spirit, you can try to secure a cabin aboard a freighter. Passage on a freighter tends to be less expensive than on a passenger ship, but this requires a little comparison shopping. For example, a budget accommodation aboard the *QE2* can cost less money and require less time than passage on a freighter. For legal reasons, no freighter can carry more than 12 passengers (more than that would require a full-time ship's doctor). Your cabin might be adequate, but there is little organized activity.

Most freighters dock at Le Havre, Rotterdam, or Bremerhaven, but a limited number make stops at such unlikely British ports as Felixstowe. The voyage takes from 7 days to 12 days. Sometimes the final port will change during crossing, throwing prearranged itineraries into confusion.

In summer, cabins tend to be fully booked for as much as a year in advance. Space is more likely to be available in winter. A typical fare for a passage from Newark (New Jersey) to Felixstowe costs from $1,400 to $1,500 per person, based on double occupancy.

For more information on freighter travel, write to Fords Freighter Travel Guide, 19448 Londelius St., Northridge CA 91324 (tel. 818/701-7414).

Two reputable booking agents for freighter travel both bemoan the lack of available space on freighters. They are **Anytime Anywhere Travel,** 35 King St., Chappaqua, NY 10514 (tel. 914/238-8800) and **Vacations Unlimited,** 136 South Orange Ave., South Orange, NJ 07079 (tel. 201/763-4800).

---

3. Traveling Within Britain

BY AIR
Although Britain enjoys one of the world's best maintained network of motorways, many visitors prefer to commute from their arrival point in London to other cities by air. **British Airways** maintains routes to more than 20 other destinations within the United Kingdom. Several flights a day leave London for such cities as Manchester (the heart of the Midlands), Glasgow, and Edinburgh. British Airways telephone representatives within North America are well qualified to give price and schedule information and to make reservations. Ask about the British Airways Supper Shuttle Saver fares. If granted one of these fares to certain key British cities you may find your ticket cost reduced by 50%. Of course, trips must be reserved and ticketed two weeks in advance and you can fly only during off-peak times. That means weekends or daily from 10 a.m. to 3:30 p.m. and after 7 p.m.

BY TRAIN
There is something magical about traveling on a train in Britain. You sit in comfortable compartments, on upholstered seats, watching the scenery pass in review. You're served your meal in the dining car, and the entire experience can become a relaxing interlude.

You should, of course, be warned that *your Eurailpass is not valid on trains in Great Britain.* But the cost of rail travel in England, Scotland, Northern Ireland, and Wales can be quite low—particularly if you take advantage of certain cost-saving travel plans, some of which can only be purchased in North America, before leaving for Great Britain.

BritRail Pass
This pass gives unlimited rail travel in England, Scotland, and Wales, and is valid on all British Rail routes. It is not valid on ships between Great Britain and the continent, the Channel Islands, or Ireland. Gold (first-class) and silver (economy-class) passes are sold for travel periods of varying lengths. An 8-day gold pass costs $250 as of 1989; a silver ticket goes for $179. For 15 days, a gold pass costs $370; silver, $259. For 22 days, gold is $470; silver, $339. For one month, gold is $540; silver, $389. Children up to 5 years of age travel free, and those 5 to 15 go for $125 gold and $90 for silver for 8 days; $185 gold and $130 silver for 15 days; $235 gold and $170 silver for 22 days; and $270 gold and $195 silver for one month.

Youth passes, all silver, are $149 for 8 days, $219 for 15 days, $289 for 22 days, and $329 for one month. The youth passes are available for persons 16 through 25 years of age, but they must pay the full adult fare if they choose to go first class.

Britrail also offers a **Senior Citizen gold pass** to those age 60 and over, costing less than the regular gold pass. Prices are $210 for 8 days, $310 for 15 days, $400 for 22 days, and $460 for one month.

Prices for BritRail Passes are higher for Canadian travelers.

BritRail Passes cannot be obtained in Britain, but should be secured before leaving North America either through travel agents or by writing or visiting BritRail Travel International, 630 Third Ave., New York, NY 10017; Suite 603, 800 S. Hope St., Los Angeles, CA 90017; or Cedar Maple Plaza, 2305 Cedar Springs, Dallas, TX 75201. Canadians can write to 94 Cumberland St., Toronto M5R 1A3, ON; or 409 Granville St., Vancouver V6C 1T2, BC.

BritRail Passes do not have to be predated. Validate your pass at any British Rail station when you start your first rail journey.

BritRail Flexipass

The Flexipass allows the traveler the same unlimited access to the British Rail network as the regular BritRail pass with these differences: The Flexipass is available only for either 8 days or for 15 days. The 8-day Flexipass can be used for any four (nonconsecutive) days. The 15-day Flexipass can be used for any eight (nonconsecutive) days of travel out of 15. The 8-day pass costs $210 in first class, $149 in economy. Children 5 to 15 are charged $105 first class, $75 economy. Seniors pay $180 (first class), and youths 16 through 25 pay $129 to travel economy class. The 15-day Flexipass costs $310 first class, $219 economy. For children, the charges are $155 first class, $110 economy. First class for seniors is $270, and economy class for youths is $189.

With Flexipass, you get your money's worth. For example, to travel to York and Bath from London without the pass would cost at least $154 in economy class round trip. However, for only $149, the 8-day BritRail Flexipass buys four whole days of rail travel to any destination you choose.

Remember, you cannot purchase your Flexipass in Great Britain. You must secure it from either your travel agent or from BritRail Travel International in the U.S.

Capital Travel Pak

The Capital Travel Pak is a package offered by BritRail for purchase before you leave home, to let you see all the best of London and take easy rail trips to many nearby attractions for four days or a full week. The package combines a 4- or 7-day rail pass with a 4- or 7-day London Visitor Travelcard (see "Transportation in Greater London," Chapter III). The 4-day Travel Pak costs $99 for adults, $60 for children 5 to 15. The price of a 7-day package is $129 for adults, $65 for children. The passes and Travelcards are for consecutive days from the day of validation. Gatwick or Heathrow Airport transfers are included.

Special Bargain Fares

British Rail from time to time offers special round-trip fares for optional travel and weekend travel, which may only be purchased in Great Britain. Because of the changing nature of these fares and facilities, it is not possible to give information about them to travelers from abroad. Information may be obtained from travel agents and British Rail stations in Great Britain.

If you're in London, and want more information on transportation rates, schedules, or facilities, go to the **British Travel Centre,** Rex House, 4-12 Lower Regent St., S.W.1 (tel. 01/730-3400), only a few minutes' walk from Piccadilly Circus. This office deals only with inquiries made in person. Don't try to telephone for information. The office is open from 9 a.m. to 6:30 p.m. Monday to Saturday, 10 a.m. to 4:30 p.m. Sunday. You can also make reservations and purchase rail tickets there and at the British Travel Centres at Oxford Street, Victoria Station, the Strand, King William Street, Heathrow Airport, and the main London stations—Waterloo, King's Cross, Euston, Victoria, and Paddington—where each deals mainly with its own region. For general information, call the appropriate station. All numbers are listed in the telephone directory.

The Britainshrinkers

This is a bonanza for travelers who want to make several quickie trips into the heart of England, without having to check out of their hotel room in London. From early April to the end of October, scheduled full-day tours are operated by British Rail. You're whisked out of London by train to your destination, where you hop on a waiting bus to visit the various sights during the day. You have a light lunch in a local pub, and there is also free time to shop or explore. A guide accompanies the tour from London and back. Except for overnight trips to Scotland or Wales, your return is in time for dinner or the theater. Included in the rates are entrance fees and VAT.

On one day trip, you can visit Warwick Castle, Stratford-upon-Avon, and Coventry Cathedral, at a cost, with lunch included, of $79 for adults, $63 for children up to 16 years old, but holders of BritRail Passes pay only $56 for adults, $51 for children. One of the most heavily booked tours is to Bath and Stonehenge, taking in Salisbury Cathedral, costing $79 for adults, $62 for children for regular tickets; $51 for adults, $46 for children for BritRail Pass holders.

CAR RENTALS

Once you get over the initial awkwardness of driving on the left-hand side of the road, you will quickly discover that the best way to see the real Britain is to have a car while you're there. There is, quite simply, no substitute for the freedom and flexibility that only your own vehicle can provide.

Partly because of the huge number of visitors to the United Kingdom, the car-rental market is among the most competitive in all of Europe, with many different companies bidding avidly for the U.S.-based business. The company that you eventually select will depend on your age and the category of car you're seeking. For example, younger drivers usually gravitate to **Hertz.** because that company allows 18-year-old drivers to rent its less expensive cars if they present a credit card in their own name. Drivers must be 21 at **Avis** and 23 at **Budget.**

In overall pricing, however, in the small and medium-size categories, **Budget Rent-a-Car** is usually the least expensive choice. For example, Budget's Fiat Panda (a small car suitable for two passengers and a modest amount of luggage) costs, as of this writing, £79 ($138.25) a week with unlimited mileage. Similar or comparable cars at Avis and Hertz rent for £91 ($159.25) and £98 ($171.50), respectively. Budget tends to be the most competitively priced in the medium-size market as well. However, as the size, power, accessories, and extra features of rental vehicles increase, the price advantages at all three major chains become blurred.

In brief, it's best to shop around, compare prices, and have a clear idea of your automotive needs before you reserve a car. All three companies give the best rates to clients who reserve at least two business days in advance and who agree to return the car to its point of origin. It is also an advantage to keep the car for at least one week, as opposed to three or four days. Be warned that all car rentals in the U.K. attach a 15% extra government tax.

When you reserve a car, ask about the availability of a 24-hour-a-day number within Britain that you can call for emergency assistance if your vehicle breaks down.

For reservations and information, you can call either of the major players by dialing toll-free from within the U.S. at the following numbers: Budget at 800/527-0700, Avis at 800/331-2112, and Hertz at 800/654-3001.

A less well-known car-rental company, which does brisk business in the U.K., is **Kenning Car Rental,** affiliated in North America with General Rent-a-Car. This company sometimes offers attractive promotional rates that merit a second look. For reservations and information, contact their Florida sales office by dialing 800/227-8990.

Car Insurance

With the rise in inflation and a staggering increase in the cost of car repairs, the price of insurance premiums are going up worldwide. Several years ago, far more insurance protection was automatically factored into the average car-rental contract. Today, however, many benefits have been decreased, and it's more important than ever to purchase additional insurance to avoid financial liability in the event of an accident.

In other words, it pays to ask questions—lots of them—before renting a car. You can purchase a waiver at each of the major car-rental companies for around £10 ($17.50) a day. Without it, you might be responsible for up to the full cost of the eventual repairs to the vehicle. Considering the unfamiliarity of driving on the left, different road practices, and roads that tend to be narrow and sometimes thickly congested, I consider the purchase of an optional collision damage waiver almost essential. Additional personal accident insurance (which covers unforeseen medical costs in the event of an accident) costs around £2 ($3.60) a day.

Driving Requirements

To drive a car in Britain, your passport and your own driver's license must be presented along with your deposit; no special British license is needed. The prudent driver will secure a copy of the *British Highway Code,* available from almost any stationer or news agent.

Although not mandatory, a membership in one of the two major auto clubs in England can be helpful: the **Automobile Association** and the **Royal Automobile Club.** The headquarters of the AA are at Fanum House, Basingstoke, Hampshire RG21 2EA (tel. 0256/20123); the RAC offices are in London at RAC House, Landsdowne Road, Croydon, Surrey CR9 2JA (tel. 01/686-2525). Membership in one of these clubs is usually handled by the agent from whom you rent your car. Upon joining, you'll be given a key to the many telephone boxes you see along the road, so that you can phone for help in an emergency.

Warning: Pedestrian crossings are marked by striped lines (zebra striping) on the road. Also, flashing lights near the curb indicate that drivers *must* stop and yield the right of way if a pedestrian has stepped out into the zebra zone to cross the street.

Wearing seatbelts is mandatory in the British Isles.

Fuel

Gasoline, called petrol by the British, is usually sold by the liter, with 4.5 liters making up their imperial gallon. Most pumps show a list of prices and measures. The prices, incidentally, will be much higher than you are used to paying. You'll probably have to serve yourself at the petrol station. In some remote areas, especially in Scotland, stations are few and far between, and many all over the country are closed on Sunday.

BUSES IN BRITAIN

For the traveler who wants to see the country as even a train cannot reveal it, but who can't afford to rent a car, the old, reliable, and inexpensive (at least half the cost of railway fares) bus offers a fine form of transportation. While the trains do go everywhere, passing through towns and villages, they rarely bring you into contact with country life, and they almost never carry you across the high (main) streets of the villages, as the buses do. Moreover, distances between towns in England are usually short, so your chances of tiring are lessened. Every remote village is reachable by a bus.

The **express motorcoach network** covers the greater part of Britain and is operated by National and Scottish Citylink Coaches. It links many villages and most towns and cities with frequent schedules, convenient timetables, and efficient operation in all seasons. Most places off the main route can be easily reached by stopping and switching to a local bus. Fares are relatively cheap, making travel on the express motorcoach network economical.

The departure point from London for most of the bus lines is **Victoria Coach Station,** Buckingham Palace Road, S.W.1 (tel. 01/730-0202), a block up from Victoria Railroad Station. It is the hub of Britain's largest coach operators, National Express, whose long-distance coach network covers England and Wales with connections to Scotland, Ireland, and the continent. You need reservations for some express buses.

National Express Rapides are luxurious coaches doing long-distance runs with reclining seats, light refreshments, video, and no-smoking areas. To phone them, call 01/730-0202 from 8 a.m. to 10 p.m. daily. The National Express ticket office for England and Wales is open daily from 6 a.m. to midnight. The ticket bureau for Scotland, Ireland, and the continent is open daily from 7:30 a.m. to 10:30 p.m. You can also arrange coach excursions here, as well as sightseeing tours, and purchase rail and ferry travel tickets, even get hotel accommodations.

From 9:15 a.m. to 5:30 p.m. it is also possible to visit the **Air & Holiday Centre** for air travel, inclusive holidays, and coach tours of Britain. Telephone sales can be made if you have a MasterCard or VISA by calling 01/730-3499 for destinations in the United Kingdom and Ireland from 8 a.m. to 9 p.m. Air and holiday bookings can be secured by calling 01/730-3466 from 9:15 a.m. to 5:30 p.m. Monday to Saturday.

For journeys within roughly a 35-mile radius of London, including such major attractions as Windsor, Hampton Court and Chartwell, try the **Green Line** bus service. The Green Line Enquiry Office is at Eccleston Bridge, Victoria, S.W.1 (off Buckingham Palace Road), and can be phoned at 01/668-7261.

Golden Rover Tickets cost £4.50 ($7.90) per person, available for one day's travel on most London Country and Green Line routes, but not their Jetlink and Flightline buses connecting London and the airports. It is possible to cover quite a large area around London and into the country for a very small cost. For more precise information on routes, fares, and schedules, write to **Green Line Travel Ltd.,** Lesbourne Road, Reigate, Surrey RH2 7LE (tel. 01/668-7261).

Britexpress Card

This offers one-third off all adult trip tickets purchased on Britain's Express Coach Network of National Express and Scottish Citylink coaches, valid for a 30-day period throughout the year. Travel where and when you wish with a choice of 1,500 destinations. All it costs is £9 ($15.75). The Britexpress Card can be purchased from your U.S. travel agent or on your arrival in London at Victoria Coach Station on 13 Regent St. Examples of some approximate one-way fares and travel times are: London-Edinburgh, (Cordon Bleu service), £17 ($29.75), time 7 hours, 45 minutes; London-Stratford-upon-Avon, £9 ($15.75), time 3 hours, 5 minutes; London-York (Rapide service), £16 ($28), time 4 hours, 20 minutes; London-Cambridge, £6 ($10.50), time 1 hour, 50 minutes. Trip tickets can be purchased in the United Kingdom from 2,500 agents nationwide.

Tourist Trail Pass

This provides unlimited travel on the nationwide National Express and Scottish Citylink bus network and is available for either 5, 8, 15, 22, or 30 days. Prices start at £48 ($84), with a one-third discount for senior citizens and children. The pass can be purchased where the Britexpress Card (above) is sold. The general sales agent in the U.S. is Worldwide Marketing Associates, 909 W. Vista Way, Vista, CA 92083.

BICYCLES

This is the cheapest transportation apart from walking, and you can get a wealth of assistance from the **Cyclists' Touring Club,** Cotterell House, 69 Meadrow,

Godalming, Surrey GU7 3HS (tel. 04868/7217). It costs £17.50 ($30.65) to join, and membership is good for one year. The club helps with information and provides maps, insurance, touring routes, and a list of low-cost accommodations, including farmhouses, inns, guesthouses, and private homes that cater especially to cyclists.

BARGAIN SIGHTSEEING TIP

If you plan to do extensive sightseeing in Britain, consider the **Great Britain Heritage Pass.** Information about it can be obtained by calling 01/846-9000. The pass grants you entrance to 600 properties within the country, including Edinburgh Castle, Churchill's Chartwell, Woburn Abbey, Hampton Court Palace, and Windsor Castle. The ticket covers all properties in care of the National Trust and those run by the Department of the Environment. It is estimated that anyone visiting as many as five of these sightseeing attractions will get back the initial outlay of £16 ($28) for a 15-day pass and £24 ($42) for a one-month pass. In the United States you can purchase this pass at any branch office of British Airways or its specially appointed travel agents. In Great Britain, it can be purchased at any tourist office in the country.

The **National Trust** specializes in historic and stately homes. They offer a year-long membership in the Royal Oak Foundation for £16 ($28). This can be purchased at the National Trust, 36 Queen Anne's Gate, London SW1H 9AS (tel. 01/222-9251). Tube to St. James's Park. Hours are weekdays, 9:30 a.m. to 5:30 p.m.

The U.S. headquarters for Royal Oak is at 285 West Broadway, New York, NY 10013 (tel. 212/966-6565). Membership can be purchased here, and it's considered a tax-deductible charitable contribution. The purpose of the Royal Oak Foundation is the maintenance and continued exposure of British monuments and stately homes to the public. With membership, you're entitled to visit properties in Great Britain administered by the National Trust.

TOURS

Is this the year for your trip to England and Scotland? If this is to be your first trip to the British Isles, you probably have many questions. You may not be fully sure of what you really want to see, aside, of course, from the Tower of London and Big Ben. Troublesome thoughts can be: How do I plan my trip to be sure of seeing the most outstanding sights? How much of a problem will I have in going from place to place with my luggage? Am I too old to embark on such a journey, perhaps alone? Will I meet people who share my interests with whom to chat and compare notes?

To people going to England and Scotland, as well as to other European countries for the first time, I simply say: Go on a good tour. By this I don't mean simply a tour of one city or of one building. I refer to a vacation tour where you and your needs will be looked after from your arrival in the country of your choice to your departure en route back to the United States. Choose a tour suited to the length of time you have for your trip, the money you can spend, and the places you want to go. If you go on your own, the fluctuating currency situation might force you to stay in undesirable hotels and to search long and hard for inexpensive eating places abroad, but a good tour group can allow you to make an affordable trip, staying in first-class hotels, dining well, and visiting the outstanding attractions of England and Scotland. Because you pay the set price for your tour package in advance, with a good tour group, you can know ahead just what your visit will cost, and, in addition, you won't be bothered by such matters as having to arrange your own transportation, look after your own luggage, or see to other requirements of travel.

Any good travel agent can help you select the tour most suited to your needs.

It will help you enjoy your tour more if you take along a copy of this guide, which gives the background of areas you'll see, where to shop, and other practical information. You may please your fellow tour members by taking them to a cozy pub you find recommended in these pages.

MILEAGE BETWEEN MAJOR CITIES
(Distance in Miles)

	Aberdeen	Brighton	Cambridge	Coventry	Edinburgh	Glasgow	Inverness	Liverpool	LONDON	Newcastle	Norwich	Nottingham	Oban	Oxford	Plymouth	Southampton
Aberdeen		616	500	461	130	150	107	368	558	235	527	432	180	509	641	583
Ayr	196	467	351	311	81	35	207	219	409	150	377	282	127	360	492	434
Brighton	616		117	158	475	474	642	277	53	349	170	193	574	105	222	81
Bristol	526	157	166	96	385	384	552	187	121	297	225	149	484	73	124	79
Cambridge	500	117		88	335	358	526	208	55	230	61	88	458	100	287	128
Coventry	461	158	88		319	318	487	121	100	208	149	52	419	54	211	118
Dover	637	84	199	179	458	459	663	186	298	354	173	214	595	146	320	152
Dumfries	231	408	292	252	80	79	247	160	350	91	318	223	179	301	433	375
Dundee	67	594	433	394	63	83	134	301	491	168	460	365	116	442	574	516
Edinburgh	130	475	335	319		46	156	227	417	105	361	266	123	368	500	442
Glasgow	150	474	358	318	46		172	226	416	157	384	289	93	367	499	411
Inverness	107	642	526	487	156	172		394	584	261	553	458	118	535	667	609
Leicester	470	165	74	24	293	327	496	130	107	188	117	26	428	70	236	166
Liverpool	368	277	208	121	227	226	394		219	170	235	130	326	170	302	244
LONDON	558	53	55	100	417	416	584	219		276	109	135	516	59	242	87
Manchester	363	260	163	105	222	221	389	35	202	139	190	72	321	153	285	277
Newcastle	235	349	230	208	105	157	261	170	276		256	161	258	254	412	350
Norwich	527	170	61	149	361	384	553	235	109	256		120	485	160	346	188
Nottingham	432	193	88	52	266	289	458	130	135	161	120		390	98	264	194
Oban	180	574	458	419	123	93	118	326	516	258	485	390		467	599	541
Oxford	509	105	100	54	368	367	535	170	59	254	160	98	467		194	64
Plymouth	641	222	287	211	500	499	667	302	242	412	346	264	599	194		161
Portsmouth	604	48	133	139	463	462	630	265	78	354	192	199	562	85	182	21
Southampton	583	81	128	118	442	441	609	244	87	350	188	194	541	64	161	
Stoke-on-Trent	397	220	133	85	256	255	423	58	182	190	177	50	355	113	187	187

4. Alternative and Special-Interest Travel

Mass tourism of the kind that has transported vast numbers of North Americans to the most obscure corners of the map has been a by-product of the affluence, technology, and democratization that only the last half of the 20th century was able to produce.

With the advent of the 1990s, and the changes they promise to bring, some of America's most respected travel visionaries have perceived a change in the needs of many of the world's most experienced (and sometimes jaded) travelers. There has emerged a demand for specialized travel experiences whose goals and objectives are clearly defined well in advance of an actual departure. There is also an increased demand for organizations that can provide like-minded companions to share and participate in increasingly esoteric travel plans.

This yearning for a special-interest vacation might be especially intense for a frequent traveler whose expectations have already been defined by earlier exposure to foreign cultures.

Caveat: Under no circumstances is the inclusion of an organization to be interpreted as a guarantee either of its credit-worthiness or its competency. Information about the organizations coming up is presented only as a preliminary preview, to be followed by your own investigation should you be interested.

INTERNATIONAL UNDERSTANDING

About the only thing the following organizations have in common is reflected by the headline. These organizations not only promote trips to increase international understanding, but they often encourage and advocate what might be called "intelligent travel."

The Friendship Force was founded in Atlanta, Georgia, under the leadership of former President Jimmy Carter during his tenure as governor of that state. This nonprofit organization exists for the sole purpose of fostering and encouraging friendship among disparate peoples around the world. The dozens of branch offices lie throughout North America, meet regularly for meetings of goodwill, and appoint a volunteer director whose responsibility it is to recruit new members and cultivate potential destinations for en masse visits.

These visits usually occur once a year. Because of group bookings by the Friendship Force, the price of air fare to the host country is usually less than an individual APEX ticket. Each participant is required to spend two weeks in the host country (primarily in Europe, but also throughout the world). One stringent requirement is the need for a participant to spend one full week in the home of a family as a guest, supposedly to further the potential for meaningful friendships between the host family and the participants. Most volunteers spend the second week traveling in the host country.

It should be noted that no particular study regime or work program is expected of participants, but only a decorum and interest level that speaks well of America and its residents. Again, the goal and aim of this group is to further friendship in a nonpolitical, nonreligious context of cooperation and good will. For more information, contact The Friendship Force, 575 South Tower, 1 CNN Center, Atlanta, GA 30303 (tel. 404/522-9490).

People to People International, 501 E. Armour Blvd., Kansas City, MO 64109 (tel. 816/531-4701). Defining its purpose as the promotion of world peace through increased understanding among individuals, this philanthropic nonprofit organization was established in the early 1950s by Dwight D. Eisenhower. People to People organizes collegiate ambassador programs, where participants spend a month in Europe studying with an American professor for college credit. Similar programs exist for high school students as well. Programs have been offered, for example, for students of corporate or public administration to spend two unpaid months watching the interior workings of a British corporation or a British government agency.

There is also a department to facilitate visits by North American professionals to their counterparts in countries around the world. This usually occurs in a convention setting, requires time away of two or three weeks, and can include a wide array of highly specialized careers. Membership in this organization qualifies newcomers to a newsletter and costs $15 a year for individuals, $25 for families, and $10 for students.

World Wide Christian Tours, P.O. 506 Box, Elizabethtown, KY 42701 (tel. 502/769-5900 or toll free 800/732-7920), focuses on Christian travel. These trips include ecumenical tours of England and golf-related tours of Scotland. This organization will tailor-make tours for special interest and church groups of two to well over 200. World Wide Christian Tours is bonded and approved by ARC and IATA and also has a bus brokerage license.

Servas, 11 John St., New York, NY 10038 (tel. 212/267-0252). Founded in 1948 by an American-born conscientious objector living in Denmark, this organization grew slowly from a collection of index cards kept in a friend's kitchen to one of the most prominent collections of people of goodwill in the world. Servas (translated from the Esperanto, it means "to serve") is a nonprofit, nongovernmental, international, interfaith network of travelers and hosts whose goal is to help build world peace, goodwill, and understanding. Servas travelers are invited to share living space in a privately owned home within a community, normally staying without charge for visits lasting a maximum of two days. Day visits as well as a single shared meal can also be arranged. Visitors pay a $45 annual membership fee, fill out an application, and are interviewed for suitability by one of more than 200 Servas interviewers throughout the country. They then receive a Servas directory listing the names and addresses of Servas hosts on six continents who welcome visitors into their homes. What's amazing is that with all the potential problems that an organization this diverse might have, there seem to be surprisingly few trouble zones.

International Visitors Information Service, 733 15th St. NW, Suite 300, Washington, DC 20005 (tel. 202/783-6540). For $4.95, this organization will mail anyone a booklet listing opportunities someone might use for contact with local residents in foreign countries. Europe is heavily featured. Checks should be made out to Meridian House/IVIS.

Staying with a British Family

An ideal way to find out about the British way of life is provided by a number of hosts operating under a code of conduct set up by the British Tourist Authority. For information on this program, a booklet is available published by the BTA listing dozens of agencies and services offering help in finding the place where you might like to stay for a happy British holiday.

If possible, interested persons should call in person at the **British Travel Centre,** 12 Regent St., Piccadilly Circus, in London. In the U.S. write to any of the following **British Tourist Authority** offices: Third Floor, 40 West 57th St., New York, NY 10019; John Hancock Center, Suite 3320, 875 North Michigan Ave., Chicago, IL 60611; Cedar Maple Plaza, 2305 Cedar Springs Rd., Dallas, TX 75201-1814; or World Trade Center, 350 South Figueroa St., Suite 450, Los Angeles, CA 90071.

ADVENTURE/WILDERNESS TRAVEL

Whether by bicycle or on foot, the following organizations offer tours for the athletic who want to explore "the wilds," or at least country roads, before they disappear forever.

Outward Bound, 383 Field Point Rd., Greenwich, CT 06830 (tel. 203/661-0797, or toll free 800/243-8520 outside Connecticut). Considered the oldest and most experienced wilderness survival school in America, Outward Bound was founded in 1941 by a German-English educator, Kurt Hahn. Its goal is to help people "go beyond their self-imposed limits, to use the wilderness as a metaphor for personal growth and self-discovery." Training sessions last from three days to three months. A three-month course will sometimes be accepted for college credits toward a degree. The location of these courses is usually in a wilderness setting near the sea or high in the mountains. Outward Bound maintains 35 different schools and centers throughout the world.

   Wilderness Travel, Inc., 801 Allston Way, Berkeley, CA 94710 (tel. 415/548-0420, or toll free 800/247-6700 outside California), specializes in mountain tours and bicycle tours. It also offers walking tours of Cornwall and the Cotswolds as well as Wales and Scotland. Call or write for more information.

   Country Cycling Tours, 140 W. 83rd St., New York, NY 10024 (tel. 212/874-5151). One of New York's largest tour operators for bicyclists, this company has tours of the back roads of England and Ireland, as well as walking tours in England. Tours (costing from $1,395 to $1,795) include overnight accommodations in charming three-star hotels, breakfast, and most dinners, and last 10 to 13 days. Luggage precedes you in a van. Cyclists can bring their own bicycles or rent them on site.

   The American company referred to as "the granddaddy of cycle tour operators" is **Vermont Bicycle Touring,** P.O. Box 711, Bristol, VT 05443 (tel. 802/453-4811). Tours range from 25 to 40 miles a day, and a van transports luggage. The tours allow flexibility for individual levels of cycling experience, but additional guidance, assistance, and services are always available. Most of this group's tours are in England.

   For trekking and backpacking tours, get in touch with **Outdoor Bound,** 18 Stuyvesant Oval, No. 1A, New York, NY 10009 (tel. 212/505-1020). Founded by Seth Steiner, it leads walking tours through the Lake District of England. Tours last up to two weeks, covering five to ten miles a day. Accommodations are based in a 17th-century country inn near Ambleside and Windermere. A minibus takes walkers to an embarkation point noted for scenic beauty. Depending on the tour and options, charges are $1,000 to $2,000.

INLAND WATERWAYS

   For a completely new angle on travel in the British Isles, visitors can take boat trips on the network of inland waterways threading through the country. You can choose between a skipper-yourself boat, equipped with food, comprehensive instructions, and suggested routes, or else a hotel boat, where you get good food, a helpful crew, and the companionship of fellow passengers. Waterways holidays make sightseeing easy, allowing you to leave your luggage aboard as you spend the days exploring. Some places allow you to take your boat right into the center of a city, as at Chester, Stratford-upon-Avon, Norwich, Cambridge, York, and Windsor.

   Cruising areas include the Norfolk Broads, canals, the River Thames, Scottish and Irish lochs, and the fascinating Cambridgeshire rivers: Ouse, Cam, and Nene. For information and reservations, contact **UK Waterway Holidays Ltd.,** Welton Hythe, Daventry, Northamptonshire NN11 5LG (tel. 0327/843773).

SENIOR CITIZEN VACATIONS

   One of the most dynamic organizations in the world of postretirement studies for senior citizens is **Elderhostel,** 80 Boylston St., Boston, MA 02116 (tel. 617/426-7788). Established in 1975 by Martin Knowlton, a retired engineer and professor of political science, Elderhostel maintains a dazzling array of university-based summer educational programs for senior citizens throughout the world, including England, Scotland, and all major countries on the continent. Most courses last around three weeks, representing remarkable value, considering that air fare, hotel accommodations in student dormitories or modest inns, all meals, and tuition are included. Currently, three weeks with all of these included cost a surprisingly low

$1,992 for a program in England, for example. Courses involve no homework, are ungraded, and are especially focused on the liberal arts. Even field trips are related to the academic discipline being studied in the classroom.

In no way is this to be considered a luxury vacation, but rather an adventure in academic fulfillment for senior citizens. Participants must be over 60 years of age. However, if a pair of members goes as a couple, only one member needs to be older than 60. Meals are the kind of solid, no-frills fare typical of educational institutions worldwide. A frequently unpublicized side benefit of this program is the safety in which many older single women can travel. Some 70% of the participants are women, who understandably prefer to travel with a goal, an orientation, amid like-minded individuals waiting for them at the end of their transatlantic airplane ride.

Anyone interested in participating in one of Elderhostel's programs should write for their free newsletter and a list of upcoming courses and destinations.

One company that has made a reputation exclusively because of its quality tours for senior citizens is **Saga International Holidays,** established in the 1950s as a sensitive and highly appealing outlet for tour participants at least 60 years of age or older. Insurance and air fare are included in the net price of all of their tours, which encompass dozens of locations in Europe and usually last for an average of 17 nights. For more information, get in touch with Saga International Holidays, 120 Boylston St., Boston, MA 02116 (tel. toll free 800/343-0273).

EDUCATIONAL AND STUDY TRAVEL

University vacations, or **UNIVAC,** offers a wealth of study opportunities at Oxford and Cambridge, where participants find themselves surrounded by history in a rich atmosphere of culture and academic excellence spanning more than 700 years. These cultural vacations combine relaxation with the stimulus of an academic purpose, wherein you can explore history, literature, and the arts through lectures, excursions, and guided walking tours, with no pressures such as exams or papers to prepare. There are no formal academic requirements for participation in UNIVAC —all adults over 18 are invited to share in the programs, living in one of the colleges, eating in an elaborate dining hall or intimate private Fellows' dining rooms.

Programs, lasting 7 to 12 days, include university architecture, history, art, and literature, among other English treasures. North American headquarters for UNIVAC is the International Building, 9602 N.W. 13th St., Miami, FL 33172 (tel. 305/591-1736, or toll free 800/792-0100). In the United Kingdom, its headquarters is at 8 Beaufort Pl., Cambridge, England CB5 8AG; in summer, Brasenose College, Oxford, England OX1 4AJ, or Corpus Christi College, Cambridge, England CN2 1RH.

British Universities Summer Schools, University of Oxford, Department for External Studies, Rewley House, Wellington Square, Oxford OX1 2JA, England, offers academic programs in literature and history related to the cultural resources of the universities of Birmingham (at its Stratford-upon-Avon center), London, and Oxford. These programs are designed for graduates, particularly teachers, for graduating seniors, and some undergraduates.

The **Institute of International Education,** the largest U.S. organization in the field of international higher education, administers a variety of postsecondary academic, training, and grant programs. It is best known for administering the USIA predoctoral and collaborative Fulbright grants. For information on IIE-administered programs for U.S. citizens, contact the U.S. Student Programs Division of IIE, 809 United Nations Plaza, New York, NY 10017 (tel. 212/984-5330). College students, teachers, university faculty, adults, and professionals looking for study opportunities abroad can visit the IIE Information Center at 809 United Nations Plaza (First Avenue at 45th Street).

If you're interested in participating in scientific discoveries in Europe, you might look into **Earthwatch,** P.O. Box 403N, Watertown, MA 02271 (tel. 617-/ 926-8200). It organizes scientific projects throughout the world, including several in Europe. Most expeditions are organized into two-week work teams, in which participants interested in a "hands-on study project" each contribute to the cost of that project. Examples of studies include surveys of birds, glaciers, architectural history, and marine ecology, as well as archeological excavations.

Earthwatch is a nonprofit organization to which university professors from around the world apply for paying volunteers for their research projects. Payments that volunteers make are considered tax-deductible contributions to a scientific project. Only 7% of the volunteers are students. A work project with Earthwatch offers a "chance to pursue for a brief while the path not taken." It has also been defined as a "scientific short-term Peace Corps." About a third of the 350 college professors who apply yearly are accepted on the basis of the research merits of their projects. Tasks include everything from weighing a wolf pup to measuring turtle eggs to researching genealogical records. The organization publishes a magazine six times a year, listing the dozens of unusual opportunities.

HEALTH AND FITNESS FACILITIES

A wide range of health and fitness facilities is offered at a number of hotels in England and Scotland, together with sporting amenities, such as golf, riding, and fishing at some places. Included in the hotels' offerings are saunas, solariums, gymnasiums, whirlpools, steam cabinets, massage facilities, slimming and beauty treatments, jogging tracks, squash and tennis courts, and indoor or outdoor heated swimming pools. Health farms and hydros are also available, with a selection of therapies and treatments, such as Swedish, gyratory, and underwater massages, deep-cleansing facials, hair removal by waxing, manicure, and pedicure.

For information on locations and offerings, write to the **British Tourist Authority,** 64 St. James's St., London SW1A 1NF, and ask for the brochure they publish on these facilities, or ask at any BTA office.

OPERA TOURS

On a cultural note, **Dailey-Thorp,** 315 W. 57th St., New York, NY 10019 (tel. 212/307-1555), is probably the best-regarded organizer of music and opera tours in America. Because of its "favored" relation with European box offices, it's often able to purchase blocks of otherwise unavailable tickets to such events as the Salzburg Festival, the Vienna, Milan, Paris, and London operas, or the Bayreuth Festival in Germany. Tours range from 7 to 21 days, including first-class or deluxe accommodations and meals in top-rated European restaurants. Dailey-Thorp is also known for its breakthrough visits to operas in Eastern Europe and regional operas of Italy.

A TRAVEL COMPANION

A recent American census showed that 77 million Americans more than 15 years of age are single. However, the travel industry is far better geared for double occupancy of hotel rooms. One company that has made heroic efforts to match single travelers with like-minded companions is headed by Jens Jurgen, who charges between $29 and $66 for a six-month listing in his well-publicized records. New applicants desiring a travel companion fill out a form stating their preferences and needs. They then receive a mini-listing of potential traveling partners. Companions of the same or opposite sex can be requested. Because of the large number of listings, success is often a reality.

For an application and more information, get in touch with Jens Jurgen, **Travel Companion,** P.O. Box P-833, Amityville, NY 11701 (tel. 516/454-0880).

5. The ABCs of Britain

The aim of this "grab bag" section—dealing with the minutiae of your stay—is to make your adjustment to the British way of life easier. It is maddening to have your trip marred by an incident that could have been avoided had you been tipped off earlier. To prevent this from happening, I'll try to anticipate the addresses, data, and information that might come in handy on all manner of occasions.

For more specific information on two particular areas, refer to "Practical Facts" under the Orientation section on London, Chapter III, and on Edinburgh in Chapter XX.

BABYSITTERS: These are hard to find, and the safest way is to get your hotel to recommend someone—possibly a staff member. Expect to pay the cost of travel to and from your hotel by taxi. There are a number of organizations advertised in the Yellow Pages of the telephone directory that provide sitters, usually registered nurses and carefully checked mothers, as well as trained nannies.

CIGARETTES: Most U.S. brands are available in major towns. *Warning:* Smoking is banned at an increasing number of places. Make sure you enter a "smoker" on the train or Underground, and only smoke on the upper decks of buses or in the smoking area of single-deckers, theaters, and other public places. Some restaurants restrict smoking, as do many bed-and-breakfast houses.

CLIMATE: British temperatures can range from 30° to 110° Fahrenheit. The British Isles, however, have a temperate climate with no real extremes, and even in summer evenings are cool. No Britisher will ever really advise you about the weather—it is far too uncertain. If you come here from a hot area, bring some warm clothes. If you're from cooler climes, you should be all right.

CRIME: Whenever you're traveling in an unfamiliar city or country, stay alert. Be aware of your immediate surroundings. Wear a moneybelt and don't sling your camera or purse over your shoulder; wear the strap diagonally across your body. Always lock your car and protect your valuables. Stay in well-lit areas and out of questionable neighborhoods. This will minimize the possibility of becoming a victim of crime. Every society has its criminals. It's your responsibility to be aware and alert even in the most heavily touristed areas.

CURRENCY: At the time of writing this book, the **pound (£)** was worth $1.75. Each pound breaks down into 100 **pence (p)**. There are now £1 coins as well as banknotes, plus coins of 20p, 10p, 2p, and 1p.

CUSTOMS: Visitors from overseas may bring in 400 cigarettes and one quart of liquor. If you come from the European Economic Community (EEC, or Common Market) area, you are allowed to bring in 300 cigarettes and one quart of liquor, provided you bought them and paid tax on them in that EEC country. If you have obtained your allowance on a ship or plane, then you may import only 200 cigarettes and one liter of liquor. There is no limit on money, film, or other items for your own use, except that all drugs other than medical supplies are illegal. Obviously, commercial goods such as video films and nonpersonal items will require payment of a bond and will take a number of hours to clear Customs. Do not try to import live birds or animals. You may be subject to heavy fines if you try to sneak one through, and the pet will be destroyed.

When you return home, you may take $400 worth of merchandise duty free if you have been outside the U.S. for 48 hours or more. A flat 10% duty is charged on your next $1,000 worth of purchases. Keep your receipts to prove the value of various items. On gifts, the duty-free limit is $50.

DENTIST: Outside London, ask the nearest sympathetic local resident—perhaps your hotelier—for information.

DOCTORS: Hotels have their own lists of local practitioners for whom you'll have to pay. Outside London, dial 100 and ask the operator for the local police, who will give you the name, address, and telephone number of a doctor in your area. Emergency treatment is free, but if you visit a doctor at his or her surgery (office) or if he or she makes a "house call" to your hotel, you will have to pay. It's wise to take out adequate medical/accident insurance coverage before you leave home.

DOCUMENTS FOR ENTRY: U.S. citizens, Canadians, Australians, New Zealanders, and South Africans all fall under the same category for entry into the United Kingdom. A passport is definitely required, but no visa is necessary. Immigration officers prefer to see a passport with two months' remaining validity. Much depends on the criteria and observations of Immigration officers. The one checking you through will want to be satisfied that you have the means to return to your original destination (usually a round-trip ticket) and visible means of support while you're in Britain. If you are planning to fly from, say, the U.S. to the U.K. and then on to a country that requires a visa (India, for example), it's wise to secure the Indian visa before your arrival in Britain. Even the amount of time spent in the British Isles depends for holiday-makers on the Immigration officer.

DRUGSTORES: In Britain, they are called chemist shops. Every police station in the country has a list of emergency chemists. Dial "0" (zero) and ask the operator for the local police, who will give you information as to a druggist you can reach.

ELECTRICAL APPLIANCES: The current is 240 volts AC, 50 cycles (Hz). Buy a transformer and an adapter before leaving home, as they are not readily available in Britain. A good adapter will convert your plug to almost any other sort of plug. If it's just a question of an electric razor, most hotel rooms have special sockets that can be changed from 240V to 110V at the flick of a switch. These are not suitable, however, for hairdryers and some other electrical appliances.

EMBASSY AND HIGH COMMISSION: For passport or other problems, you can visit the **U.S. Embassy,** 24 Grosvenor Square, London W1A 1AE (tel. 01/499-9000). The **Canadian High Commission** is at MacDonald House, 1 Grosvenor Square, London W1X 0AB (tel. 01/629-9492). The entrance for visitors is around the corner at 38 Grosvenor St. Tube: Bond Street.

EMERGENCY: For police, fire, or ambulance, dial 999. Give your name and address, plus the telephone number, and state the nature of the emergency. Misuse of the 999 service will result in a heavy fine. Cardiac arrest, yes. Sprained ankle, no. Accident injury, yes. Dented fender, no.

ETIQUETTE: Be normal, be quiet. The British do not like hearing other people's conversations. In pubs you are not expected to buy a round of drinks unless someone has bought you a drink. Don't talk politics or religion in pubs.

FILM: All types are available, especially in large cities. Processing takes about 24 hours although many places, particularly in London, will do it almost while you wait. There are few restrictions on the use of your camera, except where notices are posted, as in churches, theaters, and certain museums. If in doubt, ask.

HAIRDRESSING: Ask at your hotel. It may even have its own salon. You should tip the hairwasher 50p (90¢) and the stylist £1.25 ($2.25) or more if you have a tint or permanent. Hairdressing services are available in most department stores. For men, barbershops are to be found at the main railway stations in London.

HITCHHIKING: It is not illegal and is normally safe and practical. However, it is illegal for pedestrians to be on motorways. The cleaner and tidier you look, the better your chances of getting a ride. Have a board with your destination written on it to hold up for drivers to see.

HOLIDAYS AND FESTIVALS: Christmas Day, Boxing Day (December 26), New Year's Day, Good Friday, Easter Monday, May Day, and spring and summer bank holidays (the last Monday in May and August respectively) are observed. Scotland also takes January 2 as a holiday but does not recognize the summer bank holiday, taking the first Monday in August instead of the last for a holiday. Scotland does not observe Easter Monday as a bank holiday.

LAUNDRY AND DRY CLEANING: Most places take two days to complete the job and most hotels require the same length of time. London and most provincial towns have launderettes where you can wash and dry your own clothes, but there are no facilities for ironing. Many launderettes also have dry-cleaning machines. Otherwise, there are establishments that will do dry-cleaning for you with one-day service. The **Association of British Laundry Cleaning and Rental Services,** 7 Churchill Court, 58 Station Rd., North Harrow, Middlesex HA2 7SA, will give you a list if you can't find a facility close to you. For information about dry cleaners, phone 01/863-8658, and about launderers, 01/863-9178.

LIBRARIES: Every town has a public library, and as a visitor you can use the reference sections. The borrowing of volumes, however, is restricted to local citizens.

LIQUOR LAWS: No alcohol is served to anyone under the age of 18. Children under 16 are not allowed in pubs except in special rooms. In 1988, laws that had been on the books since the Industrial Revolution were altered. About time, serious beer drinkers said. Before that time, British drinking laws were considered hopelessly antiquated, at least by continental standards. Today, there is confusion in the land. Opening hours in England are left to the discretion of the innkeeper, although he or she can't exceed certain prescribed limits. The law allows a pub to serve liquor or beer from 11 a.m. to 11 p.m. Monday to Saturday and noon to 2 p.m. and 7 to 10:30 p.m. on Sunday. Guests are expected to "drink up" and leave the premises within 20 minutes of the last order. Many publicans in the countryside of England have decided to retain some semblance of the older and more limited pub hours and so may be closed between 2:30 and 6 p.m. Monday to Saturday. Hours in Scotland are more "flexible" and have always been more enlightened and liberal than those in England. Hotel residents can usually purchase alcoholic drinks outside the regular pub hours.

LITERATURE: If you're really dedicated in your exploring, I suggest Churchill's *History of the English Speaking Peoples* (four volumes) and Trevelyan's *History of England*. These tomes will help you to understand a lot more about what you'll be seeing. Otherwise, just read this guidebook, and use a good map if you are touring. I recommend the Collins *Road Atlas of Britain,* which makes a good souvenir.

LOST PROPERTY: For help in finding items lost in London, see "Practical Facts," Chapter III. Wherever you are in England, report your loss to the nearest police station, which will help you if possible. For items lost on British Rail, go to the Euston Lost Property Office in London at Euston Station (tel. 01/922-6477).

For lost passports, credit cards, or money, report the loss and circumstances immediately to the nearest police station. For lost passports, you should then go directly to your embassy. The address will be in the telephone book (and see "Embassy and High Commission," above). For lost credit cards, report to the appropriate organization; the same holds true for lost traveler's checks.

NEWSPAPERS: *The Times* is the top, then the *Telegraph,* the *Daily Mail,* and the *Guardian,* but all papers carry the latest news. Others have some news but rely on gimmicks to sell. The *International Herald Tribune,* published in Paris, and an international edition of *USA Today* are available daily.

OFFICE HOURS: Business hours are 9 a.m. to 5 p.m. Monday to Friday. The lunch break lasts an hour, but most offices stay open all day.

PETS: See "Customs." It is illegal to bring in pets, except with veterinary documents. Most are subject to six months in quarantine. Hotels have their own rules, but usually dogs are not allowed in restaurants or public rooms, and often not in bedrooms.

POLICE: The best source of help and advice in emergencies is the police. Stop a "bobby" in the street, or dial 999 if the matter is serious. If the local force cannot help, they will know the address of the person who can. Losses, theft, and other criminal matters should be reported to the police immediately.

POSTAL SERVICE: Letters and parcels to be called for may, as a rule, be addressed to you at any post office except a town sub-office. The words "To Be Called For" or "Poste Restante" must appear in the address. When claiming your mail, always carry some sort of identification. Letters generally take seven to ten days to arrive from the U.S. Post Restante service is provided solely for the convenience of travelers, and it may not be used in the same town for more than three months. It can be redirected, upon request, for a one-month period, unless you specify a longer time, not to exceed three months, on the application form you will be asked to fill out. Post offices and sub-post offices are centrally located and open from 9 a.m. to 5:30 p.m. Monday to Friday, 9:30 a.m. to noon on Saturday; closed Sunday.

RADIO AND TELEVISION: There are 24-hour radio channels operating throughout the United Kingdom, with mostly pop music and chat shows during the night. TV starts around 6 a.m. with breakfast TV and educational programs. Lighter entertainment begins around 4 or 5 p.m., after the children's programs, and continues until around midnight. There are now four television channels—two commercial and two BBC without commercials.

RELIGIOUS SERVICES: Times of services are posted outside the various places of worship. Almost every creed is catered to in London and other large cities, but in the smaller towns and villages you are likely to find only Anglican (Episcopalian), Roman Catholic, Baptist, and Nonconformist forms of worship. Scotland is mainly a Protestant country, its Church of Scotland being the leading faith.

REST ROOMS: These are usually found at signs saying "Public Toilets." Expect to put 5p (10¢) in the slot to enter a stall if you're a woman. Men usually go free. Hotel facilities can be used, but they discourage nonresidents. Garages (filling stations) also have facilities for the use of customers only, and the key is often kept by the cash register. There's no need to tip except in hotels where there is an attendant.

SENIOR DISCOUNTS: These are only available to holders of a British Pension book.

SHOE REPAIRS: Many of the large department stores in Britain have "Shoe Bars" where repairs are done while you wait.

STORE HOURS: In general, stores are open from 9 a.m. to 5:30 p.m. Monday to Saturday. In country towns, there is usually an early-closing day when the shops shut down at 1 p.m. The day varies from town to town.

TAXES: As part of an energy-saving program, the British government has added a special 25% tax on gasoline (petrol). There is no local sales tax in cities and towns, but 15% Value Added Tax (VAT) is added to all hotel and restaurant bills. VAT is also included in the cost of many of the items you purchase to take home with you.

At shops that participate in the Retail Export Scheme, it is possible to get a refund sent to you at home for the amount of the VAT tax on your purchases. Ask the salesperson for a Retail Export Scheme form (Form VAT 407) and a stamped, pre-addressed envelope to return it in. Save the VAT form along with your sales receipt to show at Customs. You may also have to show the actual purchases to Customs officials at airports or other ports of departure. After the form has been stamped by Customs, mail it back to the shop in the envelope provided.

Here are three organizing tips to help you through the Customs procedures: Keep your VAT forms with your passport as Customs is often located near passport control; pack your purchases in a carry-on bag so you will have them handy after you've checked your other luggage; and allow yourself enough time at your departure point to find a mailbox.

TELEGRAMS: Depending on your message's destination, you can send a telegram, a telemessage, or a mailgram. Any of these methods can be arranged by dialing 190, 193, or 100 from any phone in Britain. Costs for these messages can be charged to any private or business phone or paid through your hotel switchboard. Less conveniently, the cost can be paid at once by dropping coins in most pay phones (a phone company employee will give you the costs). A telemessage sent within the U.K. costs £5 ($8.75) for up to 50 words, including the address. After that, a block of 50 additional words costs another £2.50 ($4.40), plus VAT. A telemessage or telegram sent to the U.S. requires a first-time flat fee of £2.50 ($4.40), plus 38p (65¢) for each word, including the address. Most visitors find that a mailgram (delivered the next day if received before 10 p.m.) to be less expensive. It costs a flat £8 ($14) for up to 50 words. You'll probably be advised at the post office that it's less expensive simply to call your party if you keep your message brief enough.

TELEPHONES: British TeleCom is carrying out a massive improvement program to its public pay-phone service. During the transitional period, you could encounter four types of pay phones. The old-style (gray) pay phone is being phased out, but there are a lot still in use. You will need 10p (20¢) coins to operate such phones, but you should not use this type for overseas calls. Its replacement is a blue-and-silver pushbutton model that accepts coins of any denomination. The other two types of phone require cards instead of coins to operate. The Cardphone uses distinctive green cards especially designed for it. They are available in five values—£1 ($1.75), £2 ($3.50), £4 ($7), £10 ($17.50), and £20 ($35)—and they are reusable until the total value has expired. Cards can be purchased from news agencies and post offices. Finally, the Creditcall pay phone operates on credit cards—Access, VISA, American Express, and Diners—and is most common at airports and large railway stations.

Phone numbers in Britain outside of the major cities consist of an exchange name (like the U.S. area code) plus telephone number. In order to dial the number, you will need the code of the exchange being called. Information sheets on call box walls give the codes in most instances. If your code is not there, however, call the operator by dialing 100. In major cities, phone numbers consist of the exchange code and number (seven digits in all). These seven digits are all you need to dial if you are calling from within the same city. If you are calling from elsewhere, you will need to prefix them with the dialing code for the city. Again, you will find these codes on the call box information sheets. If you do not have the telephone number of the person you want to call, dial 192 or 142 for either London or elsewhere in the country. Give the operator the name of the town and then the person's name and address.

A guide to telephone costs: A call at noon from London to Reading, 40 miles away, lasting three minutes costs 80p ($1.40). This charge is more than halved between 6 p.m. and 8 a.m. and on Saturday and Sunday. A local call costs 20p (35¢) for three minutes at all times. The charges quoted are for pay phones. You will have to pay far more if you use a hotel operator at any time.

TELEX AND FAX: Telexes are very common in offices and hotels. If your hotel has a telex, they will send it for you. Fax is less common, but can be found, for instance, at large post offices. Refer to the yellow pages for telex bureaux or dial 100 and ask for Freefone Intelpost for information on fax.

TIME: England and Scotland are based on Greenwich Mean Time, five hours ahead of the U.S. East Coast, with British Summer Time (GMT + 1 hour) during the summer, roughly from the end of March to the end of October.

TIPPING: Many establishments add a service charge. If the service has been good, it's usual to add an additional 5% to that. If no service is added to the bill, give 10% for poor service, 15% or more for good. If the service is bad, make it known and don't tip. Taxi drivers expect about 20%.

TOURIST INFORMATION: The British Tourist Authority has a **British Travel Centre** at Rex House, 4-12 Lower Regent St., London S.W.1 (tel. 01/730-3400). This center offers a full information service on all parts of Britain, a British Rail ticket office, a travel agency, a theater ticket agency, hotel booking service, a bookshop, and a souvenir shop, all under one roof. Hours are 9 a.m. to 6:30 p.m. Monday to Friday and 10 a.m. to 4 p.m. on Saturday and Sunday, with extended hours on Saturday in June, July, August, and September. Telephone information is available Monday to Saturday.

Detailed information on various areas of the British Isles is available in London from: the **Wales Tourist Board,** 34 Piccadilly, S.W.1 (tel. 01/409-0969); the **Scottish Tourist Board,** 19 Cockspur St., S.W.1 (tel. 01/930-8661); and the **Northern Ireland Tourist Board,** 11 Berkeley St., W.1 (tel. 01/493-0601).

For various sources of information on London itself, see Section 1 of Chapter III.

WEATHER: For London, telephone 01/246-8091; for Devon and Cornwall, 0392/8091; for the Midlands, 021/8091; for the Scottish Highlands, 0224/8091; and for Edinburgh and Lothian, 031/8091.

WEIGHTS AND MEASURES: In England and Scotland you will run into the metric system, so become familiar with the equivalents, or follow the formula instructions if you feel the need to convert.

Length
1 millimeter = 0.04 inches (*or* less than ¹⁄₁₆ in)
1 centimeter = 0.39 inches (*or* just under ½ in)
1 meter   = 1.09 yards (*or* about 39 inches)
1 kilometer = 0.62 mile (*or* about ⅔ mile)

To convert kilometers to miles, take the number of kilometers and multiply by .62 (for example, 25 km × .62 = 15.5 mi).

To convert miles to kilometers, take the number of miles and multiply by 1.61 (for example, 50 mi × 1.61 = 80.5 km).

Capacity
1 liter = 33.92 ounces
       = 1.06 quarts
       = 0.26 gallons

To convert liters to gallons, take the number of liters and multiply by .26 (for example, 50 liters × .26 = 13 gallons).

To convert gallons to liters, take the number of gallons and multiply by 3.79 (for example, 10 gal × 3.79 = 37.9 l).

Weight
1 gram   = 0.04 ounces (*or* about a paperclip's weight)
1 kilogram = 2.2 pounds

To convert kilograms to pounds, take the number of kilos and multiply by 2.2 (for example, 75 kg × 2.2 = 165 pounds).

To convert pounds to kilograms, take the number of pounds and multiply by .45 (for example, 90 lb × .45 = 40.5 kg).

Area
1 hectare (100m²) = 2.47 acres

To convert hectares to acres, take the number of hectares and multiply by 2.47 (for example, 20 ha × 2.47 = 49.4 acres).

To convert acres to hectares, take the number of acres and multiply by .41 (for example, 40 acres × .41 = 16.4 hectares).

Temperature

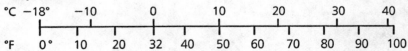

To convert degrees C to degrees F, multiply degrees C by 9, divide by 5, then add 32 (for example 9/5 × 20°C + 32 = 68°F).

To convert degrees F to degrees C, subtract 32 from degrees F, then multiply by 5, and divide by 9 (for example, 85°F − 32 × 5/9 = 29°C).

PART ONE

ENGLAND

ENGLAND

SCOTLAND

N

Solway Firth

Isle of Man

Irish Sea

Anglesey

M 6

Leeds

M 62

Liverpool

Manchester

Sheffield

M 1

Derby

Nottingham

M 6

Leicester

Birmingham

WALES

Northampton

Cambridge

Norwich

Ipswich

ENGLAND

Oxford

M 40

M 1

Cardiff

M 4

Reading

London

Bristol Channel

Bristol

M 20

M 5

M 3

Strait of Dover

Southampton

Brighton

Isle of Wight

Plymouth

English Channel

FRANCE

Channel Islands

0   Miles   50
0 Kilometers 80

INTRODUCING ENGLAND

1. THE ENGLISH
2. THE CULTURE
3. FOOD AND DRINK

Why go to England? This question inspires a variety of answers, many brought out by the greatest writers of the world who have placed this little country at or near the top of the list of places to savor and explore in a lifetime. I must speak of my own deeply felt enthusiasm. I have ancestral roots in England—as do many readers of this book—but my affection and interest are also colored by other "roots." Many of the world's greatest Anglophiles have no ancestral link to England at all, but they are inspired and ensnared by its cultural, historical, and spiritual heritage, which has shaped civilizations of the world.

The people of this little bit of land, relying largely on their wits—perhaps their most important resource—have played a dynamic role in world history, shaping the character, customs, and even the major language of many countries besides their own.

To travel in England is like experiencing a living, illustrated history book, so clear is the trail of former glory. You can ponder over the ancient mystery of Stonehenge, relive the days of Roman Britain when you walk through an excavated villa, and hear the linguistic influence of languages such as Celtic, Norse, and Norman in words and place names. Assimilation rather than genocide has developed the race of the English today.

The very smallness of the landmass of England makes it possible to see a lot in a comparatively short time. You can stand in the inner courtyard of the Tower of London where Lady Jane Grey was beheaded, walk through Westminster Abbey on the stone grave markers of such figures as Disraeli, Newton, Darwin, Chaucer, and Kipling, or visit the homes where Samuel Johnson, Charles Dickens, and Emily Brontë lived and worked and where Shakespeare wooed Anne Hathaway. Courts of law, great colleges of the world at Oxford and Cambridge, and monuments all are here to illustrate the vastness and richness of the English heritage. Innumerable museums and libraries hold treasures of the British Isles and far-flung places and long-buried civilizations. Here are early Bibles, the Magna Carta, and countless priceless documents of musical, literary, and political greats.

Unlike travel in the huge area of the United States, a trip through England takes you to fishing hamlets, villages, along country lanes, to cathedral cities, moving into an entirely different region in the short space of minutes or an hour, in this land of widely varying geography and topography. Move from the mountainous Lake District, through the rolling hills of the Cotswolds, past the Holland-like canals of Lincoln and the fens of the Norfolk Broads, to moody Lorna Doone country in North Devon with rugged hills and coastline.

From imposing and romantic moated castles to splendid country manor houses, half-timbered Tudor dwellings, thatch-roofed cottages with gardens riotous with bright flowers, and humble cottages—the habitations in England reflect the lifestyle of the people of history and today. The architecture of England is a reflection of the inner spirit, shown in churches and cathedrals with soaring Gothic arches and stained-glass windows to be seen in nearly every city.

Whatever your major interest, you'll probably find an occasion for its pursuit in the English calendar of events. Attend one of the Bard's plays at Stratford-upon-Avon, go through the Midlands on a canal boat or a houseboat, or spend time at a West Country farm riding over hill and moor on horseback. Watch boat races at Henley-on-Thames or walk through the Yorkshire Dales. You can sample true English "fayre" at ancient pubs and inns, visit spectacular gardens at stately homes and parks, even swim in a hidden cove off Cornwall.

The theater of London is stimulating and refreshing, and there are concerts, festivals, country fairs, ballet, and opera at many places throughout the country, not just in the capital. Visitors are often fascinated with the English fascination with their sports—cricket, football (soccer and rugby), tennis, skating, sailing, hockey, or hiking.

Best of all is getting to know the English people, who are usually warm and gracious. Of course, just like everywhere else in the world, England has its share of cranks, but the average man or woman is a pleasure to know and a helpful host to better acquaint you with the country.

Certainly you won't be able to do everything and go everyplace in just one trip. You'll most definitely want to come back for a second visit—and then for a third, and more.

WHERE TO GO

It takes weeks to tour England thoroughly, and many readers do just that, either by car, train, or bus. However, others are much more rushed and will need to direct their limited sightseeing time carefully. London is targeted at the top of every first-time visitor's list. Even those on the most rushed of schedules generally fit in Windsor Castle, lying about an hour's train ride from central London. For many, that's it. Then they're off to Paris or other places on the continent.

However, those with more time will want to go to the south of England, the cradle of English history, centering their exploration around the cathedral city of Canterbury, some 65 miles southeast of London. It can be done on a rushed day trip. I'd suggest two nights there, however: one day for Canterbury; another day for exploring some of the historic homes of Kent, including Knole, a showplace of England, lying in the village of Sevenoaks, about 25 miles from central London; and Churchill's home, Chartwell, 1½ miles south of Westerham. Those with yet a third night to spend in the south can go to Rye, the old Cinque port near the English Channel, 65 miles south of London.

The second most popular jaunt is to Stratford-upon-Avon and the university city of Oxford. At minimum, this should take two nights. The first night can be spent at Oxford, 57 miles northwest of London, and the second night at Stratford-upon-Avon, 40 miles northwest from Oxford, a total distance of 92 miles from London. Those with one or two more nights to spend in Stratford-upon-Avon can use it as a base for day trips to Warwick Castle, Kenilworth Castle, Sulgrave Manor (ancestral home of George Washington), and Coventry Cathedral.

My favorite tour—and perhaps yours too—might be to the fabled West Country of England, taking in Winchester, Salisbury, the New Forest, and the old spa at

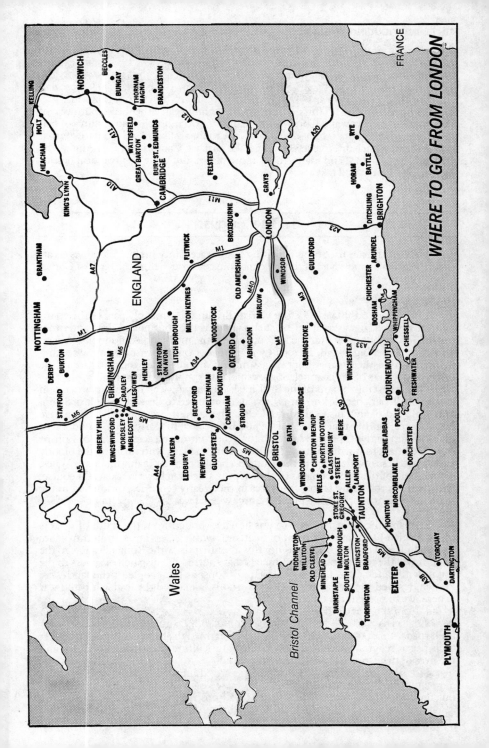

WHERE TO GO FROM LONDON

Bath. Bath is considered by many to be the most outstanding place to visit in the west of England. Your first night can be spent in Salisbury, which is a base for exploring the prehistoric ruins of Stonehenge on the Salisbury Plain. Salisbury is an 83-mile drive from London. From Salisbury, you can head north to Bath, that Georgian city on a bend of the River Avon, a distance of some 115 miles from London.

After that, those with three or four days remaining can either head southwest of Bath, taking in Devon and Cornwall, perhaps the two most charming shires of England, or can head north to the Cotswolds, the rolling hills and old wool towns that always seem to enchant. I've left out the Lake District, Cambridge, East Anglia, the cathedral city of York, and many, many more places. But there's a great deal here to take in. As I said, it will take weeks.

1. The English

The British Isles have been a melting pot of races since prehistoric times, as attested by artifacts and traces of settlements from centuries before the birth of Christ.

HISTORY

Until about 6,000 years before Christ, Britain was probably part of the continent of Europe. It was split off by such factors as the continental drift and other natural forces, but even after the split people on the mainland could look across to what was now a big island. Pressed by marauders from the east or simply seeking living room for their increasing tribes, some brave souls made their way across the often wild waters of the channel. Some came, too, simply seeking plunder.

The earliest inhabitants of the British Isles about which archeologists are certain are the small, dark people known as Iberians (connected to the early people of Spain, Portugal, and Sicily), also called pre-Celts. These are the people believed to have been the creators of Stonehenge before 500 B.C., when the early Celts, blond, often blue-eyed immigrants poured in from along the continental coastal areas of Europe from Denmark to northern Italy. The little, dark Iberians who survived the bloody assaults of these invaders fled to the Scottish Highlands and the mountains of Wales, where some of their descendants of almost pure stock can be seen today. Of course, there was interbreeding among the races in those early centuries, producing in the main the type of people living in the country when it was invaded by Julius Caesar in 54 B.C.

The land the Romans came to was heavily wooded from the south of what is today England to the north coast of Scotland, with treeless areas around marshes and on hills and moors. But it was not this asset that drew the Roman leaders to the land. It was the reports of precious metals that spurred the dispatch of scouts to the unknown island across the channel. The Britons, as the people of the land were known, resisted the onslaught of Roman troops but lacked the leadership and war experience to prevent the takeover. The Romans took all of the southern part of the island, from the Cheviot Hills in Scotland to the English Channel, and added it to the Roman Empire by A.D. 43. During almost four centuries of occupation, they built roads, villas, towns, walls, and fortresses, farmed the land, and introduced first their pagan religions and then Christianity. Agriculture and trade flourished, and the lives of the people were lastingly influenced.

After the withdrawal of Roman legions around A.D. 410, waves of Jutes, Angles, and Saxons flocked in, establishing themselves in small "kingdoms" throughout the formerly Roman colony. From the 8th through the 11th centuries, they came into conflict with Danish raiders for control of the land, now with one on top, then with another.

In 1066 William the Conqueror invaded from Normandy and defeated and slew the last Anglo-Saxon king, Harold, at the Battle of Hastings. The Norman rulers were on the throne from 1066 to 1154, when the first of the Plantagenets, Henry II (that "friend" of Thomas à Becket), was crowned. That line held power until 1399. A notable date here is 1215 when King John was forced by his nobles to sign the Magna Carta at Runnymede, guaranteeing certain rights and the rule of law, and leading eventually to the development of the foundations of the parliamentary system.

In 1399 the Lancastrians took the throne, their reign marked by defeat in the Hundred Years' War in which they tried to cement claims they had to lands in France. Opposing the Lancastrians at home and wanting the crown for themselves were the Yorkists. Dissension between these claimants led to the War of the Roses, the red rose representing Lancaster and the white rose York. By 1461 the House of York had seized power, but the war continued. It was during this time that the boy king, Edward V, and his younger brother were murdered in the Tower of London, a crime still laid by some at the door of their uncle, Richard III, who later became king.

Richard III was slain at the Battle of Bosworth Field in 1485, ending the War of the Roses and placing the first Tudor on the throne. That king, Henry VII, was followed by his son, Henry VIII, whose daughter, Elizabeth I, eventually succeeded to the crown. Henry VII curbed the powers of the barons, established reforms of the legal system, gave more importance to the landed gentry, and improved England's economic situation. Henry VIII established himself in history in disparate ways. He married six times, and he split with the Roman Catholic Church, establishing the Church of England. Of his wives, two were beheaded, two were set aside, one died in childbirth, and one survived him. The Dissolution of the Monasteries left an indelible mark on the nation, as the riches of the abbots and bishops poured into the coffers of Henry and his associates, and the rich property formerly owned by the church was placed mostly into lay ownership.

Under Elizabeth I, who managed to walk a risky line between Catholic and Protestant dissidents but held to the latter faith, England became a major naval power, defeating the Spanish Armada. The first colonies were founded in the New World, and a vigorous trade was established with the Orient and Europe. Also Scotland was united with England, and the son of Mary Queen of Scots, the queen whom Elizabeth had had beheaded, came to the throne as James I of England and James VI of Scotland.

Thus ended the Tudor dynasty, and the Stuarts came to power in the year 1603, holding it until Charles I was beheaded in 1649. During this era, the *Mayflower* sailed for the New World, and dissatisfaction with the established Church of England, as well as with what many saw as Papist leanings by the monarchs, created a time of great stress in England. Parliament and the Stuart kings came into conflict, resulting in a bloody Civil War between Parliamentarian troops led by Oliver Cromwell and Royalists who were on the side of King Charles. The Royalists lost the war, the king lost his head, and in 1649 the Puritan Commonwealth was established, with Cromwell as Lord Protector, a situation that lasted until 1660.

With the restoration of the monarchy in 1660, Charles II, a Stuart, came to the throne, but troubles still beset the people of the country. The Great Plague wiped out thousands of lives in 1665–1666, and the Great Fire destroyed large portions of London in 1666.

Then in 1688—after what was called the "Glorious Revolution," removing Catholic King James II from the throne and crowning in his place William of Orange and his wife, Mary, James's daughter—a Bill of Rights was signed by the monarchs, settling once and for all the question that had been at the very root of the Civil War: the king was king by will of Parliament, not by divine right from God.

The Hanoverian dynasty, which began its 110-year reign in 1727, had many ups and downs. Canada was won from the French, the British Indian Empire was firmly entrenched through the redoubtable Clive of India, the Boston Tea Party marked the start of the American Revolution, Captain Cook claimed Australia and New Zealand for England, and the British became embroiled in the Napoleonic Wars in France and Spain—a time of glory for two of the country's great leaders, Admiral Lord Horatio Nelson at Trafalgar, and the Duke of Wellington at Waterloo.

Perhaps the single most important thing in all this period, from the point of view of the common man, was the Industrial Revolution, which forever changed the lives of the laboring class and brought great wealth to people of the middle class.

The reign of Queen Victoria, which began in 1837, also saw great changes in her country. Trade unions were formed, a universal public school system was developed, industrialization and urbanization spread, and railroads were extended to almost every section of the British Isles. So impressed were they with the glories of the empire that Parliament declared Victoria empress, not just queen, recognizing the acquisition of large parts of Africa and Asia as subjects of the crown. When Edward VII succeeded to the throne in 1901, the country entered the 20th century with the advent of the telephone and the motorcar, which again changed everybody's lifestyle and thinking.

Edward's son, George V, ascended to the throne in 1910, and led the nation through World War I. During this conflict, he patriotically dropped his German titles and changed the name of the royal house to Windsor. His oldest son, Edward VIII, abdicated before his coronation (he became the Duke of Windsor in order to marry the American divorcée, Wallis Simpson), so George VI became king.

Then, in 1939, came World War II. The Blitz, the Dunkirk evacuation in 1941, and the successful D-Day operation that placed the Allies firmly on the road to defeat Hitler have all been kept alive through documentaries, movies, and memories of those who participated. Winston Churchill had his finest hour as prime minister in those perilous times.

After World War II, Labor came into power and the welfare state set up. At present, under Conservative Margaret Thatcher, England is undergoing a rethinking of those socialist measures.

Queen Elizabeth II came to the throne on the death of her father in 1952. Since then, Britain has joined the NATO alliance and the Common Market—and Big Ben still chimes the hours outside the Houses of Parliament.

GOVERNMENT

The United Kingdom of Great Britain and Northern Ireland (that's its name), comprises England, Wales, Scotland, and Northern Ireland. It is governed by a constitutional monarchy, the present head of state being Queen Elizabeth II. The head of government, however, is the prime minister, who is selected by the majority party in Parliament but is then requested by the queen to form a government, that is, to take charge and name cabinet members to head the various branches of that government.

Parliament is technically three separate entities: the sovereign, the House of Lords, and the House of Commons. The "government" consists of the prime minister and the cabinet members (who must be members of Parliament). The sovereign's function is chiefly ceremonial.

There are two main political parties, Conservative and Labour. The Conservatives, currently led by England's first woman prime minister, Margaret Thatcher, believe in free enterprise and freedom of the individual to make his or her own decisions, with some government support. Labour believes in state ownership and control, with the state providing maximum support for the individual. The Liberals and the Social Democrat party have joined in an uneasy alliance to form the Social Democratic and Liberal party, which is beginning to have some impact.

2. The Culture

The English are friendly people, happy to share their music, art, literature, and other cultural benefits with people who come from what was, after all, once a colonial possession of Great Britain (and Canada still is a member of the Commonwealth). With no language barrier—except for a dialect here and there—this is an opportunity for English speaking visitors to easily enjoy a great cultural experience.

LITERATURE

The most outstanding figure of all in England's literary tapestry is—who dare say me nay?—William Shakespeare (1564–1616). But if England had had no Shakespeare, that tapestry would still be a rich and glowing panoply of artists with words—oral, written, sung, in poetry, in prose, in drama. From the Old English epic poem, *Beowulf,* almost surely the result of centuries of verse recited through the ages by tribal bards, to the works of the post–World War II "angry young men," English literature is much too vast to approach in a limited space.

Old English poetry and historical prose (the *Anglo-Saxon Chronicle* of Alfred the Great and other works) yielded to the language called Middle English, in which the culture and tongue of the Normans enriched the speaking and writing of the old Anglo-Saxon language. Middle English was used by philosophers, historians, and romance writers from the 13th and 14th centuries. Greatest of the writers of this period was Geoffrey Chaucer, whose *Canterbury Tales* are masterfully told. The literary highlight of the 15th century was *Le Morte d'Arthur,* Sir Thomas Malory's free-handed story about the legend of King Arthur and his court. Ballads were also popular storytelling devices in that century, a sort of continuation of the bardic epic tradition.

During the Tudor (and Elizabethan) era, stars in the literary sky were Sir Thomas More (*Utopia*), Edmund Spenser (*The Faerie Queen*), and Christopher Marlowe (*The Tragical History of Dr. Faustus*). In this era the sonnet form was adopted from an Italian verse model, attracting as users a number of poets, such as Sir Philip Sidney and the greatest of them all, Shakespeare (remember "Shall I compare thee to a summer's day"?).

The coming to the throne of the Stuarts initiated the Jacobean period, which saw the best work of "rare Ben Jonson," author of satirical comedies and leader of the poets who met at the Mermaid Tavern in London, and the writings of John Donne (" . . . never send to know for whom the bell tolls . . ."). The translation of the Bible, known as the King James Version, was undertaken at this time under the auspices of James I, and assumed its immortal place in literature.

By the mid-17th century, writers, like all English people, began to be divided in allegiance between the king and Parliament. The Cavalier poets, of whom Robert Herrick heads the list, wrote lyrical verse and backed the king. The literary giant of the mid-17th century was John Milton, a pro-Parliamentarian and author of *Paradise Lost,* considered even in his lifetime to be one of the country's top geniuses. John Bunyan, a Baptist lay-preacher caught up in the Puritan cause, was sent to prison after the restoration of the monarchy where he wrote *Pilgrim's Progress,* whose powerful imagery transcended theological differences. After Charles II returned to the throne, theaters closed by Cromwell were reopened, and literature took on a lighter, more lively tone, reflected in the plays of Sheridan and the diary of Samuel Pepys.

Throughout the 18th century the literary world of England was crowded with the output of geniuses and near-geniuses from the rising middle class, much of whose work was aimed at social reform. Among these were Defoe (*Robinson Crusoe* and *Moll Flanders*), Alexander Pope (*An Essay on Man*), Fielding (*Tom Jones*), and a host of essayists and novelists. Most memorable in this period, however, is Samuel

Johnson, whose *Dictionary of the English Language* made him the premier lexicographer and man of letters. His association with James Boswell from Scotland resulted in Johnson's becoming a major figure in literary annals, albeit through Boswell's writings. In Johnson's circle of close friends was another notable literary figure of the time, Oliver Goldsmith (*She Stoops to Conquer* and *The Vicar of Wakefield*).

To enter into a dissertation on the early 19th-century literary scene in England and to try to expound on the stars in that galaxy in limited space would be to bog down utterly. So I'll just mention several names known to everyone who has ever studied literature in school: Thomas Gray, William Blake, William Wordsworth, Samuel Taylor Coleridge, Byron, Keats, Shelley, Jane Austen, and Charles Lamb—but there are oh! so many more. As you travel through the country, you will see birthplaces, familiar haunts, habitations, and burial places of many such writers.

Now to the years that challenge a student of literature—the mid- and late-1800s. These encompass the Victorian Age when storytellers developed emotional themes and reflected the stresses of their times, and poets created both romantic and humorous works. In this letters-rich age, readers devoured the works of Charles Dickens, Thackeray, the Brontë sisters, Matthew Arnold, Alfred Lord Tennyson, the Brownings, Lewis Carroll, George Eliot, George Meredith, Thomas Hardy, Swinburne, and Oscar Wilde, with a little heavier reading from John Ruskin thrown in. The great middle class had learned to read, printing was flourishing, and the union of these forces produced a literary thrust that took the country at a gallop into the 20th century.

Straddling the turn of the century but usually considered literary figures of modern times—from the early 1900s, it's true—are such notables as Kipling, H. G. Wells, Galsworthy, Maugham, Walter de la Mare, and Sir Arthur Conan Doyle. Writers of the 20th century include Robert Graves, Stephen Spender, W. H. Auden, Virginia Woolf, D. H. Lawrence, Aldous Huxley, Kingsley Amis, Graham Greene, George Orwell, E. M. Forster, Antonia Fraser, Ted Hughes, William Golding, Muriel Spark, and—not to be forgotten—Winston Churchill.

In the category of "good reads" are some of the best of mystery and suspense novels to be found. From these, you can learn about life in England from cottages to castles, in the cities and in the remote country, in the past and in the present, and a lot about the police and the crime scene from even before the Bow Street Runners to today's New Scotland Yard. Ellis Peters makes you feel at home at Shrewsbury in the 12th century, Dorothy Sayers places you in the fen country in the 1920s, and Agatha Christie brings to life village atmosphere in St. Mary Mead. There are many other writers of this ilk whose stories, whether you're a mystery fan or not, can enrich your visit to England by giving you a personal "word tour" of all the country.

I could go on and on and on—and I still might well leave out your favorite English writer. In fact, I'm sure someone will ask, "But what about Jonathan Swift? George Bernard Shaw? Sir Walter Scott? Robert Burns? Robert Louis Stevenson? Joseph Conrad? Dylan Thomas? Doris Lessing?" My only answer is that these novelists and poets are usually included and, indeed, they should be as they have certainly made their mark in English literature. I have tried to keep this list within manageable limits, because—no question about it—the British Isles are rich in literary greats, and I've only reminded you of *some* of them.

MUSIC

From the time the English monks' choirs surpassed those of Germany and France in singing the Gregorian chant (brought to this country in 597 by St. Augustine of Canterbury, Pope Gregory's missionary), and were judged second only to the choirs of Rome, music has been heard throughout England. Polyphonic music developed after the simple chant, and sacred vocal music was early accompanied by the organ. The first organ at Winchester was installed in the 10th century. One of the earliest written compositions was the polyphonic piece (a round), *Summer is icumen in,* with six parts.

Instruments commonly used in the Middle Ages, besides the organ found only in churches, were the fiddle, the lute, and the rebeck, used in court circles for the entertainment of royalty and hangers-on. Kings had musicians at court through the Plantagenets and into the time of the Tudors, with Henry VIII in particular making himself known as a composer. He wrote sonnets for his lady loves and set them to music, the best known being *Greensleeves*. The British Museum contains some 34 manuscripts of Henry's compositions. So flourishing was music in England in the 16th century that Erasmus of Rotterdam reported, after one of his visits: "They are so much occupied with music here that even the monks don't do anything else."

Music among the common people of the time may have been less polished but no less enthusiastic, as ditties and rounds were composed and heard in taverns and fields, the richness of the tunes compensating for the frequent vulgarity of the words. Some of the songs Shakespeare had his characters sing attest to the coarseness of the lyrics.

During the Tudor dynasty English cathedral music came into full flower. During these years, too, the forerunners of the opera and operetta came into being as spectacles called masques. These combined instrumental and vocal music, dancing, satire, recitations, and elaborate scenic effects—the beginning of stage design.

Musicians were persecuted in the 1600s under the Commonwealth, but they came back into glory with the restoration of the Stuart monarchy: Henry Purcell wrote the first English opera, *Dido and Aeneas*, in 1689. From this point on, a veritable galaxy of musical talent was inspired and appreciated in London, and thence in all England. Italian opera became the rage, even as Sir John Gay satirized such productions in *The Beggars' Opera* in 1728, Handel, who became an English subject, composed many operas and oratorios here, including the *Messiah,* and other musicians followed (sometimes haltingly) in his train.

All of this doubtless led to the uniquely English operettas of Gilbert and Sullivan in the 19th century.

Many great names in the 20th century music world are English: Sir Edward Elgar, Ralph Vaughan Williams, Sir William Walton, Benjamin Britten, to name just a few.

Paul McCartney and John Lennon of the Beatles began what has been called "the British invasion"—British rock music's invasion of America. Since the 1960s, English rock musicians have often dominated the American music charts. Individual vocalists such as Phil Collins, David Bowie, and Sting, and guitarists such as Eric Clapton have been leading forces in popular music. But the biggest musical influence from England has been the rock bands: The Rolling Stones, The Who, Pink Floyd, The Sex Pistols, and XTC. British rock's influence on Western popular music and culture has been and is still tremendous.

ART

From the first carved and jewel-bedecked baubles, utensils, and even weapons of prehistoric man, the craze for ornamentation continued and grew. Intricately wrought crosses, religious statuary, and illuminated manuscripts led the way to stained-glass windows, ecclesiastical paintings, and other art forms connected first with the abbeys and cathedrals that came into being over the centuries and throughout the country. Soon these were followed by decorative glorification and expansion of the homes of royal and noble personages, and then by the gentry and whoever could afford to have their persons and structures beautified.

Ornate tombs with sculptured effigies of the dead marked the resting places of the nobility and the princes of the church in the Middle Ages, and the cathedrals became art galleries of awesome beauty. Medieval painting consisted mostly of illumination of manuscripts by monks who took as models work done in European monasteries. Other art by the 13th century was in the embroidering of tapestries, metalwork, and carving, with panel painting, stained glass, and frescoes among the mediums of expression.

Art, and even beauty, were considered the work of the devil during the religious upheavals of the 16th and 17th centuries, but when peace of a sort returned, sculpture came into vogue again, and painting reached an enviable grandeur. The name of Grinling Gibbons looms large for his baroque carvings in the late 17th and early 18th centuries, but it was not really until the 20th century that sculpture became a serious competitor to painting in England. Names such as Henry Moore, Barbara Hepworth, Sir Jacob Epstein, and Kenneth Armitage are only a few of the greats connected with English sculpture of today.

By the time interest in art revived after the Reformation, painting in oils was being done on the continent, and from this arose the wealth of fine pictures, from miniatures to vast murals, that you can see today. This art reached its heights in England, and your visits to the many museums and galleries will make you conversant with the masters.

At first, perhaps reflecting the consistent picturing of people in ecclesiastical art, portraiture was *the* format in this country. Everybody who was anybody was depicted—alone, with family, with pets, whatever. The early leader in this field was Hans Holbein the Younger, a Swiss-born artist who had moved to England and who became painter to Henry VIII. Among the leading painters of the Tudor and Stuart periods, two who were outstanding were Van Dyck and Lely, neither of them English-born.

Native English painters came into their own by the 18th century, during the same era that landscape and animal painting and social satire began to vie with portraiture as recognized art forms. A roll call of the greats of that time resounds even today: Constable, Gainsborough, Hogarth, Reynolds, Romney, Turner, and many more. It was in that era that the Royal Academy of Arts was formed (1768), which you can visit in Piccadilly. (The academy is considered old hat by many artists and art critics today.)

Painters of the 19th and 20th centuries whose supremacy is recognized include Sir Edward Burne-Jones, Dante Gabriel Rossetti, W. Holman Hunt, Ben Nicholson, Augustus John, Francis Bacon, Graham Sutherland, to name a few. Some of these, it is true, are felt to be too cloyingly romantic or too iconoclastically avant-garde for all tastes, but each has earned a place in art history.

Whatever your preferences may be—old masters or 20th-century artists—you can find something to please you (and probably something to complain about) in the hundreds of galleries large and small throughout England.

ARCHITECTURE

From ancient man-made ceremonial sites such as Stonehenge, through the great minsters and cathedrals of the Middle Ages on up to the modern places of worship at Coventry and Liverpool, art has ever sought to bring a functional shape to the site where a higher power is invoked, as well as to places of human habitation.

Architecture in England has moved through many periods; examples can be seen today in preserved, restored, and reconstructed form. Separate architectural periods came after untitled eons in which humankind made do with caves, huts of wattle and daub, and whatever was at hand to work with. These designated architectural periods embrace the Anglo-Saxon, 6th to mid-11th centuries; the Norman, 11th and 12th centuries; Gothic (actually including four phases: Early English, Decorated, Perpendicular, and Tudor), 12th to 16th centuries; Renaissance (including Elizabethan, Jacobean, Palladian, and Byzantine), mid-16th to early 18th centuries; Georgian, early 18th to 19th; Regency, early 19th; Victorian, mid-19th to 20th; and the architecture of the present century, which has taken many forms.

Many examples exist of work from all these periods since the Norman, so that the interested visitor has little difficulty in finding them among the sights of England. Many of the names of the architects responsible for these lasting monuments to humanity's genius have not survived, but enough are known to make a formidable roster of greatness. From the monk, Gandulf, a stonemason credited with construction of the White Tower, the list reads through Inigo Jones, Sir Christopher Wren, Nicholas Hawksmoor, Sir John Vanbrugh, James Gibbs, John Nash, Sir Edwin Lutyens, and countless others. (Robert Adam, whose name is synonymous with handsome interiors and some exterior work, was a Scotsman, but much of his work can be seen in England.)

Not a builder of houses but a landscape architect was Lancelot ("Capability") Brown, whose work also lives on, framing the beauty of many palaces and manor houses.

The rich legacy of a millennium of builders is an integral part of the visitor's enjoyment of England.

---

3. Food and Drink

Understanding British traditional dishes will help you enjoy your visit even more. The following comments will explain a few; other "surprises" you must seek out for yourself. Many good old-fashioned dishes are available in restaurants, wine bars, and pubs—sometimes called inns or taverns, a name going back to the Middle Ages.

The most common pub meal is based on the food a farm worker took with him to work, a **ploughman's lunch.** Originally a good chunk of local cheese, a hunk of homemade crusty white or brown bread, some butter, and a pickled onion or two, it was washed down with ale. You will now find such variations as pâté and chutney replacing the onions and cheese. **Cheese** is still, however, the most common ingredient.

English **cheese** comes in many regional variations, the best known being Cheddar, a good, solid, mature cheese, as is Cheshire. Another is the semismooth-textured Caerphilly from a beautiful part of Wales, and also Stilton, a softer tangy cheese, more popular with a glass of port.

Dishes with names so perplexing you have no hint of their ingredients are found on the little Tea Shoppe menu or in pubs and the like. Perhaps the most popular is **shepherd's pie,** a deep dish of chopped cooked lamb mixed with onions and seasoning and covered with a layer of mashed potatoes and served hot. Another version is **cottage pie,** which is minced beef covered with potatoes and also served hot.

Traveling in the southeast part of England around Colchester, you will find a most prized British dish, the **oyster** for which, it is suggested, Julius Caesar really invaded Britain in 54 B.C.

As you move about England, you will come across dishes that were developed to fulfill a particular need. The **Cornish pasty** was made from the remains of the family's Sunday lunch in a Cornish fishing village: minced meat, chopped potato, carrot, onion, and seasoning mixed together and put into a pastry envelope, ready to be taken to sea by the fisherman on Monday for his lunch. In Grasmere you can buy **gingerbread cookies** made to a recipe more than 125 years old, coming in the same alphabet shapes used to teach children to read in the 19th century. A **"flitting dumpling,"** northern in origin, is made of dates, walnuts, and syrup mixed with other ingredients into a pudding. It was cut into slices and could feed a family when "flitting" from one area to another. It is said that "hurry pudding" or **hasty pudding** in some areas was invented by those avoiding the bailiff. This dish from Newcastle uses up stale bread (some dried fruit and milk were added before it was put into the oven). In the northeast you'll come across **Lancashire hotpot,** a stew of mutton, potatoes, kidneys, and onions (sometimes carrots). This concoction was originally put into a deep dish and set on the edge of the stove to cook slowly while the family went to work in a local mill.

Among the most known and traditional of English dishes is **roast beef and Yorkshire pudding.** The pudding is made with a flour base and cooked under the joint, allowing the fat from the meat to drop onto it. The beef could easily be a large "sirloin" (rolled loin) which, so the story goes, was named by King James I (not Henry VIII as some claim) when he was a guest at Hoghton Tower, Lancashire. "Arise, Sir Loin," he cried, as he knighted the joint with his dagger.

Meat left over would be eaten the next day in **"bubble and squeak"** when added to chopped cabbage and potatoes and fried together. Another dish that makes use of a batter similar to Yorkshire pudding is **"toad-in-the-hole,"** in which sausages are cooked in batter.

On the west coast you'll find a delicacy not to be missed, the Morecambe Bay shrimp. Of course, the whole coast of Britain provides a feast of **fish dishes**, the champions being cod, haddock, herring, plaice, and the aristocrat of flat fish, Dover sole. Cod and haddock are the most popular fish used in the making of that British tradition, **"fish and chips"** (chips, of course, are fried potatoes or french fries). The true Briton covers this dish with salt and vinegar. In the past the wrapping was newspaper, but now the demands of hygiene have removed the added—some say, indispensable—taste of newsprint from the dish.

Kipper, a smoked herring, is a popular breakfast dish. The finest are from the Isle of Man, Whitby, or Loch Fyne in Scotland. Herrings are split open and placed over oak chips and smoked slowly to produce a nice pale-brown smoked fish. The British eat large breakfasts, or at least many of them do. "Ham and eggs" is said to have originated in Britain. **Kedgeree** is another popular dish (haddock, egg, and rice). Some B&Bs still serve **black pudding** with breakfast items (it's made of pig's blood, oatmeal, barley, or groats, and suet—sounding rather repulsive, but loved by many).

High tea, almost unknown in the south, is common in the north of England and in Scotland. It is a meal that is a mix of hot and cold, giving the worker on his return home a combination of tea and supper. In the north the word *dinner* describes the midday meal (lunch), while in the south it means the evening meal. Supper by tradition is a meal taken late at night, usually after the theater.

Incidentally, real English **mustard** is simply the finely ground seed mixed with water, nothing else.

The East End of London has quite a few interesting old dishes, among them tripe and onions. Dr. Johnson's favorite tavern, the Cheshire Cheese on Fleet Street, still offers a **beefsteak, kidney, mushroom, and game pudding** in a suet case in winter and a pastry case in summer. The East Ender will be seen on Sunday at the Jellied Eel's stall by Petticoat Lane, eating eel or perhaps cockles, mussels, whelks, and winkles, all small shellfish eaten with a touch of vinegar. The eel-pie-and-mash shop can still be found in London. The name, **eel pie,** however, is misleading, because it is really a minced-beef pie topped with flaky pastry and served with mashed potatoes and accompanied by a portion of jellied eel.

It is a misconception to believe that "everything" stops for tea. People in Britain drink an average of four cups of **tea** a day, mainly at work. The real delight is to visit the little country tea shops where you can enjoy a pot of tea, some toasted tea cake (currant bun), or a crumpet (sometimes confused with the rarely found muffin), bread and butter, or sandwiches, and good homemade cakes, all enjoyed while listening to the conversation at the next table.

A word about the **wine** of the country: Britain does not produce much real wine. It does produce some very pleasant white wine on the medium-sweet side and quite fruity in taste. The real "wines" are cider and beer, both of which go well with the traditional dishes mentioned earlier.

Beer is served in all pubs. Draft beer is traditionally served at cellar temperature; the British like to taste their beer so they prefer it on the warm side of cold. Most bottled beer, however, is similar to light lager beers and is served cold. Draft beer comes in several different tastes, the most common being called "bitter," which is light in color and taste, not really bitter. A half pint is the equivalent in strength to a single measure of scotch. Others are mild ale, which is full flavored, and brown ale, which is dark and flavorsome. Stout is a strong, rich dark beer, often mixed with champagne to make "black velvet." The most famous stout is called Guinness, and it is strong tasting and very dark with a good white head (froth). **Cider** made from apples and fermented can be stronger than expected.

However, after saying all the above, I can still assure you that the food and drink (including French and Italian wines) served in most restaurants will be international in scope, with some traditional British dishes. The reputation that Britain had for years for its soggy cabbage and tasteless dishes is no longer deserved. If you pick and choose carefully, and use this guide to help you seek out the finer dining rooms, you can enjoy some of the finest food in Europe while touring the British Isles.

SETTLING INTO LONDON

London is a hybrid, a gathering place for people from the far corners of a once-great Empire. People from country villages and provincial towns visit London in the mood of going abroad. But British and foreign visitors alike come to admire its magnificent synthesis of historic city and contemporary life.

The true Londoner, usually from the East End, is called a Cockney, the name for a person born within the sound of the Bow Bells, the chimes of a church in Cheapside. But the city is also the home of the well-bred English lady who has had to sell her family estate of 400 years and take meager lodgings in Earl's Court; of the expatriate Hollywood actress living in elegance in a Georgian town house; of the islander from Jamaica who comes seeking a new life and ends up collecting fares on one of London's red double-decker buses; of the young playwright from Liverpool whose art reflects the outlook of the working class.

Cosmopolitan or not, Europe's largest city is still like a great wheel, with Piccadilly Circus at the hub and dozens of communities branching out from it. Since London is such a conglomeration of sections—each having its own life (hotels, restaurants, pubs)—the first-time visitor may be intimidated until he gets the hang of it. In this chapter, I'll concentrate on the so-called West End, although nobody has been able to come up with a satisfactory explanation as to what that entails. For the most part, a visitor will live and eat in the West End, except when he or she ventures into the old and historic part of London known as "The City," or goes on a tour to the Tower of London, or seeks lodgings in the remote villages such as Hampstead Heath.

1. Orientation

London is a city that has never quite made up its mind about its own size. The "City of London" proper is merely one square mile of (very expensive) real estate around the Bank of England. All the gargantuan rest is made up of separate cities, towns, boroughs, and corporations, called Westminster, Chelsea, Hampstead, Kensington, Camden Town, and so forth, each with its own mayor and administration and ready to fight for its independent status at the drop of an ordinance. These were once separate villages entirely, but through the centuries, the growth of Greater London has filled in the fields and woods that once separated them. Together, they add up to a mammoth metropolis—once the largest city on the globe, now dropped to 16th in a United Nations survey of population.

The millions of people loosely governed by the Greater London Council live spread out over 609 square miles. Luckily, only a minute fraction of this territory need concern us. The rest is simply suburbs, stretching endlessly to the horizon, red-roofed and bristling with TV antennas. But the heart, the brick and mortar core of this giant, is perhaps the most fascinating area on earth. For about a century, one quarter of the world was ruled from there, and with every step you take, you'll come across some sign of the tremendous influence this city has exerted over our thoughts and past actions—and still wields today.

HISTORY

London is a very old city, even by European standards. The Roman conquerors of Britain founded Londinium in A.D. 43 by settling and fortifying two small hills on the north bank of the River Thames and linking them via a military road network with the rest of the island.

More than a thousand years later, another conqueror turned the city into his capital. This was William II, Duke of Normandy, who defeated the last Saxon ruler of England, Harold Godwin, in 1066. There isn't much remaining of the Roman period, but William the Conqueror left his imprint on London for all time to come. For a start, he completed and had himself crowned in Westminster Abbey. Every British monarch since has been crowned there, right up to the present Queen Elizabeth II. William also built the White Tower, which today forms part of the Tower of London, and did even more to transform London (or rather, Westminster) into a royal capital. He and his nobles superimposed their Norman French on the country's original Anglo-Saxon language and thus concocted English as we speak it today. Both the richness and the maddening illogicality of our tongue are direct results of that transplant.

The Normans weren't exactly gentle rulers, but the nation they created did pretty well. No one, for instance, has ever successfully invaded Britain since William's time—unless you count North American visitors and others from all nations.

Royal but Democratic

London is a mass of contradictions, some of them dating far back in her history. On the one hand, she's decidedly a royal city, studded with palaces, court gardens, coats-of-arms, and other royal paraphernalia. Yet she is also the home of mankind's second-oldest parliamentary assembly (Iceland has the oldest). When handsome and rash King Charles I tried to defy its representatives, he found himself swept off his throne and into the hands of the headsman (1649) long before the French got around to dealing likewise with their anointed monarch.

The huge gray building that houses the "Mother of Parliaments," with its famous clock, Big Ben, is more truly symbolic of London than is Buckingham Palace. It was there that Prime Minister William Pitt intoned, "You cannot make peace with dictators—you have to defeat them," at a time when England stood alone against the might of Napoleon. It was there, too, that Sir Winston Churchill repeated these sentiments in even better phrases when England—alone again—stood up against Hitler. It was also in Parliament that "His Majesty's Loyal Opposition" stood up to give a rousing cheer for Gen. George Washington's army, which had just whipped His Majesty's Hessian mercenaries—whom the English detested every ounce as much as did the American colonists.

Nevertheless, London itself was largely shaped by the monarchs who ruled her —imposingly by the tough Tudors, beautifully by the wicked Georges, clumsily by the worthy Victoria.

Bouncing Back from Disasters

Much of London is also the result of disasters, both accidental and premeditated. The first was the Great Fire of 1666, which swept away most of the old wooden Tudor houses and resulted in a new city built of brick. The cause of the fire remains forever unknown, but considering the fire hazards of those tightly packed, timbered dwellings, the remarkable thing is that the town didn't burn down annually. As it was, the blaze gutted three-quarters of London—about 13,300 homes, churches, and public buildings. But it also gave England's greatest architect, Christopher Wren, the chance to design St. Paul's Cathedral as it stands today, as well as 51 other superb churches, plus the magnificent Royal Hospitals in Chelsea and Greenwich.

The blitz Hitler unleashed on the city during 1940–1941 also had one beneficial result. Along with wiping out beautiful structures, the rain of incendiary bombs demolished vast patches of the pestilential slum areas around Whitechapel in the East End. The region—made famous equally by Charles Dickens and Jack the Ripper—had been London's festering sore, boasting possibly the worst housing conditions in the Western world. With slum clearance courtesy of the Luftwaffe, the London County Council rebuilt most of the area into rather drab but infinitely superior apartment blocks.

There was something else the blitz gave London: a world image as the embattled fortress of freedom, caught unforgettably by the wartime news photo showing the white dome of St. Paul's silhouetted against the black smoke of a dozen simultaneous fires.

The postwar building boom may have made London a little less "quaint," but it also made her a very much healthier, happier place to live in, and it provided the overture of her present phase, which is that of a lively, cosmopolitan city.

A BIT OF GEOGRAPHY

There is, fortunately, an immense difference between the sprawling vastness of Greater London and the pocket-size chunk that might be called "Tourist Country." For a start, practically all of the latter is north of the River Thames, but make no mistake—this is still a hefty portion of land to cover and a really thorough exploration of it would take a couple of years. But it has the advantage of being flat and eminently walkable, besides boasting one of the best transport systems ever devised.

The local but not the geographical center of our "Tourist Country" is **Trafalgar Square,** which we'll therefore take as our orientation point. The huge, thronged, fountain-splashed square was named for the battle in which Nelson destroyed the combined French and Spanish fleets and lost his own life. His statue tops the towering pillar in the center, and local residents maintain that the reason he's been up there all these years is that nobody has told him the lions at the base are made of stone. If you stand in the square facing the imposing **National Gallery,** you're looking northwest. That is the direction of **Piccadilly Circus,** which is the real core of tourist London, as well as the maze of streets that make up **Soho.** Farther north runs **Oxford Street,** London's gift to moderately priced shopping, and still farther northwest lies **Regent's Park** with its zoo.

At your back—that is, south—runs **Whitehall,** which houses or skirts nearly every British government building, from the Ministry of Defence to the official residence of the prime minister on **Downing Street.** In the same direction, a bit farther south, stand the **Houses of Parliament** and **Westminster Abbey.**

Flowing southwest from Trafalgar Square is the table-smooth **Mall,** flanked by magnificent parks and mansions and leading to **Buckingham Palace,** residence of the queen. Farther in the same direction lie **Belgravia** and **Knightsbridge,** the city's poshest residential areas, and south of them **Chelsea,** with its chic flavor, plus **Kings Road,** the boutique-filled shopping drag.

Due west from where you're standing stretches the superb and distinctly high-priced shopping area bordered by **Regent Street** and **Piccadilly** (the street, not the Circus). Farther west lie the equally elegant shops and even more elegant homes of **Mayfair.** Then come **Park Lane** and on the other side **Hyde Park,** the biggest park in London and one of the largest in the world.

Running north from Trafalgar Square is **Charing Cross Road,** past **Leicester Square** and intersecting with **Shaftesbury Avenue.** This is London's theaterland, boasting an astonishing number of live shows as well as first-run movie houses. A bit farther along, Charing Cross Road turns into a browser's paradise, lined with bookshops selling both new and secondhand books. Finally, it funnels into **St. Giles Circus.** This is where you enter **Bloomsbury,** site of the University of London, the awesome **British Museum,** and erstwhile stamping ground of the famed "Bloomsbury Group," led by Virginia Woolf. Northeast of your position lies **Covent Garden,** known for its **Royal Opera House.**

Follow **the Strand** eastward from Trafalgar Square, and you'll come into **Fleet Street.** Beginning in the 19th century, this corner of London became the most concentrated newspaper district in the world. But over the decades, the newspapers folded or moved away. The last newspaper edition was published on Fleet Street in 1989. At the end of Fleet Street lies **Ludgate Circus**—and only there do you enter the actual City of London. This was the original walled settlement and is today what the locals mean when they refer to **"The City."** Its focal point and shrine is the Bank of England on **Threadneedle Street** with the Stock Exchange next door and the Royal Exchange across the road.

"The City" is unique in that it retains its own separate police force (distinguished by a crest on their helmets) and its own Lord Mayor. Its 677 acres are an ant heap of jammed cars and rushing clerks during the week and totally deserted on Sunday, because hardly a soul lives within its boundaries. Its streets are winding, narrow, and fairly devoid of charm. But it has more bankers and stockbrokers per square inch than any other place on the globe. In the midst of all the hustle rises **St. Paul's Cathedral,** a monument to beauty and tranquility. At the far eastern fringe of the City looms the **Tower of London,** shrouded in legend, blood, and history. It is permanently besieged by battalions of visitors.

Designed to Confuse

I'd like to tell you that London's thoroughfares follow a recognizable pattern in which, with a little intelligence, even a stranger can find his or her way around. Unfortunately, they don't and you can't. London's streets follow no pattern whatsoever, and both their naming and numbering seem to have been perpetrated by a bunch of xenophobes with an equal grudge against postal carriers and foreigners.

Be warned that the use of logic and common sense will get you nowhere. Don't think, for instance, that Southampton Row is anywhere near Southampton Street and that either of these places has any connection with Southampton Road. This is only a mild example. London is checkered with innumerable squares, mews, closes, and terraces, which jut into or cross or overlap or interrupt whatever street you're trying to follow, usually without the slightest warning. You may be walking along ruler-straight Albany Street and suddenly find that you are on Colosseum Terrace, according to the signs (with a different numbering system). Just keep on walking and after a couple of blocks you're right back on Albany Street (and the original house numbers), without having encountered the faintest reason for the sudden change in labels.

House numbers run in odds or evens, clockwise or counterclockwise as the wind blows—that is, when they exist at all, and frequently they don't. Every so often you'll come upon a square that is called a square on the south side, a road on the north, a park on the east, and possibly a something-or-other close on the west side. Your only chance is to consult a map or ask your way along. Most of the time, you'll probably end up doing both.

But there are a couple of consoling factors. One is the legibility of the street signs. The other is the extraordinary helpfulness of the locals, who sometimes pass you from guide to guide like a bucket in a fire chain.

TRANSPORTATION IN GREATER LONDON

If you know the ropes, transportation within London can be unusually easy and inexpensive, because London enjoys one of the best subway and bus systems in the world. The **Underground,** as the subways are called, and the buses are operated by **London Regional Transport,** which has **Travel Information Centres** in the Underground stations at King's Cross, Oxford Circus, and Piccadilly Circus, and also in the British Rail stations at Euston and Victoria and each of the terminals at Heathrow Airport.

Travelcards, for use on bus, Underground, and British Rail services are available for any combination of adjacent zones from the transport service. The cost of a Travelcard good for 7 days in the Central Zone is £6.40 ($11.20) for adults, £2.50 ($4.40) for children. For two zones, the charge is £6.80 ($11.90) for adults, £2.50 ($4.40) for children; for three zones, £11.20 ($19.60) for adults, £2.80 ($4.90) for children; for four zones, £14 ($24.50) for adults, £5 ($8.75) for children; and for all zones, £17.70 ($31) for adults, £5 ($8.75) for children.

To purchase a Travelcard, you must present a **Photocard.** For persons 16 years old or older, the Photocard is easy to get. Just take a passport-type picture of yourself when you buy your first Travelcard, and the Photocard will be issued free of charge. Travelcards are not issued at child rates unless supported by a Photocard. Child-rate Photocards are available at post offices in the London area, at bus garages, or at British Rail stations, as well as the Travel Information Centres listed above. In addition to a passport-type photograph, proof of age is required (for example, a passport or a birth certificate). Older children (14 or 15) are charged adult fares on *all* services unless in possession of a child-rate cards.

For shorter stays in London, you may want to consider the **One-Day Off-Peak Travelcard.** This ticket can be used on most bus, Underground, and British Rail services throughout Greater London after 9:30 a.m. Monday to Friday and at any time Saturday, Sunday, and bank holidays. The ticket is available from Underground ticket offices, bus garages, Travel Information Centres, and some news agencies. It costs £2.30 ($4.05) for adults, 80p ($1.40) for children 14 or 15.

These fares, although valid at the time of writing, will very likely change during the lifetime of this edition and are therefore presented only for general background information so that you will know the range of travel options open to you.

The London Transport Information Centres provide information on a wide range of facilities and places of interest in addition to data on bus and Underground services. They take reservations for London Transport's guided tours (see "Taking the Tours," Chapter V, Section 2), and have free Underground and bus maps and other information leaflets. A 24-hour telephone information service is available (tel. 222-1234).

In addition to the information obtainable from any of the Travel Information Centres, London Regional Transport has a Travel Information Service at 55 Broadway, London SW1H 0BD.

Airports

London has two main airports, **Heathrow** and **Gatwick.** It takes 35 to 45 minutes by Underground train from Heathrow Central to central London, costing £1.70 ($3) for adults and 60p ($1.05) for children. From Heathrow, you can also take an airbus, which gets you into central London in about an hour. The cost is £4 ($7) for adults, £2 ($3.50) for children.

Gatwick Airport, where many charter and some scheduled flights come in, lies 30 miles south of London. Trains leave from there every 15 minutes 6:30 a.m. to midnight, and every hour after midnight. Also, there is an express bus from Gatwick to Victoria Station every half hour from 6:30 a.m. to 8 p.m. and every hour from 8 to 11 p.m., Flightline bus 777; it costs £4 ($7) per person.

The Underground, airbus, and train are, of course, far cheaper means of transport than a private taxi. For example, a taxi from Heathrow into central London is likely to cost more than £20 ($35).

A bus service connects the two airports, leaving every hour for the 70-minute trip. In addition, there is also an expensive helicopter service that takes only 15 minutes between airports.

For **flight information,** telephone Heathrow at 759-4321 or Gatwick at 0293/31299.

London's newest airport is called **London City Airport** (tel. 474-5555), lying about six miles from "The City." It's reached by the District Line of the Underground (get off at Plaistow). Once leaving the underground, you can take a taxi the rest of the way to the airport. The airport specializes in STOL (short takeoff and landing), and commuter-like flights whisk you to Amsterdam, Brussels, or Paris. Leading airlines using this airport include Euro City Express (linked with Sabena) and Brymon Airways (with ties to Air France). The airport lies in the old Docklands along the Thames east of London.

The Underground

Londoners usually refer to the Underground as the "tube." Stations are identified by a distinctive sign, a red circle with blue crossbar, and the words "London Underground." If you ask for a "subway," you risk ending up in a tunnel for pedestrians running beneath the road. Destinations are listed on ticket machines, or you can buy your tickets from a booking office if you don't have the correct change. Maps showing the Underground network are displayed in every station, on each platform, and in Underground train cars. You can transfer as many times as you like so long as you stay in the Underground and don't leave the network on ground level.

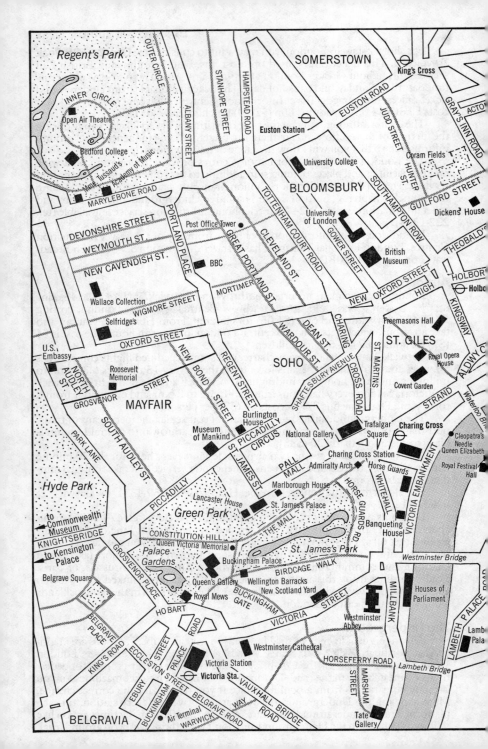

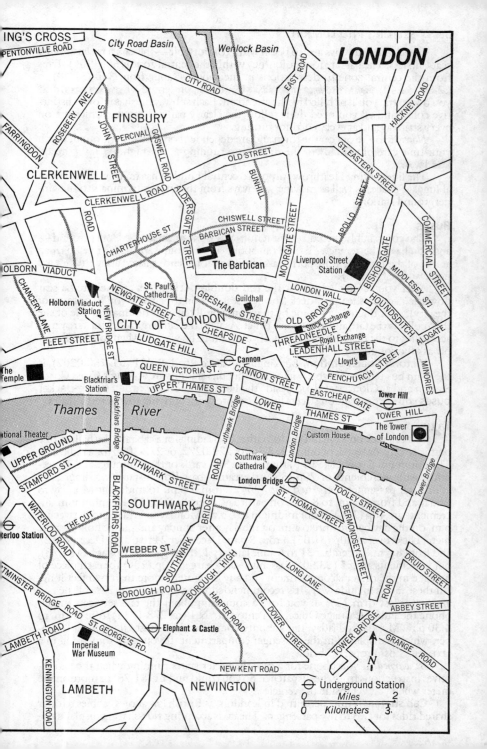

The electric subways are, to begin with, comfortable—the cars have cushioned seats, no less. The flat fare for one journey within the central zone is 50p (90¢). Trips from the central zone to destinations in the suburbs range from 80p ($1.40) to £2.50 ($4.40). *Be sure to keep your ticket;* it must be presented when you get off. If you owe extra, you'll be billed by the attendant. Each subway line has its own distinctive color, and all you need do is follow the clearly painted arrows, which are on every stairway and at every corridor turning.

Note: If you're out on the town and are dependent on the Underground, watch your time carefully. Many of the trains stop running at midnight (11:30 p.m. on Sunday).

The line serving Heathrow Airport to central London has trains with additional luggage space, as well as moving walkways from the airport terminals to the Underground station.

Buses

The comparably priced bus system is almost as good as the Underground—and you have a better view. To find out about current routes, pick up a free bus map at one of the London Transport Travel Information Centres listed above. (They are not available by mail.)

After you've queued up for the **red double-decker bus** and selected a seat downstairs or on the upper deck (the best seats are on top, where you'll see more of the city), a conductor will come by to whom you'll tell your destination. He or she then collects the fare and gives you a ticket. As with the Underground, the fare varies according to the distance you travel. If you want to be warned when to get off, simply ask the conductor.

Victoria Coach Station, Buckingham Palace Road, S.W.1 (tel. 750-0202), is the main bus terminal. Tube: Victoria. Other bus stations are at King's Cross Coach Station and at Gloucester Road beside the Forum Hotel. The **green single-decker buses** you see on London streets link the center with outlying towns and villages.

Taxis

You can pick up a cab in London either by heading for a cab rank, by hailing one on the streets, or by telephoning 253-5000, 272-0272, or 272-3030 for a radio cab. The minimum fare is £1 ($1.75) for the first 924 yards or three minutes and 18 seconds, with increments of 20p (35¢) thereafter, based on distance or time. Each additional passenger is charged 20p (35¢). From 8 p.m. to midnight Monday to Friday and from 6 a.m. to 8 p.m. on Saturday, after the 80p ($1.40) minimum, increments are 40p (70¢). From midnight to 6 a.m. Monday to Friday and between 8 p.m. on the day before until 6 a.m. on the day after Sunday and public holidays, the meter clicks over at 60p ($1.05). From 8 p.m. December 24 to 6 a.m. December 27 and from 8 p.m. December 31 to 6 a.m. January 1, the flag still drops at £1 ($1.75), but increments are £2 ($3.50). Passengers are charged 10p (20¢) for each piece of luggage in the driver's compartment and any other item more than two feet long. All these tariffs include VAT. It's recommended that you tip about 20% of the fare and never less than 15%. If you have a complaint about the taxi service you get, phone the Public Carriage Office, 15 Penton St., N.1 (tel 278-1744) from 9 a.m. to 4:30 p.m. Monday to Friday. If it's about a complaint, you must know the cab number, which is displayed in the passenger compartment. If you leave something in a taxi, see "Lost Property" below.

Be warned: If you phone for a cab, the meter starts running when the taxi receives instructions from the dispatcher. So you could find £1 ($1.75) or more on the meter when you get inside the vehicle.

Cab sharing is now permitted in London, as British law allows cabbies to offer shared rides for two to five passengers. The taxis accepting ride-sharing display a no-

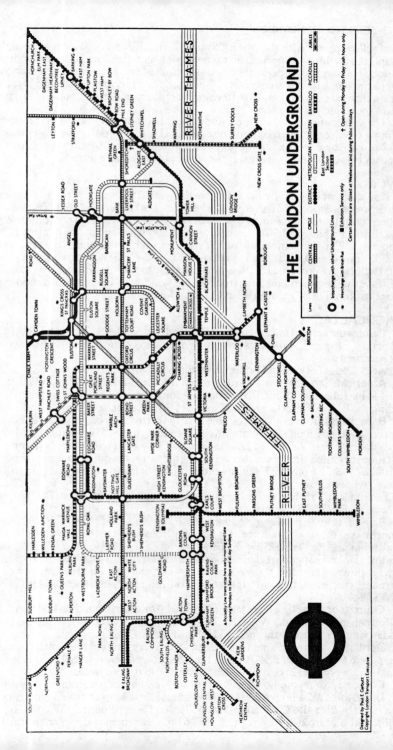

THE LONDON UNDERGROUND

Designed by Paul E. Garbutt
Copyright London Transport Executive

tice of yellow plastic with the words "Shared Taxi." These shared rides are mainly available at Heathrow Airport, main train stations, and the some 200 taxi stands in London. The savings per person is as follows: Each of two riders sharing is charged 65% of the fare a lone passenger would be charged. Three persons pay 55% each, four are charged 45% each, and five (the seating capacity of all new London cabs) pay 40% of the single-passenger fare.

The journey between Heathrow and central London costs £20 ($35) or more. If you are traveling between central London and Gatwick Airport, you must negotiate a fare with the driver before you get in the cab, as the meter does not apply. This is necessary because Gatwick is outside the Metropolitan Police District.

Bicycles

You can rent bicycles by the day or by the week from a number of businesses, such as **Savile's Stores,** 97 Battersea Rise, Battersea, S.W.11 (tel. 228-4279), which has been renting bikes for some 75 years. Stan Savile's father started the company in 1912. Prices are £30 ($52.50) per week, which is about half the charge of many of its competitors. This firm is not only one of the cheapest but also one of the most reliable bike companies I have found. A deposit of £25 ($43.75) is required with a passport. Padlocks are provided free. It is open Monday to Saturday from 9 a.m. to 5:30 p.m. Take the Northern Line tube from central London to Clapham Common and change to bus 35 or 37, getting off at Clapham Junction.

PRACTICAL FACTS

Besides the general information on England and Scotland given in "The ABCs of Britain," Chapter I, some facts pertaining mainly to London may help make your visit here better.

Area Code: For calling London from out of town, dial 01 first.

American Express: It has its main office at 6 Haymarket, London, S.W.1 (tel. 930-4411). Tube: Piccadilly Circus. There are some ten other London locations, including the British Travel Centre, 4 Regent St., S.W.1, open seven days a week.

Babysitters: Your hotel may be able to help you to find a babysitter in London. Another good possibility is **Childminders,** 9 Paddington St., W.1 (tel. 935-2049). Tube: Baker Street. Visitors to London can pay a £4 ($7) temporary booking fee each time they hire a sitter from the agency, or, if they prefer, the annual membership fee is £25 ($43.75), plus VAT. The membership fee or booking charge is paid to the agency, while pay for the job goes to the employee. Evening sitters cost £2.20 ($3.85) to £2.95 ($5.15) per hour, depending on the day of the week. The daytime charge is £3.50 ($6.15) per hour.

Banks: Hours generally are 9:30 a.m. to 3:30 p.m. Monday to Friday, although some banks in the suburbs are open on Saturday from 9:30 a.m. to 12:30 p.m. There are also Bureaux de Change, which charge high fees for cashing traveler's checks or personal (United Kingdom) checks and for changing foreign currency into pounds sterling. Bureaux are often open seven days a week, at least 12 hours or more a day. There are branches of the main banks at London's airports. You'll always get the best rates at banks.

Church services: The interdenominational **American Church in London** is at 79 Tottenham Court Rd., W.1 (tel. 580-2791). Two services are usually held on Sunday, one at 9:45 a.m., another at 11:45 a.m. Tube: Goodge Street.

Dentist: If you need emergency dental treatment, to find the dentist nearest you, phone 677-6363 or 584-1008 in London. You will be directed to whichever dental surgery (office) in or near your area can attend to your needs.

Doctors: Ask at your hotel, which probably has a list of practitioners available.

Drugstore: A 24-hour drugstore (chemist, in Britain) operation is maintained in London by **Bliss the Chemist,** 50-56 Willesden Lane, Kilburn, N.W.6 (tel. 624-8000), and 5 Marble Arch, W.1 (tel. 723-6116). Emergency drugs are normally available at most hospitals, but you'll be examined to see that the medication you request is really necessary.

Emergencies: To call for police, fire, or ambulance, dial 999.

Eyeglasses: If your glasses get lost or broken, try **Imperial Optical of Selfridges,** a branch of the well-known Canadian optical company, at Selfridges Department Store, 400 Oxford St., W.1 (tel. 629-1234, ext. 3889). An eye exam costs from £20 ($35), and the least expensive pair of eyeglasses with an uncomplicated prescription costs an additional £56 ($98). Multifocal lenses sometimes take two to three working days to complete, but simple prescriptions may be filled in two to three hours. You will pay more for designer frames. It's always wise to take a copy of your lens prescription with you when you travel. Tube: Bond Street.

Hospitals: Among hospitals offering emergency care in London 24 hours a day are the **Royal Free Hospital,** Pond Street, N.W.3 (tel. 794-0500; tube: Belsize Park), and the **University College Hospital,** Gower Street, W.C.1 (tel. 387-9300; tube: Euston Square or Warren Street). The first treatment is free under the National Health Service. Many other London hospitals also have Accident and Emergency Departments, including St. Mary's Hospital, Paddington; London Hospital, Whitechapel; King's College Hospital, Denmark Hill; Charing Cross Hospital; and St. Bartholomew's Hospital. Only emergency treatment is free.

Lost property: For finding items you may have left on the tube or in a taxi in London, report the loss to the police first, and they will advise you where to apply for its return. Taxi drivers are required to hand property left in their vehicles to the nearest police station. For items lost on the Underground or on a bus, London Transport's Lost Property Office will try to assist personal callers only at their office at the Baker Underground station. For information on items lost on British Rail trains, lost passports, and lost credit cards, see "Lost Property" in "The ABCs of Britain" section of Chapter I.

If you leave something in a taxi, you can notify the Public Carriage Office's Lost Property Office, 15 Penton St., N.1 (tel. 833-0996). While taxi drivers are required to check their cabs after dropping off each fare and to turn in any lost property at the nearest police station, it can take up to seven days for items to reach the Public Carriage Office. If you know which police station you were nearest when you lost your property, you could call them. However, if you put a note as to where you are staying in your wallet, briefcase, luggage, and coat pocket, should these items be lost you may hear of their whereabouts by the time you return to your lodgings.

Luggage shipping: This can relieve you of a lot of worry about how to get all your souvenirs home. **London Baggage Company Ltd.,** 262 Vauxhall Bridge Rd., S.W.1 (tel. 828-2400), offers worldwide service for shipping unaccompanied luggage, at rates usually below the normal excess baggage charges of airlines. They collect your extras from your London hotel and deal with all documentation and shipping. Prices vary according to weight and destination, but the charge for picking up your parcels, doing the paperwork, and delivering everything to the airport is about £18 ($31.50), plus insurance. Tube: Pimlico Station.

Medical service: Medical Express, Chapel Place, W.1 (tel. 499-1991), just off Oxford Street, is almost equidistant between the Oxford Circus and Bond Street tube stations. It's a medical center where you can have a consultation and full medical/clinical examination, such as a blood-pressure check, an ECG, and X-rays. The cost is £45 ($78.75) for a general consultation. For £20 ($35), you can get the British equivalent of your U.S. prescription here, if they decide that it's bona fide. The center is open Monday to Friday from 9 a.m. to 7 p.m. and on Saturday from 10 a.m. to 5 p.m. Full specialist services available by appointment include E.G., gynecology, ENT, dermatology, and cardiology, among others, at consultation fees of £50 ($87.50).

Post offices: Hours for the **Chief Post Office** in London, King Edward Street, EC1A 1AA, near St. Paul's Cathedral, are from 8:30 a.m. to 6:30 p.m. Monday to

Friday (to 9 p.m. Wednesday); closed Saturday and Sunday. Tube: St. Paul's. The **Trafalgar Square Post Office,** 24/28 William IV St., WC2N 4DL, operates as three separate businesses: inland and international postal services and banking, open from 8 a.m. to 8 p.m. Monday to Saturday; philatelic sales, open from 10 a.m. to 7 p.m. Monday to Friday and 10 a.m. to 4:30 p.m. Saturday; and the post shop selling greeting cards and stationery, open from 9 a.m. to 6:30 p.m. Monday to Friday and 9:30 a.m. to 5 p.m. Saturday. Tube: Charing Cross. Other post offices and sub-post offices are open from 9 a.m. to 5:30 p.m. Monday to Friday and 9 a.m. to 12:30 p.m. Saturday. Many sub-post offices and some main post offices close for one hour at lunchtime.

Telecommunications: To make telephone calls: The **Westminster Communications Center,** 1A Broadway, S.W.1, is open daily except Sunday from 9 a.m. to 7 p.m. Here you can call all countries not available from a call box. Receptionists are available to help you in case of difficulty and to take your payment once your call is finished. You can pay in cash, check, credit card, or traveler's checks in pounds sterling. A range of other services is also available, including telex, telegrams, telemessages, word processing, photocopying, radio paging, voice bank, cellular radio rental, and facsimile. Call 222-4444 for details. Remember the phone area code for London is 01, but, as in the U.S. and Canada, you don't use the area code while you're in the city, only when you're calling within the country but outside your current area code. Tube: St. James's Park.

LONDON INFORMATION

Tourist information is available from the London Tourist Board's facilities. The **Tourist Information Centre,** Victoria Station Forecourt, S.W.1 (tube: Victoria Station), can and will help you with almost anything of interest to a tourist in the U.K. capital. The center deals chiefly with accommodations in all size and price categories, from single travelers, family groups, and students to large-scale conventions. They also arrange for tour ticket sales and theater reservations and operate a bookshop. Hours are 9 a.m. to 8:30 p.m. daily from early April to the end of October; 9 a.m. to 7 p.m. Monday to Saturday and 9 a.m. to 5 p.m. on Sunday from November to April. The bookshop is open from 9 a.m. to 7 p.m. Monday to Saturday and 9 a.m. to 4 p.m. on Sunday, and these hours are extended in July and August. For most types of service, you must apply in person.

The center also has offices at:

Harrods, Knightsbridge, S.W.3, on the fourth floor. Open during store hours. Tube: Knightsbridge.

Selfridges, Oxford Street, W.1, basement services area, Duke Street entrance. Open during store hours. Tube: Bond Street.

The Tower of London, West Gate, E.C.3. Open early April to the end of October from 10 a.m. to 6 p.m. daily. Tube: Tower Hill Station.

Heathrow Airport Terminals 1, 2, and 3, Underground Concourse, open from 9 a.m. to 6 p.m.; and Terminal 2, Arrivals Concourse, open from 9 a.m. to 7 p.m. daily.

Telephone inquiries may be made to the center by calling 730-3488 Monday to Friday from 9 a.m. to 6 p.m. Written inquiries should be addressed to the London Tourist Board and Convention Bureau, Correspondence Assistant, 26 Grosvenor Gardens, London SW1W 0DU.

For **riverboat information,** phone 730-4812.

The British Tourist Authority has a **British Travel Centre** at Rex House, 4–12 Lower Regent St., SW1Y 4PQ (tel. 01/730-3400). This center offers a full information service on all parts of Britain, a British Rail ticket office, a travel agency, a theater ticket agency, hotel booking service, a bookshop, and a souvenir shop, all under one roof. Hours are 9 a.m. to 6:30 p.m. Monday to Friday and 10 a.m. to 4 p.m. Saturday and Sunday. Tube: Piccadilly Circus.

THE HOTEL OUTLOOK

The hotel picture has changed drastically since the 19th century, when the Hotel Victoria had only four bathrooms for its 500 guests. London now offers accommodations to satisfy all purposes, tastes, and pocketbooks—ranging from the deluxe suites to army cots that rent to students in hostels.

New hotels sprout up every year, and others are on the drawing boards. For too long London hotels seemed lost in the days of Victoria (many still are). Now, increased pressure from overseas has brought about a discernible upgrading. Of course, in the name of progress Edwardian architectural features have often given way to the worst and most impersonal of modern, and showers (even bedrooms) are placed in broom closets best left to serve their original functions. Nevertheless, a hotel revolution is in the air.

Before launching into actual recommendations, I should issue a . . .

Warning: July and August are the vacation months in England, when nearly two-thirds of the population strikes out for a long-awaited holiday. Many head for the capital, further exacerbating what has become a crowded hotel situation at all price levels. That doesn't mean you won't get a room if you should arrive at this peak time. There are so many hotels nowadays you can almost always find a room, but perhaps it won't be in the price bracket you want.

When the summer vacations are over, the "season" in London begins, lasting through October. Therefore, in September and October, as in June, low-budget hotels are tight—although nothing like they are in the peak summer months. It is recommended that you nail down a reservation before arriving in London. If you don't like to book a blind date, then by all means arrive early to begin your search for a room. Many of the West End hotels have vacancies, even in peak season, between 9 and 11 a.m., but by noon they are often packed solidly again with fresh arrivals.

Hotels in Four Price Ranges

All hotels, motels, inns, and guesthouses in Britain with four bedrooms or more (including self-catering accommodations) are required to display notices showing minimum and maximum overnight charges. The notice must be displayed in a prominent position in the reception area or at the entrance. The prices shown *must* include any service charge and *may* include VAT. If VAT is not included, then it must be shown separately. If meals are provided with the accommodation, this must be made clear too.

The hotels of London we have selected are listed here according to districts, such as Mayfair, Belgravia, Bloomsbury. I have further broken them down into categories, beginning with the deluxe and following with the upper bracket, the latter with first-class amenities. The medium-priced or middle bracket range follows with a listing of the best of London's moderately priced hotels with or without private baths. Finally, for those who want to keep travel costs bone-trimmed, I'll list budget-range choices wherever possible. Establishments in this category are most often converted town houses.

But I should issue a strong warning. What is considered "moderate" in price in London may not be moderate to you in terms of your hometown rates. The prices are "moderate" in London terms, and London is one of the most expensive cities on earth, especially in its tab-happy hotel tariffs. Likewise, actual "budget choices" are few. You can be almost assured that any really good budget hotel in London is likely to be full 12 months a year, because the demand is so great for low-priced rooms. Mind you, a so-called low-priced accommodation in London might be viewed in the deluxe hotel range in a country such as India.

First-class hotels in London have generally abandoned the time-honored English tradition of serving you a full English breakfast (bacon and eggs) for the price of the room. The hotels in the medium-priced range are a toss-up—the majority still maintain this custom, although many establishments rely on skimpy continental fare instead of the works, while some serve an in-between meal they call a London breakfast.

Some budget hotels in London still provide a full English breakfast for the price of the room. Because the policy of charging extra for breakfast is so erratic, always inquire when making a reservation or before checking in.

---

2. Mayfair

Mayfair, W.1, bounded by Piccadilly, Hyde Park, and Oxford and Regent Streets, is an elegant section of London. Luxury hotels exist side by side with Georgian town houses and swank shops. Here are the parks, names, and streets that have snob appeal the world over, including Grosvenor Square (pronounced Grohv-nor) and Berkeley Square (pronounced Barkley).

DELUXE CHOICES

An outstanding place to stay, **Claridge's**, Brook Street, London W1A 2JQ (tel. 01/629-8860), in Mayfair, dates from the mid-Victorian age. It has cocooned royal visitors in an ambience of discreet elegance since the time of the Battle of Waterloo. Queen Victoria visited the Empress Eugénie of France here, and thereafter, Claridge's lent respectability to the idea of ladies dining out in public. During World War II, Claridge's came to be known as "the annex of Buckingham Palace," from the royalty and heads of state staying there. Today such figures still appear, as well as top-echelon members of the financial, diplomatic, business, and cultural worlds.

Furnished with antiques as well as television sets, the 209 bedrooms (55 are suites) are spacious, many having generous-size bathrooms complete with dressing rooms and numerous amenities. Suites can be separated by private foyers from the main corridors, providing self-contained, large units suitable for a sultan and his entourage. Tariffs, including VAT and service, are £150 ($262.50) to £170 ($297.50) daily in a single, £190 ($332.50) to £215 ($376.25) in a double (twin-bedded). It's necessary to reserve a room at Claridge's far in advance.

Excellent food is stylishly served in the intimacy of the Causerie, renowned for its lunchtime smörgåsbord and pre-theater suppers, and in the more formal restaurant with English and French specialties. From the restaurant, the strains of the Hungarian Quartet, a Claridge's institution since 1902, can be heard from the adjacent foyer during luncheon and dinner. Both the Causerie and the restaurant are open from noon to 3 p.m. The Causerie serves evening meals from 5:30 to 11 p.m., and dinner is offered in the restaurant from 7:30 to 11 p.m. Tube: Bond Street.

The Dorchester, Park Lane, W.1 (tel. 01/629-8888), long known for its elegance and service, is closed for a complete refurbishment as we go to press. It is scheduled to reopen in the spring of 1990.

Inn on the Park, Hamilton Place, Park Lane, London W1A 1AZ (tel. 01/499-0888), has captured the imagination of the glamour-mongers of the world ever since it was inaugurated by Princess Alexandra in 1970. Bordered with a smallish triangular-shaped garden and ringed by one of the most expensive neighborhoods in the world, it sits behind a tastefully modern façade. Its clientele includes heads of state, superstars, and business executives. The hotel's acres of superbly crafted paneling and opulently conservative décor create the impression that the building is far older than it is. Piano music accompanies afternoon tea, served on excellent copies of Chippendale and Queen Anne furniture. A pair of restaurants creates a most alluring rendezvous, including the highly starred Four Seasons, which is both elegant and stylish, with views opening onto Park Lane. The finest wines and continental specialties dazzle guests either at lunch or at dinner, which is served until 11 p.m. The alternative dining choice is the less expensive Lanes Restaurant where many members of London's business community come to partake of the hors d'oeuvres table. Open from 6 p.m. to midnight daily, it offers pre- and post-theater suppers.

The hotel's 228 rooms are large and beautifully outfitted with well-chosen chintz patterns, reproduction antiques, and plush upholstery, along with dozens of well-concealed electronic extras. On the second floor of the inn, the owners have created 16 unique rooms, each with its own private glass conservatory. The hotel, a member of the Four Seasons group, has one of the highest occupancy rates in London. Singles cost £160 ($280) to £175 ($306.25) daily, and doubles begin at £190 ($332.50). Tube: Hyde Park Corner.

The Connaught, Carlos Place, London W1Y 6AL (tel. 01/499-7070), perhaps more than any other hotel in London, captures an elegant old English atmosphere. Located in the center of Mayfair, two short blocks from both Berkeley and Grosvenor Squares, it ranks at the top with Claridge's for prestige and character. The Connaught is a 19th-century architectural treasure house of a way of life fast disappearing. It's a brick structure, with a formal entrance, and its tall French windows overlook two curved, tree-lined streets. As you enter, the staircase reminds you of an estate in the English countryside. Throughout the hotel are antiques, such as in the drawing room with its formal fireplace, soft lustrous draperies at high windows, and bowls of fresh flowers. The cost of staying here is the same year round: a single with bath from £126 ($220.50) to £131 ($229.25) daily, a double or twin with bath from £128 ($224) to £175 ($306.25), inclusive of VAT. All meals are extra, and the service charge is 15%. The bedrooms vary in size but all are furnished with well-selected antiques and tasteful reproductions. It is imperative to reserve well in advance.

The paneled bar-lounge is old-school-tie conservative; the fashionable (with everybody from movie stars to bestselling novelists) dining room is also wood paneled, but it glitters with mirrors and crystal. The chef has perfected the English cuisine and a selection of French dishes. Attentive waiters and fresh flowers set the proper mood. Luncheon or dinner from the á la carte menu will cost £35 ($61.25) to £70 ($122.50) per person. The food lives up to its reputation as superb. Reservations are essential for nonresidents of the hotel. Tube: Bond Street.

Grosvenor House, Park Lane, London W1A 3AA (tel. 01/499-6363), is an art deco palace, a bastion of tradition and elegance, the flagship of Trusthouse Forte. It was named after the famous residence of the Duke and Duchess of Westminster, which around the turn of the century occupied this frontage along Hyde Park. To build the hotel, the efforts of the architects were spearheaded by Sir Edwin Lutyens, whose domestic architecture redefined the concept of how a fine house should be erected. The Grosvenor House came into being from 1927 to 1929, and today it is practically a miniature city unto itself, with 160 apartments (which lie within a separate tower) and 454 bedrooms and suites. Along the hallways lie many spacious accommodations, each different from its neighbor, filled with English chintz, inlaid headboards, and traditional furnishings. Accommodations contain large tile or marble bath, color TV, radio, trouser press, mini-bar, and phone. Singles rent for £160 ($280) to £195 ($341.25) daily and doubles or twins £185 ($323.75) to £205 ($358.75).

The hotel has an array of dining and drinking facilities for any occasion, plus a modern health club in its basement with a 65-foot swimming pool, a sauna, steambath, and exercise and aerobics room. Tube: Marble Arch.

THE UPPER BRACKET

The tallest building along Park Lane, and indeed one of the tallest structures in London, **London Hilton on Park Lane,** Park Lane, London W1A 2HH (tel. 01/493-8000), created an uproar when it was constructed in 1963. Persistent allegations accused residents of its uppermost floors of being able to spy into the boudoirs of faraway Buckingham Palace.

Now considered a linchpin of the London hotel scene, and currently owned by

Britain's Ladbroke chain, the Hilton is stylish and sophisticated. There's a roof-top restaurant on the 28th floor, with sweeping views over London. Facilities at the hotel include a sauna and a massage service. Graced with large picture windows over London and Hyde Park, the bedrooms are outfitted in tastefully restful colors, plush upholstery, and fine copies of Georgian furniture. Each has a color TV, mini-bar, marble-sheathed bath, and other amenities. Rooms on floors 22 through 27 tend to be at the more expensive end of the price scale. Depending on the accommodation, singles rent from £165 ($288.75) to £200 ($350) daily, with doubles going for £190 ($332.50) to £225 ($393.75). VAT and breakfast are extra. Tube: Hyde Park Corner.

The **Park Lane Hotel,** Piccadilly, London W1Y 8BX (tel. 01/499-6321), is one of the long-established Park Lane deluxe hotels, having its own loyal clients and winning new converts all the time. An intensely English hotel, it sits behind a discreet stone-block façade. One of its gateways, the Silver Entrance, is considered such an art deco marvel that its soaring columns have been used in many films, including *Brideshead Revisited, The Winds of War,* and *Shanghai Surprise* with Madonna. The hotel's restaurant, Bracewell's, is recommended separately (see Chapter IV). The hotel also operates the Brasserie on the Park, with daily changing table d'hôte menus plus á la carte. It's in a subtle pink and gray decor. Afternoon tea is served in the beautifully decorated yellow-and-white lobby, capped by a glass ceiling and filled with palms evoking the Edwardian era.

Designed in a U shape, with a view overlooking Green Park, it has more than 320 luxurious and comfortable accommodations, which are among the least expensive of the other major Park Lane hotels. Each contains a private bath, color TV, radio, mini-bar, phone, and double glazed windows for interior peace and quiet. Many of the suites offer marble fireplaces and the original marble bathrooms. Depending on the season and the accommodation, singles cost £120 ($210) to £139 ($243.25) daily, and doubles or twins go for £140 ($245) to £159 ($278.25). The hotel also offers up-to-date fitness and business centers. Tube: Hyde Park Corner.

London Marriott, Grosvenor Square, London W1A 4AW (tel. 01/493-1232). Built in a grander era as the conservative Hotel Europa, Marriott has poured millions of dollars into its refurbishment, retaining only the very best elements and, of course, much of the tradition. It sits proudly behind a red-brick and stone Georgian façade on Grosvenor Square. The American Embassy is just a few doors away.

Throughout the hotel's interior, the same colors are consistently used in combinations of pink, peach, ivory, and virgin green. The breakfast room is delightful with chintz and Chippendale antiques. In the Diplomat Bar, well-rubbed paneling and oil portraits of Edwardian statesmen lend the air of an exclusive club. Rolling silver trolleys serve elegant meals in the adjacent Diplomat Restaurant. The hotel's 223 accommodations are plushly upholstered in Georgian design, and contain all the electronic extras you'd expect. Singles cost £166.75 ($291.80) to £178.25 ($224.45) daily, and doubles go for £189.75 ($332.05) to £201.25 ($352.20). Tube: Bond Street.

Brown's Hotel, Dover Street and Albemarle Street, London W1A 4SW (tel. 01/493-6020), is recommended for those who want a fine hotel among the top traditional choices. This upper-crust, prestigious establishment was created by James Brown, a former manservant of Lord Byron. He and his wife, Sarah, who had been Lady Byron's personal maid, wanted to go into business for themselves. Brown knew the tastes of gentlemen of breeding and wanted to open a dignified, club-like place for them, his dream culminating in the opening of the hotel in a town house at 23 Dover St. in 1837, the year Queen Victoria ascended the throne of England. Today Brown's Hotel occupies some 14 historic houses on two streets, in an appropriate location—in Mayfair, just off Berkeley Square. To this day, old-fashioned comfort is dispensed with courtesy. A liveried doorman ushers you to an antique reception desk where you check in. The lounges on the street floor are inviting, including the Roosevelt Room, the Rudyard Kipling Room (the famous author was a frequent visitor here), and the paneled St. George's Bar for the drinking of "spirits." A good, old-fashioned English tea is served in the Albemarle Room. Men are required to wear jackets and ties for teas and for dining in the dining room.

The bedrooms vary considerably and are a tangible record of the past history of England. Even the wash basins are semi-antiques. The rooms show restrained taste in decoration and appointments, with good soft beds and phones. The rates for a single room are £120 ($210) to £140 ($245) daily, a double renting for £150 ($262.50) to £175 ($306.25). All rates include VAT and service. Tube: Green Park.

THE MIDDLE BRACKET

Something of a discovery, **Green Park Hotel,** Half Moon Street, London, W1Y 8BP (tel. 01/629-7522), lies on one of those narrow, almost "hidden" streets of Mayfair, yet the location is just off busy Piccadilly, near Park Lane. In this ideal location, Green Park was created from a series of period houses and converted into one of the most select of London's moderate range hotels. Designer decorated and furnished throughout, it offers 160 tasteful, often stylish, bedrooms that come in a variety of sizes and layouts, ranging from singles, doubles (also twins) to triple rooms ideal for families. The most expensive are a series of deluxe rooms and individually designed suites. All accommodations have direct-dial phone, trouser press, private bath, color TV, and 24-hour room service. Singles range from £75 ($131.25) to £85 ($148.75) daily, with doubles or twins costing from £95 ($166.25). The traditionally designed Claudes Restaurant offers a first-rate cuisine inspired by recipes from the French Riviera. Tube: Green Park.

A traditional accommodation, **Flemings Hotel,** 7-12 Half Moon St., London W1Y 7RA (tel. 01/499-2964), is set in a quiet street off Piccadilly. The reception area and spacious lounge have an air of peaceful charm and elegance with elaborate chandeliers and period furniture. The Langoustine Restaurant and Claridge Bar offer a wide choice from à la carte and table d'hôte menus served in a warm and relaxing atmosphere. There are 137 charmingly decorated rooms, all with private bath, color TV with in-house movies, radio, direct-dial phone, refrigerator, and hairdryer. Rates are £82.50 ($144.40) to £90 ($157.50) daily for a single, rising to £106 ($185.50) to £115 ($201.25) for a double or twin. Executive twins cost £125 ($218.75). Tariffs include service and VAT. Tube: Green Park.

---

3. St. James's

This section, the beginning of Royal London, starts at Piccadilly Circus and moves southwest. It's frightfully convenient, as the English say, enclosing a number of important locations such as American Express on Haymarket, many of the leading stores (Burberry of raincoat wear), and Buckingham Palace.

It basks in its associations with royalty—it was the "merrie monarch" himself, Charles II, the famous skirt chaser (Nell Gwynne the favorite), who founded St. James's Park. And it was in St. James's Palace that his father, Charles I, spent his last troubled night, awaiting his beheading the following morning. At one time the palace was a hunting lodge of Henry VIII's and his wife of the moment, Anne Boleyn.

For the traditionalist in particular, living in the heart of aristocratic London has many advantages—none more important than its well-run and discriminating hotels themselves. Their number is limited, but their addresses are most fashionable, just as they were in the society heyday of the 18th century.

A DELUXE CHOICE

Along with its namesake on the Place Vendôme in Paris, the **Ritz Hotel,** Piccadilly, London W1V 9DG (tel. 01/493-8181), made the word "ritzy" synonymous in the English vernacular with luxury. Of the Ritz in the "other city," a French writer once said, "It isn't a hotel, it isn't even a big hotel, it's a monument." Much the same can be said of the London Ritz. The Ritz world is one of crystal, gilt, Italian marble, all that epitomizes the frivolous comfort of Edwardian high life.

Through extensive renovation, Cunard Leisure has restored the lovely hotel to much of its original elegance, the way César Ritz wanted it back in 1906. The hotel has had a long and colorful history since then. The cream of London society has wined, dined, or whatever here. Pavlova danced here for the amusement of the Prince of Wales. Noël Coward wrote the lyrics for his song "Children of the Ritz". In 1931 the Aga Khan greeted Mahatma Gandhi in his familiar loincloth, and years later, De Gaulle, Churchill, and Eisenhower met in the Marie Antoinette Suite. The public places are spacious. The Palm Court is like a stage setting: oval shaped, with its centerpiece the sculptured fountain in exhellon marble, adorned by the gilt figure *La Source*. The restaurant has a paneled wall lining of melting marbles and a hand-painted ceiling depicting skies with billowing clouds. The sumptuous chandeliers are linked to each other around the room by a chain of gilt bronze garlands, so that the dining area appears to be permanently *en fête*.

Staying here costs from £150 ($262.50) in a single, from £185 ($323.75) to £230 ($402.50) in a double or twin, VAT and service included. The 128 bedrooms and suites are traditionally decorated in pastel shades. Some of the original Victorian brass beds, Carrara marble fireplaces, and crystal lighting fixtures are found in the rooms, giving them the look of an English stately home. In other words, it's for people who enjoy "Putting on the Ritz." Tube: Green Park.

THE UPPER BRACKET

Created in the Victorian era, **Dukes Hotel,** 35 St. James's Pl., London SW1A 1NY (tel. 01/491-4840), is a small hotel in the St. James's district, only a five-minute walk from Piccadilly, a hundred feet or so from Green Park (which abuts Buckingham Palace) and near St. James's Palace. It sits on a postage-stamp square lit by gas lamps and adorned with flowers. It's all pure Regency, and frequented mainly by gentry who avoid the large impersonal hotels and gravitate to an establishment where the staff knows their quirks. There is central heating throughout, every bedroom has its own private bath and direct-dial phone. A total renovation has made rooms brighter and more spacious than ever, with classical furnishings. A single rents for £140 ($245) daily, a double or twin for £170 ($297.50) to £200 ($350) for a four-poster room, inclusive of service and VAT. Main meals are served in Dukes Restaurant from 12:30 to 2:30 p.m. and 6 to 10:30 p.m. daily. Room service functions 24 hours a day. Tube: Piccadilly Circus.

Stafford Hotel, 16-18 St. James's Pl., London SW1A 1NJ (tel. 01/493-0111), dating from Edwardian days as a hostelry, lies in a cul-de-sac off St. James's Street and Green Park. It can be entered via St. James's Place or else through the Blue Ball Yard (but only when the hotel's cocktail bar is open). Built in the 19th century as a private home, the Stafford has retained a home-like, country-house atmosphere, which has made it a favorite London address for visitors looking for something elegant and comfortable, with modern amenities yet without the cold anonymity of big, chain hotels, although it is owned by the Cunard group. Comfort is the keynote in the tastefully decorated public rooms. The dining room, lighted by a chandelier and wall sconces, plus candles on the tables, gleams with silver. Here you can lunch or dine on classic dishes prepared with fresh, select ingredients and practiced know-how. The bar of the hotel is a cozy attraction.

The 62 bedrooms are individually decorated and of varying shapes, in keeping with the private-home background of the structure. Rates are £150 ($262.50) daily in a single, £155 ($271.25) to £186 ($325.50) in a double, including VAT and service. Tube: Green Park.

THE MIDDLE BRACKET

Dating from 1910, the **Goring Hotel,** Beeston Place, Grosvenor Gardens, London SW1W 0JW (tel. 01/834-8211), achieves the seemingly impossible: it provides the charm of traditional, dignified English living and at the same time offers all modern comforts. Hotelier Goring built the establishment in 1910 with "revolutionary ideas"—that is, that every room should have a private bath, foyer, and central heating. His grandson, George Goring, continues to provide top service. The 100 rooms (here they are called apartments) rent for £95 ($166.25) daily in a single, £138 ($241.50) in a double or twin. Rates include color TV, service, and VAT. You can have a three-course table d'hôte luncheon for £16.75 ($29.30), and dinner from £19 ($33.25). Afternoon teas are served by waiters from a trolley in the large, paneled Garden Lounge, where you can sit and view the garden or take cocktails before meals in a bar by the window. The dining room reflects the charm and elegance of an English country hotel. The Goring's situation is choice, close to Victoria Station, and a ten-minute walk from Buckingham Palace, Westminster Abbey, and the Houses of Parliament. Tube: Victoria Station.

Royal Westminster Thistle Hotel, 49 Buckingham Palace Rd., London SW1W 0QT (tel. 01/834-1821), lies within minutes of Buckingham Palace (in fact, this hotel is passed during the Changing of the Guard). Built originally in the 1960s as a department store, in 1972, two of its lower floors were converted into a hotel, while several floors above it were sold as up-market private apartments (called "flats" here). The elegantly furnished Royal Westminster charges £130 ($227.50) to £140 ($245) daily in a double or twin, £105 ($183.75) to £139 ($243.25) in a single. Rates include service charge and VAT. Each bedroom is spacious, with individually controlled air-conditioning, double glazing, direct-dial phone with extensions at the bedside, on the writing desk, and in the bath, radio, color TV, hairdryer, trouser press, mini-bar, and personal safe. In the bathrooms are bathrobes and toiletries. There is 24-hour room service.

THE BUDGET RANGE

Composed of early Victorian houses, **Hamilton House,** 62 Warwick Way, London SW1V 1SA (tel. 01/821-7113), has had its units joined and recently modernized. James Burns, the owner, was born in Pimlico, a few yards from the hotel. Since buying the property with his Danish wife, who was a TWA flight attendant, he has constantly improved the facilities. There are now 45 rooms of which 30 have private bath and toilet, renting for £33 ($57.75) in a single without bath, £45 ($78.75) in a bathless twin, and £50 ($87.50) in a twin with bath, breakfast and tax included. All rooms have phone, radio, and TV. There is a residents' bar on the premises, and a fine restaurant. Open to the public, it serves traditional English dishes and American fast foods. Tube: Victoria Station.

---

4. Piccadilly

If you want to be in the middle of the West End, right at Piccadilly Circus and Leicester Square, then the following recommendations will appeal to you. Most of London's theaters, Soho, Regent Street, and many famous restaurants and pubs will be at your doorstep.

A DELUXE CHOICE

First built in 1908, **Le Meridien London,** 21 Piccadilly, London W1V 0BH (tel. 01/734-8000), is now happily enjoying its reincarnation. At the time of its original opening, the Ionic arcade capping the limestone of its arched neoclassical façade was considered the height of Edwardian extravagance. It was instantly pro-

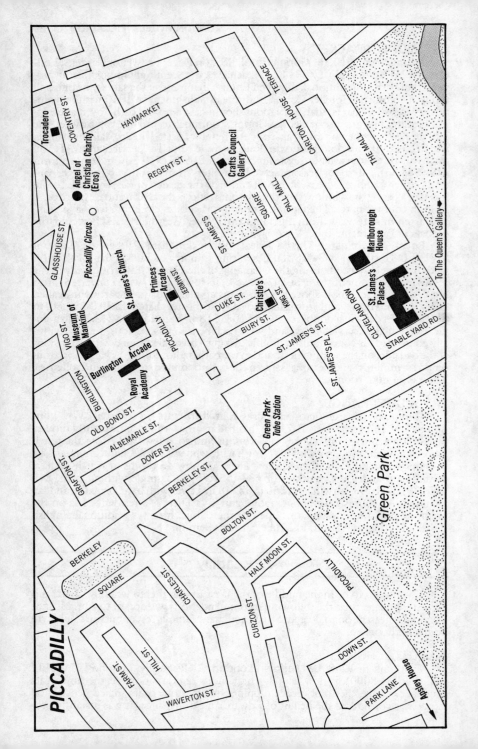

nounced the grandest hotel in London, but its huge expense bankrupted its creator. New owners continued to make the hotel one of the most stylish in the world, receiving such luminaries as Mary Pickford accompanied by Douglas Fairbanks, and much earlier, Edward VII. After World War II the hotel sank into a kind of musty obscurity until the revitalization of the Piccadilly theater district and the lavish refurbishment of the hotel, both of which coincided. Today, after the expenditure of some $30 million, the hotel is considered the European flagship of the French-owned Meridien chain. It has enough elaborately detailed plasterwork, stained glass, and burnished oak paneling to make any Francophile feel at home, yet offers enough old-world service and style to satisfy even the most discerning British. Except for the intricate beauty of the skylit reception area, the centerpiece of the hotel is the soaring grandeur of its oak-paneled tea room, where gilded sculptures and chandeliers of shimmering Venetian glass re-create Edwardian styles.

The hotel offers a formal and very elegant restaurant, the Oak Room (more about this later), and a less formal, sun-flooded eyrie under the greenhouse walls of the façade's massive Ionic portico (the Terrace Restaurant). There is, as well, a very British bar sheathed in hardwoods and featuring a live pianist. The hotel is also proud of Champney's, one of the most exotic health clubs in London. Graced with a pool almost 50 feet long, whose tilework looks like something from the grand art deco days of Budapest, it features saunas, steambaths, aerobic workshops, squash courts, billiard tables, and a private membership clientele. Each of the nearly 300 handsome bedrooms contains ample amounts of space, private bath, TV, radio, phone, and a mini-bar, plus a chosen array of fine and conservatively tasteful furniture. Singles rent for £140 ($245) to £160 ($280) daily and doubles or twins for £160 ($280) to £180 ($315). Tube: Piccadilly Circus.

THE MEDIUM-PRICED RANGE

One of the largest hotels in Europe, the **Regent Palace Hotel,** Piccadilly Circus, London W1A 4BZ (tel. 01/734-7000), has 1,034 bedrooms, all with hot-beverage facilities, radios, and color TVs. It stands in the center of London, with theaterland around the corner and Oxford Circus a five-minute walk away. It charges £44 ($77) daily in a single, £59 ($103.25) in a twin- or double-bedded room. Rates include an English breakfast, VAT, and service. The hotel's Carvery is a good place to dine, and the Café at the Regent is open for pre-theater meals. Drinks are served in the Half Sovereign bar and the Planters bar. Tube: Piccadilly Circus.

---

5. The Strand and Covent Garden

Beginning at Trafalgar Square, the Strand runs east into Fleet Street. Londoners used to be able to walk along the Strand and see the Thames, but the river has receded. In the 17th century the wealthy built their homes on the Strand, their gardens stretching to the Thames. But today it's changing to something less grand—flanked as it is with theaters, shops, hotels, and such landmarks as Somerset House.

Lanes jut off from the Strand, leading to the Victoria Embankment Gardens along the river. Opposite the gardens is Cleopatra's Needle, an ancient Egyptian obelisk, now London's oldest monument. You might want to stroll along the river if weather permits. You may also want to book a hotel along the Strand.

DELUXE CHOICES

A landmark hotel, the **Savoy,** The Strand, London WC2R 0EU (tel. 01/836-4343), with eight stories behind a façade of light terracotta glazed tiles, stands majestically between the Strand and the Thames. Opened in 1889, it was built by Richard D'Oyly Carte for the use of people going to his theater to see the Gilbert and Sullivan operas. Seven of the rooms for private parties are named for works of those masters of light opera. Through the Savoy's portals have walked famous personages of yesterday and today, everybody from royalty to political leaders to stars of stage, screen, TV, and rock. The hotel has 200 bedrooms, many with sitting rooms. Each has a different decor, but all have private bath, comfortable chairs, solid furniture, and large closets. The units contain a blend of antiques, an eclectic combination of such pieces as gilt mirrors, Queen Anne chairs, and Victorian sofas. Singles cost from £120 ($210) daily. Doubles and twins go for £160 ($280) to £225 ($393.75).

The Savoy Grill has long been popular with a theatrical clientele. The room has wood paneling, and a harpist plays in the evening. The even more elegant Savoy Restaurant is in a prime position, with tables looking toward the Thames. A four-person band plays in the evening for dancing on the intimate dance floor surrounded by tables. Tube: Temple, Embankment, or Covent Garden.

The **Howard Hotel,** Temple Place, The Strand, London WC2R 2PR (tel. 01/836-3555), is a unique luxury hotel overlooking the Embankment between Blackfriars and Waterloo bridges, at a point where the City meets the West End. The façade of the building that contains this hotel is very modern, but its public rooms are authentic late-18th-century, Adam-style fantasies. So what you'll see is a forest of Ionic columns, Savonnerie-style carpets in vivid pinks, blues, and golds, elaborate plaster detailing, and walls the color of cotton candy. A terraced courtyard with masses of seasonal flowers and cascades of water can be seen from the high-ceilinged bar, whose walls are adorned with a spun-sugar lacework of pink and turquoise. There's an elegant restaurant in the basement. Also overlooking the same terraced garden, is the acclaimed Quai d'Or Restaurant, with its domed ceiling and Renaissance-style decor, which offers a classic menu of French haute cuisine. The 135 semi-rococo bedrooms are filled with copies of marquetry-covered antiques. Each room is air-conditioned, with private bath, and many open onto a view of the Thames. Singles rent for £165 ($288.75) daily, and doubles go for £180 ($315), including service and VAT. Tube: Temple.

THE UPPER BRACKET

Born in Edwardian days, **The Waldorf,** Aldwych, London WC2B 4DD (tel. 01/836-2400), is alive and well today. Its art nouveau tea garden, the Palm Court, has become one of London's most sought-after places for a "cuppa," consumed to the music of a resident orchestra. The glass canopy that covers its marble floor illuminates what used to be an outdoor flower market. It is said that in the 1600s King Charles II's favorite mistress, "sweet Nell Gwynn," used to sell oranges here. Its proximity to the five largest theaters in London almost guaranteed a full roster of visiting stars and celebrities. After a long period of tattiness it was renovated. Today the vaudevillian theatricality of yesteryear lives on in the old photographs ringing the reception area. A brasserie serves informal French meals in a belle époque setting for after-theater suppers. The Palm Court reverberates again to the strains of music every day at teatime. Each of the 310 bedrooms is comfortably upholstered in chintz and a conservative blend of new and old furniture. They rent for £108 ($189) daily in a single, £139 ($243.25) in a double, VAT included. Tube: Aldwych.

THE MIDDLE BRACKET

Ideally situated for those who want to be in the theater district, the **Strand Palace Hotel,** The Strand, London WC2R 0JJ (tel. 01/836-8080), is near points such as Trafalgar Square and Covent Garden, yet within a block of the Thames Embankment. Rooms are comfortably furnished and decorated in colors ranging from cool pastel to warm sun-bright shades and have a number of facilities, including tea/coffee-makers and remote-control TV. Rates are £69 ($120.75) daily in a single, £82 ($143.50) in a double, and £94 ($164.50) in a triple. VAT and service are included, and all rooms have baths and showers. Among the assets of the Strand Palace are its restaurants that include a Carvery where every day, you can feast on England's finest roasts at £11.95 ($20.90) per person, including VAT and service. There is also the

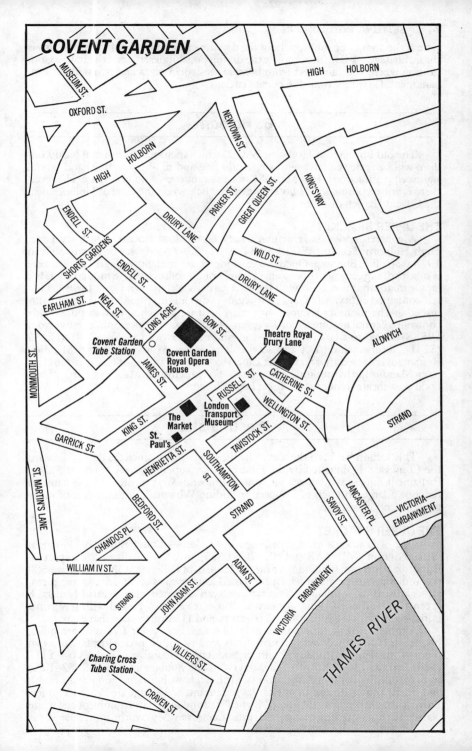

Café at the Strand, open throughout the day attracting show people. Favored also is the intimate Mask Bar. To complete the dining possibilities, there is the Italian Connection where you can select from homemade Italian pizza and pasta. Tube: Embankment, Charing Cross, or Covent Garden.

6. Holborn

The old borough of Holborn, W.C.2, which includes the heart of legal London, will be reviewed later with some drinking and dining selections and several sightseeing attractions. It is normally not thought of as a hotel district. However, there is one recommendable hotel (previewed below) on the edge of Holborn near the Covent Garden district.

THE UPPER BRACKET

A concrete-and-glass structure, **Drury Lane Moat House,** 10 Drury Lane, High Holborn, London WC2B 5RE (tel. 01/836-6666), was originally built in 1978 as an office building. Once you're inside its confines, however, the atmosphere is subdued, suggesting neither a chain hotel nor one of such severe modernity as the façade might indicate. Built with terraced gardens and its own plaza, the hotel is a self-contained entity. All of its 153 spacious bedrooms have good views and are furnished in a harmonious fashion, with many luxurious touches, such as individually controlled central heating, color TV, even 24-hour room service. Singles range from £95 ($166.25) to £102 ($178.50) daily and doubles from £120 ($210) to £132 ($231). Tariffs include VAT and service. The bedrooms have tile baths. Maudie's Restaurant is named after Sir Osbert Lancaster's famous arbiter-of-chic cartoon character Maudie Littlehampton, and offers a French cuisine. Maudie's Bar makes a good post-theater rendezvous. Tube: High Holborn.

7. Westminster

This section has been the seat of British government since the days of Edward the Confessor. Dominated by the Houses of Parliament and Westminster Abbey, Parliament Square symbolizes the soul of England. Westminster is a big name to describe a large borough of London, including Whitehall, headquarters of many government offices.

THE UPPER BRACKET

One of London's most stylish hotels, **St. James Court Hotel,** Buckingham Gate, London SW1 6AF (tel. 01/824-6655), was carved from a complex of Edwardian apartment buildings near the Houses of Parliament. Its more than 500 accommodations (some of which are rented long term as apartments) wrap themselves around the fountain of a central courtyard adorned with caryatids, emerald-green tiles, and neo-Gothic stonework. You enter a lobby ringed with travertine, burnished walnut, 18th-century oil portraits, and a Georgian-era sedan chair.

Although no two rooms are exactly alike, each has a color TV, mini-bar, radio, phone, and full bath. More expensive units are air-conditioned. Most fall into two types—"transitional modern" and reproduction Georgian. Singles cost £115 ($201.25) to £130 ($227.50) daily, and twins and doubles go for £138 ($241.50) to £160 ($280). Among its attractions, the hotel has a business center and a health and fitness center for use of guests. Its restaurant, L'Auberge de Provence, offers Provençal cuisine prepared by an all-French staff and served in an ambience of white plaster, tile floors, ceiling beams, and rustic accessories. My favorite spot, however, is the hotel's elegantly formal Chinese restaurant, whose walls are covered with hand-painted murals in motifs of ferns and flowers. The Restaurant St. Germain is the hotel's à la carte restaurant. The cuisine is mainly French and international. Le Café next to the restaurant is open all day. Tube: Victoria Station.

In a turn-of-the-century, red-brick building, **Stakis St. Ermins Hotel,** Caxton Street, London SW1H 0QW (tel. 01/222-7888), stands in the heart of Westminster and only a few minutes' walk from Buckingham Palace, the Houses of Parliament, and Westminster Abbey. Its 296 bedrooms all have private bath, radio, TV, and individually controlled central heating, with 24-hour room service. The hotel has two restaurants: the Caxton Grill offers an à la carte menu, while the Carving Table has a set price for lunch and dinner, serving a selection of roast meats. The lounge bar offers an alternative, serving light snacks 24 hours a day. The rates at the hotel are £99 ($173.25) daily in a single, rising to £144 ($252) for a twin-bedded room. These rates include VAT. The hotel is near New Scotland Yard and Buckingham Palace, halfway between Victoria Station and Big Ben. Tube: St. James's Park.

THE MEDIUM-PRICED RANGE

One of the largest block of flats (apartments) in all of Europe, **Dolphin Square,** Dolphin Square, London SW1 V3LX (tel. 01/834-3800), while not a traditional hotel, offers one of the best values in the city. The location, if not prestigious, is interesting—set back from Thames-bordering Grosvenor Road, between Chelsea and the Tate Gallery. Dolphin Square, an "instant home in London," has a vast inner courtyard and lots of gardens and lawns. A guest room with phone and a shared bath costs £26 ($45.50) nightly in a single and £38 ($66.50) in a double. Prices of studios and one-bedroom apartments, suitable for two guests, vary in price according to their size and view (those on the fifth and sixth floors are better decorated and offer more scenery). Doubles with private baths and kitchens cost from £75 ($131.25) to £90 ($157.50) daily. Even larger suites and apartments are also available at much higher prices. A restaurant overlooks a heated swimming pool. Sauna baths are available for both men and women. For those who want to go English all the way, eight squash courts beckon. Tube: Pimlico Station.

---

8. Victoria

Directly south of Buckingham Palace is a section of Westminster and Pimlico often referred to as "Victoria," with its namesake—sprawling, bustling Victoria Station—as its center. Known as "the Gateway to the Continent," Victoria Station is where you get boat trains to Dover and Folkestone for that trip across the Channel to France.

The area also has many other advantages from the standpoint of location, as the British Airways Terminal, the Green Line Coach Station, and the Victoria Coach Station are all just five minutes from Victoria Station. From the bus stations, you can board many a Green Line coach for the suburbs. And an inexpensive bus tour of London departs from a point on Buckingham Palace Road, just behind Victoria Station. From Grosvenor Gardens, you can get a bus direct to Heathrow Airport, and from Victoria Station, trains to Gatwick Airport.

Your best bet in this area is to walk about Ebury Street, which lies directly to the east of Victoria Station and Buckingham Palace Road. There you'll find some of the best reasonably priced lodgings in central London. The following are my favorite recommendations along this street.

THE BUDGET RANGE

Created out of a group of small town houses, **Ebury Court,** 26 Ebury St., London SW1W 0LU (tel. 01/730-8147), has a country-house flavor; it's brightly painted (turquoise and white), with railings to match and flower-filled window boxes. The little reception rooms are informal and decorated with flowery chintz and quite good antiques. Best of all, it has a cordial and informal staff. The hotel is close to the airline terminals. Terms quoted include an English breakfast and VAT. The rate in a single ranges from £42 ($73.50) to £45 ($78.75) daily, from £65 ($113.75) in a bathless twin-bedded room or a double. Doubles with private bathrooms cost from £75 ($131.25). Each of the rooms has hot and cold running water, as well as a telephone and radio. In the small restaurant, you can order either a lunch or dinner. A special feature of this establishment is the bar, which caters only to guests and to members of the Ebury Court Club, a group of local people who enjoy their drinks in a congenial atmosphere. A night porter is on duty to look after late arrivals.

The A1 bus, which goes to Heathrow every 20 minutes, leaves from Grosvenor Gardens, approximately a 1½ minute walk from the Ebury Court. Porters from the hotel will help visitors with their luggage on a trolley if required. Tube: Victoria Station.

Overlooking the attractive, quiet gardens of a stately square, the **Elizabeth Hotel,** 37 Eccleston Square, London SW1V 1PB (tel. 01/828-6812), is an intimate, privately owned establishment and an excellent place to stay, convenient to Belgravia, Chelsea, and Westminster, and not far from Buckingham Palace. Of its 24 rooms, three have bath or shower, and good facilities are available for bathless rooms, which have hot and cold water basins. Singles cost from £26 ($45.50) daily without bath, and bathless twins or doubles are priced from £40 ($70). Doubles with shower (no toilet) cost from £44 ($77). A large double or twin room with bath or shower, toilet, color TV, and refrigerator rents from £57 ($99.75), and a family room costs from £50 ($87.50) to house three persons, from £56 ($98) for four persons. Prices include either an English or a continental breakfast. The friendly reception staff will help guests find good pubs and restaurants in the neighborhood, as well as advising on how to enjoy London. Tube: Victoria Station.

Collin House, 104 Ebury St., London SW1W 9QD (tel. 01/730-8031), provides a good, clean B&B under the watchful eye of its resident proprietors, Mr. and Mrs. D. L. Thomas. Everything is well maintained here, and the majority of bedrooms have private showers and toilets, something of a rarity for a B&B. Singles with private bath/shower and toilet cost £30 ($52.50) per night, doubles renting for £36 ($63) without bath, £42 ($73.50) with bath. All rates are inclusive of a full English breakfast, VAT, and the use of showers and toilets for those who don't have private facilities. There are a number of family rooms here. The main bus, rail, and Underground terminals are about a five-minute walk from the hotel. Tube: Victoria Station.

Lewis House Hotel, 111 Ebury St., London SW1W 9QU (tel. 01/730-2094), is a town house that was the home of playwright Sir Noël Coward from 1917 to 1930. It was his parents who opened this place to paying guests. During World War II, military leaders were housed here, each with a direct phone link to the Admiralty and the War Office. Today, this family-run hotel is managed by John Evans and offers rooms with or without showers, costing £38 ($66.50) to £42 ($73.50) daily for two persons, including a full English breakfast and VAT. The family suite, for four or five persons, rents for £85 ($148.75) and has bath facilities. Breakfast is taken in the large Noël Coward room, which has many pictures of "the master" and assorted memorabilia on the walls. Tube: Victoria Station.

---

9. Belgravia

Belgravia, south of Hyde Park, is the aristocratic quarter of London, challenging Mayfair for grandness. It reigned in glory along with Queen Victoria, but today's aristocrats are likely to be the top echelon in foreign embassies, along with a rising new-money class of actors and models.

Belgravia is near Buckingham Palace Gardens and Brompton Road. Its center is Belgrave Square, one of the more attractive plazas in London. A few town houses once occupied by eminent Edwardians have been discreetly turned into hotels (others were built specifically for that purpose). For those who prefer a residential address, Belgravia is choice real estate.

A DELUXE CHOICE

An elegant place to stay is the **Berkeley Hotel,** Wilton Place, London SW1X 7RL (tel. 01/235-6000). The original hotel so beloved by Noël Coward was moved, along with the loyalty of its well-heeled clients, to a travertine-faced building near Hyde Park in 1972. Its French-inspired façade conceals a world of impeccable service, flickering fireplaces and richly textured oak paneling, as well as a news-service telex machine between the Ionic marble columns of the lobby, formally dressed receptionists, a penthouse swimming pool designed like a modernized Roman bath, and lots of hideaway corners for drinks and conversations in elegant surroundings. The Restaurant, as it is called, serves a superb French cuisine in a decor of bleached paneling, masses of flowers, gracious proportions, and English chintz. Each of the accommodations is comfortable, but the hotel is perhaps best known for its opulent suites, many of which contain exquisite paneling and a gargantuan bathroom. With VAT included, singles cost £130 ($227.50) to £185 ($323.75) daily, while doubles go for £185 ($323.75) to £230 ($402.50). Tube: Knightsbridge.

THE MODERATE RANGE

For best all around value, the **Diplomat Hotel,** 2 Chesham St., London SW1X 8DT (tel. 01/235-1544), is a leader in its field. Part of its multiple allure lies in its status as a small, reasonably priced family-operated hotel in an otherwise prohibitively expensive neighborhood filled with privately owned Victorian homes and high-rise first-class hotels. You register at a desk whose borders are framed by the sweep of a partially gilded circular staircase beneath the benign gaze of cherubs gazing down from the borders of a Regency-era chandelier.

The 28 comfortable bedrooms have modern baths, color TVs, phones, high ceilings, and well-chosen wallpaper in vibrant Victorian-inspired colors, as well as such extra touches as a hairdryer and morning newspapers. Each is named after one of the famous streets in this posh district. Singles rent for £49.95 ($87.40) daily and doubles for £64.95 ($113.65). A sumptuous English buffet breakfast is served in a private dining room. Tube: Sloane Square.

---

10. Knightsbridge

Adjoining Belgravia is Knightsbridge, another top residential and shopping district of London. Just south of Hyde Park, Knightsbridge is close in character to Belgravia, although much of this section to the west of Sloane Street is older—dating back in architecture and layout to the 18th century. Several of the major department stores, such as Harrods, are here (take the Piccadilly Underground line to Knightsbridge). Since Knightsbridge is not principally a hotel district, my recommendations are limited.

THE UPPER BRACKET

Rising like a concrete cylinder, the **Sheraton Park Tower,** 101 Knightsbridge, London SW1X 7RN (tel. 01/235-8050), is not only one of the most convenient hotels in London, virtually at the doorstep of Harrods, but one of the best. It rises with its unusual circular architecture in contrast to the well-heeled 19th-century neighborhood around it. From its windows guests have a landscaped view of Hyde Park. The front door is unexpectedly and discreetly placed in the rear of the building, where taxis can deposit guests more conveniently. Managed by the Sheraton group as the flagship for their European enterprises, they have tried to make it, in the words of one spokesperson, "a modern version of the Connaught."

Designers have decorated each of the rooms in a tastefully international kind of plushness. Each of the accommodations, 295 in all, contains air conditioning, central heating, soundproof windows, in-house movies, radio, and phone. Room service and babysitting are also available. Commercial travelers, along with visiting diplomats and military delegations, often book the rooms, which are, incidentally, opposite the French Embassy. Singles range from £154 ($269.50) to £180 ($315) daily, and doubles or twins go for £170 ($297.50) to £180 ($315).

Its travertine-covered lobby bustles with scores of international clients who congregate on the well-upholstered sofas or in the Edwardian comfort of the hideaway bar. In the rotunda, near the ground-floor kiosks, you can be served afternoon tea. The champagne bar offers you a choice of either a glass or a silver tankard filled with bubbly, along with oysters, dollops of caviar, and iced vodka. "The Restaurant" is open from 7 a.m. to midnight, ideal for an after-theater supper. There you can dine on such dishes as English crab, medallions of venison, and Scottish lamb. The restaurant has its own entrance on Knightsbridge. Tube: Knightsbridge.

One of the most personalized hotels in the West End is **The Capital,** 22 Basil St., London SW3 1AT (tel. 01/589-5171). Small and modern, it's a stone's throw from Harrods. It has a warm town-house ambience, a result of an extensive refurbishment program. The elegant *fin de siècle* decoration is matched by the courtesy and professionalism of the staff. From the lobby, an elevator takes guests to each floor, where the corridors and staircase are all treated as an art gallery. Each of its 60 rooms have air conditioning, direct-dial phone, full audio and video service, and twin or king-size beds. Singles rent for £135 ($236.25) daily and doubles for £150 ($262.50). The Capital Restaurant is among the finest in London. The chef is Philip Britten, who formerly operated Chez Nico. His food is outstanding, and he ranks as one of the best British chefs today. Tube: Knightsbridge.

THE MEDIUM-PRICED RANGE

One of London's most charming small hotels, **The Beaufort,** 33 Beaufort Gardens, London SW3 1PP (tel. 01/584-5252), sits behind two Victorian porticos. You register at a small alcove extending off a bay-windowed parlor, and later you climb the stairway used by the Queen of Sweden during a stay here. Each of the 29 bedrooms contains at least one painting by an art student, a modern color scheme, and plush carpeting. Amenities include a private bath, color TV, earphone radio, and phone. With a continental breakfast and VAT included, singles cost from £100 ($175) daily, and doubles or twins go for £120 ($210) to £150 ($262.50). Suites are more expensive. One added advantage of this place is the pleasant staff and the inspired direction of its owner, Diana Wallis, a television producer. She did everything she could to create the feeling of a private house in the heart of London. Tube: Knightsbridge.

Basil Hotel, Basil Street, London SW3 1AH (tel. 01/581-3311), has long been a favorite little hotel of discerning British, who make an annual pilgrimage to London to shop at Harrods and perhaps attend the Chelsea Flower Show. This Edwardian charmer is totally unmarred by pseudo-modernization, and guests who can appreciate this individualistic hotel are preferred. The open mahogany staircase seems ideal as a setting for the entrance line of a drawing room play: "You're just in time for tea, Braddie." There are several spacious and comfortable lounges, appropriately furnished with 18th- and 19th-century decorative accessories. Off the many rambling corridors are smaller sitting rooms. The pleasantly furnished bedrooms are priced according to size and location. Single rooms range from £45 ($78.75) to

£85 ($148.75) daily, the latter with private baths. Doubles without bath go for £69 ($120.75), increasing to £110 ($192.50) with bath. A three-course table d'hôte luncheon is served in the dining room, and dinner is à la carte. Candlelight and piano music re-create the atmosphere of a bygone era. The Upstairs Restaurant is suitable for lighter meals and snacks, and Basil's Wine Bar, in a basement adjoining the hotel, offers a selection of wines and good food. Tube: Knightsbridge.

L'Hotel, 28 Basil St., London SW3 1AT (tel. 01/589-6286), has been converted by David and Margaret Levin, owners of the nearby Capital Hotel in Basil Street, into a 12-room inn with countrified bedrooms and modern baths. Downstairs is the Metro, a café/wine bar where breakfasts are served, with dishes of the day offered later. You can rent a room, either single or double occupancy, for £110 ($192.50) per night, which includes a continental breakfast. If you'd like an excellent gourmet meal, try the Capital Hotel's well-known restaurant, just down the street. Tube: Knightsbridge.

THE BUDGET RANGE

Built in 1870, **The Executive Hotel,** 57 Pont St., London SW1X 0BD (tel. 01/581-2424), was originally a private home behind an ornate neo-Romanesque façade of red brick. After costly renovation by a hard-working and savvy entrepreneur, it was restored and is now one of the most appealing and convenient small hotels in the district. Part of its charm lies in the Adam-style frieze that ascends and curves around the high ceilings and graceful stairway of the main entrance. From the front you see only a discreet metal plaque announcing the establishment's status as a hotel. But once inside, you find 29 comfortable, modernized bedrooms, each containing simple built-in furniture, a high ceiling, radio, color TV, phone, private bath, and central heating. With a full English breakfast included, singles cost £49.95 ($87.40) daily, with a double or twin costing £64.95 ($113.65). An extra bed can be added to a double for £19.95 ($34.90). A cozy modern bar occupies one of the rooms off the lobby, and the location, near the attractions of Knightsbridge (the nearest tube stop), make the Executive very, very central.

Claverley House Hotel, 13-14 Beaufort Gardens, London SW3 1PS (tel. 01/589-8541), is an award-winning hotel lying just a few blocks from Harrods. In many ways it's one of the best hotels in the neighborhood, especially considering its price. It's a small cozy place with Georgian-era accessories. The lounge is one of the hotel's most interesting features, containing 19th-century oil portraits, a Regency fireplace, and a collection of antiques and leather-covered sofas much like an ensemble you'd find in a private country house. Of the 36 bedrooms, all but six have a private bath and several contain open-air balconies overlooking a wide-angle view of the rear end of Harrods. Decorated with frilly Victorian wallpaper and wall-to-wall carpeting, they all have comfortable armchairs, direct-dial phones, color TV, and in-house movies. With VAT and a full English breakfast, singles cost £45 ($78.75) to £50 ($87.50) daily, and doubles or twins rent for £50 ($87.50) to £60 ($105). Tube: Knightsbridge.

Knightsbridge Hotel, 10 Beaufort Gardens, London SW3 1FT (tel. 01/589-9271), sandwiched between the restaurants and fashionable boutiques of Beauchamp Place and Harrods, still retains the feeling of a traditional British hotel. On a tree-lined square that is peaceful and tranquil, and free from traffic, it has a subdued Victorian charm. The place is small—only 20 bedrooms. Units have phones, radios, and central heating, and there's a lounge with a color "telly" and a bar on the premises. Rooms come with and without bath, with singles costing £29 ($50.75) to £40 ($70) daily, and doubles going for £41 ($71.75) to £65 ($113.75). All tariffs include a continental breakfast, VAT, and service charge. Tube: Knightsbridge.

Knightsbridge Green Hotel, 159 Knightsbridge, London SW1X 7PD (tel. 01/584-6274), is an unusual establishment in a building constructed in the 1890s a block from Harrods. In 1966, when it was converted into a hotel, the developers were careful to retain the wide baseboards, cove molding, high ceilings, and spacious proportions of the dignified old structure. None of the accommodations contains a kitchen, but the result comes close to apartment-style living. Many of the doubles or twins are suites, each well furnished with access to the second-floor "club room" where coffee and pastries are available throughout the day. Each of the units contains a private bath, phone, and TV. Singles rent for £55 ($96.25) daily, doubles or twins from £70 ($122.50), and 16 suites for two persons for £85 ($148.75), VAT included. Reservations are important here. Tube: Knightsbridge.

11. Chelsea

This stylish district stretches along the Thames, south of Hyde Park and South Kensington. Beginning at Sloane Square, it runs westward toward the periphery of Earl's Court and Brompton. Its spinal cord: King's Road, center for boutique hopping. The little streets and squares on either side of King's Road have hundreds of tiny cottages used formerly by the toiling underprivileged of the 18th and 19th centuries (although Carlyle lived there—see "Homes of Famous Writers" in Chapter V). Now, except for Belgravia and Mayfair, Chelsea couldn't be more chic. To become a part of the scene, you can, like Carlyle, "take up abode" in one of the following recommendations.

A DELUXE CHOICE

One of the most plushly decorated and best-maintained hotels in London is the **Hyatt Carlton Tower,** 2 Cadogan Pl., London SW1X 9PY (tel. 01/235-5411). Its location and its height made this luxurious hotel a landmark even before Hyatt transformed it into their European flagship. It overlooks one of the most civilized gardens in London, whose Regency-era town houses were originally built as part of an 18th-century plan. Its marble-floored lobby, with a resident harpist, looks a lot like the private salon of an 18th-century merchant, complete with the lacquered and enameled treasures he might have brought back from the Far East. A massive bouquet of flowers almost, but not quite, dominates the clusters of Chippendale-style chairs and sideboards, creating a haven for breakfast, light lunches, afternoon tea, and nightcaps. In fact, after the publicity it generated once as "Britain's Tea Place of the Year," the hotel has been considered one of the capital's most fashionable corners in which to enjoy a midafternoon pick-me-up. The hotel contains a few hideaway bars, the Rib Room for relatively informal meals in a warmly atmospheric setting and the Chelsea Room, considered one of the great restaurants of London (both covered in the dining chapter).

Bedrooms are opulently outfitted, the beneficiary of the more than $30 million that Hyatt spent. Each contains all the modern comforts you'd expect, as well as a marble-lined bathroom, artwork, air conditioning, and in-house movies. For either single or double occupancy, the charges range from £170 ($297.50) to £190 ($332.50) nightly. Suites are more expensive, of course. A family plan allows children under 18 sharing a room with their parents to stay free. Of particular note is a chic and desirable health club, whose two stories of shimmering glass encompass a sweeping panorama of the old trees of Cadogan Place. It is filled with the most up-to-date exercise machines and staffed by a bevy of health and beauty experts. On its upper floor, a neo-Grecian bar serves health-conscious light meals, and it's also preferred as an early rendezvous place for its breakfast buffet. Tube: Knightsbridge.

The small, elegant **Cadogan Thistle Hotel,** 75 Sloane St., London SW1X 9SG (tel. 01/235-7141), has a history dating back to the middle of the 19th century. Although recently refurbished, the Edwardian style of the interior has been retained and is complemented by well-chosen antiques. The oak-paneled drawing room leads through to Langtry's Restaurant, which is open from noon to 10 p.m. daily for dining. Bedrooms are comfortable, well furnished, and modernized. Guests can stay in Lillie Langtry's suite (once occupied by the mistress of Edward VII) or the room lived in by Oscar Wilde, writer and wit, who was a frequent guest at the hotel until he was arrested in these same quarters. Rates are £115 ($201.25) to £145 ($253.75) daily for a single and from £135 ($236.25) to £160 ($280) for a twin room, inclusive of VAT and service. Tube: Sloane Square or Knightsbridge.

THE MIDDLE BRACKET

Chic and welcoming, **The Fenja,** 69 Cadogan Gardens, London SW3 2RB (tel. 01/589-7333), is one of the most luxurious upmarket B&Bs in London. It stands in a highly desirable location, close to the Peter Jones Department Store and the boutiques of King's Road. Only 13 bedrooms are offered in this restored Victorian townhouse. Each is decorated tastefully in traditional English styling and furnished in part with antiques. Each accommodation, which contains a modern bath with all the amenities, honors a writer or painter, everybody from Jane Austen to Henry James. Prices are from £80 ($140) daily in a single, rising to £155 ($271.25) in a double. Drinks can be ordered in a small drawing room; otherwise, meals are served in your room. Tube: Sloane Square.

THE BUDGET RANGE

A 19th-century town house opening onto gardens, **The Willett,** 32 Sloane Gardens, Sloane Square, London SW1W 8DJ (tel. 01/824-8415), is one of the nuggets of Chelsea. It has many architectural curiosities, including a Dutch roof and bay windows. While retaining its traditional charm, the hotel has been fully renovated with new furnishings in all the well-equipped bedrooms and in the public lounge areas. The breakfast room is especially inviting, with plush red velvet chairs. In fact, the hotel has rapidly become a favorite address with many discriminating English people who like a town house address and who prefer being close to the restaurants, attractions, and good shops of Chelsea. Singles with private bath cost £49.95 ($97.40) daily, with a double or twin-bedded room, also with bath, renting for £59.95 ($104.91). An extra bed can be added to a bedroom for £19.95 ($34.91) per person. VAT is added to all tariffs. Tube: Sloane Square.

As dyed-in-the-wool British as you can get is the **Wilbraham Hotel,** Wilbraham Place, off Sloane Street, London SW1X 9AE (tel. 01/730-8296). On this quiet little street, just a few hundred yards from busy Sloane Square, three Victorian town houses have been joined together as one hotel. It has an intimate sitting room and an attractively old-fashioned bar/lounge where you can have simple meals at both lunch and dinnertime. There are 57 rooms in all, plus 42 baths, and prices range according to plumbing. Singles go for £33 ($57.75) to £47 ($82.25) daily and doubles or twins for £48 ($84) to £70 ($122.50), the latter for a deluxe chamber. Tube: Sloane Square.

Blair House Hotel, 34 Draycott Pl., London SW3 2SA (tel. 01/581-2323), is a good, moderately priced choice for those who'd like to anchor deep in the heart of Chelsea. In a building of architectural interest, it has been modernized and completely refurnished. Rooms are usually small but still comfortable, and contain such conveniences as direct-dial phones, radios, and facilities for making tea or coffee, along with TVs. Most rooms contain a private bath or shower, and, naturally, those are more expensive. Depending on the plumbing, singles cost £33 ($57.75) to £47 ($82.25) daily, doubles and twins going for £48 ($84) to £60 ($105), the prices including a continental breakfast and VAT. Tube: Sloane Square.

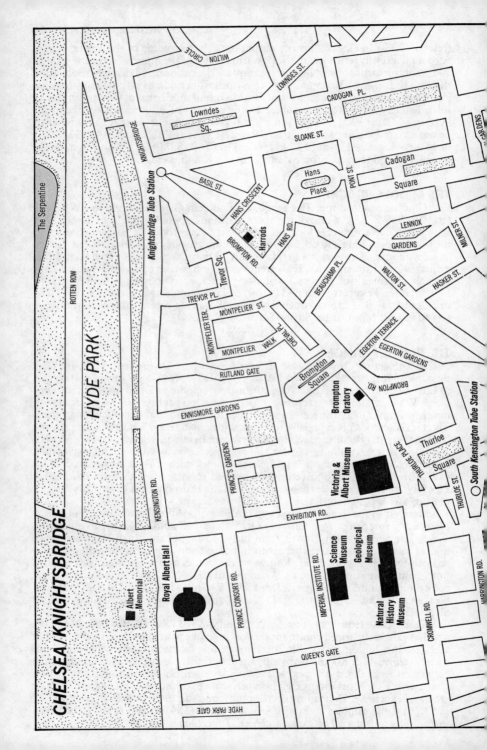

CHELSEA / KNIGHTSBRIDGE

The Serpentine

HYDE PARK

ROTTEN ROW

Albert Memorial

Royal Albert Hall

HYDE PARK GATE

KENSINGTON RD.

PRINCE CONSORT RD.

QUEEN'S GATE

CROMWELL RD.

HARRINGTON RD.

EXHIBITION RD.

IMPERIAL INSTITUTE RD.

Science Museum

Geological Museum

Natural History Museum

PRINCE'S GARDENS

ENNISMORE GARDENS

RUTLAND GATE

Victoria & Albert Museum

Brompton Square

Brompton Oratory

BROMPTON RD.

THURLOE PLACE

Thurloe Square

THURLOE ST.

South Kensington Tube Station

MONTPELIER WALK

MONTPELIER ST.

MONTPELIER TER.

MONTPELIER PL.

CHEVAL PL.

TREVOR PL.

Trevor Sq.

BROMPTON RD.

Harrods

HANS CRESCENT

BASIL ST.

Knightsbridge Tube Station

KNIGHTSBRIDGE

Lowndes Sq.

WILTON CIRCLE

LOWNDES ST.

CADOGAN PL.

SLOANE ST.

Hans Place

HANS RD.

PONT ST.

Cadogan Square

LENNOX GARDENS

BEAUCHAMP PL.

WALTON ST.

MILNER ST.

HASKER ST.

EGERTON TERRACE

EGERTON GARDENS

GARDENS

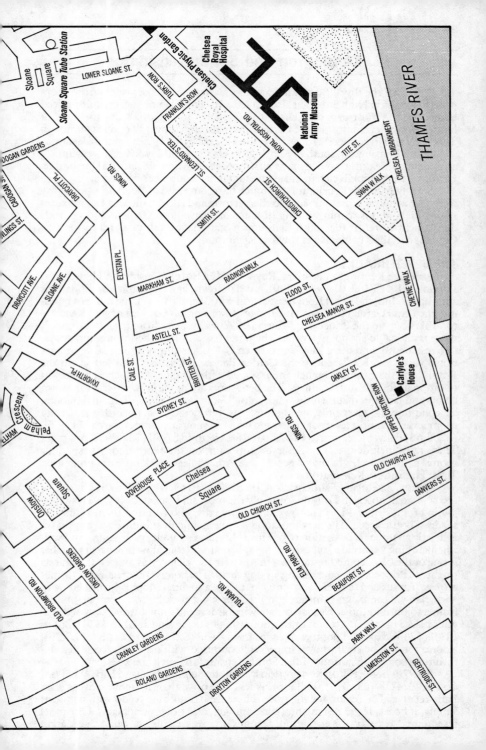

12. Kensington and South Kensington

Although the Royal Borough draws its greatest number of visitors from shoppers (Kensington High Street), it also attracts with a number of fine, medium-priced hotels, for the most part on Kensington Gardens. In Victoria's day the rows of houses along Kensington Palace Gardens were inhabited by millionaires (although Thackeray also lived there). Today the houses are occupied largely by ambassadors.

South Kensington, south of Kensington Gardens and Hyde Park, is essentially a residential area, not as elegant as that bordering Belgravia and Knightsbridge. However, the section is rich in museums, and it has a number of colleges.

Staying in South Kensington has much to recommend it. Besides its proximity to the Kensington museums, such as the Victoria and Albert, the area encompasses Albert Hall, and is within walking distance of Kensington Gardens and Harrods department store. At the South Kensington Station, you can catch trains for Kew Gardens and the Thames River town of Richmond.

THE UPPER BRACKET

A deluxe Kensington hostelry, **Royal Garden Hotel,** Kensington High Street, London W8 4PT (tel. 01/937-8000), is well known for its stylish accommodations and supper club, the Royal Roof (see Section 4 in Chapter V). A large modern building, the Royal Garden towers on the fringe of Kensington Gardens next to Kensington Palace where the Prince and Princess of Wales live, and fronts one of London's most fashionable shopping streets. The hotel has 384 large bedrooms and suites, two restaurants, and three bars. The Garden Café offers all-day dining of an international flavor and is adjacent to the Garden Bar, a sunken area with settees. In the Royal Roof, the cuisine is French and is served with a choice of well-chosen wines in traditional English surroundings. The bedrooms are modern, with decor in warm colors and facilities that include radio, color TV, in-house films, direct-dial phones, air conditioning, electronic message systems, refrigerated bars, hairdryers, sitting room areas, dressing rooms, and private baths or showers. Singles start at £117.50 ($205.65) daily, increasing to £147.50 ($258.15) to £157.50 ($275.65) for a twin. These rates include tax. The Reserve Club wing on the tenth floor has spacious rooms patronized by business people and other guests seeking extra amenities. Tube: High Street Kensington.

Blakes, 33 Roland Gardens, London SW7 3PF (tel. 01/370-6701), is one of the best small hotels in London, certainly the most sophisticated. It was created by joining four former Victorian town houses together and painting them a uniform shade of bottle green. The neighborhood may be staunchly middle class, but Blakes is strictly an upper-class bastion of privilege. London's parade of the young and stylish, including "rag trade" types, photographers, and actors, dine downstairs in what is one of the best-reputed restaurants in town. It's so glamorous, in fact, that guests might see Princess Margaret dining among them. The hotel is the creation of former actress, Anouska Hempel. You enter a richly appointed lobby furnished with Victorian-era campaign furniture, probably brought back by some empire-builder from a sojourn in India. Near an ornate wire birdcage (a miniature version of a mogul's palace in itself), a receptionist quotes singles beginning at £115 ($201.25) to £140 ($245) daily and doubles or twins from £155 ($271.35) to £165 ($288.75). Rooms tend to be smallish, yet impeccably outfitted with unusual accessories and furniture, some of it antique. Tube: South Kensington (but a taxi's better).

A 1970s hotel, **Hilton Kensington International,** 179 Holland Park Ave. London W11 4UL (tel. 01/603-3355), is less expensive than its more famous Park Lane relative. The reason for the price difference has nothing to do with comfort: simply, it boasts fewer restaurants, bars, lounges, and other peripherals. One of its restaurants, Hiroko of Kensington, features a Japanese cuisine, while the Market

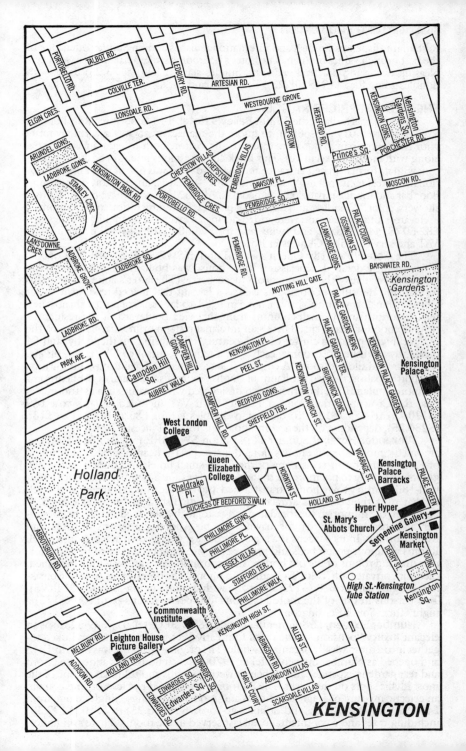

KENSINGTON

Restaurant dispenses English and international dishes and on Sunday offers one of the best brunch values in town. The hotel's bedrooms strike a balance between eye-pleasing decor and practical gadgetry. Singles start at £99 ($173.25) daily, with doubles going for £119 ($208.25). Tube: Holland Park.

THE MEDIUM-PRICED RANGE

When it was built in the 1880s, **Bailey's Hotel,** 140 Gloucester Rd., London SW7 4QH (tel. 01/373-6000), to quote the management, was a "firm favourite with the squirearchy," but now caters to the visitor, both foreign and domestic, along with budding executives. This brick corner establishment in South Kensington, with its formal arched entrance and mansard roof, was one of those first revolutionary hotels to install an "ascending room"—that is, an elevator. The ground floor bar and lounge is paneled in limed oak. All 162 bedrooms have private baths/showers, color TV, radios, and direct-dial phones. Many amenities, such as automatic elevators and a restaurant, were added during an extensive upgrading. Singles cost £82.50 ($144.40) daily, and twins rent for £96.50 ($168.88). All prices include VAT and service. Tube: Gloucester Road.

The **Gore Hotel,** 189 Queen's Gate, London SW7 5EX (tel. 01/584-6601). This elegantly detailed neoclassical town house was built in 1870 as the private home of a relative of the Marquess of Queensberry. (The latter's fame resides in his formalizing the rules of boxing as well as a lawsuit that helped to destroy Oscar Wilde.) Transformed into a private hotel in 1908, today banks of potted shrubs shelter its Corinthian-style half-columns from the wide boulevard of the residential neighborhood where it sits. There's an informal restaurant in what used to be the high-ceilinged parlor, a cluster of 19th-century oil paintings in the lobby, and 54 pleasantly furnished bedrooms, each with a remote-controlled TV, radio, phone, hairdryer, and tile bathroom. A comfortable bar, lined with paintings, gilt mirrors, and potted palms, is often the haunt of English journalists. Several of the bedrooms are more opulent than the others, each designated with a name such as Tudor, Venus, the Crown, or the Consort Room. With VAT included, singles cost £69 ($120.75) to £79 ($138.25) daily, and doubles go for £85 ($148.75) to £135 ($236.25), depending on the accommodation. Tube: Gloucester Road.

Alexander Hotel, 9 Sumner Pl., London SW7 3EE (tel. 01/581-1591), is among the most expensive hotels along this street in the heart of the Royal Borough of Kensington, but it is also one of the finest small hotels in London, and many guests are willing to pay more for the added luxuries and amenities. Made up of four mid-18th-century town houses transformed into a single unit, it is an elegant hostelry that over the years has attracted many distinguished guests, including S. J. Perelman, the humorist. Restored in good taste, with a subdued decor, the Alexander also has won awards for having the best hotel garden in Chelsea and Knightsbridge. In its gardens is a separate cottage with its own access to the hotel. Rooms with four-poster beds and private balconies have been created from the former drawing rooms of the old house. All accommodations are tastefully furnished, each with private bath, color TV, radio, and phone. The hotel serves an ample breakfast. Singles start at £70 ($122.50) daily, with doubles going for £85 ($148.75). Two persons in one of the more luxurious four-poster rooms pay £100 ($175) a night. Tube: South Kensington.

Number Sixteen, 16 Sumner Pl., London SW7 3EG (tel. 01/589-5232), is an elegant luxury "pension" made up of four early Victorian town houses linked together into a dramatically organized whole. The original structure was built in 1848 and opened as Number Sixteen hotel in 1970. As each house was added, the front and rear gardens expanded, until their flowering shrubs and tulips create one of the most idyllic spots on the street. The 33 rooms are reached by elevator, and contain an eclectic mixture of English antiques and modern paintings. Singles range from £40 ($70) to £60 ($105), and doubles go for £95 ($166.25) to £110 ($192.50) including taxes and a continental breakfast served in the rooms. There's an honor-system self-service bar in one of the elegantly formal sitting rooms, where a blazing fire is lit on cool nights and days to take off the chill. Many of the clients of Number Sixteen are tied into the arts in some way. Tube: South Kensington.

The Regency Hotel, 100 Queen's Gate, London SW7 5AG (tel. 01/370-5555), takes its name from the Prince Regent, later George IV. The hotel used this leading figure to set the style for its gracious living close to museums, Kensington, and Knightsbridge. The decor of the public rooms includes silk tapestries, Oriental rugs, and crystal chandeliers. There is a set price carvery in the Pavilion restaurant with a choice of hot roasts and fish (also vegetarian options). The hotel offers 192 well-furnished bedrooms, each with direct-dial phone, color TV, trouser press, and hairdryer. Singles rent for £79 ($138.25) daily, with doubles costing £94 ($164.50). The Elysium health spa is beneath the hotel, offering a solarium, floatarium, a vibro-sauna, and steam rooms, along with a staff of beauty therapists and masseuses. Tube: Gloucester Road or South Kensington.

One Cranley Place, 1 Cranley Pl., London SW7 3AB (tel. 01/589-7704), is one of the little nuggets of London, a "secret address." Lying on a little mews behind a Regency-style Victorian row house, this well-accessorized hotel offers only ten bedrooms, but each is tastefully furnished, evoking the aura of an elegant country home filled with summertime colors. A front parlor, for example, is embellished with Turkish kilim weavings, Chinese vases, and a scattering of antiques. A fireplace is lit in the reception, and a stairway takes you to the gallery-windowed alcoves, carpeted hallways, and the bedrooms. Doubles range from £75 ($131.25) to £120 ($210) daily. Breakfast is served in a blue-and-white country-style kitchen, skylit from above, with views of a well-maintained garden. Tube: South Kensington.

Onslow Hotel, 109-113 Queen's Gate, London SW7 5LR (tel. 01/589-6300), was originally built in the 1860s. Its dignified facade is accented with a pair of marble columns supporting a front portico and jet-black iron railings. Completely renovated, it has regained some of its old allure. There is a resident pianist in the bar, and a popular Brasserie open daily from noon to 11 p.m. The hotel contains 174 comfortable bedrooms, each with private bath. For one, you pay £70 ($122.50) daily in a single and £91 ($159.25) in a double. Breakfast is extra. Bedrooms have such amenities as direct-dial phones, color TVs, and hairdryers. Tube: South Kensington.

THE BUDGET RANGE

Behind an early Victorian façade, **Aster House,** 3 Sumner Pl., London SW7 3EE (tel. 01/581-5888), is the smallest hotel on this unusual street of hotels. Rachel and Peter Caraplet are the owners, and their guests come from around the world. Peter, an architect, has built l'Orangerie over the adjacent garage, adding a glassed-in conservatory that doubles as a breakfast room and lounge. All 12 of the hotel's rooms have private baths, color TVs, mini-bars, direct-dial phones, and central heating. Two of the attractive units are on the ground floor, one with a fireplace and a curtained four-poster. Singles cost £42 ($73.50) to £52 ($91), while doubles and twins go for £68 ($119) to £82 ($143.50). Tube: South Kensington.

Number Eight, 8 Emperor's Gate, London SW7 4HH (tel. 01/370-7516), is a hotel in a cul-de-sac, offering warmth and elegance in a stately Victorian building. Bedrooms in this small hotel are of individual decor, each one named after a county of England. Most of the 14 units have bath or shower, and all have direct-dial phone, color TV, radio, hairdryer, and other modern amenities. Buffet breakfast is served. There is a 24-hour private bar, with room service. Depending on the plumbing, singles range from £40 ($70) to £45.95 ($80.40) nightly, with doubles costing from £50 ($87.50) to £56 ($98). Personal service of a high standard is the keynote of Number Eight. Tube: Gloucester Road.

Aston's Budget Studios, Designer Studios and Luxury Apartments, 39 Rosary Gardens, London SW7 4NQ (tel. 01/370-0737), combines the elegance of a Victorian home with the convenience and economy of self-catering, in a quiet residential street of South Kensington, only minutes from Hyde Park, Harrods, and the

Underground and buses. Each budget studio has fresh decor. Concealed behind double doors is a compact, complete kitchenette, and each of the immaculate, fully serviced baths is shared by only a few guests. The budget studios range in size from singles to large family units. Prices per week are from £160 ($280) for one person, from £130 ($227.50) per person for three, and from £105 ($183.75) per person for four guests. Designer studios for double occupancy are reminiscent of an English country home with understated luxury. Vibrant colors, mirrored walls, and a marble shower room, a high-tech fully equipped kitchenette, and a direct-dial phone meet the needs of the budget-conscious luxury market, at a rental of from £450 ($787.50) per week. Luxury apartments are one-bedroom, spacious, designer-decorated, self-contained facilities, offering Old World charm with modern conveniences. Sleeping up to four people, they cost from £650 ($1,137.50) per week. Aston's is personally managed by Shelagh King. Tube: Gloucester Road.

13. Notting Hill Gate

Increasingly gaining in fashion and frequented by such personages as the Princess of Wales, Notting Hill Gate is bounded on the south by Bayswater Road and on the east by Gloucester Terrace. It is hemmed in on the north by West Way and on the west by the Shepherds Bush ramp leading to the M40. It has many turn-of-the-century mansions and small houses that sit on quiet, leafy streets.

THE MIDDLE BRACKET
It refers to itself as a "Bed and Breakfast Hotel," but **Abbey Court,** 20 Pembridge Gardens, London W2 4DU (tel. 01/221-7518), is more luxurious than that name suggests. In furnishings and decor, it is strictly up-market. Contained within a white-fronted mid-Victorian town house, it has a flowery patio in front and a small garden in back. The lobby is graciously decorated with a sunny bay window, flower-patterned draperies, and comfortable sofa and chairs. Breakfast served in the 22 bedrooms is included in the price of £70 ($122.50) daily in a single, £95 ($166.25) in a double, and £120 ($210) for a larger than usual four-poster bed suitable for two. Each accommodation offers carefully coordinated fabrics and a scattering of fine furniture. You'll find fresh flowers in the hallways and the reception area, and within each room is a full bath with Jacuzzi jets, heated towel racks, and a bath lined with brownish-beige Italian marble. Kensington Gardens is a short walk away, as are the antique stores along Portobello Road. Tube: Notting Hill Gate.

14. Holland Park

About a ten-minute taxi ride from the heart of the West End, this was once meadowland belonging to Lady Holland. In time it became a fashionable address for upper-class Victorians. The park grew up around a 1606 Jacobean structure, Holland House, which was a beehive of social and political activity at the dawn of the 19th century. In the closing years of the Victorian era it was the scene of some of the most fashionable garden parties and masquerade balls in London. Although heavily bombed during the Luftwaffe attack on London in the early 1940s, the formally laid-out gardens have been restored, and in summer this is a rendezvous for concerts and open-air plays.

THE UPPER BRACKET
Called "by far the grandest of London's small hotels," the **Halcyon Hotel,** 81 Holland Park, London W11 3RZ (tel. 01/727-7288), was formed from a pair of

Victorian mansions originally built in 1860 by upper-class Londoners wanting to live on former meadowland owned by Lady Holland. Today their successful union contains a hotel of charm, class, fashion, urban sophistication, and much comfort. Since it opened in 1985 its clientele has included a bevy of international film and recording stars who like the privacy and anonymity provided by this place, where maids, dressed in black with starched white pinafores, glide silently through the corridors. More than half of the 44 accommodations are classified as suites, and each unit is outfitted with the kinds of furnishings and textiles you might find in an Edwardian country house. Several accommodations are filled with such whimsical touches as tented ceilings, and each contains all the modern luxuries you'd expect in a hotel of this caliber. Singles cost from £125 ($218.75) to £140 ($245) nightly, doubles from £175 ($306.25) to £195 ($341.25), and suites for two from £250 ($437.50) to £400 ($700), prices including VAT and service. The public rooms are inviting oases, with trompe-l'oeil paintings against backgrounds of turquoise. A complimentary limousine service takes clients to and from the West End, and there's a host of extras, including 24-hour room service, one-hour pressing of clothes, and a message-paging system that extends 20 miles from the hotel. The hotel's restaurant, Kingfisher, is recommended in the next chapter. Tube: Holland Park.

---

15. Lancaster Gate

North of Kensington Gardens and Hyde Park stands Lancaster Gate, a highly desirable section of London south of Paddington Station. It grew into prominence when residential development at Marble Arch pushed westward at the beginning of the 1800s. In time this area grew seedy, but with much restoration it has come back, as exemplified by the following selection in—

THE UPPER BRACKET

A classic town house hotel right in the center of London, **Whites Hotel,** Lancaster Gate, London W2 3NR (tel. 01/262-2711), is a home for the discerning. A trio of French Renaissance style terraced private residences were joined together to form this engaging hotel. The entrance, through a courtyard with limited parking, leads into a series of beautifully decorated public rooms, with a connecting bar and restaurant (perhaps the most elegant in Bayswater). Overlooking Kensington Gardens, the 54 bedrooms are designed in exquisite English taste, with swagged moiré draperies and soft muted colors, along with marble baths imported from Italy. Such luxury commands a price tag, with singles renting for £125 ($218.75) daily, and doubles climbing the scale from £160 ($280) to £215 ($376.25) at this five-star winner. In a setting of gleaming silver place settings and crystal chandeliers, you can enjoy a carefully chosen English cuisine, with traditional grills and flambé dishes, along with such seasonal produce as grilled saddle of Highland venison in its own juices laced with Scotch malt whisky. Tube: Lancaster Gate.

---

16. Paddington/Bayswater

A popular hotel area, particularly for budget travelers, is the Paddington section, around Paddington Station, just to the northwest of Kensington Gardens and Hyde Park. Here you'll be within walking distance of the great Marble Arch, the entrance to Hyde Park. The main Paddington avenue, Sussex Gardens, has been known for years to pence-shy travelers who seek out its bed-and-breakfast houses. But as more and more town houses are being razed on Sussex Gardens to make way for expensive flats, Norfolk Square is gaining importance as the area in which to shop for budget hotels. Allowed to deteriorate after World War II, the square was formerly one of the most prestigious squares of London, especially in the reign of Victoria when the eminent built large, beautiful town houses ideal for big families, maids, and nannies.

Lying just north of Bayswater Road and Kensington Gardens, slightly to the west of Hyde Park, Bayswater is an unofficial district with a number of decently priced lodgings. Many former town houses—converted into guesthouses or private hotels—date back to the days when Bayswater spelled the good life to a prosperous upper middle class. Some of these houses, often lined up in rows, open onto pleasant squares.

Tube stops serving the Bayswater and Paddington areas are Paddington, Bayswater, Queensway, Notting Hill Gate, and Ladbroke.

THE MEDIUM-PRICED RANGE

For those seeking a moderately priced accommodation overlooking Kensington Gardens, **The Coburg Hotel,** 129 Bayswater Rd., London W2 4RJ (tel. 01/229-3654), is an ideal choice. With that view, you feel almost as if you are in the country. Yet a walk around the corner will put you on one of the most popular budget restaurant streets of London, Queensway. There you can take either the Queensway or Bayswater tubes, which will whisk you into the heart of the West End in minutes. The hotel, a landmark on the Bayswater skyline, has been massively renovated. Its motto is delivering "value for money," and in that it succeeds admirably, as evidenced by many repeat customers.

A wide number of accommodations are offered, 125 bedrooms in all, including some family rooms. Many bedrooms are quite spacious, and others, such as singles, are snugly cozy with all the necessary amenities, such as TV, phone, and radio. Most of them also have a color TV, private bath, and an electric trouser press. Rooms at the front, overlooking busy Bayswater Road, are double-glazed for tranquility's sake. Depending on the plumbing, rates in a single range from £39.95 ($69.90) to £59.95 ($105.91) daily and from £59.95 ($105.91) to £79.95 ($139.90) in a double or twin, including a large buffet English breakfast. VAT is extra. The hotel also offers a good restaurant downstairs, serving an excellent British cuisine, which always includes a roast of the day as well as a number of international dishes.

In a residential area, **Colonnade Hotel,** 2 Warrington Crescent, London W9 1ER (tel. 01/286-1052), is an imposing town house built in 1853 as two private homes, just a block from the Warwick Avenue tube station. The bedrooms are spacious (some with balconies) and are equipped with either private baths/showers or hot-and cold-water basins. All have TVs, videos, radios, phones, hairdryers, and trouser presses. There are 16 special rooms with four-poster beds. Some are airconditioned and some have Jacuzzis. The rates are £35 ($61.25) to £50 ($87.50) daily in a single and from £65 ($113.75) to £85 ($148.75) in a double. Tariffs depend on the plumbing. A full English breakfast and VAT are included. The hotel has a restaurant and a cocktail piano bar called Cascades, which has become so popular that you need to have a reservation even to get a martini.

Mornington Hotel, 12 Lancaster Gate, London W2 3LG (tel. 01/262-7361), brings a touch of Swedish hospitality to the center of London. Just north of Hyde Park and Kensington Gardens, the hotel has been completely redecorated with a Scandinavian-designed interior. The bedrooms, 70 in all, are not only tastefully conceived and most comfortable, but each unit is complete with private bath and shower, a color TV, a phone, and a radio. Rates are £59 ($103.25) daily in a single, rising to £70 ($122.50) to £78 ($136.50) in a double or twin. If you're traveling with a child, the Swedish-speaking staff will place an extra bed in your room for an additional charge. Tariffs include a Scandinavian buffet breakfast, service, and VAT. Naturally, there's a genuine Finnish sauna, but you'll also find a well-stocked bar where you can order snacks and, if you're in time, afternoon tea. Tube: Lancaster Gate.

17. St. Marylebone

Below Regent's Park, northwest of Piccadilly Circus, is the district of St. Marylebone (pronounced Mar-li-bone), primarily a residential section that faces Mayfair to the south and extends north of Marble Arch. A number of gracious town houses in this section have been converted into private hotels.

THE UPPER BRACKET

A grand English country house, the **Dorset Square Hotel,** 39-40 Dorset Square, London NW1 6QN (tel. 01/723-7874), is made up of four Georgian Regency town houses similar to their neighbors on the small square near Regent's Park. Hotelier Tim Kemp and his wife, Kit, have transformed the former dwellings into a hotel with 37 bedrooms and 12 suites, with an interior so designed that the public rooms, bedrooms, and baths still give the impression of being in an elegant private home. The bedrooms are decorated in chintz or print materials that complement the furniture, a mix of antiques and reproductions. Rates are £65 ($113.75) daily in a single, from £80 ($140) to £100 ($175) in a double, and £125 ($218.75) for two in a top luxury room. The handsome restaurant, Country Manners, is graced by a mural showing Dorset Square when it was the home of the Marylebone Cricket Club. The menu, featuring the best of English cuisine, changes daily, offering such dishes as Stilton soup and venison in season and poached Scottish salmon with hollandaise sauce. Tube: Baker Street or Marylebone.

Hotel Montcalm, 33 Great Cumberland Pl., London W1A 2LF (tel. 01/402-4288). Set near Marble Arch, along the inner curve of a Georgian-era crescent of identical town houses, this hotel is a favorite of visiting rock stars and international celebrities. The guests who have registered at the lobby's vintage Louis XVI writing table have included everyone from Michael Jackson to Duran Duran to Stevie Wonder. This is the first Nikko Hotel (fully owned by Japan Air Lines) in London, but the decor includes only a hint of Oriental flavor. The public rooms are plushly upholstered with brown carpeting and brown leather sofas whose modern lines are attractively compatible with an overall flavor of 18th-century opulence. The polite staff is formally dressed, sometimes in amusing contrast to the blue jeans and sneakers of the musical artists who make this place a favorite. Because the Georgian lines of the building's façade couldn't be altered, some of the biggest accommodations are duplexes, connected upstairs and down by circular metal staircases. Each accommodation contains air conditioning, security locks, color TV, in-house movies, and dozens of extra touches. Singles cost £138 ($241.50) daily, and doubles go for £158 ($276.50) to £195 ($341.25), with service and VAT included. Tube: Marble Arch.

THE MEDIUM-PRICED RANGE

A 200-year-old hostelry, **Durrants Hotel,** George Street, London W1H 6BJ (tel. 01/935-8131), has a sprawling Georgian façade of brown brick incorporating several neighboring houses. A walk through the pine- and mahogany-paneled public rooms is like a tour through another century. Its restaurant serves full afternoon teas and satisfying meals in one of the most beautiful Georgian decors in the neighborhood. The less formal breakfast room is ringed with 19th-century political cartoons by the noted Victorian artist, Spy.

The 18th-century niceties include a letter-writing room sheathed with old paneling, plus a popular neighborhood pub with Windsor chairs, an open fireplace, and a decor that probably hasn't changed much in 200 years. The establishment's oldest bedrooms face the front and have slightly higher ceilings than the newer ones. Even

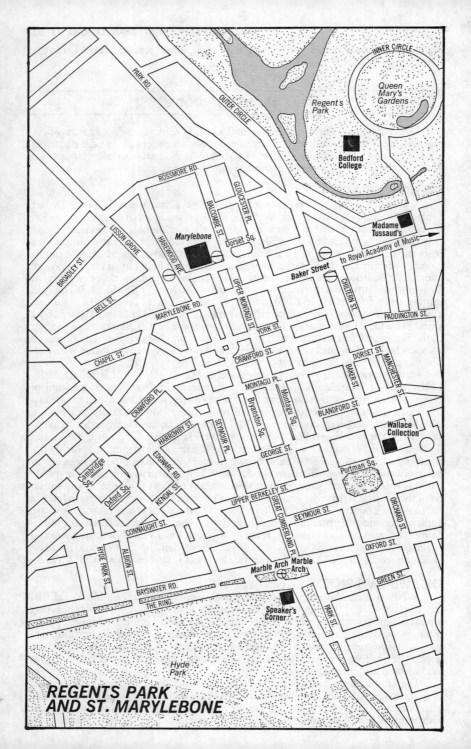

REGENTS PARK
AND ST. MARYLEBONE

the most recent accommodations, however, have elaborate cover moldings, comfortable furnishings, and a solid feeling of well-being. Each has color TV, phone, radio, and private bath. Singles cost £45 ($78.75) to £60 ($105), and doubles rent for £68 ($119) to £90 ($157.50). Tube: Bond Street.

THE BUDGET RANGE

A well-preserved building, **Hart House Hotel,** 51 Gloucester Pl., Portman Square, London W1H 3PE (tel. 01/935-2288), is part of a group of Georgian mansions occupied by the French nobility during the French Revolution. The hotel is in the heart of the West End and is convenient for shopping, theaters, and sightseeing. It is within a few minutes' walk of Oxford Street, Selfridges, Marble Arch, Hyde Park, Regent's Park, and the zoo, as well as Madame Tussaud's and the Planetarium. Run by the Bowden family, Hart House is centrally heated, and all 15 bedrooms have hot and cold running water, color TV, radio, and phone. Prices, which include an English breakfast, are £25 ($43.75) daily for a single, £35 ($61.25) to £44 ($77) in a twin or double, and £52 ($91) to £60 ($105) in a triple, the rate depending on the plumbing. Tube: Marble Arch or Baker Street.

Bryanston Court Hotel, 56-60 Great Cumberland Pl., London W1H 8DD (tel. 01/262-3141), is composed of three individual houses, each around 190 years old, which were joined together. Owned by the Theodore family, today it is one of the most elegant hotels on the street, with gas fireplace in the Chesterfield-style bar, plus a stairway leading up to the 56 bedrooms. Each of these contains a private bath, color TV, phone, and radio. Singles cost £55 ($96.25) daily, and doubles or twins go for £60 ($105) to £68 ($119). VAT and a continental breakfast are included in the prices. The opulent red dining room, the Brunswick Restaurant, is furnished in an early 19th-century style, with antiques and oil paintings. Tube: Marble Arch.

A small hotel with style, the **Hotel Concorde,** 50 Great Cumberland Pl., London W1H 8DD (tel. 01/402-6316), is housed in a building that was once a private home, now converted into a 28-room hostelry. The reception desk, nearby chairs, and part of the tiny bar area were once part of a London church. A display case in the lobby contains an array of reproduction English silver, each piece for sale. The accommodations are pleasant, with flowered wallpaper, color TVs, direct-dial phones, and private baths. Singles rent for £55 ($96.25) daily, while doubles or twins cost £65 ($113.75). A continental breakfast, included in the rates, is the only meal served. Guests may wish to patronize the recommended Bryanston Court for à la carte lunches and dinner. Tube: Marble Arch.

Edward Lear Hotel, 28-30 Seymour St., London W1H 5WD (tel. 01/402-5401), is a popular hotel, made all the more desirable by the bouquets of fresh flowers set up around the public rooms. It's one city block from Marble Arch in a pair of brick town houses, both of which date from 1780. The western house was the London home of the 19th-century artist and poet Edward Lear, whose illustrated limericks and original lithographs adorn the walls of one of the sitting rooms. Steep stairs lead to the 30 bedrooms, 11 of which contain a private bath. The cozy units are fairly small but have all the usual amenities, including color TVs, radios, phones, and hot beverage facilities. Singles cost from £29 ($50.75) daily, doubles and twins from £39 ($68.25), and triples from £48 ($84). Tariffs include VAT and a large English breakfast. The owner, Peter Evans, is helpful to guests. Tube: Marble Arch.

Hallam Hotel, 12 Hallam St., Portland Place, London W1N 5LJ (tel. 01/580-1166), is a heavily ornamented stone-and-brick Victorian house, one of the few on the street to escape bombing in World War II. Today it's the property of Earl Baker and his sons, Grant and David, who maintain it well. The bright breakfast room overlooks a pleasant patio. There is also a bar for residents. An elevator leads to the 23 simple but comfortable bedrooms, each with TV, phone, radio, and 24-hour room service. VAT and a light English breakfast are included in the price of the rooms, which cost £34 ($59.50) to £41 ($71.75) in a single, £57 ($99.75) to £62 ($108.50) in a double. Tube: Oxford Circus.

18. Bloomsbury

To the northeast of Piccadilly Circus, beyond Soho, is Bloomsbury, a world unto itself. It is, among other things, the academic heart of London, where you'll find London University, several other colleges, the British Museum, and many bookstores. Despite its student overtones, the section is fairly staid and quiet. Its reputation has been fanned by such writers as Virginia Woolf (it figures in her novel *Jacob's Room*). She and her husband, Leonard, were once the unofficial leaders of a coterie of artists and writers known as the Bloomsbury Group, nicknamed Bloomsberries.

The exact heart of Bloomsbury is difficult to pinpoint. There are those who say it is Russell Square, with its university buildings, private homes, and hotels. Others feel it is the nearby British Museum. Still others are convinced it's the sprawling University of London, which also contains the Royal Academy of Dramatic Art on Gower Street. In any case there are at least four other old tree-filled squares—Bloomsbury, Bedford, Gordon, and Tavistock—each one an oasis of green in the midst of some of London's finest buildings. The unquestioned northern border is Euston Road, with its three railway stations—St. Pancras, King's Cross, and Euston—and its southern border is New Oxford Street.

THE UPPER BRACKET

Within easy reach of theaters and shopping, **Hotel Russell,** Russell Square, London WC1 5BE (tel. 01/837-6470), is a late Victorian red-brick hotel facing the gardens of Russell Square. It offers 328 rooms, all with private bath or shower. Masses of visitors seem to move in and out of here, as fast as the reservations system can process them. Rates for a single begin at £90 ($157.50) daily and at £110 ($192.50) for a twin. The public rooms have been refurbished and include a Carvery Restaurant and the Brasserie. The Kings Bar serves cocktails in the atmosphere of a London club, and you can order draft beer in a country-pub ambience at Benjamin's Bar. The hotel has 24-hour room service. Other facilities include a theater-ticket agency, secretarial services, and car rental. Tube: Russell Square.

THE MEDIUM-PRICED RANGE

In the heart of London, the **"Y" Hotel,** 112 Great Russell St., London WC1B 3NQ (tel. 01/636-8616), is actually a modern accommodation. It was built by the London Central Young Men's Christian Association for men and women of all ages. At the Oxford Street end of Tottenham Court Road, this "Y" Hotel may not be like any you've ever seen before. Its facilities include squash courts, a gymnasium, a swimming pool, a shop, and an underground garage for car parking. Other facilities include a lounge and bar, plus a restaurant. Every bedroom has a private shower, central heating, color TV, and radio. The furnishings are up-to-date and comfortable, and there's even wall-to-wall carpeting. Single rooms with showers rent for £39 ($68.25) daily, the price rising to £59 ($103.25) in a double or twin-bedded room with shower, VAT and service included. Tube: Tottenham Court Road.

THE BUDGET RANGE

One of a row of similar buildings, the **Morgan Hotel,** 24 Bloomsbury St., London WC1B 3QJ (tel. 01/636-3735), is distinguished by its gold-tipped iron fence railings. Several of the 14 rooms overlook the British Museum, and the whole establishment is very much part of the international scholastic scene of Bloomsbury. The lobby is a bit cramped, the stairs rather steep, but the rooms are pleasant and the atmosphere congenial; consequently, the hotel is unusually heavily booked. The bedrooms in this completely refurbished hotel are well carpeted and have private

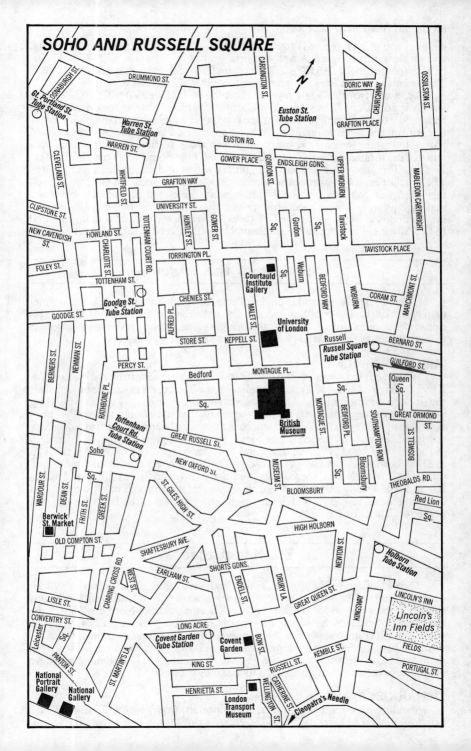

SOHO AND RUSSELL SQUARE

OSNABURGH ST.

DRUMMOND ST.

CARDINGTON ST.

DORIC WAY

CHURCHWAY

OSSULSTON ST.

Gt. Portland St. Tube Station

WARREN ST.

Warren St. Tube Station

Euston St. Tube Station

GRAFTON PLACE

CLEVELAND ST.

WHITFIELD ST.

TOTTENHAM COURT RD.

EUSTON RD.

GOWER PLACE

ENDSLEIGH GDNS.

GORDON ST.

UPPER WOBURN

MABLEDON

CARTWRIGHT

CLIPSTON E.

GRAFTON WAY

UNIVERSITY ST.

HUNTLEY ST.

GOWER ST.

Gordon Sq.

Woburn Sq.

Tavistock Sq.

TAVISTOCK PLACE

NEW CAVENDISH ST.

HOWLAND ST.

CHARLOTTE ST.

FOLEY ST.

TOTTENHAM ST.

FORRINGTON PL.

CHENIES ST.

Courtauld Institute Gallery

MALET ST.

BEDFORD WAY

WOBURN

CORAM ST.

MARCHMONT ST.

GOODGE ST.

Goodge St. Tube Station

ALFRED PL.

STORE ST.

KEPPELL ST.

University of London

Russell Sq.

Russell Square Tube Station

BERNARD ST.

BERNERS ST.

NEWMAN ST.

RATHBONE PL.

PERCY ST.

Bedford Sq.

MONTAGUE PL.

MONTAGUE ST.

BEDFORD PL.

GUILFORD ST.

Queen Sq.

GREAT ORMOND ST.

BOSWELL ST.

SOUTHAMPTON ROW

WARDOUR ST.

DEAN ST.

FRITH ST.

GREEK ST.

Soho Sq.

Tottenham Court Rd. Tube Station

GREAT RUSSELL ST.

NEW OXFORD ST.

British Museum

MUSEUM ST.

Bloomsbury Sq.

THEOBALDS RD.

Red Lion Sq.

Berwick St. Market

OLD COMPTON ST.

ST. GILES HIGH ST.

BLOOMSBURY

HIGH HOLBORN

NEWTON ST.

Holborn Tube Station

SHAFTESBURY AVE.

EARLHAM ST.

SHORTS GDNS.

DRURY LA.

GREAT QUEEN ST.

KINGSWAY

LINCOLN'S INN

LISLE ST.

WEST ST.

CHARING CROSS RD.

ENDELL ST.

Lincoln's Inn Fields

CONVENTRY ST.

Leicester Sq.

PANTON ST.

ST. MARTIN'S LA.

LONG ACRE

Covent Garden Tube Station

Covent Garden

BOW ST.

RUSSELL ST.

KEMBLE ST.

FIELDS

PORTUGAL ST.

National Portrait Gallery

National Gallery

KING ST.

HENRIETTA ST.

London Transport Museum

CATHERINE ST.

WELLINGTON ST.

Cleopatra's Needle

showers and toilets, big beds (by British standards), dressing tables with mirrors, and ample wardrobe space, as well as central heating. Singles cost £30 ($52.50) daily, and doubles go for £45 ($78.75). Prices include a full English breakfast and VAT. The nearest tubes are Russell Square and Tottenham Court Road.

Academy Hotel, 17-21 Gower St., London, WC1E 6HG (tel. 01/634-4115), is a joining of three 1776 Georgian row houses that retain many of the original architectural details. Substantially modernized and stylishly refurbished in 1987, it is different from the usual standard chain hotel and a good choice for travelers tired of paying four-star prices for two-star comforts (if that). It stands within walking distance of the theater section, Covent Garden, and other points of interest in the West End. Facilities include an elegant bar, library room, and a secluded patio garden. The hotel offers 24-hour room service, and each accommodation is not only well furnished but contains a color TV and radio, direct-dial phone, and beverage-making equipment. Most rooms have private showers and toilets, but public plumbing is adequate. Singles rent for £55 ($96.25) daily, with doubles going for £70 ($122.50), including tax and a continental breakfast. Tube: Euston Square.

---

19. East of the Tower

Carefully developed and thoughtfully restored, St. Katharine's Dock is immediately east of the Tower of London and Tower Bridge. In the once-dilapidated section are boutiques, pubs, walkways, and bridges surrounding the docks where yachts from many ports tie up. Many visitors prefer to stay in this area, too.

THE UPPER BRACKET

With sweeping views, the **Tower Thistle Hotel,** St. Katharine's Way, London E1 9LD (tel. 01/488-4134), stands tall, with the Tower and its bridge on one side, the dock on another, and the Thames on yet another. A strikingly modern building with 826 bedrooms, the hotel has its own parking facility, a bonus in crowded London. The units are air-conditioned and have private baths and TV with in-house video, in addition to the spectacular views from all angles. Singles rent for £95 ($166.25) to £110 ($192.50) daily, and doubles go for £105 ($183.75) to £125 ($218.75), with VAT and service included. The Tower offers a choice of three restaurants, the Princes Room, the Carvery, and the Which Way West Café. The Thames Bar and The Lounge both are relaxing ambiences in which to enjoy drinks with sweeping views of the river. For late night entertainment, the hotel has its own nightclub. Tube: Tower Hill.

---

20. Hampstead

The old village of Hampstead, sitting high on a hill, is the most desirable residential suburb of London. The village borders a wild heathland, which contains sprawling acres of wooded dells and fields of heather. Yet the Northern Line of the Underground reaches the edges of the heath, making it possible for Londoners to enjoy isolated countryside while living only 20 minutes from city center. These advantages have caused many young artists to discover what Keats could have told them years ago—Hampstead is the place to live. The little Georgian houses have never received so much attention and love as they get now.

THE BUDGET RANGE

Standing on a residential street, **Sandringham (Igar) Hotel,** 3 Holford Rd., London NW3 1AD (tel. 01/435-1569), is in one of the best parts of London.

Coming out of the Hampstead tube station, you'll be on Heath Street. Turn right and walk up toward the hill, past interesting shops, restaurants, and pubs. On the fourth turning to the right, you enter Hampstead Square, which leads to Holford Road. If you have a car, you can park in the driveway. Comfortable rooms often house professional people who want to be near the center of London while retaining the feel of rural life. From the upper rooms, you will have a view over Hampstead Heath and the heart of London. The hotel has a comfortable lounge with a color TV. The B&B charge in rooms without bath are £23 ($40.25) daily in a single, £39 ($68.25) in a double, and £48 ($84) for a four-bedded room. A double with a private bath or shower costs £45 ($78.75), rising to £50 ($87.50) in a triple and £55 ($96.25) in a four-bedded room. VAT is included. Breakfast is served in a pretty room that has a view of the well-kept garden.

21. Swiss Cottage

For another place to stay on a tree-lined residential street in north London, the following choice may appeal to you. It lies only ten minutes by Underground from the heart of the West End.

THE MIDDLE RANGE

Named for the district in which it stands, the **Swiss Cottage Hotel,** 4 Adamson Rd., London NW3 3HP (tel. 01/722-2281), consists of four late-Victorian houses that were joined to create the intriguing accommodations. The result is a maze of halls and staircases, with varying floor levels and bedrooms of different sizes and decor. Throughout, however, you'll find paintings and antique furniture, Persian rugs, chandeliers, wood inlay writing desks or bureaus, and patterned wallpaper. The glass-fronted reception desk contains a fine collection of porcelain figures. There is a quiet bar, a dining room where à la carte meals are served, a sauna, and 24-hour room service. Behind the hotel is a small formal town garden, plus the Tea House area. This is the honeymoon suite, but you need not be on honeymoon to rent it. Bedrooms in the main hotel are comfortable and, except for some singles, have modern showers or bathrooms. All have TV and phones. Singles cost £40 ($70) daily in a room whose occupant shares a shower with the guests of some of the other rooms. The most expensive singles go for £69 ($120.75) to £88 ($154) for a large deluxe unit with private bath. Doubles or twins rent for £68 ($119) to £96 ($168). Tariffs include a continental breakfast and VAT. Tube: Swiss Cottage.

22. Wimbledon

Wimbledon, in south London, has been linked with the history of the British capital for centuries, particularly its High Street at the top of Wimbledon Hill, but little is left from the days of yore. Today it's known for its international tennis championships, as the world's premier tennis competition is held here over a two-week period each summer. Also famous is the 1,000-acre Wimbledon Common, one of the largest green areas in the London environs.

THE UPPER BRACKET

Providing Georgian country-house elegance, **Cannizaro House,** West Side, Wimbledon Common, London SW19 4UF (tel. 01/879-1464), is an oasis of tranquility only a short distance from the center of London. Built in the 1720s, the house took its name from the Duke of Cannizaro, a Sicilian nobleman whose wife sponsored musical recitals here in the 1830s, establishing a lasting tradition. The house has had as residents and guests the rich and famous since its construction. The structure, with stone walls, painted ceilings, and a mansard roof, is set in parkland overlooking the Common. Individually furnished bedrooms offer luxury accommodations with a decor reflecting the colors and scents of gardens. Singles rent for £79 ($138.25) to £90 ($157.50) daily, and doubles go for £95 ($166.25) to £130 ($227.50). The restaurant looks out on lawns, a sunken garden, and woodlands. Tube: Wimbledon.

---

23. Airport Hotels

As one of the major gateways to Europe (not to mention England), London's two major airports are among the busiest in the world. Many readers have expressed a desire to be near their point of departure, spending the night in ease before "taking off." With that in mind, I'd suggest the following accommodations, beginning—

AT OR NEAR GATWICK

The airport's most convenient resting place is the **Gatwick Hilton International,** Gatwick Airport, Horley, Surrey RH6 0LL (tel. 0293/518080), a deluxe, five-floor hotel of the Hilton chain. A covered footbridge links the hotel and air terminal with a five-minute walk. You can also obtain porterage to the airport, and there are trolleys and electric cars if you can't cope with a walk. In the first-floor lobby, a glass-covered portico rises through four floors, containing a full-scale replica of the de Havilland Gypsy Moth airplane, *Jason,* used by Amy Johnson on her solo flight from England to Australia in 1930. The reception is close by, an area of much greenery, trees, and flowering shrubs. There is a health club with a sauna, massage room, Jacuzzi, a large gymnasium, and a heated indoor swimming pool. On the ground floor is a restaurant serving both English and continental dishes. The Jockey bar serves snacks, and there is also a cozy lounge bar, where refreshments are available 24 hours a day.

Rooms have full air conditioning, double-glazed windows, phone, radio, and color TV with a full-length feature film shown daily and a mini-bar. Laundry and dry cleaning are returned within the day if collected at 9 a.m. The 552 bedrooms, each with private bath and shower, cost from £92 ($161) daily in a single and from £97 ($169.75) in a double. Up-to-date flight information is flashed on the TV screen.

Gravetye Manor, near East Grinstead, West Sussex RH19 4LJ (tel. 0342/810567), is a 16th-century Elizabethan manor just 12 miles from Gatwick, part of an estate set in the hills, standing in its own 30 acres of woods, orchards, and a trout lake. It's approached by a mile-long winding driveway leading into an entrance courtyard. Later, you can discover the restored formal gardens, the lifetime creation of one of England's leading horticulturists, William Robinson, pioneer of the English natural garden. The spacious drawing room has tasteful furnishings, oak-paneled walls, and many antiques. Guests and area residents gather in the sitting room, warmed by a large oak fireplace, for apéritifs before dinner. All the 14 bed-chambers are different, named after trees on the estate: ash, bay, beech, whatever. My favorite is the Willow, an elegant, comfortable double with Tudor windows in both bedroom and bath from which you have a panorama of the gardens. Doubles or twin-bedded rooms range in price from £75 ($131.25) to £130 ($227.50) nightly. One is the former master bedroom, with a massive carved four-poster and, over the fireplace, wood-carved portraits of the original owners (Richard and Katherine Infield in 1598). The rates in a single with private bath are from £65 ($113.75). These prices are inclusive of a continental breakfast. Service is also included, but VAT is added to the entire account. Write well in advance for reservations in high season.

Dinner is to be savored, not rushed. The restaurant has the best wine cellar in England, with some 500 listings. They smoke their own salmon and venison in a smokehouse on the estate. Expect to spend from £35 ($61.25) for a complete meal. Luncheon is served daily from 12:30 to 2 p.m. and dinner from 7:30 to 9:30 p.m.

Cisswood House Hotel, Lower Beeding, near Horsham, West Sussex RH13 6NF (tel. 040/376-216), was called "Harrods in the country" by the locals when it was built in the late 1920s for Sir Woodman Burbidge, chairman of Harrods store. Craftsmen from the Harrods workshops were employed to create the wood and plasterwork and give the house its character, even if it is mock country Tudor. It is surrounded by traditional gardens with shrubs and flowering creepers, herbaceous borders, and well-kept lawns, with dovecotes and trees.

Othmar and Elizabeth Illes have owned Cisswood since 1979 and have built a reputation for their high-quality cooking and the comfort of their rooms. The dining room is beamed, and there is a cheerful bar. The bedrooms are all individually designed and have flower prints, potted plants, modern baths, and direct-dial phones. Four have four-poster beds. Prices range from £49 ($85.75) daily in a single and £65 ($113.75) in a double. The hotel also has an indoor swimming pool with exercise equipment. Cisswood lies about 12 minutes from Gatwick Airport, and you can order a taxi for an early departure if necessary.

Gatwick Copthorne Hotel, Copthorne, near Crawley, West Sussex RH10 3PG (tel. 0342/714971), is a 16th-century farmhouse with various additions, set in a large garden with a lake. A garden room overlooks the central patio with its fountains and weeping willows. The bar and many of the bedrooms in the old part of the house have ancient beams. Floral bedspreads and chintz curtains add to the ambience. Bathrooms are modern, but most singles have showers only. The restaurant is dark, with a low beamed ceiling and wooden balustrades. Meals include mainly French dishes, such as onion soup and bouillabaisse. The vegetables are fresh, and you have a good choice of desserts from the trolley. A set dinner costs £11.95 ($20.90), with an à la carte meal going for about £30 ($52.50) for three courses. As befits an airport hotel, food is available from 6:30 a.m. to 10:45 p.m. A single bedroom with a shower rents for £70 ($122.50) to £75 ($131.25) daily, while doubles go for £80 ($140) to £100 ($175). There are some ground-floor rooms suitable for the handicapped. Transportation to nearby Gatwick is available.

Langshott Manor, Horley, Surrey RH6 9LN (tel. 0293/786680), may lie only minutes from the modernity of Gatwick Airport, but it is a manor house dating from the 1700s. In the small market town of Horley, the location is about half an hour from the heart of London on the Gatwick-Victoria Express. Geoffrey and Rish Noble took over this manor standing on a 2½ acre estate and have painstakingly restored it. They rent five individually decorated bedrooms, decorated with porcelain, print wallpaper and fabrics from old designs, and antiques. The bedrooms have adjoining bathrooms luxuriously appointed with extra amenities such as bubble bath in an apothecary jar. Charges for overnight stays range from £65 ($113.75) daily in a single to £75 ($131.25) in a double. A traditional English cuisine is also served here.

AT OR NEAR HEATHROW

If you've got an overnight wait between planes, you might consider **Sheraton Skyline,** Bath Road (A4), Hayes, Middlesex UB3 5BP (tel. 01/759-2535), a leading airport hotel. The hotel operates on an international schedule, with travelers from around the world checking in around the clock. The hotel, which opened in 1971, offers 352 well-furnished bedrooms. Charges are £110 ($192.50) daily in a single and from £121 ($211.17) in a double. Facilities include an indoor swimming pool and a tropical patio. The Colony Room Restaurant offers an acceptable cuisine, and a club called Diamond Lil's might be amusing.

Heathrow Penta Hotel, Bath Road, Hounslow, Middlesex TW6 2AQ (tel. 01/897-6363), is within the perimeter of the airport, so many of the rooms have fantastic views of Concorde and jumbo-jet takeoffs, with double-glazed windows protecting your ears from the sound. The bedrooms have up-to-date amenities such as tea- and coffee-making equipment, mini-bars, TVs, and in-house movies. All units have a bathroom, and there is an indoor swimming pool and health center, plus a hairdresser and 24-hour laundry service. Singles are £83 ($145.25) daily, twins and doubles cost £94 ($164.50), including VAT and service. Besides the 24-hour coffeeshop, there is a restaurant, as well as a Flying Machine Bar decorated with flying prints and models.

Another convenient choice for a first or last night near the airport is the **Post House Hotel,** Sipson Road, West Drayton, Middlesex UB7 0JU (tel. 01/759-2323). This modern ten-story building is conveniently situated just off the M4 motorway, only minutes from the airport. The hotel has its own private car park and also offers frequent coach service to and from all airport terminals. The Post House has 580 bedrooms, with 160 on the two Executive Club floors offering club guests the use of the solaria, sauna, Jacuzzi, and fitness room. All the bedrooms have remote-control TVs, radios, direct-dial phones, mini-bars, private baths, and hot beverage facilities, and are fully air-conditioned. The prices are £77 ($134.75) daily for a standard single, £85 ($148.75) for an executive single. Doubles and twins cost £89 ($155.75) in a standard room, £97 ($169.75) in executive quarters. The hotel has two bars, as well as a choice of restaurants.

LONDON'S RESTAURANTS AND PUBS

1. THE WEST END
2. OTHER LOCALES
3. A DINING MISCELLANY
4. THE PUBS OF LONDON
5. THE WINE BARS

With the pressure of tourism and the influx of foreign chefs, the reputation of English cuisine has risen considerably. There also exists now a wave of English-born, -bred, and -trained chefs who have set a superb standard of cookery, using high-quality ingredients. One food writer called this new breed "the very professional amateur."

In the snackeries of suburbia the vegetables may still taste as if they had a grudge against you and the soup may remain reminiscent of flavored tapwater. But in the central sections of London—where you'll probably do your eating—the fare has improved immeasurably. This is largely because of intense competition from foreign establishments, plus the introduction of espresso machines, which make English coffee now resemble—well, coffee.

In the upper brackets, London has always boasted magnificent restaurants, several of which have achieved world renown. But these were the preserve of the middling wealthy, who have had their palates polished by travel abroad. Those less fortunate enjoyed a diet akin to parboiled blotting paper. For about a century the staple meal of the working class consisted of fish 'n' chips—and in my opinion, they still haven't learned to properly fry either the fish *or* the chips (potatoes). There are some dishes, however—mostly connected with breakfast—at which the English have always excelled. The traditional morning repast of eggs and bacon (imported from Denmark) or kippers (smoked herring, of Scottish origin) is a tasty starter for the day, and locally brewed tea beats any American bag concoction. It's with the other meals that you have to use a little caution. If you want to splurge in a big way, you have the London "greats" at your disposal. But if these eateries are too expensive for you, you'll find dozens of good moderately priced restaurants. And then I'll turn to the budget establishments that charge even less for a three-courser.

What may astonish you is the profusion of international restaurants. London offers a fantastic array of Italian, Indian, Chinese, French, German, Swiss, Greek, Russian, Jewish, and Middle Eastern dineries, which probably outnumber the native establishments. You'll find them heavily represented on my list.

If you're a vegetarian, as more and more people are these days, you will find it no longer necessary to seek out a specific vegetarian restaurant as most now provide vegetarian dishes. One, for example, has a special menu for vegetarians, another menu for meat-eaters. In fact, that health-conscious individual can find something good to eat in almost any place he or she selects. Even restaurants with a very limited table d'hôte menu of only three or four main courses usually reserves one of those courses for the vegetarian.

The prevailing mealtimes are much the same as in the U.S. You can get lunch from about midday onward and dinner until about 11 p.m., until midnight in the Soho area. The difference is that fewer Londoners go in for the "business lunch." They'll either make do with sandwiches or take a snack in a pub. The once-hallowed custom of taking afternoon tea became for many years the preserve of matrons unworried about their waistlines. However, in the past few years it is having a renaissance. Viewed as a civilized pause in the day's activities, it's particularly appealing to those who didn't have time for lunch or who plan an early theater engagement.

Most of the restaurants I mention serve the same meals for lunch or dinner, so they're easily interchangeable. Most—but not all—add a 10% to 15% service charge to your bill. You'll have to look at your check to make sure about that. If nothing has been added, leave a 12% to 15% tip.

All restaurants and cafés in Britain are required to display the prices of the food and drink they offer, in a place where the customer can see them before entering the eating area. If an establishment has an extensive à la carte menu, the prices of a representative selection of food and drink currently available must be displayed, as must the table d'hôte menu, if one is offered. Charges for service and any minimum or cover charge must also be made clear. The prices shown must be inclusive of VAT.

Finally, there's the matter of location. Once upon a time, London had two traditional dining areas: Soho for Italian and Chinese fare, Mayfair and Belgravia for French cuisine. Today the gastronomical legions have conquered the entire heart of the metropolis. You're likely to find any type of eatery anywhere from Chelsea to Hampstead. The majority of my selections are in the West End region, but only because this happens to be the handiest for visitors.

Note: If you wish to phone ahead from out of town for reservations at the more popular restaurants, remember the **area code for London is 01.**

---

1. The West End

I'll begin the pleasant task of exploring the cuisine in the major districts of the West End:

MAYFAIR
Stick a few extra pounds in your pocket and join the swells for a memorable meal in chic, high-priced Mayfair.

London's Leading Restaurant
Le Gavroche, 43 Upper Brook St., W.1 (tel. 408-0881), has long stood for the finest quality French cuisine in Great Britain. It's the creation of two Burgundy-born brothers, Michel and Albert Roux. Service is faultless; the ambience chic and formal, but not stuffy. The menu changes constantly, depending on the availability of the freshest produce of the season, but more important, on the inspiration of the Roux brothers, who began modestly in London at another location and have gone on to world fame in the culinary world.

Their wine cellar is among the most interesting in London, with many quality burgundies and bordeaux. Try, if featured, their stuffed smoked salmon and their mousseline of lobster. Most main courses are served on a silver tray covered with a silver dome. The lid is lifted off with great flourish, and the platters, like a stage play, are artistically arranged. You can enjoy an apéritif upstairs while perusing the menu and enjoying the delectable canapés. A set luncheon is offered at a relatively modest price of £19.50 ($34.15), with a table d'hôte dinner costing £45 ($78.75). To order à la carte in the evening will cost from £50 ($87.50) per person. Lunch is presented from noon to 2 p.m. and dinner from 7 to 10:30 p.m. Closed Saturday and Sunday. To be assured of a table, reserve well in advance. Tube: Bond Street or Marble Arch.

Mayfair's Grand Hotel Restaurants
The Oak Room, Le Meridien London, 21 Piccadilly, W.1 (tel. 734-8000), is one of the finest restaurants in London. The setting alone—said to be the most beautiful dining room in the center of London—would be worth the trip. But it is the refined cuisine that is the draw. Lavish in its appointments, this splendid period room where the greats of the world have dined (then and now) has been restored to all its gilded splendor, including the ceiling and the original oak paneling. Averting your eye a moment from this gilded magnificence, you can then preview the menu, a creation of an award-winning French chef, Michel Loraine (decorated with stars and toques), and David Chambers, who is as equally at home with the English culinary repertoire as in the most exacting French kitchen.

You can select from cuisine créative or cuisine traditionnelle, enjoying such dishes as filet of red mullet and scallops poached in stock enhanced with fennel or roast pigeon served warm on a French salad with crayfish. The set lunch at £18.50 ($32.40) is acclaimed as one of the food bargains of London, considering the quality of ingredients that go into it. It's a loss leader for the hotel, but a magnet for the movers and shakers of the West End business world who dine here weekly. A set dinner is also presented in the evening, costing from £27 ($47.25) and you can also peruse the à la carte selections. Reservations are vital, and service is Monday to Saturday (dinner only on Saturday) from noon to 2 p.m. and 7 to 10:30 p.m. Tube: Piccadilly Circus.

Bracewell's, Park Lane Hotel, Piccadilly, W.1 (tel. 499-3621). Sheltered by the thick fortresslike walls of this previously recommended hotel, Bracewell's is one of chic London's better-kept secrets. The cuisine prepared by English-born chef David Ryan is among the best in the capital, and the decor and the five-star service are worthy of its distinguished clientele. You might begin with a drink among the gilded torchères and comfortable armchairs of Bracewell's Bar. Later you will be ushered into an intimately illuminated room whose deeply grained paneling was long ago removed from a château in France by industrial magnate Pierpont Morgan. In the 1920s it was reinstalled at the Park Lane.

Full meals from Mr. Ryan's repertoire are served from noon to 2:30 p.m. and 7 to 10:30 p.m. daily except Saturday at lunch and all day Sunday. A fixed-price lunch costs £15 ($26.25), a set dinner going for £22 ($38.50). À la carte meals are around £40 ($70). The specialties are based on the freshest ingredients in any season. Examples of Mr. Ryan's talents are reflected by such dishes as slices of lobster encased in puff pastry with herb butter, terrine of wild duck with a reduced sauce of button onions, suprême of turbot topped with pike mousse and a carrot sauce, sliced breast of wild duck (cooked pink) and garnished with orange-and-basil sauce, and roasted boneless quail filled with foie gras and served on a bed of celeriac with red wine sauce. Reservations are needed. Tube: Hyde Park Corner.

London's Leading Fish Restaurants
Bentley's, 11 Swallow St., W.1 (tel. 734-4756), in business since 1916, lies just off Piccadilly Circus in the heart of London. There used to be a certain type of Englishman who emerged only in the early evening to head for Bentley's where he

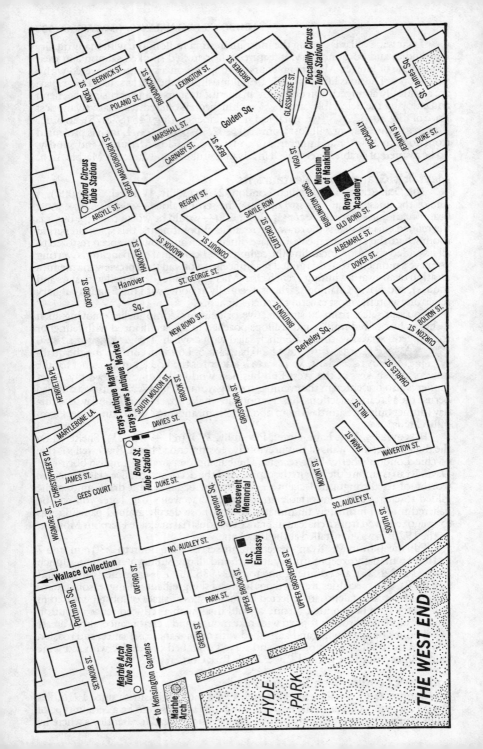

THE WEST END

would down his daily quota of oysters. If such a creature still exists, Bentley's, English to the core, is there to serve him. The oysters here, in fact, are considered among the best in London. You can also order such fare as home-smoked eel, sole Bentley, and salmon fishcakes. On the ground floor is a marble-topped oyster bar (the elegant restaurant is upstairs). Meals cost from £28 ($49) and are served from noon to 3 p.m. and 6 to 10:30 p.m. (closed Sunday). Tube: Piccadilly Circus.

Scotts, 20 Mount St., W.1 (tel. 629-5248), is considered the most noted restaurant in the world for oysters, lobster, and caviar. It is the most expensive fish restaurant in London. In addition to its regular spacious restaurant and cocktail bar, it has a special caviar bar and an oyster bar. Its origins were humble, going back to a fishmonger in 1851 in Coventry Street. However, its fame rests on its heyday at Piccadilly Circus when it often entertained Edward VII and his guests in private dining rooms. It has been at its present reincarnation since 1967, enjoying a chic address in the neighborhood of the swank Connaught Hotel and Berkeley Square. Its decor, with its terracotta walls, has been called "Assyrian Monumental," the wall panels hung with English primitive pictures.

The restaurant's chef believes in British produce, and he handles the kitchen with consummate skill and authority. You get top-notch quality and ingredients, but at a price—around £45 ($78.75) per person. Lobster is prepared "three ways," and you might also order smoked Ellingham eel. The eel comes from Suffolk where it is "swum" (that is, kept alive) until it's ready for smoking. Dover sole is prepared "any way." The English prefer it "on the bone," considering filleted fish for sissies. A favorite beginning is terrine de canard, and more down-to-earth dishes, such as fish cakes, appear regularly (or at least weekly) on the luncheon menu. Meals are served Monday through Saturday from 12:30 to 2:45 p.m. and 6 to 10:45 p.m. On Sunday only dinner is offered, from 7 to 10 p.m. Tube: Green Park.

The Medium-Priced Range

Langan's Brasserie, Stratton Street, W.1 (tel. 491-8822), has maintained its popularity since its opening in late 1976. The café is reminiscent of a Parisian bistro. The walls are covered with pictures, and the combination of overhead fans and potted palms creates a 1930s atmosphere. A complete meal, including wine, VAT, and service, comes to about £25 ($43.75). The long menu always has a good choice of English dishes, such as duck pâté and roast joints and pies, along with the classic French dishes. Live music is played during the dinner hour. Lunch is served from 12:30 to 2:45 p.m. and dinner from 7 to 11:45 p.m. Monday to Friday. On Saturday, hours are 8 p.m. to 12:45 a.m., and the restaurant is closed on Sunday. Upstairs is a more intimate dining room, although prices are the same as downstairs. The Venetian decor was the work of Patrick Proctor, the artist. Tube: Green Park.

Al Hamra, 31 Shepherd Market, W.1 (tel. 493-1954), is the premier Lebanese restaurant in London. You get good value, impeccable service, and food that delights the palate. As for the staff, Beirut's loss was London's gain. Nostalgic refugees —those who managed to get out with their money—come here for a taste of the old country, and they rarely leave disappointed. To begin with, you are faced with a dazzling selection of mezes, or appetizers. There are at least five dozen, both hot and cold, ranging from the inevitable hummus (chick peas) to such delights as shinklish (cheese salad of Lebanon). A salad of fresh vegetables is placed on each table, and you are to help yourself. For a main course, you can select from such dishes as grilled quail in garlic sauce and succulent grilled meats on a skewer. The bread, baked on the premises, is an important part of the ritual of dining here. Likewise, the Lebanese who frequent the place like the honeyed sweets, but a member of the staff assured me that these desserts are "adjusted" for English diners—that is, they are prepared with less sugar than is customary. Hours are noon to midnight daily, and the cost is £20 ($35) per head, which is reasonable, considering the quality of the fresh ingredients and the time-consuming preparation they take. Sometimes it's very difficult to get a table, so call early for a reservation. Tube: Green Park.

The Veeraswamy, 99-101 Regent St., W.1 (tel. 734-1401), is London's oldest and most famous Indian restaurant, having opened in 1927. Now beautifully restored in muted tones, it is still a leading choice for Indian regional and tribal dishes. In the kitchen each chef is a specialist in his particular region of the subcontinent. In the past, kings and show business personalities have flocked here, learning a lesson in gastronomic geography. From Gujarat to Goa (try the fiery coconut-flavored chicken), the cuisine is often mouth tingling. Vegetarians will delight in the thalis and home-baked breads. The best bargain, popular with the Regent Street business crowd, is the all-you-can-eat luncheon buffet at £12.50 ($21.90), a price rising to £20 ($35) and up for an à la carte dinner. Service is daily from noon to 3 p.m. and 6 to 11:30 p.m. Tube: Piccadilly Circus.

Coconut Grove, 3-5 Barrett St., W.1 (tel. 486-5269), is a bright, shiny restaurant at the end of St. Christopher's Place, just off Oxford Street. The restaurant has an art deco mood with subtle pastel shades and large palm trees. The restaurant has two levels: the ground floor favored by high-profile customers and the basement, preferred for business or more intimate lunches or dinners. A chef's specialty of the day accompanies the large and varied menu. Half a dozen or so salads are offered, including avocado and bacon, spinach, and chicken and walnut. Vegetarian dishes are an important part of the menu, particular favorites being vegetable pancakes, guacamole, and crudités. You might like the Coconut Grove fresh pasta or the broiled halibut with ratatouille. A lunch costs from £10 ($17.50), with dinners averaging around £16 ($28) per person. Hours are from noon to 11:30 p.m. Monday to Thursday and from noon to midnight Friday to Sunday. Sunday brunch is also popular, offered from noon to 4 p.m. Adjoining the restaurant is the Polo Bar, serving superb cocktails. During the summer months, tables are placed outside the bar on the pavement overlooking St. Christopher's Place walkway. Tube: Bond Street.

The Budget Range

Gaylord Mayfair, 16 Albemarle St., W.1 (tel. 629-9802), has established an enviable reputation among local connoisseurs of Indian cuisine. An elegant Oriental atmosphere pervades the restaurant, creating an air of festive expectancy. And the delicacies on which you dine do not disappoint you. So many regional dishes are available that one hardly knows where to begin. The restaurant features three different types of regional cooking: tandoori centers on the tandoor, an oven of Indian clay that is used for cooking foods while retaining the flavor and natural moisture. Mughlai cooking dates from the Moghul period of Indian history in which exotic dishes were prepared with rich combinations of spices. Kashmiri specialties frequently include combinations of lamb and yogurt. A set meal of tandoori mix or other meat costs £11.25 ($19.70), and a vegetarian fixed-price menu goes for £9.25 ($16.20). The Gaylord is open daily for lunch from noon to 3 p.m. and for dinner from 6 to 11:30 p.m. (to 11 p.m. on Sunday). Tube: Green Park.

CHELSEA

In this area, comparable to the Left Bank of Paris or the more elegant parts of Greenwich Village, even the simplest stable has glamour. Here the diplomats and wealthy-chic, the stars of stage and screen, and successful sculptors and painters long ago replaced the struggling artists. To reach the area, take the Circle or District Line to Sloane Square.

King's Road (named after Charles II) is the main street of Chelsea, and activity is lively here both day and night. On Saturday morning, Chelsea boutiques blossom with London's flamboyantly attired. What were once stables and garages (mews), built for the town houses nearby, have been converted and practically rebuilt, so that you see little alleyways with two-story houses, all brightly painted.

In the Mauve Era, Chelsea became popular with artists and writers. Oscar Wilde found refuge here, as did Henry James, Whistler, George Eliot, and many more. The Chelsea Embankment, an esplanade along the Thames, is also found here. The best-known and most interesting part of the embankment, Cheyne Walk (pronounced Chain-y), contains some Georgian town houses. It's a good place to go for a stroll around dusk.

This district boasts some of the city's finest restaurants, but not cheap ones.

Two Top Restaurants of London

La Tante Claire, 68 Royal Hospital Rd., S.W.3 (tel. 352-6045). The quality of its cuisine is so legendary that this "Aunt Claire" has become one of the grande dames of the capital's gaggle of French restaurants. It's considered a culinary monument of the highest order. The waiting list for an available table continues to make a meal here one of the more sought-after status symbols of London. A discreet doorbell, set into the Aegean-blue and white of the façade, prompts an employee to usher you politely inside. There, birchwood and chrome trim, bouquets of flowers, and a modernized, vaguely Hellenistic décor complement an array of paintings that might have been inspired by Jean Cocteau. Pierre Koffman, the celebrated chef, creates such specialties as galette de foie gras, turbot served with a cinnamon and lemon sauce, and pistachio-nut soufflé with pistachio ice cream. Every gastronome in London talks about his pigs' trotters stuffed with morels and the exquisite sauces that complement many of his dishes. A set luncheon is good value at £19 ($33.25). However, in the evening, expect to pay around £55 ($96.25) per person for dinner, from 12:30 to 2 p.m. and 7 to 11 p.m.; closed Saturday, Sunday, and for three weeks in August. You have a better chance of getting a table if you dine very early or very late. Tube: Sloane Square.

Chelsea Room, Hyatt Carlton Tower, 2 Cadogan Pl., S.W.1 (tel. 235-5411), is a superb restaurant, one of the best in London, located inside one of Hyatt's finest international properties (recommended in the previous chapter). The dining room's combination of haute cuisine, stylish clientele, and elegant decor make it a much-sought-after place for lunch or dinner. The location is one floor above lobby level of the hotel, at the end of a paneled hallway reminiscent of something in a private Edwardian house. The color scheme is tasteful and subdued in grays, beiges, and soft greens. Artwork, from contemporary Oriental watercolors to original 18th-century oils, was chosen with taste and an eye to beauty, and everywhere you look are fresh flowers and plants. The dining room is run by a winning team: maître cuisinier de France, Bernard Gaume, and the long-standing maître d'hôtel, Jean Quero. Original offerings, time-tested classics, and very fresh ingredients are the chef's forte. The menu will change by the time of your visit, but to give you an idea, you are likely to be served baked sea bass in a light sauce with leeks and a garnish of salmon and Russian caviar, roast partridge served on a bed of savoy cabbage, or small filets of venison in a game sauce with port and a medley of multicolored peppercorns with juniper berries. His desserts require a separate menu. Wedgwood plates with the restaurant's cockerel motif adorn each place setting. The average lunch costs from £22 ($38.50); dinners, from £40 ($70). The room is open daily from 12:30 to 2:45 p.m. and 7 to 11:15 p.m. (to 10:45 p.m. on Sunday). Tube: Sloane Square.

The Medium-Priced Range

Rib Room, Hyatt Carlton Tower, 2 Cadogan Pl., S.W.1 (tel. 235-5411). Many of the residents of the well-heeled neighborhood surrounding this five-star hotel drop in just for drinks and to enjoy the warmly intimate russet-colored decor. It sits on the ground floor of Hyatt's premier European hotel, behind glass windows allowing light to stream in from Cadogan Place. The place is richly textured with rust-colored marble, deeply grained hardwoods, subtle lighting, and brass trim. The food served here includes the very finest of Scottish beef along with fresh fish. Both the preparation and the service are excellent. You might ask for one of the seafood trays, including the "Billingsgate," containing two kinds of oysters, clams, shrimp, and crab, among other offerings. The traditional specialties include roast prime rib of Aberdeen Angus, New Yorker sirloin, roast rack of English lamb with rosemary, and a special mixed grill. Meals cost from £22 ($38.50) and are served Monday to Saturday from 12:30 to 2:45 p.m. and 7 to 11:15 p.m., on Sunday to 10:45 p.m. Tube: Sloane Square.

The English House, 3 Milner St., S.W.3 (tel. 584-3002), is a tiny restaurant in the heart of Chelsea, where dining is like being a guest in an elegant private house. Its decor, in which blues and terracotta predominate, provides both spectacle and atmosphere. The walls are clad in a printed cotton and are a traditional English design of autumn leaves and black currants. The fireplace and the collection of beautiful furniture adds to the background. The food is British with such succulent offerings as home oak-smoked pigeon breast, Old English steak pie with pickled walnuts, and Welsh rarebit made by a new recipe based on the time-honored ingredients: beer, mustard, cheese, and egg yolks. The chef's daily choices are included in a special luncheon menu at £10.50 ($18.40) for two courses and coffee. À la carte dinners average £30 ($52.50), all prices inclusive of VAT and service. The restaurant is open daily for lunch from 12:30 to 2:30 p.m. (on Sunday to 2 p.m.), and for dinner from 7:30 to 11:30 p.m., to 10 p.m. on Sunday. Tube: Sloane Square.

The English Garden, 10 Lincoln St., S.W.3 (tel. 584-7272), is pretty and light-hearted. The Garden Room on the ground floor is whitewashed brick with panels of large stylish flowers and stark white curtains. Rattan chairs in a Gothic theme and candy-pink napery complete the scene. With the domed conservatory roofs and banks of plants, the atmosphere lives up to its namesake. The menu is extensive and includes plenty of salads and fish. Interesting dishes are a checkerboard of freshwater fish (an intricately patterned mousse of salmon, carp, and pike), collops of beef with plum brandy, and lemon flummery, a deceptively rich confection of lemon and eggs, adapted from an 18th-century recipe, served with ratafia biscuits. The chef's daily choices are included in a special luncheon menu at £12.50 ($21.90) for three courses and coffee. À la carte dinners average £25 ($43.75), and all prices include VAT and service. A comprehensive wine list is available, with an excellent French house wine always obtainable. The restaurant is open daily for lunch from 12:30 to 2:30 p.m. (to 2 p.m. on Sunday) and for dinner from 7:30 to 10 p.m. Tube: Sloane Square.

Drakes, 2a Pond Pl., S.W.3 (tel. 584-4555), bears a resemblance to the hall of a grand Tudor house, with its bare brick walls, brass chandeliers, tapestries, and fine oil paintings of ducks. It has a visible kitchen where you can see baby lamb, game, and ducklings being spit-roasted over a charcoal grill. All main dishes are complemented by fine, fresh English produce. Typical English favorites such as Dover sole, smoked salmon, and roast beef with Yorkshire pudding are always available. There is a 100-bin wine list to represent the most outstanding wine regions. A three-course evening meal averages £25 ($43.75), with VAT and service included. Drakes is open for dinner seven days a week from 6:30 to 11 p.m. (from 7 to 10:30 p.m. on Sunday). Sunday lunch is served from 12:30 to 3 p.m. Drakes is fully air-conditioned and has a no-smoking area. Tube: South Kensington.

VICTORIA
This area, popularly called "Victoria," is in Westminster.

The Medium-Priced Range
Eatons Restaurant, 49 Elizabeth St., S.W.1 (tel. 730-0074). Finding a reasonably priced restaurant serving good food in expensive Belgravia is a bit of a trick. Long a reliable choice, Eatons is right near Victoria Station and that street of moderately priced small hotels, Ebury. Guests enter into a narrow room with a clublike ambience, where the service is first rate. The cuisine has been called "enlightened English" with French overtones. Translated, that means you are likely to be served

such dishes as grilled Scottish beef with herb butter, chicken suprême, or roast English lamb flavored with rosemary. Meals cost from £18 ($31.50) and up and are served daily except Saturday and Sunday from noon to 2 p.m. and 7 to 11:15 p.m. Tube: Sloane Square or Victoria.

Very Simply Nico, 48a Rochester Row, S.W.1 (tel. 630-8061), was created in a moment of whimsy by Nico Ladenis, considered by many as the finest chef in London. His grander and more expensive restaurant is at 35 Great Portland St., Fitzrovia (but more about that later). Run by his sous chef, Very Simply Nico, is in the words of Nico, "cheap and cheerful." Nevertheless, you can expect to spend from £22 ($38.50) per person. Wood floors seem to reverberate with the noise of contented diners, who pack in here daily at snug tables and chairs. The food is often simply prepared and invariably French inspired, with fresh ingredients handled deftly in the kitchen. The menu changes frequently. It is open Monday to Friday from noon to 2 p.m. and 6 to 11:15 p.m. On Saturday it serves dinner only and it is closed all day Sunday. Tube: Victoria.

ST. JAMES'S

Already described and previewed as a hotel district (see the previous chapter), elegant, aristocratic St. James's has for decades been known as a center of gastronomy. Its cookery can be either the best of British or the best of Japanese, as exemplified by the two restaurants previewed below in—

The Upper Bracket

Wiltons, 55 Jermyn St., S.W.1 (tel. 629-9955), is one of the leading exponents of cookery called "as British as a nanny." In spite of its move into new quarters, its developers re-created the ambience of the original premises. You might be tempted to have an apéritif or drink in the bar near the entrance, where photos of the royal family are alternated with oil portraits of the original owners.

The thoroughly British menu of this restaurant is known for its fish and game. You might begin with an oyster cocktail and follow with Dover sole, plaice, salmon, or lobster, prepared in any number of ways. In season you can enjoy such delights as roast partridge, roast pheasant, or roast grouse properly hung. The chef might ask you if you want them "blue" or "black," a reference to roasting times. If, after a dessert of, say, of sherry trifle or syllabub, you wish to be truly British, you may order a savory such as Welsh rarebit or soft roes, even anchovies. Dinners cost from £38 ($66.50) and reservations are vital. Lunch hours are 12:30 to 2 p.m. Monday to Friday; dinner, 6:30 to 10:30 p.m. Monday to Saturday. Tube: Green Park or Piccadilly Circus.

Suntory, 72 St. James's St., S.W.1 (tel. 409-0201), is the most elite, expensive, and best Japanese restaurant in London. Owned and operated by the Japanese distillers and brewers, it offers a choice of dining rooms. First-time visitors seem to prefer the Teppan-Yaki dining room downstairs, where iron grills are set in each table and you share the masterful skills of the high-hatted chef, who is frighteningly familiar with a knife. You can also dine in other rooms on fare such as sukiyaki and tempura, perhaps selecting sushi, especially the fresh raw tuna fish delicately sliced. You can also enter one of the private dining rooms, but only if shoeless. Waitresses in regional dress serve you with all the highly refined rituals of the Japanese, including the presentation of hot towels. You may prefer a salad of shellfish and seaweed or a superb squid. Appetizers are artful and delicate, and even the tea is superior. Japanese businessmen on expense accounts like the hushed tone of the place, and the elegant decor, which is said to evoke the quality of a Japanese manor hours. The least expensive way to eat here is to order the £12 ($21) set lunch. Dinners begin at £23 ($40.25). Suntory is open Monday to Saturday from noon to 1:30 p.m. and 7 to 9:30 p.m. Tube: Green Park.

LEICESTER SQUARE

Named for the Earl of Leicester, and once the site of the home of Sir Joshua Reynolds, Leicester Square has since become the movie center of London. The 19th-century square is a congested area of stores, theaters, movie houses, even churches. It also has some moderately priced restaurants and pubs (popular with West End actors) in its little offshot lanes and alleyways.

The Medium-Priced Range

Chez Solange, 35 Cranbourne St., W.C.2 (tel. 836-0542), is crowded and cozy, and has a loyal following. Located near the Wyndham Theatre, it's still run by René and Thérèse Rochon, and the kitchen still specializes in traditional bourgeois French cuisine, such as cassoulet Toulousain and blanquette de veau. Open daily except Sunday from noon to 2 a.m., the best value is its pre-theater menu, costing £13.50 ($23.65) per person, but watch those supplements. The average à la carte meal will cost £25 ($43.75). Try the breast of chicken stuffed with mushrooms and baked in puff pastry, with truffles and a sherry sauce. Piano entertainment is provided in the evening, and it's vital to reserve if you're dining after the theater, as Chez Solange is at its most popular then. Tube: Leicester Square.

J. Sheekey Ltd., 29-31 St. Martin's Court, W.C.2 (tel. 240-2565), is an 1896 restaurant and an art nouveau oyster bar that over the years has been a gathering place for show people (autographed celebrity photos on the wall). Trying to get a table may make you feel like a salmon going upstream, but it's worth it. Sheekey serves a pre- and after-theater meal. For a beginning, I suggest native oysters. Most fish dishes are either grilled or poached. The fish cakes are now classic, and if you want to know how the British used to dine, ask for the "stewed eels and mash." A complete meal will cost £24 ($42) to £30 ($52.50), more if you order lobster. The restaurant is open Monday to Saturday from 12:30 to 3 p.m. and 5:30 to 11:30 p.m. It faces the stage doors of the Albury and Wyndham theaters and is around the corner from the English National Opera. Tube: Leicester Square.

ON THE STRAND

In another major geographic and tourist center, the Strand, you can sample "English fayre" or else have a nostalgic taste of American food.

The Medium-Priced Range

Simpson's-in-the-Strand, 100 The Strand, W.C.2 (tel. 836-9112), is more of an institution than a restaurant. Next to the Savoy Hotel, it has been doing business since 1828. All this very Victorian place needs is an Empire. It has everything else: Adam paneling, crystal, and an army of grandly formal waiters hovering about. On most first-time visitors' lists, there is this notation: "See the changing of the guard, then lunch at Simpson's." It's that popular, so make a reservation. There is one point on which most diners agree: Simpson's serves the best roasts (joints) in London. One food critic wrote that "nouvelle cuisine here means anything after Henry VIII." Huge roasts are trolleyed to your table and you can have slabs of beef carved for you and served with traditional Yorkshire pudding. The classic dishes are roast sirloin of beef, roast saddle of mutton with red currant jelly, roast Aylesbury duckling, and steak, kidney, and mushroom pie. Remember to tip the tail-coated carver. For dessert, you might order the treacle roll and custard or else Stilton with a vintage port. Meals cost £18 ($31.50) to £25 ($43.75). Service is Monday to Saturday from noon to 2:45 p.m. and 6 to 9:45 p.m. From 6 to 7 p.m., an early evening dinner is offered for £13 ($22.75), with three courses and coffee, including VAT and service. Tube: Covent Garden.

Joe Allen's, 13 Exeter St., W.C.2 (tel. 836-0651), long ago invaded London with its red-checked tablecloths, barbecued ribs, and bowls of chili. The food is solid, reliable, and rarely disappointing. Try the other familiar specialties: black-bean soup, calves' liver and onions, steak, and the really tasty pecan pie. Expect to spend at least £12 ($21) to £22 ($38.50). Show business posters adorn the walls and service is by waiters and waitresses who just may be out-of-work actors and actresses. The guests are also often people connected with the world of the theater and after-theater crowds. Joe Allen's is open from noon to 1 a.m. every day (till midnight on Sunday). Tube: Covent Garden or Embankment.

COVENT GARDEN

In 1970 London's flower, fruit, and veg market celebrated its 300th anniversary. But "Auld Lang Syne" should have been the theme song that day, as the historic, congested market was transferred in 1974 to a 64-acre site at Nine Elms, in the suburb of Vauxhall, 2½ miles away, across the Thames.

Covent Garden was originally designed in the 1630s by Inigo Jones, using the Florentine style he imported to England. The Covent Garden Market was established in 1671 by Charles II on the site of the abbot of Westminster's convent garden (hence its name). The king's mistress, Nell Gwynne, once peddled oranges on the market's Drury Lane (and later appeared on the stage of the Drury Lane Theatre).

All that remains of the original buildings is the church of **St. Paul's Covent Garden,** where the English actress, Dame Ellen Terry (noted in particular for her letters to G. B. Shaw), is buried. In fact, St. Paul's eastern face looks down on the market where Professor Higgins from Shaw's *Pygmalion* met his "squashed cabbage leaf," Eliza Doolittle. On the wall of St. Paul's Church is a carving commemorating the first performance in England of Punch's Puppet Show, witnessed in 1662 by Samuel Pepys. Nowadays there are often guitarists, flautists, and violinists playing in the area for their own pleasure, generally the center of an admiring crowd. Also nearby is the **Royal Opera House** on Bow Street, housing the Royal Ballet and the Royal Opera Company. On nearby Russell Street, Samuel Johnson met his admirer, Boswell, and coffeehouses in the district were once patronized by Addison and Steele.

Covent Garden has now been turned into a commercial and entertainment district, complete with restaurants, hotels, and a convention center. An old cabbage warehouse was reopened as the Jubilee Market. Monday is the antique market, and Saturday and Sunday are the days of a crafts market. Cockney costermongers (vegetable traders) have moved in in force, including the fastest apple polisher in the business and a purveyor of jellied eels.

The area also attracts art galleries, as is appropriate in Covent Garden. In the 18th century it was a beehive of artists, including Lely and Kneller (famous portrait painters, the latter of whom is buried at St. Paul's Church, around the corner). Others who lived here were Thornhill, Richard Wilson, Fuseli, Daniel Mytens, the sculptor Roubiliac, Zoffany, and Flaxman. The American painter Benjamin West also lived here after he got out of jail for trying to study in London during the Revolution.

The Upper Bracket

Inigo Jones, 14 Garrick St. (tel. 836-6456), is one of the lights of Covent Garden, and although it has been around for more than a quarter of a century, it's better than ever. But what has made the restaurant such a renewed success is the cookery of the chef de cuisine, Paul Gayler. I can't recommend any specialties, because he depends for his inspiration on the daily offerings of the marketplace. For example, you might be served breast of new season grouse with a red wine and black currant sauce or roast "best end" of lamb with fresh herbs. The average price for an à la carte meal is £45 ($78.75), served from 7 to 11:30 p.m. A fixed-price meal, costing £18.25 ($31.95), is offered at lunchtime and from 5:30 to 7 p.m. All prices include VAT and service. Hours are 12:30 to 2:30 p.m. Monday to Friday for lunch and 5:30 to 11:30 p.m. Monday to Saturday for dinner; closed Sunday. It's imperative to telephone for a reservation. Tube: Covent Garden.

Boulestin, 1A Henrietta St., W.C.2 (tel. 836-7061). This famous old restaurant was founded by Marcel Boulestin, the first Fleet Street restaurant critic, more than half a century ago. It's reached by a side door that leads down into the basement beneath a bank. Kevin Kennedy, who is both the manager and the chef, is one of the new British-bred cuisine experts who has style, flair, and imagination in the kitchen. The chandeliers are still there, and the menu still has many of the old Boulestin dishes, including crab with artichaut, coquilles St-Jacques, and magret de canard. You might also try the tulipe de sorbets maison. But Mr. Kennedy is also free to experiment—much to the pleasure of his guests. He offers a set lunch for £18 ($31.50), but dinner could run higher than £45 ($78.95) per person, including some wine. The restaurant is open from 12:30 to 2:30 p.m. and 7:30 to 11:15 p.m. It is closed for lunch on Saturday, all day Sunday, on bank holidays, and during most of the month of August. Tube: Covent Garden.

The Medium-Priced Range

Poons of Covent Garden, 41 King St., W.C.2 (tel. 240-1743), is one of the best Chinese restaurants in London. The place is run by Wai-Lim (Bill) Poon. Mr. Poon's great-great-grandfather cooked for the Chinese emperors, and succeeding generations of the family have all interested themselves in traditional Chinese cookery. The decor is reminiscent of *The World of Suzie Wong*. Tables surround an island see-through kitchen. The house specializes in wind-dried meat, including sausage, which is quite different in flavor from smoked. Two of the most recommendable courses include Poons special crispy duck and Poons special wind-dried meat with seasonal greens. If you're a serious and dedicated gourmet of Chinese cuisine, Poons will provide you with some rare and delectable specialties, providing you give them 24 hours' notice. Ever had stewed duck's feet with fish lips? An à la carte meal averages £25 ($43.75), with a table d'hôte menu costing £16.50 ($28.90). The restaurant is open from noon to 11:30 p.m. daily except Sunday. Tube: Covent Garden.

Rules, 35 Maiden Lane, off the Strand, W.C.2 (tel. 836-5314), dates from 1798 when it made its debut as an oyster bar. As such, it lays claim to being the oldest restaurant in London still operating on the original premises. Over its long and legendary history, it has been the steady haunt of actors and actresses, newspaper columnists, barristers, and such literary giants as Thackeray, John Galsworthy, H. G. Wells, and Graham Greene. In the Gay '90s the Prince of Wales (later Edward VII) was its most famous patron, accompanied, as always, by the Jersey Lillie. The prince dined on the second floor, now the Edward VII Room. Pictures of Lillie hang in the alcove where they used to sit. Another alcove honors Charles Dickens, who used to dine and do some of his writing at Rules. You enter via the front bar, with its red plush settees. The walls are hung with cartoons George Whitelaw did in the '20s and '30s. Rules has both a summer and a winter menu. You can order such classic dishes as Loch Fyne oysters, jugged hare, and Aylesbury duckling in orange sauce. Depending on the season, you might have game fish, such as wild Scottish salmon or wild sea trout, or game birds, perhaps grouse, snipe, partridge, pheasant, and woodcock. You can also order those unusual British savories, such as angels on horseback (oysters wrapped in bacon on toast). Meals begin at £18 ($31.50) per person, plus the cost of your drink. A pre-theater dinner is available for £13 ($22.75), served from 3 to 6:30 p.m. Rules is open for lunch and dinner from noon to midnight Monday to Saturday. Reservations are important. The restaurant is closed on Sunday. Tube: Covent Garden.

The Budget Range

Porter's English Restaurant, 17 Henrietta St., W.C.2 (tel. 836-6466), owned by the Earl of Bradford, who is a frequent visitor, has an informal and lively atmosphere in comfortable surroundings. Known as a "pie and pudding" restaurant, it specializes in classic English pies, including steak and kidney, lamb and apricot, chicken and asparagus, and steak, oyster, and clam. The traditional roast beef with

Yorkshire pudding is served on weekends. With whipped cream or custard, the "puddings" come hot or cold, including bread-and-butter pudding and a steamed syrup sponge. Count on a bill of around £12 ($21). The bar does quite a few exotic cocktails, and you can also order Westons Farmhouse Draught cider by the half pint, even English wines or traditional English mead. It is open from noon to 3 p.m. and 5:30 to 11:30 p.m. Monday to Friday, from noon to 11:30 p.m. Saturday, and from noon to 10:30 p.m. Sunday. Tube: Covent Garden.

BLOOMSBURY

In the academic heart of London, you may wish to stop for a meal after spending time at the British Museum or browsing through the many bookstores.

For a very special meal in truly British surroundings, try **Winstons Restaurant and Wine Bar,** 24 Coptic St., W.C.1 (tel. 580-3422), named in honor of Winston Spencer Churchill. Winstons offers good food and wine in a unique traditional but informal way. The restaurant is set in an original 18th-century Bloomsbury house full of Churchill mementos, whose first-floor dining room is decorated in Edwardian club style. Your meal might begin with a Stilton or Brie wrapped in pastry and deep-fried, served with fresh cranberries, followed by Scottish salmon, steak, or filet of beef Wellington. Desserts include the old favorite English apple pie. The average price for a meal, including wine, is £25 ($43.75). The restaurant is open for lunch from 11 a.m. to 3 p.m. Monday to Friday and for dinner from 5:30 to 11 p.m. Monday to Saturday. On the ground floor, the wine and piano bar offers a unique Churchillian meeting place with an extensive wine list. The establishment, which is closed Sunday, is fully air-conditioned. Tube: Tottenham Court Road.

WESTMINSTER

Our dining expedition to Westminster will take us to the Tate Gallery among other places.

The Medium-Priced Range

Pomegranates, 94 Grosvenor Rd., S.W.1 (tel. 828-6560). The owner of this basement restaurant, Patrick Gwynn-Jones, has traveled far and collected dishes from throughout the world. Asian and Indonesian delicacies vie for a place on the menu with European and North American dishes, offering such choices as Scandinavian gravad lax, Mexican baked crab with avocado and tequila, West Indian peppered filet of beef, and English game pie. The decor consists of soft amber lights, mirrors, and well-laid tables. Bread is baked twice a day, and vegetables are fresh, adding to the pleasure. You should get away for about £30 ($52.50) a person for dinner, including wine, but if you start on the luscious desserts—fresh mango sorbet, honey and brandy ice cream—it will cost more. The place is open for lunch from 12:30 to 2:15 p.m. Monday to Friday and for dinner from 7:30 to 11:15 p.m. Monday to Saturday. There is a good wine list and some reasonably priced house wines. Special luncheons are featured for £10.50 ($18.38), £13.50 ($23.65), and £16 ($28). It's best reached by taxi.

The **Tate Gallery Restaurant,** Millbank, S.W.1 (tel. 834-6754), is better than ever. Even if it weren't, it would still be a viable choice as the Whistler Room contains the famous murals by Rex Whistler. The menu undergoes seasonal changes, but you can count on good, wholesome food in the British tradition. Some recipes, I suspect, were in use in Victoria's time, and the lamb chops, for example, are likely to be named after Lord Nelson. The wine list is extensive, and the restaurant is widely praised for its moderate tabs on some excellent vintages. It's essential to reserve a table (many in-the-know locals call ahead and even order their wine so that it can be at the right temperature upon their arrival). Costing from £15 ($26.25), lunches in this highly unusual setting are served from noon to 3 p.m. Monday to Saturday. Tube: Pimlico. Bus: 88.

BELGRAVIA

Belgravia after dark used to be a gastronomic wilderness. Happily, that situation changed long ago.

The Medium-Priced Range

Ciboure, 21 Eccleston St., S.W.1 (tel. 730-2505). The artfully simple decor mingles elements of hi-tech with clear colors, unusual flowers, and imaginative lighting. Even the menu is abbreviated and enlightened, offering flavorful combinations of food whose ingredients are impeccably fresh. The vegetables, too often neglected in England, are perfectly cooked. It lies on the periphery of Belgravia. A set lunch is offered for £14 ($24.50), and à la carte dinners go for around £30 ($52.50). An after-the-theater fixed-price menu is priced at £14 ($24.50). Specialties include a papillote of barbue aux légumes fondants, spring lamb with a duxelle of mushrooms, and filets of red snapper with a rosemary-cream sauce. Lunch is served daily except Saturday from noon to 2:30 p.m. and dinner from 7 to 11:30 p.m. Reservations are necessary, and the restaurant is closed on Sunday. Tube: Victoria Station.

Drones, 1 Pont St., S.W.1 (tel. 235-9638), was labeled by one newspaper columnist the "unofficial club for the bright people, at least half of whom seem to know each other." Long ago, David Niven (now deceased) & Friends launched this two-floor restaurant, and its reputation for charm and chic spread. Reservations are imperative, preferably a day in advance. There's no elaborate menu, just simple but good food. At lunch, have the cheese soufflé or oysters. For dinner, the calves' liver with bacon will be cooked pink if you prefer. Main dish specialties are veal Pojarsky Palace, entrecôte de boeuf au poivre, and fish cakes. The menu is wisely limited and seldom changes, although plats du jour are featured. A meal costs from £19 ($33.25). You sit on bentwood armchairs at white wrought-iron tables. The white walls are perfect foils for patchwork quilts. Drones is open from 12:30 to 3 p.m. and 7:30 p.m. to midnight seven days a week. Tube: Sloane Square.

KNIGHTSBRIDGE—BROMPTON ROAD

After splurging at the high-priced shops of Knightsbridge, these choices will make you feel better.

The Upper Bracket

Turner's, 87 Walton St., S.W.3 (tel. 584-6711), is named for Brian J. Turner, one of the most accomplished chefs of London who gained fame at a number of establishments he didn't own. As one critic aptly put it, his food comes not only fresh from the market that day but "from the heart." He had early roots in Yorkshire, but surely he didn't learn his refined cuisine working in his father's transport "caff" in Leeds. His cooking has been called "cuisine à la Brian Turner," meaning he doesn't seem to imitate anyone but sets his own standards. Try, for example, his marinated raw scallops with shredded gherkins, sea bass with fresh tomato-and-basil dressing, or a roast rack of lamb with a herb crust. He seems to view cooking as a "performance," and sometimes he'll make an appearance in the dining room, asking about his food and how it is perceived. A four-course menu is offered for £22.50 ($39.40), but you will more likely spend from £35 ($61.25). A table d'hôte lunch is a superb bargain at £15 ($26.25). Lunch is served from 12:30 to 2:45 p.m. Monday to Friday and from 12:30 to 2:45 p.m. Sunday. Dinner is offered seven days a week from 7:30 to 11 p.m. Tube: Knightsbridge.

Waltons Restaurant, 121 Walton St., S.W.3 (tel. 584-5297), is now deep into its second decade. A rendezvous of posh, it offers the best quality fresh produce from local and European markets served with flair in elegant surroundings. Its chefs prepare a refined international cuisine, featuring such British dishes as roast breast of Norfolk duckling or roast filet of Welsh lamb with crab. Waltons, long a favorite with the Harrods lady shoppers' crowd, has a reputation for being expensive. However, its "Simply Waltons" lunch at £13 ($22.75) offers three courses and is considered one of London's best dining values. For theater-goers and late eaters, a late night supper, available from 10 p.m., goes for £19.50 ($34.15). Sunday lunch is only £15 ($26.25) for three courses and offers the traditional Sunday roast. Otherwise, à la carte orders can range from £45 ($78.75) per person. The wine list, which features the best champagne list in London, is wide ranging, from Australia to California. The restaurant is open daily, including Sunday, from 12:30 to 2:30 p.m. (Sunday until 2 p.m.) and 7:30 to 11:30 p.m. (Sunday until 10:30 p.m.). Tube: Knightsbridge.

The Medium-Priced Range

San Lorenzo, 22 Beauchamp Pl., S.W.3 (tel. 584-1074). This is the kind of fashionable, young, modern place that has a two-level dining room capped with a glass canopy that is pulled back on sunny days. Reliability is the hallmark of the cuisine, that and good-quality produce, often seasoned with fresh herbs. Nearly everything you order seems delectable, from the homemade fettuccine with salmon to the carpaccio, and certainly the risotto with fresh asparagus. Meals, costing from £25 ($43.75), are served from 12:30 to 3 p.m. and 7:30 to 11:30 p.m. Monday to Saturday. Always make a reservation, and even then, it may be hard to get a table when you show up. Tube: Knightsbridge.

Shezan, 16-22 Cheval Pl., off Montpelier Street, S.W.7 (tel. 589-7918), is a leading Indian/Pakistani restaurant a five-minute walk from Harrods. This brick-and-tile establishment in Kensington turns out zesty dishes from its clay tandoor ovens. Murgh tikki lahori (marinated tandoori chicken) is usually served slightly pink. Another specialty is bhuna gosht (lamb cooked with tomatoes and spices). Tandoori charcoal barbecues and grills are always featured as are kebabs. The tandoori breads are excellent, especially roti, a dark wholewheat bread. Expect to spend from £18 ($31.50) for a complete dinner. However, a set lunch costs only £9.50 ($16.65). Food is served from noon to 2:30 p.m. and 7 to 11:30 p.m. daily except Sunday. Tube: Knightsbridge.

The Budget Range

Harvey's at the Top, the rooftop restaurant above Harvey Nichols store, Knightsbridge, S.W.1 (tel. 235-5000, ext. 2149, for table reservations), is a light, airy place among the rooftops of Knightsbridge. In summer you can eat in the open air, but there is also a large restaurant inside. The day starts with a continental breakfast at 10 a.m., costing £2.50 ($4.40). The staff serves morning coffee, luncheon, then afternoon tea until 5:30 p.m. when the store closes. There is a selection of appetizers, main courses, desserts, cheese, and coffee, or you can help yourself from the cold buffet. The average cost is around £12 ($21). They also do a real old cream tea, with homemade scones, strawberry jam, and clotted Devon cream to revive the flagging shopper. Tube: Knightsbridge.

KENSINGTON

If Princess Di didn't ask you to stay to dinner at Kensington Palace, you'll be just as happy with:

The Upper Bracket

La Ruelle, 14 Wrights Lane, W.8 (tel. 937-8525), is one of the top restaurants in Kensington. Lying off Kensington High Street, the restaurant has a pretty color scheme in a subtle pink and gray-blue. Shoppers and business people predominate at lunch, but the evening draws a sophisticated crowd. The food is prepared by a French staff that offers cuisine moderne. Set business lunches cost from £13.50 ($23.65), and an evening table d'hôte menu goes for £19 ($33.25). À la carte meals, however, may go as high as £50 ($87.50). Hours are from noon to 2:30 p.m. and

6:30 to 11:30 p.m. Tuesday to Saturday. The restaurant is closed Sunday and Monday as well as on major holidays. Tube: High Street Kensington.

Launceston Place Restaurant, la Launceston Pl., W.8 (tel. 937-6912), has a kind of urban chic, lying in an affluent, almost village-like neighborhood. The restaurant is a series of uncluttered Victorian parlors illuminated in the rear by a skylight at lunch. Lying off Gloucester Road, it stands next to Lady Eden's School, which is known for training what used to be called—and still is around here—debutantes. Since its opening in 1986 Launceston Place has been known for its food. You get a classic British cuisine, including such dishes as steamed mussels in cider with spring onions, liver with red onion marmalade and "bubble and squeak," and a casserole of pheasant with wild mushrooms. Set menus, served from 12:30 to 2:30 p.m. and 7 to 8 p.m., cost £9.50 ($16.65) for two courses, £11.50 ($20.15) for three courses. A fixed-price Sunday lunch menu always includes traditional roast beef with Yorkshire pudding as well as a choice of other dishes. The price for the Sunday lunch is £11.50 ($21.90). À la carte dinners cost from £22 ($38.50). Hours are from 12:30 to 2:30 p.m. and 7 to 11:30 p.m. It is closed for lunch on Saturday and for dinner on Sunday night. Tube: Gloucester Road.

The Middle Bracket

Clarke's, 124 Kensington Church St., W.8 (tel. 221-9225), is named after English chef Sally Clarke, who is considered one of the finest in London. She trained in California at Michael's in Santa Monica and the River Café in Venice (California, that is). Everything is bright and modern, with wood floors, discreet lighting, and additional tables in the basement. You get a set menu with a very limited choice at this excellent Anglo-French restaurant, but the food is so well prepared "in the new style" that diners rarely object. A set two-course lunch costs £14 ($24.50) and a table d'hôte dinner £25 ($43.75). Lunch hours are 12:30 to 2 p.m., and dinner or supper, from 7:30 to 11 p.m. Monday to Friday; closed Saturday and Sunday. You might begin with such appetizers as a hot cream soup of roasted red peppers with parmesan and rosemary breadsticks, then follow with pork filet marinated in sesame oil, ginger, and mint, which is grilled and served with a light mint sauce. Desserts are likely to include a strawberry-and-vanilla ice cream trifle. Tube: Notting Hill Gate or High Street Kensington.

Boyd's Glass Garden, 135 Kensington Church St., W.8 (tel. 727-5452), is one of the stellar lights along this street of antique shops, which is also becoming known for its outstanding English restaurants. Small, cozy, and intimate, Boyd's is named for its chef and owner, Boyd Gilmour, who has stylishly decorated the place with the look of a Victorian conservatory. The menu he conceives is always one of the most imaginative on the street—light-hearted fare prepared with fresh, carefully chosen ingredients. Try, for example, char-grilled salmon marinated in balsamic vinegar. A set luncheon is offered for £14.75 ($25.80), but an à la carte dinner is likely to cost from £25 ($44.65). Hours are Tuesday to Friday from 12:30 to 2:30 p.m. and Tuesday to Saturday from 7:30 to 10:30 p.m. Tube: Notting Hill Gate.

SOUTH KENSINGTON

When you're exhausted from South Kensington's museums, try a feast at the following:

The Upper Bracket

Bibendum, Michelin House, 81 Fulham Rd., S.W.3 (tel. 581-5817), is a fashionable restaurant in a whimsical art nouveau style. On the ground level is a more affordable Oyster Bar, and upstairs is an elegant restaurant attracting the glitterati, everybody from Fergie to Dustin Hoffman. At the Oyster Bar you can order wine by the glass along with oysters from Colchester in East Anglia or West Cork in Ireland, plus an array of seafood. A meal here just begins at £12 ($21) but could easily run two or three times that. No reservations are accepted: you just show up and hope for a seat. Upstairs, reservations (as far in advance as possible) are mandatory if you wish to taste the viands prepared by Simon Hopkinson, one of the most outstanding chefs on the London scene. Hearty regional French cooking is all the rage here, some critics calling the fare *cuisine bourgeoise*. A set lunch goes for £18.50 ($32.40), with à la carte dinners costing from £35 ($61.25) per person. Hours are Monday to Friday from 12:30 to 2:30 p.m. and 7 to 11:30 p.m.; on Saturday from 12:30 to 3:30 p.m. Closed Sunday. Tube: South Kensington.

The Medium-Priced Range

Bombay Brasserie, Courtfield Close, S.W.7 (tel. 370-4040), is the finest, most popular, and most talked-about Indian restaurant in London. Established in 1982, with a cavernous trio of rooms, it is staffed by one of the capital's most accommodating teams of Indian-born waiters, each of whom is willing to advise you on the spice-laden delicacies that thousands of years of Indian culinary tradition have developed. Lattices cover the windows, dhurrie rugs the floors, and sepia photographs of imperial Britain at its Asian height adorn the walls. You might order a drink amid the wicker chairs of the pink-and-white bar before heading into dinner. The atmosphere there has often been compared to Singapore's Raffles. One of the two dining rooms curves like a half moon beneath a glass-covered ceiling to create an Edwardian conservatory. A buffet lunch costs around £11.50 ($20.15) and, considering its quality, is one of the best food values in London. It's served daily from 12:30 to 3 p.m. and is especially popular on Sunday, so reservations are important. À la carte meals, costing from £18 ($31.50) each, are served nightly from 7:30 p.m. to midnight. One look at the menu, and you're launched on "A Passage to India," a grand culinary tour of the subcontinent: every dish from tandoori scallops to chicken tikki (a dish from the Hindukush mountains). Whole meals for vegetarians are also served. One corner of the menu is reserved for the cookery of Goa. Tube: Gloucester Road.

Hilaire, 68 Old Brompton Rd., S.W.7 (tel. 584-8993), is a jovially cramped restaurant, housed in what was originally built as a Victorian storefront. Ceiling fans, apple-green walls, fresh flowers, and twin Corinthian columns form the framework for elegant French specialties. There is no à la carte menu here, since both lunch at £15.50 ($27.15) and dinner at £23.50 ($41.15) are offered at a fixed price. Bryan Webb prepares a mixture of classical French and cuisine moderne that has made this one of the most stylish restaurants in London. Menu items include calves' brains with capers, roast end of lamb with grilled kidneys and béarnaise sauce, and filet of veal with morels, followed by a choice of luscious desserts. Reservations are absolutely necessary for meals served daily from 12:30 to 2:30 p.m. and 7:30 to 11 p.m. Hilaire is closed Saturday at lunch and all day Sunday. Tube: South Kensington.

Eleven Park Walk, 11 Park Walk, S.W.10 (tel. 352-3449), is a high-key, smart little restaurant drawing a bevy of chic Londoners, including many from the art, fashion, and photography worlds. Modern and beautiful, it has big mirrors and three skylights. In addition to being seen, you can also order some good food. The restaurant's owners serve mainly northern Italian dishes, beginning with minestrone primavera, and a number of good pasta dishes, principally ravioli with ricotta and fettuccine with salmon. Fish specialties include calamari fritti and sea bass with herbs. Main meat courses include bollito misto with green sauce. A three-course meal, including half a liter of wine, costs from £20 ($35) per person. Hours are 12:30 to 3 p.m. and 7 p.m. to midnight daily except Sunday. Tube: South Kensington or Gloucester Road. Bus: 14.

WEST BROMPTON

South of Earl's Court and Kensington, in the general vicinity of the Earl's Court Exhibition Hall, is an increasingly fashionable area sometimes called West

Brompton. Once, in this neighborhood, the best cuisine you could hope to find was "bangers and mash." But today some of the most fashionable members of young London gravitate here, drawn by shops selling some of the most exclusive and costly goods in London. Many young Londoners are attracted to this area's restaurants and pubs in the evening also. To the southwest of West Brompton is a section known as Fulham, which is beginning to distinguish itself for restaurants.

The Medium-Priced Range

Brinkley's, 47 Hollywood Rd., S.W.10 (tel. 351-1683), in West Brompton, is rumored to be a favorite of the Princess of Wales. It has a small garden terrace in back, although London's gray skies usually encourage diners to head for the lower dining room instead. There, one of the waiters will serve a three-course, fixed-price meal for £16 ($28), although if you go after 10 p.m. the cost for the same meal is only £13 ($22.75). The menu changes regularly but is likely to include such appetizers as a hot terrine of wild mushrooms, fish pâté with watercress sauce, or saffron-flavored fish soup. Main courses might feature a breast of chicken with fresh mussels and herbs, marinated venison steak with truffle sauce, and several temptingly prepared fish dishes. Dinner is served from 7:30 to 11:30 p.m. Monday to Saturday. Reservations are necessary. Tube: Earls Court.

La Croisette, 168 Ifield Rd., S.W. 10 (tel. 373-3694), lies in an unlikely neighborhood in southwest London. Yet because of its French decor you might believe you're in the south of France once you go inside. You enter a turn-of-the-century apéritif bar, then descend a wrap-around iron staircase into an intimate dining room inspired by Cannes. The £22 ($38.50) set menu offers a wide choice of seafood. For example, your first course might include one of five different kinds of oysters. Most visitors opt for the plateau des fruits de mer, where all the bounty of the sea's shellfish is served from a cork platter dripping with garlands of seaweed and fresh crustaceans. The establishment is closed all day Monday and every Tuesday at lunch. Lunch is served otherwise from 12:30 to 2:30 p.m., and dinner, from 7 to 11:30 p.m. Tube: Earls Court.

Blue Elephant, 4-5 Fulham Broadway, S.W.6 (tel. 385-6595), is the sister of the famous l'Eléphant Bleu in Brussels. In a converted factory building, London's Blue Elephant has been all the rage since it opened in 1986. It is the leading Thai restaurant of London, where the competition is growing. In an almost magical garden setting of lush tropical foliage, Londoners and foreign visitors alike are treated to an array of ancient and modern Thai food. You can begin with a "floating market" (shellfish in clear broth flavored with chili paste and lemon grass), and then go on to a splendid and varied selection of main courses, for which many of the ingredients were flown in from Thailand. For a main course, you might try roasted duck curry served in a clay cooking pot. The average price for dinner is from £20 ($35), and hours are daily except Saturday lunch from noon to 2:30 p.m. and 7 to 11:30 p.m. It is important to reserve a table. Tube: Fulham Broadway.

Reads, 152 Old Brompton Rd., S.W.5 (tel. 373-2445), is known for serving food that is "English with imagination." The decor is smartly sophisticated, with apricot-colored walls, potted trees, and bamboo chairs. There are also silkscreen depictions of birds and flowers. The cookery has individuality, and dishes are light and stylish, with swift, attentive service. The best bargain is the £11.50 ($20.15) lunchtime menu served from 12:30 to 2:30 p.m. Monday to Saturday. The menu changes daily, but is likely to include a ragoût of monkfish, salmon, redfish, and plaice, or homemade venison sausages with rosemary and juniper berries. A table d'hôte dinner menu is more elaborate, and might offer, for example, loin of Highland venison or wild Exe salmon. On Sunday you get a traditional roast of Angus beef with Yorkshire pudding on the fixed-price menu of £14 ($24.50). Hours then are noon to 2:45 p.m. Otherwise dinner is served Monday to Saturday from 7:30 to 10:45 p.m. Tube: Gloucester Road.

ST. MARYLEBONE
In Mar-li-bone you're in for a treat when you visit choices in:

The Medium-Priced Range
Odin's, 27 Devonshire St., W.1 (tel. 935-7296). Amid an eclectic decor of gilt-touched walls, art deco armchairs, Japanese screens, ceiling fans, and evocative paintings and prints, you can enjoy the well-prepared specialties of the owner-chef Christopher German. The menu offers an excellent wine list and selections from many culinary traditions. Dishes change every day, depending on the shopping and the availability of fresh ingredients. You might begin your meal with pigeon breast in puff pastry. Main courses include a filet of turbot with prawns from Dublin Bay and a Scottish sirloin with garlic and breadcrumbs. Meals cost from £35 ($61.25) and are served from 12:30 to 2:30 p.m., with dinner offered from 7 to 11:30 p.m. The restaurant is closed every Saturday for lunch and all day Sunday. Tube: Baker Street.

Langan's Bistro, 26 Devonshire St., W.1 (tel. 935-4531), has been a busy fixture on the London restaurant scene since the mid-1960s. Set next to Odin's Restaurant (recommended just above), the bistro is less expensive than the better-known Langan's Brasserie in Mayfair. You'll find it behind a storefront in a residential neighborhood. Inside, almost every square inch of the high ceiling is covered with fanciful clusters of Japanese parasols. Rococo mirrors accent the black walls, setting off surrealistic paintings and old photos. The French-inspired menu changes frequently, and only the best and freshest seasonal ingredients are used in the specialties. These include roast guinea fowl, veal with Pommery mustard and tarragon, and pork with a honey-flavored ginger sauce. The dessert extravaganza is known as "Langan's chocolate pudding." Full meals cost from £20 ($35) and are served from 12:30 to 2:30 p.m. and 7 to 11:30 p.m. The restaurant is closed Saturday at lunchtime and all day on Sunday. Tube: Regent's Park.

BAYSWATER
Along Queensway in Bayswater, the children of a once far-flung empire have come back to the mother country to open restaurants, or so it would seem. As you wander up and down this street, you'll think you are in Hong Kong perhaps. The street is filled with restaurants of many nationalities, not all offering a reliable cuisine. An exception to that follows.

Mandarin Kitchen, 14 Queensway, W.2 (tel. 727-9012), serves some of the best Chinese-style fish dishes in London. Sometimes rather elegantly dressed members of the Mayfair crowd journey out to Queensway to sample the kettle of fish simmering in this mandarin's kitchen. Sometimes dishes such as live eels or live carp, take longer in preparation. You can also feast on seabass, Dover sole, monkfish, Chinese pomfret, and yellow croaker, prepared, it would seem, in an infinite number of ways. Barbecued Peking duck is another specialty. It'll take a good half hour to make it through the menu, as you carefully study items such as mussels in a black bean and chili sauce, trying to make up your mind for that final order. The restaurant is rather large, and reservations are rarely needed. Set menus begin at £7.50 ($13.50) but, chances are, you'll spend from £18 ($31.50) if ordering an à la carte Chinese feast. You can go almost any time seven days a week from noon to 11:30 p.m. Tube: Queensway.

NOTTING HILL GATE
For a gourmet treat in an increasingly fashionable area, try the following.

The Upper Bracket
Leiths, 92 Kensington Park Rd., £.11 (tel. 229-4481). Prudence Leith, a lovely woman from South Africa, long ago brought her culinary talents to the unlikely Notting Hill Gate district of London, a few blocks from the Portobello Road Market

and near the Portobello Hotel. Prue, studied at the Cordon Bleu in Paris and also at the Cordon Bleu in London. At Leiths, you dine with French silver, Darlington crystal, and beautiful English crockery, along with luxurious furnishings. Special features of the establishment are the first-course, dessert, and cheese trolleys, the latter bearing a variety of both traditional and new British cheeses. There are four seasonal menus, from which guests are free to select only two courses if they wish. Prices are based on the number of courses: two go for £26 ($45.50), three for £32.50 ($56.90), and four for £36 ($63), including coffee, petits fours, service, and VAT. One recent autumn menu included seared brill filet with beetroot-butter sauce, smoked breast of chicken with a chive-and-cream sauce, and saddle of venison. To end your meal, you might select a ginger syllabub from the dessert trolley. An ambitious wine list *carte* offers wines from all over the world. The restaurant is open daily from 7:30 p.m. to midnight. Tube: Notting Hill Gate.

The Middle Bracket

L'Artiste Assoiffe, 122 Kensington Park Rd., W.11 (tel. 727-4714), is housed in a handsome Georgian building in Kensington Park, near Portobello Road. Charles Dickens used to stop here to pick up his prescriptions when this was a drugstore, but there's no hint of that use of the location in the charming restaurant of today. Paintings and murals by Liz Reber (whose art also decorates the menus), statues, carousel horses, old washing equipment, and parrots create a pleasing ambience in which diners can relax and enjoy their meals and drinks. As the name of the place leads you to expect, the cuisine is mainly French, but with interesting additions. The menu is geared to what was the freshest at the market on any given day. You might start with avocado mousse in smoked salmon. Main courses include calves' liver cooked with sage and filet Dijon (steak caramelized and served with Dijon mustard). If you're not tempted by one of the luscious desserts, you might choose from the cheeses brought from France on a weekly basis. Dinner costs £20 ($35) and up. Hours are 7:30 to 11 p.m. Monday to Friday, and lunch is served only on Saturday, from noon to 3 p.m.; closed Sunday. Tube: Notting Hill Gate.

HOLLAND PARK

This park grew up around Holland House, a Jacobean building from 1606. Once it was fashionable, and now it's becoming so again, thanks a lot to this restaurant in a chic hotel.

The Upper Bracket

Kingfisher, Halcyon Hotel, 81 Holland Park. W.11 (tel. 727-7288), previously recommended as a hotel, is an exciting dining possibility, and worth the ten-minute taxi ride from the heart of the West End. Peter James has not only created a small hotel of charm and taste, but on the lower level he has installed a restaurant that attracts the rich and famous, including royalty, perhaps Princess Michael. To reach the restaurant, you pass a medley of trompe-l'oeil murals with color and whimsy. You might enjoy an apéritif in the pink-tinted bar before heading for a meal in the tastefully uncluttered restaurant. Lattices and views of a garden create an image of springtime even in winter.

The menu is sophisticated and highly individualized, the work of James Robins, formerly of Blakes Hotel, to which this restaurant bears some resemblance, at least in its superb food. One food critic wrote that a menu by Robins "reads like a United Nations of cuisine." The menu is based on the inspiration of the chef and the shopping, as only the freshest ingredients are used. You might begin with a crab, coriander, and ricotta ravioli before going on to roast breast of guinea fowl with noodles, prunes, and leek, or salmon baked in pastry with pesto. Desserts are worth saving room for, as reflected by a ginger parfait with mango coulis. A three-course set luncheon costs £19 ($33.25), dinner is from £25 ($43.75), and hours are daily from

12:30 to 2:30 p.m. and 7:30 to 11:30 p.m. Reservations are necessary. Tube: Holland Park.

SOHO

This section of narrow lanes and crooked streets is the main foreign quarter of London, where some of the city's best international restaurants reside. The life of the continent echoes throughout Soho. Large numbers of French people are found here, and so are Italians and all other European nationalities, as well as Orientals.

One writer wrote of Gerrard Street: "The smell of pickled ginger and roast duckling seeps from restaurant doors. The men scurry into stores from afternoon games of fan-tan and mah-jongg. A lilting twang of Chinese rock'n'roll envelops the downtown street." Gerrard Street has succeeded in becoming London's Chinatown. Strip shows and honky-tonk clubs have given way to Chinese restaurants and bookstores keeping you informed of the latest developments in Hong Kong.

Soho starts at Piccadilly Circus, spreading out like a peacock and ending at Oxford Street. From Piccadilly Circus, walk northeast and you'll come to Soho, to the left of the theater center on Shaftesbury Avenue. This jumbled section can also be approached from the Tottenham Court Road tube station. Walk south along Charing Cross Road and Soho will be to your right.

The Upper Bracket

The Lindsay House, 21 Romilly St., W.1 (tel. 439-0450), bases many of its dishes on 18th-century English recipes. Other platters have been called Tudor and cuisine moderne. Everyone from royalty to film stars, from diplomats to regular people, shows up here. The owners, Roger Wren and Malcolm Livingston, who already run some of the most fashionable restaurants in London, selected a 19th-century house in the heart of Soho and converted it tastefully and dramatically with rich colors and fabrics, a medley of greens and reds. For what is called "first dishes," you might begin with Hannah Glasse's stewed "scollops" with oranges, based on an old recipe. To follow, you might try roast rack of Southdown lamb or a traditional fish pie with cubes of halibut, salmon, scallops, and quail eggs in a creamy sauce. Summer puddings are often featured—packed with such traditional fruits as strawberries, red currants, and raspberries, all served with a raspberry "cullis" with Devonshire clotted cream. A set lunch costs £13.50 ($23.65), and dinner may go as high as £40 ($70) per person. The restaurant, which is on an upstairs floor, is open daily for lunch from 12:30 to 2:30 p.m. and for dinner from 6 p.m. to midnight. On Sunday lunch is from 12:30 to 2 p.m.; dinner, 7 to 10 p.m. Tube: Leicester Square or Tottenham Court Road.

The Middle and Budget Range

Gay Hussar, 2 Greek St., W.1 (tel. 437-0973), is called the "last of the great Soho restaurants." The cuisine of Central Europe is served in this intimate, cozy rendezvous where diners can begin with the chilled wild-cherry soup or perhaps a hot spicy red-fish soup in the style of Szeged in Hungary's southern Great Plain. Main courses may include stuffed cabbage or roast saddle of carp. A set lunch costs £12.50 ($21.90), and dinners go for £20 ($35) to £25 ($43.75). Meals are served daily except Sunday from 12:30 to 2:30 p.m. and 5:30 to 10:45 p.m. Tube: Tottenham Court Road.

The Ivy, 1-5 West St., W.C.2 (tel. 836-4751), now part of the Wheeler's fish restaurant group, is strong on tradition, an entrenched London eating place since World War I. In the past it drew such regulars as Prime Ministers Lloyd George and Sir Winston Churchill, who knew his French viands and wines. Over the years it became a rendezvous for show folk—Noël Coward, Gracie Fields, Dame Sybil Thorndike, Rex Harrison used to be habitués. The interior captures the luster of Paris—paneled walls with old paintings, bronze lamps, cut-plush chairs, art nouveau bronze figures set in window ledges. The menu tends to be a little old-fashioned in its length and detail. The cuisine is basic English/French. Sole is available with 13 different sauces and garnishes. Other Ivy seafood specialties include filet of sea bass steamed with ginger and spring onion. You can also order traditional Ivy meat and poultry dishes, including charcoal-grilled steaks. À la carte meals begin at £20 ($35), and a set lunch costs £12.50 ($21.90). It's open for lunch from 12:15 to 2:30 p.m. and for dinner from 6 to 11:15 p.m. No lunch is served on Saturday, and it's closed all day Sunday. Tube: Leicester Square or Covent Garden.

Au Jardin des Gourmets, 5 Greek St., W.1 (tel. 437-1816), is an "Île de France" off Soho Square, where devotees of the Gallic cuisine gather for their pâté maison. There is an à la carte menu with a comprehensive selection offering such house specialties as noisettes d'agneau "Riches," roast breast of duck in red wine with fresh cranberries, and a selection of fish and seafood dishes. The average price of a meal, including half a bottle of house wine, is £25 ($43.75) per person. A set lunch or dinner is offered for £14 ($24.50). The wine list is reputed to be one of the best in London, with burgundies and clarets of old vintages, plus two excellent house wines, red and white, which you can order by the glass. The restaurant is open from 12:30 to 2:30 p.m. and 6:30 to 11:30 p.m. Monday to Friday, only from 6:30 to 11:30 Saturday. Closed Sunday. Tube: Tottenham Court Road.

Jamdani, 34 Charlotte St., W.1 (tel. 636-1178), brings a fresh, healthy approach to Indian cuisine. Operated by the same people who run Red Fort (one of the finest Indian restaurants in London), Jamdani was inspired by the fine muslin of that name, woven in Bangladesh and described as "woven air" because of its quality and delicacy. That delicacy is also apparent in the food served here seven days a week from noon to 3 p.m. and 6 to 11:30 p.m. The restaurant is air conditioned, with meals averaging £18 ($31.50). Featuring the cookery of rural India, most specifically that of Bangladesh, among the dishes offered here are tandoori specialties from the north, fisk tikka, even cashew rolls in a date sauce. Lentils (called *dal*) are used in many dishes, and vegetables are fresh and expertly handled. In effect, this is a lighter, more enjoyable cuisine than that served in your typical street corner Indian restaurant that hasn't varied any recipes in 30 years. The setting for such delectable dishes as eggplant flavored with yogurt and spices or fish amritsari with coriander and mint is modern and stylized, with unpainted wood and rough plaster in abundance. Call for a reservation. Tube: Goodge Street.

Dragon's Nest, 58-60 Shaftesbury Ave., W.1 (tel. 437-3119), just might be the finest Chinese restaurant in Soho. Much newer than most of its nearby competitors, it has a distinct flavor and zesty seasonings in most of its northern Chinese dishes, with an emphasis on the spicy, hot food of Szechuan province. Satisfy both Chinese and European tastes, the largely Taiwan kitchen staff offer a long menu and often feature unusual combinations of dishes, prepared with fresh, crispy ingredients. Try the sweet-and-sour fish, squid in green peppers, and the garlic-laden Szechuan eggplant, a favorite with vegetarian diners who will find many dishes here to satisfy their tastes. The Dragon takes diners into its nest seven days a week from noon to 11:30 p.m. A set lunch is a remarkable value at £5 ($8.75). Most à la carte orders cost from £12 ($21) and up. Tube: Piccadilly Circus.

Chuen Cheng Ku, 17 Wardour St., W.1 (tel. 437-1398), is one of the best eateries in Soho's "New China." A large restaurant seating 400 on several floors, Chuen Cheng Ku is noted for its Cantonese food and is said to have the longest and most interesting menu in London. Specialties are paper-wrapped prawns, steamed spareribs in black-bean sauce, and shredded pork with cashew nuts, all served in generous portions. Dim sum (dumplings) are served from 11 a.m. to 6 p.m. The Singapore noodles, reflecting one of the Chinese-Malaysian inspirations, are thin rice noodles, sometimes mixed with curry and pork or else shrimp with red and green peppers. A set lunch or dinner costs from £13 ($22.75) per person. The average à la carte meal costs from £15 ($26.25). The restaurant is open daily from 11 a.m. to 11:45 p.m. Tube: Leicester Square or Piccadilly Circus.

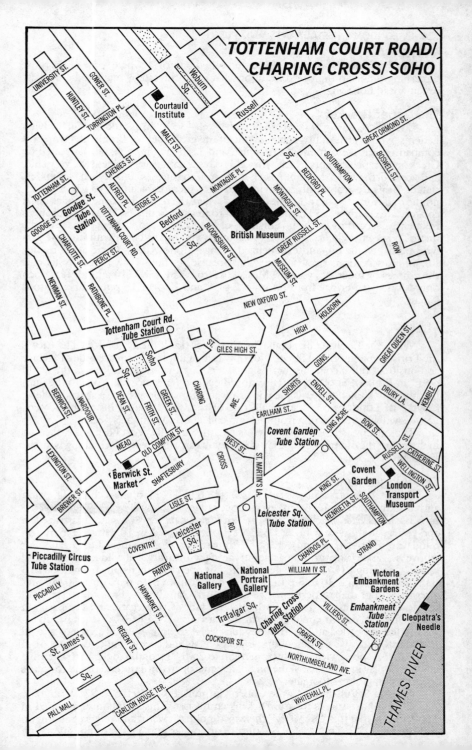

TOTTENHAM COURT ROAD/ CHARING CROSS/ SOHO

UNIVERSITY ST.
GOWER ST.
HUNTLEY ST.
TORRINGTON PL.
Woburn Sq.
MALET ST.
Courtauld Institute
Russell Sq.
GREAT ORMOND ST.
BOSWELL ST.
SOUTHAMPTON
ROW
TOTTENHAM ST.
GOODGE ST.
Goodge St. Tube Station
CHENIES ST.
ALFRED PL.
STORE ST.
MONTAGUE PL.
MONTAGUE ST.
BEDFORD PL.
CHARLOTTE ST.
PERCY ST.
TOTTENHAM COURT RD.
Bedford Sq.
BLOOMSBURY ST.
GREAT RUSSELL ST.
British Museum
NEWMAN ST.
RATHBONE PL.
Tottenham Court Rd. Tube Station
MUSEUM ST.
NEW OXFORD ST.
HIGH HOLBORN
GREAT QUEEN ST.
BERWICK ST.
WARDOUR
DEAN ST.
FRITH ST.
GREEN ST.
Soho Sq.
CHARING
ST. GILES HIGH ST.
AVE.
SHORTS GDNS.
ENDELL ST.
LONG ACRE
DRURY LA.
KEMBLE
LEXINGTON ST.
MEAD
OLD COMPTON ST.
EARLHAM ST.
BOW ST.
RUSSELL ST.
CATHERINE ST.
Berwick St. Market
SHAFTESBURY
WEST ST.
Covent Garden Tube Station
Covent Garden
London Transport Museum
WELLINGTON ST.
BREWER ST.
LISLE ST.
CROSS
ST. MARTIN'S LA.
KING ST.
HENRIETTA ST.
SOUTHAMPTON
COVENTRY
Leicester Sq.
Leicester Sq. Tube Station
RD.
Piccadilly Circus Tube Station
PANTON
CHANDOS PL.
STRAND
PICCADILLY
HAYMARKET ST.
National Gallery
National Portrait Gallery
WILLIAM IV ST.
Victoria Embankment Gardens
St. James's Sq.
REGENT ST.
Trafalgar Sq.
Charing Cross Tube Station
VILLIERS ST.
Embankment Tube Station
Cleopatra's Needle
PALL MALL
CARLTON HOUSE TER.
COCKSPUR ST.
CRAVEN ST.
NORTHUMBERLAND AVE.
WHITEHALL PL.
THAMES RIVER

FITZROVIA

North of Soho is a section of London called Fitzrovia, where some of the most discerning diners in the world head for what is considered by many to be the best restaurant in London.

The Upper Bracket

Chez Nico, 35 Great Portland St., W.1 (tel. 436-8846), is the domain of Nico Ladenis, who is firmly entrenched as one of the great chefs of Britain. A former oil company executive, a trained economist, and a self-taught cook, he was reared by Greek and French parents in East Africa. His restaurant is very expensive, very chic, and very Nico, with a decor of pastels and art deco touches. It is stylish, yet understated. Meals are profoundly satisfying and often memorable in the very best gastronomic tradition of "post nouvelle cuisine," where the tenets and benefits of classical cookery are creatively and flexibly adapted to fresh ingredients. The menu changes frequently, according to the imagination of Mr. Ladenis, so some patrons leave the menu choice entirely up to him. For example, you might begin with hot foie gras with beans, truffle oil, and caramelized oranges, followed by a pair of tournedos Rossini. Reservations are absolutely vital because he could easily fill this restaurant three times or more every night. Meals cost from £50 ($87.50) a head. It is open only Monday to Friday from noon to 2 p.m. and 7 to 11:15 p.m. Tube: Oxford Circus.

THE CITY

When the English talk about The City, they don't mean London. The City is the British version of Wall Street. Not only is it an important square mile of finance and business, but it contains many sights. Here are the buildings known the world over: the **Bank of England** on Threadneedle Street (entrance hall open to the public); the **Stock Exchange,** where you can watch transactions from a special gallery; **Lloyd's of London,** on Leadenhall, one of the world's great insurance centers. Lloyd's will insure anything from a stamp collection to a giraffe's neck.

Typical English food—shepherd's pie, mixed grills, roast beef—is dished up in dozens of the old pubs of The City. Here you can eat inexpensively along with the English.

The Budget Range

Barbican Centre, Silk Street, E.C.2 (tel. 638-4141), offers a choice of eating and drinking establishments in several price ranges. On Level 5, the Waterside Cafeteria is self-service, offering a range of hot meals, salads, sandwiches, pastries, tea, and coffee, along with wine and beer. It is open daily from 10 a.m. to 8 p.m. (on Sunday from noon to 8 p.m.), charging from £5 ($8.75) for a meal. On Level 7, Cut Above is a carvery, featuring roast joints, along with an array of cold meats, fish, and salads. Charging £17 ($29.75) per person, it is open for lunch daily from noon to 3 p.m., for tea from 3:30 to 5 p.m., and for dinner from 5:45 p.m. until 30 minutes after the end of the last performance within Barbican Centre. From the restaurant, windows open onto St. Paul's Cathedral, St. Giles Cripplegate, and the Barbican Lake. On Level 6, you might also want to patronize Wine on Six, which has an extensive list of bottled and draft wines and beers, accompanied by a variety of cold meats, fish, and salads, along with specialty breads and cheese. Full meals cost from £7 ($12.25), and service is daily from noon to 2:30 p.m. and 5 to 8 p.m. If there is a concert or play in progress, Wine on Six remains open until the end of the concert's intermission. Tube: Moorgate.

George & Vulture, 3 Castle Court, Cornhill, E.C.3 (tel. 626-9710), an olde Pickwickian hostelrie, is for the Dickens enthusiast. This chophouse, founded in 1660, claims that it is "probably" the world's oldest tavern, and refers to an inn on this spot in 1175. The George & Vulture no longer puts up overnight guests (al-

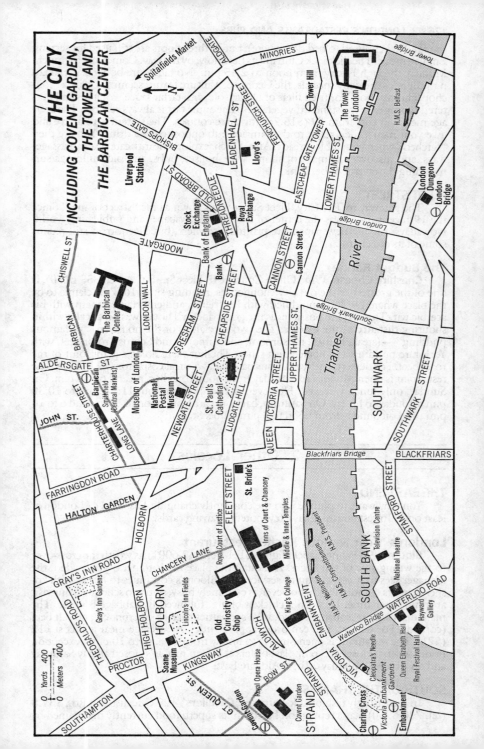

though Dickens used to bed down here), but its three floors are still used for serving English meals. The Pickwick Club meets here now, by the way. Come here for lunch, Monday through Friday from noon to 2:45 p.m. No tables are booked after 1:20 p.m. Besides the daily specials, the George & Vulture features a mixed grill, a "loin chop, chump chop," or fried filets of Dover sole with tartar sauce. Potatoes and buttered cabbage are the standard vegetables. The apple tart is always reliable. The average meal will cost from £9 ($15.75) for three courses. The system is to arrive and give your name, then retire to the Jamaica pub opposite for a drink. You are then "fetched" when your table is ready. After lunch, explore the intricate nearby passageways, and discover the maze of shops, wine houses, pubs, and old buildings surrounding the tavern. Tube: Bank.

FLEET STREET
The gateway to The City, Fleet Street was known as the "street of ink." Since the 19th century, it was the center of London's newspaper and publishing world. Nowadays, the big newspapers are printed elsewhere, but Fleet Street still retains some of its old charm.

The Budget Range
Cheshire Cheese, Wine Office Court, 145 Fleet St., E.C.4 (tel. 353-6170), is one of the greatest of the old city chophouses, running since 1667. It claims to be the place where Dr. Johnson dined with his friends and entertained them with his acerbic wit. This is quite possible, as the good doctor's house was practically within shouting distance of the Cheese. The two specialties of the house are "ye famous pudding"—(steak, kidney, mushroom, and game)—and Scottish roast beef, with Yorkshire pudding and horseradish sauce. The hot plate holds a giant joint of the roast beef. For dessert, try "ye famous pancake." A meal costs from £12 ($21). The restaurant is open Monday to Saturday from noon to 2:30 p.m. and 6 to 8 p.m. On Sunday, only lunch is served. However, the bar is open from 11:30 a.m. to 10:30 p.m. Monday to Friday. On Saturday, bar hours are from noon to 3 p.m. and 6 to 10 p.m., and on Sunday from noon to 3 p.m. Tube: St. Paul's.

2. Other Locales

THE EAST END
You may want to plunge into the constantly changing East End of London at least once. In restaurants it has a few potent drawing cards.

London's Most Famous Kosher Restaurant
Bloom's, 90 Whitechapel High St., E.1 (tel. 247-6001), is worth the cross-over to the wrong side of the tracks. Although the place tends to get overcrowded, the manager sees to it you get quick service, and Bloom's continues to tempt with kosher delights. Sunday lunch, however, is extremely busy, so try to schedule your visit at some other time. Feast on a chicken blintz, followed by cabbage borscht. The main dishes are reasonably priced, with specialties such as sauerbraten and salt beef (corned). For dessert, you can order apple strudel. An average meal will cost £12 ($21). The restaurant is open Sunday to Friday from 11 a.m. to 10 p.m., except on Friday when it closes at 3 p.m. (last orders at 2:30 p.m.). It's closed all day Saturday and on all Jewish holidays. Tube: Aldgate East.

SOUTH OF THE THAMES
In increasingly fashionable Battersea, **Cavaliers',** 129 Queenstown Rd., S.W.8 (tel. 720-6960), has a reputation based on its superb food currently maintained by

its new owner, David Cavalier, a chef of remarkable ability. In an L-shaped dining room ringed with natural pine and pastel shades, you can enjoy such specialties as roast lobster encased in puff pastry with tomato and tarragon, and pot-roasted Highland grouse with orange and thyme pasties. A three-course dinner is offered for £23.50 ($41.15), and a special lunchtime menu goes for £15.50 ($27.15). The restaurant is open for lunch from noon to 2 p.m., and for dinner from 7:15 to 10:30 p.m. Tuesday to Saturday. Because of the location, this establishment is best reached by taxi.

South of the Border, 8-10 Joan St., S.E.1 (tel. 928-6374). The name reflects the attitude a lot of people have toward London "South of the River," as the locals say, and it's rare to find a fashionable place to eat after a visit to the Royal Festival Hall, National Theatre, and Young Vic Theatre. Joan Street is at the junction of the Cut and Blackfriars, within easy reach of all. Once a mattress factory, the ground floor and gallery can seat more than 80 people, and in summer there are also tables on the outdoor terrace. The decor is French style with whitewashed walls. The menu is changed frequently, a vegetarian dish is included, and Indonesian and South Pacific dishes are featured. Chef John Donton, an Australian, has quite a flair for soufflés and for tempura dishes. He is open for lunch from noon to 2:30 p.m. Monday to Friday and for dinner from 6 to 11:30 p.m. Monday to Saturday. He is closed for lunch on Saturday and all day Sunday. The average meal will cost from £18 ($31.50). Tube: Waterloo.

HAMPSTEAD

In the footsteps of Keats, you can head for a dining adventure in the north of London. Try **Le Cellier du Midi,** 28 Church Row, N.W.3 (tel. 435-9998), something of a paradox—a basement French bistro that's crisp, light, and comfortable—off Hampstead Heath Street. It's decorated with Victorian knickknacks and its rough wooden tables are covered with red cloths. The kitchen offers classic French cooking with the day's specialties shown on the blackboard. For £16.75 ($29.30), you're given a four-course meal, which may also seem paradoxical—a fixed-price repast ordered à la carte. You get your choice of appetizer, perhaps choosing escargots de Bourgogne. Main courses include beef filet, lamb, duck, veal, chicken, or fish, served with vegetables or salad, and then comes a selection of desserts. Coffee and wine are extra, of course, but VAT and the cover charge are included in the price. Le Cellier is open daily for dinner from 7 to 11:30 p.m. It is wise to reserve, particularly on Saturday and Sunday. Tube: Hampstead.

ISLINGTON

This is the area for the antique hunter, so you may find yourself there with time to enjoy a meal at **Frederick's Restaurant,** Camden Passage, N.1 (tel. 359-2888). Originally, in 1789, the building was a pub called the Gun. Then in 1834 it was rebuilt and renamed "The Duke of Sussex" in honor of George III's sixth son, Prince Augustus Frederick. So when the restaurant opened in 1970, what more natural than to name it after the prince? You can eat in the Garden Room, designed like a Victorian glasshouse with a domed ceiling, as well as tables inside. Glass doors lead to a terrace and the large garden. The French cuisine changes every fortnight. The menu has six main-dish selections—fish, poultry, meat, specialties (noisettes d'agneau au strudel, for instance), vegetarian, game in season—and sometimes a cuisine minceur selection. Desserts are all homemade, and there is a good cheese board. A three-course meal with coffee will cost from £22 ($38.50), including VAT. Wine is extra. There is a long excellent wine list and a palatable house wine. If you are in the area on Saturday, they do a set luncheon for £9.75 ($17.05), offering a choice of three appetizers, two main dishes with vegetable, and a trio of desserts. VAT and service are included. Hours are noon to 2:30 p.m. and 7 to 11:30 p.m. Monday to Saturday. Tube: Angel.

3. A Dining Miscellany

For a memorable experience, take a taxi, tube, or bus to Aldgate East and spend a hectic hour or so at **Petticoat Lane.** That's the street market where, on Sunday, even if you don't want to buy the goods, you can see the full wit and expertise of the Cockney street vendors. Look for the one who sells tea services, buy a toffee apple or a hot dog, and then go around the corner to **Club Row,** a street market for animals and birds.

A short walk will bring you down to the Tower of London and, right beside it, just below Tower Bridge, **St. Katharine's Dock.** After you've had a look around, you may be interested in dining or just having a snack to tide you over. Some places you'll see are overpriced and have become careless about the quality of their cuisine, while others still provide good food and good value.

Tower Thistle Hotel, St. Katharine's Way, E.1 (tel. 481-2575). At the Carvery Restaurant in this modern hotel built overlooking the Thames, you can enjoy all you want of some of the most tempting roasts in the Commonwealth. For example, you can select (rare, medium, or well done) from a standing rib of prime beef with Yorkshire pudding, horseradish sauce, and the juice; or from tender roast pork with crackling accompanied by a spiced bread dressing and apple sauce; or perhaps the roast spring Southdown lamb with mint sauce. Then you help yourself to the vegetables. Perhaps you'll prefer a selection of cold meats and salads from the buffet table. No one counts—even if you go back for seconds or thirds. Before going to the carving table, you will be served either a shrimp cocktail, a bowl of soup, or a cold slice of melon. Afterward, you can end the meal with a selection from the dessert trolley (especially recommended is the fresh fruit salad, ladled out with thick country cream poured over). You also receive a large cup of American-style coffee. Lunch costs £12.75 ($22.30), going up to £13.75 ($24.05) at dinner. Hours are daily from 12:15 to 2:30 p.m. and 6 to 10 p.m. Bus: 15.

Before or after dinner you might want to visit the Thames Bar, which has a nautical theme and a full panoramic view of its namesake, along with Tower Bridge and the river traffic. There is a small balcony outside for drinks in summer.

Nearby is the **Dickens Inn by the Tower,** St. Katharine's Way, E.1 (tel. 488-2208), a very carefully reconstructed 19th-century warehouse. Incorporating the original redwood beams, stock bricks, and ironworks, it is a balconied pub/restaurant on three levels. Sitting on a wooden chair at an old table, you can enjoy such bar snacks as cockles, mussels, rollmops, and a ploughman's lunch. In the restaurant, the choice is seafood or traditional English meat dishes. Prices begin at £2.50 ($4.40) for one of the snacks, around £4 ($7) for the hot dish of the day accompanied by a vegetable. A three-course meal in the restaurant begins at around £15 ($26.25). The inn is open daily for lunch from 11:30 a.m. to 2:30 p.m. Hours for the pub are from 11 a.m. to 1 p.m. and 6:30 to 10:30 p.m. Monday to Saturday, from noon to 3 p.m. and 7 to 10:30 p.m. Sunday. Tube: Tower Hill.

CRUISE AND DINE

You can explore the waterways of London while you dine and cruise along historic Regent's Canal aboard **My Fair Lady.** You go all the way to Robert Browning's island at Little Venice before returning. A three-course meal, freshly cooked in the galley, is served, and you also have a well-stocked open bar during the cruise. The dinner cruise boards Tuesday to Saturday at 7:30 p.m., sailing at 8 with a return at 11. The price is £16.95 ($29.65) including tax. It's also possible to take a Sunday lunch cruise, with a boarding at 12:30 p.m. Leaving at 1 p.m., the cruise takes 2½ hours, costing £12.75 ($22.30) for a menu of traditional English food. The location is at 250 Camden High St., N.W.1 (tel. 485-4433), 200 yards from Camden Town tube station (Northern line).

R.S. (restaurant ship) *Hispaniola,* moored on the Thames at Victoria Embankment, Charing Cross, is a large and luxurious air-conditioned ship offering a splendid view of the heart of London from Big Ben to St. Paul's, armchair comfort at the tables, and two cocktail bars for other brands of comfort. Meals are served on both the upper and lower decks, and at night the sparkling lights along the banks turn the entire area into a romantic scene. The menu offers many meat and vegetarian dishes, and the cost without service is £15.50 ($27.15) for lunch, £20 ($35) for dinner. Lunch is served Monday to Friday and on Sunday from noon to 2 p.m. On Sunday and Monday, dinner is served from 6:30 to 10 p.m., to midnight Tuesday to Saturday. For reservations, telephone 839-3011. Tube: Embankment.

TIME OUT FOR TEA

During the 18th century the English from every class became enamored of a caffeine-rich brew finding its way into London from far-away colonies. Tea-drinking became the rage. The great craftsmen of England designed furniture, porcelain, and silver services for the elaborate ritual, and the schedule of aristocrats became increasingly centered around teatime as a mandatory obligation. Even Alexander Pope found it expedient to be witty publicly as he satirized teatime as something uniquely English. The most dramatic way to enjoy this custom is to experience tea at the Ritz Palm Court, a gold and white room like a soaring stage set. That's the **Ritz Hotel,** Piccaddilly, W.1 (tel. 493-8181). The hotel has afternoon tea dances, where gentlemen are requested to wear jackets and ties and ladies are encouraged to wear hats—those little ones with veils. Tea is served daily at 3:15 and 4:30 p.m. You must phone and reserve a table, and count on spending £10.50 ($18.40) per person. Tube: Green Park.

Le Meridien London, Piccadilly, W.1 (tel. 734-8000). From 3 to 6 p.m. daily, the bleached oak perimeters of the vast and lavishly decorated hall of this previously recommended hotel welcome nonresidents for the very British tradition of tea. Here, perhaps more than at any other London hotel, it comes with a certain Gallic flair. But that may be only perceived thanks to the resident harpist, the masses of flowers, and the formal service. A complete tea, accompanied by a selection of sandwiches and tarts, costs from £8 ($14) per person. The menu lists a bewildering array of exotic teas, several of which you may never have tried. Tube: Piccadilly Circus.

DINING OUTSIDE OF LONDON

In a red-brick early-Victorian vicarage near Reading, in Berkshire, sits one of the finest dining rooms in the London environs. It's **L'Ortolan,** The Old Vicarage, Church Lane, Shinfield (tel. 0734/883783), which is worth the effort to get there. This once was an out-of-the-way hamlet: now the world comes to the door of this restaurant, named for a game bird. It seems to breathe both material warmth and a seriousness about gastronomy, which implies almost at once that this is one of the culinary citadels of England. You might be offered a table in an alcove: the glass-enclosed conservatory. The cuisine is self-styled as "contemporary classic." The menu changes constantly, based on seasonal produce and inspirations of the chef. A set lunch costs £18.50 ($32.40), and a set dinner goes for £28.50 ($49.90), but you are likely to spend far more, of course. Hours are from 12:15 to 2:15 p.m. and 7:15 to 10:15 p.m. Reservations are essential. The restaurant is closed Sunday evening, all day Monday, and for the last two weeks in August.

---

4. The Pubs of London

No activity is more typically British than to head for that venerated institution, the Public House, affectionately known as pub. Many are dreary Victorian monstrosities, patronized by the working men and women in the neighborhood. Others, particularly those in the West End, have glamour, basking in associations real (Charles Dickens, Samuel Johnson) or imagined (Sherlock Holmes). Pub crawling is a real part of your English experience.

Many North American visitors who don't usually go to bars at home become rabid enthusiasts of the English pub. And most single women feel comfortable in them.

The most noticeable change in English pubs, especially those in the West End, is in the improved standard of food served. However, many pubs still rely on snacks, as typified by the little meat pies, drab dough wrapped around last week's pork roast. Others serve superb sandwiches (fresh salmon stuffed between healthy slices of brown bread), even hot dishes, such as shepherd's pie. Some London pubs are offering a fine cuisine in a separate dining room on their premises—the fare ranging from lobster soup to river trout grilled in butter to roast Aylesbury duckling in orange sauce.

My pub recommendations in the major tourist centers of the West End follow, with the emphasis on those having historic interest (The Prospect of Whitby, Ye Olde Cock Tavern) or else those catering to special-interest groups, such as theater buffs and actors (Salisbury).

ST. JAMES'S

A short walk from Piccadilly Circus is the **Red Lion,** 2 Duke of York St., St. James's Square, S.W.1 (tel. 930-2030). Ian Nairn compared its spirit to that of Edouard Manet's painting *A Bar at the Folies-Bergère* (see the collection at the Courtauld Institute Galleries). Try to avoid peak hours. The owners, Michael and Elfriede Brown, offer pub lunches at noon, with traditional fish 'n' chips on Friday. Roasts are regularly featured. A simple meal costs from £4 ($7). Everything is washed down with Ind Coope's fine ales in this little Victorian pub, with its posh turn-of-the-century decorations—patterned glass, deep-mahogany curlicues—that recapture the gin-palace atmosphere. Food is more copious at lunch than at dinner, with only sandwiches and "pasties" being offered in the evening. The Red Lion roars from 11 a.m. to 11 p.m. Single women can be at ease here. Tube: Piccadilly Circus.

LEICESTER SQUARE

One of the most famous Victorian pubs of London is the **Salisbury,** 90 St. Martin's Lane, W.C.2 (tel. 836-5863). Its glittering cut-glass mirrors reflect the faces of English stage stars (and would-be stars) sitting around the curved buffet-style bar, having a cold joint snack. A plate of the roast leg of pork on the buffet, plus a salad, costs from £4 ($7). If you want a less prominent place to dine or to nibble oysters, choose the old-fashioned wall banquette with its copper-topped tables, and art nouveau decor. The light fixtures, veiled bronze girls in flowing togas holding up clusters of electric lights concealed in bronze roses, are appropriate. It is open from 11 a.m. to 11 p.m. Monday to Saturday, from noon to 3 p.m. and 7 to 10:30 p.m. on Sunday. Tube: Leicester Square.

TRAFALGAR SQUARE

A perennial favorite is the **Sherlock Holmes,** 10 Northumberland St., W.C.2 (tel. 930-2644), especially for fans of the legendary English detective and his creator, Arthur Conan Doyle. You can order your mug of beer and then look at the re-creation upstairs of 221B Baker Street's living room, where get-togethers of "The Baker Street Irregulars" are held. Such Holmesiana are included as the cobra of *The Speckled Band* and the head of *The Hound of the Baskervilles.* The food served upstairs reflects both an English and a continental influence. Main-dish specialties include roast beef with Yorkshire pudding, chef's homemade steak-and-kidney pie, veal Cordon Bleu, and poached trout. Or why not cook your own steak on a granite stone at your table. A three-course meal with coffee comes to around £11 ($19.25). In the snackbar downstairs, you can have a salad with a wide variety of traditional English meat pies or choose a hot dish from one of the chef's specialties. Hours are from 11 a.m. to 11 p.m. Monday to Saturday, from noon to 3 p.m. and 7 to 10:30 p.m. Sunday. Tube: Charing Cross or Embankment.

CHELSEA

In a fashionable residential district of London, **King's Head and Eight Bells,** 50 Cheyne Walk, S.W.3 (tel. 353-1820), is a historic Thames-side pub. It's popular with stage and TV personalities as well as writers. Many distinguished personalities once lived in this area. A short stroll in the neighborhood will take you to the former homes of such personages as Carlyle, Swinburne, and George Eliot. Press gangs used to roam these parts of Chelsea seeking lone travelers who were abducted for a life at sea. The snack bar has been upgraded to Cordon Bleu standards at pub prices. The best English beers are served here, as well as a goodly selection of wines and liquors. A large plate of rare roast beef is a favorite selection, followed by a choice of salad from the salad bar. Other tasty dishes include homemade game pie, if featured, or else steak-and-kidney pie. Everything is displayed on a large old table in the corner. Meals cost from £7 ($12.25). It is open Monday to Saturday from 11 a.m. to 3 p.m. and 5:30 to 11 p.m. (on Sunday from noon to 3 p.m. and 7 to 10:30 p.m.). Food is served from 30 minutes after each opening until one hour before closing. It's a long walk from the Sloane Square tube stop.

BELGRAVIA

Protected from the noise of traffic, **The Grenadier,** Wilton Row, S.W.1 (tel. 235-3074), is an oldtime pub on a cobblestone street, sheltered by higher buildings. The Grenadier is one of the special pubs of London—associated with the Iron Duke (Wellington). But today it's filled with a sophisticated crowd of Belgravia flatmates and chic mews-dwellers. At the entrance to Wilton Row (in the vicinity of Belgrave Square), a special guard ("good evening, guv'nor") was once stationed to raise and lower a barrier for those arriving by carriage. The guard's booth is still there. A gentle ghost is said to haunt the premises, that of a Grenadier guard who was caught cheating at cards and died of the flogging given as punishment. Pub enthusiasts are fanatic about the Grenadier. If anyone tries to tear it down, he may meet his Waterloo.

You can lunch or dine as well as drink here. English meals are served in front of fireplaces in two of the small rooms behind the front bar. Lunch is available daily from noon to 2:30 p.m. and dinner from 6 to 9:45 p.m. Monday to Saturday, from 7 to 9:45 p.m. Sunday. A soup of the day might be followed by baked Virginia ham, steak-kidney-and-mushroom pie, guinea fowl, or, in honor of the former patron, beef Wellington. A table d'hôte menu, costing £14 ($24.50), gives you a choice from among three appetizers and three main dishes, plus coffee. If you order à la carte, expect to spend from £12 ($21) to £16 ($28), depending on whether you include an appetizer and dessert. Reservations are required for dinner and Sunday lunch. Bar snacks are available during the same hours the restaurant serves. The bar is open from 11 a.m. to 3 p.m. and 5:30 to 11 p.m. Monday to Saturday, from 11 a.m. to 3 p.m. and 7 to 10 p.m. Sunday. The Grenadier is known for its Bloody Marys, with a Bloody Mary bar being operated during lunchtime Saturday and Sunday. The pub is closed only on Christmas Day. Tube: Hyde Park Corner.

The **Antelope,** 22 Eaton Terrace, S.W.1 (tel. 730-7781), is on the fringe of Belgravia, at the gateway to Chelsea. This eatery caters to a hodgepodge of clients, aptly described as "people of all classes, colours, and creeds who repair for interesting discussion on a whole gamut of subjects, ranging from port to medieval, mid-European wicker-work, bed-bug traps, and for both mental and physical refreshment." It is also a base for English rugby aficionados (not to be confused with those who follow soccer). Rugby is a game not unlike American football, but it is played continuously for 80 minutes, and the players wear no bodily protection. The trappings here have long since mellowed as the Antelope goes back to about 1800. You can take lunch in a ground-floor bar that provides hot and cold pub food. On the second floor (British first floor), food is served at a wine bar both morning and evening. The ground floor is devoted at night to drinks only. The food is principally English, with steak-and-kidney pie and jugged hare among the specialties. Steaks are also served. Meals are offered daily except Sunday from 11 a.m. to 3 p.m., costing from £10 ($17.50). Pub hours are from 11 a.m. to 11 p.m. Monday to Saturday and from noon to 3 p.m. and 7:30 to 10:30 p.m. Sunday. Tube: Sloane Square.

Star Tavern, 6 Belgrave Mews West, S.W.1 (tel. 235-3019), is famous. Set in a Georgian mews, it is one of the most colorful pubs in the West End, lying behind a picture-postcard-type façade. In winter it's one of the coziest havens around, with two fireplaces going. Groups of office workers descend after work, staking out their territory. The place is attractive inside, with olive-green Victorian walls and banquettes beneath the 19th-century Victorian moldings. You can order plates of food for £4 ($7), including such dishes as baby spring chicken, sirloin steak, or perhaps a vegetable quiche. Food is served daily at lunch from 11:30 a.m. to 3 p.m., but dinner is offered only Monday to Friday. The pub is open Monday to Thursday from 11:30 a.m. to 3 p.m. and 5 to 11 p.m., Friday from 11:30 a.m. to 11 p.m., Saturday from 11:30 a.m. to 3 p.m. and 6:30 to 11 p.m., and Sunday from noon to 3 p.m. and 7 to 10:30 p.m. Tube: Knightsbridge.

SHEPHERD MARKET

Considered *the* pub of Mayfair, **Shepherds Tavern,** 50 Hertford St., W.1 (tel. 499-3017), is a nugget, attracting a congenial mixture of patrons. There are many luxurious touches, including a collection of antique furniture. Chief among these is a sedan chair that once belonged to the son of George III, the Duke of Cumberland. Many of the local habitués recall the tavern's association with the pilots of the Battle of Britain. Bar snacks and hot dishes include shepherd's pie or fish pie with vegetables. Upstairs, the owners operate a cozy restaurant, Georgian in style with cedar paneling. There they serve staunchly British food, with a three-course fixed meal costing £14 ($24.50). You can also order à la carte. Meals are served from noon to 3 p.m., and 6 to 10:30 p.m. Monday to Saturday. On Sunday, only dinner is offered from 6 to 10:30 p.m. The street-level pub is open 11 a.m. to 11 p.m. Monday to Saturday and from noon to 3 p.m. and 7 to 10:30 p.m. on Sunday. Tube: Green Park.

BLOOMSBURY

Opposite the British Museum, **Museum Tavern,** 49 Great Russell St., W.C.1 (tel. 242-8987), is a turn-of-the-century pub, with all the trappings: velvet, oak paneling, and cut glass. It's right in the center of the London University area and popular with writers and publishers. Very crowded at lunchtime, it is also popular with researchers from the museum. It is said that Karl Marx wrote in the pub over a meal. Traditional English food is served, with steak-and-kidney pie, beef-in-ale casserole, sausages cooked in English cider, and chef's specials on the hot-food menu. Cold food includes turkey and ham pie, ploughman's lunches, cheeses, salads, and quiches. A hot-food meal costs from £4 ($7), a menu of cold food going for £3 ($5.25) and up. Beverages offered are several different real English ales, cold lagers, cider, Guinness, wines, and spirits. The tavern is open from 11 a.m. to 11 p.m. Monday to Saturday, from noon to 10:30 p.m. Sunday. Food and coffee are served all day. Tube: Holborn or Tottenham Court Road.

THE CITY

Associated with Sir Christopher Wren, **Ye Olde Watling,** 29 Watling St., E.C.4 (tel. 248-6252), was built after the Great Fire of London in 1666. On the ground level is a mellow pub, with an intimate restaurant upstairs that serves lunch from noon to 2 p.m. Monday through Friday. Under oak beams and on trestle tables, you can have a good choice of English food, with such traditional dishes as homemade steak-and-kidney pie, shepherd's pie, and pork chops in cider. You'll be charged from £4.50 ($7.90) for a meal. Bar snacks are served throughout the day during regular pub hours of 11 a.m. to 9 p.m. Monday to Friday only. Tube: Mansion House.

Dating from 1549, **Ye Olde Cock Tavern,** 22 Fleet St., E.C.4 (tel. 353-3454), boasts a long line of ghostly literary comrades, such as Dickens, who have favored this ancient pub with their presence in life. Downstairs, you can order a pint as well as snackbar food. You can also order steak-and-kidney pie or a cold chicken and beef plate with salad. Light meals cost from £4 ($7). At the Carvery upstairs, a meal goes for £7.25 ($12.70) and includes a choice of appetizers, followed by all the roasts you can carve—beef, lamb, pork, or turkey. The Carvery serves only lunch, from noon to 3 p.m., and the street-level pub's hours are from 10 a.m. to 11 p.m. The place is closed Saturday and Sunday. Tube: Temple or Chancery Lane.

ALONG THE THAMES

One of London's oldest riverside pubs, **The Prospect of Whitby,** 75 Wapping Wall, E.1 (tel. 481-1095), was founded originally in the days of the Tudors. The Prospect has many associations—it was visited by Dickens, Turner, Whistler, in search of local "colour." Come here for a "tot," a "noggin," or whatever it is that you drink. The Pepys Room honors the diarist, who may—just may—have visited the Prospect back in its rowdier days, when the seamy side of London dock life held sway here. The pub is named after a ship, the *Prospect,* which sailed from its home port of Whitby and used to drop anchor outside the pub. Live music is presented Thursday to Sunday from 8:30 to 11 p.m. At the restaurant upstairs, you should reserve early and ask for the bow-window table with fine views over the Thames. Here, a meal will cost you from £14 ($24.50). In the bar, you can have snacks.

The street-level pub is open from 11:30 a.m. to 3 p.m. and 5:30 to 11 p.m. six days a week and from noon to 3 p.m. and 7 to 10:30 p.m. on Sunday. The upstairs restaurant's hours are noon to 2 p.m. and 7 to 10 p.m. daily. No lunch is served on Saturday and no dinner on Sunday evening. To get there, take the Metropolitan Line to Wapping station. When you emerge onto Wapping High Street, turn right and head down the road along the river. Wapping Wall will be on your right, running parallel to the Thames. It's about a five-minute walk.

City Barge, 27 Strand-on-the-Green, Chiswick, W.4 (tel. 994-2148). Londoners head here for an outing and an evening pint of ale on a summer night. A little country pub, a nostalgic link with the past—it can be reached in 45 minutes from the center of London. Take the tube to Hammersmith, then change to bus 27 and get off at the beginning of Kew Bridge (during the day this can be combined with a visit to Kew Gardens). Then walk down a townpath (about a five-minute jaunt), past moored boats and a row of little Regency, Queen Anne, Georgian, and Dutch houses, till you reach the pub. Or you can go by boat from Westminster Pier to Kew Gardens, then visit the City Barge, and return to London by train. Regulars often bypass the little tables set outside (in summer) so as to have their pint while sitting on the embankment wall under a willow tree, and enjoying the boats chugging or gliding by. The kitchen makes good sandwiches and also offers hot dishes such as moussaka or steak-and-kidney pie, with meals costing from £4 ($7). Hours are 11 a.m. to 3 p.m. and 5:30 to 11 p.m. daily (closes at 10:30 p.m. Sunday).

The Anchor, 1 Bankside, Southwark, S.E.1 (tel. 407-1577), is steeped in atmosphere, standing near what used to be the infamous debtors' prison, Clink (hence, the expression—"putting a man in the clink"). The original Anchor burned down in 1676 but was rebuilt and survived the bombs of World War II. Much of the present tavern, however, is aptly described by the management as "Elizabeth II." After getting off at the tube stop, you pass by Southwark Cathedral through a warehouse district that looks at night like Jack the Ripper country till you reach the riverside tavern. There's a viewing platform—especially popular during the day—right on the Thames. You'll find a number of bars named after the historical associations of the inn (Thrale Room, Dr. Johnson's Room, the Globe Bar, the Clink Bar, and the Boswell Bar). In addition, you can dine either upstairs or down in such "parlours" as the Globe Bar, the Chart Rooms, or the Georgian pine-paneled Shakespeare Room. The food is good, and meals begin at £15 ($26.25) in the Chart Rooms. Sunday lunch costs £9.50 ($16.65). From May to October, there is an outdoor barbecue area. The Anchor is open from noon to 2 p.m. for lunch and from 7 to 10 p.m. for dinner Monday through Saturday. On Sunday, lunch is from noon to 2 p.m.; dinner, 7 to 9 p.m. Tube: London Bridge.

ELEPHANT & CASTLE
South of the Thames, the following pub is easily reached by Underground train to Elephant & Castle. From the station where you get off, it's a five-minute walk.
Goose and Firkin, 47 Borough Rd., S.E.1 (tel. 403-3590), is a pub that brews its own beer. The owner of this enterprise is David Bruce, who worked as a brewer for one of the big companies for many years and has now expanded his operation to include ten other London pubs. A large mirror proclaims "Bruce's Brewery, established 1979." David brews three special strengths: Goose at £1 ($1.75) for a pint; Borough Bitter at £1.12 ($1.95) a pint; and Dogbolter, £1.26 ($2.20) a pint. For special occasions, he produces a variety of strong ales with names such as Earthstopper, Kneetrambler, Gobstopper, and for Christmas, Slay Belles, all costing £2.65 ($4.65) a pint. Be warned: these latter brews are macho beers and are extremely potent. Food is also available in this lovely old London pub. Each day, there is a different hot dish. Or else you can order extra large baps (bread buns) filled with your choice of meat and salad. A meal will cost from £2.50 ($4.40). Most evenings, a pianist plays all the old numbers in a good old "knees up" style. The place is open seven days a week from 11:30 a.m. to 3 p.m. and 5:30 to 11 p.m.

HAMPSTEAD
This residential suburb of London, beloved by Keats and Hogarth, is a favorite excursion spot for Londoners on the weekend. Take the Northern Line of the Underground to the Hampstead Heath station.
Spaniards Inn, Spaniards Lane, N.W.3 (tel. 455-3276), is a Hampstead Heath landmark, opposite the old tollhouse, a bottleneck in the road where people had to pay a toll to enter the country park of the Bishop of London. The pub, built in 1630, still contains some antique benches, open fireplaces, and cozy nooks in the rooms with their low, beamed ceilings and oak paneling. Old muskets on the walls are mute survivors of the time of the Gordon Riots of 1780, when a mob stopped in for drinks on their way to burn nearby Kenwood House, property of Lord Mansfield. The innkeeper set up so many free drinks that when the Horse Guards arrived, they found many of the rioters *hors de combat* from too much libation and relieved them of their weapons.
The pub serves traditional but above-average food. A light repast begins at £2.75 ($4.80). Hot dishes are served 9:30 p.m. Pub hours are 11 a.m. to 11 p.m. Monday to Saturday, from noon to 3 p.m. and 7 to 11:30 p.m. on Sunday. In summer, customers can sit at slat tables in a pleasant garden beside a flower-bordered lawn, with an aviary. The pub and garden were known to Byron, Dickens, Galsworthy, Shelley, and David Garrick.

5. The Wine Bars

For years, the stark, atmospheric, and ancient wine cellars of the old City have been patronized by businessmen in bowlers, and were almost a well-kept secret, as you never ran into a tourist or a woman there. However, that has long ago changed.

Wine bars are the fashion, and the pub no longer dominates the drinking scene in the English capital.

With the coming of the newer wine bars, London's drinking habits have undergone significant change. Wine bars are not only places at which to drink, but also to meet friends and enjoy good food. A few of the older, more established ones still offer only wine, but in today's terms a wine bar is likely to mean anything, including a disco!

The English taste for wine has increased, hence the number of wine bars springing up in all parts of the city. Nearly all the establishments recommended below sell wine by the glass, although if you're traveling in a party you may want to order by the bottle and share as it's less expensive that way.

I'll lead off with the most interesting collection of wine bars that still lie in the City and are best visited Monday to Friday for lunch. In the other sections of town you can go for both lunch and dinner.

THE CITY

Dating from 1663, the **Olde Wine Shades,** 6 Martin Lane, off Cannon Street, E.C.4 (tel. 626-6876), is the oldest wine house in the City. It was the only City tavern to survive the Great Fire of 1666, not to mention the Blitz of 1940. Only 100 yards from the Monument, the Olde Wine Shades used to attract Charles Dickens who enjoyed its fine wines. In the smoking room the old oil paintings have darkened with age, and the 19th-century satirical political cartoons remain enigmatic to most of today's generation. Some of the fine wines of Europe are served here, and port and sherry are drawn directly from an array of casks behind the counter. A candlewick bar and restaurant is found downstairs, but upstairs, along with your wine, you can order French bread with ham off the bone. Breton pâté, sandwiches, jacket potatoes filled with cheese, venison pie with salad garnish, and a large beef salad. Meals range from £7.50 ($13.25). Jackets, collars, and ties are required for men. Hours are 11:30 a.m. to 3 p.m. and 5 to 8 p.m.; closed Saturday, Sunday, and bank holidays. Tube: Monument or Cannon Street.

Bow Wine Vaults, 10 Bow Churchyard, E.C.4 (tel. 248-1121), has existed since long before the current wine bar fad. The atmosphere is staunchly masculine in the "Old Bar," but the clientele in the "New Bar" is fairly mixed. Sherries, port, and madeira are available by the glass, as are an assortment of table wines beginning at £1.25 ($2.20) by the glass. Sandwiches, cheeses, and fruitcake are available in the Old Bar, varying salads and hot dishes in the New Bar. A bustling cellar restaurant completes the range of public services. The New Bar is open Monday to Friday from 11:30 a.m. to 3 p.m., and the Old Bar is open Monday to Friday from 11:30 a.m. to around 8 p.m., depending on business. The restaurant mentioned charges from £8 ($14) for a full meal, which is served as two different sittings Monday to Friday at 12:15 p.m. and again at 1:30 p.m. Tube: Mansion House or Bank.

Jamaica Wine House, St. Michael's Alley, off Cornhill, E.C.3 (tel. 626-9496), lies in a tangle of City alleyways, and if you do manage to find it, you'll be at one of the first coffeehouses to be opened in England. In fact, the Jamaica Wine House is reputed to be the first coffeehouse in the Western World. Pepys used to visit it and mentioned the event in his Diary. The coffeehouse was destroyed in the Great Fire of 1666, rebuilt in 1674, and has remained, more or less, in its present form ever since. For years London merchants and daring sea captains came here to lace deals with rum and coffee. Nowadays, the two-level house dispenses beer, ale, lager, and fine wines, among them a variety of ports, to appreciative drinkers. The oak-paneled bar at street level is for the money-makers, the jacket-and-tie crowd of investment bankers, whereas the basement bar is rowdier, patronized by the City's messengers and service personnel. The basement bar's beer is on draft, cheaper and less prestige-conscious than the imported bottled beer served upstairs. You can order a glass of wine from £1.10 ($1.95), along with light snacks such as pork pie, stuffed baked potatoes with various fillings, and toasted sandwiches. Light meals cost from £3.50

($6.15). It is open Monday to Friday only from 11:30 a.m. to 8 p.m. without interruption. The Bank of England is only a stone's throw away. Tube: Bank.

SOUTH OF PICCADILLY

Among the many wine bars in London, **Greens Restaurant and Oyster Bar,** 36 Duke St., S.W.1 (tel. 930-4566), is a good choice for the excellence of its menu, the charm of its staff, and its central location. A busy place, it has a cluttered entrance leading to a crowded bar, where you can stand at what the English call "rat-catcher counters" if the tables are full, there to sip fine wines and, from September to May, enjoy oysters. Other foods to encourage the consumption of the wines are quails' eggs, king prawns, smoked Scottish salmon, crab, and baby lobsters. If you choose to go into the dining room, you can select from a long menu, choosing from a number of fish dishes or grilled foods. Meals cost from £20 ($35). Greens is open for lunch from 11:30 a.m. to 3 p.m. Monday to Saturday and from 11:30 a.m. to 4 p.m. Sunday. Dinner is served Monday to Saturday from 5:30 to 11 p.m. It's best to reserve a table if you are not planning to arrive early in the evening. Tube: Piccadilly Circus or Green Park.

NEAR LEICESTER SQUARE

In the theater district, **Cork and Bottle Wine Bar,** 44–46 Cranbourn St., W.C.2 (tel. 734-7807), is just off Leicester Square. Don Hewitson, the owner, has revitalized the food, with a wide range of hot dishes, so that it is not a typical "glass of wine and slice of pâté" type of bistro. The most successful dish is a raised cheese-and-ham pie. In just one week the bar sold 500 portions of this alone. It has a cream-cheesy filling, and the well-buttered pastry is crisp—not your typical quiche. Don also offers a mâchon lyonnaise, a traditional worker's lunch in Lyon. He imports his own saucisson from a charcuterie in Lyon, serving it hot with warm potato salad, a mixed green salad, spicy Dijon mustard, and French bread. You can also order an "American gourmet salad," consisting of lettuce, tomato, avocado, green beans, and croutons, in a spicy red Stilton dressing. Meals cost from £9 ($15.75). Don has expanded the wine list, and he doubts if anyone in the U.K. has a better selection of beaujolais cru and wines from Alsace. He also stocks a good selection of California labels. The bar is open Monday to Saturday from 11 a.m. to 3 p.m. and 5:30 to 11 p.m. and on Sunday from noon to 2 p.m. and 7 to 10:30 p.m. Tube: Leicester Square.

MAYFAIR

A good choice is **Shampers,** 4 Kingly St., W.1 (tel. 437-1692), where you get an excellent selection of wines and imaginatively prepared food. Australian and New Zealand wines are a specialty. Full meals in the street-level bar cost from £5 ($8.75) each, and typical dishes include cheese and ham pie, pastas, and a vegetarian dish of the day. At lunch only, from noon to 3 p.m. Monday to Friday, the cellar serves as a Provençal-inspired brasserie. The food is robust and spicy, including sausages and ratatouille. Here it costs around £10 ($17.50) for a meal. At night, however, the cellar serves only as an overflow for the less pretentious food in the wine bar. Hours are Monday to Friday from 11 a.m. to 11 p.m. and on Saturday from 11 a.m. to 3 p.m. Closing is Saturday night and all day Sunday. Tube: Oxford Circus.

NEAR VICTORIA STATION

On one of London's most popular streets for budget hotels, the **Ebury Wine Bar,** 139 Ebury St., S.W.1 (tel. 530-5447), is convenient for dining or drinking. This wine bar and bistro attracts a youthful crowd to its atmospheric precincts. Wine is sold either by the glass or bottle. A cold table is offered daily, and you can always get an enticing plat du jour, such as beef braised in beer, preceded perhaps by orange and carrot soup. The menu invariably includes grilled steaks and lamb cutlets. All the food is prepared fresh daily. Sunday lunch costs £7.95 ($13.90). Otherwise, meals go for around £12 ($21). The wine bar is open seven days a week, serving food from noon to 2:45 p.m. and 6 to 10 p.m. Monday to Saturday, from noon to 2:30 p.m. and 7 to 10 p.m. Sunday. Tube: Victoria Station.

Methuselah's, 29 Victoria St., S.W.1 (tel. 222-1750), opposite New Scotland Yard, is popular with MPs from the House of Commons. It not only has an excellent cellar of wines, but a sophisticated menu to back it up, along with attractive surroundings. Called "Bourgeois," with a devotion to Provence, the day's specialties are written on the blackboard. There is a ground-floor bar, along with a cellar buffet and wine bar, plus a more formal dining room, the Burgundy Room, on the mezzanine. Meals cost from £11 ($19.25) and are served Monday to Friday only, from 11:30 a.m. to 3 p.m. and 5:30 to 11 p.m. Tube: Victoria.

KNIGHTSBRIDGE

Said by some people who know about such matters to be the finest wine bar in London, **Le Métro Wine Bar,** 28 Basil St., S.W.3 (tel. 589-6286), around the corner from Harrods Department Store, draws a fashionable crowd to its precincts in the basement. You can order special wines by the glass instead of by the bottle, thanks to a cruover machine that stands in a position of honor behind the bar. This machine keeps the wine in perfect condition even after it is opened. As the wine is drawn, the vacuum is replaced by an inert gas that prevents oxidization. The food served at Le Métro is good, solid, and reliable, and it's also prepared with a certain flair. Typical dishes include a ragoût of "sea fruit," smoked chicken salad, and a confit of duckling. Meals cost from £12 ($21). It is open from 7:30 a.m. to 10:30 p.m. Monday to Friday, and from 7:30 a.m. to 6 p.m. on Saturday; closed Sunday. Tube: Knightsbridge.

Bill Bentley's, 31 Beauchamp Pl., S.W.3 (tel. 589-5080), stands on this restaurant-and boutique-lined street near Harrods. A small Georgian house, it offers many ground-floor rooms and a little sun-filled patio in back. Cozy and atmospheric, it presents a varied list of reasonably priced wines, including a fine selection of bordeaux. If you're in the neighborhood, you can enjoy a pub-style lunch, such as ham and salad. Hot main dishes are likely to include Bill Bentley's fish cakes and grilled sirloin steak. The oysters are the special treat here. Menus change frequently. Meals cost from £15 ($26.25). It's open from 11 a.m. to 11 p.m. Monday to Saturday; closed Sunday and bank holidays. Tube: Knightsbridge.

CHELSEA

One of the most frequented of the Chelsea wine bars, **Blushes,** 52 King's Rd., S.W.3 (tel. 589-6640), stands across from the Duke of York's headquarters. (That's not Fergie's husband, but a long-ago ancestor. Built in 1801, it is now the barracks of several London regiments of the Territorial Army.) Behind its pink and white façade, a lively King's Road crowd enjoys food and drink. Full meals, including such dishes as Dover sole, freshly made salads, and steaks, cost from £10 ($17.50) per person. Many patrons visit just to drink, enjoying a glass of house wine from £1.50 ($2.65). It opens every day of the week in time for an early Chelsea breakfast, closing at 11:30 p.m. Its presentation changes throughout the day from a breakfast café to a restaurant to a wine bar. The lunch and dinner menu is available from noon to 11 p.m. A cocktail bar in the cellar is open only at night from 6 to 11 Monday to Friday, from 1 to 11 p.m. on Saturday, and closed on Sunday. Tube: Sloane Square.

WHAT TO SEE AND DO IN LONDON

Dr. Johnson said: "When a man is tired of London, he is tired of life, for there is in London all that life can afford." And that holds true today.

Come along with me as we survey only a fraction of that life: ancient monuments, boutiques, debates in Parliament, art galleries, Soho dives, museums, theaters, flea markets, and castles. Some of what we're about to see was known to Johnson and Boswell, even Shakespeare, but much of it is new.

1. Seeing the Sights

London is not a city to visit hurriedly. It is so vast, so stocked with treasures that, on a cursory visit, a person will not only miss many of the highlights but will also fail to grasp the spirit of London and to absorb fully its special flavor, which is unique among cities. Still, faced with an infinite number of important places to visit and a time clock running out, the visitor will have to concentrate on a manageable group.

THE TOP TEN SIGHTS

Here is a list of the top ten sights of London. Try to see them even if you have to skip all the rest, saving them for "next time."

(1) The Tower of London

This ancient fortress on the north bank of the Thames continues to pack 'em in because of its macabre associations with all the legendary figures who were either imprisoned or executed here, or both. James Street once wrote, " . . . there are more spooks to the square foot than in any other building in the whole of haunted Britain. Headless bodies, bodiless heads, phantom soldiers, icy blasts, clanking chains—you name them, the Tower's got them."

Back in the days of the axman, London was "swinging" long before *Time* magazine discovered that fact in the 1960s. Ranking in interest are the colorful attending Yeoman Warders, the so-called Beefeaters, in Tudor dress, who look as if they are on the payroll for gin advertisements (but don't like to be reminded of it).

Many visitors consider a visit to the Tower to be the highlight of their sightseeing in London—so schedule plenty of time for it. You don't have to stay as long as Sir Walter Raleigh (released after some 13 years), but give it an afternoon. Take either the Circle or District Line to Tower Hill station (the site is only a short walk away). Or on a sunny day, why not take a boat instead, leaving from Westminster Pier?

Admission to the Tower, including the Jewel House, is £4.50 ($7.90) for adults, £2 ($3.50) for children except in February, when the Jewel House is closed for the annual cleaning and maintenance, and prices are reduced to £3.50 ($6.15) for adults, £1.50 ($2.75) for children. Those under 5 are admitted free. The Tower and all its buildings are closed on New Year's Day, Good Friday, the Christmas holidays, and on Sunday from November through February. The gates open at 9:30 a.m. Monday to Saturday all year and at 2 p.m. on Sunday from March to the end of October (closed Sunday the remainder of the year). The last tickets are sold at 5 p.m. from March to the end of October and at 4 p.m. from November to the end of February, with actual closing at 5:45 p.m. in summer, 4:30 p.m. in winter. The Tower Wharf, entered by the East or West Gate, is open daily except Christmas Day from 7 a.m. Monday to Saturday, from 10 a.m. on Sunday. Closing times vary depending on the season but never earlier than 6:30 p.m.

Tours of approximately an hour in length are given by the Yeoman Warders at about 30-minute intervals, starting from the Middle Tower near the main entrance. The tours include the Chapel Royal of St. Peter ad Vincula. The last guided walk starts about 3:30 p.m. in summer, 2:30 p.m. in winter. For further information about opening times and visiting privileges, telephone 709-0765, ext. 235.

Don't expect to find only one tower. The fortress is actually a compound, in which the oldest and finest structure is the White Tower, begun by William the Conqueror. Here you can view the Armouries, the present collection dating back to the reign of Henry VIII. A display of instruments of torture and execution will recall some of the most ghastly moments in the history of the Tower. At the Bloody Tower, the Little Princes (Edward V and the Duke of York) were allegedly murdered by their uncle, Richard III.

The hospitality today far excels that of years ago, when many of the visitors left their cells only to walk to the headsman's block on Tower Hill. Through Traitors' Gate passed such ill-fated, but romantic, figures as Robert Devereux, a favorite of Elizabeth I, known as the second Earl of Essex. Elizabeth herself, when a princess, was once imprisoned briefly in Bell Tower. At Tower Green, Anne Boleyn and Katharine Howard, two wives of Henry VIII, lost their lives. The nine-day queen, Lady Jane Grey, and her husband, Dudley, also were executed, along with such figures as Sir Thomas More.

According to legend, the disappearance of the well-protected ravens at the Tower will presage the collapse of the British Empire (seen any around lately?).

To see the **Jewel House,** where the Crown Jewels are kept, go early in the day during summer, as long lines usually form by late morning. Get a Beefeater to tell you how Colonel Blood almost made off with the crown and regalia in the late 17th century. Of the three English crowns, the Imperial State Crown is the most important—in fact, it's probably the most famous crown on earth. Made for Victoria for her coronation in 1838, it is today worn by Queen Elizabeth when she opens Parliament. Studded with some 3,000 jewels (principally diamonds), it contains the Black Prince's Ruby, worn by Henry V at Agincourt, the battle in 1415 when the English defeated the French. Don't miss the 530-carat Star of Africa, a cut diamond on the Royal Sceptre with Cross.

The Tower of London has an evening ceremony called the **Ceremony of the Keys.** It is, in fact, the ceremonial locking up of the Tower for yet another day in its 900 years. Nothing stops the ceremony. During World War II, a bomb fell within the castle walls during the ceremony and nobody flinched—but the Tower was locked up two minutes late. Rumor has it that the guard that night was censured for tardiness, the pilot of the plane that dropped the bomb blamed as the culprit. The Beefeater will explain to guests the significance of the ceremony. For free tickets, write to the Resident Governor, Tower of London, London EC3N 4AB, requesting a specific date but also giving alternative dates you'd like to attend. At least six weeks' notice is required. All requests must be accompanied by a stamped, self-addressed envelope (*British stamps only*) or two International Reply Coupons. With ticket in hand, you'll be admitted by a Yeoman Warder around 9:35 p.m.

(2) Westminster Abbey

No less an illustrious figure than St. Peter is supposed to have left his calling card at the abbey. If it's true, I wouldn't be surprised—for nearly everybody else, at least nearly everybody in English history, has left his mark. But what is known for certain is that in 1065 the Saxon king, Edward the Confessor, rebuilt the old minster church on this spot, overlooking Parliament Square, and founded the Benedictine abbey.

The first English king crowned in the abbey was Harold in 1066, who was killed at the Battle of Hastings that same year. The man who defeated him, Edward's cousin, William the Conqueror, was also crowned at the abbey; the coronation tradition has continued to the present day, broken only twice (Edward V and Edward VIII). The essentially Early English Gothic structure existing today owes more to Henry III's plans than to any other sovereign, although many architects, including Wren, have contributed to the abbey.

Adults pay £2 ($3.50) and children pay 50p (90¢) to visit the Royal Chapel, the Royal Tombs, the Coronation Chair, and the Henry VII Chapel. Hours are Monday to Friday from 9 a.m. to 4:45 p.m., and on Saturday from 9 a.m. to 2:45 p.m. and 3:45 to 5:45 p.m. On Wednesday, the Royal Chapels are open with free admission from 6 to 7:45 p.m. This is the only time photography is allowed in the abbey. On Sunday, the Royal Chapels are closed, but the rest of the church, at Broad Sanctuary, S.W.1, is open between services.

Built on the site of the ancient Lady Chapel in the early 16th century, the Henry VII Chapel is one of the loveliest in Europe, with its fan vaulting, Knights of Bath banners, and Torrigiani-designed tomb of the king himself over which is placed a 15th-century Vivarini painting of *Madonna and Child*. The chapel represents the flowering of the Perpendicular Gothic style. Also buried here are those feuding half-sisters, Elizabeth I and Mary Tudor ("Bloody Mary"). Elizabeth I was always vain and adored jewelry. The effigy that lies on top of her tomb has been fitted with a new set of jewelry, a gilded collar and pendant, a modern copy derived from a painting now at Hatfield House. The originals were stolen by souvenir hunters in the early 18th century. Her orb and sceptre were added earlier. In one end of the chapel you can stand on Cromwell's memorial stone and view the R.A.F. chapel containing the Battle of Britain memorial stained-glass window, unveiled in 1947 to honor the R.A.F.

You can also visit the most hallowed spot in the abbey, the shrine of Edward the Confessor (canonized in the 12th century). In the saint's chapel is the Coronation Chair, made at the command of Edward I in 1300 to contain the Stone of Scone. Scottish kings were once crowned on this stone (in 1950 the Scots stole it back, but it was later returned to its position in the abbey).

Another noted spot in the abbey is Poets' Corner, to the right of the entrance to the Royal Chapel, with its monuments to everybody from Chaucer on down—the Brontë sisters, Shakespeare, Tennyson, Dickens, Kipling, Thackeray, Samuel Johnson, "O Rare Ben Johnson" (his name misspelled), even the American Longfellow. The most stylized and controversial monument is Sir Jacob Epstein's sculptured bust of William Blake. One of the more recent tablets commemorates the poet Dylan Thomas.

Statesmen and men of science—such as Disraeli, Newton, Charles Darwin—are also either interred in the abbey or honored by monuments. Near the west door is the 1965 memorial to Sir Winston Churchill. In the vicinity of this memorial is the tomb of the Unknown Soldier, symbol of British dead in World War I. Surprisingly, some of the most totally obscure personages are buried in the abbey, including an abbey plumber.

Many visitors overlook such sights as the 13th-century Chapter House, where Parliament used to meet. The Chapter House in the Great Cloister is open from 9:30 a.m. till 6 p.m. (closed on Sunday) from March through September. It shuts down at 3:30 p.m. off-season.

Even more fascinating are the treasures in the museum in the Norman undercroft (crypt), part of the monastic buildings erected between 1066 and 1100. The collection includes effigies—figures in wax, such as that of Nelson, and woodcarvings of early English royalty. Along with the wax figures—the abbey's answer to Madame Tussaud—are ancient documents, seals, replicas of coronation regalia, old religious vestments (such as the cope worn at the coronation of Charles II), the sword of Henry V, and the famous Essex Ring that Elizabeth I is supposed to have given to her favorite earl. The museum is open daily from 10 a.m. to 4 p.m. Admission is £1.50 ($2.65) for adults, 40p (70¢) for children. This also provides visits to the Chapter House and the Pyx Chamber (containing a Treasury).

For tours of the abbey with an expert guide, the cost is £4 ($7) per person. These tours operate Monday to Friday from 10 a.m. to the last tour at 3 p.m. On Saturday, the hours are 10 a.m., 11 a.m., and 12:30 p.m. Inquire at the West Door for the meeting point. For times of services and other information, phone the Chapter Office (tel. 222-5152).

Off the Cloisters, **College Garden** is the oldest garden in England, under cultivation for more than 900 years. Surrounded by high walls, flowering trees dot the lawns, and park benches provide comfort where you can hardly hear the roar of passing traffic. It is open on Thursday throughout the year, from 10 a.m. to 4 p.m. in winter, to 6 p.m. in summer. In August and September, band concerts are held at lunchtime from 12:30 to 2 p.m. Admission is free. Tube: Westminster.

(3) Houses of Parliament

These are the spiritual opposite of the Tower, the stronghold of Britain's democracy, the assemblies that effectively trimmed the sails of royal power. Both Houses (Commons and Lords) are in the formerly royal Palace of Westminster, the king's residence until Henry VIII moved to Whitehall.

Although I can't assure you of the oratory of a Charles James Fox or a William Pitt the Elder, the debates are often lively and controversial in the House of Commons (seats are at a premium during crises). The chances of getting into the House of Lords when it's in session are generally better than they are in the more popular House of Commons, where even the Queen isn't allowed. The old guard of the palace informs me that the peerage speak their minds more freely and are less likely to adhere to party line than their counterparts in the Commons.

The general public is admitted to the Strangers' Gallery in the House of Commons on "sitting days"—normally from about 4:15 p.m. Monday to Thursday and from about 9:30 a.m. on Friday. You have to join a public queue outside the St. Stephen's entrance on the day in question. Often there is considerable delay before the head of the public queue is admitted. You might speed matters up somewhat by applying at the American Embassy or the Canadian High Commission for a special pass, but this is too cumbersome for many people. Besides, the embassy has only four tickets for daily distribution, so probably you might as well stand in line. It is usually easier to get in after about 6 p.m. The head of the queue is normally admitted to the Strangers' Gallery of the House of Lords after 2:40 p.m. Monday to Wednesday (often at 3 p.m. on Thursday).

The present House of Commons was built in 1840, but the chamber was bombed and destroyed by the German air force in 1941. The 320-foot tower that houses Big Ben, however, remained standing and the celebrated clock continued to strike its chimes—the signature tune of Britain's wartime news broadcasts. "Big Ben," incidentally, was named after Sir Benjamin Hall, a cabinet minister distinguished only by his long-windedness.

Except for the Strangers' Galleries, the two Houses of Parliament and Westminster Palace are presently closed to the public.

Further information about the work of the House of Commons is available by phoning 219-4272; House of Lords, 219-3107; or on the Post Office Prestel Viewdata system, frame 5,000. Tube: Westminster.

(4) The British Museum

Within its imposing citadel on Great Russell Street, W.C.1, in Bloomsbury (tel. 636-1555), the British Museum shelters one of the most catholic collections of art and artifacts in the world, containing countless treasures of ancient and modern civilizations. To storm this bastion in a day is a formidable task, but there are riches to see even on a cursory first visit, among them the Oriental collections (the finest assembly of Islamic pottery outside the Islamic world), the finest collection of Chinese porcelain in Europe, the best holdings of Indian sculpture outside India and Pakistan, and the Prehistoric and Romano-British collections, among many others. Basically, the overall storehouse splits into the national collections of antiquities; prints and drawings; coins, medals, and banknotes; and ethnography.

As you enter the front hall, you may want to head first to the Assyrian Transept on the ground floor, where you'll find the winged and human-headed bulls and lions that once guarded the gateways to the palaces of Assyrian kings. Nearby is the Black Obelisk of Shalmaneser III (858–824 B.C.), tribute from Jehu, King of Israel. From here you can continue into the angular hall of Egyptian sculpture to see the Rosetta Stone, whose discovery led to the deciphering of the mysterious hieroglyphs, explained in a wall display behind the stone.

Also on the ground floor is the Duveen Gallery, housing the Elgin Marbles, consisting chiefly of sculptures from the Parthenon. The frieze shows a ceremonial procession that took place in Athens every four years. Of the 92 metopes from the Parthenon, 15 are housed today in the British Museum. These depict the to-the-death struggle between the handsome Lapiths and the grotesque, drunken Centaurs. The head of the horse from the chariot of Selene, goddess of the moon, is one of the pediment sculptures.

The classical sculpture galleries also hold a caryatid from the Erechtheum, a temple started in 421 B.C. and dedicated to Athena and Poseidon. Displayed here, too, are sculptures from the Mausoleum at Halicarnassus (one of the Seven Wonders of the Ancient World), built for Maussollos, ruler of Caria, who died around 350 B.C. Look also for the blue-and-white Portland Vase, considered the finest example of ancient cameo carving, having been made in the 1st century B.C. or A.D.

The Department of Medieval and Later Antiquities has its galleries on the first floor (second floor to Americans), reached by the main staircase. Of its exhibitions, the Sutton Hoo Anglo-Saxon ship burial, discovered in Suffolk, is, in the words of an expert, "the richest treasure ever dug from English soil," containing gold jewelry, armor, weapons, bronze bowls and cauldrons, silverware, and the inevitable drinking horn of the Norse culture. No body was found, although the tomb is believed to be that of a king of East Anglia who died in the 7th century A.D. You'll also see the bulging-eyed Lewis chessmen, Romanesque carvings in Scandinavian style of the 12th century, and the Ilbert collection of clocks and watches.

The featured attractions of the upper floor are the Egyptian Galleries, especially the mummies. Egyptian room 63 is extraordinary, looking like the props for *Cleopatra*, with its cosmetics, domestic utensils, toys, tools, and other work. Some items of Sumerian art, unearthed from the Royal Cemetery at Ur (southern Iraq), lie in a room beyond: a queen's bull-headed harp (oldest ever discovered); a queen's sledge (oldest known example of a land vehicle); and a figure of a he-goat on its hind legs, crafted about 2500 B.C. In the Iranian room rests "The Treasure of the Oxus," a hoard of riches, perhaps a temple deposit, ranging in date from the 6th to the 3rd century B.C., containing a unique collections of goldsmith work, such as a nude youth, signet rings, a fish-shaped vase, and votive plaques.

If your visit to the museum makes you want to know more about this treasure trove, I recommend a book by M. L. Caygill of the museum director's office, *Treasures of the British Museum,* which gives detailed account of the major treasures and summaries of departmental collections.

The museum is open Monday to Saturday from 10 a.m. to 5 p.m. and on Sunday from 2:30 to 6 p.m. (The galleries start to close ten minutes earlier.) It is closed Good Friday, December 24, 25, and 26, New Year's Day, and the first Monday in May. Admission to the entire museum is free. Tube: Holborn or Tottenham Court Road.

THE BRITISH LIBRARY: Some of the treasures from the collections of the British Library (tel. 636-1544), one of the world's greatest libraries, are on display in the exhibition galleries in the east wing of the British Museum building. In the Grenville Library are displayed western illuminated manuscripts. Notable exhibits are the Benedictional (in Latin) of St. Ethelwold, Bishop of Winchester (963–984), the Luttrell Psalter, and the Harley Golden Gospels of about 800.

In the Manuscript Saloon are manuscripts of historical and literary interest. Items include two of the four surviving copies of King John's Magna Carta (1215) and the Lindisfarne Gospels (an outstanding example of the work of Northumbrian artists in the earliest period of English Christianity, written and illustrated about 698). Almost every major literary figure, such as Dickens, Jane Austen, Charlotte Brontë, Yeats, is represented in the English literature section. Also on display are historical autographs, including Nelson's last letter to Lady Hamilton and the journals of Captain Cook.

In the King's Library, so called because this is where the library of King George III is housed, the history of the book is illustrated by notable specimens of early printing, including the Diamond Sutra of 868, the first dated example of printing, as well as the Gutenberg Bible, the first book ever printed from movable type, 1455.

In the center of the gallery is an exhibition of fine bookbindings dating from the 16th century. Beneath Roubiliac's 1758 statue of Shakespeare is a case of documents relating to the Bard, including a mortgage bearing his signature and a copy of the First Folio of 1623. The library's unrivaled collection of philatelic items, including such things as the 1840 Great British Penny Black and the rare 1847 Post Office issues of Mauritius, are also to be seen.

The library regularly mounts special temporary exhibitions, usually in the Crawford Room off the Manuscript Saloon. The opening times of the British Library's exhibition galleries are the same as those of the museum. Admission is free.

THE MUSEUM OF MANKIND: The Museum of Mankind, the Ethnography Department of the British Museum, is housed at 6 Burlington Gardens, W.1 (tel. 437-2224), where the galleries are open to the public during the same hours as those of the Bloomsbury museum. It has the world's largest collections of art and material culture from tribal societies. A selection of treasures from five continents is displayed, and a number of exhibitions show the life, art, and technology of selected cultures. New exhibitions are mounted every year. There is no admission charged. Tube: Piccadilly Circus.

(5) Madame Tussaud's

In 1770 an exhibition of life-size wax figures was opened in Paris by Dr. Curtius. He was soon joined by his niece, Strasbourg-born Marie Tussaud, who learned the secret of making lifelike replicas of the famous and the infamous. During the French Revolution, the head of almost every distinguished victim of the guillotine was molded by Madame Tussaud or her uncle.

After the death of Curtius, Madame Tussaud inherited the exhibition, and in 1802 she left France for England. For 33 years she toured the United Kingdom with her exhibition, and in 1835 she settled on Baker Street. The exhibition was such a success that it practically immortalized her in her day; she continued to make portraits until she was 81 (she died in 1850).

While some of the figures still on display today come from molds taken by the incomparable Madame Tussaud, the exhibition also introduces new images of whoever is *au courant.* An enlarged Grand Hall continues to house years of royalty and old favorites such as Winston Churchill, as well as many of today's heads of state and political leaders. In the Chamber of Horrors you can have the vicarious thrill of meeting such types as Dr. Crippen, and walking through a Victorian London street where special effects include the shadow terror of Jack the Ripper. The instruments and victims of death penalties contrast with present-day criminals portrayed within the confines of prison. You are invited to mingle with the more current stars in the Conservatory, as well as see the Beatles relaxing.

"Super Stars" offers latest technologies in sound, light, and special effects combined with new figures in a celebration of success in the fields of film and sports. On the ground floor you can relive the Battle of Trafalgar on the gun deck of Nelson's flagship, *Victory.*

Madame Tussaud's, air-conditioned throughout, is open daily, including Saturday and Sunday, year round (closed on Christmas Day only). Open hours are 10 a.m. to 5:30 p.m. Monday to Friday and 9:30 a.m. to 5:30 p.m. Saturday and Sunday. Doors open earlier throughout the summer season. Admission for adults is £4.80 ($8.40) and £3.15 ($5.50) for children under 16. Prices are slightly lower in the off-season.

The **London Planetarium** is right next door, costing £2.65 ($4.65) for adults and £1.70 ($3) for children. A combined ticket, costing £6.10 ($10.70) for adults and £3.80 ($6.65) for children, for both the Planetarium and Madame Tussaud's will save you money. For information, phone 935-6861. The entrance to Madame Tussaud's is on Marylebone Road, N.W.1. Tube: Baker Street.

(6) Tate Gallery

This building, beside the Thames on Millbank, S.W.1 (tel. 821-1313), houses the best grouping of British paintings from the 16th century on, as well as England's finest collection of modern art, the works of British artists born after 1860, together with foreign art from the impressionists onward. The Tate is open from 10 a.m. to 5:50 p.m. daily (on Sunday from 2 to 5:50 p.m.). To reach it, take the tube to Pimlico or bus 88 or 77A. The number of paintings is staggering. If time permits, try to schedule at least two visits—the first to see the classic English works, the second to take in the modern collection. Since only a portion of the collections, can be shown simultaneously, the works on display vary from time to time. However, the most time-pressed individual may not want to miss the following, which are almost invariably on view:

The first giant among English painters, William Hogarth (1697–1764), is well represented, particularly by his satirical *O the Roast Beef of Old England* (known as *Calais Gate*), with its caricatured figures, such as the gluttonous monk. The ruby-eyed *Satan, Sin, and Death* remains one of his most imaginative works.

Two other famous British painters of the 18th century are Sir Joshua Reynolds (1723–1792) and Thomas Gainsborough (1727–1788). Reynolds, the portrait painter, shines brightest when he's painting himself (three self-portraits hang side by side). Two other portraits, of Francis and Suzanna Beckford, are typical of his early work. His rival, Gainsborough, is noted for his portraits too, and also landscapes ("my real love"). His landscapes with gypsies are subdued, mysterious; *Wooded Landscape with Peasant Resting* is more representative. One of Gainsborough's most celebrated portraits is *Edward Richard Gardiner*, a handsome boy in blue (the more famous *Blue Boy* is in California). Two extremely fine Gainsborough portraits have recently been acquired: *Sir Benjamin Truman*, the notable brewer, and *Giovanna Baccelli* (1782), who was well known both as a dancer and as the mistress of the third Earl of Dorset.

In the art of J. M. W. Turner (1775–1851), the Tate possesses its greatest collection of the works of a single artist. Most of the paintings and watercolors exhibited here were willed to the nation by Turner. His studio at the time held 282 oils and more than 19,000 drawings, watercolors, and sketches. In 1987, a new wing at the Tate, called Clore Gallery, was opened so that the entire bequest of the artist can be seen. Of his paintings of stormy seas, none is more horrifying than *Shipwreck* (1805). In the Petworth series he broke from realism (see his *Interior at Petworth*). His delicate impressionism is best conveyed in his sunset and sunrise pictures, with their vivid reds and yellows. Turner's vortex paintings, inspired by color theories of Goethe, are *Light and Color—the Morning After the Deluge* and *Shade and Darkness —the Evening of the Deluge*.

In a nation of landscape painters, John Constable (1776–1837) stands out. Some of his finest works include *Flatford Mill*, a scene from his native East Anglia, and in a different mood, the stormy sketch for *Hadleigh Castle*.

American-born Sir Jacob Epstein became one of England's greatest sculptors, and some of his bronzes are owned and occasionally displayed by the Tate. Augustus John, who painted everybody from G. B. Shaw to Tallulah Bankhead, is also represented here with portraits and sketches.

The Tate owns some of the finest works of the Pre-Raphaelite period of the mid-19th century. One of the best of the English artists of the 20th century, Sir Stanley Spencer (1891–1959) is best represented by his two versions of *Resurrection* and three remarkable self-portraits.

The Tate has many major paintings from both the 19th and 20th centuries, including Wyndham Lewis's portraits of Edith Sitwell and of Ezra Pound, and Paul Nash's *Voyages of the Moon*. But the drawings of William Blake (1757–1827) attract the most attention. Blake, of course, was the incomparable mystical poet and illustrator of such works as *The Book of Job*, *The Divine Comedy*, and *Paradise Lost*.

In the modern collections, the Tate contains Matisse's *L'Escargot* and *The Inattentive Reader*, along with works by Dali, Chagall, Modigliani, Munch, Ben Nicholson (large collection of his works), and Dubuffet. The different periods of Picasso bloom in *Woman in a Chemise* (1905), *Three Dancers* (1925), *Nude Woman in a Red Armchair* (1932), *Goat's Skull, Bottle, and Candle* (1952), and *Reclining Nude* (1968).

Truly remarkable is the room devoted to several enormous, somber, but rich abstract canvases by Mark Rothko, the group of paintings by Giacometti and sculptures by Giacometti (1901–1966), and the paintings of two of England's best-known modern artists, Francis Bacon (especially gruesome, *Three Studies for Figures at the Base of a Crucifixion*) and Graham Sutherland (see his portrait of W. Somerset Maugham).

Rodin's *The Kiss*, a world-famous piece of sculpture, is on show. In addition, sculptures by Henry Moore and Barbara Hepworth are displayed.

Downstairs is the internationally renowned restaurant (see Chapter IV), with murals by Rex Whistler, as well as a coffeeshop.

(7) National Gallery

On the north side of Trafalgar Square, W.C.2, in an impressive neoclassic building, the National Gallery (tel. 839-3321) houses one of the most comprehensive collections of Western paintings, representing all the major schools from the 13th to the early 20th century. The largest part of the collection is devoted to the Italians, including the Sienese, Venetian, and Florentine masters.

Of the early Gothic works, the *Wilton Diptych* (French school, late 14th century) is the rarest treasure. It depicts Richard II being introduced to the Madonna and Child by such good contacts as John the Baptist and the Saxon king, Edward the Confessor.

A Florentine gem, a Virgin and grape-eating Bambino, by Masaccio (one of the founders of Renaissance painting) is displayed, as are notable works by Piero della Francesca, particularly his linear *The Baptism*.

Matter and spirit meet in the haunting nether world of the *Virgin of the Rocks,* a Leonardo da Vinci painting. Also shown are two other giants of the Renaissance— Michelangelo (represented by an unfinished painting, *The Entombment*), and Raphael (*The Ansidei Madonna,* among others).

Among the Venetian masters of the 16th century, to whom color was paramount, the most notable works include a rare *Adoration of the Kings* by Giorgione, *Bacchus and Ariadne* by Titian, *The Origin of the Milky Way* by Tintoretto (a lush galaxy, with milk streaming from Juno's breasts), and *The Family of Darius Before Alexander* by Veronese (one of the best paintings at the National). A number of satellite rooms are filled with works by major Italian masters of the 15th century— artists such as Andrea Mantegna of Padua (*Agony in the Garden*); his brother-in-law, Giovanni Bellini (his portrait of the Venetian doge, Leonardo Loredano, provided a change of pace from his many interpretations of Madonnas); and finally, Botticelli, represented by *Mars and Venus, Adoration of the Magi,* and *Portrait of a Young Man.*

The painters of northern Europe are well represented. For example, there is Jan van Eyck's portrait of G. Arnolfini and his bride, plus Pieter Brueghel the Elder's Bosch-influenced *Adoration,* with its unkingly kings and ghoul-like onlookers. The 17th-century pauper, Vermeer, is rich on canvas in a *Young Woman at a Virginal,* a favorite theme of his. Fellow Delft-ite Pieter de Hooch comes on sublimely in a *Patio in a House in Delft.*

One of the big drawing cards of the National is its collection of Rembrandts. Rembrandt, the son of a miller, became the greatest painter in the Netherlands in the 17th century. His *Self-Portrait at the Age of 34* shows him at the pinnacle of his life; his *Self-Portrait at the Age of 63* is more deeply moving and revealing. For another Rembrandt study in old age, see his *Portrait of Margaretha Trip. The Woman Taken in Adultery* shows the artist's human sympathy. Rembrandt's portrait of his mistress, Hendrickje Stoffels, is also displayed. The picture is signed and dates from 1659.

Part of the prolific output of Peter Paul Rubens is to be seen, notably his *Peace and War* and *The Rape of the Sabine Women.* A recent Rubens acquisition is *Samson and Delilah,* a little-known painting. It cost $5.4 million and has been described as the most important Rubens to come on the market for many years.

Five of the greatest of the home-grown artists—Constable, Turner, Reynolds, Gainsborough, and Hogarth—have masterpieces here. Constable's *Cornfield* is another scene of East Anglia, along with *Haywain,* a harmony of light and atmosphere. Completely different from Constable is the work of Turner, including his dreamy *Fighting Téméraire* and *Rain, Steam, and Speed.* In what is essentially a portrait gallery, you can see several works by Sir Joshua Reynolds, along with a Gainsborough masterpiece. *The Morning Walk,* an idealistic blending of portraiture with landscape. Finally, in a completely different brush stroke, Hogarth's *Marriage à la Mode* caricatures the marriages of convenience of the upper class of the 18th century.

The three giants of Spanish painting are represented by Velázquez's portrait of the sunken-faced Philip IV, El Greco's *Christ Driving the Traders from the Temple,* and Goya's portrait of the Duke of Wellington (once stolen) and his mantilla-wearing *Doña Isabel de Porcel.*

Other rooms are devoted to early 19th-century French painters such as Delacroix and Ingres; the later 19th-century French impressionists such as Manet, Monet, Renoir, and Degas; and post-impressionists such as Cézanne, Seurat, and Van Gogh.

The National Gallery (tube to Charing Cross or Leicester Square) is open Monday to Saturday from 10 a.m. to 6 p.m., on Sunday from 2 to 6 p.m. It is closed on January 1, Good Friday, Christmas Eve, Christmas Day, Boxing Day, and May bank holiday. Admission is free.

(8) Kensington Palace

Home of the State Apartments, some of which were used by Queen Victoria, this is another of the major attractions of the city, at the far western end of Kensington Gardens. The palace was acquired by asthma-suffering William III (William of Orange) in 1689, and was remodeled by Sir Christopher Wren. George II, who died in 1760, was the last king to use it as a royal residence.

The most interesting chamber to visit is Queen Victoria's bedroom. In this room, on the morning of June 20, 1837, she was aroused from her sleep with the news that she had ascended the throne, following the death of her uncle, William IV. Thus the woman who was to become the symbol of the British Empire and the Empress of India began the longest reign in the history of England. In the anteroom are memorabilia from Victoria's childhood—a dollhouse and a collection of her toys.

A special attraction is the Court Dress Collection, which shows restored rooms from the 19th century, including Queen Victoria's birthroom and a series of room settings with the appropriate court dress of the day, from 1760 to 1950. However, a more modern dress captures the attention of most visitors—the wedding dress worn by the Princess of Wales on July 29, 1981.

As you wander through the apartments, you can admire many fine paintings from the Royal Collection. The State Apartments are open Monday to Saturday from 9 a.m. to 5 p.m., on Sunday from 1 to 5 p.m. Adults pay an admission of £2.60 ($4.55), and children pay £1.30 ($2.30). You enter from the Broad Walk, and you reach the building by taking the tube either to Queensway or Bayswater on the north side of the gardens, or High Street Kensington on the south side. You'll have to walk a bit from there, however. For more information, telephone 937-9561.

The palace gardens, originally the private park of royalty, are also open to the public for daily strolls around Round Pond, near the heart of Kensington Gardens. The gardens adjoin Hyde Park. Also in Kensington Gardens is the Albert Memorial honoring Queen Victoria's consort. Facing Royal Albert Hall, the statue reflects all the opulent vulgarity of the Victorian era—it's fascinating, nonetheless.

(9) St. Paul's Cathedral

During World War II, newsreel footage reaching America showed the dome of St. Paul's Cathedral, St. Paul's Church yard, E.C.4 (tel. 236-4128), lit by bombs exploding all around it. That it survived at all is miraculous, as it was hit badly twice in the early years of the Nazi bombardment of London. But St. Paul's is accustomed to calamity, having been burned down three times and destroyed once by invading Norsemen. It was in the Great Fire of 1666 that the old St. Paul's was razed, making way for a new Renaissance structure designed (after many mishaps and rejections) by Sir Christopher Wren.

The masterpiece of this great architect was erected between 1675 and 1710. Its classical dome dominates the City's square mile. Inside, the cathedral is laid out like a Latin cross, containing few art treasures (Grinling Gibbons's choir stalls are an exception) and many monuments, including one to the "Iron Duke" and a memorial chapel to American servicepersonnel who lost their lives in World War II while stationed in the United Kingdom. Encircling the dome is the Whispering Gallery, where discretion in speech is advised. In the crypt lie not only Wren but the Duke of Wellington and Lord Nelson. A fascinating Diocesan Treasury was opened in 1981.

The cathedral (tube to St. Paul's) is open daily from 8 a.m. to 6 p.m. The crypt and galleries, including the Whispering Gallery, are open only from 10 a.m. to 4:15 p.m. Monday to Friday, from 11 a.m. on Saturday. Guided tours, lasting 1½ hours, and including the crypt and parts of St. Paul's not normally open to the public, take place at 11 and 11:30 a.m. and 2 and 2:30 p.m. when the cathedral is open (except Sunday), costing £3.60 ($6.30) for adults, £1.60 ($3.80) for children.

St. Paul's is an Anglican cathedral with daily services held at 8 a.m. and 5 p.m. On Sunday, services are at 10:30 and 11:30 a.m. and 3:15 p.m. In addition, you can climb to the very top of the dome for a spectacular 360° view of all of London, costing £1 ($1.75) per person.

(10) Victoria and Albert Museum

When Queen Victoria asked that this museum be named after herself and her consort, she could not have selected a more fitting memorial. The Victoria and Albert is one of the finest museums in the world, devoted to fine and applied art of many nations and periods, including the Orient. In many respects, it's one of the most difficult for viewing, as many of the most important exhibits are so small they can easily be overlooked. To reach the museum on Cromwell Road, S.W.7 (tel. 938-8500), take the tube to the South Kensington stop. The museum is open Monday to Saturday from 10 a.m. to 5:50 p.m., on Sunday from 2:30 to 5:50 p.m.

I have space only to suggest some of its finest art. The medieval holdings include many treasures, such as the Eltenberg Reliquary (Rhenish, second half of the 12th century). In the shape of a domed, copper-gilt church, it is enriched with champlevé enamel and set with walrus-ivory carvings of Christ and the Apostles. Other exhibits in this same salon include the Early English Gloucester Candlestick, the Byzantine Veroli Casket, with its ivory panels based on Greek plays, and the Syon Cope, made in the early 14th century, an example of the highly valued embroidery produced in England at that time. The Gothic tapestries, including the Devonshire ones depicting hunting scenes, are displayed in another gallery. An area devoted to Islamic art contains the Ardabil carpet from 16th-century Persia (320 knots per square inch).

Renaissance art in Italy includes such works as a Donatello marble relief, *The Ascension;* a small terracotta statue of the Madonna and Child by Antonio Rossellino; a marble group, *Samson and a Philistine,* by Giovanni Bologna; and a wax model of a slave by Michelangelo. The highlight of 16th-century art from the continent is the marble group *Neptune with Triton,* by Bernini.

The cartoons by Raphael, which are owned by the Queen, can be seen here. These cartoons—conceived as designs for tapestries for the Sistine Chapel—include scenes such as *The Sacrifice of Lystra* and *Paul Preaching at Athens.*

A most unusual, huge, and impressive exhibit is the Cast Rooms, with life-size plaster models of ancient and medieval statuary and architecture, made from molds formed over the originals.

Of the rooms devoted to English furniture and decorative art during the period from the 16th to the mid-18th century, the most outstanding exhibit is the Bed of Ware, big enough for eight. In the galleries of portrait miniatures, two of the rarest ones are by Hans Holbein the Younger (one of Anne of Cleves, another of a Mrs. Pemberton). In the painting galleries are many works by Constable. His *Flatford Mill* represents a well-known scene from his native East Anglia. All paintings, prints, drawings, and photographs are in the new Henry Cole wing.

No admission is charged, but they suggest a donation of £2 ($3.50) for adults, 50p (90¢) for children under 12.

A restaurant serving wholesome traditional English snacks and meals is open from 10 a.m. to 5 p.m. Monday to Saturday, from 2:30 to 5 p.m. on Sunday. Two museum shops, with gifts, posters, cards, and books, are open from 10 a.m. to 5:30 p.m. Monday to Saturday and 2:30 to 5:30 p.m. on Sunday.

THE BEST OF THE REST

Now, for those with more time to get acquainted with London, we'll continue our exploration of this sight-filled city.

Royal London

From Trafalgar Square, you can stroll down the wide, tree-flanked avenue known as The Mall. It leads to **Buckingham Palace,** the heart of Royal London (English kings and queens have lived here since the days of Victoria). Three parks—St. James's, Green, and the Buckingham Palace Gardens (private)—converge at the center of this area, where you'll find a memorial honoring Victoria.

London's most popular daily pageant, particularly with North American tourists, is the **Changing of the Queen's Guard** in the forecourt of Buckingham Palace. The regiments of the Guard's Division, in their bearskins and red tunics, actually are five regiments in one, including the Scots, Irish, and Welsh. The guards march to the palace from either the Wellington or Chelsea barracks, arriving around 11:30 a.m. for the half-hour ceremony. To get the full effect, go somewhat earlier. There is usually no ceremony when the weather is what the English call "inclement." But remember that your idea of inclement may not be a weather-toughened Londoner's idea of inclement. These ceremonies are curtailed in winter, between October 1 and March 31. During those months, the official schedule is that the changing of the guard takes place on even calendar days in October, December, and February, and on odd calendar days in November, January, and March. When in doubt, phone 730-3488 for information; tube to St. James's Park or Green Park.

You can't visit the palace, of course, without an invitation, but you can inspect the **Queen's Gallery,** S.W.1 (tel. 930-4832), entrance on Buckingham Palace Road. The picture gallery can be visited from 10:30 a.m. to 5 p.m. Tuesday to Saturday and bank holidays, from 2 to 5 p.m. Sunday. Closed Monday except bank holidays. Admission is £1.20 ($2.10) for adults, 60p ($1.05) for children. As is known, all the royal families of Europe have art collections—some including acquisitions from centuries ago. The English sovereign has one of the finest, and has consented to share it with the public. I can't predict what exhibition you're likely to see, as they are changed yearly at the gallery. You may find a selection of incomparable works by old masters, and sometimes furniture and objets d'art. The Queen's collection contains an unsurpassed range of royal portraits, from the well-known profile of Henry V, through the late Plantagenets, the companion portraits of Elizabeth I as a girl and her brother, Edward VI, and four fine Georgian pictures by Zoffany, to recent works including two portraits of Queen Alexandria from Sandringham and paintings of Queen Elizabeth II and other members of the royal family. Tube: Green Park or St. James's.

You can get a close look at Queen Elizabeth's coronation carriage at the **Royal Mews,** on Buckingham Palace Road, S.W.1 (tel. 930-4832). Her Majesty's State Coach, built in 1761 to the designs of Sir William Chambers, contains emblematic and other paintings on the panels. Its doors were executed by Cipriani. It was formerly used by sovereigns when they traveled to open Parliament in person and on other state occasions. Queen Elizabeth used it upon her coronation in 1953 and in 1977 for her Silver Jubilee Procession. It was traditionally drawn by eight gray horses. Many other official carriages are housed here as well, including the Scottish and Irish state coaches. The Queen's carriage horses are also housed here. The mews is open to the public on Wednesday and Thursday from 2 to 4 p.m. and charges an admission of £1 ($1.75) for adults, 50p (90¢) for children. It is closed during Ascot week in June and at some other times as announced. Tube: Green Park or St. James's.

Official London

Whitehall, S.W.1, the seat of the British government, grew up on the grounds of Whitehall Palace and was turned into a royal residence by Henry VIII, who snatched it from its former occupant, Cardinal Wolsey. Beginning at Trafalgar Square, Whitehall extends southward to Parliament Square (Houses of Parliament and Westminster Abbey, described earlier). Along it you'll find the Home Office, the Old Admiralty Building, and the Ministry of Defense.

Visitors today can see the **Cabinet War Rooms,** the bomb-proof bunker, that suite of rooms, large and small, just as they were left by Winston Churchill in September 1945 at the end of World War II. Many objects were moved only for dusting, and the Imperial War Museum studied photographs to replace everything exactly as it had been, including notepads, files, and typewriters—right down to pencils, pins, and clips. You can see the Map Room with its huge wall maps, the Atlantic map a mass of pinholes. Each hole represents at least one convoy. Next door is Churchill's bedroom-cum-office, reinforced with stout wood beams. It has a very basic bed and a desk with two BBC microphones on it for his broadcasts of those famous speeches that stirred the nation.

The Transatlantic Telephone Room, to give it its full title, is little more than a broom cupboard, but it had the Bell Telephone Company's special scrambler phone by the name of Sig-Saly. From here, Churchill and Roosevelt conferred. The scrambler equipment was actually too large to house in the bunker, so it was placed in the basement of Selfridges Department Store on Oxford Street. The actual telephone was still classified at the end of the war and was removed. So far below ground level, it was impossible to know the world's weather conditions. Therefore a system of boards, rather like old railway-station boards, was used, with such laconic phrases as "wet," "very wet," "hot and sunny," "dry and dull".

The entrance to the war rooms is by Clive Steps at the end of King Charles Street off Whitehall near Big Ben, S.W.1 (tube: Westminster). The rooms are open every day except New Year's Day and Christmas holidays, from 10 a.m. to 5:50 p.m. (last admission at 5:15 p.m.). They may be closed at short notice on certain state occasions. Admission is £2.80 ($4.90) for adults, £1.50 ($2.65) for children. For further information, phone 930-6961.

At the **Cenotaph** (honoring the dead in two world wars), turn down unpretentious Downing Street to the modest little town house at **No. 10,** flanked by two bobbies. Walpole was the first prime minister to live here: Churchill the most famous.

Nearby is the **Horse Guards Building,** Whitehall, S.W.1(tel. 930-4466, ext. 2396), which is now the headquarters, Household Division & London District. There has been a guard change here since 1649 when the site was the entrance to the old Palace of Whitehall. You can watch the Queen's Lifeguards in the mounted guard change ceremony at 11 a.m. (at 10 a.m. on Sunday) when 12 mounted troopers arrive from Knightsbridge Barracks. Photographers can get a good view of the London traffic halted for this troop to cross out of Hyde Park, past the Wellington Arch. They proceed down Constitution Hill and the Mall. If you are at Hyde Park Corner at 10:30 a.m., you can follow them. You can also see the smaller change of the guard hourly when mounted troopers are changed. At 4 p.m. you can watch the evening inspection when ten unmounted troopers and two mounted troopers assemble in the courtyard. Tube: Westminster.

Across the street is Inigo Jones's **Banqueting House,** Palace of Whitehall, S.W.1 (tel. 930-4179), site of the execution of Charles I. William and Mary accepted the crown of England here, but preferred to live at Kensington Palace. The Banqueting House was part of Whitehall Palace, which burned to the ground in 1698. The ceremonial hall escaped razing. Its most notable feature today is an allegorical ceiling painted by Peter Paul Rubens. The Banqueting House may be visited Tuesday to Saturday from 10 a.m. to 5 p.m., on Sunday from 2 to 5 p.m. Admission is 80p ($1.40) for adults, 40p (70¢) for children.

Finally, you may want to stroll to Parliament Square for a view of **Big Ben,** the world's most famous timepiece, the very symbol of the heart and soul of England. Big Ben is actually the name of the deepest and loudest bell, although it's also the common name for the clock tower on the Houses of Parliament. Opposite, in the gardens of Parliament Square, stands the statue of Churchill by Oscar Nemon. Tube: Westminster.

Legal London

The smallest borough in London, bustling **Holborn** (pronounced Hoburn) is often referred to as Legal London, the home of the city's barristers, solicitors, and law clerks. It also embraces the university district of Bloomsbury. Holburn, which houses the ancient Inns of Court—Gray's Inn, Lincoln's Inn, Middle Temple, and Inner Temple—was severely damaged in World War II bombing raids. The razed buildings were replaced with modern offices housing insurance brokers, realtors, whatever. But the borough still retains quadrangled pockets of its former days.

Going from the Victoria Embankment, Middle Temple Lane leads between Middle and Inner Temple Gardens in the area known as **The Temple,** E.C.4 (tel. 353-4366; tube: Temple), named after the medieval order of the Knights Templar (originally formed by the Crusaders in Jerusalem in the 12th century). It was in Temple Gardens that Henry II's barons are supposed to have picked the blooms of red and white roses and started the War of the Roses in 1430. Today only members of the Temples and their guests are allowed to enter the Inner Temple Gardens. The Middle Temple contains a Tudor hall completed in 1570 with a double hammer-beam roof. It is believed that Shakespeare's troupe played *Twelfth Night* here in 1602. A table on view is said to have come from timber from Sir Francis Drake's *The Golden Hind.* The hall may be visited from 10 a.m. to noon and 3 to 4:30 p.m. Monday to Saturday. Within the precincts of the Inner Temple is the **Temple Church,** one of three Norman "round churches" left in England. First completed in the 12th century, it has been restored. Look for the knightly effigies and the Norman door any time from 10 a.m. to 5 p.m. (to 4 p.m. in winter). Take note of the circle of grotesque portrait heads, including a goat in a mortar board. A caretaker can show you a "dungeon" one flight up. Continue north on Middle Temple Lane to about where the Strand becomes Fleet Street going east. Look for the memorial pillar called Temple Bar, marking the boundary of the City.

North across the Strand stand the **Royal Courts of Justice,** W.C.2 (tel. 405-7641, ext. 3439; tube to Temple), which are open Monday to Friday from 10 a.m. to 4 p.m. You can go through its main doorway on the Strand and on through the building, which was completed in 1882 but designed in the style of the 13th century. This is the home of such courts as admiralty, divorce, probate, chancery, appeals, and Queen's Bench. Leave the Royal Courts building by the rear door and you'll be on Carey Street, not far from New Square. From there, you're in the near vicinity of **Lincoln's Inn,** W.C.2 (tube: Holborn), another of the famous inns of court, and **Lincoln's Inn Fields.** Lincoln's Inn, founded in the 14th century, evokes colleges at Cambridge or Oxford. This ancient inn forms an important link in the architectural maze of London. Its chapel and gardens are open to the public between noon and 2:30 p.m., and they're well worth seeing. The chapel was rebuilt around 1620 by Inigo Jones. Cromwell lived here at one time. To the west of the inn lies the late 17th-century square, one of the few such London areas still complete, called Lincoln's Inn Fields. Near the south of the fields on Kingsway is the **Old Curiosity Shop,** immortalized by Charles Dickens.

If you proceed north on Chancery Lane to High Holborn, W.C.1, heading toward **Gray's Inn,** the fourth of the ancient Inns of Court still in operation, take a look at the old **Staple Inn,** near the Chancery Lane tube stop. This half-timbered edifice and eight other former Inns of Chancery are no longer in use in the legal world. Now lined with shops, it was built and rebuilt many times, originally having come into existence between 1545 and 1589. Dr. Johnson moved here in 1759, the year *Rasselas* was published.

Gray's Inn, on Gray's Inn Road north of High Holborn, is entered from Theobald's Road. As you enter, you'll see a late-Georgian terrace lined with buildings that, like many of the other houses in the inns, are combined residences and offices. Gray's has been restored after being heavily damaged by World War II bombings. Francis Bacon, scientist and philosopher (1561–1626), was the most eminent tenant who resided here in other days. The inn contains a rebuilt Tudor Hall, but its greatest attraction is the plane-tree–shaded lawn and handsome gardens, considered the best in the inns. The 17th-century atmosphere exists today only in the square.

When Horace Rumpole, known to readers and TV audiences as *Rumpole of the Bailey,* leaves his chambers in one of the Temple Inns of Court to go to court, he usually heads not for the Royal Courts of Justice mentioned above, which are involved with civil cases, but to the **Central Criminal Court,** better known as **Old Bailey,** on the corner of Old Bailey and Newgate Street, E.C.4. To reach it, go east on Fleet Street, which along the way becomes Ludgate Hill. Cross Ludgate Circus and turn left to the Old Bailey, a domed structure with the figure of Justice standing atop it. The courthouse replaced the infamous Newgate Prison, once the scene of public hangings and other forms of public "entertainment." The public is permitted to enter from 10:20 a.m. to 1 p.m. and 1:50 to 4 p.m. Monday to Friday. Entry is strictly on a first-arrival basis. Guests queue up outside (where, incidentally, the final public execution took place in the 1860s). Courts 1 to 4, 17, and 18 are entered from Newgate Street, and the balance from Old Bailey (the street). No one under 14 is admitted, and teenagers from 14 to 17 must be accompanied by a responsible adult. No cameras or tape recorders are allowed. Tube: Temple, Chancery Lane, or St. Paul's.

Other Museums

The present **Guildhall,** King Street in Cheapside, The City, E.C.2 (tel. 606-3030; tube: Bank), was built in 1411. But the Civic Hall of the Corporation of London has had a rough time, notably in the Great Fire of 1666 and the 1940 Blitz. The most famous tenants of the rebuilt Guildhall are *Gog* and *Magog,* two giants standing over nine feet high. The original effigies, burned in the London fire, were rebuilt only to be destroyed again in 1940. The present giants are third generation. Restoration has returned the Gothic grandeur to the hall, which is replete with a medieval porch entranceway; monuments to Wellington, Churchill, and Nelson; stained glass commemorating lord mayors and mayors; the standards of length; and shields honoring fishmongers, haberdashers, merchant tailors, ironmongers, and skinners— some of the major Livery Companies. The Guildhall may be visited Monday to Saturday from 2 to 5 p.m. (on Sunday, May to September only, from 10 a.m. to 5 p.m.) Admission is free.

Sir John Soane's Museum, 13 Lincoln's Inn Fields, W.C.2 (tel. 405-2107), is the former home of an architect who lived from 1753 to 1837. Sir John, who rebuilt the Bank of England (not the present structure, however), was a "spaceman" in a different era. With his multilevels, fool-the-eye mirrors, flying arches, and domes, Soane was a master of perspective, a genius of interior space (his picture gallery, for example, is filled with three times the number of paintings a room of similar dimensions would be likely to hold). That he could do all this—and still not prove a demon to claustrophobia victims—was proof of his remarkable talent. Even if you don't like Soane (he was reportedly a cranky fellow), you may still want to visit this museum to see William Hogarth's satirical series, *The Rake's Progress,* containing his much reproduced *Orgy,* and the satire on politics in the mid-18th century, *The Election.* Soane also filled his house with paintings (Watteau's *Les Noces,* Canaletto's large *Venetian Scene*) and classical sculpture. Finally, be sure to see the sarcophagus of Pharaoh Seti I found in a burial chamber in the Valley of the Kings. The museum is open Tuesday to Saturday from 10 a.m. to 5 p.m. A guided tour is given at 2:30 p.m. on Saturday. Take the tube to Chancery Lane or Holborn.

Royal Academy of Arts, Piccadilly, W.1 (tel. 734-9052; 439-4996 for recorded information), founded in 1768, is the oldest established society in Great Britain devoted solely to the fine arts. The academy is made up of a self-supporting, self-governing body of artists, who conduct art schools, hold exhibitions of the work of living artists, and organize loan exhibits of the arts of past and present periods. A summer exhibition, which has been held annually for an unbroken 200 years, presents contemporary paintings, drawings, engravings, sculpture, and architecture.

Occupying old Burlington House, which was built in Piccadilly in the 1600s, the Royal Academy's first president was Sir Joshua Reynolds. The program of loan exhibitions provides opportunities to see fine art examples on an international scale. The Royal Academy Shop and a restaurant are open during exhibition hours, usually 10 a.m. to 6 p.m. daily, and the framing workshop can be visited from 10 a.m. to 5 p.m. Monday to Saturday. Admission is free. Burlington House is opposite Fortnum and Mason. Tube: Piccadilly Circus or Green Park. Buses 9, 14, 19, 22, and 38 stop outside.

Just across the Thames on Lambeth Road, S.E.1, is the **Imperial War Museum** (tel. 735-8922; tube to Lambeth North or Elephant & Castle). Built around 1815, this large domed building, the former Bethlehem Royal Hospital for the Insane, or Bedlam, houses the museum's collections relating to the two world wars and other military operations involving the British and the Commonwealth since 1914.

A wide range of weapons and equipment is on display, along with models, decorations, uniforms, posters, photographs, and paintings. You can see a Mark V tank, a Battle of Britain Spitfire, a German one-man submarine, and the rifle carried by Lawrence of Arabia, as well as the German surrender document and Hitler's political testament. While preparations are under way for the redevelopment of the museum, the galleries have been reorganized on a chronological basis covering the two world wars and more recent conflicts. In addition, regular art exhibitions are being shown during redevelopment. The museum is open seven days a week from 10 a.m. to 6 p.m. Admission is £2.50 ($4.40) for adults, £1.25 ($2.20) for children.

National Army Museum, Royal Hospital Road, S.W.3 (tel. 730-0717), in Chelsea, traces the history of the British land forces from 1485 to 1982, as well as the Indian Army, and Colonial land forces. The museum backers agreed to begin the collection at the year 1485, because that was the date of the formation of the Yeomen of the Guard. The saga of the forces of the East India Company is also traced, beginning in 1602 and going up to Indian independence in 1947. The gory and the glory —it's all here, everything from Florence Nightingale's lamp to the French Eagle captured in a cavalry charge at Waterloo, even the staff cloak wrapped around the dying Wolfe at Québec. Naturally, there are the "cases of the heroes," mementos of such outstanding men as the Dukes of Marlborough and Wellington. But the field soldier isn't neglected either. The Flanders to the Falklands gallery tells the soldier's story from the 1914–1918 war through World War II and on to the conflict in the Falklands in 1982. The admission-free museum is open Monday to Saturday from 10 a.m. to 5:30 p.m., on Sunday from 2 to 5:30 p.m. It is closed on New Year's Day, Good Friday, from December 24 to 26, and on the May bank holiday. Tube: Sloane Square.

Apsley House, The Wellington Museum, 149 Piccadilly, Hyde Park Corner, W.1 (tel. 499-5676), takes us into the former town house of the Iron Duke, the British general (1769–1852) who defeated Napoleon at the Battle of Waterloo. Designed by Robert Adam and built in the late 18th century, Wellington's London residence was opened as a public museum in 1952. Once Wellington had to retreat behind the walls of Apsley House—even securing it in fear of a possible attack from Englishmen outraged by his autocratic opposition as prime minister to reform. In the vestibule you'll find a colossal statue in marble of Napoleon by Canova—ironic, to say the least. Completely idealized, it was presented to the duke by King George IV. In addition to the famous *Waterseller of Seville* by Velázquez, the Wellington collection includes Correggio's *Agony in the Garden,* Jan Steen's *The Egg Dance,* and Pieter de Hooch's *A Musical Party.* You can see the gallery where Wellington used to invite his officers for the annual Waterloo banquet. The house also contains a large porcelain and china collection, including a magnificent Sèvres porcelain Egyptian service, made originally for Empress Josephine and given by Louis XVIII to Wellington. In addition, superb English silver and the extraordinary Portuguese center-piece, a present from a grateful Portugal to its liberator, are exhibited. The house is open from 11 a.m. to 5 p.m. Tuesday to Sunday; closed Monday, Christmas holidays, and New Year's Day. Admission is £2 ($3.50) for adults, £($1.75) for children. Tube: Hyde Park Corner.

In London's Barbican district near St. Paul's Cathedral, the **Museum of London** at 150 London Wall, E.C.2 (tel. 600-3699), allows visitors to trace the history of London from prehistoric times to the present—through relics, costumes, household effects, maps, and models. Exhibits are arranged so that visitors can begin and end their chronological stroll through 250,000 years at the main entrance to the museum. You can see the death mask of Oliver Cromwell, but the pièce de résistance is the Lord Mayor's coach, built in 1757 and weighing in at three tons. Still used each November in the Lord Mayor's Procession, this gilt-and-red, horse-drawn vehicle is like a fairytale coach. Visitors can also see the Great Fire of London in living color and sound; reconstructed Roman dining rooms with the kitchen and utensils; cell doors from Newgate Prison made famous by Charles Dickens; and most amazing of all, a shop counter with pre–World War II prices on the items.

The museum, opened in 1976, overlooks London's Roman and medieval walls and, in all, has something from every era before and after—including little Victorian shops and re-creations of what life was like during the Iron Age in what is now the London area. Anglo-Saxons, Vikings, Normans—they're all there, arranged on two floors around a central courtyard. With quick labels for museum sprinters, more extensive ones for those who want to study, and still deeper details for scholars, this museum, built at a cost of some $18 million, is an enriching experience for *everybody*.

At least an hour should be allowed for a full (but still quick) visit to the museum. Free lectures on London's past are given during lunch hours. These aren't given daily, but it's worth inquiring at the entrance hall. You can reach the museum by going up to the elevated pedestrian precinct at the corner of London Wall and Aldersgate, five minutes from St. Paul's. Admission free, the museum is open Tuesday to Saturday from 10 a.m. to 6 p.m., on Sunday from 2 to 6 p.m.; closed Monday. A restaurant overlooks a garden. Tube: St. Paul's, Barbican, or Moorgate.

London Transport Museum, Covent Garden, W.C.2 (tel. 379-6344), is in a splendidly restored Victorian building that formerly housed the flower market. Horse buses, motorbuses, trams, trolley buses, railway vehicles, models, maps, posters, photographs, and audio-visual displays illustrate the fascinating story of the evolution of London's transport systems and how this has affected the growth of London. There are also a number of unique working displays. You can "drive" a tube train, a tram, and a bus, and also operate full-size signaling equipment. The exhibits include a reconstruction of George Shillibeer's omnibus of 1829, a steam locomotive that ran on the world's first underground railway, and a coach from the first deep-level electric railway. The museum is open every day of the year except December 24, 25, and 26, from 10 a.m. to 6 p.m. (last admission at 5:15 p.m.). Admission charges are £2.40 ($4.20) for adults, £1.10 ($1.95) for children. A family ticket for two adults and two children is £5.50 ($9.95). The museum sells a variety of souvenirs of London Transport, (see Shopping section under "Posters"). Tube: Covent Garden.

National Postal Museum, King Edward Building, King Edward Street, E.C.1 (tel. 239-5420), attracts philatelists from all over the world. Actually part of the Post Office, it features permanent exhibitions of the stamps of Great Britain and the world and special displays of stamps and postal history, changing every few months according to certain themes. For example, one exhibition featured "Crossing the Atlantic." The museum is open from 10 a.m. to 4:30 p.m. Monday to Thursday, to 4 p.m. on Friday. Admission is free. Tube: St. Paul's or Barbican.

Royal Air Force Museum, Grahame Park Way, Hendon, N.W.7 (tel. 205-2266), contains one of the world's finest collections of historic aircraft illustrating all aspects of the history of the Royal Air Force and much of the history of aviation in general. The museum stands on ten acres of the former historic airfield at Hendon in North London, and its main Aircraft Hall occupies two hangars dating from World War I. From the museum's collection of more than 100 aircraft, some 60 machines are displayed, including the legendary Spitfire and Lancaster, plus German and American aircraft. On a site adjacent to the main building is the Battle of Britain Hall, containing a unique collection of British, German, and Italian aircraft that were engaged in the great air battle of 1940. The museum is a national memorial to the victorious forces and especially to "The Few." Machines include the Spitfire, Hurricane, Gladiator, Defiant, Blenheim, and Messerschmitt BF 109. A central feature of the exhibition is a replica of the No. 11 Group Operations Room at RAF Uxbridge. Equipment, uniforms, medals, documents, relics, works of art, and other memorabilia of the period are included in the permanent memorial to the men, women, and machines involved in the air battle.

Also in the same complex is the massive **Bomber Command Hall,** with its striking display of famous bomber aircraft, including the Lancaster, Wellington, B17 Flying Fortress, Mosquito, and Vulcan.

Admission to the entire complex is £3 ($5.25) for adults, £1.50 ($2.65) for children. Hours are from 10 a.m. to 6 p.m. daily except New Year's Day and from December 24 to December 26. The nearest underground is Colindale on the Northern Line, and the nearest British Rail station is Mill Hill Broadway. Access by road is via the A41 from the M1 at junction 4, the A1, and North Circular Road.

The Science Museum, Exhibition Road, S.W.7 (tel. 938-8000), traces the development of both science and industry and their influence in everyday life. The collections are among the largest, most comprehensive, and most significant anywhere. On display is Stephenson's original *Rocket,* the tiny locomotive that won a race against all competitors in the Rainhill Trials and became the world's prototype railroad engine. You can also see Whittle's original jet engine and the Gloster aircraft, the first jet-powered British plane. A cavalcade of antique cars from the Stanley steam car to the yellow Rolls-Royce can be seen, side by side with carriages and vintage bicycles and motorcycles. To aid the visitor's understanding of many scientific and technological principles, working models and video displays are here, including a hands-on gallery called Launch Pad. Here you can take part in experiments and demonstrations and discover that science can be fun. The recently designed East Hall welcomes visitors with an audio-visual slide show and the soothing sound of a huge Lancashire Hill engine of 1903, running on steam. A shopping concourse provides the opportunity of taking home a souvenir. The museum is open from 10 a.m. to 6 p.m. Monday to Saturday, from 11 a.m. to 6 p.m. Sunday. Admission is £2 ($3.50) for adults, £1 ($1.75) for children 5 to 15. Take the tube to South Kensington or bus 14.

You can step back into the days of Queen Victoria when you visit the **Linley Sambourne House,** 18 Stafford Terrace, W.8 (tel. 994-1019), which has remained unchanged for more than a century. The house, part of a terrace built between 1868 and 1874, is a five-story, Suffolk brick structure to which Linley Sambourne brought his bride. Sambourne was a draftsman who later became a cartoonist for *Punch.* The Sambourne family owned and occupied the house until 1980, when it was purchased by the Greater London Council and leased to the Victorian Society. From the moment you step into the entrance hall, you see a mixture of styles and clutter that typified Victorian decor, with a plush portière, a fireplace valance, stained glass in the backdoor depicting an orange tree in a blue-and-white bowl, and a large set of antlers vying for attention. The drawing room alone contains an incredible number of items. Admission to the house, which is open on Wednesday from 10 a.m. to 4 p.m. and on Sunday from 2 to 5 p.m. March 1 to October 31, is £2 ($3.50). Tube: High Street Kensington.

The major communal building for English Jewry is **Woburn House,** Tavistock Square, W.C.1, near Euston Station, the nearest tube stop. In these precincts you'll also come upon the hard-to-find **Jewish Museum** (tel. 388-4525), tucked away on a lovely square. Walk along Euston Road, and turn right onto Upper Woburn Place. When you reach Tavistock Square, turn right again, and there's the entrance. After entering, you're invited to sign a guest book, then you're guided up to the museum, a large salon filled with antiques relating to the history of the Jews. You'll come across many artifacts used in Jewish rituals and other exhibits of interest to those concerned with Anglo-Judaica. It is open from 10 a.m. to 4 p.m. Sunday and Tuesday to Thursday as well as Friday in summer. In winter, Friday hours are from 10 a.m. to 12:45 p.m. It is closed Monday, Saturday, public holidays, and Jewish holidays.

Other Galleries

National Portrait Gallery, St. Martin's Place, W.C.2 (tel. 930-1552; entrance around the corner from the National Gallery on Trafalgar Square), gives you a chance to outstare the stiff-necked greats and not-so-greats of English history. In a gallery of remarkable and unremarkable portraits, a few paintings tower over the rest, including Sir Joshua Reynolds's first portrait of Samuel Johnson ("a man of most dreadful appearance"). Among the best are Nicholas Hilliard's miniature of a handsome Sir Walter Raleigh and a full-length Elizabeth I (painted to commemorate her visit to Sir Henry Lee at Ditchley in 1592), along with the Holbein cartoon of Henry VIII (sketched for a family portrait that hung, before it was burned, in the Privy Chamber in Whitehall Palace). You'll also see a portrait of William Shakespeare (with gold earring, no less) which is claimed to be the most "authentic contemporary likeness" of its subject of any work yet known. The John Hayls portrait of Samuel Pepys adorns one wall. Whistler could not only paint a portrait, he could also be the subject of one, as shown here. One of the most unusual pictures in the gallery—a group of the three Brontë sisters (Charlotte, Emily, Anne)—was painted by their brother, Branwell. An idealized portrait of Lord Byron by Thomas Phillips is pleased with itself, and you can treat yourself to the likeness of the incomparable Aubrey Beardsley. For a finale, Princess Diana is on the Royal Landing. The gallery is open from 10 a.m. to 5 p.m. Monday to Friday, to 6 p.m. on Saturday, and from 2 to 6 p.m. on Sunday. Admission is free except for special exhibitions held at the gallery throughout the year. Tube: Charing Cross or Leicester Square.

The **Wallace Collection,** Manchester Square, W.1 (tel. 935-0687), off Wigmore Street, has an outstanding collection of works of art of all kinds bequeathed to the nation by Lady Wallace in 1897 and still displayed in the house of its founders. There are important pictures by artists of all European schools, including Titian, Rubens, Van Dyck, Rembrandt, Hals, Velázquez, Murillo, Reynolds, Gainsborough, and Delacroix. Representing the art of France in the 18th century are paintings by Watteau, Boucher, and Fragonard, and sculpture, furniture, goldsmiths' work, and Sèvres porcelain. Also found are valuable collections of majolica and European and Oriental arms and armor. Frans Hals's *Laughing Cavalier* is the most celebrated painting in the collection, but Pieter de Hooch's *A Boy Bringing Pomegranates* and Watteau's *The Music Party* are also well known. Other notable works include Canaletto's views of Venice (especially *Bacino di San Marco*), Rembrandt's *Titus,* and Gainsborough's *Mrs. Robinson (Perdita).* Boucher's portrait of the Marquise de Pompadour is also worthy. The Wallace Collection may be viewed daily from 10 a.m. to 5 p.m. (from 2 p.m. on Sunday); closed Christmas Eve, Christmas Day, Boxing Day, New Year's Day, Good Friday, and the first Monday in May. Admission free. Tube: Bond Street.

The **Courtauld Institute Galleries,** Somerset House, The Strand, W.C.2 (tel. 580-1015), is the home of the art collection of London University—noted chiefly for its superb impressionist and post-impressionist works. It has eight works by Cézanne alone, including his *A Man with a Pipe.* Other notable art includes Seurat's *La Poudreuse,* Van Gogh's self-portrait (with ear bandaged), a nude by Modigliani, Gauguin's *Day-Dreaming,* Monet's *Fall at Argenteuil,* Toulouse-Lautrec's delicious

Tête-a-Tête, and Manet's *Bar at the Folies Bergère.* The galleries also feature classical works, including a *Virgin and Child* by Bernardino Luini, a Botticelli, a Giovanni Bellini, a Veronese, a triptych by the Master of Flémâlle, works by Pieter Brueghel, Massys, Parmigianino, 32 oils by Rubens, oil sketches by Tiepolo, three landscapes by Kokoschka, and wonderful old master drawings (especially Michelangelo and Rembrandt). The artworks may be viewed Monday to Saturday from 10 a.m. to 5 p.m. and on Sunday from 2 to 5 p.m. Admission is £1.50 ($2.75) for adults, 50p (90¢) for children. Tube: Charing Cross.

The **Hayward Gallery,** South Bank, S.E.1 (tel. 928-3144), presents a changing program of major exhibitions. The gallery forms part of the South Bank Centre, which also includes the Royal Festival Hall, the Queen Elizabeth Hall, the Purcell Room, the National Film Theatre, and the National Theatre. Admission to the gallery varies according to exhibitions from £2.50 ($4.40) to £4 ($7), with the cheaper entry all day Monday, and from 6 to 8 p.m.; on Tuesday and Wednesday. Hours are Monday to Wednesday from 10 a.m. to 8 p.m.; Thursday, Friday, and Saturday from 10 a.m. to 6 p.m.; and on Sunday from noon to 6 p.m. The gallery is closed between exhibitions, so check the listings before crossing the Thames. For recorded information, phone 261-0127. Tube: Waterloo Station.

Homes of Famous Writers

Dr. Johnson's House: The Queen Anne house of the famed lexicographer is at 17 Gough Square (tel. 353-3745). It'll cost you £1.50 ($2.65), and it's well worth it. Children £1 ($1.75). It was there that Dr. Johnson and his copyists compiled his famous dictionary. The 17th-century building has been painstakingly restored (surely "Dear Tetty," if not Boswell, would approve). Although Johnson lived at Staple Inn in Holborn and at a number of other houses, the Gough Square house is the only one of his residences remaining in London. He occupied it from 1748 to 1759. It is open from 11 a.m. to 5:30 p.m. Monday through Saturday, May through September, closing half an hour earlier off-season. Take the tube to Blackfriars, then walk up New Bridge Street, turning left onto Fleet. Gough Square is a tiny, hidden square, north of the "street of ink."

Carlyle's House: 24 Cheyne Row, S.W.3 (tel. 352-7087), in Chelsea (bus 11, 19, 22, or 39). For nearly half a century, from 1834 to 1881, the handsome author of *The French Revolution* and other works, along with his letter-writing wife, took up abode in this modest 1708 terraced house, about three-quarters of a block from the Thames, near the Chelsea Embankment. Still standing and furnished essentially as it was in Carlyle's day, the house was described by his wife as being "of most antique physiognomy, quite to our humour; all wainscotted, carved and queer-looking, roomy, substantial, commodious, with closets to satisfy any Bluebeard." Now who could improve on that? The second floor contains the drawing room of Mrs. Carlyle. But the most interesting chamber is the not-so-soundproof "soundproof" study in the skylit attic. Filled with Carlyle memorabilia—his books, a letter from Disraeli, a writing chair, even his death mask—this is the cell where the author labored over his *Frederick the Great* manuscript. The Cheyne (pronounced chainey) Row house is open daily from 11 a.m. to 5 p.m. from Easter Saturday to the end of October except Monday and Tuesday. Admission is £1.60 ($2.80) for adults and half price for accompanied children. The nearest tube, Sloane Square, is a long way off.

Dickens's House: In Bloomsbury stands the house of the great English author Charles Dickens, accused in his time of "supping on the horrors" of Victoriana. Born in 1812 in what is now Portsmouth, Dickens is known to have lived at 48 Doughty St., W.C.1 (tel. 405-2127; tube to Russell Square), from 1837 to 1839. Unlike some of the London town houses of famous men (Wellington, Soane), the Bloomsbury house is simple, the embodiment of middle-class restraint. The house contains an extensive library of Dickensiana, including manuscripts and letters second in importance only to the Forster Collection in the Victoria and Albert Museum. In his study are his desk and chair from the study at Gad's Hill Place, Rochester, on which he wrote the last two letters before he died (also the table from his Swiss chalet on which he wrote the last unfinished fragment of *The Mystery of Edwin Drood*). Dickens's drawing room on the first floor has been reconstructed, as have the still room, wash house, and wine cellar in the basement. The house is open daily, except Sunday and bank holidays, from 10 a.m. to 5 p.m. Admission is £1.50 ($2.65) for adults, 75p ($1.30) for children, and £3 ($5.25) for families.

Hampstead and Highgate

Hampstead Heath is hundreds of acres of wild and unfenced royal parkland about four miles north from the center of London, so elevated that on a clear day you can see St. Paul's Cathedral and even the hills of Kent south of the Thames. It is the scene of big one-day fairs in good weather, and it has for years drawn Londoners on such weekend pursuits as kite-flying, sunning, fishing in the ponds, swimming, and picnicking, and it is a favorite place for joggers. It was the common of Hampstead Manor in the time of King Charles II, a good ride out from London. Tube: Hampstead Heath.

Hampstead Village developed from the rural area around some of the substantial houses built in the area. From a village, a fashionable spa town developed in the 18th century, giving the name to Well Walk and other parts of the growing town. With the coming of the Underground in 1907, its attractions as a place to live, even for those who went frequently into the City, became widely known, and writers, artists, architects, musicians, and scientists came to join earlier residents, some of their own kind.

Among the many eminent figures in the literary world who have lived in Hampstead, either full time or part time were Keats, D. H. Lawrence, Rabindranath Tagore, Shelley, and Robert Louis Stevenson and some (such as Kingsley Amis, and John Le Carré) still do. Regency and Georgian houses were built in this village just 20 minutes by tube from Piccadilly Circus, with its palatable mix of history-rich pubs, toy shops, and chic boutiques, as seen along Flask Walk, a pedestrian mall. The original village, on the side of a hill, still has pleasing features such as the old roads, lanes, places, alleys, steps, rises, courts, and groves to be strolled through.

Keats's House: The darling of romantics, John Keats lived for only two years at Wentworth Place, Keats Grove, Hampstead, N.W.3 (tel. 435-2062; take the tube to Belsize Park or Hampstead or bus 24 from Trafalgar Square). But for the poet, that was something like two-fifths of his creative life, as he died in Rome of tuberculosis at the age of 25 (1821). In Hampstead, Keats wrote some of his most celebrated *Odes*—in praise of a Grecian urn and to the nightingale. In the garden stands an ancient mulberry tree that the poet must have known. His Regency house is well preserved, and contains the manuscripts of his last sonnet ("Bright star, would I were steadfast as thou art"), a final letter to the mother of Fanny Brawne (his correspondence to his Hampstead neighbor, who nursed him while he was ill, forms part of his legend), and a portrait of him on his death bed in a house on the Spanish Steps in Rome. Wentworth Place is open from 2 to 6 p.m. Monday to Friday, 10 a.m. to 5 p.m. Saturday, and 2 to 5 p.m. Sunday and bank holidays April to October. From November to March, hours are from 1 to 5 p.m. Monday to Friday, 10 a.m. to 5 p.m. Saturday, and 2 to 5 p.m. Sunday. However, call to confirm hours as they may be changed in the lifetime of this edition. Closed Christmas holidays, New Year's Day, Easter holidays, and May Day. Admission is free.

The Iveagh Bequest, **Kenwood,** Hampstead Lane, N.W.3 (tel. 348-1286), handsome with its columned portico, was built as a gentleman's country home around the start of the 18th century. It became the seat of Lord Mansfield in 1754 and was enlarged and decorated by the famous Scottish architect, Robert Adam from 1764. In 1927 it was given to the nation by Lord Iveagh, together with his collection of pictures. The Adam stamp is strongest in the restored oval library, painted in rose, blue, white, and gold. The rooms contain some fine neoclassical furniture, but the main attractions are the old masters and the work of British artists. You can see paintings by Rembrandt (*Self-Portrait in Old Age*), Vermeer, Turner, Franz Hals, Cuyp, Crome, Gainsborough, Reynolds, Romney, Raeburn, Guardi, and Angelica Kauffmann, plus a portrait of the *Earl of Mansfield, Lord Chief Justice,* who made Kenwood such an important home. In the Coach House, where there is a cafeteria, stands a 19th-century family coach that carried 15 people comfortably. The house is open daily from 10 a.m. to 6 p.m. Easter Saturday to September 30, 10 a.m. to 4 p.m. October 1 to Maundy Thursday; closed Christmas Eve, Christmas Day, and Good Friday.

Fenton House, Windmill Hill, N.W.3 (tel. 435-3471), a National Trust property, is in a village area on the west side of Hampstead Grove, just a short distance north of Hampstead Village. You pass through beautiful wrought-iron gates to reach the red-brick house in a fine walled garden. Built in 1693, it is one of the earliest, largest, and finest houses in the Hampstead section. The south front is striking, with a central pediment and seven bays. The original main staircase, some door frames, and chimney pieces remain of the early construction. Paneled rooms contain furniture, pictures, English, German, and French porcelain from the 18th century, and the outstanding Benton-Fletcher collection of early keyboard musical instruments. Exhibits of these date from 1540 to 1805, including a 17th-century Flemish harpsichord on loan from the Queen Mother. On the second floor you'll see harpsichords, spinets, square pianos, clavichords, and also a virginal. There are also some fine needlework pictures on the walls. The house is open on Saturday and Sunday from 2 to 6 p.m. in March; Saturday to Wednesday from 2 to 6 p.m. April to October. Last admission is at 5 p.m. It's closed on Good Friday. Admission is £2 ($3.50) for adults, £1 ($1.75) for children. Occasional concerts are held at the house.

The Freud Museum, 20 Maresfield Gardens, N.W.3 (tel. 435-2002), is a spacious, three-story red-brick house in which Sigmund Freud, father of psychoanalysis, lived, worked, and died after escaping with his family and possessions from Nazi-occupied Vienna. On view are rooms containing original furniture, letters, photographs, paintings, and personal effects of Freud and his daughter, Anna. A focal point of the museum is the study in which you can see the famous couch and large collection of Egyptian, Roman, and Oriental antiquities. The museum is developing as a research archive, educational resource, and cultural center. Temporary exhibitions, continuous guided tours, and an archive film program are available, plus a shop. Hours are from noon to 5 p.m. Wednesday to Sunday. Admission is £2 ($3.50). Tube: Finchley Road.

Burgh House, New End Square, N.W.3 (tel. 431-0144), is a Queen Anne structure built in 1703 in the middle of the village, the home of professional men and later the residence of the daughter and son-in-law of Rudyard Kipling, who often visited here. It is now used for local arts exhibits, concerts, recitals, and talks and public meetings on many subjects. The house is also the home of several local societies including the Hampstead Music Club and the Hampstead Scientific Society. The Heath & Old Hampstead (Conservation) Society holds regular meetings here, and their Heath walks start from the house. The **Hampstead Museum** is in Burgh House. Both are open from noon to 5 p.m. Wednesday to Sunday and from 2 to 5 p.m. on bank holidays Monday. They are closed Good Friday, two weeks around Christmas, and New Year bank holiday. Admission is free except for talks, recitals, and other entertainment. Just ask one of the mums pushing her pram or a passing villager walking his or her dog to direct you to the place.

Highgate Village, a stone's throw east of Hampstead Heath, has a number of mansions from the 16th and 17th centuries, as well as small cottages lining three sides of the now pondless Pond Square. Its most outstanding feature, however, is **Highgate Cemetery,** which is entered from Swain's Lane, N.6. This cemetery is the ideal setting for a collection of Victorian sculpture. Described as everything from "walled romantic rubble" to "an anthology of horror," the 37-acre burial ground attracts tombstone fanciers. Highgate's most famous grave is that of Karl Marx, the founder of modern Communism, who died in Hampstead in 1883. On the tomb is a huge bust of Marx, inscribed with his quotation, "Workers of the world, unite." The grave is seldom without a wreath or bouquet of red flowers, usually placed there by an Eastern embassy or a local Communist group. For further information, phone 348-0808.

The Parks of London

London's parklands easily rate as the greatest, most wonderful system of "green lungs" of any large city on the globe. Not as rigidly artificial as the parks of Paris, those in London are maintained with a loving care and lavish artistry that puts their American equivalents to shame. Above all, they've been kept safe from land-hungry building firms and city councils, and still offer patches of real countryside right in the heart of the metropolis. Maybe there's something to be said for inviolate "royal" property, after all. Because that's what most of London's parks are.

Largest of them—and one of the biggest in the world—is **Hyde Park,** W.2. With the adjoining Kensington Gardens, it covers 636 acres of central London with velvety lawns interspersed with ponds, flowerbeds, and trees. Hyde Park was once a favorite deer-hunting ground of Henry VIII. Running through the width is a 41-acre lake known as the Serpentine. Rotten Row, a 1½-mile sand track, is reserved for horseback riding and on Sunday attracts some skilled equestrians.

Kensington Gardens, W.2, blending with Hyde Park, border on the grounds of Kensington Palace. Kensington Gardens also contain the celebrated statue of Peter Pan, with the bronze rabbits that toddlers are always trying to kidnap. The Albert Memorial, that previously mentioned Victorian extravaganza, is also here.

East of Hyde Park, across Piccadilly, stretch **Green Park** and **St. James's Park,** W.1, forming an almost unbroken chain of landscaped beauty. This is an ideal area for picnics, and you'll find it hard to believe that this was once a festering piece of swamp near the leper hospital. There is a romantic lake, stocked with a variety of ducks and pelicans, descendants of the pair that the Russian ambassador presented to Charles II in 1662.

Regent's Park, N.W.1, covers most of the district by that name, north of Baker Street and Marylebone Road. Designed by the 18th-century genius John Nash to surround a palace of the prince regent that never materialized, this is the most classically beautiful of London's parks. The core is a rose garden planted around a small lake alive with waterfowl and spanned by humped Japanese bridges. In early summer, the rose perfume in the air is as heady as wine.

Regent's Park also contains the Open-Air Theater and the London Zoo. Also— as in all the local parks—there are hundreds of deckchairs on the lawns in which to sunbathe. The deckchair attendants, who collect a small fee, are mostly college students on vacation.

London Zoo

One of the greatest zoos in the world, the London Zoo is more than a century and a half old. Run by the Zoological Society of London, Regent's Park, N.W.1 (tel. 722-3333), with an equal measure of showmanship and scholarly know-how, this 36-acre garden houses some 8,000 animals, including some of the rarest species on earth. One of the most fascinating exhibits in the Snowdon Aviary. Separate houses are reserved for some species: the insect house (incredible bird-eating spiders, a leafcutter ant colony), the reptile house (huge dragon-like monitor lizards and a fantastic 15-foot python), and other additions, such as the Sobell Pavilion for Apes and Monkeys and the Lion Terraces.

Designed for the largest collection of small mammals in the world, the Clore Pavilion has a basement called the Moonlight World, where special lighting effects simulate night for the nocturnal beasties, while rendering them clearly visible to onlookers. You can see all the night rovers in action: leaping bush babies, a fierce Tasmanian devil, and the giant Indian fruit bats with heads like prehistoric dogs.

The zoo is open daily from 9 a.m. in summer and from 10 a.m. in winter, until 6 p.m. or dusk, whichever is earlier. Last admission is a half hour before closing. Admission is £4.30 ($7.55) for adults, £2.60 ($4.55) for children 4 to 15 (under 4, free). On the grounds are two fully licensed restaurants, one self-service, the other with waitresses. Take the tube to Baker Street or Camden Town, then take bus 74 (Camden Town is nearer and an easy ten-minute walk).

Landmark Churches

St. Martin-in-the-Fields, overlooking Trafalgar Square, W.C.2 (tel. 839-4342), is the Royal Parish Church, dear to the hearts of many an English person, and especially the homeless. The present classically inspired church, with its famous steeple, dates back to 1726. James Gibbs, a pupil of Wren's, is listed as its architect. The origins of the church go back to the 11th century. Among the congregation in years past was George I, who was actually a churchwarden, unique for an English sovereign. From St. Martin's vantage position in the theater district, it has drawn many actors to its door—none more notable than Nell Gwynne, the mistress of Charles II. On her death in 1687, she was buried in the crypt. Throughout the war, many Londoners rode out an uneasy night in the crypt, while Blitz bombs rained down overhead. One, in 1940, blasted out all the windows. The crypt contains a pleasant restaurant, a bookshop, and a gallery. Tube: Charing Cross.

St. Etheldreda's, Britain's oldest Roman Catholic church, lies on Ely Place, Clerkenwell, E.C.1 (tel. 405-1061), leading off Charterhouse Street at Holborn Circus. Built in 1251, it was mentioned by the Bard in both *Richard II* and *Richard III*. One of the survivors of the Great Fire of 1666, the church was built by and was the property of the Diocese of Ely in the days when many bishops had their episcopal houses in London rather than in the actual cathedral cities in which they held their sees. Until this century, the landlord of Ye Olde Mitre public house near Ely Place where the church stands had to obtain his license from the Justices of Cambridgeshire rather than in London, and even today the place is still a private road, with impressive iron gates and a lodge for the gate-keeper, all administered by six commissioners who are elected. St. Etheldreda, whose name is sometimes shortened to St. Audrey, was a 7th-century king's daughter who left her husband and turned to religion, establishing an abbey on the Isle of Ely. The name St. Audrey is the source of the word *tawdry,* from cheap trinkets sold at the annual fair honoring the saint. St. Etheldreda's is made up of a crypt and an upper church, catering to working people and visitors who come to pray. It has a distinguished musical tradition, with the 11 a.m. mass on Sunday sung in Latin. Other mass times are 9 a.m. and 6 p.m. on Sunday and at 8 a.m. and 1 p.m. Monday to Friday. Lunches are served from noon to 2 p.m. Monday to Friday in The Pantry, with a varied choice of hot and cold dishes. Meals cost from £4 ($7). Tube: Farringdon.

Along the Thames

There is a row of fascinating attractions lying on, across, and alongside the River Thames. All of London's history and development is linked with this winding ribbon of water. The Thames connects the city with the sea, from which it drew its wealth and its power. For centuries the river was London's highway and main street.

Some of the bridges that span the Thames are household words. London Bridge, which, contrary to the nursery rhyme, has never "fallen down," but was dismantled and shipped to the United States, ran from the Monument (a tall pillar commemorating the Great Fire of 1666) to Southwark Cathedral, parts of which date back to 1207.

Its neighbor to the east is the still-standing **Tower Bridge,** E.1 (tel. 407-0922), one of the city's most celebrated landmarks and possibly the most photographed and painted bridge on earth. Tower Bridge was built during 1886–1894 with two towers 200 feet apart, joined by footbridges that provide glass-covered walkways for the public who can enter the north tower, take the elevator to the walkway, cross the river to the south tower, and return to street level. It's a photographer's dream, with interesting views of St. Paul's, the Tower of London, and in the distance, a part of the Houses of Parliament. You can also visit the main engine room with its Victorian boilers and steam-pumping engines, which used to raise and lower the roadway across the river.

There are models showing how the 1,000-ton arms of the bridge can be raised in 1½ minutes to allow ships passage upstream, among the exhibitions that trace the history and operation of this unique bridge. Nowadays, electric power is used to raise the bridge, an occurrence that usually happens on an average of once a day, more often in summer. You'll know if it is going to open, however, as a bell sounds throughout the bridge and road traffic is stopped. Admission to exhibits is £2.50 ($4.40), £1 ($1.75) for children. It is open daily in summer from 10 a.m. to 6:30 p.m. (to 4:45 p.m. in winter). Tube: Tower Hill.

The piece of river between the site of the old London Bridge and the Tower Bridge marks the city end of the immense row of docks stretching 26 miles to the coast. Although most of them are no longer in use, they have long been known as the Port of London.

Particular note should be taken of the striking removal of pollution from the Thames in the past decades. The river, so polluted in the 1950s that no marine life could exist in it, can now lay claim to being "the cleanest metropolitan estuary in the world," with many varieties of fish, even salmon, back as happy denizens of these waters.

The Thames Flood Barrier

Since its official opening in 1984, the engineering spectacle known as the Thames Flood Barrier has drawn increasing crowds to the site, at a point in the river known as Woolwich Reach in east London, where the Thames is a straight stretch about a third of a mile in width. For centuries the Thames estuary has from time to time brought tidal surges that have on occasion caused disastrous flooding at Woolwich, Hammersmith, Whitehall, and Westminster, and elsewhere within the river's flood reaches. The flooding peril has increased during this century due to a number of natural causes, including the unstoppable rise of tide levels in the Thames, surge tides from the Atlantic, and the down-tilt of the country by some 12 inches a century.

All this led to the construction, beginning in 1975, of a great barrier with huge piers linking mammoth rising sector gates, smaller rising sector gates, and falling radial gates, all of which when in use make a solid steel wall about the height of a five-story building, which completely dams the waters of the Thames, keeping the surge tides from passage up the estuary. The gates are operated every month to remove river silt and be sure they work smoothly.

London Launches offers trips to the barrier, operating from Westminster Pier. Four trips sail daily in summer, at 10 and 11:15 a.m. and at 1:30 and 2:45 p.m. Except on the last trip, passengers can get off at the barrier pier, visit the Barrier Centre, and return by a later boat or by bus. An audio-visual show depicting the need for the barrier and it's operation is presented at the center, where there are also a souvenir shop, a snackbar, and a cafeteria. Round-trip fare from Westminster Pier is £3.50 ($6.15) for adults, £2 ($3.50) for children. For further information, phone 854-1373.

A Floating Museum

H.M.S. *Belfast*, Morgan's Lane, Tooley Street (tel. 407-6434), Europe's largest historic warship, is permanently moored on the Thames, opposite the Tower of

London. This World War II veteran was among the first to open fire against German fortifications on D-Day. She also served with distinction during the Korean War, where she earned the name, "that straight-shooting ship," from the United States Navy. By exploring the ship from the bridge right down to her engine and boiler rooms, seven decks below, you can discover how Royal Navy sailors lived and fought during the past 50 years. Among the many areas to be visited aboard are the bridge, operations room, 6-inch gun turrets, living quarters, galley, and the D-Day exhibition. H.M.S. *Belfast* is open daily from 11 a.m. to 6 p.m. in summer and from 11 a.m. to 4:30 p.m. in winter. Last boardings are 30 minutes before closing. Admission is £3 ($5.25) for adults, £1.50 ($2.65) for children. Nearest tube stop: London Bridge or Tower Hill. A ferry runs daily from Tower Pier (Tower of London) directly to the ship. It operates only on Saturday and Sunday in winter.

London Docklands

What was a dilapidated eight square miles of property surrounded by water—some 55 miles of waterfront acreage within a sailor's cry of London's major attractions—has been reclaimed, restored, rejuvenated, whatever, until now London Docklands is coming into its own as a leisure, residential, and commercial lure.

Included in this complex are Wapping, the Isle of Dogs, the Surrey and Royal Docks, and more, all with Limehouse at its heart. The former urban wasteland of deserted warehouses and derelict wharves and the many facilities already completed can be visited by taking the **Docklands Light Railway** that links the Isle of Dogs and London Underground's Tower Hill station, via several new local stations. To see the whole complex, take the railway at the Tower Gateway near Tower Bridge for a short journey through Wapping and the Isle of Dogs. You can get off at Island Gardens and then cross through the 100-year-old Greenwich Tunnel under the Thames to see the attractions at Greenwich described in Section 5 of this chapter, "One-Day Trips from London." A regular water-bus service connects Greenwich with Charing Cross in a river voyage of about half an hour, and other tunnels are planned to link the Docklands with port points and motorways.

A visit to the **Exhibition Centre** on the Isle of Dogs offers an opportunity to see what the Docklands past, present, and future include. Already the area has provided space for overflow from the City of London's square mile, and it looks as though the growth and development is more than promising. A shopping Village at Tobacco Dock, a new home at Shadwell Basin for the Academy of St. Martin-in-the-Fields Orchestra, and the London Arena (largest man-made sport and leisure complex in the country) at the tip of the Isle of Dogs are being joined by luxury condominiums, offices, hotels, museums, and theaters; these and all the other amenities aimed at making the East End of London a shining star have been or soon will be completed.

Free Sights—London in Action

Those who have grown museum-weary might like to see workaday London engaged in its task of, say, trying to start a revolution at Speakers Corner or sentencing a modern-day Jack the Ripper at Old Bailey. Here are a few of the action items available:

First, at the northwest extremity of Mayfair, head for **Marble Arch,** an enormous *faux pas* that the English didn't try to hide but turned into a monument. Originally it was built by John Nash as the entrance to Buckingham Palace, until it was discovered that it was too small for carriages to pass through. If you see a crowd of people nearby who look as if they are plotting revolution, you might be right. In this part of Hyde Park (tube to Marble Arch) is **Speakers Corner,** where you will see English free speech in action. Everybody from terrorists to Orgone theorists mounts the soapbox to speak his or her mind. The speeches reach their most violent pitch on Sunday, the best day to visit Marble Arch.

The **Stock Exchange** is, in terms of the number of stocks and shares listed, the largest in the world. From the Visitors' Gallery, you can watch the dealers on the trading floor below you, and guides are in attendance to give talks and to explain the functions and operations of the stock market. After each talk, there is a film in the adjoining cinema, which gives an insight into the financial world. The Visitors' Gallery entrance is in Old Broad Street, E.C.2. For the film, reservations are necessary, to be made by calling the Publicity Department (tel. 588-2355). Tube: Bank.

Historic **Lloyd's of London,** 1 Lime St., E.C.3 (tel. 623-7100), opened its doors to visitors in 1986, and already thousands of people have come to see the workings of the world's biggest insurance market in its new headquarters in the financial district of London. The visitors' gallery on the fourth floor contains a multimedia display depicting the market's history and a reconstruction of the 17th-century coffeehouse of Edward Lloyd, where it all started. Guides explain how risks are placed and discuss the worldwide intelligence service operated for Lloyd's. A gallery lets you look down into an atrium to the underwriting room below, which is centered by the rostrum bearing the famous Lutine Bell, that used to be sounded when a ship disaster occurred at sea. The Visitors' Gallery is open Monday to Friday from 10 a.m. to 2:30 p.m. Admission is free. There is a room where afternoon tea is served, as well as a gift shop. Tube: Bank, Monument, or Aldgate.

2. Taking the Tours

In addition to the sights you can see in London by foot, or by using the tubes, there are numerous attractions that can be reached via several coach tours. As an added bonus, there are dozens of fascinating trips that can be made on the Thames.

EASIEST WAY TO SEE LONDON

For the first-timer, the quickest and most economical way to bring the big city into focus is to take a two-hour, 20-mile circular tour of the West End and The City, the guided **Original London Sightseeing Tour,** which passes virtually all the major places of interest in central London. Operated by London Transport Tours, part of the city's official bus company, the journeys leave at frequent intervals daily from Victoria, Piccadilly Circus, Marble Arch, and Baker Street. Tickets cost £6 ($10.50) for adults and £4 ($7) for children under 16 and are available from the driver. Tickets can also be purchased from London Regional Transport Travel Information Centres, where you can get a discount of £1 ($1.75) off each ticket. Locations of the travel centers are given under "Transportation," in Section 1 of Chapter III of this book.

LONDON'S WEST END AND THE CITY

If you prefer a more detailed look at the city's sights, then **London Transport** offers two highly regarded conducted coach tours.

For a look at the West End, a three-hour tour is offered, passing Westminster Abbey (guided tour), Houses of Parliament, Horse Guards, Trafalgar Square, and Piccadilly Circus, including the changing of the guard. The tour starts at 10 a.m. every day except Sunday, and the fare is £10.50 ($18.40) for adults and £8.50 ($14.90) for children under 14.

London Transport's other popular three-hour tour is of The City, and includes guided trips to the Tower of London and St. Paul's Cathedral. The fare for this is £15 ($26.25) for adults, £12 ($21) for children. The tour is operated Monday to Saturday at 2 p.m. In summer the tour also runs on Sunday.

These two tours are combined to form the London Day Tour, which costs £29.50 ($51.65) for adults, £24.50 ($42.90) for children under 14, including lunch. The tour leaves at 10 a.m. The tours begin at Victoria Coach Station, at the corner of Buckingham Palace Road and Elizabeth Street.

For details of London Transport's half- or full-day tours, phone 227-3456.

BOAT TRIPS

Touring boats operate on the Thames all year, taking you various places within Greater London. Main embarkation points are Westminster Pier, Charing Cross Pier, and Tower Pier—a system that enables you, for instance, to take a "water taxi" from the Tower of London to Westminster Abbey. Not only are the boats energy-saving, bringing you painlessly to your destination, but they permit you to sit back in comfort as you see London from the river.

Pleasure boats operate down the Thames from Westminster Pier to the Tower of London and Greenwich and the Thames Barrier all year, departing every 20 minutes in summer, from 10 a.m. to 4 p.m., and every 30 minutes in winter. It takes 20 minutes to reach the Tower and 40 minutes to arrive at Greenwich. In the summer, services operate upriver to Kew, Richmond, and Hampton Court from Westminster Pier. There are departures every 30 minutes from 10:30 a.m. to 4 p.m. for the 1½-hour journey to Kew and three departures daily for the 2½-hour Richmond trip as well as to Hampton Court, a 3- to 5-hour trip each way.

The multitude of small companies operating boat services from Westminster Pier have organized themselves into the **Westminster Passenger Service Association,** Westminster Pier, Victoria Embankment, S.W.1 (tel. 930-4721). Boats leave the pier for cruises of varying length throughout the day and evening.

A CANAL BOAT IN LITTLE VENICE

When you get tired of fighting the London traffic, you might want to come here and take a peaceful trip (1½ hours) aboard the traditionally painted Narrow Boat *Jason* and her butty boat *Serpens.* Come for lunch along the most colorful part of the Regent's Canal in the heart of London. The boat is moored in Blomfield Road, just off Edgware Road in Maida Vale. Little Venice is the junction of two canals and was given its name by Lord Byron.

To inquire about bookings, including the Boatman's Basket Luncheon Trip, get in touch with **Jason's Trip,** Opp. No. 60 Blomfield Rd., Little Venice, W.9 (tel. 286-3428). Advance booking is essential during high season. If you come by tube, take the Bakerloo Line to Warwick Avenue. Face the church, turn left, and walk up Clifton Villas to the end and turn right (about two minutes). If you arrive early, you can browse around the shop, which sells many brightly colored traditionally painted canal wares.

On the trip you'll pass through the long Maida Hill tunnel under Edgware Road, through Regent's Park, the Mosque, the Zoo, Lord Snowdon's Aviary, past the Pirate's Castle to Camden Lock and return to Little Venice. The season begins Good Friday and lasts through September. During April and May, the boats run daily at 12:30 and 2:30 p.m. In June, July, August, and September, there are additional trips at 10:30 a.m. to 4:30 p.m. daily. Always telephone first. Refreshments are served on all trips: prebooked lunches on the 12:30 and 2:30 p.m. cruises, and a cream tea on the 4:30 p.m. voyage. The fare is £2.95 ($5.15) for adults, £1.75 ($3.05) for children.

ORGANIZED LONDON WALKS

Hunt for ghosts or walk in the steps of Jack the Ripper, the infamous East End murderer of prostitutes in the 1880s. Retrace the history of The City from the Romans to the Blitz. Visit glamorous Chelsea or elegant Mayfair. Investigate the London of Shakespeare, Dickens, and Sherlock Holmes, or taste the delights of an evening's drinking in four historic pubs. These and many other walks are included in the program of unusual and historical walks organized by **London Walks,** 10 Greenbrook Ave., Hadley Wood, Hertfordshire EN4 0LS (tel. 441-8906). Walks take place on Saturday and Sunday throughout the year and also during the week from April to October. The cost is £3 ($5.25); £2.50 ($4.40) for students with ID cards; children under 14 go free. No reservation is required. If you want to write for information from abroad send an International Reply Coupon for their answer.

Another small and enthusiastic company, a husband-and-wife team, offering a vast variety of London walks, is **Discovering London.** It's operated by a Scot, Alex Cobban, a historian of some note whose guides are professionals. Mainly on Saturday and Sunday, but during the week as well, scheduled walks are planned, starting at easily found Underground stations, to Dickens's London, Roman London, Ghosts of the City, the Inns of Court–Lawyers' London, Jack the Ripper. Mr. Cobban's knowledge of Sherlock Holmes is immense. No advance booking is necessary, and the walks cost £3 ($5.25) for adults; children under 16 go free, and students with ID cards are charged £2.75 ($4.80). Each walk takes about 1½ to 2 hours. Write, enclosing an International Reply Coupon, for a detailed schedule of the walks available during your stay in London. The address is Discovering London, 11 Pennyfields, Warley, Brentwood, Essex CM14 5JP (tel. 0277/213-704).

3. Shopping for Value

In London, this "nation of shopkeepers" displays an enormous variety of wares. You can pick up bargains ranging from a still-functioning hurdy-gurdy to a replica of the crown jewels. For the best buys, search out new styles in clothing, as well as traditional and well-tailored men's and women's suits, small antiques and curios, woolens, tweeds, tartans, rare books, Liberty silks, Burberrys, English china, silver, even arms and armor, to name just a few.

Most stores are open from 9 a.m. to 5:30 p.m. Monday to Saturday, with late shopping until 8 p.m. on Thursday. In the East End, around Aldgate and Whitechapel, many shops are open on Sunday from 9 a.m. to 2 p.m. There are a few all-night stores, mostly in the Bayswater section.

Here is a brief survey of some of the more attractive merchandise offered:

ANTIQUE MARKETS—FOR CURIOS

Sheltered in a rambling old building, the **Chelsea Antiques Market,** 245-253 King's Rd., S.W.3 (tel. 352-1720), is a gold mine where you can pan for some hidden little treasure. It offers endless browsing possibilities for the curio addict. In this ever-changing display you're likely to run across Staffordshire dogs, shaving mugs, Edwardian buckles and clasps, ivory-handled razors, old velours and lace gowns, wooden tea caddies, antique pocket watches, wormy Tudoresque chests, silver snuff boxes, grandfather clocks, and jewelry of all periods. It is open Monday through Saturday from 8 a.m. to 6 p.m.; closed Sunday. Tube: Sloane Square.

Grays and **Grays in the Mews Antique Markets,** 58 Davies St. and 1-7 Davies Mews, W.1 (tel. 629-7034), just south of Oxford Street and opposite Bond Street tube station, are in a triangle formed by Davies Street, South Molton Lane, and Davies Mews. The two old buildings have been converted into walk-in stands with independent dealers. The term "antique" here covers items from oil paintings to, say, the 1894 edition of the *Encyclopaedia Britannica.* Also sold here are exquisite antique jewelry, silver, gold, maps and prints, bronzes and ivories, arms and armor, Victorian and Edwardian toys, furniture, art nouveau and art deco items, antique luggage, antique lace, scientific instruments, crafting tools, and Oriental, Persian, and Islamic pottery, porcelain, miniatures, and antiquities. There is also a whole floor of repair workshops, an engraver, and a Bureau de Change.

Alfies Antique Market, 13-25 Church St., N.W.8 (tel. 723-6066), is the biggest and one of the cheapest covered markets in London, and it's where many dealers come to buy. Alfies is named after the father of Bennie Gray, the owner of Grays and Grays in the Mews Antique Markets and former owner of the Antique Hypermarket Kensington and Antiquarius. The market contains more than 370 stalls, showrooms, and workshops on 35,000 square feet of floor, plus an enormous, 70-unit basement area. Tube: Edgware Road.

Antiquarius, 131-141 King's Rd., S.W.3 (tel. 351-5353), echoes the artistic diversity of the street on which it is located. More than 200 standholders offer specialized and general antiques of all periods from ancient times to the 1950s, including statuary and metalwork, early domestic and crafting tools, timepieces, silver and silver plate, precious and costume jewelry, period clothes, lace, theatrical items, porcelain, glass, early writing and travel accessories, tiles, ethnic items, Delft and faïence, antiquarian books and prints, fine paintings, and small furniture. It's open Monday to Saturday from 10 a.m. to 6 p.m. Tube: Sloane Square. Bus 11, 19, or 22 will also take you there.

Chenil Galleries, 181-183 King's Rd., S.W.3 (tel. 351-5353), offers a unique blend of fine art and antiques set in spacious surroundings. A permanent exhibit of an Epstein statue reflects the long association with the arts, which is also recorded on a rotunda mural. Here you can find 17th- and 18th-century paintings, long case clocks, scientific instruments, antiquarian books, prints and maps, fine porcelain, silverware, art nouveau and art deco items, jewelry boxes, chess sets, fine period furniture, and objets d'art. Here also you'll find Oriental carpets, collector's dolls, and teddy bears. The gallery also contains the Chenil Garden Restaurant, which serves food throughout the day, and the Chenil Art Gallery with changing exhibitions of contemporary art. It's open Monday to Saturday from 10 a.m. to 6 p.m. Tube: Sloane Square.

ARTS AND CRAFTS

On a Sunday morning along **Bayswater Road,** for more than a mile, pictures, collages, and craft items are hung on the railings along the edge of Hyde Park and Kensington Gardens. If the weather is right, start at Marble Arch and walk and walk, shopping or just sightseeing as you go along. Along Piccadilly, you'll see much of the same thing by walking along the railings of **Green Park** on a Saturday afternoon.

The **Crafts Council,** 12 Waterloo Pl., S.W.1 (tel. 930-4811), is a public body that exists to promote crafts in England and Wales. It has galleries that offer a broad program of changing crafts exhibitions from British domestic pottery to American traditional patchwork. Most exhibitions are free; concessions are available. Other facilities include a lively information center, which can direct you to craft events throughout Britain, a slide library, and a bookstall. (*Note:* The Crafts Council runs a quality craft shop at the Victoria and Albert Museum, South Kensington.) The galleries and information center are open Tuesday to Saturday from 10 a.m. to 5 p.m. and on Sunday from 2 to 5 p.m. Tube: Piccadilly Circus.

BEAUCHAMP PLACE

This is one of London's top shopping streets. Beauchamp Place (pronounced Beecham) is a block off Brompton Road, near Harrods Department Store. The *International Herald Tribune* called it "a higgledy-piggledy of old-fashioned and trendy, quaint and with-it, expensive and cheap. It is deliciously unspecialized." Whatever you're looking for—from a pâté de marcassin to a carved pine mantelpiece—you are likely to find it here. Reject china, crystal, and pottery, secondhand silver, old alligator bags, collages, custom-tailored men's shirts—whatever. It's pure fun even if you don't buy anything.

BOOKS

Claiming to be the world's largest bookstore, **W. & G. Foyle Ltd.,** 113-119 Charing Cross Rd., W.C.2 (tel. 439-8501), has an impressive array of hardcovers and paperbacks, including travel maps. The shop includes records, videotapes, and sheet music. Tube: Leicester Square.

Hatchards Ltd., 187-188 Piccadilly, W.1 (tel. 439-9921), is an old-fashioned-looking place on the south side of Piccadilly stuffed with books ranging from popular fiction and specialist reference books to paperbacks. There are shelves of guidebooks and atlases, cookbooks, and books of puzzles to occupy you on train and plane trips. Tube: Piccadilly Circus.

BRASS RUBBING

Formerly at St. James's Church in Piccadilly, the **London Brass Rubbing Centre** is now at St. Martin-in-the-Fields Church, Trafalgar Square, W.C.2 (tel. 437-6023), in the big brick-vaulted 1730s crypt. The center has 70 exact copies of celebrated bronze portraits ready for use. Paper, rubbing materials, and instructions on how to begin are furnished. Classical music is played as visitors work at the task. The charges range from 50p (90¢) for a small copy to £12 ($21) for the largest, a life-size Crusader knight. The center is open all year except Christmas Day and Easter Thursday to Easter Sunday. Hours are from 10 a.m. to 6 p.m. Monday to Saturday, noon to 6 p.m. on Sunday. A gift area is open, selling unusual historical goods, brass-rubbing kits for children, budget-priced ready-made rubbings, plaques, model knights, jewelry, souvenirs with a heritage theme, replica brasses, posters, and postcards. In the same attractive crypt area, the center has a brasserie-style restaurant, bookshop, exhibition area, and original craft market. Free lunchtime concerts can be heard in the famous church. Tube: Embankment or Charing Cross.

The same company operates a brass-rubbing center at **All Hallows Church by the Tower,** Byward Street, E.C.3 (tel. 481-2928), where material and instruction are supplied. It is open on the same schedule and prices are the same as given above. Next door to the Tower, this center is a quiet place to relax. The church is a fascinating place with a crypt museum, Roman remains, and traces of early London, including a Saxon wall pre-dating the Tower. Samuel Pepys, famed diarist, climbed to the spire of this church to watch the raging fire of London in 1666. The center has a bookshop and restaurant that is open from noon to 2 p.m. Monday to Friday. Tube: Tower Hill.

BRITISH DESIGN

Exhibitions in **The Design Centre,** 28 Haymarket, S.1.1 (tel. 839-8000), deal with topical design subjects of all kinds. There is an innovation center that provides a showcase for new ideas and prototypes to attract potential manufacturers and a related materials information center offering advice and information. The Design Council Bookshop stocks a wide range of publications related to design, architecture, and crafts. In 1989, the Young Designers' Centre opened, providing the first permanent year-round national exhibition area dedicated to the work of design students and graduates. The Design Centre is open from 10 a.m. to 6 p.m. Monday and Tuesday, from 10 a.m. to 8 p.m. Wednesday to Saturday, and from 1 to 6 p.m. Sunday. Tube: Piccadilly Circus.

BURLINGTON ARCADE

Next door to the Royal Academy of Arts is the Burlington Arcade, W.1 (tel. 427-3568), which is more than 150 years old. It was built in 1819 by Lord George Cavendish. The bawdy Londoners of those days threw rubbish over the garden wall, particularly oyster shells, so he built the arcade as a deterrent, history's most expensive antigarbage campaign. The arcade is now an ancient monument protected by Her Majesty. You can wander at leisure through this holdover from Regency London, checking out each of its 38 shops for some antique or bric-a-brac. It's a concentrated bit of luxury. Who knows what might happen? Mary Ann Evans—alias George Eliot, the novelist—met the journalist, George Lewes, in Jeff's Bookshop and they were lovers until he died in 1866. Eliot, of course, wrote *The Mill on the Floss* and *Silas Marner.* Even the famous novelist, Charles Dickens, commented on the arcade and its double row of shops, "like a Parisian passage," in his 1879 guide to London.

Pomp and ceremony may be departing, but if you linger in the arcade until 5:30

in the afternoon, you can watch the beadles, those ever-present attendants, in their black-and-yellow livery and top hats, ceremoniously put in place the iron grills that block off the arcade until 9 the next morning, when they just as ceremoniously remove them, marking the start of a new business day. Also at 5:30 p.m., a hand bell called the Burlington Bell is sounded, signaling the end of trading. It's rung by one of the beadles, the last of London's top-hatted policemen and Britain's oldest police force. There are only three of these constables remaining. Tube: Piccadilly Circus.

CARNABY STREET

You may be too young to remember Mary Quant, but in the 1960s she launched Carnaby Street with her daring fashions that helped earn London the title of "swinging." Well, Carnaby Street is still here, and it's a vehicle-free pedestrian shopping mall today, displaying shop after shop of fashions for the young. And even Mary Quant (who has dozens and dozens of shops in Japan today) has returned with the **Mary Quant Colour Shop,** 21 Carnaby St., W.1 (tel. 494-3277). Her shop sells cosmetics and accessories, along with some clothing, especially provocative swimwear. Even if you don't buy anything (highly unlikely), Carnaby Street is still good for an afternoon stroll. Treat it like a sightseeing attraction if nothing else. Tube: Oxford Circus.

CHILDREN

The largest specialist children's bookshop in Britain is the **Children's Book Centre Ltd.,** 237 Kensington High St., W.8 (tel. 937-7497). A feature of the shop is that fiction, both hardcover and paperback, is arranged according to age including the young-adult reader in the 14 to 16 age group. The shop is open from 9:30 a.m. to 6 p.m. Monday to Saturday. Tube: High Street Kensington.

Hamleys of Regent Street, 188-196 Regent St., W.1 (tel. 734-3161), is an Ali Baba's cave of children's treasures ranging from electronic games and *Star Wars* robots on the ground floor to different toys on each of the other floors—table and card games, teddy bears, nursery animals, dolls, and outdoor playthings. The Hamleys train races around the walls. Tube: Oxford Circus.

CHINA

A wide range of English bone china, as well as crystal and giftware, is sold at **Lawleys,** 154 Regent St., W.1 (tel. 734-8184). The firm specializes in Royal Doulton, Minton, Royal Crown Derby, Wedgwood, and Aynsley porcelain; Webb Corbett, Stuart, Waterford, Brierley, and Edinburgh crystal; and Lladró figures. They also sell cutlery. Tube: Piccadilly Circus or Oxford Circus.

The legendary merchandise of **Wedgwood** is in plentiful supply in London. Waterford Wedgwood has three large shops, all within a few hundred yards of Piccadilly Circus. There you can see a huge range of Wedgwood tableware, including Jasper, and Waterford crystal, along with giftware in bone china. Wedgwood porcelain figures are always popular, as are cameos in classical motifs (often dating from the 1700s). The shops are Waterford Wedgwood, 266 Regent St., W.1 (tel. 734-5656), Waterford Wedgwood, 158 Regent St., W.1 (tel. 734-7262), and Gered Wedgwood, 173-174 Piccadilly, W.1 (tel. 629-2614). Tube: Piccadilly Circus.

Goodes, 19 S. Audley St., Grosvenor Square, W.1 (tel. 499-2823), a fine glass and china shop with three Royal Warrants, has Minton majolica elephants gracing its front windows. The main entrance, with its famous mechanical doors, gives access to the china, glass, and silverware displayed in 14 showrooms. You can choose a small gift or purchase a unique dinner service with cresting and a monogram. A Goodes catalog is available. Tube: Hyde Park Corner.

CHOCOLATES

What may be the finest chocolates in the world are made by **Charbonnel et Walker Ltd.,** 28 Old Bond St., W.1 (tel. 491-0939). They will send messages of thanks or love, spelled out on the chocolates themselves. The staff of this bow-fronted shop on the corner of the Royal Arcade off Old Bond Street will help you choose from the variety of centers. A box will be priced by weight. They have ready-made presentation boxes as well. Tube: Green Park.

Prestat, 14 Princes Arcade, S.W.1 (tel. 629-4838), is chocolate maker "to Her Majesty the Queen by appointment." Why not impress your friends by taking home a box of assorted Napoleon truffles? Coffee or double mints and brandy cherries may also tempt you. All boxes are gift wrapped with an extra touch of elegance. Tube: Bond Street.

CLOCKS

In the heart of the Camden Passage Antiques Village in Islington, **Strike One Limited,** 51 Camden Passage, N.1 (tel. 226-9709), sells clocks and barometers. Strike One clearly dates and prices each old clock, and every clock is guaranteed worldwide for a year against faulty workmanship. A wide selection of clocks is displayed, ranging from Victorian dial clocks to early English long-case timepieces. Strike One specializes in Act of Parliament clocks. They issue an illustrated catalog, which is mailed internationally to all serious clock collectors. They also undertake to find any clock a customer might request, if they do not have a suitable example in stock. The shop is open daily except Sunday from 9 a.m. to 5 p.m. (at other times by appointment). Tube: Angel.

CONTEMPORARY ART

Originally established as a branch office of Christie's, specializing in modern art, **CCA Galleries,** 8 Dover St., W.1 (tel. 499-6701), in 1987 broke away from its illustrious mother. Today it offers etchings, lithographs, and screenprints by up-and-coming artists. It also offers major works by such world masters as Henry Moore. The gallery is considered innovative and creative even within the competitive world of London galleries. Tube: Green Park.

COVENT GARDEN ENTERPRISES

In the Central Market Building an impressive array of shops, pubs, and other attractions can be found. For the shops listed below, take the tube, of course, to Covent Garden.

Contemporary Applied Arts, 43 Earlham St., W.C.2 (tel. 836-6993), is an association of craftspeople that is pioneering in its energetic encouragement of contemporary artwork, both traditional and progressive. The galleries at the center house a diverse retail display of members' work that includes glass, rugs, lights, ceramics for both use and decoration, fabric, clothing, paper, metalwork, and jewelry —all selected from the work of the most outstanding artisans currently producing in the country. There is also a program of special exhibitions that focus on innovations in the crafts. These are lone or small-group shows from the membership. Many of Britain's best-established makers are represented, as well as promising, lesser-known ones. The center is open Monday to Saturday from 10 a.m. to 5:30 p.m.

The **General Store,** 111 Long Acre, W.C.2 (tel. 240-0331), offers thousands of ideas for gifts and souvenirs with prices of a few pence to several pounds. It is ideally situated in Covent Garden, and because of the entertainment nature of the area, the store offers extended trading hours: from 10 a.m. to 11:30 Monday to Saturday and 11 a.m. to 7 p.m. on Sunday. The store also features the Green & Pleasant soup-and-salad restaurant.

At 21 Neal St., W.C.2 (tel. 836-5254), the **Natural Shoe Store** sells all manner of comfortable and quality footwear from Birkenstock to the best of the British classics.

Neal Street East, 5 Neal St., W.C.2 (tel. 240-0135), is a vast shop devoted to Oriental or Orient-inspired merchandise. Here you can find artificial flowers, pottery, baskets, chinoiserie, and toys, as well as calligraphy, modern and antique clothing, textiles, and jewelry. There is also an extensive cookware section and a bookshop. Open from 10 a.m. to 7 p.m. Monday to Saturday.

The **Tea House,** 15a Neal St., W.C.2 (tel. 240-7539), is a shop devoted to tea and "teaphernalia," anything associated with tea, tea drinking, and tea time, including 45 different teas and more than 250 teapots.

Naturally British, 13 New Row (by Covent Garden), W.C.2 (tel. 240-0551), specializes in items handmade in Britain and displayed on excellent antique furniture of oak, pine, yew, and fruitwood. Naturally British aims to present the best of contemporary craft works from many fields: pottery, jewelry, glass, clothes from Ireland, Wales, and Scotland, cosmetics, rocking horses, games, puzzles, painted firescreens, and iron works, as well as soft toys. There is a wide range of prices. Open Monday to Saturday from 10:30 a.m. to 6:45 p.m., and on Sunday in summer.

The Glasshouse, 65 Long Acre, W.C.2 (tel. 836-9785), sells beautiful glass, and also invites visitors into the workshops to see the craftspeople producing their wares. At street level, passersby can see glassblowers at work.

Penhaligon's, 41 Wellington St., W.C.2 (tel. 836-2150), established in 1870 as a Victorian perfumery, holds Royal Warrants to H.R.H. the Duke of Edinburgh and H.R.H. the Prince of Wales. It offers a large selection of perfumes, aftershave, soap, and bath oils for men and women. Perfect gifts include antique silver perfume bottles.

The **Royal School of Needlework,** 5 King St. W.C.2 (tel. 240-3186), offers in kit form many of the great number of almost classic tapestry designs bequeathed to them by such designers as Burne-Jones and William Morris. The school also has a design studio that will undertake special commissions and a workroom that repairs and restores historic textiles. An appointment is necessary to visit the workroom or design studio. Classes and courses are available either full- or part-time, covering all aspects of embroidery and related textile skills, art and design, the history of textiles and textile techniques, textile conservation and restoration, and youth training in needle skills. The school is open from 10 a.m. to 5:30 p.m. Monday to Friday. Numerous books on the subject of needlework, as well as materials, are for sale through the mail-order service. A full-color catalog is available for £2.25 ($3.95).

Behind the Warehouse off Neal Street runs a narrow road leading to **Neal's Yard,** a mews of warehouses that seem to retain some of the old London atmosphere. The open warehouses display such goods as vegetables, health foods, fresh-baked breads, cakes, sandwiches, and in an immaculate dairy, the largest variety of flavored cream cheeses you are likely to encounter.

DEPARTMENT STORES

The department store to end all department stores is **Harrods,** Brompton Road, at Knightsbridge, S.W.1 (tel. 730-1234). As firmly entrenched in English life as Buckingham Palace and the Ascot Races, it is an elaborate emporium, at times as fascinating as a museum. In a magazine article about Harrods, a salesperson was quoted as saying: "It's more of a sort of way of life than a shop, really." The store is undergoing refurbishing to restore it to the elegance and luxury of the '20s and '30s. Aside from the fashion department (including high-level tailoring and a "Way In" section for young people), you'll find such incongruous sections as a cathedral-ceilinged and arcaded meat market, even a funeral service. Harrods has everything: men's custom-tailored suits, tweed overcoats, cashmere or lambswool sweaters for both men and women, hand-stitched traveling bags, raincoats, mohair jackets, patterned ski sweaters, scarves of hand-woven Irish wool, pewter reproductions, a perfumery department, "lifetime" leather suitcases, pianos. There is a choice of ten restaurants and bars in the store. Tube: Knightsbridge.

Much more economical, however, is **Selfridges,** on Oxford Street W.1 (tel. 629-1234), one of the biggest department stores in Europe, with more than 300 divisions, selling everything from artificial flowers to groceries. The specialty shops are particularly enticing, with good buys in Irish linen, Wedgwood, leather goods, silver-plated goblets, cashmere and woolen scarves. There's also the Miss Selfridge Boutique, for the young or those who'd like to be. To help you travel light, the Export Bureau will air freight your purchases to anywhere in the world, completely tax free. In the basement Services Arcade, the London Tourist Board will help you find your way around London's sights with plenty of maps, tips, and friendly advice. Tube: Bond Street.

Liberty & Company Limited, Regent Street, W.1 (tel. 734-1234), is renowned worldwide for selling high-quality, stylish merchandise in charming surroundings. Its flagship store on Regent Street houses six floors of fashion, fabrics, china, and home furnishings, plus the Oriental department in the basement. As well as the famous Liberty Print fashion fabrics, furnishing fabrics, scarves, ties, luggage, and gifts, the shop sells well-designed high-quality merchandise from all over the world. Liberty offers a personal "corner shop" service with helpful and informed assistants selling its stylish and often unique merchandise. Tube: Oxford Street. The company has outlets in Bath, Cambridge, Canterbury, Chelsea, Edinburgh, Glasgow, Manchester, Norwich, York, and Oxford.

Marks & Spencer has several branches in London, attracting the thrifty British, who get fine buys, especially in woolen goods. The main department store is at 458 Oxford St., W.1 (tel. 935-7954), three short blocks from Marble Arch. Tube: Marble Arch. However, there are a number of branches in London as well as in most towns of any size in Britain. This chain has built a reputation for quality and value, and now clothes some 70% of British workers—wholly or partially. It is said that 25% of the socks worn by men in Britain come from M&S. The prices are competitive even when you go as far as cashmere sweaters for women.

Simpson's, 203 Piccadilly, W.1 (tel. 734-2002), opened in 1936 as the home of DAKS clothing, and it's been going strong ever since. It is known not only for men's wear, but women's fashions, perfume, jewelry, and lingerie. The clothes are of the highest quality and exude elegance and style, from casual weekend wear to a wide selection of evening dress. Tube: Piccadilly Circus.

DESIGNER CLOTHING (SECOND HAND)

A London institution since it was first established in the 1940s, **Pandora,** 16-22 Cheval Pl., S.W.7 (tel. 589-5289), stands in fashionable Knightsbridge, a stone's throw from Harrods. It features dozens of hand-me-down designer dresses, and it is generally acknowledged that this store carries the finest such merchandise in London. Several times a week, chauffeurs will drive up with bundles packed by the anonymous gentry of England. These are likely to include dresses, jackets, suits, and gowns that the ladies wish to sell. Entire generations of London women have clothed themselves at this store. One woman, voted best dressed at Ascot several years ago, was wearing a secondhand dress acquired at Pandora's. Identities of the owners are strictly guarded. But many buyers are titillated at the thought they might be wearing a hand-me-down from a royal person, perhaps Princess Di. Prices are generally one third to one half of their retail value. Chanel, Yves St. Laurent, and Valentino are among the designers represented. Yes, Pandora is also the drag queen's emporium. Tube: Knightsbridge.

GROCERY STORE WITH ELEGANCE

Down the street from the Ritz, **Fortnum and Mason Ltd.,** 181 Piccadilly, W.1 (tel. 734-8040), draws the carriage trade, the well-heeled dowager from Mayfair or Belgravia who comes seeking such tinned treasures as pâté de foie gras or a boar's head. She would never set foot in a regular grocery store, but Fortnum and Mason, with its swallow-tailed attendants, is no mere grocery store—it's a British tradition dating back to 1707. In fact, the establishment likes to think that Mr. Fortnum and Mr. Mason "created a union surpassed in its importance to the human race only by the meeting of Adam and Eve." Today this store exemplifies the elegance and style one would expect from an establishment with two Royal Warrants. Enter the doors and be transported to another world of deep-red carpets, crystal chandeliers, spiraling wooden staircases, and unobtrusive tail-coated assistants.

The grocery department is renowned for its impressive selection of the finest foods from around the world—the best champagne, the most scrumptious Belgian chocolates, and succulent Scottish smoked salmon. You might choose one of their wicker baskets of exclusive foods to have shipped home, perhaps through their telephone and mail order service. You can wander through the other four floors and consider the purchase of bone china and crystal cut glass, perhaps find the perfect present in the leather or stationery departments or reflect on the changing history of furniture, paintings, and ornaments in the antiques department.

At the Patio & Buttery restaurant on the mezzanine, open from 9:30 a.m. to 5 p.m., you can mingle at lunch with the caviar-and-champagne shoppers, choosing from a menu that ranges from soup and sandwiches to chicken pie and steak-and-kidney pie. American-style milkshakes, sundaes, and ice-cream sodas are also available here, as well as at the Fountain Restaurant on the ground level. With entrances from both the store and Jermyn Street, the Fountain stays open from 9:30 a.m. until 11:30 p.m. and is a popular after-theater place for snacks or light meals. The elegant St. James's Restaurant on the fourth floor is open from 9:30 a.m. to 5 p.m., offering a more extensive and more expensive menu than the other two restaurants. Look for the ornate Fortnum and Mason clock outside on the front of the store. Tube: Piccadilly Circus or Green Park.

IRISH WARES

Northern Ireland and the Republic of Ireland are united in the stock of a wide variety of stuff in a small area at the **Irish Shop,** 11 Duke St., W.1 (tel. 935-1366). Prices are reportedly as close to those you'd pay in Ireland as possible. Merchandise ranges from china to woolens, from "tea cosies" to Celtic-designed jewelry, to Irish linen. Waterford crystal comes in all styles and types. Belleek china and Gaelic coffee glasses—single or in a set—are also featured. You can purchase hand-woven tweed by the yard. A 45-inch by 45-inch Irish linen tablecloth, hand-embroidered, will be yours for £42 ($73.50) and up. As the jerseys are all hand-knitted, you have to rummage to find the exact one to suit your particular shape and size. Women's suits and men's jackets in fine Donegal tweeds are offered as well. Duke Street is off Wigmore, a street running alongside Selfridges from Oxford Street. Tube: Bond Street or Marble Arch.

JEWELRY

A family firm, **Sanford Brothers Ltd.,** 3 Holborn Bars, Old Elizabethan Houses, E.C.1 (tel. 405-2352), has been in business since 1923. They sell anything in jewelry, both modern and Victorian, silver of all kinds, and a fine selection of clocks and watches. The old Elizabethan buildings are one of the sights of Old London. Tube: Chancery Lane.

London Diamond Centre, 10 Hanover St., W.1 (tel. 629-5511), offers organized tours of a permanent exhibition showing how diamonds are mined, cut, polished, and made into exclusive jewelry, as well as a visit to the showroom where unmounted diamonds and ready-to-wear diamond jewelry, as well as other gem jewelry from costly to inexpensive can be purchased or ordered to your requirements. Hours are from 9:30 a.m. to 5:30 p.m. Monday to Friday, from 9:30 a.m. to 1:30 p.m. Saturday. Admission is £3.45 ($6.05) per person, the fee including a souvenir brilliant-cut zirconium (not a diamond), which you can have mounted in a 9-karat gold setting of your choice at modest cost.

KING'S ROAD

The formerly village-like main street of Chelsea, although still the cutting edge for fashion trends, has undergone yet another metamorphosis—the trendies of the '70s, who replaced the hippies and mod Mary Quant, of the '60s, have been pushed aside by the punk scene. Numerous stores sporting American clothes have sprung up along its length.

King's Road starts at Sloane Square (with Peter Jones's classy department store) and meanders on for a mile before losing its personality and dissolving into drabness at a sharp bend appropriately known as World's End. Along the way you'll see the tokens of Chelsea's former claims to fame—cozy pubs, smart nightclubs and discos, coffee bars, and cosmopolitan restaurants. More and more, however, King's Road is becoming a lineup of markets and "multistores," large or small conglomerations of in- and outdoor stands, stalls, and booths fulfilling half a dozen different functions within one building or enclosure. They spring up so fast that it's impossible to keep them tabulated.

MAPS AND ENGRAVINGS

An ideal place to find an offbeat souvenir of your visit to London is **The Map House,** 54 Beauchamp Pl., S.W.3 (tel. 589-4325), selling antique maps and engravings. The shop also has a vast selection of old prints of London and England, both in the original and in reproduction. An original engraving, guaranteed genuinely more than 100 years old, can cost from as little as £1 ($1.75) to a massive £10,000 ($17,500). The Map House is open from 9:45 a.m. to 5:45 p.m. Monday to Friday, and from 10:30 a.m. to 5 p.m. on Saturday. Tube: Knightsbridge.

The **Greater London Record Office and History Library** (administered by the Corporation of the City of London), 40 Northampton Rd., E.C.1 (tel. 633-6851), in Clerkenwell, sells reproductions of old maps and prints of London. The office has archives, maps, history books, and photographs. Open Tuesday to Friday. Tube: Farringdon.

MEN'S CLOTHING

Offering both British and international designers, **Austin Reed,** 113 Regent St., W.1 (tel. 734-6789), has long stood for quality men's wear. The suits of Chester Barrie, for example, are said to fit like bespoke models. The polite employees are usually honest about telling you what looks good on you. The store always stocks top-notch but expensive cashmere jackets, along with well-made conventional clothes. Men can outfit themselves from dressing gowns to gloves to overcoats. The Cue Shop is aimed at a young, fashion-conscious man-about-town. An entire floor, the third, is devoted to the clothing needs of women, with carefully selected suits, separates, coats, shoes, shirts, knitwear, and accessories offered. Tube: Piccadilly Circus.

MILITARY MINIATURES

A bewildering array of military miniatures, perfect in every detail, is sold at **Tradition,** 5a Shepherd St., W.1 (tel. 439-7452). You name it, Tradition makes it. It has a vast stock of French cavalry figures, all sorts of British soldiers from the Napoleonic Wars, U.S. Cavalrymen from the War of 1812 and the Civil War, to name but a few. What more fitting souvenir of London than a British Grenadier, a Beefeater, or a Chelsea Pensioner? The range is enormous, and the shop will sell you figures painted or unpainted, marching, running, firing, kneeling, even dying. Tube: Green Park.

NOTIONS

A variety of toilet articles and fragrances is found at **Floris,** 89 Jermyn St., S.W.1 (tel. 930-2885). The floor-to-ceiling mahogany cabinets that line its walls are considered architectural curiosities in their own right. They were installed relatively late in the establishment's history (that is, 1851), long after the shop had received its Royal Warrants as suppliers of toilet articles to the king and queen. The business was established in 1730 by a Minorcan entrepreneur, Juan Floris, who brought from his Mediterranean home a technique for extracting fragrances from local flowers. Fashionable residents of St. James's flocked to his shop, purchasing his soaps, perfumes, and grooming aids. Today you can buy essences of flowers grown in English gardens, including stephanotis, rose geranium, lily of the valley, violet, Madagascar white jasmine, and carnation. Other items include cologne for gentlemen, badger-hair shaving brushes, ivory comb-and-brush sets, Chinese cloisonné dressing table items, and combs made of wood. Open from 9:30 a.m. to 5:30 p.m. Monday to Friday, 9:30 a.m. to 4 p.m. Saturday. Tube: Piccadilly Circus.

PHILATELY

Interested in stamps? The **National Postal Museum,** King Edward Building, King Edward Street, E.C.1 (tel. 239-5420), is open Monday to Thursday from 9:30 a.m. to 4:30 p.m. (to 4 p.m. on Friday), and houses a magnificent collection of postage stamps and allied material. It also sells postcards illustrating the collection and has a distinctive Maltese Cross postmark first used on the Penny Black.

A letter mailed from Heathrow Airport is franked at Hounslow with an attractive Concorde cancellation. In country areas, the post office provides a postbus service between many remote and otherwise isolated villages. Often passenger tickets are cancelled with a special stamp of collector interest, and postcards depicting places of interest along the routes are issued and mailed from these buses. More specialized, many of the narrow-gauge and privately owned railroads in the country issue and cancel their own stamps. Among these are the Ravenglass and Eskdale, the Keighley and Worth Valley Light Railway, and the Bluebell Railway, along with the Romney, Hythe, and Dymchurch Railway. Tube: St. Paul's.

PIPE SMOKERS

A pipe-smoker's paradise, **Astleys,** 109 Jermyn St., S.W.1 (tel. 930-1687), is masculine to the core. Apart from selling superb pipes (some of them special freehand models) and virtually every conceivable blend of their own tobaccos, Astleys features a kind of pipe museum, consisting of antique smoking utensils that tell the history of the ancient and noble art of "tobacco drinking."

POSTERS

For a fine souvenir of your visit to London, try the **London Transport Museum Shop,** Covent Garden, W.C.2 (tel. 379-6344), open daily from 10 a.m. to 5:45 p.m. except Christmas Day and Boxing Day. This unique shop carries a fine selection of a wide range of posters. The London Underground maps can be purchased here, as well as massive pictorial posters as seen at tube stations (size 40 inches by 60 inches). The shop also carries books, cards, T-shirts, and other souvenir items. Tube: Covent Garden.

PRINCES ARCADE

If you like "one-stop" shopping, you may be drawn to the Princes Arcade, which was opened by Edward VII in 1883, when he was Prince of Wales. Between Jermyn Street and Piccadilly, in the heart of London, it has been restored. Wrought-iron lamps light your way as you search through some 20 bow-fronted shops, looking for that special curio (say, a 16th-century nightcap) or a pair of shoes made by people who have been satisfying royal tastes since 1847. A small sign hanging from a metal rod indicates what kind of merchandise a particular store sells. Tube: Piccadilly Circus.

RAINCOATS

Where else but **Burberry,** 18 Haymarket, S.W.1 (tel. 930-3343), near the London offices of American Express? The word Burberry has been synonymous with raincoats ever since King Edward VII publicly ordered his valet to "bring my Burberry" when the skies threatened rain. Its circa-1912 Haymarket store connects three lavishly stocked floors to an oak-lined staircase upon which have trod some of the biggest names in politics, the stage, and screen. An impeccably trained staff sells the famous raincoat, along with a collection of excellent men's shirts, sportswear, knitwear, and accessories. Raincoats are available in women's sizes and styles as well as men's. Don't think you'll get anything cheap from such a world-famous retailer. You get prestige and quality. Tube: Piccadilly Circus.

SAINT CHRISTOPHER'S PLACE

One of London's most interesting and little-known (to the foreign visitor) shopping streets is Saint Christopher's Place, W.1. It lies just off Oxford Street—walk down Oxford from Selfridges toward Oxford Circus, ducking north along Gees Court across Barrett Street. There you will be surrounded by antique markets and good shops for women's clothing and accessories. The nearest tube is Bond Street.

SILVER

Established in Victoria's day (1882), the **London Silver Vaults,** Chancery Lane, W.C.2 (tel. 242-3844), soon became the largest silver vaults in the world. You can actually go shopping in vault after vault for that special treasure. The vaults are open Monday to Friday from 9 a.m. to 5:30 p.m., on Saturday to 12:30 p.m. Tube: Chancery Lane.

A very special place is **Stanley Leslie,** 15 Beauchamp Pl., S.W.3 (tel. 589-2333). Behind a cramped and black-painted, big-windowed storefront lies a staggering array of Georgian, Victorian, and early 20th-century silver. It's just the place to spend hours ferreting around for a special present. The quality is very high—and it's amazing that Mr. Leslie, a lovely London character, knows what he's got there and how much is a fair price. Tube: Knightsbridge.

SOUVENIRS

Closely linked to Charles Dickens, **The Old Curiosity Shop,** 13-14 Portsmouth St., off Lincoln's Inn Fields, W.C.2 (tel. 405-9891), was used by the writer as the abode of Little Nell. One of the old Tudor buildings still remaining in London, dating from 1567, the shop crams every nook and cranny with general knickknackery, whatnots, china, silver, pewter, prints, and souvenirs—even Charles Dickens first editions. A popular item is an unframed silhouette of a Dickens character. Horse brasses are also sold, as are Old Curiosity Shop bookmarks and ashtrays with Dickensian engravings. The shop is open every day of the week, including Sunday and holidays. Tube: Holborn.

SPORTS GOODS

Britain's biggest sports store, **Lillywhites Ltd.,** Piccadilly Circus, S.W.1 (tel. 930-3181), has floor after floor of sports clothing, equipment, and footwear. Established in 1863 and Europe's most renowned sports store, Lillywhites offers everything connected with sport, together with new and exciting ranges of stylish and fashionable leisure-wear for both men and women. Lillywhites Special Orders and International Departments offer a worldwide service. Tube: Piccadilly Circus.

STEAM ENGINE MINIATURES

For steam engine buffs, **Steam Age,** 19 Abingdon Rd., W.8 (tel. 938-1982), offers a rare selection of miniature but accurately scaled models of locomotives and stationary, marine, and traction engines permanently on display. They also stock a large range of steam fittings for model engineers. It's open Monday through Friday from 9:30 a.m. to 5:30 p.m., on Saturday to 1 p.m. Tube: High Street Kensington.

STREET MARKETS

Street markets have played an important part in the life of London. They are recommended not only for bric-a-brac but as a low-cost adventure. In fact, you don't have to buy a thing. But be warned—some of the stallkeepers are mighty convincing. Here are the best ones:

Portobello Road Market: This Saturday market is one of the city's most popular flea markets. Take the Notting Hill Gate tube to Portobello Road, W.11. Here you'll enter a hurly-burly world where stall after stall selling curios may tempt you. Items include everything from the military uniforms worn by the Third Bavarian Lancers to English soul food. Some of the stallholders are antiquarians, with shops in fashionable Kensington, Belgravia, and Chelsea—and they know the price of everything. Feel free to bargain, however. A pastime is dropping in for a pint of ale at one of the Portobello pubs. The best time to visit is on a Saturday, although the market is open Monday to Saturday from 7 a.m. to 6 p.m. (on Thursday to 1 p.m.).

New Caledonian Market: Commonly known as the **Bermondsey Market** because of its location, it's on the corner of Long Lane and Bermondsey Street. At its extreme east end, it begins at Tower Bridge Road. This is one of Europe's outstanding street markets in size and quality of goods offered. The stalls are well known, and many dealers come into London from the country. The market gets under way on Friday at 7 a.m. The most serious bargain hunters are the early birds. Antiques and other items are generally lower in price here than at Portobello Road and the other street markets, but bargains are gone by 9 a.m. The market closes at noon. It's best reached by taking the Underground to London Bridge station, then get bus 78 or walk down Bermondsey Street.

Petticoat Lane: On Sunday between 9 a.m. and 2 p.m. (go before noon), throngs of shoppers join the crowds on Petticoat Lane (also known as Middlesex Street, E.1; tube to Liverpool Street, Aldgate, or Aldgate East). It is surrounded by a maze of lanes that begin at the Liverpool Street station on the Bishopsgate side where you can buy clothing, food, antiques, and plenty of junk.

Camden Passage: This antique bric-a-brac market in Islington, N.1 (in back of the Angel), northeast of Bloomsbury, is open from 9 a.m. to 6 p.m. The best time to visit is on Saturday market day. On all days, the emphasis is on books, prints, drawings, paintings, antiques, and similar hard items. Prices are not inexpensive, but there are bargains to be found if you look carefully through the more than 50 shops and 20 boutiques. Take the Northern-line tube to the Angel stop.

Jubilee Market: At Covent Garden Piazza, W.C.2, this is a small general market operating from 9 a.m. to 5 p.m. Monday to Saturday. Antiques are sold on Monday, crafts on Saturday, and various other items on other days. Tube: Covent Garden.

Leather Lane: A daily market, reached by taking the tube to Chancery Lane, it's open Monday to Saturday from 11 a.m. to 3 p.m. At this lively market, you'll find a good variety of items for sale: fruit from carts, vegetables, books, men's shirts and sweaters, and women's clothing. There are no try-ons at this outdoor market, so make sure of the size clothing you want before buying.

WOOLENS

For top-quality woolen fabric and garments, go to the **Scotch House,** 84 Regent St., S.W.1 (tel. 734-0203), renowned worldwide for its comprehensive selection of cashmere and wool knitwear for both men and women. Also available is a wide range of tartan garments and accessories, as well as Scottish tweed classics. The children's collection covers ages 2 to 13 and also offers excellent value and quality. Tube: Piccadilly Circus. The Scotch House has stores also at 191 Regent St., W.1; 2 Brompton Rd., S.W.1; and 187 Oxford St., W.1.

Westaway & Westaway, opposite the British Museum at 62-65 Great Russell St., W.C.1 (tel. 405-4479), is a substitute for a shopping trip to Scotland. They stock an enormous range of kilts, scarves, waistcoats, capes, dressing gowns, and rugs in authentic clan tartans. What's more, they are knowledgeable on the subject of these minutely intricate clan symbols. They also sell superb—and untartaned—cashmere, camel-hair, and Shetland knitwear, along with Harris tweed jackets, Burberry raincoats, and cashmere overcoats for men. Tube: Tottenham Court Road. Another branch is at 92-93 Great Russell St., W.C.1.

Berk, 46 Burlington Arcade, W.1 (tel. 493-0028), the cashmere specialist, is one of those irresistible "fancy shops" for which London is famous. To shelter your precious cashmere from the elements, Berk also carries Burberry raincoats, golf jackets and caps, and rain hats. And all this is displayed in the 150-year-old Burlington Arcade, an attraction in its own right. Tube: Piccadilly Circus.

4. London After Dark

London is crammed with nighttime entertainment. You'll have a wide choice of action—from the dives of Soho to elegant clubs. So much depends on your taste, pocketbook, and even the time of year. Nowhere else will you find such a panorama of legitimate theaters, operas, concerts, gambling clubs, discos, vaudeville at Victorian music halls, striptease joints, jazz clubs, folkmusic cafés, nightclubs, and ballrooms. For information about any of these events, ask a newsstand dealer for a copy of *Time Out* or *What's On in London* containing listings of restaurants, theaters, and nightclubs.

THEATERS

The fame of the English theater has spread far and wide. In London, you'll have a chance to see it on its home ground. You may want to spend a classical evening with the National Theatre Company (formerly the Old Vic), or you may settle for a new play. You might even want to catch up on that Broadway musical you missed in New York, or be an advance talent scout for next year's big Stateside hit.

You can either purchase your ticket from the theater's box office (the most recommended method), or else from a ticket agent, such as the one at the reservations desk of American Express (with agent's fee charges, however). Many theaters will accept bookings by telephone if you give your name and credit-card number when you call. Then all you have to do is go along before the performance to collect your tickets, which will be sold at the theater price. All theater booking agencies charge a fee. Once confirmed, the booking will be charged to your account even if you don't use the tickets. Only cardholders can collect the tickets charged to their accounts. Remember, if you are calling ahead from out of town, the area code for London is 01. In a few theaters, you can reserve your spot in the gallery, the cheapest seats of all, but in some cases the inexpensive seats are sold only on the day of performance. This means that you'll have to buy your ticket earlier in the day, and—as you don't get a reserved seat—return about an hour before the performance and queue up for the best gallery seats.

If you want to see two shows in one day, you'll find that Wednesday, Thursday, and Saturday are always crammed with matinee performances. Many West End theaters begin their evening performances at 7:30.

Discounted tickets are sometimes offered, but only to long-running plays on their last legs or to new "dogs," which you may not want to see anyway. A really hot musical in its early life will almost never offer discounted tickets. Discounted tickets are more likely to be available for matinees.

For full details on West End productions, pick up a free biweekly *London Theatre Guide* at the Booth or at any West End theater, tourist or travel information center, hotel, or library on your arrival in London.

Of London's many theaters, these are particularly outstanding:

The **National Theatre,** South Bank, S.E.1 (tel. 633-0880; for tickets, 928-2252), is in a concrete cubist fortress—a three-theater complex that stands as a $32-million landmark beside the Waterloo Bridge on the south bank of the Thames. It was first suggested in 1848, and it took Parliament 101 years to pass a bill vowing government support. Flaring out like a fan, the most thrilling theater in this complex is the **Olivier,** named after Lord Laurence Olivier, its first director when the company was born in 1962. The Olivier Theatre bears a resemblance in miniature to an ancient Greek theater: it's an open-stage, 1,160-seat house. The **Cottesloe** is a simple box theater for 400 people. Finally, the 890-seat **Lyttelton** is a traditional proscenium-arch house that doesn't have one bad seat. In the foyers there are three bookshops, eight bars, a restaurant, and five self-service buffets (some open all day except Sunday), and many outside terraces with river views. For everyone, with or without tickets for a play, there is live foyer music, free, before evening performances and Saturday matinees, and free exhibitions. The foyers are open from 10 a.m. to 11 p.m. daily except Sunday. Also, guided theater tours are available daily, including backstage areas, for £2.50 ($4.40).

Tickets range from £6.50 ($11.40) to £14 ($24.50), and midweek matinees are £5 ($8.75). Some tickets are available on the day of the performance, at £6.50 ($11.40) and £9 ($15.75). You can have a meal in the National Theatre Restaurant for around £13.50 ($23.65), or at one of the coffee bars a snack will cost around £4.50 ($7.90). Tube: Waterloo Station.

You may also be interested in the activities of the **National Film Theatre,** S.E.1 (tel. 928-3232), in the same South Bank complex. More than 2,000 films a year from all over the world are shown here, including features, shorts, animation, and documentaries. A visitor can obtain daily membership at 40p (70¢). If booked in advance, tickets cost £3.25 ($5.70), or standby tickets can be obtained half an hour before a performance at £3 ($5.25). Tube: Waterloo Station.

MOMI, the Museum of the Moving Image, underneath Waterloo Bridge, S.E.1 (tel. 401-2636), is also part of the South Bank complex. Tracing the history of the development of cinema and television, MOMI takes the visitor on an incredible journey from cinema's earliest experiments to modern animation, from Charlie Chaplin to the operation of a TV studio. There are artifacts to handle, buttons to push, and a cast of actors to tell visitors more. Admission is £3.25 ($5.70) for adults and £2.50 ($4.40) for children. There is also a £10 ($17.50) family ticket. The museum is open from 10 a.m. to 8 p.m. Tuesday to Saturday, from 10 a.m. to 6 p.m. Sunday and bank holidays. Closed Monday. Allow two hours for a visit. Tube: Waterloo Station.

The Old Vic, a 170-year-old theater on Waterloo Road, S.E.1 (tel. 928-2651, or the box office at 928-7616), underwent a mammoth facelift and modernization. The façade and much of the interior were restored in their original early 19th-century style, and most of the modernization was behind the scenes. The proscenium arch was moved back, and the stage trebled in size, and more seats and stage boxes added. It is air-conditioned and contains five bars. There are short seasons of varied plays, and several subscription offers have been introduced with reductions of up to 55% of regular prices. Otherwise, top prices vary, with the best stalls or dress circle seats going for about £15 ($26.25) a ticket. Tube: Waterloo Station.

The **Royal Shakespeare Company** has its famous theater in Stratford-upon-Avon and is also housed in the Barbican Centre, E.C.2 (tube to Barbican or Moorgate; tel. 638-8891 in London or 0789/295623 in Stratford-upon-Avon). This is the single theater group in Britain that most seriously concentrates on the theatrical works of the Bard, although it presents works by such relatively modern playwrights as Jean Genet. Plays run in repertoire and are presented two or three times a week each. The company also has three smaller theaters where new and experimental plays are performed as well as classics: The Other Place and the new Swan Theatre are in Stratford-upon-Avon and The Pit is at the Barbican Centre. Travel to Stratford from London's Euston Station is possible via the Shakespeare Connection, plus a theater/hotel/restaurant package available through the Shakespeare Stopover (tel. 0789/414999).

Royal Court Theatre, Sloane Square, S.W. 1 (tel. 730-1745; tube to Sloane Square). The English Stage Company has operated this theater for more than 30 years. The emphasis is on new playwrights (John Osborne got his start here with the 1956 production of *Look Back in Anger*). Also on the premises is the Theatre Upstairs, a studio theater also devoted to the work of new playwrights. Prices of tickets are £5 ($8.75), £7 ($12.25), £9 ($15.75), and £12 ($21). At the Theatre Upstairs, the tickets go for £3 ($5.25) to £6 ($10.50). Shows are at 8 p.m. daily, 4 and 8 p.m. on Saturday downstairs; 7:30 p.m. daily and 3:30 and 7:30 p.m. on Saturday for the Theatre Upstairs. Closed Monday.

The Young Vic, 66 The Cut, Waterloo, S.E.1 (tel. 928-6363), aims primarily at the 15 to 25 age group, but many older and younger people use the theater as well. The Young Vic's repertoire includes such authors as Shakespeare, Ben Jonson, Arthur Miller, and Harold Pinter, plus specially written new plays. Performances normally begin at 7:30 p.m. Seats cost £7.50 ($13.15), reduced to £3.75 ($6.55) for students and children. Tube: Waterloo Station.

Sadler's Wells Theatre, Rosebery Avenue, E.C.1 (tel. 278-8916 for the box office), is on a site where a theater has stood since 1683, a short walk from Camden Passage. The resident companies are the Sadler's Wells Royal Ballet and the New Sadler's Wells Opera, which produces light opera, operetta, and fresh productions of that most English of theatrical institutions, the work of Gilbert and Sullivan. They are complemented by a program of British and foreign dance, opera, and ballet. Seats are offered at prices ranging from £4 ($7) to £20 ($35), the average cost being £16 ($28). Performances generally begin at 7:30 p.m. Reach the theater by the Angel tube, or bus 19 or 38 from Piccadilly, Charing Cross, or Holborn. A theater buffet (hot and cold) is open from 6:30 p.m. on performance days, from 1:30 p.m. on matinee days.

OPERA AND BALLET

You may be getting a little tired of superlatives, but in this particular chapter they're unavoidable. For in the operatic and ballet field, as well as in legitimate theater, the British currently lead the world. In a way this is rather strange, because historically neither singing nor dancing has been a particularly English talent. But over the past few decades (and with a strong influx of foreigners), both have developed in an almost breathtaking fashion.

The central shrine is the **Royal Opera House,** a classical building on Bow Street, W.C.2, actually the northeast corner of Covent Garden, which was London's first square, laid out by Inigo Jones as a residential piazza. Until a few years ago the whole area was a thriving fruit and vegetable market, originally started by nuns selling surplus stocks from their convent garden. In the 16th century the section became fashionable to live in and was soon to become one of the centers of London nightlife. The first theater was built on the present site in 1732. The existing opera house, one of the most beautiful theaters in Europe, was built in 1858 and is now the home of the Royal Opera and Royal Ballet, the leading international opera and ballet companies. Newspapers give full details of performances.

The Opera House advance box office, at 48 Floral St., W.C.2 (tel. 240-1066), is open from 10 a.m. to 8 p.m. Monday to Saturday. Seat prices range from £1 ($1.75) to £37 ($64.75) for ballet, from £2.50 ($4.40) to £75 ($131.25) for opera. Tube: Covent Garden.

English National Opera, London Coliseum, St. Martin's Lane, W.C.2 (tel. 836-3161 for reservations or 240-5258 for inquiries and credit-card booking). The London Coliseum, built in 1904 as a variety theater and converted into an opera house in 1968, is London's largest and most splendid theater. The English National Opera is one of the two national opera companies. It performs a wide range of works, from great classics to operetta to world premieres, and every performance is in English. A repertory of 18 to 20 productions is presented five or six nights a week for 11 months of the year. Balcony tickets are available for as little as £2.50 ($4.40), but many visitors prefer the Upper Circle or Dress Circle at about £12.50 ($21.90) to £14 ($24.50). During the opera season, usually from August to June, about 100 cheap seats in the balcony are held for sale on the day of performance, from 10 a.m. Tube: Charing Cross or Leicester Square.

The **Barbican Centre,** The Barbican, E.C.2, is considered the largest art and exhibition center in Western Europe. It was created to make a perfect setting in which to enjoy good music and theater from comfortable, roomy seating. The theater is now the London home of the Royal Shakespeare Company (see description above). The Concert Hall is the permanent home of the London Symphony Orchestra and host to visiting orchestras and performers. As well as the art gallery, there are free foyer exhibitions and performances including jazz at lunchtime Sunday. For quieter moments, the center has a rare and beautiful conservatory open to the public Saturday, Sunday, and some other days. Hall seat prices range from £4 ($7) to £18.50 ($32.40). Theater matinee prices go from £5 ($8.75) to £13 ($22.75), and evening prices are from £6 ($10.50) to £15 ($26.25).

There are several bars, a self-service café with a lakeside terrace, and a restaurant (see my restaurant recommendations in Chapter IV). The following numbers will be useful: 638-8891 for the box office, 628-9760 or 628-2295 for 24-hour recorded information about the performances, and 638-4141, ext. 218 for general help from the information desk. Tube: Moorgate or Barbican. (Barbican tube is closed Sunday and public holidays.)

CONCERTS

In recent years, the musical focal point in London has shifted to a superbly specialized complex of buildings on the South Bank side of Waterloo Bridge, called the **South Bank Centre,** at South Bank, S.E.1. It includes the Hayward Gallery and houses three of the most stylish, comfortable, and acoustically perfect concert structures in the world: the **Royal Festival Hall,** the **Queen Elizabeth Hall,** and the **Purcell Room.** Here, more than 1,200 performances a year are presented, and it's not all classical music: included are ballet, jazz, popular classics, pop, and folk. The Royal Festival Hall is open from 10 a.m. every day and offers an extensive range of things to see and do. There are free exhibitions in the foyers and free lunchtime music from 12:30 to 2 p.m., plus guided tours of the building, and book, record, and gift shops. The Festival Buffet has a wide selection of food at reasonable prices, and there are a number of bars throughout the foyers. The office that prebooks with credit cards is open daily from 10 a.m. to 9 p.m. (tel. 928-8800). Tickets range from £4 ($7) to £20 ($35). Tube: Waterloo Station.

Royal Albert Hall, Kensington Gore, S.W.7 (tel. 589-8218), opened in 1871, dedicated to the memory of Queen Victoria's consort, Prince Albert. The building encircles one of the world's largest and finest auditoriums with a seating capacity of 5,500. Home since 1941 to the BBC Promenade Concerts, the famous eight-week annual festival of classical music, it is also a popular venue for light music by stars such as Frank Sinatra and Johnny Mathis plus the latest in rock and pop. Sport and pageantry figure strongly. Boxing events are held here as well as covered court lawn tennis, with the Masters Doubles Championship being played here a month after the annual Royal British Legion Festival of Remembrance. A daily guided tour costs £2.50 ($4.40). Tube: South Kensington, High Street Kensington, or Knightsbridge.

Wigmore Hall, 36 Wigmore St., W.1 (tel. 935-2141). At this intimate auditorium, you'll hear excellent recitals and concerts. There are regular series, master concerts by chamber music groups and instrumentalists, song recital series, and concerts featuring special composers or themes throughout the year. There are nightly performances, plus Sunday Morning Coffee Concerts and also concerts on Sunday at 4 and 7 p.m. Many good seats are in the £4 ($7) range. A free list of the month's program is available from the hall. Tube: Bond Street or Oxford Circus.

GILBERT AND SULLIVAN EVENINGS

The English Heritage Singers present Gilbert and Sullivan programs at the **Mansion House at Grim's Dyke,** Old Redding, Harrow Weald, Middlesex HA3 6SH (tel. 954-4227), every other Sunday in winter and every Sunday the rest of the year. This is a dinner event, costing £25 ($43.75) per person. You arrive for cocktails in the Library Bar of the house where Gilbert once lived and where he and Sullivan worked on their charming operettas—when they were at peace with each other. A full Edwardian-style dinner is served at 8 p.m., with costumed performances of the most beloved of Gilbert and Sullivan songs both during and after the meal. You can request favorite melodies from the Gilbert and Sullivan works. The singers know them all.

OPEN-AIR THEATER

As the name indicates, **Regent's Park,** N.W.1 (tel. 486-2431), is an outdoor theater, right in the center of Regent's Park. The setting is idyllic, and the longest theater bar in London provides both drink and food. Performances are given in June, July, August, and the first half of September, evenings at 7:45, matinees on Wednesday, Thursday, and Saturday at 2:30 p.m. Presentations are mainly Shakespeare, usually in period costume. Both seating and acoustics are excellent. If it rains, you're given tickets for another performance. Prices are £4.50 ($7.90) to £11 ($19.25). Tube: Baker Street.

MUSIC HALLS

The atmosphere of a Victorian music hall is recaptured at **The Cockney Club,** 18 Charing Cross Rd., W.C.2 (tel. 408-1001). At the whisky and gin reception, you'll have the cockles of your heart warmed and learn about "mother's ruin" (large gins). The lively waiters and waitresses join guests to sing along to the sounds of a honky-tonk piano. An East End meal, four courses of Cockney nosh, is served, along with unlimited beer and wine during dinner. Music for singing and dancing marks the evening. The show is divided into two parts, featuring cabaret with both production numbers and solo performances. The hall is open daily from 8 p.m., with dancing until midnight. The charge is £25 ($43.75) per person Sunday to Friday, £27 ($47.25) per person Saturday. Phone for reservations. Tube: Leicester Square.

The **Rheingold Club** thrives in a century-old wine cellar at Sedley Place, just off 361 Oxford St., W.1 (tel. 629-5343), and has a restaurant, two bars, and a good-size dance floor. The main attraction is a top-class band playing daily except Sunday and bank holidays, from 9:30 p.m. to about 2 a.m. There is also an occasional cabaret, usually with big-time guest stars, but most of the entertainment is created by the patrons themselves. The Rheingold, founded in 1959, is the oldest and most successful "singles club" in London, existing long before the term had been coined. It is a safe place for men to take their wives or girlfriends, and single women are welcome and safe here. The club serves Viennese, German, and English food with a selection of German and French wines. The price of a three-course meal is about £8 ($14) per person, and membership for overseas visitors is available at the door at a charge of £5 ($8.75) for men and £4 ($7) for women. The club is open from 8 p.m. to 1:30 a.m. Monday and Tuesday, to 2 a.m. on Wednesday, Thursday, and cabaret nights, and to 2:30 a.m. on Friday and Saturday. Take the tube to Bond Street station, use the main exit to Oxford Street, turn right and turn right again to Sedley Place. It's only 40 yards from the station.

The **Water Rats,** 328 Grays Inn Road, W.C.1 (tel. 837-7269), perpetuates the world of Victorian music hall entertainment, and it's contained within a London pub famous since 1655. It is the headquarters of the Grand Order of Water Rats, a charitable organization of Britain's top variety performers. The cost of dinner and a music hall type show is £17.50 ($30.63). If you want to go only for the show, the price is £8.50 ($14.90). It is open Monday to Saturday, with dinner served at 7:30 p.m., the show presented at 9 p.m. On Sunday, dinner is at 7 p.m., with the show beginning at 8:30 p.m. Tube: Kings Cross.

A CABARET RIVER CRUISE

The **Romance of London,** a cabaret river cruise, complete with commentary, takes you all the way through the heart of London to the Thames Barrier. A superior three-course meal is served with wine shortly after boarding, while musicians stroll among the tables. A barbershop quartet, cabaret, and dancing are also featured. The Romance of London cruises are available on Sunday from May to September and also on Tuesday from June to September. They depart from Westminster Pier at 7 p.m., returning at 10:30 p.m. The price is £28.75 ($50.30) per person. For information and reservations, call 620-0474.

NIGHTCLUBS

There are several kinds of nightclubs where you can eat or drink, be entertained, dance—even gamble. Most often these clubs are private—but don't turn away yet. The private club came into existence to avoid the unpopular early closing hour of 11 p.m. for licensed public establishments, and may stay open till 3 or 4 a.m. In most cases the clubs welcome overseas visitors showing passports, granting them a temporary membership. The cost of a temporary membership may even be deducted from the price of dinner; however, there is no hard-and-fast rule. Many clubs offer dinner, a show, and dancing. No visitor to London should be afraid to ask about membership in a private club. After all, most of the clubs are in business to make money and welcome foreign patronage.

Comedy Store, 28a Leicester Square, W.C.2 (tel. 839-6665), is London's most visible showcase of rising and emerging comedic talent. Set in the heart of the city's nighttime district, it announces by means of a prerecorded telephone message the various comedians and musicians who are scheduled to appear during the upcoming week. Even if the names of the performers are unfamiliar to you (highly likely), you will still enjoy the spontaneity of live comedy performed before a live British audience. Shows (subject to change) are currently performed Thursday at 9 p.m., Friday and Saturday at 8 p.m. and midnight, and Sunday at 8:30 p.m. No reservations are accepted in advance, and tickets are sold only on the same day of the performance. The club opens one hour prior to each show. There are two bars. Entrance ranges from £5 ($8.75) to £6 ($10.50). Tube: Leicester Square.

Tiddy Dols Eating House, 55 Shepherd Market, W.1 (tel. 499-2357), in the heart of Mayfair, is named for an eccentric gingerbread maker. Guests come to this old-timey eating house to enjoy such dishes as jugged hare, Aylesbury pie, game soup, and plum pudding and the original gingerbread of Tiddy Dol. While dining, they are entertained by madrigals, music hall fare, Noël Coward, Gilbert and Sullivan, whatever. Strolling players perform on reproduced instruments used during the Renaissance. Dinner, costing around £25 ($43.75), is served nightly from 6 p.m. to midnight. Dancing goes on until 2 a.m. Tube: Green Park.

Eve, 189 Regent St., W.1 (tel. 734-0557), is London's longest established late-night club. Doyen of London's nightlife, owner Jimmy O'Brien launched it in 1953. International variety cabaret entertainment (at 1 a.m.) has replaced the floor shows previously presented. Dancing is to disco, alternating with live music of a high standard. Eve is open Monday to Friday from 10 p.m. to 3:30 a.m. Admittance is by membership only. There is an annual subscription of £8 ($14), but a special temporary membership for overseas visitors, valid for one night only, is granted for £2 ($3.50). Only one person in a party need be a member, and overseas visitors may be admitted on application without waiting the customary 48 hours. There is an entrance fee or cover charge of £8 ($14) for a member and each guest. An à la carte menu is offered throughout the night. All prices include VAT. Female escorts, many of whom speak more than one language, are available as dining or dancing partners for unaccompanied men. Tube: Oxford Circus.

Royal Roof Restaurant, Royal Garden Hotel, Kensington High Street, W.8 (tel. 937-8000), on the top floor of the hotel, is elegant and refined, and overlooks Kensington Gardens and Hyde Park. From your table you will see the lights of Kensington and Knightsbridge, with a view of London's West End skyline. In a romantic candlelit aura, you can enjoy a three-course dinner costing around £26 ($45.50). The restaurant is open from 7 p.m. to 1 a.m. Monday to Saturday (last orders taken at 11:30 p.m.). A live band plays for dancing. Reservations are necessary. Tube: High Street Kensington.

L'Hirondelle, Swallow Street, W.1 (tel. 734-6666), is a small but popular nightspot just off Regent Street. The spectacular hour-long stage shows are performed in what appears to be an all-gold environment, complete with gold-colored wallpaper, accessories, and sparkling chandeliers to reflect the entire scene. The company of glamorous showgirls go skillfully through their routines in colorful—and often scanty—costumes with overwhelming headdresses. Singers and dancers add their talents to the hour of variety and music. Two bands assure you of constant music for dancing throughout the rest of the evening. You'll pay a minimum charge of £10.50 ($18.40) if you don't dine here, but L'Hirondelle offers a set dinner for £22.50 ($39.40), which allows you to choose from a number of items in each course. The club is open from 8:30 p.m. to 3:30 a.m., and dancing is from 9 p.m. The floor shows are at 11 p.m. and 1 a.m. It's closed Sunday. Tube: Piccadilly Circus.

Stork Club, 99 Regent St., W.1 (tel. 734-3686), is a first-class night club offering cabaret acts and a line-up of girls who don't believe in overdressing. Two cabaret shows are staged nightly, one at 11 p.m., another at 1 a.m. Foreign visitors don't have to go through the tedium of obtaining membership. You can order a table d'hôte menu for £25 ($43.75), plus a 15% service charge. The club is open nightly from 8:30 p.m. to 3:30 a.m. (however, the last food orders go in shortly before 3 a.m.). If you don't want to order dinner, you can see the show from the cocktail bar. Near the corner of Swallow Street, in the heart of Mayfair, this club is reached by taking the underground to Piccadilly Circus.

Bouzouki

The **Elysée,** 13 Percy St., W.1 (tel. 636-4804), is for *Never on Sunday* devotees who like the reverberations of bouzouki and the smashing of plates. The domain of the Karegeorgis brothers—Michael, Ulysses, and the incomparable George—it offers hearty fun at moderate tabs. You can dance nightly except Sunday (until 3 a.m.), to the music by Greeks. At two different intervals (last one at 1 a.m.) a cabaret is provided, highlighted by brother George's altogether amusing act of balancing wine glasses (I'd hate to pay his breakage bill). You can book a table on either the ground floor or the second floor, but the Roof Garden is a magnet in summer. The food is good too, including the house specialty, the classic moussaka, and the kebabs from the charcoal grill. Expect to pay about £25 ($43.75) each for a complete meal, including a bottle of wine. Dinner is served from 7 p.m. to 2:45 a.m. There's a £3 ($5.25) cover charge. Tube: Goodge Street or Tottenham Court Road.

A Theater Restaurant

A unique theater restaurant in a unique setting, that's **The Talk of London** (tel. 408-1001), in the New London Theatre, an entertainment complex at Parker Street, off Drury Lane, W.C.2, the heart and soul of the city's theaterland. The restaurant is ingeniously designed so that every guest gets "the best seat in the house." By using a circular layout and varying floor levels, everyone has an uninterrupted view of the show. The Talk of London offers a complete evening's entertainment from 8 p.m. to 1 a.m.: a four-course dinner of your choice, dancing to the Johnny Howard orchestra, Europe's top show band, Afrodisiac, and an international cabaret at 10:30 p.m. All this and coffee, service, and VAT are included in the price of £23 ($40.25) Monday to Friday and on Sunday, £25 ($43.75) on Saturday. Drinks are extra. Phone for reservations, which are essential. Tube: Covent Garden or Holborn.

LONDON SPECTACLES

Take a trip back in time to where **Shakespeare's Feast,** 6 Hanover St., W.1 (tel. 408-1001), pays tribute to the Bard. Here, many of the most famous characters from Shakespeare's plays are re-created for a riotous night of fun, aided in no small part by jugglers, jesters, and magicians. There are even duellists. The costumed staff serves traditional honeyed wines, followed by a five-course banquet with unlimited wines and ale during the meal. The wine serving begins at 8 p.m. daily, and there is dancing until midnight. The cost is £25 ($43.75) per person Sunday to Friday, rising to £27 ($47.25) on Saturday night. At the same address is the **Caledonian,** where guests enjoy an evening of Scottish hospitality. A "Tilt o' the Kilt" takes you to the land of the Highland fling. Kilts are supplied free to "men of courage," and whisky is served at 8 p.m. nightly, followed by dancing until midnight. In between there is the traditional ceremony of the haggis, as well as a five-course meal with unlimited wines. The cost is £25 ($43.75) per person Sunday to Friday, rising to £27 ($47.25) per person on Saturday night. Tube: Oxford Circus.

Beefeater Club by the Tower of London, St. Katharine's Yacht Marina, E.1 (tel. 408-1001), offers traditional feasting and continuous entertainment at the Court of Henry VIII in the historic vaults of Ivory House, surrounded on three sides by the Thames. British pageantry is re-created here, complete with jesters, knights, wenches, and royal entertainers. Traditional honeyed wine is served at 8 nightly, with dancing until 11:30 p.m. During a five-course medieval feast, guests are given unlimited wines and ale. The cost is £25 ($43.75) per person Sunday to Friday, rising to £27 ($47.25) per person on Saturday. Tube: Tower Hill.

Eroticism in Soho

Once upon a time, Britain's film censors were kept busy snipping the bare patches out of those "daring" French movies, and London's stage regulations permitted braless belles only on condition that they didn't move a limb while thus exposed. All this might just as well have happened in the last century for all the relevance it has today. Sheer acreage of undress currently on view in London outshows anything in Paris, New York, San Francisco, or Hamburg. Only Tokyo might be on a par. The big, plush establishments have regular and highly paid casts, and among the most spectacular is—

Raymond Revuebar, Walker's Court, Brewer Street, W.1 (tel. 734-1593). Proprietor Paul Raymond is considered the doyen of strip society, and his young, beautiful, hand-picked women are among the best in Europe. The stage show, "Festival of Erotica," is presented Monday to Saturday at 8 and 10 p.m. There are licensed bars, and patrons may take their drinks into the theater. The price of admission is £15 ($26.25), and there is no membership fee. Whisky is around £1.50 ($2.65) per large measure. Tube: Piccadilly Circus.

THE DISCOS

Disco life still holds forth. Many clubs open, enjoy a quick but fast-fading popularity, then close. Some possible favorites that may still be going strong upon your arrival are the following:

Stringfellows, 16-19 Upper St. Martins Lane, W.C.2 (tel. 240-5534), is one of London's most elegant nighttime rendezvous spots, the creation of its owner and manager, Peter Stringfellow of the Hippodrome fame (see below). It is said to have £1 million worth of velvet and hi-tech gloss and glitter. In theory it's a members-only club, but, and only at the discretion of management, nonmembers may be admitted. It offers two lively bars, a first-class restaurant, and a theater. It's been called "an exquisite oasis of elegance," and its nightclub food "the best in London"—for a nightclub, that is. Dancing starts at 11 p.m., dinner at 8 p.m., and the fun continues until 3:30 a.m. daily except Sunday. Prices start at £8 ($14) for entrance Monday to Thursday and £15 ($26.25) on Friday and Saturday; closed Sunday. Tube: Leicester Square or Covent Garden.

The Hippodrome, at the Hippodrome corner of Charing Cross Road and Leicester Square, W.C.2 (tel. 437-4311). Here Peter Stringfellow has created one of London's greatest discos, an enormous place where light and sound beam in on you from all directions. Revolving speakers even descend from the roof to deafen you in patches, and you can watch yourself on closed-circuit video. There are six bars, together with a balcony restaurant, where well-prepared food is served. Lasers and a hydraulically controlled stage for visiting international performers are only part of the attraction of this place. Monday is "gay night" at the Hippodrome. Depending on the night of the week, admission prices at the door range from £6 ($10.50) to £12 ($21) per person. The Hippodrome is open Monday to Saturday from 9 p.m. to 3:30 a.m. Tube: Leicester Square or Covent Garden.

Limelight, 136 Shaftesbury Ave., W.1 (tel. 434-1761), was originally built in the 1880s by the Welsh Presbyterian Church. It was deconsecrated and subsequently sold in the early 1980s, reopening as a disco in 1986. You can dance beneath the soaring dome of the interior, or sip iced vodka or champagne in the circular gallery high above the spectacle. You can also sample a French-inspired cuisine in what used to be the crypt. The average age of the clients in this unusual place is between 25 and 30 years old. Entrance fees range from £5 ($8.75) to £10 ($17.50), depending on the night of the week. A pint of lager costs £1.50 ($2.65). The music covers a broad range of electronically impulsed styles. Tube: Leicester Square.

Camden Palace, la Camden High St., N.1 (tel. 387-0428), is housed inside what was originally a theater. It draws an over-18 crowd who flock in various costumes and energy levels according to the night of the week. It is open nightly except Sunday from 9 p.m. to 2:30 a.m., offering a rotating style of music. It's best to phone in advance to see if that evening's musical genre appeals to your taste. Styles range from rhythm and blues to what young rock experts call "boilerhouse," "garage music," "acid funk," "hip-hop," and "twist & shout." There's also a restaurant if you get the munchies. Tube: Camden Town or Mornington Crescent.

Barbarella 2, 43 Thurloe St., S.W.7 (tel. 584-2000), combines a first-class Italian restaurant with a carefully controlled disco. So that diners can converse in normal tones, the flashing lights and electronic music of the disco are separated from the dining area by thick sheets of glass. Full meals, costing from £20 ($35), include an array of Neapolitan-inspired dishes. Only clients of the restaurant are allowed into the disco, which prevents hordes of late-night revelers from cramming into the place when the regular pubs close. It is open every night but Sunday from 7:30 p.m. to 3 a.m., with the last food orders going in at 12:45 p.m. Tube: South Kensington.

Samantha's, 3 New Burlington St., W.1 (tel. 734-6249), lies just off Regent Street and has been one of London's most popular discos for nearly 30 years. Actually, it's two separate discos on the same premises. At street level you can drink in the cocktail lounge or else order complete meals in Rocky's Restaurant, which is open from 6 p.m. to 6:30 a.m. The club itself is open from 9 p.m. to 3:30 a.m. except Sunday. Admission ranges from £4 ($7) to £7 ($12.25) per person. Tube: Oxford Circus.

FOR DANCING TO LIVE MUSIC

A legendary setting is the **Café de Paris,** 3 Coventry St., off Piccadilly Circus, W.1 (tel. 437-2036). Once Robert Graves considered it a worthy subject for a book, and the Duke of Windsor went here to see Noël Coward perform. But those days are long gone. The place is almost unique in London in that it draws an older patronage who like to dance the way they did in the 50s to live bands and records. Admission ranges from £2 ($3.50) to £7 ($12.25), depending on what time you choose to enter. A half pint of lager costs £1.20 ($2.10) once you're inside. Hours are Monday and Thursday from 7:30 p.m. to 1 a.m., Friday and Saturday from 7:30 a.m. to 3 a.m., and Sunday from 7:30 p.m. to midnight. It is closed Tuesday and Wednesday evenings. Afternoon tea dances draw a nostalgic crowd on Wednesday, Thursday, Saturday, and Sunday from 3 to 5:45 p.m. Tube: Piccadilly Circus or Leicester Square.

Empire, Leicester Square, W.C.1 (tel. 437-1446), was originally built in the 1880s, and it's been revamped and rebuilt so many times since then, going in and out of style, that today it is considered a virtual cultural monument. The bandstand is a leaping, revolving, and ever-changing spectrum of light. In the heart of London's entertainment district, the Empire features top caliber live bands along with music by DJs. It is closed on Sunday but open Monday to Saturday at 8 p.m., closing at either 2 a.m. or 3 a.m., depending on the night of the week. Live music begins at 10:30 p.m. nightly except Monday. Admission ranges from £5 ($8.75) to £8 ($14). There are six bars to quench your thirst between dances. Tube: Leicester Square.

ROCK

In the Covent Garden area, the place where new bands are launched is the **Rock Garden,** 6-7 The Piazza, W.C.2 (tel. 240-3961), which offers live music every night of the week and at lunchtime Saturday and Sunday. Dire Straits, The Police, U2, Talking Heads, and T'Pau, to name a few, played here before they found fame. From noon to 3 p.m., three bands play on Saturday and top jazz musicians gather for jam sessions on Sunday. The music venue is open from 7:30 p.m. to 3 a.m. every day. In the Rock Garden Restaurant, open from noon to midnight Sunday to Thursday and noon to 1 a.m. Friday and Saturday, they serve a wide range of dishes, from swordfish to steak. A two-course meal costs around £10 ($17.50). In summer, you can dine al fresco in the heart of Covent Garden. Both the restaurant and music venue have licensed bars. Tube: Covent Garden. At night, buses run from neighboring Trafalgar Square.

The Marquee, 105 Charing Cross Rd., W.C.2 (tel. 437-6601). Despite a move to a new address in 1988, this is still considered one of the best-known centers for rock music in Europe. Its reputation goes back to the 1950s. Since that time, many groups, such as the Rolling Stones, have gotten their starts at The Marquee. Admission ranges from £2 ($3.50) to £6 ($10.50) depending on who is playing at the time of your visit. Within a former movie theater, the club welcomes visitors on two different floors, the lower of which slopes toward the stage to permit everyone a view of the performers. It is open nightly at 7, with a relatively early closing of 11 p.m. Tube: Leicester Square.

JAZZ

Mention the word "jazz" in London and people immediately think of **Ronnie Scott's,** 47 Frith St., W.1 (tel. 439-0747), long the citadel of modern jazz in Europe where the best English and American groups are booked. Featured on almost every bill is an American band, often with a top-notch singer. It's in the heart of Soho, a ten-minute walk from Piccadilly Circus via Shaftesbury Avenue, and worth an entire evening. You can not only saturate yourself in the best of jazz, but get reasonably priced drinks and dinners as well. There are three separate areas: the Main Room, the Upstairs Room, and the Downstairs Bar. You don't have to be a member, although you can join if you wish. The nightly entrance fee is about £10 ($17.50), depending on who is appearing. If you have a student ID you are granted considerable reductions on entrance fees. The Main Room is open Monday through Saturday from 8:30 p.m. to 3 a.m. You can either stand at the bar to watch the show or sit at a table, where you can order dinner. The Downstairs Bar is more intimate, a quiet rendezvous where you can meet and talk with the regulars, usually some of the world's most talented musicians. The Upstairs Room is separate. It has a disco called The

Tango and is open from 8:30 p.m. to 2 a.m. Monday to Thursday, from 8:30 p.m. to 3 a.m. Friday and Saturday. On most nights a live band is featured. Tube: Tottenham Court Road or Leicester Square.

The **100 Club,** 100 Oxford St., W.1 (tel. 636-0933), is a serious contender for the title of London's finest jazz center. The emphasis here is strictly on the music, which begins each evening at 7:30 p.m. and lasts until midnight. Admission is usually between £2.50 ($4.40) to £5 ($8.75), depending on which artist is appearing. The club's musical policy consists of jazz (traditional to contemporary), blues, rhythm and blues, jump-jive, whatever. Most of Britain's top performers play here as well as many visiting musicians from Europe. The club's restaurant features a comprehensive menu. There's also a fully licensed bar, serving liquor, wine, and beer. Tube: Tottenham Court Road or Oxford Circus.

The **Bull's Head,** 373 Lonsdale Rd., Barnes Bridge, S.W.13 (tel. 876-5241), has presented live modern jazz concerts every night of the week for more than 30 years. One of the oldest hostelries in the area, it was a staging post in the mid-19th century where travelers on their way to Hampton Court and beyond could eat, drink, and rest while the coach horses were changed. The place is known today for its jazz, performed by musicians from all over the world. It's said by many to be the best in town. Jazz concerts are presented on Sunday from noon to 2:30 p.m. and 8:30 to 10:30 p.m. From Monday to Saturday, you can hear the music from 8:30 to 11 p.m. You can order good food at the Carvery in the Saloon Bar daily and dine in the 17th-century Stable Restaurant. The restaurant, in the original, restored stables, specializes in steaks, fish, and other traditional fare. It is open daily from 7 p.m. and on Sunday from noon. Meals cost £4 ($7) and up. To get there, take the tube to Hammersmith, then bus 9 the rest of the way.

VAUDEVILLE
Virtually extinct in America, the variety stage not only lives but flourishes in London. Streamlined and updated, it has dropped most of the corn and preserved all the excitement of the old vaudeville fare.

Top house in the field (not merely in London but in the world) is the **London Palladium,** Argyle Street, W.1 (tel. 437-7373), although it presents more than just vaudeville. It's hard to encapsulate the prestige of this establishment in a paragraph. Performers from Britain, Europe, and America consider that they have "arrived" when they've appeared here. Highlight of the season is the "Royal Command Performance" held before the queen, which includes an introduction of the artists to Her Majesty. It's amazing to watch hard-boiled showbiz champions moved close to tears after receiving the royal handshake.

Over the years, the Palladium has starred such aces as Frank Sinatra, Shirley MacLaine, Andy Williams, Perry Como, Julie Andrews, Tom Jones, Sammy Davis, Jr., and so on, like the Milky Way of stardom. Second-line program attractions are likely to include, say, "Los Paraguayos" and the Ukrainian Cossack Ensemble. Ticket prices are usually in the £8 ($14) to £17 ($29.75) range, and show times vary. Tube: Oxford Circus.

A FAMOUS BAR
For those who like bars instead of pubs, **Jules,** 85 Jermyn St., S.W.1 (tel. 930-4700), is the best-known watering hole in St. James's. It was constructed originally as the Waterloo Hotel in 1830. After Jules Ribstein bought it in 1903, he turned it into a ground-floor restaurant, and in time it became a rendezvous for the "bucks and blades." Today it serves many purposes. It will even serve you lunch, from 11 a.m. to 3 p.m. But it's known mainly for its cocktails, some 50 in all, ranging from those made with champagne to Hawaiian dream. "Godfather" is scotch and amaretto; "Godmother," vodka and amaretto. Cocktails cost from £2.90 ($5.10). At the restaurant in back, you can order such treats as smoked salmon pâté, or salm-

on and sole "as you like it," perhaps one of a variety of steaks, with meals costing from £18 ($31.50). Evening hours are 5:30 to 11 Monday to Saturday. Tube: Piccadilly Circus.

GAY NIGHTLIFE

The most reliable source of information on all gay clubs and activities is the **Gay Switchboard** (tel. 837-7324). The staff there runs a 24-hour service of information on places and activities catering openly to homosexual men and women.

For both men and women who aren't interested in bars or discos, the **London Lesbian & Gay Centre**, 67 Cowcross St., E.C.1 (tel. 608-1471), is the best bet. It's open on Tuesday from 5:30 to 11 p.m., Wednesday, Thursday, and Sunday from noon to 11 p.m., Friday from noon to midnight, and Saturday from noon to 2 a.m. Closed Monday. Entrance is 30p (55¢). Annual membership is £15 ($26.25), but you don't have to be a member to use the facilities. A women-only disco is held Saturday night and a mixed disco (called a tea dance) Sunday night. Different courses, meetings, and activities take place in meeting rooms, and the café and bar area is open all the time. Tube: Farringdon.

Here are some other suggestions; most are membership clubs that, nevertheless, welcome overseas visitors.

Roy's, 206 Fulham Rd., S.W.10 (tel. 352-6828), is the leading gay restaurant of London. People come here not only for the good food, but the entertaining and relaxing ambience. The set menu of freshly prepared ingredients is only £11.50 ($20.15) at this basement restaurant. Dinner is Monday to Saturday from 7:30 to 11:30 p.m. and Sunday from 1:30 to 3 p.m. and 8 to 11:30 p.m. Tube: Earl's Court or South Kensington.

One club that welcomes overseas visitors, **The Heaven,** The Arches, Villiers Street, Charing Cross, W.C.2 (tel. 839-3852), is still considered the largest and most high energy disco in Europe. It is a world of fantastic lasers, lights, and sounds. Unlike many other discos, which make Monday night gay night, Heaven makes every Monday straight night. Tuesday through Saturday is gay, although straight couples are welcomed and admitted as well. It is closed on Sunday. The entrance fee ranges from £2 ($3.50) to £5 ($8.75). Tube: Charing Cross Road.

Madame Jo Jo's, 8 Brewer St., W.1 (tel. 734-2473), is set side by side with some of Soho's more explicit girlie shows. Madame Jo Jo also presents "girls," but they are likely to be in drag. This is London's most popular transvestite show, with revues staged nightly at 12:15 a.m. and 1:15 a.m. The club itself, with its popular piano bar, is open Monday to Saturday from 10 p.m. to 3 a.m. Entrance ranges from £6 ($10.50) to £8 ($14) per person, depending on the night of the week, and drinks cost around £3.50 ($6.15) each. Tube: Piccadilly Circus.

GAMBLING

London was a gambling metropolis long before anyone had ever heard of Monte Carlo and when Las Vegas was an anonymous sandpile in the desert. From the Regency period until halfway into the 19th century, Britain was more or less governed by gamblers. Lord Sandwich invented the snack named after him so he wouldn't have to leave the card table for a meal. Prime Minister Fox was so addicted that he frequently went to a cabinet meeting straight from the green baize table.

Queen Victoria's reign changed all that, as usual, by jumping to the other extreme. For more than a century games of chance were so rigorously outlawed that no barmaid dared to keep a dice cup on the counter. The pendulum swung again in 1960 when the present queen gave her Royal Assent to the new "Betting and Gaming Act." According to this legislation, gambling was again permitted in "bona fide clubs" by members and their guests.

Since London's definition of a "club" is as loose as a rusty screw in a cardboard wall, this immediately gave rise to the current situation, which continues to startle,

nd bewilder foreign visitors. For the fact is that you come across gambling
n the most unlikely spots, such as discos, social clubs, and cabaret restau-
...ts. All of which may, by the haziest definition, qualify as "clubs." The more legitimate gambling clubs offer pleasant trimmings in the shape of bars and restaurants,
but their central theme is unequivocally the flirtation with Lady Luck. There are at
least 25 of them in the West End alone, with many scattered through the suburbs.
And the contrasts between them are much sharper than you find in the Nevada casinos.

Owing to a new law, casinos are not allowed to advertise, and if they do, they
are likely to lose their licenses. Their appearance in a travel guide is still considered
"advertising"—hence, I cannot recommend specific clubs. However, most hall
porters can tell you where you can gamble in London. It's not illegal to gamble, just
to advertise it. You'll be required to become a member of your chosen club, and
must wait 24 hours before you can play the tables, then strictly for cash. The most
common games are roulette, blackjack, punto banco, and baccarat.

---

5. One-Day Trips from London

It would be sad to leave England without ever having ventured into the countryside, at least for a day. The English are the greatest excursion travelers in the
world, forever dipping into their own rural areas to discover ancient abbeys, 17th-
century village lanes, shady woods for picnic lunches, and stately mansions. From
London, it's possible to take advantage of countless tours—either by conducted
coach, boat, or via a do-it-yourself method on bus or train. On many trips, you can
combine two or more methods of transportation; for example, you can go to Windsor by boat and return by coach or train.

Highly recommended are the previously described Green Line Coaches, operated by London Country Bus Services Ltd. (see Chapter I, Section 3, "Traveling
Within Britain" section).

For longer tours, say, to Stratford-upon-Avon, you will find the trains much
more convenient. Often you can take advantage of the many bargain tickets outlined
in Chapter I. For further information about trains to a specific location, go to the
British Rail offices on Lower Regent Street.

The **London Regional Transport** system has conducted tours of places of interest in and around London. For example, a day tour (operating in summer) visits
Windsor and Hampton Court Palace Monday to Saturday, departing Wilton Road
Coach Station at 9:15 a.m. The return to Victoria Station is at 5:15 p.m. Adults pay
£25 ($43.75) and children are charged £20 ($35). Operating all year, an afternoon
tour visits Windsor and goes on a river cruise to Runnymede. Departures are from
Wilton Road Coach Station on Tuesday, Wednesday, Friday, Saturday, and Sunday
at 1 p.m., with a return to Victoria Station at 6:15 p.m. The price is £14 ($24.50) for
adults and £12 ($21) for children. For details on the transport system's information
and ticket centers, see "Transportation in Greater London" in section 1 of Chapter
III.

HAMPTON COURT

On the north side of the Thames, 13 miles west of London in East Molesey,
Surrey (tel. 930-0921), this 16th-century palace of Cardinal Wolsey can teach us a
lesson. Don't try to outdo your boss—particularly if he happens to be Henry VIII.
The rich cardinal did just that. But the king had a lean and hungry eye. Wolsey, who
eventually lost his fortune, power, and prestige, ended up giving his lavish palace to
the Tudor monarch. In a stroke of one-upmanship, Henry took over, even outdoing
the Wolsey embellishments. The Tudor additions included the Anne Boleyn gate-

way, with its 16th-century astronomical clock that even tells the high-water mark at London Bridge. From Clock Court, you can see one of Henry's major contributions, the aptly named Great Hall, with its hammer-beam ceiling. Also added by Henry were the tiltyard, a tennis court, and kitchen.

To judge from the movie *A Man for All Seasons,* Hampton Court had quite a retinue to feed. Cooking was done in the Great Kitchens. Henry cavorted through the various apartments with his wives of the moment—everybody from Anne Boleyn to Catherine Parr (the latter reversed things and lived to bury her erstwhile spouse). Charles I was imprisoned here at one time, and temporarily managed to escape his jailers.

Although the palace enjoyed prestige and pomp in Elizabethan days, it owes much of its present look to William and Mary of Orange—or rather to Sir Christopher Wren, who designed and had built the Northern or Lion Gates, intended to be the main entrance to the new parts of the palace. The fine wrought-iron screen at the south end of the south gardens was made by Jean Tijou around 1694 for William and Mary. You can parade through the apartments today, filled as they are with porcelain, furniture, paintings, and tapestries. The King's Dressing Room is graced with some of the best art. In Queen Mary's closet, you'll find Pieter Brueghel the Elder's macabre *Massacre of the Innocents.* Tintoretto and Titian deck the halls of the King's Drawing Room. Finally, be sure to inspect the Royal Chapel (Wolsey wouldn't recognize it). To confound yourself totally, you may want to get lost in the serpentine shrubbery Maze in the garden, also the work of Sir Christopher Wren.

The gardens, including the Great Vine, King's Privy Garden, Great Fountain Gardens, Tudor and Elizabethan Knot Gardens, Broad Walk, Tiltyard, and Wilderness, are open daily year round from 7 a.m. until dusk (but not later than 9 p.m.), and can be visited free. Cloisters, courtyards, and State Apartments are open from 9:30 a.m. to 5 p.m. weekdays, from 2 to 7 p.m. on Sunday, January 2 to March 31 and October 1 to December 31, closing at 6 p.m. from April 1 to September 30. The Great Kitchen and cellars, Tudor tennis court, king's private apartments, Hampton Court exhibition, and Mantegna paintings gallery are open the same hours as above, but only from April to September. The Maze is open daily from 10 a.m. to 5 p.m. March to October 31. The year-round price for an all-inclusive ticket (except the Maze) costs £3.40 ($5.95) for adults and £1.70 ($3) for children. Tickets for the Maze cost an additional £1 ($1.75) for adults and 50p (90¢) for children. It is easiest to reach Hampton Court by frequent train service from Waterloo Station in London. You can also go by bus, but many prefer in summer to take a boat in either direction. From Easter until late September, Westminster Passenger Services, Westminster Pier, Victoria Embankment, London, S.W.1 (tel. 930-4721) operates as many as four boats a day in either direction. The cost is £7 ($12.25) for adults round trip or £5.50 ($9.65) one way. *Be warned:* rides to Hampton Court from Central London are always slower (2 to 4½ hours depending on the tides) than downstream rides back to the city. Always ask about river conditions before booking a ticket, and plan your schedule accordingly.

Where to Dine

After visiting the palace, lunch at **Bastians,** Hampton Court Road, in East Molesey, Surrey (tel. 977-6074), an attractive old building with a large stone-floored hall, roaring log fire, and comfortable chairs. Here you order an apéritif and select your meal. Then you go into the simple dining room or, in summer, into the tiny garden to eat al fresco.

The French menu includes such appetizers as an enormous platter of moules marinières in season, or trout mousse. Main dishes include filet steak and lamb cutlets in a light mustard sauce. These courses are served with a variety of sauces and well-cooked vegetables, depending on the season and availability. A carafe of house wine is always available. Expect to spend from £18 ($31.50) to £25 ($43.75), plus wine. Prices include VAT but not the 12½% service charge. The restaurant is open

Monday to Friday from 12:30 to 3 p.m. for lunch, Monday to Saturday from 7:30 to 11:30 p.m. for dinner.

KEW

Nine miles southwest of central London at Kew, near Richmond, are the **Royal Botanic Gardens,** better known as Kew Gardens (tel. 940-1171), among the best known in Europe, containing thousands of varieties of plants. But Kew is no mere pleasure garden—rather, it is essentially a vast scientific research center that happens to be beautiful. A pagoda, erected in 1761–1762, represents the "flowering" of chinoiserie. One of the oddities of Kew is a Douglas-fir flagstaff, more than 220 feet high. The classical Orangery, near the main gate on Kew Green, houses an exhibit telling the story of Kew, as well as a bookshop where guides to the garden are available.

The gardens cover a 300-acre site encompassing lakes, greenhouses, walks, garden pavilions, and museums, together with fine examples of the architecture of Sir William Chambers. At whatever season you visit Kew, there's always something to see: in spring, the daffodils and bluebells, through to the coldest months when the Heath Garden is at its best. Among the 50,000 plant species are notable collections of arum lilies, ferns, orchids, aquatic plants, cacti, mountain plants, palms, and tropical water lilies. The gardens are open daily except Christmas and New Year's Day from 9:30 a.m. to no later than 4 to 6:30 p.m. (8 p.m. on Sunday and public holidays), depending on the season. The entrance fee has gone above the traditional "one penny" in effect for a couple of centuries and is now £1 ($1.75).

Much interest focuses on the red-brick **Kew Palace** (dubbed the Dutch House), a former residence of King George III and Queen Charlotte. It is reached by walking to the northern tip of the Broad Walk. Now a museum, it was built in 1631 and contains memorabilia of the reign of George III, along with a royal collection of furniture and paintings. It is open only April to September from 11 a.m. to 5:30 p.m. daily. Admission is 80p ($1.40) for adults, 40p (70¢) for children.

At the gardens, **Queen Charlotte's Cottage** has been restored to its original splendor. Built in 1772, it is half-timbered and thatched. George III is believed to have been the architect. The house has been restored in great detail, including the original Hogarth prints that hung on the downstairs walls. The cottage is open April to September on weekends and bank holidays. The least expensive and most convenient way to visit the gardens is to take the District Line subway to Kew. The most romantic way to come in summer is via a steamer from Westminster Bridge to Kew Pier. Admission is 40p (70¢) for adults, 20p (35¢) for children.

Kew Bridge Steam Museum, Green Dragon Lane, Brentford, Middlesex (tel. 568-4757), houses what is probably the world's largest collection of steam-powered beam engines. These were used in the Victorian era and up to the 1940s to pump London's water, and one engine has a capacity of 700 gallons per stroke. There are six restored engines that are steamed on weekends, plus other unrestored engines, a steam railway, and a working forge. The museum has a tea room, plus free parking for cars. It's open and in steam on Saturday, Sunday, and Monday when it falls on a holiday, from 11 a.m. to 5 p.m. From Monday to Friday, you can see it as a static exhibition during the same time period. Admission on steam days is £1.80 ($3.15) for adults, 90p ($1.60) for children, with a family price of £5 ($8.75). On other days, adults are charged £1 ($1.75) and children 50p (90¢), with the family rate being £2.75 ($4.80). The museum is north of Kew Bridge, under the tower, a ten-minute walk from Kew Gardens. You can reach it by a Southern Region British Rail train from Waterloo Station to Kew Bridge Station; by buses 27, 65, 237, or 267 (7 on Sunday); or by Gunnersbury or South Ealing tube and thence by bus.

GREENWICH

Greenwich Mean Time, of course, is the basis of standard time throughout most of the world, the zero point used in the reckoning of terrestrial longitudes since 1884. But Greenwich is also home of the Royal Naval College, the National Maritime Museum, and the Old Royal Observatory. In drydock at Greenwich Pier is the clipper ship *Cutty Sark,* as well as Sir Francis Chichester's *Gipsy Moth IV.*

About four miles from The City, Greenwich is reached by a number of methods, and part of the fun of making the jaunt is getting there. Ideally, you'll arrive by boat, as Henry VIII preferred to do on one of his hunting expeditions. In summer, launches leave at regular intervals from either the pier at Charing Cross, Tower Bridge, or Westminster. The boats leave daily for Greenwich about every half hour from 10 a.m. to 7 p.m. (times are approximate, depending on the tides). Bus 1 runs from Trafalgar Square to Greenwich; bus 188 goes from Euston through Waterloo to Greenwich. From Charing Cross station, the British Rail train takes 15 minutes to reach Greenwich, and there is now the new Docklands Light Railway, running from Tower Gateway to Island Gardens on the Isle of Dogs. A short walk under the Thames through a foot tunnel brings you out in Greenwich opposite the *Cutty Sark.*

Unquestionably, the *Cutty Sark*—last of the great clippers—holds the most interest, having been seen by millions. At the spot where the vessel is now berthed stood the Ship Inn of the 19th century (Victorians came here for whitebait dinners, as they did to the Trafalgar Tavern). Ordered built by Capt. Jock Willis ("Old White Hat"), the clipper was launched in 1869 to sail the China tea trade route. It was named after the Witch Nannie in Robert Burns's *Tam o' Shanter* (note the figurehead). Yielding to the more efficient steamers, the *Cutty Sark* later was converted to a wool-carrying clipper, plying the route between Australia and England. Before her retirement she knew many owners, even different names, eventually coming to drydock at Cutty Sark Gardens, Greenwich Pier, S.E.10 (tel. 858-3445), in 1954. For £1.30 ($2.30) for adults, 70p ($1.25) for children, the vessel may be boarded Monday to Saturday from 10 a.m. to 6 p.m., on Sunday from noon to 6 p.m. It closes at 5 p.m. in winter.

Next to the clipper—and looking like a sardine beside a shark—lies the equally famous *Gipsy Moth IV* (also tel. 858-3445). This was the ridiculously tiny sailing craft in which Sir Francis Chichester circumnavigated the globe—solo! You can go on board and marvel at the minuteness of the vessel in which the gray-haired old seadog made his incredible 119-day journey. His chief worry—or so he claimed—was running out of ale before he reached land. The admission to go aboard is 20p (35¢) for adults, 10p (20¢) for children under 16. The *Gipsy* keeps the same hours as the *Cutty Sark* in summer, closed in winter.

The **Royal Naval College** (tel. 858-2154) grew up on the site of the Tudor palace in Greenwich in which Henry VIII and Elizabeth I were born. William and Mary commissioned Wren to design the present buildings in 1695 to house naval pensioners, and these became the Royal Naval College in 1873. The buildings are baroque masterpieces, in which the Painted Hall (by Thornhill from 1708 to 1727) and the chapel are outstanding. It is normally open to visitors between 2:30 and 5 p.m. (latest time of entrance, 4:30 p.m.) daily, except Thursday and certain public holidays. These days are published in daily papers. Admission is free.

The **National Maritime Museum** (tel. 858-4422, ext. 221), built around Inigo Jones's 17th-century Palladian Queen's House, portrays Britain's maritime heritage. Actual craft, marine paintings, ship models, and scientific instruments are displayed, including the full-dress uniform coat that Lord Nelson wore at the Battle of Trafalgar. Other curiosities include the chronometer (or sea watch) used by Captain Cook when he made his Pacific explorations in the 1770s. The museum is open from 10 a.m. to 6 p.m. Monday to Saturday, from 2 to 6 p.m. on Sunday in summer, closing at 5 p.m. in winter. It is closed January 1, Good Friday, May bank holiday, and the Christmas holidays. A combined ticket to the main buildings and the Old Royal Observatory (see below) costs £3 ($5.25) for adults, £1.50 ($2.65) for children aged 7 to 16. A £7.50 ($13.15) family ticket admits two adults and up to five children. There is a licensed restaurant in the west wing.

The **Old Royal Observatory** (tel. 858-4422, ext. 221) is worth exploring. Sir

Christopher Wren was the architect—after all, he was interested in astronomy even before he became famous. The observatory overlooks Greenwich and the Maritime Museum from a park laid out to the design of Le Nôtre, the French landscaper. Here you can stand at 0° longitude, as the Greenwich Meridian, or prime meridian, marks the first of the globe's vertical divisions. See also the big red time-ball used in olden days by ships sailing down the river from London to set their timepieces by. There is a fascinating bewilderment of astronomical and navigational instruments, and time and travel become more realistic after a visit here. Hours and prices are the same as for the National Maritime Museum, of which the observatory is a part.

On Saturday and Sunday in Greenwich, there are arts, crafts, and antique markets. Ask at the **Tourist Information Centre,** by the pier and *Cutty Sark* (tel. 858-6376), open daily except Thursday from 2:30 to 5 p.m.

Eating in Greenwich

Trafalgar Tavern, Park Row, S.E.10 (tel. 858-2437), overlooks the Thames at Greenwich and is surrounded by many attractions. Directly opposite the tavern is the Royal Naval College. Ringed with nautical paintings and engravings, lots of heavy dark wood, and brass artifacts, the restaurant invites you to enjoy traditional English specialties that go well with the 18th-century naval memorabilia. Try the steak-and-kidney pie, one of the succulent steaks, or duck in orange sauce. You can also order daily specials, including fish pie. It is open from noon to 2 p.m. and 7:30 to 10:30 p.m. No dinner is served on Monday, but Monday lunch is available in summer. Meals cost from £15 ($26.25) each.

RUNNYMEDE

Two miles outside Windsor is the meadow on the south side of the Thames, in Surrey, where King John put his seal on the Great Charter. John may have signed the document up the river on a little island, but that's being technical. Today, Runnymede is also the site of the John F. Kennedy Memorial, one acre of English ground given to the United States by the people of Britain. The memorial, a large block of white stone, is hard to see from the road. The pagoda you can see from the road was placed there by the American Bar Association to acknowledge the fact that American law stems from the English system.

In accommodations, the **Runnymede Hotel,** Windsor Road, Egham, Surrey TW20 0AG (tel. 0784/36171), stands in ten acres of landscaped grounds on the Thames, bordering the Mede. The setting, near the spot where King John signed the Magna Carta, is just 17 miles from the heart of London (Waterloo Station can be reached by fast train in about half an hour). The water-view garden hotel, built in 1973, with a new wing (filled with executive doubles) opened in 1985, has a clean-cut freshness and big-windowed lounges. The 126 bedrooms each have private baths or showers. Charges are £78 ($136.50) daily in a single, £98 ($171.50) in doubles, with breakfast and VAT included. English and continental cuisines are served in the River Room, which is built on two levels, giving every table a view of the garden and river. A set dinner costs from £14 ($24.50). Two bars, the Anglers and the Magna Carta, are very attractive.

SYON PARK

Just nine miles from Piccadilly Circus, on 55 acres of the Duke of Northumberland's Thames-side estate, is one of the most beautiful spots in all of Great Britain. There's always something in bloom. Called "The Showplace of the Nation in a Great English Garden," Syon Park was opened to the public in 1968. A nation of green-thumbed gardeners is dazzled here, and the park is also educational, showing amateurs how to get the most out of their small gardens. The vast flower- and plant-studded acreage betrays the influence of "Capability" Brown, who laid out the grounds in the 18th century. Particular highlights include a six-acre rose garden, a butterfly house, and the Great Conservatory, one of the earliest and most famous buildings of its type, built 1822–1829. There is a quarter-mile-long ornamental lake studded with waterlilies and silhouetted by cypresses and willows, even a gardening supermarket, and the Motor Museum, with the Heritage Collection of British cars. With some 90 vehicles, from the earliest 1895 Wolseley to the present day, it has the largest collection of British cars anywhere. Syon is also the site of the first botanical garden in England, created by the father of English botany, Dr. William Turner in 1548. Trees include a 200-year-old Chinese juniper, an Afghan ash, Indian bean trees, and liquidambars.

On the grounds is **Syon House,** built in 1431, the original structure incorporated into the Duke of Northumberland's present home. The house was later remade to the specifications of the first Duke of Northumberland in 1762–1769. The battlemented façade is that of the original Tudor mansion, but the interior is from the 18th century, the design of Robert Adam. Basil Taylor said of the interior feeling: "You're almost in the middle of a jewel box." In the Middle Ages, Syon was a monastery, later suppressed by Henry VIII. Katherine Howard, the king's fifth wife, was imprisoned in the house before her scheduled beheading in 1542.

The house is open from Easter to the end of September from noon to 5 p.m. daily except Friday and Saturday. The gardens are open all year except for Christmas and Boxing Day. The gates open at 10 a.m. and close at dusk or 6 p.m. After October, the winter closing hour is 4 p.m. Admission to the gardens is £1.50 ($2.65) for adults and £1 ($1.75) for children. Admission to Syon House is £1.75 ($3.05) for adults, £1.25 ($2.20) for children. A combined ticket for house and gardens is £3 ($5.25) for adults, £2 ($3.50) for children. A separate ticket is required for entrance to the Motor Museum, costing £2 ($3.50) for adults, £1.25 ($2.20) for children. For more information, phone 560-0882.

THORPE PARK

One of Europe's leading family leisure parks, Thorpe Park, Staines Road, Chertsey, Surrey (tel. 0932/562633), lies only 21 miles from Central London on the A320 between Staines and Chertsey, with easy access from junctions 11 and 13 on the M25. The entrance fee of £7 ($12.25) for adults and £6.50 ($11.40) for children under 14 includes all rides, shows, attractions, and exhibits. Additional charges are made only for water sports, rollerskate rental, and coin-operated amusements. Just a few of the favorite rides and shows are Treasure Island, Magic Mill, Phantom Fantasia, Thunder River, Space Station Zero, the Family Teacup ride, Cinema 180, Palladium Theatre, and Loggers Leap. Free transport is provided around the 500 acres by railway and waterbus. Guests can picnic on the grounds or patronize one of the restaurants or fast food areas, such as La Fontana, the French Café, Bavarian Festhalle, or the popular Mississippi Riverboat. The park is open from 10 a.m. to 6 p.m. daily from March 23 to October 29, except from July 22 to August 10 when it remains open until 8 p.m. To avoid the busiest times, Monday to Saturday are recommended for visits from April to July and in September. The nearest mainline station is Staines from Waterloo, and many bus services operate directly to Thorpe Park.

WINDSOR, OXFORD, AND THE HOME COUNTIES

Within easy reach of London, the Thames Valley and the Chiltern Hills are history-rich parts of England, and they lie so close to the capital they can be easily reached by automobile or Green Line coach. You can explore here during the day and return in time to see a show in the West End.

Here are some of the most-visited historic sites in England: the former homes of Disraeli and Elizabeth I, the estate of the Duke of Bedford, and of course, Windsor Castle, 22 miles from London, one of the most famous castles in Europe and the most popular day trip for those visitors venturing out of London for the first time.

Of course, your principal reason for coming to Oxfordshire is to explore the university city of Oxford, about an hour's drive from London. But Oxford is not the only attraction in the country, as you'll soon discover as you make your way through Henley-on-Thames. The shire is a land of great mansions, old churches of widely varying architectural styles, and rolling farmland.

In a sense, Oxfordshire is a kind of buffer zone between the easy living in the southern towns and the industrialized cities of the heartland. In the southeast are the chalky Chilterns, and in the west you'll be moving toward the wool towns of the Cotswolds. In fact, Burford, an unspoiled medieval town west of Oxford, is one of the traditional gateways to the Cotswolds (dealt with in Chapter XII). The Upper Thames winds its way across the southern parts of the county.

The "Home Counties" are characterized by their river valleys and gentle hills. The beech-clad Chiltern Hills are at their most beautiful in spring and fall. This 40-

mile chalk ridge extends in an arc from the Thames Valley to the old Roman city of St. Albans in Hertfordshire. The whole region is popular for boating holidays, as it contains a 200-mile network of canals.

1. Windsor

A Green Line bus from London will deliver you in about an hour to Windsor, site of England's greatest castle and its most famous boys' school. Green Line buses 700, 702, and 704 leave from Eccleston Bridge behind Victoria Station (see "Buses in Britain," Chapter I, Section 3). Buses 700 and 702 are express service. For the return journey, you can either go straight back into London or stop at Hampton Court. Take bus 726 or 718 from Windsor. For further information, telephone 668-7261.

Windsor was called "Windlesore" by the ancient Britons who derived the name from winding shore—so noticeable as you walk along the Thames here.

THE SIGHTS

Your bus will drop you near the Town Guildhall, to which Wren applied the finishing touches. It's only a short walk up Castle Hill to the following sights:

Windsor Castle

William the Conqueror ordered a castle built on this spot, beginning a legend and a link with English sovereignty that has known many vicissitudes. King John cooled his heels at Windsor while waiting to put his signature on the Magna Carta at nearby Runnymede; Charles I was imprisoned here before losing his head; Queen Bess did some renovations; Victoria mourned her beloved Albert, who died at the castle in 1861; the royal family rode out much of World War II behind its sheltering walls. When Queen Elizabeth II is in residence, the royal standard flies. The State Apartments may usually be visited except for about six weeks at Easter, all of June, and three weeks in December, when the court is at Windsor. At other times, the apartments are open during January, February, early March, November, and early December from 10:30 a.m. to 3 p.m. daily except Sunday, and July to late October from 10:30 a.m. to 5 p.m. daily, 1:30 to 5 p.m. on Sunday. Ticket sales cease about 30 minutes before closing, and last admissions are 15 minutes before closing time. The price of admission is £2 ($3.50) for adults, £1 ($1.75) for children. It is always advisable to check what is open before visiting by telephoning 0753/868286.

The apartments contain many works of art, porcelain, armor, furniture, three Verrio ceilings, and several Gibbons carvings from the 17th century. The world of Rubens adorns the King's Drawing Room and in his relatively small dressing room is a Dürer, along with Rembrandt's portrait of his mother, and Van Dyck's triple look at Charles I. Of the apartments, the grand reception room, with its Gobelin tapestries, is the most spectacular.

The changing of the guard ceremony takes place at 11 a.m. daily except Sunday, from May to August. In winter, the guard is changed every 48 hours except Sunday, so unless you plan to visit in summer, it's wise to phone in advance for information, at the number listed above, extension 252. The Windsor changing of the guard is a much more exciting and moving experience, in my opinion, than the London exercises. In Windsor the guard marches through the town, stopping the traffic as it wheels into the castle to the tune of a full regimental band when the court is in residence. When the Queen is not there, a drum and pipe band is mustered.

Old Master Drawings

The royal family possesses a rare collection of drawings by old masters that are shown at Windsor. Notably among them are a number by Leonardo da Vinci. One

Leonardo sketch, for example, shows a cat in 20 different positions; another is a study of a horse; still a third is that of Saint Matthew, a warmup for the head used in *The Last Supper*. In addition, you'll find sketches by William Blake, Thomas Rowlandson, and 12 Holbeins (don't miss his sketch of Sir John Godsalve). The drawing exhibition may be visited at the same time as the State Apartments for an admission of 80p ($1.40) for adults, 40p (70¢) for children. Unlike the State Apartments, it remains open when the Court is in residence.

Queen Mary's Dollhouse

Just about the greatest dollhouse in the world is at Windsor. Presented to the late Queen Mary as a gift, and later used to raise money for charity, the dollhouse is a remarkable achievement and re-creation of what a great royal mansion of the 1920s looked like—complete with a fleet of cars, including a Rolls-Royce. The house is perfect for Tom Thumb and family and a retinue of servants. All is done with the most exacting detail—even the champagne bottles in the wine cellar contain vintage wine of that era. There's a toothbrush suitable for an ant. A minuscule electric iron really works. For late-night reading, you'll find volumes ranging from Hardy to Housman. In addition, you'll see a collection of dolls presented to the monarchy from nearly every nation of the Commonwealth. The dollhouse may be viewed for an admission of 80p ($1.40) for adults, 40p (70¢) for children, even when the State Apartments are closed.

St. George's Chapel

A gem of the Perpendicular style, this chapel shares the distinction with Westminster Abbey of being a pantheon of English monarchs (Victoria is a notable exception). The present St. George's was founded in the late 15th century by Edward IV on the site of the original Chapel of the Order of the Garter (Edward III, 1348). You enter the nave first with its fan vaulting (a remarkable achievement in English architecture). The nave contains the tomb of George V and Queen Mary, designed by Sir William Reid Dick. Off the nave in the Urswick Chapel, the Princess Charlotte memorial provides an ironic touch. If she had survived childbirth in 1817, she—not her cousin Victoria—would have ruled the British Empire. In the aisle are the tombs of George VI and Edward IV. The Edward IV "Quire," with its imaginatively carved 15th-century choir stalls (crowned by lacy canopies and Knights of the Garter banners), evokes the pomp and pageantry of medieval days. In the center is a flat tomb, containing the vault of the beheaded Charles I, along with Henry VIII and one of his wives (no. 3, Jane Seymour). The chapel is closed during services, and it's advisable to telephone to check opening hours at other times (tel. 0753/ 865538). The chapel is usually open from 10:45 a.m. to 3:45 or 4 p.m. Monday to Saturday, and from 2 to 3:45 or 4 p.m. on Sunday. The price of admission is £1.50 ($2.65) for adults, 60p ($1.05) for children. Closed for a few days in early January and in mid-June.

Footnote: Queen Victoria died on January 22, 1901, and was buried beside her beloved Prince Albert in a mausoleum at **Frogmore** (a private estate), near Windsor (open only two days a year, in May). The Prince Consort died in December 1861.

The Royal Mews

Entered from St. Albans Street, the red-brick buildings of the Royal Mews and Burford House were built for Nell Gwynne in the 1670s. They were named for King Charles II's natural son by her, the Earl of Burford. When the child was 14 years old, he was created Duke of St. Albans, from which the street outside takes its name.

Housed in the mews is the exhibition of the Queen's Presents and Royal Carriages. Displayed are pictures of several members of the royal family, including those of Queen Elizabeth II as colonel-in-chief of the Coldstream Guards riding in the grounds of Buckingham Palace, the Duke of Edinburgh driving his horses through a water obstacle at Windsor, and the Queen Mother with Prince Edward, Viscount Linley, and Lady Sarah Armstrong-Jones in the Scottish State Coach. There is also a full-size stable with model horses showing stable kit, harnesses, and riding equipment. In the coach house is a magnificent display of coaches and carriages kept in mint condition and in frequent use. The exhibition of the Queen's Presents includes unique items of interest given to Her Majesty and the Duke of Edinburgh throughout her reign. There is also a collection of pencil drawings of the Queen and family with horses and dogs.

The exhibition is open in November and December and January to March from 10:30 a.m. to 3 p.m. Monday to Saturday. April to October, hours are 10:30 a.m. to 5 p.m. It's also open on Sunday from 10:30 a.m. to 3 p.m. May to October. Admission is £1 ($1.75) for adults, 50p (90¢) for children.

Royalty and Empire

The famous company founded by Madame Tussaud in 1802 has taken over part of the Windsor Town railway station to present an exhibition of "Queen Victoria's Diamond Jubilee 1837–1897." It's at the Windsor and Eton Central Railway Station on Thames Street (tel. 0753/857837). At one of the station platforms is a replica of *The Queen,* the engine used to draw the royal coaches, disembarking the life-size wax figures of guests arriving at Windsor for the Jubilee celebration. Seated in the Royal Waiting Room are Queen Victoria (in wax, of course), and her family. In one of the carriages, the Day Saloon, are Grand Duke Serge and the Grand Duchess Elizabeth (the queen's granddaughter) of Russia. Waiting in the anteroom is the queen's faithful Indian servant, Hafiz Abdul Karim, the Munshi. Among the famous guests portrayed are the Prince and Princess of Wales (Edward VII and Alexandra), the Empress Frederick of Prussia (Queen Victoria's eldest daughter), and the prime minister, Lord Salisbury. The platform is busy with royal servants, a flower seller, a newsboy, an Italian with a barrel organ, and others who have come to see the arrival of the train. Drawn up on the ceremonial parade ground are the troops of the Coldstream Guards and the horse-drawn carriage that would take the party to the castle. With the sound of military bands in the background and the voices of officers commanding their troops, you really feel you are present for Her Majesty's arrival.

Afterward, at the end of the walkway through the Victorian Conservatory, you reach the 260-seat theater where a short audio-visual presentation with life-size animated models gives further glimpses of life during Victoria's reign. The entire visit takes about 45 minutes. The exhibition is open daily from 9:30 a.m. to 5:30 p.m. (closed Christmas Day). Admission is £3.55 ($6.20) for adults, £2.55 ($4.45) for children.

Sunday Entertainment

There are often polo matches in **Windsor Great Park**—and at Ham Common —and you may see Prince Charles playing and Prince Philip serving as umpire. The Queen often watches. For more information, telephone 0753/860633.

The Town Itself

Windsor is largely a Victorian town, with lots of brick buildings and a few remnants of Georgian architecture. In and around the castle are two cobblestone streets, **Church** and **Market,** with their antique shops, silversmiths, and pubs. One shop on Church Street was supposedly occupied by Nell Gwynne who needed to be within call of Charles II's chambers. After lunch or tea, you may want to stroll along the three-mile, aptly named Long Walk.

Around Windsor Sightseeing Tours

A 35-minute tour of Windsor and the surrounding countryside is offered in an open-top, double-deck bus with commentary. The ten-mile drive starts from Windsor Castle and passes the Royal Mews, the Long Walk, the Royal Farms, Albert Bridge, Eton College, and the Theatre Royal. The departure point is Castle Hill, near the King Henry VIII Gateway to Windsor Castle. Adults pay £3 ($5.25) and children, £2 ($3.50). Tickets, along with information about dates of operation and departure times, are available from **Windsorian Coaches,** 17 Alma Rd. (tel. 0753/856841).

Guided Tours

A 1½-hour guided tour of Windsor Castle and the town leaves from the **Tourist Information Centre** (tel. 0753/852010) in the Central Station, the one opposite the castle. The walking tour includes a look at the Long Walk, then the Guildhall and Market Cross House, along with the changing of the guard when possible. In the castle precincts you'll visit the Cloistersand the Albert Memorial Chapel, finishing in the State Apartments where no guiding is allowed. Subject to demand, the tours leave at 10:45 a.m. and 1:45 p.m. Monday to Saturday and at 1:45 p.m. on Sunday, costing £2 ($3.50) for adults and £1.50 ($2.65) for children. All tours are accompanied by a licensed guide.

STAYING OVER AT WINDSOR

If you don't have an engraved invitation to overnight at the castle, there's always room at one of the inns, except during Ascot Races and the Windsor Horse Show.

For those who decide to stay in Windsor and use it as a base for London sightseeing, trains run from Windsor Town Station and from Windsor and Eton Riverside Station to London. Trains leave London as late as 10:30 or 11 p.m., so it's quite easy to take in an early theater and dinner before returning to Windsor for overnight.

The Upper Bracket

The **Castle Hotel,** High Street, Windsor, Berkshire SL4 1LJ (tel. 0753/851011), near Windsor Castle, is a solid and well-established hotel originally built in the 15th century as a shelter to feed and house the hundreds of workers laboring on the city's foundations and royal buildings. By the 17th century it had changed its name from the Mermaid to the Castle and benefited from the heavy stagecoach traffic that often deposited visitors at its doorstep. In 1986 the entourage of the royal family of Spain was housed in 17 of its best rooms, Princess Anne has dropped in for breakfast, and the Duke of Edinburgh has been a guest speaker at functions. The Windsor Bar is airily decorated in soft tones of pink and green. Centuries ago the grounds in back of the hotel's dignified Georgian façade served as the stable yards for Windsor Castle, but now they support a modern wing belonging to the hotel, containing 46 of the hotel's 85 bedrooms. Each of the accommodations is complete with private bath or shower, color TV, radio, phone, and mini-bar. Singles rent for £74 ($129.50) daily and doubles or twins for £94 ($164.50). The castle also has a car park.

Sir Christopher Wren's House Hotel, Thames Street, Windsor, Berkshire SL4 1PX (tel. 0753/861354), was designed and lived in by Christopher Wren in 1676. Between Eton and Windsor, the former town house occupies a prime position on the Thames, its gardens overlooking the swans and boats. The central hall is impressive, with a Queen Anne black marble refectory table. Wren's former study is inviting: it's in apricot and white paneling, with his Empire desk, along with a fireplace and shield-back Hepplewhite chairs. The bay-windowed main drawing room, decorated with mirrors, sconces, and a formal marble fireplace, opens into a garden and a riverside flagstone terrace for after-dinner coffee and drinks. All of the 38 bedrooms contain a private bath. Some have fine old furniture, and all are equipped with color

TV, direct-dial phone, and trouser press. Several units overlook the river. Room 2, which was Sir Christopher Wren's bedroom, is said to be haunted. Singles with bath range from £80 ($140) daily, and doubles or twins with bath, from £118 ($206.50). Open to nonresidents, the hotel restaurant, the Orangerie, is recommended separately.

The Medium-Priced Range

Ye Harte & Garter Hotel, 21 High St., Windsor, Berkshire SL4 1LR (tel. 0753/863426), stands on Castle Hill opposite Windsor Castle. An impressive building, the hotel is a combination of two separate inns dating back to the time of Henry VIII. The old Garter Inn burned down in the 1800s and was rebuilt as part of one hostelry that included the Hart. The old Garter, named for the Knights of the Garter, was the setting for scenes in Shakespeare's *Merry Wives of Windsor.* The present hotel is characteristic of the Victorian era, having been rebuilt in 1890 of red brick. From the front bedrooms you can watch the guards marching up High Street every morning on their way to change the guard at the castle. Singles cost £42 ($73.50) daily. Doubles go for £65 ($113.75). Breakfast is included. Rooms contain color TV, direct-dial phone, trouser press, hot beverage equipment, and other amenities. You can dine in the Henry VIII or Apéritif Restaurants, or have a drink in the Grape Press Wine Bar.

Royal Adelaide Hotel, Kings Road, Windsor Berkshire SL4 2AG (tel. 0753/863916), is opposite the famous Long Walk leading to Windsor Castle, five minutes away. An interesting Georgian building, it offers single rooms costing from £55 ($96.25) to £67 ($117.25) daily and doubles and twins from £65 ($113.75) to £80 ($140), and all rates include breakfast. All units, which vary in size, have private baths, radios, phones, alarms, and hot beverage facilities. There is car parking at the rear for guests, and the hotel is well furnished. A set dinner is available at £10.75 ($18.80) for three courses.

On the Outskirts

On the river road, the A308, from Windsor to Maidenhead, the motorist comes across the **Oakley Court Hotel,** Windsor Road, Water Oakley, Windsor, Berkshire SL4 5UR (tel. 0628/74141), three miles from Windsor and about 20 minutes from Heathrow. This Victorian manor house emerged from a semiretirement and blossoms as a most attractive riverside hotel. The Gothic house with its turrets and chimneys contains the reception and the living rooms, and the restaurant. One modern wing of bedrooms extends from the old house; another, built beside the river, is a 30-foot walk from the main building. Of the 92 rooms, those in the old house have high ceilings, interesting shapes, big baths, and one still contains the original paneling. In the two modern wings, the rooms are of generous size and have baths. All have color TV and radio with remote control and phone. There is full room service. Singles rent for £92 ($161) to £98 ($171.50) daily, and doubles cost £106 ($185.50) to £115 ($201.25), including an English breakfast, VAT, and service.

At Oakley Court's Oak Leaf Restaurant, you can enjoy such specialties as terrine de homard et turbot (terrine of lobster and turbot encased in spinach and served with a mint-and-honey cream) and suprême de volaille blanquette (suprême of chicken stuffed with a chicken mousse, prunes, and orange zest, served with a cream and white wine sauce). A set lunch costs £15.50 ($27.15), and a set dinner goes for £22 ($38.50). If you order à la carte, expect to pay from £35 ($61.25). The culinary expertise of MacSween has made this a popular dining spot, with such notables as Prince Charles and Prince Philip among the customers.

DINING AT WINDSOR

At Sir Christopher Wren's House Hotel, Thames Street (tel. 0753/861354), already recommended as a hotel, **The Orangerie** is the most elegant and charming restaurant in Windsor with garden terraces. Its anterooms contain nymphs whose carved heads gaze out from either side of a neoclassical mantelpiece. The dining room is designed a bit like a greenhouse, with cabriole-legged furniture, lots of chintz, and views through tall French windows of the garden. At dinner a live pianist entertains. Full meals, costing from £25 ($43.75), might include a terrine of guinea fowl with macadamia nuts and avocado sauce, mignons of veal filet roasted in a cabbage and cider sauce, or a pair of wood pigeon breasts fermented in port and served with a plum and blood-orange sauce. Meals are offered daily from 12:30 to 2 p.m. and 7:30 to 10:30 p.m. In summer, guests can dine in the garden beside the Thames.

Many guests prefer some excellent hotel dining rooms, but if not, there are several independent candidates. One is **Cope's Oyster House,** 6 Church St. (tel. 0753/850929), a seafood restaurant in a house that dates from the 15th century. Once it was owned by Nell Gwynne. A tunnel in the cellar, now bricked up, leads through to Windsor Castle (apparently, it was used for the secret visits of the king with his mistress). Fresh oysters are always available on the menu, as well as lobster, crab, scampi, salmon, and oysters. Meals at this fully licensed restaurant average £28 ($49) per person. There is a good selection of wines to go with your seafood. Hours are from noon to 2:30 p.m. and 7 to 10:30 p.m. except Saturday at lunch and all day Sunday.

ETON

To visit Eton, home of what is arguably the most famous public school in the world (Americans would call it a private school), you can take a train from Paddington Station, go by car, or take the Green Line bus to Windsor. If you go by car, you can take the M4 motorway, leaving it at exit 5 to go straight to Eton. However, parking is likely to be a problem, so I advise turning off the M4 at exit 6 to Windsor. You can park there and take an easy stroll past Windsor Castle and across the Thames bridge. Follow Eton High Street to the college. From Windsor Castle's ramparts, you can look down on the river and on the famous playing fields of Eton.

Eton College

Largest and best known of the public (private) schools of England, Eton College was founded by a teenage boy himself, Henry VI, in 1440. Some of England's greatest men, notably the Duke of Wellington, have played on the fields of Eton. Twenty prime ministers were educated here, as well as such literary figures as George Orwell and Aldous Huxley. Even the late Ian Fleming, creator of James Bond, attended. If it's open, take a look at the Perpendicular chapel, with its 15th-century paintings and reconstructed fan vaulting. Visits to the school are possible from Easter to the end of September from 2 to 4:30 p.m. daily, with guided tours being given at 2:15 and 3:15 p.m. During the summer holidays, it is also open from 10:30 a.m. The guided tours of the school and museum (see below) cost £2.40 ($4.20) for adults, £1.80 ($3.15) for children. For information regarding visits, phone 0753/863593.

The Museum of Eton Life

The history of Eton College since its inception in 1440 is depicted in the museum located in vaulted wine cellars under College Hall, which were originally the storehouse for use of the college's masters. The displays, ranging from formal to extremely informal, include a turn-of-the-century boy's room, schoolbooks, sports trophies, canes used by senior boys to apply punishment they felt needful to their juniors, and birch sticks used by masters for the same purpose. Also to be seen are letters written home by students describing day-to-day life at the school, as well as samples of the numerous magazines produced by students over the centuries, known as ephemera because of the changing writers and ideas. Many of the items to be seen were provided by Old Etonians, with collections formerly scattered throughout various buildings of the school also being included. The museum schedule is based on the school year, with hours varying widely (see above). For information, contact the Custodian, Eton College (tel. 0753/863593).

Dining at Eton

House on the Bridge, 71 High St. (tel. 0753/860914), is charmingly contained within a red-brick and terracotta Victorian house set adjacent to the bridge beside the river at the edge of Eton. Near the handful of outdoor tables is an almost vertical garden whose plants cascade into the Thames. Food is well prepared here, with an array of British and international dishes. Full meals, costing from £18 ($31.50) to £22 ($38.50) per person, are served daily from noon to 2:30 p.m. and 6 and 11 p.m. Menu choices include steak Diane, roast Aylesbury duckling, grilled Dover sole, and crêpes suzette. Many of the most interesting dishes are prepared only for two diners, so it's best to bring a friend.

Eton Wine Bar, High Street (tel. 0753/854921), just across the bridge from Windsor, it is a charming place set among the antique shops with pinewood tables and old church pews and chairs. There is a small garden out back. Soups of the day are often imaginative and sophisticated (ever had watercress vichyssoise?). Another "starter" might be mussels marinated in a roquefort dressing. Main dishes include such treats as stuffed eggplant with a Provençal tomato sauce and rice. Each day, two special dishes are featured, and desserts include pineapple and almond flan and damson crunch. Meals cost from £10 ($17.50) up. Wine can be ordered by the glass. Food is served from noon to 2:30 p.m. and 6 to 10:30 p.m. Monday to Thursday, to 11 p.m. Friday and Saturday. Sunday hours are from noon to 2 p.m. and 7 to 10 p.m.

Antico, 42 High St. (tel. 0753/863977), is an old building with beams spreading through several rooms. On your way to the tiny bar you pass a cold table, displaying an array of hors d'oeuvres, fresh fish, and cold meats. Grilled fresh sardines are also a feature. There is a wide choice of fish dishes, such as sole grilled, Colbert, or with mushrooms, capers, and prawns. Beef filet is a favorite dish. Desserts from the trolley are offered. Meals range from £20 ($35) to £25 ($43.75), including VAT and service. The restaurant is open for lunch daily except Saturday, from noon to 2:30 p.m. Dinner is nightly from 7 to 11. Closed Sunday and bank holidays.

NEARBY SIGHTS

Several attractions of interest are in the surrounding area.

One of England's Great Gardens

Savill Garden, Wick Lane, Englefield Green (tel. 0753/860222), is in Windsor Great Park and signposted from Windsor, Egham, and Ascot. Started in 1932, the garden is considered one of the finest of its type in the northern hemisphere. The display starts in spring with rhododendrons, camellias, and daffodils beneath the trees; then throughout the summer are spectacular displays of flowers and shrubs presented in a natural and wild state. It is open all year except at Christmas, from 10 a.m. to 6 or 7 p.m., and the admission is £1.80 ($3.15) for adults; accompanied children under 16 are admitted free. There is a licensed, self-service restaurant on the premises.

Adjoining the Savill Garden are the **Valley Gardens,** full of shrubs and trees in a series of wooded natural valleys running down to Virginia water. It's open daily, free, throughout the year.

Windsor Safari Park

Two miles southwest of Windsor Castle lies Windsor Safari Park, Winkfield Road (tel. 0753/869841), perhaps Britain's most exciting such park, with a killer whale/dolphin/sea lion show, plus shows of birds of prey, parrots, and a computer-animated Tiki show. There is an exciting twin-track alpine toboggan run. You can see the Tropical World of plants, alligators, butterflies, chimpanzees, and a host of other animals in drive-through reserves—tigers, lions, bears, wolves, baboons, and zebras among them. Open from 10 a.m. to dusk daily except Christmas Day, the park has catering facilities, picnic areas, soft play centers, and adventure playgrounds. If you have a soft-top car or come on public transport, there is free safari-bus service to take you through the reserves. The all-inclusive admission (for entrance and all shows and attractions) is £6.50 ($11.40) for adults, £5.50 ($9.65) for children. The park is 20 miles from London. Take the M4 motorway, leaving it at junction 6 and following the signs.

The Wellington Ducal Estate

If you'd like to make an interesting day trip in Berkshire, I'd suggest **Stratfield Saye House** (tel. 0256/882882), between Reading and Basingstoke on the A33. It has been the home of the Duke of Wellington since 1817 when the 17th-century house was bought for the Iron Duke to celebrate his victory over Napoleon at the Battle of Waterloo. Many memories of the first duke remain in the house, including his billiard table, battle spoils, and pictures. The funeral carriage that since 1860 had rested in St. Paul's Cathedral crypt is now in the ducal collection. In the gardens is the grave of Copenhagen, the charger ridden to battle at Waterloo by the first duke. There are also extensive pleasure grounds together with a licensed restaurant and gift shop.

A short drive away is the **Wellington Country Park** (tel. 0734/326444) with the fascinating National Dairy Museum where you can see relics of 150 years of dairying. Other attractions include a riding school, nature trails, and boating and sailing on the lake. In addition, there are a miniature steam railway, the Thames Valley Time Trail, and a deer park.

Stratfield Saye is open from 11:30 a.m. to 5 p.m. daily except Friday from May 1 to the last Sunday in September. Admission is £3 ($5.25) for adults and £1.50 ($2.65) for children. Wellington Country Park is open from 10 a.m. to 5 p.m. daily from March to September. Admission is £2 ($3.50) for adults, £1 ($1.75) for children. A combined ticket for the house and park cost £4 ($7) for adults, £2 ($3.50) for children.

Mapledurham House on the Thames

The Elizabethan mansion home of the Blount family (tel. 0734/723350) lies beside the Thames in the unspoiled village of Mapledurham and can be reached by car from the A4074 Oxford–Reading road. A much more romantic way of reaching the lovely old house is to take the boat that leaves the promenade next to Caversham Bridge at 2:15 p.m. on Saturday, Sunday, and bank holidays from Easter to the end of September. The journey upstream takes about 40 minutes, and the boat leaves Mapledurham again at 5 p.m. for the journey back to Caversham. This gives you plenty of time to walk through the house and see the Elizabethan ceilings and the great oak staircase, as well as the portraits of the two beautiful sisters with whom the poet Alexander Pope, a frequent visitor here, fell in love. The family chapel, built in 1789, is a fine example of modern Gothic. Cream teas with homemade cakes are available at the house. On the grounds, the last working watermill on the Thames still produces flour.

The house is open from 2:30 to 5 p.m. Saturday, Sunday, and public holidays from Easter to the end of September; the mill, from 1:30 to 5 p.m. on the same days in summer and on Sunday from 2 to 4 p.m. in winter. Entrance to the house costs £2 ($3.50) for adults, £1 ($1.75) for children. To the mill, the charge is £1 ($1.75) adults, 50p (90¢) for children.

The boat ride from Caversham costs £2.75 ($4.80) for adults, £1.95 ($3.40) for children for the round trip. Further details about the boat can be obtained from

D&T Scenics Ltd., Pipers Island, Bridge Street, Caversham Bridge, Reading, Berkshire RG4 8AH (tel. 0734/481088).

2. Ascot

While following the royal buckhounds through Windsor Forest, Queen Anne decided to have a racecourse on Ascot Heath. The first race meeting at Ascot was inaugurated in 1711. Since then, the Ascot Racecourse has been a symbol of chic as pictures of the Royal Family, including the Queen and Prince Philip, have been flashed around the world. Nowadays instead of Queen Anne, you are likely to see Princess Anne, an avid horsewoman.

Ascot lies only 28 miles west of London, directly south of Windsor at the southern end of Windsor Great Park (take the A332). There is frequent rail service in London from Waterloo to Ascot Station, which lies about ten minutes from the racecourse.

The **Ascot Racecourse** (tel. 0344/322211) is open throughout the year except for the months of March and August. There are three enclosures: Tattersalls is the largest, Silver Ring the least expensive, and the third is the Members Enclosure. Plenty of bars and restaurants exist to suit a wide range of pocketbooks. Tickets cost adults £3 ($5.25) to £17 ($29.75); children under 16 are admitted free if accompanied by an adult. The highlight of the Ascot social season—complete with fancy hats and white gloves—is Royal Week, in late June, but there is excellent racing on the third Saturday in July and the last Saturday in September, with more than three-quarters of a million pounds in prize money. The races here are flat races, unlike some of the other famous English races which are steeplechases.

FOOD AND LODGING

One of the most elegant hotels in the region, the **Royal Berkshire,** London Road, Sunninghill, Ascot, Berkshire SL5 0PP (tel. 0344/23322), lies two miles northeast of Ascot on A322. Its interior decor does justice to its history. Built of russet-colored bricks in the Queen Anne style in 1705, it was lived in for many years by relatives of Sir Winston Churchill. Bedrooms, 82 in all, are often spacious, with a number of amenities including private baths or showers. A single is priced at £71 ($124.25) to £76 ($133) daily, and doubles go for £106 ($185.50) to £121 ($211.75). Many people visit only for a meal in the Stateroom Restaurant overlooking the lawns and gardens of the hotel. The food is some of the finest in the area, made with quality ingredients and often reflecting artistic flair. Lunch costs from £18 ($31.50) and dinner from £20 ($35). There is a good à la carte menu that changes frequently and offers a range of contemporary English dishes. Meals are served daily from 12:30 to 2:30 p.m. and 7:30 to 9:30 p.m.

Berystede Country House Hotel, Bagshot Road, Ascot, Berkshire SL5 9JH (tel. 0344/23311), was built by the Victorians, including re-creations of medieval towers, half-timbering, steeply pitched roofs covered with slates and tiles, and a landscaped garden. The entrance hall incorporates the massive lintel and Ionic pilasters of a pseudo-Gothic stone fireplace that, if the weather's cool enough, might be blazing. Upgraded, enlarged, and redecorated, the hotel is filled with original deep-relief half-paneling left over from its original construction. Seating nooks are scattered about. Bedrooms, with their high ceilings and chintzes, evoke the aura of rooms in a private country house. Each contains a private bath, phone, and color TV, and the more expensive suites boast mahogany reproductions of 18th-century antiques. The rooms, 91 in all, rent for £71 ($124.25) to £77 ($134.75) daily in a single, £91 ($159.25) to £135 ($236.25) in a double or twin.

3. Henley-on-Thames

At the eastern edge of Oxfordshire, only 35 miles from London, Henley-on-Thames is a small town and resort on the river. At the foothills of the Chilterns, it is the headquarters of the Royal Regatta held annually in July, the Number One event among European oarsmen. The regatta dates back to the first years of the reign of Victoria.

The Elizabethan buildings, the tea rooms, and the inns along the town's High Street live up to one's conception of what an English country town looks like—or should look like. The life here is serene, and Henley-on-Thames makes for an excellent stopover en route to Oxford. **Warning:** During the Royal Regatta, rooms are virtually impossible to get at the fashionable inns of Henley, unless you've made reservations months in advance.

FOOD AND LODGING

Dating from the 16th century, the **Red Lion Hotel,** Henley Bridge, Henley-on-Thames, Oxfordshire RG9 2AR (tel. 0491/572161), is a former coaching inn. A bedchamber used to be kept ready for the Duke of Marlborough, who would stop over on his way to his palace at Blenheim. The guest list reads like a hall of fame, including such notables as Johnson and Boswell, even George IV who, it is said, downed more than a dozen lamb chops one night. The red-brick façade, with its climbing wisteria, remains untouched, but most of the interior has been renovated and modernized. A bathless single costs £30 ($52.50) daily, rising to £50 ($87.50) with bath, and bathless doubles go for £60 ($105), increasing to £70 ($122.50) with bath. Guests congregate in the low-beamed lounge and take meals in the Riverside Restaurant that serves an à la carte lunch or dinner for £20 ($35).

4. Inns Along the Thames

For those who want to anchor into riverside villages with old inns along the Thames, I offer the following suggestions for the motorist. You can watch the peaceful river making its way between the history-laden banks, lined with trees, gardens, and buildings lying somnolent under the English skies.

BRAY-ON-THAMES

Twenty-eight miles from London, you come upon this attractive Thames-side village, with its beautiful old almshouses, timbered cottages, and small period houses. Windsor Castle is just a short jaunt away. The town was once famous for its 16th-century "Vicar of Bray" who couldn't make up his mind about his religious or political affiliations.

In what was a traditional English riverside pub on an attractive stretch of the river, the Roux Brothers operate the **Waterside Inn,** Ferry Road (tel. 0628/20691), known for its impeccable cooking (and also for its astronomical prices). The restaurant has been given almost every superlative in the book. The Roux Brothers were brought up in the Saône et Loire region of France and first started serious cooking at the age of 14. Their father had a charcuterie (delicatessen), and the boys learned the basic skills from him and from their mother. Both went into private service in England and France, working in some of the best-known homes and at embassies. They then opened a London restaurant, Le Gavroche, and later came to the Waterside. Michel Roux is in charge of this operation.

If you select from the à la carte menu, expect to pay around £43 ($75.25) per person, plus wine, if you have been extravagant in your choice of dishes. Actually, you can dine well by ordering the set dinner at £42.50 ($74.40). At lunchtime, you can enjoy the set meal at £20.50 ($35.90) Monday to Friday, £23.50 ($41.15) Saturday and Sunday. Chef Michel has developed some interesting combinations, such as salmon and brill with ginger, a mousse using three different fish, and fileted young rabbit with marrons glacés. Recently I feasted happily on the mousseline of volaille au roquefort, a cassoulette d'écrevisses aux tagliatelles with sauce Nantua, and Harlem sauce Drambuie. Roughly, in English that's a fine game pâté with roquefort cheese, baked crayfish with tagliatelli, and a tasty dessert. The Waterside is open from Tuesday dinner to Sunday lunchtime; closed in January and for the Christmas holiday. Hours for lunch are noon to 2 p.m.; dinner, 7:30 to 10 p.m. Reservations are essential.

If the Waterside is too rich for your pocketbook's blood, you should be well pleased with the following, more modestly priced recommendation.

Hinds Head Hotel, High Street (tel. 0628/26151), lies on the bend of a very busy, narrow road, but there's ample parking in front of the restaurant. Although calling itself a hotel, the Hinds has no rooms to rent. There is a bar and you can take your pint in with you if you wish, as the wine list is expensive. A three-course weekday lunch costs £17.50 ($30.65), going up to £19.50 ($34.15) on Sunday. A dinner goes for £25 ($43.75). There is a fish course before the roast beef, pork, or lamb, with all the trimmings. Be warned, the waitresses bring around three sorts of potatoes and then about four different green vegetables. Hours are 12:30 to 2 p.m. and 7:30 to 10 p.m. except Sunday evening. This is the sort of place to come to on a nice Sunday for a good old English "blow-out" lunch. The portions are large, and the standard of cuisine pretty high on the plainer dishes.

STREATLEY-ON-THAMES

This Thamesside village has some old buildings and a fine Priory Church. And it has **The Swan at Streatley,** High Street, Streatley-on-Thames, Berkshire RG8 9HR (tel. 0491/873737), a riverside inn. The Swan has now been much enlarged, but still it retains much of its old charm. It would take a lot to ruin the tranquility and eternity of the River Thames. Gardens slope down to the water. The menu offers a high standard of food at a variety of prices. Set lunches cost £11 ($19.25) and £13.50 ($23.65), or you can order à la carte. A specialty three-course, fixed-price dinner goes for £17 ($29.75), with a seven-course gourmet repast offered for £26 ($45.50). Expect to pay from £18 ($31.50) if you order your evening meal à la carte. Whether you're touring or just spending a last night before going to Heathrow, this is a good choice. All the rooms, each individually designed, have private baths, and a full English breakfast, service, and VAT are included in the rates. The most desirable rooms open onto views of the Thames. Singles cost from £65 ($113.75) daily and doubles from £85 ($148.75). A boathouse bar and a leisure club are added features.

---

5. Oxford

A walk down the long sweep of The High, one of the most striking streets in England; a mug of cider in one of the old student pubs; the sound of a May Day dawn when choristers sing in Latin from Magdalen Tower; the Great Tom bell from Tom Tower, whose 101 peals traditionally signal the closing of the college gates; towers and spires rising majestically; the barges on the upper reaches of the Thames; nude swimming at Parson's Pleasure; the roar of a cannon launching the bumping races; a tiny, dusty bookstall where you can pick up a valuable first edition. All that is Oxford—57 miles from London and home of one of the greatest universities in the world. An industrial city, the center of a large automobile business, as well as a university town, Oxford is better for sightseeing in summer. That's when the students are wherever Oxford scholars go for vacation and the city is less crowded.

However, at any time of the year you can enjoy a tour of the colleges, many of them representing a peak in England's architectural kingdom, as well as a valley of Victorian contributions. The Oxford Information Centre (see below) offers guided walking tours daily in summer and on Saturday in winter. Just don't mention the other place (Cambridge) and you shouldn't have any trouble.

The city predates the university—in fact, it was a Saxon town in the early part of the 10th century. And by the 12th century Oxford was growing in reputation as a seat of learning—at the expense of Paris. The first colleges were founded in the 13th century. The story of Oxford is filled with conflicts too complex and detailed to elaborate here. Suffice it to say, the relationship between town and gown wasn't as peaceful as it is today. Riots often flared, and both sides were guilty of abuses.

Nowadays, the young people of Oxford take out their aggressiveness in sporting competitions, with the different colleges zealously competing in such games as cricket and soccer. However, all colleges unite into a powerful university when they face matches with their traditional rival, Cambridge.

Ultimately, the test of a great university lies in the caliber of the people it turns out. Oxford can name-drop a mouthful: Roger Bacon, Samuel Johnson, William Penn, John Wesley, Sir Walter Raleigh, Edward Gibbon, T. E. Lawrence, Sir Christopher Wren, John Donne, William Pitt, Matthew Arnold, Arnold Toynbee, Harold Macmillan, Graham Greene, A. E. Housman, Lewis Carroll, and even Dean Rusk.

Many Americans arriving in Oxford ask, "Where's the campus?" If an Oxonian shows amusement when answering, it's understandable. Oxford University is, in fact, made up of 35 colleges. To tour all of these would be a formidable task. Besides, a few are of such interest they overshadow the rest.

PARK AND RIDE

Traffic and parking are a disaster in Oxford, and not just during rush hours. However, there are three large car parks on the north, south, and west of the city's ring road, all well marked. Car parking is free at all times, but at any time from 9:30 a.m. on, and all day on Saturday, you pay 60p ($1.05) for a bus ride into the city, getting off at St. Aldates or Queen Street to see the city center. The buses run every eight to ten minutes in each direction. There is no service on Sunday. The car parks are on the Woodstock road near the Peartree roundabout, on the Botley road toward Faringdon, and on the Abingdon road in the southeast.

TOURS AND TOURIST SERVICES

A tourist reception center for Oxford is operated by **Guide Friday Ltd.,** railway station, Oxford. Their office dispenses free maps and brochures on the town and area, and operates tours. Also available is a full range of tourist services, including accommodation references and car rental. In summer, the office is open daily from 9 a.m. to 6 p.m. In winter, hours are daily from 9 a.m. to 4 p.m. Guided tours of Oxford and the colleges leave from the railway station daily. In summer, when open-top double-decker buses are used, departures are every 15 minutes. The tour can be a 45-minute panoramic ride, or you can get off at any of the stops in the city. The ticket is valid all day. The tour price is £3 ($5.25).

THE SIGHTS

In season (from Easter through October), the best way to get a running commentary on the important sightseeing attractions is to go to the **Oxford Information Centre,** St. Aldate's Chambers, St. Aldate's, opposite the Town Hall, near Carfax (tel. 0865/726871). Walking tours through the major colleges leave daily both morning and afternoon, last two hours, and cost £2.40 ($4.20). The tour does not include New College or Christ Church. These open-top bus tours of Oxford leave St. Aldate's every 45 minutes and cost £2.40 ($4.20). Minibus tours are offered daily to tour the Cotswolds. You can also get reservations for entertainment facilities, as well as for Stratford-upon-Avon and London West End theaters (tel. 0865/727855).

Because there are so many well-known buildings in Oxford (Radcliffe Camera, whose dome competes in a city of spires; Sheldonian Theatre, an early work of Wren's; the Bodleian Library, one of the most important in the world), I have narrowed down the sights to a representative list of a few colleges.

For a bird's-eye view of the city and the colleges, climb Carfax Tower. This is the one with the clock and figures that strike the hours. Admission is 40p (70¢) for adults, 10p (20¢) for children.

To help with an understanding of the university complex, **Heritage Projects Ltd.,** Broad Street (tel. 0865/728822), presents "The Oxford Story." It provides an insight into the structure of the colleges, with a look behind the portals at some of the architectural and historical features that might otherwise be missed. It also fills you in on the general background of the colleges and highlights the deeds of some of the famous personalities who have passed through its portals. The audio-visual presentation is given daily from 9 a.m. to 5 p.m., with an admission charge of £3 ($5.25) for adults and £1.50 ($2.65) for children.

At **Punt Station,** Cherwell Boathouse, Bardwell Road (tel. 0865/515978), you can rent a punt at a cost of £4 ($7) per hour, plus a £25 ($43.75) deposit that must be posted. Similar charges are made on rentals at Magdalen Bridge Boathouse and at the Folly Bridge Boathouse. Hours are 10 a.m. to 10 p.m. daily.

A Word of Warning

The main business of a university, is, of course, to educate—and unfortunately this function at Oxford has been severely interfered with by the number of visitors who have been disturbing the academic work of the university. So, with deep regret, visiting is now restricted to certain hours and small groups of six or fewer. In addition, there are areas where visitors are not allowed at all, but the tourist office will be happy to advise you when and where you may "take in" the sights of this great institution.

Christ Church

Begun by Cardinal Wolsey as Cardinal College in 1525, Christ Church, known as The House, was founded by Henry VIII in 1546. Facing St. Aldate's Street, Christ Church has the largest quadrangle of any college in Oxford.

Tom Tower houses Great Tom, the 18,000-pound bell referred to earlier. It rings at 9:05 nightly, signaling the closing of the college gates. The 101 times it peals originally signified the number of students in residence at the time of the founding of the college. The student body number changed, but Oxford traditions live on forever. In the 16th-century Great Hall, with its hammer-beam ceiling, are some interesting portraits, including works by those old reliables, Gainsborough and Reynolds. Prime ministers are pictured, as Christ Church was the training ground for 13 prime ministers: men such as Gladstone and George Canning. There is a separate picture gallery.

The cathedral, dating from the 12th century, was built over a period of centuries. (Incidentally, it's not only the college chapel, but the cathedral of the diocese of Oxford.) The cathedral's most distinguishing features are its Norman pillars and the vaulting of the choir, dating from the 15th century. In the center of the Great Quadrangle is a statue of Mercury mounted in the center of a fish pond. The college and cathedral can be visited from 9:30 a.m. to noon and 2 to 6 p.m. in summer, to 4:30 p.m. in winter. Entrance fee is £1 ($1.75).

Magdalen College

Pronounced "maud-len," this college was founded in 1458 by William of Waynflete, bishop of Winchester and later chancellor of England. Its alumni range from Wolsey to Wilde. Opposite the botanic garden, the oldest in England, is the bell tower, where the choristers sing in Latin at dawn on May Day. The reflection of the 15th-century tower is cast in the waters of the Cherwell below. On a not-so-happy day, Charles I—his days numbered—watched the oncoming Roundheads. Visit the 15th-century chapel, in spite of many of its latter-day trappings. Ask when the hall and other places of special interest are open.

A favorite pastime is to take Addison's Walk through the water meadows. The stroll is so named after a former alumnus, Joseph Addison, the 18th-century writer and poet noted for his contributions to *The Spectator* and *The Tatler*. The grounds of Magdalen are the most extensive of any Oxford college, even containing a deer park. You can visit Magdalen each day from 2 to 6:15 p.m.

Merton College

Founded in 1264, this college (tel. 0865/276310) is among the trio of the most ancient at the university. It stands near Corpus Christi College on Merton Street, the sole survivor of Oxford's medieval cobbled streets. Merton College is noted for its library, said to be the oldest college library in England, having been built between 1371 and 1379. There was once a tradition of keeping some of its most valuable books chained. Now only one book is so secured, to show what the custom was like. One of the treasures of the library is an astrolabe (astronomical instrument used for measuring the altitude of the sun and stars), thought to have belonged to Chaucer. You pay only 30p (55¢) to visit the ancient library, as well as the Max Beerbohm Room (the satirical English caricaturist who died in 1956). Both are open from 2 to 4 p.m. (4:30 p.m. March to October) Monday to Saturday except between Christmas and the end of the second week in February and for a week at Easter. In addition, the college is open from 10 a.m. to noon on Saturday and Sunday only. You can also visit the chapel, dating from the 13th century, at these times.

University College

On The High, University College (tel. 0865/276602) is the oldest one at Oxford, tracing its history back to 1249 when money was donated by an ecclesiastic William of Durham. More fanciful is the old claim that the real founder was Alfred the Great. Don't jump to any conclusions about the age of the buildings when you see the present Gothic-esque look. The original structures have all disappeared, and what remains today represents essentially the architecture of the 17th century, with subsequent additions in Victoria's day, as well as in more recent times. For example, the Goodhart Quadrangle was added as late as 1962. Its most famous alumnus, Shelley, was "sent down" for his part in collaborating on a pamphlet on atheism. However, all is forgiven today, as the romantic poet is honored by a memorial erected in 1894. The hall and chapel of the University College can be visited during vacations from 2 to 4 p.m.

New College

New College was founded in 1379 by William of Wykeham, bishop of Winchester and later lord chancellor of England. The college at Winchester supplied a constant stream of candidates. The first quadrangle, dating from before the end of the 14th century, was the initial quadrangle to be built in Oxford, forming the architectural design for the other colleges. In the ante-chapel is Sir Jacob Epstein's remarkable modern sculpture of *Lazarus* and a fine El Greco painting of St. James. One of the treasures of the college is a crosier (pastoral staff of a bishop) belonging to the founding father. In the garden you can see the remains of the old city wall and the mound. The college (entered at New College Lane) can be visited free from 2 to 5 p.m. daily at term time (otherwise, from 11 a.m. to 5 p.m.). Admission is 50p (90¢).

OXFORD

KEY TO NUMBERED SIGHTS:

1. Somerville College
2. Keble College
3. Mansfield College
4. Ruskin College
5. St. John's College
6. Trinity College
7. Wadham College
8. Manchester College
9. St. Catherine's College
10. Worcester College
11. Balliol College
12. New College
13. Nutfield College
14. St. Peter's College
15. Jesus College
16. Exeter College
17. Lincoln College
18. Brasenose College
19. Hertford College
20. All Souls College
21. Queen's College
22. Magdalene College
23. Oriel College
24. University College
25. Corpus Christi College
26. Christ Church College
27. St. Hilda's College

Salter's River Thames Services

From mid-May until mid-September, Salter Brothers run daily passenger boat services on many reaches of the River Thames. Trips are to or from Oxford, Abingdon, Reading, Henley, Marlow, Cookham, Maidenhead, Windsor, Runnymede, and Staines. Combined outings from London can be made in conjunction with train or bus services. Full details can be obtained from **Salter Bros. Ltd.,** Folly Bridge, Oxford (tel. 0865/243421).

WHERE TO STAY

The accommodations in Oxford are limited, although the addition of motels on the outskirts has aided the plight of those who require modern amenities. Recently, some of the more stalwart candidates in the city center have been refurbished as well. In addition, motorists may want to consider some grand country houses on the outskirts of town, which offer the best living in Oxford if you don't mind commuting.

The **Oxford Information Centre,** St. Aldate's Chambers, St. Aldate's (tel. 0865/726871), operates a year-round room-booking service for a fee of £2 ($3.50) and a 7% refundable deposit. If you'd like to seek out lodgings on your own, the staff at the center will provide a list of accommodations for 30p (55¢), maps, and guidebooks, or you may try one of the following recommendations:

The Upper Bracket

Randolph Hotel, Beaumont Street, Oxford, Oxfordshire OX1 2LN (tel. 0865/247481), is a refurbished Gothic-Victorian hotel, dating from 1864. For more than a century it has been overlooking St. Giles, the Ashmolean Museum, and the Cornmarket. The lounges, although modernized, are still cavernous enough for dozens of separate conversational groupings, and the furnishings are contemporary. The hotel contains 109 rooms, all with private baths, direct-dial phones, radios, and color TV. Singles cost £69 ($120.75) per night, and doubles rent for £89 ($155.75). The hotel's Spires Restaurant presents the time-tested and the nouvelle in a high-ceilinged Victorian dining room. An à la carte dinner costs about £30 ($52.50) per person, while a set dinner goes for £18 ($31.50) and a set lunch for £14.50 ($25.40). Hours are daily from 12:30 to 2 p.m. and 7 to 10 p.m. There is also a coffeeshop with an entrance off the street. The hotel's Chapters bar has a tradition-laden atmosphere. The drink list offers everything from "textbook classics" to "epilogue."

The Medium-Priced Range

Cotswold Lodge Hotel, 66a Banbury Rd., Oxford, Oxfordshire OX2 6JP (tel. 0865/512121), is a 19th-century building that stands in the midst of several Victorian houses used for housing by Oxford University. The hotel is set on a wide avenue lined with stately trees, in a conservative area about a mile from the town center. The outside has Victorian detailing, but the interior has been renovated into functional modern. A newer wing from the 1970s contains additional and comfortable accommodations, each well scrubbed and very pleasant. In the older section, a scattering of units have flowered wallpaper and some Victoriana. With private bath and direct-dial phone, singles cost £68 ($119) to £78 ($136.50). Set-price lunches and dinners are served in the hotel's restaurant.

Welcome Lodge, Peartree Roundabout, Woodstock Road, Oxford, Oxfordshire OX2 8JZ (tel. 0865/54301), is suitable for motorists who want to be within easy reach of the university and shopping districts of Oxford, two miles away, yet set apart at the city edge. Easy to spot, near a large bus stop, the lodge invites with international flags fluttering in the breezes. Its lower-level bedrooms open onto private terraces. The furnishings are in the typical motel style, with compact, built-in necessities. Each of the rooms has a picture-window wall, a private bath with shower, TV, radio, individually controlled heating, and tea-making facilities. Room rates in a single are £50 ($87.50) to £55 ($96.25) daily and £57 ($99.75) to £62 ($108.50) in a double or twin. Special rooms for nonsmokers are also offered. A full English breakfast is included in the tariffs. On the grounds are a swimming pool (summer only), the Lodgekeepers Restaurant and bar, the Little Chef Grill, the Granary Self-Service Restaurant, a family shop, and a 24-hour garage.

Oxford Moat House, Godstow Road, Wolvercote Roundabout, Oxford, Oxfordshire OX2 8AL (tel. 0865/59933), one of the Queens Moat Houses Group, incorporates the principles of motel design, with an emphasis on spacious, glassed-in areas and streamlined bedrooms. Its position, at the northern edge of Oxford two miles away, is hidden from the traffic at the junction of the A40 and the A34. Although generally patronized by motorists, it can also be reached by bus. In a double or twin, with a full breakfast, you pay £84 ($147) daily for two, £69 ($120.75) in a single. Units contain private baths or showers, radios, color TVs, videos, phones, trouser presses, and hot beverage equipment. The Moat House has a swimming pool, squash courts, a whirlpool bath, a sauna, a solarium, a hairdressing and beauty salon, and a snooker room.

Eastgate Hotel, Merton Street, The High, Oxford, Oxfordshire OX1 4BE (tel. 0865/248244), stands opposite the ancient Examination Halls and lies within walking distance of Oxford colleges and the city center. Recently refurbished, the Eastgate offers modern facilities while retaining somewhat the atmosphere of an English country house. All rooms have baths, direct-dial phones, color TV, radios, and tea/coffee-makers. Singles cost from £60 ($105) daily, and twins or doubles go from £75 ($131.25). Prices include VAT and service. The Ruskin Restaurant offers a selection of roasts and traditional English "fayre," complemented by a choice of wines. A three-course table d'hôte meal is modestly priced at £10.50 ($18.40).

Royal Oxford Hotel, Park End Street, Oxford, Oxfordshire OX1 1HR (tel. 0865/248432), is an oldish establishment given a new lease on life by a renovation of its interior. Near Oxford Station, about a ten-minute walk from the center of the city, it is a comfortable and convenient place at which to stay. Of its 25 bedrooms, 12 have private bath, and all have color TV, phone, and radio. A bathless single goes for £32 ($56) daily, a single with bath costing £45 ($78.75). Doubles or twins rent for £43 ($75.25) bathless, £55 ($96.25) with bath. Prices include service and VAT. The bedrooms are well kept, with modern, compact furnishings. Ask about "weekend breaks" when booking.

The Budget Range

Old Parsonage Hotel, 3 Banbury Rd., Oxford, Oxfordshire OX2 6NN (tel. 0865/310210), is so old it looks like an extension of one of the ancient colleges. Originally a 13th-century hospital named Bethleen, it was restored in the early 17th century. Near St. Giles Church, it is set back from the street behind a low stone wall and sheltered by surrounding trees and shrubbery. However, most of the rooms are in a residential wing that is more institutional in character. The owners charge from £25 ($43.75) per person nightly for B&B in a single, from £38 ($66.50) in a twin or double. Should you want a private shower, the price is increased to £48 ($84) for two persons. Some of the large front rooms in the older part, with leaded-glass windows, are set aside for travelers. You have breakfast in a pleasant dining room, overlooking the garden. A licensed restaurant and bar are on the premises.

Belmont Guest House, 182 Woodstock Rd., Oxford, Oxfordshire OX2 7NG (tel. 0865/53698), is on a tree-lined avenue in the residential part of Oxford, about one mile from the city center. All rooms have central heating, hot and cold running water, and tea/coffee-makers. A few have private showers. Most rooms can be used as either doubles, twins, or family rooms. The owners, Mr. and Mrs. J. Deadman, charge from £13 ($22.75) per person daily for B&B.

LIVING ON THE OUTSKIRTS

A moated stone edifice, **Weston Manor,** Weston-on-the-Green, Oxfordshire OX6 8QL (tel. 0869/50621), is only eight miles from Oxford, on the A43 Oxford–Northampton road, ideal as a center for touring the district (Blenheim Palace is only five miles away). The manor, owned and run by the Osborn family, is rooted in the 11th century; portions of the present building date from the 14th and 16th centuries, with later additions in Victoria's day. Although long owned by noblemen, the estate was an abbey until they were abolished by Henry VIII. Of course, there are ghosts, such as Mad Maude, the naughty nun who was burned at the stake for her "indecent and immoral" behavior. She returns to haunt the Oak Bedrooms. Prince Rupert, son of Charles II, hid from Cromwell's soldiers in one of the fireplaces, eventually escaping in drag as the "maiden of the milk bucket."

As you enter the driveway, you pass two elm trees, dating back to 1672, and proceed into a formal car-park area. The reception lounge is furnished with antiques, dominated by a Tudor fireplace and a long refectory table. The various lounges have fine old pieces. Most of the bedrooms are spacious, furnished with antiques (often four-posters), old dressing tables, and chests. The cost of staying here is from £62.50 ($109.40) daily in a single, from £79.50 ($139.15) in a double. Two persons in a room with a four-poster pay £95 ($166.25). Tariffs include an English breakfast and VAT. In the Great Hall, one of the most beautiful dining rooms in England, you'll be served your meals. It's like a chapel, with an open-rafter and beamed ceiling, the lower portion solidly paneled with a rare example of linenfold. There's a minstrels' gallery and a large wrought-iron chandelier. The English food is first rate. À la carte meals average £16 ($28), and the big Sunday lunch costs £12.50 ($21.90). In warm weather, you can enjoy the open-air swimming pool surrounded by gardens.

Studley Priory Hotel, Horton-cum-Studley, Oxfordshire OX9 1AZ (tel. 086735/203), may be remembered by those who saw *A Man for All Seasons.* The former Benedictine priory, a hotel since 1961, was used for background shots for the private residence of Sir Thomas More. It is a stunning example of Elizabethan architecture, although it originally dates from the 12th century. Set in 13 acres of wooded grounds and lived in for around 300 years by the Croke family, the manor, only seven miles from Oxford, is built of stone in the manorial style, with large halls and long bedroom wings and gable with mullioned windows. The rooms are large and the furnishings tasteful. Guests are received for £55 ($96.25) daily in a single, £55 ($96.25) to £100 ($175) in a double. All the rooms have private baths. Even if you're not staying over, you may want to visit for lunch or dinner, with a four-course, rather sophisticated meal averaging around £20 ($35). Getting here is a bit complicated—so be armed with a good map when you strike out from Oxford.

WHERE TO DINE

A dining and lodging choice supreme, **Le Manoir aux Quat' Saisons,** Great Milton, Oxfordshire OX9 7PD (tel. 08446/278881), 12 miles southeast of Oxford, enjoys a reputation for offering the finest cuisine in the Midlands. The gray and honey-colored stones of this manor house were originally assembled by a Norman nobleman in the early 1300s. In this way, the property established a connection with France, which the Gallic owner and chef, Raymond Blanc, masterfully continues to this day. His reputation for comfort and cuisine attracts guests from as far away as London—gastronomes who regard the one-hour trek as a delicious excuse for a day in the country. The gabled house that rises today from a mature garden and lawns was built in the 1500s and improved and enlarged in 1908. An outdoor swimming pool, still in use, was added much later. Inside, ten luxurious rooms, each decorated boudoir-style with lots of flowery draperies, ruffled canopies, radio, color TV, springtime colors, and high-quality antique reproductions, cost £110 ($192.50) to £250 ($437.50) daily, double occupancy.

The main focus of the establishment is a pair of beamed-ceiling dining rooms whose mullioned windows offer pleasant views of the garden. You can enjoy such specialties as a soup of Cornish lobster with cumin, a mousse of asparagus with chervil sauce, zucchini flowers stuffed with a sabayon of wild mushrooms, veal cutlet with truffles, breast of wild duck with pear and apples, and scallops poached with herbs. A menu du jour costs £19.50 ($34.15), £25.50 ($44.65) on Saturday. A menu gourmand is £44 ($77). You can also order à la carte. Coffee is served beside the fire in the comfortable lounge after your meal. Reservations are a necessity. If you call, an employee will guide you with directions. Exit from the artery connecting London with Oxford (the M40) at exit 7. Head along the A329 in the direction of Wallingford, Thame, and Milton Common. Look carefully for signs about a mile later directing you to the manor. It is closed all day Monday and at lunchtime on Tuesday. Otherwise, lunch is offered from 12:15 to 2:30 p.m. and dinner from 7:15 to 10:30 p.m.

Restaurant Elizabeth, 84 St. Aldate's (tel. 0865/242230), is an intimate and special restaurant that (in spite of its name) owes the inspiration of its cuisine to the continent, notably Spain, France, and Greece. Under the watchful eye of Antonio Lopez, it attracts Oxonians who appreciate good food served in an inviting atmosphere. For appetizers, try either the ttoro (a Basque fish soup served with aïoli), or avgolemono (the Greek national soup—chicken bouillon laced with a beaten egg and lemon juice). Favorite main dishes that I highly recommend include trout stuffed with seafood mousse and coq au vin. Including wine and coffee, plus all the extras, the cost of a dinner is about £28 ($49) per person. Wine by the liter, both bourgogne and bordeaux, is available. The restaurant is open for lunch, costing about £12 ($21), from 12:30 to 2:30 p.m., and for dinner from 6:30 to 11 p.m. every day except Monday. Sunday dinner is from 7 to 10:30 p.m.

La Sorbonne, 130A High St. (tel. 0865/241320), in a 17th-century building, is tucked away on a narrow lane off The High, one minute's walk from Carfax. True to its name, it provides exceptional French meals and has done so since 1966. Diners have included Dame Margot Fonteyn, Paul McCartney, and the Princess of Wales. A good beginning is the chef's special, moules marinières, offered from October to March only. An alternative suggestion is escargots bourguignon. André Chavagnon, the chef de cuisine and proprietor, offers not only the usual French dishes, but the following specialties as well: jugged hare, wild duck, and tarragon-flavored chicken suprême. A soufflé for two is a specialty. Mr. Chavagnon says: "Soufflés are expensive, but they require a lot of care and attention. When we tried to charge less, everybody wanted one and we couldn't cope." Expect to pay, on an average, about £23 ($40.25) per head. The restaurant is open from noon to 2:30 p.m. and 7 to 11 p.m. seven days a week.

Downstairs in the Croûte Room, you can eat for about £12 ($21), dining on such meals as, for example, onion soup, a dish of the day including vegetables and potatoes, crème caramel, coffee, and a glass of wine. Hours are the same as for the upstairs restaurant.

Saraceno, 15 Magdalen St. (tel. 0865/249171), is rather unobtrusive, hidden around the corner from the Randolph Hotel and opposite St. Mary Magdalen Church. It's in the basement so only the door and a small sign announce its presence. The kitchen is separated from the dining room by vast red-glass panes, behind which a puppet show of figures dance and weave among the pots and pans. Saraceno is, after all, an Italian restaurant, and all the usual pasta dishes are available with just the right sauces. After ordering one, you might settle later for scaloppine with sage and olives or rainbow trout with almonds. Appetizers include scrambled eggs with caviar and smoked mackerel. They have a very special dish of quail served in a rich wine sauce with plain cooked vegetables or salad. With ample portions of the Italian house wine, a meal will cost about £16 ($28) to £22 ($38.50) per person, including a creamy dessert from the trolley. The restaurant is open for lunch from 12:30 to 2:30 p.m. and for dinner from 7 to 11:30 p.m.; closed Sunday.

15 North Parade, at (you guessed it) 15 North Parade (tel. 0865/513773), continues to win respect and praise from its patrons as the cookery here is first rate. Wicker chairs, subtle lighting, and plenty of photos provide the proper background for the presentation of the ever-changing cuisine. You might begin with a fish soup (similar to what you'd be served in Nice), then follow with roast guinea fowl in a sherry sauce. Care also goes into the vegetables, such as French beans, which are fresh and cooked crisp. Meals are served from noon to 2 p.m. and 7 to 10:30 p.m. Monday to Saturday. A set lunch is a bargain at £9.75 ($17.05), but count on spending £26 ($45.50) and up for dinner. Wines, which are extra, are reasonably priced for the most part.

Michel's Brasserie, 10 Little Clarendon (tel. 0865/52142), is a cherished little Gallic brasserie in a section of Oxford that has increasingly become an after-dark rendezvous spot. The preparation of the food, which is done with style, and the freshness of the ingredients, along with the alert attention from the staff have combined to make this one a winner. The menu changes frequently, but typical dishes are likely to include fresh river trout, lamb kidneys in a mustard sauce, and breast of chicken in a tarragon sauce. A three-course lunch goes for £9.75 ($17.05), with a set dinner of three courses costing £13.95 ($24.40). From clusters of items on the menu, you can select from a choice of eight appetizers, ten main courses, and eight desserts. The brasserie is open daily from noon to 2:30 p.m. and 7 to 11 p.m. (Sunday lunch begins at 12:30 p.m.).

THE SPECIAL PUBS OF OXFORD

A short block from the High, overlooking the north side of Christ Church College, **Bear Inn,** Alfred Street (tel. 0865/244680), is an Oxford tradition. It's the village pub. Its swinging inn sign depicts the bear and ragged staff, old insignia of the earls of Warwick, who were among the early patrons. Built in the 13th century, the inn has been known to many famous people who have lived and studied at Oxford. Over the years it's been mentioned time and time again in English literature.

The Bear has served a useful purpose in breaking down social barriers, bringing a wide variety of people together in a relaxed and friendly way. You might talk with a rajah from India, a university don, a titled gentleman—and the latest in a line of owners that goes back more than 700 years. Some former owners developed an astonishing habit: clipping neckties. Around the lounge bar you'll see thousands of the remains of ties, which have been labeled with their owners' names. For those of you who want to leave a bit of yourself, a thin strip of the bottom of your tie will be cut off (with your permission, of course) with a huge pair of ceremonial scissors. Then you, as the donor, will be given a free drink on the house. After this initiation, you may want to join in some of the informal songfests of the undergraduates. The shelves behind the bar are stacked and piled with items to nibble on: cheese, crisp rolls, cold meats, flans. Light meals cost from £3.50 ($6.15). Hours are from 11 a.m. to 2:30 p.m. and 5:30 to 11 p.m. Monday to Saturday, from noon to 3 p.m. and 7 to 10:30 p.m. Sunday.

Trout Inn, 195 Godstow Rd., near Wolvercote (tel. 0865/54485), lies on the outskirts of Oxford. Hidden away from visitors and townspeople, the Trout is a private world where you can get ale and beer—and top-notch meals. Have your drink in one of the historic rooms, with their settles, brass, and old prints, or go out in sunny weather to sit on a stone wall. On the grounds are peacocks, as well as ducks, swans, and herons that live in and around the river and an adjacent weir pool, who will join with a shoal of chubb fish in turning up for a free feast if you're handing out crumbs. Take an arched stone bridge, stone terraces, architecture with wildly pitched roofs and gables, add the Thames River, and you have the Trout. The Stable Bar, the original 12th-century part, complements the inn's relatively new 16th-century bars. Daily specials are featured, and there is an excellent cold snack bar, with prices ranging from £1.50 ($2.65) to £4.85 ($8.50), the charge for a smoked salmon salad. Hot meals are served all day in the restaurant. You can dine well for £4.50 ($7.80), up to £8.15 ($14.25), the latter price buying a 16-ounce T-bone steak. Salads are served in summer and grills in winter. The Trout is open from 11 a.m. to 2:30 p.m. and 6 to 11 p.m. Monday to Saturday and from noon to 2 p.m. and 7 to 10:30 p.m. Sunday. If you don't have a car, take bus 520 or 521 to Wolvercote, then walk to the pub. On your way there and back, look for the view of Oxford from the bridge.

A SHOPPING NOTE

An arcade of first-class shops and boutiques, the **Golden Cross** lies between Cornmarket Street and the Covered Market (or between High Street and Market Street). Parts of the arcade date from the 12th century. Many buildings remain from the medieval era, along with some 15th and 17th century structures. The market also has a reputation as the Covent Garden of Oxford, where live entertainment takes place on Saturday morning in summer. In the arcade shops you'll find a wide selection of merchandise, including handmade Belgian chocolates, specialty gifts, clothing for both women and men, and luxury leather goods.

EATING AND DRINKING NEAR OXFORD

Seven miles along the A420 Oxford/Swindon/West Country road, the **White Hart,** Fyfield (tel. 0865/390585), is high on the list of Oxford students who want to celebrate by taking their friends to a romantic inn—once the Fyfield Chantry—for a superb dinner. It's a public house, dating from the early 15th century, and owned since 1580 by St. John's College (although the present building is leased). In the 1960s the college renovated the inn, successfully restoring its old-world charm. It was once the home of a chantry priest and five almsmen until it was dissolved under Henry VIII. What was the lower chamber for the priest has now been transformed into a raftered dining room; and the ancient kitchen is the beamed lounge bar. The menu consists of house specialties, plus the dishes of the day. At lunchtime and in the evening, a wide range of bar snacks is offered. From the à la carte menu, you can order meals ranging in price from £12 ($21). The wines, an excellent selection, are extra. Specialties of the White Hart include traditional English food, with emphasis on game. The restaurant is open daily except Sunday, and reservations are advised. Hours are 10:30 a.m. to 2:30 p.m. and 6 to 11 p.m.

DIDCOT

A little town ten miles south of Oxford near the Berkshire border, east of the A34, Didcot is served by trains from Paddington Station in London. Didcot Parkway is a principal intercity station, with good connections to Oxford, Bristol, Reading, and the south coast. Didcot Halt is a typical small country station.

For the railway buff, this place is paradise, the home of the **Didcot Railway Centre** (tel. 0235/817200). In the engine sheds are steam locomotives, and on "steaming days" you can roll gently along in a Great Western Railway train running on a re-creation of Brunel's original broad-gauge Great Western track. In season, various other preserved railways in the country send visiting locomotives. The center is open on Saturday, Sunday, and bank holidays from 11 a.m. to 5 p.m. March to mid-December and daily from Easter to the beginning of September. Admission charges are £2 ($3.50) to £3.50 ($6.15), depending on the event.

6. Woodstock (Blenheim Palace)

The small country town of Woodstock, the birthplace in 1330 of the Black Prince, ill-fated son of King Edward III, lies on the edge of the Cotswolds. Some of the stone houses here were constructed when Woodstock was the site of a royal palace, which had so suffered the ravages of time that its remains were demolished when

Blenheim Palace was built. Woodstock was once the seat of a flourishing glove industry.

Some eight miles north of Oxford on the A34 road to Stratford-upon-Avon, Woodstock's main claim to fame today is—

BLENHEIM PALACE

This extravagant baroque palace regards itself as England's answer to Versailles. Blenheim is the home of the 11th Duke of Marlborough, a descendant of the first Duke of Marlborough (John Churchill), an on-again, off-again favorite of Queen Anne's. In his day (1650–1722) the first duke became the supreme military figure in Europe. Fighting on the Danube near a village named Blenheim, Churchill defeated the forces of Louis XIV. The lavish palace of Blenheim was built for the duke as a gift from the queen. It was designed by Sir John Vanbrugh, who was also the architect of Castle Howard. Landscaping was carried out by Capability Brown.

The palace is loaded with riches: antiques, porcelain, oil paintings, tapestries, and chinoiserie. But more North Americans know Blenheim as the birthplace of Sir Winston Churchill. His birthroom forms part of the palace tour, as does the Churchill exhibition, four rooms of letters, books, photographs, and other Churchilliana. Today the former prime minister lies buried in Bladon Churchyard, near the palace.

Blenheim Palace is open every day from mid-March to October, inclusive, from 10:30 a.m. to 5:30 p.m. The last admittance to the palace is at 4:30 p.m. The admission fee is £4.50 ($7.90) for adults, £2.20 ($3.85) for children.

In the park is the Blenheim Butterfly and Plant Centre. The complex contains a Butterfly House containing tropical moths and butterflies in free flight in a virtually natural habitat, an Adventure Play Area, a Garden Café, a gift shop, and a shop for plants and gardening requirements. The palace is at Woodstock, eight miles north of Oxford on the A34 road to Stratford-upon-Avon. From Oxford, there is a "Blenheim Palace and Historic Woodstock" open-top bus, which runs every 70 minutes from Beaumont Street. Tickets, which include the palace tour, may be purchased on the bus or, including rail travel, at any main-line railway station. For information, telephone 0993/811325.

FOOD AND LODGING IN WOODSTOCK

An ancient coaching inn, the **Bear Hotel,** Park Street, Woodstock, Oxfordshire OX7 1SZ (tel. 0993/811511), is reputed to be one of the six oldest such caravanseries in England, dating from the 16th century. The half-stone structure stands in the center of Woodstock, with its courtyard now being used for car parking rather than the rumbling coaches of old. Look for the sign in front with the picture of a huge brown bear. History surrounds you in the 45-bedroom hotel, even such relatively recent history as the hiding away here of Richard Burton and Elizabeth Taylor during one of their marriages. They stayed in the Marlborough suite, an attractively decorated sitting room with a mini-bar, plus a bedroom and bath. One of the chambers of the hotel is haunted, legend says. Modern amenities are combined with antiques in the bedrooms, which have hairdryers and trouser presses, as well as bathrooms in 41 of the units, radios, color TVs, and phones. The charge is from £65 ($113.75) daily in a single, from £105 ($183.75) in a double. Blazing hearth fires are found throughout the hotel when the days and nights are cool. You can relax in the big, black-beamed bar or the comfortable lounge for drinks, and enjoy traditional dishes in the dining room. Meals range in price from £16 ($28) to £17.50 ($30.65).

There is also the beautifully furnished **Feathers,** Market Street, Woodstock, Oxfordshire OX7 1SX (tel. 0993/812291), a red-brick building where Gordon Campbell-Gray receives guests for his 15 individually decorated bedrooms, all of which have a complete bath.

Along with antiques and pictures, the units also are equipped with color TV and direct-dial phone. Singles in this excellent hotel cost from £48 ($84) daily, and doubles, £98 ($171.50). The two lounges have wood fires. One boasts fine china and valuable old books; the other is oak-paneled with sturdy beams. A multitude of stuffed birds from which the house gets its name adorn the bar, from which you can go into the delightful garden in the courtyard. The food at Feathers is of high quality, served in the elegant dining room. Whether you are here for lunch, from 12:30 to 2:15 p.m., or for a candlelit dinner, 7:30 to 9:45 p.m., you're sure to enjoy the imaginative, well-prepared food, either simple dishes or such specialties as hot lobster soufflé, or English game pie. An exceptionally good set lunch costs £12.50 ($21.90), while complete à la carte dinners go for £18 ($31.50) and up. In summer, you can have a light lunch or afternoon tea in the courtyard garden.

7. Hertfordshire

Like a giant jellyfish, the frontier of Greater London spills over into this county, once described by Charles Lamb as "hearty, homely, loving Hertfordshire." This fertile land lies northwest of London and supplies much of that city's food, although industry has crept in. Hertfordshire is sometimes called "the market basket of England."

Its most important tourist attraction, which is usually visited on a day trip from London, is:

HATFIELD HOUSE

One of the chief attractions of Hertfordshire, and one of the greatest of all English country houses, Hatfield House (tel. 07072/62055) is just 21 miles north of London on the A1, close to the M1. To build what is now the E-shaped Hatfield House, the old Tudor palace at Hatfield was mostly demolished. The Banqueting Hall, however, remains.

Hatfield was much a part of the lives of both Henry VIII and his daughter, Elizabeth I. In the old palace, built in the 15th century, Elizabeth romped and played as a child. Although Henry was married to her mother, Anne Boleyn, at the time of Elizabeth's birth, the marriage was later nullified (Anne lost her head and Elizabeth her legitimacy). Henry also used to stash away his oldest daughter, Mary Tudor, at Hatfield. But when Mary became Queen of England, and set about earning the dubious distinction of "Bloody Mary," she found Elizabeth a problem. For a while she kept her in the Tower of London, but she eventually let her return to Hatfield (Elizabeth's loyalty to Catholicism was seriously doubted). In 1558, while at Hatfield, Elizabeth learned of her ascension to the throne of England.

The Jacobean house that exists today contains much antique furniture, tapestries, and paintings as well as three much-reproduced portraits, including the ermine and rainbow portraits of Elizabeth I. The Great Hall is suitably medieval, complete with a minstrel's gallery. One of the rarest exhibits is a pair of silk stockings, said to have been worn by Elizabeth herself, the first lady in England to don such apparel. The park and the gardens are also worth exploring. The Riding School and Palace Stables contain an interesting vehicle exhibition and the National (North) Collection of Model Soldiers.

Hatfield is usually open from March 25 to the second Sunday in October daily, except on Monday and Good Friday, from noon to 5 p.m. (on Sunday, from 1 to 5 p.m., and on bank holiday Mondays from 11 a.m. to 5 p.m.). Admission is £3.20 ($5.60) for adults, £2.25 ($3.95) for children. The house is across from the station in Hatfield. From London, take Green Line coach 794 or 797, or the fast trains from King's Cross. Luncheons and teas are available in the converted coach house in the Old Palace yard.

Elizabethan banquets are staged on Tuesday, Thursday, Friday, and Saturday, with much gaiety and music. Guests are invited to drink in an anteroom, then join the long tables for a feast of five courses with continuous entertainment from a group of Elizabethan players, minstrels, and jesters. Wine is included in the cost of the meal, but you're expected to pay for your before-dinner drinks yourself. The best way to get there from London for the feast is to book a coach tour for an inclusive fee starting at £29.50 ($51.65). The Evan Evans agency has tours leaving from Russell Square or even from 41 Tottenham Court Rd. The coach returns to London after midnight. If you get there under your own steam, the cost is £19.50 ($31.15) on Tuesday, Thursday, and Friday, and £20.50 ($35.90) on Saturday. For reservations, telephone 07072/62055.

HERTFORD

This old Saxon city is the county town, containing many fine examples of domestic architecture, some of which date from the 16th century. Hertford is reached via the A1 or A10 from London. Samuel Stone, founder of Hartford, Connecticut, was born here. The town's Norman castle has long been in ruins, although part of the still-standing keep dates from the 16th century.

For food and lodging, try the **Salisbury Arms Hotel,** Fore Street, Hertford, Hertfordshire SG14 1BZ (tel. 0992/583091), which has been called "always Hertford's principal inn." For 400 years it's been feeding and providing lodgings to wayfarers, or giving a hot grog to the coachman, a stable for his horses. Although the stables have long given way to a car park, a sense of history still prevails. In the cellar is medieval masonry pre-dating the 16th-century structure around it. Cromwell is said to have lodged here, and both Royalists and Roundheads have mounted the Jacobean staircase. Bedrooms now spill over into a modern extension. All have private baths, TV, phones, and tea/coffee-makers. Singles cost £40.50 ($70.90) daily, with doubles or twins renting for £44.50 ($77.90) to £58 ($101.50). On Friday and Saturday, prices are lowered to £29.50 ($51.65) per night in a single, £32.50 ($56.90) to £45 ($78.75) in a double or twin. Good, wholesome English "fayre" is provided. The dining room is paneled and intimately partitioned. There is, as well, a well-stocked cellar. Dinners are from £12 ($21).

FABDENS PARK

Norman Swallow, artist turned chef/restaurateur, has created **Fabdens Park,** Cold Christmas, near Ware, Hertfordshire SG12 0UE (tel. 0920/463484), 20 miles north of London. This small hotel and restaurant in a lovely 15th-century home has a small, opulent dining room with only five tables. It is open for dinner only from 7 to 10:30 p.m. Tuesday to Saturday, with emphasis on top-quality cuisine. Mr. Swallow prepares food with care and flair, traveling to London markets daily to secure the best produce possible. He says he cooks the kind of food he would choose for himself, classical English and French cuisine mainly. You can dine at leisure, and then take coffee in one of the three sitting rooms. A complete meal costs £30 ($52.50) to £35 ($61.25) per person. Reservations are essential. There are also four suites for rent, all offering the services you would find in a large deluxe hotel. Each unit has a bedroom, bath, and sitting room and is decorated in an individual, romantic style. Each also has a direct-dial phone, color TV, and other amenities, including a full English or a continental breakfast. Butler and maid service is provided all day and most of the night, and Mr. Swallow is on hand to take a personal interest in his guests' well-being. Prices are from £65 ($113.75) daily in a double.

ST. ALBANS

This cathedral city, just 21 miles northeast of London, dates back 2,000 years. It was named after a Roman soldier, the first Christian martyr in England. Don't ask a resident to show you to the **Cathedral of St. Albans.** Here it's still known as "The Abbey," even though Henry VIII dissolved it as such in 1539. Construction on the cathedral was launched in 1077, making it one of the early Norman churches of England. The bricks, especially visible in the tower, came from the old Roman city of Verulamium at the foot of the hill. The nave and west front date from 1235.

The new Chapter House, the first modern building beside a great medieval cathedral in the country, which also serves as a pilgrim/visitor center, was opened by the Queen in 1982.

The **Verulamium Museum** at St. Michael's (tel. 0727/54659) stands on the site of the Roman city. Here you'll view some of the finest Roman mosaics in Britain. Part of the Roman town wall, a hypocaust, and houses and shops are still visible. Visit in summer from 10 a.m. to 5:30 p.m. Monday to Saturday (on Sunday from 2 to 5:30 p.m.), and in winter from 10 a.m. to 4 p.m. Monday to Saturday, 2 to 4 p.m. on Sunday, paying £1 ($1.75) for adults, 50p (90¢) for children and students.

The **Clock Tower** at Market Place was built in 1402, standing 77 feet high, a total of five floors. It is open from Easter to mid-September on Saturday and Sunday from 10:30 a.m. to 5 p.m.

From St. Albans you can visit **Gorhambury,** a classic-style mansion built in 1777, containing 16th-century enameled glass and historic portraits. It's open, May to September, only on Thursday (2 to 5 p.m.), charging adults £2 ($3.50) for admission; children pay £1 ($1.75). The location is 2½ miles west of St. Albans near the A5.

On the outskirts, the **Mosquito Aircraft Museum,** the oldest aircraft museum in Britain, lies on the grounds of Salisbury Hall, just off the main M25 London–St. Albans road (turn off at junction 22) at London Colney, about five miles south of St. Albans. The museum is on the B556. The hall is no longer open to the public, but the museum can be visited from Easter Sunday to the end of October on Sunday and bank holidays from 10:30 a.m. to 5:30 p.m.; on Thursday from July to the end of September from 2 to 5:30 p.m. Displayed is the prototype of the de Havilland "Mosquito" aircraft, which was designed and built at Salisbury Hall in World War II, plus 18 other de Havilland aircraft, memorabilia, and relics. Admission is £1 ($1.75) for adults, 40p (70¢) for children. For more information, telephone 0727/22051.

Food and Lodging

St. Michael's Manor Hotel, Fishpool Street, St. Albans, Hertfordshire AL3 4RY (tel. 0727/64444), stands in five acres of landscaped gardens, with a private lake, about a ten-minute walk from the heart of St. Albans. At its core is an original manor house dating from the 16th century. To the original structure a William and Mary bow-fronted center section has been added, along with a Georgian-style extension. The grounds of the hotel contain such trees as cedars of Lebanon, hornbeam, and Wellingtonia, and all 26 attractively furnished bedrooms are named after the trees in the garden. The Lilac honeymoon suite, complete with a four-poster bed and lilac decor, is most impressive, as are the other three four-poster accommodations. All the bedrooms have baths or showers. A single costs £49.50 ($86.65); doubles or twins, £75 ($131.25). Prices include a full English breakfast and VAT. Special bed-and-breakfast terms are offered on weekends. All rooms have direct-dial phone, color TV, and radio. A well-prepared international menu is presented for both luncheon and dinner to residents and nonresidents. A lunchtime table d'hôte meal with coffee costs £12.50 ($21.90), and a "chef recommends" dinner goes for £15 ($26.25).

Sopwell House, Cottonmill Lane, St. Albans, Hertfordshire AL1 2HQ (tel. 0727/64477), affiliated with the Best Western reservation system, is a private mansion from the days of George III. Over the years it has known a number of royal personages as guests. Now converted into a hotel of superb taste and comfort, it occupies nearly a dozen Hertfordshire acres. Some guests in the 32 attractively furnished bedrooms, each with private bath, come here to play golf at the neighboring Verulam course, home of the Ryder Cup. Many visitors prefer to anchor in here instead of London, so that they can explore some of the grand mansions previewed in this chapter, notably Hatfield House of Elizabeth I fame and Woburn Abbey. Amenities in the bedrooms include direct-dial phone, trouser press, hairdryer, and beverage-making equipment. B&B costs from £63 ($110.25) daily in a single, rising to £78 ($136.50) in a double, with set dinners going for £15 ($26.25). The public rooms in the grand 18th-century style are the finest in St. Albans, including the Park Room restaurant with a conservatory opening onto a terrace and the gardens. The location is off A1018, within easy access to M1, M10, A1, and M25, an easy commute from London.

SHAW'S CORNER

In the village of **Ayot St. Lawrence,** three miles northwest of Welwyn, stands the home where George Bernard Shaw lived from 1906 to 1950. The house is practically as he left it at his death. In the hall, for example, his hats are still hanging, as if ready for him to don one. His personal mementos are in his study, drawing room, dining room, and writing hut. The kitchen and scullery are also open to view as well as some first floor rooms on some days. The house is open from 2 to 6 p.m. Wednesday to Saturday April to the end of October, from noon to 6 p.m. on Sunday and bank holiday Mondays; closed Good Friday. Admission is £1.80 ($3.15) for adults, 90p ($1.60) for children. For more information, phone 0438/820307.

---

8. Buckinghamshire

This is a leafy county, lying north of the Thames and somewhat to the west of London. Its identifying marks are the wide Vale of Aylesbury, with its sprawling fields and tiny villages, and the long chalk range of the Chilterns. Going south from the range, you see what is left of a once-great beech forest.

AYLESBURY

The county town of Buckingham, Aylesbury has retained much of its ancient character, especially around the town center with its narrow Tudor alleyways as well as several 17th-century houses. The parish church, St. Mary's, dates from the 13th century and has an unusual spirelet. A short walk from the church takes you to Hickman's Almshouses and the Prebendal Houses, both from the 17th century.

Less than 40 miles from London, Aylesbury is a market town, with Wednesday and Saturday markets held in Friars Square. Gourmets still speak of the succulent Aylesbury ducks and ducklings, a prize-winning dish on any table, although fowls bearing that name are usually raised elsewhere these days.

Six miles northwest of Aylesbury on the Bicester road (A41), **Waddesdon Manor** contains an outstanding collection of French royal decorative art of the 17th and 18th centuries, including furniture, Sèvres porcelain, and Savonnerie carpets. Among the paintings are portraits by Reynolds, Gainsborough, and Romney. The manor was built in the late 19th century for Baron Ferdinand de Rothschild and stands in 150 acres of grounds with rare trees, an aviary, and a herd of Sika deer. Visiting times are from the end of March until the middle of October, Wednesday to Sunday from 1 to 5 p.m. It costs £3 ($5.25) to enter the house, grounds, and aviary. For information, apply to the administrator, Aylesbury (tel. 0296/651282).

Food and Lodging

The Bell, Market Square, Aylesbury, Buckinghamshire HP20 1TX (tel. 0296/89835), adjacent to the county hall of Aylesbury, is the best inn in town. An old coaching house, it sits in the center of this market town. The 17 bedrooms all have private baths and showers, color TVs, radios, phones, and hot beverage facilities. Singles rent for £52 ($91) daily, and doubles go for £63 ($110.25). The cuisine offered here is traditional English cooking. The public bar is cozy with beams and a log fire in cool weather. Cold and hot snacks are available weekdays in the Market Bar. Don't confuse this Bell in the center of town with the Bell Inn at Aston Clinton, just outside Aylesbury, recommended below.

The best restaurant in Aylesbury is **Peebles**, Pebble Lane (tel. 0296/86622), which is run by Jeremy Blake O'Connor, the capable chef. Part of his success is based on his clever use of fresh ingredients, which are subtly flavored and cooked, then attractively presented. The low-ceilinged, wooden beamed restaurant is reached by walking up a cobblestone-paved lane. There is very limited seating in either of the two dining rooms, one with a Victorian stove, so reservations are imperative. A set luncheon goes for £11.50 ($20.15), and dinner costs from £20 ($35) per person. Hours are from noon to 2:15 p.m. and 7 to 11 p.m. On Sunday, lunch is from 12:30 to 3 p.m. The restaurant is closed Monday and for dinner Sunday.

On the Outskirts
The Bell Inn, Aston Clinton, Buckinghamshire HP22 5HP (tel. 0296/ 630252), a *Relais & Chateaux* since 1955, is a former coaching inn believed to have been built at the end of the 18th century. Under the guidance of the Harris family, the inn has won extraordinary acclaim for its cuisine. Advertised by a large bell instead of an inn sign, it stands unobtrusively by the road 40 miles from London and four miles from Aylesbury. It's a mossy brick structure, with crisp white windows and a Georgian portico. Inside, antiques are used. The dining room, with its Four Seasons murals, is cooly elegant, with polished wood and sparkling glass and silver. You select your meal in a large stone-floored bar while having a drink. Lunch or dinner is a special event. For a beginning, try the "smokies," then go on to the civet de homard or gâteau de gibier or some such dish. The price of a typical meal is about £35 ($61.25), including half a bottle of the house wine. There are six bedrooms in the original inn, all with private bath, refrigerator, and mini-bar, and all tastefully decorated. Converted from a stable block are 15 more comfortable rooms, arranged around a courtyard across a narrow road from the inn. Such thoughtful touches have been added as bathrobes, bubble-bath powder, shampoo, whatever, all included in the luxuriously appointed baths. Room rates range from £69 ($120.75) to £84 ($147) daily in a single, from £83 ($145.25) to £120 ($210) for a double, including a continental breakfast, VAT, and service. A log fire in the lounge makes for a warm welcome to this old coaching inn.

CLIVEDEN
The former home of Nancy, Lady Astor, now a National Trust property, has been turned into a fabulous deluxe hotel (see below). But the grounds and some of the sumptuously decorated rooms are on view to the public at certain times, if you can't afford to stay here. The garden features a rose garden, a magnificent parterre, and an amphitheater where "Rule Britannia" was played for the first time. There are 375 acres of garden and woodland to explore. The house is open from the first of April to October only on Thursday and Sunday from 3 to 6 p.m. The grounds are open March to December daily from 11 a.m. to 6 p.m. or sunset if earlier. Admission to the grounds is £2.40 ($4.20); to the house, 80p ($1.40). Cliveden is 20 miles west of London, lying two miles north of Taplow on the B476, off the A40.

Cliveden House, Cliveden, Taplow, Maidenhead, Berkshire SL6 0JB (tel. 06286/68561). Among the dozens of country-house hotels that have opened their antique-filled premises, none inspired such acclaim in England as Cliveden. Its stratospherically expensive tariffs haven't daunted the hosts of hotel connoisseurs who pay dearly for a glimpse into the lifestyle once maintained by the Astors. The house stands on a man-made terrace of mature gardens high above the Thames, about a 20-minute drive from Heathrow Airport. The estate's original mansion as well as the vast sweep of the lawns was created by William Winde in 1666 for the second Duke of Buckingham. Later, the father of King George III reared his sons here during moments of refuge from the politics of London. After a fire in 1795, the house was redesigned by Sir Charles Barry, the architect of the Houses of Parliament, into its present gracefully symmetrical form. A soaring clock tower was added to one side as a late Victorian folly. When the house was sold by the Duke of Sutherland to the Astors in 1893, Queen Victoria lamented the passage. The house remained as part of the Astor legacy until 1966, serving as a repository of some of the most stunning antiques and paintings in Europe. After the Viscount Astor died in 1966, the house was briefly occupied by the English branch of Stanford University. In 1984 the National Trust leased the hotel to Blakeney Hotels, a firm that turned it into one of the world's most beautiful hotels and the most luxurious in England.

The surrounding gardens show a distinguished variety of plantings, ranging from Renaissance-style topiary to meandering forest paths with vistas of statuary and flowering shrubs. The staff-to-bedroom ratio is two to one. Depending on the accommodation, twins and doubles range from £170 ($297.50) to £235 ($411.25) daily. There is only one single room, renting for £125 ($218.75). Breakfast and taxes are included in the rates. Meals, costing from £40 ($70), are served dining-room style in the gilt, mauve, and cream-colored room that is almost ecstatically beautiful. An English breakfast is consumed in a green-and-gold breakfast room fit for Versailles.

MARLOW

This Thames-side town, 35 miles from London, stands on a great loop of the riverbank between Maidenhead and Oxford. Here, along this middle reach of the Thames, is some of the most beautiful rural scenery in England, a land of green fields and deep woods, of stately mansions and parks. It was in these surroundings that Izaak Walton wrote his immortal work on fishing some 350 years ago, *The Compleat Angler*. On the south bank of the river facing Marlow itself stood the inn in which he stayed. That inn still stands and is named after his work. It's the best bet for—

Food and Lodging

Just 30 miles west of London, **The Compleat Angler Hotel,** Marlow Bridge, Bisham Road, Marlow, Buckinghamshire SL7 1RG (tel. 06284/4444), occupies an emerald-colored swath of lawns stretching down to the banks of the Thames. One of the most distinguished country hotels of England, it has had an equally distinguished list of clients, including Percy Shelley and his wife, Mary, along with Dame Nellie Melba (for whom the peach dessert was named), J. M. Barrie (author of *Peter Pan*), F. Scott Fitzgerald, and Noël Coward. The reddish brick of its façade incorporates both Georgian and Edwardian elements. Inside, the hotel is a well-organized and impeccably polite world of English chintz, mahogany and oaken antiques, plush carpeting, predictably elegant bars, and very fine dining. Each of the 42 bedrooms is outfitted a lot like those in an elegant private country home, with real antiques or reproductions, deeply comfortable armchairs and beds, private baths, color TVs, radios, and direct-dial phones. Singles cost £86 ($151.50) daily, and doubles or twins go for £106 ($185.50) to £116 ($203), with service and VAT included.

JORDANS VILLAGE

A peaceful place, **Old Jordans,** Jordans Lane, Jordans Village, Buckinghamshire HP9 2SW (tel. 02407/4586), is a farm dating back to the Middle Ages. But its recorded history starts in the early 17th century when one Thomas Russell, sitting tenant, bought the freehold, signing the deed with his thumbprint. The house was added to over the years, and in the mid-17th century William Penn, founder of Pennsylvania, and other well-known Dissenters stayed here and worshipped. It's full of history, perhaps a little isolated from today's bustle but easily accessible to London and Oxford. Now the property of the Quakers, the house is run as a conference center, but they have 30 simply furnished rooms available for overnight guests. Bathless rooms cost £20 ($35) daily in a single, £33.50 ($58.65) in a double. Rooms with bath rent for £30 ($52.50) in a single and £46.50 ($81.40) in a double. All tariffs include a full English breakfast. Lunch, served at 1 p.m., costs £5 ($8.75) Monday to Saturday, £6 ($10.50) on Sunday.

On the grounds is the Mayflower Barn, built almost indisputably from timbers from the ship *Mayflower* in which the first Pilgrims sailed to the New World. These days the beams ring to the strains of concert music and recitals performed by top-notch artists.

MILTON'S COTTAGE

The modern residential town of Gerrards Cross is often called the Beverly Hills of England, as it attracts many wealthy people who settle here in the many beautiful homes. Surrounding this plush section are several tucked-away hamlets, including **Chalfont St. Giles,** where the poet Milton lived during the Great Plague in 1665. He completed *Paradise Lost* here. In this 16th-century cottage are two museum rooms containing 93 rare books, including first editions of *Paradise Lost* and *Paradise Regained* and other Miltoniana, with exhibits of interest to young and old. A beautiful cottage garden is a further attraction. The house is open from 10 a.m. to 1 p.m. and 2 to 6 p.m. Tuesday to Saturday and on spring and summer bank holiday Mondays and from 2 to 6 p.m. on Sunday from March 1 to October 31. Admission is £1 ($1.75) for adults, 40p (70¢) for children. Closed Monday and in November, December, January, and February. For information, write to Milton's Cottage, Dean Way, Chalfont St. Giles, Bucks, HP8 4JH, U.K. (tel. 02407/2313).

West of Gerrards Cross, the town of Beaconsfield, with its broad, tree-lined High Street, enjoys many associations with Disraeli. Visitors pass through here en route to—

HUGHENDEN MANOR

Outside High Wycombe, in Buckinghamshire, sits a country manor that gives us not only an insight into the age of Victoria, but acquaints us with a remarkable man. In Benjamin Disraeli we meet one of the most enigmatic figures of 19th-century England. At age 21, Dizzy published anonymously his five-volume novel *Vivian Grey.* But it wasn't his shining hour. He went on to other things, marrying an older widow for her money, although they developed, apparently, a most successful relationship. He entered politics and continued writing novels, his later ones meeting with more acclaim.

In 1848 Disraeli acquired Hughenden Manor, a country house that befitted his fast-rising political and social position. He served briefly as prime minister in 1868, but his political fame rests on his stewardship as prime minister from 1874 to 1880. He became Queen Victoria's friend, and in 1877 she paid him a rare honor by visiting him at Hughenden. In 1876 Disraeli became the Earl of Beaconsfield: he had arrived, but his wife was dead, and he was to die in 1881. Instead of being buried at Westminster Abbey, he preferred the simple little graveyard of Hughenden Church.

Hughenden contains an odd assortment of memorabilia, including a lock of Disraeli's hair, letters from Victoria, autographed books, and especially a portrait of Lord Byron, known to Disraeli's father, are of interest.

If you're driving to Hughenden Manor on the way to Oxford, continue north of High Wycombe on the A4128 for about 1½ miles. If you're relying on public transportation from London, take coach 711 to High Wycombe, then board a Bee Line bus (High Wycombe-Aylesbury 323 or 324). The manor house and garden are open from 2 to 6 p.m. Wednesday to Saturday from Easter Saturday to October, from noon to 6 p.m. Sunday and bank holiday Mondays. It is open only on Saturday and Sunday from March 4 to March 19 from 2 to 6 p.m. It is closed from November to the end of March and on Good Friday. Admission is £2 ($3.50) for adults, £1 ($1.75) for children. For more information, phone 0494/32580.

WEST WYCOMBE

Snuggled in the Chiltern Hills 30 miles west of London, the village of West Wycombe still has an atmosphere of the early 18th century. The thatched roofs have been replaced by tiles, and some of the buildings have been removed or replaced, but the village is still two centuries removed from the present day.

In the mid-18th century Sir Francis Dashwood began an ambitious building program at West Wycombe. His strong interest in architecture and design led Sir Francis to undertake a series of monuments and parks that are still among the finest in the country today. He also sponsored the building of a road using the chalk quarries on the hill to aid in the support of the poverty-stricken villagers. The resulting caves of "The Knights of St. Francis of Wycombe," became later known as **The Hellfire Club.** The Knights consisted of a number of illustrious men drawn from the social circle surrounding the Prince of Wales. Its members "gourmandized," swilling claret and enjoying the company of women "of a cheerful, lively disposition . . . who considered themselves lawful wives of the brethren during their stay."

A visit to West Wycombe wouldn't be complete without a tour of **West Wycombe Park,** seat of the Dashwood family, of both historical and architectural interest. Both George III and Ben Franklin stayed here, but not at the same time. The house is one of the best examples of Palladian-style architecture in England. The interior is lavishly decorated with paintings and antiques from the 18th century. It is owned by the National Trust.

The caves, café, and gift shop are open Monday to Saturday March until late May from 1 to 6 p.m.; Monday to Saturday late May to early September from 11 a.m. to 6 p.m.; plus Sunday and bank holidays early April to late October from 11 a.m. to 6 p.m. In winter they are open only on Saturday and Sunday from 1 to 5 p.m. The house and grounds are open from 2 to 6 p.m. Monday to Friday in June, with Sunday included in July and August. Admission to the caves is £2 ($3.50) for adults, £1 ($1.75) for children. To visit the house and grounds costs £2.60 ($4.55) for adults, £1.60 ($2.80).

For information on the caves, house, and grounds, call the **West Wycombe Park Office,** West Wycombe (tel. 0494/24411).

Other sights at West Wycombe include the **Church of St. Lawrence,** perched atop West Wycombe Hill and topped by a huge golden ball. Parts of the church date from the 13th century; its richly decorated interior was copied from a 3rd-century Syrian sun temple. The view from the hill is worth the trek up. Near the church stands the **Dashwood Mausoleum,** built in a style derived from Constantine's Arch in Rome.

---

9. Bedfordshire (Woburn Abbey)

This county contains the fertile, rich Vale of Bedford, crossed by the River Ouse. Most visitors from London head here on a day trip to visit historic Woburn Abbey (previewed below). Others know of its county town—

BEDFORD

On the Ouse, Bedford contains many riverside parks and gardens, but is better known for its associations with John Bunyan. In Mill Street stands the 1850 **Bunyan Free Church** (tel. 0234/58075), erected on the site of a barn where Bunyan used to preach. The bronze doors, considered to be artistically outstanding, illustrate ten scenes from *Pilgrim's Progress.* The Bunyan Museum contains the surviving relics of Bunyan and a famous collection of *Pilgrim's Progress* in 400 foreign-language editions. Open Tuesday to Saturday April to September from 2 to 4 p.m., it charges 50p (90¢) for adults, 20p (35¢) for children.

About a mile south of Bedford lies Elstow, close to Bunyan's reputed birthplace. Here you can visit **Elstow Moot Hall,** a medieval timber-frame building originally used as a market hall, now managed as a museum containing a permanent display relating to the life of John Bunyan, including various editions of his work. It is open Tuesday to Saturday and bank holidays from 2 to 5 p.m. and on Sunday from 2 to 5:30 p.m. from April to October. It is closed in winter. Admission is 35p (60¢) for adults, 20p (35¢) for children. For more information, telephone 0234/228330.

The **Swiss Garden,** Old Warden, near Biggleswade, is an unusual romantic site dating from the early 19th century. It contains the original period buildings and features, together with many interesting plants and trees, some of great rarity. A lakeside picnic area in adjoining woodlands is open at all times. Hours for the garden are 2 to 6 p.m. (last admission at 5:15 p.m.) on Wednesday, Thursday, Saturday, and Sunday from April to October. The garden lies approximately 2½ miles west of Biggleswade adjoining the Biggleswade–Old Warden road about two miles west of the A1. For more information, telephone 0234/228330.

WOBURN ABBEY

Few tourists visiting Bedfordshire miss the Georgian mansion of **Woburn Abbey,** the seat of the dukes of Bedford for more than three centuries. The much-publicized 18th-century estate is about 42 miles from London and half a mile from the village of Woburn, which lies 13 miles southwest of Bedford. Its State Apartments are rich in furniture, porcelain, tapestries, silver, and a valuable art collection, including paintings by Van Dyck, Holbein, Rembrandt, Gainsborough, and Reynolds. A series of paintings by Canaletto, showing his continuing views of Venice, grace the walls of the Canaletto Room, an intimate dining room. (Prince Philip said the duke's collection was superior to the Canalettos at Windsor—but Her Royal Highness quickly corrected him.) Of all the paintings, one of the most notable from a historical point of view is the *Armada Portrait* of Elizabeth I. Her hand rests on the globe, as Philip's invincible armada perishes in the background.

Queen Victoria and Prince Albert visited Woburn Abbey in 1841. Victoria slept in an opulently decorated bedroom. Victoria's Dressing Room contains a fine collection of 17th-century paintings from the Netherlands. Among the oddities and treasures at Woburn Abbey are a Grotto of Shells, a Sèvres dinner service (gift of Louis XV), and a chamber devoted to memorabilia of "The Flying Duchess." Wife of the 11th Duke of Bedford, she was a remarkable woman who disappeared on a solo flight in 1937 (the same year as Amelia Earhart). The duchess, however, was 72 years old at the time.

In the 1950s the present Duke of Bedford opened Woburn Abbey to the public to pay off some $15 million in inheritance taxes. In 1974 he turned the estate over to his son and daughter-in-law, the Marquess and Marchioness of Tavistock, who reluctantly took on the business of running the 75-room mansion. And what a business it is, drawing hundreds of thousands of visitors a year and employing more than 300 people to staff the shops and grounds.

Today Woburn Abbey is surrounded by a 3,000-acre Deer Park that includes the famous Père David deer herd, originally from China and saved from extinction at Woburn. The Woburn Wild Animal Kingdom contains lions, tigers, giraffe, camels, monkeys, Prevalski horses, bongos, elephants, and other animals. What would Humphry Repton, the designer of the estate's park in the 19th century, say?

In January, February, and March, the park is open only on Saturday and Sunday from 10:30 a.m. to 3:40 p.m. and the abbey from 11 a.m. to 4:45 p.m. From April to October, the park hours are 10 a.m. to 4:45 p.m. daily, 10 a.m. to 5:45 p.m. on Sunday, while the abbey is open from 11 a.m. to 5:45 p.m. daily and 11 a.m. to 6:15 p.m. on Sunday. The last admission to the abbey is 45 minutes before closing time.

The charge to enter the park is £2 ($3.50) for a car and passengers, 50p (90¢) per person for cyclists and pedestrians. Admission to the abbey is £4 ($7) for adults, £1.50 ($2.65) for children 7 to 16. To economize, if it fits your needs I suggest a family ticket, going for £9 ($15.75) and admitting two adults and two children, with similar reductions for more children.

The deer park admission charge does not apply to visitors purchasing the abbey entrance ticket as they enter the park. When not in use by the duke's family, visitors may see the private apartments at an additional charge of 30p (55¢) for adults, 10p (20¢) for children. For more information, telephone 0525/290666.

As mentioned, Woburn Abbey is outside Woburn, near Dunstable. It is hard to reach by public transportation from London, so you may prefer to take one of the organized tours.

Food and Lodging

After visiting the abbey, a good spot for both food and lodgings is **Bedford Arms**, 1 George St., Woburn, Bedfordshire MK17 9PX (tel. 0525/290441). This is a Georgian coaching inn with a checkered history that blends the old and new at the gates of the estate of the Duke of Bedford. Tastefully modernized, it still preserves a mellow charm. Its 75-seat Georgian dining room, Hollands, was designed by Henry Holland, architect of Woburn Abbey. Guests are housed in one of the pleasantly furnished bedrooms, all of which contain private bath or shower. Singles cost £62 ($108.50) daily; doubles or twins, £78 ($136.50). Each unit contains coffee-making facilities, radio, phone, automatic alarm system, and color TV. A more recent block provides executive bedrooms furnished and decorated to high standards. All these rooms have private bath, color TV, radio, hairdryer, trouser press, and drinks facilities. This block brings the hotel's complement of bedrooms to 55. The Tavistock adjoining the hotel's main restaurant has been restored, its old beams exposed as well as its inglenook fireplaces. By contrast, a cocktail bar has been designed as an ideal place for a before-dinner drink or cocktail. The bar creates an atmosphere of luxury.

Paris House, Woburn Park (tel. 0525/290692), lies about two miles from Woburn on the B528 and is reached by going through the park with grazing deer. On the grounds of the abbey, it is not only scenically located but is without challenge the grandest dining choice in the area. The chef de cuisine and owner, Peter Chandler, selected a black-and-white timbered structure said to have been constructed for the Paris Exhibition in the 1870s. His cookery is heavily influenced by that of the Roux brothers, the famous master chefs of England. Paris House is a citadel of fine French cuisine, making use of very fresh ingredients deftly handled by a well-trained kitchen staff. The menu is always changing, so it would be useless to recommend specific dishes. However, in times past, favorite main courses have included a scallop cassolette, chicken suprême with confit d'ail, or rabbit in cider. The chef has long been known for his tulipe en fantaisie, which is a "sugar fairy" fantasy with fruit and ice cream. Set lunches cost from £15 ($26.25); a table d'hôte dinner, £22 ($38.50). The menu is backed up by a good wine list. The restaurant, for which reservations are necessary, is open Tuesday to Sunday from 12:30 to 2:30 p.m. and 7 to 10 p.m. On Sunday, only lunch is served, from noon to 2 p.m. Closed in February.

On the Outskirts

Moore Place Hotel, The Square, Aspley Guise, near Woburn, Bedfordshire, MK17 8DW (tel. 0908/282000), is a gracious Georgian era mansion constructed by Francis Moore in 1786 in this old village 13 miles from Woburn. Exit at junction 13 from the M1. Set in landscaped grounds and restored with sensitivity, Moore Place is a citadel of the good life. Decorations are generally modern but in a style in keeping with the age of the house. A Victorian-style conservatory (all the rage nowadays) was added, along with a block of contemporary bedrooms. This makes for a courtyard effect, with a rock garden and water cascade. The 54 beautifully furnished bedrooms, each with private bath, rent for £65 ($113.75) daily in a single, rising to £85 ($148.75) in a double. In an elegantly modernized setting, the restaurant at the hotel is among the finest in Bedfordshire. Yet its continental and English cookery comes at a relatively modest price: £9.50 ($16.35) for lunch and £12.50 ($21.90) for dinner, with meal service daily except Saturday lunch from 12:30 to 2:15 p.m. and 7:30 to 10 p.m.

WHIPSNADE WILD ANIMAL PARK

This is the country breeding park of the Zoological Society of London (which also operates the London Zoo), where the animals roam free in large paddocks and certain species even wander among visitors. On the edge of the Chiltern escarpment in Bedfordshire, Whipsnade lays claim to being the world's first open-air zoo. Many endangered species are here, including the cheetah, Père David deer, oryx, and Indian and white rhinos. There are also 24 species of crane, including the rare and beautiful red-naped or Manchurian crane. There is a lot of walking here to see everything in a single day, but the opportunities for photography are second to none. Exhibits include sea lions, a steam railway, a birds of prey show, a Discovery Centre, and a family center. Animals are in geographical groupings. Cars are admitted for £5 ($8.75) except from November 1 to February 28 when they are admitted free. In addition, you must pay £3.90 ($6.85) for adults and £2.40 ($4.20) for children. Children under the age of 4 are admitted free. The zoo is open daily from 10 a.m. to 6 p.m. or sunset, whichever is earlier. Take the train from St. Pancras to Luton, then a number 43 bus to Whipsnade Park.

KENT, SURREY, AND THE SUSSEXES

Lying to the South and southeast of London are the shires (counties) of Kent, Surrey, and the Sussexes. Combined, they form a most fascinating part of England to explore, and are easy to reach, within commuting distance of the capital.

Of all the centers, **Canterbury** in Kent is of foremost interest, but the old Cinque ports of **Rye** and **Winchelsea** in East Sussex are equally exciting, as is **Brighton** in its own distinctive way. In and around these major meccas are dozens of castles and vast estates, monuments, homes of celebrated men and women, cathedrals, yachting harbors, and little villages of thatched cottages.

The range of accommodations varies from an old-world smugglers' inn at the ancient seaport of Rye to a 16th-century house in Canterbury featured in *David Copperfield*. Throughout the counties of the south coast, you'll discover some superb bargains, as the English themselves come to these coastal shires for the sun and are accustomed to paying reasonable rates.

In the fog-choked cities of northern England, the great dream for retirement is to find a little rose-covered cottage in the south, where the living's easier.

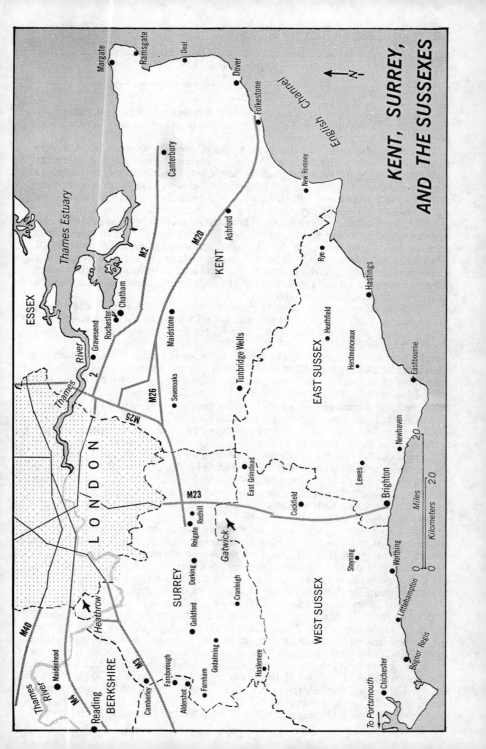

KENT, SURREY, AND THE SUSSEXES

KENT

Fresh from his cherry orchard, the Kentish farmer heads for his snug spot by an inglenook, with its bright-burning fire, for his glass of cherry brandy. The day's work is done. All's right with the world.

We're in what was once the ancient Anglo-Saxon kingdom of Kent, on the fringes of London yet far removed in spirit and scenery. Since the days of the Tudors, cherry blossoms have pinkened the fertile landscape. Not only orchards, but hop fields abound. The conically shaped oasthouses with kilns for drying the hops dot the rolling countryside. Both the hops and orchards have earned for Kent the title of the garden of England. And in England the competition's rough.

Kent suffered severe destruction in World War II, as it was the virtual alley over which the Luftwaffe flew in its blitz of London. After the fall of France, a German invasion was feared imminent. Shortly after becoming prime minister in 1940, Churchill sped to Dover, with his bowler, stogie, walking cane, and pin-striped suit. Once there, he inspected the coastal defense and gave encouragement to the men digging in to fight off the attack. But Hitler's "Sea Lion" (code name for the invasion) turned out to be a paper tiger.

In spite of much devastation, Kent is filled with interesting old towns, mansions, and castles. The country is also rich in Dickensian associations—in fact, Kent is sometimes known as Dickens Country. His family once lived near the naval dockyard at Chatham.

In the cathedral city of Rochester, 30 miles from London, you can visit the **Charles Dickens Centre** and **Dickens Chalet** in Eastgate House, built in 1590. This center, on High Street in Rochester, is open seven days a week from 10 a.m. to 5 p.m. Admission is £1.60 ($2.80) for adults, £1 ($1.75) for children. The museum has tableaux depicting various scenes from Dickens's novels, including a Pickwickian Christmas scene, then the fever-ridden graveyard of *Bleak House,* scenes from *The Old Curiosity Shop* and *Great Expectations, Oliver Twist,* and *David Copperfield.* There is clever use of sound and light. Information is also available at the center on various other sights in Rochester associated with Dickens, including Eastgate House and, in the garden, the chalet transported from Gad's Hill Place, where Dickens died, as well as the Guildhall Museum, Rochester Cathedral, and the mysterious "6 Poor Travelers' House." Pick up a brochure that includes a map featuring the various places and the novels with which each is associated. For further information, telephone 0634/44176.

Canterbury, the road to Dover, the byways of Kent, were all known to the Victorian novelist. At Broadstairs, his favorite seaside resort, what is now **Dickens House Museum** (tel. 0843/62853), on the main seafront, was once the home of Mary Pearson Strong, on whom he based much of the character of Betsey Trotwood, David Copperfield's aunt. It is open daily from 2:30 to 5:30 p.m. from April to October, charging 50p (90¢) admission for adults, 25p (45¢) for children.

At Broadstairs, you can also visit **Bleak House,** Fort Road (tel. 0843/62224), high up on the cliffs. At the peak of his fame, this mansion was occupied by Dickens and inspired the title of one of his greatest works, *Bleak House.* Here he entertained many men famous in art and literature, and he wrote the greater part of *David Copperfield* during his sojourn here. It is open seven days a week Easter to November from 10 a.m. to 6 p.m. From July through September hours are 10 a.m. to 9 p.m. The property also contains a Maritime Museum. Admission is £1.50 ($2.65) for adults, 85p ($1.50) for children under 12. An exhibit, "The Golden Age of Smuggling, 1780–1830," is in the cellar.

At Westerham, at the junction of the Edenbridge and Sevenoaks roads (the A25 and the B2026), an attraction for Canadian readers in particular is the square, red-brick, gabled house where James Wolfe, the English general who defeated the French in the battle for Québec, lived until he was 11 years old. Called **Québec House** (tel. 0959/62206), a National Trust property, it contains an exhibition about the capture of Québec and memorabilia associated with the military hero, who was born in Westerham on January 2, 1727. The house can be visited from 2 to 6 p.m. daily except Thursday and Saturday, April to October, for an admission of £1.40 ($2.45) for adults, 70p ($1.23) for children.

1. Kent's Country Houses, Castles, and Gardens

CHURCHILL'S HOME

For many years, Sir Winston lived at **Chartwell** (tel. 0732/866368), which lies 1½ miles south of Westerham in Kent. Churchill, a descendant of the first Duke of Marlborough, was born in grand style at Blenheim Palace on November 30, 1874. Chartwell doesn't pretend to be as grand a place as Blenheim, but it's been preserved as a memorial, administered by the National Trust. The rooms remain as Churchill left them, including maps, documents, photographs, pictures, and other personal mementos. In two rooms are displayed a selection of gifts that the prime minister received from people all over the world. There is also a selection of many of his well-known uniforms. Terraced gardens descend toward the lake with its black swans. In a garden studio are many of Churchill's paintings. Go if you want to see where a giant of a man lived and worked.

The house is open April to October from noon to 5 p.m. on Tuesday, Wednesday, and Thursday; from 11 a.m. to 5 p.m. on Saturday and Sunday. In March and November, hours are 11 a.m. to 4 p.m. on Wednesday, Saturday, and Sunday. The gardens and studio are not open in March and November, at which time admission to the house only is £1.80 ($3.15). Otherwise, you pay £3 ($5.25) to visit the house and garden, £1.20 ($2.10) to see the garden only, and 40p (70¢) for a visit to the studio. Children are charged half price. The restaurant offers light meals, salads, sandwiches, cakes, and a few hot dishes. It's open from 10:30 a.m. on the days the house is receiving visitors.

KNOLE

Begun in the mid-15th century by Thomas Bourchier, archbishop of Canterbury, Knole, at the Tonbridge end of the town of Sevenoaks, just off the A225 (tel. 0732/450608), is one of the largest private houses in England and is considered one of the finest examples of purely British Tudor style architecture. It is set in a 1,000-acre deer park.

Henry VIII liberated the former archbishop's palace from the church in 1537. He spent considerable sums of money on Knole, but there is little record of his spending much time here after extracting the place from the reluctant Archbishop Cranmer. History records one visit only, in 1541. It was then a royal palace until Queen Elizabeth I granted it to Thomas Sackville, first Earl of Dorset, whose descendants have lived here ever since. Virginia Woolf, often a guest of the Sackvilles, used Knole as the location for her novel *Orlando*. The building was given to the National Trust in 1946. The Great Hall and the Brown Gallery are Bourchier rooms, early 15th century, both much altered by the Earl of Dorset, who made other additions in about 1603. The earl was also responsible for the Great Painted Staircase. The house covers seven acres and has 365 rooms, 52 staircases, and seven courts. The elaborate paneling and plasterwork provide a background for the 17th- and 18th-century tapestries and rugs, Elizabethan and Jacobean furniture, and the collection of family portraits.

234 □ KENT, SURREY, AND THE SUSSEXES

Knole is open from Good Friday to the end of October, Wednesday to Saturday and bank holiday Mondays from 11 a.m. to 5 p.m., on Sunday from 2 to 5 p.m.; closed November to March. Last admission is an hour before closing. The gardens are open May to September only on the first Wednesday of the month. Admission to the house is £2.50 ($4.40) for adults, £1.30 ($2.30) for children. On Friday (except Good Friday), extra rooms in Lord Sackville's private apartments are shown, costing £3 ($5.25) for adults, £1.50 ($2.65) for children. To visit the gardens only costs adults 50p (90¢); children, 25p (45¢). The park is open daily to pedestrians; cars are allowed to enter when the house is open.

Knole is five miles north of Tonbridge and 25 miles from London. Frequent train service is available from London (about every 30 minutes), and then you can take a taxi or walk the remaining 1½ miles to Knole.

IGHTHAM MOTE

A National Trust property, Ightham Mote, Ivy Hatch, Sevenoaks (tel. 0732/810378), is well worth a stop if you're in the area visiting other stately homes and castles. It was extensively remodeled in the early 16th century. The Tudor chapel with its painted ceiling, the timbered outer walls, and the ornate chimneys reflect that period. A stone bridge crosses the moat and leads into the central courtyard overlooked by the magnificent windows of the Great Hall. The rest of the house is built around the courtyard. From the Great Hall, a Jacobean staircase leads to the old chapel on the first floor, where you go through the solarium, with an oriel window, to the Tudor chapel.

Unlike many other ancient houses of England lived in by the same family for centuries, Ightham Mote passed from owner to owner, each family leaving its mark on the place. When the last private owner, an American who was responsible for a lot of the restoration, died, he bequeathed the house to the National Trust. It's open from 11 a.m. to 5 p.m. daily except Tuesday and Friday. Admission is £2.50 ($4.40) for adults, £1.50 ($2.65) for children. Ightham Mote is 2½ miles south of Ightham, off the A227, 6 miles east of Sevenoaks.

SQUERRYES COURT

At Westerham, west of Sevenoaks on the A25, is Squerryes Court (tel. 0959/62345), a William and Mary–period manor house built in 1681 and owned by the Warde family for 250 years. Besides a fine collection of paintings, tapestries, and furniture, in the Wolfe Room is a collection of pictures and relics of the family of General Wolfe. The general received his military commission in the grounds of the house at a spot marked by a cenotaph. The house and grounds are open from March to September (on Sunday only during March). From April to September you can visit on Wednesday, Saturday, Sunday, and bank holiday Mondays from 2 to 6 p.m. Admission is £2.20 ($3.85) for adults, £1.20 ($2.10) for children.

DOWN HOUSE

North of the M25 motorway, Squerryes Court, and Chartwell, Down House, Luxted Road, Downe, Orpington (tel. 0689/59119), was the home of Charles Darwin for some 40 years. It was in this 18th-century house that he wrote *Origin of Species*. Visitors can see his memorial and the museum containing personal articles including relics from the *Beagle* and other interesting items and pictures. Attractive gardens and the Sandwalk Wood are preserved. The house is open daily from 1 to 6 p.m. except Monday and Friday (open bank holidays); closed in February and Good Friday. Admission is £1.50 ($2.65) for adults, 30p (55¢) for children. The village of Downe is 5½ miles south of Bromley off the A233.

HEVER CASTLE

Built at the end of the 13th century, Hever Castle was then just a fortified farmhouse surrounded by a moat. A dwelling house was added within the fortifications some 200 years later by the Bullen family. In 1506 the property was inherited by Sir Thomas Bullen, father of Anne Boleyn. It was here that Henry VIII courted Anne for six years before she became his second wife and later mother of Elizabeth, who became Queen Elizabeth I of England. In 1538 Hever Castle was acquired by Henry VIII, who granted it to his proxy (fourth) wife, the "great Flanders mare," Anne of Cleves, when he discovered that his mail-order bride did not live up to her Holbein portrait. This luckier Anne did not seem to mind, however. She owned this comfortable castle for 17 years supported by Henry with plenty of money.

In 1903 the castle was purchased by William Waldorf Astor, who spent five years restoring and redecorating it, as well as building the unique village of Tudor-style cottages connected to the castle, for use by his guests. Astor was responsible also for the construction of the spectacular Italian gardens with fountains, classical statuary, a maze, and an avenue of yew trees trimmed into fantastic shapes. He also had a 35-acre lake put in, through which the River Eden flows. The castle and its grounds have been used as locations for a number of motion pictures. The forecourt and the gardens were used in filming *Anne of a Thousand Days* in 1969. More recently, Hever Castle was used in *Lady Jane*. Two permanent exhibitions here are "Henry VIII and Anne Boleyn at Hever Castle" and "The Astors of Hever."

The castle and grounds are open from Good Friday until the end of October. The gardens can be entered daily from 11 a.m. to 6 p.m. (last entry at 5 p.m.). The castle opens at noon. Admission is £3.70 ($6.50) for adults, £1.90 ($3.35) for children, to both the castle and the gardens. To visit the gardens only, adults pay £2.50 ($4.40); children £1.50 ($2.65). For further information, call the Hever Castle Estate Office, Hever, near Edenbridge (tel. 0732/865224). The castle is three miles southeast of Edenbridge, midway between Sevenoaks and East Grinstead, 20 minutes from the M25 junction 6.

PENSHURST PLACE

A magnificent English Gothic mansion, Penshurst Place, at Penshurst, near Tonbridge (tel. 0892/870307), is one of the outstanding country houses in Britain. In 1338 Sir John de Pulteney, four times lord mayor of London, built the manor house whose Great Hall forms the heart of Penshurst still, after more than 600 years. The boy king, Edward VI, presented the house to Sir William Sidney, and it has remained in that family ever since. It was the birthplace in 1554 of Sir Philip Sidney, the soldier-poet. In the first half of the 17th century Penshurst was known as a center of literature, attracting such personages as Ben Jonson. Today it is the home of William Philip Sidney, the Viscount De L'Isle, and Lady De L'Isle. Lord De L'Isle was in Winston Churchill's cabinet in the 1950s and governor-general of Australia in the 1960s.

The Nether Gallery, below the Long Gallery, which contains a suite of ebony and ivory furniture from Goa, houses the Sidney family collection of armor. Visitors can also view the splendid State Dining Room and Queen Elizabeth's Room. In the Stable Wing is an interesting Toy Museum. The place is open daily except Monday from April to the first Sunday in October. It is also open on Good Friday and all bank holiday Mondays. The gardens, home park, Venture Playground, nature trail, and countryside exhibition are open from 12:30 to 6 p.m., the house from 1 to 5:30 last entry at 5 p.m. Admission to the house and grounds is £3 ($5.25) for adults, £1.60 ($2.80) for children. Penshurst Place is 33 miles from London and 6 miles west of Tonbridge.

SISSINGHURST CASTLE GARDEN

V. Sackville-West and her husband, Harold Nicolson, created the celebrated Sissinghurst Castle Garden, Sissinghurst, two miles northeast of Cranbrook (tel. 0580/712850), on view between the surviving parts of an Elizabethan mansion. The gardens are worth a visit at all seasons. There is a spring garden where bulb flowers flourish, a summer garden, and an autumn garden with flowering shrubs, as well as a large herb garden. The place is open Easter to mid-October, Tuesday to Friday from 1 to 6:30 p.m. and on Saturday, Sunday, and Good Friday from 10 a.m. to 6:30 p.m. Admission is £3.50 ($6.15) for adults and £1.80 ($3.15) for children on Sunday, dropping to £3 ($5.25) for adults and £1.50 ($2.65) for children Tuesday to Saturday. Meals are available in the Granary Restaurant, open Good Friday to mid-October from noon to 6 p.m. Tuesday to Friday, from 10 a.m. to 6 p.m. Saturday and Sunday.

LEEDS CASTLE

Once described by Lord Conway as the loveliest castle in the world, Leeds Castle, Maidstone (tel. 0622/65400), dates from A.D. 857. Originally built of wood, it was rebuilt in 1119 in its present stone structure on two small islands in the middle of the lake, and it was an almost impregnable fortress before the invention of gunpowder. Henry VIII converted it to a royal palace.

The castle has strong links with America through the sixth Lord Fairfax who, as well as owning the castle, owned five million acres in Virginia and was a close friend and mentor of the young George Washington. The last private owner, the Hon. Lady Baillie, who lovingly restored the castle with a superb collection of fine art, furniture, and tapestries, bequeathed it to the Leeds Castle Foundation. Since then, royal apartments, known as "Les Chambres de la Reine" (the chambers of the queen), in the Gloriette, the oldest part of the castle, have been open to the public. The Gloriette, the last stronghold against attack, dates from Norman and Plantagenet times, with later additions by Henry VIII.

Within the surrounding parkland is a wildwood garden and duckery where rare swans, geese, and ducks can be seen. The redesigned aviaries contain a superb collection of birds, including parakeets and cockatoos. Dogs are not allowed here, but dog lovers will enjoy the Great Danes of the castle and the Dog Collar Museum at the Gatehouse, with a unique collection of collars dating from the Middle Ages. A nine-hole golf course is open to the public. The Culpeper Garden is a delightful English country flower garden. Beyond are the castle greenhouses, the maze centered by a beautiful underground grotto, and the vineyard recorded in the *Domesday Book* and now again producing Leeds Castle English white wine.

In the summer, from April to October, Leeds Castle is open daily from 11 a.m. to 5 p.m. From November to March, it is open from noon to 4 p.m. Saturday and Sunday. It is closed on the first Saturday in July for the annual open-air concert and on a Saturday in early November for the grand fireworks display. Admission to the castle and grounds is £4.80 ($8.40) for adults and £3.30 ($5.80) for children. If you want to visit only the grounds, the charge is £3.80 ($6.65) for adults, £2.30 ($4.05) for children. Car parking is free, with a free ride on a tractor-trailer available for persons who cannot manage the half-mile or so walk from the car park to the castle.

Snacks, salads, cream teas, and hot meals are offered daily at a number of places on the estate, including Fairfax Hall, a restored 17th-century tithe barn with a self-service carvery restaurant and bar. There are special combined Sunday lunch/ entrance tickets available during the winter (these should be reserved in advance), but traditional roast beef lunches are always available for about £12 ($21) for three courses.

Kentish Evenings are presented in Fairfax Hall every Saturday throughout the year, starting at 7 p.m., with a sherry cocktail reception, then a guided tour of the castle. Guests feast on Kentish pâté, followed by broth and roast beef carved at the table, plus seasonal vegetables. The meal is rounded off by dessert, cheese, and coffee. A half bottle of wine is included in the overall price of £25.50 ($44.65) per person. During the meal, musicians play a selection of music suitable to the surroundings and the occasion. Advance reservations are required, made by calling the castle. Kentish Evenings finish at 12:30 a.m., and accommodation is available locally.

If you are not driving during your trip, British Rail and several London-based bus tour operators offer inclusive day excursions to Leeds Castle. The castle is four miles east of Maidstone at the junction of the A20 and the M20 London–Folkestone roads.

The Leeds Castle Foundation also owns the Park Gate Inn, Hollingbourne (tel. 062780/582), built during the last year of the reign of Charles I, on the site of an earlier building dating back to the Middle Ages. The structure was originally a store and domestic quarters for Leeds Castle, being adjacent to the entrance to the castle, later changed.

CHILHAM CASTLE GARDENS

In Chilham Village, six miles west of Canterbury, Chilham Castle Gardens (tel. 0227/730319), were originally laid out by Tradescant and later landscaped by Lancelot "Capability" Brown. On a former royal property, the gardens are visually magnificent, looking out over the Stour Valley. A Norman castle used as a hunting lodge once stood here. It was frequented by more than one royal personage until King Henry VIII sold it. The Jacobean castle, built between 1603 and 1616 by Sir Dudley Digges (whose descendant was governor-general of Virginia), was reputedly designed by Inigo Jones. It is one of the best examples extant of the architecture of its day and is built around a hexagonal open-ended courtyard. Medieval banquets are held in the Gothic Hall throughout the year.

The castle is not open to the public—only the gardens. They are open from mid-March to mid-October daily from 11 a.m. to 6 p.m. (last entry at 5 p.m.). Admission is £2 ($3.50) for adults and £1 ($1.75) for children Tuesday, Wednesday, Thursday, and Saturday; £1.80 ($3.15) for adults and 90p ($1.60) for children Monday and Friday. On Sunday, with jousting included, the charge is £3 ($5.25) for adults and £1.50 ($2.65) for children. On bank holiday Sundays and Mondays, the prices are £4 ($7) for adults, £1.50 ($2.65) for children. You can also visit Petland and the old Norman castle keep.

The little village of Chilham has a lovely small square with a church at one end, the castle at the other, and a mass of half-timbered buildings interspersed with old red-brick houses. It is on the A252 Canterbury–Maidstone road and the A28 Canterbury–Ashford road.

---

2. Canterbury

Under the arch of the ancient West Gate journeyed Chaucer's knight, solicitor, nun, squire, parson, merchant, miller, and cook—spinning racy tales. They were bound for the shrine of Thomas à Becket, archbishop of Canterbury, who was slain by four knights of Henry II on December 29, 1170. (The king later walked barefoot from Harbledown to the tomb of his former friend, where he allowed himself to be flogged in penance.) The shrine was finally torn down in 1538 by Henry VIII, as part of his campaign to destroy the monasteries and graven images. Canterbury, by then, had already been an attraction of long standing.

The medieval Kentish city, on the Stour River, is the mother city of England, its ecclesiastical capital. Mother city is an apt title, as Canterbury was known to have been inhabited centuries before the birth of Jesus Christ. Julius Caesar once went on a rampage near it. Although its most famous incident was the murder of Becket, the medieval city witnessed other major moments in English history—including Bloody Mary's ordering of nearly 40 victims to be burned at the stake. Richard the Lion-Hearted came back this way from crusading, and Charles II passed through on the way to claim his crown.

Canterbury was once completely walled, and many traces of its old fortifications remain. In the 16th century, weavers, mostly Huguenots from northern France and the Low Countries, fled to Canterbury to escape religious persecution.

They started a weaving industry that flourished until the expanding silk trade with India ruined it.

The old city is much easier to reach today than it was in Chaucer's time. As it lies 56 miles from London, it is within a 1½-hour train ride from Victoria Station. The city center is closed to cars, but it's only a short walk from several car parks to the cathedral or walking-tour starting point.

From just below the Weavers House, boats leave for half-hour trips on the river with a commentary on the history of the buildings you pass. Umbrellas are provided to protect you against inclement weather. You can get more precise information from the **Tourist Office,** 34 St. Margaret's St. (tel. 0227/766567), a few doors away from St. Margaret's Church.

Now, as in the Middle Ages, the goal of the pilgrim remains:

CANTERBURY CATHEDRAL

The foundation of this splendid cathedral (tel. 0227/762862) dates back to the coming of the first archbishop, Augustine, from Rome in A.D. 597, but the earliest part of the present building is the great Romanesque crypt built circa 1100. The monastic choir erected on top of this at the same time was destroyed by fire in 1174, only four years after the murder of Thomas à Becket on a dark December evening in the northwest transept, still one of the most famous places of pilgrimage in Europe. The destroyed choir was immediately replaced by a magnificent early Gothic one, and first used for worship in 1185. The cathedral was the first great church in the Gothic style to be erected in England and set a fashion for the whole country. Its architects were the Frenchman, William of Sens, and "English" William who took Sens's place after the Frenchman was crippled in an accident in 1178 that later proved fatal.

This part of the church is noteworthy for its medieval tombs of royal personages such as King Henry IV and Edward the Black Prince, as well as numerous archbishops. To the later Middle Ages belongs the great 14th-century nave and the famous central "Bell Harry Tower." The cathedral stands in spacious precincts amid the remains of the buildings of the monastery—cloisters, chapter house, and Norman water tower, which have survived intact from the Dissolution in the time of King Henry VIII to the present day.

Becket's shrine was destroyed by the Tudor king, but the site of that tomb is in Trinity Chapel, near the High Altar. The saint is said to have worked miracles, and the cathedral contains some rare stained glass depicting those feats. Perhaps the most miraculous thing is that the windows escaped Henry VIII's agents of destruction and Hitler's bombs as well (part of the cathedral was hit in World War II), having been removed as a precaution at the beginning of the war. The cathedral library was damaged by a German air raid in 1942, but the main body of the church was unharmed, although a large area of the town of Canterbury was flattened. The replacement windows of the cathedral were blown in, proving the wisdom of having the medieval glass safely stored away. East of the Trinity Chapel is "Becket's Crown," in which is a chapel dedicated to "Martyrs and Saints of Our Own Time." St. Augustine's Chair, one of the symbols of the authority of the archbishop of Canterbury, stands behind the high altar. The cathedral is open daily from 8:45 a.m. to 7 p.m. in summer (closes at 5 p.m. in winter).

ROMAN PAVEMENT

This site is off High Street down Butchery Lane. It contains some fine mosaic pavement remains and treasures from excavations in the city. The pavement is open daily from 10 a.m. to 1 p.m. and 2 to 4 p.m. (afternoon only, in winter). The entrance charge is 55p (95¢), which also includes access to the West Gate Towers Museum that has the same hours. For information, call 0227/452747.

PILGRIM'S WAY

Re-creating the Thomas à Becket pilgrimage of Chaucerian England, **Canterbury Pilgrim's Way,** St. Margaret's Street (tel. 0227/454888), is open daily from 9 a.m. to 5 p.m., costing adults £3 ($5.25) and children £1.50 ($2.65). Visitors are taken on a tour through England of the Middle Ages, and they meet some of Chaucer's pilgrims, including the Wife of Bath. Audio-visual techniques bring these characters to life. Stories of jealousy, pride, avarice, and romance, certainly chivalry, are recounted.

GUIDED TOURS

Guided tours of Canterbury are organized by the **Guild of Guides,** Arnett House, Hawks Lane (tel. 0227/459779), costing £1.50 ($2.65) with daily tours from April to October.

WHERE TO STAY

Before you can begin any serious exploring, you'll need to find a hotel. You have several possibilities, both in the city and on the outskirts, ranging from craggy Elizabethan houses of historic interest to modern studio-type bedrooms with private baths.

County Hotel, High Street, Canterbury, Kent CT1 2RX (tel. 0227/66266), has been a hotel since the closing years of the reign of Victoria. But its recorded history goes back to the end of the 12th century, when a man named Jacob built a private town house on the spot. Over the years it has undergone many changes and alterations, in both its structure and its name. It was first licensed in 1629. Today considered the best in town, it offers 73 bedrooms fully equipped with private bathrooms and showers, color TVs, tea/coffee-makers, radios, phones, and bowls of fruit. The rate for a single is £48 ($84) daily, and a twin or double goes for £70 ($122.50). Period rooms—that is, with a Georgian or Tudor four-poster—are more expensive. All prices include a full English breakfast, service, and VAT. For gourmet dining, go to Sullys Restaurant, the hotel's fully air-conditioned dining room (see below). For snacks, vegetarian specialties, salads, and hot dishes, the Coffee Shop may be your best best. There is also the Tudor Bar, where you can have apéritifs or after-dinner libations. The hotel has both covered and open car parking.

Chaucer Hotel, Ivy Lane, Canterbury, Kent CT1 1TT (tel. 0227/464427), was originally built as a coaching inn around the time of the American Revolution and became known throughout Kent as one of the rowdiest hotels in town. That's but a memory today. The location is on a historic street within a few minutes' walk of the cathedral and the Micawber House made famous in *David Copperfield.* You register at a reception desk flanked with grandfather clocks and centuries-old paneling. Your room will lie at the end of a labyrinth of stairs, narrow hallways, and doors; however, the hotel staff will carry luggage and park your car. The most appealing bedrooms are the large ones under the eaves, with exposed hand-hewn timbers, slanted ceilings, and a modernized format of comfortable furniture and tile baths. Each unit has a color TV, phone, radio, and coffee-making equipment. With service and VAT, singles cost £55 ($96.25) daily; doubles or twins, £70 ($122.50). Don't overlook the possibility of a drink in one of the Chesterfield chairs in the Pilgrim's Bar, where fires heat Regency mantelpieces and French windows open to outdoor terraces in summer. Meals are served in a restaurant filled with exposed beams, banquettes, and an array of menu specialties named after characters in *The Canterbury Tales.*

Howfield Manor, Chartham Hatch, Canterbury, Kent CT4 7HG (tel. 0227/738294), stands 3¼ miles from Canterbury by the A28. The Dutch-style gables of this brick manor house rise impressively behind a holly and a low enclosing wall of local stone. The oldest section, which dates from 1181, is now used as a restaurant. An ancient well remains from when the manor house was built as a chapel for an

Augustinian Priory. When Henry VIII suppressed the monasteries of England, the property fell into private hands. It was enlarged in the 17th century, eventually serving as the farmhouse of a large landowner. Set on five acres of rolling meadows, the house offers 13 tastefully furnished bedrooms that contain such amenities as private baths, alarm clocks, trouser presses, and hair dryers. For a bed and a full English breakfast, the charge is £60 ($105) daily in a single, £65 ($113.75) in a twin or double. Drinks are served from the Priory Bar and can be taken into the lounge where guests enjoy the plush upholstery and the warmth from a fireplace lined with hand-made bricks and dotted with well-polished antique accessories. A set dinner served in the restaurant costs from £18.95 ($33.15).

Slatters, St. Margaret's Street, Canterbury, Kent CT1 1AA (tel. 0227/ 463271), is a record of the city's changing past. Originally, its Jolly Miller Restaurant was built in the 17th century, and many of its old beams and stones are intact. The structure stands on ground once occupied by buildings bombed in World War II. The contemporary bedrooms, most with private bath, are motel-like. Most of the rooms convert into sitting areas during the day, with armchairs, a radio, and television. All rates include breakfast. Singles rent for £36 ($63) daily and doubles go for £52 ($91), all with bath, these tariffs including an English breakfast, service, and VAT. Parking is available even though you're in the heart of Canterbury, a five-minute stroll from the cathedral. The fully licensed French restaurant serves lunch and dinner. Bar snacks are also available at lunchtime.

Three Tuns, 24 Watling St., Canterbury, Kent CT1 2UD (tel. 0227/67371), is a fine old building that began life as three separate 15th-century houses, built on what was the site of a Roman theater. Additions were made to the structures in the 16th and 17th centuries, and during the 1700s the tavern became known as a coaching inn, popular with people traveling from London to Folkestone and Dover. William and Mary, who later became King and Queen of England, stopped over here in 1679, and you can follow their example, even going so far as to stay in the same room, attractively furnished and with a four-poster bed. Depending on the plumbing, singles cost £28 ($49) daily, and doubles run £38 ($66.50) to £42 ($73.50), with breakfast and VAT included. Each room is equipped with a TV, phone, and hot beverage facilities. The Chapel Restaurant, which serves good fixed-price meals costing £9.50 ($16.65) and £13 ($22.75), is open daily from noon to 2 p.m. and 6:30 to 9 p.m. The restaurant was the setting for illegal masses during the Civil War, with a secret passage whose entrance can be seen.

Cathedral Gate Hotel, 36 Burgate, Canterbury, Kent CT1 2HA (tel. 0227/ 464381), is for modern-day pilgrims who want to rest their bones at an inn shouldering up to the cathedral's gateway. Built in 1438, adjoining Christchurch Gate and overlooking the Buttermarket, the hotel has views of the cathedral. In 1620 this former hospice became one of the earliest of the fashionable coffeehouses and tea houses of England. Its façade was added in the 19th century, however. The interior reveals many architectural features of the 17th century. Two curved bay windows overlook the little square in front of the gateway, and rear access leads directly into the cathedral precincts. Mr. and Mrs. A. C. Jubber and their children own the hotel and welcome guests to their 26 comfortably furnished rooms, many with private baths. Singles cost £16 ($28) to £32 ($56) daily, and doubles or twins go for £30 ($52.50) to £47.50 ($83.15). Tariffs include a continental breakfast, and you can also have afternoon tea or supper.

WHERE TO DINE

The most distinguished restaurant in town, **Sully's,** High Street (tel. 0227/ 66266), is at the most distinguished hotel in Canterbury, the County (already previewed). The seating and comfort level are first rate, and both visitors and locals (the latter usually celebrating some special occasion) frequent this establishment. Considering the quality of the ingredients, the menu offers good value, especially if you stick to the table d'hôte menus: £10.50 ($18.40) for lunch and £14 ($24.50) for dinner. If you order à la carte, expect to spend from £18 ($31.50) per head. Food service is daily from 12:30 to 2:30 p.m. and 7 to 10 p.m. You can always count on a selection of plainer, traditional dishes, but might settle for one of the more imaginatively conceived platters instead. Both English and a continental cuisine are served, and dishes are backed up by a respectable wine list. It's best to call for a table.

Waterfield's Restaurant, 5a Best Lane (tel.0227/450276), is a 17th-century house with a light, bright dining room and attractive views across the river to the ancient houses beyond. Pine wood and white-painted brick walls make for a perfect setting for the expert cuisine of Michael Waterfield. There is a choice of different priced menus, ranging from saffron soup, kipper pâté, and terrine of eel to tournedos Rossini. All main courses are accompanied by fresh vegetables or potatoes and salad. One specialty is roast guinea fowl stuffed with cream cheese and salmon, en croûte. Set lunch is £8.50 ($14.90). À la carte dinners average £20 ($35) per person. The restaurant is open from noon to 2:30 p.m. and 7 to 10:45 p.m. It's closed all day Sunday and at lunchtime Monday.

Tuo e Mio, 16 The Borough (tel. 0227/61471), is a bastion of zesty Italian cookery, the finest in town in its category. Signor R. P. M. Greggio sets the style and plans the menu at his casual bistro. Some dishes are standard, including the pastas, beef, and veal found on most Italian menus. However, a certain flair is shown in the daily specials, based on the shopping for fresh and good quality ingredients on any given day. Try especially the fish dishes including skate, which is regularly featured. A set lunch is modestly priced at £8 ($14) but in the evening you'll spend from £12 ($21) and up. A selection of reasonably priced Italian wines is there to accompany your food selection. The restaurant is open Tuesday to Sunday (no lunch on Tuesday) from noon to 2:30 p.m. and 7 to 10:45 p.m. (until 10 p.m. on Sunday). Call for a table, especially at lunch.

RIDE THE RAILS

In the area is the **Romney, Hythe & Dymchurch Light Railway Co.,** New Romney Station, New Romney (tel. 0679/62353), the world's smallest public railway. The engines are all steam driven, the carriages covered so there's no fear of getting wet. The line is 13½ miles long from Hythe (Kent) to New Romney and Dungeness, and the trains are one-third-size miniature versions of the kind of trains that ran on English or North American mainline railways in the 1920s. Fares depend on the distance traveled. An ordinary round-trip ticket costs £5.40 ($9.45) for adults. Otherwise, you can purchase a runabout ticket valid for unlimited travel, costing about £8 ($14) per day. Children travel for one-third the adult fare. It operates daily from Easter to the end of September, with service in March and October on Saturday and Sunday only. The railway is reached by road along the A259. The ride takes about an hour. Naturally, the ticket includes freedom to travel for a whole day as services permit on the R.H.&D. Railway. Telephone for train times. The terminal of the railway, Hythe, is near Folkestone, which can be reached by frequent trains from London.

By car, leave Canterbury on the Dover road; five miles out turn right and Elham's five miles farther. A right turn and another five miles will take you to Hythe.

---

3. Dover

Dover, one of the ancient Cinque ports, is famed for its white cliffs. In Victoria's day, it basked in popularity as a seaside resort. Today it is of importance mainly because it is a port for major cross-Channel car and passenger traffic between England and France (usually Calais). Sitting in the open jaws of the white cliffs, Dover was one of England's most vulnerable and easy-to-hit targets in World War II and suffered repeated bombings that destroyed much of its harbor.

Hovering nearly 400 feet above the port is **Dover Castle** (tel. 0304/201628), one of the oldest and best known in England. Its keep was built at the command of Becket's fair-weather friend, Henry II, in the 12th century. You can visit the keep year round, generally daily from 9:30 a.m. to 6:30 p.m. in summer (it closes earlier off-season), for an admission of £2.50 ($4.40) for adults, £1.30 ($2.30) for children. The castle houses a military museum and a film center. The restaurant is open all year. The ancient castle was called back to active duty as late as World War II. The "Pharos" on the grounds is a lighthouse built by the Romans in the first half of the 1st century. The Romans landed at nearby Deal in 55 B.C. and 54 B.C. The first landing was not successful. The second in 54 B.C. was more so, but after six months they departed, and did not return until nearly 100 years later, in A.D. 43, when they occupied the country and stayed 400 years.

This seaport handles more visitors from abroad than any other point of entry to Great Britain. At the **National Tourist Information Centre,** Townwall Street (tel. 0304/205108), I found a small band of dedicated workers tirelessly answering questions and booking accommodations. It is easy to be casual and offhand when dealing with the same old questions time and time again, but these people treat each inquiry as something of vital interest and importance and give endless helpful advice. I am sure they will solve any problem you may have.

WHERE TO STAY

The traditional choice is **The White Cliffs,** Waterloo Crescent Dover, Kent CT17 9BP (tel. 0304/203633), many of whose bedrooms face the Channel. Clinging to the past, its façade is impressive, built like a string of attached town houses, with an unbroken seafront balcony and a glass-enclosed front veranda. The bedrooms are comfortable and tranquil. All units have private baths or showers, color TVs, radios, direct-dial phones, and hot beverage facilities. Singles cost from £38 ($66.50) daily, and doubles begin at £60 ($105). Rates include breakfast and VAT. Meals and light snacks are available 24 hours a day: dinner costs from £7.50 ($13.15). A covered garage is available. The hotel is close to the eastern and western docks and the hoverport for travel to and from France and Belgium.

Dover Moat House, Townwall Street, Dover, Kent CT16 1SZ (tel. 0304/203270), stands in the center of town, just a few minutes away from the railway station, the seafront, and the international ferry terminal and hoverport. Its 80 rooms are furnished to a good standard, with queen-size beds, private baths with showers, color TVs, radios, in-house movies, direct-dial phones, hairdryers, mini-bars, and individually controlled air conditioning and heating. Singles begin at £55 ($96.25) nightly, while the charge is £69 ($120.75) for a twin with up to four persons sharing. On the premises are an indoor heated swimming pool and a restaurant with a carvery and salad bar, plus coffeeshop facilities and an English-style bar.

WHERE TO EAT

Finding a good place to eat in Dover is not easy. One of the most reliable establishments is **Britannia,** Townwall Street (tel. 0304/203248), across from the Dover Stage Coachotel, near the seafront. It has a bow window, along with gilt and brass nautical accents on its black façade. The restaurant is one floor above street level, with a popular pub on the ground floor. A large menu of international favorites is featured, including beef Stroganoff, chicken Kiev, and duck à l'orange. Naturally, Dover sole is served (the chef grills it or prepares it Véronique style). Meals cost from £8 ($14). The restaurant is open from noon to 2:30 p.m. and 7 to 10 p.m. Monday to Saturday, from noon to 2 p.m. and 7 to 10 p.m. Sunday. A popular pub on the premises serves from 11 a.m. to 11 p.m. Monday to Saturday, from noon to 3 p.m. and 7 to 10:30 p.m. Sunday.

Ristorante al Porto, 43 Townwall St. (tel. 0304/204615), brings a continental flair to Dover. One block from the landing dock of the ferry boats, this Italian-owned restaurant is decorated in a nautical style, with fish nets hanging from the ceiling. It offers one of the largest menus in town, featuring such specialties as steak in a black-pepper, cream, and brandy sauce, along with cannelloni or succulent veal in a sauce of mushrooms, garlic, and tomatoes. Try the gelati misti (mixed ice cream) for dessert and a cup of espresso. Expect to pay from £10 ($17.50) for a meal here. However, an à la carte lunch goes for £4.75 ($8.30). Hours are noon to 2:30 p.m. and 7 to 10:15 p.m. daily except Sunday.

For our next and final stopover in Kent, we go inland, 37 miles from London, to a once-fashionable resort.

4. Royal Tunbridge Wells

Dudley, Lord North, courtier to James I, is credited with the discovery in 1606 of the mineral spring that started it all. His accidental find led to the creation of a fashionable resort 36 miles south of London that reached its peak in the mid-18th century under the foppish leadership of "Beau" Nash. Beau or Richard Nash (1674–1761) was a dandy in his day, the final arbiter of what to wear and what to say—even how to act (for example, he got men to take off their boots and put on stockings). But, of course, most of his time was devoted to Bath. Even so, Tunbridge Wells enjoyed a prime spa reputation from the days of Charles II through Victoria. Because so many monarchs visited it, Edward VII named it Royal Tunbridge Wells in 1919. Over the years the cure was considered the answer for everything from too many days of wine and roses to failing sexual prowess.

The most remarkable feature of Royal Tunbridge Wells is its Pantiles, a colonnaded walkway for shoppers, tea-drinkers, and diners, built near the wells. At the Assembly Hall, entertainment such as opera or vaudeville is presented.

Alas, there's nothing sadder in tourism than a resort that's seen its day. Still, it's worth a visit—just for a fleeting glimpse of the 18th century.

Canadians touring in the area may want to seek out the grave of the founder of their country's capital. Lt. Col. John By of the Royal Engineers (1779–1836) died at Shernfold Park in Frant East Sussex, near Tunbridge Wells, and is buried in the churchyard there. His principal claim to fame is that he built the Rideau Canal in Upper Canada and established what was later to be the capital of the Dominion of Canada, the city of Ottawa.

The Rideau Canal, some 124 miles long, links the city of Kingston on the St. Lawrence River with the city of Ottawa on the Ottawa River. Between 1826 and 1832 John By successfully constructed this canal through an unexplored wilderness for the British government. At the northern end of the canal he laid out "Bytown." Twenty years later this was renamed Ottawa, and it became the capital of a united Canada. His grave near Royal Tunbridge Wells is marked by a plaque erected by the Historical Society of Ottawa in 1979.

FOOD AND LODGING

The leading place to stay is the **Spa Hotel,** Mount Ephraim, Royal Tunbridge Wells, Kent TN4 8XJ (tel. 0892/20331). Privately owned, it still retains many of its Georgian charms, although modern amenities have been installed. Standing in 14 acres of its own grounds, this hotel dates back to 1766. Today it is the property of the Goring family. The owners rent 76 well-maintained and comfortably appointed bedrooms, charging from £55 ($96.25) daily in a single, from £68 ($119) in a double. Each of these accommodations contains a private bath. This is the kind of place where guests often check in for long stays, as opposed to using it as an overnight stopover. Originally a private home, it was converted to a hotel in 1880. The Chandelier Restaurant serves a combination English and French cuisine, with a set lunch at £14 ($24.50), an à la carte dinner going for £20 ($35). Facilities include a sauna, a solarium, tennis, and an indoor swimming pool.

Calverley Hotel, Crescent Road, Royal Tunbridge Wells, Kent TN1 2LY (tel. 0892/26455), is an old stone hotel facing Calverley Park, gardens of special interest in themselves. The hotel's large lounge, furnished with comfortable chairs, opens onto the terrace and gardens. The dining room also overlooks the gardens. The bedrooms, on the upper floors, are reached by elevator. Each room has central heating, phone, and radio, and many have private bath or shower. Guests frequently meet in the cocktail bar for drinks before dinner. Overnight rates at the Calverley are £34 ($59.50) in a bathless single, £38 ($66.50) in a single with bath. Doubles or twins cost £52 ($91) bathless, £54 ($94.50) with bath. VAT and breakfast are included, but you pay an additional £7 ($12.25) for the table d'hôte luncheon and about £8 ($14) for dinner, also with VAT included.

Wellington Hotel, Mount Ephraim, Royal Tunbridge Wells, Kent TV4 8BU (tel. 0892/42911), enjoys a regal position, overlooking the common. The Regency hotel suggests a Charles Addams drawing, with its mansard roof, rows of dormers, and original balconies. Catering mainly to business people and families, it is in an ideal position to be used as a base for visiting the southeast of England. For a luxury period double room with private bath, the charge is from £60 ($105) per night, including VAT and service. Less expensive doubles go for £55 ($96.25). A four-course dinner costs from £12 ($21).

Russell, 80 London Rd., Royal Tunbridge Wells, Kent TN1 1DZ (tel. 0892/44833), is one of the best places for accommodations at the old spa. It is also reasonable in price. Within an easy walk of the Pantiles, it is run by Toni and Kevin Wilkinson. All the pleasant and comfortable bedrooms have private bath. Singles cost from £48 ($84) daily, with doubles or twins going for £60 ($105), including a full breakfast and VAT. Units have color TV and direct-dial phone. You should take your meals here, as they are good tasting and offer value for money. A four-course dinner, for example, costs £15 ($26.25).

Thackeray's House, 85 London Rd. (tel. 0892/37558), serves the finest food in Royal Tunbridge Wells, and you get a little history as well, as this is the second-oldest house in the spa and it was once inhabited by the novelist, William Makepeace Thackeray. Bruce Wass, the owner-chef, once worked at one of my favorite restaurants in London, Odin's, before coming here to set up his own place. He has created an elegant atmosphere, backed up by attentive service, for his specialties, which are served from 12:30 to 2:30 p.m. and 7 to 10 p.m. He is closed both Sunday and Monday and also takes a two-week vacation some time in summer. A table d'hôte lunch begins at £15.75 ($27.55), and a set dinner is offered at £19 ($33.25). Care goes into all his dishes, and many have flair, including an occasional salad with fresh flowers. He reaches perfection with such dishes as tender duck breast served with citrus, or lamb, which comes with baby turnips and is flavored with fresh herbs. For dessert, he is most often cited for his chocolate armagnac loaf, served with a walnut liqueur sauce.

At a bistro, Downstairs at Thackeray's, slightly simpler fare is offered in an informal, friendly atmosphere complete with an inglenook fireplace and an open fire in winter or courtyard dining in summer. Average prices downstairs are around £7 ($12.25) for lunch, £10 ($17.50) for dinner. Meals are served from 12:30 to 2:30 p.m. and 7 to 11 p.m. except Sunday and Monday.

Instead of leaving London for Kent, you might head directly south of the capital to inviting Surrey.

SURREY

This tiny county has for some time been in danger of being gobbled up by the growing boundaries of London and turned into a sprawling suburb. Already some of the densely populated area in Surrey is now part of Greater London. But Surrey still retains much unspoiled countryside, largely because its many heaths and commons do not make good land for postwar suburbanite houses. Essentially, Surrey is a county of commuters (Alfred, Lord Tennyson was among the first), since a worker in the city can practically travel to the remotest corner of Surrey from London in anywhere from 45 minutes to an hour.

Long before William the Conqueror marched his pillaging Normans across its chalky North Downs, Surrey was important to the Saxons. In fact, early Saxon kings were once crowned at what is now **Kingston-on-Thames** (their Coronation Stone is still preserved near the Guildhall).

LIVING IN TUDOR SPLENDOR

The best of England—the best living accommodations, in particular—are to be found in the countryside. There you can sometimes live like a duke or duchess. Transportation facilities are often so good that you can enjoy the best of two worlds, darting into London for all its attractions, while enjoying better surroundings of rural England. For those who want to be in the vicinity of Heathrow Airport, yet within easy access of central London, I have the following recommendation in the upper bracket:

Great Fosters, Egham, Surrey TW20 9UR (tel. 0784/33822), is one of the most impressive old manor houses of England. It was built in 1550 and in its day belonged to Elizabeth I and was a hunting lodge in Windsor's Royal Forest. Only 18 miles from London, it still preserves the link to its past. A red-brick Tudor building, with stone-mullioned windows, many gables, and towering chimneys, it is placed in a private garden, where paths cut through formal grounds of clipped yew hedges, roses, and rhododendrons—and a swimming pool. The architectural features of the interior are in the grand style, as witness the main hall with its carved black oak Jacobean fireplace. In the 15th-century Tithe Barn, with its high vaulted and raftered oak beams, meals are served and an orchestra plays for dancing on Saturday night. Some of the master bedrooms are in a period style. For example, the gilt-paneled Italian bedroom contains an overscale bed with hand-carved cherubs on the posts. Period-style rooms for two people rent from £90 ($157.50) daily, doubles and twins from £72.50 ($126.90), and singles from £50 ($87.50). These room rates include a full English breakfast, service, and VAT. Great Fosters is only a half mile from Runnymede and the Kennedy Memorial, and only seven miles in different directions from Windsor Castle and Hampton Court Palace.

5. Richmond

Want to spend an afternoon in a Thames river town? Richmond in Surrey is only a 30-minute ride from London, and can easily be reached by the Underground trains, or else Green Line coaches 716 or 716a from Hyde Park Corner. The old town, popular in Victorian times, has good public rail links with London, and it offers the escape many seek from the rush and bustle of the metropolis. If you're feeling light-hearted, take the boat trip down the Thames. Turner himself, art materials in hand, came here for inspiration.

THE SIGHTS

Richmond is only one mile from Kew and its botanical gardens. You may prefer a combined excursion to Kew Gardens and Richmond on the same day. One of the attractions of the Thames town is the 2,500-acre **Richmond Park,** first staked out by Charles I in 1637. It is filled with photogenic deer and waterfowl. Richmond has long enjoyed associations with royalty, as Henry VII's Richmond Palace stood there (an even earlier manor was razed). Queen Elizabeth I died in the old palace in 1603. Somebody's short-sightedness led to the palace's being carted away, and only a carriageway remains.

If you want to be like the English, you'll climb **Richmond Hill** for a view of the Thames considered by some to be one of the ten best views in the world. The scene reminded William Byrd of a similar view near his home on the James River in Virginia, inspiring him to name the city founded there in 1737 Richmond.

There are good shops and an excellent theater facing the green on which, in summertime, cricket matches are played. There's also boating on the river. Richmond Park has a public golf course, and you can rent a horse from the local stables. The Richmond Ice Skating Rink has been the nursery of many of England's skating champions. Wimbledon and the Tennis Championships are within easy reach, as is Hampton Court Palace.

At Petersham, the 13th-century **St. Peter's Church** is the burial place of Capt. George Vancouver. The Queen Mother's parents, Lord and Lady Glamis, were married there. It also has some very old wooden box pews. At **St. Anne's Church** at Kew Green, the painters Gainsborough and Zoffany were buried.

From Richmond, you can take bus 65 or 71 to visit historic **Ham House** (disembark at the Fox and Duck Pub across from the grounds of the Ham Polo Club), eight miles from the heart of London. The house offers an amazing look into the lives of the aristocracy of 17th-century England. Unlike most such houses in Britain, this one has been maintained almost intact. Much of the house, especially the kitchen (modern for its time), was the work of Elizabeth Murray, Duchess of Maitland and Countess of Dysart. Her aim was to create the most sumptuous private residence in Restoration England, complete with elegant French upholstered pieces and ceilings depicting mythological scenes. One of the first private bathrooms in England was installed at Ham House. The house is open daily from 11 a.m. to 5 p.m., charging an admission of £2 ($3.50) for adults, £1 ($1.75) for children. In summer, you can order tea in the 17th-century garden. For more information, phone 01/ 940-1950.

WHERE TO STAY

Two privately owned hotels at the top of Richmond Hill, **The Petersham,** Nightingale Lane, Richmond Hill, Richmond, Surrey TW10 6UZ (tel. 01/940-7471), and the **Richmond Gate,** Richmond Hill, Richmond, Surrey TW10 6RP (tel. 01/940-0061), 200 yards apart, are operated and managed as one hostelry. Both enjoy a view of the Thames that has attracted artists for centuries, and both have interesting historical features. The Petersham, built as a hotel in 1864, has a spiral stone staircase dominated by ceiling murals of Renaissance painters, and the Richmond Gate comprises two adjoining Georgian buildings, one originally occupied by a member of the Penn family. Bedrooms in both hotels are a blend of old and new, and all have private baths, color TVs, radios, and direct-dial phones. Room service is offered until 10:45 p.m. Singles at the Petersham cost £75 ($131.25) daily, £65 ($113.75) at the Richmond Gate. Luxury river-view and four-poster rooms for two persons are offered at both places for £75 ($131.25) to £110 ($192.50). Rates are reduced at both hotels on weekends. At the Petersham, a "value for money" weekend package is available at £90 ($157.50) and £120 ($210), with two meals included. The Richmond Gate is operated on a B&B basis. For lunch and dinner, guests can take a courtesy minibus to the Petersham, where Nightingales Restaurant enjoys panoramic views over the river. Both fixed-price and à la carte menus are available. The three-course set menu offers a wide choice of international dishes with wines from the hotel's private cellar. Lunch costs £14 ($24.50); dinner, £17 ($29.75); and a traditional Sunday lunch, £15 ($26.25).

WHERE TO EAT

Londoners often go down to Richmond for the day, browse through its art galleries, and then dine out—which must account for the town's number of good restaurants. My recommendation follows:

Kew Rendezvous, 110 Kew Rd. (tel. 01/940-1334), billing itself with some justification as "the leading Peking-style restaurant in the United Kingdom," is in a building of unique architectural design, just down the road from Kew Gardens. The food is superb, especially if you stick to the chef's specialties and avoid the routine Chinese restaurant fare. Three dishes, designed to delight, include barbecued Peking duck, crispy duck, or a variety of meats on a sizzling iron plate. Also recommended are hot-and-sour Peking soup, scampi Peking style, sliced beef in oyster sauce, and diced chicken in yellow-bean sauce. If there are six people in your party, you can forgo the above and leave it to the chef, who will prepare you a Peking dinner at £18 ($31.50) per person. Lunches cost from £13 ($22.75). Hours are from noon to 2:30 p.m. and 6 to 11:30 p.m. daily.

---

6. Haslemere

A quiet, sleepy town, Haslemere attracts because early English musical instruments are made by hand there. Ever heard a harpsichord concert? An annual music festival (see below) is the town's main drawing card. Over the years, the Dolmetsch family has been responsible for the acclaim that has come to this otherwise unheralded little Surrey town, which lies in the midst of some of the shire's finest scenery. Haslemere is only an hour's train ride from Waterloo Station in London, about 42 miles away.

THE FESTIVAL

It isn't often that one can hear such exquisite music played so skillfully on the harpsichord, the recorder, the lute, or any of the instruments designed so painstakingly to interpret the music of earlier centuries. Throughout the year the Dolmetsch family makes and repairs these instruments, welcoming visitors to their place on the edge of Haslemere. They rehearse constantly, preparing for the concerts that are held in July and last nine days.

You can get specific information by writing to the **Haslemere Festival Office,** Jesses, Grayswood Road, Haslemere, Surrey GU27 2BS (or telephone 0428/2161 between 9 a.m. and 12:30 p.m. daily). During the festival, matinees begin at 3:15 p.m., evening performances at 7:30 p.m. For seats in the balcony, prices range from £4 ($7) to £6 ($10.50), with stall seats going for £2.50 ($4.40) to £5 ($8.75).

WHERE TO STAY

On the outskirts of Haslemere, the **Lythe Hill Hotel,** Petworth Road, Haslemere, Surrey GU27 3BQ (tel. 0428/51251), is a 14th-century farmhouse of historic interest set in 14 acres of parkland overlooking National Trust woodlands and just one hour from London, Heathrow, and Gatwick. Across the courtyard is the main hotel, with 32 luxuriously appointed bedrooms and suites, as well as an English restaurant. In the black-and-white timbered farmhouse are five elegant period units, with marble-tile baths. One has a four-poster bed dated 1614. Singles cost from £55 ($96.25) daily, twins and doubles rent for £95 ($166.25), and 12 suites are priced at £115 ($201.25) to £150 ($262.50) for two. All tariffs include a continental breakfast and VAT. Downstairs in the farmhouse is the renowned oak-beamed and paneled Auberge de France Restaurant, offering a classic French cuisine served on polished oak tables by candlelight. Specialties include turbot, fresh Scottish salmon, tournedos de boeuf, and a cellar of fine wines. Dinner, served from 7 to 9:45

p.m., costs around £40 ($70) for two persons. The restaurant is open for dinner Tuesday to Sunday.

WHERE TO DINE

Considered the most outstanding French restaurant in Surrey, **Morels,** 25-27 Lower St. (tel. 0428/51462), showcases the talents of a remarkable chef, Jean-Yves Morel. He represents the best of yesterday while at the same time is not afraid to experiment with new ideas (mainly those that work). He doesn't represent excess in experimental cookery. His main street establishment is bright and furnished in modern overtones, but there's nothing about the decor that detracts from the cuisine. Londoners flock here.

Monsieur Morel uses morels in some of his concoctions, perhaps in honor or respect for his own name. His menu, adjusted to the seasons and market conditions, changes every 30 days or so, so it's difficult to recommend specific dishes. A typical one might be char-grilled pigeon breast subtly flavored with a light sauce made with a light sauce made with juices of langoustine. Vegetables are almost invariably done to perfection, and diners have been enthusiastic about the cheeseboard selection, which rivals those of France. The assiette du chef is a feast for the palate, a perfectly balanced selection of his finest desserts. A set lunch, from 12:30 to 2 p.m., costs £12 ($21), and a table d'hôte dinner, from 7 to 10 p.m., goes for £15 ($26.25). Count on spending from £30 ($52.50) if dining à la carte. The restaurant is closed for lunch on Saturday and all day Sunday and Monday.

---

7. Guildford

The old and new meet in the county town on the Wey River, 40 minutes by train from Waterloo Station in London. Charles Dickens believed that its High Street, which slopes to the river, was one of the most beautiful in England. The Guildhall has an ornamental projecting clock that dates back to 1683.

Lying 2½ miles southwest of the city, **Loseley House** (tel. 0483/571881), a beautiful and historic Elizabethan mansion visited by Queen Elizabeth I, James I, and Queen Mary, has been featured on TV and in five films. Its works of art include paneling from Henry VIII's Nonsuch Palace, period furniture, a unique carved chalk chimney-piece, magnificent ceilings, and cushions made by the first Queen Elizabeth. The mansion is open from the end of May to the end of September on Wednesday, Thursday, Friday, and Saturday from 2 to 5 p.m., charging £2.80 ($4.90) for adults, £1.50 ($2.65) for children. Lunches and teas are served in the 17th-century Tithe barn from noon to 5 p.m., and you can tour the farm and visit the farm shop.

FOOD AND LODGING

About two miles southwest of the center of Guildford, the **Post House Hotel,** Egerton Road, Guildford, Surrey GU2 5XZ (tel. 0483/574444), opened in 1987, is surrounded by landscaped grounds, just off the A3 London–Portsmouth road. In the 119-bedroom hostelry, a feeling of heritage is conveyed by natural wood joinery in red elm, polished brass fittings, and marble floors. Bedrooms incorporate both living and sleeping areas, and all contain baths and showers, remote-control TVs, radios, direct-dial phones, hot beverage facilities, and private bars. The needs of disabled guests have been taken into consideration. Rates range from £74 ($129.50) daily in singles, from £90 ($157.50) in doubles. The restaurant features traditional English roasts and international dishes. Guests find the hot and cold buffet good value. The coffeeshop, open from 6:30 a.m. to 11 p.m., offers family favorities served in an informal atmosphere.

Angel Hotel, High Street, Guildford, Surrey GU1 3DR (tel. 0483/64555), is an old coaching inn in the middle of the cobbled main street of town. Its entrance and part of its courtyard are Tudor, and many other original features of this once-busy hostelry have been maintained. Inside, there is lavish paneling, plus a huge, open fireplace as well as exposed beams. Great oak timbers from old ships at Portsmouth were used to support the gallery. Most of the 25 bedrooms, including two family rooms, are simply furnished, although some are quite attractively decorated (these disappear first to those who reserve ahead). Each has a private bath, as well as a phone, radio, TV, and coffee maker. Rates begin at £58 ($101.50) daily in a single, going up to £75 ($131.25) in a double or twin; including VAT and service. In addition to a well-decorated bar, the hotel has a quick-service coffeeshop as well as a 13th-century restaurant in the crypt, with medieval architecture making for cozy surroundings. The restaurant offers a wide range of dishes, including English roasts, at an average price of £16 ($28) per person.

GODALMING

Five miles from Guildford, **Inn on the Lake,** Ockford Road, Godalming, Surrey GU7 1RH (tel. 04868/5575), is a haven of landscaped gardens with ducks drowsing on pools beside the lake. Rooms are decorated with pretty country prints and simple furniture, each having TV, tea- and coffee-making equipment, and radio. Charges are from £40 ($70) daily for a single, £60 ($105) for a double, including VAT and a large breakfast. Excellent snacks are served in a real old-world bar, where some of the timbers date from Tudor times. In summer, barbecues are held in the garden. For more substantial dinners, three fixed-price menus are offered at £11.50 ($20.15), £13.50 ($23.65), and £15.50 ($27.15) for five courses, with a varied selection of grills, English, and continental dishes. The house was listed in the *Domesday Book* and has Tudor, Georgian, and Victorian associations. Godalming was the starting point for the emigrés who eventually settled Allenton, Georgia, after landing in Savannah.

WISLEY GARDEN

One of the great gardens of England and the world, Wisley Garden (The Royal Horticultural Society), in Wisley near Ripley (tel. 0483/224234), lies just off the M25 (junction 10) on the A3 London–Portsmouth Road. Every season of the year, this 250-acre garden has a profusion of flowers and shrubbery, ranging from the New Alpine House with its delicate blossoms in spring to the Walled Garden with formal flowerbeds in summer to the Heather Garden's colorful foliage in the fall and a riot of exotic plants in the glasshouses in winter. This garden is the site of a laboratory where botanists, plant pathologists, and an entomologist experiment and assist amateur gardeners. Hours year round are from 10 a.m. to 7 p.m. (or sunset if earlier) Monday to Saturday. Closed Sunday. Admission is £2.50 ($4.40) for adults, £1 ($1.75) for children 6 to 14.

---

8. Dorking

This town, birthplace of Lord Laurence Olivier, lies on the Mole River, at the foot of the North Downs. Within easy reach are some of the most scenic spots in the shire, including Silent Pool, Box Hill, and Leith Hill. Three miles to the northwest and 1½ miles south of Great Bookham, off the A246 Leatherford–Guildford road, stands **Polesden Lacey** (tel. 0372/52048), a former Regency villa containing the Greville collection of antiques, paintings, and tapestries. In the early part of this century it was enlarged to become a comfortable Edwardian country house when it was the home of a celebrated hostess, who frequently entertained royalty there. The 18th-century garden is filled with herbaceous borders, a rose garden, and beech walks, and in all the estate consists of 1,000 acres. The house is open from 1:30 to

5:30 p.m. daily except Monday and Tuesday from April to the end of October, from 1:30 to 4:30 p.m. on Saturday and Sunday only in March and November. The charge to visit both the house and garden is £3.20 ($5.60) on Sunday and bank holidays, £2.50 ($4.40) on other days for adults, with children paying half price. The garden is open daily all year from 11 a.m. to sunset. To visit just the gardens, adults are charged £1.20 ($210) and children pay 60p ($1.05). A licensed restaurant on the grounds is open from 11 a.m. on the days the house can be visited.

FOOD AND LODGING

Back in Dorking, **Burford Bridge Hotel,** Box Hill, Dorking, Surrey RH5 6BX (tel. 0306/884561), offers stylish living in a rural town from which a train will zip you into London in less than half an hour. At the foot of the beauty spot of Box Hill, the hotel has a lot of historical associations. Lord Nelson was a frequent patron, and Keats completed *Endymion* here in 1817. Everyone from Wordsworth to Robert Louis Stevenson also frequented the place. You get the best of both the old and the new here, including a tithe barn (circa 1600) as well as 48 large bedrooms, renting for £70 ($122.50) daily in a single, from £92 ($161) in a double. Each room has its own bath or shower, plus a phone and color TV. The restaurant serves good English food, and a bar opens onto a flowered patio with a fountain. In summer, you can enjoy the garden swimming pool and frequent barbecues.

White Horse Hotel, High Street, Dorking, Surrey, RH4 1BE (tel. 0306/ 881138). Just ten miles from Gatwick Airport, you can dine or lodge at a hotel that dates in part from 1500. Once the vicarage of Dorking, the White Horse by tradition was supposed to have been the "Marquis of Granby" in the *Pickwick Papers*. At least Dickens was known to have frequented the bar parlor. An atmospheric place of creaking timbers and low beamed ceilings, the inn offers 68 bedrooms, including 18 family units, each with private bath or shower, phone, radio, TV, and coffee maker. Some are in a modern annex. A single with bath costs from £54 ($94.50) daily, and a double rents for £70 ($122.50), including VAT and service. Often called "the most interesting house in Dorking," the inn has a restaurant as well as a Pickwick bar offering à la carte meals for £12 ($21) and up. There is also a heated pool.

After visiting Surrey, you can head south toward the English Channel and the sprawling shires of Sussex.

THE SUSSEXES

If King Harold hadn't loved Sussex so much, the course of English history might have been changed forever. Had the brave Saxon waited longer in the north, he could have marshaled more adequate reinforcements before striking south to meet the Normans. But Duke William's soldiers were ravaging the countryside he knew so well, and Harold rushed down to counter them.

Harold's enthusiasm for Sussex is understandable. The landscape rises and falls like waves. The country is known for its Downlands and tree-thickened Weald, from which came the timbers to build England's mighty fleet in days gone by. The shires lie south of London and Surrey, bordering Kent in the east, Hampshire in the west, and opening directly onto the sometimes sunny, resort-dotted English Channel.

Like the other sections in the vulnerable south of England, the Sussexes witnessed some of the biggest moments in the country's history. Apart from the Norman landings at Hastings, the most life-changing transfusion of plasma occurred in the 19th century, as middle-class Victorians flocked to the seashore, pumping new spirit into Eastbourne, Worthing, Brighton, even old Hastings. The cult of the saltwater worshippers flourished, and has to this day. Although **Eastbourne** and **Worthing** are much frequented by the English, I'd place them several fathoms below **Brighton** and **Hastings**, which are much more suitable if you're seeking a holiday by the sea.

Far more than the resorts, the old towns and villages of the Sussexes are intriguing, particularly **Rye** and **Winchelsea**, the ancient towns of the Cinque Port Confederation. No Sussex village is lovelier than **Alfriston** (and the innkeepers know it too); **Arundel** is noted for its castle; the cathedral city of **Chichester** is a mecca for theater buffs. Traditionally, and for purposes of government, Sussex is divided into East Sussex and West Sussex. I've adhered to that convenient dichotomy.

I'll begin in East Sussex, where you'll find many of the inns and hotels within commuting distance of London.

9. Rye and Winchelsea

"Nothing more recent than a Cavalier's Cloak, Hat and Ruffles should be seen in the streets of Rye," said Louis Jennings. He's so right. This ancient town, formerly an island, was chartered back in 1229. Rye, 65 miles below London, near the English Channel, and neighboring Winchelsea were once part of the ancient Cinque Ports Confederation. Rye flourished as a smuggling center, its denizens sneaking in contraband from the marshes to stash away in little nooks (even John Wesley's firm chastisements couldn't stop what was a strongly entrenched tradition).

But the sea receded from **Rye,** leaving it perched like a giant whale out of water, two miles from the Channel. Its narrow, cobblestone streets twist and turn like a labyrinth, with buildings jumbled along them whose sagging roofs and crooked chimneys indicate the town's medieval origins. The old town's entrance is **Land Gate,** where a single lane of traffic passes between massive, 40-foot-high stone towers. The parapet of the gate contains holes through which boiling oil used to be poured on unwelcome visitors such as French raiding parties.

Attacked several times by French fleets, Rye was practically razed in 1377. But it rebuilt sufficiently, decking itself out in the Elizabethan style so that Queen Elizabeth I, during her visit in 1573, bestowed upon the town the distinction of Royal Rye. This has long been considered a special place, having attracted any number of famous men, including Charles Lamb (who considered the smugglers "honest thieves") and Henry James, who lived in **Lamb House** on West Street at the top of Mermaid Street from 1898 to 1916. There are many James mementos in the house, which is set in walled gardens. It is open April through October from 2 to 5:30 p.m. on Wednesday and Saturday, charging an admission of £1 ($1.75).

THE SIGHTS

Today the city has any number of specific buildings and sites of architectural interest, notably the 15th-century **St. Mary's Parish Church,** with its clock flanked by two gilded cherubs, known as the Quarter Boys from their striking of the bells on the quarter hour. If you're courageous, you can climb a set of wooden stairs and ladders to the bell tower of the church, from which an impressive view is afforded.

Rye Museum, 4 Church Square (tel. 0797/223254), is housed in the Ypres Tower, a fortification built circa 1250 by order of Henry III as a defense against French raiders. In this ancient building, the museum contains collections of military objects, shipping artifacts, toys, Cinque Ports relics, Victoriana, inn lore, and pottery. From Easter to mid-October, its hours are daily 10:30 a.m. to 1 p.m. and 2:15 to 5:30 p.m. Monday to Saturday (opens at 11:30 a.m. on Sunday). Admission is 75p ($1.30).

The sister Cinque Federation port to Rye, neighboring **Winchelsea** has also witnessed the water's ebb. It traces its history back to Edward I, and has experienced many dramatic moments, such as sacking by the French. Today it is a dignified residential town. In the words of one 19th-century writer, Winchelsea is "a sunny cream of centuries ago." Its finest sight is a badly damaged 14th-century church, containing a number of remarkable tombs.

On the outskirts, you can visit **Smallhythe Place,** at Tenterden (tel. 05806/2334), which for 30 years was the country house of Dame Ellen Terry. Ellen Terry, of course, was the English actress acclaimed for her Shakespearean roles who had a long theatrical association with Sir Henry Irving. She died in the house in 1928. This timber-framed house, of a type known as a "continuous-jetty house," was built in the first half of the 16th century. It is filled with Terry memorabilia. The house is on the B2082 near Tenterden, about six miles to the north of Rye. The house is open April to October daily except on Thursday and Friday, from 2 to 6 p.m. Adults pay £1.40 ($2.45) admission; children, 70p ($1.25).

WHERE TO STAY

The leading choice is **Mermaid Inn,** Mermaid Street, Rye, East Sussex TN31 7EU (tel. 0797/223065), one of the most famous of the old smugglers' inns of England, known to that band of cutthroats, the reallife Hawkhurst Gang, as well as to Russell Thorndike's fictional character, Dr. Syn. One of the present rooms, in fact, is called Dr. Syn's Bedchamber, and is connected by a secret staircase—set in the thickness of the wall—to the bar. That room, with a private bath, rents for £34 ($59.50) per person nightly, as does the Elizabethan Chamber (with four-poster and private bath). Two other special rooms—the Fleur-de-Lys Chamber and the Tudor Rose Chamber—contain private baths and twin beds, and also cost £34 ($59.50) per person. Terms include breakfast, and a 10% service charge is added. The best rooms are in the main building overlooking the cobblestone street. One, the Smugglers Room, has an oak four-poster. The Mermaid has sheltered everybody from Queen Elizabeth I to George Arliss. When Elizabeth came to Rye in 1573, the inn had already been operating nearly 150 years. A covered carriageway leads to the car park. In the center of the hotel is a courtyard, where you'll see a pedestal fountain with water flowing down on the heads of water lilies. The Mermaid has also taken over the 16th-century Ship Inn at the foot of Mermaid Street, which, with its 12 bedrooms and restaurant on the first floor, complements the Mermaid.

The George, High Street, Rye, East Sussex, TN31 7JP (tel. 0797/22114) is a former coaching inn with a history going back 400 years. It's composed of a trio of 14th-century buildings whose boundaries over the years have grown less distinct. In the 18th century it drew a clientele of passengers traveling by horse-drawn carriage and packet boat between London and France. This is one of the most charming small inns in the region. Winding hallways lead to the 16 bedrooms and to a Georgian salon, reserved only for the use of guests, one flight above the antique-laden lobby. Each of the bedrooms contains a private bath, TV, radio, and phone, and has a half-timbered kind of charm. Some of the timbers capping the ceilings are said to have come from the wreck of an English ship broken up in Rye Harbour after the defeat of the Spanish Armada. Singles cost from £52 ($91) daily; doubles or twins, £68 ($119). On the premises, tucked away at the ends of narrow hallways and twisted stairwells, is the John Crouch pub, with about eight different kinds of beer and cider on tap. The hotel also has an old-fashioned restaurant and at least two blazing fireplaces in cold weather.

Hope Anchor Hotel, Watchbell Street, Rye, East Sussex TN31 7HA (tel. 0797/222216), at the end of a cobblestone street, is a 17th-century hostelry enjoying panoramic views of the surrounding countryside and overlooking the Strand Quay where yachts can be seen at their moorings. Oak beams and open fires in winter make this a most inviting place to spend a few days. The 17 bedrooms—seven with private bath—are comfortable, all with color TV and hot beverage facilities. With a full English breakfast included, doubles cost from £45 ($78.75) daily, and singles begin at £28 ($49). VAT is included. Bar meals are served at lunchtime, and the restaurant offers English cuisine, especially fresh fish caught locally. A traditional roast lunch with fresh local vegetables is served on Sunday. A fixed-price dinner in the restaurant is attractively priced at £10 ($17.50).

Durrant House Hotel, East Street, Rye, East Sussex TN31 7LA (tel. 0797/ 223182), is a beautiful Georgian house set on a quiet residential street in the old town behind a cream-colored façade at the end of Market Street. Over the years it has attracted many famous personages, including John Wesley during his evangelistic tours. In more recent times, the renowned artist Paul Nash lived next door until his death in 1946. In fact his celebrated view, as seen in his painting, *View of the Rother,* can be enjoyed from the River Room of the hotel. Sir William Durrant, a friend of the Duke of Wellington, acquired the house, which is now named after him. In time it was used as a relay station for carrier pigeons; these birds brought news of the victory at Waterloo. The hotel possesses much charm and character. There is a cozy lounge with an arched brick fireplace and, across the hall, a residents' bar. Nine comfortably furnished bedrooms, seven with private baths, are rented. Depending on the plumbing, singles cost from £15 ($26.25) to £25 ($43.75) daily, and doubles go for £24 ($42) to £50 ($87.50), with an English breakfast included.

WHERE TO DINE

Built in the Georgian era as one of the vicarages for St. Mary's Anglican Church, **The Old Vicarage in East Street,** East Street, Rye, East Sussex TN31 7JY (tel. 0797/225131), is a charming establishment that was converted into a French-style *restaurant avec chambres* in 1979. Although the owners, Sarah and Bill Foster, maintain four beautifully decorated bedrooms upstairs, two of which have Regency four-poster beds with ornate canopies, the establishment is best known for its elegant restaurant. Each of the rooms is suitable for one or two persons and rents, with breakfast included, for £22 ($38.50) to £27 ($47.25) daily per person. Units contain private bath, color TV, phone, and a carefully assembled kind of panache.

After an apéritif in the cocktail bar, dinner guests proceed into the elegant blue-and-white dining room, which has many antique pieces and old silver. There, within sight of a carved fireplace, ringed with French chairs and Doric columns, guests enjoy selection of dishes from the classic cuisine. The menu changes monthly to make the most of the best in local fish and meat. A typical meal listing might include shrimp-and-spinach soup, hot devilled crab, Romney Marsh lamb grilled with rosemary, filet of Rye Bay plaice stuffed with prawns in a fresh cream-and-herb sauce, and escalope of pork in a vermouth sauce, followed by desserts such as vacherin aux fruits and a selection of unusual homemade ice creams. A la carte three-course meals range from £12 ($21) to £15 ($26.25). Dinner is served every night from 7 to 9 p.m. This establishment is not to be confused with a nearby B&B also called the Old Vicarage.

The **Flushing Inn,** Market Street (tel. 0797/223292), is in a 16th-century inn on a cobblestreet. It has preserved the best of the past, including a wall-size fresco in the restaurant dating from 1544 and depicting a menagerie of birds and heraldic beasts. A rear dining room overlooks a carefully tended flower garden. A special feature is the Sea Food Lounge Bar, where sandwiches and plates of seafood are available from £5 ($8.75) to £9 ($15.75). In the main restaurant, luncheons are offered beginning at £8.50 ($14.90); dinners run from £15 ($26.25). Besides these lunches and dinners, gastronomic evenings are held at regular intervals between October and April. For one of these specially prepared meals, including your apéritif, wine, and after-dinner brandy, you pay £33 ($57.75) per person. Fine Wine evenings cost £40 ($70) to £50 ($87.50). Hours are 12:30 to 1:45 p.m. and 7:30 to 9 p.m. The inn is closed Monday night, all day Tuesday, for two weeks after Christmas, and for the first two weeks in June. The Flushing Inn has been run by the Mann family since 1960, with the second generation now fully active in the business in the persons of a daughter and son-in-law.

Another choice is offered at the **Landgate Bistro,** 5 Landgate (tel. 0797/ 222829). Nick Parkin and Toni Ferguson-Lees are known for their fresh local fish, wild duck, rabbit, pigeon, and jugged hare. It's all there in pies, casseroles, and stews, accompanied by fresh seasonal vegetables properly cooked or a salad. A meal will cost £15 ($26.50). Food is served Tuesday to Saturday from 7 to 9:30 p.m. only.

---

10. Hastings and St. Leonard's

The world has seen bigger battles, but few are as well remembered as the Battle of Hastings in 1066. When William, Duke of Normandy, landed on the Sussex coast and lured King Harold (already fighting Vikings in Yorkshire) southward to defeat, the destiny of the English-speaking people was changed forever. It was D-Day in reverse. The actual battle occurred at what is now Battle Abbey (nine miles away), but the Norman duke used Hastings as his base of operation.

Hastings suffered other invasions—it was razed by the French in the 14th century. But after that blow a Tudor town grew up in the eastern sector, and it makes for a good stroll today. The more recent invasion threat, that of Hitler's armies, never came to pass, although the dragons' dentures put up across the countryside stood waiting to bite into Nazi tanks.

Linked by a three-mile promenade along the sea, Hastings and St. Leonard's were given a considerable boost in the 19th century by that eminent tripper Queen Victoria, who visited several times. Both towns no longer enjoy such royal patronage; rather, they do a thriving business with Midlanders on vacation. Hastings and St. Leonard's have the usual shops and English sea-resort amusements. Only 63 miles from London, they are serviced by fast trains from Victoria Station.

The two chief attractions are:

HASTINGS CASTLE

In ruins now, the first of the Norman castles to be built in England sprouted up on a western hill overlooking Hastings, circa 1067. Precious little is left to remind us of the days when proud knights, imbued with a spirit of pomp and spectacle, wore bonnets and girdles. The fortress was ordered torn down by King John in 1216, and later served as a church and monastery until it felt Henry VIII's ire. Owned by the Pelham dynasty from the latter 16th century to modern times, the ruins have been turned over to Hastings. It is open from 10 a.m. to 5 p.m. daily from mid-March to the end of October. Admission is £1.30 ($2.30) for adults, 80p ($1.40) for children. A family ticket, for two adults and up to four children, costs £3.75 ($6.55). From the mount, you'll have a good view of the coast and promenade.

THE HASTINGS EMBROIDERY

A commemorative work, the Hastings Embroidery was first exhibited in 1966. It is a remarkable achievement that traces 900 years of English history through needlework. Depicted are some of the nation's greatest moments (the Battle of Hastings, the coronation of William the Conqueror) and its legends (Robin Hood). In all, 27 panels, 243 feet in length, depicting 81 historic scenes, are exhibited at the Town Hall, Queen's Road (tel. 0424/722026). The history of Britain comes alive —the murder of Thomas à Becket, King John signing the Magna Carta, the Black Plague, Chaucer's pilgrims going to Canterbury, the Battle of Agincourt with the victorious Henry V, the War of the Roses, the Little Princes in the Tower, Bloody Mary's reign, Drake's *Golden Hind,* the arrival of Philip's ill-fated Armada, Guy Fawkes's gunpowder plot, the sailing of the *Mayflower,* the disastrous plague of 1665 and the great London fire of the following year, Nelson at Trafalgar, the Battle of Waterloo, the Battle of Britain, and the D-Day landings at Normandy. Also exhibited is a scale model of the battlefield at Battle, depicting William's one-inch men doing in Harold's mini-soldiers. Admission is 75p ($1.30) for adults, 40p (70¢) for children.

A SMUGGLER'S ADVENTURE

You can descend into underground haunts of smugglers in days of yore at **St. Clements Caves.** The caves cover four acres of passages, caverns, and secret chambers 60 feet below ground. You descend 140 feet down the monk's walk, a candlelit passage into the depths of the caves. There you'll find an exhibition of costumes, weapons, artifacts, and "tools of the trade," which tell the story of smuggling in the 18th century. More than 50 life-size figures are brought to life. It is open from mid-March until the end of October daily from 10 a.m. to 6 p.m., charging adults £1.80 ($3.15) and children £1.30 ($2.30).

WHERE TO STAY

The most desirable accommodation at either resort is **Royal Victoria,** Marina, St. Leonard's, East Sussex TN38 0BD (tel. 0424/445544). The hotel, constructed in 1829, has the most impressive architecture of any establishment in town. It was long a landmark on the seafront, occupying a formidable position, but it needed complete refurbishing. That was done in 1988, and now Royal Victoria is back to its premier position. The hotel offers 28 well-furnished bedrooms, along with 31 impressive, sometimes regal, suites. Standard singles rent for £45 ($78.75) daily, with doubles costing £58 ($101.50). The hotel is attractively furnished and decorated, and bedrooms, each with private bath, contain all the modern amenities. The restaurant of the Royal Victoria offers some of the best food in the area, with meals beginning at £12.50 ($21.90).

On the outskirts, one of the best places to stay in the Hastings-Battle district is **Beauport Park Hotel,** Battle Road, Rte. A2100, Hastings, East Sussex TN38 8EA (tel. 0424/51222). It looks much older than it is. It was originally erected as the private estate of General Murray, once the governor of Québec (he had previously served under General Wolfe). However, a fire in 1923 swept over it, and it was later reconstructed in the old style. Run as a hotel accommodating 30 guests, it is surrounded by beautiful gardens (the Italian-style grounds in the rear contain statuary and flowering shrubbery). The living room and drinking lounge are tastefully furnished, and the French windows in the dining room open onto the parklike rear. The B&B rate is £45 ($78.75) daily in a single, £75 ($131.25) in a double. All units have private bath with shower, direct-dial, phone, and TV. The hotel offers well-prepared and handsomely served cuisine. Some of the produce comes from the hotel's own gardens. A set lunch is featured for £9.50 ($16.65) at which a varied choice is available. The set dinner is £11.50 ($20.15), and again the choice is wide.

WHERE TO DINE

The leading restaurant, **Röser's,** 64 Eversfield Pl. (tel. 0424/712218), is a relief to find in what is often considered one of the gastronomic wastelands of southern England. Most diners come here to enjoy the seafood dishes of Gerald Röser, who shows considerable skill in his choice of food offerings, including everything from the classic Dover sole to lamb from Romney Marsh. In season, game dishes are also featured. The cuisine is French inspired, and service is first rate. A set lunch is good value at £13.50 ($23.65), but you will more likely spend £25 ($43.75) enjoying the evening's à la carte selections. Service is from noon to 2 p.m. and 7 to 10 p.m. except Saturday lunch and all day Sunday. The wine list is chosen with discretion, and prices tend to be reasonable, as this is not a resort for big spenders.

---

11. Battle

Nine miles from Hastings, in the heart of the Sussex countryside, is the old market town of Battle, famed in history as the setting for the Battle of Hastings in

1066. King Harold, last of the English kings, encircled by his housecarls, fought bravely, not only for his kingdom but for his life. In the battle, Harold was killed by William, Duke of Normandy, and his body was dismembered. To commemorate the victory, William the Conqueror founded **Battle Abbey,** High Street (tel. 0426/3792), some of the stone for which was shipped from his own lands at Caen in northern France.

During the dissolution of the monasteries in 1537 by King Henry VIII, the church of the abbey was largely destroyed. Some buildings and ruins, however, remain in what Tennyson called "O Garden, blossoming out of English blood." The principal building still standing is the Abbot's House, which is leased to a private school for girls and not open to the general public. Of architectural interest is the Gatehouse, with its octagonal towers, standing at the top of the Market Square. All of the north Precinct Mall is still standing, and one of the most interesting sights of the ruins is the ancient Dorter Range, where the monks once slept.

The town of Battle grew up around the abbey, but even though it has remained a medieval market town, many of the old half-timbered buildings regrettably have lost much of their original character because of stucco plastering carried on by past generations. The abbey is open from 9:30 a.m. to 6:30 p.m. Monday to Saturday and 2 to 6:30 p.m. Sunday from March 15 to October 15. Hours are from 9:30 a.m. to 4 p.m. Monday to Saturday and 2 to 4:30 p.m. Sunday from October 16 to March 14. It is also open from 9:30 a.m. Sunday from April 1 to September 30. Admission is £1.60 ($2.80) for adults, 80p ($1.40) for children.

WHERE TO STAY

Standing in 30 acres of parkland, **Netherfield Place,** Netherfield Road, Battle, East Sussex TN33 9PP (tel. 04246/4455), built in 1924, is 1¾ miles outside Battle on the A2100, and it's by far the best place to stay. The symmetrical wings of this brick-fronted Georgian mansion extend toward flowering gardens on all sides. Once you pass beneath the cornices of the entrance, you'll discover a world of plush upholstery, comfortable bedrooms, and sun-flooded panoramas. You can enjoy tea or a drink in the glassed-in lounge overlooking the trees outside. The hotel offers cozy bedrooms, each with full carpeted bath, attractive wallpaper, and tasteful curtains. Each accommodation also has a private bath or shower, phone, and TV. The costs begin at £45 ($78.75) daily in a single, £70 ($122.50) in a double. The food is also good and carefully served, prepared with fresh, wholesome produce. Fresh fruit and vegetables come from their own garden. Dinners cost from £15 ($26.25).

George Hotel, 23 High St., Battle, East Sussex TN33 0EA (tel. 04246/4466), is an old coaching inn in the center of historic Battle. An inn has stood on this site for more than 600 years, and today the George combines modern comfort and a historic, listed building. Yolanda and Dennis Laybourne, the resident owners, have 21 bedrooms, all with private baths, TVs, and hot beverage facilities. Prices, with a continental breakfast included, are £26 ($45.50) daily in singles, £36 ($63) to £38 ($66.50) in doubles. The traditional four-poster bedroom rents for £44 ($77) per night. Saturday and Sunday breaks are offered, with £26 ($45.50) per person charged for B&B. The hotel has a comfortable bar, with a full bar snack menu. Open log fires make the place cozy in winter. The spacious restaurant features English and continental dishes. Lunch costs from £5.50 ($9.65), and dinner, from £9.90 ($17.35). There is a private parking area.

WHERE TO DINE

Once a smithy for the village and the 11th-century manor house, the **Blacksmith's Restaurant,** 43 High St. (tel. 04246/3200), is in an oak-beamed building dating back to the 15th century. Owned by Martin and Christine Howe, the restaurant they have created here since 1981 has become a much-talked-of place. Martin was head chef at London's well-known Gay Hussar for 14 years before finding this location in Battle when he felt the need of a place of his own. The result is a friendly, low-windowed restaurant with wheel-back chairs and gleaming silver, decorated with antique blacksmith's tools and a large pair of bellows in one corner.

There is a small bar where Christine or one of the pleasant local women will take your order from the à la carte menu, costing £14 ($24.50) to £18 ($31.50) for dinner. I sampled roast duck Blacksmith's style, crispy and coated with honey, served with cherry sauce accompanied by vegetables, and finished off with a homemade dessert from the trolley. The meal was not only a delight, but reasonably priced for the generous portions served. Tuesday to Saturday, a two-course lunch is offered for just £5.50 ($9.65), and a set dinner costs £12 ($21). Lunch is served Tuesday to Sunday from noon to 2:30 p.m., and dinner is offered Tuesday to Saturday from 7 to 10:30 p.m. You must reserve a table.

KIPLING'S HOME IN SUSSEX

Rudyard Kipling, the British writer famous for his stories about the days of empire in India, lived his last 34 years—1902 to 1936—at **Bateman's,** a country house half a mile south of Burwash, on the A265, the Lewes–Etchingham road (tel. 0435/882302). The sandstone house, built in 1634, was bequeathed, together with its 300 acres of land and its contents, to the National Trust by Kipling's widow. East and West meet within the house, in Oriental rugs, antique bronzes, and other mementos the writer collected in India and elsewhere. Kipling's library is among the points of interest to be visited. The house is open from April to the end of October daily except Thursday and Friday from 11 a.m. to 6 p.m. (last admissions at 5:30 p.m.). Admission to the house, a restored watermill, and the attractive garden is £2.50 ($4.40) for adults, £1.30 ($2.30) for children Monday to Friday, £2.80 ($4.90) for adults, £1.40 ($2.45) for children Saturday, Sunday, and bank holidays.

12. Alfriston and Lewes

Nestled on the Cuckmere River, **Alfriston** is one of the most beautiful villages of England. Its High Street, with its old market cross, looks like one's fantasy of what an English village should be. Some of the old houses still have hidden chambers where smugglers stored their loot. Alfriston has several old inns.

During the day Alfriston is likely to be overrun by coach tours (it's that lovely, and that popular). The village lies about 60 miles from London, northeast of Seaford on the English Channel, in the general vicinity of the resort of Eastbourne and the modern port of Newhaven.

You can visit **Drusilla's Zoo Park** (tel. 0323/870234), on the outskirts. This zoo has won awards. It is not large, but fascinating nonetheless with a flamingo lake, Japanese garden, and unusual breeds of some domestic animals, among other attractions. Children are especially delighted, as there is a playland covering more than one acre. An English Wine and Food Centre is also part of the complex. The park is open from late March until October daily from 11 a.m. to 5:30 p.m. (until dusk in winter), charging adults £2.50 ($4.38) and children the same.

Only about a dozen miles along the A27 toward Brighton lies **Lewes,** an ancient Sussex town worth exploring. Centered in the South Downs, Lewes is 51 miles from London. Since the home of the Glyndebourne Opera is only five miles to the east, the accommodations of Lewes are often frequented by cultured guests and are difficult during the Glyndebourne Opera festival, but adequate at other times.

The county town has many historical associations, listing such residents as Thomas Paine who lived at Bull House, High Street, now a restaurant. The half-timbered **Anne of Cleves House** (tel. 0273/474610), so named because it formed part of that queen's divorce settlement from Henry VIII, is now a Museum of Local History and is cared for by the Sussex Archaeological Society. (Anne of Cleves never lived in the Anne of Cleves House, and there is no proof that she ever visited Lewes.)

258 □ KENT, SURREY, AND THE SUSSEXES

The museum has a furnished bedroom and kitchen and displays of furniture, local history, the Wealden iron industry, and other local crafts. It is on Southover High Street and is open Monday to Saturday from mid-February to mid-November from 10 a.m. to 5 p.m.; on Sunday, April to October, from 2 to 5 p.m. Admission is £1.10 ($1.95) for adults, 55p (95¢) for children.

Lewes, of course, grew up around its Norman castle. From the tower you can obtain a fine view of the countryside. To visit **Lewes Castle and Museum** (tel. 0273/474379), a joint ticket costs adults £1.30 ($2.30); children, 65p ($1.15). The castle and museum are open all year from 10 a.m. to 5:30 p.m. Monday through Saturday (also on Sunday, April to October, from 2 to 5:30 p.m.).

FOOD AND LODGING IN ALFRISTON

The most desirable place to stay is **Deans Place,** Alfriston, Polegate, East Sussex BN26 5TW (tel. 0323/870248), a historic country home with a modern wing set on its own five acres of grounds, with a swimming pool and tennis courts. On the banks of the Cuckmere River, the house lies about five miles from the coast. Lounges are spacious and comfortable. Each of the 40 bedrooms is attractively decorated and furnished, with private bath, phone, beverage-making equipment, hairdryer, and TV. Janet and Michael Pritchard are the thoughtful hosts, welcoming guests at the rate of £47 ($82.52) to £52 ($91) daily in a single, the tariff going up to £75 ($131.25) to £81 ($141.75) in a double. Bar lunches are excellent at midday, and a set dinner is offered for only £11.50 ($20.15), plus an à la carte selection as well.

White Lodge Country House Hotel, Sloe Lane, Alfriston, East Sussex BN26 5UR (tel. 0323/870265). For some 20 years Don and Maureen Denyer lived within its Edwardian era walls with their children. It was their private home. But in 1984, three weeks after Don retired from a career as a property developer, he transformed his home into one of the most opulently furnished hotels in the region. It stands on five acres of gardens, about a five-minute walk from the center. The public rooms are outfitted like French salons, with carved 18th- and 19th-century antiques, many of them gilded. Bronze statues inspired by classical Greek myths are placed about. The daytime dining room is French with Louis XV furniture, centered around a chiseled fireplace of violet-tinged marble. Dinner is served below the reception area in an Edwardian room. A four-course lunch, served daily from 12:15 to 2:15 p.m., goes for £9.95 ($17.40); a four-course dinner, from 7:15 to 9:45 p.m., costs £14.95 ($26.15). Menu specialties, prepared by a trio of chefs, include cornets of smoked salmon, grilled lemon sole, and in season, marinated venison. Each of the beautifully furnished bedrooms has a private bath, color TV, hairdryer, phone, lots of flounced and tasseled curtains, and countryside views. Singles rent for £40 ($70) daily and doubles or twins for £65 ($113.75).

Star Inn, High Street, Alfriston, East Sussex BN26 5TA (tel. 0323/870495), occupies a building dating from 1450, although it was originally founded in the 1200s, perhaps to house pilgrims en route to Chichester and the shrine of St. Richard. In the center of the village, its carved front still unchanged, it boasts an overhanging second story of black and white timbers and bay windows. The lounges are on several levels, a forest of old timbers. Out back is a motel wing, with studio rooms all of which have private baths. Each has a radio, phone, heating, and built-in wardrobe. A single costs £52 ($91) daily, and a double or twin goes for £72 ($126). These rates include VAT and service. A three-course dinner is priced from £12 ($21).

Moonrakers, High Street (tel. 0323/870472), offers the best food in town. The welcome is warm at this charming little 16th-century restaurant with old beams and a well-prepared cuisine where a homemade taste is emphasized. Elaine Wilkinson is the chef, and she operates the restaurant with her husband, Barry. The menu is changed every few weeks, so I can't recommend specific dishes with any guarantee that they will be served. Fresh fish appears frequently on the menu, and chicken dishes are prepared with flair. Count yourself lucky if you're there on the night Elaine decides to prepare beef Wellington. Fresh herbs are used discreetly. A set dinner is served for £17.50 ($30.65). Dinner is served from 7 to 9 p.m. (slightly later on Saturday). The Moonrakers' wine list is the finest in town. The restaurant is closed for lunch and shuts down completely on Sunday and Monday. Its annual closing is from mid-January to mid-February, and reservations are essential.

FOOD AND LODGING IN LEWES

Dating back to 1526. **Shelleys Hotel,** High Street, Lewes, East Sussex BN7 1XS (tel. 0273/472361) is a manor house owned by the Earl of Dorset, before it was sold to the Shelley family, distant relatives of the poet. Radical changes were made to the architecture in the 18th century. Nowadays, the standards of the management are reflected in the fine antiques, the bowls of flowers, the paintings and prints, the well-kept gardens, and most important, the staff. In the rear is a sun terrace and lawn for tea and drinks. Horse chestnuts and copper beech shade the grounds. The central hall is characterized by Ionic columns, a domed ceiling, and the coat-of-arms of the Shelley family. The bay windows of the front drawing room open onto the rear gardens, and the drinking lounge is paneled. The 21 bedrooms are personal, individually furnished, usually spacious and most comfortable. Singles with shower cost from £54 ($94.50) daily; doubles with bath/shower, £78 ($136.50). Service and VAT are included in all charges. Room 11 has a 16th-century frieze of Bacchanalian figures and a design of entwining grapes and flowers. You can order meals at Shelleys. Lunch costs from £9.50 ($16.65); dinner is from £12 ($21).

Kenwards, Pipe Passage, 151a High St. (tel. 0273/472343), stands near the Bull House where Thomas Paine lived. It's across the street, a stone-and-brick building reached by a very narrow passage. John and Caroline Kenward welcome you into their little enclave, which was a converted mid-16th-century brewery. In fair weather, you can enjoy a drink in their garden. Under a beamed ceiling, you can later partake of their menu, which uses only fresh seasonal produce. The chef's talent is reflected in such dishes as venison with juniper berries and chicken with orange and coriander. The lemon sole is always reliable. The menu is small, but as Spencer Tracy said of Katharine Hepburn, "it's choice." You can order one of their "surprises" for dessert. The wine list is reasonably priced. Dinner is likely to cost from £18 ($31.50) per person. Only dinner is served, from 7:30 to 9:30 p.m. The restaurant is closed on Sunday and Monday, and also on Tuesday in winter.

---

13. Brighton and Hove

In 1753, when Dr. Russell propounded the seawater cure—even to the point of advocating the drinking of an "oceanic cocktail"—he launched a movement that was to change the life of the average English person, at least his or her vacation plans. Brighton, 53 miles south of London, was one of the first of the great seaside resorts of Europe. The village on the sea from which the present town grew was named Brighthelmstone, and the English eventually shortened it to Brighton.

The original swinger who was to shape so much of its destiny arrived in 1783, after just turning voting age; he was the then Prince of Wales, whose presence and patronage gave immediate status to the seaside town.

Fashionable dandies from London, including Beau Brummell, turned up. The construction business boomed, as Brighton blossomed with charming and attractive town houses, well-planned squares and crescents. From the Prince Regent's title came the voguish word "Regency," which was to characterize an era, but more specifically refers to the period between 1811 and 1820. Under Victoria, and in spite of her cutting off the patronage of her presence, Brighton continued to flourish.

Alas, in this century, as the English began to discover more glamorous spots on the continent, Brighton lost much of its old joie de vivre. It became more aptly tabbed as tatty, featuring the usual run of fun-fair-type English seaside amusements ("let's go down to Brighton, ducky"). Happily, that state of affairs has changed, owing largely to the huge numbers of Londoners moving in (some of whom have taken to commuting, as Brighton lies only one hour with frequent train service from Victoria Station). The invasion is making Brighton increasingly light-hearted and sophisticated. A beach east of the town attracts nude bathers, Britain's first such venture. Introduction of real-life attractions of the flesh has certainly made passé such pictorial representations as were once the big draw on penny machines by the seafront. These, however, still clank and grind away in a museum, where you can take a trip back in time by means of an old penny purchased at the museum's kiosk.

The Lanes, a closely knit section of alleyways off North Street in Brighton (many of the present shops were formerly fisherman's cottages), were frequented in Victoria's day by style-setting curio and antique collectors. Some are still there, although sharing space with boutiques.

At **Hove,** once a separate town but now a part of the Greater Brighton complex, of special interest is the **Engineerium,** in a building that used to house a waterworks. Here you can see a little steam launch, models of engines and steam trucks, old motorbikes, and the Victorian waterworks kept in operative condition.

THE ROYAL PAVILION

Among the royal residences of Europe, the Pavilion at Brighton (tel. 0273/603005), a John Nash version of an Indian mogul's palace, is unique. Ornate and exotic, it has been subjected over the years to the most devastating wit of English satirists and pundits. But today we can examine it more objectively as one of the outstanding examples of the orientalizing tendencies of the romantic movement in England.

Originally the pavilion was built in 1787 by Henry Holland. But it no more resembled its present look than a caterpillar does a butterfly. By the time Nash had transformed it from a simple classical villa into an Oriental fantasy, the Prince Regent had become King George IV. He and one of his mistresses, Lady Conyngham, lived in the palace until 1827.

A decade passed before Victoria, then queen, arrived in Brighton. Although she was to bring Albert and the children on a number of occasions, the monarch and Brighton just didn't mix. The very air of the resort seemed too flippant for her—and the latter-day sea-bathing disciples of Dr. Russell trailed Victoria as if she were a stage actress. Further, the chinoiseries of the interior and the mogul domes and cupolas on the exterior didn't sit too well with her firm tastes—even though the pavilion would have been a fitting abode for a woman who was to bear the title Empress of India.

By 1845 Victoria and Brighton had had it. She began packing, and the royal furniture was carted off. Its tenants gone, the pavilion was in serious peril of being torn down. By a narrow vote, Brightonians agreed to purchase it. Gradually, it is being restored to its former splendor, enhanced in no small part by the return of much of its original furniture on loan by the present tenant at Buckingham Palace.

Of exceptional interest is the domed **Banqueting Hall,** with a chandelier of bronze dragons supporting lily-like glass globes. In the Great Kitchen, with its old revolving spits, is a collection of Wellington's pots and pans, his *batterie de cuisine,* from his town house at Hyde Park Corner. In the State Apartments, particularly the domed Salon, dragons wink at you, serpents entwine, lacquered doors shine. The Music Room, with its scalloped ceiling, is a salon of water lilies, flying dragons, sunflowers, reptilian paintings, bamboo, silk, and satin.

In the second-floor gallery, look for Nash's views of the pavilion in its elegant heyday. There is also an exhibition of pavilion history, illustrating the damage caused by rainwater, frequent alterations, and the impressive program of repair and reclamation in progress. Currently, the Royal Pavilion is undergoing an extensive program of structural and decorative restoration. This inevitably results in occasional inconvenience to visitors, although the work is, in its own right, absolutely fascinating. The pavilion is open daily from 10 a.m. to 5 p.m. October to May, to 6 p.m. June to September; closed Christmas and Boxing Day. Admission is £2.30 ($4.05) for adults, £1.20 ($2.10) for children 5 to 15. A family ticket for one adult and up to four children costs £3.50 ($6.15), for two adults and up to four children £5.75 ($10.05).

SEEING BRIGHTON

A walking tour costs £1 ($1.75) for adults, 50p (90¢) for children. Tours are offered from March to December, but hours are subject to change. For times and places of departure, consult the **Tourist Information Centre**, Marlborough House, 54 Old Steine (tel. 0273/23755), by the Royal Albion Hotel and the bus terminal. You can also get help here if you have accommodations problems.

WHERE TO STAY

Dozens of accommodations are to be found in all price ranges. Regrettably, many are establishments, to quote Norman Mailer, "where elderly retired India colonels brood through dinner. . . ." However, that situation is changing now, as the most celebrated relics of yesteryear are experiencing (or have experienced) extensive overhauling. I'll survey the leading hotels, then proceed to a representative sampling of the accommodations awaiting those who must keep expenses trimmed.

The Upper Bracket

The Grand, Kings Road, Brighton, East Sussex BN1 2FW (tel. 0273/21188), is the premier hotel of Brighton. The original Grand was constructed in 1864, and in time entertained some of the most eminent of the Victorians and the Edwardians. Tragically, this landmark was massively damaged following a terrorist attack on Margaret Thatcher and key figures in the British government. Several colleagues were killed, Mrs. Thatcher narrowly escaped, and entire sections of the hotel looked as if hit by an air raid. That gave its present owners, De Vere Hotels, the challenge to create a new Grand rising from the ashes. Frankly, the new one is better than the old one. It's the most elegant Georgian re-creation in town.

You enter via a glassed-in conservatory and register in public rooms with soaring ceilings, elaborate moldings, and grandiose proportions. The hotel has plushly comfortable furniture in traditional tastes with well-chosen accessories. The rooms, of a very high standard, from a single to the presidential suite, are generally spacious with many amenities, including a private bath, color TV, radio, direct-dial phone, hospitality tray, trouser press, and hairdryer. A special feature, the sea-view rooms contain refrigerators. There are also units designed for "lady executives," as well as "romantic rooms" with double whirlpool baths. Thoughtfully, some accommodations have been provided with additional facilities for the disabled. Singles rent for £90 ($157.50) daily, and doubles or twins go for £125 ($218.75) to £170 ($297.50), including a full English breakfast and VAT. Hobden's Health Spa is complete with spa pool, steamroom, sauna, solarium, and massage and exercise arena. There is also a hairdressing salon and beautician. Both British and continental cuisine are served in King's Restaurant. The food uses superb ingredients masterfully handled by the kitchen staff. The Victoria Bar is an elegant rendezvous, and Midnight Blues is considered the most sophisticated club at the resort.

Ramada Renaissance, King's Road, Brighton, East Sussex BN1 2GS (tel. 0273/206700), is one of the finest accommodations in the south of England. Rising from the seafront, it has been stylishly and often rather luxuriously designed for maximum comfort. Guests wander at leisure through an array of tastefully furnished public rooms, complete with a well-decorated sunken bar lounge. The hotel is perhaps the best equipped in town, certainly for the athletic, with a whirlpool bath, gym, indoor swimming pool, along with a solarium and sauna. Several thoughtful extras with today's modern client in mind were added, including a laundry service and a coffee shop that remains open until 11 p.m. for late arrivals. In all, 204 well-furnished and attractively decorated bedrooms are rented, each with private shower and bath. The air-conditioned bedrooms, which offer mini-bars, cost from £95 ($166.25) daily in a single, rising to £150 ($262.50) in a double. Its restaurant, La Noblesse, is outstanding, with a set lunch menu going for £15.50 ($27.15). A table d'hôte dinner costs £20 ($35), plus à la carte selections. Imaginative but not overly ambitious cooking is the rule here, and menus are well planned. Nonresidents might enjoy partaking of the viands any time from noon to 2 p.m. and 7 to 11 p.m. except Sunday.

Brighton Metropole, King's Road, Brighton, East Sussex BN1 2FU (tel. 0273/775432), rises in a neo-Romanesque red-brick style from a central location on the seafront. The lobby is in a neutral modern style, and the 328 recently refurbished and luxurious bedrooms offer such amenities as private baths and showers, color TV, radios, direct-dial phones, in-house movies, hairdryers, trouser presses, and tea/coffee-makers. Singles cost £95 ($166.25) daily, and doubles and twins go for £115 ($201.25). The hotel also offers 16 suites. On the premises is a Leisure Club, including indoor swimming pool, plus an array of dining and drinking facilities, among them the Arundel and Windsor Restaurants, the Canon Pub, and the Metro Night Club.

Queens Hotel, 1-5 King's Rd., Brighton, East Sussex BN1 1NS (tel. 0273/727316), one of Brighton's most prestigious hotels, occupies possibly the finest position on the seafront, reputedly on the site of Sake Deen Mahomet's "Indian Vapour Baths," where the first Turkish baths in Britain stood and where the word *shampoo* originated. This first-class hotel became famous in the 19th century and has had many distinguished guests, even royalty. Each bedroom has a private bath, color TV, radio, direct-dial phone, mini-bar, and personalized safe. Rates are from £70 ($122.50) daily in a single, £85 ($148.75) in a twin or double. Tariffs include a full English breakfast and VAT. The sea-facing restaurant offers table d'hôte and à la carte menus. Snacks are also available all day in the Atrium lounge. Hotel facilities include a deluxe nightclub and the Royales Health Club with pool, Jacuzzi, mini-gym, sunbeds, massage, and Turkish bath.

Sheridan Hotel, 64 King's Rd., Brighton, East Sussex BN1 1NA (tel. 0273/23221). Named after the supremely witty friend of the prince who made Brighton famous, the hotel is built of Edwardian brick. The property juts above the beachfront. Its whimsically ornate façade is composed of two tones of brick, capped with hexagonal towers, bulky chimneys, and Dutch-style gables. Inside, the old-fashioned proportions of the bedrooms offer a tastefully updated kind of modern comfort, always with a full bath, radio, color TV, and phone. The 34 bedrooms rent for £57 ($99.75) daily in a single, £76 ($133) in a double. A full English breakfast, served in the room, and VAT are included in the tariffs. A multilevel car park is nearby.

The Medium-Priced Range

The **Granville Hotel,** 125 King's Rd., Brighton, East Sussex BN1 2FA (tel. 0273/26302), on Brighton's seafront, with views over the West Pier and the channel. The 25-room hotel has a black-and-white reception area and lounge reminiscent of Raffles Hotel in Singapore, complete with an elevator and a restaurant. The bedrooms are all comfortably furnished, and some can even be called luxurious. For example, the Granville Room has a handmade pine four-poster antique double bed, sea views, and private bathroom with a double Grecian bath. You may even have a room with a family-size Jacuzzi. Décor by Laura Ashley and Mary Quant occurs throughout the hotel. All the units have color TV, radio, and phone. The charge in a single is from £55 ($96.25) daily, from £80 ($140) in a double. For a room with double bed, private balcony, and a double bathroom with Jacuzzi, you'll pay £120 ($210), while the Granville Room, described above, costs £103 ($180.25). The hotel's Trogs Restaurant is previewed below.

Old Ship Hotel, King's Road, Brighton, East Sussex BN1 1NR (tel. 0273/

29001), in a central position on the seafront, has a paneled interior with comfortable sea-view lounges, an oak-paneled bar, and a spacious sea-facing restaurant. A well-organized kitchen serves good-tasting meals with selections from an impressive wine list. Each of the accommodations has a color TV, radio, direct-dial phone, and full private bath. Singles cost £60 ($105) daily; doubles, £80 ($140). All tariffs include an English breakfast and VAT. In 1651 the owner of an earlier manifestation of this hotel saved the life of King Charles II by spiriting him away in his ship.

The Budget Range

Twenty-One Hotel, 21 Charlotte St., Marine Parade, Brighton, East Sussex BN2 1AG (tel. 0273/686450), is one of the most sophisticated—perhaps *the* most sophisticated—of the smaller hotels of Brighton. It also serves some of the best food (some say *the* best) at the resort, but regrettably the dining room isn't open to nonresidents. In other words, to enjoy the full experience of the place, you'd better try to get a room here. Stuart Farquharson and Simon Ward rent only seven bedrooms in this early-Victorian white-fronted house a block from the sea. Five of their attractive and well-furnished bedrooms contain private baths, and all units offer color TVs, direct-dial phones, radios, and hot beverage facilities. Each accommodation has a different color scheme, often in green, pink, or terracotta. The basement-level garden suite opens directly onto an ivy-clad courtyard. Singles rent for £30 ($52.50) to £40 ($70) daily and doubles go for £40 ($70) to £65 ($113.75), including VAT, breakfast, and service. A menu degustation of four courses, costing £22 ($38.50), is written in French and translated into English. Main courses are likely to include such subtle dishes as sliced breast of duck served pink with a lime sauce or wild poached salmon with fine strips of vegetables.

Topps Hotel, 17 Regency Square, Brighton, East Sussex BN1 2FG (tel. 0273/729334), enjoys a diagonal view of the sea from its position beside the sloping lawn of Regency Square. Flowerboxes fill the windows of this cream-colored town house, whose owners, Paul and Pauline Collins, have devoted years to upgrading it. The establishment contains a dozen rooms, all with private baths. Each accommodation is of a different shape and is furnished individually, sometimes with neo-Elizabethan furniture and early 19th-century moldings. Each contains a TV, radio, mini-bar, phone, and trouser press. The hotel charges £35 ($61.25) to £45 ($78.75) daily in a single and £65 ($113.75) to £75 ($131.25) in a double, with an English breakfast and VAT included. A small restaurant in the basement serves dinners to clients who reserve by noon. Closed during Christmas and the first week in January.

The **Regency Hotel,** 28 Regency Square, Brighton, East Sussex BN1 2FH (tel. 0275/202690), is in a circa 1815 town house with bay windows, a carved door, and a canopied balcony facing south across the square toward the sea. Owners Ambrose and Gail Simons have extensively renovated the establishment. The ground floor contains a high-ceilinged lounge with period furniture, Waterford chandeliers, and an original coal-burning fireplace. The 14 bedrooms, ten of which have private showers and toilets, rent for £26 ($45.50) to £33 ($57.75) daily in a single, £44 ($77) to £52 ($91) in a double, with VAT and a full English breakfast included. For something romantic, you can reserve the Regency Suite whose half-tester bed, private balcony, complete bath, and formal furniture look like something out of the Royal Pavilion. It rents for £65 ($113.75) for two. All rooms have color TV, direct-dial phones, hairdryers, radios, and tea/coffee-makers. The higher up you go, the simpler the bedrooms become. The hotel has a licensed bar, and there is underground parking available in the square. The beach is 200 yards away.

DINING OUT IN BRIGHTON

In a well-preserved, 19th-century building conveniently opening into The Lanes, **English's Oyster Bar and Seafood Restaurant,** 29-31 East St. (tel. 0273/27980), is my leading choice for superbly cooked fish. It combines an inviting setting with good food. For years diners have been making such wise selections as half a dozen Colchester native oysters or a hot seafood en croûte with lobster sauce. The chef is known for such specialties as Dover sole English's and fresh, locally caught plaice. He also offers a seasonal menu, which is available for lunch and dinner every day. You're given a selection of appetizers, plus a choice from at least six main courses. Expect to spend from £18 ($31.50) if you order à la carte. The restaurant is open Monday to Saturday from noon to 10:15 p.m. and on Sunday from 12:30 to 4 p.m.

French Cellar, 37 New England Rd. (tel. 0273/603643), provides the resort's best French cuisine. In the kitchen, Jean-Claude Rozard presides with a certain flair, a style also possessed by Mrs. Rozard who is likely to welcome you up front. Their "cellar" is home to Monsieur's concerned, thoughtful cooking. As many times as he's prepared a certain dish, he seems to approach the challenge first again, as if he must make his reputation. Many of the dishes, such as stuffed mussels and a classic onion soup, are familiar fare on old French menus. Other dishes are more stylized in keeping with today's modern cuisine. Fish dishes are generally excellent. You can order a modestly priced house wine from France. Service is Monday to Saturday for dinner only from 7:15 to 10 p.m. You'll spend from £16 ($28) and up, and reservations are needed.

La Marinade, 77 St. George's Rd., Kemp Town (tel. 0273/600992), is another French restaurant, this one the domain of Yves Volant whose cuisine is inspired by the regions of Normandy and Brittany. A two-story restaurant, La Marinade offers a menu showing a certain subtle sophistication in cookery. You get a good range of sensitively cooked dishes, where care has been taken to preserve natural flavors. The white butter sauce, for example, on my recently sampled fish dish was just as good as any served in the Loire Valley. Lunch is from 12:15 to 2 p.m. and dinner from 7:15 to 10 p.m. except when it is closed for lunch Saturday, dinner Sunday, and all day Monday. The set lunch menu for £9 ($15.75) is one of the best food values of Brighton. However, should you visit for dinner, count on spending from £20 ($35) or more.

China Garden, 88 Preston St. (tel. 0273/251124), The menu is large and satisfying to most diners, and you can eat almost any time—that is, from noon to 11 p.m. daily. Dim sum, however, is offered only until 4 p.m., and makes a popular luncheon choice. Try such dishes as chicken feet in a black bean sauce, duck's web and mixed meat, perhaps sliced pork Szechuan style. A set dinner is excellent value at £9.50 ($16.35) or you can order à la carte at £20 ($35) per person.

Trogs, 125 King's Rd. (tel. 0273/26302), is a charming restaurant in the semibasement of the Granville Hotel and under the same ownership. Its name is short for *troglodytes* (cave dwellers), but the little bistro eating place is far from cavelike, being a sunny place opening onto King's Road. Under an arched ceiling, bentwood chairs and potted palms against rough plaster walls provide a pleasing ambience in which to enjoy the French cuisine. Some dishes depend for their ingredients on the best produce found in the market that day. A fixed-price lunch costs £9.95 ($17.40), including VAT, and might offer such food as crêpes filled with creamed mushrooms (for vegetarians), lamb noisette gingered and grilled, or grilled trout with sesame seeds. A three-course dinner, costing £16.95 ($29.65) might include crudités and garlic dip, pâté, porc en croûte (filet of pork stuffed with pâté, wrapped in a puff pastry, and baked), and a dessert or cheeseboard selection. À la carte meals cost from £16 ($28) up. Lunch is served from noon to 2:30 p.m. and dinner from 7 to 10:30 p.m. daily.

STAYING AT HOVE

The leading hotel is **The Dudley,** Lansdowne Place, Hove, Brighton, East Sussex BN3 1HQ (tel. 0273/736266), set near the seafront just a few blocks from the resort's bronze statue of Queen Victoria. Going up marble steps, you register at a carved mahogany desk in the Chippendale style beneath crystal chandeliers and within view of 18th-century antiques and oil portraits of Edwardian-era debutantes.

The large and high-ceilinged public rooms emphasize the deeply comfortable chairs, the thick cove moldings, and the chandeliers. The hotel was created when three neighboring houses, each built with bow-fronted façades in the 1820s, were combined into one unit. A bar precedes the entrance to the dining room, where candles and paneling add to the allure of the British and international cuisine. The 80 bedrooms contain private bath, color TV, radio, phone, and coffee-making equipment, along with high ceilings, tall windows, and conservatively stylish furniture. Depending on the accommodation, singles cost £56 ($98) to £59 ($103.25) daily, and doubles or twins go for £71 ($124.25) to £75 ($131.25).

The **Alexandra Hotel,** 42 Brunswick Terrace, Hove, Brighton, East Sussex BN3 1HA (tel. 0273/202722), was built in 1830 at the height of the Regency period. On the Hove seafront, it was at the heart of the Brunswick Estate, which was a small cluster of residences for "people of quality." Before being established as a hotel by a special Act of Parliament, the structure at this address was the home of the exiled Austrian diplomat, Prince Metternich. It was one of the first houses in England to have hot and cold running water. The hotel has been fully modernized without detracting from its period atmosphere, with care taken to restore windows and exterior ironwork in the Regency style. Each of the 60 bedrooms has a private bath, color TV, radio and alarm clock, direct-dial phone, tea/coffee-makers, hairdryers, and central heating. Many rooms enjoy sea views. A single costs £46 ($80.50) daily, while a double or twin goes for £64 ($112), including service and VAT. You can enjoy choice Sussex ale in Alex's Bar and have meals of English or continental cuisine in the 1830 Restaurant, with its Regency ambience. A table d'hôte luncheon costs around £8 ($14), with dinner from £10 ($17.50).

Sackville Hotel, 189 Kingsway, Hove, Brighton, East Sussex BN3 4GU (tel. 0273/736292). Its lime- and cream-colored, neo-baroque façade was built across the road from the beach in 1902. Today, in a comfortably updated form, it welcomes visitors into a high-ceilinged collection of bedrooms with big windows, sea views, and a collection of Queen Anne furnishings. Each of the 45 bedrooms contains a private bath, color TV, phone, radio, and reminders of yesteryear. Singles rent for £47 ($82.25) to £54 ($94.50) daily, and doubles for £60 ($105) to £72 ($126). A few units have terraces. A large ground-floor dining room offers a warmly masculine kind of formality with views of the sea and good service and food. An adjacent bar, Winston's, is filled with photographs of Churchill in war and peace.

Courtlands Hotel, 19-27 The Drive, Brighton, East Sussex BN3 3JE (tel. 0273/731055), lies 400 yards from the sea, opening onto the wide thoroughfare known as "The Drive," about a mile from the center of Brighton. It is a comfortable Victorian building, recently modernized, with 56 rooms, all with private bath or shower and color TV. This includes units in the Courtlands complex—five particularly agreeable rooms in the cottage and coach house annex, which possess mini-bars, direct-dial phones, and tea- and coffee-making facilities. Bedrooms are spacious and harmonious, with prices set according to plumbing. Rates include a full English breakfast, service, and VAT. Singles cost £52 ($91) daily. Doubles rent for £68 ($119). This traditional hotel has more than adequate facilities, including the Golden Dolphin lounge bar and a dining room opening onto gardens. A good cuisine, both international and English, is assured. The hotel has a small children's playground, a solarium, and a heated swimming pool, as well as a games room, and adequate parking is provided.

14. Arundel

This small town in West Sussex, only 58 miles from London, four miles from the English Channel, nestles at the foot of one of England's most spectacular castles. The town was once an Arun River port, its denizens enjoying the prosperity of considerable trade and commerce. The harbor traffic is gone, replaced by buses filled with visitors who come to visit the castle.

ARUNDEL CASTLE

The ancestral home of the Dukes of Norfolk, this baronial estate (tel. 0903/883136) is a much-restored mansion of considerable importance. Its legend is associated with some of the great families of England—the Fitzalans and the powerful Howards of Norfolk. Arundel Castle traces its history back to King Alfred; its keep goes back to around the Conquest.

Over the years Arundel Castle suffered destruction, particularly during the Civil War when Cromwell's troops stormed its walls, perhaps in retaliation for the 14th Earl of Arundel's (Thomas Howard) sizable contribution to Charles I. In the early 18th century the castle virtually had to be rebuilt. In late Victorian times it was remodeled and extensively restored again. Today it is filled, as you'd expect, with a good collection of antiques, along with an assortment of paintings by old masters such as Van Dyck and Gainsborough.

The castle is open from 1 to 5 p.m. Sunday to Friday from March 24 to the last Friday in October, opening at noon in June, July, August, and on bank holidays. Last admission is at 4 p.m. Closed Saturday. Admission is £3 ($5.25) for adults, £2 ($3.50) for children 5 to 15 years of age. Surrounding the castle is a 1,100 acre park (scenic highlight: Swanbourne Lake).

OTHER SIGHTS

In a Georgian cottage in the heart of historic Arundel, the **Arundel Toy and Military Museum** at "Doll's House," 23 High St. (tel. 0903/882908), displays a delightful and intriguing family collection spanning many generations of old toys and games, small militaria, dolls, dollhouses, tin toys, musical toys, famous teddy bears, frogs, Britain's animals and soldiers, arks, boats, rocking horses, and crested military models. It is open most days from Easter to October (in winter, Saturday and Sunday only), or it may be seen at any time by arrangement. Admission is £1 ($1.75) for adults, 75p ($1.30) for children. The museum is opposite Treasure House Antiques Market.

Arundel Cathedral (the Cathedral of Our Lady and St. Philip Howard), London Road (tel. 0903/882297), stands at the highest point in town. A Roman Catholic cathedral, it was constructed for the 15th Duke of Norfolk by A.J. Hansom, who invented the Hansom taxi. However, it was not consecrated as a cathedral until 1965. The interior includes the shrine of St. Philip Howard, featuring Sussex wrought ironwork. Admission is free, it is open daily from 9 a.m. to 6 p.m. (closes at dusk in winter). Donations are appreciated.

FOOD AND LODGING

A former Georgian coaching inn in the center of town, the **Norfolk Arms,** 22 High St., Arundel, West Sussex BN18 9AD (tel. 0903/882101), is just a short walk from the castle. The lounges and dining room are in the typically English country-inn style—that is, unostentatious but unquestionably comfortable. The hotel has been restored with many modern amenities blending with the old architecture. The bedrooms are handsomely maintained and furnished, each with personal touches. Most rooms have a private bathroom, and all have color television. It is a medium-priced place. The B&B rate is £39.50 ($69.15) to £44 ($77) daily for singles, £56 ($98) to £60 ($105) for doubles. In the restaurant you can order good English cooking with a luncheon for £9 ($15.75). When available, fresh local produce is offered. You can also dine on a specialty menu for £12 ($21), which includes many traditional English dishes.

Pogey's, 25 Tarrant Street (tel. 0903/882222), has brought new life and vitality to what had traditionally been considered a dull restaurant town. In an art deco setting with chrome, you get English food with a flair here. Perhaps lamb with red currant sauce will be featured or perhaps magret of duckling in an orange and Cointreau sauce. Try, if offered, suprême of chicken with an asparagus and sweet corn sauce. Full à la carte meals cost from £10 ($17.50) to £20 ($35). A fixed price lunch, when offered, goes for £5 ($8.75) Tuesday to Saturday, going up to £7 ($12.25) on Sunday. Hours are daily except Monday from noon to 3 p.m. and 7 to 11 p.m.

---

15. Chichester

According to one newspaper, Chichester might have been just a market town if the Chichester Festival Theatre had not been established in its midst. One of the oldest Roman cities in England, Chichester is in vogue, drawing a crowd from all over the world who come to see its theater's presentations.

Only a five-minute walk from the Chichester Cathedral and the old Market Cross, the 1,400-seat theater, with its apron stage, stands on the edge of Oaklands Park. It opened in 1962 (first director: Lord Laurence Olivier), and its reputation has grown steadily, pumping new vigor and life into the former walled city.

THE FESTIVAL THEATRE

Booking opens in March, and the season runs from the middle of April until late September. The price of seats ranges from £6.50 ($11.38) to £14 ($24.50) for the finest tickets in the house. A limited number of £3 ($5.25) seats go on sale at the box office on the day of each performance, sold on a first-come, first-served basis. Reservations made over the phone will be held for a maximum of four days (call 0243/781312). It's better to mail inquiries and checks to the box office, **Chichester Festival Theatre,** Oaklands Park, Chichester. Matinee performances begin at 2:30 p.m., evening shows at 7:30 p.m., except "First Nights," which are at 7 p.m.

How to get there: If you would like to come down from London, 62 miles away, for a matinee, catch the 11:21 a.m. train from Victoria Station, which will deliver you to Chichester by 1:01 p.m., in plenty of time. For an evening performance, board the 4:21 p.m. train from Victoria Station, arriving at 6:06 p.m. Regrettably, there is no direct late train back to London after the show. Visitors who must return can make a connection via Brighton, arriving at Victoria Station shortly after midnight.

WHERE TO STAY

In Chichester, you have a choice of living either at one of the old inns inside the city or on the outskirts.

Dolphin & Anchor, West Street, Chichester, West Sussex PO19 1QE (tel. 0243/785121), is two old inns joined together. The situation is prime, right at the historic 15th-century Market Cross and opposite the Chichester Cathedral, a ten-minute walk from the Festival Theatre. The setting blends 19th-century architectural features, including an old coaching entrance, with 20th-century comforts. A more up-to-date wing of bedrooms is also offered. The two-in-one inn has 51 bedrooms, all with bath, TV, radio, and phone. A single is £54 ($94.50) daily, a twin going for £68 ($119), these tariffs including service and VAT. A few deluxe rooms rent for £79 ($138.25) for two people. There are lounges, bars, the Whig and Tory Restaurant, and the Roussillon Coffee Shop, which serves light meals and grills until 10 p.m.

Ship Hotel, North Street, Chichester, West Sussex PO19 1NH (tel. 0243/782028), is one of the classic Georgian buildings of the city, only a few minutes' walk from the cathedral, the Chichester Festival Theatre, and many fine antique shops. The Ship was built as a private house in 1790 for Admiral Sir George Murray (one of Nelson's commanders) and still remains an air of elegance and comfort. A grand Adam staircase leads from the main entrance to the bedrooms (most with private bathroom), which are all named after historic ships. Single-room prices are £28 ($49) to £48 ($84) daily, and doubles cost £42 ($73.50) to £63 ($110.25). A full English breakfast is included. Good pub lunches are offered. The Victory Bar is one of Chichester's most popular meeting places. The welcoming restaurant offers excellent value for money with its à la carte and special four-course dinner menus each evening from £11 ($19.25).

Chichester Resort Hotel, Westhampnett, Chichester, West Sussex PO19 4UL (tel. 0243/786351), is a boon to motorists because it's a mile from the city center on the main A27 with large car-parking facilities. A covered passageway connects it to the older White Swan Inn nearby. The attractively styled hotel offers 43 modern bedrooms tastefully furnished, each containing private bathroom, telephone, radio, tea-making facilities, and color TV. The rate is £62 ($108.50) daily for a double and £47 ($82.25) for a single, including VAT, service, and a full English breakfast. The hotel has a cocktail bar and restaurant serving a set lunch for £10 ($17.50), a table d'hôte dinner for £12 ($21), VAT and service included. There is also an à la carte menu. A health club and swimming pool are on the premises.

WHERE TO DINE
In contrast to its limited number of accommodations, Chichester abounds with good restaurants. I find the following establishments superior, both for food and value.

Comme Ça, 149 St. Pancras (tel. 0243/788724), is the best French restaurant in town. In fact, it's the best restaurant period. The decor is unpretentious, with a certain French provincial quality. The chef is French, as a look at the menu offerings will reveal. Try feuillete of salmon with chives, sole Comme Ça, perhaps filet of beef with a Dijon mustard sauce. Good quality ingredients are used. Meals cost from £20 ($35), and are served from 12:15 to 2 p.m. and 7:15 to 9:30 or 10 p.m., depending on business. It is closed for lunch Saturday, dinner Sunday, and all day Monday. Reservations are needed.

White Horse, 1 High St. (tel. 024359/219), lies 6½ miles north of Chichester by the B2141 road to Petersfield. The wine cellar at this informally elegant country restaurant is believed to be one of the most comprehensive in Britain. This is partly because of the careful attention the owners, Barry and Dorothea Phillips, pay to the details of their 18th-century inn, whose patina has been burnished every day since it was first built in 1765. The trio of dining rooms contains old beams, lots of hardwood, and a close attention to the gleaming silver of the table settings. Open daily except Sunday and Monday, the establishment serves lunch from noon to 1:45 p.m. and dinner from 7 to 9 p.m. Specialties include wild duck with a black-cherry and port sauce, wild mushroom and chicken vol-au-vent, and veal with a vermouth-and-sorrel sauce. A set lunch costs £12.95 ($22.65), a set dinner going for £16.95 ($29.65). The restaurant is closed in February.

WEALD AND DOWNLAND OPEN AIR MUSEUM
In the beautiful Sussex countryside at Singleton, six miles north of Chichester on the A286 (London road), historic buildings that have been saved from destruction are being reconstructed on a 40-acre Downland site. The structures show the development of traditional building from medieval times to the 19th century in the Weald and Downland area of southeast England. The museum is open every day from 11 a.m. to 6 p.m. April to October 31. From November to March, it is open only on Wednesday and Sunday from 11 a.m. to 5 p.m. Admission is £2.50 ($4.40) for adults, £1.25 ($2.20) for children. Still developing, the museum shows the history of traditional buildings in southeast England. Exhibits include a Tudor market hall; timber-frame medieval houses dating from the 14th to the 16th centuries with wattle-and-daub walls; a working watermill producing stone-ground flour; a black-

smith's forge; plumbers' and carpenters' workshops; a toll cottage; a 17th-century treadwheel; agricultural buildings, including thatched barns and an 18th-century granary; a charcoal burner's camp; and a 19th-century village school. For further information, phone 024363/348.

FISHBOURNE

A worthwhile visit only two miles from Chichester is to the remains of the **Roman Palace,** Salthill Road (tel. 0243/785859), the largest Roman residence yet discovered in Britain. Built around A.D. 75 in Italianate style, it has many mosaic-floored rooms and even an underfloor heating system. The gardens have been restored to their original 1st-century plan. The story of the site is told both by an audio-visual program and by text in the museum. There is free parking and a cafeteria. The museum is open from March through November. Admission is £1.80 ($3.15) for adults, £1 ($1.75) for children.

LIVING ON THE OUTSKIRTS

One of the most interesting ways to attend the theater in Chichester is from a base on the outskirts. That way, you get to enjoy the best of English village life, but can conveniently go into the city whenever you want. Some recommendations follow.

Old Bosham

One of the most charming little villages of West Sussex, Bosham was the site of the first establishment of Christianity on the Sussex coast. The Danish King Canute made it one of the seats of his North Sea empire, and it was the site of a manor (now gone) of the last of England's Saxon kings, Harold, who sailed from here to France on a journey that finally culminated in the invasion of England by William the Conqueror in 1066. Bosham's little church was depicted in the Bayeux Tapestry. Near the harbor, it is reached by a narrow lane. Its graveyard overlooks the boats (a daughter of King Canute is buried inside). The church is filled with ship models and relics, showing the villagers' link to the sea. Bosham is principally a sailing resort, linked by bus service to Chichester.

Millstream Hotel, Bosham Lane, Bosham, Chichester, West Sussex PO18 8HL (tel. 0243/573234), is set on the road to the village of Bosham and its harbor, off the A27. Completely redecorated, the rooms have different colors, but all are outfitted with floral-patterned wallpaper. The decor is in keeping with the country cottage-type hotel. Beds are comfortable, and each of the 29 rooms has a private bath. The charge is £70 ($122.50) daily for a double or twin, £42 ($73.50) in a single, with breakfast included in the rates. The cocktail bar at the entrance to the restaurant is tastefully furnished with white bamboo chairs and tables. At the adjoining restaurant, you can order such à la carte dishes as moules marinières and roast Sussex lamb with fresh herbs. Dinner costs from £12 ($21).

Midhurst

Spread Eagle Hotel, South Street, Midhurst, West Sussex GU29 9NH (tel. 073081/6911), started life as a 15th-century coaching inn, and has been much lived in, altered, and loved ever since. The inn and the market town of Midhurst are so steeped in history that the room you sleep in and the pavement you walk on have a thousand tales to tell. The rooms have beams, small mullioned windows, and unexpected corners, as well as having been modernized with baths, along with radios, color TVs, and phones. The Queen's Suite with four-poster bed goes for £140 ($245) a night. However, you can rent a double or twin room from £70 ($122.50) to £100 ($175) or a single from £60 ($105), including VAT, service, and a large English breakfast.

Dinner is served in the dining hall, lit by candles that flicker on the gleaming tables. In the winter, log fires blaze. The lounge with its timbered ceiling is where

Queen Elizabeth I and her court might have sat to watch festivities in the Market Square outside. The eagle in the lounge is the actual one that decorated the back of Hermann Goering's chair in the Reichstag. It was acquired for its apt illustration of the hotel's name. There are several bars. Midhurst lies only 12 miles from Chichester, only a bit farther from Arundel and Bosham; Brighton is just 36 miles down the road. It's also quite a good place for a first or last night for those boarding a flight at Gatwick Airport outside London.

HAMPSHIRE AND DORSET

Stone farmhouses—Burke's Landed Gentry—all this belongs to the countryside of the 17th century. Fireplaces where stacks of logs burn merrily. Wicker baskets of apples freshly brought in from the orchard (ever had homemade apple butter?). Chickens stuffed with dressing and roasted with strips of bacon on top to keep them tender and juicy. Milk that doesn't come from bottles. Old village houses, now run as hotels, possessing quality and charm. Beyond the pear trees, on the crest of a hill, the ruins of a Roman camp. A village pub, with two rows of kegs filled with varieties of cider, where the hunt gathers.

You're in Hampshire and Dorset, two shires guarded zealously by the English, who protect their special rural treasures. Everybody knows of Southampton and Bournemouth, but less known is the undulating countryside lying inland. Your car will take you through endless lanes, revealing tiny villages and thatched cottages untouched by the industrial invasion.

The area is rich with legend and in literary and historical associations. Here Jane Austin and Thomas Hardy wrote—and set their novels. Here, too, King Arthur held court around his Round Table. And from here sailed such memorable ships as the *Mayflower*, Lord Nelson's *Victory*, the D Day invasion flotilla, and the *QE2*.

HAMPSHIRE

This is Jane Austen country—firmly middle class, largely agricultural, its inhabitants doggedly convinced that Hampshire is the greatest spot on earth. Austen wrote six novels of manners, including *Pride and Prejudice* and *Sense and Sensibility*, that earned her a room at the top among 19th-century writers. Her books provided a keen insight into the solid middle-class English who were to build such a powerful Empire. Although the details of the life she described have now largely faded ("At five o'clock the two ladies retired to dress, and at half-past six Elizabeth was summoned to dinner"), much of the mood and spirit of Hampshire depicted in her books remains.

Born in 1775, Jane Austen was the daughter of the Oxford-educated rector, the Reverend Mr. George Austen, a typical Hampshire country gentleman, who had much charm but little money. In keeping with a custom of the time, the Austens gave their second son, Edward, to a wealthy, childless family connection, Thomas Knight, whose heir the young man became. It was Edward who gave to his mother and sisters **Chawton Cottage,** Chawton near Alton (tel. 0420/83262), where visitors can see the surroundings in which the novelist of manners spent the last 7½ years of her life, her period of greatest creation. In the unpretentious but pleasant cottage, you can see the table on which Jane Austen penned new versions of three of her books and wrote three more, including *Emma* (her "handsome, clever, and rich" heroine, Emma Woodhouse). You can also see the rector's George III mahogany bookcase and a silhouette likeness of the Reverend Austen presenting his son to the Knights. It was in this cottage that Jane Austen became ill in 1816 of what would have been diagnosed by the middle of the 19th century as Addison's disease.

There is an attractive garden in which visitors are invited to have picnics, and an old bakehouse with Miss Austen's donkey cart. About two miles from the station, the home is open daily April to October, including Sunday, from 11 a.m. to 4:30 p.m., for £1 ($1.75) admission; children under 14, 50p (90¢). It is closed Monday and Tuesday in November, December, and March; Monday to Friday in January and February; and Christmas Day and Boxing Day.

Hampshire embraces the **New Forest** (don't expect anything in England labeled "new" to be new), the **South Downs,** the **Isle of Wight** (Victoria's favorite retreat), the passenger port and gateway city of **Southampton,** and the naval city of **Portsmouth.**

Going west from Southampton, you'll come to the New Forest, more than 90,000 acres selfishly preserved by William the Conqueror as a private hunting ground (poachers met with the death penalty). William lost two of his sons in the New Forest—one killed by an animal, the other by an arrow. Today it is a vast woodland and heath, ideal for walking and exploring.

Although Hampshire is filled with many places of interest, for our purposes I've concentrated on two major areas that seem to hold the most appeal for visitors: Southampton for convenience of transportation and accommodations and Winchester for history.

1. Portsmouth and Southsea

Virginia, New Hampshire, even Ohio, may have their Portsmouths, but the daddy of them all is the old port and naval base on the Hampshire coast, 70 miles south of London. German bombers in World War II virtually leveled the city, hitting about nine-tenths of its buildings. But the seaport has recovered admirably.

Its maritime associations are known around the world. From Sally Port, the most interesting district in the **Old Town,** "Naval heroes innumerable have embarked to fight their country's battles." That was certainly true on June 6, 1944, when Allied troops set sail to invade occupied France.

Southsea, adjoining Portsmouth, is a popular seaside resort with fine sands, gardens, bright lights, and a host of holiday attractions. Many historic monuments can be seen along the stretches of open space where you can walk on the Clarence Esplanade and look out on the Solent, viewing the busy shipping activities of Portsmouth harbor.

THE SIGHTS

Some 400 years earlier, an English navy ship didn't fare so well. The **Mary Rose,** flagship of the fleet of wooden men-o'-war of King Henry VIII, sank in the Solent in 1545 in full view of the king. In 1982 a descendant of that monarch, and heir to the throne, Charles, Prince of Wales, watched the *Mary Rose* break the water's surface after almost four centuries spent lying on the sea bottom, not exactly shipshape and Bristol fashion but surprisingly well-preserved nonetheless. Now the remains are on view, but the hull must be kept permanently wet. The hull and the more than 10,000 items brought up by divers constitute one of the major archeological discoveries of England in many years. Among the artifacts on permanent exhibit are almost the complete equipment of the ship's barber, with surgeon's cabin saws, knives, ointments, and plaster all ready for use; long bows and arrows, some still in shooting order; carpenters' tools; leather jackets; and some fine lace and silk. Close beside the dock where the hull lies is the *Mary Rose* exhibition in Boathouse 5. The artifacts rescued from the ship are stored there. It contains an audio-visual theater and a spectacular two-deck reconstruction of a segment of the ship, including the original guns. A display with sound effects recalls the sinking of the vessel.

To see the *Mary Rose* Ship Hall and Exhibition (tel. 0705/750521), use the entrance to the Portsmouth Naval Base through the Victory Gate (as for H.M.S. *Victory*), and follow the signs. It is open every day from 10:30 a.m. to 5:30 p.m. (closed Christmas Day). Admission is £2.80 ($4.90) for adults and £1.80 ($3.15) for children. Family tickets cost £7.40 ($12.95). For information, write to the *Mary Rose* Trust, College Road, H.M. Naval Base, Portsmouth, Hampshire PO1 3LX.

Of major interest is Lord Nelson's flagship, **H.M.S. Victory,** a 104-gun, first-rate ship of the line, now at No. 2 Dry Dock in Portsmouth Naval Base (tel. 0705/826682). Although she first saw action in 1778, her fame was earned on October 21, 1805, in the Battle of Trafalgar when the English scored a victory over the combined Spanish and French fleets. It was in this battle that Lord Nelson lost his life. The flagship, after being taken to Gibraltar for repairs, returned to Portsmouth with Nelson's body on board (he was later buried at St. Paul's in London). It is open from 10:30 a.m. to 5 p.m. Monday to Saturday, from 1 to 5 p.m. on Sunday; closed Christmas Day. Admission is £2.80 ($4.90) for adults, £1 ($1.75) for children, and £4.60 ($8.05) for a family (of four).

The **Royal Naval Museum** (tel. 0705/733060) stands next to Nelson's flagship, H.M.S. *Victory,* and the *Mary Rose* in the heart of Portsmouth's historic naval dockyard. The only museum in Britain devoted exclusively to the general history of the Royal Navy, it contains relics of Nelson and his associates, together with unique collections of ship models, naval ceramics, figureheads, medals, uniforms, weapons, and other naval memorabilia. Special displays feature "The Rise of the Royal Navy" and "H.M.S. *Victory* and the Campaign of Trafalgar." Other exhibits include the Victorian navy, the navy in the 20th century, and the modern navy. The museum is open daily from 10:30 a.m. to 5 p.m. (with some seasonal variations). Admission is £1 ($1.75) for adults, 75p ($1.30) for children. The museum complex includes a buffet and a souvenir shop.

Portsmouth was the birthplace of Charles Dickens, and the small terrace house of 1805 in which the famous novelist made his appearance on February 7, 1812, and

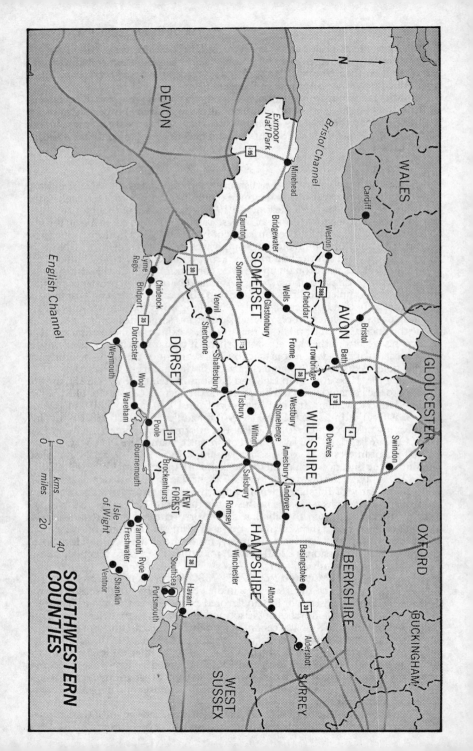

SOUTHWESTERN COUNTIES

lived for a short time, was restored and furnished to illustrate the middle-class taste of the early 19th century. Called **Charles Dickens's Birthplace Museum,** it is at 393 Old Commercial Rd., Mile End (tel. 0705/827261). It is open daily from 10:30 a.m. to 5:30 p.m. (closed November 1 to the end of February). Admission is 50p (90¢) for adults, 25p (45¢) for students and children. Family tickets (four persons) are available for £1.25 ($2.20). Last tickets are sold at 5 p.m.

On the Southsea front, you can see a number of naval monuments, including the big anchor from Nelson's ship, *Victory,* a commemoration of the officers and men of H.M.S. *Shannon* for heroism in the Indian Mutiny, an obelisk with a naval crown in memory of the crew of H.M.S. *Chesapeake,* and a massive column, the **Royal Naval memorial** honoring those lost at sea in the two world wars, as well as a shaft dedicated to men killed in the Crimean War. There are also commemorations of persons who fell victim to yellow fever in Queen Victoria's service in Sierra Leone and Jamaica. The **Southsea Common,** between the coast and houses of the area, known in the 13th century as Froddington Heath and used for army bivouacs, is a picnic and play area today. Walks can be taken along Ladies' Mile if you want to be away from the common's tennis courts, skateboard and roller-skating rinks, and other activities.

Southsea Castle, built in 1545 as part of the coastal defenses ordered by King Henry VIII, and the D-Day Museum, devoted to the Normandy landings 399 years later, are next door to each other on the Clarence Esplanade of Southsea. The castle, a fortress built of stones from Beaulieu Abbey, houses a museum with displays tracing the development of Portsmouth as a military stronghold, as well as naval history and the archeology of the area. The castle is open daily from 10:30 a.m. to 5:30 p.m. except on Christmas Eve, Christmas Day, and Boxing Day. Admission is 50p (90¢) for adults, 25p (45¢) for children.

The **D-Day Museum** contains the Overlord Embroidery, showing the complete story of Operation Overlord, as the D-Day action was designated, the men, and the machines that were featured in the invasion operation. The appliquéd embroidery, believed to be the largest of its kind (272 feet long and three feet high), was designed by Sandra Lawrence and took 20 women of the Royal School of Needlework five years to complete. There is a special audio-visual program with displays, including reconstructions of various stages of the mission with models and maps. You'll see a Sherman tank in working order, Jeeps, field guns, and even a DUKW (popularly called a Duck), that incredibly useful amphibious truck that operated on land and sea. The museum is open seven days a week from 10:30 a.m. to 5:30 p.m. except during the three-day Christmas holiday. Admission is £2 ($3.50) for adults, £1.20 ($2.10) for children, and £5.20 ($9.10) for families to two adults and two children. For information on both Southsea Castle and the D-Day Museum, phone the Visitors Services Organizer at the City Museums office (tel. 0705/827261).

On the northern side of Portsmouth Harbour on a spit of land are the remains of **Portchester Castle** (tel. 0705/378291), built in the late 12th century by King Henry II, plus a Norman church. It is set inside the impressive walls of a 3rd-century Roman fort built as a defense against Saxon pirates when this was the northwest frontier of the declining Roman Empire. By the end of the 14th century Richard II had modernized the castle, making it a secure small palace. Among the ruins are the hall, kitchen, and great chamber of this palace. Portchester was popular with medieval kings, who stayed here when they visited Portsmouth. The last official use of the castle was as a prison for French seamen during the Napoleonic wars. It is open from 10 a.m. to 6 p.m. daily except Monday from Good Friday to the end of September, charging an admission of £1.10 ($1.95) for adults and 55p (95¢) for children.

Cross Portsmouth Harbour by one of the ferries that bustle back and forth all day to Gosport. Some departures go directly from the station pontoon to H.M.S. *Alliance* for a visit to the **Royal Navy Submarine Museum** (tel. 0705/529217).

The museum traces the story of underwater warfare and life below the seas from the earliest days to the present nuclear age, and contains excellent models, dioramas, medals, and displays from all ages. There is also as much about submariners themselves as about the steel tubes in which they make their homes, and although the museum focuses on British boats, it includes much of international interest. The principal exhibit is H.M.S. *Alliance,* and after a brief audio-visual presentation, visitors are guided through the boat by ex-submariners, experiencing the true feeling of life on board in the artificial world beneath the sea. Midget submarines, both British and others, including an X-craft, can be seen outside the museum. Also on display is H.M. *Torpedo Boat No. 1,* better known as *Holland I,* launched in 1901, which sank under tow to the breaker's yard in 1913 and was salvaged in 1982. Admission to the museum is £2 ($3.50) for adults, £1.20 ($2.10) for children.

WHERE TO STAY

With fine views of the sea, **The Pendragon,** Clarence Parade, Southsea, Hampshire PO5 2HY (tel. 0705/823201), is a comfortable hotel. All of the bedrooms have color TVs, radios, phones, and hot beverage facilities, and many have private baths. Rent in a single begins at £49 ($85.75) daily, and doubles cost from £62 ($108.50). The Camelot Restaurant specializes in traditional English food and wines. The Skylark Bar, whose nautical theme is reflected by a counter resembling a rowboat, attracts both hotel guests and local residents, offering a buffet table at lunchtime. For a quiet drink, however, you might prefer the Camelot Bar.

Hospitality Inn, South Parade, Southsea, Hampshire PO4 0RN (tel. 0705/731281). Its balconied façade rises above the boulevard running beside the sea. Restored by its owners, the hotel contains an interior decor that, depending on your room assignment, ranges from contemporary to full-curtained traditional. Each of the spacious bedrooms has been renovated with built-in furniture and tile bath and equipped with such extras as a trouser press and tea-making facilities. The cost is £54 ($94.50) daily, in a single, £67 ($117.25) in a double. A restaurant serves dinners for £10 ($17.50).

WHERE TO DINE AT SOUTHSEA

In Old Southsea, **Bistro Montparnasse,** 103 Palmerston Rd. (tel. 0705/816754) comes as a bit of surprise. It is generally conceded to serve the best food in the area. This is a French bistro enclave, with candles glowing on the tables and music played in the background to get you in the mood for a well-rounded selection of dishes. Fresh produce is competently and delicately prepared. The cooking is familiar fare, the menu a sort of list of the way we used to eat. Some of the dishes, such as veal flavored with Calvados and cream, betray a Norman influence. Meals cost from £12 ($21) to £16 ($28), and service is only at dinner and never on Sunday. Hours are from 7 to 10:30 p.m. Some good house wine is available by the carafe.

WHERE TO STAY AND DINE IN THE ENVIRONS

Dating from 1715, **The Old House Hotel,** The Square, Wickham, Fareham, Hampshire PO17 5JG (tel. 0329/833049), nine miles from Portsmouth, is a handsome early Georgian house. It is thought to have been the first house of its architectural type built in the village, surrounded by low, medieval timber structures around the square. The paneled Georgian rooms on the ground and first floors of the hotel contrast with the beamed bedrooms on the upper floors, once the servants' quarters. All the bedrooms contain period furniture, many pieces original antiques. The individually decorated units have private baths, radios, phones, and TVs. Singles are priced at £60 ($105) and doubles at £80 ($140) for B&B, service, and VAT. Hotel bedrooms are available only Monday to Friday. The restaurant occupies what was once a timber-frame outbuilding with stables, adjacent to a garden overlooking the Meon River. It serves a French provincial cuisine, a complete meal costing from £21 ($36.75). The menu changes weekly, and care goes into the selection of the freshest vegetables and seasonal produce. The restaurant is closed Saturday at lunch, all day Sunday, and on Monday night. Otherwise, lunch is served from 12:30 to 2 p.m. and dinner from 7:30 to 9:30 p.m. The hotel's bar, with a French provincial ambience, is open exclusively for hotel and restaurant guests. Owners Richard and Annie Skipwith, who converted a private residence into this fine hotel in 1970, recommend making reservations in advance.

Between Portsmouth and Southampton lies an attraction in this part of the country—

BROADLANDS

The home of Earl Mountbatten of Burma until his assassination in 1979, Broadlands, Romsey (tel. 0794/516878), lies on the A31, 72 miles southwest of London. Lord Mountbatten lent the house to the then Princess Elizabeth and Prince Philip, Mountbatten's nephew, as a honeymoon haven in 1947, and in 1981 Prince Charles and Princess Diana spent the first nights of their honeymoon here. Broadlands is owned by Lord Romsey, Lord Mountbatten's eldest grandson, who has created a fine exhibition and audio-visual show depicting the highlights of the brilliant career as a sailor and statesman of his grandfather, who has been called "the last war hero." The house, originally linked to Romsey Abbey, was purchased by Lord Palmerston in 1736. It was later transformed into an elegant Palladian mansion by Capability Brown and Henry Holland. Brown landscaped the parkland and grounds, making the river (the Test) the main object of pleasure. The house, the Mountbatten Exhibition, and the riverside lawns are open daily from 10 a.m. to 4 p.m. from March 23 to October 1. Closed Monday except in August, September, and on bank holidays. Admission is £3.95 ($6.90) for adults, £2.25 ($3.95) for children.

2. Southampton

To many North Americans, England's No. 1 passenger port, home base for the *Queen Elizabeth 2*, is the gateway to Britain. Southampton is a city of wide boulevards, parks, and shopping centers. It was rebuilt after German bomb damage, which destroyed hundreds of its old buildings.

In World War II, some 3½ million men embarked from here (in the First World War, more than twice that number passed through Southampton). Its supremacy as a port has long been recognized and dates from Saxon times when the Danish conqueror, Canute, was proclaimed king here in 1017.

Southampton was especially important to the Normans and kept them in touch with their homeland. It shares the dubious distinction of having imported the bubonic plague in the mid-14th century that wiped out a quarter of the English population. On the Western Esplanade is a memorial tower to the Pilgrims, who set out on their voyage to the New World from Southampton on August 15, 1620. Both the *Mayflower* and the *Speedwell* sailed from here but were forced by storm damages to put in at Plymouth, where the *Speedwell* was abandoned. The memorial is a tall column with an iron basket on top—the type used as a beacon before lighthouses.

If you're waiting in Southampton between boats, you may want to use the time to explore some of the major sights of Hampshire that lie on the periphery of the port—the New Forest, Winchester, the Isle of Wight, and Bournemouth in neighboring Dorset.

WHERE TO STAY

Considered the finest hotel in Southampton, **Polygon Hotel,** Cumberland Place, Southampton, Hampshire SO9 4GP (tel. 0703/330055), is a favorite with tourists and business travelers. It bears the name of a district known as the Polygon that was popular with visiting nobility in the 18th century. The present hotel was built in the early part of this century to replace a 19th-century hostelry. The Polygon has been modernized and refurbished to a good standard. The bedrooms all have private baths, mini-bars, color TVs, radios, phones, and hot beverage facilities. They rent for £62 ($108.50) daily for a single, £78 ($136.50) for a twin-bedded room. The Polygon overlooks the town's Watts Park and Civic Centre, and is within easy reach of the main shopping area.

Post House, Herbert Walker Avenue, Southampton, Hampshire SO1 0HJ (tel. 0703/228081), rises ten floors tall. It was built near the New Docks to overlook the harbor, but is only five minutes away from the city center. You can unload your luggage under a sheltered drive and walk into the reception area. The rooms, 135 in all (nine studio and eight syndicate accommodations), are handsome and spacious, with fine built-in pieces, picture-window walls, private baths, phones, radios, and TVs. Twin or double rooms cost £75 ($131.25) daily, and singles go for £59 ($103.25). Rates include service and VAT. Among the facilities of the hotel are a heated open-air swimming pool and a residents' lounge with color TV. The Harbour Bar adjacent to the restaurant offers an intimate atmosphere.

Dolphin Hotel, 35 High St., Southampton, Hampshire SO9 2DS (tel. 0703/339955), which dates back to the 13th century, was Jane Austen's choice, and even Thackeray's when he was writing *Pendennis*. In time, Queen Victoria arrived in a horse-drawn carriage at this Georgian inn and coaching house. A classic brick building, with a pair of bow windows, it is in the center of the city, and is approached through an arched entrance, over which rests a coat-of-arms of William IV and Queen Adelaide. The 74 bedrooms vary widely in size, but are generally spacious and well furnished. All have private bath. Singles cost £52 ($91) daily; doubles and twins, £65 ($113.75). The lounge is nicely paneled. The open staircase holds a rare collection of naval uniform prints. Meals at the Dolphin are quite good, with a table d'hôte dinner beginning at £11 ($19.25). Drinks are served in the Nelson Bar.

Southampton Moat House, 119 Highfield Lane, Portswood, Southampton, Hampshire SO9 1YQ (tel. 0703/559555), stands in a residential area on the outskirts of the city. This modern hotel, a member of Queens Moat Houses group, offers comfortable accommodations and efficient service. Its restaurant, Hamilton's, serves both table d'hôte and à la carte menus, which are complemented by a comprehensive wine list. Lunch and dinner will cost from £10 ($17.50) for a three-course meal. Rooms are from £50 ($87.50) daily in a single and £65 ($113.75) in a double, including an English breakfast and VAT.

WHERE TO DINE

Southampton isn't distinguished for its gastronomy. However, there have been some improvements, as exemplified by the selections below.

Geddes, Town Quay (tel. 0703/221159), is the best restaurant in town. Contained within the red-brick walls of a historic warehouse, it was originally designed by Scottish architect John Geddes as a ship's chandler and warehouse. Back then, the sea came up to its foundations. In spite of the rustic exterior, the interior is decorated in a French Regency style. There is a wine cellar with 600-year-old walls, once part of the medieval Southampton Wall. Meals are offered daily except Saturday lunch and all day Sunday. A fixed price three-course lunch goes for £12.50 ($21.90), with à la carte dinners ranging from £18 ($31.50) per person without wine. Specialties include a timbale of seafood mousse wrapped in smoked salmon, venison in red currant sauce, and breast of chicken with a blue cheese mousse stuffing. Lunch is from noon to 2:30 p.m. and dinner from 7 to 10:30 p.m.

Kuti's, 70 London Rd. (tel. 0703/221585), is the best Indian restaurant in all of Hampshire. Decorated in a flamboyant style, with murals from India, it invites you to partake of its wares. It pays homage to the many different cuisines of India, giving you a wide choice. You can visit seven days a week from noon to 2:30 p.m. (at which time a buffet lunch is served) or from 6 p.m. to midnight. Lunch costs from £6.50 ($11.40), with dinners averaging around £12 ($21). Sample a vegetarian thali or tandoori chicken, along with a host of other dishes. Some items may be familiar to you; others come as delightful, zesty surprises.

---

3. The New Forest

The New Forest came into the limelight in the times of Henry VIII, who loved to hunt here, as venison abounded. Also, with his enthusiasm for building up the British naval fleet, he saw his opportunity to supply oak and other hard timbers to the boatyards at Buckler's Hard on the Beaulieu River for the building of stout-hearted men-o'-war. Today you can visit the old shipyards, the museum with its fine models of men-o'-war, pictures of the old yard, and dioramas showing the building of these ships, their construction, and their launching. It took 2,000 trees to build one man-o'-war.

Stretching for about 92,000 acres, the New Forest is a large tract, 14 miles wide and 20 miles long. William the Conqueror laid out the limits of this then-private hunting preserve. Those who hunted without a license faced the executioner if they were caught, and those who hunted but missed had their hands severed.

Nowadays, the New Forest is one of those places traversed by a motorway by those motorists bound for the southwest. However, I'd suggest you stop a moment and relax.

This used to be a forest, but now the groves of oak trees are separated by wide tracts of common land that is grazed by ponies and cows, hummocked with heather and gorse, and frequented by rabbits. Away from the main arterial roads, where signs warn of wild ponies and deer, there is a private world of peace and quiet.

BEAULIEU ABBEY—PALACE HOUSE

This stately home is in the New Forest (tel. 590/612345). The abbey and house, as well as the National Motor Museum, are on the property of Lord Montagu of Beaulieu, at Beaulieu, 5 miles southeast of Lyndhurst and 14 miles south of Southampton. A Cistercian abbey was founded on this spot in 1204, and the ruins can be explored today. The Palace House was the great gatehouse of the abbey before it was converted into a private residence in 1538. The house is surrounded by gardens.

On the grounds, the **National Motor Museum,** one of the best and most comprehensive motor museums in the world, with more than 250 vehicles, is open to the public. It traces the story of motoring from 1895 to the present. Famous autos include four land-speed record-holders, among them Donald Campbell's *Bluebird*. The collection was built on the foundation of Lord Montagu's family collection of vintage cars. A special feature is called "Wheels." In a darkened environment, visitors can travel in specially designed "pods," each of which carries up to two adults and one child along a silent electric track. They move at a predetermined but variable speed, and each pod is capable of rotating almost 360°. This provides a means by which the visitor is introduced to a variety of displays spanning 100 years of motor development. Sound and visual effects are integrated into individual displays. In one sequence, visitors experience the smell, noise, and visual thrill of being involved in a Grand Prix race.

All facilities are open daily from 10 a.m. to 6 p.m. Easter to September, from 10 a.m. to 5 p.m. October to Easter. Closed Christmas Day. Admission to the motor museum, palace and gardens, abbey ruins, and exhibition of monastic life costs £5.25 ($9.20) for adults, £3.50 ($6.15) for children. For further information, contact the Visitor Reception Manager, John Montagu Building, at the number above.

BUCKLER'S HARD

This historic 18th-century village on the banks of the River Beaulieu is where ships for Nelson's fleet were built, including the admiral's favorite, *Agamemnon*, as well as *Eurylus* and *Swiftsure*. The **Maritime Museum** (tel. 059063/203) reflects the shipbuilding history of the village. Its displays include shipbuilding at Buckler's Hard; Henry Adams, master shipbuilder; Nelson's favorite ship; Buckler's Hard and Trafalgar; and models of Sir Francis Chichester's yachts and items of his equipment. The cottage exhibits are a re-creation of 18th-century life in Buckler's Hard. Here you can stroll through the New Inn of 1793 and a shipwright's cottage of the same period, or look in on the family of a poor laborer at home. All these displays include village residents and visitors of the late 18th century.

The museum is open daily from 10 a.m. to 6 p.m. Easter to May, to 9 p.m. June to September, and to 4:30 p.m. October to Easter. Admission is £1.85 ($3.25) for adults, £1.10 ($1.95) for children. The walk back to Beaulieu, 2½ miles along the riverbank, is well marked through the woodlands. During the summer you can take a half-hour cruise on the River Beaulieu in the present *Swiftsure*, an all-weather catamaran cruiser.

FOOD AND LODGING

My recommendations for food and lodging follow, beginning with the finest establishment in the entire area.

New Milton

Chewton Glen Hotel, Christchurch Road, New Milton, Hampshire BH25 6QS (tel. 0425/275341) is a gracious country house on the fringe of the New Forest. It's within easy reach of Southampton and Bournemouth. After leaving the village of Walkford, follow the signpost off the A35 New Milton–Christchurch road, through parkland to a private car park. Rooms are either in the old house or in the new wing. In the old house, you take the magnificent staircase to one of the well-furnished chambers opening onto lovely views over the spacious grounds. In the new wing, you find yourself on the ground level with French doors opening onto your own private patio. Here the decor is in muted colors, the rooms named for the heroes of novels written by Captain Marryat (he was the author of *The Children of the New Forest*). Everywhere log fires burn and fresh flowers add fragrance. Guests can swim in an open-air heated swimming pool. The garden sweeps down to a stream and then to rhododendron woods. In addition there are a tennis court and a nine-hole golf course.

In the dining room, the standard of cooking and the presentation of the food is high. Particular emphasis is placed on fresh ingredients. The chef favors a modern cuisine, complemented by excellent sauces and velvety-smooth desserts. The set meal of three courses is changed daily. A set lunch is £16 ($28), going up to £20 ($35) on Sunday. A set dinner costs £32.50 ($56.90). The price to stay here begins at £125 ($218.75) daily for two persons, including VAT, service, and a continental breakfast. Suites are more expensive.

Lyndhurst

Lyndhurst Park Hotel, High Street, Lyndhurst, Hampshire SO43 7NL (tel. 042128/3923), is a large old country house set in five acres of beautiful gardens, with an outdoor heated swimming pool and all-weather tennis court. The 59 bedrooms all have private baths, color TV with in-house video, direct-dial phones, radio-alarms, tea/coffee-makers, hairdryers, and trouser presses. They rent for £49.50 ($86.65) to £56.50 ($98.90) daily in a single, £60 ($105) to £80 ($140) in a double, including VAT and an English breakfast. There are two bars, one with beams, high-backed settles, and harnesses decorating the brick walls. The hotel has an oak-paneled restaurant, where a wide selection of dishes is offered at both lunch and dinner. A four-course dinner with coffee will cost about £14 ($24.50).

Crown Hotel, High Street, Lyndhurst, Hampshire SO43 7NF (tel. 042128/ 2722), stands on a spot where there has been a hostelry for centuries, on the main street of the village opposite the church with its tall spire. The present building is a mere 100 years old, and the bedrooms are snug with color TV, radio, phone, and a drink cabinet. Singles cost from £40 ($70) daily, and doubles or twins, from £60 ($105), including VAT and a full English breakfast. Much local produce is used in the dining room, including venison. This specialty is a rich concoction of meat, mushrooms, and onions cooked in red wine and cream with red currants and brandy. A set lunch or dinner costs from £12.25 ($21.45). There are also à la carte selections. Sunday lunch is well patronized by the local people. They also do substantial bar meals.

Brockenhurst

New Park Manor, Lyndhurst Road, Brockenhurst, Hampshire SO42 7QH (tel. 0590/23467), is a former royal hunting lodge dating from the days of William the Conqueror. It is the only hotel in the New Forest itself. In 1666 King Charles made New Park his favorite hunting lodge on his return from exile in France, and came here accompanied by Nell Gwynne. Now a modern country hotel, the manor has some 30 bedrooms. The original rooms have been preserved, including such features as beams and open log fires. The owners have installed central heating throughout, and the bedrooms contain baths, color TVs, and tea- and coffee-making facilities. The price for B&B in a single is £39.50 ($69.15) to £44.50 ($77.90) daily; in a double, £28 ($49) to £32 ($56) per person. Included in the tariff is the use of a swimming pool, in a sheltered corner of the garden (heated in summer), and a hard tennis court. Riding from the hotel's stables is available. The candlelit restaurant, with its log fire, specializes in flambé cookery. Backed up by a good wine list, the chef often uses fresh garden produce. The hotel lies half a mile off the A337 Lyndhurst–Brockenhurst road past the 500-year-old thatched lodge to the manor.

Carey's Manor, Lyndhurst Road, Brockenhurst, Hampshire SO42 7RH (tel. 0590/23551), is a manor house built of red brick. Its origins were in the days of Charles II, who used to come here when Carey's was a hunting lodge. Greatly extended in 1888, the building became a country hotel in the 1930s. Much improved in recent years, it is better than ever. The old house is still filled with character, as exemplified by its mellow, time-worn paneling and carved oak staircase. The bedrooms, 80 in all, are well furnished, although they differ in style and location. Some are in the restored main building, while others are in the garden wing. Each accommodation contains private bath or shower, phone, radio, hairdryer, and trouser press. Singles cost from £60 ($105) daily, with doubles renting for £90 ($157.50). The hotel also serves good food, a modern British and French cuisine. Carey's is ideal as a resort, with an indoor swimming pool, gym, solarium, and sauna. The hotel, about a 90-minute drive from London, stands on five acres of landscaped grounds.

Balmer Lawn Hotel, Lyndhurst Road, Brockenhurst, Hampshire SO42 7ZB (tel. 0590/23116), is a sophisticated place, with grounds blending with those of New Forest, a heated swimming pool, and comfortable lounges. Lunch costs from £8.50 ($14.90); dinner from £12 ($21). The menu offers many interesting selections. After a local fish or venison, you might try, for example, a date-and-ginger pie. Rooms rent for £57 ($99.75) daily in singles, £82 ($143.50) in doubles, including VAT and a full breakfast. The hotel lies on the A337, the Lyndhurst–Lymington road, about a mile outside of Brockenhurst.

Beaulieu

Montagu Arms, Beaulieu, Hampshire SO42 7ZL (tel. 0590/612324), was built with locally made bricks and tiles as well as timbers from the New Forest. Its origins are from the 13th century. This time-tested favorite combines the comfort of a country manor house with the cozy hospitality of a mellow wayside inn. The hotel staff keeps up an old English garden, which is well sheltered and filled with some rare plants. The main lounge overlooks this garden, and the dining room, serving good food and wine, is oak beamed and paneled. In one of the three bars, the counter was fashioned from an old wine press. The bedrooms are immaculately kept and modernized, all with private baths. Singles cost £52 ($91) to £56 ($98) daily, and twins and doubles go for £65 ($113.75) to £98 ($171.50), including VAT, service, and a full English breakfast. The rates vary according to season and type of room. You can have a set lunch in the dining room for £15 ($26.25); a set dinner, from £18 ($31.50).

Buckler's Hard

Master Builders House Hotel, Buckler's Hard, Beaulieu, Hampshire SO4 7XB (tel. 0590/63253), 2½ miles south of Beaulieu, is a lovely 18th-century main house that was once the home of master shipbuilder Henry Adams, who was responsible for many of the wooden walls that dominate the seaways of the world. Today there is a wing that accommodates guests in pleasant double rooms with bath, color TV, and tea- and coffee-making facilities. Singles rent for £17 ($29.75) to £35 ($61.25) doubles and twins for £55 ($96.25), including VAT and a full English breakfast. The space in the main building is devoted to the Yachtsman Buffet Bar, which provides good, ample snack meals, and to the restaurant with its wide windows overlooking the busy river.

---

4. Isle of Wight

Four miles across the Solent from the south coast towns of Southampton, Lymington, and Portsmouth, the Isle of Wight is known for its sandy beaches and its ports, favored by the yachting set. The island, which long attracted such literary figures as Alfred Tennyson and Charles Dickens, is compact in size, measuring 23 miles from east to west, 13 miles from north to south. You can take regular ferryboats over, and hydrofoils cross the Solent in just 20 minutes from Southampton.

The price of a round-trip ticket on the ferry from Southampton to Cowes is from £3.40 ($5.95) to £4.30 ($7.55) per passenger. Taking a car over for the day costs from £17 ($29.75) to £25 ($43.75), depending on the size of the vehicle.

The ferry from Lymington to Yarmouth for a day round trip costs £3.40 ($5.95) for adults, £1.85 ($3.25) for children. Transport of an average car, round trip, is £26 ($45.50).

The more usual way of reaching the island from London is by ferry from Portsmouth Harbour or by Hovercraft from Southsea, both of which take you to Ryde, the railhead for the island's communications system. A train that services the island meets the ferry at the end of an 800-yard pier. Arriving in Yarmouth, via Lymington, however, is something else—a busy little harbor providing a mooring for yachts and also for one of the lifeboats in the Solent area.

Visitors who'd like to explore the Isle of Wight just for the day can take an **Around the Island Rover** bus trip, for which tickets may be purchased on the bus. This enables anyone to board and leave the buses at any stop on the island. The price is £4 ($7) for adults per day and £2 ($3.50) for children. It also gives passage on the island's only railway, running from the dock at Ryde to the center of Shanklin, a distance of 12 miles. For further information, phone 0938/523821.

Ryde is on the northeast of the island. It was established as a seaside resort in Victorian times. The Church of All Saints, designed by Sir Gilbert Scott, dominates the town with its 200-foot spire.

Cowes is the premier port for yachting in Britain. Henry VIII ordered the castle built there, but it is now the headquarters of the Royal Yacht Squadron. The seafront, the Prince's Green, and the high cliff road are worth exploring. Hovercraft are built in the town, and it's also the home and birthplace of the well-known maritime photographer, Beken of Cowes. It's almost *de rigueur* to wear oilskins and wellies, leaving a wet trail behind you.

Along the southeast coast are the twin resorts of **Sandown,** with its new pier complex and theater, and **Shanklin,** at the southern end of Sandown Bay, which has held the British annual sunshine record more times than any other resort. Keats once lived in Shanklin's Old Village.

Farther along the coast, **Ventnor** is called the "Madeira of England," because it rises from the sea in a series of steep hills.

On the west coast, the sand cliffs of **Alum Bay** are a blend of many different colors, a total of 21 claimed. The Needles, three giant chalk rocks, and the Needles Lighthouse, are further features of interest at this end of the island. If you want to stay at the western end of Wight, consider **Freshwater Bay.**

Newport is the capital, a bustling market town lying in the heart of the island.

Long a favorite of British royalty, the island has as its major attraction **Osborne House,** Queen Victoria's most cherished residence, lying a mile southeast of East Cowes. Prince Albert, with his characteristic thoroughness, contributed to many aspects of the design of the Italian-inspired mansion, which stands in lush gardens, right outside the village of Whippingham. The rooms have remained as Victoria knew them, right down to the French piano she used to play and with all the cozy clutter of her sitting room. Grief-stricken at the death of Albert in 1861, she asked that Osborne House remain as it was, and so it has been. Even the turquoise scent bottles he gave her, decorated with cupids and cherubs, are still in place. It was in her bedroom at Osborne House that the queen died on January 22, 1901. The house is open from Easter to the end of October daily from 10 a.m. to 5 p.m. Admission is £3 ($5.25) for adults, £1.50 ($2.65) for children.

A completely different attraction, **Carisbrooke Castle** (tel. 0983/522107) is where Charles I was imprisoned by the Roundheads in 1647. This fine medieval castle is in the center of the island, 1½ miles southwest of Newport. Everybody heads for the Well House, concealed inside a 16th-century stone building. Donkeys take turns treading a large wooden wheel connected to a rope that hauls up buckets of water. The castle is open from mid-March to mid-October Monday to Saturday from 9:30 a.m. to 6:30 p.m. In winter it closes at 4 p.m. On Sunday in season its hours are 9:30 a.m. to 6:30 p.m., but 2 to 4 p.m. in the other months. Admission is £2.20 ($3.85) for adults, £1.10 ($1.95) for children.

You have a choice of several bases on the Isle of Wight unless you're what the English call a "day-tripper."

RYDE

A good anchor on the Isle of Wight is **Hotel Ryde Castle,** Esplanade, Ryde, Isle of Wight PO33 1JA (tel. 0983/63755), an accommodation on the seafront, looking out on the Solent. The original castle (circa 1540) was ordered built by Henry VIII as part of the defenses against the Armada. With its crenellated, ivy-clad exterior and its well-kept public rooms and bedrooms, the hotel attracts families as well as single visitors. The 17 units have private baths, color TV, phones, radios, hairdryers, and tea/coffee-makers. Double bedrooms have four-poster beds. The charge for B&B is £28.80 ($49.15) per person daily, with half board costing £37.90 ($66.35). Both table d'hôte and à la carte meals are offered in the dining room, where full use is made of fresh fish caught locally and island farm produce. The bar lounge offers a wide range of snacks for lunch.

Some of the best dining on the island is at **Biskra House,** 17 St. Thomas's St., Isle of Wight PO33 2XX (tel. 0983/67913), which also offers rooms, nine in all. Each has a TV, phone, and either a shower or bathtub. Singles rent for £28 ($49) daily, with doubles costing from £46 ($80.50) to £56 ($98) with VAT and breakfast included. There are two restaurants within Biskra House. A cellar restaurant is Italian, serving full meals seven days a week from noon to 2 p.m. and 7 to 10:30 p.m., costing from £10 ($17.50) to £12 ($21) per person. On the street level is a French restaurant, which has a fixed price menu at £12.50 ($21.90). Service is daily except Sunday night and Monday night from noon to 2 p.m. and 7 to 9:30 p.m. Fresh lobster is often featured, and steak Diane is prepared at your table.

SHANKLIN

A good bargain is provided by **Bourne Hall Country Hotel,** Luccombe Road, Shanklin, Isle of Wight PO37 6RR (tel. 0983/862820). Because of the Old Village, with its thatched cottages, and The Chine, two of the leading attractions on the island, many visitors prefer to make their base at Shanklin. At Bourne Hall they receive a warm welcome from Mr. and Mrs. Douglas, who have one of the best equipped houses in the area, complete with two swimming pools along with a Jacuzzi and solarium. Rooms, 28 in all, are comfortably furnished with private bath, phone, and TV. From February to November, guests are received and charged from £26 ($45.50) daily in a single, rising to £60 ($105) in a double.

Luccombe Chine House, Luccombe Chine, Shanklin, Isle of Wight PO37 GRH (tel. 0983/862037), stands on about 10 acres of grounds opening onto Luccombe Bay. It's small and choice, with only eight bedrooms, half a dozen of which contain four-poster beds. Each room is immaculately kept and well furnished, containing a private bath or shower, beverage-making equipment, TV, and hairdryer. Singles cost from £35 ($61.25) daily, with doubles renting for £58 ($101.50). It's a good base from which to explore Isle of Wight. The food is also good, with meals costing from £10 ($17.50).

SANDOWN

Standing in its own garden, **St. Catherine's Hotel,** 1 Winchester Park Rd., Sandown, Isle of Wight PO36 8HJ (tel. 0983/402392), is just a few minutes' walk from Sandown's sandy beach, leisure center, and pier complex, with its sun lounges and theater. St. Catherine's was built in 1860 of creamy Purbeck stone and white trim, for the dean of Winchester College; a modern extension was added for streamlined and sunny bedrooms. The brightly redecorated lounge has matching draperies at the wide bay windows. There are card tables and a small library of books. Adjacent is a cozy, fully stocked bar and a spacious comfortable dining room. Bedrooms have duvets, white furniture, and built-in headboards. All of the rooms contain private baths or showers. Stuart and Marlene Barker welcome you, charging £24.50 ($42.90) per person per night for half board in a room with color TV and phone, £17.50 ($30.65) per person for B&B. VAT is included in the rates.

FRESHWATER BAY

Once the home of Alfred Lord Tennyson, **Farringford Hotel,** Bedbury Lane, Freshwater Bay, Isle of Wight PO40 9PE (tel. 0983/752500), has an old-fashioned country ambience. A holiday, recreational estate, it has at its core a fine stone manor house and is surrounded by cottages on attractively landscaped grounds. It's adapted to the taste of the English who are accepted from March until after Christmas. Half board goes from £34 ($59.50) to £44 ($77) per person daily including VAT and service. Dinner is four courses of well-cooked simple dishes, and lunch can be a snack in the bar lounge. There is a nine-hole golf course free to hotel guests, as well as tennis courts, a swimming pool, a croquet lawn, and a sports pavilion.

CHALE

A 17th-century coaching inn, **The Clarendon Hotel and Wight Mouse Inn,** Newport Road, Chale, Isle of Wight PO38 2HA (tel. 0983/730431), lies on the most southerly part of the island, where the vegetation is almost tropical. From here, you have views over the Channel to the mainland coast. The Clarendon is a cheerful

place at which to spend the night. The rooms are beautifully furnished with antiques, and all have color TV as well as tea/coffee-makers. John and Jean Bradshaw
offer a half-board rate of £28 ($49) per person daily. The meals are ample, with many
fresh ingredients. In their pub, the Wight Mouse Inn, they serve a large selection of
beers, including real ales, and 150 malt whiskies, in addition to the more usual
drinks. Live entertainment is provided nightly year round. Children are welcome
here.

TOTLAND BAY

With the colored sands of Alum Bay and the Needles nearby (two of the attractions of the Isle of Wight), **Country Garden,** Church Hill, Totland Bay, Isle of
Wight PO39 0ET (tel. 0983/754521), is ideally situated. It's the most charming
place to stay at Totland Bay (and about this there is little dispute). It also has a restaurant open to the public, with meals costing from £12 ($21) and up. The food is
good, and local produce is used whenever possible. From its well-landscaped, two-
acre garden, you'll have views of the Dorset coastline (coming up in the next section). The hotel and restaurant was successfully converted from a once-private Victorian home. Eight bedrooms, each attractively and comfortably furnished, are
rented to guests at a rate of £27 ($47.25) daily in a single, going up to £75
($131.25) for the best doubles. Each accommodation has a private bath as well as
many up-to-date amenities. Other facilities include an indoor swimming pool, sauna, and solarium.

---

5. Winchester

The most historical city in all of Hampshire, Winchester is big on legends—it's
even associated with King Arthur and the Knights of the Round Table. In the Great
Hall, all that remains of Winchester Castle, a round oak table, with space for King
Arthur and his 24 knights, hangs on the wall. But all that spells undocumented romance. What is known, however, is that when the Saxons ruled the ancient kingdom of Wessex, Winchester was the capital.

The city is also linked with King Alfred, who is honored today by a statue, and is
believed to have been crowned here. The Danish conqueror, Canute, came this way
too, as did the king he ousted, Ethelred the Unready (Canute got his wife, Emma, in
the bargain). The city is the seat of the well-known Winchester College, whose
founding father was the bishop of Winchester, William of Wykeham. Established in
1382, it lays claim to being the oldest public (private) school in England.

Traditions are strong in Winchester. It is said (although I've never confirmed
the assertion) that if you go to St. Cross Hospital, now an almshouse, dating from
the 12th century, you'll get ye olde pilgrim's dole of ale and bread (and if there's no
bread, you can eat cake!). Winchester, 65 miles from London, is essentially a market
town, on the Downs on the Itchen River.

WINCHESTER CATHEDRAL

For centuries Winchester Cathedral (tel. 0962/53137) has been one of the
great mother churches of England. The present building, the longest cathedral in
Britain, dates from 1079, and its Norman heritage is still in evidence. When a Saxon
church stood on this spot, St. Swithun, bishop of Winchester and tutor to young
King Alfred, suggested modestly that he be buried outside. When he was later buried inside, it rained for 40 days. The legend lives on: just ask a resident of Winchester
what will happen if it rains on St. Swithun's Day, July 15.

Of the present building, the nave with its two aisles is most impressive, as are
the chantries, the reredos (late 15th century), and the elaborately carved choir stalls.
Of the chantries, that of William of Wykeham, founder of Winchester College, is

perhaps the most visited (it's found in the south aisle of the nave). The cathedral also contains a number of other tombs, notably those of Jane Austen and Izaak Walton (exponent of the merits of the pastoral life—*The Compleat Angler*). The latter's tomb is to be found in the Prior Silkestede's Chapel in the South Transept. Jane Austen's grave is marked with a commemorative plaque. Winchester Cathedral contains in chests the bones of many of the Saxon kings and the remains of the Viking conqueror, Canute, and his wife, Emma, in the presbytery. The son of William the Conqueror, William Rufus (who reigned as William II), is also believed to have been buried at the cathedral. There are free guided tours Monday to Saturday at 11 a.m. and 3 p.m. from April to the end of October.

The Crypt is flooded for a large part of the year, and at such times it is closed to the public. When it's not flooded, there are regular tours at 10:30 a.m. and 2:30 p.m. daily except Sunday. The Library, in which is displayed the Winchester Bible and other ancient manuscripts, is open for limited hours throughout the summer season (except Monday morning and Sunday) and on Wednesday and Saturday for the rest of the year. In January the library is open on Saturday only. The Treasury is open during the summer season from 11 a.m. to 5 p.m. It is small and does not require a guide. No admission fee is charged, but a donation of £1 ($1.75) for the upkeep of the cathedral is suggested. A Triforium Gallery Museum and Library ticket costs £1 ($1.75).

WHERE TO STAY

Accommodations are limited, but adequate. I'll survey the most expensive recommendations first.

The Upper Bracket

Lainston House, Sparsholt, Winchester, Hampshire SO21 2LT (tel. 0962/ 63588), is a fine, restored 17th-century William and Mary manor house, lying 3½ miles northwest of Winchester, along the A272. Visitors are struck with the beauty of the red-brick structure as they approach via a long, curving, tree-lined drive. It sits in 63 acres of rolling land, linked with the name Lainston in the *Domesday Book* of 1086. Inside the stately house, elegance is the keynote, with Delft-tile fireplaces, oak and cedar paneling, molding, and cornices of the original owners preserved, set off with period pieces. From the reception areas, done in soft pastels and antiques, you go up the mahogany and oak staircase to some of the 32 bedrooms, which are equally attractive. These and the units in the annex are carpeted and have well-equipped bathrooms, plus radios, color TVs, and mini-bars. Charges are £70 ($122.50) daily in a single, £89 ($155.75) to 135 ($236.25) in a double. In either of the two dining rooms, you can order such specialties as veal with wild-mushroom stuffing and smoked salmon with a hazelnut-and-lemon dressing. Meals cost £20 ($35) to £25 ($43.75).

Wessex Hotel, Paternoster Row, Winchester, Hampshire SO23 9LQ (tel. 0962/61611), is a modern structure adjacent to the grounds of Winchester Cathedral. Two stories high, built of natural brick, it turns most of its walls of windows toward a view of the Norman Tower. The lounges and reception areas are built on several open levels. The coffeeshop is contemporary in design, and the cocktail lounge and restaurant are traditional with leather furniture, mahogany and brass. The hotel has 93 bedrooms and one suite, with 27 accommodations facing the cathedral. The rooms are warmed by soft materials and have such amenities as direct-dial phones, color TVs, radios, hairdryers, and 24-hour room service. A single rent begins at £65 ($113.75) daily and a double at £80 ($140). The coffeeshop is open from 10 a.m. until 10 p.m. daily, and the main restaurant has large picture windows overlooking the cathedral and its grounds. Both traditional English and French cuisine are served.

The Middle Bracket

Royal Hotel, St. Peter Street, Winchester, Hampshire SO23 8BS (tel. 0962/
53468) is a fine old hotel, built at the end of the 17th century as a private house. It
has a modern extension overlooking gardens. For 50 years it was used by nuns from
Brussels as a convent before being turned into a hotel. As a hotel, however, it soon
became the center of the city's social life. It's only a few minutes' walk to the cathedral, yet still enjoys a secluded position. Best of all is the garden hidden behind high
walls. Singles go for £56 ($98) daily and the best doubles for £92 ($161). These
prices include a traditional English breakfast, VAT, and service. Meals are served in a
small, formal dining room, with a view of the private garden. A set dinner costs £15
($26.25).

The Budget Range

Stratton House, Stratton Road, St. Giles Hill, Winchester, Hampshire SO23
8JQ (tel. 0962/63919), is a lovely old Victorian house (circa 1890) set in an acre of
ground in an elevated position on St. Giles Hill, overlooking the city. It is about a
five- to ten-minute walk from the center. Single, double, twin-bedded, and family
units are available throughout the year. The charge for B&B is from £16 ($28) daily
in a single, £30 ($52.50) to £34 ($59.50) in a double. All bedrooms have TV and
hot-drink facilities. An evening meal can be arranged for another £7.50 ($13.15).
There is ample parking in a private courtyard, and free pick-up is possible if you arrive at the train or bus station.

WHERE TO DINE

The best restaurant in town, **Brann's,** 9 Great Minster St. (tel. 0962/64004),
overlooks Winchester Cathedral. It is both a restaurant (upstairs) and a wine bar
downstairs. At the wine bar customers may enjoy lighter meals at less expensive
prices. David C. Brann, who has had a long and distinguished history in the restaurant business, is aided by his wife and business partner, Barbara, a former actress.
Their aim is to produce high quality, affordable meals using fresh, seasonal ingredients. In that, they succeed admirably. There are always daily specials to look forward
to that prevent the menu from becoming dull, even to diners who eat at Brann's
every day. The welcome is always courteous, but never stuffy or pretentious. The
decor is elegant but comfortable. Casual dress is not frowned upon, but they do like
guests in the restaurant upstairs to wear a jacket and tie in the evening. Service is
Monday to Saturday from noon to 3 p.m. and 6 to 10:30 p.m. They are closed on
bank holidays and for the first two weeks in January. The wine bar menu features
excellent dishes such as Brann's fish chowder followed by tandoori chicken with
dark almond sauce. Meals here cost from £8 ($14). In the restaurant a lunch goes for
£12.50 ($21.90), with dinner costing £18.50 ($32.40). Typical dishes are likely to
include chicken breast stuffed with tarragon and lemon and glazed with Pernod,
roast best end of English lamb with rosemary sauce and spinach mousse, or grilled
breast of English duckling, marinated with soy, ginger, and honey. Reservations are
needed upstairs.

In an atmosphere of another century, **Elizabethan Restaurant,** 18 Jewry St.
(tel. 0962/53566), offers you an opportunity to dine under hand-hewn beams by
candlelight. The street-level bar is for drinks and snacks, while the more formal dining room is one floor above. The restaurant sits in the upper reaches of the village, in
a building originally dating from 1509. Well run, the kitchen offers an excellent English cuisine with many French-inspired dishes, Try, for example, roast beef or lobster thermidor. A tourist menu costs only £7.95 ($13.90) for three courses, but you
must order it by 8 p.m. After that, à la carte dinners cost from £17 ($29.75). Meals
are served daily from noon to 2:30 p.m. and 6 to 10:30 p.m.

The Old Chesil Rectory Restaurant, 1 Chesil St. (tel. 0962/53177), is just a
short walk from the cathedral. Once a rectory, the unusual timber-and-stucco build-

ing, constructed in 1450, is the oldest building in Winchester. Inside and out, The Old Chesil exudes an air of "merrie olde England." Likewise, the menu is "olde English," with such dishes as homemade soup and "Old English" roast beef and Durkan's Delight. The restaurant is open daily from 10:30 a.m. to 10:30 p.m., serving morning coffee, light luncheons and snacks costing from £1.75 ($3.05), full à la carte luncheons, afternoon teas, light suppers, and complete à la carte dinners, averaging around £14 ($24.50).

DORSET

This is Thomas Hardy country. You may have read *Far from the Madding Crowd* or *Tess of the D'Urbervilles* (or seen the movies based on them), and know Dorset is the Wessex of Hardy novels. Some of the towns and villages, although altered considerably, are still recognizable from his descriptions. However, he changed the names to protect the innocent. Bournemouth, for example, became Poole, Weymouth converted to Budmouth. "The last of the great Victorians," as he was called, died in 1928 at the age of 88. While his tomb rests in a position of honor in Westminster Abbey, his heart was cut out and buried in his beloved Dorsetshire.

One of England's smallest shires, Dorset stretches all the way from the old seaport of **Poole** in the east to **Lyme Regis** in the west (known to Jane Austen). Dorset is a southwestern county, bordering the English Channel. It's big on cows, and Dorset butter is served at many an afternoon tea. Mainly, it is a land of farms and pastures, with plenty of sandy heaths and chalky downs.

The most prominent tourist center of Dorset is the Victorian seaside resort of **Bournemouth.** If you don't anchor there, you might also try a number of Dorset's other seaports, villages, and country towns. For the most part, we'll hug closely to the impressive coastline.

Incidentally, Dorset, as the vacation-wise English might tell you if they wanted to divulge a secret, is a budget traveler's friend.

6. Bournemouth

The south coast resort at the doorstep of the New Forest didn't just happen: it was carefully planned and manicured, a true city in a garden. Flower-filled, park-dotted Bournemouth contains great globs of architecture inherited from those arbiters of taste, Victoria and her son, Edward. Its most distinguished feature is its Chines (narrow, shrub-filled, steep-sided ravines) along the zigzag coastline. The real walking English strike out at, say, Hengistbury Head, making their way past sandy beaches, both the Boscombe and Bournemouth Piers, to Alum Chine, a distance of six miles, and a traffic-free walk to remember.

It is estimated that of the nearly 12,000 acres that Bournemouth claims for its own, about one-sixth is turned over to green parks and flowerbeds, such as the Pavilion Rock Garden, through which amblers pass both day and night. The total effect, especially in spring, is striking, and helps explain Bournemouth's long-established popularity with the garden-loving English. Bournemouth was discovered back in Victoria's day, when sea-bathing became a firmly entrenched institution, often practiced with great ritual. Many of the comparatively elegant villas that exist today (now largely bed-and-breakfast houses and hotels) were once private homes.

Bournemouth, which along with Poole and Christchurch forms the largest urban area in the south of England, is not as sophisticated as Brighton. Increasingly, it is becoming a retirement place for widowed or single English ladies. But Bournemouth and its neighbors also have some 20,000 students attending the various schools or colleges, who explore, in their off-hours, places written about or painted by such poets and artists as Shelley, Beardsley, and Turner.

The resort's amusements are wide and varied. At the Pavilion Theatre, for example, you can see West End–type productions from London. The Bournemouth Symphony Orchestra is justly famous in Europe. And there's the usual run of golf courses, band concerts, variety shows, and dancing.

Bournemouth is about 104 miles from London, easily reached in about one hour and 40 minutes on an express train from Waterloo Station. It makes a good base for exploring a historically rich part of England. On its outskirts are the New Forest, Salisbury, and Winchester, and the Isle of Wight (15 miles away, the former seaside retreat of Victoria).

WHERE TO STAY

Bournemouth offers accommodation choices in all price ranges. I'll begin with—

The Upper Bracket

The Carlton Hotel, Meyrick Road, East Overcliff, Bournemouth, Dorset BH1 3DN (tel. 0202/22011). Its staff defines it as Edwardian, although in parts it evokes art deco with its rounded balconies and horizontal detailing. More easily defined as a vacation resort than just an ordinary hotel, it sits atop a seaside cliff lined with private homes and other hotels. The Carlton boasts a luxury restaurant and cocktail bar, elegant lounges, a boutique, a swimming pool, and a health and beauty spa. There, a sudsy whirlpool, a gymnasium, and a trained staff contribute to healthy vacations. The hotel contains 66 comfortably modernized bedrooms, each with private bath, radio, and color TV. Double occupancy costs £126.50 ($221.40) daily, with singles at £87.45 ($153.05). Lunch goes for £14.50 ($25.38), and dinner costs £21.50 ($37.65).

Royal Bath Hotel, Bath Road, Bournemouth, Dorset BH1 2EW (tel. 0202/25555), was built in the Victorian era to simulate a French château, with towers and bay windows looking out over the bay and Purbeck Hills. It's opening date in fact was June 28, 1838, the day of Victoria's coronation. After the teenage Prince of Wales (later—a long time later—Edward VII) stayed here, the hotel added "royal" to its name. Over the years it has attracted everybody from Oscar Wilde to Rudolf Nureyev, and most definitely the great prime minister, Disraeli. In its own three acres of cliff-top gardens is a heated swimming pool. The rate is £67 ($117.25) to £77 ($134.75) daily in a single, £112 ($196) to £150 ($262.50) in a twin, inclusive of breakfast, service, and taxes. The table d'hôte lunch is £13 ($22.75), and dinner is £20 ($35). The resident band plays for a dinner-dance Saturday evenings. For health enthusiasts, there is a sauna bath, as well as Swedish massages and special diets. Every bedroom, 135 in all, has a private bath and television (the large accommodations contain sitting areas as well).

The Medium-Priced Range

Highcliff Hotel, 105 St. Michael's Rd., West Cliff, Bournemouth, Dorset BH2 5DU (tel. 0202/27702). Built by the Victorians along a clifftop at the edge of the sea, this hotel boasts a rhythmically massive façade dotted with jutting bay windows and a glassed-in conservatory. Its high-ceilinged interior has been tastefully renovated into a subtly updated format, retaining most of the elegant ceiling moldings but replacing the antiques with conservatively modern counterparts. The hotel premises offer a heated swimming pool, tennis court, sauna, solarium, putting green, and games room. A tastefully elegant restaurant serves well-prepared food in a grand manner, with formal service. The refurbished bedrooms contain private baths, phones, and TVs, with singles costing £48 ($84) daily; doubles, £96 ($168).

The Norfolk Royale Hotel, Richmond Hill, Bournemouth, Dorset BH2 6EN (tel. 0202/21521), one of the oldest prestige hotels of the resort, built a few blocks from the seafront and the shopping area in the center of town, has undergone a major £5-million renovation program, restoring it to its former Edwardian elegance. Disregarding what lies on its periphery, it is like a country estate, with a formal entrance and a rear garden and fountain shaded by trees. The public rooms are geared to holiday guests, with two drinking bars. The bedrooms and suites have been luxuriously appointed with the traditional styles of the Edwardian period blending with modern comforts. Rates start at £65 ($113.75) per person daily for bed and an English breakfast, with special weekend rates from £45 ($78.75) per person. Among the special features of the hotel are the swimming pool covered with a glass dome and the Orangery restaurant set in the terraced gardens.

Langtry Manor Hotel, 26 Derby Rd., East Cliff, Bournemouth, Dorset BH1 3QB (tel. 0202/23887), originally called the Red House, was built in 1877 for Lillie Langtry, the famous Jersey Lily, as a gift from Edward VII to his favorite mistress. The house contains all sorts of reminders of its illustrious inhabitants, including initials scratched on a windowpane and carvings on a beam of the entrance hall. On the half-landing is the peephole through which the prince could scrutinize the assembled company before coming down to dine, and one of the fireplaces bears his initials. Mrs. Pamela Hamilton Howard, the present owner, has furnished the hotel in the Edwardian style, and on Saturday she has six-course Edwardian dinner parties. There is no menu; the dishes are just produced for inspection. Other evenings, dinner is a more usual three-course affair at £12 ($21). Bedrooms range from ordinary twins with bathroom from £34.50 ($60.40) per person daily, including breakfast. The Lillie Langtry suite, Lillie's own room, with a four-poster bed draped in Nottingham lace and a double heart-shaped bathtub (not to mention the more modern refinements of color TV, refrigerated bar, and toilet), goes from £49.50 ($86.65), or you can rent the Edward VII suite, furnished as it was when His Royal Highness lived in this spacious room. The huge, carved oak fireplace has hand-painted tiles showing scenes from Shakespeare. The four-poster bed can be made up as either twins or a large double bed, and you have a private bath, color TV, a refrigerated room-bar, and a phone. The cost is £65.50 ($114.65) per person nightly. All rates include VAT.

WHERE TO DINE

You may want to go more than once to **Sophisticats,** 43 Charminster Rd. (tel. 0202/291019), which is among the leading restaurants at this south coast resort. Lying in a shopping section, about 1½ miles from the heart of Bournemouth, Sophisticats tempts its diners with its excellent fresh fish, among other good main dishes. While seated in a cozy booth, you can peruse the menu of international dishes. In this former shop, you can order any number of veal and beef dishes (sometimes the latter will be prepared in the Indonesian style). Appetizers are filled with flavor and texture, and a highly desirable finish to a meal is to order a dessert soufflé (but let the waiter know in time). Service is Tuesday to Saturday from 7 to 10 p.m., with meals costing from £15 ($26.25). Make sure you reserve a table.

Crust, Hampshire House, Bourne Avenue, The Square (tel. 0202/21430), is one of the best bistros in Bournemouth, waking up sleepy local tastebuds with some really good food at fair prices. Paul Harper and his wife, Tricia, the owners, keep their pleasant little place open daily from noon to 2:30 p.m. and 6:30 to 11 p.m., offering a set lunch for £6.50 ($11.40), with dinner priced from £12 ($21) to £20 ($35). Look for the daily specials on a blackboard menu. You might begin with a freshly made quiche, a hearty soup, or pâté, then follow with Moroccan lamb or fresh grilled fish cooked just right.

FOOD AND LODGING AT POOLE

An iron fence separates the flower-filled urns of the flagstone forecourt of the **Mansion House,** 11 Thames St., Poole, BH15 1JN (tel. 0202/685666), from the street. The neoclassical detailing and fan-shaped windows that pierce the red brick of the establishment's façade are the pride and well-maintained joy of the owners, Robert and Valerie Leonard. You'll probably be offered a glass of sherry as you register near the sweeping staircase of the entrance vestibule. A pair of bars offers both formal and rustic decors. An upstairs lounge and graciously furnished bedrooms provide plenty of quiet, well-decorated corners for relaxation. The 19 bedrooms come with many thoughtful extras and cost £70 ($122.50) daily in a single, £102 ($178.50) in a double. Excellent modern English cuisine is served at around £16 ($28) per meal. The house was built more than 200 years ago by an English entrepreneur engaged in cod-fishing off the coast of Newfoundland.

KINGSTON LACY

An imposing 17th-century mansion, Kingston Lacy, at Wimborne Minster, on the B3082 Wimborne–Blandford road, 1½ miles west of Wimborne, was the home for more than 300 years of the Bankes family, who had as guests such distinguished persons as King Edward VII, Kaiser Wilhelm, Thomas Hardy, George V, and Wellington. The house contains a magnificent collection of artworks, tapestries, and furnishings brought from abroad by Sir Charles Barry (designer of the House of Commons) at the request of William Bankes, a friend of Lord Byron's. The present house was built to replace Corfe Castle, the Bankes family's home that was destroyed in the Civil War. During her husband's absence in pursuit of duties as chief justice to King Charles I, Lady Bankes led in the defense of the castle, withstanding two sieges before being forced to surrender to Cromwell's forces in 1646 through actions of a treacherous follower. The keys of Corfe Castle hang in the library at Kingston Lacy. The house, set in 250 acres of wooded park, is open from noon to 5 p.m. daily except Thursday and Friday from April to the end of October. The park is open from noon to 6 p.m. Admission to the house and garden is £3.50 ($6.15) for adults, £1.75 ($3.05) for children. The park and garden can be visited for £1 ($1.75) for adults, 50p (90¢) for children.

7. Shaftesbury

The origins of this typical Dorsetshire market town date back to the 9th century when King Alfred founded the abbey and made his daughter the first abbess. King Edward the Martyr was buried there, and King Canute died in the abbey but was buried in Winchester. Little now remains of the abbey, but the ruins are beautifully laid out. The museum adjoining St. Peter's Church at the top of Gold Hill gives a good idea of what the ancient Saxon hilltop town was like.

Today, ancient cottages and hostelries cling to the steep cobbled streets, thatched roofs frown above tiny paned windows, and modern stores vie with the street market in the High Street and the cattle market off Christy's Lane.

The town, right on the A30 from London, is an excellent center from which to visit Hardy Country (it appears as Chaston in *Jude the Obscure*), Stourhead Gardens, and Longleat House.

FOOD AND LODGING

A Georgian house with Victorian additions, **The Royal Chase Hotel,** Shaftesbury, Dorset SP7 8DB (tel. 0747/3355), has had varied occupants. Once a button-making factory and then a monastery, it is now a delightfully informal Best Western hotel run by George and Rosemary Hunt. All rooms have private baths and go for £31 ($54.25) per person per night, including a full breakfast, early-morning tea, newspaper, service, and VAT. The hotel offers an indoor swimming pool, a leisure center, and a Turkish steam room.

A meal in the elegant Byzant Restaurant will cost from £15 ($26.25) and includes several local dishes such as local trout, seasonal game, and venison marinated in sherry. Dinner is served nightly from 7 to 9:30. Every day throughout the year, the Country Kitchen with its gingham cloths and hoop-backed chairs provides an informal style of dining at lunchtime and in the evening if you don't want a full meal in the main restaurant. Meals cost from £7 ($12.25). They serve Thomas Hardy's Ale, featured in the *Guinness Book of Records* as the strongest beer brewed in a bottle. Even for less fanatical drinkers, the bar, dominated by an open-kitchen range and decorated with Dorsetshire bygones, is an attraction. There are traditional bar games, shove ha'penny, and table skittles at which to pitch your skill. On weekends the Cellar Bar also offers snacks and a wide selection of wines at lunchtime and in the evening if you don't want a full meal in the restaurant.

In the Environs

Plumber Manor, Sturminster Newton, Dorset DT10 2AF (tel. 0258/72507), a Jacobean manor house in 600 acres of farmland, has been lived in by the Prideaux-Brune family since the early 17th century. The present inhabitants, Richard Prideaux-Brune and his wife, Alison, open the lovely old place to guests. Downstairs, a large hall from which the staircase rises is decorated with family portraits. A comfortable lounge is furnished with antiques. There's a bar to serve the restaurant, made up of three connecting dining rooms where guests can sample the excellent cooking of Brian Prideaux-Brune, Richard's brother. Upstairs, a gallery leads to six of the bedrooms, all with private bath and views over the gardens and the countryside. Six more large units in a long, low stone barn across the stable block (large umbrellas are provided to make the crossing if necessary) are well designed, with wide window seats and views over the gardens, modern baths, and well-chosen furnishings. A small double-bedded room costs £47.50 ($83.15) for single occupancy, £60 ($105) for double. A standard double- or twin-bedded room, based on single or double occupancy, costs £50 ($87.50) to £70 ($122.50), and a superior unit, on the same basis, rents for £60 ($105) to £80 ($140). All rates include a full English or a continental breakfast, VAT, and service. Dinner is a three-course meal costing from £17.50 ($30.65), including VAT. Try the English lamb or roast pheasant in port sauce. All main courses are served with fresh vegetables. The restaurant is closed to nonresidents on Monday in winter. On those days, a set meal is served for residents. Plumber Manor has a family atmosphere, with the Prideaux-Brunes treating their clientele as house guests.

---

8. Wareham

This historic little town on the Frome River is about a mile west of Poole Harbor. Many find it a good center for touring the South Dorset coast and the Purbeck Hills. It contains remains of early Anglo-Saxon and Roman town walls, plus the Saxon church of St. Martin with its effigy of Lawrence of Arabia.

The district was known to T.E. Lawrence (Lawrence of Arabia), who died in a motorcycle crash in 1935. His former home, **Clouds Hill,** lies a few miles to the west (one mile north of Bovington Camp). It is open Wednesday to Friday (also Sunday) from April until the end of September, from 2 to 5 p.m. (from October until the end of March, it is open only on Sunday, from 1 to 4 p.m.), charging an admission of £1.50 ($2.65).

FOOD AND LODGING

In what was a 16th-century priory, the **Priory Hotel,** Church Green, Wareham, Dorset BH20 4ND (tel. 09295/2772), has as a backdrop the rectangular bulk of the nearby village church. Beside the River Frome, the hotel has a well-tended garden adorned by graceful trees. Inside, a warmly paneled bar and a sumptuous lounge filled with antiques open onto views of the lawn. The 15 bedrooms are tastefully furnished with antiques and complementary textiles. Each has its own bath, mini-bar, direct-dial phone, and many extras. Singles go for £40 ($70) to £65 ($113.75) daily and doubles for £50 ($87.50) to £150 ($262.50), with breakfast included. French-inspired meals are served in the wood-ringed dining room, while less formal fare is featured in the basement restaurant.

9. Dorchester

Thomas Hardy, in his 1886 novel *The Mayor of Casterbridge,* gave Dorchester literary fame. But it was known to the Romans; in fact, its Maumbury Rings, south of the town, is considered the best Roman amphitheater in Britain, having once re-sounded with the shouts of 12,000 spectators screaming for gladiator blood. Dorchester, a country town, was the setting of another bloodletting, the "Bloody Assize" of 1685, when Judge Jeffreys condemned to death the supporters of the Duke of Monmouth's rebellion against James II.

But it is mostly through Hardy that the world knows Dorchester. Many of his major scenes of love and intrigue took place on the periphery of Dorchester. The land was best known to Hardy, since he was born in 1840 at **Higher Bockhampton,** three miles northeast of Dorchester. His home, now a National Trust property, may be visited by the public March to October daily from 11 a.m. to 6 p.m. or dusk, whichever is earlier. But to go inside, you must make an appointment with the ten-ant. You may write in advance to **Hardy's Cottage,** Higher Bockhampton, Dorchester, Dorset, England, or telephone 0305/62366. You approach the cottage on foot, a ten-minute walk after parking your vehicle in the space provided in the wood. The admission is £1.50 ($2.65).

You may also want to browse around the **Dorset County Museum,** High West Street (next to St. Peter's Church), with its gallery devoted to memorabilia of Thom-as Hardy. In addition, you'll find an archeological gallery with displays and finds from Maiden Castle, Britain's largest Iron Age hill fort, plus galleries on the geolo-gy, local history, and natural history of Dorset. The museum is open Monday to Saturday from 10 a.m. to 5 p.m. Admission is £1.20 ($2.10) for adults, 60p ($1.05) for children 5 to 16 years of age (children under 5, free).

FOOD AND LODGING

In business more than three centuries, **Kings Arms Hotel,** 30 High East St., Dorchester, Dorset DT1 1HF (tel. 0305/65353), has great bow windows above the porch and a swinging sign hanging over the road, a legacy left over from its days as a coaching inn. An archway leads to the courtyard and parking area at the back of the hotel. All the rooms have been refurbished and have private baths, radios, TVs, phones, and hot beverage facilities. An overnight stay will cost £45 ($78.75) daily in a single, from £65 ($113.75) in a twin or double. A full English breakfast and VAT are included in the tariffs. In addition to the main bar, there is a bistro overlooking the conservatory. Lunchtime snacks are served in both the bar and the bistro. Lunch and dinner are available in the restaurant, where the price for dinner is £11.55 ($20.20), including VAT.

On the Outskirts

Summer Lodge, Evershot, Dorset DT2 0JR (tel. 0935/83424), is a country-house hotel 12 miles north of Dorchester, where its resident owners, Nigel and Mar-garet Corbett, provide care, courtesy, and comfort. Once home to the heirs of the Earls of Ilchester, the country house, in the village of Evershot, stands on four acres of secluded gardens. Evershot appears as Evershed in *Tess of the D'Urbervilles,* and author Thomas Hardy designed a wing of the house. In this relaxed, informal atmosphere, guests rent rooms with views either of the garden or over the village rooftops to the fields beyond. Although centrally heated, the hotel offers log fires in winter. Guests sit around the fire getting to know each other in a convivial atmosphere. All rooms have private baths. Rates range from £45 ($78.75) to £60 ($105) per person daily, including a full English breakfast, afternoon tea, a five-course dinner with coffee, and VAT. Mrs. Corbett, who does the cooking, specializes in traditional English dishes the way they should be done, placing the emphasis on home-grown and local produce. In addition to the dining room with its French windows opening onto a terrace, the Corbetts have a bar and a TV room, plus a heated outdoor pool.

Yalbury Cottage, Lower Bockhampton, Dorchester, Dorset DT2 8PZ (tel. 0305/62382), is a small country house hotel and restaurant lying only two miles from Dorchester. In a village, it offers eight beautifully furnished bedrooms, each with private bath. These rooms were added to the original old thatched cottage, but the modern extension was designed in keeping with the style. Rolf and Pauline Voss give personal attention to each of their guests. All bedrooms contain a phone, hairdryer, color TV, and beverage-making equipment. Depending on the room asignment, two persons pay from £35.50 ($62.15) to £39.50 ($69.15) per person nightly. Special winter breaks, featuring price reductions, are offered. Tariffs quoted include not only the bed and a continental breakfast, but dinner as well. Dinner for nonresidents ranges from £15.50 ($27.15) to £16.50 ($28.90) per person. Traditional English and continental dishes are offered at this hotel with its beamed ceilings and inglenook fireplaces. The restaurant is open only in the evening. Lower Bockhampton, incidentally, was called "Melstock" in the fiction of Thomas Hardy (his cottage is just up the road).

10. Bridport

In Thomas Hardy's fictional Wessex terrain, Bridport was Port Bredy. The town lies inland, although there is a harbor one mile away at the holiday resort of West Bay, near the end of Chesil Beach. Ropes and fishing nets are Bridport specialties. Many a man dangled from the end of a Bridport dagger—that is, a rope—especially when some home-grown rebels were carted off to Dorchester to face Hanging Judge Jeffreys.

An interesting excursion from Bridport is to visit **Parnham** at Beaminster (tel. 0308/862204). One of the loveliest houses in Dorset, it stands in a wooded valley beside the River Brit. Since Tudor times it has been surrounded by sweeping lawns and magnificent trees, along with terraces and falling water. In 1976 John Makepeace, internationally known designer and furniture maker, bought Parnham, made it his home, and set up his workshop in the former stables. Here his team of artisans make the unique pieces of exquisite commissioned furniture Makepeace designs and on which his reputation is based. The well-restored rooms of the great house display recently completed pieces from the workshop, and there are monthly exhibitions by Britain's leading contemporary artists, designers, and artisans. The ornate plastered ceilings, paneled walls, and stone fireplaces are a splendid setting for the best of 20th-century design and craftsmanship.

Light lunches and teas with homemade cakes and local clotted cream are served in the 17th-century licensed buttery. The house, gardens, exhibitions, and workshop are open from 10 a.m. to 5 p.m. on Wednesday, Sunday, and bank holiday from Easter to October. Admission is £2.50 ($4.40) for adults, £1.20 ($2.10) for children. Parnham is on the A3066, five miles north of Bridport.

FOOD AND LODGING

One of the most desirable places to stay in Bridport just happens to be a bargain as well. From February to October, **Roundham House**, Roundham Gardens, West Bay Road, Bridport, Dorset DT6 4BD (tel. 0308/22753), receives guests. It lies one mile south of Bridport by B3157. Near the sea, Roundham may be your sunny dream of a Dorset holiday. A beautifully kept country home, it rents a total of only eight bedrooms. Each is well furnished with either a private bath or shower, as well as a number of other amenities including hairdryers and TVs. Your hosts, Mr. and Mrs. Moody, provide many thoughtful extras for their guests, charging from £22 ($38.50) daily in a single, the cost rising to £45 ($78.75) in a double. Some accommodations are suitable for families. A table d'hôte menu at £12.50 ($21.90) provides good value and is made with fresh ingredients.

Haddon House, West Bay, Bridport, Dorset DT6 4EL (tel. 0308/23626), in the environs of Bridport, was built in the Regency style. It lies within a short walk of the harbor and the beaches of West Bay, which is about 1½ miles south of Bridport on B3157. Wing Commander and Mrs. W. W. J. Loud are superb hosts, seeing to the needs of their guests and welcoming them into a homelike setting. They have 13 well furnished bedrooms to rent, each with private bath or shower and many amenities such as phone, TV, and beverage-making equipment, along with trouser press and hairdryer. At this fully licensed hotel, they receive guests all year, charging from £31 ($54.25) daily in a single, rising to £45 ($78.75) in a double. The hotel adjoins an 18-hole golf course. Haddon House also offers good food with meals ranging from £8.50 ($14.90) to £12.50 ($21.90).

---

11. Chideock

Chideock is a charming village one mile west of Bridport. It's a hamlet of thatched houses, with a dairy farm found in the center. About a mile away from the coast, it's a gem of a place for overnight stopovers, or especially longer stays. The countryside, with its rolling hills, makes excursions a temptation.

Chideock came into the world limelight when the Duke and Duchess of York (Andrew and Fergie) purchased Chideock Manor, a handsome old stone structure, as their country home.

FOOD AND LODGING

In this village of winners, the 15th-century **Chideock House Hotel,** Chideock, Dorset DT6 6JN (tel. 0297/89242), is perhaps the prettiest thatched house. Set near the road, with a protective stone wall, the house opens onto a rear garden of flowers, shrubs, and fruit trees. A driveway through the gardens leads to a large car park. You go directly into the beamed lounge with its two fireplaces, one an Adam fireplace with a wood-burning blaze on cool days. Most of the bedrooms have private baths, and all have TV and tea/coffee-makers. You can stay here on a B&B basis at a cost beginning at £18 ($31.50) per person daily. The cuisine is a local favorite with the best dessert table in town and offers a good table d'hôte or à la carte menu, served from 7 to 9 p.m. daily. The house quartered the Roundheads in 1645, and the ghosts of the village martyrs still haunt, as their trial was held at the hotel. Resident owners are Derek and Jenny Hammond.

The **Thatch Cottage,** Chideock, Dorset DT6 6JE (tel. 0297/89794). You'd never suspect that under the thatch of this 17th-century cottage are the comforts of home. The owner, Phil Hughes, accepts paying guests year round. While this is essentially a summer resort, there are those who welcome the idea of staying winter weekends, snugly sitting in front of the fireplace after enjoying good home-cooking. Fresh local produce is a specialty. A table d'hôte dinner at £8 ($14) is featured. Most of the year the charge is £12.50 ($21.90) per person daily for B&B. With dinner, the rate becomes £19 ($33.25) per person. If you want to walk to the beach, you can ask your host to pack a picnic lunch. It's best to make Chideock your center for a week, exploring the many sights in the area on day trips. Reservations are necessary from June to September.

12. Charmouth

On Lyme Bay, Charmouth, like Chideock, is another winner. A village of Georgian houses and thatched cottages, Charmouth contains some of the most dramatic coastal scenery in West Dorset. The village lies to the west of Golden Cap, which is, according to the adventurers who measure such things, the highest cliff along the coast of southern England.

FOOD AND LODGING

The most desirable place to stay is **White House,** 2 Hillside, Charmouth, Bridport, Dorset DT66PJ (tel. 0297/60411). It lies in this small coastal town once visited by Jane Austen gathering material for *Persuasion.* The White House is a Georgian home, with much of its period architecture, including bow doors, well preserved. It is tastefully furnished in a traditional style in keeping with the character of the house. Mr. and Mrs. Balfour took this place, constructed in 1827, and turned it into a most comfortable place at which to stay. Each of their seven handsomely furnished bedrooms has a private bath or shower, along with direct-dial phone, color TV, and beverage-making equipment. For B&B, a single person pays from £28 ($49) nightly, with a double going for £56 ($98). Bar lunches are available during the day, and at night home-cooked dishes, with a selection of carefully chosen wines, are offered.

13. Lyme Regis

On Lyme Bay near the Devonshire border, the resort of Lyme Regis is one of the most attractive centers along the south coast. For those who shun such big, commercial holiday centers as Torquay or Bournemouth, Lyme Regis is ideal—the true English coastal town, with a highly praised mild climate. Seagulls fly overhead: the streets are steep and winding; walks along Cobb Beach brisk and stimulating; the views, particularly of the craft in the harbor, photogenic. Following Lyme Regis's career as a major seaport (the Duke of Monmouth landed here to begin his unsuccessful attempt to become king), one finds it was a small spa for a while, catering to such visitors as Jane Austen.

The seaside town was the location of the film *The French Lieutenant's Woman,* and the actors stayed in the town's two main hotels.

The town also boasts the 1979–1981 world champion and best-dressed town crier four different years, the latest being 1987. Richard Fox is just maintaining a tradition that has been handed down for 1,000 years in Lyme Regis when he announces the local news. He'll also take visitors on a two-hour tour of the resort on Tuesday at 3 p.m. to see the Cobb, the harbor from which ships sailed to fight the Spanish Armada. The walk heads up old Broad Street. Mr. Fox can be reached at Flat 2, 22a Broad Street. (tel. 02974/3568).

The surrounding area is a fascinating place for fossilism. Mary Anning discovered in 1810 at the age of 11 one of the first articulated ichthyosaur skeletons. She went on to become one of the first professional fossilists in the country. Books telling of walks in the area and the regions where fossils can be seen are available at the local **Information Bureau** in the Guildhall on Bridge Street (tel. 02974/2138).

FOOD AND LODGING

The most desirable place to stay is **Alexandra Hotel,** Pound Street, Lyme Regis, Dorset DT7 3HZ (tel. 02974/2010). Once a dower house, it was converted into a successful hotel with some two dozen bedrooms, nearly all of which have a private bath or shower. The bedrooms in front open onto the Cobb. Mr. and Mrs. David Haskins welcome guests, charging from £29 ($50.75) daily in a single, the tariff rising to £75 ($131.25) for the best doubles. Rooms are well cared for and offer such standard amenities as beverage-making equipment, phone, and TV. Guests are received every month but January. Menus are limited but varied each night, and are reasonable in price, costing from £7.50 ($13.15) to £13 ($22.75), remarkably good value for what you get. Guests can unwind in a sun lounge.

An impressive Regency house, **High Cliff Hotel,** Sidmouth Road, Lyme Regis, Dorset DT7 3EH (tel. 02974/2300), is placed in the midst of surrounding gardens on the edge of a cliff, providing views of the coast. Formerly the home of Lord Lister, the doctor who pioneered antiseptic surgery, it accepts paying guests. High Cliff was opened in 1935. Inside, the central formal hallway, lounges, and dining room are tastefully decorated, with a sprinkling of antiques. Bedrooms are appropriately homelike, with good beds, hot and cold running water, and comfortable furnishings, and most have private baths or showers. The charge is £32 ($56) daily in a single, £42 ($73.50) in a double. A table d'hôte dinner costs from £10.50 ($18.40), and an à la carte menu is also offered. All the food is fresh, especially the local fish and other seafood as well as vegetables from the hotel's garden. The hotel is open from March to November.

Mariners Hotel, Silver Street, Lyme Regis, Dorset DT7 3HS (tel. 02974/2753), a coaching inn dating from 1641, has been preserved and refurbished to become a fine hotel. The resident proprietors, Stewart and Lesley Preston, are proud, and rightly so, of the view from their lounge and some of the bedrooms of the Dorset coastline and all the way to the lighthouse at Portland Bill, 25 miles away. All the bedrooms have private baths within or outside the units. Although modernized, the accommodations retain their 17th-century charm of crooked beams and irregularly shaped rooms. The daily rate based on a minimum two-day stay is from £30 ($52.50) per person for room, breakfast, and a four-course dinner. In the restaurant, you can either order table d'hôte or à la carte menus. The floodlit garden features a 340-year-old tulip tree, the third oldest in the country. The building occupied by the hotel was immortalized by Beatrix Potter in her painting of "Susan the Cat and Stumpy the Dog" and featured in *Tales of Little Pig Robinson* published in 1902.

Kersbrook Hotel, Pound Road, Lyme Regis, Dorset DT7 3HX (tel. 02974/2596), was built of stone in 1790 and is crowned by a thatch roof. It sits on a ledge above the village, which provides a panoramic view of the coast, on its 1½ acres of gardens redone according to the original 18th-century plans. The public rooms have been refurnished with antique furniture, recreating old-world charm yet with all modern facilities. Mr. and Mrs. Eric Hall Stephenson are the resident proprietors of Kersbrook, charging from £19 ($33.25) to £26 ($45.50) per person daily for B&B, £31 ($54.25) to £38 ($66.50) per person for half board. All rooms have private baths and showers. There is a good choice of an evening meal, with an extensive trolley. Booking is essential for dinner.

Royal Lion, Broad Street, Lyme Regis, Dorset DT7 3QF (tel. 02974/5622), is an old coaching inn, once known as the White Lion. On the side of a hill, it climbs up from the sea, with country furnishings in the oak-beamed bar and lounge. The bedrooms are also country style, including one with a canopied bed used regularly by Edward VII when he was Prince of Wales (his mistress, Lillie Langtry, was born in Lyme Regis). A room and a large breakfast costs from £25 ($43.75) per person daily, including VAT and an early-morning cup of tea brought up with the daily papers. Ordered separately, a dinner will cost around £10 ($17.50), and you're given a choice of fresh local fish along with grilled meat dishes. There is a separate buffet bar.

14. Chedington

Chedington is known to mapmakers and geologists as the meeting place of two of England's famous streams, the Axe and the Parrett. Motorists can more easily locate it near Winyard's Gap, a few yards from the A3565, which stretches between Crewkerne and Dorchester. The legendary King Alfred is said to have found solace in this countryside from the pressures of ruling his feudal kingdom. For a visit here, the following hotel is recommended.

Chedington Court, Chedington, near Beaminster, Dorset DT8 3HY (tel. 093589/265), is a Jacobean manor house set in ten acres of terraces, gardens, and lawns. It contains mullioned windows, boldly angled gables, and steep slate roofs. This manor was converted into an eight-room hotel in 1981 by the establishment's owners, Philip and Hilary Chapman. Much of the style and some of the grandeur of the Victorians have been preserved. There's a glassed-in conservatory laden with mimosa and plumbago. The bedrooms are individually furnished, sometimes with antiques, canopied beds, and fireplaces, along with some elegant accessories. One contains satinwood furniture that long ago was contained in an oceangoing suite aboard the *Queen Mary*. Doubles cost £46 ($80.50) to £65 ($113.75) per person daily for half board, including service and VAT. The fresh and flavorful meals served in the dining room from 7 to 9 p.m. are a high point of the day. Each is personally and carefully prepared by Hilary and served in a room with a panoramic view over the Dorset Hills.

15. Sherborne

A little gem of a town, with well-preserved medieval, Tudor, Stuart, and Georgian buildings, Sherborne is in the heart of Dorset in a setting of wooded hills, valleys, and chalk downs. It was here that Sir Walter Raleigh lived before the vicissitudes of power dislodged him forever.

Sherborne Old Castle (tel. 0935/812730), half a mile east of the town, was built in the early 12th century by the powerful Bishop Roger de Caen, but it was soon seized by the Crown about the time of the death of King Henry I in 1135 and the troubled accession to the throne of Stephen. The castle was given to Sir Walter Raleigh by Queen Elizabeth I. The gallant knight built Sherborne Lodge on the grounds. The buildings were mostly destroyed in the Civil War, but you can still see a gatehouse, some graceful arcades, and decorative windows. The castle ruins can be visited from 10 a.m. to 6 p.m. daily from March 17 to October 14. From October 15 to March 16, hours are from 10 a.m. to 4 p.m. Closed three days at Christmas and New Year's Day.

Sherborne Castle (tel. 0935/813182) was built by Sir Walter Raleigh in 1594, when he decided that it would not be feasible to restore the old castle to suit him. His new home was an Elizabethan residence, a square mansion, which later owners gussied up with four Jacobean wings to make it more palatial. After King James I had Raleigh imprisoned in the Tower of London, the monarch gave the castle to a favorite Scot, Robert Carr, so that the Raleighs were banished from their home. It became the property of Sir John Digby, first Earl of Bristol, in 1617 and has been the Digby family home ever since. The mansion was enlarged by Sir John in 1625, and in the 18th century the formal Elizabethan gardens and fountains of the Raleighs were altered by Capability Brown, who created a serpentine lake between the two castles. The 20 acres of lawns and pleasure grounds around the 50-acre lake are open to the public. In the house are fine furniture, china, and paintings by Gainsborough, Lely, Reynolds, Kneller, and Van Dyck, among other artists. From Easter Saturday to the end of September the house is open on Thursday, Saturday, Sunday, and bank holiday Mondays from 2 to 6 p.m. Admission to the castle is £2.70 ($4.75) for adults, £1.35 ($2.35) for children; to the grounds only, £1 ($1.75) for adults, 50p (90¢) for children.

Sherborne Abbey is worth visiting to see the splendid fan vaulting of the roof, as well as the many monuments, including Purbeck marble effigies of medieval abbots and the Elizabethan four-posters and canopied Renaissance tombs. A baroque statue of the Earl of Bristol, standing between his two wives, was carved in 1698. The church is open daily until 6 p.m. in summer, 4 p.m. in winter. Many of the abbey's medieval monastic buildings are still in existence, used today to house a school. This British public school was the setting of a novel by Alec Waugh, *The Loom of Youth,* and for M.G.M.'s film *Goodbye, Mr. Chips.*

At **Cerne Abbas,** a village south of Sherborne, stands the Pitchmarket, where Thomas and Maria Washington, uncle and aunt of America's George Washington, once lived.

FOOD AND LODGING

Convenient to motorists because of its location at the side of the A30, the **Post House Hotel,** Horsecastles Lane, Sherborne, Dorset DT9 6BB (tel. 0935/813191), is a modern hotel offering standardized comfort and renewed bathrooms. Accommodations are carpeted and attractively upholstered, containing mini-bars, tea makers, and color TVs. Singles rent for £52 ($91) daily and doubles for £63 ($110.25), with breakfast included. A bar and restaurant are on the premises.

Eastbury Hotel, Long Street, Sherborne, Dorset DT9 3BY (tel. 0935/813131), is a 12-room Georgian town house hotel, lying in its own walled garden close to the 8th century abbey and Sherborne's two castles. Built in 1740 in the reign of George II, it has a traditional ambience, with its own library of antiquarian books. Beautifully restored, it still maintains its 18th-century character. Bedrooms, each with its own bath, color TV, direct-dial phone, along with several other amenities, maintains its own character. The charge is from £40 ($70) daily in a single, rising to £66 ($115.50) in a double. The best fresh English produce is served in the dining room, which has an extensive wine list.

DEVON

The Great Patchwork Quilt area of the southwest of England, part of the "West Countree," abounds with cliffside farms, rolling hills, foreboding moors, semitropical plants, and fishing villages—all of which combine to provide some of the finest scenery in England. The British approach sunny Devon with the same kind of excitement one would normally reserve for hopping over to the continent. Especially along the coastline, the British Riviera, many of the names of the seaports, villages, and resorts have been synonymous with holidays in the sun: Torbay, Clovelly, Lynton-Lynmouth.

Many small towns and fishing villages do not allow cars to enter. These towns provide car parks on their outskirts, but this can involve a long walk to reach the center of the harbor. In high season, from mid-July to mid-September, the more popular villages get quite crowded, and one needs reservations in the limited number of hotels available.

It's easy to involve yourself in the West Country life, as lived by the British vacationers. Perhaps you'll go pony trekking across moor and woodland, past streams and sheep-dotted fields, stopping at local pubs to soak up atmosphere and ale. Chances are your oddly shaped bedroom will be in a barton (farm) mentioned in the *Domesday Book* or in a thatch cottage neither straight, level, nor true.

When a Devonian invites you to walk down the primrose path, he or she means just that. The primrose is practically the shire flower of this most beautiful of countries. Devon is a land of jagged coasts—the red cliffs in the south facing the English Channel, the gray cliffs in the north opening onto the Bristol Channel.

Aside from the shores, a great many of the scenic highlights appear in the two national parks, **Dartmoor** in the south, **Exmoor** in the north. First, we'll explore:

SOUTH DEVON

It's the lazy life in South Devon, as you sit in the orchard, enjoying the view of the coast from which Raleigh and Drake set sail. Almost every little hamlet, on some level, is geared to accommodate tourists, who flock here in great numbers from early spring to late fall. There is much to see and explore. The tranquil life prevails.

1. Exeter

The county town of Devonshire, on the banks of the River Exe, Exeter was a Roman city founded in the 1st century A.D. Two centuries later it was encircled by a mighty stone wall, traces of which remain today. Conquerors and would-be conquerors, especially the Vikings, stormed the fortress in the centuries to come. None was more notable than William the Conqueror. Irked at Exeter's refusal to capitulate (perhaps also because it sheltered Gytha, mother of the slain Harold), the Norman duke brought Exeter to its knees on short notice.

Under the Tudors, the city grew and prospered. The cocky Sir Walter Raleigh and Sir Francis Drake cut striking figures strolling through Exeter's streets. In May 1942 the Germans bombed Exeter, destroying many of the city's architectural treasures. Exeter was rebuilt, but the new, impersonal-looking shops and offices couldn't replace the Georgian crescents and the black-and-white timbered buildings with their plastered walls. Fortunately, much was spared, including the major architectural treasure—

EXETER CATHEDRAL

Owing its present look to the Decorated style of the 13th and 14th centuries, the Exeter Cathedral of St. Peter actually goes back to Saxon times. Even Canute, the Viking conqueror, got in on the act of rebuilding around 1017. The cathedral of Bishop Warelwast came into being in the early 12th century, and the north and south towers serve as reminders of the Norman period. The remarkable feature of the present Gothic building is the tierceron vaulting of the nave and quire, 300 feet long and unbroken by any central tower or spire. The cathedral did suffer damage in the 1942 German bombings, losing its St. James's Chapel, which subsequently has been restored. But most of the treasures remained intact, including the rows of sculpture along the west front; the 14th-century Minstrels' Gallery, its angelic figures with Early English musical instruments in hand; and the carved oak 14th-century bishop's throne. The Dean and Chapter, who own the cathedral, request that visitors make a donation of at least £1 ($1.75) per adult.

EXETER MARITIME MUSEUM

At the Haven (tel. 0392/58075), the maritime museum has a collection of more than 160 small craft, many of which are on display, and shelters the world's largest collection of English and foreign craft, coming from places that range from the Congo to Corfu. The larger boats afloat in the canal basin can be boarded. There are canoes, proas, and boats that have been rowed across the Atlantic, and you can go aboard the oldest working steamboat or even picnic on a Hong Kong junk or an Arab dhow. This is an active museum, and the ISCA members who maintain the boats sail some of them during the summer months. Five colorful Portuguese chatas that carry a maximum of six passengers are available for rent at the museum from May to September. The boats are rowed along the three miles of navigable water on the historic canal at a charge of £2 ($3.50) per hour. The museum is open every day of the year except Christmas and Boxing Day, from 10 a.m. to 5 p.m. October to June, to 6 p.m. July to September. Adults pay an admission of £3 ($5.25); children, £1.50 ($2.65). *Note:* Occasionally, individual boats used for special events or sailing may not be on display.

OTHER ATTRACTIONS

Much of the old remains. The **Exeter Guildhall,** a colonnade building on High Street (tel. 0392/265500), is regarded as the oldest municipal building in the kingdom. The earliest reference to the Guildhall is contained in a deed of 1160. The Tudor front that straddles the pavement was added in 1593. Inside is a fine display of silver in the gallery. It contains a number of paintings as well, including one of Henrietta Anne, daughter of Charles I (she was born in Exeter in 1644). The ancient hall is paneled in oak. Subject to mayoral commitments, the Guildhall is open throughout the year, Monday to Saturday, from 10:30 a.m. to 5 p.m., and admission is free.

Just off "The High" is a green historic oasis. At the top of Castle Street stands an impressive Norman Gate House from William the Conqueror's Castle. Although only the house and walls survive, the view from here and the surrounding gardens is spectacular. Just by the Gate House is a charming Regency villa, adapted from an earlier house, which is now the **Rougemont House Museum of Costume and Lace,** Castle Street (tel. 0392/265858), open daily from 10 a.m. to 5:30 p.m. The museum features costumes displayed in period rooms (these change twice a year), along with one of the largest lace collections in Europe. It charges £1.70 ($3) for adults and 70p ($1.25) for children.

On the way to the Quay you will pass the Underground Passages, the subterranean water supply channels of medieval times. **St. Nicholas Priory,** The Mint, off Fore Street (tel. 0392/265858), is open Tuesday to Saturday from 10 a.m. to 5:30 p.m., charging adults 60p ($1.05) and children 30p (55¢). This is the guest wing of a Benedictine priory founded in 1070. You'll see fine plaster ceilings and period furniture.

On the Outskirts

Powderham Castle, Powderham (tel. 0626/890243), lies eight miles south of Exeter off the A379 Dawlish road. A castle was built here in the late 14th century by Sir Philip Courtenay, sixth son of the second Earl of Devon, and his wife, Margaret, granddaughter of Edward I. Their magnificent tomb is in the south transept of Exeter Cathedral. The castle suffered damage during the Civil War and was restored and altered in the 18th and 19th centuries, but its towers and battlements are still pure 14th century. The castle contains much fine furniture, including a remarkable clock that plays full tunes at 4, 8, and 12 o'clock, some 17th-century tapestries, and a chair used by William III for his first Council of State at Newton Abbot. The staircase hall contains some remarkable plasterwork set in bold relief against a brilliant turquoise background, more than two centuries old, as well as a detailed pedigree of the Courtenay family, a document more than 12 feet high. The chapel dates from the 15th century, with hand-hewn roof timbers and carved pew ends. Powderham Castle is a private house lived in by Lord and Lady Courtenay and family. From May to early September the castle is open daily except Friday and Saturday from 2 to 5:30 p.m. Admission is £2.75 ($4.80) for adults, £1.75 ($3.05) for children 8 to 16. There is a tea room for light refreshments.

WHERE TO STAY

In accommodations, Exeter has a number of comfortable choices.

Buckerell Lodge, Topsham Road, Exeter, Devon EX2 4SQ (tel. 0392/ 52451), is about the finest place to stay in the area, lying a mile southeast of the center on the B3182. The origins of the house go back to the 12th century, but it has been altered and changed beyond recognition over the years. Often a choice of commercial travelers, it's also a tourist favorite, especially in summer. The look today is

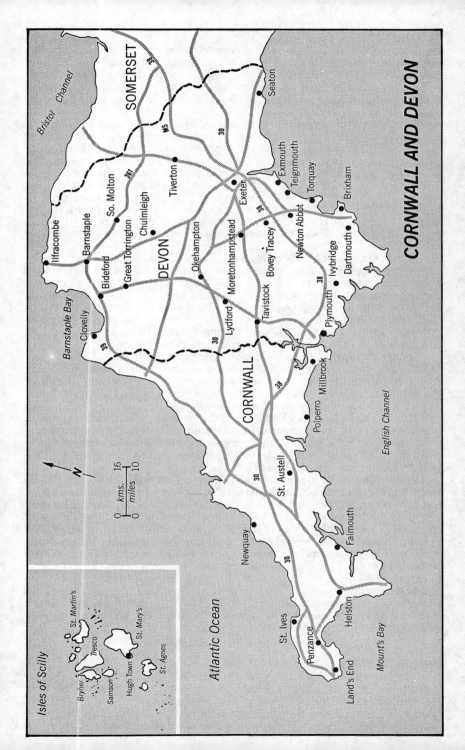

CORNWALL AND DEVON

Bristol Channel

SOMERSET

M5

Isles of Scilly

St. Martin's
Tresco
Bryher
Samson
Hugh Town
St. Mary's
St. Agnes

Ilfracombe

Barnstaple

Bideford

Great Torrington

Clovelly

Barnstaple Bay

So. Molton

Chulmleigh

Tiverton

DEVON

Okehampton

Moretonhampstead

Lydford

Tavistock

CORNWALL

Bovey Tracey

Exeter

Exmouth

Teignmouth

Torquay

Brixham

Newton Abbot

Ivybridge

Dartmouth

Plymouth

Millbrook

Polperro

English Channel

Seaton

St. Austell

Newquay

Falmouth

St. Ives

Penzance

Helston

Land's End

Mount's Bay

Atlantic Ocean

N

kms. 16
miles 10
0   0

361

30

38

30

29

30

38

30

38

30

Regency, and the bedrooms are well decorated and nicely equipped, coming in a range of styles and sizes. In all, 54 bedrooms are rented, costing £60 ($105) daily in a single, £78 ($136.50) in a double. During the day you can dine on lighter fare such as soups and salads, and in the evening you can order such traditional English fare as roast beef and Yorkshire pudding, served from 7 to 9:45 p.m., costing £20 ($35) for a complete meal.

Rougemont Hotel, Queen Street, Exeter, Devon EX4 3SP (tel. 0392/54982), is imbued with a stylish flair that none of its competitors provides. Fairly recently, this great, old-fashioned Victorian hotel, opposite the Central Railway Station, underwent a metamorphosis, emerging as a solid place at which to stay. Its neoclassic architecture is a background for the contemporary furnishings. Much of the comfort and tasteful decor are found in the bedrooms. Singles rent from £50 ($87.50) daily and doubles from £60 ($105), including VAT and an English breakfast. Amenities include telephones, radios, TVs, and private baths. Dinner is à la carte, beginning at £10 ($17.50). Guests gather in the Adam-style Cavendish Bar for drinks. A good stock of wines comes from the cellar, which, incidentally, was once used as a debtor's prison.

Royal Clarence Hotel, Cathedral Yard, Exeter, Devon EX1 1HD (tel. 0392/58464), a Georgian building, escaped destruction during the war. It is a hotel full of history, recently refurbished. All of the 56 bedrooms have private baths, and many overlook the 14th-century cathedral. A single rents for £60 ($105) to £65 ($113.75) daily, a double going for £75 ($131.25) to £120 ($210), with VAT included. Comfortable lounges display a mixture of antiques, gilt mirrors, and modern pieces. In the restaurant, a table d'hôte lunch costs £12.50 ($21.90) and a set dinner costs £15 ($26.25). You can also order à la carte.

Devon Motel, Exeter Bypass, Matford, Exeter, Devon EX32 8XU (tel. 0392/59268), lies on the outskirts of the city at the western sector of the bypass on the A38. It is convenient to the airport and as a stopping-off point for those headed for the West Country. You drive your car into your own open garage, and your bedroom and private bath are directly overhead. Singles pay £38 ($66.50) daily and doubles £49 ($85.75), including a full English breakfast and VAT. Some cheaper singles are in the old part of the hotel and are without bath, but all doubles and units in the new wing have a private bath. Inside, all is compact and built-in, with a picture window overlooking the meadows beyond. On the premises are a restaurant and drinking bars. An à la carte dinner is around £12 ($21).

White Hart Hotel, 65-66 South St., Exeter, Devon EX1 1EE (tel. 0392/79897), is one of the oldest inns in the city, having been a coaching inn in the 17th and 18th centuries. The hotel is a mass of polished wood, slate floors, oak beams, and gleaming brass and copper. The comfortable sitting rooms are bright with chintz. Bedrooms combine old and new. Most have color TV, a bath or shower, and a phone. Guests are housed in either the old wing or a more modern one. Some units are considered deluxe, and the most expensive are private suites. The single rate begins at £27 ($47.25) daily with bath or shower, going up to £40 ($70). Doubles or twins with bath cost from £58 ($101.50). All tariffs include a full English breakfast. Suites are more expensive. The dining room offers good English and continental dishes in a well-appointed atmosphere. The hotel has a good wine cellar, which supplies the Ale & Port House (a bar with waiter service where you can feast on traditional English fare), plus the well-known Bottlescreu Bills wine bar, which offers beefsteak-and-oyster pie or, in summer, barbecued steak in the wine garden.

WHERE TO EAT

A short walk from the cathedral, the **Ship Inn,** Martin's Lane (tel. 0392/72040), was often visited by Sir Francis Drake, Sir Walter Raleigh, and Sir John Hawkins. Of it Drake wrote: "Next to mine own shippe, I do most love that old 'Shippe' in Exon, a tavern in Fyssh Street, as the people call it, or as the clergie will have it, St. Martin's Lane." The pub still provides tankards of real ales, lager, and stout and is still loved by both young and old. A large selection of snacks is offered in the bar every day, while the restaurant upstairs provides more substantial English fare. At either lunch or dinner, you can order from a wide selection including French onion soup, whole grilled lemon sole, and five different steaks. The price of the main courses includes vegetables, roll, and butter. Portions are large, as in Elizabethan times. Expect to spend from £6 ($10.50) to £10 ($17.50) for a three-course meal. The restaurant is open from noon to 2 p.m. Monday to Saturday and from 6:30 to 10 p.m. Monday to Thursday, 6:30 to 10:30 p.m. Friday and Saturday. Closed Sunday and bank holidays. The bar is open from 11 a.m. to 2:30 p.m. and 5 to 11 p.m. Monday to Saturday, from noon to 2 p.m. and 7 to 10:30 p.m. Sunday.

Coolings Wine Bar, 11 Gandy St. (tel. 0392/434183). In one of the older and more interesting little streets of the city, this is a beckoning place with beams above the checked cloths of the tables. Some of the dining space is in the cellars of the old building. All the food is prepared on the premises, and that includes a good selection of cold meats, pies, and quiches, as well as chicken Waldorf and sugar-baked ham, each served with a variety of salads, then two or three daily hot dishes, chalked up on the blackboard. Meals cost around £6 ($10.50). D.C. Belford is the proprietor. He keeps the place open from 11 a.m. to 11 p.m. Monday to Saturday, from noon to 3 p.m. and 7 to 10:30 p.m. Sunday.

Port Royal Inn, The Quay (tel. 0392/72360), stands close to the Maritime Museum, along the edge of the River Exe, a two-minute walk from the quay. In fair weather, tables are placed outside overlooking the river. This is a real ale house, also known for its ports and sherries. With such a name, the pub reminds one of smugglers in the Caribbean, intrepid explorers, and the famous navigators. The bar food offered will revive the inner person in a more modern way. Salads are tempting, and you can also order a ploughman's lunch or pâté and toast. Sandwiches made from granary bread are filled with meat or cheese. There are also mini-loaves of white or granary bread filled with salad, cheese, or meat. Each day they do two or three hot specials such as seafood, roast chicken, and roast lamb. There are also desserts and coffee with cream, and the pub serves several real ales from various breweries. All food is ordered at the pub but will be delivered to your table by a waitress. Lunch is served daily from 11 a.m. to 2:30 p.m. and dinner from 6 to 10 p.m. The inn is open seven days a week.

FOOD AND LODGING OUTSIDE EXETER

Perhaps the finest way to enjoy the cathedral city of Exeter, especially if you have a car, is to live on the outskirts, from 10 to 19 miles from the heart of the city.

At Bickleigh

In the Exe Valley, four miles south of Tiverton and ten miles north of Exeter, lies Bickleigh, a hamlet with a river, an arched stone bridge, a mill pond, and thatch-roofed cottages—a cliché of English charm, one of the finest spots in all of Devon.

The Fisherman's Cot, Bickleigh, near Tiverton, Devon EX16 8RW (tel. 08845/237), sits like a picture postcard across the way from Bickleigh Bridge. This beautiful thatched hotel offers accommodations with private baths, TVs, direct-dial phones, and hot beverage facilities. Rates are £30 ($52.50) daily in a single, £40 ($70) in a double. A traditional English breakfast and VAT are included. An extensive menu is available every day for lunch and dinner. You can choose from bar snacks, with fresh home-baked bread, grills, fish dishes, or roast beef from the carvery. You can help yourself from the salad buffet, perhaps choosing locally caught River Exe salmon. The hotel is fully licensed and has a lovely bar overlooking the bridge and river.

At Ottery St. Mary

The sleepy little market town, where the incomparable Coleridge (*The Rime of the Ancient Mariner, Kubla Khan*) was born, lies in the Otter River Valley, only ten miles east of Exeter. See the almost perfectly preserved church from the 14th century. The old cloth town makes a good base for exploring the South Devon coastline, particularly if you center at the following medium-priced recommendation:

Salston Hotel, Ottery St. Mary, near Exeter, Devon EX11 1RQ (tel. 04081/ 5581), an old manor house, lies 1½ miles off the main A30 London road, and a mile from Ottery St. Mary. The hotel is officially listed as a building of historical and architectural interest. It was once the home of the Coleridge family. Even though it has lost most of its acreage and original furnishings, the exterior is intact—a rambling three-story brick hotel with chimneys and gables. The lounge is large, with two bay windows opening onto the gardens. A ballroom, built for the visit of Princess Alexandra of Teck (that name may send you rushing to your history books), has a Tudor fireplace. The Salston has added a 12-bedroom extension with luxury rooms, each with shower, hairdryer, refrigerated mini-bar, and a double and single bed. B&B charges are from £40 ($70) per person daily. Spa fans will find a health studio run in conjunction with the Salston, plus two squash courts. There is a 20- by 48-foot swimming pool, plus an adjoining Norwegian pine cabin with sauna, solarium, and a massage and relaxing room.

At South Zeal

South Zeal lies 17 miles from Exeter. The village is signposted from the old A30, near Sticklepath.

The Oxenham Arms, South Zeal, Okehampton, Devon EX20 2JT (tel. 0837/ 840244). Its conversion to an inn in 1487 earmarks this place as one of the oldest continuously licensed inns in England. Its history predates that era by hundreds of years, however, as a massive Celtic standing-stone testifies. The establishment is owned by Louisiana-born James Henry and his English wife, Patricia. The carefully preserved inn was originally built in the 12th century as a monastery. The mullioned windows and chiseled granite of the façade, coupled with the beamed and paneled interior, hint that this is no ordinary pub. Inside, clusters of antiques and open fireplaces add a note of charm. Nature lovers appreciate the garden, whose shrubs are accessible via the old monastery's steps. All but a few of the eight rooms contain private bath. For stays of one or two nights, the rate for B&B ranges from £16 ($28) to £20 ($36) per person daily, depending on the plumbing. The half-board tariff is also attractively priced at £26 ($45.50) to £30 ($52.50) per person daily. The dining room is open to nonresidents, the charge being £8.50 ($14.90) to £12.50 ($21.90) for a fixed-price lunch or dinners. Menu specialties include tasty bar food as well as more formal dishes such as pot pie of mixed shellfish, Devonshire squab pie, and fresh fish. There's a dart board, plus several kinds of English ale in the atmospheric bar.

2. Dartmoor

Antiquity-rich Dartmoor lies in the southern part of the shire. The land of this granite mass sometimes rises to a height of 2,000 feet above sea level. The national park is a patchwork quilt of mood changes: gorse and purple heather, Dartmoor ponies, a foreboding landscape for the experienced walker only, gorges with rushing water.

Accommodation information is operated by the **Dartmoor Tourist Association,** 8 Fitzford Cottages, Tavistock (tel. 0252/3501). Local information centers will also provide a list of accommodations.

Some 13 miles west from Exeter, the peaceful little town of **Moretonhampstead,** perched on the edge of Dartmoor, makes a good center. Moretonhampstead contains much that is old, including a market cross and several 17th-century colonnaded almshouses.

The much visited Dartmoor village of **Widecombe-in-the-Moor** is only seven miles from Moretonhampstead. The fame of the village of Widecombe-in-the-Moor stems from an old folksong about Tom Pearce and his gray mare, listing the men who were supposed to be on their way to Widecombe Fair when they met with disaster: Bill Brewer, Jan Stewer, Peter Gurney, Peter Davy, Daniel Whiddon, Harry Hawke, and Old Uncle Tom Cobley. Widecombe also has a parish church worth visiting. Called the **Cathedral of the Moor,** with a roster of vicars beginning in 1253, the house of worship in a green valley is surrounded by legends. When the building was restored, a wall-plate was found bearing the badge of Richard II (1377–1399), the figure of a white hart.

A summer bus service provides an ideal way to get onto the moor in order to hike some of the 500 miles of foot- and bridlepaths. The country is rough, and on the high moor you should always make sure you have good maps, a compass, and suitable clothing and shoes. Don't be put off, however. Unless you are a professional hiker, it is unlikely that you will go very far from the well-trodden paths. The park authority also runs guided walks from selected starting points.

Information on the bus links between various villages and towns on Dartmoor is available from **Plymouth CityBus,** Milehouse, Plymouth (tel. 0752/264888), and from **Devon General,** Exeter Bus Station, Paris Street, Exeter (tel. 0392/219911).

The guided walking tours are of varying difficulty, ranging from one hour up to six hours for a trek of some 9 to 12 miles. All you have to do is turn up suitably clad at your selected starting point, and there you are. Details are available from the **Dartmoor National Park Information Centres** or from the **Dartmoor National Park Authority,** Parke, Haytor Road, Bovey Tracey, Newton Abbot, Devon TQ13 9JQ (tel. 0626/832093). The charge for walks is 75p ($1.30) for 1½ hours, £1 ($1.75) for up to three hours, or £1.50 ($2.65) for six hours.

Throughout the area are stables where you can arrange for a day's trek on horseback across the moors. For horse-riding on Dartmoor, there are too many establishments to list. All are licensed, and you are accompanied by an experienced rider/guide. The moor can be dangerous, with sudden fogs descending without warning on treacherous marshlands. All horse-rental stables are listed in a useful free publication, the *Dartmoor Visitor,* obtainable from tourist and visitor centers or by mail. Send an International Reply Coupon to the Dartmoor National Park Authority (address above). Prices for horse rental are around £3 ($5.25) per hour, £8 ($14) for a half day, and £14 ($24.50) for a full day.

The **Museum of Dartmoor Life,** The Dartmoor Centre, West Street, Okehampton (tel. 0837/53020). The market town of Okehampton owes its existence to the Norman castle built by Baldwin de Bryonis, sheriff of Devon, under orders from his uncle, William the Conqueror, in 1068, just two years after the conquest. The Courtenay family lived there for many generations until Henry VIII beheaded one of them and dismantled the castle in 1538. The museum is housed in an old mill with a waterwheel and is part of the Dartmoor Centre, a group of attractions around an old courtyard. Also here are working craft studios, a Victorian Cottage Tea Room, and a Dartmoor National Park Tourist Information Centre. Museum displays cover all aspects of Dartmoor's history from prehistoric times, including geology, industries, living conditions, crafts, farm tools and machinery, and some old vehicles—a Devon box wagon of 1875, a 1922 Bullnose Morris motorcar, a 1937 motorcycle. There is a reconstructed cider press and a blacksmithy, and much more. The museum is open from 10 a.m. to 5 p.m. (to 4 p.m. in winter) Monday to Saturday from March to December and also on Sunday in July and August. Admission is 50p (90¢) for adults, 30p (55¢) for children.

FOOD AND LODGING

A Jacobean-style mansion, the **Manor House Hotel,** Moretonhampstead, Devon TQ13 8RE (tel. 0647/40355), is set in 270 acres of private parkland on the edge of the Dartmoor National Park. In the grounds are an excellent 18-hole championship golf course, a par-3 course, a putting green, and tennis and squash courts. Built by the second Viscount Hambledon as a hunting lodge in 1907, the hotel is renowned for its open log fires, oak paneling, and superb cuisine. All of the 69 bedrooms have private baths, color TVs, radios, direct-dial phones, trouser presses, and hot beverage facilities. Prices quoted for half board are £75 ($131.25) to £82 ($143.50) daily for singles in high season, £50 ($87.50) to £65 ($113.75) in low season. Doubles and twins, also for half board, pay £130 ($227.50) to £150 ($262.50) in high season, £90 ($157.50) to £115 ($201.25) off-season. Prices include VAT, service charge, and golf privileges. Bar snacks can be enjoyed at lunchtime, and Devonshire cream teas are available every afternoon. From the terrace, you can watch the River Bovey meandering through the grounds or set out on a walk along its banks to the lakes and gardens.

Moorwood Cottage Restaurant, Lustleigh, near Newton Abbot (tel. 06477/341). It's easy to drive past the small 17th-century cottage with bettling thatch and leaded windows on the A382 highway between Moretonhampstead and Bovey Tracey. However, it serves some of the finest dinners in Dartmoor. The dining room is in a William and Mary style synchronized with the age of the house (1640). Mick and Lisa Daymond once catered to racecar drivers competing in the Grand Prix, but now their pots, pans, and skills operate from this address. They serve dinner nightly except Monday from 6:30 to 9 p.m., costing from £25 ($43.75) per person. Specialties change with the season but might include noisettes of lamb in Pernod sauce, turbot in puff pastry, or beef Stroganoff. Six fresh vegetables are served al dente. Reservations are needed.

The Castle Inn, Lydford, near Okehampton, Devon EX20 4BH (tel. 082282/242), is a 16th-century inn next to Lydford Castle. The low inn, with its pink façade and row of rose trellises, is the hub of the village, along with the all-purpose grocery store and post office. The inn's owners, David and Susan Grey, have maintained the character of the commodious rustic lounge, with its valuable collection of old furniture and accessories, including wing chairs, grandfather clocks, and antique prints. One room is called the "Snug," containing a group of high-backed oak settles arranged in a circle. The inn is the home of the famous Lydford pennies, hammered out in an old Saxon mint in the reign of Ethelred the Unready (circa A.D. 1000). Seven of the pennies are displayed in the Foresters' Bar. In this bar, with its lamplit beams, collection of old plates, and Norman fireplace, meals are served buffet style, from noon to 2 p.m. daily, a great spread set out on a long table. The cost depends on your selection of a main course. The salads are on a help-yourself basis. Buffet salads at lunch cost about £4 ($7) with a main course. Snacks are available as well, and you can take your plate, along with a lager, and sneak off to an inviting nook. A three-course dinner will run about £14 ($24.50). For a bed and a large country-style breakfast, the charge is £20 ($35) daily in a single, £25 ($43.75) to £35 ($61.25) in a double or twin, depending on the plumbing. The bedrooms are not large but are well planned and attractively furnished, often with mahogany and marble Victorian pieces, each room with its own color scheme.

Holne Chase Hotel, Ashburton, near Newton Abbot, Devon TQ13 7NS (tel. 03643/471), is a white-gabled country house, within sight of trout- and salmon-fishing waters. You can catch your lunch and take it back to the kitchen to be cooked. Although the mood of the moor predominates, Holne Chase is surrounded by trees, lawns, and pastures, a perfect setting for walks along the Dart. It's off the main Ashburton–Princetown road, between Holne Bridge and New Bridge. Holne Chase is run by Mary and Kenneth Bromage and their son, Hugh, who returned to their native Devon to preserve the house "as a sanctuary of peace and hospitality." Every bedroom in the house is named after a tributary of the River Dart. The best way to stay here is to take the half-board rate, available for stays of two nights or more, costing £42.50 ($74.40) to £57.50 ($100.65) daily in singles, depending on the season. Doubles, on the two-day basis, rent for £56 ($98) to £66 ($115.50) in low season, rising to £80 ($140) to £90 ($157.50) in summer. A suite for two, with a four-poster bed, costs £81 ($141.75) in winter, £105 ($183.75) in summer. The house is furnished in period style, a refurbished bar also being done in the style of the rest of the hotel. The cooking combines the best of English fare with specialty dishes that are made all the better whenever produce from the gardens is used or fresh fish from the Dart River and Torbay. Devon beef and lamb are also featured. The old cellars hold a good selection of wines.

Cherrybrook Hotel, Two Bridges, Yelverton, Devon PL20 6SP (tel. 0822/88260), is a small family-run hotel in the center of the Dartmoor National Park, on the high moor but within easy driving distance of Exeter and Plymouth. It was built in the early 19th century by a friend of the Prince Regent, given permission to enclose a large area of the forest of Dartmoor for farming. Part of the farm was later leased to a gunpowder-manufacturing company, whose remains can still be seen. The lounge and bar with their beamed ceiling and slate floors are a reminder of these times. John and Susan Reynolds rent double, single, and family rooms, all of which have private showers and toilets, charging £18.50 ($32.40) per person daily for B&B. You can dine here also, paying around £8.50 ($14.90) for a four-course dinner and coffee.

A VISIT TO AN ABBEY

Constructed in 1278, **Sir Francis Drake's House,** Buckland Abbey, Yelverton (tel. 0822/853607), was originally a Cistercian monastery. It was dissolved in 1539 and became the country seat of Sir Richard Grenville and later Sir Francis Drake (two great sailors). It remained in the Drake family until 1946 when the abbey and grounds were given to the National Trust. The abbey is now a museum, housing exhibits including Drake's drum, banners, and other artifacts. (You probably won't get a chance to beat Drake's drum, but if you do, remember the words of Henry Newbold's poem: "Drake will quit the port of heaven and come to England's aid once more.") The abbey lies three miles west of Yelverton off the A386. It is open daily from 11 a.m. to 6 p.m. from April to the end of October. The rest of the year it is open only on Wednesday, Saturday, and Sunday from 2 to 5 p.m. Admission is £2.80 ($4.90) for adults, £1.40 ($2.45) for children. Light snacks are available when the abbey is open daily.

3. Chagford

Six hundred feet above sea level, Chagford is an ancient Stannary Town. With the moors all around, it is a good base for your exploration of the region of North Dartmoor. It is 20 miles from Exeter, Torquay, and Plymouth. Chagford overlooks the Teign River in its deep valley and is itself overlooked by the high granite tors. There's good fishing in the Teign (ask at your hotel). From Chagford, the most popular excursion is to **Postbridge,** six miles to the southwest, a village with a prehistoric clapper bridge.

Near Chagford stands **Castle Drogo,** in the hamlet of Drewsteignton (tel. 06473/3306). This massive granite castle was designed and built by Sir Edwin Lutyens and the castle's owner, Julius Drewe, in the early 20th century. It stands high above the River Teign, with views over the moors. The family can trace its origins back to the Norman Conquest. Drewe, who wanted to create a home worthy of his noble ancestors, found the bleak site high above the moors, and he and Lutyens created a splendid modern castle. The tour includes the elegant library, the drawing room, the dining room with fine paintings and mirrors, and a chapel, along with a vaulted-roof gunroom and a garden. There is a restaurant open daily from 11 a.m. to 5:30 p.m. The castle is open from April to October from 11 a.m. to 5:30 p.m., to 4:30 p.m. in October, charging an admission of £2.80 ($4.90) for adults, half price for children. If you wish to visit only the grounds, the fee is £1.30 ($2.30) for adults, half that for children.

WHERE TO STAY AND DINE

A mile from the edge of Dartmoor in beautiful countryside, the **Gidleigh Park Hotel,** Chagford, Devon TQ13 8HH (tel. 06473/2367), is two miles from Chagford, northwest by Gidleigh Road. A visit to this hotel, a *Relais & Chateaux,* is highly recommended. Its American owners, Kay and Paul Henderson, have renovated and refurnished the house with flair and imagination. In a park of 40 acres, the mansion is Tudor style. Large beech and oak trees abound. Inside, the oak-paneled public rooms and the open log fires invite a return to yesterday. The windows open onto views of the garden and the Teign Valley, with Dartmoor lying beyond. Most of the bedrooms, 14 in all, are on the second floor and are approached by a grand staircase. All rooms contain private bath, color TV, and phone. Half board ranges from £70 ($122.50) to £119 ($208.25) per person nightly. Good-tasting meals are served in an oak-paneled dining room. The menu is changed daily, and only the best and freshest products are used. Dining here has been called "a memorable experience." In fact, the restaurant here has been called "one of the best in the West Country."

How to get there: From Chagford Square turn right into Mill Street at Lloyds Bank. After 200 yards, fork right and down the hill to the crossroads. Cross straight over onto Holy Street, following the lane passing Holy Street Manor on your right and shifting into low gear to negotiate two sharp bends on a steep hill. Over Leigh Bridge, turn a sharp right into Gidleigh Park. A half-mile drive will bring you to the hotel.

Teignworthy Hotel, Frenchbeer, Chagford, Devon TQ13 8EX (tel. 06473/3355), 2½ miles down the south Teign Valley by the Fernworthy and Thornworthy road, is an attractive granite and slate country house where John and Gillian Newell welcome you as guests. Teignworthy stands 1,000 feet up on Dartmoor with a view. The house has central heating, but log fires in the main living rooms add to the ambience. There are nine comfortable and individual double bedrooms, six in the main house and three in the hayloft. All bedrooms have bath, color TV, and phone, and there is room to relax in privacy. They have a drawing room with an open log fire and a small bar for before-dinner drinks. Dinner can include local corn-fed guinea fowl, filets of John Dory with beurre blanc, and noisettes of Devon lamb. A complete dinner costs about £30 ($52.50), with VAT included. Wherever possible, local fresh produce is used. There is also a good, well-thought-out wine list. Overnight stays, including an English breakfast and dinner, will cost £73 ($127.75) per person daily in a double, £80 ($140) in a single, including VAT.

Great Tree Hotel, Sandy Park, Chagford, Devon TQ13 8JS (tel. 06475/2491), lies 1½ miles northeast of Chagford. Formerly an old hunting lodge, it is a comfortable country house set in 20 acres of private grounds. Bedrooms are country style, with private baths or showers, TV, radios, phones, and tea/coffee-makers. The charge is from £30 ($52.50) per person daily, with a full English breakfast included. Bev and Nigel Eaton-Gray, the proprietors, offer a four-course dinner made with home grown produce, so far as possible, costing £15.50 ($27.15). There are bar snacks at lunchtime and Devonshire cream teas later.

Easton Court Hotel, Easton Cross, Chagford, Devon TQ13 8JL (tel. 06473/3469), an oldtime favorite of mine, is still going strong. It is known to many a discerning visitor, and ever since it was established as a hotel in the 1920s by an American, Carolyn Cobb, this Tudor house has known its share of literary and theatrical celebrities. Alec Waugh wrote *Thirteen Such Years* here, and Patrick Leigh Fermor penned *The Traveller's Tree.* But it is best known as the place where Evelyn Waugh wrote *Brideshead Revisited.* An 11-hour video cassette of the entire TV series is available to guests. The guest book reads like a Who's Who of yesteryear: Robert Donat, Margaret Mead, Ralph Richardson, C. P. Snow, Richard Widmark, John Steinbeck.

Here is the atmosphere that usually fits in with a preconceived impression of a country place in England: an ancient stone house with a thatch roof, heavy oak beams, an inglenook where log fires burn in cold weather, and a high-walled flower garden. The eight bedrooms are snug and comfortable, sheltering 15 guests at a time with private baths or showers. Your hosts charge £40 ($70) per person daily for half board, depending on the season. British and international dishes are served, including coq au vin, steak-and-mushroom pie, and curried prawns. Meals, open to non-residents who reserve, cost from £15 ($26.25).

---

4. Torbay (Torquay)

In April 1968 the towns of Torquay, Paignton, and Brixham combined to form the "County Borough of Torbay," as part of a plan to turn the area into one of the super three-in-one resorts of Europe. Vacationers from the factories of the Midlands find it easier to bask in the home-grown Devonshire sunshine than to make the pilgrimage to Rimini or the Costa del Sol.

Torquay, set against a backdrop of the red cliffs of Devon, contains 11 miles of coastline, with many sheltered pebbly coves and sandy beaches. With its parks and gardens (including numerous subtropical plants and palm trees), it isn't hard to envision it as a Mediterranean-type resort (and its retired residents are fond of making this comparison, especially in postcards sent back to their cousins in Manchester). At night, concerts, productions from the West End (the D'Oyly Carte Opera appears occasionally at the Princess Theatre), vaudeville shows, and ballroom dancing keep the holiday-makers—and many honeymooners—entertained.

If you suddenly long for an old Devonshire village, you can always ride the short distance to **Cockington,** still in the same borough, which contains thatched cottages, an old mill, a forge, and a 12th-century church. Furthermore, if you want to visit one of the great homes of England, you can call on **Oldway,** in the heart of Paignton (tel. 0803/296244). Started by the founder of the Singer sewing-machine dynasty, Isaac Merritt Singer, and completed the year after he died (1875), the neoclassic mansion is surrounded by about 20 acres of grounds and Italian-style gardens. Inside, if you get the feeling you're at Versailles, you're almost right, as some of the rooms were copied. Open all year, Oldway may be visited Monday to Saturday from 9 a.m. to 1 p.m. and 2 to 5:15 p.m. (on Saturday and Sunday from 2:30 to 5 p.m., May to September only). Admission is free. The gardens are always open.

WHERE TO STAY

The leading five-star hotel in the West Country, **The Imperial,** Park Hill Road, Torquay, Devon TQ1 2DG (tel. 0803/294301), dates from the 1860s. Ever since then, it's always been known as the finest hotel along the south coast of England. It sits within 5½ acres of subtropical gardens opening onto rocky cliffs, with views of the Channel. Inside, a world unfolds of soaring ceilings, marble columns, and ornate plasterwork, enough to make a former visitor, Edward VII, feel at home. Its exterior, however, makes it look far younger than its years, as it was sheathed in the mid-1950s in a weatherproof shell of aluminum and concrete. Each of the 163 bedrooms enjoys lots of well-ordered space, traditional furniture, a private bath, phone, TV, radio, and mini-bar. Each accommodation enjoys a private balcony suspended high above a view taking in offshore islands with black rocks and sheer sides. Singles rent for £78 ($136.50) daily and doubles or twins for £67 ($117.25) per person. Included in the rates are the full use of the sporting facilities, dancing in the ballroom every night except Sunday, and entrance to La Pigalle nightclub.

The Ballroom Restaurant is a world of crystal chandeliers and tasteful decor, serving a menu, either table d'hôte or à la carte, of both British and international dishes, backed up by a fine wine list. Hours are daily from 12:30 to 2:30 p.m. for lunch. If you go for dinner, served from 7 to 9 p.m., it's important to reserve a table. The hotel also contains one of the most modern sports facilities in town, complete with Jacuzzi, a pair of all-weather tennis courts, a "pitch and putt" machine, two squash courts, and an exercise room.

Palace, Babbacombe Road, Torquay, Devon TQ1 3TG (tel. 0803/299799), ranks along with the Imperial as the most desirable accommodation at this seaside resort. This Victorian hotel was built when life was on a grand scale, as reflected by its spacious public rooms with their molded ceilings and columns. With all its many improvements in recent years, it should ride into the next century in a premier position. A four-star hotel, it is luxurious in appointments and facilities. Its public facilities, in fact, are the most impressive in Torquay, with both in- and outdoor swimming pools along with in- and outdoor tennis courts, even a nine hole golf course. All its bedrooms, some 135 in all, not counting suites, are well furnished, with private baths and other amenities. Singles rent for £46 ($80.50) and up on a daily rate, with doubles costing from £66 ($115.50). The hotel occupies 25 choice acres of real estate in Torquay, sweeping down to Anstey's Cove.

Palm Court Hotel, Sea Front, Torquay, Devon TQ2 5HW (tel. 0803/284881), a Victorian crescent built facing south onto the esplanade overlooking Torbay, offers style and good living. Two lounges are wood-paneled with leaded-glass windows. In the dining room is a minstrels' gallery. There are two up-to-date bars and a coffeeshop, open all day. All rooms have been modernized and have color TV, tea- and coffee-making facilities, central heating, telephone, and radio. Of the bedrooms, 53 have private baths. The highest tariffs are charged from July to September. Depending on the plumbing, B&B costs £20.50 ($35) to £23.50 ($41.15) per person per night. The half-board rate is £28 ($49) to £31 ($54.25) per person. The hotel has an elevator. With garden chairs and tables on the sun terrace outside the coffeeshop, the Palm Court becomes a social center. At night the colored floodlighting around the bay evokes a Riviera atmosphere.

Homers, Warren Road, Torquay, Devon TQ2 5TN (tel. 0803/213456). The Victorians who built this house set it near the top of steeply inclined gardens overlooking Tor Bay. The 14 bedrooms are furnished with mini-bars, phones, color TVs, private baths, and such touches as antique mirrors and patterned wallpaper. The accommodating owners charge £30 ($52.50) daily in a single, £60 ($105) in a double, with a full breakfast. English and French specialties are served in the hotel's restaurant, the dishes prepared with fresh ingredients. A fixed-price lunch costs £9 ($15.75); dinner, £19 ($33.75).

On the outskirts, **Orestone Manor,** Rockhouse Lane, Maidencombe, Torquay, Devon TQ1 4SX (tel. 0803/38098), lies in this small village about 3½ miles north of Torquay by A379. Sometimes the best way to enjoy a bustling seaside resort is from afar, nestling in a country home. Orestone Manor provides such an opportunity from March to December. In one of the loveliest valleys in South Devon, this gabled manor house was constructed in the early 17th century as a private home. Janet and John Flude now operate it as one of the finest small hotels in the area. This Georgian manor enjoys a tranquil rural setting, standing on two acres of well-landscaped gardens. Bedrooms are handsomely and comfortably furnished, with private baths and several amenities such as phone and beverage-making equipment. The single rate is from £29 ($50.75) nightly, rising to £70 ($122.50) in a double. Good and tasty bar lunches are provided Monday to Saturday, and a set dinner, correctly prepared and using fresh ingredients, is a bargain at £11.50 ($20.15). The staff is most helpful.

WHERE TO DINE

Considered by some as the finest independent dining spot in town, **Remy's,** 3 Croft Rd. (tel. 0803/292359), serves food at reasonable prices. The name of the place, in a Victorian building, comes from its owner and chef de cuisine, Remy Bopp of France. Here is a chef who sets great store by his raw ingredients, whether they be fresh fish from a local fisherman or vegetables from the market. Food-wise guests also enjoy his carefully selected collection of French wines. Meals are served Monday to Saturday from 7 to 9:30 p.m., costing from £15 ($26.25) and up. It is closed Sunday, Monday, and for the first two weeks in August.

Mulberry Room, 1 Scarborough Rd., Torquay, Devon TQ2 5UJ (tel. 0803/213639). Lesley Cooper is one of those inspired cooks, and she'll feed you well in her little dining room, seating some two dozen diners at midday. In fact, you can even stay here in one of the trio of bedrooms, each simply but comfortably furnished and well kept. B&B charges range from £10.50 ($18.40) to £13.50 ($23.65) daily, making it one of the bargains of the resort. The vegetarian will find comfort here, while regular diners feast on her baked lamb or honey-roasted chicken among other dishes. Traditional roasts draw the Sunday crowds. The choice is wisely limited so that everything served will be fresh. She is open for lunch only Wednesday to Sunday from 12:15 to 2:30 p.m. and serves dinner only on Saturday from 7:30 to 9 p.m. when reservations are essential. A set lunch ranges in price from £6 ($10.50) to £8.50 ($14.90), with Saturday dinner going for £10 ($17.50) to £12.50 ($21.90).

---

5. Totnes

One of the oldest towns in the West Country, the ancient borough of Totnes rests quietly in the past, seemingly content to let the Torbay area remain in the vanguard of the building boom. On the River Dart, 12 miles upstream from Dartmouth, Totnes is so totally removed in character from Torquay that the two towns could be in different countries. Totnes has several old historic buildings, notably the ruins of a Norman castle, an ancient guildhall, and the 15th-century church of St. Mary, made of red sandstone. In the Middle Ages, the old cloth town was encircled by walls, and the North Gate serves as a reminder of that period.

WHERE TO STAY

A historic former coaching inn, **Royal Seven Stars Hotel,** Totnes, Devon TQ9 5DD (tel. 0803/862125) dates for the most part back to 1660, although its origins go back 500 years before that. The hotel has an interesting porch over its entrance and overlooks a square in the town center, near the banks of the River Dart. The interior courtyard, once used for horses and carriages, is now enclosed in glass, with an old pine staircase. With antiques and paintings, the hotel's own heraldic shield, hand-carved chests, and a grandfather clock, the courtyard forms an inviting entrance to the inn. The bedrooms have been modernized, and most have private baths, built-in furniture, and comfortable beds. All have color TVs, phones, hot beverage facilities, and central heating. Charges, which include a big English breakfast, are £28 ($49) to £38 ($66.50) daily in a single, £40 ($70) to £48 ($84) for a double, with VAT included. A buffet bar is open for lunch all year as well as for supper May to September. A three-course lunch or four-course dinner can be enjoyed in the Brutus Room, open all year. Lunch costs £7 ($12.25), and dinner, around £12.50 ($14.90) for nonresidents. A dinner-dance and cabaret show is presented in the Star-lite Room most Saturdays.

WHERE TO DINE

An intimate rendezvous for diners, **The Elbow Room,** 6 North St. (tel. 0803/863480), is in a converted one-time cider press and adjoining cottage. The original 300-year-old stone walls have been retained and decor matched to them to give a unique atmosphere. Mr. and Mrs. R.J. Savin provide a standard of food and service that attracts gourmets. Mrs. Savin combines technical skill with inspiration and a flair for the unusual in the selection, preparation, and presentation of her appetizers, main courses, and homemade desserts. Main courses are accompanied by, and inclusive of, fresh vegetables. The menu is restricted to a maximum of ten international dishes, ranging from chicken with almonds (a suprême of fresh chicken served in a fresh cream and Grand Marnier sauce, garnished with flaked almonds and apple) to whisky steak Dijonnaise (prime filet of English beef served in a whisky, herb mist, and mushroom sauce). A lunchtime carvery, with a selection of roasts, charges £7.50 ($13.15) for three courses. In the evening, à la carte meals range from £12 ($21) to £19 ($33.25) for three courses. The restaurant is open from noon to 2 p.m. and 6:30 to 9:30 p.m. Tuesday to Saturday. Mr. Savin presides over the restaurant with charm and expertise.

WHERE TO STAY AND EAT ON THE OUTSKIRTS

In and around this area is some of South Devon's finest scenery. The hamlets are especially pleasing.

At North Huish

Just 2½ miles south of the A38, near Avonwick, Charles and Carol Trevor-Roper welcome guests to **Brookdale House,** North Huish, South Brent, Devon TQ10 9NR (tel. 054882/402), a comfortable hotel decorated in traditional country-house style to match the elegance of the large marble open fireplaces and decorative plaster cornice work in the spacious public rooms. The six bedrooms in the main house and two in adjacent Brookdale cottage all contain bathrooms and are tastefully furnished, with easy chairs, color TVs, direct-dial phones, hairdryers, trouser presses, and hot beverage facilities. The charge for B&B is £60 ($105) daily for single occupancy, £70 ($122.50) to £90 ($157.50) in a double or twin. The house has a large, comfortable lounge, a reading room, and a cozy paneled bar where you can order a snack lunch and drinks. The restaurant offers dishes making use of local produce, including Devon lamb and beef, game, salmon from the River Dart, and fresh fish from Brixham and Plymouth, together with fresh vegetables, clotted cream, local cheeses, and stone-ground flour. A set dinner costs £21 ($36.75). Brookdale House is closed in January.

At Stoke Gabriel

About four miles southeast of Totnes sits the little village of Stoke Gabriel, one of the loveliest in Devon. Famous as a fishing hamlet, it lies on a creek of the River Dart. Dartmouth is only six miles south of the village (equidistant to Torquay). Desirable as a base is:

The **Gabriel Court Hotel,** Stoke Gabriel, near Totnes, Devon TQ9 6SF (tel. 080/428206), is a manor house that until recent times had been owned by one family since 1485. What must the ghosts have thought when Michael and Eryl Beacom acquired it and guests started to fill up the rooms, chasing away the cobwebs of the past? The gleaming white house is surrounded by gardens, hedges, and magnolia trees. A heated swimming pool has been added. B&B rates are from £26 ($45.50) per person daily. You might get a room in the newer wing, containing eight bedrooms. All of the hotel's comfortable rooms have a private bath or shower and toilet facilities, TV, phones, and tea/coffee-makers. Gabriel Court enjoys a reputation for its well-cooked English food, enhanced all the more by fruit and vegetables from the garden, as well as trout and salmon from the Dart and poultry from nearby farms. The hotel has a bar. In winter, there are log fires in the lounges, and the house is also centrally heated.

---

6. Dartmouth

At the mouth of the River Dart, this ancient seaport, 36 miles from Exeter, is the home of the Royal Naval College. Traditionally linked to England's maritime greatness, Dartmouth sent out the young midshipmen who ensured that Britannia ruled the waves. You can take a river steamer up the Dart to Totnes (book at the kiosk at the harbor). The view along the way is of Devon's most beautiful river.

Dartmouth's 15th-century castle was built during the reign of Edward IV. The town's most noted architectural feature is the Butterwalk, lying below Tudor houses. The Flemish influence in some of the houses is pronounced.

WHERE TO STAY

A coaching inn since 1639, the **Royal Castle Hotel,** The Quay, Dartmouth, Devon TQ6 9PS (tel. 08043/4004), has slept a host of visitors, including Sir Francis Drake, Queen Victoria, Charles II, and Edward VII (bedrooms named after them commemorate their visits). Horse-drawn carriages (as late as 1910) would dispatch their passengers in a carriageway, now enclosed to make the reception hall. Everywhere you look, you see reminders of the inn's rich past. The glassed-in courtyard, with its winding wooden staircase, has the original coaching horn and a set of 20 antique spring bells connected to the bedrooms. Many of the rooms opening off the covered courtyard and the rambling corridors have antiques. All the units have been recently restored and have private baths, color TVs, direct-dial phones, and central heating. Prices range from £29.50 ($51.65) daily in a single, from £59 ($103.25) in a double, including the Royal Castle breakfast and VAT. The meals, taken in the restaurant under a beautiful Adam ceiling are excellent, in the best English tradition. A set lunch goes for £6.50 ($11.40), a set dinner for £9.50 ($16.65). A favorite place to settle in is the Galleon Bar, once two old kitchens, with double fireplaces and large hand-hewn beams said to have been rescued from Armada ships. There is another pub-style bar, with settles, popular with the locals. Guests lounge on the second floor in a room with a bay window overlooking the harbor.

Dart Marina Hotel, Sandquay, Dartmouth, Devon TQ6 9PS (tel. 08043/2580), is an ochre-walled establishment at the edge of its own marina, within a three-minute walk of the center of town. It was originally built as a clubhouse for the marina, but was expanded into a full-fledged hotel. Warmly masculine, its public rooms are sheathed with paneling crafted from glowing pine interspersed with yard upon yard of upholstery. From the bar, the yachting set can view their craft through large windows. Of the 33 comfortable bedrooms, most have a private bath, several contain balconies, and each has a color TV, radio, phone, and coffee-making equipment. Singles cost from £48 ($84) daily, and doubles or twins go for £65 ($113.75).

WHERE TO DINE

Considered the best restaurant in town, **The Carved Angel,** 2 South Embankment (tel. 08043/2465), serves specialties that are usually more akin to the creative cuisine of the continent than to the traditional cookery of England. Co-owner and chef Joyce Molyneux welcomes visitors to her stylishly simple riverside restaurant, the kitchen of which is partially screened from the dining room by plants. It was a former Victorian storefront. Typical dishes include beef marinated in orange and ginger and served with bay leaves on a skewer, and black bream with fennel and a sauce made of lemons and onions. The fish soup Provence style is superb. Full meals cost £27.50 ($48.15) to £32 ($56), with a fixed-price lunch going for £7.50 ($13.15) to £21 ($36.75). Meals are served from 12:30 to 1:45 p.m. and 7:30 to 9:30 p.m. daily except Sunday night and all day Monday. The restaurant is behind a half-timbered, heavily carved façade rising opposite the harbor. Inside, a central statue of a carved angel is ringed with a decor of neutral colors.

Bistro 33, 33 Lower St. (tel. 08043/2882), stands near the ferry stop from Kingswear (if you're coming from Torquay). It enjoys a bistro atmosphere under the direction of the chef and co-owner, Richard Cranfield. Capably prepared food is imaginatively presented on a well-balanced menu that, naturally, leans heavily toward fish, as reflected in the ragoût of seafood with a Provençal sauce. You might also try one of the meat or pasta dishes, including homemade green peppercorn noodles with smoked ham and cream, or else lamb tournedos coated with mushrooms and served in an onion sauce. Service is Tuesday to Sunday from 7 to 10 p.m., with meals costing from £20 ($35).

Horn of Plenty, Gulworthy, Devon PL19 8JD (tel. 0822/832528), is three miles west of Tavistock on the A390. As you drive along that road from Tavistock to Callington, you will see a small sign pointing north along a leafy drive to the solid Regency house where Sonia Stevenson operates what the French call a *restaurant avec chambres.* You can stay in one of the spacious, warm, and elegant bedrooms that have been installed over the old stables of the house, paying £52 ($91) daily in a single, £68 ($119) in a double. All accommodations have color TV, tea-and coffee-making facilities, phone, and a well-stocked mini-bar. You can return after a day of touring around the country to enjoy one of Sonia's dinners served in the cool dining room. Her well-prepared dishes might include young grouse with red-currant jelly or an Alsatian choucroute with boiled bacon and frankfurters, served with Alsatian wines. You can expect to pay from £25 ($43.75) for dinner. Lunch at £15 ($26.25) is served from noon to 2 p.m. except on Thursday, Friday, and Christmas Day. Dinner is from 7 to 9:30 p.m. every day except Christmas.

---

7. Plymouth

The historic seaport of Plymouth is more romantic in legend than in reality. But this was not always so. In World War II, the blitzed area of greater Plymouth lost at least 75,000 buildings. The heart of present-day Plymouth, including the municipal civic center on the Royal Parade, has been entirely rebuilt—the way that it was done the subject of much controversy.

For the old you must go to the Elizabethan section, known as the **Barbican,** and walk along the quay in the footsteps of Sir Francis Drake (once the mayor of Plymouth) and other Elizabethan seafarers, such as Sir John Hawkins, English naval commander and slave trader. It was from here in 1577 that Drake set sail on his round-the-world voyage. An even more famous sailing took place in 1620 when the Pilgrim Fathers left their final port in England for the New World. That fact is commemorated by a plaque at the harbor.

Legend has it that while playing bowls on Plymouth Hoe (Celtic for "high place"), Drake was told that the Spanish Armada had entered the sound and, in a masterful display of confidence, finished the game before going into battle. A local historian questions the location of the bowls game, if indeed it happened, starring Sir Francis. I am told that the Hoe in the 16th century was only gorse-covered scrubland outside tiny Plymouth and that it is more likely that the officers of the Royal Navy would have been bowling (then played on a shorter green than today) while awaiting the Armada arrival at the Minerva Inn, Looe Street, 20 yards from the house where Sir Francis lived, about two minutes' walk from the Barbican. My informant says that other captains, knowing that it would take about 20 minutes to ready their ships to sail against the Spanish, may have sent their executive officers to prepare while they finished their drinks and game. Doubt is cast on Drake's display of such insouciance, however, the feeling being that "5 feet 2 inches of red-haired impetuosity as he was, he'd have been off like a flash!"

Of special interest to visitors from the U.S. is the final departure point of the Pilgrim Fathers in 1620, the already-mentioned Barbican. The two ships, *Mayflower* and *Speedwell,* that sailed from Southampton in August of that year, put into Plymouth after they suffered storm damage. Here the *Speedwell,* was abandoned as unseaworthy, and the *Mayflower* made the trip to the New World alone. The Memorial Gateway to the Waterside on the Barbican marks the place, tradition says, whence the Pilgrims' ship sailed.

The Barbican is a mass of narrow streets, old houses, and quayside shops selling antiques, brasswork, old prints, and books. Fishing boats still unload their catch at the wharves, and passenger-carrying ferryboats run short harbor cruises. A trip includes a visit to Drake's Island in the Sound, the dockyards, and naval vessels, plus a view of the Hoe from the water.

A cruise of Plymouth Harbour costs £2 ($3.50) for adults and £1 ($1.75) for children. Departures are from February to November, with cruises leaving every half hour from 10 a.m. to 4 p.m. daily. These **Plymouth Boat Cruises** are booked at the Phoenix Wharf, the Barbican (tel. 0752/662338).

The **Barbican Craft Centre,** White Lane (tel. 0752/662338), in the Barbican, has workshops and showrooms where you can watch and talk to the people engaged in crafts. You'll see such sights as a potter throwing a special design or a glass-blower fashioning a particular glass. Woodcarvers, leather workers, and weavers are also busy, and you can buy their products at reasonable prices, even commissioning your own design if you're lucky.

WHERE TO STAY

Still a major base for the British navy, Plymouth makes for an interesting stopover. The pick of the lot in accommodations follows.

Duke of Cornwall Hotel, Millbay Road, Plymouth, Devon PL1 3LG (tel. 0752/266256), is a Victorian Gothic building that survived World War I bombings. The 70 accommodations, all with private baths, have been refurbished. Nine are master bedrooms, one with an antique four-poster bed. A single costs £45 ($78.75) daily, and a double goes for £55 ($96.25). Tariffs include a full English breakfast and VAT. The paneled Clan Bar provides an ideal setting for a drink, and the Spider's Web Bistro in the cellar offers a wide selection of bar snacks. The hotel dining room is of an elegant contemporary style with a circular ceiling supporting a fine chandelier. A set lunch costs £7.50 ($13.15), and a fixed-price dinner goes for £10.50 ($13.40).

Holiday Inn, Armada Way, Plymouth, Devon PL1 2HJ (tel. 0752/662866), might have upset the departure plans of our forefathers. If they'd known how luxurious the Holiday Inn would be, they might never have sailed. It's one of the most distinguished hotels in the West Country, overlooking the harbor and the Hoe. Rising like a midget skyscraper, it contains 217 good-size bedrooms with long double beds. Singles cost £70 ($122.50) daily, and doubles go for £85 ($148.75). The rooms are well-furnished with air conditioning, wide picture windows, TVs, radios, phones, and private baths. Babysitting is available. A covered swimming pool is on the grounds, and there's a sauna and sun terrace as well, with garden tables set up for poolside refreshments. On the top floor is the Penthouse, with views across Plymouth Sound, and on the ground floor there's a specialty fish and meat restaurant, Mongers.

Astor Hotel, 14 Elliott St., The Hoe, Plymouth, Devon PL1 2PS (tel. 0752/225511), was originally built by Victorians as the private home of a prosperous sea captain. In 1987 it received a major restoration, and today it contains 56 comfortable bedrooms, each with private bath, radio, color TV, phone, and coffee-making equipment. With breakfast included, singles cost £45 ($78.75) daily; doubles or twins, £60 ($105). Reduced rates can be arranged for stays of two nights or more, providing that half board is accepted. The hotel lies near The Hoe on a street lined with 19th-century buildings. On the premises is a series of well-decorated public lounges, plus a cozy and accommodating pub separated from the reception desk by a fan-shaped trio of glass doors.

Mayflower Post House, Cliff Road, The Hoe, Plymouth, Devon PL1 3DL (tel. 0752/662828), is situated on a hilltop above the bay. This nine-story hotel was constructed in 1970, its clientele divided equally between tourists and business-related travelers. The hotel contains 106 bedrooms, all but a dozen of which face the sea. Each unit has a TV, radio, private bath, mini-bar, and phone. Singles cost £59

($103.25) daily, and doubles or twins rent for £69 ($120.75), with VAT and service included. On the premises is a pub, the Boston Bar, with a separate entrance, along with a free-form heated outdoor pool (open only from April to October) and a restaurant with wide-angle views of the sea.

WHERE TO DINE

The most distinguished restaurant in Plymouth is **Chez Nous,** 13 Frankfort Gate (tel. 0752/266793). The owner and chef, Jacques Marchal, is a master in the kitchen, borrowing heavily from the past if he wants to, but also daring to express his creative talent by showing diners what he is capable of. Chez Nous is quite pretty and cozy, lying in a shopping complex. French posters decorate the walls, and you look for the specials of the day on the blackboard menu. Aided by a classic and rather elegant wine list, the food is likely to include such dishes as scallops steamed with ginger, seaman's pie, and pork with prunes. Fish, generally, is the preferred main dish to order here. Desserts and appetizers are also prepared with care. Fresh, quality ingredients are a hallmark of the cuisine. Lunch or dinner costs from £18.50 ($32.40) on the table d'hôte, with most à la carte meals going for £25 ($43.75) and up. It is open Tuesday to Saturday from 12:30 to 2 p.m. and 7 to 10:30 p.m., but closed for the first three weeks in September and again in February.

The **Barbican Wine Lodge,** The Quay Barbican (tel. 0752/660875), lies right on the quayside, across the water from the Customs House. Owned and run by Peter Stadnyk, the lodge is an old building with wooden floors softened by sawdust. Vintage wines are stacked in racks behind the bar under an oak-beamed ceiling. There is a good ambience, plus a set lunch menu, or you can order à la carte. The lodge specializes in fish bought locally each day, including brill, turbot, red mullet, John Dory, oysters, and mussels when in season. Live music is presented each evening and jazz on Sunday at lunchtime. The Wine Lodge is open from noon to 2:15 p.m. and 7 to 11 p.m. daily. Meals cost from £10 ($17.50). Parking is available on the quay.

For a change of pace, try **China Garden,** 17 Derry's Cross (tel. 0752/664472), which is the finest Chinese restaurant in the area, charging remarkably low prices, considering the quality of its cookery. The cooking is inspired by the cuisine of Peking (now Beijing), and you get the legendary Peking duck, along with tasty spareribs and other delicacies—even that which is not so delicate (beef and red-hot peppers). In addition to à la carte items, the menu is divided into a series of "feasts," beginning at £10.50 ($18.40) per head. Service is efficient and accurate, and lunch is from noon to 2:30 p.m., dinner 6 to 11:30 p.m. On Friday and Saturday, only dinner is served, 6 to midnight, and Sunday hours are only from 6 to 11 p.m. It's highly recommended, and located just outside the center of town.

NORTH DEVON

"Lorna, Lorna . . . Lorna Doone, my lifelong darling," is the wailing cry you'll think of as you lie abed in your North Devon farmhouse. A wildness seems to enter the air at night on the edge of the moody Doone Valley. Much of the district is already known to those who have read Victorian novelist R. D. Blackmore's romance of the West Country, *Lorna Doone.*

The bay-studded coastline is mysterious. Pirates and smugglers used to find havens in crooked creeks and rocky coves. The ocean crashes against the rocks, and the meadows approach so close to the cliff's edge that you wonder why they don't go spilling into the sea, sheep and all. The heather-clad uplands of Exmoor, with its red deer, extend into North Devon from Somerset, a perfect setting for an English mystery. Favorite bases are Clovelly and the twin resorts of Lynton and Lynmouth.

8. Milton Damerel

You may want to visit Cornwall before heading north along the Devonshire coastline. If you do, and if you're taking the A39 north from Cornwall, consider a stopover deep in the heart of North Devon in the hamlet of Milton Damerel. As you reach the junction with A3072, head eastward to Holsworthy. There you will connect with the A388 going north. The turnoff for Milton Damerel is signposted.

FOOD AND LODGING

A mile north on the A388, the **Woodford Bridge Hotel,** Milton Damerel, Holsworthy, Devon EX22 7LL (tel. 040926/481) is a pretty, 15th-century white-washed inn with thatch roof, lots of wood paneling, and comfortable chairs and bedrooms. The bar, where a good selection of snacks is offered, is popular with the locals. There is also an elegant dining room, where you can enjoy well-prepared dishes, including fresh local produce, game, sea bass, and other courses. A table d'hôte dinner with three choices for each course goes for £11.95 ($20.90), while a meal chosen à la carte can cost £12.50 ($21.90) to £25 ($43.75). The hotel's owner has decorated the accommodations (many of which have a modern bath) with chintz and dainty lamps. Rents are £28 ($49) to £40 ($70) daily in a single, depending on the plumbing. Doubles or twins on the same basis cost £55 ($96.25) to £64 ($112). Breakfast and VAT are included in the tariffs.

---

9. Clovelly

This is the most charming of all Devon villages and is one of the main attractions of the West Country. Starting at a great height, the village cascades down the mountainside, with its narrow, cobblestone High that makes travel by car impossible. (You park your car at the top and make the trip by foot.) Supplies are carried down by donkeys. Every yard of the way provides views of tiny cottages, with their terraces of flowers lining the main street. The village fleet is sheltered at the stone quay at the bottom.

To avoid the climb back up the slippery incline, go to the rear of the Red Lion Inn and "queue up" for a Land Rover. In summer, the line is often long, but considering the alternative, it's worth the wait. Two Land Rovers make continuous round trips, costing 40p (70¢) per person each way.

Tip: To avoid the flock of tourists, stay out of Clovelly from around 11 in the morning till teatime. After tea, settle in your room, and have dinner, perhaps spend the night in peace and contentment. The next morning after breakfast, you walk around the village or go for a swim in the harbor, then visit the nearby villages during the middle of the day when the congestion sets in. Bideford, incidentally, is 11 miles away.

WHERE TO STAY

A warning: It's hard to get a room in Clovelly. Advance reservations, with a deposit, are imperative during the peak summer months, although you can always telephone in advance and just possibly get a bed.

New Inn, Main Street, Clovelly, Devon EX39 5TQ (tel. 02373/303), about halfway down the High Street, is the village pub, a good meeting place at sundown. It offers the best lodgings in the village, in two buildings on opposite sides of the steep street (but only a 12-foot leap between their balconies). B&B ranges from £15 ($26.25) per person daily, inclusive. If you're only stopping over, then this little country inn is recommended for meals. A wide choice of moderately priced meals is offered in the oak-beamed dining room. The local fare, including Devonshire cream, is featured whenever possible. Locally caught lobsters are also prepared by the chef. Motorists can park in the car park. It is advisable to pack an overnight case, as the luggage has to be carried down (but is returned to the top by donkey).

Red Lion, The Quay, Clovelly, near Bideford EX39 5TF (tel. 02373/237), may well have the best location in the village—at the bottom of the steep cobbled street, right on the stone seawall of the little harbor. Rising three stories, it is an unspoiled country inn, the life centering on an antique pub where the villagers gather to satisfy their thirsts over pints of ale. Most of the bedrooms look directly onto the sea. All have hot and cold running water and adequate furnishings. The cost is £14.50 ($25.40) per person nightly, including breakfast. Other meals are available in the sea-view dining room, where lunch is served from noon to 2 p.m. and dinner from 7 to 8 p.m. The manager can arrange for boating in the bay, and suggests that the Red Lion is not suitable for children under 7 years of age.

---

10. Lynton-Lynmouth

The north coast of Devon is set off most dramatically in Lynton, a village some 500 feet high. It is a good center for exploring the Doone Valley and that part of Exmoor that spills into the shire from neighboring Somerset. The Valley of Rocks, west of Lynton, offers the most spectacular scenery.

The town is joined by a cliff railway to its sister, Lynmouth, about 500 feet lower. The rivers of East and West Lyn meet in Lynmouth, a resort popular with the English. For a panoramic view of the rugged coastline, you can walk on a path halfway between the two towns that runs along the cliff. From Lynton, or rather from Hollerday Hill, you can look out onto Lynmouth Bay, Countisbury Foreland, and Woody Bays in the west.

FOOD AND LODGING

Set high on a cliff, **Tors Hotel,** Lynmouth, Lynton EX35 6NA (tel. 0598/53236), opens onto a view of the coastline and the bay of Lynmouth. It was built in the fashion of a Swiss château, with more than 40 gables, Tyrolean balconies jutting out to capture the sun (or the moon), black-and-white timbered wings, and some 30 chimneys. Surrounding the hotel are a terrace and a heated swimming pool. The interior has been modernized, and much attention has been paid to the comfortable bedrooms. Singles rent for £28 ($49) daily, and doubles cost £65 ($113.75). All tariffs include VAT and a full English breakfast. A set lunch costs £7 ($12.25), a set dinner going for £14 ($24.50). The hotel is open from March to mid-November.

Hewitt's Hotel and Restaurant, North Walk, Lynton, Devon EX35 6HJ (tel. 0598/52293), is named for the gentleman, Sir Thomas Hewitt, who helped construct the funicular rail that links the twin resorts. In the latter 19th century, he also built a home for himself, and that place today is one of the most successful little inns in Lynton, operated by Susan and Robert Mahon. Lying in some two dozen acres of grounds, it opens onto beautiful vistas of Lynmouth Bay (best enjoyed while seated on a sunny terrace). The old house is filled with architectural character, as exemplified by its grand staircase, time-mellowed paneling, antiques, and stained-glass windows. The most desirable bedrooms have private balconies, although all of them are well furnished and comfortably appointed. Most of them also contain private baths. The hotel is "for all seasons," and the country house atmosphere can be enjoyed for £26 ($45.50) daily in a single, rising to £66 ($115.50) in the best doubles. Bar lunches are far above average, and dinner is among the best served at the resort. In fact, it is reason enough to stay here, and you won't be overcharged either, as meals cost from £15 ($26.25). A medley of British and continental dishes are served.

The **Rising Sun Hotel,** The Harbour, Lynmouth, Lynton, Devon EX35 6EQ (tel. 0598/53223) is perhaps one of the most colorful thatched inns in England, especially as it's right at the end of the quay at the mouth of the Lyn River. Not only is the harbor life spread before you, but you can bask in the wonder and warmth of an inn in business for more than 600 years. In bedroom after bedroom, with crazy levels and sloping ceilings, you'll have views of the water, the changing tides, and bobbing boats. It is a lovely old place, where the staircase is so narrow and twisting that it requires care to negotiate. Ceilings are low and floorboards creak. Behind the inn, halfway up the cliff, is a tiny garden bright with flowers in summer, where you can sit and gaze out over the thatch roofs to the sea. Hugo Jeune, the owner, has refurbished the place and added more rooms by joining two adjacent properties, and he has rooms available nearby in Shelley's Cottage, where the poet honeymooned with Harriet in 1812. R. D. Blackmore wrote part of *Lorna Doone* while staying at the hotel. Guests are charged from £25.59 ($44.65) to £28.50 ($51.65) per person daily for B&B, service, and VAT. Mr. Jeune has supplied 16 of the bedrooms with private baths or showers. Half board is available for £36 ($63) to £50 ($43.75) per person daily. It's a delight dining at the Rising Sun, as everything is 101% British in the dining room, with its deeply set window and fireplace. See the original 14th-century fireplace in the bar.

Bath Hotel, Lynmouth, Lynton, Devon EX35 6EL (tel. 0598/52238), is a solid building between the busy street and the towering cliffs. B&B begins at $17 ($29.75) per person daily in a bathless room and £25 ($43.75) per person in a room with bath. Many of the units have views over the river and out to the sea. A good set dinner is served in the restaurant for £10.25 ($17.95), with lobster and salmon specialties, plus a full à la carte menu. Sunday lunch, offers cuts from a roast, traditional vegetables, and an old-fashioned dessert.

---

11. The Taw Valley

The River Taw rises high on Dartmoor, as do many other West Country rivers, and makes its way northwest through beautiful moorland scenery and mid-Devon farmlands, finally emptying into the sea at Barnstaple. The river and area are the settings for Henry Williamson's world-renowned books, *Salar the Salmon* and *Tarka the Otter,* as well as being highly productive of sea trout, salmon, and brown trout. This is an unspoiled rural valley between Exmoor and Dartmoor. It retains a peaceful atmosphere away from the pressures of modern life, and it's populated with hospitable people.

Many visitors have never heard of such little towns as Crawleigh, Chulmleigh, Winkleigh, Crediton, and Eggesford, so I recommend a trip through the valley. Fishing opportunities abound.

FOOD AND LODGING

An old coaching inn built in the early 1800s is now the **Eggesford House Hotel** (Fox and Hounds), Eggesford, Chulmleigh, Devon EX18 7JZ (tel. 0769/80345). The coaching inn formed part of the large Eggesford Country Estate, home of the earls of Portsmouth. The Forestry Commission presently owns the majority of the estate's 7,000 acres, with beautiful walks and scenery provided. The hotel, set in its own grounds of some 30 acres, is approached by a sweeping drive through woodlands. Owned by David and Sheila Ingyon and their family, it has recently undergone considerable renovation but retains its attractive inherent characteristics. All 18 bedrooms are beautifully appointed and have baths. B&B costs from £20 ($35) per person daily, rising to £30 ($52.50) for half board. If your heart is set on experiencing the peace and tranquility of the mid-Devon countryside, sampling some of the best salmon and trout fishing in the whole area, and spending the autumn and winter evenings beside a crackling fire, eating and drinking with locals, or experiencing the pleasure of sleeping in a four-poster bed, this is the place for you. Fishermen and early risers can select their accommodations from a range of fully modernized country cottages adjacent to the main hotel buildings. The hotel is open all year.

CORNWALL

The ancient Duchy of Cornwall is the extreme southwestern part of England, often called "the toe." But Cornwall is one toe that's always wanted to dance away from the foot. Although a peninsula, it is a virtual island—if not geographically, then spiritually. Encircled by coastline, it abounds with rugged cliffs, hidden bays, fishing villages, sandy beaches, and sheltered coves where smuggling was once practiced with consummate skill. Many of the little seaports with their hillside-clinging cottages resemble towns along the Mediterranean, yet Cornwall retains its own distinctive flavor.

The true Cornish people are generally darker and shorter than the English. Their Celtic origin still lives on in superstition, folklore, and fairy tales. King Arthur, of course, is the most vital legend of all. When Cornish people speak of King Arthur and his Knights of the Round Table, they're not just handing out a line to tourists. To them, Arthur and his knights really existed, romping around Tintagel Castle, now in ruins—Norman ruins, that is—lying 300 feet above the sea, 19 miles from Bude.

The ancient land had its own language up until about 250 years ago, and some of the old words ("pol" for pool, "tre" for house) still survive. The Cornish dialect is more easily understood by the Welsh than by those who speak the Queen's English.

The Cornish, like the Welsh, are great miners (tin and copper), and they're fond of the tall tale. Sometimes it's difficult to tell when they're serious. One resident, for example, told me that he and his wife had been walking in the woods at twilight, but had lost their way. He claimed that the former owner of the estate (in Victoria's day) appeared suddenly in a dog-carriage and guided them back to where they'd taken the wrong turn. If this really had happened, I wouldn't be surprised—at least not in Cornwall.

I suggest berthing at one of the smaller fishing villages, such as East and West Looe, Polperro, Mousehole, or Portloe—where you'll experience the true charm of the duchy. Many of the villages, such as St. Ives, are artists' colonies. Except for St. Ives and Port Isaac, most of my recommendations lie on the southern coast, often called the Cornish Riviera, which strikes many foreign visitors as being the most intriguing. However, the north coast has its own peculiar charm.

---

1. Looe

After your visit to Plymouth, about 15 miles away in Devon, you can either take the Tamar Suspension Bridge to Cornwall, or else cross by ferry from Plymouth. You'll soon arrive in the ancient twin towns of East and West Looe, connected by a seven-arched stone bridge that spans the river. In the jaws of shrub-dotted cliffs, the fishing villages present a stark contrast to Plymouth. Houses scale the hills, stacked one on top of the other in terrace fashion.

In both fishing villages you can find good accommodations. Fishing and sailing are two of the major sports, and the sandy coves, as well as East Looe Beach, are spots for seabathing. Beyond the towns are cliff paths and downs worth a ramble.

Looe is noted for its shark-angling, but you may prefer simply walking the narrow, crooked medieval streets of East Looe, with its old harbor and 17th-century guildhall.

If you wish, you can strike out from Looe on the cliff walk, a distance of 4½ miles, to Polperro. The less adventurous will drive.

WHERE TO STAY

Space and prices are at a premium in July and August. Some hotels are so heavily booked that they can demand Saturday-to-Saturday clients only.

Hannafore Point Hotel, Marine Drive, Hannafore, West Looe, Cornwall PL13 2DG (tel. 05036/3273), is a rambling, many-gabled structure commanding an advantageous view of the harbor, overlooking miles of Cornish coastline and one of the most beautiful bays in England. In addition to the older bay-windowed chambers, newer sections have walls of glass for viewing the harbor and St. George's Island. The entrance opens onto several levels of comfortable lounges and bars, with cantilevered stairs and balconies. The modern bedrooms all include either private bath or shower, and most of the front rooms have their own balcony. B&B rates vary depending on the view, location of the room, and the time of year. From May to the end of October, a single costs from £36 ($63) daily, and a double or twin go for £60 ($105) to £80 ($140). That panoramic view adds to the pleasure of dining in the St. George's Restaurant, where fresh ingredients are used in the fine Cornish and French cuisine. The hotel has an elevator, and there is a comprehensive leisure center with an indoor pool on the premises. Hannafore Point is in the main center for shark and deep-sea fishing, and is ideal for exploring either Cornwall or parts of Devon.

Fieldhead Hotel, Hannafore, West Looe, Cornwall PL13 2DR (tel. 05036/2689), was originally built in 1896 as a private home. Now operated as a hotel, one of the most recommendable in the area, it sits in two acres of gardens opening onto a view of the sea. Closed in January, it otherwise receives guests in its 14 well-furnished bedrooms. Nine of these accommodations offer private baths. Depending on the season, B&B overnight rates range from £18 ($31.50) to £25 ($44.75) per person for occupancy of a double or twin room. Single residents pay a daily supplement of £5 ($8.75).

Talland Bay Hotel, Talland-by-Looe, Cornwall PL13 2JB (tel. 0503/72667), lies four miles southwest of Looe by the A387. A country house dating from the 16th century, set on 2½ acres, it is under the domain of Polly and Ian Mayman, who will indicate local beaches and the croquet lawn. Its thick, white walls shelter two sides of a rectangular swimming pool whose borders are ringed with flagstones and a semitropical garden. Views from the 23 tastefully furnished bedrooms include the sea and rocky coastline. Most units contain a private bath, color TV, radio, and phone. Some of the bedrooms are in an annex. The charge for half board is from £33 ($57.75) to £57.50 ($100.65) per person daily. The food is the best in the area, featuring excellently prepared seafood, and even if you aren't staying here, you may want to reserve a table. À la carte meals cost around £20 ($35) per person. A much frequented buffet lunch is served by the pool in summer. The restaurant is open from 12:30 to 2 p.m. Monday to Saturday, from 12:45 to 1:30 p.m. Sunday, and from 7:15 to 9 p.m. seven days a week. The hotel is closed from January to mid-February.

Commonwealth Manor Hotel, St. Martins Road, East Looe, Cornwall, PL13 1LP (tel. 05036/2929), is a family-operated country house hotel, about a 12-minute walk from the harbor and the center of the resort. Well maintained, it operates like a little inn, containing 11 bedrooms with private baths. From March to October, guests receive a warm welcome here and are shown to one of the well-furnished and comfortably appointed bedrooms. With a full English breakfast included, charges are from £27 ($47.25) to £32 ($56) daily in a single, going up to £44 ($77) to £52 ($91) in a double. Opening onto the Looe River Valley, Commonwealth Manor stands on a wooded hillside in some three acres of private grounds, with a heated swimming pool. Meals are good, using fresh ingredients, with dinners going for about £8 ($14) to £12 ($21).

WHERE TO STAY AND DINE OUTSIDE LOOE

Peacefully secluded five miles from Looe, the **Old Rectory Country House Hotel,** St. Keyne, near Liskeard, Cornwall PL14 4RL (tel. 0579/42617), is in the countryside of southeast Cornwall, which is known for its natural beauty. The owners have brought the hotel to a high standard to complement the original architecture, with use of paneled doors, marble fireplaces, Persian rugs, velvet sofas, and crystal. Meals are served on Wedgwood china in the elegant dining room. All the bedrooms have baths or showers, color TVs, electric blankets, and hot beverage facilities. The charge for B&B is £28 ($49) daily in a single, £45 ($78.75) in a double. A five-course dinner costs £10.50 ($18.40). The approach to the hotel is by a winding drive off the little-used B3254 to the rear of the house. The hotel overlooks three acres of gardens with views across the valley.

Well House, St. Keyne, Liskeard, Cornwall PL14 4RN (tel. 0579/42001), is another one of those *restaurant avec chambres* found occasionally in the West Country. This one, in fact, surfaces near the top. Lying about three miles from Liskeard, Well House stands in five acres of gardens opening onto vistas of St. Keyne Valley. It offers an all-weather tennis court and a swimming pool, as well as seven beautifully furnished bedrooms, each with private bath or shower. Overnight B&B charges are from £45 ($78.75) daily in a single, rising to £82 ($143.50) in a double. Nicholas Wainford, the owner, provides many thoughtful extras, such as fresh flowers in the bedrooms. But it is mainly for the cuisine that guests flock to the place, which they can do any day of the week except Monday from 12:30 to 2 p.m. and 7 to 9 p.m. A set luncheon goes for £14.50 ($25.40), with a table d'hôte dinner offered for £20 ($35). You're ushered into a grand contemporary dining room, with an almost formal staff where you can peruse the brief but delectable menu, which changes every 30 days or so. Carefully prepared and elegantly presented, tip-top ingredients are used in the food that combines the best of both British and continental dishes. The menu is imaginative but not dangerously so. You feel that each dish was carefully thought out and perfected before appearing on the menu.

---

2. Polperro

This ancient fishing village is reached by a steep descent from the top of a hill. Motorists in summer are forbidden to take their cars down unless they are booked in a hotel. Why? Because otherwise they'd create too much of a traffic bottleneck in July and August. At one time it was estimated that nearly every man, woman, and child in the village spent time salting down pilchards for the winter or smuggling. Today, tourists have replaced the contraband.

You'd have to search every cove and bay in Cornwall to turn up a village as handsome as Polperro, which looks almost as if it had been removed intact from the 17th century. The village is tucked in between some cliffs. Its houses—really no more than fishermen's cottages—are bathed in pastel-wash. A small river, actually a stream called the Pol, cuts its way through Polperro. The heart of the village is its much photographed, much painted fishing harbor, where the pilchard boats, loaded to the gunnels, used to dock.

There's a large car park, the price based according to the length of your stay. For those unable to walk, a horse-drawn bus carries visitors to the town center.

WHERE TO STAY

Receiving guests from March to October, **Lanhael House,** Langreek Road, Polperro, Cornwall PL13 2PW (tel. 0503/72428), is one of the best of the moderately priced accommodations at the resort. Roy and Sandra Pauls's modernized house dates from the 17th century, but today it has many amenities, including a swimming pool and a terrace to capture the sun of the Cornish coast. The six bedrooms are comfortable and attractively furnished, and two contain private bath. The charge, depending on the plumbing, ranges from £18 ($31.50) daily in a single and from £30 ($52.50) in a double. There is limited car parking as well.

Claremont, Fore Street, Polperro, Cornwall PL13 2RG (tel. 0503/72241), is a 17th-century cottage with postwar additions. It lies behind a white façade on the main street leading to the center of the village. Service and access to the owners of this pleasant hotel are probably the most compelling reasons to check in. It sits above the village, offering a view over its rooftops for guests to enjoy between Easter and October. The ten bedrooms are all comfortably furnished and have private baths, costing £34 ($59.50) daily for doubles, £15 ($26.25) for singles. The French owners, Nellie Peyrin and Gilles Couturier, serve genuine French cooking from 7:30 to 9 p.m., a dinner costing from £8.50 ($14.90).

WHERE TO EAT

Good English cookery is offered at **The Kitchen,** Fish na Bridge (tel. 0503/72780), a pink cottage about half way down to the harbor from the car park. Once a wagon builder's shop, it is now a restaurant, run by Vanessa and Ian Bateson. Ian is the chef, except Vanessa makes all the homemade desserts, as well as bakes the bread. Reservations are essential. Everything is homemade from the best fresh ingredients available. The menu changes seasonally and is biased toward local fresh fish. Typical dishes include crab in filo pastry, seafood provençale, and roasted garlic monkfish. Lunch is from 12:30 to 2:30 p.m. daily, two courses costing from £6 ($10.50). Dinner, nightly in summer from 7 to 9:30, costs from £9.50 ($16.35), although you can order a house menu at £12 ($21) and a vegetarian menu at £8 ($14). In winter, service is offered only on Friday and Saturday.

The **Captain's Cabin,** Lansallos Street (tel. 0503/72292), in one of the mellow old structures of town, a 16th-century fisherman's cottage, invites you to dine among antiques and brass in the beamed low-ceilinged dining room. The owner, Lesley Jacobs, and her staff offer a comprehensive cuisine. The chef has a fine reputation for his local fish dishes, from among which you might choose crab mornay, lobster thermidor, or grilled lemon sole. The wide variety of fresh local fish is brought in daily by the fishermen of Polperro. At lunchtime, 11:30 a.m. to 2:30 p.m., you can order à la carte meals for around £6 ($10.50), or special snacks and sandwiches such as fresh crab and salad. At dinner there are à la carte listings and chef's specials, as well as two set meals: three courses for £7.95 ($13.90), and four courses for £10.95 ($19.15) and £12.95 ($22.65). Dinner is served from 7 to 11 p.m. The Cabin is open daily all year, including holidays.

WHERE TO STAY AND EAT ON THE OUTSKIRTS

If you find the busy activity of the two little harbors of Looe and Polperro too much for you, then you can live in far greater style at two of England's outstanding inns, just outside. **Pelynt,** about three miles north of Polperro, is a small, sleepy village; and **Lanreath,** lying off the road to West Looe, is another peaceful, pleasant community.

Jubilee Inn, Jubilee Hill, Pelynt, Cornwall PL13 2JZ (tel. 0503/20312), was built in the 16th century, but it took its name from the time it was restored in connection with the tribute paid to Queen Victoria's Jubilee celebration. Only the best handmade Victorian furnishings were used in the restoration, even in the bedrooms. Ten well-furnished rooms are rented, costing £21.40 ($37.45) per person nightly for B&B or £30.90 ($54.10) for half board. Single occupancy is another £4.50 ($7.90) per person daily. The food is good, and the vegetables come fresh from the inn's own garden. Sunday lunch is served for £8.50 ($14.90). Otherwise, you have lunch in the bar, where hot and cold dishes are offered. Dinner is à la carte and will cost £15 ($26.25) to £20 ($35), depending on what you choose and how much. The inn is a comment on, rather than a monument to, the past. The lounge has a hooded fireplace, with a raised hearth, Windsor armchairs, antique porcelain, and copper bowls filled with flowers cut from the garden behind the building. The dining room is elegantly Victorian, with mahogany chairs and tables. A circular, glass-enclosed staircase takes you to the bedrooms. Fitting onto the outside, the winding stairway has been built to serve as a combined tower and hothouse.

Punch Bowl Inn, Lanreath, near Looe, Cornwall PL13 2NX (tel. 0503/20218), has had a checkered career since 1920, serving in turn as a courthouse, coaching inn, and rendezvous for smugglers. Today, its old fireplaces and high-backed settles, as well as its bedrooms (some with four-posters), provide hospitality to travelers from abroad and to the English. The B&B rate is from £16.50 ($28.90) to £21.50 ($37.65) per person daily with bath, from £12 ($21) to £17.50 ($30.65) per person without bath. There is a modern lounge, TV room, air-conditioned cocktail bar, and an additional bedroom wing. Even if you're not stopping over, owners Harvey and Sylvia Frith invite you to sample the fare or drinks in one of the kitchens (really bars, among the few "kitchens" licensed in Britain as "bars"). In the Stable Restaurant, with its Tudor beams and fireplace, you eat à la carte, choosing to have just a bowl of soup, or perhaps you'd like a steak. Meals cost £6 ($10.50) to £15 ($26.25). Food is served from noon to 2 p.m. and 7 to 9:30 p.m. daily.

3. Fowey

Called the Dartmouth of Cornwall, Fowey is a town of historical interest (one of the most ancient seaports in the West Country). Once the Fowey Gallants sailed the seas and were considered invincible when raiding French coastal towns. However, occasional retaliation was inevitable. At the time of the Armada, Fowey sent more ships than London. With its narrow streets and white-washed houses, it has remained unspoiled over the years, enjoying a sheltered position on a deep-water channel. Its creeks and estuary attract sailors and fishermen. If you climb to St. Catherine's Point, you'll be rewarded with a view of the harbor. Sandy beaches and coves are there to explore as well (there's also an 18-hole golf course within easy reach of Carlyon Bay).

FOOD AND LODGING

A Georgian house, **Marina Hotel,** The Esplanade, Fowey, Cornwall PL23 1HY (tel. 072683/3315), has shutters and sweeping verandas stretching across its symmetrical façade. It is under the direction of David and Sheila Johns. Originally built for a bishop of Truro, the house sits on top of a well-constructed retaining wall that rises steeply above the boats moored in the estuary of the Fowey (pronounced "Foy") River. The modernized interior still retains some of the best of the original architectural features, as well as a walled garden running to the water's edge. A well-managed restaurant is on the premises, and if by chance you arrive by boat, the hotel will provide you with a mooring. Some of the comfortable and big-windowed bedrooms have a private balcony. Half-board rates range from £32 ($56) to £41 ($71.75) per person daily, but for stays of two days or longer, prices are reduced by around 12%.

Food for Thought, Town Quay (tel. 072683/2221). The sprawling stone walls that contain this establishment were originally built as the village Customs house. Since its renovation by Martin Billingsley, this warmly decorated restaurant has been known for some of the best seafood in town. Directly on the water, the snug-ceilinged dining room serves succulent lobster and Scottish crayfish. The dishes are usually inspired by recipes prepared in neighboring France and include crab-stuffed chicken breast served with a saffron sauce, a mixed fish tart, and grilled fresh Fowey sea bass. Full à la carte meals cost from £25 ($43.75), and a three-course fixed-price dinner, with service, drinks, and VAT included, comes to £15 ($26.25). Meals are served only from 7 to 9:30 p.m. daily except Sunday. Reservations are necessary. The restaurant is closed from Christmas until early March.

4. Truro

This ancient town on the Truro River is the only cathedral city in Cornwall, the ecclesiastical center of Cornwall. The cathedral church of St. Mary was begun in 1880 in the Early English style (the spires are in the Norman Gothic design). The town is within 8 to 20 miles of the Cornish beaches. It can be used as a base to explore the countryside, which ranges from bleak Bodmin Moor to fertile farmland and the Winter Roseland of the Falmouth Estuary.

Trelissick Garden (tel. 0872/862090) lies on both sides of the B3289 south of Truro, overlooking King Harry Passage. The entrance is just off the King Harry Ferry up the hill and beyond the circular tower. In this beautiful wooded park with peaceful walks through the well-tended trees and shrubs, the rhododendrons are a splash of color in early summer. Upon arrival, you pick up a map and set out on a woodland walk that will take you through the plantations to the banks of Lamouth Creek and all along the edge of the River Fal and Channals Creek before you return to the center of the garden, about a one-hour stroll. Then you can visit the gardens where the vegetation is more controlled and see the special plant section where experiments on acclimatization are made.

The restaurant here (tel. 0872/863486) is open daily at 11 a.m. for coffee and from 12:15 to 2:15 p.m. for lunch, with afternoon teas served until 6 p.m. The emphasis is on wholesome, fresh food, such as homemade soup and Cornish ice creams and clotted cream. A lunch costs £6 ($10.50) Monday to Saturday, £8.25 ($14.45) for a three-course meal on Sunday, which includes a roast and coffee. You can also have sherry Cornish cider or one of the various lagers.

The garden is open April to October from 11 a.m. to 6 p.m. Monday to Saturday, 1 to 6 p.m. (or to sunset if earlier) on Sunday. Entry to the park and woodland walk is free. To visit the gardens costs adults £1.90 ($3.35), and children pay half price.

FOOD AND LODGING

A very special and charming place is **Alverton Manor,** Tregolls Road, Truro, Cornwall TR1 1XQ (tel. 0872/76633), which was originally built around 1820 and later became an Anglican convent. Built of honey-colored stone and capped with a slate roof, it was in derelict condition until its restoration began in 1987. After its transformation, it has been turned into the finest hotel and restaurant in Cornwall. The manor sits on sloping land in a garden of six acres, less than a mile north of the center of Truro. Open all year, it contains 25 carefully decorated bedrooms, most with high ceilings and either arched or rectangular mullioned leaded windows. All accommodations have private bath and come with a continental breakfast included. Singles range from £63 ($110.25) to £85 ($148.75) daily, with doubles costing from £85 ($148.75) to £100 ($175). Meals are a delight, a sophisticated continental cuisine using top quality ingredients deftly handled by an accomplished chef. A full à la carte lunch costs from £12 ($21), with dinners going from £15 ($26.25). A five-course surprise menu showcases the chef's considerable talents at a cost of £22 ($38.50). The dining room is pastel colored and often sunny, and filled with French-inspired furniture in cherrywood. Reservations are needed.

A gracefully detailed late Victorian house, the **Carlton Hotel,** 49 Falmouth Rd., Truro, Cornwall TR1 2HL (tel. 0872/72450), has twin gables overlooking a pleasant garden and a spacious modern bedroom wing. Most of the establishment's 31 rooms contain private baths and color TVs. Conveniently close to the center of town, the hotel charges £25 ($43.75) daily in a single, £39 ($68.25) in a double, with breakfast included. Snacks as well as more formal lunches and dinners are available.

---

5. Portloe

If you really want to get away from it all and go to that hidden-away Cornish fishing village, then Portloe is for you. It lies 15 miles from Truro. On the slope of a hill, opening onto Veryan Bay, it is reached by a road suitable for cars—but chances are you may get sidetracked and spend the rest of the afternoon on byways, opening and closing gates to keep the cattle from straying.

Portloe is an ideal stopover on the south Cornish coast if you're traveling in July and August, when the popular tourist centers, such as Looe and St. Ives, are overrun.

WHERE TO STAY

A prestigious inn, the **Lugger Hotel,** Portloe, Cornwall TR2 5RD (tel. 0872/501322), is a 17th-century establishment at the top of the harbor slip, with a bay and boats as part of the scene. It is believed to have been a smugglers' hideaway in its early days, but today, the Powell family runs it as a modernized, sparkling clean hotel on the water's edge. The 20 bedrooms all have private baths or showers and toilets, color TV, radios, central heating, tea/coffee-makers, and direct-dial phones. The charges are from £39.50 ($69.15) to £44 ($77) per person daily for a bed, an English breakfast, dinner, and VAT. Accommodations in the main building and the 19th-century bedroom wing are traditionally furnished in Tudor or Victorian style. The restaurant, which is open to nonresidents for dinner, has a panoramic view of the cove. A cocktail bar occupies the original inn parlor, and the hotel also has lounges, a sauna, and a solarium. Guests are allowed reduced greens fees at nearby Truro Golf Club. The hotel is open from mid-March to early November, with room rates reduced for stays of more than two days.

6. St. Mawes

Overlooking the mouth of the Fal River, St. Mawes is often compared to a port on the French Riviera. Because it's sheltered from northern winds, subtropical plants grow here. From the town quay, you can take a boat to Frenchman's Creek, Helford River, and other places. St. Mawes is noted for its sailing, boating, fishing, and yachting. Half a dozen sandy coves lie within 15 minutes by car from the port. The town, built on the Roseland Peninsula, makes for interesting walks, with its color-washed cottages and sheltered harbor. On Castle Point, Henry VIII ordered the construction of St. Mawes Castle. Falmouth, across the water, is only two miles away.

FOOD AND LODGING

The highest-rated hotel is the **Tresanton,** 27 Lower Castle Rd., St. Mawes, Cornwall TR2 5DR (tel. 0326/270544). It is really three buildings, the oldest one dating from the 18th century. One is on the roadside, another halfway up, and the third—the main part of the hotel—on top of the hill and away from the traffic noise. The upper level has spacious veranda terraces—so there are a lot of places to sit outside among the flowers, looking across the bay. To quote a reader, it's "quite simply the most charming and delightful hotel I have ever stayed in." The owners are Graham and Maureen Brockton. The bedrooms are fresh and bright, furnished for the most part in the French country-house manner. All have private baths and are stocked with sewing kits, tissues, books to read, whatever. All accommodations face the sea. A single with dinner and B&B rents from £55 ($96.25) daily, while a similar double goes for £125 ($218.75). The lounge has an open fireplace and comfortable chairs. The dining room, also overlooking the sea, has attractive murals and a decor designed to carry the eye from the house to the sun terraces, the subtropical gardens, and the sea beyond. The menu wisely emphasizes fish dishes.

The **Idle Rocks,** Tredenham Road, St. Mawes, Cornwall TR2 5AN (tel. 0326/270771), is a solid old building right on the sea wall, with gaily colored umbrellas and tables lining the terrace. Water laps at the wall, and the site opens onto views over the river and the constant traffic of sailing boats and dinghies. The bar serves tasty lunchtime snacks, including fresh seafood caught locally. The bedrooms mostly have sea or river views, and they're equipped with central heating, tea- or coffee-making facilities, color TV, radio, and intercom. The main hotel building contains 15 of the rooms, with nine more being in an annex. All of them contain private baths or showers. Singles rent for £38 ($66.50) to £40 ($70) daily, depending on the location of the room. Doubles cost from £76 ($133) to £80 ($140). The higher priced units are in the main building. Tariffs include a full English breakfast and VAT. Half board is offered for £43 ($75.25) to £45 ($78.75) per person. The hotel is open from mid-March to the first of January. Golf is available at Truro Golf Club at reduced greens fees.

A colorful inn on the seafront, **The Rising Sun,** The Square, St. Mawes, Cornwall TR2 5DJ (tel. 0326/170233), is made of a row of fishermen's cottages with a flagstone terrace out front. It oozes with tasteful charm. Known as one of Cornwall's best inns, it was recently redecorated. B&B charges in a single are £30 ($52.50) per day, rising to £35 ($61.25) per person in a double, the latter with private bath or shower. The inn also has a reputation for good food, and you may want to patronize its facilities even if you don't spend the night. The dining room is tastefully decorated, and a table d'hôte dinner costs from £14 ($24.50). During the day you can enjoy tasty bar meals, and, on Sunday, of course, a traditional roast. There are both a sophisticated cocktail bar and a public bar, the latter enjoyed by the locals.

7. Falmouth

A lot of cutthroat ship wreckers used to live in the area. In fact, when John Killigrew, a leading citizen, started to build a lighthouse on Lizard Head, they protested that the beacon in the night would deprive them of their livelihood and "take away God's Grace from us." Falmouth, 26 miles from Penzance, is today a favorite base for the yachting set, who consider it one of the most beautiful harbors in Europe. On a small peninsula, Falmouth's old section overlooks the land-locked inner harbor. The newer part, center for most of the hotels, faces the bay and commands a panorama from St. Anthony's Lighthouse to Pendennis Castle. Warmed in winter by the Gulf Stream, Falmouth has become a year-round resort. Built on a promontory overlooking the estuary of the Fal, it was once occupied in part by the captains of old mail-carrying packet ships. Many find it a good center for touring the rugged Cornish coastline. It's possible, for example, to take a ferry from Falmouth to St. Mawes, a 20-minute ride.

Pendennis Castle, once part of Henry VIII's coastal defense system, dates from 1544, when the central circular keep was completed on the site of a prehistoric fortress. Since Tudor days it has protected the entrance to Falmouth Harbour. Youth Hostels Association runs a hostel in the old barrack block, but the castle can be visited daily from Good Friday to the end of September from 10 a.m. to 6 p.m., from 10 a.m. to 4 p.m. the remainder of the year. Admission is £1.30 ($2.30) for adults, 65p ($1.15) for children. For information, phone 0326/316594.

During most of the year, sightseeing craft ply up and down the River Fal from the Prince of Wales Pier in Falmouth to the Town Quay in Truro.

WHERE TO STAY

From its five acres of gardens, the **Falmouth Hotel,** Castle Beach, Seafront, Falmouth, Cornwall TR11 4NZ (tel. 0326/312671), rises in an impressively eclectic mélange of 19th-century styles. Considered the biggest and most important hotel in town, it contains 80 comfortably modernized rooms, each with its own bath, phone, radio, and color TV. Singles or doubles rent for £28 ($49) per person daily, with breakfast included. There's a choice of bars and restaurants, plus a heated swimming pool and a desirable position bordering the water. The hotel often hosts business conferences for local companies.

Greenbank Hotel, Harbourside, Falmouth, Cornwall TR11 2SR (tel. 0326/312440), hangs tenaciously to the old days of the Post Office Packet Services (1688–1850). Beside the shore road, this hotel overlooks the water with its own landing pier. Over the years it has been expanded, but it remains traditional, having attracted many famous guests, including Florence Nightingale. The spacious lounges have views of the harbor, and the rooms are comfortably furnished. In a single, the rate ranges from £45 ($78.75) daily, increasing to £92 ($161) in a double or twin. The hotel has a hairdressing and beauty salon, as well as a water-view dining room favored by local yachting people and serving old-fashioned English food. Lunches cost from £8 ($14); dinners, from £12 ($21).

Penmere Manor Hotel, Mongleath Road, Falmouth, Cornwall TR11 4PN (tel. 0326/211411), is an 18th-century Georgian mansion one mile from the center of Falmouth. After David and Rachel Pope acquired the property, they embarked on an enthusiastic campaign to upgrade it, and today they work hard to make their guests happy, serving flavorful meals in the dining room and arranging a variety of outside activities for their guests. There are 42 rooms in the main building and extensions. Each accommodation has a private bath, radio, phone, and color TV. Singles cost £35 ($61.25) daily, and doubles go for £56 ($98), with a full breakfast included. The Fountain Leisure Club provides guests with indoor and outdoor heated swimming pools, spa bath, sauna, mini-gym, croquet lawn, and even giant chess. The view from the trio of lounges includes five acres of woodland and of Falmouth Bay.

On the Outskirts

Budock Vean Hotel, Golf and Country Club, Mawnan Smith, Falmouth, Cornwall TR11 5LG (tel. 0326/250288), five miles southwest by Trescobeas Road (off the B3291), stands among the pines and subtropical vegetation sloping sharply to the Helford River. You come to an old stone house with a stout front door and bright welcoming hall. Some bedrooms are in the old house, others in the new wing, and all have bath and toilet. A few units have views over the gardens and down to the distant river, and others overlook the private golf course. B&B costs £38 ($66.50) daily in a single, £105 ($183.75) in a double. VAT is included in the tariffs. Meals are a selection of international and English dishes. The hotel has an indoor, heated swimming pool. In winter, a log fire burns on the open grate. The main attraction for many guests is the 18-hole golf course free to residents. Closed in January and February.

Riverside, Helford, near Helston, Cornwall, TR12 6JU (tel. 032623/443), owned by Susan Darrell, is a small, French provincial-style restaurant in two 18th-century cottages beside the Helford River. There are 12 tables with a capacity of 36 diners. Furnishings are in keeping with the cottage style of the house. Try the bourride, a Provençal fish stew with aïoli and rouille. Main courses include chicken Georgian style, with grapes and oranges, or guinea fowl with rosemary. Desserts offers such fare as a toothsome walnut treacle tart and iced lemon soufflé. The set price of £25 ($43.75) includes VAT and service. A table is yours for the evening, so there's no rushing to clear up for the next serving. Reservations are essential. Meals are served daily from 7:30 to 9:30 p.m. Closed from November to early March. Riverside also has overnight accommodations. The seven double rooms have private baths, and there are some with TV and some with fine views. The charge is £75 ($131.25) to £90 ($157.50) per night for two persons, with a continental breakfast, VAT, and service all included.

POLDARK MINE

Three miles north of Helston on the B3297 is the **Poldark Mine and Heritage Complex,** Wendron 0326/573173). As you have driven around Cornwall, the old workings of the tin mines will have been evident everywhere. Here you have the chance of visiting a mine and walking through the old workings, which extend for several miles beneath the surface. Recent extension of the area open to the public into newly discovered caverns has made the tour of the mine last well over an hour. There are extensive Heritage Museums depicting the living conditions of the 18th-century mining community, the history of tin, and the famous Holman collection. One museum houses the largest collection of flatirons in Europe and perhaps the world. Amid prize-winning gardens are restaurants, Cornish craft shops, picnic areas, and children's play areas. The mine and heritage complex is open from 10 a.m. to 6 p.m. daily April to October (to 8 p.m. in August). The last mine tour is one hour before closing. Admission to the mine is £3.30 ($5.80) for adults, £2 ($3.50) for children.

The mine and surrounding area are of particular interest to readers and television viewers of the "Poldark" series, filmed from novels by Winston Graham.

8. Penzance

This little Gilbert and Sullivan harbor town is the end of the line for the Cornish Riviera Express. A full 280 miles southwest from London, it is noted for its equable climate (it's one of the first towns in England to blossom with spring flowers), and summer throngs descend for fishing, sailing, and swimming. Overlooking Mount's Bay, Penzance is graced in places with subtropical plants, as well as palm trees.

The harbor is used to activity of one sort or another. Those pirates in *The Pirates of Penzance* were not entirely fictional. The town was raided by Barbary pirates, destroyed in part by Cromwell's troops, sacked and burnt by the Spaniards, and bombed by the Germans. In spite of its turbulent past, it offers tranquil resort living today.

The most westerly town in England, Penzance makes a good base for exploring Land's End, The Lizard peninsula, St. Michael's Mount, the old fishing ports and artists' colonies of St. Ives, Newlyn, and Mousehole—even the Isles of Scilly.

THE SIGHTS

Three miles east of Penzance, **St. Michael's Mount** is reached at low tide by a causeway. Rising about 250 feet from the sea, St. Michael's Mount is topped by a partially medieval, partially 17th-century castle. At high tide the mount becomes an island, reached only by motor launch from Marazion. A Benedictine monastery, the gift of Edward the Confessor, stood on this spot in the 11th century. The castle, with its collections of armor and antique furniture, is open, weather and tide permitting, from 10:30 a.m. to 5:45 p.m. Monday to Friday from the end of March to the end of October. It charges £2.50 ($4.40) for adults and £1.25 ($2.20) for children. In winter, you can only go over when the causeway is dry. There is a tea garden on the island, as well as a National Trust restaurant, both of which are open in summer. *Warning:* The steps up to the castle are steep and rough, so wear stout shoes.

From Penzance, take bus 20, 21, or 22, then get off at Marazion, the town opposite St. Michael's Mount. To avoid disappointment, it is a good idea to telephone the office of St. Michael's Mount (tel. 0736/710507) to learn the state of the tides, especially during the winter months when a regular ferry service does not operate.

The **Minack Theatre** in Porthcurno, nine miles from Penzance, is unique. It's carved out of the Cornish cliff-face with the Atlantic as its impressive backdrop. In tiered seating, similar to that of the theaters of ancient Greece, 550 people can watch the show and the rocky coast beyond the stage. The theater's season of plays and musical shows begins at the end of May and continues until mid-September. There is an exhibition hall that houses a permanent record of the life and work of Rowena Cade. This exhibition center is open from Easter to October 31 and includes a chance to visit the theater outside of performance times. Seats cost around £3 ($5.25) purchased at the box office. The price includes a free visit to the exhibition center. When no performance is on, admission to the center and to see the theater is £1 ($1.75). For details, phone 0736/810471 during the season. To reach Minack, leave Penzance on the A30 heading toward Land's End. After three miles, bear left onto the B3283 and follow signposts to Porthcurno.

WHERE TO STAY

Back in Penzance, it is time to find a room.

The Queen's Hotel, The Promenade, Penzance, Cornwall TR18 4HG (tel. 0736/62371), opens onto good views across Mounts Bay. Lying on the only promenade in Cornwall, this Victorian hotel is decorated and furnished with many antiques. Paintings from Newlyn Art School adorn many of the walls. The hotel offers

71 comfortably furnished bedrooms with private baths and such amenities as color TV, free in-house video system, direct-dial phone, and beverage-making equipment. A single begins at £32 ($56) nightly, with doubles going for £58 ($101.50). Fresh local seafood is a specialty of the Promenade Restaurant where dinners cost from £14 ($24.50). A bar buffet is offered daily except Sunday for £3.25 ($5.70). Or else you can dine in the hotel's bar, brasserie, and restaurant, the Strollers. The hotel also has such health facilities as a gymnasium, sauna, and Jacuzzi, as well as a hairdressing salon.

Built in 1660, the **Abbey Hotel,** Abbey Street, Penzance, Cornwall TR18 4AR (tel. 0736/66906), is a well-preserved place that is frequented by discerning guests. The bonus is its situation—on a narrow side street on several terraces directly over-looking Penzance Harbour. Bedrooms and baths are stylishly furnished. You can take only your room and breakfast at the Abbey, or have dinner in the restaurant downstairs. Singles cost from £40 ($70) to £45 ($78.75) daily per day, a double or twin going from £55 ($96.25) to £75 ($131.25), including a full English breakfast and VAT. Behind the hotel, which is built close to the street, is a tiny formal garden on two tiers, each with a view of the water. Here the herbs are grown that are used to spice the delicately flavored meats in the restaurant downstairs. The owners, Michael and Jean Cox, have brought their vitality, style, and charm into the hotel business. Mrs. Cox is the former international model, Jean Shrimpton. Sample dishes from their dinner menu include homemade soups, mackerel paté, fresh local fish dishes, and generally a roast joint. Everything is fresh and delicately cooked, a dinner costing from £13.50 ($23.65).

The **Georgian House,** Chapel Street, Penzance, Cornwall TR18 4AE (tel. 0736/65664), once the home of the mayors of Penzance, and reputedly haunted by the ghost of Mrs. Baines, who owned it hundreds of years ago, has been completely renovated into a cozy, intimate hotel. Denise and Michael Hardman welcome guests to their bright, clean bedrooms, all with hot and cold water basins, color TV, and tea/coffee-makers. Most of the rooms contain private baths or showers and toilets. Rates are £11.50 ($20.15) per person daily for B&B in a bathless room, rising to £14.95 ($43.65) with private bath. The house is centrally heated, with a comfortable reading lounge, a licensed bar with a nautical motif, and an intimate dining room where good Cornish meals are served from April to October, although the house takes guests all year. Parking is available in the courtyard at the rear of the premises.

WHERE TO DINE

Down a narrow cobblestone street opposite Lloyds Bank, **Harris's Restaurant,** 46 New St. (tel. 0736/64408), is owned and run by a husband-and-wife team, Roger and Anne Harris. It's a warm, candlelit place with a relaxed atmosphere. Light lunches, costing from £8 ($14), served upstairs, include crab Florentine, lobster salad, and salad niçoise. Dinner is more elaborate, offering such dishes as breast of duckling in a port wine sauce, filet steak with a red wine and wild-mushroom sauce, or veal served with a marsala-and-cream sauce. Expect to pay up to £20 ($35) for a complete dinner. Lunch is served from noon to 1:45 p.m., and dinner from 7 to 10 p.m. daily except Sunday all year and on Monday in winter.

Berkeley, Abbey Street (tel. 0736/62541), lies on a side street near the Abbey Hotel. It was designed and built by the Morris family at the rear of Admiral Benbow's Restaurant and Bar. A sophisticated rendezvous, it has exposed stone, plush banquettes, and touches of glitter. Some of the taped music and much of the atmosphere will evoke a setting of some 50 years ago. You get good honest cookery here, not flights of fancy. For example, try the whole Dover sole cooked in butter with lemon juice or breast of chicken fried in butter and seasoned with fresh sage, perhaps scallops Breton style. The restaurant only serves dinner, and is open nightly except Sunday (also closed on off-season Mondays) from 7:30 to 10:30 p.m. A set meal costs £15 ($26.25), or you can have a full à la carte dinner for around £20 ($35).

9. The Isles of Scilly

Perhaps the most interesting and scenic excursion from Penzance is a day trip to the Isles of Scilly, which lie off the Cornish coast about 27 miles west-southwest of Land's End. There are five inhabited and more than 100 uninhabited islands in the group, some consisting merely of a few square miles of land while others, such as the largest, St. Mary's, encompass some 30 square miles. Two of these islands attract tourists, St. Mary's and Tresco.

These islands were known to the early Greeks and the Romans, and in Celtic legend they were inhabited entirely by holy men. There are more ancient burial mounds on these islands than anywhere else in southern England, and artifacts found establish clearly that people lived here more than 4,000 years ago.

Today there is little left of this long history to show the visitor. Now these are islands of peace and beauty where early flowers are the main export and tourism the main industry.

St. Mary's is the capital, with about seven-eighths of the total population of all the islands, and it is here that the ship from the mainland docks at Hugh Town. However, for the day visitor, I recommend the helicopter flight from Penzance to **Tresco,** the neighboring island, where you can enjoy a day's walk through the 735 acres, mostly occupied by the **Abbey Gardens.**

HOW TO GET THERE

You can travel via the **Isles of Scilly Steamship Company Ltd.,** Quay Street, Penzance (tel. 0736/62009), with daily departures from March to October. The trip from Penzance to Hugh Town, St. Mary's, takes about three hours. Steamships leave Penzance daily at 9:15 a.m. and return from Scilly at 4:45 p.m. In winter, there is a restricted service. A same-day round-trip ticket costs £22 ($38.50) in summer for adults, £10 ($17.50) for children. You can buy an onward ticket for Tresco, including the ferry and landing charges, at £3.50 ($6.25).

British International Helicopters, at the Penzance Heliport (tel. 0736/63871), operates a year-round helicopter service between Penzance and St. Mary's, and to Tresco from March to October. Flight time is 20 minutes. The standard fare from Penzance to the islands is £24 ($42) each way. Flights start at 7:50 a.m. in high season, July to September, and at 8:45 a.m. the remainder of the year. They continue regularly throughout the day, with the last flight back to Penzance at 6:15 p.m. in high season, 4:10 p.m. otherwise. For people arriving in Penzance on the train, there is a bus service between the railway station and the heliport. The cost is £1 ($1.75), and travel time is about five minutes.

British Rail runs express trains from Paddington Station, London, to Penzance. BritRail Passes can be used. Travel time is about five hours. There are special offers on the Night Riviera Express.

For those who wish to travel to Penzance by road, there is good express bus service. The Rapide costs from around £23.50 ($41.15) round trip for the journey from London, about eight hours each way. The buses are fitted with toilets and have reclining seats and a hostess who dispenses coffee, tea, and sandwiches. The buses are run by **National Express** from Victoria Coach Station, 172 Buckingham Palace Rd., London, S.W.1 (tel. 01/730-0202).

WHAT TO SEE AND DO ON TRESCO

No cars or motorbikes are allowed on the island, but walking or bicycling is pleasant. Bikes can be rented by the day. The hotels use a special wagon towed by a farm tractor to transport guests and luggage from the harbor.

The **Abbey Gardens,** mentioned above, are the most outstanding features of Tresco. Here you can enjoy a day's walk through the 735 acres. These gardens were started by Augustus Smith in the mid-1830s. When he began work, the area was a barren hillside, a fact visitors find hard to believe.

The gardens are a collector's dream, with more than 5,000 species of plants from some 100 different countries. The old abbey, or priory, is a ruin said to have been founded by Benedictine monks in the 11th century, although some historians date it from A.D. 964. Of special interest in the gardens is **Valhalla,** a collection of nearly 60 figureheads from ships wrecked around the islands. There is a rather eerie atmosphere surrounding these gaily painted figures from the past, each one a ghost with a different story to tell. Hours are 10 a.m. to 4 p.m. daily. Admission is £2.50 ($4.40).

After a visit to the gardens, walk through the fields, along paths, and across dunes thick with heather. Flowers, birds, shells, and fish are so abundant that Tresco is a naturalist's dream and a walker's paradise. Birds are so unafraid that they land within a foot or so of you and feed happily.

The phone number for **information** to do with Tresco is 0720/22849. Call it to find out about boat schedules, possible changes in hours and prices at the abbey, and other matters.

WHERE TO STAY ON TRESCO

The top hostelry here is the **Island Hotel,** Tresco, Isles of Scilly, Cornwall TR24 0PU (tel. 0720/22883), a modern establishment on the northeast side of the island with views that have been compared to those seen in the Greek islands. The building blends with the sea and the rocks, and long, low extensions have been added to an original cottage. Some rooms overlook the sea, some face inland. All the units are comfortably furnished with easy chairs and storage space, private baths, toilets, drying racks, color TVs, phones, and razor points. Managers John and Wendy Pyatt charge rates that vary considerably, according to location and time of year. The tariffs for half board are £64 ($112) to £75 ($131.25) daily in a single, £54 ($94.50) to £95 ($166.25) per person for doubles or twins, the higher the rate for a suite. A room with sea view in the Cottage or Garden wings of the hotel costs £67 ($117.25) per person for half board in high season. Understandably, one-night stays are not encouraged, a three-night minimum being preferred. The hotel is closed from October to March.

The only other hotel on Tresco is the **New Inn,** Tresco, Isles of Scilly, Cornwall TR24 0PU (tel. 0720/22844). This pub, built of stone and standing on the island's road, has an outdoor area for those who wish to picnic and drink a glass of ale. Inside, the bar is the meeting place for locals and tourists alike. Lunch snacks are available, a bar meal costing £6 ($10.50) for two courses. Dinners are £13 ($22.75) to £15 ($26.25). The pictures in the bar are worth a look. They show many of the ships that sank or foundered around the islands in the past, as well as some of the gigs used in pilotage, rescue, smuggling, and pillage. The inn has 12 rooms, all twins and doubles with private bathrooms. Here, too, there is a wide range of prices. Accommodation prices vary from £15 ($26.25) per person daily for B&B until mid-April, after which a dinner, bed, and breakfast tariff applies until mid-October. The prices range from £30 ($52.50) to £40.50 ($70.90) during that time. The inn has a heated outdoor swimming pool.

WHAT TO DO AND SEE ON ST. MARY'S

Expert diver Mark Groves who runs **Underwater Island Safaris,** "Nowhere," Old Town (tel. 0720/22732), has worked as a diver in both the Caribbean and the Red Sea. He can entertain both the experienced and the inexperienced diver. A diving safari costs from £20 ($35) for three hours of instruction and diving, including gear rental. Diving for qualified persons takes place on many of the historic and beautiful drop-offs. Waterskiing is also offered.

Cars are available but hardly necessary. The **Island Bus Service** has a basic charge of 50p (90¢) from one island point to another. However, sightseers can circumnavigate the island, paying £1 ($1.75) for the privilege. Children are charged half fare.

Bicycles are one of the most practical means of transport. **Buccabu Bicycle Rentals,** The Strand, St. Mary's (tel. 0720/22289), is the major rental agency. The cost, depending on the type of bicycle you want, ranges from £3.40 ($5.95) to £10 ($17.50) per day, the latter the price for a tandem bike.

The **Isles of Scilly Museum** on St. Mary's (tel. 0720/22337) is open Monday to Saturday from 10 a.m. to noon, 1:30 to 4:30 p.m., and 7:30 to 9 p.m. in summer. Winter hours are from 2 to 4 p.m. Wednesday. Admission is 40p (70¢). The museum shows the history of the islands from 1500 B.C. with artifacts from wrecked ships, drawings, and relics discovered in the Scillies.

The **Tourist Information Office** on St. Mary's offers service (tel. 0720/22536).

WHERE TO STAY ON ST. MARY'S

A substantial stone structure, the **Hotel Godolphin,** St. Mary's, Isles of Scilly, Cornwall TR21 0JR (tel. 0720/22316) gives the impression, as you approach, of being a private house—which is what it was until the Mumford family, who own and operate it, decided to make it into a hotel. This they have done with skillful additions, creating a fine hostelry in the town. There are 31 bedrooms, 29 of which have private baths. All have color TVs, radios, intercoms, phones, hot beverage facilities, and central heating. The best rooms overlook the garden. Open March to October, the hotel charges £34 ($59.50) to £50 ($87.50) daily in a double. Incidentally, the hotel's name comes from the name of the estate on which the building stands, originating in the reign of Queen Elizabeth I, who gave the island to Francis Godolphin in 1571.

Star Castle Hotel (tel. 0720/22317) is in a structure built as a castle in 1593 in the shape of an eight-pointed star. It was erected for the defense of the Isles of Scilly against attacks by Spain in retaliation for the 1588 defeat of the Armada. Because of the purpose of the original building, the hotel has views out to sea as well as over the town and the harbor. The great kitchen has a huge fireplace where a whole ox could be roasted. An early Prince of Wales (later King Charles II) took shelter here in 1643 when he was being hunted by Cromwell and his parliamentary forces. In 1933 another Prince of Wales was here to officiate at the opening of the castle as a hotel. This was the man who succeeded to the throne as King Edward VIII but was never crowned.

The hotel has 24 bedrooms, 16 of which are in the garden annex comprising two wings facing each other across the lawns. These are extra-large units, each with bath and opening directly onto the gardens. Of the eight double or twin rooms in the castle, five have private baths and the remainder have hot and cold running water and include the rampart guard house. These are much favored for their isolation, in the points of the star overlooking the sea and the town, although the bathroom is a few yards away—across the ramparts. Single rates begin at £33 ($57.75) daily, with a double costing up to £100 ($175). All tariffs include a full English breakfast and dinner. There is a glass-covered, heated swimming pool, and the garden has many sheltered places for you to relax. Lunch and dinner orders are taken in the Cellar Bar. A four-course dinner costs £11 ($19.25). Typical English food is served daily, from noon to 1:30 p.m. and 6:45 to 8 p.m., and many of the vegetables come from the hotel's large gardens.

Carnwethers Country Guest House, Pelistry Bay, St. Mary's, Isles of Scilly, Cornwall TR21 0NX (tel. 0720/22415), is a modernized, two-story farmhouse with a one-story extension, standing on top of a hill looking down to fields, beach, and the sea. Pelistry Bay is a secluded part of St. Mary's island, the sandy beach well sheltered. You can walk at low tide across to the nearby uninhabited island of Tolls.

The hostelry is owned and operated by Roy and Joyce Graham, with Joyce personally supervising the kitchen. For dinner, although the choice is limited, traditional English fare is offered. Dinner, served at 6:30 p.m. includes only fresh local produce and home-grown vegetables. Breakfast is a substantial meal, the marmalade being a particular pride of the house. Half board costs £22 ($39.40) to £25 ($43.75) per person daily in spring and fall, £25 ($43.75) to £28 ($49) in high season. Most of the rooms have private baths, £3 ($5.25) extra being charged for a unit so equipped. VAT is included in the rates. All the rooms are spotless, warm, and comfortable. The main lounge is in two parts, one for conversation and reading, the other containing a library full of books about the island. There is a separate bar lounge in its own grounds with a croquet lawn. A heated outdoor swimming pool is in operation in summer.

10. Newlyn, Mousehole, and Land's End

Back at Penzance, we head south to two of the most charming villages of Cornwall.

NEWLYN

From Penzance, a promenade leads to Newlyn, a mile away, another fishing village on Mount's Bay. Stanhope Forbes, now dead, founded an art school in Newlyn. The village has an artists' colony, attracting both the serious painter and the amateur sketcher. From Penzance, Newlyn is reached by taking bus 1 or 1B. For a dining or overnighting recommendation, try the following.

Food and Lodging

Higher Faugan Hotel, Newlyn, Penzance, Cornwall TR18 5NS (tel. 0736/ 62076), lies three-quarters of a mile south of Penzance on the B3315. The structure was built in 1904 by painter Alexander Stanhope Forbes, whose work is now in demand, commanding high prices, as does that of his wife, Elizabeth Adela Forbes, and many other artists from the "Newlyn" school. The spacious country-house hotel is the property of Michael and Christine Churchman. The building's granite walls, big windows, and steep roofs are surrounded by ten acres of lawn, garden, and woodland, all of which can be covered on foot by adventurous visitors. The amenities include a heated outdoor swimming pool, putting green, a hard tennis court, a well-furnished lounge, a billiards room, and a cultivated dining room serving beautifully prepared specialties. A dozen well-furnished bedrooms are offered, each with private bath, TV, and coffee-making facilities. B&B is priced at £25 ($43.75) to £32 ($56) per person daily, and half board goes for £32 ($56) to £42 ($73.50) per person.

MOUSEHOLE

Still another Cornish fishing village, Mousehole lies three miles south of Penzance. The hordes of tourists who flock here haven't changed it drastically: the gulls still squawk, the cottages still huddle close to the harbor wall (although they look as if they were built more to be photographed than lived in), the fishermen still bring in the day's catch, the salts sit around with their pipes talking about the good old days, and the lanes are as narrow as ever. About the most exciting thing that's occurred around here was the arrival in the late 16th century of Spanish galleons, whose sailors sacked and burned the village. In a sheltered cove, off Mount's Bay, Mousehole (pronounced mou-zel) long ago developed an artists' colony, which is home to both painters and potters.

The village's odd name, according to linguistic historians, is derived from a now-extinct Mediterranean language probably used by the Phoenicians when they landed here more than 2,000 years ago. Roughly translated, it means "watering place."

Food and Lodging

Carn Du Hotel, Raginnis Hill, Mousehole, Cornwall TR19 6SS (tel. 0736/ 731233), has twin bay windows gazing over the top of the village onto the harbor with its bobbing fishing vessels. Andrew and Sigrid Field are the rulers of this panoramic aerie, whose seven bedrooms offer private baths, radios, and much comfort. Half board in low season is £27.50 ($48.15) daily per person, rising to £30.70 ($53.75) in high season. The meals, going for £10.50 ($18.40), are straightforward and fresh, usually accompanied by a bottle of wine from the cellars. You might precede your meal with a drink in one of the lounges. The Fields will arrange sporting options for active vacationers but won't mind if you prefer to sit and relax. The establishment is open from March to mid-January.

Tavis Vor Hotel, The Parade, Mousehole, near Penzance Cornwall TR19 6PR (tel. 0736/731306), opens onto a marvelous view overlooking the harbor and St. Michael's Mount. Almost directly opposite is a small island on which there are the remains of a monastery. The first building on the sea side when you enter Mousehole, Tavis Vor is a nine-bedroom hotel set on its own grounds. Ample parking is provided (a rarity in Mousehole), and there is direct access to the beach from the grounds of the hotel. Most of the bedrooms contain a private bath. Overnight tariffs for B&B range from £14.50 ($25.50) to £18.50 ($32.40) per person. The hotel, which remains open all year, specializes in traditional English cooking.

Food and Lodging on the Outskirts

Lamorna Cove Hotel, Lamorna Cove, Cornwall TR19 6XH (tel. 0736/ 731411), lies five miles from Penzance. This is one of the most perfect Cornish coves, seemingly inaccessible down a winding, narrow road, dropping always toward the sea until you suddenly emerge onto the sea wall of the tiny cove. The owners have added to the old stone building, once a tiny chapel with a bell tower. They once even blasted several tons of rock from the cliff face to provide more room. The bar is in the chapel. A large dining room runs the length of the building, and there are several lounges full of comfortable chairs, with a log fire in winter. Accommodations are in the main hotel with bath or shower, some with balcony. There are also two cottages, one suitable for four, the other for five persons. A rocky garden clings to the cliffside and then surrounds a small swimming pool with a sun terrace overlooking the sea. In high season, a single costs from £35 ($61.25) daily, and a double or twin begins at £89 ($155.75), these tariffs including a full breakfast, VAT, and service. If you don't have the time to stay at the hotel, their bar lunches can be well recommended. On Sunday, a traditional luncheon is served. Dinners, at £13.50 ($23.65) are quite a feast.

LAND'S END

Craggy Land's End, where England comes to a stop, is where you'll find the last of everything. It lies nine miles west of Penzance and is reached by bus. America's coast is 3,291 miles away to the west of the rugged rocks that tumble into the sea beneath Land's End.

Publicity says that "Everyone should stand here, at least once." Given the romantic concept that this is the piece of England closest to America, the most distant point you can go on mainland England, this is so. It must still retain some of its mystique, even if "big business" has now opened the Land's End Heritage Museum, the Man and the Sea Exhibition, and the Worzel Gummidge Exhibition, not to mention a Video Theatre with continuous performances and the First and Last Craft Workshop from which to buy your first and "last" souvenirs. True, the area needs an injection of money. As anyone standing on those jagged cliffs can see, the pounding they take causes much damage to the coastline. Better to ignore the commercial aspect and enjoy the cliff walks and spectacular views. If you want to research the ancient traditions of Cornish folklore, there are other places far more dedicated to research than this tourist trap.

Food and Lodging

State House Hotel, Land's End, Sennen, Cornwall TR19 7AA (tel. 0736/ 871844), is set behind a white façade within a complex of buildings rising from the scrubby landscape at the very tip of England. The hotel has a panoramic clifftop position, exposed to the wind and sea spray. Each of its 34 bedrooms is handsomely furnished with a private bath, beverage-making equipment, phone, and TV. The price of the rooms is £90 ($157.50) daily in a double and £50 ($87.50) in a single. In winter, these tariffs include dinner and B&B. However, in summer it includes only B&B. Singles occupying a double room pay a surcharge costing from £10 ($17.50) to £15 ($26.25) daily. A fixed price lunch is served daily from noon to 2 p.m., costing £7.25 ($12.70), with a table d'hôte dinner from 7 to 9:30 p.m. going for £12.50 ($21.90).

11. St. Just-in-Penwith

Between Sennen and St. Ives lie some of the finest dining recommendations in the area. Actually, there are two places in Cornwall called St. Just. This one is St. Just-in-Penwith. (The other, outside St. Mawes, is St. Just-in-Roseland.) St. Just-in-Penwith was a tin-mining town in the last century. Its main attraction is its church, lying just off a triangle-shaped square and containing a pinnacled tower from the 15th century. The town is named for St. Just-in-Penwith, a saint of the mid-5th century.

DINING AT BOTALLACK

The following recommendation lies 2¼ miles northwest of St. Just-in-Penwith by the B3306.

The **Count House Restaurant,** Botallack, near St. Just-in-Penwith (tel. 0736/ 788588), is the most southwesterly place to eat on the English mainland to be recommended in this guide. Overlooking the Atlantic, the building occupied today by the restaurant was constructed around 1820 as a carpenter's workshop for the nearby tin mine, with the adjoining Georgian house, formerly the counting house for the mine, being the private home of owners Graham and Helen Ashton. The restaurant is constructed from local stone with a high-beamed roof. Paintings by local artists and antique prints displayed in the restaurant can be purchased. You dine at well-spaced tables, choosing from a menu that changes weekly and features fresh fish and produce from local farms and markets. Full dinners cost from £15 ($26.25) to £20 ($35) per person. From April to October, hours are from 7:30 to 9:30 p.m. daily except Sunday night and Monday. From November to March, food is served from 7:30 to 9:30 p.m. Wednesday, Thursday, Friday, and Saturday. All year, Sunday lunch is served from 12:30 to 2:30 p.m.

12. St. Ives

This north coast fishing village, with its sandy beaches, is England's most famous art colony. Only 20 miles from Land's End, 10 from Penzance, it is a village of narrow streets and well-kept cottages. The artists settled in many years ago and have integrated with the fishermen and their families.

The art colony was established long enough ago to have developed several schools or "splits," and they almost never overlap—except in a pub where the artists hang out, or where classes are held. The old battle continues between the followers of the representational and the devotees of the abstract in art, with each group recruiting young artists all the time. In addition, there are the potters, weavers, and other craftspeople—all working, exhibiting, and selling in this area. There are several galleries to visit, with such names as the Sail Loft.

A word of warning: St. Ives becomes virtually impossible to visit in August, when you're likely to be trampled underfoot by busloads of tourists, mostly the English themselves. However, in spring and early fall, the pace is much more relaxed, and a visitor can have the true experience of the art colony.

PARK AND RIDE

During the summer months, many of the streets in the center of town are closed to vehicles. You may want to leave your car in the **Lelant Saltings Car Park,** three miles from St. Ives on the A3074, and take the regular train service into town, an 11-minute journey. Departures are every half hour. It's free to all car passengers and drivers, and the car-park charge is £2 ($3.50) per day. Or you can use the large **Trenwith Car Park,** close to the town center, for 35p (60¢) and then walk down to the shops and harbor or take a bus, costing 30p (55¢) for adults and 15p (25¢) for children.

BARBARA HEPWORTH MUSEUM

At Trewyn Studio and Garden, on Barnoon Hill (tel. 0736/796226), the former home of Dame Barbara Hepworth contains a museum of sculpture by the artist from 1929 until her death in 1975, together with photographs, letters, and other papers documenting her life and background. The garden, too, contains sculpture and is well worth a visit. The museum is open daily from 10 a.m. to 5:30 p.m. in summer, to 4:30 p.m. in winter. Admission is 50p (90¢) for adults, 25p (45¢) for children. There is limited parking some 200 yards away.

WHERE TO STAY

Standing on its own 70 acres, **Tregenna Castle Hotel,** St. Ives, Cornwall TR26 2DE (tel. 0736/795254), was really once a castle. It was optimistically earmarked by Von Ribbentrop to be Hitler's British Berchtesgaden. Approached by a long driveway, it crowns a hill high above the fishing village of St. Ives. While the interior is spacious and a good background for gracious living, the grounds contain gardens and lawns, an open-air, heated swimming pool with a flagstone edging for sunbathers, three lawn tennis courts, three hard courts, and an 18-hole golf course. The bedrooms usually are of good size, handsomely maintained with contemporary furniture, and more than 80% have private bath. They rent for £28 ($49) daily in a single, £44 ($77) in a double.

Porthminster Hotel, The Terrace, St. Ives, Cornwall TR26 2BN (tel. 0736/ 795221), has long been a leading Cornish Riviera resort. On the main road into town, it is set in a beautiful garden, within an easy walk of Porthminster Beach. Large and imposing, Porthminster, like Tregenna Castle, has long been the traditional choice for visitors to St. Ives. With its staunchly Victorian architecture, it is warm and inviting. The hotel, a Best Western affiliate, offers 50 well-furnished bedrooms, each with private bath or shower. Singles rent from £29 ($50.75) to £35.50 ($62.15) daily, with doubles costing £57 ($99.75) to £70 ($122.50). Rooms contain color TV, radio, and direct-dial phone. Extra facilities at the hotel include a sun lounge, solarium, and a sauna, as well as a swimming pool that sees action from June to September. Bar lunches go for £4.50 ($7.90), with dinners costing from £12 ($21).

Pedn-Olva Hotel, The Warren, St. Ives, Cornwall TR26 2EA (tel. 0736/ 796222). From the car park above, all you can see of the hotel is the roof and chimneys, and then you pass through the practical lobby to the lounges and restaurant before coming on the magnificent view over the bay that is the outstanding feature of this establishment. There are sun terraces with lounges and umbrellas and a swimming pool for those who do not wish to walk down the rocky path to Porthminster Beach. If you crave solitude, however, scramble down the rocks to sunbathe just above the gentle rise and fall of the sea. Most bedrooms have sea views and private baths. The half-board rate ranges from £34 ($59.50) daily in a single, going up to £74 ($129.50) in a double.

Garrack Hotel, Higher Ayr, Burthallan Lane, St. Ives, Cornwall TR26 3AA (tel. 0736/796199), from its two-acre knoll, commands a panoramic view of St. Ives and Portmeor Beach. The vine-covered little hotel, once a private home, is reached by heading up a narrow lane. It's one of the friendliest and most efficiently run small medium-priced hotels on the entire coast, with every room furnished in a warm, homey manner. The atmosphere in the living room is inviting, with a log-burning fireplace, antiques, and comfortable chairs. The Garrack belongs to Mr. and Mrs. Kilby, who are proud of their meals (see my dining recommendations). The Kilbys have added a wooden leisure building to the hotel with a swimming pool that has a Jacuzzi whirlpool and swim jet, a solarium, and a sauna, all with changing rooms and a small bar overlooking the lovely bay. On a patio, you can sunbathe. There is a honeymoon suite, plus a mini-launderette. Rates range from £20 ($35) to £25 ($43.75) per person daily for B&B without bath, from £23 ($40.25) to £31 ($54.25) per person with bath or shower. Half-board terms are quoted on stays of more than three days.

WHERE TO EAT

The dining room at the **Garrack Hotel,** Higher Ayr, Burthallan Lane (tel. 0736/796199), the domain of Mr. and Mrs. Kilby, is outstanding, producing an excellent cuisine and, when possible, using fresh ingredients from their own garden. The hotel dining room, open to non-residents, offers regular à la carte listings, plus a cold buffet or snacks at the bar, and an £11 ($19.25) dinner from 7 to 8:30 p.m. The menu features some of the finest of English dishes, such as roast shoulder of lamb with mint sauce, fried fillet of plaice, and a wide sampling of continental fare, such as filet of bass meunière and escalopes de veau Cordon Bleu. Live lobsters swim in the Kilbys' seawater tank until being removed for preparation and cooking to order. Of course, if you order cold lobster salad, a little prior notice is required. Two trolleys are at your service, one with continental cheeses and two antique cheeseballs covering half a Stilton wheel or a farmhouse Cheddar cheese, and the other with a wide choice of desserts. (You can have Cornish cream with any dessert, if you wish.) The Kilbys' son Michael joined his parents in the operation of the hotel and restaurant after completing a training period with Claridges in London.

---

13. Port Isaac

The most unspoiled fishing village on the north Cornish coastline is Port Isaac, nine miles from Wadebridge. This Atlantic coastal resort retains its original character, in spite of the intrusions of large numbers of summer visitors. By all means wander through its winding, narrow lanes, gazing at the whitewashed fishermen's cottages with their rainbow trims.

FOOD AND LODGING

The leading choice is **Port Gaverne Hotel,** Port Gaverne, Port Isaac, Cornwall PL29 3SQ (tel. 0208/880244), which was built in the 17th century as a coastal inn sheltering fishermen looking for refuge from their seagoing labors. Today, under the gracious administration of Frederick and Marjorie Ross, it caters to vacationing families and holidaying couples. It boasts a sheltered cove for boating and swimming, and can arrange shark fishing, pony trekking, and country hikes. Its painted façade is draped with vines, and inside you'll find a trio of comfortably atmospheric bars for relaxing beside a fireplace (one of them is a modified baking oven). Clusters of antiques, stained glass, and early photographs of Cornwall add sometimes bittersweet grace notes. Dinners are served by candlelight and include locally caught lobster, fish, or crab in season, as well as locally raised lamb and beef. Bar snacks are also available, with dinners costing from £13 ($22.75). The comfortably furnished bedrooms rent for £31 ($54.25) to £33 ($57.75) per person daily. Tariffs include a full English breakfast. Each unit has its own bath. The hotel is closed from mid-January to mid-February.

Slipway Hotel, Harbourfront, Port Isaac, Cornwall PL29 3RH (tel. 0208/880747), was originally built in 1527, with major additions added in the early 1700s. This waterside building has seen more uses than any other structure in town, everything from fisherman's cottages to the headquarters of the first bank here. Once the building was a lifeboat station for rescuing sailors stranded on stormy seas. This establishment is one of the few at Port Isaac that offers private parking. The Slipway rents only a few bedrooms, charging half-board tariffs of £27 ($47.25) to £31 ($54.25) per person daily, depending on the accommodation, the view, and the plumbing. It is better known as a restaurant. Its main dining room is high ceilinged and contains a minstrel's gallery, occupying the cellar and part of the ground floor. A table d'hôte dinner is served nightly from 7:30 to 9:30 p.m., costing £9.75 ($17.05), with à la carte meals priced from £14 ($24.50). Bar snacks are served at lunch from noon to 2 p.m., costing from £3 ($5.25).

---

14. Tintagel

On a wild stretch of the Atlantic coast, Tintagel is forever linked with the legends of King Arthur, Lancelot, and Merlin. The 13th-century ruins of **Tintagel Castle** (tel. 0840/770328), popularly known as King Arthur's Castle, stand 300 feet above the sea on a rocky promontory. It is open from 10 a.m. to 6 p.m. daily from Good Friday to September 30. Hours off-season are from 10 a.m. to 4 p.m. Closed Monday. Admission is £1.30 ($2.30) for adults, 65p ($1.15) for children. The colorful writing of Lord Tennyson in *Idylls of the King* greatly increased the interest in Tintagel, as had the works of Geoffrey of Monmouth. The ruins, which date from Geoffrey's time, are what remains of a castle built on the foundations of a Celtic monastery from the sixth century, a long, steep, tortuous walk from the car park. In summer, many visitors make the ascent to Arthur's lair, 100 rock-cut steps. You can also visit Merlin's Cave.

The **Old Post Office** (tel. 0208/4281) at Tintagel is a National Trust property. It was once a 14th-century manor, but since the 19th century it has had connections with the post office. In the village center, it has a genuine Victorian post room that is open, April to October, daily from 11 a.m. to last admission at 5:45 p.m., or sunset if earlier. Admission is £1 ($1.75) for adults, 50p (90¢) for children.

If you become excited by legends of Knights of the Round Table, you can go to **Camelford,** five miles inland from Tintagel. The market hall there dates from 1790, but more interestingly, the town claims to be Camelot.

WHERE TO STAY

As you approach Tintagel from Boscastle, **Bossiney House Hotel,** Bossiney, Tintagel, Cornwall PL34 0AX (tel. 0840/770240), stands in an inviting spot on the right. Two brothers, Colin and Bob Savage, and their families operate the hotel, and everybody combines to make guests feel welcome. The hotel is comfortable, with a TV lounge and a well-stocked bar/lounge, which has a fine view of surrounding meadows marching right up to the tops of the cliff as well as of the wide expanse of lawn with a putting green. Rooms are comfortably furnished and have private baths and central heating. The large dining room, where a big English breakfast is served and you can enjoy other well-prepared meals brought to you by smiling Cornish women, is so situated as to give a view of the front, side, and back lawns. Guests pay from £27 ($47.25) to £29 ($50.75) per person daily for a room and half board, depending on the season. The proprietors will direct you to interesting places you might otherwise miss seeing in the area. The hotel is closed from the end of October to Easter.

Trebrea Lodge, Trenale, near Tintagel, Cornwall PL34 0HR (tel. 0840/770410), may appear a dignified stately home, but in truth it looks and feels inside like an old Cornish farmhouse. It dates back to 1315, and was lived in by the same family for more than 600 years. The house, owned by Jill and Richard Radford, looks straight out across fields to the sea, and each bedroom has a good view. Rooms are available in many sizes, and each has a private bath, color TV, radio, intercom, and even a baby-listening service. Evenings are cozy in the drawing room around an open fire. The original first-floor drawing room has been restored, and there is a traditional Victorian smoking room in addition to the bar. You can have drinks in another lounge with a fireplace. Dining is most informal, and all food is homemade by Mrs. Radford, who has mastered true English recipes. The cost is £30 ($52.50) per person daily for half board. The lodge is open from February to mid-November.

---

15. Bolventor

This village in central Cornwall near Launceston is visited by the fans of Daphne du Maurier, as it was the setting for her novel *Jamaica Inn* (see below). The inn is named for the Caribbean island where the one-time owner of the inn had become prosperous from sugar on his plantation there. Opposite the inn, a small road leads to Dozmary Pool where the "waves wap and the winds wan" into which Sir Bedivere threw Excalibur at King Arthur's behest.

Jamaica Inn, Bolventor, Launceston, Cornwall PL15 7TS (tel. 056686/250) is a long, low building beside the main road across Bodmin Moor, an ideal spot on the desolate moor for a smugglers' den in other times. Busy throughout most of the day with passing trade, it has welcoming bars where food and soft drinks are dispensed along with local beer and cider. Bedrooms with private bath rent for £35 ($61.25) daily for double occupancy, with singles going for £20 ($35). There is a restaurant with waitress service open in the evening and a potters museum in the courtyard. The bar is open from 11 a.m. to 11 p.m., with a food bar serving from 9:30 a.m. to 10 p.m. Hours are more limited in winter.

XI

WILTSHIRE, SOMERSET, AND AVON

1. SALISBURY
2. CASTLE COMBE
3. LACOCK
4. EXMOOR NATIONAL PARK
5. DUNSTER
6. TAUNTON
7. GLASTONBURY
8. WELLS
9. THE CAVES OF MENDIP
10. BATH
11. BRISTOL
12. THORNBURY

For our final look at the "West Countree," we move now into Wiltshire, Somerset, and Avon, the most antiquity-rich shires of England. When we reach this area of woodland and pastoral scenes, London seems far removed—even divorced from the bucolic life here.

On cold, windswept nights in unrecorded times, the Druids used to steal across these plains, armed with twigs. Sheltered by boulders, they'd burn their sloe with rosemary to ward off the danger of witchcraft.

Most people seem to agree that the West Country, a loose geographical term, begins at Salisbury, with its Early English cathedral. Nearby is Stonehenge, England's oldest prehistoric monument. Both Stonehenge and Salisbury are in Wiltshire.

Somerset is even more varied—the diet richer not only in historical cities, but in wild scenic grandeur, especially in Exmoor, the home of the red deer. The legendary burial place of King Arthur at Glastonbury and the cathedral city of Wells also await you on your visit to Somerset. The old Roman city of Bath and the seaport of Bristol are the main targets in the county of Avon.

WILTSHIRE

When you cross into Wiltshire, you'll be entering a county of chalky, grassy uplands and rolling plains. Much of the shire is agricultural, and a large part is devoted to pastureland. Wiltshire produces an abundance of England's dairy products, and is noted for its sheep raising. In this western shire, you'll traverse the Salisbury Plain, the Vale of Pewsey, and the Marlborough Downs (the last gobbling up the greater part of the land mass). Unquestionably, the crowning achievement of Wiltshire is:

1. Salisbury

Long before you've come to the end of the 83-mile trek from London, the spire of Salisbury Cathedral comes into view—just as John Constable painted it so many times. The 404-foot pinnacle of the Early English and Gothic cathedral is the tallest in England. But Salisbury is also a fine base for touring such sights as Stonehenge.

Salisbury, or New Sarum, lies in the valley of the Avon River. Filled with Tudor inns and tea rooms, it is known to readers of Thomas Hardy as Melchester and to the Victorian fans of Anthony Trollope as Barchester.

SALISBURY CATHEDRAL

You can search all of England, but you'll find no purer example of the Early English, or pointed, style than Salisbury Cathedral. Its graceful spire has already been mentioned, but the ecclesiastical building doesn't depend totally on the tower for its appeal. Construction began as early as 1220, then took 38 years to complete, which was jet-age speed in those days (it was customary to drag out cathedral-building for three centuries at least). The spire began soaring at the end of the 13th century. Despite an ill-conceived attempt at revamping in the 18th century, the architectural harmony of the cathedral was retained.

The cathedral's octagonal Chapter House (note the fine sculpture) is especially attractive, dating from the 13th century. It also contains one of the four surviving original texts of Magna Carta, together with treasures from the diocese of Salisbury and manuscripts and artifacts belonging to the cathedral. There is a charge of 25p (45¢) per person to visit the Chapter House. The cloisters enhance the beauty of the cathedral. The Close, with at least 75 buildings in its compound (some from the early 18th century and others predating that), is exceptionally large, setting off the cathedral most fittingly. A donation of 75p ($1.30) is asked of each visitor.

The cathedral has a good **Brass Rubbing Centre** where you can choose from a selection of exact replicas molded perfectly from the original brasses. The small charge made for each rubbing includes the cost of materials and a donation to the church from which it comes. The center is open at the cathedral from early June to early September Monday to Saturday from 10 a.m. to 5 p.m., from 2 to 5 p.m. on Sunday.

One of the most distinguished houses in the Close is **Mompesson House,** built by Charles Mompesson in 1701, while he was Member of Parliament for Old Sarum. An outstandingly beautiful example of the Queen Anne style, it is well known for its fine plasterwork ceilings and paneling. There is also a magnificent collection of 18th-century drinking glasses. It is open April to October daily except Thursday and Friday, from 12:30 to 6 p.m. or dusk, charging an admission of £1.50 ($2.65) for adults, 75p ($1.30) for children.

Also in the Close is the **Regimental Museum of the Duke of Edinburgh's Royal Regiment (Berkshire and Wiltshire),** The Wardrobe, 58 The Close (tel.

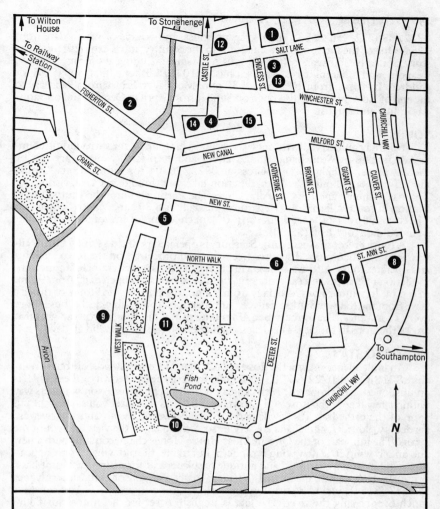

SALISBURY

0	meters 250
0	feet 750

KEY TO NUMBERED SIGHTS:

1. Shoemakers' Hall
2. Theatre
3. Bus Station
4. St. Thomas' Church
5. North Gate
6. St. Ann's Gate
7. Museum
8. Joiners' Hall
9. King's House
10. Harnham Gate
11. Salisbury Cathedral
12. Post Office
13. Tourist Information Centre
14. Market Place
15. Guildhall

0722/336222, ext. 2683), in an elegant house, the origins of which date from 1254. One of the finest military museums in the country, it has exhibits telling the story of nearly 250 years of this famous regiment, including uniforms, pictures, weapons, and other militaria. Admission is £1.10 ($1.95) for adults, 50p (90¢) for children. It is open from 10 a.m. to 4:30 p.m. Monday to Friday from February to the end of November. It is also open on Sunday from April to October and on Saturday in July and August.

TOURS

Leisurely guided walks through the city and car tours of the surrounding countryside, including Stonehenge and Avebury and even farther afield, are run by **Wessexplore.** Telephone Don Cross at 0722/26304 for information. Regular guided walks of about 1½ hours' duration take you through the city, visiting St. Thomas's Church and the Cathedral Close. The starting point is the **Tourist Information Bureau** in Fish Row. Departures are daily at 8:30 a.m. May to September. The cost is 90p ($1.60) for adults 40p (70¢) for children. An entire family can go for a guided walk for £1.60 ($2.80).

A tourist reception center for Salisbury is operated by **Guide Friday Ltd.,** Railway Station. Their office dispenses free maps and brochures on the town and area and operates tours. Also available is a full range of tourist services, including accommodation references and car rental. In summer, the office is open daily from 9 a.m. to 6 p.m. In winter, hours are daily from 9 a.m. to 4 p.m. Guided tours of the city leave from the Railway Station daily. In summer open-top double-decker buses leave every 15 minutes. The tour can be a 45-minute panoramic ride, or you can get off at any of the stops in the city. The ticket, costing £3.50 ($6.15), is valid all day.

WHERE TO STAY

An inn-collector's gem, the **Rose and Crown,** Harnham Road, Salisbury, Wiltshire SP2 8JQ (tel. 0722/27908), 1½ miles from the heart of town by the A3094, is an unspoiled, half-timbered, 13th-century hostelry. The River Avon winds its way within a few feet of the Rose and Crown, and beyond the water you can see the tall spire of the cathedral. The lawns and gardens between the inn and the river are shaded by old trees, and chairs are set out so you can enjoy the view and count the swans. The inn, part of the Queens Moat House Hotels chain, contains both a new and an old wing. The new wing is modern, but to me, the old wing is more appealing, with its sloping ceilings, and antique fireplaces and furniture. Each unit has a private bath. A single rents for £61 ($106.75) daily, a double or twin with bath goes for £88 ($154), including an English breakfast, service, and VAT. You can have lunch overlooking the river. The fare is English. A set luncheon goes for £8.50 ($14.90) and a dinner from £12 ($21). Across the courtyard (where there's free parking) are two taverns. You can easily walk over the arched stone bridge to the center of Salisbury from here in ten minutes or so.

Grasmere, 70 Harnham Rd., Salisbury, Wiltshire SP2 8JN (tel. 0722/338388), is a late Victorian house beautifully restored and operated by the previously recommended Rose and Crown. It stands near the confluence of the Nadder and Avon rivers in 1½ acres of grounds. Constructed in 1896 for Salisbury merchants, the house still suggests a family home. Architectural features were retained as much as possible, including a "calling box" for servants in the dining room. Grasmere rents only five bedrooms, but each is rather luxuriously furnished and contains private baths. A trio of them overlook the Cathedral, a view witnessed by John Constable. Singles rent for £30 ($52.50) nightly, with doubles going for £48 ($84).

White Hart, 1 St. John's St., Salisbury, Wiltshire SP1 2SD (tel. 0722/27476), combines the best of the old and the new worlds. The White Hart has been a Salisbury landmark since Georgian times. Its classic façade is intact, with tall columns crowning a life-size effigy of a hart. The older accommodations are traditional, but a new part has been added making a total of 68 bedrooms. It's in the rear, opening onto a large car park—like a motel. New-wing units are tastefully conceived and decorated. The highest prices are charged from April to the end of October. Singles cost from £56 ($98) daily and doubles from £72 ($126). Service and VAT are included in the tariffs. You can have your before-dinner drink in Wavell's Bar, followed by a meal for around £11.25 ($19.70).

King's Arms Hotel, 9 St. John's St., Salisbury, Wiltshire SP1 2SB (tel. 0722/27629), is a former coaching inn, in black-and-white Tudor style, with leaded-glass windows, an old pub sign out front, and a covered entrance, formerly a coach setting-down point. It is unsophisticated without being self-consciously so. The King's Arms charges from £34 ($59.50) daily for a single room, from £50 ($87.50) for a double with bath and separate shower. A special feature of the hotel is the William and Mary four-poster suite. No one seems to know the age of the inn, although it is generally recognized that it was built at the same time as the cathedral. Conspirators helping Charles II flee to France were thought to have met here in the mid-17th century. The hotel contains fine old oak beams, the original ironwork, a priest's hiding hole, and the Elizabethan fireplace. Have a pint of ale in the oak-beamed pub, sitting in a high-backed settle, warming yourself in front of the open fire.

Cathedral Hotel, 7 Milford St., Salisbury, Wiltshire SP1 2AJ (tel. 0722/20144), is in the heart of Salisbury, across the street from the old Red Lion. An 18th-century building, it lies near the cathedral and shops, and is family owned and managed. Its bedrooms have been renovated, and all 30 of them have color TVs, radios, direct-dial phones, and intercoms, and most have private baths. Singles are priced at £26 ($45.50) daily, and doubles rent for £60 ($105). The rooms are large and well furnished and maintained. Add to that an elevator to take your luggage upstairs, plus helpful personnel, and you have a good place to stay, with a full English breakfast, VAT, and service charge included in the rates. The Cathedral Bar, with traditional pub atmosphere, serves a hot and cold buffet at lunchtime, and the restaurant offers good food. You can have drinks in either the Cathedral Bar or the Milford Lounge Bar.

The New Inn, 43 New St., Salisbury, Wiltshire SP1 2PH (tel. 0722/27679), is an upmarket B&B, one of the finest in Salisbury. But, contrary to its name, it isn't new at all. It's a 15th-century building whose walled garden backs up to the Cathedral Close wall. The center of the inn is the serving bar, which is a common counter for three outer rooms—one, a tiny sitting area; another, a tavern with high-backed settles and a fireplace, and the third, a lounge. In addition to serving food and drink, it rents eight bedrooms, each attractively and comfortably furnished, with a private bath. Only nonsmokers are accepted, however. B&B costs from £30 ($52.50) daily in a single, rising to £40 ($70) to £46 ($80.50) in a double.

WHERE TO DINE

The best restaurant in town is **Crustaceans,** 2 Ivy St. (tel. 0722/333948), which, as the name suggests, specializes in fish. From the north of Scotland all the way to the Isles of Scilly (off the coast of Cornwall), an array of fresh fish tempts diners nightly except Sunday from 7 to 10:30 p.m. Meals cost from £20 ($35) and up, and reservations are needed. Roy Thwaites makes good use of the fish he buys, and tries to preserve its flavor while awakening the tastebuds with various sauces and means of preparation. Lemon and Dover sole are specialties. But you'll find the complete array of fish here, everything from langoustines and tiger prawns to Devonshire turbot.

Haunch of Venison, Minster Street (tel. 0722/22024), deserves its popularity. Right in the heart of Salisbury, this creaky-timbered, 1320 chophouse serves some excellent dishes, especially English roasts and grills. Stick to its specialties and you'll rarely go wrong. Diners with more adventurous palates will sample a bowl of game soup. The pièce de résistance of the inn is its local New Forest haunch of venison, with chestnut purée and red-currant jelly. Meals cost from £12 ($21) up. For a bargain lunch, enjoy the bar snacks, including game pie made with venison. The centuries have given a gleam to the oak furnishings, and years of polishing have worn down the brass. Twisting steps lead to tiny, cozy rooms (there is one small room with space for about four to sit where you can saturate yourself in the best of England's yesterdays and todays). Two windows of the barroom overlook St. Thomas's cloisters. Dancing fires are kept burning in the old fireplace; heavy beams are overhead; antique chairs encircle the tables. The restaurant is open daily for lunch from noon to 2 p.m. and in the evening from 7 to 10:30 p.m., except Sunday night when only the bar is open and no food is served.

On the Outskirts

Silver Plough, Pitton, near Salisbury (tel. 072272/266), lies just off the A30 road from London to Salisbury. Originally a farmhouse, it's a pretty country pub with a restaurant added. The pub has a reputation for country wines and English cheeses. You can sup at least 17 varieties and eat home-baked cottage loaves with a wide selection of cheese for your lunch, in the beamed lounge bar, hung with tankards, coachhorns, and other country memorabilia. In addition to the cheese served for lunch in the pub, the restaurant is also open. The bar, incidentally, serves a full snack menu of homemade dishes, featuring steak-and-kidney pie, grilled steak, and various pastas. There is also a dining room, where the chef does succulent grills and roasts for the set meals or else provides you with an à la carte dinner. He prepares smoked salmon, pheasant, and fish dishes. The owners pride themselves on providing everything from a simple ploughman's lunch to a full meal, a set dinner costing from £17.50 ($30.65). Hours are 11:30 a.m. to 2:30 p.m. and 6:30 to 10 p.m. daily. The Silver Plough has known many famous visitors, but apart from displaying a signed letter from Queen Victoria, the management prefers to stick to its quiet country atmosphere and to concentrate on making its guests feel at home.

SIDE TRIPS FROM SALISBURY

In this area rich in reminders of England's heritage, traces have been found of human occupation long beyond the dawn of history—Neolithic man, Iron Age habitation, Romans, Saxons, Danes, Normans, and English people of today, all have left their mark on the land and can be visited during your stay at Salisbury.

Old Sarum

About 2 miles north of Salisbury off the A345 is Old Sarum (tel. 0722/335398), the remains of what is believed to have been an Iron Age fortification. The earthworks were known to the Romans as Sorbiodunum, and later to the Saxons. The Normans, in fact, built a cathedral and a castle in what was then a walled town of the Middle Ages. Parts of the old cathedral were disassembled to erect the cathedral at New Sarum. It is open daily from 10 a.m. to 6 p.m. from Good Friday to the end of September; from 10 a.m. to 4 p.m. off-season. Closed Monday.

Wilton House

In the town of Wilton, less than three miles to the west of Salisbury, is one of England's great country estates, Wilton House (tel. 0722/743115), the home of the Earl of Pembroke. The stately house dates from the 16th century, but has seen modifications over the years, as late as Victoria's day. It is noted for its 17th-century state rooms by Inigo Jones. Many famous personages have either lived at or visited Wilton. It is believed that Shakespeare's troupe entertained here. Plans for the D-Day landings at Normandy were laid out here by Eisenhower and his advisers, in the utmost secrecy, with only the silent Van Dycks in the Double Cube room as witnesses. The house is filled with beautifully maintained furnishings and displays some of the finest paintings in England, including works by Rembrandt, Rubens, and Reynolds. There are exhibitions of 7,000 model soldiers; the Pembroke Palace dollhouse; a historic tableau of dolls and toys through the ages, together with a unique collection of tiny dolls' clothes; and a 400-foot-square model railway with models of

Salisbury Cathedral and Wilton House. There is also a huge adventure play
for children.

The estate lies in the midst of 20 acres of grounds, with giant cedars of Lebanon, the oldest of which were planted in 1630. The Palladian Bridge was built in
1737 by the ninth Earl of Pembroke and Roger Morris. Wilton House can be visited
from Easter to mid-October, Tuesday to Saturday and on bank holiday Mondays
from 11 a.m. to 6 p.m. and on Sunday from 1 to 6 p.m. Last admission is 5:15 p.m.
Guided tours are given daily except Sunday and special days. Admission to the house
and grounds is £2.40 ($4.20) for adults, £2 ($3.50) for children. An inclusive ticket
to the house, grounds, and exhibitions is £3.40 ($5.95) for adults, £2.50 ($4.40) for
children.

Stonehenge

Two miles west of Amesbury, at the junction of the A303 and the A344/A360,
and about nine miles north of Salisbury is the renowned Stonehenge, believed to be
anywhere from 3,500 to 5,000 years old. This huge circle of lintels and megalithic
pillars is the most important prehistoric monument in Britain.

Some Americans have expressed their disappointment after seeing the concen-
tric circles of stones. Admittedly, they are not the pyramids, and some imagination
has to be brought to bear on them. Pyramids or not, they represent an amazing engineering feat. Many of the boulders, the bluestones in particular, were moved many
miles (perhaps from southern Wales) to this site by the ancients. If you're more fanciful, you can always credit Merlin with delivering them on clouds from Ireland.

The widely held view of the 18th- and 19th-century romantics that Stonehenge
was the work of the Druids is without foundation. The boulders, many weighing
several tons, are believed to have predated the arrival in Britain of that Celtic cult.
Recent excavations continue to bring new evidence to bear on the origin and purpose of Stonehenge. Controversy surrounds the prehistoric site especially since the
publication of *Stonehenge Decoded* by Gerald S. Hawkins and John B. White, which
maintains that Stonehenge was an astronomical observatory—that is, a Neolithic
"computing machine" capable of predicting eclipses.

Others who discount this theory adopt Henry James's approach to Stonehenge, which regards it as "lonely in history," its origins and purposes (burial
ground? sunworshipping site? human sacrificial temple?) the secret of the silent,
mysterious Salisbury Plain.

Admission is £1.60 ($2.80) for adults, 80p ($1.40) for children. From Good
Friday to September 30, hours are daily from 10 a.m. to 6 p.m. From October to
Maundy Thursday, hours are daily from 10 a.m. to 4 p.m. Your ticket permits you to
go inside the fence surrounding the site to protect the stones from vandals and souvenir hunters. You can go all the way up to a short rope barrier about 50 feet from the
stones. If you don't have a car, you can take a bus from the Salisbury train station.
There are also organized bus tours out of Salisbury.

Longleat House

Between Bath and Salisbury, Longleat House (tel. 09853/551), owned by the
sixth Marquess of Bath, lies four miles southwest of Warminster, 4½ miles southeast
of Frome on the A362. The first view of this magnificent Elizabethan house, built in
the early Renaissance style, is romantic enough, but the wealth of paintings and furnishings within its lofty rooms is enough to dazzle.

A tour of the house, from the Elizabethan Great Hall, through the Library, the
State Rooms, and the Grand Staircase, is awe-inspiring in its variety and splendor.
The State Dining Room is full of silver and plate, and fine tapestries and paintings
adorn the walls in rich profusion. The Library represents the finest private collection
in the country. The Victorian kitchens are open during the summer months, offering a glimpse of life below the stairs in a well-ordered country home. Various exhibitions are mounted in the Stable Yard. Events are staged frequently in the grounds,

and the Safari Park contains a vast array of animals in open parklands, including Britain's only white tiger.

A maze, believed to be the largest in the world, was added to the attractions by Lord Weymouth, son of the marquess. It has more than 1½ miles of paths among yew trees. The first part is comparatively easy, but the second part is very complicated, with bridges adding to the confusion. It knocks the Hampton Court maze into a cocked hat, as the British say.

Longleat House is open daily from 10 a.m. to 6 p.m. from Easter to the end of September, to 4 p.m. the rest of the year. Safari Park is open mid-March to early November from 10 a.m. to 6 p.m. (last cars admitted at 5:30 p.m. or sunset if earlier). Admission to Longleat House is around £3 ($5.25), £1 ($1.75) for children. The Safari Park costs around £3.80 ($6.65) for adults, £2.50 ($4.40) for children. Special exhibitions and rides require separate admission tickets. Discount tickets for all attractions cost £8 ($14) for adults, £5 ($8.75) for children.

Stourhead

After Longleat, you can drive six miles down Rte. 3092 to Stourton, a village just off the B3092, three miles northwest of Mere (A303). Stourhead (tel. 0747/840348), a Palladian house, was created in the 18th century by the banking family of Hoare. The magnificent gardens became known as *le jardin anglais* in that they blended art and nature. Set around an artificial lake, the grounds are decorated with temples, bridges, islands, and grottoes, as well as statuary. The house is open from March 25 to November 5. Hours are 2 to 6 p.m. Saturday to Wednesday from March 25 to April 1 and October 1 to November 5. From May to the end of September, it is also open on Thursday from 2 to 6 p.m. It's always closed on Friday. Last admission is at 5:30 p.m. Admission is £2.50 ($4.40) for adults and £1.30 ($2.30) for children 5 to 16. The gardens are open daily from 8 a.m. to 7 p.m. (until dusk if earlier) all year. Admission to the gardens is £2 ($3.50) for adults and £1 ($1.75) for children. In May and June, adults are charged £2.50 ($4.40), and children pay £1.30 ($2.30). From November to February, admission is £1.50 ($2.65) for adults, 70p ($1.25) for children.

Avebury

One of the largest prehistoric sites in Europe, Avebury lies about six miles west of Marlborough, on the Kennet River. It gained in popularity with visitors once the government had to rope off the sarsen circle at Stonehenge (see above). Explorers are able to walk the 28-acre site at Avebury, winding in and out of the circle of more than 100 stones, some weighing up to 50 tons. They are made of sarsen, a sandstone found in Wiltshire. Inside this large circle are two smaller ones, each with about 30 stones standing upright. Native Neolithic tribes are believed to have built these circles. The village of Avebury, some of which is in the ownership of the National Trust, has been called the Ancient Capital of England.

Dating from before the Conquest, **Avebury Manor** (tel. 06723/203) was built on the site of a Benedictine cell. An early Elizabethan manor house, it stands beside the great stone circle of Avebury. Original oak-paneled rooms and plasterwork ceilings, fine oak furniture, and early paintings fill the house. The manor is steeped in history. The attic and anterooms have been chosen to take you back in time. There you will see wax figures of the notorious William Sharington, the staunch royalist Sir John Stawell, and Sir Richard Holford, all once owners of the house. Additional attractions include Sir John Stawell's armory, supplied by the Tower of London. Replica jewelry and dress of the Elizabethan period, artifacts of torture, and exhibitions of civil war arms are displayed. Within the grounds, visitors can see an Elizabethan market square full of craft workshops, music-making minstrels, jugglers, strolling players, lords and ladies, and jesters. There is also an adventure playground, plus falconry demonstrations. Surrounding gardens and parkland are equally intriguing. The manor is open from 11:30 a.m. to 6 p.m. Monday to

Saturday and 1:30 to 6 p.m. Sunday from March 24 to October 8. Admission is £3.50 ($6.15) for adults, £2.50 ($4.40) for children 4 to 14. The manor lies 1½ miles from the A4 London-to-Bath road, 9 miles from junction 15 (Swindon exit) on the M4, and 6 miles from Marlborough.

Avebury Museum (tel. 0672/3250), founded by Alexander Keiller, houses one of Britain's most important archeological collections. It began with Keiller's material from excavations at Windmill Hill and Avebury, and now includes artifacts from other prehistoric digs at West Kennet, Long Barrow, Silbury Hill, West Kennet Avenue, and the Sanctuary. It is open from 10 a.m. to 6 p.m. from Good Friday to the end of September; from 10 a.m. to 4 p.m. off-season. Closed Monday. Admission is 80p ($1.40) for adults and 40p (70¢) for children.

The **Great Barn Museum of Wiltshire Folk Life** (tel. 06723/555), housed in a 17th-century thatched barn, is a center for the display and interpretation of Wiltshire life during the last three centuries. There are displays on cheese making, blacksmithing, thatching, sheep and shepherds, the wheelwright and other rural crafts, as well as local geology and domestic life. From mid-March to the end of October, it is open daily from 10 a.m. to 5:30 p.m. The remainder of the year, it is open on Saturday from 1 to 4:30 p.m. and on Sunday from 11 a.m. to 4:30 p.m. Admission is 95p ($1.65) for adults, 50p (90¢) for children, and £2.25 ($3.95) for a family ticket.

After sightseeing—and still in the same vicinity—you may be ready for a bite to eat. The **Stones Restaurant,** High Street (tel. 06723/514), has made an impact on the palates in the area since its opening in 1984 by Dr. Hilary Howard and Michael Pitts. They specialize in freshly made, original, high-quality food (no additives), served in friendly and attractive surroundings at reasonable prices. You can have a meal for around £5 ($8.75), including drinks. A wide range of cakes, desserts, and cold savories is available throughout the day, supplemented at lunchtime by a full hot-food menu, which can be accompanied by the local prize-winning ale, Wadsworth's 6X. Other drinks are available, including coffee, tea by the pot, fruit juices, and bottled beer. There is an exceptional range of handmade unpasteurized English and Welsh cheeses. In summer, queues get long at lunchtime, so it's best to arrive early (lunch starts at noon), and to avoid Sunday lunchtime entirely. Cream teas at Stones are famous, with their own scones and jam plus clotted cream brought from Cornwall. Stones is open April to mid-October from 10 a.m. to 6 p.m. seven days a week.

2. Castle Combe

Once voted Britain's prettiest village, Castle Combe was used for location shots for *Dr. Dolittle,* with Rex Harrison. About 9½ miles from Bath, this little Cotswold village is filled with shops selling souvenirs and antiques. The village cottages are often set beside a trout stream, and are made of stone with roofs laden with moss. The church is unremarkable except for its 15th-century tower. An old market cross and a triple-arched bridge are much photographed.

FOOD AND LODGING

Set in 26 acres of gardens and parkland, the **Manor House,** Castle Combe, Wiltshire SN14 7HR (tel. 0249/782206) is on a country estate whose original manor was a 14th-century baronial seat in Castle Combe. To the south, the lawns sweep down to the trout-stocked Bybrook River where fishing is permitted for a fee. Antiques and period pieces adorn the oak-paneled public rooms, with the main lounge having an 18th-century frieze depicting Shakespeare's Falstaff. The 35 bedrooms, all with private baths or showers, are individually furnished. Some are in the Cotswold Mews cottages at the entrance to the grounds. A double costs £75

($131.25) to £125 ($218.75) daily, and a single goes for £65 ($113.75). The hotel offers an extensive menu, with dinner costing from £23.50 ($41.15). Although casual informality prevails during the day, the general manager requests that men wear jackets and ties for dinner. The hotel has an outdoor heated swimming pool and an all-year tennis court.

3. Lacock

This is a National Trust village, with a 13th-century abbey in ruins and adjoining 16th-century houses and gardens. Within an easy drive of Bath, it contains a delightful 14th-century inn, **Sign of the Angel,** 6 Church St., Lacock, Wiltshire SN15 2LA (tel. 024973/230), ideal for a meal. This small inn offers good meals in an atmosphere that makes one feel he or she has stepped back into Shakespeare's time. Before an open fire on nippy days, food is served under a heavily beamed ceiling. Roasts are often featured on the menu. A set dinner runs from £20 ($35) per person, and a reservation is essential. Lunch is served from 1 to 1:30 p.m. and dinner from 7:30 to 8 p.m. (one sitting only). The Sign of the Angel is closed for luncheon on Saturday and for dinner on Sunday (also it shuts down for the Christmas holidays). In addition, you'll find six "quaint" rooms, some with patchwork quilts and all with private baths. Bed and full English breakfast ranges from £45 ($78.75) daily per person to £70 ($122.50) in a double room, including VAT and service. In all, it's an overnight stop that can be one of lasting memories (no guests under 12 are permitted, however).

SOMERSET

When writing about Somerset, it's difficult to avoid sounding like the editor of *The Countryside Companion,* waxing poetic over hills and valleys, dale and field. The shire embraces some of nature's most masterly scenic touches in England. Mendip's limestone hills undulate across the countryside (ever had a pot-holing holiday?). The irresistible Quantocks are the pride of the west, especially lovely in spring and fall. Here, too, is the heather-clad **Exmoor National Park,** a wooded area abounding in red deer and wild ponies, much of its moorland 1,200 feet above sea level. Somerset opens onto the Bristol Channel, with Minehead the chief resort, catering primarily to the English.

Somerset is rich in legend and history, and is particularly fanciful about its associations with King Arthur and Queen Guinevere, along with Camelot and Alfred the Great. Its villages are noted for the tall towers of their parish churches.

A quiet, unspoiled life characterizes Somerset. You're likely to end up in an ivy-covered old inn, talking with the regulars, and being served broiled salmon that night by the fireside. Or you may stop at a large estate that stands in a woodland setting, surrounded by bridle paths and sheep walks (Somerset was once a great wool center). Maybe you'll settle down in a 16th-century thatched stone farmhouse, set in the midst of orchards in a vale. Somerset is reputed (and I heartily concur) to have the best cider anywhere. When you lounge under a shady Somerset apple tree, downing a tankard of refreshingly chilled golden cider, all the types you've drunk in the past taste like apple juice.

My notes on Somerset, accumulated over many a year, would easily fill a book. But because space is limited I've confined myself in the main to just some of the highlights.

4. Exmoor National Park

The far west of Somerset forms most of the Exmoor National Park. In addition to the moor, the park includes the wooded valleys of the Rivers Exe and Barle, the Brendon Hills, and the sweeping stretch of coast from Minehead to the boundary of Devon. This is more of the land of Blackmore's *Lorna Doone*. You can walk up Badgworthy Water from Malmsmead to Doone Valley, divided by the Somerset-Devon line, or visit tiny Oare Church and see the window through which Carver Doone shot Lorna at her wedding. The moors, which rise to 1,707 feet at Dunkery Beacon, are inviting to walkers and pony trekkers, with ponies and wild deer roaming freely.

Visit England's smallest complete church at Culbone and the centuries-old clapper bridge over the River Barle at Tarr Steps. Some of England's prettiest villages are within the national park, and some lie along its borders. Selworthy, an idyllic little town, is in Exmoor, as is Allerford, with its pack-horse bridge and its walnut tree, both of them owned and preserved by the National Trust.

Minehead, a fine resort, is just outside the park's northeastern boundary, but in some ways, the little villages which have that town as a focal point have more charm.

Below are recommendations for those wishing to prolong their visit to this area.

BILBROOK

Near Washford, **Dragon House,** Bilbrook, Somerset TA24 6HQ (tel. 0984/40215), is reached by driving from the A39 a short distance southeast of Minehead, then through a wide gateway into the inn's driveway and walking into the charming house, with a comfortable lounge and cozy bar. Everything is spotlessly clean, with old furniture lovingly polished and gleaming in the firelight. The beamed bedrooms are individually furnished in country-cottage style, with good beds and some antiques. One has a half-tester bed. All the units have a radio, and some also have TV. Most of the rooms have a bath or shower and views over the moors or the garden. From the elegant hall, an ancient staircase leads to a gallery around the first floor off which many of the bedrooms open. Staircases lead to other units with dormer windows in the roof. B&B is £28 ($49) daily in a single, £62 ($108.50) in a double. At lunchtime, excellent bar meals are served. For dinner in the antique-furnished dining room, a good selection is offered on the à la carte menu, including local trout with white wine sauce or honey-roast duck taken off the bone. An à la carte four-course dinner goes for £15 ($26.25).

MIDDLECOMBE

About 1½ miles west of Minehead on the A39, **Periton Park,** Middlecombe, Minehead, Somerset TA24 8SW (tel. 0643/6885), is reached by a long, winding drive through rhododendron clumps and tall trees. The Victorian house is set high above its 30 acres of pasture and woodland. The house has seven units for guests, each with its own character. Perhaps you'll be fortunate enough to have the spacious ground-floor quarters from which you can walk in the garden without disturbing the rest of the house. An overnight stay here costs £48 ($84) daily in a single, £66 ($115.50) in a double. Dinner is another £15 ($26.25). Breakfast, which you can order the night before, is served in your room.

WINSFORD

Actually in Exmoor National Park but near Minehead is the **Royal Oak Inn,** Winsford, Somerset TA24 7JE (tel. 064385/455). This thatched 15th-century inn facing the village green is to many the epitome of West Country inns, catering to a farming-hunting-shooting population from near and far. If you're there on a Tuesday, you get a sense of the requirements and nature of local farmers and residents through observation of those who attend a meeting of the National Westminster Bank officials in a part of the lounge. In season, the bar and restaurant teem with elegantly dressed hunters and shooters who descend on the moors annually, interspersed with locals in sensible tweeds, moor-walkers with backpacks and heavy boots, and tourists trying to blend into the landscape. Double rooms with bath cost from £60 ($105) per night, with breakfast included. Perhaps you might prefer the Royal Oak Suite if it's available; minor royalty often stays here, and the charge is £100 ($175) for two. Some rooms are across the courtyard. The restaurant offers such selections as fisherman's pot and a choice of fresh or saltwater fish. Roast rack of Exmoor lamb is a specialty. Meals cost from £17 ($29.75).

5. Dunster

The village of Dunster lies in Somerset near the eastern edge of Exmoor National Park, three miles southeast of Minehead, just off the A39. It grew up around the original Dunster Castle, constructed as a fortress for the de Mohun family whose progenitor came to England with William the Conqueror. The village, about four miles from the Cistercian monastery at Cleeve, has an ancient priory church and dovecote, a 17th-century gabled Yarn Market, and little cobbled streets along which whitewashed cottages gleam proudly.

FOOD AND LODGING

On the site of what has been a hostelry for weary travelers for more than 600 years, **Luttrell Arms,** 36 High St., Dunster, Somerset TA24 6SG (tel. 0643/821555), is the outgrowth of a guesthouse the Cistercian abbots at Cleeve had built in the village of Dunster. It was named for the Luttrell lords of the manor, who bought Dunster Castle and the property attached to it in the 14th century. The hotel has, of course, been provided with the amenities expected by modern travelers, but from its stone porch to the 15th-century Gothic hall with hammer-beam roof (now divided), it still retains a feeling of antiquity. The 25 bedrooms, all with private baths or showers, are for the most part comfortably appointed and attractively decorated in keeping with the hotel's long history. Four of the accommodations have four-poster beds. Singles rent for £56 ($98) daily, and doubles, for £78 ($136.50). A lounge is upstairs, while downstairs you can enjoy a drink in the Tudor-timbered bar, with its large inglenook fireplace. This was once the kitchen of the hostelry. A meal in the dining room, costing from £12 ($21), can be ordered from a varied menu. Depending on the season, you might choose guinea fowl or baked sugared ham with Somerset cider sauce. A buffet lunch is offered Monday to Saturday. You can also order bar food.

DUNSTER CASTLE

On a tor (high hill) from which you can see the Bristol Channel, Dunster Castle (tel. 0643/821314) stands on the site of a Norman castle granted to William de Mohun of Normandy by William the Conqueror shortly after the conquest of England. The 13th-century gateway built by the de Mohuns is all that remains of the original fortress. In 1376 the castle and its lands were bought by Lady Elizabeth Luttrell and belonged to her family until given to the National Trust in 1976, together with 30 acres of surrounding parkland. The first castle was largely demolished during the Civil War, and the present Dunster Castle is a Jacobean house built in the lower ward of the original fortifications in 1620, then rebuilt by Salvin in 1870 to look like a castle. Terraced walks and gardens command good views of Exmoor and the Quantock Hills.

Outstanding among the contents within are the 17th-century panels of embossed painted and gilded leather depicting the story of Antony and Cleopatra, and a remarkable allegorical 16th-century portrait of Sir John Luttrell shown wading naked through the sea with a female figure of peace and a wrecked ship in the background. The 17th-century plasterwork ceilings of the dining room and staircase and the finely carved staircase balustrade of cavorting huntsmen, hounds, and stags are also particularly noteworthy. The castle and grounds can be visited from April to the end of September every day except Friday and Saturday from 11 a.m. to 5 p.m. (last admission at 4:30 p.m.). In October it is open daily except Friday and Saturday from 2 to 4 p.m. (last admission at 3:30 p.m.). Admission to both the castle and grounds is £3 ($5.25) for adults, £1.50 ($2.65) for children. To the grounds only, admission is £1.50 ($2.65) for adults, 50p (90¢) for children.

COMBE SYDENHAM HALL

Between Dunster and Taunton, on the B3188 just south of Monksilver, you can visit Combe Sydenham Hall (tel. 0984/56284), which was the home of Elizabeth Sydenham, wife of Sir Francis Drake. It stands on the ruins of monastic buildings that were associated with nearby Cleeve Abbey. At the hall, you can see a cannon ball that legend says halted the wedding of Lady Elizabeth to a rival suitor in 1585. The gardens include Lady Elizabeth's Walk, which circles around ponds originally laid out when the knight was courting his bride-to-be. The valley ponds are fed by springwater full of rainbow trout (ask about the fly-fishing and tuition). Woodland walks are possible to Long Meadow with its host of wildflowers. Also to be seen are a deserted hamlet whose population reputedly was wiped out by the Black Death and a historic corn mill, presently being restored. In the hall's tea room, smoked trout and pâté are produced on oak chips, as in days of yore, and there are a shop and car park. The hall is open from 11 a.m. to 4 p.m. in July, August, and September and from 11 a.m. to 3 p.m. April, May, June, and October except on Saturday and Sunday. The country park hours are from 11 a.m. to 6 p.m. in July, August, and September, from 11 a.m. to 5 p.m. April, May, June, and October except on Saturday. Admission is £2.20 ($3.85) for adults, £1.50 ($2.65) for children.

Combe Sydenham is five miles south of Watchet on the B3188 road between Monksilver and Elsworthy. Incidentally, it was from Watchet, a few miles east of Minehead along the coast, that Coleridge's Ancient Mariner sailed.

COLERIDGE COTTAGE

Across the Quantock Hills to the east of the area just previewed, the hamlet of Nether Stowey lies on the A39, at the northern edge of Quantock Forest. Here you can visit Coleridge Cottage (tel. 0278/732662), home of Samuel Taylor Coleridge when he wrote *The Rime of the Ancient Mariner*. During his 1797–1800 sojourn here, he and his friends, William Wordsworth and sister Dorothy, enjoyed exploring the Quantock woods. The cottage, at the west end of Nether Stowey on the south side of the A39 and eight miles west of Bridgwater, has its parlor and reading room open to visitors from April to the end of September from 2 to 5 p.m. Tuesday to Thursday and on Sunday. Admission to the National Trust property is £1 ($1.75).

---

6. Taunton

The historic county town of Somerset in the Vale of Taunton Deane, Taunton is one of the best centers for exploring West Somerset. Taunton Castle was the scene of Judge Jeffreys' Bloody Assize after the end of the Monmouth rebellion at the Battle of Sedgemoor. The castle dates from the 11th and 12th centuries, and the east gatehouse is now a hotel (see below). The castle also houses a museum (look for the picture of Judge Jeffreys in the Great Hall). Even more interesting than the castle is the Church of St. Mary Magdalene, with its soaring tower, completed in 1514.

FOOD AND LODGING

Beauty and history are combined at the **Castle Hotel,** Castle Green, Taunton, Somerset TA1 1NF (tel. 0823/272671), in the center of Taunton. Nature lovers usually opt for one of this establishment's four garden suites, whose windows look out over a landscape originally designed in the 12th century. The plantings and nearby archeological ruins are not the only attraction here. Some of the hotel's thick walls were built as part of a Norman fortress. Later architects designed the newer sections in a crenellated pattern whose windows barely peek out from behind cascades of climbing wisteria. The 35 bedrooms benefit from a recent upgrading, which filled most with softly upholstered, tasteful furniture and many amenities of modern life. The Chapman family charges £52 ($91) daily in a single, £89 ($155.75) in a double. After an apéritif in the Rose Room, you can head for the elegant restaurant. There the chef applies French-inspired nouvelle cuisine techniques to traditional English ingredients for such imaginative specialties as rabbit pithivier, red mullet, and succulent lamb, beef, and venison dishes. Open daily, the restaurant charges £10.50 ($18.40) to £21 ($36.75) for fixed-price lunches and dinners, or else you might pay up to £35 ($61.25) for an elaborate à la carte meal. Hours are from 7:45 a.m. to 10 p.m. Monday to Saturday, 8:15 a.m. to 10 p.m. Sunday.

7. Glastonbury

The goal of the medieval pilgrim, **Glastonbury Abbey** (tel. 0458/32267), once one of the wealthiest and most prestigious monasteries in England, is no more than a ruined sanctuary today. But it provides Glastonbury's claim to historical greatness, an assertion augmented by legendary links to such figures as Joseph of Arimathea, King Arthur, Queen Guinevere, and St. Patrick.

It is said that Joseph of Arimathea journeyed to what was then the Isle of Avalon, with the Holy Grail in his possession. According to tradition, he buried the chalice at the foot of the conically shaped Glastonbury Tor, and a stream of blood burst forth. (You can scale this more than 500-foot-high hill today, on which rests a 15th-century tower.)

At one point, the saint is said to have leaned against his staff, which immediately was transformed into a fully blossoming tree. A cutting alleged to have survived from the Holy Thorn can be seen on the abbey grounds today. It blooms at Christmastime. Some historians have traced this particular story back to Tudor times.

Joseph, so it goes, erected a church of wattle in Glastonbury. The town, in fact, may have had the oldest church in England, as excavations have shown.

The most famous link—popularized for Arthurian fans in the Victorian era by Tennyson—concerns the burial of King Arthur and Queen Guinevere on the abbey grounds. In 1191 the monks dug up the skeletons of two bodies on the south side of the Lady Chapel, said to be those of the king and queen. In 1278, in the presence of Edward I, the bodies were removed and transferred to a black marble tomb in the choir. Both the burial spot and the shrine are marked today.

A large Benedictine Abbey of St. Mary grew out of the early wattle church. St. Dunstan, who was born nearby, was the abbot in the 10th century, later becoming archbishop of Canterbury. Edmund, Edgar, and Edmund "Ironside," three early English kings, were buried at the abbey.

In 1184 a fire destroyed most of the abbey and its vast treasures. It was eventually rebuilt after much difficulty, only to be dissolved by Henry VIII. Its last abbot, Richard Whiting, was hanged by the neck at Glastonbury Tor. Like the Roman forum, the abbey for years later was used as a stone quarry.

The modern-day pilgrim to Glastonbury can visit the ruins of the Lady Chapel, linked by an Early English "Galilee" to the nave of the abbey. The best-preserved building on the grounds is a 14th-century octagonal Abbot's Kitchen, where oxen were once roasted whole to feed the wealthier of the pilgrims (that is, the biggest donors). You can visit the ruins and museum from 9:30 a.m. till dusk for £1 ($1.75) for adults, 50p (90¢) for children under 16.

Glastonbury may be one of the oldest inhabited sites in Britain. Excavations have revealed Iron Age lakeside villages on its periphery. Some of the discoveries dug up may be viewed in a little museum in the High Street.

After the destruction of its once-great abbey, the town lost prestige. It is a market town today. The ancient gatehouse entry to the abbey is a museum, its principal exhibit a scale model of the abbey and its community buildings as they stood in 1539, at the time of the dissolution.

SOMERSET RURAL LIFE MUSEUM

The history of the Somerset countryside over the last 100 or so years is explained in a museum, **Abbey Farm,** Chilkwell Street (tel. 0458/32903). The main part of the exhibition is Abbey Barn, the home barn of the abbey, built in 1370. The magnificent timbered roof, the stone tiles, and the sculptures outside, including the head of Edward III, make it special. There are also a Victorian farmhouse and various other exhibits illustrating farming in Somerset during the "horse age" and domestic and social life in Victorian times. In summer they have demonstrations of butter-making, weaving, basketwork—anything that has reference to the rural life of the country, now rapidly disappearing with the invention of the engine, the freezer, and the instant meal. The museum is open in summer from 10 a.m. to 5 p.m. Monday to Friday, from 2 p.m. to 6 p.m. Saturday and Sunday. Winter hours are from 2:30 to 5 p.m. daily. Admission is 70p ($1.25) for adults, 20p (35¢) for children.

FOOD AND LODGING

If you're one of the lucky few who can stay over in this town rich in history, you can lodge where the wealthy pilgrim of yore did.

The George & Pilgrims Inn, 1 High St., Glastonbury, Somerset BA6 9DP (tel. 0458/31146), is one of the few pre-Reformation hostelries still left in England. Once it offered hospitality to Glastonbury pilgrims; now it accepts modern travelers. In the center of town, the inn has a façade that looks like a medieval castle, with stone-mullioned windows with leaded glass. Some of the bedrooms are former monks' cells; others have four-posters, carved monuments of oak. You may be given the Henry VIII Room, where the king watched the burning of the abbey in 1539. The owners charge £38 ($66.50) daily for a single, from £50 ($87.50) to £70 ($122.50) in a double, all rooms with private bath, direct-dial phone, and TV. VAT and an English breakfast are included. You could be drawn to the old kitchen, which is now the Pilgrim's Bar with its old oak beams. Even if you don't stay over, you may want to stop in for lunch or dinner in the Georgian Restaurant to enjoy the à la carte or table d'hôte menus, both of which feature traditional local dishes, or homemade fare in the snackbar. A set luncheon goes for £9.50 ($16.65); a dinner, £15 ($26.25).

Number 3, 3 Magdalene St., Glastonbury, Somerset BA6 9EW (tel. 0458/32129). With the exception of Sunday at lunchtime, only dinner is served in this pleasant family-run restaurant. That makes an evening meal here something of an event for the loyal clientele of this Georgian-style dining room, run by John and Ann Tynan. Specialties include several lobster dishes (they have their own tanks), scallops in Smitain sauce topped with langoustine, loin of Somerset lamb served with orange-and-ginger sauce, venison with blackberry and port wine sauce, and wild Scottish salmon with lime sauce. There are also special vegetarian dishes. Fixed-price meals begin at £13 ($22.75) for Sunday lunch, £21 ($36.75) for dinner. A "super" wine list contains descriptions of each of the carefully selected vintages. There are two outdoor tables for warm-weather dining. The restaurant also has three cozy double bedrooms, tastefully and individually decorated and with private baths, costing £35 ($61.25) to £45 ($78.75) daily, breakfast included.

8. Wells

To the south of the Mendip Hills, the cathedral town of Wells is a medieval gem. It lies only 21 miles from Bath, 123 from London. Wells was a vital link in the Saxon kingdom of Wessex—that is, important in England long before the arrival of William the Conqueror. Once the seat of a bishopric, it was eventually toppled from its ecclesiastical hegemony by the rival city of Bath. But the subsequent loss of prestige has paid off handsomely in Wells today. After experiencing the pinnacle of prestige, it fell into a slumber—hence, much of its old look remains. Wells was named after wells in the town, which were often visited by pilgrims to Glastonbury in the hope that their gout could be eased by its supposedly curative waters.

The crowning achievement of the town is:

WELLS CATHEDRAL

Begun in the 12th century, Wells Cathedral is a well-preserved example of the Early English style of architecture. The medieval sculpture (six tiers of hundreds of statues recently restored) of its west front is without peer in England. The western façade was completed in the mid-13th century. The landmark central tower was erected in the 14th century, with its attractive fan vaulting attached later. The inverted arches were added to strengthen the top-heavy structure.

Much of the stained glass dates from the 14th century. The fan-vaulted Lady Chapel, also from the 14th century, is in the Decorated style. To the north is the vaulted Chapter House, built in the 13th century. Look also for a medieval astronomical clock in the north transept. There is no charge to enter the cathedral. However, visitors are asked to make voluntary donations of £1 ($1.75) for adults, 50p (90¢) for students and children. For information, telephone the cathedral offices (tel. 0749/74483).

After a visit to the cathedral, walk along its cloisters to the moated Bishop's Palace. The swans in the moat ring a bell when they are hungry. The Great Hall, built in the 13th century, is in ruins. Finally, the street known as the Vicars' Close is one of the most beautifully preserved streets in Europe.

WHERE TO STAY

Your best choice is the **Swan Hotel,** Sadler Street, Wells, Somerset BA5 2RX (tel. 0749/78877). Set behind a stucco façade on one of the town's main arteries, this place was originally built in the 15th century as a coaching inn. It faces the west front of Wells Cathedral. The inn offers 32 comfortable and attractive bedrooms, each with private bath, color TV, phone, and a refreshing color scheme. Several of the accommodations contain four-poster beds. Depending on the accommodation, singles cost from £45 ($78.75) daily, and doubles or twins run £63.50 ($111.15), with a full English breakfast included. The spacious and elegantly accessorized public rooms stretch out to the left and right of the entrance as you enter. Both ends contain a blazing and baronial fireplace, beamed ceilings, and paneling. The restaurant, the Bishop's Kitchen, is recommended separately.

Star Hotel, 14 High St., Wells, Somerset BA5 2SQ (tel. 0749/73055), had its origins somewhere in the 16th century, but it is best associated with the great coaching era. The cobbled carriageway is still a feature and leads to the dining room— once the stables. The hotel front was restored in the Georgian period. The hotel has been modernized, yet retains its old charm and unhurried pace. Copper and brass are extensively used for decoration, and several original stone walls and timbers have been exposed. A single costs from £25 ($43.75) daily with bath or shower, and a double with the same plumbing goes for £40 ($70). Tariffs include VAT and an English breakfast. The inn has a reputation for good food, a set dinner costing £9.95 ($17.40).

Crown Hotel, Market Place, Wells, Somerset BA5 2RP (tel. 0749/73457), was built in the 15th century as a coaching inn. In Elizabethan times it witnessed a number of additions. William Penn, the founder of Pennsylvania, preached from a bedroom window here in 1685. A plaque commemorating this is on the hotel wall. You'll find open beams in at least one of the bedrooms. All accommodations contain private bath and cost £30 ($52.50) to £34 ($59.50) daily in a single, £43 ($75.25) to £55 ($96.25) in a double. These terms include a full English breakfast and VAT. Tea/coffee-makers and color TV are in all the rooms. A cold buffet in the restaurant costs from £9 ($15.75) at lunch, a dinner in the evening going for £15 ($26.25). They also have a coffeeshop serving light snacks. The Crown is just two minutes from Wells Cathedral.

Red Lion Hotel, Market Place, Wells, Somerset BA5 2RP (tel. 0749/72616), is an early 15th-century coaching inn close to the cathedral and the Bishop's Palace. A bathless single costs £28 ($49) per day, a single with bath going for £31 ($54.25). Doubles are priced at £39 ($68.25) bathless, £45 ($78.75) with bath. The dining room serves good English cooking, charging £10.50 ($18.40) for dinner. There is a pretty courtyard with tables and chairs for bar snacks at lunch or an evening drink.

WHERE TO DINE

One of the leading choices is **The Bishop's Kitchen** (Ridènes Restaurant), the Swan Hotel, Sadler Street (tel. 0749/77312). Owned and operated by this previously recommended hotel, the restaurant is reached via a separate entrance that funnels in from an alleyway in back. Of the several cozy rooms, some are heated with stone-sided fireplaces. Many visitors claim that the most charming pub in town can be found here, and you might be tempted to linger for a drink before heading in for dinner. In a warmly decorated room redolent of antique paneling and beamed ceilings, you can enjoy full meals priced from £13.50 ($23.65) at dinner, but only £9 ($15.75) for lunch. These are served daily from 11:30 a.m. to 3 p.m. and 7 p.m. to midnight. Typical menu items include filet steak Diane, veal marsala, and darne of salmon.

9. The Caves of Mendip

The Caves of Mendip are two exciting natural sightseeing attractions in Somerset—the great caves of Cheddar and Wookey Hole, both easily reached by heading west out of Wells.

THE CAVES

After leaving Wells, you'll first come to **Wookey Hole** (tel. 0749/72243), less than two miles away, the source of the River Axe. In the first chamber of the caves you can see, as legend has it, the Witch of Wookey turned to stone. These caves are believed to have been inhabited by prehistoric people at least 60,000 years ago. Even in those days there was a housing problem, with hyenas moving in and upsetting real-estate values. A tunnel opened in 1975 leads to chambers unknown to early man and previously accessible only to divers.

In 1973 Madame Tussaud's bought the ravine and joined the celebrated caves and old paper mill into one remarkable sequence. Leaving the caves, you follow a canal path to the mill, where paper has been made by hand since the 17th century. Here you can watch the best-quality paper being made by skilled men according to the traditions of their ancient craft. Also in the mill is housed a "Fairground by Night" exhibition, an extraordinary and colorful assembly of relics from the world's fairgrounds, and Madame Tussaud's Cabinet of Curiosities, a re-creation of her traveling exhibition. Visit the seaside at the Edwardian Penny Pier Arcade, still using "old pennies." Adults pay £3.70 ($6.50) and children under 17 £2.60 ($4.55) for a guided tour lasting about two hours. Free parking is provided, and visitors can use a cafeteria and a picnic area. Wookey Hole is open every day from 9:30 a.m. to 5:30 p.m. in summer, from 10:30 a.m. to 4:30 p.m. in winter.

A short distance from Bath, Bristol, and Wells is the village of **Cheddar,** birthplace of Cheddar cheese. It lies at the foot of Cheddar Gorge. A climb up the 274 steps of Jacob's Ladder offers views of the Mendip Hills and over Somerset. On a clear day, you may even see as far as Wales. Within the gorge are the **Cheddar Showcaves,** with impressive formations and a museum displaying prehistoric artifacts dating from when the caves were the home of Cheddar Man, whose skeleton is also on display. The caves are open all year except Christmas Eve and Christmas Day. Hours are from 10 a.m. to 5:30 p.m. Easter to the end of September, from 10:30 a.m. to 4:30 p.m. the remainder of the year. Admission to all attractions is £3.10 ($5.45) for adults, £1.70 ($3) for children. If you are more than 12 years of age, fit, and bold, you can take one of the Adventure Caving Expeditions. It costs £4.25 ($7.45) per person and takes you beyond the showcave on a tour of discovery lasting 1½ hours. Overalls, helmets, and lamps are supplied.

AVON

Avon is the name that has been given to the area around the old port of Bristol and the spa at Bath, an area that used to be in Somerset.

10. Bath

Victoria didn't start everything. In 1702 Queen Anne made the 115-mile trek from London to the mineral springs of Bath, thereby launching a fad that was to make the city the most celebrated spa in England. Of course, Victoria-come-lately eventually hiked up too, to sample a medicinal cocktail (which you can still do today), but Bath by then had passed its zenith.

The most famous personage connected with Bath's scaling the pinnacle of fashion was the 18th-century dandy, Beau Nash. He was the final arbiter of taste and manners (one example: he made dueling déclassé). The master of ceremonies of Bath, he cut a striking figure as he made his way across the city, with all the plumage of a bird of paradise. While dispensing (at a price) trinkets to the courtiers and aspirant gentlemen of his day, Beau was carted around in a liveried carriage. The gambler was given the proper setting for his considerable social talents by the 18th-century architects John Wood the Elder and his son. These architects designed a city of stone from the nearby hills, a feat so substantial and lasting that Bath today is the most harmoniously laid-out city in England.

Their work done, the Georgian city on a bend of the Avon River was to attract a following among leading political and literary figures—Dickens, Thackeray, Nelson, Pitt. Canadians may already know that General Wolfe lived on Trim Street, and Australians may want to visit the house at 19 Bennett St. where their founding father, Admiral Philip, lived. Even Henry Fielding came this way, observing in *Tom Jones* that the ladies of Bath "endeavour to appear as ugly as possible in the morning, in order to set off that beauty which they intend to show you in the evening."

Bath has had two lives. Long before its Queen Anne, Georgian, and Victorian popularity, it was known to the Romans as Aquae Sulis. The foreign legions founded their baths here (which may be visited today), so they might ease rheumatism in the curative mineral springs.

Remarkable restoration and careful planning have ensured that Bath retains its handsome look today. The city suffered devastating destruction from the infamous Baedeker air raids of 1942, when Luftwaffe pilots seemed more bent on bombing historical buildings than in hitting any military target.

THE SIGHTS

The major sights today are the abbey and the Pump Room and Roman baths. But if you're intrigued by architecture and city planning, you may want to visit some of the buildings, crescents, and squares. The North Parade, where Goldsmith lived, and the South Parade, where Fanny Burney (English novelist and diarist) once resided, represent harmony, the work of John Wood the Elder. The younger Wood, on the other hand, designed the Royal Crescent, an elegant half-moon row of town houses copied by Astor architects for their colonnade in New York City in the 1830s. Queen Square is one of the most beautiful (Jane Austen and Wordsworth used to live here—but hardly together), showing off quite well the work of Wood the Elder. And don't miss his Circus, built in 1754, as well as the shop-flanked Pulteney Bridge, designed by Robert Adam and compared aptly to the Ponte Vecchio of Florence.

Bath Abbey

Built on the site of a much larger Norman cathedral, the present-day abbey is a fine example of the late Perpendicular style. When Queen Elizabeth I came to Bath in 1574, she ordered that a national fund be set up to restore the abbey. The west front is the sculptural embodiment of a Jacob's Ladder dream of a 15th-century bishop. When you go inside and see its many windows, you'll understand why the abbey is called the "Lantern of the West." Note the superb fan vaulting, achieving at times a scalloped effect. Beau Nash was buried in the nave and is honored by a simple monument totally out of keeping with his flamboyant character.

Pump Room and Roman Baths

Founded in A.D. 75 by the Romans, the baths were dedicated to the goddess Sul Minerva. In their day they were an engineering feat, and even today are considered among the finest Roman remains in the country. They are still fed by the only hot spring water in Britain. After centuries of decay, the baths were rediscovered in Victoria's reign, and the site of the Temple of Sulis Minerva has been recently excavated and is now open to view. The museum connected to the baths contains many interesting objects from Victorian and recent digs (look for the head of Minerva). Coffee, lunch, and tea, usually with music from the Pump Room Trio, can be enjoyed in the 18th-century Pump Room, overlooking the hot springs. There's a drinking fountain serving hot mineral water. The Pump Room, Roman baths, excavations, and museum are open daily in summer from 9 a.m. to 6 p.m. In winter, hours are 9 a.m. to 5 p.m., on Sunday from 10 a.m. to 5 p.m. Admission is £2.70 ($4.75) for adults, £1.40 ($2.45) for children. For more information, phone 0225/461111) Monday to Friday.

Bath International Festival

Bath's graceful Georgian architecture provides the setting for one of Europe's most prestigious international festivals of music and the arts. For 17 days in late May and early June each year the city is filled with more than 1,000 performers. The festival is built around a base of classical music, jazz, and the contemporary visual arts, with orchestras, soloists, and artists from all over the world. In addition to the main music and art program, there is all the best in films, talks, tours, and the festival fringe. Ticket prices are £3 ($5.25) for lunchtime recitals and range from £3 ($5.25) to £20 ($35) for evening concerts and operas. Full details can be obtained from Bath Festival, 1 Pierrepont Place, Bath BA1 1JY (tel. 0225/462231). In the U.S., full details and tickets are available from Keith Prowse, 234 W. 44th St., New York, NY 10036 (tel. 212/398-1430).

The Theatre Royal

The Theatre Royal, Saw Close, has been restored and refurbished with plush red-velvet seats, red carpets, and a painted proscenium arch and ceiling, and is now regarded as the most beautiful theater in Britain. It is a 1,000-seat theater with a small pit and then grand circles rising to the upper circle. Beneath the theater, reached from the back of the stalls or by a side door, are the theater vaults. There you will find a pleasant bar in one of the curved vaults with stone walls. In the next vault is the Brasserie, and a Japanese restaurant is beside the stage door.

The theater advertises a sophisticated list of forthcoming events with a repertoire that includes, among other offerings, West End shows. The box office (tel. 0225/448844) is open from 9:30 a.m. to 8 p.m. Monday to Saturday.

A Georgian House

No. 1 Royal Crescent (tel. 0225/28126) gives you the chance to see inside a Bath town house that has been redecorated and furnished by the Bath Preservation Trust so that it appears as it might have toward the end of the 18th century. The house is in a splendid position at one end of Bath's most magnificent crescent. It is open to the public from March to the end of October from 11 a.m. to 5 p.m. Tuesday to Saturday and from November to Christmas from 11 a.m. to 3 p.m. Saturday and Sunday. Last admissions are 30 minutes before closing. Closed Monday except bank holidays and during the Bath Festival. Admission is £1.50 ($2.65) for adults, £1 ($1.75) for children.

The American Museum

Some 2½ miles outside Bath you get a glimpse of life as lived by a diversified segment of American settlers until Lincoln's day. It was the first American museum established outside the United States. In a Greek Revival house, designed by a Georgian architect, Claverton Manor, the museum (tel. 0225/60503) sits proudly in its own extensive grounds high above the Avon valley. Among the authentic exhibits— shipped over from the States—are a New Mexico room, a Conestoga wagon, an early American beehive oven (ever had gingerbread baked from the recipe of George Washington's mother?), the dining room of a New York town house of the early 19th century, and (on the grounds) a copy of Washington's flower garden at Mount Vernon. You can visit the museum from the end of March to the end of October, daily except Monday from 2 to 5 p.m. There is an American arboretum on the grounds. Admission to the house and gardens is £3 ($5.25) for adults, £2.50 ($4.40) for children.

Walking Tours

A good look at Bath is provided by the **Mayor's Corps of Honorary Guides** in the free walking tours of the city. The guides are all unpaid volunteers acting in an honorary capacity to point out the beauties of their city. They don't accept tips. Tours, lasting about two hours, leave from the abbey churchyard, outside the Pump Room. Visitors see the historical and architectural features of the city, but are not shown into any buildings. From May to October, tours are offered at 10:30 a.m. Sunday to Friday, at 2:30 p.m. on Sunday and Wednesday, and at 7 p.m. on Tuesday and Friday except in October. Saturday tours are at 6 p.m. except in October. From November to April, the walks are Sunday to Friday at 10:30 a.m. and on Sunday at 2:30 p.m. The tours are arranged by the guides corps in conjunction with the Bath City Council (tel. 0225/461111, ext. 2785).

Tours and Tourist Services

A reception center for Bath is operated by **Guide Friday Ltd.,** railway station (tel. 0225/444102). Their office dispenses free maps and brochures on the town and area and provides tours. Also available is a full range of tourist services, including accommodation references and car rental. In summer, the office is open daily from 9 a.m. to 6 p.m. In winter, hours are from 9 a.m. to 4 p.m. daily. Guided tours of Bath leave the railway station daily. In summer, open-top double-decker buses depart every 15 minutes. The tour can be a one-hour panoramic ride, or you can get off at any of the stops in the city. The ticket, costing £3 ($5.25), is valid all day.

WHERE TO STAY

In accommodations, Bath offers a wide choice—some in architectural landmarks.

The Upper Bracket

The Priory Hotel, Weston Road, Bath, Avon BA1 2XT (tel. 0225/331922), was converted from one of Bath's Georgian houses in 1969. It stands in two acres of formal gardens with manicured lawns and flowerbeds, a swimming pool, and a croquet lawn. The 21 bedrooms are individually decorated and furnished with antiques, and each has color TV, direct-dial phone, and easy chairs. My personal favorite is Clivia (all rooms are named after flowers or shrubs), a nicely appointed duplex within a circular turret. Prices start at £72 ($126) daily for singles, with standard twins and doubles renting from £105 ($183.75). Deluxe rooms for two cost from £140 ($245). All tariffs include a full English breakfast and VAT. The restaurant consists of three separate dining rooms, one in a small salon in the original building. The others have views over the garden. The menu is varied and reflects seasonal availability. Grouse, partridge, hare, and venison are served in several recipes in season as is the succulent best end of lamb roasted with herb-flavored breadcrumbs. The average dinner price is £28 ($49). A three-course luncheon is offered for £16 ($28), and on Sunday traditional roast meats are featured. The Priory is known for its wine list.

Six Kings Circus, 6 The Circus, Bath, Avon BA1 2EW (tel. 0225/28288). Rarely can a visitor find such exquisitely ornamented public rooms, coupled with the charm and the trappings of a private home. They're contained in one of the nearly identical town houses that a Georgian architect arranged in a symmetrical ring around quintuplicate plane trees. Its owner just after it was built in 1756 was Lady Stanhope, who embellished her entrance vestibule for the lavish entertaining she did. The hotel offers four doubles or twins with private baths plus one suite, also with its own bath. Rates are £120 ($210) daily for a double or twin, £65 ($113.75) for single occupancy. All rates include a full English breakfast and VAT. The true grandeur of the place, however, is in the antique-filled public rooms, each of which looks like the setting for a Restoration comedy. Guests serve their own drinks from an antique Dutch sideboard. Breakfast is the only meal served.

Queensberry Hotel, Russel Street, Bath, Avon BA1 2QT (tel. 0225/447928). Much of the beauty of this place derives from the many original fireplaces, ornate ceilings, and antiques, which the creators of the property, Stephen and Penny Ross, have preserved. Each of three interconnected town houses that form this hotel was constructed in the early Georgian era. Today, 27 bedrooms are rented, each with a private bath, antique furniture, and carefully chosen upholstery in keeping with the character of the house. Open since 1988, Queensberry has already become one of Bath's most important hotels. Depending on their location, doubles cost from £70 ($122.50) to £105 ($183.75) daily, with singles going for £65 ($113.75). The least expensive doubles, although spacious, are in the basement. VAT and a continental breakfast are included in the price.

Fountain House, 9-11 Fountain Buildings, Lansdown Road, Bath, Avon BA1

5DV (tel. 0225/338622). The three buildings that compose this hotel are a trio of Regency neoclassic white-fronted structures, each of which dates from 1735. British entrepreneur Robin Bryan created an all-suite hotel that has been favorably compared to the most prestigious properties in the region. Each suite contains reproduction antiques, lots of color-coordinated chintz, at least one bedroom, a sitting room, and a private bath, as well as all the electronic equipment you'd expect in such an elegant hotel. The 14 suites cost £86 ($151.50) daily for two persons, whereas a two-bedroom suite, suitable for four persons, rents for £122 ($213.50). The hotel stands within 100 yards of Milsom Street, the city's main shopping and historical thoroughfare. It doesn't serve a formal breakfast. Instead, all ingredients are delivered in a basket to the door, and clients prepare their own breakfasts at their own pace.

The Moderate Range

Lansdown Grove Hotel, Lansdown Road, Bath, Avon BA1 5EH (tel. 0225/ 315891), is a well-run hotel outside the center of the city, set on the northern slopes with views, 600 feet above sea level. Its drawing room is informal, with flowering chintz draperies, a large gilt-and-marble console, and comfortable armchairs. The bedrooms all have private baths or showers, color TVs, mini-bars, hairdryers, and trouser presses. Singles cost from £50 ($87.50) daily, and doubles from £66 ($115.50). All rates include VAT and a full English breakfast. It's a pleasure to eat in the sunny dining room, with its bay window that opens onto the garden. Before-dinner drinks are available in the cocktail bar. The hotel, a Best Western affiliate, offers a car park as well as a covered garage.

The Francis Hotel, Queen Square, Bath, Avon BA1 2HH (tel. 0225/24257), was created during the intensive rebuilding following the bombings of World War II when a quartet of neighboring Regency-era town houses were destroyed in a single air raid. An entrepreneur purchased the four lots, removed the rubble, and rebuilt nearly exact copies of the original buildings. Of course, modern amenities and comforts were added in the process. The public rooms contain shell-shaped niches, moldings, some 18th-century antiques, and a cocktail bar. The Edgar restaurant offers a wide array of both British and international food. Each of the well-furnished bedrooms, 94 in all, has a private bath, color TV, phone, and radio. Singles cost £67 ($117.25) daily, and doubles or twins rent for £97 ($169.75). Rooms are reached by following a labyrinth of halls and stairs.

Duke's Hotel, Great Pulteney Street, Bath, Avon BA2 4DN (tel. 0225/ 63512). A short walk from the heart of Bath, this building dates from 1780 but has been completely restored and rather elegantly furnished and modernized. Many of the original Georgian features, including cornices and moldings, have been retained. Twenty-two attractively furnished bedrooms are rented, and all but two have a complete private bath. Amenities include electric trouser press, direct-dial phone, color TV, and hairdryer. The owner, Peter F. Yarker, charges from £30 ($52.50) to £50 ($87.50) daily in a single and £50 ($87.50) to £80 ($140) in a double, depending on the room assignment. Guests can relax in a refined drawing room or else patronize the cozy bar. A varied menu is also offered.

Pratt's Hotel, South Parade, Bath, Avon BA2 4AB (tel. 0225/60441), once the home of Sir Walter Scott, is convenient for sightseeing, on a wide street with a large car park close by. Several elegant terraced Georgian town houses were joined into a comfortable place with warm, cheerful lounges, a bar, and a high-ceilinged dining room. Bedrooms all have private bath, color TV with in-house movies, radio, telephone, trouser presses, and tea/coffee-makers. A single goes for £52.50 ($91.90) daily and a twin or double for £65 ($113.75). All rates include a full English breakfast and VAT. Children under 15 sharing a room with two adults stay free. English and French cuisine is served in the dining room, where dinner costs from £12 ($21).

Apsley House Hotel, 141 Newbridge Hill, Bath, Avon BA1 3PT (tel. 0225/ 336966), is a charming private hotel in a building dating back to the reign of William IV, just a mile from the center of Bath. It's set in its own gardens, stately, with a square tower, arched windows, and a walled garden with south views. All rooms have private bath and are luxuriously appointed. The Alpine and Romantic Rooms cost from £95 ($166.25) daily for two people, while the Champagne, Gold, Melissa, Ondine, and Ballerina Rooms go for £75 ($131.25). Tariffs include a full English breakfast, service, and VAT. If you would like to have dinner in the handsome dining room, expect to spend £20 ($35) for the three-course menu. Drinks are served in an intimate cocktail bar, and there is a comfortable lounge. To reach the hotel, take the A4 to Upper Bristol 1 Road and fork right at traffic signals into Newbridge Hill.

Number Nine, 9 Miles Buildings, George Street, Bath, Avon BA1 2QS (tel. 0225/25462), is one of the most delightful small hotels of Bath, personally cared for by the owners, Sue and Paul Hayward. The hotel dates from the 18th century, when it was built according to the plans of the celebrated architect John Wood the Elder. The Haywards have taken care to retain its Georgian overtones, selecting furniture appropriate to the era. In the center of Bath, near the Royal Crescent, the Assembly Rooms, and the Circus, the little hotel lies on one of the city's walkways, cut off from the roar of traffic. Parking space is available nearby. Rooms are attractively furnished and individually decorated, often with half-tester beds. The cost is £65 ($113.75) daily and up in a double or twin with a private bathroom. A single with bath begins at £50 ($87.50). The hotel, incidentally, does not cater to children. The bay-windowed public rooms look out onto an old-world garden. Guests who cannot be accommodated in the main building are housed in a mews cottage nearby. Ask about the membership arrangement with the Bath House, where you can enjoy steambaths, saunas, and a Jacuzzi.

Laura Place Hotel, 3 Laura Place, Great Pulteney Street, Bath, Avon BA2 4BH (tel. 0225/463815), was built the same year as the French Revolution (1789). The hotel won a civic award for the restoration of its stone façade. Set on a corner on a residential street overlooking a public fountain, it lies within a four-minute walk of the Roman Baths and Bath Abbey. The place is skillfully decorated with antique furniture and fabrics evocative of the 18th century. The house is owned by Patricia Bull, who rents 10 comfortable bedrooms. Seven of these offer a private bath. With VAT and breakfast included, singles range from £18 ($31.50) to £25 ($43.72) daily, with doubles going for £50 ($87.50) to £60 ($105).

Luxury Living on the Outskirts

Ston Easton Park, Ston Easton, near Farrington Gurney BA3 4DF (tel. 076121/631), lies 1¼ miles south of Farrington Gurney on the A37. From the moment you pass a collection of stone out-buildings and the century-old beeches of its 30-acre park, you know you've come to a very special place. The mansion was created in the mid-1700s from the shell of an existing Elizabethan house, and in 1793 Sir Humphry Repton designed the landscape. In 1977, after long years of neglect, Peter and Christine Smedley acquired the property and poured money, love, and labor into its restoration. Now, it is one of the great country hotels of England. A pair of carved mahogany staircases ringed with ornate plaster detailing might be considered works of sculpture. A sunflower-colored, formal dining room contains museum-quality oil portraits, grandeur, and exquisite attention to detail. The chef prepares superb food, offering imaginative menus. A lunch costs £17 ($29.75), and a dinner goes for £28 ($49). Guests who return early from sightseeing enjoy tea in the hotel garden beside one of the four cascades. The sheer volume of antiques filling the place is staggering. There's a manorial library, as well as a drawing room suitable for a diplomatic reception and 20 tasteful bedrooms filled with flowers, plus upholstery and antiques. Singles cost from £60 ($105) daily, doubles and twins rent for £105 ($183.75) to £185 ($323.75), and junior suites for two persons are priced at

£220 ($385) to £260 ($455). Children under 12 aren't accepted. The hotel is 11 miles southwest of Bath, 13 miles southeast of Bristol, and 5 miles north of Wells.

Hunstrete House, Chelwood, near Bristol, Avon BS18 4NS (tel. 07618/578), is a *Relais & Chateaux*, lying 8½ miles west of Bath. It is operated by Thea and John Dupays, who ran a rather exclusive school in Bath before they found this 18th-century house set in 90 acres of private parkland. It provides a setting for pursuing their hobby of antique collecting. The village of Hunstrete was first recorded in A.D. 936 when King Athelstan passed through on his way to the abbey in Glastonbury. The fine Georgian house has 24 bedrooms with private baths. Six units are in the Courtyard House, attached to the main structure and overlooking a paved courtyard with its Italian fountain and flower-filled tubs. Swallow Cottage, which also adjoins the main house, has its own private sitting room, double bedroom, and bath. Units in the main house are individually decorated and furnished in attractive colors. They vary in size as reflected by the rates. A small double is £90 ($157.50) daily, rising to £105 ($183.75) to £175 ($306.25) in a four-poster room, and £165 ($288.75) in a cottage. A single person will pay from £80 ($140). Tariffs include a continental breakfast, VAT, and service. Part of the pleasure of staying at Hunstrete is the food, contemporary and classical cuisine. A three-course dinner at £25 ($43.75) gives diners a wide and delectable choice. A heated swimming pool lies in a sheltered corner of the walled garden.

Homewood Park, Hinton Charterhouse, Bath, Avon BA3 6BB (tel. 022122/3731), is set in ten acres of garden, just five miles south of Bath on the A36 Bath–Warminster road. Stephen and Penny Ross, who ran the successful Popjoy's restaurant in Bath, have converted the property and now offer 15 bedrooms with private bath. This small, family-run hotel was built in the 18th century, then subsequently enlarged in the 19th century. Overlooking the Limpley Stoke Valley, it is a large Victorian house, its grounds adjoining the 13th-century ruin of Hinton Priory. The B&B rate is from £50 ($87.50) per person nightly. Of course, most visitors come here for the cuisine, served in a dining room facing south, overlooking the gardens. The French and English cooking is prepared with skill and flair, and you should expect to spend from £16.50 ($28.90) for lunch, £27.50 ($48.15) for a three-course dinner. You can play tennis and croquet in the garden. Riding and golfing are nearby, and beautiful walks in the Limpley-Stoke Valley lure guests.

WHERE TO DINE

Bath enjoys a reputation as a gourmet citadel of Britain.

Popjoy's, Beau Nash House, Sawclose (tel. 0225/460494), is housed in a 1720 Georgian building that was once the home of the notorious Beau Nash, the "King of Bath." The restaurant is named after Julianna Popjoy, Nash's last mistress. Her ghost is said to haunt the drawing room. When Nash died in 1761, Julianna vowed never again to sleep in a bed, and spent the rest of her life gathering herbs and living in a hollow tree in Wiltshire. In 1982 Popjoy's was restored exactly as it had been in 1720, even down to scraping the centuries of paint from the walls to discover the original colors. Everything is freshly prepared in the basement kitchen. A set dinner is priced at £18.50 ($32.40), while à la carte meals cost from £25 ($43.75). A set lunch goes for £11.50 ($20.15). Meat comes from Devon, fish daily from Cornwall, and fresh vegetables from local farmers. Menus lean toward the new way of cooking using less fat, less cream, and no flour in sauces. The wine list (they buy their wine from 16 different wine merchants) is more than 100 strong. The menu is changed every eight weeks, and ever since the place reopened in 1983, there has hardly been an empty seat. The house wine is specially bottled in France and imported for the restaurant. It is open from noon to 2 p.m. and 6 to 10:30 p.m. Tuesday to Saturday (except Saturday lunch).

Hole in the Wall, 16 George St. (tel. 0225/25242). You enter what looks like the living room of a Georgian town house, where a hostess greets you, takes your name and order for a drink, and presents you with the impressive menu. She'll even help plan your meal if you prefer. All the selections are especially prepared for you. When your table is ready, you descend into an old-world dining room, with an attractive decor that includes a great "dungeon" fireplace. The benches, tables, and chairs are antiques. The menu is changed frequently. The cooking is both English and cuisine moderne, with a superb use made of fresh ingredients. A two-course meal costs £18.50 ($32.40), and a three-course repast goes for £22 ($38.50). Lunch is served from 12:30 to 2 p.m. and dinner from 7 to 10 p.m. Closed at lunchtime on Sunday.

Tarts, 8 Pierrepont Place (tel. 0225/330280), is a bistrolike place located on two different levels of a rustic cellar. It offers French-inspired cuisine, with full meals costing from £17 ($29.75), which many diners consider worth the splurge. That is, after they've sampled the chef's filet of beef with peppercorns flambéed in cognac, suprême of ginger with fresh coriander and tomatoes, or sautéed medallions of pork with sage butter and sautéed sage. A vegetarian specialty might be a buttered brioche filled with quick steamed fresh vegetables. The bistro contains room for only 20 diners, so reservations are important. Tarts is open daily except Sunday from noon to 2:30 p.m. and 7 to 10:30 p.m.

Woods, 9-13 Alfred St. (tel. 0225/314812). The elegant Georgian building that contains this restaurant is also the home of one of Bath's antique emporiums. Diners climb a flight of steps to reach this restaurant, and once inside find carefully prepared daily specials described on a blackboard. American jazz from the 1930s might accompany a meal here, which is consumed in a pine-ringed dining room filled with springtime colors. The chef offers a vegetarian dish of the day in addition to regular meat and fish specialties. These might include calves' liver with kidneys and coriander, filet of English lamb cooked pink, and a homemade fish pie. Full meals, costing from £15 ($26.25), are served at lunch and dinner daily except Sunday from noon to 2:15 p.m. and 6:45 to 10:15 p.m.

Chikako's, Theatre Royal, Saw Close (tel. 0225/664125). Its intimacy, coupled with its flavorfully light-textured Japanese specialties, attracts a clientele that ranges far beyond the patrons of the theater in which it is housed. The low-slung lacquered tables make one believe that diners are sitting cross-legged, Japanese style, but the depressions beneath the table allow all the leg-dangling comfort of the West. Some of the meals are cooked on a hotplate plugged directly into your table. A bevy of waitresses bring fresh slices of prawn, halibut, mackerel, seasonal vegetables, chicken, pork, salmon, and beef. Sake, tea, and Japanese beer are the preferred drinks, but wine is also available. The menu includes a full range of Japanese cuisine (teriyaki is a favorite). Food is served amid a simple decor of bamboo, rice paper, and lacquerwork. Meals cost £10 ($17.50) to £18 ($31.50). It is open daily from 6 to 11 p.m.

---

11. Bristol

Bristol, the largest city in the West Country, is a good center for touring western Britain. Its location is 10 miles west of Bath, just across the Bristol Channel from Wales, 20 miles from the Cotswolds, and 30 miles from Stonehenge. This historic inland port is linked to the sea by seven miles of the navigable Avon River. Bristol has long been rich in seafaring traditions and has many links with the early colonization of America. In fact, some claim that the new continent was named after a Bristol town clerk, Richard Ameryke. In 1497 John Cabot sailed from Bristol, which led to the discovery of the northern half of the New World.

THE SIGHTS

In Bristol, the world's first iron steamship and luxury liner has been restored to her 1840 glory. She's the 3,000-ton **S.S. Great Britain,** and was created by Isambard

Brunel, a Victorian engineer. Visitors can go aboard this "floating palace" daily from 10 a.m. to 6 p.m. in summer, to 5 p.m. in winter, for an admission of £1.90 ($3.35) for adults, 90p ($1.60) for children. For information, phone 0272/ 260680.

At the age of 25 in 1831, Brunel began a Bristol landmark, a suspension bridge over the 250-foot-deep Avon Gorge at Clifton.

Bristol Cathedral, College Green (tel. 0272/264879), was begun in the 12th century and was once an Augustinian abbey. The central tower was added in 1466. The Chapter House and Gatehouse are good examples of late Norman architecture, and the choir is magnificent. The cathedral's interior was singled out for praise by Sir John Betjeman, the late poet laureate.

Another church, **St. Mary Redcliffe,** 10 Redcliffe Parade West (tel. 0272/ 291962), was called "the fairest, the goodliest, and most famous parish church in England" by such an authority as Elizabeth I. Built in the 14th century, it has been carefully restored. One of the chapels is called "The American Chapel," where the kneelers show the emblems of all the states of the U.S.A. The tomb and armor of Admiral Sir William Penn, father of the founder of Pennsylvania, are in the church.

Cobbled King Street is known for its **Theatre Royal,** built in 1776 and now the oldest working playhouse in the United Kingdom. It is the home of the Bristol Old Vic. Backstage tours leave the foyer at noon every Friday and Saturday. Phone 0272/250250, box office, or 0272/277466, administration.

Guided walking tours are conducted in summer, and these last about 1½ hours, leaving from Neptune's Statue. The tour departs daily at 11 a.m. and 2:30 p.m. On Sunday, guided tours are also conducted through Clifton, a suburb of Bristol, which has more Georgian houses than the just-previewed Bath.

Additional information on special walks is provided by **Bristol Tourist Information,** 14 Narrow Quay (tel. 0272/260767).

WHERE TO STAY

A modern city-center hotel, the **Holiday Inn,** Lower Castle Street, Bristol, Avon BS1 3AD (tel. 0272/294281), is ideal for the business traveler, but also suitable to the visitor who makes it to this part of the West Country. The heated swimming pool is impressive, and the foyer is spacious. Public areas are comfortable and stylish, in the tradition of this popular chain. The Restaurant Panache serves an à la carte menu as well as snacks from 7 a.m. to 10 p.m. Bedrooms are uniformly furnished, bright, and cheerful, with double beds (doubles have two) and good tile bathrooms. Singles cost £77 ($134.75) daily, and the double tariff is £84 ($147).

Grand Hotel, Broad Street, Bristol, Avon BS1 2EL (tel. 0272/291645). Built by the Victorians in the grand manner, this 178-room hotel sits on a street in the commercial heart of town. The architectural detailing that causes it to be considered one of the most noteworthy hotels in town includes rows of fan-shaped windows, intricate exterior corniches, lavishly ornate crystal chandeliers, two bars (one in a nautical theme), and a pair of comfortable restaurants, including the Brass Nails, serving good food. Dinners cost from £10.50 ($18.40). Each of the refurbished bedrooms has a TV, radio, phone, and private bath, as well as coordinated fabrics. Singles cost from £59 ($103.25) daily, and doubles £69 ($120.75), with breakfast included.

Hilton International, Redcliff Way, Bristol, Avon BS1 6NJ (tel. 0272/ 260041). Set conveniently amid the commercial bustle of the center of town, this modern hotel offers an imaginative decor. Its multilevel restaurant is set inside the brick-lined walls of a former 16th-century glass kiln refurbished in the style of a French brasserie offering both lunch and dinner and featuring English and French specialties. Lunch costs from £14 ($24.50) and dinner from £21 ($36.75). Many of the 194 bedrooms are outfitted in pastels, and all contain private baths, radios, phones, in-house video, and tea/coffee-makers. Singles cost £75 ($131.25) daily, and doubles go for £100 ($175).

WHERE TO DINE

In cellars once used by monks, **Harvey's Restaurant,** 12a Denmark St. (tel. 0272/277665), is in a house which has belonged to Harvey's since the company was founded in 1796. The cellars date from far earlier, as they were originally part of a monastery dissolved and sacked by order of Henry VIII. Today the subterranean chambers house what is arguably the best restaurant in Bristol, with one of the finest, longest wine lists in Europe. The French chef, Thierry Rouvrais, offers a lunchtime selection for £13.50 ($23.65), and an à la carte dinner can cost from £20 ($35). Specialties include beef Wellington, roast ribs of lamb with garlic and herbs, and veal medallions Normand. Food is served from noon to 2:30 p.m. and 7 to 11:15 p.m. Monday to Friday from 6:30 to 11:15 p.m. on Saturday; closed Sunday.

The rest of the historic building is Harvey's Wine Museum, which contains a collection of exhibits connected with the production and enjoyment of wine. Aside from the main gallery lined with huge sherry butts, there are displays of silver decanter labels and old wine bottles. The glass gallery contains many engraved and decorated glasses and goblets. There are family documents, passports, and watches belonging to Victorian and Edwardian Harveys. In the Unicorn, a reconstructed medieval inn, visitors are sustained with a glass of sherry. The museum is open on Friday from 10 a.m. to noon or by appointment. If you lunch here, you may be able to arrange a visit to this place.

Lettonie, 9 Druid Hill, Stoke Bishop (tel. 0272/686456), is run by Martin Blunos and Sian Williams who insist on high quality ingredients. Both imbue their subtle restaurant with a simple elegance, and they are known for producing some of the most memorable meals in the area. Try, as for example, guinea fowl in a prune and brandy sauce, followed by one of their luscious desserts, perhaps a terrine of mixed chocolates. Service is top rate, as is the welcome. Lunch is served from noon to 2 p.m. costing £10.50 ($18.40), with a set dinner offered at £18 ($31.50) from 7 to 10:30 p.m. They are closed for dinner on Sunday and all day Monday. It's possible to dine à la carte for about £22 ($38.50) per person. Reservations are essential. The wine list is carefully selected and moderate in price.

Some of the most creative cookery in town is found at **Michael's,** 129 Hotwell Rd., Bristol, Avon BS8 4RU (tel. 0272/276190), run by Michael McGowan. His charming and well-patronized restaurant is near Clifton, on a highway leading toward the Avon Gorge. In his pleasant bar, decorated like an Edwardian parlor, an open fire burns. The dining room is also bright and inviting. Michael's menu is imaginative, and he likes to change it, depending on the availability of seasonal produce. Service is informal and enthusiastic. Sunday lunch is offered in winter only, for £7.95 ($13.90) and up from noon to 2:30 p.m. Dinner is served Monday to Saturday from 7 to 11:30 p.m. Expect to pay about £20 ($35) per person. Always call for a table. There's no smoking in the dining room. If you want a cigarette, stick to the bar. Michael offers simple, bathless accommodations in a five-story Regency house overlooking the Avon Gorge and Suspension Bridge. Rooms have hot and cold running water, and guests can use a kitchen and communal lounge. The price is from £15 ($26.25) per person per night.

12. Thornbury

Twelve miles from Bristol, Thornbury is known for its castle (now a hotel, see below). Many of the crenellations and towers were built in 1511 as the last defensible castle ever constructed in England. Tragically, its owner was beheaded by Henry VIII for "certain words" spoken in haste. Henry confiscated the lands and, to celebrate, stayed here for ten days with an equally doomed Anne Boleyn in 1535. Later, Mary Tudor spent three years of her adolescence here.

Thornbury Castle, Thornbury, near Bristol, Avon BS12 1HH (tel. 0454/ 418511), is a genuine Tudor Castle (built 1511) and once owned by Henry VIII. It is surrounded by trees and almost impenetrable stone walls. Maurice C. R. Taylor, who was a music publisher, TV producer, and real estate developer, has brought many improvements to the property. He rents 18 bedchambers, four of which contain four-posters. Rooms, which have private baths, are superbly accessorized with fine furniture and many amenities. Singles rent for £70 ($122.50) daily, with doubles costing £145 ($253.75) to £170 ($297.50). Dining is some of the finest in Avon in one of the hotel's two dining rooms. Lunch costs from £12.50 ($21.90) per person and is served from noon to 2 p.m. daily. Dinner, from £22.50 ($39.40) per person, is served from 7 to 9:30 p.m. Specialties include Scottish smoked salmon with a salad dressed in walnut oil, breast of chicken with an apricot and basil filling, and hot butterscotch pudding.

XII

THE COTSWOLDS

1. **TETBURY**
2. **MALMESBURY**
3. **CIRENCESTER**
4. **PAINSWICK**
5. **CHELTENHAM**
6. **ROYAL SUDELEY CASTLE**
7. **BIBURY**
8. **CLANFIELD**
9. **BURFORD AND MINSTER LOVELL**
10. **SHIPTON-UNDER-WYCHWOOD**
11. **CHIPPING NORTON**
12. **BOURTON-ON-THE-WATER**
13. **STOW-ON-THE-WOLD**
14. **LOWER SWELL**
15. **UPPER AND LOWER SLAUGHTER**
16. **MORETON-IN-MARSH**
17. **BROADWAY**
18. **CHIPPING CAMPDEN**

The Cotswolds, a stretch of limestone hills sometimes covered by grass, often barren plateaus known as wolds, is a pastoral land dotted by ancient villages and deep wooded ravines. This bucolic scene in the middle of southwest England, about a two-hour drive from London, is found mainly in Gloucestershire, with portions in Oxfordshire, Wiltshire, and Worcestershire. The wolds or plateaus led to this area's being given the name Cotswold, old English for "God's high open land."

Cotswold lambs used to produce so much wool they made their owners very rich—wealth they invested in some of the finest domestic architecture in Europe, made out of honey-brown Cotswold stone. The wool-rich gentry didn't neglect their church contributions either. Often the simplest of villages will have a church that in style and architectural detail seems to rank far beyond the means of the hamlet.

If possible, try to explore the area by car. That way, you can spend hours surveying the land of winding goat paths, rolling hills, and sleepy hamlets, with names such as Stow-on-the Wold, Wotton-under-Edge, Moreton-in-Marsh, Old Sodbury, Chipping Campden, Shipton-under-Wychwood, Upper and Lower Swell, and Upper and Lower Slaughter, often called "The Slaughters." These most beautiful of English villages keep popping up on book jackets and calendars. The adventure begins in:

1. Tetbury

In the rolling Cotswolds, Tetbury was never in the mainstream of tourism with places like Oxford or Stratford-upon-Avon. However, ever since an attractive man and his lovely bride moved there and took up residence in the Macmillan place, a Georgian building on nearly 350 acres, it is now drawing crowds from all over the world. Charles and Diana may one day be King and Queen of England. Their nine-bedroom mansion, Highgrove, lies just outside the town on the way to Westonbirt Arboretum. The house cannot be seen from the road, but you might see Princess Di shopping in the village.

The town has a 17th-century Market Hall and a lot of antique shops, along with trendy boutiques (one called Diana's). Its inns, even before the royal couple moved in, were not cheap, and the prices have certainly not dropped since that time.

WHERE TO STAY AND DINE

Dating from 1596, **The Close,** 8 Long St., Tetbury, Gloucestershire GL8 8AQ (tel. 0666/52272), takes its name from a Cistercian monastery that was on this site. It was once the home of a wealthy Cotswold wool merchant. Architecturally, it is built of warm honey-brown Cotswold stone, with gables and stone-mullioned windows. The ecclesiastical-type windows in the rear overlook a garden with a reflection pool, a haven for doves. Inside, you'll find a Georgian room with a domed ceiling (once it was an open courtyard), where before-dinner drinks are served and you can peruse the menu. Dining is in one of two rooms. Candlelight on winter evenings, floral arrangements, sparkling silver and glass are just the background for the fine food. The cooking is superb, and an à la carte menu offers specialty dishes. A set dinner costs from £22 ($38.50) per person. Fixed-price menus are also offered for lunch for £10.95 ($19.15) to £12.95 ($22.65). Most of the ten bedrooms, all with private bath, are spacious and handsomely furnished with antiques. A single room is priced at £55 ($96.25) daily and a double at £130 ($227.50). A continental breakfast, service, and VAT are included.

The Snooty Fox, Market Place, Tetbury, Gloucestershire GL8 8DD (tel. 0666/52436), is one of the most desirable hotels in the commercial heart of Tetbury. It was originally built in the 16th century as a coaching inn. The Victorians added a high front porch under which flowers grow in what used to be watering troughs for horses. A stone-walled lounge with comfortable chairs and a Gothic fireplace opens off the reception area. There's a popular pub inside, with an amusing caricature of a snooty fox in full riding regalia, and one of the most elegant restaurants in town. In warm weather, tables are set at the edge of the market square beneath the 19th-century iron overhang. Three of the hotel's dozen bedrooms contain antique beds with canopies, and the rest are comfortably and tastefully furnished in a more modern style. Each has a private bathroom, color TV, radio, phone, hairdryer, trouser press, and tea- and coffee-making facilities. Singles cost from £62 ($108.50) daily and doubles from £84 ($147). VAT and a continental breakfast are included.

Calcot Manor, Calcot, Tetbury, Gloucestershire GL8 8YJ (tel. 066689/391), stands 3½ miles west of Tetbury on the A4135. It was originally a farmhouse, and on the grounds is a 14th-century tithe barn, among the oldest in Britain. The thick stone walls of the main house shelter a flowering terrace where tea and drinks are served in good weather. Tastefully decorated public rooms mix touches of modernism with clusters of flowers and English antiques. Meals are relaxing, with continental touches gathered from the Ball family's combined catering experience in Switzerland and France. The food is the finest served in the area. Dinner, daily from 7:30 to 9:30 p.m., goes for around £28 ($49). Wife and mother Barbara, husband Brian, and son Richard add gracious touches to the establishment. The 13 bedrooms are furnished with antiques, rich fabrics, and modern conveniences. Four contain whirlpool baths, and one has a four-poster bed. Views from many of the rooms encompass a sweep of lawn and the Cotswold countryside. With early morning tea and a full English breakfast, singles cost £65 ($113.75) daily, and doubles rent for £85 ($148.75) to £110 ($192.50). Each accommodation has color TV and a direct-dial phone. Only children over age 12 are accepted.

---

2. Malmesbury

At the southern tip of the Cotswolds, the old hill town of Malmesbury is encircled by the Avon River. In the center of England's "Middle West," it makes a good base for touring the Cotswolds. Cirencester is just 12 miles away; Bibury, 19 miles; and Cheltenham, 28 miles. Malmesbury is a market town, with a fine market cross. Its historical fame is reflected by the Norman abbey built there on the site of King Athelstan's grave.

Malmesbury is considered the oldest "borough" in England, as it was granted its charter by Alfred the Great in 880. In 1980 it celebrated its 1,300th anniversary. Some 400 years ago the Washington family lived there, leaving their star-and-stripe coat-of-arms on the church wall. In addition, Nancy Hanks, Abraham Lincoln's mother, came from Malmesbury. The town still has members of the family, noted for their lean features and tallness. The Penns of Pennsylvania also originally came from Malmesbury.

FOOD AND LODGING

In the heart of town adjoining the 13th-century Norman abbey, **The Old Bell,** Abbey Row, Malmesbury, Wiltshire SN16 0BW (tel. 0666/822344), is arguably the oldest hotel in England, having been a hostelry for more than 700 years. Historical connections link it with Nancy Hanks, mother of Abraham Lincoln, and also with the family of George Washington. Its façade is wisteria-covered stone, with six gables and three towering chimneys; an iron picket fence guards the flowers and shrubbery. The inn opens onto a formal garden, with graveled monks' walks leading to the rear back wall, with its little stone gazebo bordering the Avon below. Architecturally, much remains of the original building, including a 13th-century window. There are 37 bedrooms, and all are individually styled and have private baths, color TVs, hairdryers, trouser presses, and hot beverage facilities. With breakfast, singles cost £52 ($91) daily, and doubles run £95 ($166.25), including VAT. The inn is often used by sportsmen, especially during Saturday hunts. Guests congregate in the dining room and the informal lounges and bars. The dining room is more modern (Regency), serving lunch for £9.50 ($16.65), and dinner for £16.50 ($28.90).

An even better accommodation is found on the outskirts at **Whatley Manor,** Easton Grey, Malmesbury, Wiltshire SN16 0RB (tel. 0666/8222888), which lies about half a mile east of Easton Grey on B4040. Easton Grey itself is two miles west of Malmesbury on B4040. This 18th-century manor house is one of the most desirable country house hotels in Wiltshire. By the River Avon, it was once a farmhouse but has been successfully converted into an upmarket Cotswold stone manor hotel. It rents 26 well-furnished, often most spacious, bedrooms, each with private bath or shower. Some of the accommodations are found in the old Court House on the grounds. The tariff in a single is from £58 ($101.50) nightly, with doubles costing £92 ($161). The hotel has formal gardens, beautifully kept, on ten acre acres of land. Facilities include an outdoor swimming pool, a sauna, and solarium, plus an all-weather tennis court. Even if you aren't staying here, consider candlelight dining nightly from 7:30 to 9, with a set dinner going for £19 ($33.25). You can also visit for lunch, with set meals costing from £9 ($15.75) to £10.50 ($18.40). Service is from 12:30 to 1:45 p.m. The cooking is both British and international.

---

3. Cirencester

Don't worry about how to pronounce the name of the town. Even the English are in disagreement. Just say "siren-sess-ter" and you won't go too far wrong. Cirencester is often considered the unofficial capital of the Cotswolds, probably a throwback to its reputation in the Middle Ages when it flourished as the center of the great wool industry.

Even in Roman Britain, five roads converged on Cirencester, which was called Corinium in those days. In size, it ranked second only to London. Today it is chiefly a market town, a good base for touring, as it lies 34 miles from Bath, 16 from the former Regency spa at Cheltenham, 17 from Gloucester, 36 from Oxford, and 38 from Stratford-upon-Avon. The trip from London is 89 miles. In the heart of the town itself are two important sights:

Corinium Museum, Park Street (tel. 0285/655611), houses one of the finest collections of archeological remains from the Roman occupation, all found locally in and around Cirencester. Mosaic pavements found here on Dyer Street in 1849 and other mosaics are the most important exhibits. Provincial Roman sculpture, such as figures of Minerva and Mercury, pottery, and artifacts salvaged from long-decayed buildings provide a link with the remote civilization that once flourished here. The museum has been completely modernized to include full-scale reconstructions and special exhibitions on local history and conservation. It is open from 10 a.m. to 5:30 p.m. Monday to Saturday, from 2 to 5:30 p.m. Sunday. Admission is 60p ($1.05) for adults, 30p (55¢) for children.

The restored 19th-century, two-cell jail, or **Cirencester Lock-up** as it was called in its heyday, on Trinity Road (tel. 0285/65561), is open daily by arrangement, so visitors can see interpretive displays including architectural conservation in the Cotswolds. Details of the exhibits here may be acquired at the Corinium Museum (see above).

Cirencester Parish Church, dating back to Norman times and Henry I, is the Church of John the Baptist, overlooking Market Place. (Actually, a church may have stood on this spot in Saxon times.) In size, the Cirencester church appears to be a cathedral—not a mere parish church. The present building represents a variety of styles, largely Perpendicular, as in the early-15th-century tower. Among the treasures inside are a 15th-century pulpit and a silver-gilt cup given to Queen Anne Boleyn two years before her execution.

WHERE TO STAY AND EAT

A delightful country-house atmosphere prevails at **Stratton House Hotel,** Gloucester Road, Stratton, Cirencester, Gloucestershire GL7 2LE (tel. 0285/651761), at Stratton, 1¼ miles northwest on the A417, a building that is part Jacobean and part Georgian. This mellow old house, which stands in its own beautiful grounds with a walled garden and herbaceous borders, is inviting and comfortable. The bedrooms are large and most have private bath. In the dining and drawing rooms, some fine antique furniture and oil paintings may be seen. The half-board rates range from £49.50 ($86.65) to £76 ($133) per person daily. These tariffs include an English breakfast and a well-served dinner with a wide choice of British dishes. There is a timbered-beam bar, and in winter log fires blaze in this bar and in the main hall.

The **Fleece Hotel,** Market Place, Cirencester, Gloucestershire GL7 2NZ (tel. 0285/68507). Its half-timbered façade hints at its origins as an Elizabethan coaching inn. Later it was enlarged by the Georgians. On warm days its flowering courtyard offers one of the most pleasant dining spots in town. Inside, a handful of open fireplaces warm the beamed interior whenever it's chilly. The staff offers diners French-inspired dinners priced from £18.50 ($32.40), enjoyed in an attractive restaurant or in the establishment's congenial wine bar, where local residents shuffle through a dusting of sawdust. The 23 comfortably modernized bedrooms contain old-fashioned hints of yesteryear such as quilted bedcoverings. Each has a private bath, color TV, radio, and coffee-making facilities, with B&B costing £40 ($70) daily in a single, £75 ($131.25) in a double.

4. Painswick

The sleepy little town of Painswick, four miles northeast of Stroud, is considered a model village. All of its houses, while erected at different periods, blend harmoniously, as the villagers used only Cotswold stone as their building material. The one distinctive feature on the Painswick skyline is the spire of its 15th-century parish church. The church is linked with the legend of 99 yew trees, as well as its annual Clipping Feast (not the yew trees—rather, the congregation joins hands and circles around the church as if it were a Maypole, singing hymns as they do). Ancient tombstones dot the churchyard.

WHERE TO STAY

At the rear of the Painswick church stands the **Painswick Hotel,** Kemps Lane, Painswick, Gloucestershire GL6 6YB (tel. 0452/812160). Completely refurbished, this beautiful Georgian house, with a 19th-century façade, was once a royal vicarage and is encircled by terraces of formal gardens. The hotel reception area was once the private chapel. I think this hotel offers exceptional value. Many readers have reported it to be the highlight of their Cotswold tour. In rooms, cuisine, and service, it merits consideration enough to rate a major detour from wherever else you were going. All the rooms have private baths. Rates for bed and an English breakfast are £39 ($68.25) daily in a single, £56 ($98) in a double, with VAT included. Guests booking in to stay Friday and Saturday nights or Saturday and Sunday are offered a special rate of £75 ($131.25) per night for two persons, inclusive of breakfast, a table d'hôte dinner, and VAT. There are 16 rooms in all, spread among a newer wing and those in the main building, the latter with classical proportions. The hotel has high standards of cuisine and service in its half-paneled dining room. It is managed by resident proprietors Mrs. Jacqueline Ash and her mother, Mrs. Kay Hardy, who give particular attention to their North American guests.

Before Columbus sailed on his quest for a new route to China, there was a Market Hall in Painswick, supported by stone pillars. In Shakespeare's time, Gloucestershire stone masons turned the hall into one of the most beautiful houses in the town. Today, right in the middle of Painswick, that Market Hall is **Thorne,** Friday Street, Painswick, Gloucestershire, GL6 6QJ (tel. 0452/812476), the home of Barbara and Roy Blatchley (he's a retired country doctor). Barbara welcomes guests to this handsome, beautifully appointed house on a fairly selective basis, as she has only two twin guest rooms, complete with bathrooms and central heating. The charge is from £36 ($63) per person per day for bed, breakfast, and dinner, with wine and cocktails. Meals are served in the beam-ceilinged dining room, where two of the market pillars dating from 1400 are part of the wall. Top-quality farm produce and fresh vegetables are used in the preparation of meals. If you arrive at the railway station in Stroud,

Barbara will arrange to have you picked up at no extra charge. Car guide service is also available.

WHERE TO DINE

An excellent restaurant, **The Country Elephant,** New Street (tel. 0452/813564), serves fine, English country-style cuisine. Owned and operated by Kenneth and Marril Gibson, the restaurant has a distinct personal touch. Marril does the cooking, buying the freshest ingredients locally. There is a cozy bar with an open log fire, and in the pleasantly decorated dining room you may enjoy filet of beef with oysters, fresh trout or sole, or pork filet with apricot and Stilton mousse, all cooked to order and served with a selection of fresh seasonal vegetables. Appetizers, both hot and cold, are imaginative. The dessert trolley is tempting. Meals cost from £18.50 ($32.40). Kenneth has composed an interesting and reasonably priced wine list to suit most palates. The restaurant is open for dinner from 7 to 9:30 p.m. except Sunday and Monday.

---

5. Cheltenham

In a sheltered area between the Cotswolds and the Severn Vale, a mineral spring was discovered by chance. Legend has it that the Cheltenham villagers noticed pigeons drinking from a spring and observed how healthy they were. The pigeon has therefore been incorporated into the town's crest.

Always seeking a new spa, George III arrived in 1788 and launched the town. The Duke of Wellington also came to ease his liver disorder. Even Lord Byron came this way too, proposing marriage to Miss Millbanke.

Some 100 miles from London, Cheltenham is one of England's most fashionable spas. Its architecture is mainly Regency, with lots of ironwork, balconies, and verandas. Attractive parks and open spaces of greenery make the town especially inviting.

The main street, the Promenade, has been called "the most beautiful thoroughfare in Britain." Rather similar are such thoroughfares as Lansdowne Place and Montpelier Parade. The design for the dome of the Rotunda was based on the Pantheon in Rome. Montpelier Walk, with its shops separated by caryatids, is one of the most interesting shopping centers in England.

You can take guided tours of Cheltenham on foot by checking in at the **Tourist Information Centre** on the Promenade (tel. 0242/522878). However, an advance notice of at least two days is required.

WHERE TO STAY

The best hostelry at the spa is **Queens Hotel,** Promenade, Cheltenham, Gloucestershire GL50 1NN (tel. 0242/514724). At the head of the Regency Promenade, this upper-bracket hotel looks down on the gardens. Architecturally, it is imposing, built in 1838 in the style of the Roman temple of Jupiter. This distinguished hotel has a Regency decor and an unusually fine staircase. There are 77 bedrooms, all with private bath, radio, and color TV. Accommodations at the back are quieter. Everything is well furnished, although decidedly old-fashioned. A single rents for £65 ($113.75) daily, and a double for £85 ($148.75), including service and VAT. The restaurant serves a luncheon from £10 ($17.50). A complete set dinner is £18 ($31.50).

Hotel De la Bere and Country Club, Southam, Cheltenham, Gloucestershire GL52 3NH (tel. 0242/37771), lies two miles northeast on the A46. The year A.D. 1500 is a long time ago. This beautiful house was built at the turn of the century and was owned by the De la Bere family for three centuries. It was converted into a hotel in 1972, and every effort has been made to ensure that the original charm of the building still remains. The restaurant, the Elizabethan Room, and the Royalist Room are all paneled in oak, and there is also a Great Hall, complete with its minstrel's gallery. The menu is impressive, and there are some interesting first courses. Dinner à la carte costs £18 ($31.50), with a fixed-price menu available for lunch at £8.50 ($14.90) and for dinner at £15 ($26.25). The bedrooms, five of which boast double four-poster beds, all have private bath, color TV, and tea- and coffee-making facilities. They have all been tastefully decorated and furnished to preserve their individual charm and character. Single bedrooms cost from £59 ($103.25) daily, and doubles or twins go for £90 ($157.50).

Greenway, Shurdington, near Cheltenham, Gloucestershire GL51 5UG (tel. 0242/862352), is an elegant and beautifully furnished Cotswold country house in a garden setting lying in the village of Shurdington, less than four miles southwest of Cheltenham on A46. Ivy clad, this is a Cotswold showpiece. Restored with sensitivity and decorated and furnished to a high standard, Greenway rents rooms in both its main house and in a converted coach house. Original paintings and antiques abound throughout the hotel. On a chilly day, open fires beckon. Guests are almost assured of comfort here. Some 18 well-furnished bedrooms are rented, each with private bath or shower. Singles cost £75 ($131.25) daily, with doubles going for £95 ($166.25) to £170 ($297.50). The dining room is elegantly appointed with an extension added in the Victorian conservatory style. The cooking is superb, using quality produce and good, fresh ingredients that are handled deftly. Lunch is from 12:30 to 2 p.m. Sunday to Friday, and dinner is Monday to Saturday from 7:30 to 9:30 p.m. (on Sunday at 7:30 p.m. only). A set lunch goes for £14.50 ($25.40), with a table d'hôte dinner costing £20 ($35). You can also order à la carte. Service is formal, on target, and polite, all at the same time.

WHERE TO DINE

A good place to eat along the A40 is **Twelve Suffolk Parade,** 12 Suffolk Parade (tel. 0242/584544). Norman Young, the owner, shares chef duties with David Harker, the two of them turning out meals worthy of being served in the charming French restaurant. Under the giant basket of ferns hanging in the center of the dining room, you can enjoy such specialties as chicken breast with curried mango sauce and rice flavored with cardamom and coriander, individual casseroles of sole with shrimp, and fresh, hot homemade garlic bread, while you sip one of the excellent French wines. Set lunches, served from noon to 2 p.m. Tuesday to Sunday (but not on Saturday), cost £9 ($15.75). Dinners go for around £18 ($31.50) and are served from 7:30 to 10 p.m. Tuesday to Thursday, to 10:30 p.m. on Friday and Saturday, with no dinner service on Sunday.

Le Champignon Sauvage, 24 Suffolk Rd. (tel. 0242/573449), is one of the leading restaurants of this old spa. David Matthias is a chef of considerable talent. He wisely limits his selection of dishes every night for better quality control. The style is French with English overtones. On some nights Mr. Matthias allows his imagination to roam a bit, so dining here is always a surprise, a pleasant one usually. He might stuff a wild rabbit with herbs or stuff a lamb with offal and eggplant, whatever. This "wild mushroom" serves lunch from 12:30 to 2:30 p.m. and dinner from 7:30 to 10:45 p.m. It is closed for lunch on Saturday and all day Sunday. Count on spending from £25 ($43.75) per person. Reservations are essential.

Redmond's, 12 Suffolk Rd. (tel. 0242/580323), is a premier dining room of Cheltenham. Many of its devotees rank it as the very best. Redmond Hayward, for whom this choice dining spot is named, keeps his selections of food items limited. That way, he can give his discriminating diners the best of local produce and well-chosen ingredients to go with his fine wine list. His constantly changing menu reflects the wide range of his repertoire and offers a true international flavor. Whatever your selection of a main course—perhaps chicken breast with an orange-flavored vanilla sauce—save room for one of his soufflés, which tend to be light-as-a-feather delights. Everything, certainly the soufflés, is prepared fresh and to order. Dinner, nightly from 7:15 to 10:30, offers both a table d'hôte at £17.50 ($30.65) and à la carte for around £25 ($43.75) per person. Lunch is provided at £12.50 ($21.90) only on Saturday and Sunday from noon to 2 p.m.

---

6. Royal Sudeley Castle

Sudeley is a 15th-century castle in the Cotswolds village of Winchcombe, six miles northeast of Cheltenham. The history of the castle dates back to Saxon times, when the village was the capital of the Mercian kings.

One of England's finer stately homes, Sudeley Castle attracts visitors from all over the world. There are works of art by Constable, Turner, Rubens, Van Dyck, and many others. The gardens are formal and surrounded by rolling farms and parkland. The Queen's Garden (replanted with old-fashioned roses) dates from the time when Katherine Parr, sixth wife of Henry VIII, lived and died at Sudeley. There are several permanent exhibitions, some magnificent furniture and glass, and many relics from the castle's past. Waterfowl are to be found on the Moat Pond and peacocks strut around the grounds.

In an area to the right of the keep as you enter the castle are workshops for talented local artisans who use traditional skills to produce stained glass, textiles, wood and leather articles, and marbled paper, among other items. There is also a design exhibition illustrating the use of craftsmanship in country houses.

The castle is open daily from noon to 5 p.m. Easter to the end of October. The grounds are open from 11 a.m. Admission to the castle, exhibitions, and grounds is £3.25 ($5.70) for adults, £1.74 ($3.05) for children. A family ticket for two adults and two children costs £8 ($14). For more information, phone 0242/602308.

The present owner of Sudeley Castle, Lady Ashcombe, an American by birth, has lived here for more than 25 years.

If you feel like a meal after visiting the castle, wander down to the village and to **Isbourne House,** Castle Street, Winchcombe, Cheltenham, Gloucestershire GL54 5JA (tel. 0242/602281). This is a lovely period Cotswold stone house surrounded by a well-kept garden, stone walls, and wrought-iron gates. Here Ted Saunders and his friend and colleague, Dick Whittamore, provide elegant dinners for £16 ($28) per person for three or four courses. Dinner might include hot smokies (a smoked haddock dish), Camembert frits, mushroom hors d'oeuvres, or prawns for appetizers, followed by filet de porc aux herbs, truite au four, or whole pheasant for two people. Meals for nonresidents are provided by arrangement only. If you ring Ted at least 24 hours ahead, he will be prepared to discuss the menu with you, advising on local products, what's in season, and what he can order fresh as required. In the house, part Elizabethan, part Georgian, you can have B&B for £32 ($56) to £40 ($70) per night for two, depending on whether you have the room with bath and toilet or just a shower and hand basin. The breakfast, however, will make your stay worthwhile. They begin with fruit juice and cereal, then proceed to a full platter carrying most of the following: eggs, bacon, tomatoes, lambs' kidneys, mushrooms, and sausages, along with croissants or brioche with jams and marmalade, as well as tea or coffee. Ted and Dick like to introduce guests to the local scene according to what's on the calendar, perhaps foxhunting.

---

7. Bibury

On the road from Burford to Cirencester, Bibury is one of the loveliest spots in the Cotswolds. In fact, the utopian romancer of Victoria's day, poet William Morris, called it England's most beautiful village. On the banks of the tiny Coln River,

Bibury is noted for **Arlington Row,** a gabled group of 15th-century cottages, its biggest and most-photographed drawing card. The row is protected by the National Trust.

Arlington Mill Museum (tel. 028574/368) dates from the 17th century and was in use as a mill until 1914. Mill machinery, agricultural implements, cobbler's and blacksmith's equipment, printing and weaving devices, and Victorian costumes and wedding finery are on display. There are William Morris and John Keble rooms, and you can see arts and crafts exhibits, including furniture. There is also pottery for sale. The museum is open from 10:30 a.m. to 7 p.m. (or dusk, if earlier) from mid-March to October daily, from November to February on Saturday and Sunday. Admission is £1.50 ($2.65) for adults, 70p ($1.25) for children.

WHERE TO STAY

Bibury is a good base for touring the old wool towns of the North Cotswolds. For those who prefer a secluded roadside oasis, I have the following recommendations:

Bibury Court Hotel, Bibury, Gloucestershire GL7 5NT (tel. 028574/337), is a Jacobean manor house built by Sir Thomas Sackville in 1633 (parts of it date from Tudor times). Its eight acres of grounds are approached through a large gateway, the lawn extending to the encircling Coln River. The house was privately owned until it was turned into a hotel in 1968. The structure is built of Cotswold stone, with many gables, huge chimneys, leaded-glass stone-mullioned windows, and a formal graveled entryway. Inside there are many country manor furnishings, and antiques, as well as an open stone log-burning fireplace. In rooms with bath, the rent is from £36 ($63) daily in a single, £48 ($84) to £56 ($98) in a double. Many of the rooms have four-poster beds, original oak paneling, and antiques. Meals are an event in the stately dining room, where dinners are priced from £14 ($24.50). Lunchtime bar meals cost from £4 ($7). After tea and biscuits in the drawing room, walk across the lawn along the river where you'll find a doorway leading to a little church. On your return, head for one of the coaching houses that has been converted into a drinking lounge, a restful place for a glass of stout.

Swan Hotel, Bibury, Gloucestershire GL7 5NW (tel. 028574/204), is a scene-stealer. Before you cross over the arched stone bridge spanning the Coln, pause and look at the vine-covered façade. Yes, it's the same view that has appeared on many a calendar. The former coaching inn will bed you down for the night in one of its handsomely appointed chambers, all with bath or shower, charging £35 ($61.25) in a single, £62.50 ($109.40) in a double. A traditional English breakfast and VAT are included. All of the rooms have been modernized, and there are many comforts. The special feature of the Swan is the small stretch of trout stream reserved for guests. If you're just passing through for the day, you may want to stop over and order the £11.50 ($20.15) lunch or the £15.25 ($26.70) dinner. When you see the gardens at the Swan, your exploring days may be over.

---

8. Clanfield

Clanfield lies at the foot of the Cotswolds, near the upper reaches of the Thames. In the heart of "hunting country," it is convenient to Cheltenham and the Newbury race courses. Golf and fishing are available nearby. Clanfield lies 20 miles from Oxford, 8 miles from our last stopover in Burford, and 16 miles from Swindon, and also makes a center for visits to Blenheim Palace, Stratford-upon-Avon, Henley-on-Thames, and the Cotswold Wild Life Park, only a ten-minute drive from the following recommendation.

FOOD AND LODGING

A fine example of a 16th-century manor house, **The Plough,** Bourton Road, Clanfield, Oxfordshire OX8 2RB (tel. 036781/222), is widely considered to be the most attractive building in this area. The first-class restaurant is decorated in soft pastel shades, complemented by fine crystal and silver settings. A set three-course lunch is offered, costing £15 ($26.25), and dinners can be ordered à la carte for around £26 ($45.50), VAT included. The restaurant is open seven days a week, with last orders taken at 9:30 p.m. You can enjoy drinks in the charming lounge bar in front of a huge fireplace, amid a wealth of beams and lots of old-world charm. The Plough has eight beautiful, individually decorated bedrooms, two with showers in the bathrooms and the remaining six with whirlpool baths. One room, Honeysuckle, has a four-poster bed, and another, Primrose, is made elegant by a canopied bed. All rooms have color TV, trouser press, hairdryer, and direct-dial phone. Bed and a full English breakfast costs £66 ($115.50) daily in a single, £105 ($183.75) in a double, with VAT included.

9. Burford and Minster Lovell

In Oxfordshire, as you go east or west along the A40, you can make interesting stops at Burford, right on the highway, or Minster Lovell, a short distance to the north of the main road.

BURFORD

The gateway to the Cotswolds, this unspoiled medieval town, built of Cotswold stone, is 19 miles to the west of Oxford, 31 miles from Stratford-upon-Avon, 14 miles from Blenheim Palace, and 75 miles from London. Its fame rests largely on its early Norman church (c. 1116) and its High Street, lined with coaching inns. Oliver Cromwell passed this way, as did Charles II and Nell Gwynne. Burford was one of the last of the great wool centers, the industry surviving into Victoria's reign. You may want to photograph the bridge across the Windrush River, where Queen Elizabeth I once stood. Burford is definitely equipped for tourists, as the antique shops along The High will testify.

Food and Lodging

Whether you're staying over or simply stopping off for lunch, there's a choice of some romantic old inns.

Bay Tree Hotel, Sheep Street, Burford, Oxfordshire OX8 4LW (tel. 099382/3137), would astonish the former owner of this 400-year-old, stone-gabled home. Surely Sir Lawrence Tanfield would never have predicted that this stately old house would become a peaceful setting for retreat-seekers. In his time, he was the unpopular Lord Chief Baron of the Exchequer to Elizabeth I—and was not noted for his hospitality. But time has erased the bad memory, and the splendor of this Cotswold manor house remains. The house has oak-paneled rooms with stone fireplaces, where logs burn in chilly weather. There is a high-beamed hall with a minstrel's gallery. Room after room is furnished tastefully. The 20th-century comforts, such as central heating and bathrooms in all 22 bedrooms, have been discreetly installed. And the beds are a far cry from the old rope-bottom contraptions of the days of Queen Elizabeth I. Try to get one of the rooms overlooking the terraced gardens at the rear of the house. The charge is £35 ($61.25) daily in singles, £80 ($140) in doubles.

Lamb Inn, Sheep Street, Burford, Oxfordshire OX8 4LR (tel. 099382/3155), is a thoroughbred Cotswold house, built solidly in 1430 of thick stones, with mullioned and leaded windows, many chimneys and gables, and a slate roof mossy with age. It opens onto a stone-paved rear garden, with a rose-lined walk and a shaded lawn. B&B costs from £35 ($61.25) per person daily. The bedrooms are a mixture of today's comforts, such as good beds and plentiful hot water, and antiques. The public living rooms contain heavy oak beams, stone floors, window seats, Oriental rugs, and fine antiques (Chippendale, Tudor, Adam, Georgian, Jacobean). In the drinking lounge, a special beer, made in an adjoining brewery, is served. Light lunches and snacks are served in the bars and lounges, or in the garden in summer. Dinner as well as a traditional Sunday lunch are served in the beamed dining room with a garden view. If you're dining here in the right season, you can feast on treats of the rivers or forest, such as salmon, trout, and venison.

Golden Pheasant Hotel, High Street, Burford, Oxfordshire OX8 4RV (tel. 099382/3223), has both the oldest set of property deeds surviving in Burford, as well as a location on main street. In the 1400s it was the private home of a prosperous wool merchant, but began serving food and drink in the 1730s when it used to both brew and serve beer. Like many of its neighbors, it is capped with a slate roof and fronted with light-gray hand-chiseled stones. Inside, within view of dozens of old beams and a blazing fireplace, a candlelit restaurant serves both French and English specialties. The hotel offers a dozen bedrooms, a pair with four-poster beds, but each with private bath, radio, TV, phone, time-blackened ceiling beams, and coffee-making equipment. Depending on the season, and with an English breakfast included, singles range from £36 ($63) to £42 ($73.50) daily and doubles or twins from £49 ($85.75) to £69 ($120.75).

MINSTER LOVELL

From Oxford along the A40, you pass through Witney. Soon after, you turn right at the Minster Lovell signpost, about half a mile off the highway between Witney and Burford. Long since passed by the main road, the village is visited because of **Minster Lovell Hall and Dovecote** (tel. 0993/775315). In ruins, the hall dates from the 1400s. The medieval dovecote with nesting boxes survives. An early Lovell is said to have hidden in the moated manor house and subsequently starved to death after a battle in the area. The hall and dovecote can be visited daily from 10 a.m. to 6 p.m. from Good Friday to the end of September, from 10 a.m. to 4 p.m. off-season. Closed Monday. Admission is 80p ($1.40) for adults, 40p (70¢) for children. The legend of the mistletoe bough originated in the village by the Windrush River. Minster Lovell is mainly built of Cotswold stone, with thatch or stone-slate roofs. It's rather a pity that there is a forest of TV antennas, but the place is still attractive to photographers.

Food and Lodging

The Old Swan Hotel, Main Street, Old Minster, Minster Lovell, Oxfordshire OX8 5RN (tel. 0993/775614), has been an inn for some 600 years. It offers a unique blend of Cotswold stone and half-timbering. The Swan and the manor house (now in ruins) were once the two most important buildings in the village. The manor house was the home of the Lovell family, close friends of Richard III, whom they entertained there while his servants slept at the Swan. Polished flagstone floors and traditional log fires are reminders of those times. Today the Old Swan offers 20th-century comfort in historic surroundings. All ten bedrooms have private bath, phone, and color TV, and are individually furnished. There's even an impressive four-poster suite. A twin- or double-bedded room costs from £54 ($94.50) daily and a single from £43 ($75.25). The price includes VAT and a full English breakfast. In the beamed candlelit restaurant you can enjoy fine food, some of which is grown in the gardens of the hotel. Luncheon is £8.50 ($14.90), to £10.50 ($18.40), dinner from about £18 ($31.50), and a light snack is available in the bar during the week.

10. Shipton-under-Wychwood

Taking the A361 road, en route from Burford to Chipping Norton, you arrive after a turn-off at the little village of Shipton-under-Wychwood in Oxfordshire. It's about four miles north of Burford; but don't blink or you'll pass it right by.

WHERE TO STAY AND DINE

The site of a hospice for dispensing aid to the poor operated by monks as part of the Bruern Abbey in the 13th century, **The Shaven Crown,** High Street, Shipton-under-Wychwood, Oxfordshire OX7 6BA (tel. 0993/830330), was built of rugged Cotswold stone during the reign of Queen Elizabeth I. It is on the main village road, and opens onto a triangular village green in the shadow of a church. Most of the rooms overlook a cobblestone courtyard and garden and have some antiques. Private baths have been installed in every bedroom. The charge for B&B is £24 ($42) daily in a single and £56 ($98) in a double. Half board is offered for £33 ($57.75) per person per day if you stay two or more days.

11. Chipping Norton

Just inside the Oxfordshire border is Chipping Norton, another gateway town to the Cotswolds. Since the days of Henry IV it has been an important market town, and its main street is a curiosity as it's built on a slope, making one side higher than the other.

Chipping Norton was long known for its tweed mills. Also seek out its Guild-hall, its church, and its handsome almshouses. If you're touring, you can search for the nearby prehistoric Rollright Stones, more than 75 stones forming a circle 100 feet in diameter—the "Stonehenge of the Cotswolds." Chipping Norton lies 11 miles from Burford, 20 miles from Oxford, and 21 miles from Stratford-upon-Avon.

WHERE TO STAY AND DINE

The town's best-known inn is the **White Hart,** High Street, Chipping Norton, Oxfordshire OX7 5AD (tel. 0608/2572), which stands in the center of this Cotswold town. Its façade overlooking the Market Place, the White Hart traces its origins to Richard II in the 13th century. However, its stone exterior is from the 18th century. Once it was a favorite stopover for wayfarers between London and Worcester. The hotel still retains many of its historical mementos in its public rooms. In winter, fires still greet guests as they did when this was a stopover for the coaching trade. The hotel has been modernized with many amenities, yet some of its Regency style is still intact. Guests gather for drinks in a stone-clad bar, with a log fire, before heading for the restaurant, serving British cookery. The bedrooms, 22 in all, are well furnished and comfortably appointed. Six contain private baths, and two are fitted with four-poster beds. Each unit contains color TV, phone, and either electric fires or central heating. Singles range from £30 ($52.50) to £45 ($78.75) daily, and doubles cost £58 ($101.50) to £88 ($154).

The leading restaurant in town is **La Madonette,** 7 Horsefair (tel. 0608/2320), which is a Cotswold stone cottage, graced with a bay window, lying only a short walk from the Market Place. A Frenchman, Alain Ritter, maintains this oasis of grace and quality cooking in an area where men often ask for a "gin and tonic, tomato soup, and a good steak." in that order. This is the type of restaurant you expect to encounter in a charming little French village. Under a beamed ceiling, often with a fire going, you can peruse the menu. He handles fish with style and flair, as exemplified by my most recently sampled salmon steak with langoustine tails. My dining companion that evening ordered venison steak cooked pink with an armagnac sauce, and it was delectable. On other occasions I have enjoyed spring lamb cooked with fresh tarragon. Whatever you are likely to be served on any given evening, know that care and concern will go into the dish, beginning with the shopping earlier that day. Only dinner, costing from £25 ($43.75), is served, and it's offered from 7:30 to 9:45 p.m. Closed Sunday and Monday.

An Old Mill on the Outskirts

Mill House Hotel & Restaurant, Kingham, Oxfordshire, OX7 6UH (tel. 060871/8188). In A.D. 1086 reference was made in the *Domesday Book* to a mill worth 44 pence in lease value situated at "Corsingham of the King." This same mill on the Cornwell Brook at Kingham in Oxfordshire turns leisurely today as the centerpiece in one of rural England's finest regional hotels, where the nostalgia of days gone by merges with today. The Mill House Hotel envelops all that was charming of the original mill and bakehouse, and it has been possible to infuse modern amenities without detracting from the original purpose of the buildings. There are comfortable lounges with log fires and old stone floors and oak beams. In the Lounge Bar, the original ovens of the old bakehouse line the wall. The bedrooms, all with private bath and shower, color TV, radio, and phone, have been refurbished to a high standard as has the enlarged restaurant, now one of the finest in the Cotswolds. The B&B rate is £55 ($96.25) daily in a double, £45 ($78.75) in a single. The hotel has an award-winning chef, who offers excellent à la carte and fixed-price menus, and the wine list is based on some 175 bins. Even if you're not a resident, you may want to call for a reservation. Lunch is daily from 12:30 to 2 p.m., with dinner served from 7 to 9:45 p.m. Meals begin at £12 ($21), going up. Guests at this establishment, standing in some ten acres of ground bounded by a trout stream, will be warmly welcomed by John and Valerie Barnett, the resident owners.

12. Bourton-on-the-Water

In this most scenic Cotswold village, you can be like Gulliver, voyaging first to Brobdingnag, then to Lilliput. Brobdingnag is Bourton-on-the-Water, lying 85 miles from London, on the banks of the tiny Windrush River.

To see Lilliput, you have to visit the **Old New Inn** (tel. 0451/20467). In the garden is a near-perfect and most realistic model village. It's open daily from 9:30 a.m. till dusk, and costs 90p ($1.60) for adults, 80p ($1.40) for children.

If you're coming to the Cotswolds by train from London, the nearest rail station is in Moreton-on-Marsh, eight miles away. Buses make connections with the trains, however.

Among the attractions in the area, **Birdland** (tel. 0451/20689) is a handsomely designed garden set on about five acres, containing some 1,200 birds of 362 different species. Included is the largest and most varied collection of penguins in any zoo, with underwater viewing. In the tropical house are hummingbirds. Many of the birds are on view in captivity for the first time. From March to November the hours for seeing these exotic birds and flowers are 10:30 a.m. to 5 p.m.; other months, 10:30 a.m. to 4 p.m. Admission is £1.75 ($3.05) for adults and £1 ($1.75) for children up to 14 years old.

WHERE TO STAY AND EAT

Bourton-on-the-Water offers a handful of quite good accommodations, all of them inexpensive in spite of its reputation as a tourist attraction.

The **Old New Inn,** High Street, Bourton-on-the-Water, Cheltenham, Gloucestershire GL54 2AF (tel. 0451/20467), can lay claim to being the leading hostelry in the village. Right in the center, overlooking the river, it's a good example of Queen Anne design. But it is mostly visited because of the miniature model village in its garden (referred to earlier). Hungry or tired travelers are drawn to the old-fashioned comforts and cuisine of this most English inn. The B&B rate is from £22 ($38.50) per person nightly, including service charge and VAT. The rooms are comfortable, with homelike furnishings, soft beds, and eight with private bath. Nonresidents are also welcome here for meals, with lunches at £5 ($8.75) and dinners from £12 ($21). You may want to spend an evening in the pub lounge, playing darts or chatting with the villagers.

On the outskirts, **Farncombe,** Clapton, Bourton-on-the-Water, Cheltenham, Gloucestershire GL54 2LG (tel. 0451/20120), lies about 2½ miles from Bourton-on-the-Water. The little hamlet is a "secret address" known to the discerning English who stay here when the more popular and more famous place is overrun with tourists. Mrs. J. M. Wright receives guests from April to October. She rents only three rooms, each suitable for two persons, charging from £22 ($38.50) for B&B. Considering the hospitality and the comfort, the rooms are worth far more. Try to make this place your center for touring the Cotswolds, branching out on day trips. The property opens onto views of the Windrush Valley.

Old Manse Hotel, Victoria Street, Bourton-on-the-Water, Cheltenham, Gloucestershire GL54 2BX (tel. 0451/20082), is reminiscent of the setting of Nathaniel Hawthorne's *Mosses from an Old Manse.* A gem architecturally, the ivy-covered hotel is by the slow-moving river that wanders through the village green. Built of Cotswold stone, with chimneys, dormers, and small-paned windows, it has been modernized inside, and all rooms have color TVs, radios, and central heating. The charge is £46 ($80.50) to £60 ($105) daily for two persons in a twin with private bath, £35 ($61.25) to £41 ($71.75) in a single. A continental breakfast is included in the rates. The inn's best feature is the stone fireplace in the dining room, and the wood-paneled bar is nice too. Dining is a treat here. The manse is closed during the first week in January.

Rose Tree, Riverside (tel. 0451/20635), has a setting like a stage designer's fantasy of the perfect English weekend retreat. It includes a 300-year-old cottage on a village green near the mossy vegetation of a nearby stream. Those elements, combined with the culinary specialties, create an ambience that's hard to resist. A small but carefully researched menu changes with the availability of the ingredients. Try fresh baked trout, seasonal pot roast of venison, or any of several preparations of English lamb. If it's warm enough, you might want to sit at one of the outdoor tables. A set dinner costs £17.50 ($30.65). The restaurant is open for dinner from 7:30 to 8:30 p.m. daily except Sunday and Monday. The only day lunch is served is on Sunday, from 12:30 to 2 p.m., when a traditional midday meal costs £10 ($17.50). Reservations are suggested. Closed from mid-January to mid-February.

A MUSEUM AT NORTHLEACH

Opened in 1981, the **Cotswold Countryside Collection,** Fosseway (Cotswold District Council) (tel. 0451/60715), is a museum of rural life displays. You can see the Lloyd-Baker collection of agricultural history, including wagons, horse-drawn implements, and tools, as well as a "seasons of the year" display. A Cotswold gallery records the social history of the area. "Below Stairs" is an exhibition of laundry, dairy, and kitchen. The museum's home was a House of Correction, and its history is displayed in the reconstructed cellblock and courtroom. The museum is open daily from 10 a.m. to 5:30 p.m. (from 2 to 5:30 p.m. on Sunday). Admission is 75p ($1.30) for adults, 45p (80¢) for children. Northleach lies off the A40 between Burford and Cheltenham.

13. Stow-on-the-Wold

This Cotswold market town is unspoiled, in spite of the busloads of tourists who stop off en route to Broadway and Chipping Campden, about ten miles away. The town is the highest in the Cotswolds, built on a wold about 800 feet above sea level. In its open market square, you can still see the stocks where offenders in days gone by were jeered at and punished by the townspeople with a rotten egg in the face. The final battle between the Roundheads and the Royalists took place in Stow-on-the-Wold. The town, which is really like a village, is used by many for exploring not only the Cotswold wool towns but also Stratford-upon-Avon, 21 miles away. The nearest rail station is at Moreton-in-Marsh, four miles away.

WHERE TO STAY AND DINE

A wealth of old inns is to be found here.

Wyck Hill House, Burford Road, Stow-on-the-Wold, Cheltenham, Gloucestershire GL54 1HY (tel. 0451/31936), dates from 1720 when its stone walls were begun as the manor house for the parish church of Wyck-Rissington. After a long and varied history, it was discovered in 1984 by two Texas-born Anglophiles who restored it to elegance before selling it to a London travel company. One wing of the manor house, it was discovered, rested on the foundations of a Roman villa. Today, Wyck Hill is one of the most sophisticated country hotels in the region, lying on 33 acres of grounds and gardens two miles south of Stow-on-the-Wold. The opulent interior pays attention to 18th-century authenticity. Room after room leads into paneled libraries, Adam sitting rooms, and a sun-flooded bay-windowed dining room. Sixteen well-furnished bedrooms are in the hotel, ten in the coach house annex, and six in the orangery. Accommodations range in price from £70 ($122.50) to £145 ($253.75) for two persons daily. Excellent food is also served, a three-course luncheon costing £13.50 ($23.65), an à la carte dinner going for around £26 ($45.50).

Stow Lodge Hotel, The Square, Stow-on-the-Wold, Cheltenham, Gloucestershire GL54 1AB (tel. 0451/30485), dominates the Market Place, but is set back far enough to maintain its aloofness. Its gardens, honeysuckle growing over the stone walls, diamond-shaped windows, gables, and many chimneys, capture the best of country living, while letting you anchor right into the heart of town. Mr. and Mrs. Jux, the owners, who are partners with their daughter and son-in-law, Mr. and Mrs. Hartley, offer 22 ample, well-furnished bedrooms, all with private bath, radio, TV, B&B, central heating, and tea- and coffee-making facilities. Depending on the season, the daily rate in a double or twin ranges from £47 ($82.25) to £52 ($91) with a full English breakfast included. Arrange to have your afternoon tea out back by the flower garden. The owners discovered an old (approximately 1770) open stone fireplace in their lounge and since have offered log fires as an added attraction.

The Grapevine Hotel, Sheep Street, Stow-on-the-Wold, Cheltenham, Gloucestershire GL54 1AU (tel. 0451/30344), mingles urban sophistication with reasonable prices, rural charm, and intimacy. Known both for its hotel and restaurant, it is one of the most innovative and charming places to stay in this much-visited village. It was named after the ancient vine whose tendrils shade and shelter the beautiful conservatory restaurant. The reading room, comfortable lounge, and cozy bar with Victorian accessories create a warm ambience for tea, bar snacks, or dinner. Full meals feature English, French, and Italian cuisine and are served from 7 to 9 p.m. daily. Bar snacks are served at midday. Dinners are more elaborate, costing from £15.95 ($27.90) and including, perhaps, turkey scallops with white wine sauce, beef filet topped with Stilton, or, for the vegetarian, garlic mushroom mille-feuilles.

The transformation of a pair of Cotswold stone-sided houses into this hotel was the personal statement of Sandra Elliott. She supervised the decor of the 18 bedrooms, each with a private bath or shower, tasteful furnishings, color TV, phone, radio, hairdryer, and tea/coffee-makers. The dinner, bed, and breakfast rate is £39.95 ($69.90) per person daily, with B&B going for £30 ($52.50) per person. A "bargain break" rate is also available.

The Fosse Manor Hotel, Fosse Way, Stow-on-the-Wold, Cheltenham, Gloucestershire GL54 1AX (tel. 0451/30354). Its stone walls and neo-Gothic gables are almost concealed by strands of ivy, which threaten to engulf even the windows. It lies about a mile south of Stow-on-the-Wold along the A429 near the site of an ancient Roman road that used to bisect England. From your high stone-sided window, you might enjoy a view of a landscaped garden with a sunken lily pond, flagstone walks, and an old-fashioned sundial. Inside, the interior is conservatively modernized with such touches as a padded and upholstered bar and a dining room. Bedrooms are home-like, with matching fabrics and wallpaper. Many contain a private bath or shower, and two of the rooms are favorites of honeymooners. Overnight rates are £35 ($61.25) in a single, £53 ($92.75) to £75 ($131.25) in a double, including breakfast, VAT, and service.

14. Lower Swell

Near Stow-on-the-Wold, Lower Swell is a twin. Both it and Upper Swell, its sister, are small villages of the Cotswolds. The hamlets are not to be confused with Upper and Lower Slaughter.

WHERE TO STAY AND DINE

You may want to anchor in for the night or stop for a meal at the following recommendation:

The **Old Farmhouse Hotel,** Lower Swell, Stow-on-the-Wold, Cheltenham, Gloucestershire GL54 1LF (tel. 0451/30232), is a small, intimate 16th-century hotel in the heart of the Cotswolds, one mile west of Stow-on-the-Wold. It was converted from a 16th-century farmhouse. The hotel has been completely refurbished and the original fireplaces restored, once again blazing with log fires. The relaxed, friendly atmosphere, together with excellent food and wine, has made this a popular stop for visitors, so reserving a room before arrival is strongly recommended. Rollo and Rosemary Belsham have 13 bedrooms to rent, all with color TV and 11 with private bath. Two accommodations under the eaves share a bath. All the units are different because of the building's farmhouse origin, so there are two price levels for B&B with private bath according to room quality, plus a third for the two four-poster bedrooms. All prices include a cooked English breakfast. The B&B rate in a double or twin-bedded room ranges from £39 ($68.25) daily with a shared bath up to £60 ($105) with a four-poster bed and a private bath. Dinner is served daily from 7 p.m., with last orders taken at 9 p.m. The table d'hôte menu is changed daily, costing £10.50 ($18.40). The hotel has a secluded walled garden and ample private parking. It is closed from Christmas to mid-January.

15. Upper and Lower Slaughter

Midway between Bourton-on-the-Water and Stow-on-the-Wold are the twin villages of Upper and Lower Slaughter. Don't be put off by the name because these are two of the prettiest villages in the Cotswolds. Actually the name "Slaughter" was a corruption of "de Sclotre," the original Norman landowner. The houses are constructed of honey-colored Cotswold stone, and a stream meanders right through the street, providing a home for the ducks that wander freely about, begging scraps from kindly visitors. In Upper Slaughter you can visit a fine example of a 17th-century Cotswold manor house.

WHERE TO STAY AND DINE

In its own private grounds, surrounded by flower beds and shady trees, the **Lower Slaughter Manor,** Lower Slaughter, Cheltenham, Gloucestershire GL54 2HP (tel. 0451/20456), is steeped in a thousand years of history, yet it offers the facilities of a modern, first-class hotel. Even before the Norman conquest a manor house stood on this spot, becoming at some period a convent housing the nuns of the Bridgetine Order of Syon for a few centuries. A reminder of those days is a decorated ceiling on which pious words are used as a motif. After the break-up of religious houses and expulsion of the nuns, the house was given to the high sheriff of Gloucestershire in 1608, and he rebuilt it much as it is today. The west wing was added, as was the stable block with its central clock tower and the great stone fireplace.

The bedrooms are handsome and spacious, all with baths, color TVs, radios, and direct-dial phones. Some have four-poster beds. Double rooms are rented for single occupancy for £60 ($105) to £80 ($140) nightly for bed, early morning tea, a continental breakfast, and VAT. As a double, the charge is £70 ($122.50) to £85 ($148.75). The four-poster rooms costs £90 ($157.50) to £145 ($253.75). In the manor's restaurant you can enjoy traditional English country cooking, with each meal cooked fresh using locally grown produce, herbs from the house's gardens, honey from Cotswold bees, local free-range eggs, and homemade preserves. Guests can use the heated indoor swimming pool with a sauna and a solarium, or in good weather, the croquet lawn and tennis court.

Lords of the Manor Hotel, Upper Slaughter, Cheltenham, Gloucestershire GL54 2JD (tel. 0451/20243), is a 17th-century house standing on several acres of rolling fields and gardens that include a stream flowing through the grounds in which guests fish for brown trout. Modernized in its amenities, the hotel has still been successful in maintaining the quiet country-house atmosphere of 300 years ago. The 15 guest rooms are equipped with private bath, and many rooms have views of the Cotswold hills. Rates, which include a full English breakfast, VAT, and service, range from £80 ($140) to £115 ($201.25) daily for a double, depending on the plumbing. Singles cost from £55 ($96.25). The walls in the lounge bar are hung with family portraits of the original lords of the manor. Another bar overlooks the garden, and chintz and antiques are everywhere. The country atmosphere is carried into the dining room as well, with its antiques and mullioned windows. All the well-prepared dishes are fresh and home-cooked. You'll pay an average of about £23 ($40.25) for an à la carte dinner with dessert and coffee. The cooking is modern English with some French influence.

---

16. Moreton-in-Marsh

As it's connected by rail to Paddington Station in London (83 miles away), Moreton-in-Marsh is an important center for train passengers headed for the Cotswolds. It is very near many of the villages of interest—Bourton-on-the-Water, 8 miles; Stow-on-the-Wold, 4 miles; Broadway, 8 miles; Chipping Campden, 7 miles; Stratford-upon-Avon, 17 miles away.

Each of the Cotswold towns has its distinctive characteristics. In Moreton-in-Marsh, look for the 17th-century Market Hall and its old Curfew Tower, and then walk down its High Street, where Roman legions trudged centuries ago (the town once lay on the ancient Fosse Way). Incidentally, if you base here, don't take the name Moreton-in-Marsh too literally. Marsh derives from an old word meaning border.

WHERE TO STAY

In a 300-year-old structure, the **Manor House Hotel,** High Street, Moreton-in-Marsh, Gloucestershire GL56 0LJ (tel. 0608/50501), is complete with its own ghost, a priest's hiding hole, a secret passage, and a Moot Room used centuries ago by local merchants to settle arguments over wool exchanges. On the main street, it is formal, yet gracious, and its rear portions reveal varying architectural periods of design. Here, the vine-covered walls protect the garden. Inside are many living rooms, one especially intimate with leather chairs and a fireplace-within-a-fireplace, ideal for drinks and the exchange of "bump-in-the-night" stories. Mr. and Mrs. Fentum, the owners, who have been joined by their Swiss-hotel-trained daughter and son-in-law, have instructed the staff to keep the log fires burning—"never spare the woodpile." They have added a heated indoor pool, a spa bath, and a sauna. You can't miss on most of the bedrooms, as they are tastefully furnished, often with antiques or fine reproductions. Many have fine old desks set in front of window ledges, with a view of the garden and ornamental pond. All contain color TV. A single without bath costs £27 ($47.25) daily, increasing to £45 ($78.75) with bath. In a bathless double the tariff is £55 ($96.25), going up to £72.50 ($126.90) with bath, all prices including breakfast and VAT. In addition, Apple House, between the garden and the hotel orchard, contains three double bedrooms, each with shower, toilet, and basin. The cost is £55 ($96.25) per room, with breakfast and VAT included. A favorite nook is the bar-lounge, with its garden view through leaded Gothic windows. Evening meals in the two-level dining room are candlelit. A table d'hôte lunch goes for £8 ($14), and dinner is £17 ($29.75).

Redesdale Arms, High Street, Moreton-in-Marsh, Gloucestershire GL56 0AN (tel. 0608/50308), owned by Michael C. Elvis and Patricia M. Seedhouse, a long-enduring favorite, is one of the best-kept coaching inns in the Cotswolds. It has been a landmark along the old Fosse Way for some two centuries. Some of the look of the 1700s is still evident, but the inn has been considerably upgraded. Guests gravitate to the bar lounge, where drinks are served in front of a six-foot-high stone fireplace in winter. In warmer months, the courtyard is a favorite spot for having a leisurely snack or drink. Each bedroom is tastefully and individually furnished. The majority of the units contain private baths. A bathless single costs £35 ($61.25) daily, and a double or twin without bath costs £49.75 ($87.05). With bath, a double or twin goes for £57.50 ($100.65). All prices include an English breakfast and VAT. The inn is also well known for its meals: a three-course dinner costs £11 ($19.25); a full à la carte menu is also offered. Bar snacks are available at lunchtime and in the evening, and on Sunday, you can enjoy the classic English roast lunch in full for £8.95 ($15.65). The dining room is open seven days a week.

The White Hart Royal Hotel, High Street, Moreton-in-Marsh, Gloucestershire GL56 0BA (tel. 0608/50731), is a mellow old Cotswold inn. It's also another one of the hostelries graced by Charles I (in 1644), who did a lot of sleeping around. The inn provides the amenities of today without compromising the personality of yesteryear. There are 18 well-furnished bedrooms, with hot and cold running water (some with private bath), innerspring mattresses, and a few antiques intermixed with basic 20th-century pieces. Singles cost £52 ($91) daily, and twins or doubles with bath go for £75 ($131.25). All rates include service and VAT. The bar lounge is built of irregular Cotswold stone. You can have drinks in front of the ten-foot open fireplace.

---

17. Broadway

This is the best-known Cotswold village. Its wide and beautiful High Street is flanked with honey-colored stone buildings with mullioned windows remarkable for the harmony of their style and design. Overlooking the Vale of Evesham, Broadway is virtually mobbed with tourists in summer, a major stopover for bus tours. That it retains its charm in spite of the invasion is a credit to its character. Broadway lies near Evesham at the southern tip of Hereford and Worcester. Many of the prime attractions of the Cotswolds as well as Shakespeare Country lie within easy reach of Broadway. Stratford-upon-Avon is only 15 miles away. The nearest rail stations are at Evesham and Moreton-in-Marsh.

WHERE TO STAY

For lodgings, Broadway has the dubious distinction of sheltering the most expensive inn in the Cotswolds. Even the guesthouses can command a good price—and get it.

Lygon Arms, High Street, Broadway, Hereford and Worcester WR12 7DU (tel. 0386/852255), a many-gabled structure whose mullioned windows look right out on the road in the center of town, basks in its reputation as one of the greatest old English inns. In the rear it opens onto a private garden, with three acres of lawns, trees, and borders of flowers, stone walls with roses, and nooks for tea or sherry. The oldest portions, built of fieldstone with a mossy slate roof, date from the 16th century, but builders many times since have made their additions. King Charles I reputedly drank with his friends in one of the oak-lined chambers, and later, his principal enemy, Oliver Cromwell, slept here on the night before the Battle of Worcester. Today, an earlier century is evoked by the almost overwhelmingly charming cluster of antique-laden public rooms. These include cavernous fireplaces, smoke-stained paneling, 18th-century pieces, and polished brass. You dine in the oak-paneled Great Hall, with a Tudor fireplace, a vaulted ceiling, and a Minstrels' Gallery. Many but not all the rooms are in the antique style. A new wing offers more 20th-century styling. If you choose to stay here, singles cost from £70 ($122.50) to £90 ($157.50) daily, and doubles, £105 ($183.75) to £195 ($341.25), with a continental breakfast and VAT included. Each room contains a radio, TV, phone, hairdryer, and trouser press.

Dormy House, Willersey Hill, Broadway, Hereford and Worcester WR12 7LF (tel. 0386/852711), two miles southeast of Broadway on the A44, is a manor house standing high on a hill above the village, with views in all directions. Its spectacular position has made it a favorite place for those who desire either a meal, afternoon tea, or lodgings. Halfway between Broadway and Chipping Campden, it was created from a sheep farm. The owners transformed it, furnishing the 17th-century farmhouse with a few antiques, good soft beds, and full central heating, extending these amenities to an old adjoining timbered barn, which they converted into studio rooms, with open-beamed ceilings. All of the accommodations have color TV, radio clock alarms, and private baths. Units in the main house include suites, even a penthouse, renting for £116 ($203). Singles cost £45 ($78.75) to £60 ($105) daily, depending on the standard of the room. Doubles, ranging from small to twin to four-poster units, are priced from £90 ($157.50) to £105 ($183.75). Rates include a full English breakfast and VAT. The establishment serves excellent cuisine, a table d'hôte luncheon costing £14.25 ($24.95), and a fixed-price dinner going for £21.75 ($38.05), both with coffee included. The cellar contains a superb selection of wines. Bar meals range from around £4 ($7). Bowls of fresh flowers adorn tables and alcoves throughout the hotel.

Buckland Manor, Buckland, Broadway, Gloucestershire WR12 7LY (tel. 0386/852626), about two miles south of Broadway via the B4632, across the county line in Gloucestershire, is an imposing slate-roofed manor house ringed with fences of Cotswold stone, green lawns, lambs, and daffodils. Its jutting chimneys rise a few steps from the Buckland church, with its darkened stone tower. The core of the manor house was erected in the 13th century, with wings added in succeeding centuries, especially the 19th. Adrienne and Barry Berman, after he retired as an accountant in London, poured labor, love, and money into making this an exquisitely furnished property, with 11 bedrooms to rent. The Oak Room, with a four-poster bed and burnished paneling, occupies what used to be a private library. In each of the rooms, leaded windows overlook lush gardens and grazing land with Highland cattle and Jacob sheep. Even the oversize bathrooms each contain at least one antique, as well as carpeting and modern plumbing, and all the rooms have color TV and phone. Singles rent for £115 ($201.25) to £130 ($227.50) daily and doubles for £125 ($218.75) to £175 ($306.25). Prices include early morning tea, a full English breakfast, and VAT. French-inspired meals, served in the elegant dining room with a baronial fireplace, cost from £20 ($35). Children under 12 are not accommodated. The hotel is closed for three weeks between January and February.

Broadway Hotel, The Green, Broadway, Hereford and Worcester WR12 7AB (tel. 0386/852401), is right on the village green, perhaps one of the most colorful houses in Broadway. It is a converted 15th-century house, formerly used by the abbots of Pershore, combining the half-timbered look of the Vale of Evesham with the stone of the Cotswolds. While keeping its old-world charm, the hotel has been modernized and converted to provide comforts. All rooms have private bath or shower, color TV, tea- and coffee-making equipment, central heating, and bedside phone. A single costs £33 ($57.75) daily, and doubles go for £62 ($108.50) to £70 ($122.50). All tariffs include an English breakfast, service, and VAT. One of the rooms with full private bath has a four-poster bed. The cooking is fine, the service personal, the dining room attractive, the bedrooms pleasantly furnished. The comfortable cocktail bar is well stocked.

Collin House Hotel & Restaurant, Collin Lane, Broadway, Hereford and Worcester WR12 7PB (tel. 0386/858354), was a 16th-century farmhouse built of Cotswold stone. Transformed into a hotel by John and Judith Mills, it sits on a country lane in eight acres of gardens and orchards. The seven cozy bedrooms are named for flowers that grow here in profusion. Large structural timbers, tasteful wallpaper, private baths, and mullioned windows make the rooms attractive. "Wild Rose," with its sloped ceiling, is probably the most romantic. Singles cost £33 ($57.75) daily, with doubles going for £61 ($106.75) to £69 ($120.75), with a full English breakfast (minimum two nights). A bar/lounge offers seating beside an inglenook fireplace. Traditional English food, flavorfully and freshly prepared by Judith, is served in the evening by candlelight. In a room with stone-rimmed windows and ceiling beams, you can enjoy such specialties as crisp duckling with kumquats and pineapple sauce and baked breast of chicken with a grape and vermouth sauce. A three-course evening meal costs £13 ($22.75) to £15.50 ($27.15). At noon informal bar lunches are served beside the fire. The hotel lies one mile west of Broadway along the A44. From Broadway, follow the signs to Evesham before turning right onto Collin Lane.

WHERE TO DINE

Set back from the main street, **Hunter's Lodge Restaurant,** High Street (tel. 0386/853247), is surrounded by its own lawns, flower beds, and shady trees. The stone gables are partially covered with ivy, and the windows are deep-set with mullions and leaded panes. There is a formal entrance, with a circular drive and a small foyer furnished with antiques. The Swiss chef/proprietor is Kurt Friedli. His wife, Dottie, greets you, discusses the menu, and makes sure you have everything you want in the way of food and service. That might include rabbit casserole, wild duck with orange and fresh cream, or two quails on a skewer grilled with bacon and apples and finished with apple brandy. In summer you can eat in the garden. Dottie says she doesn't try to make "every chair pay the maximum." If somebody wants only one course, that's all right with her. Three courses at dinnertime will cost around £20 ($35) per person. Lunch is lighter and simpler—perhaps chicken liver pâté followed by sea bream with herb butter and vegetables, topped off by a homemade dessert, a meal costing about £12 ($21). Lunch is served from 12:30 to 2 p.m., and dinner from 7:30 to 10 p.m. The Lodge is closed on Sunday night and all day Monday.

18. Chipping Campden

The English themselves, regardless of how often they visit the Cotswolds, are attracted in great numbers to this town. It's neither too large nor too small. Off the main road, it's easily accessible to major points of interest, and double-decker buses frequently run through here on their way to Oxford (36 miles away) or Stratford-upon-Avon (12 miles away).

On the northern edge of the Cotswolds above the Vale of Evesham, Campden, a Saxon settlement, was recorded in the *Domesday Book*. In medieval times, rich merchants built homes of Cotswold stone along its model High Street, described by the historian G. M. Trevelyan as "the most beautiful village street now left in the island." The houses have been so well preserved that Chipping Campden to this day remains a gem of the Middle Ages. Its church dates from the 15th century, and its old Market Hall is the loveliest in the Cotswolds. Look also for its almshouses. They and the Market Hall were built by a great wool merchant, Sir Baptist Hicks, whose tomb is in the church.

WHERE TO STAY

Here are several good choices, all in the medium-priced range:

Noel Arms Hotel, High Street, Chipping Campden, Gloucestershire GL55 6AT (tel. 0386/840317), may make you a snob. You just may assume a title for the night, dreaming that this is your personal manor house, with its staff of servants. Dating back to the 14th century, the Noel Arms is a famous establishment. All rooms have private baths, direct-dial phones, and tea/coffee-makers. Singles rent for £37.50 ($65.65) daily, doubles going for £48.75 ($85.30), and doubles with four-poster beds costing £58.50 ($102.40). Included in the prices are a full English breakfast and VAT. Be sure to ask for a room in the main building, as those in the modern annex tend to be much less attractive. You can drive your car under the covered archway and into the old posting yard, where parking is private. The food here always draws praise. Lunch averages £8 ($14) and dinner runs £13.50 ($23.65) to £16.50 ($28.90), if you order from the à la carte menus. The food is traditional English: poached salmon, roast sirloin of beef with Yorkshire pudding, roast leg of lamb with onion sauce, steak hollandaise, apple and loganberry pie. There's a private sitting room for residents, but you may prefer the lounge, with its 12-foot-wide fireplace. The adjoining room is the public tavern—public in the sense that it's frequented by the locals. It's almost too quaint: old worn curved settles where you can drink beer from mugs of pewter, and soak up an atmosphere enhanced by racks of copper, brass pans, medallions, and oak tables and chairs worn from centuries of use.

Cotswold House Hotel, The Square, Chipping Campden, Gloucestershire GL55 6AN (tel. 0386/840330), is a stately, formal Regency house dating from 1800. Right in the heart of the village, opposite the old wool market, it is run by Mr. and Mrs. Robert Greenstock. They have brought a high taste level to this handsome old house, set in 1½ acres of tended, walled garden with shaded seating. They are rightfully proud of the winding Regency staircase in the reception hall. All 15 bedrooms, each with private bath, have been renovated. They are individually furnished with themes ranging from Gothic to French to military, with many others included along the way. There is even an Indian Room complete with tiger's head. Singles rent for £40 ($70) to £47.50 ($83.15) daily, and doubles or twins run £70 ($122.50) to £90 ($157.50). All tariffs include full breakfast and VAT. You can dine either in the restaurant, which serves first-class food, a combination of the best of English and French, in a formal elegant room, or else in Greenstocks All-day Eaterie, open from 9:30 a.m. to last orders at 9:30 p.m. Here light dishes and meals are served.

Kings Arms Hotel, The Square, Chipping Campden, Gloucestershire GL55 6AW (tel. 0386/840256), stands right in the center. It is partly Georgian, partly much older, a pretty house with a large garden in which you can wander and whence come the fresh vegetables for your good dinner. All the accommodations are well furnished and spotlessly clean. The rate is £25 ($43.75) to £28 ($49) per person without bath. With a private bath, the charge goes up to £28 ($49) to £30 ($52.50) per person, including VAT and a full breakfast. This hotel has a high reputation for its cooking, and over the years has won many awards. The traditional Sunday lunch in the English style is offered at £9.95 ($17.40); however, a regular set dinner is featured at £14 ($24.50). Bar snacks, incidentally, are an inexpensive way to sample some gourmet dishes here.

On the Outskirts

Even more desirable than the accommodations of Chipping Campden are those found at **Charingworth Manor Hotel,** Charingworth, near Chipping Campden, Gloucestershire GL55 6NS (tel. 038678/555), which traces its origins back to Tudor days. Actually, a manor of some sort stood on this spot at the time of the *Domesday Book*. In the 1930s the house was host to such illustrious guests as T. S. Eliot, author of *The Wasteland*. The village of Charingworth lies 3¼ miles east of Chipping Campden. Charingworth rents only seven luxuriously furnished bedrooms, plus one sumptuous suite, and is open all year except mid-January to mid-February. Jacobean additions were made onto the manor, and today's country home has been completely restored with great sensitivity to preserve its old character. All its bedrooms have private baths and many amenities such as phones and TVs. Singles rent for £60 ($105) nightly, with doubles costing £130 ($227.50). Guests take their cocktails in the elegant drawing room and library, later enjoying a well-prepared cuisine, with first-class wines and formal service. With its honey-colored stone and slate roofs, this manor house stands on its own 55 acres of grounds.

STRATFORD AND THE HEART OF ENGLAND

So close to London, so rich in fascination, the Shakespeare Country in the heart of England is that district most visited by North Americans (other than London, of course). Many who don't recognize the county name, Warwickshire, know its foremost tourist town, Stratford-upon-Avon, the birthplace of England's greatest writer.

The county and its neighboring shires form a land of industrial cities, green fields, and sleepy market towns—dotted with buildings, some of which have changed little since Shakespeare's time. Here are many of the places that have magic for overseas visitors, not only Stratford-upon-Avon, but also Warwick and Kenilworth Castles, as well as Coventry Cathedral.

Those who have time to penetrate deeper into the chapter will find elegant spa towns, such as Great Malvern, historic cathedral cities such as Hereford and Worcester, and industrial archeology at Stoke-on-Trent (the famous potteries). Scenery in Shropshire ranges from untamed borderlands to gentle plains that give way in the north to wooded areas and meres.

---

1. Stratford-upon-Avon

This town has a phenomenal tourist trade. Actor David Garrick really launched it in 1769 when he organized the first of the Bard's birthday celebrations. It is no secret by now, of course, that William Shakespeare was born in Stratford-upon-Avon on April 23, 1564.

Surprisingly little is known about his early life, as the frankest of his biographers concede. Perhaps because documentation is so lacking about the writer, much useless conjecture has arisen (did Elizabeth I really write the plays?). But the view that

Francis Bacon wrote all of Shakespeare's work would certainly stir up *The Tempest*, if suggested to the innkeepers of Stratford-upon-Avon. Admittedly, however, some of the stories and legends connected with Shakespeare's days in Stratford are largely fanciful, invented belatedly to amuse and entertain the vast number of literary fans making the pilgrimage.

Today's magnet, in addition to Shakespeare's birthplace, is the Royal Shakespeare Theatre, where Britain's foremost actors perform during a long season that lasts from Easter until January. Stratford-upon-Avon is also a good center for trips to Warwick Castle, Kenilworth Castle, Sulgrave Manor (ancestral home of George Washington), Compton Wynyates, and Coventry Cathedral. The market town lies 92 miles from London, 40 from Oxford, and 8 from Warwick.

THE SIGHTS

Besides the attractions on the periphery of Stratford, there are many Elizabethan and Jacobean buildings in this colorful town—many of them administered by the Shakespeare Birthplace Trust. One ticket—costing £4.50 ($8) for adults, £2 ($3.50) for children—will permit you to visit the five most important sights. You should pick up the ticket if you're planning to do much sightseeing (obtainable at your first stopover at any one of the Trust properties). The properties are open all year except Good Friday morning, December 24 to December 25, and the morning of January 1. From April to September, hours are from 9 a.m. to 6 p.m. Monday to Saturday, from 10 a.m. to 6 p.m. Sunday. October opening times are the same, with closing at 5 p.m. From November to March, hours are from 9 a.m. to 4:30 p.m. Monday to Saturday. On Sunday in winter, only Shakespeare's Birthplace and Anne Hathaway's Cottage are open, hours being from 1:30 to 4:30 p.m. The other three properties (Mary Arden's House, Hall's Croft, and New Place/Nash's House) are closed on Sunday in winter. Last admissions all year are 20 minutes before closing time.

For further information concerning the Trust's activities, send a stamped (English postage, please), self-addressed envelope to the Director, the Shakespeare Centre, Henley Street, Stratford-upon-Avon, Warwickshire CV37 6QW (tel. 0789/204016).

Shakespeare's Birthplace

On Henley Street, the son of a glover and whittawer, the Bard was born on St. George's day (April 23) in 1564, and died 52 years later on the same day. Filled with Shakespeare memorabilia, including a portrait, and furnishings of the writer's time, the Trust property is a half-timbered structure, dating from the early years of the 16th century. The house was bought by public donors in 1847 and preserved as a national shrine. You can visit the oak-beamed living room, the bedroom where Shakespeare was born, a fully equipped kitchen of the period (look for the "baby-minder"), and a Shakespeare Museum, illustrating his life and times. Later, you can walk through the garden out back. It is estimated that some 660,000 visitors pass through the house annually. If visited separately, admission is £1.70 ($3) for adults, 70p ($1.25) for children. Next door to the birthplace is the modern Shakespeare Centre, built to commemorate the 400th anniversary of the Bard's birth. It serves both as the administrative headquarters of the Birthplace Trust and as a library and study center. An extension to the original center, opened in 1981, includes a Visitors' Centre providing reception facilities for all those coming to the Birthplace.

Anne Hathaway's Cottage

One mile from Stratford-upon-Avon, in the hamlet of Shottery, is the thatched, wattle-and-daub cottage where Anne Hathaway lived before her marriage to the poet. In sheer charm, it is the most interesting and most photographed, it would seem, of the Trust properties. The Hathaways were yeoman farmers, and—aside from its historical interest—the cottage provides a rare insight into the life of a fami-

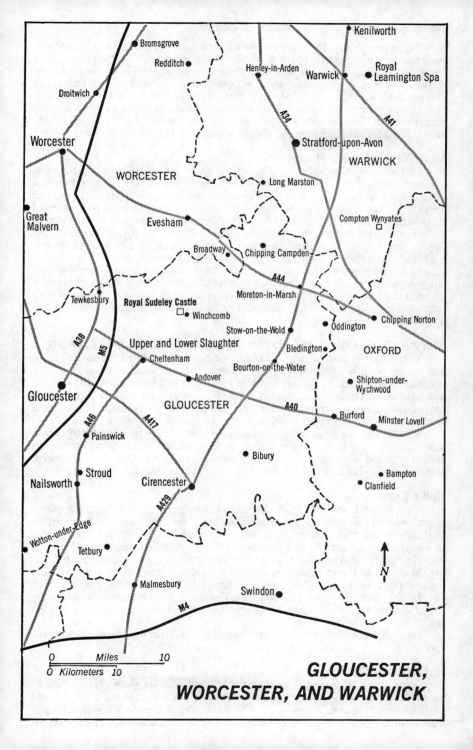

Bromsgrove
Redditch
Droitwich
Worcester
Great Malvern

WORCESTER

Kenilworth
Henley-in-Arden
Warwick
Royal Leamington Spa

A34
A41

Stratford-upon-Avon

WARWICK

Long Marston

Evesham

Broadway
Chipping Campden

Compton Wynyates

A44

Tewkesbury
Moreton-in-Marsh
Chipping Norton

Royal Sudeley Castle
Winchcomb

Stow-on-the-Wold
Oddington

A38
M5

Upper and Lower Slaughter
Cheltenham
Bledington

OXFORD

Andover
Bourton-on-the-Water

GLOUCESTER

Shipton-under-Wychwood

Gloucester

A40
Burford
Minster Lovell

A46
Painswick

A417

Bibury

Stroud
Nailsworth
Cirencester

Bampton
Clanfield

A429

Wotton-under-Edge
Tetbury

Malmesbury
Swindon

M4

N

0   Miles   10
0 Kilometers 10

*GLOUCESTER,
WORCESTER, AND WARWICK*

ly of Shakespeare's day. If the poet came a-courtin', he must have been treated as a mere teenager, as he married Miss Hathaway when he was only 18 years old and she much older. Many of the original furnishings, including the courting settle and utensils, are preserved inside the house, which was occupied by descendants of Shakespeare's wife until 1892. After a visit through the house, you'll surely want to linger in the garden and orchard. You can either walk across the meadow to Shottery from Evesham Place in Stratford (pathway marked), or else take a bus from Bridge Street. The admission is £1.60 ($2.80) for adults, 60p ($1.05) for children.

New Place / Nash's House
This site is on Chapel Street, where Shakespeare retired in 1610, a prosperous man to judge from the standards of his day. He died there six years later, at the age of 52. Regrettably, only the site of his former home remains today, as the house was torn down. You enter the gardens through Nash's House (Thomas Nash married Elizabeth Hall, a granddaughter of the poet). Nash's House has 16th-century period rooms and an exhibition illustrating the archeology and history of Stratford. The heavily visited Knott Garden adjoins the site, and represents the style of a fashionable Elizabethan garden. New Place itself has its own Great Garden, which once belonged to Shakespeare. Here, the Bard planted a mulberry tree, so popular with latter-day visitors to Stratford that the cantankerous owner of the garden chopped it down. The mulberry tree that grows there today is said to have been planted from a cutting of the original tree. The admission is £1.10 ($1.95) for adults, 60p ($1.05) for children.

Mary Arden's House and the Shakespeare Countryside Museum
This Tudor farmstead, with its old stone dovecote and various outbuildings, was the girlhood home of Shakespeare's mother. It is situated at Wilmcote, three miles from Stratford. The house contains rare pieces of country furniture and domestic utensils. The barns, stable, cowshed, and farmyard are used to display an extensive collection of farming implements and other bygones illustrating life and work in the local countryside from Shakespeare's time to the present century.

Visitors also see the neighboring Glebe Farm whose interior evokes farm life in late Victorian and Edwardian times. A working smithy and displays of country crafts are added attractions. Light refreshments are available, and there is a picnic area. Admission is £1.60 ($2.80) for adults, 70p ($1.25) for children.

Hall's Croft
This house is in Old Town, Stratford-upon-Avon, not far from the parish church, Holy Trinity. It was here that Shakespeare's daughter Susanna lived with her husband, Dr. John Hall. Apart from that association, Hall's Croft is a Tudor house of outstanding character with a particularly beautiful walled garden. Dr. Hall was widely respected and built up a large medical practice in the area. Exhibits illustrating the theory and practice of medicine in Dr. Hall's time are on view in the house, which is furnished in the style of a middle-class Tudor home. The admission is £1.10 ($1.95) for adults, 50p (90¢) for children. Visitors to the house are welcome to use the adjoining Hall's Croft Club, which serves morning coffee, lunch, and afternoon tea.

Other interesting sights not administered by the Trust foundation include the following:

Holy Trinity Church
In an attractive setting near the Avon, the parish church of Stratford-upon-Avon is distinguished mainly because Shakespeare was buried in the chancel ("and curst be he who moves my bones"). The Parish Register records his baptism and burial (copies of the original, of course). No charge is made for entry into the

church, described as "one of the most beautiful parish churches in the world," but visitors wishing to view Shakespeare's tomb are asked to donate a small sum, 40p (70¢) for adults, toward the restoration fund. Hours are from 8:30 a.m. to 6 p.m. Monday to Saturday and from noon to 5 p.m. Sunday from April to October 31; from 8:30 a.m. to 4 p.m. Monday to Saturday and 2 to 5 p.m. Sunday from November to March 31.

Harvard House

Not just of interest to Harvard students and alumni, Harvard House on High Street (tel. 0789/204507) is a fine example of an Elizabethan town house. Rebuilt in 1596, it was once the home of Katherine Rogers, mother of John Harvard, founder of Harvard University. In 1909 the house was purchased by a Chicago millionaire, Edward Morris, who presented it as a gift to the American university. With a profusion of carving, it is the most ornate house in Stratford. Its rooms are filled with period furniture, and the floors, made of the local flagstone, are authentic. Look for the Bible Chair, used for hiding the Bible during the days of Tudor persecution. Harvard House, charging admission of £1 ($1.75) for adults, 50p (90¢) for students and children, is open April through September from 9 a.m. to 1 p.m. and 2 to 6 p.m., 2 to 6 p.m. on Sunday.

A Brass-Rubbing Center

At the **Royal Shakespeare Theatre Summer House,** Avonbank Gardens (tel. 0789/297671), open seven days a week from 10 a.m. to 6 p.m. in summer, you can explore brass rubbing. Admission is free. Medieval and Tudor brasses illustrate the knights and ladies, scholars, merchants, and priests of a bygone era. The Stratford collection contains a large assortment of exact replicas of brasses. The charge made for the rubbings includes the special paper and wax required, and any instruction you might need.

GETTING THERE

A service allowing you to spend the entire day in Stratford and Shakespeare's Country is the **Shakespeare Connection "Road and Rail Link,"** leaving from London's Euston Station Monday to Friday at 8:40, 10:10, and 10:40 a.m. and 12:40, 4:40, and 5:10 p.m.; on Saturday at 8:40 and 10:40 a.m. and 12:40, 4:40, and 5:10 p.m.; and on Sunday at 9:40 a.m. and 6:10 p.m. (the 8:40 a.m. Monday to Friday and 12:40 p.m. Monday to Saturday trains do not operate in winter). This is a safe, sure way for you to attend the Royal Shakespeare Theatre and return to London on the same day. If you only want to attend the evening performance at the theater, again the Shakespeare Connection is your best bet, trains leaving London at 4:40 or 5:10 p.m. Monday to Saturday. Returns to London are timed to fit theater performances, with departure at 11:15 p.m. from either the Guide Friday Ltd. office at the Civic Hall, 14 Rother St.; or just opposite the theater. The service is the fastest way of reaching Stratford from London, journey time averaging two hours. It is operated by **British Rail** and **Guide Friday** (tel. 0789/294466). Prices are £17.75 ($31.05) for a one-way fare, £19.75 ($34.55) for a round-trip ticket valid for three months. Ask for a Shakespeare Connection ticket at London's Euston Station or at any British Rail London Travel Centre. BritRail pass holders using the service simply pay the bus fare to Stratford-upon-Avon from Coventry, £4 ($7) one way, £5.50 ($9.65) for a round-trip ticket.

TOURS AND TOURIST SERVICES

A tourist reception center for Stratford-upon-Avon and Shakespeare's Country is operated by **Guide Friday Ltd.,** the Civic Hall, 14 Rother St. (tel. 0789/294466). The center dispenses free maps and brochures on the town and area and operates tours. Also available is a full range of tourist services, including accommodation booking, car rental, and theater tickets. In summer, the center is open daily from 9 a.m. to 7 p.m. In winter, hours are from 9 a.m. to 5:30 p.m. Monday to Friday, from 9 a.m. to 4 p.m. Saturday, and from 9:30 a.m. to 4 p.m. Sunday.

Guided tours of Stratford-upon-Avon leave the Guide Friday Tourism Centre daily. In summer, aboard open-top double-decker buses, departures are every 15 minutes from 9:30 a.m. to 5:30 p.m. The tour can be a one-hour panoramic ride, or you can get off at any or all of the Shakespeare's Birthplace Trust properties. Anne Hathaway's Cottage and Mary Arden's House are the two logical stops to make outside the town. Tour tickets are valid all day for you to hop on and off the buses. The price for these tours is £3.50 ($6.15) per person. Tours are also offered to Warwick Castle, Kenilworth Castle, and Charlecote Park, costing £6.50 ($11.40) per person; Cotswold Country Villages, £9 ($15.75) per person; Cotswold Country Pubs, £6.50 ($11.40) per person; and Blenheim Palace and Bladon (the Churchill story tour), £9 ($15.75) per person. Tour prices do not include entrance fees at the stops made.

ATTENDING THE THEATER

On the banks of the Avon, the **Royal Shakespeare Theatre** (tel. 0789/ 295623) is the number one theater for Shakespearean productions. The season runs for ten months from March to late January, with a winter program in February. The present theater was opened in 1932, after the old Shakespeare Memorial Theatre, erected in Victoria's day, burned down in 1926. The theater employs the finest actors and actresses on the British stage. In an average season, six Shakespearean plays are staged.

Usually, you'll need reservations: there are two successive booking periods, each one opening about two months in advance. You can best pick these up from a North American or an English travel agent. If you wait until your arrival in Stratford, it may be too late to get a good seat. Tickets can be booked through New York agents Edwards and Edwards or Keith Prowse, or direct with the theater box office with payment by major credit card. There are eight lines in, and the number to call is listed above. The price of seats generally ranges from £4.50 ($7.90) to £22 ($38.50). A small number of tickets are always kept back for sale on the day of a performance. You can phone from anywhere and make a credit-card reservation, picking up your ticket on the day it is to be used, but there is no cancellation once your reservation is made.

In the Victorian Wing of the old Memorial Theatre, spared by the fire of 1926, is the **Swan Theatre,** opened in 1986, built in the style of an Elizabethan playhouse. Here the Royal Shakespeare Company presents plays by Shakespeare and his contemporaries, as well as Restoration and later writers. For information about performances, phone the box office number for the Royal Shakespeare (tel. 0789/ 295623). This building also houses the company's **Collection,** an exhibition of stagecraft from medieval mummers to the present day, with costumes and props from Royal Shakespeare Company productions. Backstage/RSC Collection tours are available. The Collection is open April to January from 9:15 a.m. to 6 p.m. Monday to Saturday, from noon to 5 p.m. on Sunday. Admission is £1.50 ($2.65) for adults, £1 ($1.75) for children. Backstage guided tours for the Royal Shakespeare and Swan Theatres are usually offered three times a day (including after evening performances) and four times on Sunday, production schedules permitting. Prices of such tours are £2.20 ($3.75) for adults, £1.50 ($2.75) for children.

The company has a third theater in Stratford, **The Other Place,** seating just over 100 persons, where new plays are presented.

CAUGHT WITHOUT A ROOM?

During the long theater season, the hotels in Stratford-upon-Avon are jam-packed, and you may run into difficulty if you arrive without a reservation. However, you can go to the **Tourist Information Centre** (tel. 0789/293127) from 9 a.m. to 5:30 p.m. mid-March to the end of October Monday to Saturday, from 2 to 5 p.m. on Sunday; November to mid-March, Monday to Saturday from 10:30 a.m. to 4:30 p.m. Personal callers are charged 95p ($1.65) per room. A staff person who is experienced in finding accommodation for travelers in all budget categories will get on the telephone and try to book a room for you in the price range you are seeking.

It is also possible to reserve accommodations if you write well enough in advance. By writing to the Information Centre, you'll be spared having to get in touch with several hotels on your own and running the risk of getting turned down. If you do write, specify the price range and the number of beds required. The centre often gets vague letters, and the staff doesn't know whether to book you into a private suite at the Shakespeare Hotel or else lend you a cot to put in front of the Royal Shakespeare Theatre. For this postal "book-a-bed-ahead" service, the charge is £2.50 ($4.40), payable in pounds sterling only. The complete address is **The Information Centre,** Judith Shakespeare's House, 1 High St., Stratford-upon-Avon, Warwickshire CV37 6AU.

WHERE TO STAY

For my hotel recommendations, I'll lead off with the most expensive in:

The Upper Bracket

Welcombe Hotel, Warwick Road, Stratford-upon-Avon, Warwickshire CV37 0NR (tel. 0789/295252), is one of England's great Jacobean country houses, placed about a ten-minute ride from the heart of Stratford-upon-Avon. The home once belonged to Sir Archibald Flower, the philanthropic brewer who helped create the Shakespeare Memorial Theatre. Converted into a hotel, it is surrounded by 157 acres of grounds. It is reached by a formal entrance on Warwick Road, a winding driveway leading to the main hall. There's even an 18-hole, 6,300-yard golf course on the estate. Guests gather on fair days for afternoon tea or drinks on the rear terrace, with its Italian-style garden and steps leading down to flower beds. The public rooms are heroic in size, with high mullioned windows providing views of the park. The bedrooms—some big enough for tennis matches—have pleasant furnishings. A single room with bath rents for £70 ($122.50) daily. A double with bath costs £105 ($183.75) to £160 ($280), all prices including a full breakfast, service charge, and VAT. You can order either table d'hôte meals or from the à la carte menu.

Ettington Park Hotel, Alderminster, Stratford-upon-Avon, Warwickshire CV37 8BS (tel. 0789/740740), a Victorian Gothic mansion, is one of the most sumptuous retreats in the Shakespeare Country—maybe *the* most sumptuous. This mansion opened as a hotel in 1985, but it has a history stretching over nine centuries. The land is a legacy of the Shirley family, whose 12th-century burial chapel stands near the hotel. With its baronial fireplaces and conservatory and its charming staff, the place is like a grand private home. Restorers have brought back the beauty of the Adam ceilings, the stone carvings, and the ornate staircases, transforming the Shirley family home into this deluxe retreat. A new wing, assembled with the same stone and neo-Gothic carving as that of the original house, stretches toward a Renaissance-era garden arbor entwined with vines. The giant sequoias, ancient yews, and cedars planted by long-ago inhabitants were incorporated into what became lawns and terraced gardens, whose flowers and ferns cascade into the waters of a rock-lined stream.

The 49 bedrooms contain dozens of memories of another era, yet the most modern comforts are concealed behind antique façades. With a full breakfast, doubles cost from £105 ($183.75) daily. In the dining room, the Shirley family crest is inlaid in hundreds of marquetry depictions in the carved and burnished paneling. The cuisine is a medley of English and French specialties, a fixed-price dinner costing from £25 ($43.75). The waters of a Jacuzzi foam into an indoor swimming pool under a Gothic skylight. Downstairs, there's a sauna. To get here, don't go to the village of Ettington, as the name of the hotel suggests. Head instead along the A34 between Stratford-upon-Avon and Oxford to the village of Alderminster. You can't miss the sign.

The Shakespeare, Chapel Street, Stratford-upon-Avon, Warwickshire CV37 6ER (tel. 0789/294771), is filled with historical associations. Its original core dates from the 1400s, but it has seen many additions in its long life. It's been called both the Four Gables Hotel and the Five Gables Hotel. In the 1700s a demure façade of Regency brick was added to conceal the intricately timber framing, but in the 1880s, with a rash of Shakespearean revivals, the hotel was restored to its original Tudor look. Residents relax in the post-and-timber-studded public rooms, within sight of fireplaces and playbills from 19th-century productions of Shakespeare's plays. The hotel restaurant serves well-prepared lunches and dinners, and one of the most charming pubs in town, the Froth and Elbow, lies on the hotel's street level. Many of the bedrooms, 70 in all, were named by the noted actor, David Garrick. The oldest are capped with hewn timbers, with bathrooms built between the 400-year-old timbers. Modern comforts have been added, including mini-bars and phones. Even the newer accommodations are at least 40 to 50 years old and have rose and thistle patterns carved into many of their exposed timbers. Single rooms cost from £63 ($110.25) to £71 ($124.25) daily, and doubles and twins go for £88 ($154) to £106 ($185.50).

Alveston Manor Hotel, Clopton Bridge, Stratford-upon-Avon, Warwickshire CV37 7HP (tel. 0789/204581), is a black-and-white timbered manor, conveniently placed for attending the theater, just a two-minute walk from the Avon. It has a wealth of chimneys and gables, a hodgepodge of styles, everything from an Elizabethan gazebo to Queen Anne windows. Tracing the building's ancestry involves one in early English history, as its origins predate the arrival of William the Conqueror. A Ping-Pong game of ownership has been played with Alveston, which was mentioned in the *Domesday Book.* Rooms in the Manor House are for those who gravitate to old slanted floors, overhead beams, and antique furnishings. However, in the modern block, attached by a covered walk through the rear garden, rooms have built-in pieces, baths with showers, phones, radios, dressing tables, and a color-coordinated decor. In a single room, the rate is £60 ($105) to £70 ($122.50) daily, increasing to £80 ($140) to £100 ($175) in a double or twin. Service and VAT are included. In the newer block, a number of large rooms are rented to three or four persons. The lounges are in the manor; and guests gather in the Cedar Room with a view of the centuries-old tree at the top of the garden—said to have been the background for the first presentation of *A Midsummer Night's Dream.* In the main living room, with its linenfold paneling, logs burn in the Tudor fireplace. Food is served in the softly lit Tudor Restaurant, with its oak beams and leaded-glass windows. A set dinner costs £14 ($24.50).

Moat House International, Bridgefoot, Stratford-upon-Avon, Warwickshire CV37 6YR (tel. 0789/414411), is a four-star hotel standing in five acres of landscaped lawns on the banks of the River Avon. It is one of the flagships of Queens Moat Houses, a hotel chain in Britain. The hotel has recently undergone a total refurbishment program, and now every bedroom has a high standard of comfort. Nearly 250 bedrooms are offered, each with private bath or shower, air conditioning, direct-dial phone, color TV, video, and hairdryer. Rates for a single begin at £60 ($105) nightly, going up to £82 ($143.50) in a double, with VAT and a full English breakfast included. The hotel offers an array of drinking and dining facilities, including the Warwick Grill, which features a British and continental menu. You can also dine in the Tavern, which has a carvery of hot and cold roasts. You can drink in the Tavern Pub and in the Actors, which doubles as a night club. The location overlooks the Royal Shakespeare Theatre, which can be reached by barge.

The Medium-Priced Range

White Swan, Rother Street, Stratford-upon-Avon, Warwickshire CV37 6NH (tel. 0798/297022), is a cozy, intimate hotel, one of the most atmospheric in Stratford. It was in business for more than 100 years before Shakespeare appeared on the scene. The gabled medieval front would present the Bard with no surprises, but the modern comforts inside would surely astonish him, even though many of the rooms have been preserved. Paintings dating from 1550 hang on the lounge walls. All the bedrooms are well appointed and have color TVs, radios, phones, and hot beverage facilities. Many also have private baths, and the inn is centrally heated. Singles rent for £57 ($99.75) daily, and doubles go for £73 ($127.75). The hostelry has a spacious restaurant, where good food is served. The oak-beamed bar is a popular meeting place (see "Special Pubs," below).

The Falcon, Chapel Street, Stratford-upon-Avon, Warwickshire CV37 6HA (tel. 0789/205777), is a blending of the very old and the very new. At the rear of a black-and-white timbered inn, licensed a quarter of a century after Shakespeare's death, is a contemporary bedroom extension, joined by a glass-covered passageway. In the heart of Stratford, the Falcon faces the Guild Chapel and the New Place Gardens. The bedrooms in the mellowed part have oak beams, diamond leaded-glass windows, some antique furnishings, and good reproductions. One arrives at the rear portion to unload luggage, just as horse-drawn coaches once dispatched their passengers. All bedrooms have private bath, radio, TV, phone, electric trouser press, and tea- and coffee-making equipment. Rates include accommodation, full English breakfast, space for your car, VAT, and service charge. A single with bath is £55 ($96.25) daily, and a double or twin with bath costs £74 ($129.50) to £80 ($140). The social lounges are tasteful and comfortable—some of the finest in the Midlands. In the intimate Merlin Lounge is an open copper-hooded fireplace where coal and log fires are kept burning under beams salvaged from old ships (the walls are a good example of wattle and daub, typical of Shakespeare's day). The Oak Lounge Bar is a forest of weathered beams, and on either side of the stone fireplace is the paneling removed from the poet's last home, New Place. A set luncheon costs £11 ($19.25), and a set dinner goes for £13.25 ($23.20), both tariffs including three courses, service, and VAT.

The Swans Nest, Bridgefoot, Stratford-upon-Avon, Warwickshire CV37 7LT (tel. 0789/66761), presents a Georgian façade with tall, narrow windows looking out over the Avon with its swans. Most of the bedrooms, however, are in a modern red-brick extension whose walls encircle courtyards. The complex sits in its own gardens on a low, flat area beside a canal, not far from the Royal Shakespeare Theatre. The River Bar offers a view of the planting outside. The Bewick Restaurant serves food in a room lined with early-19th-century paintings. Fixed-price lunches and dinners cost £8.75 ($15.30) and £12.50 ($21.90) respectively. Bedrooms are comfortably modern and filled with tasteful furnishings. Each unit has its private bath, color TV, radio, phone, and facilities for making tea and coffee. Singles cost £57 ($99.75) nightly and doubles from £73 ($127.75).

Arden Hotel, 44 Waterside, Stratford-upon-Avon, Warwickshire CV37 6BA (tel. 0789/294949), has a nearly symmetrical red-brick main section dating from the Regency period. Over the years, a handful of adjacent buildings and a modern extension have been added to enlarge the capacity. Today the modernized interior contains a well-upholstered cocktail lounge and pub, a dining room with big front windows, a covered garden terrace, and 45 comfortable bedrooms. Each unit has a private bath, phone, color TV, and tea- and coffee-making equipment. With an English breakfast included, singles cost £65 ($113.75) daily, and doubles go for £80 ($140). A fixed-price dinner in the restaurant goes for £17 ($30.65). The hotel is convenient for theater-goers because of its position across the street from the side entrance of the Royal Shakespeare.

Dukes, Payton Street, Stratford-upon-Avon, Warwickshire CV37 6UA (tel.

0789/69300), was formed when two Georgian town houses were united and restored to create this little charmer. In the center of Stratford, it has a large garden, yet is close to Shakespeare's birthplace. A family operated inn, Dukes offers attractively decorated public areas and bedrooms that have been restored to an impressive degree of comfort and coziness. The hotel offers 22 bedrooms, each with private bath or shower as well as a direct-dial phone and TV. Charges for an overnight stay range from £35 ($61.25) daily in a single to £55 ($96.25) to £75 ($131.25) in a double. The owners, Mr. and Mrs. Power, are helpful hosts, and the building reflects their taste in the well-chosen pieces of furniture, often antique. Dukes also serves a good English and continental cuisine.

The Budget Range

Haytor Hotel, 20 Avenue Rd., Stratford-upon-Avon, Warwickshire CV37 6UX (tel. 0789/297799), is a private Edwardian country house hotel where good service is rendered by the staff. All of the 11 rooms contain private baths and are individually furnished, fully carpeted, and have color TV. Two bedrooms, including the Green Onyx, contain four-poster beds. Charges are £29.50 ($51.65) daily in a single, £45 ($78.75) to £55 ($96.25) in a double, with an English breakfast included. Meals are served in a charming dining room, and a lounge bar, comfortable sitting room, and garden away from traffic noise can be enjoyed by guests. The hotel is only about 900 yards from the Royal Shakespeare Theatre.

Grosvenor House Hotel, 12-14 Warwick Rd., Stratford-upon-Avon, Warwickshire CV37 6YT (tel. 0789/69213), is a pair of Georgian residences joined to form a hotel of 57 bedrooms, 53 of which have private bath or shower. It is a member of the Best Western hotel group. Lawns and gardens to the rear of the hotel lend attraction. All bedrooms have color TVs, radios, tea/coffee-makers, and phones. Singles rent for £35 ($61.25) to £40 ($70) daily, and doubles go for £58 ($101.50) to £66 ($115.50), including service, VAT, and a full English breakfast. There is a large free car park for guests. The informal bar (open until midnight) and terrace offer pleasant relaxation before or after you lunch or dine in the large restaurant, whose floor-to-ceiling windows look onto the gardens. The Grosvenor is a short stroll from the intersection of Bridge Street and Waterside so that you're right at riverside Bancroft Gardens and the Royal Shakespeare Theatre.

The Stratford House, Sheep Street, Stratford-upon-Avon, Warwickshire CV37 6EF (tel. 0789/68288), a Georgian house, stands 100 yards from the River Avon and the Royal Shakespeare Theatre. It is a small hotel of only ten bedrooms, all with private bath or shower. The hotel is owned by Sylvia Adcock, who extends a warm welcome to North American clients. The house is furnished tastefully and with style, somewhat like a private home, with books and pictures along with a scattering of antiques. Everything is spotlessly maintained. On the side is a walled courtyard, with flowering plants. The B&B rate is from £32 ($56) per person daily in a double. The price includes a full English breakfast and VAT. All bedrooms have color TV and tea/coffee-makers. Both hotel guests and outsiders can dine in the garden restaurant, Shepherd's, recommended separately.

Stratheden Hotel, Chapel Street, Stratford-upon-Avon, Warwickshire CV37 6EP (tel. 0789/297119), is a small, tuck-away hotel in a building dating to 1673, with a tiny rear garden and top-floor rooms with slanted, beamed ceilings. Owned by Mr. and Mrs. Wells (she's from Northern Ireland, he's a native of Warwickshire), the house has improved in both decor and comfort, with fresh paint, curtains, and good beds. Most rooms have private shower and toilet, with B&B costing £15 ($26.25) to £21 ($36.75) per person nightly. The entry hallway has a glass cupboard, holding family heirlooms and collector tidbits. The house is sprinkled with old pieces. The dining room, with a bay window, has an overscale sideboard that once belonged to the "insanely vain" Marie Corelli, the eccentric novelist, poet, and mystic who wrote a series of seven books, beginning with *A Romance of Two Worlds* and ending with *Spirit and Power and Universal Love.* Queen Victoria was one of her avid readers. The Victorian novelist (1855–1924) was noted for her passion for pastoral paintings and objets d'art. You can see an example of her taste in bedchamber furniture: a massive mahogany tester bed in one of the rooms.

WHERE TO DINE

In the best position in town, the **Box Tree Restaurant,** Royal Shakespeare Theatre, Waterside (tel. 0789/414999), is in the theater, with walls of glass providing an unobstructed view of the Avon and its swans. The meals and service are worthy of its unique position. The restaurant is open on matinee days from noon to 2 p.m., when a three-course table d'hôte luncheon costs £10.75 ($18.80). Evening hours are 5:45 p.m. to midnight, when a three-course pre-theater dinner is featured. During intermission, there is a snack feast of smoked salmon and champagne. After each evening's performance, you can dine by flickering candlelight. Classical French, Italian, and English cuisine is served. Dinner and supper are à la carte and cost from £15.75 ($27.55) to £20 ($35) per person. Be sure to book your table in advance, especially on the days of performances (there's a special phone for reservations in the theater lobby).

Also overlooking the Avon, the **River Terrace Restaurant** in the theater is open to the general public as well as to play-goers. A colorful coffeeshop and licensed restaurant serves typical English and pasta dishes, morning coffee, and afternoon teas, which are offered on a self-service basis. Meals cost £4 ($7) to £8.50 ($14.90). It's open from 10:30 a.m. to 9:30 p.m. daily. Sunday hours are 11 a.m. to 5 p.m. The restaurant has the same phone as the Box Tree (above).

Shepherd's Garden Restaurant, Stratford House Hotel, Sheep Street (tel. 0789/68288), is appropriately stylish for its role as host to many of the directors and actors from the Royal Shakespeare Theatre. Light and airy, it has a skylit conservatory look, with draping vines and plants. Windows open onto a view of a walled garden. You are served British cookery here among the finest in Stratford-upon-Avon. For an appetizer, you might begin with smoked chicken and mango with a curried mayonnaise, going on to either fresh salmon with a chive and butter sauce or roast rack of lamb with a mild garlic sauce. These are only examples of what type of food is served, as the menu, based on the use of fresh ingredients, changes frequently. Lunch, served from noon to 2 p.m. daily, costs from £9 ($15.75), with dinner, from 6 to 9:30 p.m., going for £15 ($26.25) and up.

Hussain's, 6a Chapel St. (tel. 0789/67506), stands across from the Shakespeare Hotel and historic New Place. Dining here has been compared to a visit to a private Indian home, and the restaurant has many admirers—some of whom consider it the finest dining spot in Stratford-upon-Avon. At least it pleased Ben Kingsley, star of *Gandhi.* The owner, Noor Hussain, has selected a well-trained, alert staff, who welcome guests into their domain, often advising about special dishes. Against a setting of pink crushed-velvet paneling, you can select from an array of dishes from northern India. Herbs and spices are blended imaginatively in the kitchen to give dishes a distinctive flavor. Regular meals cost from £11 ($19.25), and set dinners are offered at £22 ($38.50) for two persons. Many tandoori dishes are offered, along with various versions of curries such as lamb and prawn. The best bargain is the Sunday luncheon buffet, an eat-all-you-want affair for £7.50 ($13.15). It's open Monday to Thursday from noon to 2 p.m. and 5:15 to 11:45 p.m., on Friday and Saturday from noon to 2 p.m. and 5 p.m. to midnight, and on Sunday from 12:30 to 2:30 p.m. and 5:30 to 11:45 p.m.

Bunbury's, 3 Greenhill St. (tel. 0789/293563), serves dishes known in Shakespeare's time. The kitchen reproduces 16th- and 17th-century recipes found in old manuscripts and cookbooks. It also creates the atmosphere of those times with barley-white and cream with black wood decor, flagstone floors, and oak tables and chairs. There is a gallery, as well as a fire in the grate to welcome you after the walk from the theater. Appetizers include Stilton-and-port pâté. Main dishes feature pork with nuts and capon with pistachios and gooseberries. For dessert, try the panperdey (cherries served on toast with egg and cream). A set lunch is modestly priced at £7 ($12.25), with a table d'hôte dinner offered for £12.50 ($21.90). Meals are served daily except Monday from noon to 2:30 p.m. and 6 to 11:30 p.m., ideal for after-theater suppers. Sunday hours are from noon to 2 p.m. and 7 to 11 p.m. (closed Sunday in off-season).

Sir Toby's, 8 Church St. (tel. 0789/68822), was discovered by several readers. Constructed of red brick, it lies away from the busy center. The setting of the place is the way dining rooms used to look in England, but that is part of the charm of Sir Toby's. It's cozy and intimate, with limited seating. In summer, a few tables are placed outside for al fresco dining. Mr. and Mrs. Watkins welcome diners to their establishment only in the evening from 5:30 to 9:30 p.m. and never on Sunday. They take pride in their good home cooking and also cater to the vegetarian palate. In their food, the best of the past is blended with the cooking techniques of today. You might also visit for a pre-theater meal because of its early opening. Meals cost from £15 ($26.25) and up.

Da Giovanni, 8 Ely St. (tel. 0789/297999), is an intimate spot, favored by actors at the theater. The yellow-brick cottage is graced with an Italianate façade that shelters the entrance to a sophisticated cocktail lounge with antiques. Da Giovanni is in the trattoria style, its cuisine beginning fittingly enough with minestrone. The classic Italian menu includes such pasta dishes as lasagne and cannelloni, and such main dishes as escalope pietmontese and scampi provençale. A good Italian dessert is the zabaglione, although at least two persons must order it. A selection of excellent continental ices is also featured, everything from Italian cassata to mela stregata. Expect to pay from £15 ($26.25) for a complete dinner. A 10% service charge is added. It's closed on Sunday, but open other days from 12:30 to 2 p.m. and 6 to 11:30 p.m.

SPECIAL PUBS

Affectionately known as the Dirty Duck, it's really the **Black Swan,** Waterside (tel. 0789/297312). By whatever bird it's called, it's been popular since the 18th century as a hangout for Stratford players. The autographed photographs of its patrons, such as Lord Laurence Olivier, line the wall. The front lounge and bar crackles with intense conversation. In the spring and fall an open fire blazes. In the Dirty Duck Grill Room, typical English grills, among other dishes are featured. You're faced with a dozen appetizers, most of which would make a meal in themselves. Main dishes include braised kidneys. Meals cost from £12 ($21). Hours are from 11 a.m. to 3 p.m. and 5:30 to 11 p.m. Monday to Saturday, from noon to 3 p.m. and 7 to 10:30 p.m. Sunday. In fair weather, you can drink while sitting in the front garden and watch the swans on the Avon glide by.

After visiting the Black Swan, you may be ready to call on the **White Swan,** Rother Street (tel. 0789/297022), one of the most atmospheric pubs in Stratford-upon-Avon, found in a hotel previously recommended. Once you step inside, you're drawn into a world of cushioned leather armchairs, old oak settles, oak paneling, and fireplaces. It is believed that Shakespeare may have come here to drink back when it was called Kings Head. Today you can go here for food and drink from 10:30 a.m. to 2:30 p.m. and 5:30 to 11 p.m. Monday to Saturday, from noon to 3 p.m. and 7 to 10:30 p.m. Sunday. At lunch you can partake of the food offerings, including hot dishes of the day along with fresh salads and sandwiches, light meals costing from £3.50 ($6.15).

FOOD AND LODGING AT ETTINGTON

Some 6½ miles southeast of Stratford-upon-Avon on the A422, **Chase Country House Hotel,** Banbury Road, Ettington, Stratford-upon-Avon, Warwickshire CV37 7NZ (tel. 0789/740000), has a somewhat notorious history as the former home of an Irish gunrunner. It's contained within a high-gabled mansion of elaborate brickwork upon which a Victorian architect unleashed Gothic fantasies in 1867.

The establishment today contains 11 comfortably traditional bedrooms, priced at £49 ($85.75) to £53 ($92.75) daily for a single and £65 ($113.75) to £69 ($120.75) for a double, with a full breakfast included. Each unit has a phone, radio alarm, color TV, and private bath. The highlight of the hotel, however, is that it provides some of the best food in the area. Typical English dishes include Wiltshire fritters with a spicy sauce, an appetizing mélange of Cotswold fish (smoked on the premises using smoldering English oak in smoke pots), and braised oxtail. A heavenly dessert is called Athol Brose, concocted from cream, whisky, and honey layered with oat flakes. Meals are priced from £18.50 ($32.40), reasonable for such a commendable restaurant. Reservations are important. Hours are 12:30 to 2:30 p.m. (to 1:30 p.m. on Sunday) and 7:30 to 9 p.m. Closed to nonresidents for lunch on Saturday and for dinner on Sunday.

STAYING AT WILMCOTE

In the tiny village where Shakespeare's mother, Mary Arden, lived stands the **Swan House Hotel,** The Green, Wilmcote, Stratford-upon-Avon, Warwickshire CV37 9XJ (tel. 0789/67030). Really an upgraded village pub-hotel, the white-painted Swan is tranquil, offering not only fresh bedrooms at low prices, but good meals as well. It's owned by Ian and Diana Sykes, who have made the inn homelike. It has 12 bedrooms, all with private baths or showers, color TVs, and hot beverage facilities. A single rents for £28 ($49) daily, and a double goes for £44 ($77). All tariffs are inclusive of an English breakfast, service, and VAT. A four-poster room is available. In the popular beamed bar with an open fire and the original well, they serve a range of homemade hot and cold bar snacks. The bar offers four real ales at lunchtime or in the evening. The restaurant is a good setting for à la carte meals. English cuisine is prepared with French overtones, using fresh local produce.

SIGHTS AND LODGING AT ALCESTER

A magnificent, 115-room Palladian country house, **Ragley Hall** (tel. 0789/762090), built in 1680, is the home of the Marquess and Marchioness of Hertford and their family, lying nine miles from Stratford-upon-Avon. The house has been lovingly restored and appears as it probably looked during the early 1700s. Great pains were taken to duplicate color patterns and in some cases even the original wallpaper patterns. Ragley Hall's vast and spacious rooms boast priceless pictures, furniture, and works of art that have been collected by ten generations of the Seymour family. While possessing a museum-like quality in the sense that its artifacts are properly displayed, lighted, and have great historical importance, Ragley Hall is indeed a private home.

Perhaps the most spectacular attraction is the lavishly painted south staircase hall. The present marquess commissioned muralist Graham Rust to paint the modern trompe l'oeil work on the subject, *The Temptation,* but this religious theme stops with the lavishly evil Devil offering a gold circlet to Christ in the central ceiling medallion.

The house is open from noon to 5:30 p.m. except Monday and Friday from Easter Saturday to the end of September. The park, gardens, Adventure Wood, and Farm and Country Trail are open from noon to 5:30 p.m. in March, April, May, and September and from 10 a.m. to 6 p.m. in June, July, and August. Admission to the house, garden, and park is £2.90 ($5.10) for adults, £1.90 ($3.35) for children. The garden, park, wood, and trail can be visited for £1.90 ($3.35) for adults, 90p ($1.65) for children.

As a luxury note, Lord and Lady Hertford also entertain guests to dinner at an all-inclusive price of £75 ($131.25) per person, which covers a champagne reception, vintage wines with dinner, and vintage port and liqueurs after.

Ten centuries of history are lodged at **Billesley Manor Hotel,** Billesley, near Alcester, Warwickshire B49 6NF (tel. 0789/499888), three miles west of Stratford-upon-Avon by the A422. Set in 11 acres of English gardens, the manor offers a traditional welcome combined with modern comfort. The old blends with the new, from the oak panels and carved fireplaces to an indoor heated swimming pool. Accommodations, 41 in all, range from four-poster to modern bedrooms, all with spacious baths, color TV, trouser presses, and direct-dial phones. Rates are from £75 ($131.25) daily in a single and from £95 ($166.25) in a double or twin. Tariffs include a full English breakfast, VAT, and service. You can relax in front of a roaring log fire in manorial splendor, and the wood-paneled restaurants serve excellent fare, backed up by a fine wine list. There are tennis courts, a croquet lawn, and a golf "pitch and putt" course. Hot air ballooning, riding, shooting, and fishing can be arranged.

2. Warwick

Most travelers approach Warwick via the A46 from Stratford-upon-Avon, 8 miles away. The town, 92 miles from London, stands on the Avon.

Visitors seem to rush through Warwick to see Warwick Castle; then they're off on their next adventure, traditionally to the ruins of Kenilworth Castle. But the historic center of medieval Warwick deserves to be treated with greater respect. It has far more to offer than a castle.

In 1694 a fire swept through Warwick, destroying large segments of the town, but it still retains a number of Elizabethan and medieval buildings—along with some fine Georgian structures. (Very few traces remain, however, of the town walls, except the East and West Gates.) Warwick looks to Ethelfleda, daughter of Alfred the Great, as its founder. But most of its history is associated with the earls of Warwick, a title created by the son of William the Conqueror in 1088. The story of those earls —the Beaumonts, the Beauchamps (such figures as "Kingmaker" Richard Neville) —makes for an exciting episode in English history too detailed to document here.

WARWICK CASTLE

Perched on a rocky cliff above the Avon, this magnificent 14th-century fortress encloses a stately mansion in the grandest late-17th-century style. The importance of the site has been recognized from earliest times. The first defense works of significance at Warwick were built by Ethelfleda, daughter of Alfred the Great, in A.D. 915. Her fortifications were further developed by the construction of a motte and bailey castle on the orders of William the Conqueror in 1068, two years after the Norman Conquest. There are now no remains of the Norman castle except the castle mound, as this was sacked by Simon de Montfort in the Barons' War of 1264.

The Beauchamp family, the most illustrious medieval earls of Warwick, are responsible for most of the castle as it is seen today, and much of the external structure remains unchanged from the mid-14th century. When the castle was granted to Sir Fulke Greville by James I in 1604, he spent £20,000 (an enormous sum in those days) converting the existing castle buildings into a luxurious mansion. The Grevilles have held the Earl of Warwick title since 1759, when it passed from the Rich family.

The State Rooms and Great Hall house fine collections of paintings, furniture, arms, and armor. The armory, dungeon, torture chamber, ghost tower, clock tower, and Guy's tower give vivid insights into the castle's turbulent past and its important part in the history of England. The private apartments of Lord Brooke and his family, who in recent years sold the castle to Madame Tussaud's company, of waxworks fame, are open to visitors to display a carefully constructed Royal Weekend House Party of 1898. The major rooms contain wax models of the time: young Winston Churchill, the Duchess of Devonshire, Winston's widowed mother, Jennie, and Clara Butt, the celebrated singer, along with the Earl and Countess of Warwick and their family. In the Kenilworth bedroom, the Prince of Wales, later to become King

Edward VII, reads a letter, and in the red bedroom, the Duchess of Marlborough prepares for her bath. Among the most lifelike of the figures is a little uniformed maid, bending over a bathtub into which the water is running, to test the temperature. Surrounded by gardens, lawns, and woodland, where peacocks roam freely, and skirted by the Avon, Warwick Castle was described by Sir Walter Scott in 1828 as "that fairest monument of ancient and chivalrous splendor which yet remains uninjured by time."

Don't miss the re-created Victorian Rose Garden, originally designed by Robert Marnock in 1868. It fell into disrepair, and a tennis court was built on the site among the trees. In 1980 it was decided to restore the garden, and as luck would have it, Marnock's original plans were discovered in the County Records Office. Close by the rose garden is a Victorian alpine rockery and water garden. The romantic castle is, throughout the year, host to various special events, colorful pageants such as those created by the members of the Sealed Knot and the French Foot Grenadiers. There are regular appearances of the magnificent Red Knight on his splendid warhorse, and traditional Morris Dancers perform on the lawns. Some form of live entertainment is presented almost every day on the grounds in summer.

Warwick Castle, Castle Hill (tel. 0926/495421), is open from 10 a.m. to 5:30 p.m. daily from March 1 to October 31 and from 10 a.m. to 4:30 p.m. from November 1 to February 28 except Christmas Day. Admission is £4.50 ($7.90) for adults, £3 ($5.25) for children.

OTHER SIGHTS

Other nearby sights worth exploring include the following:

St. Mary's Church

Destroyed in part by the fire of 1694, this church on Old Square with its rebuilt battlemented tower and nave is considered among the finest examples of the work of the late 17th and early 18th centuries. The Beauchamp Chapel, spared from the flames, encases the Purbeck marble tomb of Richard Beauchamp, a well-known Earl of Warwick who died in 1439 and is commemorated by a gilded bronze effigy. The most powerful man in the kingdom, not excepting Henry V, Beauchamp has a tomb considered one of the finest remaining examples of Perpendicular-Gothic as practiced in England in the mid-15th century. The tomb of Robert Dudley, Earl of Leicester, a favorite of Elizabeth I, is against the north wall. The Perpendicular-Gothic choir dates from the 14th century, as do the Norman crypt and the Chapter House. For more information, get in touch with the Warwick Parish Office, Old Square Warwick (tel. 0926/400771).

Lord Leycester Hospital

At the West Gate, this group of half-timbered almshouses was also spared from the Great Fire. The buildings were erected in about 1400, and the hospital was founded in 1571 by Robert Dudley, the Earl of Leicester, as a home for old soldiers. It is still in use by ex-servicemen and their wives today. On top of the West Gate is the attractive little chapel of St. James, dating from the 12th century, although much restored. The hospital, on High Street (tel. 0926/491422), can be visited from 10 a.m. to 5:30 p.m. daily except Sunday for £1.50 ($2.65) for adults, 50p (90¢) for children. Off-season, it closes at 4 p.m. Last admission is 15 minutes before closing.

Warwick Doll Museum

In one of the most charming Elizabethan buildings in Warwick, this doll museum, Oken's House, Castle Street (tel. 0926/495546), is near St. Mary's Church. Its seven rooms contain an extensive private collection of dolls in wood, wax, and porcelain. The house once belonged to Thomas Oken, a great benefactor of Warwick. The museum is open from 10 a.m. to 12:30 p.m. and 1:30 to 5 p.m. Monday to

Saturday and 2 to 5 p.m. Sunday from Easter to the end of September. Admission is 75p ($1.30) for adults, 50p (90¢) for children.

Warwickshire Museum

At the Market Place, this museum (tel. 0926/410410 ext. 2500) was established in 1836 to house a collection of geological remains, fossils, and a fine grouping of British amphibians from the Triassic period. There are also displays illustrating the history, archeology, and natural history of the country, including the famous Sheldon tapestry map. It is open Monday to Saturday from 10 a.m. to 5:30 p.m., and on Sunday in summer from 2:30 to 5 p.m.

St. John's House

At Coten End, not far from the castle gates, there is a display of domestic life and costumes, and the house in which these exhibitions are displayed is a fund of beauty itself, dating from the early 17th century. A Victorian schoolroom is furnished with original 19th century school furniture and equipment. During term time, Warwickshire children, dressed in replica costumes, can be seen enjoying Victorian-style lessons. Groups of children also use the Victorian parlor and the kitchen. As it is impossible to display more than a small amount at a time, a study room is available where you can see objects from the reserve collections. The costume collection is a particularly fine one, and visitors can study the drawings and photos that make up the costume catalog. These facilities are available by prior appointment only (see below). Upstairs is a Military Museum, tracing the history of the Royal Warwickshire Regiment from 1674 to the present day. The house is open Tuesday to Saturday from 10 a.m. to 12:30 p.m. and 1:30 to 5:30 p.m., and also on Sunday May to September from 2:30 to 5 p.m. Admission is free. For more information and for appointments in the study room, telephone the Keeper of Social History (tel. 0926/410410, ext. 2021).

WHERE TO STAY

Many prefer to seek lodgings in Warwick, then commute to Stratford-upon-Avon. If you're one of them, here are my hotel recommendations:

The **Hilton National Hotel,** Warwick Bypass, the A46 Stratford Road, Warwick, Warwickshire CV34 6RE (tel. 0926/499555), is at the elbow junction of a network of highways, making it popular with commercial travelers. It has a hutch-style, low-slung modern design of earth-colored brick, an octagonal dining room, and a functional series of interconnected bars, lounges, and public areas, as well as a heated indoor swimming pool. The establishment hosts many conferences and sales meetings for local companies. Foreign visitors find that its standardized comfort and easy-to-find location make it a good base for touring Warwick and the surrounding regions. Singles cost £63 ($110.25) daily, and doubles rent for £85 ($148.75).

The **Lord Leycester Hotel** (Calotels), Jury Street, Warwick, Warwickshire CV34 4EJ (tel. 0926/491481), was a manor house belonging in 1726 to Lord Archer of Umberslade. Years later, it was converted into an inn under the sign of the three tuns, and later still it became once more a private residence. In 1926, it was turned into a hotel, an identity it retains today. The 53 bedrooms provide comfortable accommodation, all with private baths or showers. Singles rent for £39 ($68.25) daily, and doubles or twins go for £55 ($96.25). Tariffs include a full English breakfast and VAT. All rooms have color TV, radios, phones, and tea/coffee-makers. A small à la carte menu is offered in the dining room, or you can have snacks in the Tavern Bar. A large car park is found at the rear of the hotel, whose position is central, within walking distance of the castle and other historic buildings of Warwick.

The **Westgate Arms,** 3 Old Bowling Green St., Warwick, Warwickshire CV34 4DD (tel. 0926/492362). The original structure on this site was built in 1315, but the simple black-and-white building you see today dates from 1964. Its position near the castle ensures a busy summer trade in its rambling bars, dining room, and ten comfortably refurbished bedrooms, costing £51.50 ($90.15) to £69.50 ($121.65) daily for a single and £72.50 ($126.90) to £89.50 ($156.65) for a double. If you come to dine, after passing through a loosely defined cocktail lounge/pub/social center, you enter a conservatively decorated room with tented ceiling, fabric-covered banquettes, and a vaguely heraldic theme. In the center, a service area contains facilities for chefs to prepare the popular flambéed specialties of the house. A five-course fixed-price dinner costing £16.25 ($28.45) is a traditional favorite, and a table d'hôte luncheon goes for £10.25 ($17.95). There are also some interesting à la carte dishes.

WHERE TO DINE

One of the best restaurants in town is **Randolph's,** 19-21 Coten End (tel. 0926/491292). It's in a black-and-white half-timbered building that encompasses a former cluster of narrow cottages. Within a cozily beamed dining room, Rodolf and Gillian Prymaka prepare elegantly sophisticated dishes that rely heavily on fresh ingredients and years of culinary training. You might enjoy the house-style goose in marsala wine sauce, pigeon with smoked bacon and wild mushrooms, a terrine of scallops and turbot, calves' kidneys on homemade pasta with madeira sauce, perfectly prepared vegetables, and fresh-baked bread. A favorite choice among the establishment's loyal clientele is thick-sliced beef aged three weeks. Desserts run a tempting gamut from calorie-conscious but flavorful afterthoughts to diet-breaking fantasies. Full meals, priced from £23 ($40.25), are served only in the evening from 7:45 to 9 daily except Sunday.

---

3. Kenilworth Castle

In magnificent ruins, this castle—the subject of Sir Walter Scott's romance *Kenilworth*—once had walls that enclosed an area of seven acres. It lies 5 miles north of Warwick, 13 from Stratford-upon-Avon. In 1957 Lord Kenilworth presented the decaying castle to England, and limited restoration has since been carried out.

The castle dates back to the days of Henry I, having been built by one of his lieutenants, Geoffrey de Clinton. Of the original castle, only Caesar's Tower, with its 16-foot thick walls, remains. Edward II was forced to abdicate at Kenilworth in 1327, before being carried off to Berkeley Castle in Gloucestershire, where he was undoubtedly murdered. In 1563 Elizabeth I gave the castle to her favorite, Robert Dudley, Earl of Leicester. The earl built the Gatehouse, which was visited on several occasions by the queen. After the Civil War, the Roundheads were responsible for breaching the outer walls and towers, and blowing up the north wall of the keep. This was the only damage caused following the Earl of Monmouth's plea that it be "Slighted with as little spoil to the dwellinghouse as might be."

From Good Friday to the end of September, the castle is open daily from 10 a.m. to 6 p.m. In other months, hours are from 10 a.m. to 4 p.m. daily. The castle is closed December 24 to December 26 and January 1. Admission is £1.10 ($1.95) for adults, 55p (95¢) for children under 16. For information, phone 0926/52078.

FOOD AND LODGING

In the old part of Kenilworth, **Clarendon House Hotel,** 6-8 Old High St., Kenilworth, Warwickshire CV8 1LZ (tel. 0926/57668), is a family-run hotel and restaurant. The oak tree around which the original ale house was built in 1430 is still supporting the roof of the building today. The present owners welcome guests to spend the night in any of the 30 bedrooms, all of which are tastefully decorated. Prices range from £30 ($52.50) daily for a single with shower to £38 ($66.50) for a single with shower and toilet. A twin-bedded room with complete bath goes for £50

($87.50), while a room with a four-poster bed and full plumbing facilities rents for £55 ($96.25). Tariffs include VAT, service, and a full English breakfast.

Before the evening meal, guests gather in the timbered and oak-paneled Royalist Retreat Bar and lounges. The hotel's Castle Tavern restaurant is housed in what was once the inn stable. The oddly timbered room is decorated with antique maps and armor, constant reminders that a Cromwellian garrison once stayed at the inn during a seige of Kenilworth Castle. Game is a specialty at the Clarendon House, and in season you may dine on such specialties as jugged hare, pheasant georgienne (marinated in madeira wine with oranges, grapes, and walnuts), grouse, or mallard (wild duck cooked in red wine, mushrooms, and *fines herbes*). A complete dinner, inclusive of VAT, is available for around £15 ($26.25) à la carte, but there is also an interesting table d'hôte menu of four courses for £10.50 ($18.40). You can dine from 7 to 9:30 p.m. Sunday to Thursday, from 7 to 10 p.m. on Friday and Saturday. Sunday luncheon of three courses is available at £8 ($14), served from noon to 1:30 p.m.

Restaurant Bosquet, 97A Warwick Rd. (tel. 0926/52463), is a tiny terraced town-house restaurant owned and operated by Bernard Lignier, a Frenchman, who does the cooking, and his English wife, Jane. The à la carte menu is changed with the seasons but consists mainly of French dishes, such as sweetbreads, loin of lamb with tarragon, fish according to the market, and game according to the season. There is a good selection of reasonably priced regional French wines. A meal of three courses goes for £25 ($43.75) per person. The set dinner menu, at £13 ($22.75), is changed regularly and also includes seasonal produce. The restaurant is open from 7 to 10 p.m. daily except Sunday and Monday. It is essential to make reservations, as the place is quite small. Bosquet is something of a culinary oasis in Kenilworth.

---

4. Coventry

Coventry has long been noted in legend as the ancient market town through which Lady Godiva made her famous ride, giving birth to a new name in English: Peeping Tom. The Lady Godiva story is clouded in such obscurity that the truth has probably been lost forever. It has been suggested that the good lady never appeared in the nude, but was the victim of scandalmongers, who, in their attempt to tarnish her image, unknowingly immortalized her.

Coventry is 19 miles from Stratford-upon-Avon, and only 11 from Warwick and 6 from Kenilworth.

THE SIGHTS

This Midlands city, home of motorcar and cycle manufacturing, is principally industrial, but you'll want to pay it a visit to see Sir Basil Spence's controversial **Coventry Cathedral,** consecrated in 1962. The city was partially destroyed during the blitz in the early '40s, but the rebuilding was miraculous. No city more than Coventry seems to symbolize England's power to bounce back from adversity.

The cathedral grew up on the same site as the 14th-century Perpendicular building. Many Coventry residents have maintained that the foreign visitor is more likely to admire the structure than the Britisher, who perhaps is more attached to traditional cathedral design.

Outside is Sir Jacob Epstein's bronze masterpiece, *St. Michael Slaying the Devil.* Inside, the outstanding feature is the 70-foot-high altar tapestry by Graham Sutherland, said to be the largest in the world. The floor-to-ceiling abstract stained-glass windows are the work of the Royal College of Art. The West Window is most interesting, with its engraved glass, rows of stylized saints and monarchs with angels flying around between them.

In the undercroft of the cathedral is a Visitor Centre, **The Spirit of Coventry.**

There you can see the Walkway of Holograms, three-dimensional images created with laser light, depicting the Stations of the Cross. It is an exciting walk through sound, light, and special effects, tracing the history of Coventry and the cathedral from its foundation to the present day. The treasures of the cathedral are on show. An audio-visual on the city and church includes the fact that 450 aircraft dropped 40,000 firebombs on the city in one day.

The cathedral is open daily in summer from 8:30 a.m. to 7:30 p.m., closing at 5:30 p.m. in winter. The 14th-century tower of the old cathedral costs £1 ($1.75) for adults to visit, 59p (90¢) for children. Admission to the Visitor Centre is £1.25 ($2.20) for adults, 75p ($1.30) for children 6 to 16.

After visiting the cathedral, you may want to have tea in Fraters Restaurant nearby, listening to the chimes.

St. Mary's Guildhall, Bayley Lane (tel. 0203/225555). Up a flight of steps leading from a small yard off Bayley Lane is one of the most attractive medieval guildhalls in England, dating from 1342. It was originally built as a meeting place for the guilds of St. Mary, St. John the Baptist, and St. Catherine. It is now used for the solemn election of the lord mayors of the city and for banquets and civic ceremonies. Above the north window is an arras (tapestry), added in the 15th century, and a beautiful oak ceiling with its original 14th-century carved angels, which was rebuilt in the 1950s. There is a minstrel's gallery and a treasury, and off the armoury, Caesar's Tower where Mary Queen of Scots was imprisoned in 1569. By appointment only, you can also see a magnificent collection of 42 original watercolors by H. E. Cox, depicting Coventry before the bombings of 1940. City pensioners conduct guided tours.

Ford's Hospital, Greyfriars Lane (tel. 0203/223838), is a house built in the very early 16th century to house the poor of the city. Today it is a wealth of old beams and mullioned windows restored during 1953. It is now the home once more of elderly Coventry residents. There is a beautiful inner courtyard surrounded by timbered walls hung with geraniums, ferns, and ivy in summer. It is open from 10 a.m. to 5 p.m. throughout the year, and is well worth a visit. Admission is free.

The **Museum of British Road Transport,** St. Agnes Lane, Hales Street (tel. 0203/832425), is some five minutes' walk from Coventry Cathedral in the city center. It houses the largest municipally owned collection in the United Kingdom, possibly in the world. The oldest car is an original Daimler, dating from 1897 (the first English Daimler was built in Coventry only one year before). The museum also displays some of the most antique vehicles still running—six of them are regular participants in the annual London–Brighton run (only vehicles manufactured before 1905 are eligible). Curiosities include a 1910 Humber taxi whose mileage is listed at more than one million. Exhibits are diversified, as the museum has the ambitious task of covering the total history of transport in the Midlands, internationally recognized as the home of the British transport industry. Indeed, Coventry has been the home of some 124 individual motor vehicle manufacturers, many of which are represented in the collections. Among the military vehicles is the staff car in which Montgomery rode into Berlin after the defeat of the Nazis. Special exhibitions include a period street scene for the formative years of motoring (1895–1929); a "Royalty in the Road" display featuring both Queen Mary's 1935 limousine and King George VI's 1947 state landaulette; a history of the cycle exhibit for 1818–1987; and the most recent innovation, a hi-tech audio-visual display featuring *Thrust 2,* the current holder of the world land-speed record, relating the entire history of this important story from 1898 to today. The museum is open daily throughout the summer (Easter to September) and on Friday, Saturday, and Sunday from October to March. Admission is £1 ($1.75) for adults, 75p ($1.30) for children.

FOOD AND LODGING

A modern structure, the **De Vere Hotel,** Cathedral Square, Coventry, West Midlands CV1 5RP (tel. 0203/633733), is considered the best in town, standing in a position near the cathedral. Just off the Coventry inner ring road, it is in the center of the city. For such a provincial hotel, it has a first-class standard of comfort and service. Attracting a large business clientele, the hotel sounds an elegant tone in its public rooms, including the Terrace Room, a coffeeshop-restaurant where, in summer, glass doors slide back to give access to the terrace forming one side of Cathedral Square. In addition, Daimlers, the hotel's biggest bar, is decorated in art deco style, and the Three Spires Restaurant specializes in British and continental cookery. Bedrooms are spacious and equipped with rosewood furnishings, and each unit was designed as a twin-bedded studio with private bath and double-glazed windows to keep out traffic noises. Twins range in price from £79 ($138.25) to £127 ($222.25) daily, the latter for a VIP suite, and singles pay £79 £62 ($108.50) to £109 ($190.75). These rates include breakfast and VAT.

Hotel Leofric, Broadgate, Coventry, West Midlands CV1 1LZ (tel. 0203/ 21371), named for Lady Godiva's husband, attracts far more business people than tourists. However, if you're overnighting in Coventry, it's a good choice, lying only two or three minutes from the cathedral, overlooking the famous statue of Lady Godiva. Each of the 91 bedrooms has a private bath, TV, phone, and central heating. The regular rate in a single is from £52 ($91) daily, increasing to £66 ($115.50) and up in a double or twin. Tariffs include VAT. The Leofric's Carving Room is perhaps the best value in Coventry and serves traditional English food. A three-course meal is offered for £10.50 ($18.40). The coffeeshop, Peep-in-Tom's, is named after the legendary figure who took a look at Lady Godiva. For a before-dinner drink, I'd recommend one of the specials in Ray's Bar.

On the outskirts, **Ansty Hall,** Ansty, Coventry, West Midlands CV7 9HZ (tel. 0203/612222), offers even better living, at least for the traditionalist. The location is in a 1600s house set on about nine acres of grounds at the village of Ansty, which lies about half a mile from junction 2 of the busy M6. Behind a pristine red-brick façade, the architectural character of the house is set as you enter a spacious reception hall paneled in oak. The hotel is small, with only 13 bedrooms, but each accommodation has been brought up to date with modern amenities such as a private bath or shower, direct-dial phone, and TV. Some units are more spacious than others, almost like a small suite. B&B ranges from £62 ($108.50) daily in a single, going up to £100 ($175) in a double. The hotel also serves good British food with meals costing from £15 ($26.25), but you must arrive for dinner by 9:30 p.m.

---

5. Hereford and Worcester

The Wye Valley contains some of the most beautiful river scenery in Europe. The river cuts through agricultural country, and there is no population explosion in the sleepy villages. Wool used to be its staple business. Today, fruit growing and dairy farming are important.

The old county of Herefordshire has now combined with Worcestershire to form "Hereford and Worcester"-shire. Worcestershire's name, of course, has become famous around the world because of its sauce familiar to gourmets. It is one of the most charming of Midland counties, covering a portion of the rich valleys of the Severn and Avon.

Herefordshire's Black Mountains border the Welsh Brecon Beacons National Park, and between the two cathedral cities of Hereford and Worcester the ridge of the Malverns rises from the Severn Plain.

The heart of England is the best point to travel to by train from Paddington Station in London if you wish to use your BritRail Pass. The train takes you through many of the previously mentioned towns and villages, and you can stop and visit Windsor, Henley-on-Thames, and Oxford, not to mention the numerous Cotswold villages such as Chipping Campden. It must be one of the best train rides in the country, and you can also take a side trip by bus from Evesham to Stratford-upon-Avon. Or take the bus back from Stratford to Oxford via Woodstock, then the train back into London.

HEREFORD

One of the most colorful old towns in England, the ancient Saxon city of Hereford, on the Wye River, was the birthplace of both David Garrick and Nell Gwynne. Dating from 1079, the red sandstone **Hereford Cathedral** (tel. 0432/59880) contains all styles of architecture, from Norman to Perpendicular. One of its most interesting features is a library of chained books—more than 1,600 copies—as well as one of the oldest maps in existence, the Mappa Mundi of 1290. There is also a Treasury of the crypt.

Hereford is surrounded by both orchards and rich pasturelands. Hence it has some of the finest cider in the world, best sampled in one of the city's mellow pubs. Hereford cattle sold here are some of the finest in the world too.

The Old House, High Town (tel. 0432/268121, ext. 207), is preserved as a Jacobean period museum, with the appropriate furnishings. The completely restored half-timbered structure was built in 1621. Furnished in 17th-century style on three floors, the house includes a kitchen, hall, and bedrooms with four-poster beds. It was originally part of Butcher's Row. The house is open all year from Monday to Saturday. Summer hours are from 10 a.m. to 1 p.m. and 2 to 5:30 p.m. In winter, it is open only from 10 a.m. to 1 p.m. Admission is 50p (90¢) for adults, 25p (45¢) for children. A joint ticket costing 80p ($1.40) admits you to both The Old House and Churchill Gardens Museum.

The **Cider Museum & King Offa Cider Brandy Distillery,** Pomona Place, Whitecross Road (the A438 to Brecon) (tel. 0432/354207), tells the story of traditional cider making right through to modern factory methods. Displays include orcharding, an enormous 17th-century French beam press, a cooper's shop, an old farm cider house, traveling cider makers' "tack" that used to be trundled from farm to farm, and the original champagne cider cellars with their tiers of bottles. Also on view are a 1920s press house and factory bottling line and the great oak vats of the Napoleonic period. The King Offa Distillery has been granted the first new license to distill cider brandy in the United Kingdom in more than 250 years, and visitors can see it being produced from the beautiful copper stills brought from Normandy. The museum shop sells cider, cider brandy, cider brandy liqueur, and Royal Cider, the real wine of Old England, as well as a good selection of gifts and souvenirs. The museum is open from 10 a.m. to 5:30 p.m. seven days a week from April to the end of October, from 1 to 5 p.m. Monday to Saturday from November to March. Admission is £1.20 ($2.10) for adults, 90p ($1.60) for children. The museum is five minutes' walk from the city center and a quarter of a mile from the city Ring Road on the A438 to Brecon.

Food and Lodging

Green Dragon Hotel, Broad Street, Hereford, Hereford and Worcester HR4 9BG (tel. 0432/272506), hides behind an 18th-century Georgian facade, although this former coaching inn is considerably older. Near the cathedral, it retains many traditional old features, including some early 17th-century paneling made of Herefordshire oak. Bedrooms are adequate enough, with private baths or showers, color TVs, and in-house movies. Singles cost from £35 ($61.25) nightly, with doubles beginning at £56 ($98). The paneled restaurant offers both English and continental dishes.

Effy's, 96 East St. (tel. 0432/59754), is the best independent restaurant in Hereford. Reached by heading up a narrow street (off Broad Street), it is housed behind a storefront-style façade. Inside, the atmosphere warms considerably, with a fantasy of pink-and-green latticework along with fresh flowers and a garden out back. There's even a second floor for additional seating, as there are only a few tables downstairs (which means that reservations are important). A set lunch is offered for £7.95 ($13.90) from noon to 2 p.m., and dinner, costing from £12 ($21), is served from 7 to 11 p.m. daily except Sunday and Monday. Some dishes are really excellent, and the cookery has imaginative flair. Try such offerings as pigeon breasts in garlic butter, trout meunière, or a chicken-and-zucchini casserole, finished off by, say, apple and plum pie, perhaps one of the homemade ice creams (made with fresh fruit). Dishes offered, of course, will depend on the season and what is particularly fresh on any given day.

WORCESTER

This historic cathedral city, known for its gloves and porcelain, stands 27 miles from Birmingham and 26 miles from Stratford-upon-Avon.

Worcester Cathedral, set high on the bank of the River Severn, celebrated its 900th anniversary in 1984. The original crypt is still in daily use, and the Quire, rebuilt in 1224, has contained the tomb of King John since 1216. The Chapter House, with its single central supporting column, is one of the oldest and finest in England. The cathedral, which has a long tradition of the finest choral music, is open daily from 7:45 a.m. to 6 p.m. (to 7 p.m. in summer). On Saturday and school holidays you can usually climb the tower and see the view over the city and countryside. The tower door is open from 11 a.m. to 3:30 p.m. The cost is 50p (90¢) for adults, 30p (55¢) for children.

A visit to the **Royal Worcester Porcelain Factory,** Severn Street (tel. 0905/23221), is worthwhile. A tour costs £2 ($3.50) for adults, £1 ($1.75) for children over 8, allowing you to see the craftspeople at work. Unfortunately it's necessary to book ahead if you wish to take a tour (for "same day" tour, phone before 10 a.m.), but everyone can enjoy browsing in the shop at the factory. There you can buy examples of their craft. Many pieces are "seconds," all marked as such and sold at moderate prices. Most of the time you won't be able to tell why. There is also a magnificent museum.

The city is rich in other sights, including the **Commandery** (tel. 0905/355071), founded in the 11th century as the Hospital of St. Wulstan, becoming over the years a fine 15th-century timber-frame structure that was the country home of the Wylde family. Charles II used the house as headquarters for the 1651 Battle of Worcester. The Great Hall has a hammerbeam roof and a minstrels' gallery. England's premier **Civil War Centre** is now situated here, with audio-visual displays and regular "living history" encampments with 17th-century costumes and crafts. The house is open from 10:30 a.m. to 5 p.m. Monday to Saturday and 2 to 5 p.m. on Sunday. Admission is £1.50 ($2.65) for adults, 75p ($1.30) for children, and £4 ($7) for a family ticket. The Commandery has canalside tea rooms, a picnic area, and a Garden of Fragrance.

You can also see **Queen Anne's Guildhall,** built in 1724, with statues honoring Charles I and Charles II, erected by the Royalists. Walking tours of the city are offered in summer. Pump Room teas are available on certain dates. Ask at the **Tourist Information Centre** for details (tel. 0905/723471).

Food and Lodging

Fownes, City Walls Road, Worcester, Hereford and Worcester WR1 2AP (tel. 0905/335021), is the best place to stay in town, a glove factory in the days of Queen Victoria. It has been successfully converted until now it offers 61 well-furnished bedrooms, each with private bath or shower, direct-dial phone, and TV. Within easy walking distance of Worcester Cathedral, the hotel opens onto a canal. Most bedrooms are spacious, decorated with pastel colors and containing thoughtful extras. Singles range from £60 ($105) per night, climbing to £75 ($131.25) in a double. Extra facilities include a sauna and laundry service. King's Restaurant, the hotel's dining room, is credited with offering the finest cuisine in town. Meals range from £11.50 ($20.15) to £26 ($45.50) (closed Monday lunch and Sunday dinner).

Brown's Old Cornmill, 24 Quay St. (tel. 0905/26263), is a richly atmospheric dining room in a building constructed as a grain mill in the late 1700s. Today, subtly modernized reminders of an agrarian society surround you as you enjoy flavorful meals. You might begin with a warm salad of bacon and scallops, following with roast quail garnished with cognac and grapes or a plump chicken breast loaded with herb-and-cheese stuffing. Fish is popular here, with several preparations of Dover sole, as well as imaginative dishes of salmon and turbot. Fixed-price lunches begin at £15.95 ($27.90), and dinners at £22 ($38.50). A special Sunday lunch menu is offered for £11 ($19.25). Service is from 12:30 to 1:45 p.m. and 7:30 to 9:30 p.m. Monday to Saturday, from 12:30 to 2 p.m. Sunday. Closed Saturday at lunchtime, Sunday evening, and bank holidays.

Food and Lodging at Abberley

The **Elms Hotel,** Abberley, near Worcester, Hereford and Worcester WR6 6AT (tel. 029921/666), is on the A443 12 miles northwest of Worcester on the border of the old county of Herefordshire. Queen Anne was on the throne when this magnificent country house was built in 1710. Twelve acres of rolling parkland surround formal gardens, and there are tennis courts, a putting green, and a croquet lawn for the use of the guests. This is a warm country house where open log fires burn in the comfortably furnished lounges to welcome visitors. Bedrooms are mostly large, some with four-poster beds. All have private baths or showers, radios, phones, and color TVs. Much antique and good English furniture is used. Bathrooms are supplied with such accessories as hairdryers. Rates for single rooms with bath start at £60 ($105) daily, doubles and twins from £82 ($143.50). All tariffs include a full English breakfast, VAT, and service. Brooke Room Restaurant, the restaurant at the Elms, is open daily for lunch from 12:30 to 2 p.m. and for dinner from 7:30 to 9 p.m. It's an elegant and restful place to enjoy "nouvellish" cuisine. Using only the finest and freshest ingredients and the lightly flavored sauces of nouvelle cuisine, the chef admits that larger portions are served here than are usual in such restaurants, in order to satisfy the hearty country appetites of the local clientele. You can enjoy the view of the raised gardens, floodlit at night, through the arched windows while you wait for your freshly prepared meal to be served. Luncheon is £12 ($21); dinner, £25 ($43.50). There is a good wine list.

Museums on the Outskirts

Sir Edward Elgar's Birthplace, Crown East Lane, Lower Broadheath (tel. 090566/224), about three miles west of Worcester, is a brick cottage surrounded by stables and a coach house built by his father and uncle in the early 19th century. Nowadays the house contains a museum of photographs and drawings, original musical scores, and mementos of his youth. Musicians and conductors come from afar to check his music and their interpretations of it. To reach the house, drive out of Worcester on the A44 toward Leominster. After two miles, turn off to the right at the sign. The house is in the village, half a mile along a side road. Admission is £2 ($3.50) for adults, 50p (90¢) for children. It's open daily except Wednesday from 10:30 a.m. to 6 p.m. in summer, from 1:30 to 4:30 p.m. in winter; closed from mid-January to mid-February.

Avoncroft Museum of Buildings, Stoke Heath, Bromsgrove (tel. 0527/31886), is 11 miles from Worcester and 21 miles from Stratford-upon-Avon. It is open daily from 11 a.m. to 5:30 p.m. in June, July, and August. Hours are the same in April, May, September, and October, but it's closed Monday. In March and November, it's open from 11 a.m. to 4:30 p.m. daily except Monday and Friday; closed altogether in December, January, and February. Admission is £2 ($3.50) for adults, 50p (90¢) for children. A family ticket admitting two adults and two children goes for £5.15 ($9). The museum is an open-air site where a variety of historic buildings have been saved from destruction and reconstructed. There are a windmill in working order; a merchant's timber-framed house from the 15th century; an Elizabethan house; a cockfight theater, a stable, a wagon shed, and an ice house, all from the 18th century; chain- and nailmaking workshops; a blacksmith's forge; an 18th-century dovecote with doves; a three-seater earth closet (outdoor toilet); and an early 19th-century toll house. The displays give a fascinating insight into the construction of building erected by English forefathers. The 14th-century Guesten Hall roof from Worcester is being reconstructed on a new building that, as well as displaying the roof, will serve as an exhibition hall for the museum. Free car parking is available, and there is also a picnic area.

The **Jinney Ring Craft Centre,** Hanbury, Bromsgrove (tel. 052784/272), is in the same area as Avoncroft Museum and Hanbury Hall, in the village of Hanbury on the B4091 from Bromsgrove and only 15 miles from Stratford-upon-Avon. A range of old timbered farm buildings have been carefully restored by Richard and Jenny Greatwood into eight small studio workshops, housing a potter, an artist, a woodcarver, a leather worker, a fashion designer, and a stained-glass artist. Many examples of their work can be purchased from the Exhibition Gallery, which has art and craft work from all over Great Britain. There is also a large gift shop. Coffee, tea, lunches, and evening meals are served in their 200-year-old Barn Restaurant (tel. 052784/653). There is a display of old farm tools and implements including the Jinney Ring from which the center gets its name. In season, there's a press for do-it-yourself cider making. There is ample free parking and no charge for admission. The Ring is open Wednesday to Saturday from 10:30 a.m. to 5 p.m. and on Sunday from 2 to 5:30 p.m.

Also in the area, **Hanbury Hall** (tel. 052784/214) is a Wren-style red-brick building erected in the early 18th century. It is remarkable for its painted ceilings and magnificent staircase by Thornhill. It is open from 2 to 5 p.m. Saturday and Sunday from April to October (including all of Easter weekend). From May to the end of September, hours are from 2 to 6 p.m. Wednesday to Sunday and bank holidays. Admission is £1.90 ($3.35) to 95p ($1.65) for children. Tea is served in the building.

THE MALVERNS

The beautiful, historic Malverns, once part of the ancient kingdom of Mercia, lie to the west of Worcester. Great Malvern became important in the 19th century as a spa town, and much of the Victorian splendor remains. The Malvern Hills stretch for nine miles, with six townships lying along their line, making this a splendid walking center for your visit to the shire of Hereford and Worcester. The largest Priory Church in the area dates from the 15th century and has some fine stained glass. The monks' stalls have superb misericords and medieval titles. You can wander through Great Malvern, Malvern Link, West Malvern, Malvern Wells, Little Malvern, and several other hamlets on a walking tour.

Two miles out of Great Malvern to the left as you leave on the Ledbury road is **St. Wulstan's Church** where Sir Edward Elgar, who lived throughout his life in the Malvern area, is buried with his wife and daughter. There is a bronze bust to the composer in Priory Park, and he lived at Craeglea on the Malvern Wells road and at Forli in Alexandra Road. It was here that he composed the *Enigma Variations, Sea Pictures,* and the *Dream of Gerontius.*

Water is still bottled at **Holy Well,** above Malvern Wells, and you can visit the place where monks are reputed to have wrapped the infirm in cloths steeped in the waters to cure their ills. St. Anne's Well is also open to view above the town, but you have to be hardy to climb the 200-odd steps to taste the waters.

Food and Lodging at Malvern Wells

Great Malvern has many fine accommodations, but discriminating travelers over the years have retreated instead to Malvern Wells, two miles south on the A449. There they find peace and tranquility with views over the Severn and Evesham Vales.

Not only does Malvern Wells possess one of the most charming hotels in the area, it also has the finest and most acclaimed cuisine. Both the hotel and restaurant are recommended below.

The **Cottage in the Wood Hotel,** Holywell Road, Malvern Wells, Great Malvern, Hereford and Worcester WR14 4LG (tel. 06845/3487), is considered the best place to stay at Malvern Wells. Owned and run by John and Sue Pattin, the hotel is a Georgian building originally constructed as part of a much larger estate. The property lies in seven acres of lawn, gardens, and woodlands stretching down the hillside. The public rooms are decorated with antiques and reproductions, and upholstered sofas and chairs allow for relaxing near open fires. Some 20 bedrooms are scattered through the older main house and a pair of more recently converted outer buildings. Each has a private bath, phone, and TV. Accommodations cost £46 ($80.50) daily in a single, £62 ($108.50) to £95 ($166.25) in a double. The flavorful meals served in the dining room cost £5 ($8.75) to £23 ($40.25).

Restaurant Croque-en-Bouche, 221 Wells Rd. (tel. 0684/565612), opposite the filling station, is run by Robin and Marion Jones in what was the bakery and grocer's shop in a five-story Victorian building. There is still an old oven in the basement where wine is now stored. In the nice old house is a small bar where Robin offers a list of apéritifs, including the house drink of raspberry liqueur with sparkling white burgundy. Dinner, at £23 ($40.25), starts with a huge tureen of homemade soup, followed by a choice for the fish course, such as pancakes stuffed with salmon and spinach. The main course might be venison or wild rabbit niçoise. The cheeseboard is well supplied with British products, and you can finish with a crème brûlée or sorbet made with fresh fruits. As there are only Robin and Marion to look after you, you must reserve a table. Coffee is served, and since smoking is not permitted in the dining room, smokers adjourn to the bar at this stage. The restaurant is open from 7:30 to 9:15 p.m. Wednesday to Saturday for dinner.

LEDBURY

A pleasant place to stay, the **Hope End Country House Hotel,** Hope End, Ledbury, Hereford and Worcester HR8 1JQ (tel. 0531/3613), is owned and operated by John and Patricia Hegarty, who come from local families. John's ancestor helped build the canal and bring the railway to Ledbury, and Patricia's family has lived here for more than 500 years. Tired of work as a solicitor and a schoolteacher, the Hegartys settled at Hope End, where Elizabeth Barrett Browning lived during her first 23 years. The house, refurbished in English country style, is furnished with antiques, and paintings and other art adorn the walls of the drawing room. Bedrooms are centrally heated, and all have an adjoining bath. The charge for B&B, dinner, VAT, and service ranges from £58 ($101.50) to £75 ($131.25) per person daily, the latter price for one of the larger rooms or in the suite across the courtyard under the minaret. Patricia enjoys a reputation for her cuisine and has written a widely acclaimed book on English cookery. She specializes in providing wholesome and fresh foods and bakes her own brown bread. Fresh fruit and vegetables come from the large walled garden. Fresh eggs, local beef and lamb, fish and game, and a wide selection of English cheeses make meals a pleasure. Five-course dinners include such appetizers as haddock hotpots with cider, followed by wild duck, or lamb.

EVESHAM

A delightful market town on the Avon River, Evesham is known for its riverside parks. It contains several interesting buildings, including a 16th-century bell tower. It is a center of a famous fruit- and vegetable-growing region, and in springtime the Vale of Evesham is a mass of blossoms. Six miles southeast of Broadway and 14 miles northeast of Stratford-upon-Avon, it makes a good center for touring both the Cotswolds and the Shakespeare Country.

Evesham Hotel, Coopers Lane, off Waterside, Evesham, Hereford and Worcester WR11 6DA (tel. 0386/49111), lies down a small lane just where the A44 runs beside the River Avon to Evesham. It is owned and run by the Jenkinson family. John is general manager, and there is always a Jenkinson on duty. A dwelling has stood on the site since the 16th century, and the mulberry trees and cedars of Lebanon date back almost that far. The lounges and the restaurant look out over the gardens to the trees. There is a modern bar where the usual drinks are served, plus an amazing selection of malt whiskies and brandies. In the Cedar Restaurant, dinner, from 7 to 9:30 p.m. daily, is a well-prepared à la carte event. You choose your meal from such dishes as medallions of beef with green pepper sauce or breast of chicken stuffed with Brie and deep-fried. All are served with a selection of fresh vegetables and followed by homemade desserts. The meal price for three courses is £14 ($24.50). At lunchtime, from 12:30 to 2 p.m., a buffet offers homemade soup, selections from a serve-yourself buffet, and coffee, all costing around £6 ($10.50). The bedrooms are warm and comfortable, with color TVs, radios, phones, tea- and coffee-making equipment, and private bathrooms. An added wing has 16 modern, well-equipped units with views over the garden. It's attached to the main house by a fully enclosed and heated corridor. The cost for B&B is £43 ($75.25) daily in a single, £58 ($101.50) in a double, and £78 ($136.50) in a family suite. All tariffs include VAT and a full English breakfast, or a continental breakfast served in your room if you prefer.

6. Shropshire

Immortalized by A. E. Housman's "A Shropshire Lad," this hilly county borders Wales, which accounts for its turbulent history. The bloody battles are over today, and the towns of Shropshire, with their black-and-white timbered houses, are peaceful and quiet. The county makes a good base for touring in the Welsh mountains.

When Parliament redistricted and even renamed some of the shires of England in 1973, the name of Shropshire was changed back to a much older name—Salop. However, in this case, the name just didn't catch on, and you'll find the county still called Shropshire on recent maps and by most of its inhabitants.

SHREWSBURY

Lying within a horseshoe bend of the Severn River, Shrewsbury is the capital of Shropshire. The river almost encloses the town. Known for its cakes and ale, Shrewsbury contains one of the best-known schools in England. It was also the birthplace of Charles Darwin.

Considered the finest Tudor town in England, Shrewsbury is noted for its black-and-white buildings of timber and plaster, including Abbot's House from 1450 and the tall gabled Ireland's Mansion from 1575 standing on High Street. It also has a number of Georgian and Regency mansions, some old bridges, and handsome churches, including the Abbey Church of Saint Peter and St. Mary's Church.

Shrewsbury Castle, built by the Norman earl, Roger de Montgomery, in 1083, stands in a dominating position where the River Severn almost surrounds the town. It houses the Shropshire Regimental Museum, including the collections of the King's Shropshire Light Infantry, the Shropshire Yeomanry Cavalry, and the Shropshire Royal Horse Artillery. The collections represent more than 300 years of regimental service and include a lock of Napoleon's hair and an American flag captured in 1814 when the White House was seized and burned in the War of 1812. The castle is open daily from 10 a.m. to 5 p.m. Admission is 60p ($1.05). For more information, phone 0743/58516.

Rowley's House Museum, on Barker Street (tel. 0743/61196), is housed in a fine 16th-century timber-frame house and an adjoining brick mansion. This museum includes displays on art, local history, Roman and prehistoric archeology, geology, costumes, and natural history. The great treasures include the fine Hadrianic forum inscription and silver mirror, both from the nearby Roman city of Viroconium (Wroxeter). The museum is open from 10 a.m. to 5 p.m. Monday to Saturday year round and also from noon to 5 p.m. Sunday from Easter to mid-September. Admission is 50p (90¢) for adults, 20p (35¢) for children.

Clive House Museum on College Hill (tel. 0743/54811), town house of Clive of India when he served as mayor of Shrewsbury in 1762, contains period rooms and splendid local pottery and porcelain, early watercolors, and textiles, and has a lovely garden. Hours are 2 to 5 p.m. on Monday, 10 a.m. to 1 p.m. and 2 to 5 p.m. Tuesday to Saturday. Admission is 30p (55¢) for adults, 15p (25¢) for children.

At **Coleham Pumping Station,** Longden Coleham (tel. 0743/61196), you can see displayed compound rotative pumping engines from 1900. Open by appointment only, it charges an admission of 30p (55¢) for adults, 15p (25¢) for children.

Food and Lodging

Prince Rupert Hotel, Butcher Row, Shrewsbury, Shropshire SY1 1UQ (tel. 0743/236000), is a hotel of character—part of it dating from the 15th century—right on a quiet side street in the center of town. Its front has four peaked gables and, in summer, a wealth of flower boxes. The façade is characterized by peaked gables on the Old Church Street entrance. Even though the interior has been modernized, it still has exposed beams and uneven floors. A favorite gathering spot is the lounge, which is tapestried. There are two restaurants, including the Cavalier, which has a reputation for fine cuisine. The 63 rooms are bright and fresh, with compact, well-maintained baths. Singles range in price from £50 ($87.50) daily, and doubles or twins begin at £66 ($115.50). Guests have included Margaret Thatcher and her husband, Denis, and George C. Scott, who stayed here for seven weeks when he made a film based on Dickens's *A Christmas Carol.*

Lion Hotel, Wyle Cop, Shrewsbury, Shropshire SY1 1UY (tel. 0743/53107), is a red-brick structure, once a famous posting inn, standing in the center of town near English Bridge. In part the hotel dates from the 15th century, and oak beams and paneling from that period remain. Many famous people have stayed here, including Dickens, Jenny Lind, and De Quincey, who described the hotel's Adam ballroom in his *Confessions of an Opium Eater.* Dickens stayed in what is now the beamed Dickens Suite, where you can read his comments on his sojourn here, which he described as "the strangest little rooms, the ceilings of which I can touch with my hands." The cost is £98 ($171.50) nightly for two persons. Bedrooms are well furnished, with baths or showers. Singles cost £50 ($87.50) daily, and doubles go for £65 ($113.75) to £73 ($127.75), all tariffs including VAT and service. The restaurant with its 1920s decor serves both table d'hôte and à la carte meals. Dinner is from £10.95 ($19.15). The hotel has two bars, the Oak bar featuring a buffet at lunchtime.

LUDLOW

Looking down on the Teme River, this mellow old town was once a Norman guardian of the Welsh border, with lots of history whispering through its quiet lanes and courts and the Georgian and Jacobean timbered buildings. The two little princes who were murdered in the Tower of London lived here, and it was once the refuge and home of the first wife of Henry VIII, Catherine of Aragon. You can visit the Church of St. Laurence where the unhappy queen prayed.

The most colorful street is known as "Broad," rising from the old Ludford Bridge to Broadgate, the one remaining gateway from walls erected in the Middle Ages. See, in particular, the Butter Cross and Reader's House. A. E. Housman's grave is in the cemetery here.

nd Lodging

he **Feathers,** Bull Ring, Ludlow, Shropshire SY8 1AA (tel. 0584/5261), is one of England's most famous Elizabethan inns. Built in 1603 as a private residence, it is characterized by its half-timbered front and richly decorated interior. Bedrooms are bright and cheerful, and all of them contain private bath, as well as phone, radio, television, trouser press, and tea/coffee-makers. Colors are in harmony, with Welsh tapestry bedspreads. Singles go for £49 ($85.75) nightly, and doubles and twins cost £78 ($136.50), including an English breakfast. If possible, ask for one of the units with a four-poster bed at £86 ($151.50) to £92 ($161). The Richard III restaurant, with its original fireplace, is in the old-world style, serving good food and drink. Dinners go for £15 ($26.25) and up. There are also two fully licensed bars, and polished brass and copper set the right decorative tone. In the James I lounge, you can enjoy a carved mantelpiece and an elaborately ornamented plaster ceiling.

IRONBRIDGE

Ironbridge Gorge is the location of an intriguing complex of museums, the birthplace of the Industrial Revolution.

The Iron Bridge was the first in the world made of that metal, which was cast at Coalbrookdale in 1779 and gave its name to the area. Abraham Darby I, ironmaster, first smelted iron using coke as a fuel at the Old Furnace in Coalbrookdale, thus paving the way for the first iron rails, iron bridge, iron boat, iron aqueduct, and iron-framed building. The Ironbridge Gorge Museum spreads over some six square miles of the Severn Gorge, encompassing a unique series of industrial monuments and displays.

The **Ironbridge Gorge Museum,** Ironbridge, Telford (tel. 095245/3522), includes the Blists Hill Open Air Museum with a re-creation of a 19th-century town with costumed demonstrators, the Coalbrookdale Museum and Furnace of Iron with a sound-and-light display, the Coalport China Museum, the Jackfield Tile Museum, the Severn Warehouse (now the Museum of the River), and many other smaller museums, including the Bedlam Furnaces, the 1779 Iron Bridge (first in the world) with its original toll house, Rosehill House (the restored 19th-century home of the Darby family), the Long Warehouse Library and Archives, and the Elton Gallery with changing exhibitions. A ticket to all the attractions is £5.50 ($9.65) for adults, £3.50 ($6.15) for children. A family ticket for two adults and up to five children costs £17.50 ($30.65). All the sites are open from 10 a.m. to 6 p.m. daily from mid-February to the end of October. The Ironbridge Gorge was declared a World Heritage Site by UNESCO in 1987.

---

7. Staffordshire

Stoke-on-Trent is the name of the five towns known as the Potteries, the "Five Towns" of Arnold Bennett's novels. The Potteries are known throughout the world for the excellence of their fine porcelain and china.

The so-called Black Country of steelworks and coal mines has almost disappeared, although you can visit a coal mine and descend in the "cage" to the worked-out seams.

Within easy reach of the industrial town of Dovedale is a valley with some of England's most beautiful scenery, forming part of the wild country of Peak District National Park.

STOKE-ON-TRENT

Because of the worldwide interest in the making of pottery, this town has found itself something of a tourist attraction. It's the home of the pottery made famous by Josiah Wedgwood, along with other well-known names such as Coalport, Minton, and Spode.

The **Wedgwood Visitor Centre,** at Barlaston (tel. 0782/204141), charges adults £1.75 ($3.05) and children £1 ($1.75) for admission, and is open from 9 a.m. to 5 p.m. Monday to Friday, 10 a.m. to 4 p.m. on Saturday. The center is also open on public holidays with the exception of the Christmas period. In the demonstration hall, you can watch the clay pots being formed on the potter's wheel, see how the raised motifs so well-known on Wedgwood Jasper are made and added to the pieces, as well as witness how plates are turned and fired, then painted. Craft operatives are happy to answer your questions about their special occupation. There's a continuous film show in the large cinema, and the beginning of the movie is announced on the public address system. In the shop you can see samples of all the sorts of items made at the factory and purchase souvenirs. Prices are the same as elsewhere, but they do sometimes have items of discontinued lines and some "seconds" available at reduced prices.

The fascinating museum was redesigned and enlarged in 1985 and features "living" displays including Josiah Wedgwood's Etruria factory and his Victorian showroom. Other room settings can also be seen. When you need a rest, there is a lounge with a snack cafeteria where a selection of light refreshments can be had at reasonable prices. Here you can write your postcards home and have them franked with a special stamp to say they were mailed at the Wedgwood Centre.

Royal Doulton, Nile Street, Burslem, near Stoke-on-Trent (tel. 0782/575454). You will walk for nearly a mile and negotiate some 250 steps during the tour of this pottery factory, but you will see exactly how plates, cups, and figures are made from basic raw materials. The gift shop has slightly imperfect articles on sale alongside quality goods, and you can browse through the Sir Henry Doulton Gallery, tracing the company's history since 1815 and containing a collection of Doulton's historical figures. Tours of the factory are at 10:15 a.m. and 2 p.m., costing £2 ($3.50). The gallery is open Monday to Friday from 9 a.m. to 4:15 p.m. Advance reservations are advisable. Call Sandra Baddeley, the tour organizer.

John Beswick, Gold Street, Longton, near Stoke-on-Trent (tel. 0782/313041). Since 1896, the John Beswick Studios of Royal Doulton have built a reputation for fine ceramic sculpture. Most renowned for its authentic studies of horses, birds, and animals, the studio also creates the famed Character and Toby Jugs of Royal Doulton. You may be lucky enough to see Peter Rabbit in the making during a visit. The 1½-hour tour ends in the factory shop so you can indulge your purchasing whims. Tours depart at 10:15 a.m. and 2 p.m. Monday to Friday, costing £1.50 ($2.65). Advance reservations are essential (call Joan Barker).

Spode, Church Street, Stoke-on-Trent (tel. 0782/744011), is yet another factory to offer guided tours available at 10 a.m. and 2 p.m. Monday to Thursday, only at 10 a.m. Friday. Again, advance reservations are essential. The cost is $1 ($1.75). The shop is open from 9 a.m. to 5 p.m. Monday to Thursday, from 9 a.m. to 4 p.m. Friday, and from 9 a.m. to 1 p.m. Saturday.

Moorcroft Pottery, W. Moorcroft Ltd., Sandbach Road, Burslem, Stoke-on-Trent (tel. 0782/24323), is an interesting alternative to the world-famous names. Founded in 1898 by William Moorcroft, who produced his own special brand of pottery and was his own exclusive designer until his death in 1945, the pottery is special in that decoration is part of the first firing, giving it a higher quality of color and brilliance than, say, Spode. Today, design is in the hands of William's son, John, who carries on the personal traditions of the family firm, creating clear floral designs in bright, clear colors for what has been described as the art nouveau of the pottery world. There is much to admire and buy in the Factory Seconds Shop. The factory and the restored bottle oven is open Monday to Friday from 10 a.m. to 5 p.m. and on Saturday from 9:30 a.m. to 12:30 p.m. There is always someone around to explain the various processes and to show you around the museum, with its collections of early Moorcroft. Factory tours take place on Wednesday and cost £1 ($1.75).

Afterward, a visit to the past is in order. The **Gladstone Pottery Museum,** Uttoxeter Road at Longton (tel. 0782/319232), is a 19th-century pottery factory restored as a museum, with craftspeople demonstrating daily in original workshops. Galleries depict the rise of the Staffordshire pottery industry; tile history; sanitary ware with washstand bowls and jugs plus toilets of all shapes, sizes, colors, and decoration. There are replicas of a potter's house and a factory manager's office. Admission to the museum is £2 ($3.50) for adults, £1 ($1.75) for children. It is open from 10 a.m. to 4 p.m. Monday to Saturday and 2 to 4 p.m. Sunday. It's closed Monday in winter.

Stoke-on-Trent City Museum and Art Gallery, Bethesda Street, Hanley (tel. 0782/202173), has departments of fine arts, decorative arts, natural history, archeology, and social history. In addition, it houses one of the largest and finest collections of ceramics in the world. It's open Monday to Saturday from 10:30 a.m. to 5 p.m., 2 to 5 p.m. on Sunday. Admission is free.

Minton Museum, London Road (tel. 0782/744766), is the starting point for a 1½-hour conducted tour through the major departments of the renowned pottery firm. A telephone call or a letter in advance is advised if you would like to join the £1.50 ($2.65) conducted tour, which includes a visit to the department where Minton's celebrated raised gold designs are produced. Visitors will also have the opportunity of seeing free-hand painting of the highest order. Details are available of a service offered by Minton enabling customers to commission a special hand-painted, personalized plate featuring an illustration of their own choice. The cost is around £130 ($227.50), and delivery takes three to four months. Ask the museum curator or factory guides.

Chatterley Whitfield Mining Museum, at Tunstall, Stoke-on-Trent (tel. 0782/813337), is a unique museum of mining. Tours underground are led when possible by ex-miners who vividly relate their experiences working in a coal mine. Visitors are "kitted out" with lamp and helmet, and stout shoes are recommended. Chatterley Whitfield was the first colliery to produce one million tons of coal in a year. Coal was mined for 140 years before its transformation into a museum in 1979. Other displays and attractions include a steam-winding engine, pit ponies, locomotives, and a colliery canteen and museum shop. Hours are 10 a.m. to 4 p.m. daily, with a reduced schedule in winter, depending on the demand. Tours cost £2.95 ($5.16) for adults, £1.85 ($3.25) for children.

Food and Lodging

For those who wish to visit the Staffordshire Potteries and stay overnight in this industrial part of the country, I offer the following suggestions.

Crown Hotel, 36 High St., Stone, Staffordshire ST15 8AS (tel. 0782/813535), is a solid 18th-century coaching inn, rebuilt by Henry Holland on the site of a far more ancient staging post dating to 1579 and known as one of the most important in the country in the reign of Charles II. Today the coach yard is roofed in to provide for the lofty paneled dining room. The sleek "carriages" of today's travelers are housed in a large yard behind the hotel. Some of the accommodations are in the main hotel, reached by a fine galleried oak staircase; others are in an annex at the back. All units have bath (shower only in the newer part), color TV, and coffee- and tea-making facilities. Prices run from £48 ($84) daily in a double with bath, £38 ($66.50) in a single. Prices include VAT, service, and an enormous breakfast. Dinner in the paneled dining hall incudes main-course specials such as salmon and steaks. Dinners are from £12 ($21). At lunch, a buffet provides substantial meals.

Haydon House Hotel, Haydon Street, Basford, Stoke-on-Trent, Staffordshire ST4 6JD (tel. 0782/711311), is a turn-of-the-century privately owned town house in the heart of the pottery district. It offers singles with bath for £48 ($84) daily, and doubles with bath or shower go for £60 ($105). All units have color TV, radios, and phones. Six private apartments, called Glebe Mews, have lots of antiques and cost from £88 ($154) per day for two persons. If you make a reservation in advance, you may be able to get the antique four-poster bedroom. The Townhouse bar and dining room are Victorian in style and comfort, with antique clocks (83 in all), lending a club atmosphere to the hotel. Haydon House is noted for good food prepared by an award-winning chef. A three-course luncheon chosen from the ample list of dishes will cost from £10 ($17.50) up. The table d'hôte dinner, at £12 ($21), allows you to choose from five appetizers and five main dishes, plus dessert or cheese, then coffee. The à la carte menu is more extensive, including specially prepared steak dishes. English teas are served from 3 to 5 p.m. in Sidings Conservatory.

STAFFORD

The county town of Staffordshire was the birthplace of Izaak Walton, the British writer and celebrated fisherman. Long famous as a boot-making center, it contains many historic buildings, notably St. Chad's, the town's oldest church; St. Mary's, with its unusual octagonal tower; and the Ancient High House, the largest timber-frame town house in England.

In the Staffordshire countryside at Shallowford, between Stafford and Eccleshall, lies **Izaak Walton Cottage** (tel. 0785/760278). Walton is best remembered as the author of *The Compleat Angler*. The period garden of his cottage has been planted with 17th-century herbs and flowers, as well as plants. Admission is 25p (45¢) for adults, 15p (25¢) for children. It is open from 12:30 to 5:30 p.m. Friday to Tuesday from mid-March to October. In winter, it's open only on Saturday and Sunday from 12:30 to 4:30 p.m.

Food and Lodging

Tillington Hall Hotel, Eccleshall Road, Stafford, Staffordshire ST16 1JJ (tel. 0785/53531), a country house hotel that has been extensively remodeled and renovated, stands in its own grounds just a mile from the center of the county town, yet less than half a mile from the M6 motorway (exit 14). There are 90 bedrooms, each with private bath, color TV, radio, direct-dial phone, and facilities for making tea or coffee. The charge is from £55 ($96.25) daily in a single, £70 ($122.50) for a twin-bedded room. All tariffs include a full English breakfast, service, and VAT. Luncheon and dinner in the Potters Table Restaurant costs from £10 ($17.50).

LICHFIELD

Fans of Samuel Johnson pay a pilgrimage here to this historic city where he was born in 1709, son of an unsuccessful bookseller and parchment maker. The city is noted for its cathedral, whose three spires are known as "Ladies of the Vale." The tallest spire rises more than 250 feet, and the west front of the cathedral was built from about 1280. You can walk around the beautiful close and see a bit of the Vicars Close, with its half-timbered houses, along with the 17th-century Bishops Palace.

Dr. Johnson's Birthplace on Breadmarket Street (tel. 0543/264972) contains mementos and pictures of the author and his contemporaries. It is open daily from 10 a.m. to 5 p.m. (to 4 p.m. January to March). Admission is 60p ($1.05) for adults, 30p (55¢) for children.

Across the street from Dr. Johnson's Birthplace stands the **Heritage Centre & Treasury** (tel. 0543/256611), in Lichfield's Market Square. The former parish church has been transformed into a treasury and exhibition room with a coffee shop and a gift shop. The exhibition tells the story of Lichfield through its people and events, including an audio-visual presentation of the Civil War. The treasury displays examples of the silversmithing art showing civic, regimental, and church plate. Ancient charters are displayed in the Muniment Room. The center is open daily from 10 a.m. to 5 p.m. Admission is 70p ($1.25) for adults, 30p (55¢) for children.

You can also visit the **Guildhall** behind the Heritage Exhibition. Over the city dungeons dating from the Middle Ages, the Guildhall was rebuilt in 1846. Prisoners were jailed here before they were burned at the stake in Market Square.

Incidentally, market days are Friday and Saturday in Lichfield.

Food and Lodging

The **George Hotel,** Bird Street, Lichfield, Staffordshire WS13 6PR (tel. 0543/414822), is the most desirable place to stay in town. In the center of Lichfield, this hotel has a regal look to it. In the vicinity of the cathedral, the Georgian inn offers 38 handsomely furnished and equipped bedrooms, each with its own private bath or shower as well as direct-dial phone and TV. The hotel has many amenities, including plenty of towels and toilet articles. Singles, depending on the room assignment and the plumbing, rent for £24 ($42) to £60 ($1.05) daily, and doubles cost £48 ($84) to £70 ($122.50). Have a drink in the lovely old bar before going in to dinner (but do so before 9:30 p.m.). The George is also known for serving some of the best food in town, both a British and an international menu, with dinners costing from £12 ($21).

TUTBURY

Once a stronghold of the Anglo-Saxon kings of Mercia, and mentioned in the *Domesday Book,* Tutbury is a small town on the Dove River, lying four miles north of Burton-upon-Trent. It has a fine Norman church and the ruins of Tutbury Castle.

Ye Olde Dog and Partridge, High Street, Tutbury, Staffordshire DE13 9LS (tel. 0283/813030), has been a village inn for so long there is no clear record of its beginnings. Charming in appearance, it has an ornate black-and-white timbered façade, bay windows, and leaded glass, surviving elements from the 15th century. A coaching house in the 18th and 19th centuries, it offers a more modernized hospitality today. Inside, the inn still has a wealth of old timbering and fireplaces, maintaining a traditional character. All the bedrooms have private baths. A single costs from £52 ($91) daily and a double or twin, from £70 ($122.50). All tariffs include a full breakfast and VAT. The inn has an intimate French restaurant, plus a wine bar and carvery open seven days a week.

CAMBRIDGE AND EAST ANGLIA

1. CAMBRIDGE
2. ELY
3. THAXTED
4. SAFFRON WALDEN
5. DEDHAM
6. NEWMARKET
7. CLARE
8. LONG MELFORD
9. LAVENHAM
10. WOODBRIDGE
11. ALDEBURGH
12. EAST BERGHOLT
13. NORWICH
14. SHIPDHAM
15. NORTH NORFOLK

The four counties of East Anglia—Essex, Suffolk, Norfolk, and Cambridgeshire—are essentially low-lying areas, where the bucolic life still reigns supreme in parts.

East Anglia was an ancient Anglo-Saxon kingdom, under heavy domination of the Danes for many a year. Beginning in the 12th century, it was the center of a great cloth industry that brought it prosperity, as the spires of some of its churches testify to this day. Essentially, it is a land of heathland, fens, marshes, and broads in Norfolk.

Cambridge is the most visited city in East Anglia, but don't neglect to pass through Suffolk and Essex, Constable country, containing some of the finest landscapes in England. Norwich, the seat of the Duke of Norfolk, is less visited, but the fortunate few who go that far toward the North Sea will be rewarded.

1. Cambridge

Cambridge is a collage of visual images: A young couple lying in an open green space between colleges, reading the Romantic poets; rowing under the Bridge of Sighs; spires and turrets; drooping willows that witness much punting; dusty secondhand bookshops; daffodils swaying in the meadows; carol singing on Christmas Eve in King's College Chapel; dancing till sunrise at the May balls; the sound of Elizabethan madrigals; the purchase of horse brasses at the corner stall in the open market; narrow lanes where Darwin, Newton, and Cromwell once trod; The Backs, where the lawns of the colleges sweep down to the Cam River; the tattered black robe of an upperclassman, rebelliously hanging by a thread to his shoulder as it flies in the wind.

We're in the university city of Cambridge, which, along with Oxford, is one of the ancient seats of learning in Britain. The city on the banks of the Cam River is also the county town of Cambridgeshire, 55 miles northeast of London, 80 miles from Oxford. In many ways, the stories of Oxford and Cambridge are similar—particularly the age-old conflict between town and gown (rent-gouging landlords vs. impoverished scholars). But Oxford is an industrial city, sheltering a thriving life beyond the campus. Cambridge has some industry, but if the university were removed, I suspect it would revert to an unpretentious market town.

There is much to see and explore in Cambridge—so give yourself time to wander, even aimlessly. For those pressed, I'll offer more specific direction.

A SELF-GUIDED TOUR

The center of Cambridge is pedestrianized, so park your car at one of the many car parks (they get more expensive as you get nearer the city center), and take the opportunity to visit some of the university buildings spread throughout the city. King's College might be number one on your list, especially the chapel that houses *The Adoration of the Magi* by Rubens. Follow the courtyards through to the "Backs" (the college lawns) and walk through to Trinity (where Prince Charles studied) and St. John's colleges, including the Bridge of Sighs.

There are many other historic buildings in the city center, all within walking distance, including Great St. Mary's Church (from which the original Westminster chimes come), St. Bene't's Church, the Round Church, the Fitzwilliam Museum (one of the largest and finest provincial museums), the Folk Museum, and the modern Kettles Yard Art Gallery.

For a more detailed insight into the life and times of Cambridge, both town and gown, join one of the guided tours from the **Cambridge Tourist Information Centre,** Wheeler Street (tel. 0223/322640), which is behind the Guildhall.

TOURS AND TOURIST SERVICES

A tourist reception center for Cambridge and Cambridgeshire is operated by **Guide Friday Ltd.** at Cambridge Railway Station (tel. 0223/62444). The center, on the concourse of the railway station, dispenses free maps and brochures of the city and area and operates tours. Also available is a full range of tourist services, including accommodation booking and car rental. In summer, the Tourism Centre is open daily from 9 a.m. to 6:30 p.m., closing at 4 p.m. in winter. Guided tours of Cambridge leave the center daily. In summer, aboard open-top double-decker buses, departures are every 15 minutes from 9 a.m. to 6 p.m. In winter, departures are hourly. The tour can be a one-hour panoramic ride, or you can get off at any of the many stops, such as King's College Chapel or the American Cemetery, then rejoin the tour when you wish. Tickets are valid all day for you to hop on and off the buses. The price of this tour is £3.50 ($6.15) per person.

CAMBRIDGE UNIVERSITY

Oxford University predates the one at Cambridge. But in the early 13th century scholars began coming up to Cambridge, as opposed to being "sent down." The choice of the market town as a seat of learning just happened—perhaps coming about as a result of a core of important masters, dissatisfied with Oxford, electing to live near the fens. Eventually, Cambridge won partial recognition from Henry III, rising and slumping with the approval or disdain of subsequent English monarchs. Cambridge consists of 29 colleges for both men and women. If you have time for only one sight, then make it:

King's College Chapel

The teenaged **Henry VI** founded the college on King's Parade in 1441. But most of its buildings today are from the 19th century. It is the Perpendicular Chapel that is not only the crowning glory, but one of the architectural gems in England inherited from the Middle Ages. The chapel, owing to the chaotic vicissitudes of English kings, wasn't completed until the early years of the 16th century. Its most characteristic features are its magnificent fan vaulting—all of stone—and its Great Windows, most of which were fashioned by Flemish artisans between 1515 and 1531 (the west window, however, dates from the late Victorian period). The stained glass, in hues of blues, reds, and ambers, reflects biblical stories. The long range of the windows, reading from the first on the north side at the west end right around the chapel back to the first on the south side, tells the story of the Birth of the Virgin, the Annunciation, the Birth of Christ, the Life, Ministry, and Death of Christ, the Resurrection, the Ascension, the Acts of the Apostles, and the Assumption. The upper range contains Old Testament parallels to these New Testament stories. The rood screen is from the early 16th century. Henry James called King's College Chapel "the most beautiful in England." It is open during vacation time Monday to Saturday from 9:30 a.m. to 5 p.m., and on Sunday from 10:30 a.m. to 5 p.m. During term time the public is welcome to choral services, which are at 5:30 p.m. Monday to Saturday (service said on Monday), and at 10:30 a.m. and 3:30 p.m. on Sunday. In "term" the chapel is open to visitors from 9:30 a.m. to 3:45 p.m. daily, from 2 to 3 p.m. and from 4:30 to 5:45 p.m. on Sunday. Closed December 26 to January 1. It may be closed at other times for recording sessions.

There is an exhibition in the seven northern side chapels showing why and how the chapel was built. Admission to the exhibition is £1 ($1.75) for adults, 50p (90¢) for children.

Peterhouse

This college on Trumpington Street is visited largely because it is the oldest Cambridge college, having been founded as early as 1284. The founding father was Hugh de Balsham, the bishop of Ely. Of the original buildings, only the Hall remains, but this was restored in the 19th century and now contains stained-glass windows by William Morris. Old Court was constructed in the 15th century, but refaced in 1754, and the chapel dates from 1632. Ask permission to enter at the porter's desk.

Trinity College

On Trinity Street, Trinity College—the largest at Cambridge (not to be confused with Trinity Hall)—was founded in 1546 by Henry VIII from a number of smaller colleges that had existed on the site. The courtyard is the most spacious one in Cambridge, built when Thomas Nevile was master. Sir Christopher Wren designed the Library. For admission to the college, apply at the porter's lodge, or telephone 0223/358201 for information.

Emmanuel College

On St. Andrew's Street, Emmanuel (tel. 0223/334200) was founded in 1584 by Sir Walter Mildmay, a chancellor of the exchequer to Elizabeth I. It is of interest at least to Harvard students, as John Harvard, founder of that university, studied here. With its attractive gardens, it makes for a good stroll. You might even visit the chapel designed by Sir Christopher Wren and consecrated in 1677. Both the chapel and college are open daily from 9:30 a.m. to 12:15 p.m. and 2 to 6 p.m.

Queens' College

On Queens' Lane, Queens' College (tel. 0223/335511) is considered by some old Cantabrigians as the loveliest in the architectural galaxy. Dating back to 1448, it was founded, then refounded, by two English queens, one the wife of Henry VI, the other the wife of Edward IV. Its second cloister is the most interesting, flanked with the half-timbered President's Lodge, dating from the first half of the 16th century. The college may be visited during the day from mid-March to mid-October. An admission fee of 40p (70¢) is charged and a short printed guide issued. Normally, individual visitors are admitted from 1:45 to 4:30 p.m. daily, but during July, August, and September, the college is also open to visitors from 10:15 a.m. to 12:45 p.m. daily. Entry and exit is by the Old Porters' Lodge in Queens' Lane only. The college is closed from mid-May to mid-June. The Old Hall and chapel are usually open to the public when not in use.

St. John's College

On St. John's Street, the college was founded in 1511 by Lady Margaret Beaufort, mother of Henry VII. A few years earlier she had founded Christ's College. Before her intervention, an old monk-run hospital had stood on the site of St. John's. The impressive gateway bears the Tudor coat-of-arms, and Second Court is a fine example of late Tudor brickwork. But its best-known feature is the Bridge of Sighs crossing the Cam, built as late as the 19th century, patterned after the bridge in Venice. It connects the older part of the college with New Court, a Gothic revival on the opposite bank from which there is an outstanding view of the famous "backs." The Bridge of Sighs is closed to visitors but can be viewed from the neighboring Wren Bridge. Wordsworth was an alumnus of St. John's College. The chapel is open from 9 a.m. to 4 p.m. Monday to Friday, from 9 a.m. to noon on Saturday. On Sunday, the chapel is open to visitors attending the choral service. The college is closed to visitors from late April to late June.

Other College Sights

The above are only a representative selection of some of the more interesting colleges. **Magdalen College** on Magdalene Street was founded in 1542; **Pembroke College** on Trumpington Street was founded in 1347; **Christ's College** on St. Andrew's Street was founded in 1505; and **Corpus Christi College** on Trumpington Street dates from 1352. Only someone planning to stop in Cambridge for a long time will get around to them.

A Word of Warning: Unfortunately, because of the disturbances caused by the influx of tourists to the university, Cambridge has regretfully had to limit visitors, and even exclude them from various parts of the university altogether, and, in some cases, even charge a small fee for entrance. Small groups of up to six people are generally admitted with no problem, and you can inquire from the local tourist office about visiting hours here.

OTHER SIGHTS

However, colleges aren't the only thing to see in Cambridge, as you'll assuredly agree if you explore the following attractions.

CAMBRIDGE

KEY TO NUMBERED SIGHTS

1. Jesus College
2. Magdalen College
3. St. John's College
4. Trinity College
5. Sidney Sussex College
6. Christ's College
7. Clare College
8. King's College
9. Corpus Christi College
10. Emmanuel College
11. Selwyn College
12. Peterhouse College
13. Pembroke College
14. Downing College
15. Newnham College

The Fitzwilliam Museum

On Trumpington Street, near Peterhouse, this museum (tel. 0223/332900) was the gift of the Viscount Fitzwilliam, who in 1816 gave Cambridge University his paintings and rare books—along with £100,000 to build the house in which to display them. He thereby knowingly or unknowingly immortalized himself. Other gifts have since been bequeathed to the museum, and now it is one of the finest in England. It is noted for its porcelain, old prints, archeological relics, and oils (17th-century Italian, including Titian, Veronese, and Tintoretto; Rubens; Van Dyck; French impressionists; and a superb collection of 18th- and 19th-century British paintings). The museum is open daily from 10 a.m. to 5 p.m., on Sunday from 2:15 till 5 p.m.; closed Monday, Good Friday, December 24 to 31, and New Year's Day. Admission is free.

Great St. Mary's

Great St. Mary's, opposite King's College Chapel on King's Parade, is the university church (tel. 0223/350914). It is built on the site of an 11th-century church, but the present building dates largely from 1478. It was closely associated with events of the Reformation. The cloth that covered the hearse of King Henry VII is on display in the church. A fine view of Cambridge may be obtained from the top of the tower. Admission is 50p (90¢) for adults, 20p (35¢) for children.

BOAT RENTALS

Punting on the Cam (nothing to do with football) is a traditional pursuit of students and visitors in Cambridge, but there are other types of boating available if you don't trust yourself to stand up and pole a punt under and around the weeping willow trees. Upriver, you can go all the way to Grantchester, a distance of about two miles, made so famous by Rupert Brooke. Downstream, you pass along the Backs behind the colleges of the university.

Scudamore's Boatyards, Granta Place (tel. 0223/359750), by the Anchor Pub, has been in business since 1910. All craft rent for £4 ($7) per hour, including punts, canoes, and rowboats. A £30 ($52.50) deposit, payable with cash or credit card, is required. There is a maximum of six persons per punt. Also offered is a chauffeured punt where a moonlighting student, dressed in a traditional punter's costume, rows you past the back view of several historic buildings, lecturing as he rows. The cost of this 45-minute guided tour is £3 ($5.25) per person.

PERSONALIZED TOURS

The person to know if you're in the Cambridge area is Mrs. Isobel Bryant, who operates **Heritage Tours** from her 200-year-old cottage, Manor Cottage, Swaffham Prior (tel. 0638/741440). A highly qualified expert on the region, she will arrange tours starting from your hotel or Cambridge railway station to, for instance, Lavenham with its thatched and timbered houses, to the fine medieval churches of the Suffolk villages, to Ely Cathedral, and to one of the grand mansions nearby with their many treasures. The charge of £65 ($113.75) for the day covers up to three passengers and all travel expenses, including the services of the driver/guide. Lunch in a village pub and admission fees add £4 ($7) per person.

Mrs. Bryant can also arrange accommodation with local families in their country houses. The charges range from £28 ($49) to £50 ($87.50) for two persons per night in double rooms with private bath, these tariffs including a full English breakfast. Often dinner can be arranged at around £10 ($17.50) per person, including wine. Rooms without private bath rent from £12 ($21) per person.

There are also walking tours around the colleges of Cambridge costing £18 ($31.50) for a family-size party, lasting about two hours. There is a fascinating tour of Newmarket, headquarters of the horseracing industry. That tour includes getting to watch training gallops, a visit to the Racing Museum or a stud stable, seeing the bloodstock-sales center, and being shown the Jockey Club. For a group of 12 or more persons, a whole-day tour costs £12 ($21) per person, a half-day tour going for £7 ($12.25) per person. A shorter tour can be arranged for individuals or a family group. If you want lunch at a private manor house with Cordon Bleu cooking the cost will be £8.50 ($14.90) per person, with wine included, for groups of 12 or more. All prices include VAT.

WHERE TO STAY

Accommodations are limited in scope and facilities, although generally adequate for the purpose. Much of the overload in summer is siphoned off by little guesthouses, filled at term time with scholars, but otherwise freed when most visitors arrive in July and August. I'll begin with a general survey of the best hotels in:

The Medium-Priced Range

The Garden House, Granta Place, Mill Lane, Cambridge, Cambridgeshire CB2 1RT (tel. 0223/63421), is a modern hotel set between the riverbank and a cobblestone street in the oldest part of town, a short stroll from the principal colleges. The hostelry, next door to the boatyard where you can rent punts, has a series of outdoor terraces on which drinks and afternoon tea are served in good weather. The earth-tone brick and stained-wood exterior harmonizes with the wall coverings in the bar lounge of the hotel, where comfortable sofas and chairs tempt visitors. Well-furnished bedrooms have private bath, radio, color TV, mini-bar, phone, soundproof windows, hot beverage facilities, and hairdryer. Most of the 117 rooms have balconies and river views. Standard singles cost £52 ($91) daily, with doubles going for £71 ($124.25) to £84 ($147), with VAT and a continental breakfast included. The hotel's Le Jardin Restaurant overlooks the river and gardens and offers fixed-price and à la carte menus, including vegetarian meals, at lunch and dinner. Also a selection of hot and cold light meals is available in the Riverside Lounge, accompanied in the evening by piano music. When weather permits, the Cocktail Bar serves drinks outside on the terrace and lawn. The hotel has ample free parking.

University Arms Hotel, Regent Street, Cambridge, Cambridgeshire CB2 1AD (tel. 0223/351241), is a traditional hotel near the city center and the university. The present building contains 115 tastefully decorated bedrooms, most of which overlook Parker's Place on which one of England's greatest cricketers, Sir Jack Hobbs, learned to play. Each bedroom has its own phone, central heating, private bath, electric razor outlets, radio, and color TV. The single rate is £44.50 ($77.90) daily, and a twin-bedded room is £60 ($105). These prices include service, VAT, and an English breakfast. The spacious oak-paneled restaurant features both table d'hôte and à la carte menus. Lunch costs from £7.80 ($13.65) and dinner from £10.70 ($18.75).

The Octagon Lounge, with its stained-glass domed ceiling and open log fire, is a popular place to meet for tea. *Tip:* The hotel porter can arrange a guided tour for you.

Cambridgeshire Moat House, Huntingdon Road, Bar Hill, Cambridge, Cambridgeshire CB3 8EU (tel. 0954/80555), is five miles from the center of Cambridge on the A604 road, a modern three-star hotel with heated indoor swimming pool, sauna, three squash courts, two outside tennis courts, an 18-hole championship golf course, putting green, and a helipad. There are 100 bedrooms, all with private bath, color TV, radio, direct-dial phone, hairdryer, and tea- and coffee-making facilities. Singles cost £62 ($108.50) daily, and twins go for £107 ($187.25). Prices include a full English breakfast, VAT, and the use of all sports facilities. There are both table d'hôte and à la carte menus available in the restaurant. Bar meals are also served daily.

Post House Hotel, Lakeview, Bridge Road, Impington, Cambridge, Cambridgeshire CB4 4PH (tel. 022023/7000), near a highway intersection at Impington, lies two miles north of Cambridge on the B1049 where it intersects with the A45. Its wings partially embrace a grassy courtyard, lying a short walk from a small artificial lake. Its large public rooms soar above the dozens of sofas and chairs, ending in a peaked summit. On the premises are a heated indoor swimming pool, a Jacuzzi, a sauna, and a lobby bar. The hotel restaurant, the Churchill, has mahogany paneling, reproductions of paintings created by Sir Winston himself, portrait busts, and photos of the famous statesman at various periods of his life. Each of the 120 bedrooms offers a big-windowed view of the outdoors and is equipped with a TV, phone, and mini-bar. Singles cost £68 ($119) to £78 ($136.50) daily, and doubles or twins go for £82 ($143.50) to £94 ($164.50).

The Budget Range

Arundel House, 53 Chesterton Rd., Cambridge, Cambridgeshire CB4 3AN (tel. 0223/67701), occupies one of the finest sites in Cambridge, overlooking the River Cam and open parkland. It's only a few minutes' walk from the city center and the university colleges. This 19th-century terraced hotel has 88 bedrooms, most with private baths. All have color TVs, radios, direct-dial phones, hairdryers, and hot beverage facilities, as well as a videotaped guide to Cambridge on an in-house video channel. Video films can also be played in your room. Singles cost £23.50 ($41.15) to £39 ($68.25) daily, and doubles run £35 ($61.25) to £54 ($94.50). All room rates include a continental breakfast and VAT. The hotel has a cocktail bar and a small garden with outdoor tables and an attractive Victorian-style restaurant offering table d'hôte or à la carte menus. Bar meals are also available. A fixed-price lunch is £7.25 ($12.70); a table d'hôte dinner, £9.50 ($16.65). There's a coin-operated laundromat on the premises.

The **Gonville Hotel,** Gonville Place, Cambridge, Cambridgeshire CB1 1LY (tel. 0223/66611), stands on its own grounds, opposite Parkers Place, only a five-minute walk from the center of the city. It's not unlike a country house—ivy covered, with shade trees and a formal car entry. In 1973 it was gutted and rebuilt as a commercial hotel, intending to attract business people as well as tourists in summer. Singles go for £44.50 ($77.90) daily and doubles for £60 ($105). Prices include VAT, service charge, and an English breakfast. Special three-bedded family rooms rent for £78.50 ($137.40). Central heating is provided throughout, plus air conditioning in the restaurant, where you can get a set lunch for £9 ($15.75) or dinner for about £12 ($21). You can also order à la carte. The quality of comforts is good.

May View Guest House, 12 Park Parade, Cambridge, Cambridgeshire CB5 8AL (tel. 0223/66018), was the family home of Roger Stock's grandparents from 1922. When they died, he converted the pleasant house into one of the most charming B&Bs in the county. It sits on a street corner of the old city, across from the rolling expanse of Jesus Green. Its brick exterior was built by the Victorians, but the elegantly molded front door is an antique salvaged from a Georgian house slated for demolition. This concern for the past fills every corner of Mr. Stock's guesthouse. The six bedrooms he rents all have hot and cold running water and a view of the park. The charge is from £30 ($52.50) daily for double occupancy, with VAT and an English breakfast included. The morning meal is served in a dining room ringed with antiques or in a small Italianate courtyard.

WHERE TO DINE

A few steps from the centrally located Magdalene Bridge, **Jean Louis,** 15 Magdalene St. (tel. 0223/315232), is a French restaurant serving pleasant meals in an intimate setting of bentwood chairs, exposed brick, and rustically modern detailing. There's a handful of secluded tables as well as a bar on an upper level, but the heart and soul of the place is on the ground floor, near the busy kitchens. Set lunches cost from £8 ($14) to £12 ($21), while à la carte lunches and dinners go for £20 ($35). Your meal might include sea bass with salmon mousse, fresh lobster cooked to your taste, John Dory with a sauce of saffron and watercress, or poached turbot in a pink peppercorn sauce. Food is served from noon to 2:30 p.m. and 6:30 to 10 p.m. daily except Monday.

Upstairs, 71 Castle St. (tel. 0223/312569), is an authentic Middle Eastern and Moroccan eatery, one of the best in this part of England. The location, above Waffles, lies on a hillside road above the most historic part of Cambridge, about a five-minute walk from the center. The cookery is genuine, reflecting the varied background of the kitchen staff. You might begin with the famous harira, a Moroccan beef soup with lentils. The stuffed eggplant (called aubergine on the menu) is filled with nuts and various aromatic spices and is usually a delight, as is filet of trout in a lime sauce with pistachios. The prize offering, however, is the lamb couscous, which is flavored with ginger, among other spices, and topped with a rich sauce. It's presented for your pleasure in an earthenware tajine. Meals in this former Victorian town house cost from £12 ($21) and are served Tuesday to Sunday from 6:30 to 10:30 p.m. (closes at 9:30 p.m. on Sunday). They finish your repast with a cardamom- and orange-water flavored coffee. Reservations are advised.

Charlie Chan, 14 Regent St. (tel. 0223/61763), is generally conceded to be the finest Chinese restaurant in Cambridge, although this is a debated point, other devotees of Oriental cookery having their own favorites. Nevertheless, in frequent visits on my part this place has proved to be reliable and capable in spite of its large selection of dishes. It is a long, corridor-like restaurant, with pristine decor, consisting of, among other elements, tile floors. It lies on a busy commercial street near one of its major rivals, Shao Tao. The specialties I've most enjoyed include an aromatic and crispy duck, lemon chicken, and prawn with garlic and ginger. It's best to go with a party—that way you can sample many different dishes. Meals range in price from £20 ($35) per person. Hours are noon to 2:15 p.m. and 6 to 11:15 p.m. daily.

Twenty Two, 22 Chesterton Rd. (tel. 0223/351880). Who would expect to find one of the best restaurants in Cambridge in this quiet residential and hotel district? In the vicinity of Jesus Green, it has up to now been an address jealously guarded by the locals who "don't want tourists to spoil it." Decorated in pink and gray tones, it is an exponent of the best of contemporary English and continental cookery, relying on the freshest ingredients in any season. However, it's difficult to recommend specialties, because the menu is ever-changing, based on the shopping for any given week. Michael Sharpe, the chef and owner, uses time-tested recipes along with his own inspiration of the moment. A set dinner is offered from 7:30 to 10 p.m. Tuesday to Saturday for £15 ($26.25).

Midsummer House, Midsummer Common (tel. 0223/69299), is one of the dining discoveries of Cambridge. The preferred dining is in an elegant conservatory, but you can also find a smartly laid table upstairs. The menu is wisely limited, and quality control seems much in evidence here. The chef, Hans Schweitzer, knows the French school well, except every dish seems to bear his own special imprint and that is quite good. Attired in funereal black, the waiters will come to your assistance, as you peruse the menu for the freshest or most exciting selection on any given day. Chef Schweitzer displays his considerable talents in the set luncheon going for £10.50 ($18.40) or the table d'hôte dinners costing from £18.50 ($32.40) to £25 ($43.75). The restaurant serves from noon to 2 p.m. and 6:30 to 9:30 Tuesday to Sunday. There is no dinner on Sunday and no lunch offered on Saturday.

Restaurant Angeline, 8 Market Passage (tel. 0223/60305), is set along a commercial passageway in the heart of town behind a narrow façade, found between Sidney and Market Streets, just two blocks east of Trinity College. The multiple nationalities of its owners, coupled with its French chef, make this one of the most international restaurants in town. Upstairs, there's a bar for drinking, lots of upholstery, and attractive fixed-price lunches costing from £4 ($7). The more elaborate dinners, at £15 ($26.25), might include Wiltshire roast duck, trout meunière, grilled Dover sole, fresh salmon, and several preparations of lamb. Full meals are served from noon to 2:30 p.m. and 6 to 11 p.m., except Sunday evening.

ENTERTAINMENT

An outstanding attraction in Cambridge is the **Arts Theatre,** adjacent to the city center and the Tourist Information Office, squeezed among lodging houses and shops. It provides Cambridge and the surrounding area with its most important theatrical events. Almost all the leading stars of the British stage have performed here at one time or another. Call 0223/352000 to find out what's playing. Seats for most productions are £7 ($12.25) and £7.50 ($13.15).

---

2. Ely

The top attraction in the fen country, outside of Cambridge, is Ely Cathedral. The small city of Ely lies 70 miles from London, only 16 miles north of Cambridge. Ely used to be known as the Isle of Ely, until the surrounding marshes and meres were drained. The last stronghold of Saxon England, Ely was defended by Hereward the Wake, until his capitulation to the Normans in 1071.

ELY CATHEDRAL

The near-legendary founder of the cathedral was Etheldreda, the wife of a Northumbrian king, who established a monastery on the spot in 673. The present structure dates from 1083. Seen for miles around, the landmark octagonal lantern tower is the crowning glory of the cathedral. It was erected in 1322, following the collapse of the old tower, and represents a remarkable engineering achievement. Four hundred tons of lead and wood hang in space, held there by timbers reaching to the eight pillars.

You enter the cathedral through the Galilee West Door, a good example of the Early English style of architecture. The already-mentioned lantern tower and the Octagon are the most notable features inside, but visit the Lady Chapel. Although it has lost much of its decoration over the centuries, it's still a handsome example of the Perpendicular style, having been completed in the mid-14th century. The cathedral is open from 7 a.m. to 7 p.m. daily in summer, from 7:30 a.m. to 6 p.m. daily in winter. Visitors are asked to make a donation of £2 ($3.50) to help save the cathedral from ruin. The refectory and shop are open daily. For information, telephone 0353/667735.

The city, really a market town, is interesting—at least momentarily so—as it seems to be living in the past. If you choose to lodge or dine at Ely, here are my recommendations.

WHERE TO STAY AND EAT

Right in the center of the town, **Lamb Hotel,** 2 Lynn Rd., Ely, Cambridgeshire CB7 4EJ (tel. 0353/663574), is a former coaching inn with ample car parking available. In the shadow of the cathedral, this Queens Moat House hotel offers 32 renovated bedrooms with private baths or showers, TVs, and hot beverage facilities. The B&B rate in a double or twin is £56 ($98) daily, and a single costs £45 ($78.75). Tariffs are inclusive of an English breakfast and VAT. A table d'hôte lunch or dinner costs from £10 ($17.50). Sunday lunch, at £8.75 ($15.30), is an event when a roast topside of beef in the Merrie Olde England style is wheeled out. In the 1400s this place was known as the "Holy Lambe," a stopping-off spot for wayfarers, often pilgrims, through East Anglia.

The Old Fire Engine House, St. Mary's Street (tel. 0353/2582), opposite St. Mary's Church, is one of the finer restaurants in East Anglia, worth a detour. It enjoys an interesting setting in a walled garden, in a complex of buildings with an art gallery. The restaurant was converted from a fire station. All the good English cooking is the result of the staff, a harmonious combination of unusual people who really care about food preparation. Materials are all fresh. Soups are served in huge bowls, and accompanying them is a coarse-grained crusty bread. Main dishes include duck with orange sauce, jugged hare, steak-and-kidney pie, baked stuffed pike, casserole of rabbit, and pigeon with bacon and black olives. Desserts include fruit pie and cream, although I'd recommend the syllabub. A meal costs from £13 ($22.75). In summer you can dine outside in the garden, even order a cream tea. Ann Ford owns the place, and not only does some of the cooking and serves, but still has time to talk to customers. It's open daily from 10:30 a.m. to 5:30 p.m. and 7:30 to 9 p.m. (last entry), on Sunday from 12:30 to 5 p.m. Do try for a table if you're just passing, but this place is quite popular with locals and people coming out from Cambridge, especially on weekends, so it's better to make a reservation.

A TOUR TO GRIME'S GRAVES

On the B1108, off the main A1065 from Swaffham to Mildenhall road east of Ely, you can visit Grime's Graves (tel. 0842/810656), three miles northeast of Brandon (Norfolkshire). This is well worth the short detour, as it is the largest group of Neolithic flint mines in the country. This is fir-wooded country with little population, and it's easy to imagine yourself transported back to ancient times. The mines are well signposted, and you soon find yourself at a small parking lot presided over by a custodian who will open up one or several of the shafts, allowing you to enter ancient Britain. Climb down the ladder of the pit and imagine what must have been going on even before the time of the Anglo-Saxons. Restoration has been carried out during the intervening years, and it is now possible to see where work took place and, if you're lucky, you may find a worked flint of your own to present to the custodian. It's best to have a flashlight handy. The climb down is perpendicular, so it's only for the stout-hearted.

The mines are close to the air force bases so well known to countless American air crews during World War II. Hours are daily except Monday from 10 a.m. to 6 p.m. from Good Friday to September 30, from 10 a.m. to 4 p.m. off-season. Admission is 80p ($1.40) for adults, 40p (70¢) for children.

AN AIRCRAFT MUSEUM

Part of the **Imperial War Museum** (tel. 0223/833963), on the A505 Newmarket–Royston road, is housed appropriately at Duxford Airfield, a former Battle of Britain station. In hangars that date from World War I, you'll find a huge collection of historic civil and military aircraft, including the B17 Flying Fortress, the Super Sabre, and Concorde 01, Britain's preproduction specimen of the controversial jet. Other exhibits include midget submarines, British and German tanks, and a variety of field artillery pieces. Duxford was also a U.S. Eighth Air Force base in World War II. There are now more than 90 aircraft on display, including the only B-29 Superfortress in Europe, plus a BE2c and an RE8 from World War I, a B-52, and a Spitfire. Other exhibits include a giant 140-ton coastal artillery gun from Gibraltar and a special historical display on the U.S. Eighth Air Force in World War II.

The museum is open daily from 10:30 a.m. to 5:30 p.m. (or dusk if earlier) from mid-March to early November and from 10:30 a.m. to 3:45 p.m. the remainder of the year. Closed Christmas and New Year's Day. Admission is £3.50 ($6.15) for adults and £1.80 ($3.15) for children in summer, £2.50 ($4.40) for adults and £1.25 ($2.20) for children in winter. Special charges are made for special events. Parking is free.

ESSEX

Even though it borders London, and is industrialized in places, Essex still contains unspoiled rural areas and villages. Most motorists pass through it on the way to

Cambridge. What they find, after leaving Greater London, is a land of rolling fields. In the east there are many seaside towns and villages, because Essex opens onto the North Sea.

The major city is **Colchester,** in the east, known for its oysters and roses. Fifty miles from London, it was the first Roman city in Britain, the oldest recorded town in the kingdom. Parts of its Roman fortifications remain. A Norman castle has been turned into a museum, containing a fine collection of Roman Britain. Among the former residents of Colchester were King Cole, immortalized in the nursery rhyme, and Cunobelinus, the warrior king, known to Shakespearean scholars as Cymbeline.

However, Colchester is not the pathway of most visitors—so I have concentrated instead on tiny villages in the western part of Essex, including Saffron Walden and Thaxted, which are representative of the best of the shire. You can explore all of them quite easily on your way to Cambridge or on your return trip to London. Roughly, they lie from 25 to 30 miles south of Cambridge.

A BASE OUTSIDE LONDON

Just 22 miles from London's West End, **Brentwood Moat House,** London Road, Brentwood, Essex CM14 4NR (tel. 0277/225252), is two minutes from Intersection 28 on the M25 motorway. This four-star hotel is on the London side of Brentwood, three-quarters of a mile from the center of town. The hotel, a Tudor building of historical interest, dates back to the 16th century and was associated with Catherine of Aragon and used by Henry VIII as a hunting lodge. The bedrooms offer excellent facilities, with private baths, color TVs, radios, electric trouser presses, hairdryers, and 24-hour room service. In the main building, original Tudor bedrooms include four-poster beds. There are also five family apartments. Singles are priced at £65 ($113.75) daily, and doubles go for £72 ($126) to £85 ($148.75). The special Tudor rooms are more expensive. The character of the Moat House is preserved with original oak beams, period windows, and inglenook fireplaces. A warm atmosphere prevails.

---

3. Thaxted

Some 43 miles north of London, the Saxon town of Thaxted sits on the crest of a hill. It contains the most beautiful small church in England, whose graceful spire can be seen for miles around. Its bells are heard throughout the day, ringing out special chimes to parishioners who attend their church seriously. Dating back to 1340, the church is a nearly perfect example of religious architecture.

Thaxted also has a number of well-preserved Elizabethan houses and a wooden-pillared Jacobean guildhall.

FOOD AND LODGING IN THE AREA

About four miles southwest of Thaxted, **Whitehall,** Church End, Broxted, Thaxted, Essex CM6 2BZ (tel. 0279/850603), lies on the B1051 road. In the 18th century, almost 28,000 acres of prime farmland were attached to this property. By the 1900s the Countess of Warwick, then its mistress, entertained King Edward VII within its baronial walls. Today, in an elegantly simplified format, guests are still entertained more or less royally, thanks to the dedicated efforts of Gerry Keane and his wife, Marie. Ten elegant bedrooms are rented, each differently furnished in 18th-century style. All have private bath, many thoughtful extras, and views over the 300-year-old yew trees of an ancient walled garden. Singles cost from £60 ($105) daily and doubles from £80 ($140), with full breakfast included.

A medieval brewhouse with a soaring ceiling is the setting for specialties prepared with fresh ingredients. A tempting fixed-price lunch is offered for £14

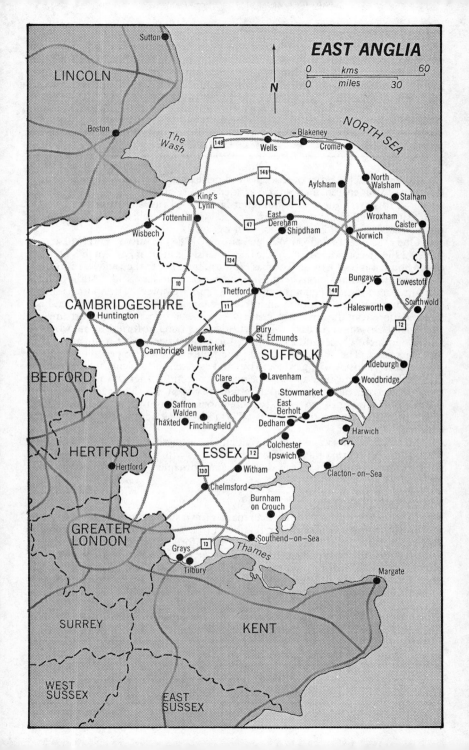

EAST ANGLIA

kms 0 — 60
miles 0 — 30

N

NORTH SEA

LINCOLN

Sutton

Boston

The Wash

Blakeney
Wells
Cromer

149

148

Aylsham
North Walsham
Stalham

King's Lynn
Tottenhill
NORFOLK
East Dereham
Shipdham
Wroxam
Caister

Wisbech

47

Norwich

134

Bungay
Lowestoft

10

Thetford
40
Halesworth
Southwold

CAMBRIDGESHIRE
11
12

Huntington

Bury St. Edmunds
SUFFOLK
Aldeburgh

Cambridge
Newmarket
Woodbridge

BEDFORD

Clare
Lavenham
Stowmarket

Sudbury
East Berholt

Saffron Walden
Harwich

Thaxted
Finchingfield
Dedham

HERTFORD
ESSEX
Colchester
12
Ipswich

Hertford
130
Witham
Clacton-on-Sea

Chelmsford

Burnham on Crouch

GREATER LONDON
Southend-on-Sea

Grays
13
Thames

Tilbury
Margate

SURREY
KENT

WEST SUSSEX

EAST SUSSEX

($24.50) but the establishment's true lure is the "menu surprise," served only at night, for around £50 ($87.50) per couple. Six lightly textured French-inspired courses depend on the availability of the finest ingredients of France and Britain. Representative dishes include brill in champagne and noisettes of lamb with zucchini in a red wine sauce.

---

4. Saffron Walden

In the northern corner of Essex, a short drive from Thaxted, is the ancient market town of Walden, renamed Saffron Walden because of the fields of autumn crocus that used to grow around it. Although it lies only 44 miles from London, it still hasn't succumbed to heavy tourist traffic. Residents of Cambridge, 15 miles to the north, escape to this old borough for their weekends.

One mile west of Saffron Walden (on the B1383) is **Audley End House** (tel. 0799/22842), considered one of the finest mansions in all of East Anglia. This Jacobean house was begun by Sir Thomas Howard, treasurer to the king, in 1605, built on the foundation of a monastery. James I is reported to have said, "Audley End is too large for a king, though it might do for a Lord Treasurer." The house has many outstanding features, including an impressive Great Hall at whose north end is a screen dating from the early 17th century, considered one of the most ornamental in England. Rooms decorated by Robert Adam contain fine furniture and works of art. A "Gothick" chapel and a charming Victorian ladies' sitting room are among the attractions. The park surrounding the house was landscaped by Capability Brown. It has a lovely rose garden, a river and cascade, and a picnic area. In the stables, built at the same time as the mansion, is a collection of agricultural machinery, a Victorian coach, old wagons, and the estate fire wagon. It's all open daily from 1 to 6 p.m. from Good Friday to the end of September. The grounds are open from noon to 7 p.m. Admission to the house is £2.50 ($4.40) for adults, £1.50 ($2.65) for children.

Many of the houses in Saffron Walden are distinctive in England, in that the 16th- and 17th-century builders faced their houses with parget—a kind of plasterwork (sometimes made with cow dung) used for ornamental façades.

FOOD AND LODGING

In the center of this Cromwellian market town stands the **Saffron Hotel,** 10–18 High St., Saffron Walden, Essex CB10 1AY (tel. 0799/22676). Dating from the 16th century, the Saffron combines modern comforts with old-world charm, as reflected by its individually designed and decorated rooms. All rooms have color TV, phone, tea/coffee-makers, and central heating, and most have private bath. Most units overlook the High Street or the inner courtyard with its patio garden. Stories abound locally about the Saffron Hotel ghost, which several of the staff claim to have seen. B&B rates are £22.50 ($39.40) daily in a bathless single, £38 ($66.50) with complete bath or shower. Doubles with full plumbing facilities cost £49 ($85.75). Prices are reduced for children sharing rooms of adults. Tariffs include a continental breakfast and VAT. The hotel's restaurant is renowned locally and is in a Regency style. Dining is by candlelight overlooking the floodlit patio garden. A three-course menu with several choices on each course costs £12.95 ($22.65). There is also an à la carte menu. The cuisine at the Saffron is among the best in the area, combining traditional dishes with more ambitious specialties. Meals are served from noon to 2 p.m. and 7:30 to 9:30 p.m. daily except Sunday. You can also order from an excellent bar menu.

5. Dedham

Remember Constable's *Vale of Dedham*? In this little Essex village on the Stour River, you're in the heart of Constable country. Flatford Mill is only a mile farther down the river. The village, with its Tudor, Georgian, and Regency house, is set in the midst of the water meadows of the Stour. Constable immortalized its church and tower. Dedham is right on the Essex-Suffolk border, and makes a good center for exploring both North Essex and the Suffolk border country.

About three-quarters of a mile from the village center is **Castle House** (tel. 0206/322127), home of Sir Alfred Munnings, the president of the Royal Academy (1944–1949) and painter extraordinaire of racehorses and animals. The house and studio contain sketches and other works, and are open early May to early October on Sunday, Wednesday, and bank holiday Mondays, as well as on Thursday and Saturday in August. Hours are 2 to 5 p.m. Admission is £1.50 ($2.65) for adults, 25p (45¢) for children.

WHERE TO STAY AND DINE

Small and exclusive, **Maison Talbooth,** Stratford Road, Dedham, Colchester, Essex CO7 6HN (tel. 0206/322367), has ten bedrooms, each really a spacious suite. This Victorian country house was handsomely restored, and each accommodation has been distinctively furnished by one of England's best-known decorators. High-fashion colors abound: antiques are mixed discreetly with reproductions—and the original architectural beauty has been preserved. The super-luxury suite, with a sunken bath, goes for £115 ($201.25) nightly for two persons and has a draped bed. Other suites, each with its own theme, start as low as £80 ($140) for two. One person pays from £70 ($122.50). When you arrive, you're welcomed by your hostess who takes you to your suite, where fresh flowers, fruit, and a private bar are standard. A continental or cooked breakfast is brought in the morning. In an informal, yet stylish, drawing room, guests mingle with the hostess, making you feel as if you're a guest in her country home.

Maison Talbooth's nearby restaurant, **Le Talbooth,** Gun Hill (tel. 0206/323150), is in a hand-hewn, hand-plastered, half-timbered weaver's house set in beautiful gardens on the banks of the River Stour in Constable country. Le Talbooth was featured in Constable's *Vale of Dedham.* You descend a sloping driveway leading past flowering terraces. A well-mannered staff will usher you to a low-ceilinged bar for an apéritif. Taller guests are cautioned to beware of low ceiling beams, which add a rich atmospheric note of another era. Owner Gerald Milsom has brought a high standard of international cooking to this rustically elegant place, where a well-chosen wine list complements the good food. An à la carte menu changes six times a year, and special dishes change daily, as they reflect the best produce available at the market. Food is cooked to order to preserve natural flavors. Main dishes are likely to range from garlic-studded Scottish beef filet to roast breast of partridge. Lunch is priced from £15 ($26.25) and dinner from £30 ($52.50). Hours are daily from noon to 2:30 p.m. and 7 to 9:30 p.m. Reservations are vital.

Dedham Vale Hotel, Stratford Road, Dedham, Colchester, Essex CO7 6HW (tel. 0206/322273), is less glamorous than owner Gerald Milsom's other hotel—the nearby Maison Talbooth, previewed above—but this vine-covered Victorian house offers half a dozen attractive bedrooms to overnight guests in a peaceful bucolic setting. Each unit has a private bath, phone, TV, radio, and a comfortable collection of traditional furniture. With a continental breakfast included, singles cost £65 ($113.75) daily, and doubles go for £75 ($131.25) to £85 ($148.75). VAT and service are included. On chilly mornings, a fire blazes in the Regency-style fireplace in the restaurant. The bar offers views of a flowering terrace and floor-to-ceiling murals of Constable's East Anglia. Many nonresidents who drop in head for the Terrace

Restaurant. There, the protective glass canopy of an Edwardian conservatory shelters the napery and cut flowers of an increasingly popular dining spot. One of Constable's great-nieces occupied one of the upstairs bedrooms here, when this was a convalescent home. The hotel is within easy reach of the ports of Harwich and Felixstowe for journeys to the continent.

SUFFOLK

The easternmost county of England—a link in the four-county chain of East Anglia—Suffolk is a refuge for artists, just as it was in the day of its famous native sons, Constable and Gainsborough. Through them, many of the Suffolk landscapes have ended up in museums on canvas.

A fast train can make it from London to East Suffolk in approximately an hour and a half. Still, its fishing villages, dozens of flint churches, historic homes, and national monuments remain relatively unvisited by overseas visitors.

The major towns of Suffolk are **Bury St. Edmunds,** the capital of West Suffolk, and **Ipswich** in the east, a port city on the Orwell River. But to capture the true charm of Suffolk, you must explore its little market towns and villages. Beginning at the Essex border, we'll strike out toward the North Sea, highlighting the most scenic villages as we move easterly across the shire.

6. Newmarket

This old Suffolk town, 62 miles from London, has been famous as a racing center since the time of King James I. Visitors can see Nell Gwynne's House, but mainly they come to visit Britain's first and only **National Horseracing Museum,** 99 High St. (tel. 0638/667333). The museum is housed in the old subscription rooms, early-19th-century rooms used for placing and settling bets. Visitors will be able to see the history of horseracing over a 300-year period. There are fine paintings of famous horses, pictures on loan from Queen Elizabeth II, and copies of old Parliamentary Acts governing races. There is also a replica of a weighing-in room, plus explanations of the signs used by the ticktack men who keep the on-course bookies informed of changes in the price of bets. A continuous 53-minute audio-visual presentation shows races and racehorses.

In order to make history come alive for the museum visitor, they offer popular tours of this historic town. You are taken by a guide to watch morning gallops on the heath, through the town where you'll see bronzes of stallions from the past, and other points of interest. An optional tour of a famous training establishment is offered, plus a visit to the Jockey Club Rooms, known for a fine collection of paintings. Reservations are necessary, but the tour, which lasts a whole morning, is always available. At a shop at the entrance you can choose from an interesting collection of small souvenirs, along with books, tankards, a Derby chart showing the male descent line of every winner of the celebrated race since 1780, and silk scarves with equine motifs. Caroline Agar is the curator of the museum, which is open from 10 a.m. to 5 p.m. Tuesday to Saturday, from 2 to 5 p.m. Sunday. Closed Monday except bank holidays in August. Equine tours are available. Admission is £1.60 ($2.80) for adults, 80p ($1.40) for children. The museum is closed from December to March, but those with a special interest in seeing it during those months can telephone.

The National Stud (tel. 0638/663464), lying beside Newmarket's July Race Course, two miles southwest of the town, is *the* place for those who wish to see some of the world's finest horseflesh, as well as watch a working thoroughbred breeding stud in operation. A tour lasting about 1¼ hours lets you see many mares and foals, plus horses in training for racing. Tours are possible at 11:15 a.m. and 2:30 p.m. Monday to Friday as well as at 11:15 a.m. Saturday when there is racing in Newmarket during the racing season, April to September. Reservations for tours must be made at The National Stud office from 9 a.m. to 1 p.m. or 2 to 5 p.m. Monday to Friday or by phoning the number given above. Admission is £2.50 ($4.40) for adults, £1.25 ($2.20).

FOOD AND LODGING

The town's best inn is the **Newmarket Moat House,** Moulton Road, Newmarket, Suffolk CB8 8DY (tel. 0638/667171), a member of Queens Moat Houses, lying near Newmarket Heath, close to the center of town. For some time now a favorite of the English horseracing world, it houses devotees of the "sport of kings" in one of its 47 well-appointed bedrooms. Contemporary in styling, it offers a private bath or shower in each of its units. Singles begin at £50 ($87.50) daily, with standard doubles priced at £65 ($113.75). The cooking is a combination of English and French, and full dinners cost from £14.95 ($26.15). You should arrive for dining no later than 9:30 p.m., however.

If you'd like to find a place in the environs, there is none better than **Swynford Paddocks,** Six Mile Bottom, Cambridgeshire CB8 0UE (tel. 063870/234), lying six miles from Newmarket on the A1304. Many guests use it as a base for exploring Cambridge. This well-appointed country house, one of the finest in the area, lies on a 60-acre stud farm surrounded by beautiful grounds. Once it was a favorite retreat of Lord Byron. But now it has been intelligently converted into a first-class hotel and restaurant (open to nonresidents, but you should call first). The hotel rents only 15 handsomely equipped and attractive bedrooms. Singles cost £50 ($87.50) daily, and doubles or twins go for £120 ($210). That's expensive, but you get a lot of quality here. A first-rate English and French cuisine is served, with dinners costing from £15 ($26.25).

---

7. Clare

Lying 58 miles from London, but only 26 miles east from Cambridge, the small town of Clare holds to the old ways of East Anglia. Many of its houses are bathed in Suffolk pink, the façades of a few demonstrating the 16th- and 17th-century plasterwork technique of pargeting. The Stour River, which has its source a few miles away, flows by, marking the boundary of Suffolk and Essex. The little rail station has fallen to the economy axe. The nearest station is now at Sudbury, where Gainsborough was born. The journey by road from London takes about two hours, unless you succumb to the scenery and the countryside along the way.

The **Ancient House Museum** (tel. 0787/277865), directly across from the churchyard, is a splendid example of pargeting and has many notable architectural features and fascinating exhibits, leading to a deeper understanding and appreciation of the rural life of Suffolk. The museum is open from Easter to October from 2:30 to 4:30 p.m. Wednesday to Sunday, as well as from 11 a.m. to 12:30 p.m. on Sunday. Admission is 60p ($1.05) for adults, 30p (55¢) for children.

FOOD AND LODGING

One of the oldest inns in England, **The Bell Hotel,** Market Hill, Clare, Sudbury, Suffolk CO10 8NN (tel. 0787/277741), was known as the Green Dragon when it served the soldiers of Richard de Clare, one of William the Conqueror's barons. Later it became a posting house, but in time the old stable became six extra bedrooms. Its owners, Brian and Gloria Miles, maintain a give-and-take with guests. B&B rates range from £25 ($43.75) to £35 ($61.25) daily for a single, £35.50

($62.15) to £52.50 ($91.90) for a double, plus service and tax. The rooms have a traditional style to them, and the beds are comfortable. Four units have four-posters. The beamed dining room, with its high-back chairs and large brick fireplace, is ideal for winter meals. Lunch costs £9 ($15.75) and dinner from £12 ($21). Afternoon teas are served, and the hotel has a cozy wine bar.

8. Long Melford

Long Melford has been famous since the days of the early clothmakers. Like its sister, Lavenham (coming up), it grew in prestige and importance in the Middle Ages. Of the old buildings remaining, the village church is often called "one of the glories of the shire." Along its three-mile-long High Street—said to boast the highest concentration of antique shops in Europe—are many private homes erected by wealthy wool merchants of yore. While London seems far removed here, it is only 61 miles to the south.

Of special interest are Long Melford's two stately homes:

Melford Hall, standing with its back to the A134 road, was favored by Beatrix Potter. Her Jemima Puddleduck still occupies a chair in one of the bedrooms upstairs, and others of her figures are on display. The house, built between 1554 and 1578, contains paintings, fine furniture, and Chinese porcelain. The principal rooms and gardens can be visited from May to the end of September from 2 to 6 p.m. Wednesday, Thursday, Saturday, Sunday, and bank holiday Mondays. From April to October, hours are from 2 to 6 p.m. only on Saturday and Sunday. Admission is £2 ($3.50) for adults, £1 ($1.75) for children. Melford Hall is a National Trust property.

Kentwell Hall, whose entrance is north of the green in Long Melford on the west side of the A134, about half a mile north of Melford Hall, has been restored by its owners, the barrister Patrick Phillips and his wife. At the end of an avenue of linden trees, the hall is a red-brick Tudor mansion surrounded by a broad moat. A 15th-century moat house, interconnecting gardens, a brick-paved maze, and a costume display are of interest, and there are also rare-breed farm animals to be seen. The public can visit this family home and its grounds over Easter weekend; on Sunday from mid-April to mid-June; and Wednesday to Sunday from mid-July to the end of September. Hours are 2 to 6 p.m. During bank holidays, when special rates apply, hours are from 11 a.m. to 6 p.m. Admission is £2.40 ($4.20) for adults, £1.40 ($2.45) for children.

WHERE TO STAY

An opportunity to experience life in one of the great old inns of East Anglia is provided at the **Bull Hotel,** Hall Street, Long Melford, Sudbury, Suffolk CO10 9JG (tel. 0787/78494). Built by a wool merchant, it is probably Long Melford's finest and best-preserved building, dating back to 1540. Improvements and interior modernization have been undertaken. Incorporated into the general hotel is a medieval weavers' gallery and the open hearth with its Elizabethan brickwork. The bedrooms are a goodly mixture of the old and new—each centrally heated, with phone and radio. A single room with bath rents for £62 ($108.50) daily, and a double with bath for £85 ($148.75). The Cordell Room is the outstanding part of the Bull, with its high beamed ceilings, trestle tables, settles, and handmade chairs, as well as a ten-foot fireplace. Food is served from noon to 2:30 p.m. and 6:30 to 9:30 p.m. daily.

Black Lion Hotel, The Green, Long Melford, Suffolk CO10 9DN (tel. 0787/312356), is a fully restored 17th-century coaching inn on the village green. The nine bedrooms are individually decorated, and all have baths, direct-dial phones, and color TVs. Singles rent for £31 ($54.25) daily, and doubles go for £55 ($96.25), all prices including either a continental or a full English breakfast. The hotel's restaurant serves good country cooking, and there is a well-chosen wine list.

WHERE TO DINE

The most highly rated restaurant in town is **Chimneys,** Hall Street (tel. 0787/79806). The guiding light behind this place is Sam Chalmers, who was chef at the highly acclaimed Le Talbooth in Dedham. Right in the heart of town, he opened this place with its oak beams and brick walls. The house is from the 16th century, and in the back is a "secret garden." This establishment represents modern British cookery at its best. With the help of a carefully chosen and reasonably priced wine list—from both California and European vineyards—guests can select from a constantly changing repertoire. On any given night you are likely to enjoy such English exotica as pressed lambs' tongues with a Cumberland sauce or wild pigeon in port wine. Try also, if featured, a smoked fish ravioli or mussels with oyster sauce. Desserts can be unusual (ever had a poppy-seed parfait?). It is closed for lunch on Monday and for dinner both Sunday and Monday. Otherwise, hours are noon to 2 p.m. and 7 to 9:30 p.m. A set lunch is good value at £10.50 ($18.40), but you can count on paying from £22 ($38.50) for an à la carte dinner.

---

9. Lavenham

Once a great wool center, Lavenham is considered a model village of East Anglia. It is filled with a number of half-timbered Tudor houses, washed in the characteristic Suffolk pink. The prosperity of the town in the days when wool was queen is reflected in the **Guildhall,** on the triangular main "square," built from wool-trading profits. Inside are exhibits on the textile industry of Lavenham, showing how yarn was spun, then "dyed in the wool" with woad (the plant used by the ancient Picts to dye themselves blue) and following on to the weaving process. There is also a display showing how half-timbered houses were constructed.

The **Church of St. Peter and St. Paul,** at the edge of Lavenham, contains interesting carvings on the misericords and the chancel screen, as well as ornate tombs. This is one of the "wool churches" of the area, built by pious merchants in the Perpendicular style with a landmark tower.

Lavenham lies only seven miles from Sudbury, 11 miles from Bury St. Edmunds. For accommodations or meals, there are the following recommendations:

WHERE TO STAY AND DINE

Linked to the Middle Ages, **The Swan,** High Street, Lavenham, Sudbury, Suffolk CO10 9QA (tel. 0787/247477), is a lavishly timbered inn, probably one of the oldest and best-preserved buildings in this relatively unmarred village. Its success has necessitated incorporating an adjoining ancient Wool Hall, which provides a high-ceilinged and timbered guesthouse and additional raftered, second-story bedrooms, opening onto a tiny cloistered garden. The Garden Bar opens onto yet another garden, with old stone walls and flowerbeds. Londoners often visit on September-to-March weekends for dinner and chamber music concerts. All the accommodations contain a private bath. A single rents for £62 ($108.50) daily and doubles, from £82 ($143.50). The bedrooms vary in size, according to the eccentricities of the architecture. Most have beamed ceilings and a mixture of traditional pieces that blend well with the old. The more expensive rooms contain four-poster beds. There are nearly enough lounges for guests to try a different one every night of the week. Meals in the raftered, two-story-high dining room have their own drama, as you sit on leather-and-oak chairs with brass studding. Even if you're not spending the night, you can sample the three-course luncheon priced at £12 ($21). Evening table d'hôte dinners go for £16 ($28). From the à la carte menu, you can order such specialties as roasted goose breast in a rich sauce with crispy bacon and mushrooms or rosettes of English lamb with avocado served with a fresh basil wine sauce with chopped tomatoes. Expect to spend from £25 ($42.75). In World War II, Allied pilots (who made The Swan their second home) carved their signatures into the bar, a longish room with a timbered ceiling and a fine weapon collection.

The Great House, Market Place, Lavenham, Sudbury, Suffolk CO10 9QZ (tel. 0787/247431), is the finest spot for dining. Behind a Georgian façade and opening onto the marketplace, it is also attractively decorated, with Laura Ashley prints, an inglenook fireplace, and old oak beams. A Texan owner, John O. Spice, has wisely hired a Frenchman, Régis Crépy as his chef-de-cuisine. He is assisted by his wife, Martine. He is an inventive chef, as reflected by such dishes as lamb with blackberries, ginger, and honey, pork filet with coconut sauce, or filet of beef with a well-flavored mushroom sauce. Meals are served from noon to 2:30 p.m. and 7 to 10:30 p.m. The least expensive way to dine here is to order the set lunch at £6.90 ($12.10) or the table d'hôte dinner at £11.75 ($20.55). À la carte menus are also available, an evening meal costing around £20 ($35). The house also rents four elegantly decorated bedrooms (suites, actually) for £40 ($70) to £50 ($87.50) daily in a single, £52 ($91) to £58 ($101.50) in a double for B&B.

---

10. Woodbridge

A yachting center, 12 miles from the North Sea, Woodbridge is a market town on a branch of the Deben River. Its best-known resident was Edward FitzGerald, the Victorian poet and translator of the *Rubáiyát* of Omar Khayyám (some critics consider the Englishman's version better than the original). The poet died in 1883 and was buried four miles away at Boulge.

Woodbridge is a good base for exploring the East Suffolk coastline and excursions to Constable's Flatford Mill, coming up. But first, a look at my medium-priced accommodation and dining recommendation, which is some 1½ miles from the Woodbridge rail station.

WHERE TO STAY AND DINE

On the A12 road near Woodbridge, **Seckford Hall,** Woodbridge, Suffolk IP13 6NU (tel. 0394/385678), captures the spirit of the days of Henry VIII and his strong-willed daughter, Elizabeth (the latter may have held court here). The estate is built of brick, now ivy covered, and adorned with crowstepped gables, mullioned windows, and ornate chimneys—pure Tudor. The hall was built in 1530 by Sir Thomas Seckford, a member of one of Suffolk's first families. You enter through a heavy, studded Tudor door into a flagstone hallway with antiques. The butler will show you to your bedroom. Owners Mr. and Mrs. Michael Bunn have seen to it that your stay is like a house party. All bedrooms have a private bath. A single room rents for £49 ($85.75) daily nightly, a double or twin for £60 ($105), and a four-poster unit for £65 ($113.75) and up. Charges include a full English breakfast, service, and tax. One room is high-ceilinged with a monumental 1587 four-poster bed. In summer, reservations are helpful for those desiring bed, breakfast, and evening dinner. (Nonguests can stop by for dinner, which is à la carte. Best to phone first.)

If you arrive before sundown, you may want to stroll through a portion of the 34-acre gardens with a rose garden, herbaceous borders, and greenhouses. At the bottom of the garden is an ornamental lake, complete with weeping willows and paddling ducks. At four o'clock, you can have a complete tea in the Great Hall. Sip your brew slowly, savoring the atmosphere of heavy beams and a stone fireplace. Your chair may be Queen Anne, your table Elizabethan. Dinner will be announced by the butler. Good English meals are served in a setting of linenfold paneling and

Chippendale and Hepplewhite chairs. After-dinner coffee and brandy are featured in the Tudor Bar. Other facilities include a heated indoor swimming pool.

---

11. Aldeburgh

Pressed against the North Sea, Aldeburgh is a favorite retreat of the in-the-know traveler, even attracting some Dutch tourists who make the sea crossing via Harwich, the British entry port for those coming from the Hook of Holland. The late composer, Sir Benjamin Britten, produced some of his most famous works while he lived here (*The Turn of the Screw, Gloriana,* and *Billy Budd*), but the festival he started at Aldeburgh in 1948 is held at Snape in June, a short drive to the west. A second festival, sponsored by British Telecon, is now held in early autumn, featuring major international singers. Less than 100 miles from London, the resort was founded in Roman times, but legionnaires have been replaced by fishermen, boatmen, and fanciers of wildfowl. A bird sanctuary, Havergate Island, lies about six miles south of the town in the River Alde.

Constructed on a shelf of land at the level of the sea, the High or main street of town runs parallel to the often-turbulent waterfront. This main street sits below a cliff face that rises some 55 feet. It has been turned in part into terraced gardens, which visitors can enter. Some take time out from their sporting activities (a golf course stretches 3½ miles) to visit the 16th-century **Moot Hall Museum** (tel. 072885/2158). The hall dates from the time of Henry VIII, but its tall, twin chimneys are Jacobean additions. The timber-frame structure contains old maps and prints. It's open from 2:30 to 5 p.m., on Saturday and Sunday only from Easter to June, and seven days a week from July to September. Admission is 25p (45¢) for adults, free to children.

Aldeburgh also contains the nation's northernmost Martello tower, erected to protect the coast from a feared invasion by Napoleon.

WHERE TO STAY AND EAT

In August, the time of the regatta, accommodations tend to be fully booked. I'll survey the pick of the lot:

Wentworth Hotel, Wentworth Road, Aldeburgh, Suffolk IP15 5BD (tel. 072885/2312), is a traditional country-house hotel, with tall chimneys and gables, overlooking the sea. Many rooms open onto good views. Since 1920 the Pritt family have welcomed the world to their hotel, including Sir Benjamin Britten and his beloved friend, Peter Pears. The novelist E. M. Forster, whose books, *Room with a View* and *Maurice,* have been filmed, also came this way. In summer tables are placed outside so guests can enjoy the sun, but in winter the open fires in the lounges, even the cozy bar, are a welcome sight. Many come here anytime except in January to enjoy the good food and wine, others seeking accommodations. The latter is housed in one of 31 bedrooms, each well appointed and centrally heated, although only about two dozen contain a private bath. Rates range from £30 ($52.50) daily in a single, £74 ($129.50) in a double.

Brudenell Hotel, The Parade, Aldeburgh, Suffolk IP15 5BU (tel. 072885/2071), is right on the waterfront. Built at the beginning of the 20th century, it was remodeled and decorated. The interior is pleasant, and from many of the bedrooms there's a view of the sea. All of the rooms have a private bath. Singles range in price from £48 ($84) daily, and twins or doubles, from £65 ($113.75), VAT and service included. Every room has TV, phone, radio, tea- and coffee-makers, and central heating, as well as good beds. The dining room with an all-glass wall overlooking the coast is an ideal spot for a three-course luncheon costing £8 ($14). Dinner goes for £13 ($22.75).

12. East Bergholt

The English landscape painter, John Constable (1776–1837), was born at East Bergholt. Near the village is **Flatford Mill** (tel. 0206/298283), subject of one of his most renowned canvases. The mill, in a scenic setting, was given to the National Trust in 1943, and since has been leased to the Field Studies Council for use as a residential college. Weekly courses are arranged on all aspects of the countryside and the environment. None of the buildings contains relics of Constable, nor are they open to the general public, but students of all ages and capabilities are welcome to courses. The fee for one week is inclusive of accommodation, meals, and tuition. Details may be obtained from The Warden, Field Studies Council, Flatford Mill Field Centre, East Bergholt, Colchester, Essex CO7 6UL.

THE LOCAL PUB
Cited by numerous writers as one of the unmarred inns of East Anglia, the **Red Lion Inn,** The Street (tel. 0206/298332), traces its ancestry back to around 1500. The family-run pub has an enclosed children's garden. There is a wide range of bar meals, costing from £1.75 ($3.05) to £5 ($8.75), including the best ploughman's lunch in the area. Steaks are offered in the evening. Hours are from noon to 3 p.m. and 7 to 11 p.m. Monday to Saturday, from noon to 3 p.m. and 7 to 10:30 p.m. Sunday. A short stroll from Flatford Mill and the heart of Constable land, the inn is opposite a historic church with a bell cage on the ground, where the bells are hand-rung. The Red Lion is reached by turning off the A12 Colchester–Ipswich road.

NORFOLK

Bounded by the North Sea, Norfolk is the biggest of the East Anglian counties. It's a low-lying area, with fens, heaths, and salt marshes. An occasional dike or wind-mill makes you think you've been delivered to the Netherlands. One of the features of Norfolk is its network of Broads, miles and miles of lagoons—shallow in parts—connected by streams.
Summer sports people flock to Norfolk to hire boats for sailing or fishing. From Norwich itself, **Wroxham,** capital of the Broads, is easily reached, only eight miles to the northeast. Motorboats regularly leave from this resort, taking parties on short trips. Some of the best scenery of the Broads is to be found on the periphery of Wroxham.

13. Norwich

Norwich, 109 miles from London and 20 miles from the North Sea, still holds to its claim as the capital city of East Anglia. The county town of Norfolk, Norwich is a charming and historic city, despite encroachments by industry. It is the most important shopping center in East Anglia and is well provided with hotels and entertainment. In addition to its cathedral, it has more than 30 medieval parish churches built of flint.
There are many interesting hotels in the narrow streets and alleyways, and a big open-air market, busy every weekday, where fruit, flowers, vegetables, and other goods are sold from stalls with colored canvas roofs.

THE SIGHTS

The **Assembly House** is a Georgian building restored to provide a splendid arts and social center. The **Maddermarket Theatre,** the home of the Norwich Players, is an 18th-century chapel converted by Nugent Monck in 1921 to an Elizabethan-style theater. On the outskirts of the city, the buildings of the University of East Anglia are modern in design and include the Sainsbury Center.

There is a **Tourist Information Centre** at the Guildhall, Gaol Hill (tel. 0603/666071).

Norwich Castle

In the center of Norwich, on a partly artificial mound, sits the castle, formerly the county gaol (jail). Its huge 12th-century Norman keep and the later prison buildings are used as a civic museum and headquarters of the county-wide Norfolk Museums Service (tel. 0603/611277). The museum houses an impressive collection of pictures by artists of the Norwich School, of whom the most distinguished were John Crome, born 1768, and John Sell Cotman, born 1782. The Castle Museum also contains a fine collection of Lowestoft porcelain and Norwich silver. These are shown in the rotunda. There are two sets of dioramas, one showing Norfolk wildlife in its natural setting, the other illustrating scenes of Norfolk life from the Old Stone Age to the early days of Norwich Castle. You can also visit a geology gallery and a permanent exhibition in the keep, "Norfolk in Europe."

The Castle Museum is open daily from 10 a.m. to 5 p.m. (on Sunday from 2 to 5 p.m.). Charges from the spring bank holiday until September are 80p ($1.40) for adults, 10p (20¢) for children. The rest of the year, adults pay 40p (70¢); children 10p (20¢). There's a cafeteria open from 10 a.m. to 4:30 p.m. Monday to Saturday, as well as a bar serving from 10:30 a.m. to 2:30 p.m.

Norwich Cathedral

Principally of Norman design, the cathedral dates from 1096. It is noted primarily for its long nave, with its lofty columns. Its spire, built in the late Perpendicular style, rises 315 feet, and shares distinction with the keep of the castle as the significant landmarks on the Norwich skyline. On the vaulted ceiling are more than 300 bosses (knob-like ornamental projections) depicting biblical scenes. The impressive choir stalls with the handsome misereres date from the 15th century. Edith Cavell—"Patriotism is not enough"—the English nurse executed by the Germans in World War I, was buried on the cathedral's Life's Green. The quadrangular cloisters go back to the 13th century, and are among the most spacious in England. A donation of 50p (90¢) is requested.

The cathedral Visitors' Centre includes a refreshment area and an exhibition and film room with tape/slide shows about the cathedral. Admission is free.

A short walk from the cathedral will take you to **Tombland,** one of the most interesting old squares in Norwich.

Sainsbury Centre for Visual Arts

In 1973 Sir Robert and Lady Sainsbury gave their private art collection to the University of East Anglia, and their son, David, gave an endowment to provide a building to house the collection. The center, designed by Foster Associates, was opened in 1978, and since then the building has won many national and international awards. Features of the structure are its flexibility, allowing solid and glass areas to be interchanged, and the superb quality of light, which allows optimum viewing of works of art. The Sainsbury Collection is one of the foremost in the country, including modern, ancient, classical, and ethnographic art. It is especially strong in works by Francis Bacon, Alberto Giacometti, and Henry Moore. Other displays at the center include the Anderson collection of art nouveau and the university aggregation of 20th-century abstract art and design. There is also a regular program of special exhibitions. The center (tel. 0603/592470) is open from noon to 5 p.m. daily except Monday. Admission is 50p (90¢) for adults, 25p (45¢) for children. The restaurant on the premises offers a self-service buffet from 10:30 a.m. to 2 p.m. Monday to Friday and a carvery service from 12:30 to 2 p.m. A conservatory coffee bar serves light lunches and refreshments from noon to 4:30 p.m. Tuesday to Sunday.

The Mustard Shop

This fascinating attraction is at 3 Bridewell Alley (tel. 0603/627889). Early in the 19th century Jeremiah Colman went into partnership with his nephew, James, and started the firm of J. & J. Colman, a name that became synonymous with mustard over the years. To mark the 150th anniversary of the business (1973), the Mustard Shop was opened in an 18th-century building up a pretty little alleyway in Norwich's old center. It is now the town's major tourist attraction after the cathedral. Here, you can learn the history of mustard and buy useful and unusual souvenirs at the same time. More than a dozen different flavors of mustard made by Colman are on sale, including horseradish, chive, and tarragon. Various mustard pots, mustard spoons, and mustard paddles are sold here. They will pack and mail to anywhere in the world. The shop and museum are open from 9 a.m. to 5:30 p.m. Monday to Wednesday and on Friday and Saturday (closed all day Thursday).

WHERE TO STAY

In business since 1272, the **Maids Head Hotel,** Tombland, Norwich, Norfolk NR3 1LB (tel. 0603/761111), claims to be the oldest continuously operated hotel in the United Kingdom. In the most ancient part of the city and next to Norwich Cathedral, it has two parts, Elizabethan and Georgian, to its architectural personality. The Georgian section has a prim white entry and small-paned windows. The 82 bedrooms offer private baths or showers, with fresh fruit, newspapers, and the traditional services such as shoe cleaning, breakfast served in bed, and afternoon cream teas. The four-poster Queen Elizabeth I room (where the Tudor monarch allegedly once slept) is much sought after, renting for £79 ($138.25) daily. Singles with shower cost £40 ($70), and singles with bath, £52 ($91). A double with bath and shower costs £64 ($112). An English breakfast is included in all the tariffs. Meals are served in the Courtyard Carvery at lunchtime, with an extensive buttery service all day. The Georgian paneled Minstrel Room offers dinner each night. Lunches cost from £7 ($12.25) and dinners from £9.75 ($17.05).

The **Post House Hotel,** Ipswich Road, Norwich, Norfolk NR4 6EP (tel. 0603/56431), is two miles from the center of the city on the A140 Ipswich road and one mile from the A11 London road. Free parking space is provided for 200 cars. The hotel charges £59 ($103.25) daily in a single, £69 ($120.75) in a double, VAT and service charge included. Executive singles cost £59 ($103.25), and executive doubles, £79 ($138.25), also including VAT and service. Each of the 120 bedrooms has a private bath, phone, TV, radio, tea/coffee-maker, and a mini-bar. The rooms have combined sitting areas, with sofas and armchairs. The coffeeshop, which stays open till 10:30 p.m., reflects Norfolk's ties with agriculture (sturdy farming tools decorate the walls); the main restaurant specializes in traditional English fare, such as game in season, smoked fish, and potted meats. The Punch Bar is decorated with early *Punch* cartoons and drawings. Guests enjoy a leisure center with indoor pool, gym, solarium, and sauna.

Hotel Nelson, Prince of Wales Road, Norwich, Norfolk, NR1 1DX (tel. 0603/760260), is modern with a waterside setting, close to Thorpe Station, behind a four-story façade pierced with horizontal rows of glass. Each of its 118 bedrooms has its own private bath, TV, phone, and a view of either the river or a pleasant courtyard. Accommodations cost £65 ($113.75) daily in a single, £72 ($126) in a double. A nautical theme is predictably carried out in most of the public rooms. There are a sauna and an exercise room on the premises, plus a cocktail lounge and two restaurants. One of these, the Quarterdeck, brings back memories of Norwich's most famous son, Horatio, Admiral Lord Nelson, after whom the hotel is named. The nautical name of the buttery also stems, of course, from the heroic naval exploits of Nelson, even up to his death at the Battle of Trafalgar. At the Quarterdeck (or should I say "on" it?), you get fast, cheerful service and a choice of dishes such as Cromer fish pie or beef-and-beer casserole with mushrooms and noodles. The restaurant is open daily from 10:30 a.m. for coffee and drinks, from noon to 2 p.m. for lunch, and from 5:30 to 10:30 p.m. for informal dinners, costing from £11 ($19.25). The hotel is near the railway station and Foundry Bridge, and there's free parking.

Embassy Lansdowne Hotel, 116 Thorpe Rd., Norwich, Norfolk NR1 1RU (tel. 0603/620302), has been refurbished and refurnished extensively, but without taking away from the previous high standards of service and atmosphere. Two semi-detached cottages on the hotel grounds have been made into luxury bedrooms and family accommodations, with modern conveniences just like in the main building, but with original features, including bay windows and wooden beams as well as a private garden. Single rooms rent for £45 ($78.75) daily, while doubles peak at £58 ($101.50). The reception area's chandeliers light the way up the elegant staircase to the restaurant.

WHERE TO DINE

The piano music probably draws as many customers to **Green's Seafood Restaurant,** 82 Upper St. Giles St. (tel. 0603/623733), as does the fresh fish. However, seafood made this establishment a social fixture in the region. By the glow of candlelight, you can enjoy a handful of well-seasoned meat dishes, as well as such specialties as smoked trout, poached scallops in red wine sauce, turbot with a creamy prawn sauce, and others. No one will mind if you forgo the creamy sauces and request a simple grilled or baked fish of your choice. Full meals cost £20 ($35). The restaurant is open for lunch, from noon to 2:30 p.m., and dinner, from 7 to 11 p.m., daily except Saturday at lunchtime and all day Sunday.

Marco's, 17 Pottergate (tel. 0603/624044), serves the best Italian food in the region, made with salad greens and herbs that owner Marco Vessalio grows in a nearby kitchen garden. The pasta is homemade and concocted into tempting specialties, including gnocchi and a range of tagliatelle. One of Signor Vessalio's chicken, veal, or beef dishes might follow a steaming bowl of minestrone or pasta. Lunch and dinner are served every day of the week except Sunday and Monday and during August, as well as some holidays. Hours are from 12:30 to 2 p.m. and 7:30 to 10 p.m. A set lunch costs £11 ($19.25), and à la carte dinners go for £21 ($36.75).

Brasted's, 8-10 St. Andrews Hill (tel. 0603/625949), offers a lovely home in the oldest part of Norwich, within an easy stroll of both the cathedral and castle (previously recommended in the introduction). After exploring the two major sights of Norwich, you can come here to sample the savory cooking of John Brasted, for whom the restaurant is named. The owner and chef de cuisine, Mr. Brasted, knows how to combine the best of yesterday with modern cooking techniques and innovations. As you enjoy the rather flamboyant interior, you can peruse the menu. You'll probably settle for one of the fresh fish dishes of East Anglia. Other dishes, including vegetables and desserts, seem equally well prepared. Brasted's is open Monday to Sunday from noon to 2 p.m. and 7 to 10:30 p.m. (however, no lunch is served on Saturday and no dinner on Sunday). Count on spending from £20 ($35) for a meal here.

14. Shipdham

As you negotiate a sharp bend around the churchyard in Shipdham village, near Thetford, you come to an open gateway leading to the wide graveled front yard of

Shipdham Place, Church Close, Shipdham, Norfolk IP25 7LX (tel. 0362/ 820303). Ring the bell, and you will be welcomed into an old country house that was once the rectory. It dates back to the 17th century, with an elegant Regency block that was added in 1800. There are two lounges with comfortable chairs and a drinks trolley. You are trusted to help yourself and enter your drinks in the book for payment at departure. Behind the house, a garden is at the disposal of guests. You can take coffee on the terrace on a warm summer evening. Upstairs, the eight bedrooms come in varying shapes and sizes. Some have sloping ceilings. All are decorated in pretty country prints, and fresh fruit and flowers are placed in your room on arrival. Rates vary from £25 ($43.75) per night for a single room to £70 ($122.50) for the big double rooms at the front of the house, which have large baths and walk-in closets. All tariffs include VAT and breakfast. It is mainly for the cuisine that Mr. and Mrs. Alan Poulton, the hosts, are known. Dishes are likely to include roast Norfolk partridge with bread sauce, potted Norfolk crab, and saddle of new-season English lamb.

---

15. North Norfolk

This part is already well known by members of the American Eighth Air Force, for many Liberators and Flying Fortresses took off and landed from this corner of the country. Their captains and crews sampled most of the local hostelries at one time or another. Now it is just feathered birds that fly overhead, and the countryside is peaceful.

THE SIGHTS

This area is of considerable scenic interest, having some very good value in its offering of accommodations and food. Norfolk especially provides an alternative to the vastly overcrowded West Country in summer, and it's extremely convenient for a weekend out of London, as it lies only a three-hour drive away.

Sandringham

Some 110 miles northeast of London, Sandringham (tel. 0553/112675) has been the country home of four generations of British monarchs, ever since the Prince of Wales (later King Edward VII) purchased it in 1861. The son of Queen Victoria, along with his Danish wife, Princess Alexandra, rebuilt the house, standing on 7,000 acres of grounds, and in time it became a fashionable rendezvous of British society. The red-brick Victorian Tudor mansion consists of more than 200 rooms, and in recent times some of these rooms have been opened to the public, including two drawing rooms and a dining room. Sandringham joins Windsor Castle and the Palace of Holyroodhouse in Edinburgh as the only British royal residences that can be examined by the public. Guests can also visit a lofty saloon with a minstrels' gallery.

A group of former coach houses has been converted into a museum of big-game trophies, plus a collection of cars, including the first vehicle purchased by a member of the royal family, a 1900 Daimler Tonneau that belonged to Edward VII. The house and grounds are open, except when the Queen or members of the royal family are there, from Easter to the last week in September daily except Friday and Saturday. Hours are 11 a.m. (noon on Sunday) to 4:45 p.m. for the house, 10:30 a.m. (11:30 a.m. on Sunday) to 5 p.m. for the grounds. Admission to the house and grounds is £2 ($3.50) for adults, £1.20 ($2.10) for children. To visit the grounds only, adults pay £1.50 ($2.65); children, 80p ($1.40). The house is closed from the third week in July to the end of the first week in August, and the grounds and house are both closed for all but the first and last three or four days of that period. The 70-acre gardens are richly planted with azaleas, rhododendrons, hydrangeas, and camellias.

Sandringham lies 50 miles from Cambridge and 10 miles from King's Lynn. There is bus service between King's Lynn and Sandringham.

Blickling Hall

A long drive, bordered by massive yew hedges towering above and framing your first view of this lovely old house, leads you to Blickling Hall, near Aylsham (tel. 0263/733471). A great Jacobean house built in the early 17th century, it is perhaps one of the finest examples of such architecture in the country. The Long Gallery has an elaborate 17th-century ceiling, and the Peter the Great Room, decorated later, has a fine tapestry on the wall. The house is set in ornamental parkland with a formal garden and an orangery. Meals and snacks are available. It is open from early April until the end of October daily except Monday and Thursday, from 1 to 5 p.m., with the gardens, shop, and restaurant opening at noon. Admission to the house and gardens is £3.50 ($6.15) for adults, £1.75 ($3.05) for children; £2 ($3.50) for adults and £1 ($1.75) for children to the gardens only.

Norfolk Lavender Ltd.

At **Caley Mill** at Heacham (tel. 0485/70384) you can see how lavender is grown, the flowers harvested, and the essence distilled before appearing prettily packaged as perfume, aftershave, and old-fashioned lavender bags to slip between your hankies. Much of the lavender is grown on the nearby Sandringham royal estate, so you may end up with a regal product. The house and grounds are open all year. Hours are from 10 a.m. to 5 p.m. Monday to Friday from January to Easter, from 10 a.m. to 5:30 p.m. daily from Easter to October, and from 10 a.m. to 5 p.m. Monday to Saturday from November to Christmas. The tours cost 75p ($1.30) for adults, free for children. The **Miller's Cottage Tea Room** serves cream teas, homemade cakes, and light lunches from Easter to the end of May in the afternoon only. From May to Christmas, the tea room is open at the same times as the shop. The best time to see the lavender in bloom is late June to mid-August.

The Thursford Collection

Just off the A148, which runs from King's Lynn to Cromer, at Thursford Green, Thursford, near Fakenham (tel. 032877/477), George Cushing has been collecting and restoring steam engines and organs for more years than you'd care to remember. His collection is now a trust, and the old painted giants are on display, a paradise of traction engines with impeccable pedigrees such as Burrells, Garretts, and Ruston Proctors. There are some static engines, the sort that run merry-go-rounds at funfairs, but the most flamboyant exhibits are the old show business musical organs, the Wurlitzers and concert organs with their brilliant decoration, moving figures, and mass of windpipes. The organs play at 3 p.m. There is a children's play area, and a Savages Venetian Gondola switchback ride with Gavoili organ, which operates daily. It was built at nearby Kings Lynn, and Disneyland has been after it for years. On many days during the summer, the two-foot-gauge steam railway, the Cackler, will take you around the wooded grounds of the museum. There is a refreshment café and a souvenir shop to buy photographs, books, and records of the steam-organ music. The collection is open daily from 2 to 5:30 p.m. from Easter until the end of October. Admission is £2.20 ($3.85) for adults, 95¢ ($1.65) for children.

The North Norfolk Railway

This steam railway plies from Sheringham to Weybourne. The station at Sheringham (0263/822045) opens daily at 10 a.m. from Easter to October. Admission to the station and museum is free from October to March. From Easter to the end of September, admission is 30p (55¢) for adults, 15p (25¢) for children. There are two museum displays of railway paraphernalia, steam locomotives, and historic rolling stock. The round trip to Weybourne by steam train takes about 45 minutes through attractive countryside. Days and times of departure vary, so you should phone between 10 a.m. and 5 p.m. before you go there. A ride on a steam train between Weybourne and Sheringham is £2.20 ($3.85) for adults for a round trip, £1.10 ($1.95) for children.

FOOD AND LODGING

Almost on the edge of the sea but protected from its worst ravages, **The Maltings,** The Street, Weybourne, near Holt, Norfolk NR25 6SY (tel. 026370/731), is a delightful country pub in the best tradition. Bedrooms are simple and comfortable with color TVs and radios, and cost £35 ($61.25) daily in a single, from £55 ($96.25) in a double. Rates include a large English breakfast, VAT, and service. The original building dates back to the 16th century, and the flint walls and stout plain exterior bear witness to those times. The elegant restaurant has à la carte choices, including most of those haute-cuisine dishes that you crave, along with a Taste of England menu when a succulent set lunch will cost £8.50 ($14.90); a set dinner, £15 ($26.25).

The Swiss Restaurant, The Street, Weybourne (tel. 026370/220), has been going for half a century. Nigel Massingham, the chef, trained here and has picked up those Swiss touches in the preparation of the dishes. The beamed dining room of the flint-and-thatch cottage is warmed by a log fire. You will be greeted as warmly by the staff as you partake of the set lunch, costing £8.45 ($14.80) for three courses. Dinner, from £14.55 ($25.45), is chosen from a similarly large menu, including roast Norfolk duckling. There is an à la carte menu where a meal will cost around £20 ($35), but I think you will find enough choices on the set menus to satisfy all tastes. The restaurant is open Tuesday to Sunday from 12:30 to 2 p.m. and 7 to 9 p.m. (closed Sunday for dinner).

Blakeney Hotel, The Quay, Blakeney, near Holt, Norfolk NR25 7NE (tel. 0263/740797). As its address indicates, the hotel is right on the quay overlooking the harbor and across the flats from Blakeney Point where migrating birds rest on their way south. The village and neighboring Cley built many of the Elizabethan sailing ships, and the hotel bar is named for one of them, *Revenge.* The 51 rooms of this hotel, built in 1923, are cozy, with private baths, color TVs, phones, and radios. Singles cost £37 ($64.75) to £45 ($78.75) daily, and doubles run £80 ($140) to £100 ($175). Breakfast is included. There is an indoor swimming pool, and the lounge has panoramic windows with views over the flats to the sea.

Congham Hall, Lynn Road, Grimston, King's Lynn, Norfolk PE32 1AH (tel. 0485/600250), is just the place if you'd like to center around the King's Lynn area. Far better than anything you'd find in town, Congham Hall lies at Grimston, more than six miles northeast by A148. One of the most scenic and beautiful of the country house hotels of East Anglia, Congham Hall is set on 40 acres of its own parklike grounds complete with paddocks and orchards. Trevor and Christine Forecast brought taste and refinement to converting this Georgian manor into a small hotel of charm and character. Their facilities include a hard tennis court and a heated swimming pool along with a sauna and solarium. The house is tastefully decorated, and the well-furnished bedrooms offer much comfort. They also contain a private bath or shower, phone, TV, and hair dryer among other amenities. They rent 10 bedrooms and one suite, with standard singles priced from £60 ($105) daily, with doubles going for £78 ($136.50). Their menu is varied, and the wine list well chosen. Meals begin at £10.50 ($18.40), going up to £28 ($49) for an elaborate repast.

Old Rectory, Great Snoring, Fakenham, Norfolk NR21 0HP (tel. 0328/820597). The history of this old house is shrouded in mystery, but in 1500 it was believed to be hexagonal with stone-mullioned windows and heraldic shields of the then owners, the Shelton family, carved on the oaken front door. The Victorians did their bit to restore the house, but it still remains a solid part of the medieval village life. Rosamond Scoles and her family have six comfortable and elegantly furnished rooms for guests. Overnight is £42 ($73.50) daily in a single, £62 ($108.50) in a double, all with bath, including a leisurely and substantial breakfast. There is a large lounge for guests, where a woodstove burns, and the light flickers on antique woodwork. Dinner is three courses, cheese, and coffee for £14 ($24.50) per person. Picnic hampers are provided for luncheon al fresco if you wish. Old Rectory is licensed, so you can enjoy a sherry before dinner or a nightcap by the fire before retiring to your bed.

Elderton Lodge, Cromer Road, Thorpe Market, North Walsham, Norfolk NR11 8TZ (tel. 026379/547). At a point 21 miles from Norwich, turn off the A149 road to the former dower house of the big estate with wide views over the farmlands. The entrance hall of the hotel is full of family memorabilia, and there's a large lounge bar, off which you'll find a conservatory in which light meals are served. Many bedrooms have a private bath, while guests in bathless units share large, elegant corridor facilities. A single costs from £20 ($35) daily, and a double begins at £46 ($80.50). All rates include a full breakfast and VAT. The set dinner menu at £10.50 ($18.40) includes grilled trout with almonds, lamb cutlets with pâté and red-currant sauce, or breast of chicken with madeira sauce.

Links Country Park Hotel and Golf Club, Sandy Lane, West Runton, near Cromer, Norfolk NR27 9QH (tel. 026375/691), is 24 miles from Norwich and 42 miles from King's Lynn. You don't need to be a golfer to enjoy this country hotel, with its large, comfortable public rooms and bars. Despite the fact that it's surrounded by the golf course, there are views out over the sea and plenty of places to walk. Bedrooms are spacious and comfortable, with TVs, radios, and tea- and coffee-making equipment. Charges are £110 ($192.50) daily in a double, £35 ($61.25) in a single. All tariffs include a full English breakfast and VAT. There is an elegant restaurant with good set menus. Next to the clubhouse is the Fairways Grill Room, a lofty place decorated with plaques and the names of past winners of golf tournaments, with plenty of tables and chairs, plus a good but simple menu. Dinners, served until 9:30 p.m., cost from £13 ($22.75).

EAST MIDLANDS

1. NORTHAMPTONSHIRE
2. LEICESTERSHIRE
3. DERBYSHIRE
4. NOTTINGHAMSHIRE
5. LINCOLNSHIRE

The East Midlands contains several widely varied counties, both in character and scenery. This part of central England, for instance, offers miles of dreary industrial sections and their offspring row-type Victorian houses, yet the district is intermixed with some of Britain's noblest scenery, such as the Peak District National Park, centered in Derbyshire. Byron said that scenes there rivaled those of Switzerland and Greece. There are, in short, many pleasant surprises in store for you, from the tulip land of Lincoln to the 18th-century spa of Buxton in Derbyshire, from George Washington's ancestral home at Sulgrave Manor in Northamptonshire to what remains of Sherwood Forest.

1. Northamptonshire

The shire of which the city of Northampton has long been the administrative center, lying in the heart of the Midlands of England, has been inhabited since Paleolithic times. Traces have been found of the Beaker and other Bronze Age people, and a number of Iron Age hill-forts existed here, remains of which can still be seen. Two main Roman roads—Watling Street and Ermine Street—ran through the county, and relics of Roman settlements have been discovered at Towcester, Whilton, Irchester, and Castor. A racial mix was contributed by the invasion in the 7th century by West Saxons and Anglians. Also in that century, in 655, the first abbey was established at Medehamstede, now Peterborough.

The Danes took over late in the 9th century, and although their stay was not long as history goes, it was under their aegis that Northampton became the seat of administration for a borough with almost the same boundaries as the shire has today and as recorded in the *Domesday Book*.

In the Middle Ages, castles and manor houses dotted the country, rich in cattle and sheep farming and leatherwork, particularly the production of boots and shoes.

SULGRAVE MANOR

On your way from Oxford to Stratford-upon-Avon, if you take the A34 north, you can visit Sulgrave Manor, the ancestral home of George Washington. First, you'll come to Banbury (see Chapter VI). Follow the A422 east from Banbury into Northamptonshire toward Brackley, but turn off to the left after a short distance onto the B4525, which will take you to the tiny village of Sulgrave. Signs will lead you to Sulgrave Manor, a small Tudor manorial house built in the mid-16th century.

As part of Henry VIII's plan to dissolve monasteries, he sold the priory-owned manor in 1539 to Lawrence Washington, who had been mayor of Northampton. George Washington was a direct descendant of Lawrence (seven generations removed). The Washington family occupied Sulgrave for more than a century. In 1656 Col. John Washington left for the New World.

In 1914 the manor was purchased by a group of English people in honor of the friendship between Britain and America. Over the years, major restoration has taken place (a whole new wing had to be added), with an eye toward returning it as much as possible to its original state. The Colonial Dames have been largely responsible for raising the money. From both sides of the Atlantic the appropriate furnishings were donated, including a number of portraits—even a Gilbert Stuart original of the first president. On the main doorway is the Washington family coat-of-arms—two bars and a trio of mullets—which is believed to have been the inspiration for the "Stars and Stripes."

The manor is open daily except Wednesday from March to December, 10:30 a.m. to 1 p.m. and 2 to 5:30 p.m. Otherwise the hours are 10:30 a.m. to 1 p.m. and 2 to 4 p.m. It's closed in January. Admission is £2 ($3.50) for adults, £1 ($1.75) for children. For more information, telephone 029576/205.

Food and Lodging

Across from Sulgrave Manor is the **Thatched House Hotel,** Manor Road, Sulgrave, near Banbury, Northamptonshire OX17 2SE (tel. 029576/232), a long, low group of thatched 17th-century cottages, with a front garden full of flowers. Even if you're just passing through, it's a good place to stop for tea following your visit to Sulgrave Manor. Cream teas, served from 3:30 to 5:30 p.m. and costing £1.65 ($2.90), consist of scones with thick cream and jam, and strawberries in season. Tea is served at a table in either the beamed living room or dining room, furnished with antiques. If you're lucky enough to stay over, Ron Walpole, the owner and manager, has modernized the bedrooms, installing private baths in all the doubles. Each unit has TV and a tea/coffee-maker. Depending on the plumbing, singles range from £23 ($40.25) to £30 ($52.50) daily, and doubles cost £50 ($90). Rates include a full English breakfast and VAT. The hotel restaurant serves meals seven days a week. Lunches cost £6.50 ($11.40) Monday to Saturday, with a traditional English roast served Sunday, lunch costing from £5.50 ($9.65) to £7.25 ($12.70). Dinner goes for £9.25 ($16.20), when you can feast on such dishes as medallion of English lamb flavored with herbs or roast guinea fowl in a sherry sauce. Food is served daily from noon to 2 p.m. and 7:30 to 9:30 p.m.

NORTHAMPTON

The administrative and political center of Northamptonshire was a favorite meeting place of Norman and Plantagenet kings, fortified after 1066 by Simon de Senlis (St. Liz). Here King John was besieged by the barons trying to force the policy changes that finally resulted in the Magna Carta. During the War of the Roses, Henry VI (before he achieved that note) was defeated and taken prisoner, and during the Civil War, Northampton stuck with Parliament and Cromwell. The town, on the River Nene, has long been an important center for the production of boots and shoes, as well as other leathercraft, pursuits that are traced in two of the city's museums.

The **Central Museum & Art Gallery,** Guildhall Road (tel. 0604/34881), displays collections of footwear through the ages, plus a re-created cobbler's shop. It also houses local archeological artifacts tracing the history of Northampton up to the Great Fire, English Oriental ceramics, Old Masters, sculpture, and British 19th-

and 20th-century art. It is open from 10 a.m. to 5 p.m. Monday to Saturday (to 8 p.m. Thursday). Admission is free.

The **Museum of Leathercraft,** The Old Blue Coat School, Bridge Street (tel. 0604/34881), traces the history of leather use from ancient Egyptian times to the present. Missal cases, 16th-century caskets, and modern saddles are displayed, with exhibits of costumes, luggage, and harnesses. Open Monday to Saturday from 10 a.m. to 5 p.m. with no admission charge.

Food and Lodging

Northampton Moat House Inn, Silver Street, Northampton, Northampton-shire NN1 2TA (tel. 0604/22441), is a concrete-and-glass structure, attracting mainly the business client, drawn to its good location just off the Inner Ring Road (West). A first-class motor hotel, it checks you in and out smoothly and efficiently. The atmosphere isn't stiff at all—in fact it's rather informal, and the public lounges are attractively decorated. You can dine in a coaching-house atmosphere in the Saddle Room, with its large stone fireplace and heavy beams. The menu is international, and guests dine by candlelight, enjoying soft music from a piano player. A resident band entertains on Saturday night from September to June. Rooms are well furnished and comfortable, each with private bath or shower and toilet, along with color TV, radio, phone, and wall-to-wall carpeting. Singles cost £62 ($108.50) daily; doubles, £78 ($136.50).

Westone Moat House, Ashley Way, Weston Favell, Northampton, Northamptonshire NN3 3EA (tel. 0604/406262), is a big 19th-century mansion that has seen much modernization. A favored spot here is the cocktail lounge, which has an elegance, its windows opening onto the terrace and grounds. All 65 bedrooms have private bath, color TV, radio, phone, and tea- and coffee-making equipment. B&B costs £54 ($94.50) daily in a single, £64 ($112) in a double or twin. Traditional English dishes are among the offerings in the restaurant which has good food, fine service, and a bright decor.

Some of the best food in town is found at **Napoleon's Bistro,** 9-11 Welford Rd., Kingsthorpe (tel. 0604/713899), lying less than two miles north by A508 on A45. Mercifully, it's not expensive either, offering one of the best value lunches in town costing only £6 ($10.50). Two former shops were taken over and converted into this bistrolike restaurant. Here you get a range of typical French dishes, beginning with onion soup and going on to boeuf bourguignon or perhaps poultry prepared in the style of Provence. At dinner expect to pay from £12 ($21) per person. Hours are noon to 2 p.m. and 7 to 10 p.m. It is closed for dinner on Tuesday, for lunch on Saturday, and all day Sunday.

THE SPENCER HOME

The mansion that was the girlhood home of the Princess of Wales, **Althorp,** Northampton (no phone calls allowed), is the residence of the Earl and Countess Spencer, parents of the former Lady Diana Spencer who married Prince Charles. The entrance lodge is five miles northwest of Northampton, beyond the village of Harlestone. Althorp is about a 1½-hour drive from London on the A428 from Northampton to Rugby. Built in 1508 by Sir John Spencer, the house has undergone many alterations over the years.

It contains a collection of pictures by Van Dyck, Reynolds, Gainsborough, and Rubens, as well as fine and rare French and English furniture, along with Sèvres, Bow, and Chelsea porcelain. The collection is quite as magnificent as that in better-known stately homes. The house is open daily from 1 to 5 p.m., except in July and August when hours are 11 a.m. to 6 p.m. Wednesday is Connoisseurs' Day, when extra rooms are shown and the tour is longer. Admission to the house and grounds on regular days is £2.75 ($4.80) for adults, £1.75 ($3.05) for children, rising to £3.75 ($6.55) for adults and £2 ($3.50) for children on Connoisseurs' Day. The grounds and lake can be visited separately for 50p (90¢) for adults, 25p (45¢) for children. A gift shop, wine shop, and tea room are maintained at Althorp. The present countess helps in the gift shop, and Lord Spencer's own favorite sideline is the excellent cellar and wine shop.

STOKE BRUERNE

On the Grand Union Canal, the **Waterways Museum,** at Stoke Bruerne near Towcester in Northamptonshire (tel. 0604/862229), is just south of the Blisworth Tunnel (take the A508 from the M1 junction 15 on the A5). The three-story grain warehouse has been restored and adapted to give an insight into the working lives of canal boatmen and their families. On display is a full-size replica of a "butty" boat cabin complete with cooking range, brassware, lace curtains, traditional ware, tools, and teapots. There is also an early semidiesel Bolinder boat engine, a boat-weighing machine once used to determine canal toll charges. You can buy posters, books, illustrations of canal life, hand-painted traditional canalware, models, and badges in a shop at the museum. It is open daily from 10 a.m. to 6 p.m.; closed on Monday from October to Easter and open till 4 p.m. Tuesday to Sunday. Admission is £1.20 ($2.10) for adults, 60p ($1.05) for children. A family ticket will cost you £2.75 ($4.80).

The Boat Inn (tel. 0604/862428) started as a row of humble cottages in the 17th century and has gradually progressed without losing its original character. It's still a limestone building with a thatched roof overlooking Grand Union Canal and the Stoke Bruerne Waterways Museum. The public house is the oldest part. It has stone floors and open fires. Bar food is served here. The restaurant offers a full range of dishes, including venison and grouse in season. A three-course meal, finished off with a choice from the dessert trolley or the cheeseboard, then coffee and mints, will cost around £15 ($26.25), including VAT. The "Great British Sunday Lunch," roast beef with Yorkshire pudding of course, costs £7.25 ($12.70) for adults, £4.95 ($8.65) for children. Hours are 11 a.m. to 3 p.m. and 6 to 11 p.m. in summer. The Woodward family has owned and run the Boat Inn since 1877.

Cruises are available on the Woodwards' canal narrow boat, *Indian Chief.* A 25-minute trip to Blisworth Tunnel Mouth and back costs 75p ($1.30) for adults, 50p (90¢) for children. The boat has music, video, a fully stocked bar, soft drinks, tea, coffee, and snacks. You can also hire a chauffeur-driven Rolls-Royce for sightseeing or for airport pick-up, costing £25 ($43.75) per hour.

AT WEEDON

True to its name, the **Crossroads Hotel,** High Street, Weedon, Northamptonshire NN7 4PX (tel. 0327/40354), lies near the M1, the A5, and A45. The owners, Richard and Wendy Amos, have created a little nook where imagination and good taste reign. The clock tower of the hotel, standing in the garden, is a sign of hospitality. Inside there is a collection of old clocks throughout the dining room and lounges. The antique collection in the dining room is enhanced with stuffed fish, horse prints, birds in cages, a Victorian carved sideboard, old bicycles hanging from the ceiling, and etched mirrors. There's a large brick oven, and best of all, excellent meals are offered. The house specialty is "Wendy's famous steak, kidney, and mushroom pie," served with vegetables. A fixed-price menu costs £12 ($21). In the Garden House, 38 first-rate rooms are offered, all with private bath, color TV, trouser press, hairdryer, and tea- and coffee-making equipment. The cost of singles at the hotel is £50 ($87.50) to £55 ($96.25) daily. Doubles range from £60 ($105) to £70 ($122.50). All tariffs include VAT and a full English breakfast. The Parlour serves breakfast, morning coffee, and afternoon tea. The Crossroads is an affiliate of Best Western.

2. Leicestershire

Virtually ignored by most North American tourists, this eastern Midland county was, according to legend, the home of King Lear. Whatever the truth of that, Leicestershire is rich in historical associations. It was at Bosworth Battlefield that the last of the Plantagenet kings, Richard III, was killed in 1485, irrevocably changing the course of English history.

LEICESTER

Although the county town is a busy industrial center, it was once a Roman settlement and has Roman remains and an archeological museum that remind one of those days.

It also has a Norman castle-hall, a period museum, a 15th-century Guildhall (Shakespeare is said to have played here), and many interesting gardens. On the Abbey Park and grounds are the remains of Leicester Abbey, Cardinal Wolsey's grave, a boating lake, paddling pool, riverside walks, ornamental gardens, and an aviary.

For details of guided tours and local excursions, ask at one of the **Tourism & Information Centres:** 2-6 St. Martin's Walk (tel. 0533/511300) or St. Margaret's Bus Station (tel. 0533/532353).

Food and Lodging

Grand Hotel, Granby Street, Leicester, Leicestershire LE1 6ES (tel. 0533/555599), is aptly named indeed. Built in 1898 when no expense was spared, the interior decoration is magnificent, oak and mahogany paneling abound, and the welcome matches the setting, with the emphasis placed on making your stay as comfortable as possible and offering you good value for money. In the Grand Carving Room, decorated in a '20s style, you can choose from succulent joints of meat generously carved by the chef to satisfy the heartiest appetite. The refurbished bedrooms have a bright, cheery decor, and all have private bath and color TV. Singles cost from £55 ($96.25) daily, and twins from £75 ($131.25).

On the Outskirts

Rothley Court Hotel, Westfield Lane, Rothley, Leicester, Leicestershire LE7 7LG (tel. 0533/374141), is five miles north of Leicester on the B5328 road, just off the A6 between Leicester and Loughborough. The hotel is on the edge of Charnwood Forest, a royal hunting ground for centuries and in the heart of the Quorn hunting area. In 1231, Henry III granted the manor and "soke" (right to hold court under feudal law) to the Knights Templar. The chapel erected next to the existing abbey around 1240 is believed to be second only to the Temple in London as the best-preserved Templar chapel in Britain. In the 16th century the Babington family bought the place, and this may be the only estate of that family to remain intact after discovery of the so-called Babington plot to overthrow Elizabeth I and put Mary Queen of Scots on the English throne. Images of Nubian slaves in the coffee lounge and on the half-landing above reflect the family's association with Kitchener of Khartoum. The hotel offers bedrooms with color TVs, radios, and direct-dial phones, as well as modern baths. Singles rent for £55 ($96.25) daily, and doubles or twins for £70 ($122.50), all tariffs including a full English breakfast and VAT. There are comfortable lounges and a bar overlooking the gardens on down to the brook. A set luncheon costs £12 ($21), while dinner goes for around £18 ($31.50), VAT included.

TOURING THE COUNTRY

As long as people continue to read Sir Walter Scott's *Ivanhoe,* they will remember **Ashby-de-la-Zouch,** a town that retains a pleasant country atmosphere. Mary Queen of Scots was imprisoned in an ancient castle here.

Belvoir Castle

On the northern border of Leicestershire overlooking the Vale of Belvoir (pronounced "beaver"), Belvoir Castle has been the seat of the dukes of Rutland since the time of Henry VIII. Rebuilt by Wyatt in 1816, the castle contains paintings by Holbein, Reynolds, and Gainsborough, as well as tapestries in its magnificent state rooms. Seven miles west-southwest of Grantham, between the A607 to Melton Mowbray and the A52 to Nottingham, the castle was the location of the movies *Little Lord Fauntleroy* and Steven Spielberg's *Young Sherlock Holmes,* and in summer it is the site of medieval jousting tournaments. From late March to early October, it is open from 11 a.m. to 6 p.m. on Tuesday, Wednesday, Thursday, and Saturday, plus Friday in June, July, and August. On Sunday, hours are from 11 a.m. to 7 p.m. During October, it is open only on Saturday and Sunday, from noon to 6 p.m. Admission is £2.60 ($4.55) for adults, £1.50 ($2.65) for children. Further details are available from Jimmy Durrands, Estate Office, Belvoir Castle, Grantham, Lincolnshire (tel. 0476/870262).

The Bosworth Battlefield

Bosworth Battlefield Visitor Centre & Country Park, Sutton Cheney, Market Bosworth, Leicestershire (tel. 0455/290429), lies between the M1 and the M6, close to Nuneaton. The 1485 battle it commemorates is considered one of England's three most important battles (the other two are the one at Hastings in 1066 and the Battle of Britain in 1940). The Battle of Bosworth ended the War of the Roses between the Houses of York and Lancaster, with the death of King Richard III, last of the Plantagenets, and the proclaiming as king the victor, Henry Tudor, a Welsh nobleman who had been banished to France to thwart his ambition. Henry landed in Wales at Milford Haven and marched cross-country to Leicester where King Richard was encamped, defeated the monarch, and became King Henry VII, first of the Tudor dynasty. Today the appropriate standards fly where the opponents had their positions, and in a 1¼-mile walk, you can see the whole scene of the battle. In the center are exhibitions, models, book and gift shops, a cafeteria, and a film theater where an audio-visual introduction, with an excerpt from the Lord Laurence Olivier film of Shakespeare's *Richard III* is presented.

The center is open from Easter to the end of October from 2 to 5:30 p.m. Monday to Saturday, from 1 to 6 p.m. Sunday and bank holiday Mondays. Admission to the exhibition is £1.20 ($2.10) for adults, 80p ($1.40) for children. The battle trails can be visited all year without charge during daylight hours. Special medieval attractions are held in July, August, and September. Special charges apply on main event days.

Melton Mowbray

Other interesting towns to visit in Leicestershire include Melton Mowbray, a market town that claims to be the original home of Stilton cheese and is renowned for its pork pies.

The **Melton Carnegie Museum,** Thorpe End (tel. 0664/69946), depicts the past and present life of the area, with special exhibits on Stilton cheese and Melton pork pies. It's open Easter to September from 10 a.m. to 5 p.m. Monday to Saturday, from 2 to 5 p.m. on Sunday. October to Easter, hours are 10 a.m. to 4:30 p.m. Monday to Friday and 10:30 a.m. to 4 p.m. on Saturday. Closed Christmas Day, Boxing Day, January 1, and Good Friday.

Hambleton Hall, Hambleton, Leicestershire LE15 8TH (tel. 0572/56991), three miles east of Oakham by the A606 road, stands on a promontory of Rutland Water, a huge man-made lake. Hambleton Hall is a century-old house built as a hunting box, now restored to a high standard of luxury and comfort. Tim and Stefa Hart run their *Relais & Châteaux* hotel more like a country home. It's a lovely, calm place, comfortably decorated and furnished, and kept supplied with fresh flowers. Terraced gardens run down to the water. The bedrooms, all with phones, radios, and color TVs, as well as private baths, cost from £100 ($175) daily for two, from £75 ($131.25) for singles. A continental breakfast is included in the rates. Guests can relax in the comfortable lounge or small bar and enjoy meals in the large dining room with fresh napery, crystal, and bright silver. A set dinner costs £25 ($43.75).

3. Derbyshire

The most magnificent scenery in the Midlands is found within the borders of this county, lying between Nottinghamshire and Staffordshire. Derbyshire has been less defaced by industry than its neighbors. The north of the county, containing the **Peak District National Park,** is by far the most exciting for touring, as it contains waterfalls, hills, moors, green valleys, and dales. In the south the land is more level, and the look becomes, in places, one of pastoral meadows.

Some tourists avoid this part of the country, because it is ringed by the industrial sprawl of Manchester, Leeds, Sheffield, and Derby. To do so, however, would be a pity, and this part of England contains the rugged peaks and leafy dales that merit a substantial detour, especially Dovedale, Chee Dale, and Millers Dale.

HISTORIC HOMES

Near Bakewell, ten miles north of Matlock, stands one of the great country houses of England, **Chatsworth,** the home of the 11th Duke of Devonshire and his Duchess, the former Deborah Mitford (sister of Nancy and Jessica). With its lavishly decorated interiors and a wealth of art treasures, it takes in 175 rooms, the most spectacular of which are open to the public. Visiting hours are 11:30 a.m. to 4:30 p.m. daily from March to October (tel. 024688/2204 for information). Admission to the house and garden is £3.75 ($6.55) for adults and £1.90 ($3.35) for children. On this spot the eccentric Bess of Hardwick built a house, which eventually held Mary Queen of Scots prisoner upon orders of Queen Elizabeth I. Most of that structure was torn down, and the present building, with many, many additions, dates from 1686. Capability Brown (who seems to have been everywhere) worked on the landscaping at one time. But it was Joseph Paxton, the gardener to the sixth duke, who turned the garden into one of the most celebrated in Europe. Queen Victoria and Prince Albert were lavishly entertained here in 1843. The house contains a great library and such paintings as the *Adoration of the Magi* by Veronese and *King Uzziah* by Rembrandt. On the grounds you can see spectacular fountains, and there is a playground for children in the farmyard.

Hardwick Hall (tel. 0246/850430) lies 9½ miles southeast of Chesterfield. The approach from M1 is at Junction 29. The house was built in 1597 for Bess of Hardwick, a woman who acquired four husbands and an estate from each of them. It is particularly noted for its architecture ("more glass than wall"). The High Great Chamber and Long Gallery crown an unparalleled series of late 16th-century interiors, including an important collection of tapestries, needlework, and furniture. The house is surrounded by a 300-acre country park, which is open daily all year. Walled gardens, orchards, and an herb garden are just part of its attractions. The house is open from the first of April until the end of October on Wednesday, Thursday, Saturday, and Sunday from 1 to 5:30 p.m. Admission to the hall and garden is £4 ($7) for adults and £2 ($3.50) for children.

Melbourne Hall, at Melbourne (tel. 0332/862502), eight miles south of Derby, originally built by the bishops of Carlisle (1133), stands in one of the most famous formal gardens in Britain. The ecclesiastical structure was restored in the 1600s by one of the cabinet ministers of Charles I and enlarged by Queen Anne's vice chamberlain. It was the home of Lord Melbourne, who was prime minister when Victoria ascended to the throne. He was born William Lamb, and Melbourne Hall was also the home of Lord Byron's friend, Lady Caroline Lamb. Lady Palmerston later inherited the house, which contains an important collection of pictures, antique furniture, and works of art. A special feature is the beautifully restored wrought-iron pergola by Robert Bakewell, noted 18th-century ironsmith. The house is open from 2 to 5 p.m. daily in August, except on August 7, 14, and 21. Admission is £1.50 ($2.65) for adults, 75p ($1.30) for children. The garden can be visited on Wednesday, Saturday, Sunday, and bank holiday Mondays from 2 to 6 p.m. April to September. Admission to the garden is £1 ($1.75).

OTHER PLACES TO SEE

In addition to majestic scenery, you may want to seek out the following sights.
Royal Crown Derby, 194 Osmaston Rd., in Derby (tel. 0332/47051). In case this is your special favorite in the pottery world, I suggest a trip into the center of Derby to take the two-hour tour of the only factory allowed to use both the words "royal" and "crown" in its name, a double honor granted by George III and Queen Victoria. At the end of the tour, you can treat yourself to a bargain in the gift shop and visit the Royal Crown Derby Museum, which is open from 9 a.m. to 12:30 p.m. and 1:30 to 4 p.m. Monday to Friday. Tours, lasting 1½ hours, take place at 10:30 a.m. and 1:45 p.m. Monday to Friday, costing £1.50 ($2.65).

National Tramway Museum, Crich, near Matlock (tel. 077385/2565). One young 70-year-old whom I know spends as much of his free time as his wife will allow in this paradise of vintage trams—electric, steam, and horse-drawn from home and overseas, including New York. Your admission ticket is £2.70 ($4.75) for adults and £1.50 ($2.65) for children. This ticket allows you unlimited rides on trams, which make the two-mile round trip to Glory Mine with scenic views over the Derwent Valley via Wakebridge, where a stop is made to visit the Peak District Mines Historical Society display of lead mining. It also includes admission to various tramway exhibitions and displays and to the tramway period street, an ongoing project. Hours are 10 a.m. to about 6 p.m. It's open Saturday and Sunday and bank holidays from early April to November, also Monday to Thursday from early May to early November, and also on Friday from mid-July to early September.

Peak District Mining Museum, The Pavilion, Matlock Bath (tel. 0629/583834), is open daily throughout the year except Christmas Day from 11 a.m. to 4 p.m. (later in high season). Admission is 80p ($1.40) for adults, 50p (90¢) for children. The exhibition traces 2,000 years of Derbyshire lead mining and has as its centerpiece a giant water-pressure engine that was used to pump water from a lead mine in the early 19th century. It was recovered from a chamber 360 feet underground by members of the society. A popular feature for young visitors is a simulated mine level and climbing shaft through which they can crawl.

BUXTON

One of the loveliest towns in Britain, Buxton was developed in the 18th century to rival the spa at Bath. However, long before that its waters were known to the Romans, whose settlement here was called Aquae Arnemetiae. The thermal waters were pretty much forgotten after that until the reign of Queen Elizabeth I, when the baths were reactivated, and even Mary Queen of Scots was brought here by her caretaker, the Earl of Shrewsbury, to "take the waters." Buxton today is mostly the result of the 18th-century development carried out under direction of the Duke of Devonshire.

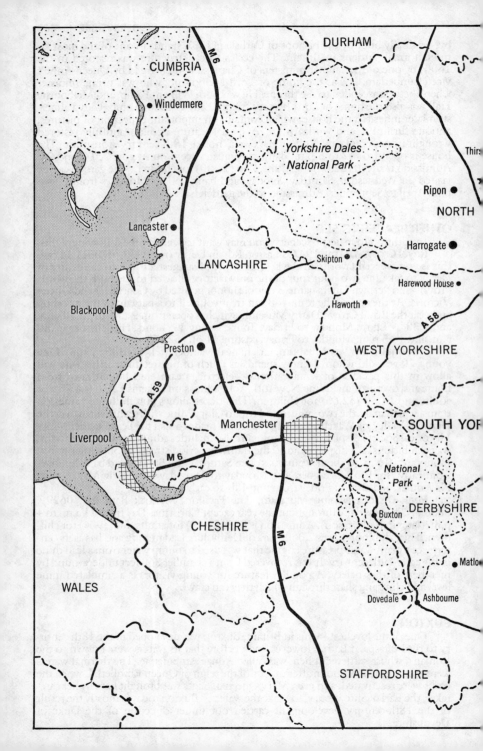

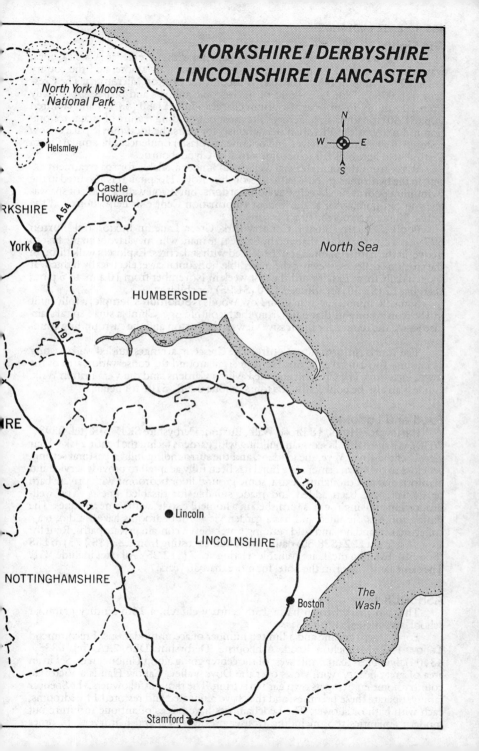

YORKSHIRE / DERBYSHIRE
LINCOLNSHIRE / LANCASTER

North York Moors
National Park

Helmsley

Castle
Howard

RKSHIRE

A 5A

York

North Sea

A 19

HUMBERSIDE

RE

A 1

A 19

Lincoln

LINCOLNSHIRE

NOTTINGHAMSHIRE

The
Wash

Boston

Stamford

The Sights

The Crescent, modeled on the one in Bath but with more elegant classical lines, was originally a hotel complex, but it is now occupied by a hotel and the county library. The Pump Room of the spa has become the **Buxton Micrarium,** The Crescent (tel. 0298/78662), a world of microscopic animals and plants. Open daily from 10 a.m. to 5 p.m., the Micrarium charges adults £1.80 ($3.15) and children 90p ($1.60) for admission. Perhaps the most outstanding feature of recent restoration in Buxton is the Victorian opera house, for years the local movie palace, now restored in all its marble, velvet, and ornamental plaster opulence. The annual Opera Festival held here bids fair to become a rival of Glyndebourne.

Water from the nine thermal wells is no longer available for spa treatment except in the hydrotherapy pool at the Devonshire Royal Hospital. It is also used in the swimming pool at the 23-acre **Pavilion Gardens,** but if you want a drink of spa water, you can purchase it at the Tourist Information Centre or help yourself at the public fountain across the street.

Poole's Cavern, Buxton Country Park, Green Lane, in Buxton (tel. Buxton 6978), is a cave that was inhabited by Stone Age man, who may have been the first to marvel at the natural vaulted roof bedecked with stalactites. Explorers walk through the spacious galleries, viewing the incredible horizontal cave, electrically lighted. It is open daily from Easter until the first week in November from 10 a.m. to 5 p.m., charging £2 ($3.50) for adults, £1.10 ($1.95) for children.

Some 20 minutes away in Grin Low Woods is **Solomon's Temple,** a folly built in 1895 on a tumulus that dates from the Neolithic Age. Climb a small spiral staircase inside the temple for impressive views over Buxton and the surrounding country.

The **Tourist Information Centre,** The Crescent, arranges guided walks lasting 1½ hours. You can take the Spa Heritage Trail around the conservation area of the town, including The Crescent and the Pavilion Gardens, and the Vera Britten Walk. Guides can also be booked for bus tours. Phone 0298/5106 for details.

Food and Lodging

Hartington Hotel, 18 Broad Walk, Buxton, Derbyshire SK17 6JR (tel. 0298/2638), is a substantial Georgian building with gardens facing the boating lake. Your view is of the River Wye, the gardens, and the surrounding hills, a pastoral setting, yet close to the town center. The hotel has been fully adapted to provide service and comfort, and as a thoughtful extra, some ground-floor bedrooms with private bath or shower have been added and made suitable for disabled guests. The well-proportioned living room is furnished in a homelike style, with some antiques. The dining room is dignified and has a garden view. All bedrooms have a radio, tea/coffee-maker, and hot and cold running water. Seven contain private baths. Rent for a single starts at £22 ($38.50) daily, with doubles costing from £33 ($57.75) to £38 ($66.50). Evening meals are available starting at £7 ($12.25). All rates include VAT. The same family has run the hotel for more than 30 years.

ASHBOURNE

This old market town has a 13th-century church, a 16th-century grammar school, and ancient almshouses.

For a superb cuisine and a limited number of accommodations, I recommend **Callow Hall,** Mappelton Road, Ashbourne, Derbyshire DE6 2AA (tel. 0335/43404), lying less than a mile west of the center going along Union Street. Set in an area of great beauty, with views over the Dove Valley, Callow Hall is a Victorian country home enjoying its own garden setting. The thoughtful owners, the Spencer family, operate these premises, and they have renovated and restored 11 bedrooms, each with bath or shower. The bedchambers have pieces of antique furniture but modern amenities too, including trouser presses, TVs, and hairdryers. In other words, you'll be looking good as you make your appearance in the dining room, one of the most outstanding in the area. The family has long been known in Ashbourne as bakers, and naturally their expertise is reflected in their dessert menu. However, appetizers and main meat courses get equal billing here. Lamb appears in imaginative ways and, in season, you can also order jugged hare. It is open Tuesday to Saturday for dinner from 7:30 to 9:30 p.m. and on Sunday for lunch from 12:30 to 2:30 p.m. A set lunch ranges in price from £9 ($15.75) to £11 ($19.25), with dinners costing from £17.50 ($30.65). The food is mainly continental with good, fresh British ingredients.

DOVEDALE

Overhung by limestone crags, this beautiful wooded valley forms part of the Peak District National Park, with its views of Thorpe Cloud, a conical hill 900 feet high. It's best explored on foot. Fishermen know of its River Dove trout stream, because of its associations with such anglers as Izaak Walton and Charles Cotton. One is honored by the hotel named after him (previewed below).

The **Izaak Walton Hotel,** Dovedale, Thorpe, Derbyshire DE6 2AY (tel. 033529/555), is a comfortable hotel in what was originally a 17th-century farmhouse. Most of the rooms have private bath, and the views over the dales and peaks of Derbyshire are unsurpassed. This is ideal rambling country, with Dovedale spreading before you. All the bedrooms have baths and have been recently refurbished. A single costs £53.50 ($93.65) daily; a double, £88 ($154). These tariffs include service, an English breakfast, and VAT. A table d'hôte luncheon costs £8.50 ($14.90) and a set dinner £12.50 ($21.90). This country is for the fisherman, but if that's not your sport, it is a good center for touring, with Haddon Hall, Chatsworth House, and Hardwick Hall, to name but a few, lying within easy reach.

FOOD AND LODGING ELSEWHERE IN DERBYSHIRE

An Elizabethan mansion house, **Riber Hall,** Riber, Matlock, Derbyshire DE4 5JU (tel. 0629/582795), three miles southeast of Matlock by the A615, is owned and operated by the Biggin family. The symmetrically gabled, stone-walled structure is ringed with acres of lawns and forests, with a walled garden closer in where guests can contemplate the foothills of the Pennines. The house was built in the 1400s, and by the 1970s it was so derelict it required massive restoration. Each of the 11 bedrooms is attractively furnished with antiques, chintz, mullioned windows, and appropriate accessories. Wedgwood bone china and cut glass are used throughout. Most units have exposed beams and carved Jacobean four-poster beds. Each has a private bath, fresh flowers, and baskets of fruit, and five have whirlpool baths. Singles cost from £53 ($92.75) daily, and doubles, from £68 ($119), with a continental breakfast included. A rather formal, elegant restaurant with an intricately carved oak mantelpiece serves outstanding meals accompanied with a selection of fine wines. Typical dishes include French-inspired versions of crêpes stuffed with foie gras, breast of partridge in puff pastry, fresh trout and salmon, and scallops with ginger. À la carte meals cost from £22 ($38.50). Guests play on an all-weather tennis court.

Rutland Arms Hotel, The Square, Bakewell, Derbyshire DE4 1BT (tel. 062981/2812), is a lovely old listed early Georgian hotel on the edge of this bustling market town. Jane Austen stayed here working on the revision of her manuscript of *Pride and Prejudice*. The most glamorous accommodation in the hotel is named after her. There is a comfortable lounge and bar, and the Four Seasons Restaurant has an excellent local reputation. All the dishes are made with fresh local produce and include local game in season. The menu lists soufflés, fresh seafood, and a vegetarian section. The chef's specialty is leg of lamb stuffed with a mushroom and ham duxelle in a pastry case, and of course, for dessert you can order the famous Bakewell pudding, created by accident in the hotel kitchens a long time ago and still prepared using a secret recipe. A number of the hotel's 36 rooms are in the courtyard. All accommodations have private baths. The charge is £40 ($70) daily in a single and £50 ($87.50) in a double, including a full English breakfast and VAT.

Cavendish Hotel, Baslow, Bakewell, Derbyshire DE4 1SP (tel. 024688/2311), built as the celebrated Peacock Inn in the 1780s, was restored in 1975 and extended in 1984. It has 23 well-equipped bedrooms, a commendable dining room, and drawing rooms with roaring log fires. The hotel is personally managed by its owner, Eric Marsh, and run by his professional staff. The Cavendish is set on the Duke of Devonshire's Chatsworth estate. You look out upon the cavern-filled Derbyshire Peak District from your room, which has such amenities as TV, clock-radio, private bar, bathroom, and shower. All rooms have twin or double beds and rent for £62.50 ($109.40) to £70 ($122.50) daily. Lunch or dinner costs £18 ($31.50) to £25 ($43.75). In the newer wing of the hotel, for which the builders found secondhand stone to match exactly that in the original old fishing inn, the Mitford Rooms were named to honor the Duchess of Devonshire, each unit named after members of her Mitford family: Deborah, Diana, Jessica, Lucy, Nancy, Pamela, Sydney, Unity, Valkyrie, and Vivian. The dutchess did the original Cavendish in 1975 and its sister hotel, the Devonshire Arms, at Bolton Abbey in 1981, borrowing furnishings from Chatsworth and also having much of the furniture made by hand in the Chatsworth workshop.

---

4. Nottinghamshire

"Notts," as it is called, was the country of Robin Hood and Lord Byron. It is also Lawrence country, as the English novelist, author of *Sons and Lovers* and *Lady Chatterley's Lover,* was also from here, born at Eastwood.

Sherwood Forest is probably the most famous woodland in the world. It isn't the green haven it used to be, but it did provide in its time excellent cover for its world-famous bandit and his band, Robin Hood and his Merry Men, including Friar Tuck and Little John. Actually very little of it was forest, even in its heyday. The area consists of woodland glades, fields, and agricultural land, along with villages and hamlets.

The **Sherwood Forest Visitor Centre,** Sherwood Forest Country Park at Edwinstowe (tel. 0623/823202), near Mansfield, stands in the area just by the Major Oak, popularly known as Robin Hood's tree. It's in the center of many marked walks and footpaths through the woodland. There's an exhibition of life-size models of Robin and the other well-known outlaws, as well as a shop with books, gifts, and souvenirs. The center, some 18 miles north of Nottingham city off the A614, will provide as much information as remains about Friar Tuck and Little John, along with Maid Marian and Alan-a-Dale, as well as the other Merry Men. Little John's grave can be seen at Hathersage, Will Scarlet's at Blidworth. Robin Hood is believed to have married Maid Marian at Edwinstowe Church, close to the Visitors Centre. The Major Oak nearby (mentioned above) is 30 feet in circumference, so that outlaws could easily have hidden in the hollow trunk.

Robin Hood's Larder offers light snacks and meals, with an emphasis on traditional English country recipes, appropriately named. It is open at various hours, depending on the center's opening days and times, but food and drinks are available from machines when the restaurant is closed.

There is a full program of events taking place on the center site and in the area. The center also contains a **Tourist Information Centre,** one of the national network in England. It's open daily from 11 a.m. to 5 p.m. in April. From May to September the hours are 11 a.m. to 5 p.m. Monday to Saturday, to 6:30 p.m. on Sunday. In March and October, it's open Tuesday to Thursday and on Saturday and Sunday from 11:30 a.m. to 4 p.m., while in January and February, it is open only on Saturday and Sunday at those same hours.

NOTTINGHAM

The county town is a busy industrial city, 121 miles north of London. On the north bank of the Trent, Nottingham is one of the most pleasant cities in the Midlands.

The Sights

Overlooking the city, **Nottingham Castle** was built by the Duke of Newcastle on the site of a Norman fortress in 1679. After restoration in 1878, it was opened as a provincial museum (tel. 0602/483504), surrounded by a charmingly laid-out garden. See, in particular, the History of Nottingham Gallery, the ceramics, and the collection of medieval Nottingham alabaster carvings. The works of Nottingham-born artists are displayed in the first-floor gallery, and you can purchase top-quality regional crafts in the museum shop. The castle is open all year, except Christmas Day, from April to September, daily from 10 a.m. to 5:45 p.m. Other months its hours are 10 a.m. to 4:45 p.m. daily from October to March. Admission is free except on Sunday and bank holidays, when adults pay 20p (35¢) and children 10p (20¢).

For 50p (90¢) you'll be taken on a conducted tour at the castle of **Mortimer's Hole** and underground passages. King Edward III is said to have led a band of noblemen through these secret passages, surprising Roger Mortimer and the queen, killing Mortimer, and putting his lady in prison. A statue of Robin Hood stands at the base of the castle.

The **Brewhouse Yard Museum** consists of five 17th-century cottages at the foot of Castle Rock, presenting a panorama of Nottingham life in a series of furnished rooms and shops. Some of them, open from cellar to attic, have much local history material on open display, and visitors are encouraged to handle these exhibits. The most interesting features are in a series of cellars cut into the rock of the castle instead of below the houses, plus an exhibition of a Nottingham shopping street, 1919–1939, with 11 shops for services that are local to the city. This is not a typical folk museum, but attempts to be as lively as possible, involving both visitors and the Nottingham community in expanding displays and altering exhibitions on a bimonthly basis. Open all year, the admission-free museum (tel. 0602/483504, ext. 48) may be visited from 10 a.m. to 5 p.m. It is closed Christmas Day.

An elegant row of Georgian terraced houses, the **Museum of Costume and Textiles,** 51 Castle Gate (tel. 0602/411881), presents costumes from the 18th century to about 1960 in period settings, textiles, embroideries, and lace (one of the city's industries). You'll see everything from the 1632 Eyre map tapestries of Nottinghamshire to "fallals and frippery." The admission-free museum is open daily from 10 a.m. to 5 p.m.

On the outskirts of Nottingham, at Ravenshead, **Newstead Abbey** (tel. 0623/793557) was once Lord Byron's home. It lies 11 miles north of Nottingham on the A60 (the Mansfield road). Some of the original Augustinian priory, bought by Sir John Byron in 1540, still survives. In the 19th century the mansion was given a neo-Gothic restoration. Mementos, including first editions and manuscripts, are displayed inside, and later you can explore a parkland of some 300 acres, with waterfalls, rose gardens, a Monk's Stew Pond, and a Japanese water garden. Admission to the grounds and gardens is 85p ($1.50) for adults, 40p (70¢) for children. To visit the abbey, the charge is $1.20 ($2.10) for adults, 20p (35¢) for children. The abbey is open from Good Friday to September 30 daily from 11:30 a.m. to 6 p.m. (last entrance at 5 p.m.). The gardens are open daily all year from 10 a.m. to dusk.

Also on the outskirts of Nottingham, **Wollaton Hall** (tel. 0602/281333) is a well-preserved Elizabethan mansion, the most ornate in England (finished in 1588), housing a natural history museum, with lots of insects, invertebrates, British mammals, birds, reptiles, amphibians, and fish. The mansion is open April to September daily from 10 a.m. to 7 p.m. (on Sunday from 2 to 5 p.m.). From October to

March, daily hours are 10 a.m. to dusk (from 1:30 to 4:30 p.m. on Sunday); closed Christmas Day. Admission is free except on Sunday and bank holidays. The hall is surrounded by a Deer Park and gardens. See the camellia house with the world's earliest (1823) cast-iron front. The bird dioramas here are among the best in Britain.

Food and Lodging

Albany Hotel, St. James's Street, Nottingham, Nottinghamshire NG1 6BN (tel. 0602/470131), is a large tower block of 160 bedrooms in the heart of the city. Flanked by multistory car parks, it offers good rooms, each with private bath, double-glazed windows, air conditioning, and central heating, as well as color TV, radio, direct-dial phone, and coffee-making facilities. Singles rent for £60 ($105) to £70 ($122.50) nightly and doubles go for £75 ($131.25) to £150 ($262.50). In the hotel's Carvery, guests can carve as much as they wish from hot and cold joints, or else patronize the more expensive Four Seasons, which, in honor of its namesakes, changes its menu and floral decorations quarterly. Along with seasonal specialties, continental dishes are featured. The Forum, the lounge and cocktail bar, is another rendezvous.

Savoy Hotel, 296 Mansfield Rd., Nottingham, Nottinghamshire NG5 2BT (tel. 0602/602621), stands on the A60 Nottingham–Mansfield road, a little less than a mile from the city center. A bustling, modern hotel, it is well maintained and run, and there's plenty of room to park your car. Attracting business people (and likely to be heavily booked on weekdays), it offers well-furnished, streamlined rooms for £45 ($78.75) daily in a single, £60 ($105) in a double, including private baths with showers, color TVs, radios, direct-dial phones, hot beverage facilities, trouser presses, and hairdryers. Have a before-dinner drink in the Savoy Bar, featuring glass domes and floral displays, before dining in the Steak Bars or the Colonial Restaurant. A meal in either costs from about £8.50 ($14.90).

Strathdon Thistle Hotel, 44 Derby Rd., Nottingham, Nottinghamshire NG1 5FT (tel. 0602/418501), a favorite of traveling business people, lies about five miles from the M1, in the center of the city. Of the 69 bedrooms (the majority of which are singles), 23 come with private tile bath, the rest with shower, although all have color TV, phone, radio, and coffee-making facilities. Singles cost £53 ($92.75) to £58 ($101.50), and doubles or twins go for £67 ($117.25) to £74 ($129.50). The rate depends on the day of the week, Saturday and Sunday being cheaper. Some rooms have shower only. Drinks are ordered in the Boston Bean Co. bar, a combination of an American saloon and a diner. In the hotel's restaurant, a good table d'hôte evening meal costs from £12 ($21), a set luncheon for £9 ($15.75), or you can order à la carte. The cuisine consists of some international dishes, along with traditional English fare.

Shogun, 95 Talbot St. (tel. 0602/475611). Someone, anybody, just had to come up with a name like this for a Japanese restaurant. Shogun is considered the leading restaurant in the Nottingham district. Yet, unlike the prices in Japan, the tariffs here are very reasonable. For example, a table d'hôte lunch goes for only £5.45 ($9.55), a set dinner costing from £11.60 ($20.30). Of course, you can spend a lot more by ordering à la carte. Service is Monday to Saturday from noon to 1:45 p.m. and 7 to 11 p.m. The chef is also the owner: Keiji Tomiyama. While admiring the samurai armor, you can order the classic dishes of the Japanese kitchen. The menu offers an imaginative choice of interesting, well-prepared dishes such as sashimi and sushi. You can also order beef, chicken, or fish teriyaki. Service is the most professional in the city. The location *could* be more convenient. It's on a road leading out of the city in the direction of the motorway (the M1) in a red-brick turn-of-the-century warehouse setting with a sophisticated decor.

SOUTHWELL

This ancient market town, about a half-hour drive from Lord Byron's Newstead Abbey, is a good center for exploring the Robin Hood country. Byron once belonged to a local amateur dramatic society here. An unexpected gem is the old twin-spired cathedral, **Southwell Minster,** which many consider the most beautiful church in England. James I found that it held up with "any other kirk in Christendom." Look for the well-proportioned Georgian houses across from the cathedral.

Saracen's Head, Market Place, Southwell, Nottinghamshire NG25 0HE (tel. 0636/812701), is a historic coaching inn, where both Charles I and James I dined. In fact, Charles I was made a prisoner here before the Scots handed him over to the Parliamentarians. After he was beheaded, the name of the inn was changed from King's Arms to Saracen's Head. Commanding the junction of the main ancient thoroughfares of the town, the old hostelry also frequently entertained Byron. Today the inn still has an old atmosphere, such as cozy bars with exposed beams and paneling. From the cellar emerges a selection of wines to complement meals, offered in the restaurant from both an à la carte and a table d'hôte menu. The redecorated and refurbished bedrooms contain a private bath with shower, TV, radio, and phone. Doubles cost from £65 ($113.75) daily, and singles rent for £50 ($87.50), including service and VAT.

East of Southwell, near the Lincolnshire border, is—

NEWARK-ON-TRENT

Here is an ancient riverside market town, on the Roman Fosse Way, lying about 15 miles across flatlands from Nottingham. King John died at **Newark Castle** in 1216. Constructed between the 12th and 15th centuries, the castle—now in ruins—survived three sieges by Cromwell's troops before falling into decay in 1646. From its parapet, you can look down on the Trent River and across to Nottingham. The delicately detailed parish church here is said to be the finest in the country. The town contains many ancient inns, reflecting its long history.

On the banks of the River Trent, a short walk from Newark Castle, is **Millgate Folk Museum** (tel. 0636/79403), in a building that housed a 19th-century oil-seed mill and then a warehouse. Today it contains portrayals of social and industrial life in the area from the turn of the century to World War II. Agricultural, malting, and printing implements are displayed, and a series of furnished rooms depicts domestic life in those times. The museum, for which there is no admission fee, is open from 10 a.m. to 5 p.m. Monday to Friday all year and from 1 to 5 p.m. on Saturday, Sunday, and bank holidays.

THE DUKERIES

In the Dukeries, portions of Sherwood Forest, legendarily associated with Robin Hood, are still preserved. These are vast country estates on the edge of industrial towns. Most of the estates have disappeared, but the park at **Clumber**—covering some 4,000 acres—is administered by the National Trust, which has preserved its 18th-century beauty, as exemplified by Lime Tree Avenue. Rolling heaths and a peaceful lake add to the charm. You can see **Clumber Chapel,** built in 1886–1889 as a chapel for the seventh Duke of Newcastle. It is open from 10 a.m. to 5 p.m. daily except Christmas Day. There is no admission charge, but entry costs £1.50 ($2.65) for cars, £2.50 ($4.40) for minibuses and house trailers. There are stables with a stable tower clock dated 1763, a classical bridge over the lake, lodges, and pleasure grounds, as well as fishing, bicycle rental, a shop, and a restaurant. The park is open all year. Clumber Park is five miles southeast of Clumber Park Stableyard, Workshop, close to the A1 (tel. 0909/476592).

EASTWOOD

Because of the increased interest in D. H. Lawrence these days, many literary fans like to make a pilgrimage to Eastwood, his hometown. The English novelist was born there on September 11, 1885. Mrs. Brown, a member of the D. H. Lawrence Society, conducts parties of visitors around the "Lawrence country," hoping, at the end, they'll make a donation to the society. If you're interested in taking a tour, write her in advance—Mrs. M. Brown, D. H. Lawrence Society, c/o 8a Victoria St., Eastwood, Nottingham (tel. 0773/718139).

The Victoria Street address is the Lawrence birthplace, which has been turned into the **D. H. Lawrence Information Centre** and **Museum** (tel. 0773/763312), now authentically depicting a miner's home as it was in 1885, with an audio-visual presentation. The Eastwood Library houses a unique collection of Lawrence's works and the headstone from his grave on the French Riviera. The museum is open daily April to October from 10 a.m. to 5 p.m., November to March from 10 a.m. to 4 p.m.; closed Christmas Eve to New Year's Day. Admission is 50p (90¢) for adults, 25p (45¢) for children.

SCROOBY

This is a tiny village of some 260 inhabitants where in 1566 William Brewster, a leader of the Pilgrim Fathers, was born. His father was bailiff of the manor and master of the postes, so it may have been in the Manor House that the infant Brewster first saw the light of day. The original house dated from the 12th century, and the present manor farm, built on the site in the 18th century, has little except historical association to attract.

Brewster Cottage, with its pinfold where stray animals were impounded, lies beside the village church of St. Wilfred. But it's uncertain whether the Pilgrim father ever lived there.

The village also contains Monks Mill on the River Ryton, now almost a backwater but once a navigable stream down which Brewster and his companions may have escaped to travel to Leyden in Holland and on to their eventual freedom.

In the 18th century the turnpike ran through the village, and there are many stories of highwaymen, robberies, and murders. The body of one John Spencer hung for more than 60 years as a reminder of the penalties of wrongdoing. He'd attempted to dispose of the bodies of the keeper of the Scrooby tollbar and his mother in the river.

Search for Pilgrim Roots

Many North Americans who trace their ancestry to the Pilgrim Fathers come to this part of England to see where it all started. The Separatist Movement had its origin in an area north of Nottingham and south of York, and the towns from which its members came are all in a small area. They include **Blyth** (the one in Nottinghamshire, not the one in Northumberland), **Scrooby, Austerfield, Bawtry,** and **Babworth.** Besides William Brewster, who is identified with Scrooby, as mentioned above, there's also William Bradford, who was born in a manor house in Austerfield, lived in and well maintained today. It can be visited by arrangement with the occupant. The churches at Scrooby and Babworth welcome North Americans.

Blyth is the most beautiful of the villages, with a green surrounded by well-kept old houses, looking a lot like a New England village, which is no surprise. The parish church was developed from the 11th-century nave of a Benedictine priory church. On the green is a 12th-century stone building which was once the Hospital of St. John.

---

5. Lincolnshire

This large East Midlands county is bordered on one side by the North Sea. Its most interesting section is Holland, in the southeast, a land known for its fields of tulips, its marshes and fens, and windmills reminiscent of the Netherlands. Although much of the shire is interesting to explore, time is too important for most visitors to linger long. Foreign tourists, particularly North Americans, generally cross the tulip fields, scheduling stopovers in the busy port of Boston before making the swing north to the cathedral city of Lincoln, lying inland.

BOSTON

This old seaport in the riding of Holland has a namesake that has gone on to greater glory, and perhaps for this reason it is visited by New Englanders. At Scotia Creek, on a riverbank near Boston, is a memorial to the early Pilgrims who made an unsuccessful attempt in 1607 to reach the promised land. They were imprisoned in the Guildhall in cells that can be visited today. A company left again in 1620—and fared better, as anybody who has ever been to Massachusetts will testify. Part of the ritual here is climbing the **Boston Stump,** a church lantern tower with a view for miles around of the all-encircling fens. In the 1930s the people of Boston, U.S.A., paid for the restoration of the tower, known officially as St. Botolph's Tower. Actually, it's not recommended that you climb the tower, as the stairs aren't in good shape. The tower, as it stands, was finished in 1460. The city fathers were going to add a spire, making it the tallest in England. But because of the wind and the weight, they feared the tower would collapse. Therefore, the tower became known as "the Boston Stump." An elderly gentleman at the tower assured me it was the tallest in England —that is, 272½ feet tall. Boston is 116 miles north from London, and 34 miles southeast of Lincoln.

The center of Boston is closed to cars, and you will have to walk to visit the church and the Guildhall.

Food and Lodging

The town's leading hotel is **White Hart,** Bridge Foot, Boston, Lincolnshire PE21 8SH (tel. 0205/64877), a Regency building constructed along the river and lying a short distance from the historic center. This old coaching inn has been newly refurbished and redecorated. Its bedrooms are pleasantly and attractively furnished, renting for £34 ($59.50) nightly in a single, the cost rising to £50 ($87.50) in a double, including an English breakfast. Most of the comfortable bedrooms have private baths or shower. There is a free car park through the coaching courtyard at the rear of the hotel. White Hart offers some of the best food and drink in town in its two bars and one restaurant, the latter specializing in steak. Bar snacks are served Monday to Saturday from noon to 2 p.m., and meals in the restaurant, costing from £15 ($26.25), are offered from noon to 2:30 p.m. and 6 to 10:30 p.m.

New England Hotel, 49 Wide Bargate, Boston, Lincolnshire PE21 6SH (tel. 0205/65255), stands in the town center and is especially busy on market days. The location is near the Market Place and the Boston Stump, opening onto a large car park. Ales and wines are dispensed in the Pilgrim Bar, and at lunchtime, the place is often a beehive of activity. This three-story Victorian building houses one of the most frequented restaurants in town, Chaucers, offering a menu that includes roasts, grills, and seafood. The average price for lunch is £8.50 ($14.90) per person, with dinner costing around £13 ($22.75). The hotel also rents 25 bedrooms, each with a private bath, color TV, phone, and tea/coffee-maker. Singles range from £44 ($77) to £49 ($85.75) daily, and doubles cost £54 ($94.50). Families are catered to, especially those with small children.

LINCOLN

One of the most ancient cities of England, and only 135 miles north of London, Lincoln was known to the Romans as Lindum. Some of the architectural glory of the Roman Empire still stands to charm the present-day visitor. The renowned **Newport Arch** (the North Gate) is the last remaining arch left in Britain that still spans a principal highway. For a look at the Roman relics excavated in and around Lincoln, head for the **City and County Museum,** Broadgate (tel. 0522/30401), open daily from 10 a.m. to 5:30 p.m. (2:30 to 5 p.m. on Sunday). Admission is 25p (45¢) for adults, 10p (20¢) for children.

Two years after the Battle of Hastings, William the Conqueror built a castle on the site of a Roman fortress. Used for administrative purposes, parts of the castle still remain, including the walls, the 12th-century keep, and fragments of the gateway tower. In addition, you can visit the High Bridge over the Witham River, with its half-timbered houses (you can have a meal in one of them). This is one of the few medieval bridges left in England that has buildings nestling on it.

Visit also the **Museum of Lincolnshire Life** (tel. 0522/28448), the largest folk museum in the area, with displays ranging from a Victorian schoolroom to locally built steam engines. It's open daily from 10 a.m. to 5:30 p.m. (from 2 to 5:30 p.m. on Sunday). Admission is 75p ($1.30) for adults, 30p (55¢) for children.

Lincoln Cathedral

No other English cathedral dominates its surroundings as does Lincoln. Visible from up to 30 miles away, the minster's three towers are an arresting sight. The central tower is 271 feet high, making it the second tallest in England, giving just one foot to its near neighbor, Boston Stump, mentioned earlier. Lincoln's central tower once carried a huge spire, which, prior to heavy gale damage in 1549, made it the tallest in the world at 525 feet. Monday to Saturday in summer, there are accompanied tower trips.

Construction on the original Norman cathedral was begun in 1072 and it was consecrated 20 years later. It sustained a major fire and then, in 1185, an earthquake. Only the central portion of the West Front and lower halves of the western towers survive from this period. The present cathedral represents the Gothic style, particularly the Early English and Decorated periods. The nave is 13th century, but the black font of tourni marble originates from the 12th century. In the Great North Transept is a rose medallion window known as the Dean's Eye. Opposite it, in the Great South Transept, is its cousin, the Bishop's Eye. East of the high altar is the Angel Choir consecrated in 1280 and so called after the sculpted angels high on the walls. The exquisite wood carving in St. Hugh's Choir dates from the 14th century. Lincoln's roof bosses, dating from the 13th and 14th centuries, are handsome. A mirror trolley assists visitors in their appreciation of these features that are some 70 feet above the floor. In the cloister are oak bosses. These are easier to see, although there is also a mirror.

In the Seamen's Chapel (Great North Transept) is a window commemorating Lincolnshire-born Captain John Smith, one of the pioneers of early settlement in America and the first Governor of Virginia. The library and north walk of the cloister were built in 1674 to designs by Sir Christopher Wren. There are fine books and manuscripts, some of which may be on view in the adjoining Mediaeval Library (1422) together with one of the four remaining originals of the 1215 Magna Carta, although this latter tours extensively throughout the world. The Cathedral Charter of 1072 and the Forester's Charter of 1225 are extant.

In the Treasury, open from 2:30 to 4:30 p.m. Monday to Saturday from Easter to the end of September, there is fine gold and silver plate from the churches of the diocese.

The cathedral is open from 7:30 a.m. It closes at 8 p.m. Monday to Saturday in summer, at 6 p.m. Monday to Saturday in winter, and at 5 p.m. on Sunday in winter. The suggested donation to the cathedral is £1 ($1.75). Guided tours, of about one hour, are available Monday to Saturday in summer. For further details, phone 0522/544544.

Where to Stay

White Hart Hotel, Bailgate, Lincoln, Lincolnshire LN1 3AR (tel. 0522/26222), was named after the emblem of Richard II because he visited the region shortly before the hotel's construction and probably stayed at an inn erected on the site. A letter from 1460 reported on a visit to the inn by a London woman who paid sixpence for her room and complained that her bed was lumpy. The façade covering the inn dates from the 1700s when it was a luxurious private home. Its life as a hotel began in 1913 when the live-in owners started accepting paying guests, but only if they came with ironclad references from mutual friends. It is surrounded by ancient cobble-covered streets usually reserved for pedestrians. The cathedral and the oldest part of Lincoln lie a short walk from the doorstep. Once through a revolving mahogany door, you enter a large and finely proportioned lounge filled with fine antiques, rare and unusual clocks, and display cabinets of rare silver, glass, and porcelain. The hotel also bears the honor of having hosted several meetings between Churchill and Eisenhower in the darkest days of World War II. The Georgian main dining room offers elegant furnishings and well-prepared lunches and dinners. If you elect to overnight here, you'll be following in the footsteps of Lloyd George, Edward VIII, and Margaret Thatcher. Each of the accommodations includes a well-accessorized private bath, phone, TV, some kind of antique furniture, and windows overlooking the old city. To reach your room, you negotiate a labyrinth of narrow halls and stairways. With breakfast included, singles cost £65 ($113.75) daily, and doubles go for £85 ($148.75).

Eastgate Post House, Eastgate, Lincoln, Lincolnshire LN2 1PN (tel. 0522/20341), is a hotel attached to a Victorian mansion (now the Eastgate Bar). Eastgate occupies a historic site: in fact, when workmen were digging its foundations in the mid-'60s, they discovered the remnants of the north tower of the East Gate of Roman Lincoln. The hotel is well sited, overlooking Lincoln Cathedral. A preserved part of the Roman city wall is included in the rear garden. All 71 bedrooms have private baths, showers, color TVs, radios, mini-bars, and hot beverage facilities. Rates are £59 ($103.25) daily in a single, £75 ($131.25) in a double or twin, including service and VAT. Breakfast, lunch, and dinner are served in the Palatinate Restaurant, which also overlooks the cathedral. The cost of a table d'hôte lunch is £9.50 ($16.65) and dinner goes for £14 ($24.50). You can choose from an à la carte menu also. The coffeeshop serves grills and snacks. Free car-parking space for up to 120 vehicles is found at the front and rear of the hotel.

Grand Hotel, St. Mary Street, Lincoln, Lincolnshire LN5 7EP (tel. 0522/24211), is an extensively remodeled hotel with a suitable amenities and a cooperative staff. You'll pay around £50 ($87.50) daily for a double with a private bath, £36 ($63) for a single with bath. The West Bar and the lounges are streamlined, but the Tudor Bar pays homage to the past. The bedrooms are compact, with many built-in features and coordinated colors. The Grand is easy to spot, as it lies opposite the bus depot. It's a long walk to the cathedral, but you can hop a bus. Its food is a top-notch bargain, both in price and taste. From 7 to 8:30 p.m., a table d'hôte dinner is offered for £9.25 ($16.20). The food is not only good and typically English, but the portions are ample. You can also lunch at the Grand daily from noon to 2 p.m. A buttery is open from 11 a.m. to 10 p.m.

D'Isney Place Hotel, Eastgate, Lincoln, Lincolnshire LN2 4AA (tel. 0522/38881), is a small, family-owned hostelry close to the cathedral, the Minster Yard, the castle, and the Bailgate shops. It was built in 1735 and later extended. The cathedral close's wall and towers, constructed in 1285, form the southern boundary of the house gardens. Each room is uniquely decorated, with a large bath, radio, phone, color TV, and tea- and coffee-making facilities. Some units have four-poster beds and Jacuzzi baths. The proprietors, David and Judy Payne, charge £39 ($68.25) daily for a single, £50 ($87.50) for a double, the latter with a Turkish steam shower and a four-poster bed. There is car-parking space in the hotel grounds.

Where to Dine

Harveys Cathedral Restaurant, 1 Exchequergate, Castle Square (tel. 0522/510333), lies in the heart of the old town, a short walk from the cathedral and the castle. My favored dining spot in the city, it is run by Adrianne and Bob Harvey. This stately Georgian building until recently was reputed to be haunted, but the cozy Victorian decor has routed any dismal spirits. The motto of the Harveys is

"Simple lunches—superb dinners," and they live up to this with a lunch menu offering traditional English dishes such as farmhouse chicken pie and beef in Guinness, followed by Victorian sherry trifle. Start with Bob's homemade pâté or warming soup, always freshly made. Lunch will cost around £9 ($15.75). In the evening the restaurant is candlelit and reservations are essential. The Harveys offer a table d'hôte menu at £18 ($31.50), fully inclusive. This consists of a special soup or fruit dish, followed by the appetizer course, with a choice of fish, savory dishes, or pâté. Then there is a selection of seven main dishes, including French and "Taste of England" specialties. A massive choice of cheeses follows, with a finale of diet-beating homemade desserts and ice creams, plus the bottomless coffee cup and mints. Almost everything the Harveys serve is homemade, and all ingredients are fresh. If you're in Lincoln over a weekend, take in a traditional Sunday lunch here. You won't taste better roast beef anywhere, but remember to reserve your table. The restaurant is open from noon to 1:45 p.m. and 7:30 to 9:30 p.m. daily.

Whites of Lincoln, The Jews House, 15 The Strait (tel. 0522/24851), is a stone-fronted building, said to be the oldest lived-in house in Europe. Dating from the 12th century, it has a low-beamed ceiling, a cast-iron fireplace, and an array of medieval features. Two of the massive ceiling beams are known to be the original, dating from 1180. The restaurant is open daily from noon to 2 p.m. for lunch, from 2 to 5 p.m. for tea, and for dinner nightly except Sunday and Monday from 7:30 to 8:45. The menu is a stylish French-inspired collection of dishes that change with the season. Typical dishes might be fresh breast of wood pigeon on a bed of artichokes or a gratin of langoustine on a bed of spinach with a champagne and port wine sauce. Desserts are much in demand here, including the special one, charlotte royale (it's filled with a double cream lemon mousse). Lunch will cost from £5 ($8.75) to £7 ($12.25), while dinners go for £15 ($26.25) to £20 ($35). Reservations are much appreciated.

STAMFORD

This charming stone-built market town, lying 89 miles from London, is visited chiefly for the following attraction:

Burghley House (tel. 0780/52451), the home of the sixth Marquess of Exeter, has been the home of the Cecil family for more than 400 years. The house, on the outskirts of Stamford, was built in 1564 on the remains of a monastery founded in 1158. Ten years later, and again in 1589, additions were made. At this magnificent Elizabethan house you will see a collection of more than 400 works of art, mainly Italian of the baroque period. There are also splendid examples of furniture, tapestries, and decoration from the 16th and 17th centuries. It is said that nobody has slept in the Queen Elizabeth I bedroom since the monarch was last here. From the window you can see a lime tree she planted in the 16th century. The present growth sprang from the roots of the original tree. The kitchen found in the oldest part of the house is huge. A whole ox could be roasted on the spit. The house is open from 11 a.m. to 5 p.m. Easter to October. Admission is £3 ($5.25) for adults, £1.70 ($3) for children.

Food and Lodging

Lady Anne's Hotel, 37-38 High St., St. Martin's without Stamford, Lincolnshire PE9 2LJ (tel. 0780/53175), is named after Lady Anne Cecil, a young and favorite sister of the ninth Earl of Exeter. She lived in the original building for many years, but it has seen many changes before emerging as a country hotel. Bedrooms come in a wide range: some have very small showers while others are light and airy with baths and toilets. Depending on the plumbing, singles range from £26 ($45.50) to £36 ($63) daily, and doubles run as high as £50 ($87.50), with more expensive suites offered. These rates are inclusive of tea or coffee, a morning paper, and a large English breakfast. Outside is a good car park, and inside there's a welcoming log fire in the bar. Bedrooms have individual TV sets, although there's a large one in the chintz-decorated lounge. The hotel has 28 bedrooms. The cottage-y dining room has a menu of grills and fish dishes, including trout cooked in white wine and butter. In season, venison pie and pheasant are specialties. Expect to spend from £10 ($17.50) for a meal.

WANSFORD-IN-ENGLAND
Instead of staying in Stamford, an ideal alternative lies just off the A1 road to the north in a village of stone houses with a wide, typical English main street.

It's the **Haycock Hotel,** Great North Road, Wansford, near Peterborough, Cambridgeshire PE8 6JA (tel. 0780/782223). A stone in the garden dates the present building from 1632, although an inn has existed on this site for many years. The inn is built around a courtyard with stone archways and mullioned windows. It is said that Mary Queen of Scots, on her way to imprisonment in 1586 at Fotheringhay, visited the inn. In later years Queen Victoria stopped by when she was still a princess. Many of the bedrooms have a four-poster, most have private bath, and all contain phone and color TV. Your overnight charge includes early-morning tea and a newspaper, then a full English breakfast. Singles ranges from £60 ($105) daily, and twins and doubles go for £90 ($157.50). Menus are à la carte in the dining room, a meal averaging about £17 ($29.75).

GRANTHAM
This market town stands in the middle of rich farming country. A corner site on North Parade was the childhood home of Britain's first woman prime minister, Margaret Thatcher. Her father, Alfred Roberts, ran a busy greengrocer's shop on the ground floor, and the family lived in rooms above the business. Daughter Margaret was born there on October 13, 1925. The family moved to a nearby house in 1944, but Mr. Roberts continued with the store until he sold it in 1959.

In the Middle Ages, Grantham was a prosperous wool-trade town. Isaac Newton attended King's School here in the 17th century, and his initials can still be seen on the wooden sill of the Old Schoolroom built of Ancaster stone. The 283-foot spire of St. Wulfram's parish church rises as a local landmark and can be seen for miles around. The town has many old inns and a medieval market cross. It's most important historical attraction is—

Belton House, a National Trust property 2½ miles north of Grantham (tel. 0476/66116), is one of the finest Restoration country houses in Britain, built in 1684. The original architect was probably William Wynde, whose work resembles that of Wren. The house today appears very much as it did originally. The saloon and red drawing room are particularly finely carpeted, and the Tyrconnel Room has a rare painted floor apparently from the early 19th century. The library contains a fine barrel-vaulted ceiling by James Wyatt. Oriental porcelain and chinoiserie are part of the attractions. Throughout the house hang portraits of the initial owners, the Brownlow family. The house is open April to October from 1 to 5:30 p.m. Wednesday to Sunday. Admission is £3 ($5.25) for adults, £1.50 ($2.65) for children.

Food and Lodging
The **Angel and Royal,** High Street, Grantham, Lincolnshire NG31 6PN (tel. 0476/65816), is reportedly one of the oldest inns in Britain, tracing its origins back to the 1100s. Today its stone façade is much more modern, at least from the 1400s. Head through an arch and you enter a stone-paved courtyard lying between two wings of the structure, with tables and chairs placed outside in fair weather. Its 13th-century stone-walled restaurant and bar is one of the most popular in town, offering lunch from 12:30 to 2 p.m. daily costing from £6 ($10.50) and dinner from 7 to 10 p.m. costing from £12 ($21) and including such classic English fare as beef sirloin with Yorkshire pudding. Tasty bar snacks are also available. The hotel rents 24 well-

appointed bedrooms, each with private bath or shower. Rates begin at £52 ($91) daily in a single, £68 ($119) in a double, but ask about weekend bargain breaks that are much cheaper.

The most desirable place to dine in the area is **Barkston House,** Barkston, Grantham, Lincolnshire NG32 2NH (tel. 0400/50555), lying less than four miles north of Grantham on A607. This is a *restaurant avec chambres.* Actually it offers only two bedrooms, so it's best to reserve well in advance. Singles pay £35 ($61.25) nightly, with doubles going for £52 ($91). Originally a Georgian farmhouse, Barkston excels in English cookery. Vegetables are perfectly crisp, and main courses are composed of fresh and well-chosen ingredients. Natural flavors are enhanced by the kitchen staff. The wine list is limited, but well chosen, and, most important, reasonable in price. Dinner is served nightly except Sunday and Monday from 7:30 to 9:15 p.m., costing from £20 ($35) for two. Lunch is from noon to 2 p.m., except on Sunday when a set menu is offered at 1 for only £8.50 ($14.90). Reservations are important.

CHESHIRE, LIVERPOOL, AND THE LAKES

The northwest of England is one of the special parts of the country. In many ways its remoteness is part of its charm. Have you ever seen one of those English-made films depicting life in the Lake District? A soft mist hovers over the hills and dells, sheep graze silently on the slope of the pasture—and a foggy enchantment fills the air.

One of England's most popular summer retreats in Victoria's day was the Lake District in the northwest. It enjoyed vogue during the flowering of the Lake Poets, including Wordsworth, who was ecstatically moved by the rugged beauty of this area. In its time the district has lured such writers as S. T. Coleridge, Charles Lamb, Shelley, Keats, Alfred Lord Tennyson, Matthew Arnold, and Charlotte Brontë.

The county of Cheshire lies south of Lancashire. I suggest that you make a pilgrimage to the ancient city of Chester, with its medieval walls, near the border of Wales.

CHESHIRE

This county is low lying and largely agricultural. The name it gave to a cheese—and a cat—(Cheshire) has spread across the world. This northwestern county borders Wales, which accounts for its turbulent history. The towns and villages of Cheshire form a good base for touring North Wales, the most beautiful part of that little country. For our headquarters in Cheshire, we'll locate at:

1. Chester

Chester is ancient, having been founded by a Roman legion on the Dee River in the 1st century A.D. It reached its pinnacle as a bustling port in the 13th and 14th centuries, declining thereafter following the gradual silting up of the river. The upstart Liverpudlians captured the sea-trafficking business. The other walled medieval cities of England were either torn down or badly fragmented, but Chester still retains two miles of fortified city walls.

The main entrance into Chester is Eastgate, itself dating back to only the 18th century. Within the walls are half-timbered houses and shops. Of course, not all of them came from the days of the Tudors. Chester is freakish architecturally in that some of its builders kept to the black-and-white timbered façades—even when erecting buildings during the Georgian and Victorian periods, with their radically different tastes.

The Rows are double-decker layers of shops—one tier on the street level, the other stacked on top and connected by a footway. The upper tier is like a continuous galleried balcony. Shopping upstairs is much more adventurous than down on the street. Rain is never a problem. Thriving establishments operate in this traffic-free paradise: tobacco shops, restaurants, department stores, china shops, jewelers, even antique dealers. For the most representative look, take an arcaded walk on Watergate Street.

At noon and at 3 p.m. daily at the City Cross, the town crier issues his news (local stuff on sales, exhibitions, and attractions in the city) at the top of his not-inconsiderable voice, to the accompaniment of a hand bell—at the junction of Watergate, Northgate, and Bridge Streets. Eastgate Street is now a pedestrian way, and musicians often play for their—and your—pleasure beside St. Peter's Church and the Town Cross.

CHESTER CATHEDRAL

The present building founded in 1092 as a Benedictine abbey was created as a cathedral church in 1541. Considerable architectural restorations were carried out in the 19th century, but older parts have been preserved. Notable features include the fine range of monastic buildings, particularly the cloisters and refectory, the chapter house, and the superb medieval woodcarving in the quire (especially the misericords). Also worth attention are the long south transept with its various chapels, the consistory court, and the medieval roof bosses in the Lady Chapel. A free-standing bell tower, the first to be built in England since the Reformation, was completed in 1975 and may be seen southeast of the main building. The cathedral is open daily from 7 a.m. to 6:30 p.m. There is a refectory, a bookshop, and an audio-visual presentation. For more information, phone 0244/324756.

DISCOVER CHESTER

In a big Victorian building opposite the amphitheater, the **Chester Visitor Centre**, Vicars Lane (tel. 0244/351609), only minutes from the city center, offers a number of services to visitors from 9 a.m. to 9 p.m. daily. A Tourist Information Centre, part of the national network, provides a wide range of services including local and national accommodations booking, maps, free leaflets, guided tours, and reservations for local attractions. You are introduced to Chester by a map and print presentation on video film. A visit to a life-size Victorian street complete with sounds and smells helps your appreciation and orientation to Chester. The center has a gift shop, a licensed restaurant serving meals and snacks all day, and a currency exchange. Guided walking tours are also offered. Admission to the center is free, but a nominal charge is made for the video theater and exhibition areas.

A WALK ON THE WALL

In the center of town, you'll see an interesting old clock mounted on a wall. Climb the stairs near it, which lead up to the top of the city wall, and you can follow it on a walk looking down on Chester today from a path of the past. The wall passes through centuries of English history. You pass a cricket field, see the River Dee, which was formerly a major trade artery, and get a look at many old buildings of the 18th century, some undergoing renovation. Flower-filled back gardens are lovely from this height. The wall also goes past some Roman ruins, and it is possible to leave the walkway to explore them. The walk is charming and free.

CHESTER ZOO

Just off the A41 on the outskirts of Chester, the Chester Zoo (tel. 0244/380280), two miles from the center of the city, is world-famous for its wide collection of mammals, birds, reptiles, and fish, as well as for its 110 acres of gardens. Many rare and endangered species breed freely in spacious enclosures, and the zoo is particularly renowned for the most successful group of chimpanzees and orangutans in Europe. The gardens are worth seeing in any season, with 160,000 plants in the spring and summer bedding displays alone. A waterbus, a popular summer feature, allows you to observe the hundreds of waterbirds who make their home here. The zoo has several facilities if you get hungry or thirsty during your visit: the licensed Oakfield Restaurant, the Jubilee self-service cafeteria, the Oasis snackbar, and the Rainbow kiosk for either meals or snacks and drinks. The zoo is open from 10 a.m. to dusk daily except Christmas Day. Admission is £3.80 ($6.65) for adults, £1.90 ($3.35) for children 3 to 15.

WHERE TO STAY

One of the most luxurious hotels in the north of England, the **Chester Grosvenor Hotel**, Eastgate Street, Chester, Cheshire CH1 1DE (tel. 0244/24024), lies in a fine, half-timbered building in the heart of Chester and has a well-deserved high reputation. It is owned and named after the family of the Duke of Westminster. The history and origin of the hotel can be traced back to the reign of Queen Elizabeth I. Started as a Tudor inn, it became a political headquarters in Hanoverian days and later went on to be a glittering mecca for the Regency and Victorian set, continuing to be a social center in the Edwardian era. Prince Albert visited here, and guests more recently have ranged from Princess Diana to Prince Rainier.

The high, marble-floored foyer of the hotel, with its 200-year-old chandelier, carved wooden staircase, and antiques, sets the tone. The bedrooms are large and well furnished, all with radios, color TVs, direct-dial phones, mini-bars, and private baths equipped with such amenities as hairdryers. All individually coordinated, 86 new bedrooms and suites were created, each offering standards of comfort as stylish as the character of the hotel itself. Marble for the bathrooms was brought in from southern Italy, handmade furniture for the bedrooms from northern Italy, fabrics and silks from France and America, carpets from the Yorkshire Dales, and soft furnishings from Monza. In all, the best of British craftsmanship abounds. Rates begin at £90 ($157.50) daily for singles, £140 ($245) for doubles or twins. VAT is included. The grand hotel has the finest drinking and dining facilities in the entire county. Its formal restaurant, Arkle, and its more informal La Brasserie will be previewed later. Other amenities include a sauna, gym, and solarium.

Crabwell Manor, Parkgate Road, Mollington, Chester, Cheshire CH1 6NE (tel. 0244/851666), is a beautifully furnished country house hotel, whose origins go back to the 16th century. Most of the present building, however, dates from the early 1800s. The location is 2¼ miles northwest of Chester on A540. Standing in about a dozen acres of private grounds and gardens, the well-managed hotel rents 32 sensitively furnished bedrooms, each with private bath or shower, direct-dial phone, and color TV. Most of the rooms are quite large and show a certain flair in their decoration, and the bathrooms are first class, with bidets and separate showers for the most part. Rates range from £65 ($113.75) daily in a single, going up to £100 ($175) in a double, with suites costing more. The finest of contemporary English and French dishes are offered in the superb split-level restaurant of Crabwell Manor. Nonresidents can also visit to enjoy the harmonious flavors, the subtle sauces, and the well-chosen meats, fowl, and fish, which are served here daily from 12:30 to 2 p.m. and 7 to 9:30 p.m. Set lunches cost £12 ($21) to £13.50 ($23.65), with a table d'hôte dinner offered for £20 ($35). You can also dine à la carte.

Mollington Banastre, Parkgate Road, Chester, Cheshire CH1 6NN (tel. 0244/851471), lies two miles northwest on A540. This successfully converted Victorian mansion, now turned into a country house hotel, one of the leading ones in Cheshire, is affiliated with the Best Western reservation system. A gabled house, it offers a health and leisure complex, along with a trio of restaurants and 67 well-furnished bedrooms. Equipped with all the modern amenities, these rent for £60 ($105) daily in a single, going up to £120 ($210) in a double. In addition, the hotel also has a pub on its grounds.

Rowton Hall Hotel, Whitchurch Road, Rowton, Chester, Cheshire CH3 6AD (tel. 0244/335262), is a stately home, two miles from the city center, which offers overnight accommodation for motorists. The gracious house, built in 1779 with a later wing added, stands in an eight-acre garden, with a formal driveway entrance. The Hall has comfortable traditional and contemporary furnishings. All bedrooms have private bath, a single renting for £58 ($101.50) daily and a double for £72 ($126). All prices include a full English breakfast and VAT. A set lunch costs £9 ($15.75), and a set dinner goes for £11 ($19.25). The good English meals are served in the oak-paneled dining room with a Tudor fireplace. The hotel stands on the site of the battle of Rowton Moor, which was fought in 1643 between the Roundheads and the Cavaliers.

Blossoms Hotel, St. John Street, Chester, Cheshire CH1 1HL (tel. 0244/323186), has been in business since the mid-17th century, although the present structure was rebuilt late in Victoria's day. Each of the traditionally furnished bedrooms is equippe¹ with central heating, and all have private bath. Each room has a phone and radio, as well as color TV and coffee maker. The price for B&B in a single begins at £61 ($106.75) daily and ʔ a double at £82 ($143.50). The old open staircase in the reception room sets the tone of the hotel. Dinner is served in the Egerton Room from 7 to 9:30 p.m. daily, offering both a carving table selection at £10.50 ($18.40) and an à la carte menu. These menus are available for lunch as well as dinner. The Snooty Fox, a traditional English pub with a hunting decor, is open for lunch from 11 a.m. to 2:30 p.m. daily and noon to 2 p.m. on Sunday.

WHERE TO DINE

The premier restaurant in this part of England is **Arkle Restaurant,** Chester Grosvenor Hotel, Eastgate Street (tel. 0244/324024), the formal restaurant of this already previewed grand hotel. This 45-seat gourmet restaurant has a superb chef de cuisine and a talented 40-strong team preparing the finest food with the freshest ingredients. Here you get modern British and continental cooking prepared with subtle touches and a certain lightness as reflected by the sauces and the cooking of meats and vegetables. For the ultimate food experience, the kitchen will prepare a special six-course dinner menu (the restaurant manager will describe the succulent feast) at a cost of £32.50 ($56.90) per person. Otherwise, a set lunch costs £15 ($26.25). To dine à la carte is about £35 ($61.25) per person. You are likely to be served such dishes as a selection of seafood with a champagne and caviar sauce, filet of beef with foie gras and a Madeira sauce, and sliced breast of guinea fowl with a poached baby pear and cinnamon sauce. Desserts are equally luscious and tempting. You can partake of this grand cuisine daily except Saturday lunch and all day Sunday from noon to 2:30 p.m. and 7:30 to 10 p.m. The tastebuds of the old city of Chester have never been this pampered.

La Brasserie, Chester Grosvenor Hotel, Eastgate Street (tel. 0244/324024), is perhaps the best all-around dining choice in Chester, not only for convenience but for price and quality. In the same building as this prestigious hotel, which has already been previewed, along with its formal restaurant, Arkle, La Brasserie is open daily from 6:30 a.m. to 11:30 p.m. Regardless of your schedule, you couldn't ask for more convenient dining hours than that. In a delightfully art nouveau setting, the Brasserie offers a three-course set lunch at £8.95 ($15.65) served from 11:30 a.m. to 2:30 p.m. and a three-course table d'hôte dinner for £12.50 ($21.90) from 6:30 to 11 p.m. Main dishes are likely to include a stew of river fish, paella valenciana, and baby chicken roasted with garlic and lemon thyme.

In the opinion of some, the leading restaurant outside the hotels is **Pippas of Chester,** 58 Watergate St. (tel. 0244/313721), where guests enjoy a good French cuisine. In a simple decor of exposed brick and racks of blue willow porcelain, this fresh, bright restaurant offers quality cuisine and good service. Lunch, served from noon to 2 p.m., is the best value, as it features an £8 ($14) set menu. A table d'hôte dinner at £14 ($24.50) is served from 7 to 10 p.m. (on Friday and Saturday until 10:30 p.m.). À la carte dinners from an extensive menu cost about the same. On occasion, a well-seasoned game soup is featured, which might be followed by, say, grilled Dover sole (served moist, not dried out), crayfish thermidor, and roast duck with a port and red-currant sauce. The restaurant is closed on Sunday.

---

2. Nantwich

The old market town on the Weaver River lies only 15 miles southeast of the county town of Chester, and can easily be tied in with a visit to that city. The town is particularly outstanding because of its black-and-white timbered houses. The most spectacular one, Churche's Mansion, is a dining recommendation.

WHERE TO STAY

With its striking appearance, **Rookery Hall,** Worleston, Nantwich, Cheshire CW5 6DQ (tel. 0270/626866), is a structure whose Italianate façade and massive proportions would appear at home in the Loire Valley in France. More a château than a manor house, it was built in the 1700s but radically altered in 1867 into the high-Victorian design that stands today. Guests are welcomed to the 11 handsomely furnished bedrooms, each with a private bath, direct-dial phone, and comfortable amenities. With a full English breakfast and a six-course dinner, single rooms cost £87.50 ($153.15) daily, and doubles rent for £150 ($262.50). While you enjoy panoramic views of the surrounding countryside, you can sample well-prepared food, which includes a combination of English dishes and modern French cuisine. The lavishly paneled dining room is a suitable setting for meals based on traditional English cookery with a modern twist. Try Cheshire sausages on a bed of leeks, rack of Welsh lamb with home-grown mustard seed sauce, and bread-and-butter pudding with honey ice cream. The location is 2½ miles north of Nantwich by the A51 and on the B5074.

WHERE TO DINE

The most enchanting old restaurant in Cheshire, **Churche's Mansion Restaurant,** Hospital Street (tel. 0270/625933), lies in Nantwich at the junction of Newcastle Road and the Chester bypass. Many years ago Dr. and Mrs. E. C. Myott learned that this historic home of a wealthy Elizabethan gentleman had been advertised for sale in America, and asked the town council to step in and save it. Alas, no English housewife wanted such a gloomy and dark home, so the Myotts attended the sale and outbid the American syndicate that wanted to transport it to the United States. Dr. Myott said that "our friends thought we were mad." They sought out the mysteries of the house: a window in the side wall, inlaid initials, a Tudor well in the garden, a long-ago love knot with a central heart (a token of Richard Churche's affection for his young wife). Today the house is widely known and recommended for its quality meals. Lunch costs from £8.50 ($14.90) and dinners from £16.50 ($28.90). Tariffs include VAT and coffee. Hours are from noon to 2 p.m. and 7 to 9:30 p.m. daily. It is advisable but not absolutely necessary to make reservations.

---

3. Liverpool

Liverpool, with its famous waterfront on the River Mersey, is a great shipping port and industrial center that gave the world everybody from the fictional Fannie Hill to the Beatles. King John launched it on its road to glory when he granted it a charter in 1207. Before that it had been a tiny 12th-century fishing village, but it quickly became a port for shipping men and materials to Ireland. In the 18th century it grew to prominence as a port as a result of the sugar, spice, and tobacco trade with the Americas. By the time Victoria came to the throne, Liverpool had become Britain's biggest commercial seaport. Recent refurbishing of the Albert Docks, establishment of a Maritime Museum, and the conversion of warehouses into little stores, similar to those in Ghirardelli Square in San Francisco, have made this an up-and-coming area once again, with many attractions for visitors.

Liverpudlians, as they are called, are rightly proud of their city, with its new hotels, two cathedrals, shopping and entertainment complexes (as exemplified by St. John's Centre, a modern pedestrian precinct), and the parks and open spaces (2,400 acres in and around the city, including Sefton Park with its Palm House). Liverpool's main shopping street, Church, is traffic-free for most of the day.

Liverpool is easily reached by car, following the M1, the M6, and the A5080 from London right to the coast city in the west where the River Mersey joins the Irish Sea. Trains go from Euston or Kensington Olympia Stations from London or the Rapide bus from Victoria Coach Station goes direct to Liverpool.

THE SIGHTS

Liverpool today has a wealth of things for the visitor to see and enjoy—major cathedrals, waterfront glories restored, cultural centers, even the places where the Beatles began their meteoric rise to fame and fortune.

The Cathedrals

Attracting many Liverpool visitors is the great new (as cathedrals go) Anglican edifice, the **Cathedral Church of Christ,** Saint James Mount (tel. 051/709-6271), largely completed 74 years after it was begun in 1903. On a rocky eminence overlooking the River Mersey, the cathedral might possibly be the last Gothic-style one to be built on earth. Dedicated in the presence of Queen Elizabeth II in 1978, it is the largest church in the country (the fifth largest in the world). England's poet laureate at the time, Sir John Betjeman, hailed it as "one of the great buildings of the world." Its vaulting under the tower is 175 feet high, the highest in the world, and its length of 619 feet is second only to that of St. Peter's in Rome. The architect, who won a competition in 1903 for the building's design, was Giles Scott. He went on to rebuild the House of Commons, gutted by bombs, after World War II. He personally laid the last stone on the highest tower pinnacle. The organ of the world's largest Anglican cathedral contains nearly 10,000 pipes, the biggest found in any church. The tower houses the highest (219 feet) and the heaviest (31 tons) ringing peals of bells in the world, and the Gothic arches are the highest ever built.

In 1984, a Visitor Centre and Refectory was opened, the dominant feature being an aerial sculpture of 12 huge sails, with a ship's bell, clock, and lights that change color on an hourly basis. Full meals may be taken in the charming refectory. The cathedral can be visited from 9 a.m. to 6 p.m. daily. Tours of the tower are offered Monday to Saturday from 10:30 a.m. to 12:30 p.m. and 2 to 4:30 p.m. and on Sunday from 4 to 5 p.m. The tours cost adults £1.50 ($2.65); children (accompanied by an adult), 50p (90¢).

Half a mile away from the Anglican cathedral stands the Roman Catholic **Metropolitan Cathedral of Christ the King,** Mount Pleasant (tel. 051/709-9222), but any notion that they glower at each other from that distance is dismissed by the name of the road that joins them—Hope Street. The sectarian strife of earlier generations has been ended, and a change in attitude, called by some the "Mersey Miracle," was illustrated clearly in 1982 when Pope John Paul II drove along Hope Street to pray in both cathedrals. The Metropolitan Cathedral is so called because Liverpool is, in Catholic terms, the mother city, the "metropolis" of the north of England. Construction of the cathedral to the design of Sir Edwin Lutyens was started in 1930, but when World War II halted progress in 1939, not even the granite and brick vaulting of the crypt was complete. At the end of the war it was estimated that the cost of completing the structure as Lutyens had designed it would be some £27 million. Architects throughout the world were invited to compete to design a more realistic project to cost about £1 million and to be completed in five years. Sir Frederick Gibberd won the competition and was commissioned to oversee the construction of the circular cathedral in concrete and glass, pitched like a tent at one end of the piazza that covered all the original site, crypt included. Between 1962 and 1967 the construction was completed, providing seating for a congregation of more than 2,000, all within 50 feet of the central altar. Above the altar rises a multicolored glass lantern weighing 2,000 tons and rising to a height of 290 feet. This has been called a "space age" cathedral.

The Metropolitan Cathedral is open daily from 8 a.m. to 6 p.m. (to 5 p.m. Sunday in winter). It has a bookshop, a tea room, and tour guides.

On the Waterfront

Albert Dock, Albert Dock Co. Ltd (tel. 051/709-9199), is the showpiece development on Liverpool's Waterfront. Built of brick, stone, and cast iron, it opened in 1846, saw a long period of decline, and has been renovated and refurbished so that the magnificent dockland warehouses now contain quality shops, restaurants, cafés, and a cellar wine bar. One pavilion houses the main building of the Merseyside Maritime Museum (see below) and another is the home of the Tate Gallery Liverpool, the national collection of modern art in the north of England (see below). Albert Dock is open daily from 10 a.m. to 8 p.m. There's no charge for going there and strolling around, and car parking is available.

Merseyside Maritime Museum, Albert Dock (tel. 051/207-0001), set in the historic heart of Liverpool's magnificent waterfront, is a large museum providing a unique blend of floating exhibits, craft demonstrations, working displays, and special events. In addition to restored waterfront buildings, exhibitions show the story of mass emigration through Liverpool in the last century, shipbuilding on

Merseyside, and other aspects of Liverpool's maritime heritage. You can see a piermaster's house and a working cooperage. The museum is open daily from 10:30 a.m. to 5:30 p.m. (last entrance at 4:30 p.m.) Admission is £1 ($1.75) for adults, 50p (90¢) for children. A smörgåsbord restaurant, a waterfront café, gift shops, and ample parking space are among the facilities.

The **Tate Gallery** at Albert Dock (tel. 051/709-3223), opened in 1988, housing the National Collection of 20th century art in the north of England. It is the first gallery in England devoted entirely to modern art. The gallery was a decision of the board of directors at the Tate Gallery in London to move more than 85 percent of its modern collections from vaults to the gallery in Liverpool where all the world could see these "hidden treasures." Lack of space in London made it impossible to show the collection. So, this new "Tate Gallery of the North" came into being. Some of the world's greatest modern artists, such as Picasso and Dali, but also Magritte and Rothko, are likely to be on display at any time, along with a changing array of temporary exhibitions and events. The gallery is open Tuesday to Sunday from 11 a.m. to 7 p.m., charging no admission. However, the price of special exhibitions is £1 ($1.75).

You can take a **Mersey Ferry** from the Pier Head to both Woodside and Seacombe, operating on a regular 20-minute schedule on Monday to Saturday and half hourly on Sunday, from early morning to late evening. Special afternoon cruises are offered along Liverpool's historic waterfront in summer. For information about times and prices, get in touch with the **Merseyside Transport Ferries Office,** Victoria Place, Seacombe, Wallasey (tel. 051/630-1030).

Where the Beatles Began

Whether or not they're Beatles fans, most visitors who come to Liverpool want to take a look at where Beatlemania began in the Swinging Sixties. Mathew Street is the heart of Beatleland, and **Cavern Walks** (tel. 051/236-9082) is a shopping development and tour service built on the site of the former Cavern Club where the Beatles performed almost 300 times. John Doubleday's controversial statue of the group is in the central piazza of the Cavern complex, surrounded by shops and restaurants. The outside of Cavern Walks was decorated by Cynthia Lennon, John's first wife. Another controversial statue of John, Paul, George, and Ringo, this one by Liverpool sculptor Arthur Dooley, is opposite the building façade. Farther along Mathew Street is the John Lennon Memorial Club and the **Beatles Shop,** 31 Mathew St. (tel. 051/236-8066), open from 9:30 a.m. to 5:30 p.m. daily except Sunday when hours are from 10:30 a.m. to 4 p.m. Around the corner on Stanley Street is a statue of Eleanor Rigby, seated on a bench.

Tours

A daily £2 ($3.50) sightseeing tour gives a brief introduction to Liverpool, while for £3.50 ($6.15), Beatles fans can take a two-hour guided tour of famous locations such as Penny Lane and Strawberry Fields. Private car tours can be arranged for £25.85 ($45.25) for up to three hours. For those who prefer to "do it themselves," a Beatles map can be purchased for £1 ($1.75). Details are available from the **Merseyside Tourism Board's** two information centers: 29 Lime St., in front of the main railway station (tel. 051/709-3631), and at the Albert Dock (tel. 051/708-8854). Both centers are open every day.

WHERE TO STAY

The "grand hotel" of Liverpool, the **Brittania Adelphi Hotel,** Ranelagh Place, Liverpool, Merseyside L3 5UL (tel. 051/709-7200), built in 1914, is known for its fine rooms and good cuisine. Past the elegant entrance, you enter a world of marble corridors, molded ceilings, and dark polished wood. However, these traditional features are complemented by a range of modern amenities, including a swimming pool. The hotel has been completely refurbished, with an increased bedroom capacity of 344 accommodations, all with private baths, color TVs, and phones. The well-furnished and attractively maintained singles cost £43 ($75.25) to £71 ($124.25) daily, and doubles go for £61 ($106.75) to £81 ($141.75). Guests have the use of an indoor swimming pool, a solarium, a whirlpool bath, a gym, and laundry service. The hotel also has a disco, a pub, and two restaurants. Parking spaces are available for 82 cars.

Liverpool Moat House, Paradise Street, Liverpool, Merseyside L1 8JD (tel. 051/7090181), is, in the opinion of some, the leading hotel of Liverpool. In the center of the city, it is one of the most comfortable hotels in Merseyside, with an efficient modernity. Bedrooms are spread across seven floors, 258 in all, each with private bath or shower, TV, and direct-dial phone. Most often favored by commercial travelers, it also lures sightseers drawn to the attractions of "new Liverpool." Singles rent for £64 ($112) nightly, with doubles costing from £84 ($147), with even more expensive suites available. The hotel has a number of facilities, including a solarium, gym, indoor swimming pool, and garden. Its coffee shop stays open until 10:30 p.m. for late arrivals. It also offers a good restaurant serving British and French dishes, with meals costing from £15 ($26.25).

Atlantic Tower, 30 Chapel St., Liverpool, Merseyside L3 9RE (tel. 051/627070), enjoys one of the most advanced architectural designs of any hotel in Liverpool. Showcased in a high rise that evokes the bows of a great luxury liner, Atlantic Tower is considered one of the two or three top hotels in the city. You check into a spacious lobby and are shown to one of the well-furnished bedrooms, each with private bath or shower, direct-dial phone, and TV. Often opening onto views of the Mersey River, bedrooms rent for £62 ($108.50) in a single and £70 ($122.50) in a double. You can dine in the Stateroom Restaurant, enjoying drinks in a bar that resembles a Pullman coach.

Trials, 62 Castle St., Liverpool, Merseyside L2 7LQ (tel. 051/2271021), is another leading hotel of Liverpool, but it's much smaller, with only 20 bedrooms. Rather luxurious, this hotel of charm and character was created from a centrally located Victorian structure that had once been a bank. Now beautifully converted to its new role, Trials is often the choice of the most discriminating visitor to Liverpool. The accommodations are split level, actually plush suites, with Jacuzzi, private bath or shower, phone, trouser press, hairdryer, and TV. Rates range from £60 ($105) daily in a single, going up to £80 ($140) in a double. Wayne Rose is the guiding hand behind this well-run place, which is a discovery for Liverpool. With a unique character, Trials Restaurant offers a grand cuisine, beautifully served in first-class surroundings.

WHERE TO DINE

Consistently good food is served at **Jenny's Seafood Restaurant,** the Old Ropery, Fenwick Street (tel. 051/236-0332). In the vicinity of the harbor, it has a basement room that is both pleasantly decorated and softly illuminated. All this forms a backdrop for the good-tasting fresh seafood that is brought in daily. Everything I've sampled has been of fine quality and well prepared. The service, on my latest rounds, was excellent. Expect to pay £11.50 ($20.15) to £21 ($36.75) for a full meal. The restaurant is closed Monday evening, for lunch Saturday, and all day Sunday, but it is open otherwise from noon to 2:15 p.m. and 7 to 10 p.m.

Far East, 27-35 Berry St. (tel. 051/7093141), is considered the finest Chinese restaurant in Liverpool. Liverpool is particularly famous for its Chinese restaurants, not surprising as the city has one of the largest Chinese populations in Europe and its own "Chinatown." Here you might enjoy a dim sum lunch, later returning in the evening for more haute Chinese fare. You face a bewildering array of Cantonese specialties, including chili-flavored large prawns. The chefs also do marvelous things with duck. You can sample its fares daily from noon to 11:30 p.m., with a set lunch offered for only £3 ($5.25) and a set dinner for £3.50 ($6.15). However, you are likely to get carried away with the à la carte specialties and spend at least £10 ($17.50).

Armadillo, 20-22 Matthew St. (tel. 051/2364123), is one of the leading independent restaurants of Liverpool. It stands across the street from the site of the famous Cavern, where the Beatles got their start. The selection of fresh, good-tasting food leans toward the vegetarian at times, but top quality meat, poultry, and fish dishes are served as well. This place, owned by Martin Cooper, seems to be near the top of everybody's list of favorite restaurants in Liverpool. A set lunch costs only £7.50 ($13.15), with à la carte dinners priced from £15 ($26.25). Hours are from 11:45 a.m. to 3 p.m. and 7:30 to 10:30 p.m. except on Sunday and dinner Monday.

CUMBRIA

Driving in the wilds of this northwestern shire is fine for a start, but the best activity is walking, which is an art—practiced here by both young and old with a crooked stick. Don't go out without a warning, however. There is a great deal of rain and heavy mist. Sunny days are few. When the mist starts to fall, try to be near an old inn or pub, where you can drop in for a visit and warm yourself beside an open fireplace. You'll be carried back to the good old days, as many places in Cumbria have valiantly resisted change. If you strike up a conversation with a local, just make sure you know something about hounds.

The far northwestern part of the shire, bordering Scotland, used to be called Cumberland. Now part of Cumbria, it is generally divided geographically into a trio of segments: the Pennines, dominating the eastern sector (loftiest point at Cross Fell, nearly 3,000 feet high); the Valley of Eden; and the lakes and secluded valleys of the west—by far the most interesting. The Lake District, so beautifully described by the Romantic Lake poets, enjoys many literary associations. Wordsworth ("when all at once I saw . . . a host of golden daffodils") was a native son, having been born at Cockermouth.

The largest town is Carlisle in the north—not a very interesting tourist center, but possible as a base for explorations to **Hadrian's Wall.** The wall stretches from Wallsend in the east to Bowness on the Solway, a distance of about 75 miles. It was built in the 2nd century A.D. by the Romans.

4. Cartmel

The village of Cartmel, lying some six miles south of the southern end of Lake Windermere, is two miles northwest of Grange-over-Sands, a resort that gained popularity in Victorian times. Cartmel's 12th-century priory and the racecourse made it an attraction then as now.

WHERE TO STAY AND DINE

Opened in 1985 by John Tovey, who created the Miller Howe Hotel in Windermere, recommended below, the **Uplands Country House Hotel,** Haggs Lane, Cartmel, near Grange-over-Sands, Cumbria LA11 6HD (tel. 05395/36248), stands in two acres of garden with views to the Morecambe Bay estuary. The hotel is run by Tom and Diana Peter in partnership with Mr. Tovey, from whom they learned their innkeeping skills in 12 years of employment at the hotel in Windermere. Uplands has four comfortable double bedrooms, all with TVs, phones, clocks, hairdryers, and private plumbing facilities. Half board costs £50 ($87.50) to

£55 ($96.25) per person daily. Tom is an excellent chef, producing country-style three-course luncheons costing £9.50 ($16.65). Even if you don't stay here, it's worth a stop just to dine, a four-course meal costing £17.50 ($30.65). You might choose as an appetizer mushroom-and-marsala quiche or stuffed cheese peach with bacon roll, followed by filet of sea bass, roast sirloin of Lakeland beef, or roast local wood pigeon. For dessert, the strawberry and kiwifruit meringue slice is just right if it's available. The hotel is closed in January and February.

5. Kendal

A market town, Kendal contains the ruins of a castle where Catherine Parr, the last wife of Henry VIII, was born. With its 13th-century parish church, Kendal makes for a good stopover en route to the lakeside resort of Windermere, about nine miles away. Kendal is 270 miles from London.

The town was also associated with George Romney, the 18th-century portrait painter (Lady Hamilton was his favorite subject) who used to travel all over the Lake District trying to get someone to sit for him. He held his first exhibition in Kendal, married and had children there. He deserted them in 1762, not returning until the end of his life. He died in Kendal in 1802.

Abbot Hall, Kirkland, a handsome stone Georgian mansion, houses the **Abbot Hall Art Gallery** and the **Museum of Lakeland Life and Industry** (tel. 0539/22646), operated by the Lake District Art Gallery and Museum Trust. The gallery, laid out in 18th-century rooms, contains portraits by Romney and Gardner and Lake District watercolors. The museum exhibits period rooms, costumes, printing, weaving, and local industries, as well as Queensgate, a reconstructed Victorian street scene, and a farming display. The gallery and museum are open Monday to Friday from 10:30 a.m. to 5:30 p.m., Saturday and Sunday from 2 to 5 p.m. They are closed for the Christmas holidays, New Year's Day, and Good Friday. Admission is £1.25 ($2.20) for adults, 65p ($1.15) for children.

The **Kendal Museum of Archaeology and Natural History,** Station Road (tel. 0539/21374), one of the oldest museums in Britain, now administered by the Abbot Hall Art Gallery, traces the story of people of the area since the Stone Age, as well as Kendal's development as a wool town. Realistic constructions take the visitor on a tour of the major wildlife habitats in the district. The museum also contains a world wildlife gallery with specimens of birds, animals, and insects, pointing out the ecological problems of the modern world. The museum is open Monday to Friday from 10:30 a.m. to 5 p.m., on Saturday and Sunday from 2 to 5 p.m. From the spring bank holiday weekend to October 31, it is open from 10:30 to 5 p.m. Saturday. It's closed during the Christmas holidays, New Year's Day, and Good Friday. Admission is £1 ($1.75) for adults, 50p (90¢) for children. Family tickets at £2.50 ($4.40) are available.

WHERE TO STAY

With a name harking back to Kendal's heyday as a wool town, the **Woolpack Hotel,** Stricklandgate, Kendal, Cumbria LA9 4ND (tel. 0539/23852), offers modern conveniences in this motel-like establishment. All 57 rooms are equipped with private bath, and some are suites, which are ideal for families of three or more. Children under 12 are accommodated at no charge when sharing their parents' rooms. All the rooms are decorated in pastel colors to add to the cheerful atmosphere. Convenient parking is provided. Singles range upward from £47 ($82.25) daily, while doubles begin at £59 ($103.25). VAT, service, and a full English breakfast are included in the tab.

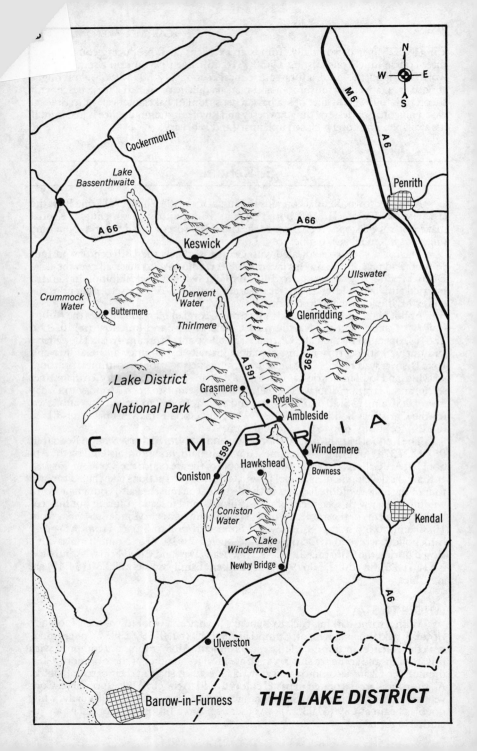

THE LAKE DISTRICT

WHERE TO DINE

In a converted former grocery store, **Moon,** 129 Highgate (tel. 0539/29254), is known for serving the best food in Kendal. Admittedly, the competition here isn't too keen, but this place excels, nevertheless. Run by Val Macconnell, the restaurant serves vegetarian and wholefood dishes, and does so exceedingly well. Good old-fashioned flavors and modern cooking techniques combine to offer a tempting array of food selections daily at dinner from 6 to 10 p.m. (it stays open until 11 p.m. on busy Friday and Saturday nights). Meals cost from £10 ($17.50) and are likely to include everything from smoked mackerel pâté with a gooseberry sauce to a vegetable ragoût. The restaurant is attractively decorated in a bistrolike format.

---

6. Windermere

The grandest of the lakes is Windermere, the largest one in England, whose shores wash up against the adjoining towns of Bowness and Windermere. Both of these lakeside resorts lie on the eastern shore of Windermere. A ferry service connects Hawkshead and Bowness. Windermere, the resort, is the end of the railway line. From either town, you can climb Orrest Head in less than an hour for a panoramic view of England's lakeland. From that vantage point, you can even see Scafell Pike, rising to a height of 3,210 feet—the peak pinnacle in all of England.

Windermere Steamboat Museum, Rayrigg Road, Windermere (tel. 09662/5565), is a delightful working museum. It was founded and developed by George Pattinson, who discovered the fascination of steam many years ago and now has probably the best and most comprehensive collection of steamboats in the country. The wet boatsheds house some dozen boats, including the veteran *Dolly,* probably the oldest mechanically powered boat in the world, dating from around 1850. It was raised from the lake bed in the early 1960s and run for several years with the original boiler and steambox.

Also displayed is the *Esperance,* an iron steam yacht registered with Lloyds in 1869, as well as many elegant Victorian and Edwardian steam launches. Attached to the boathouses is the speedboat *Jane,* dating from 1938, the first glider-plane to take off from the water in 1943, and the hydroplane racer *Cookie*—all jostling Beatrix Potter's rowing boat and other Lakeland craft for position. Boats that have been added to the collection include the steam launch *Kittiwake,* the motorboat *Lady Hamilton,* and the fast speedboat *Miss Windermere IV.*

The museum is open from Easter to October, charging an admission of £1.80 ($3.15) for adults and £1 ($1.75) for children. The *Osprey* is regularly in steam, and visitors can make a 45-minute trip on the lake at £2.25 ($3.95) for adults, £1.35 ($2.35) for children.

It's also possible to make trips on Ullswater and on Coniston, and there is regular steamer service around Windermere, the largest of the lakes, which serves the outlying villages as well as operating for visitors in summer.

WHERE TO STAY AND DINE

A clientele from all over the world comes to **Miller Howe Hotel,** Bayrigg Road, Windermere, Cumbria LA23 1EY (tel. 09662/2536), an inn bearing the unique imprint of its creator, former actor John Tovey. At the beginning of the 1970s he selected a country estate overlooking Lake Windermere, with views of the Langdale Peaks, and converted it to provide stylish accommodations and an exquisite cuisine. His large, graciously furnished rooms have names—no numbers—and he treats each guest as if he or she were invited to a house party. Each accommodation is provided with binoculars to help absorb the view better, and even copies of *Punch* from the 1890s. Antiques are used lavishly throughout the house. Rates per person, including a full English breakfast, dinner, and VAT, range from £60 ($105) to £105 ($183.75) daily, depending on the plumbing and the view. The hotel is closed from mid-December to mid-March. Dinner at Miller Howe is worth the drive up from London. While Tovey is famed as a pastry chef, he is equally known for his original appetizers and main dishes. Even if you can't stay the night, at least consider a meal here for which you must reserve. The set meal of five courses will cost £25 ($43.75) per person, including coffee and VAT. Regional dishes using local produce are a special feature. You might try Lake District lamb, fresh salmon, game pies (in season), Lancashire cheese, and Cumbria sausage. Coats and ties must be worn in the dining room. Dinners are served daily at 8:30 p.m. only, and at 7:30 and 9:30 p.m. on Saturday.

Langdale Chase Hotel, Windermere, Cumbria LA23 1LW (tel. 05394/32201), on the A591 between Windermere and Ambleside, is a great old lakeside house—built for grandeur—comparable to a villa on Lake Como, Italy. The story goes back to 1930 when the dynamic Ms. Dalzell and her mother took over the country estate, with its handsomely landscaped gardens, and decided to accept paying guests while retaining an uncommercial house-party atmosphere. Waterskiing, rowing, lake bathing, tennis, croquet on the grounds, and fishing attract the sports-minded. The rate for B&B ranges from £35 ($61.25) daily in a single. In a double or twin, the rent is £85 ($148.75). The bedrooms are furnished with excellent pieces. The interior of the Victorian stone château, with its many gables, balconies, large mullioned windows, and terraces, is a treasure house of antiques. The main lounge hall looks like a setting for one of those English drawing-room comedies. The house was built in part with bits and pieces salvaged from the destruction of a nearby abbey and castle—hence, the ecclesiastical paneling. On the walls are distinctive paintings, mostly Italian primitives, although one is alleged to be a Van Dyck. The dining room ranks among the finest in the Lake District—with guests selecting tables that are good vantage points for lake viewing. The cuisine is highly personal, mostly a liberated English fare, supported by a fine wine list. Open to nonresidents, the dining room charges from £9 ($15.75) for a set lunch, from £17 ($29.75) for a set six-course dinner.

Cedar Manor, Ambleside Road, Windermere, Cumbria LA23 1AX (tel. 09662/3192), is one of the most desirable country house hotels in the area. In Victoria's day, it was an impressive lakeside home with gables and chimneys. But since those times it was converted into a small hotel of exceptional merit. Each bedroom, containing a private bath or shower, is well furnished and maintained, renting for £40 ($70) daily in a single or £70 ($122.50) in a double. A cedar tree, perhaps from India, has grown in the garden for some two centuries, and from that tree the hotel takes its name. Meals are good and wholesome, offering excellent value at a cost of £15 ($26.25) per person for five courses.

Roger's, 4 High St. (tel. 09662/4954), is one of the most acclaimed restaurants in the Lake District. Some diners prefer it to the highly touted viands served at Miller Howe. The stellar French dining room of Cumbria, Roger's carries the name of its skilled chef de cuisine, Roger Pergl-Wilson. For almost a decade he has been going strong at this location (a part of England where restaurants seem to have a high mortality rate). That means he's doing something right. You can judge for yourself any time nightly except Sunday from 7 to 9:30. A table d'hôte dinner—superb value—costs £17.50 ($30.65), but you are more likely to spend from £20 ($35) ordering à la carte. Home-grown ingredients go into the cookery whenever possible. Regardless, everything tastes fresh here, as care goes not only into the preparation but the presentation, which is polite and efficient without being overly formal. Deer from the field, salmon from the rivers, char from Lake Windermere, and quail from the air—everything seems deftly handled here. Always call for a reservation.

7. Ambleside

A good and idyllic retreat, Ambleside is one of the major centers attracting pony-trekkers, fell-hikers, and rock-scalers. The charms are essentially there year round, even in late autumn when it's fashionable to sport a mackintosh. Ambleside is superbly perched, at the top of Lake Windermere. Traditions are entrenched, especially at the Rushbearing Festival, an annual event.

WHERE TO STAY AND DINE

Half a mile south of Ambleside, **Rothay Manor,** Rothay Bridge, Ambleside, Cumbria LA22 0EH (tel. 05394/33605), on the A593, is like a French country inn, where the star is the cuisine, combined with a dedicated chef in the kitchen, well-selected French wines, and 14 comfortable, centrally heated bedrooms and two suites with baths, showers, phones, and color TVs. The price for B&B is £55 ($96.25) daily in a single, £86 ($151.50) in a double. The rooms are individually decorated, with a free use of vibrant colors. Most of them have shuttered French doors opening onto a sun balcony, with a mountain view. Throughout the estate you'll find an eclectic combination of antiques (some Georgian blended harmoniously with Victorian), flowers, and "get-lost" armchairs. The manor is also a restaurant open to nonresidents. The spacious dining room is decked with antique tables and chairs. Appointments are flawless, and incorporate fine crystal, silver, and china. At night candles burn in silver holders. Buffet lunches are served from noon to 2 p.m. six days a week. Dinners, from 8 till 9 p.m., are more ambitious, costing £20 ($35).

Kirkstone Foot, Kirkstone Pass Road, Ambleside, Cumbria LA22 9EH (tel. 05394/32232), is a 17th-century manor house whose lodging facilities have been increased with the construction of several slate-roofed and self-catering apartments in the surrounding parklike grounds. The original building is encircled by a well-tended lawn, while the interior is cozily furnished with overstuffed chairs and English paneling. The restaurant offers home-cooked English meals under the direction of the co-owner, Jane Bateman, who personally runs this fine establishment along with her husband, Simon. Fresh produce is used whenever possible. The comfortable accommodations, either in the main house or in one of the outlying units, are tastefully decorated in a family style of coziness, with color TVs, radios, and phones. For a room with private bath or shower, a full English breakfast, and a five-course dinner, expect to pay from £32 ($56) to £38 ($66.50) per person daily. If you're staying in one of their flats, you can visit for dinner for another £14.75 ($25.80) per person.

The Riverside Hotel, near Rothay Bridge, Under Loughrigg, Ambleside, Cumbria LA22 9LJ (tel. 05394/32395), is a small country hotel, beautifully situated in a riverside setting. Secluded, on a quiet lane away from traffic noise, it is still only a few minutes' walk from the center of Ambleside. The hotel is owned and run by Jim and Jean Hainey, who accommodate guests and provide good meals. All bedrooms have private baths, color TV, radios, hairdryers, and central heating. The charge for bed and half board is £34 ($59.50) per person daily.

Nanny Brow Hotel, Clappersgate, Ambleside, Cumbria LA22 9NF (tel. 0966/32036), is set on a hill about a mile west of Ambleside off the A593. This 15-bedroom hotel was once a private home but has now been turned into one of the most successful little hotels in the Ambleside area. The Tudor-style gabled house is reached via a steep tree-flanked drive. Once you arrive, you find a country-house setting with a lovely sitting room with intricate cove moldings and, if the weather merits it, a log fire. Rooms are in both the main house and a garden wing, the latter offering first-rate accommodations (some of the suites have half-tester beds). Sixteen of the rooms contain a private bath or shower, and other amenities include coffee-making equipment and color TV along with lots of comfortable charm. B&B costs £38 ($66.50) daily in a single, £74 ($129.50) in a double. The food is well prepared, using fresh ingredients. Other facilities include a solarium and whirlpool bath.

8. Rydal

Between Ambleside (at the top of Lake Windermere) and Wordsworth's former retreat at Grasmere is Rydal, a small village on one of the smallest lakes, Rydal Water.

Rydal Mount (tel. 0966/33002) was the home of William Wordsworth from 1813 until his death in 1850. Part of the house was built as a farmer's lake cottage around 1575. A descendant of Wordsworth's still owns the property, now a museum containing many portraits, furniture, and family possessions as well as mementos and books of the poet. The 3½-acre garden was landscaped by Wordsworth and contains rare trees, shrubs, and other features of interest. The house is open daily from 9:30 a.m. to 5 p.m. from March to October, from 10 a.m. to 4 p.m. from November to February. Closed Tuesday in winter. Admission is £1.50 ($2.65) for adults, 50p (90¢) for children 5 to 16.

The village of Rydal is noted for its sheep-dog trials at the end of summer.

FOOD AND LODGING

Built in the 17th century as a wayfarer's inn, the **Glen Rothay Hotel**, Rydal, Ambleside, Cumbria LA22 9LR (tel. 0966/32524) lies between Rydal and Ambleside along the A591. Set back from the highway, it has a stucco-and-flagstone façade added by Victorians. Inside, the place has been modernized, but original detailing remains, including beamed ceilings and paneling. Much of the business derives from a popular street-level pub. There is also a more formal cocktail lounge, with a fireplace and comfortable armchairs, as well as a dining room serving solid English food. The comfortable bedrooms upstairs have private bath or shower, central heating, and coffee-making equipment, and a few offer four-poster beds. Half board ranges from £30 ($52.50) to £32.50 ($56.90) per person daily.

9. Grasmere

On a lake that bears its name, Grasmere was the home of Wordsworth from 1799 to 1808. He called this area "the loveliest spot that man hath ever known." The nature poet lived with his sister, Dorothy (the writer and diarist), at **Dove Cottage**, which is now a museum administered by the Wordsworth Trust. Wordsworth, who followed Southey as poet laureate, died in the spring of 1850, and was buried in the graveyard of the village church at Grasmere. Another tenant of Dove Cottage was Thomas De Quincey (*Confessions of an English Opium Eater*). For a combined ticket costing £2.80 ($4.90) for adults, £1.20 ($2.10) for children, you can visit both Dove Cottage and the **Wordsworth Museum.** This houses the Wordsworth treasures, manuscripts, paintings, and memorabilia. There are also various special exhibitions throughout the year, exploring the art and literature of English Romanticism. The property is open daily from 9:30 a.m. to 5:30 p.m. except from mid-January to mid-February. For further information, phone 09665/544; 09665/268 for Dove Cottage Restaurant information.

FOOD AND LODGING

In this hiking and rock-scaling center, you'll find the following recommendations, beginning first with the most expensive, then descending in price level.
Michael's Nook, Grasmere, Cumbria LA22 9RP (tel. 09665/496; turn off the

A591 at the Swan Hotel), is a country-house hotel, once a private residence, standing in its own secluded garden of three acres. A Lakeland home of stone, honoring a hill shepherd, Michael, who was immortalized by Wordsworth in a poem of the same name, it contains much fine mahogany woodwork and paneling, exemplified by its elegant staircase. Throughout the house, owned by Grasmere antiques dealer Reg Gifford and his wife, Elizabeth, are many fine antiques, enhanced by the glow of log fires or vases of flowers. The handsomely decorated bedrooms, nine doubles and two suites are individually furnished with such amenities as bath herbs, hairdryers, sandalwood sachets in drawers, and lavender-scented closets. One room, decorated with flowered chintz, has a four-poster bed. All units have private baths and showers, phones, and TVs. The minimum booking is usually three nights, but shorter visits will be accommodated where possible. The tariffs range from £160 ($280) in a standard double with bath, £212 ($371) in a superior double with bath, the rates including dinner, breakfast, service, and VAT.

Only about 20 persons are served in the intimate dining room, which accepts reservations from nonresidents for both lunch and dinner. Care and attention to detail go into preparation of the meals, with menus changing daily. You might choose from poached prawns, Loch Linnhe in cream sauce flavored with Drambuie or roast leg of lamb filled with prune-and-apple stuffing, perhaps sautéed calves' liver in shallot-and-vinegar sauce. An attractive staff serves the tables. Lunch is priced at £21 ($36.75) and is served at 12:30 p.m. daily. Dinner, at 7:30 p.m., costs £29.50 ($51.65), VAT included. In summer, dinner sittings are at 7 and 9 p.m. on Saturday.

The **Wordsworth Hotel,** Grasmere, Cumbria LA22 9RP (tel. 09665/592) stands in the heart of the village and is owned by Reg Gifford of Michael's Nook Country House Hotel. An old stone Lakeland house (once the 19th-century Rothay Hotel), the Wordsworth has been gutted and rebuilt to provide large bedrooms with views of the fells and river, as well as modern baths, TVs, phones, and comfortable chairs. The rate of £38.50 ($67.40) to £50 ($87.50) per person daily includes a full breakfast and VAT. There is a four-poster bedroom with beams and dormer windows. The original master bedroom has a Victorian bathroom, with a brass towel rail and polished pipes and taps. There are several lounges, with sink-in armchairs grouped around log fires. A buffet lunch is served in the cocktail lounge, including the chef's hot dish of the day. A set six-course dinner at £19 ($33.25) is likely to include a light fruit or vegetable appetizer, then soup, a choice of two meat dishes, followed by dessert or cheese, along with coffee and mints. The à la carte menu is more ambitious, and a three-course meal of, say, smoked-haddock and cheese soufflé, clear beef broth with quail eggs, breast of chicken stuffed with walnuts, and rich chocolate-fudge cake will cost around £20 ($35). Each dish is carefully explained on the menu so you know what you're getting. Meals are served daily from 12:30 to 2 p.m. and 7 to 9 p.m. (to 9:30 p.m. on Friday and Saturday). The hotel has a large heated swimming pool, with whirlpool, a sauna, a solarium, a games room, and a mini-gym.

The **White Moss House,** Rydal Water, Grasmere, Cumbria LA22 9SE (tel. 09665/295), is an old Lakeland cottage off the main A591 between Grasmere and Rydal Water. It overlooks the lake and the fells, where you're welcomed by Peter and Susan Dixon as a house guest to be pampered with morning tea in bed, your bedcovers turned down at night, and your culinary preferences remembered and adhered to. The rooms are comfortably furnished and well heated in nippy weather. In all there are only five accommodations, so advance booking is essential. These units have private baths, color TVs, direct-dial phones, radios, trouser presses, hairdryers, and such bathroom amenities as soap, shampoo, and herbal bath salts. The rent is £49 ($85.75) to £59 ($103.25) per person nightly including an elegant, if large, breakfast and a dinner to satisfy a gourmet. There's also Brockstone, their cottage annex, a five-minute drive along the road, where two, three, or four guests can be accommodated in utter peace. Dinner is a leisurely affair beginning at 8 p.m. You're served five courses likely to include a roast of lamb with an orange and red-currant sauce or quail with a chicken and brown-rice stuffing. For dessert, I hope Mrs. Beeton's chocolate pudding is featured. If you're not a resident, dinner will cost from £19 ($33.25), but you must reserve a table early.

The Red Lion Hotel, Grasmere, Cumbria LA22 9SS (tel. 09665/456), is a 200-year-old coaching inn in the heart of the village, owned by Westmorland Hotels. It's only a short stroll to Dove Cottage, once the home of William Wordsworth, and it's assumed that the poet often stopped for a meal, a drink, or to warm himself by the fire. Recently refurbished, the hotel offers 36 bedrooms, all with private bath. B&B costs from £24 ($42) per person daily, and half board is available for £35.50 ($62.15). Rates include VAT. There's an elevator to all floors. Enjoy a drink or lunch in the light and airy surroundings of the Easdale Bar or try the Lamb Inn and Buttery for a more traditional pub atmosphere. In the dining room, you'll be served some of the finest fare in the district, a set meal costing from £12 ($21), or you can order à la carte.

Swan Hotel, Grasmere, Cumbria LA22 9RF (tel. 09665/551), has been renovated so that only the shell of the old building remains. However, there have been inns on this site for 300 years. Sir Walter Scott used to slip in for a secret drink early in the morning, and Wordsworth mentioned the place in *The Waggoner.* In fact, in one of the lounges is the poet's tapestry chair. The 36 rooms contain built-in furniture and good beds. Singles cost from £58 ($101.50) daily, and twins begin at £75 ($131.25), with service and VAT included. The restaurant serves daily from 11 a.m. to 3 p.m. and 6 to 10:30 p.m., providing both table d'hôte and à la carte meals.

10. Hawkshead and Coniston

Discover for yourself the village of Hawkshead, with its 15th-century grammar school where Wordsworth went to school for eight years (he carved his name on a desk that still remains). Near Hawkshead, in the vicinity of Esthwaite Water, is the 17th-century **Hill Top Farm,** former home of Beatrix Potter, the author of the Peter Rabbit books, who died during World War II.

At **Coniston,** four miles away from Hawkshead, you can visit the village associated with John Ruskin. Coniston is a good base for rock climbing. The Coniston "Old Man" towers in the background at 2,633 feet, giving mountain climbers one of the finest views of the Lake District.

John Ruskin, poet, artist, and critic, was one of the great figures of the Victorian age and a prophet of social reform, inspiring such diverse men as Proust, Frank Lloyd Wright, and Gandhi. He moved to his home, **Brantwood** (tel. 05394/41396), on the east side of Coniston Water, in 1872 and lived there until his death in 1900. The house today is open for visitors to view much Ruskiniana, including some 200 pictures by him. Also displayed are his coach and boat, the *Jumping Jenny.* A video program tells the story of Ruskin's life and work.

An exhibition illustrating the work of W. J. Linton is laid out in his old printing room. Linton was born in England in 1812 and died at New Haven, Connecticut, in 1897. Well known as a wood engraver and for his private press, he lived at Brantwood, where he set up his printing business in 1853. He published *The English Republic,* a newspaper and review, before immigrating to America in 1866, where he set up his printing press in 1870. The house is owned and managed by the Education Trust, a self-supporting registered charity. It is open daily from mid-March to mid-November, and Wednesday to Sunday in winter, from 11 a.m. to 5:30 p.m. Admission is £2 ($3.50) for adults and £1 ($1.75) for children, with a family ticket costing £5.25 ($9.20). Part of the 250-acre estate is also open as a nature trail, costing 50p (90¢) for adults, 35p (55¢) for children, if the walk is taken separately. The Brantwood stables, designed by Ruskin, have been converted into a tea room and restaurant, the Jumping Jenny Also in the stable building is the Lakeland Guild

Craft Gallery, which follows the Ruskin tradition in encouraging contemporary craft work of the finest quality.

Literary fans may want to pay a pilgrimage to the graveyard of the village church, where Ruskin was buried; his family turned down a chance to have him interred at Westminster Abbey.

FOOD AND LODGING AT HAWKSHEAD

The most desirable accommodation is found at **Tarn Hows,** Hawkshead, Cumbria LA22 0PR (tel. 09666/330), which lies about 1½ miles by B5285, the Coniston Road. Secluded enough to be called a retreat, Tarns Hows is named after a scenic attraction of the Lake District. The hotel itself lies in one of the most beautiful sections of Cumbria. Operated by the Lilley family, the hotel offers 23 bedrooms, each well kept and furnished in a homelike comfortable fashion. B&B rates begin at £18 ($31.50) per person nightly. All accommodations are equipped with private bath or shower, phone, radio, and beverage-making facilities. Members of the family, based on reader reports, show a personal interest in their guests. They also serve good food. John Lilley is the chef de cuisine, and he offers fresh, correctly prepared dishes that appeal to a variety of tastes.

The best place for food in the area is **Grizedale Lodge,** Grizedale, Hawkshead, Cumbria LA22 0Q1 (tel. 09666/532), which is a Lakeside country *restaurant avec chambres.* Many people come here just to dine, as the cuisine is topnotch. Margaret Lamb is considered one of the finest chefs in the Lake District, and her considerable talents are reflected by her five-course evening meals based on the best of English and continental dishes. During the day guests order bar lunches but at night they can enjoy a memorable meal in a tranquil setting for only £13 ($22.75) per person. Service is personable. Mrs. Lamb along with her husband, Jack, also offer several handsomely furnished bedrooms for guests. Overnight charges range from £28 ($49) in a single, rising to £43 ($75.25) in a double. Guests are received every month but January.

FOOD AND LODGING AT CONISTON

The most popular, traditional, and attractive pub in the village is the **Coniston Sun Hotel,** Coniston, Cumbria LA21 8HQ (tel. 05394/41248). In reality, it is a country-house hotel of much character, dating from 1902, although the inn attached to it is from the 16th century. Standing on its own beautiful grounds above the village, it lies at the foot of "Coniston Old Man." Donald Campbell made this place his headquarters during his attempt on the world water-speed record. Each of the 11 bedrooms is decorated with style, and two of them contain four-posters. Each unit also has a private bath, color TV, and hot beverage facilities. B&B costs from £25 ($43.75) to £28.50 ($49.90) per person daily. A four-course dinner is offered for £14.50 ($35.40), including coffee and VAT. Fresh local produce is used whenever possible in the candlelit restaurant. Log fires take the chill off a winter evening, and guests relax informally in the lounge, which is like a library. Many sports can be arranged.

11. Keswick

Lying 22 miles north of Windermere, Keswick opens onto Derwentwater, one of the loveliest lakes in the district. Robert Southey, poet laureate, lived for four decades at Greta Hall, and was buried at Crosthwaite Church. Coleridge lived here too, depending on Southey for financial aid. Sir Hugh Walpole, the novelist, in a different era also resided near Keswick.

Keswick is the natural geographical starting point for car tours and walks of exploration in the northern Lake District, including the John Peel country to the north of Skiddaw (quiet and little known), Borrowdale, Buttermere, and Crummock Water, as well as Bassenthwaite, Thirlmere, and Ullswater.

WHERE TO STAY

A tranquil retreat is **Grange Country House,** Manor Brow, Ambleside Road, Keswick, Cumbria CA12 4BA (tel. 07687/72500). Set in its own gardens, it stands on a hilltop where it receives guests in every month but December and January. The hotel has 11 attractively furnished and well-kept bedrooms, each with private bath or shower. Charges are from £24 ($42) per person nightly for B&B. This charming hotel dates from the 1800s, and guests are welcome in chilly weather by log fires. Many of its rooms open onto beautiful views of the Lakeland hills. The hotel, directed by Jane and Duncan Miller, also offers a first-rate cuisine. Guests can dine here for $12.50 ($21.90) in the evening. The house is furnished in part with antiques.

The Keswick, Station Road, Keswick, Cumbria CA12 4NQ (tel. 07687/72020), set in its own 4½ acres of landscaped gardens, stands near public parks in a residential district of town, about a five-minute walk from the center. Its rhythmical bay windows and its somber stone walls evoke the very essence of a Victorian hotel. Inside, tall ceilings, a collection of blue willow porcelain, and antique reminders of a grander age lie in secluded crannies and on the landings of stairwells. The hotel contains a well-upholstered collection of high-ceilinged bedrooms with private bath or shower, color TV, radio, phone, and a welcoming tray. Singles cost from £50 ($87.50) daily, and doubles or twins go for £75 ($131.25). Many of the bedrooms, with private bath or shower, are flooded with sunlight from bay windows that encompass views of the manicured grounds. Families are especially welcomed. The restaurant, also opening onto views, serves both English and international dishes.

Skiddaw Hotel, Main Street, Keswick, Cumbria CA12 5BN (tel. 07687/72071), has an impressive face and entrance marquee built right onto the sidewalk in the heart of Keswick. The owners have refurbished the interior retaining the best features in combination with modern facilities. The bedrooms are compact and eye-catching, with phones, color TVs, and hot beverage facilities. Most have baths. They rent for £18 ($31.50) daily in a single, £32 ($56) in a double. Guests gather in the lounge or the popular but intimate cocktail bar with an art nouveau ambience. Meals feature well-prepared English cuisine, available à la carte all day. In addition, a chef's special, such as Lancashire hot pot, is offered for lunch. Dinner costs from £7 ($12.25) to £10 ($17.50). There is a wide selection of wines.

---

12. Borrowdale

If you head south from Keswick for 3½ miles along the B5289, you come to one of the most charming spots in the Lake District. This beautiful Lakeland valley begins near Great Gable at a height of 2,949 feet, opening out to enfold Derwentwater. Traditionally, it has been a center of rambling and rock climbing. It also contains one of the best-known hotels in the Lake District (see below).

FOOD AND LODGING

Since 1987, the Stakis hotel chain has run the **Stakis Lodore Swiss Hotel,** Borrowdale, Keswick, Cumbria CA12 5UX (tel. 059684/285), overlooking Derwentwater. With its spike-capped mansard tower, symmetrical gables, and balcony-embellished stone façade, it looks a lot like a hotel you might find in the foothills of Lake Geneva. When it was constructed in the 19th century, its owners were Swiss. The old tradition of good rooms, good food, and service continues today. The hotel sits amid fields where cows graze. The interior has been modernized, and each of the well-furnished bedrooms contains a direct-dial phone, hairdryer, private bath, mini-bar, radio, color TV with in-house video, and coffee-making equipment. Bed and breakfast costs £38 ($66.50) per person daily, going up to £53 ($92.75) for half board. The food is exceptional for the area, with a set dinner costing from £16 ($28). However, a menu gastronomique is offered for only £23 ($40.25). Dishes include roast topside of English beef with Yorkshire pudding, Morecambe Bay shrimp, and plaice sautéed in butter. Call for a reservation, especially at dinner. Food is served from 12:30 to 2 p.m. and 7:30 to 9:30 p.m. daily.

Borrowdale Hotel, Borrowdale, Keswick, Cumbria CA12 5UY (tel. 059684/224), is a Lakeland stone building, circa 1866, with log fires welcoming you when the weather is not kind. Its rooms are comfortable, many opening onto views. All have private bath or shower and toilet, color TV, radio, intercom, baby-listening unit, and hairdryer. Some traditional four-poster beds are available. The tariff for half board, inclusive of VAT, is £38 ($66.50) daily in a single, £85 ($148.75) in a double. The main attraction of the hotel is its restaurant. A traditional English lunch on Sunday costs from £8 ($14). During the rest of the week, bar lunches with a choice of 25 main courses cost in the £6 ($10.50) range. The seven-course dinner, consisting of appetizer, main, and dessert courses, each having a choice of at least six different dishes, starts at £13.50 ($23.65). Cuisine from all parts of the globe is offered, and the menu is changed daily. If you wish to have the daily roast, the chef will carve it at your table from a silver trolley. The hotel is owned and managed by Gunter and Jean Fidrmuc who, together with their resident manager, Christopher Carss, and his efficient, friendly staff, assure you of a warm welcome.

13. Bassenthwaite

With its fine stretch of water in the shadow of the 3,053-foot Skiddaw, Bassenthwaite makes a good center for exploring the western Lakeland.

FOOD AND LODGING
Rich in history, the **Armathwaite Hall Hotel,** Bassenthwaite, Cumbria CA12 4RE (tel. 059681/551), 1½ miles west on the B5291, was originally built in the 1300s as a house for Benedictine nuns. During the Middle Ages it was plundered frequently, leaving the sisters wretchedly poor. By the 17th century a series of wealthy landowners had completed the severe Gothic design of its stately façade, and in 1844 an architecturally compatible series of wings were added. In the 1930s it was converted into a hotel, and Sir Hugh Walpole, who once stayed here, found it "a house of perfect and irresistible charm." The Graves family, in residence since 1977, carry on in the old traditions. Ringed with almost 140 acres of woodland, some of it bordering the lake, the place offers a magnificent entrance hall filled with hunting trophies and sheathed with expensive paneling. There's also a whimsically modern cocktail lounge whose veneer-clad Gay '90s bar contrasts with one of the most neo-baroque fireplaces in the district. A Victorian billiard room is lined with old engravings, and a first-class restaurant offers a view of the lake. An indoor swimming pool is ringed with stone walls and sheltered from the rain with a roof of wooden trusses. Each of the handsomely furnished bedrooms, 42 in all, contains a private bath, color TV, radio, and phone. Singles range from £45 ($78.75) to £66 ($115.50) daily, and doubles or twins peak at £100 ($175), with breakfast included.

14. Ullswater

A seven-mile sheet of water, stretching from Pooley Bridge to Patterdale, Ullswater is the second-largest lake in the district. Incidentally, it was on the shores of Ullswater that Wordsworth saw his "host of golden daffodils." The market town of Penrith lies seven miles to the east, and while housed in the area it is easy to explore several places of archeological interest, such as Hadrian's Wall, east of Carlisle, or Long Meg stone circle near Penrith.

WHERE TO STAY AND DINE

A *Relais & Chateaux* for the past quarter of a century, **Sharrow Bay Country House Hotel,** Howtown, Lake Ullswater, near Penrith, Cumbria CA10 2LZ (tel. 08536/301), is the second oldest member of that prestigious group in Britain. It is an unusual Victorian house that was a private home until it was purchased by Francis Coulson in 1949. Realizing its potential, he began restoration work on the structure, with its low angled roof and wide eaves, sleeping on the floor while the work was in progress. Three years later he was joined by Brian Sack, and together they turned Sharrow into one of England's finest eating places. This was also the first Country House Hotel to be created in Great Britain. The hotel offers 30 antique-filled bedrooms, 18 in the gatehouse and cottages. Of these, eight units in the main house and all in the cottages have private baths. Some accommodations, as well as the drawing room, open onto views of the lakes, trees, or Martindale Fells. Each of the individually decorated bedrooms has a name rather than a number. The daily terms range from £84 ($147) to £100 ($175) per person daily for room, dinner, a full English breakfast, service, and VAT.

The six-course £31.50 ($55.15) set menu contains a formidable list of choices. I recently counted 28 appetizers, including the chef's specialty, mousseline of fresh salmon with hollandaise sauce. The carefully chosen main courses seemed designed to make the best of home-grown food items, including roast Lancashire guinea fowl, a roast stuffed shoulder of young English lamb, or even a Cumberland ham from a cold-table selection. The dessert selections are among the best you'll find in northwest England, including a fresh-strawberry, hazelnut, and brandy cream roulade. A feature as well is the Sharrow homemade cream ices, including prune and armagnac. Brian Sack is the dining room host, with a friendly and efficient staff. If you're motoring through the area, I suggest you call ahead and make a reservation for the £19.50 ($34.15) set luncheon. Meals are served from 1 to 1:45 p.m. and 8 to 8:45 p.m. Either for a meal or a room, you should write or telephone in advance. Closed December, January, and February.

---

15. Brampton

One of the best centers for the Lake District is at Brampton, which is only four miles from the Roman Wall and 11 miles from the M6 Motorway and Carlisle.

WHERE TO STAY AND DINE

On the A689 road, the **Farlam Hall Hotel,** Brampton, Cumbria CA8 2NG (tel. 06956/234), 2¾ miles south of Brampton, is a good base for visiting the Roman Wall, the Lake District, and the Yorkshire Dales. A *Relais & Chateaux,* Farlam Hall is listed as a building of architectural and historic interest. It was just a farmhouse when it was erected in the 17th century, but in 1826 it changed hands and became a noted Border manor house. It stands in four acres of grounds, with some fine old trees, a stream, and a small lake. John Wesley is said to have preached in the house, and George Stephenson, inventor of the steam railroad engine, stayed here. The hotel is run by the Quinion and Stevenson families, who have set high standards of service and cuisine. Barry, an advanced Cordon Bleu chef, is in charge of the kitchens, offering such dishes as roast Lancashire duckling with honey, almond, and raisin sauce. All ingredients are freshly brought in from the nearby coast or the local farms. Dinnertime is graced by the Quinion women, who serve the tables in full evening dress. Dinner in the formal dining room, with white linen cloths and napkins and silver table service, is at 8 p.m., costing £19.50 ($34.15). Men are expected to wear jackets and ties. Accommodations consist of 13 bedrooms, all doubles and twins, with private baths or showers, direct-dial phones, and hairdryers. Furnishings are antique, and everything is comfortable. There are views of the gardens and the lake. An overnight stay, including an English breakfast, dinner, and VAT, costs from £60 ($105) to £75 ($131.25) per person.

YORKSHIRE AND NORTHUMBRIA

For the connoisseur, the northeast of England is rich in attractions. **Yorkshire,** known to readers of *Wuthering Heights* and the works of James Herriot, embraces both the moors of North Yorkshire and the Dales. With the radical changing of the old county boundaries, the shires are now divided into North Yorkshire (the most interesting from the tourist point of view), West Yorkshire, South Yorkshire, and Humberside.

Away from the cities and towns that still carry the taint of the Industrial Revolution, the beauty of Yorkshire is wild and remote. It's characterized by limestone crags, caverns along the Pennines, many peaks, mountainous uplands, rolling hills, the chalkland wolds, heather blooming on the moorlands, broad vales, lazy rivers, and tumbling streams. Yorkshire lures not only with inland scenery but with some 100 miles of shoreline, with rocky headlands, cliffs, sandy bays, rock-strewn pools, sheltered coves, fishing villages, bird sanctuaries, former smugglers' dens, and yachting havens.

Across this vast region came the Romans, the Anglo-Saxons, the Vikings, the monks of the Middle Ages, kings of England, lords of the manor, craftspeople, hill farmers, and wool makers—all leaving their mark. You can still see Roman roads and pavements, great abbeys and castles, stately homes, open-air museums, and craft centers, along with parish churches, old villages, and cathedrals. In fact, Yorkshire's battle-scarred castles, Gothic abbeys, and great county manor houses from all periods are unrivaled anywhere in Britain.

Northumbria is made up of the counties of Northumberland, Cleveland, and Durham. Tyne and Wear is one of the more recently created counties, with Newcastle upon Tyne as its center.

The Saxons who came to northern England centuries ago carved out this kingdom, which at the time stretched from the Firth of Forth in Scotland to the banks of the Humber in Yorkshire. Vast tracts of that ancient kingdom remain natural and unspoiled. Again, this slice of England has more than its share of industrial towns, but you don't go here to see them. Set out to explore the wild hills and open spaces, crossing the dales of the eastern Pennines.

The whole area evokes ancient battles and bloody border raids. Roman relics, border castles, Saxon churches, and monastic ruins abound in Northumbria, none more notable than Hadrian's Wall, one of the wonders of the Western world. The finest stretch of the wall lies within the Northumberland National Park between the stony North Tyne River and the county boundary at Gilsland.

Let's begin our travels through this area of northeast England in its major historical and ecclesiastical center—

1. York

Few cities in England are as rich in history as York. It is still encircled by its 13th- and 14th-century city walls—about 2½ miles long—with four gates. One of these, Micklegate, once grimly greeted visitors coming up from the south with the heads of traitors. To this day, you can walk on the footpath of the walls of the Middle Ages.

The crowning achievement of York is its Minster or cathedral, which makes the city an ecclesiastical center topped only by Canterbury. In spite of this, York is one of the most overlooked cities on the cathedral circuit. Perhaps foreign visitors are intimidated by the feeling that the great city of northeastern England is too far north. Actually, it lies about 195 miles north of London on the Ouse River, and can easily be tied in with a motor trip to Edinburgh. Or after visiting Cambridge, a motorist can make a swing through a too-often-neglected cathedral circuit: Ely, Lincoln, then York.

There was a Roman York (Hadrian came this way), then a Saxon York, a Danish York, a Norman York (William the Conqueror slept here), a medieval York, a Georgian York, a Victorian York (the center of a flourishing rail business), and certainly now a 20th-century York. A generous amount of 18th-century York remains, including Richard Boyle's restored Assembly Rooms.

THE SIGHTS

The best way to see York is to go to the **Tourist Information Centre,** DeGrey Rooms, Exhibition Square (tel. 0904/621756) at 10:15 a.m. and 2:15 p.m. daily from April to the end of October, where you'll be met by a volunteer guide who will take you on a 1½-hour walking tour of the city, revealing its history and lore through numerous intriguing stories. There is no charge. Additional tours are made at 7 p.m. daily during June, July, and August. Limited winter tours may also be available.

At some point in your exploration, you may want to visit **The Shambles,** once the meat-butchering center of York, dating back before the Norman Conquest. But this messy business has given way, and the ancient street survives. It is filled with jewelry stores, cafés, and buildings that huddle so closely together you can practically stand in the middle of the pavement, arms outstretched, and touch the houses on both sides of the street.

Recently, special interest has been focused on discoveries of the Viking era, from 867 to 1066, when the city was known as Jorvik, the Viking capital and a major Scandinavian trade center (see below).

Incidentally, the suffix "gate" used for streets and sites in York is from the Scandinavian word for "street," a holdover from the era when Vikings held sway here.

York Minster

One of the great cathedrals of the world, York Minster traces its origins back to the early 7th century. The present building, however, dates from the 13th century

Like the minster at Lincoln, York Cathedral is characterized by three towers, all built in the 15th century. The central tower is lantern shaped, in the Perpendicular style.

Perhaps the distinguishing characteristic of the cathedral is its medley of stained glass from the Middle Ages—in glorious Angelico blues, ruby reds, forest greens, and ambers. See in particular the large east window, the work of a 15th-century Coventry glass painter. In the north transept is an architectural gem of the mid-13th century, the "Five Sisters," with its lancets. The choir screen, from the late 15th century, has an impressive line-up—everybody from William the Conqueror to the overthrown Henry VI.

The Chapter House is open Monday to Saturday from 10 a.m., costing adults 50p (90¢) and children 20p (35¢). The shop is open Monday to Saturday from 9 a.m. to 5 p.m. and on Sunday from 1:30 to 4 p.m. The refurbished Undercroft is open Monday to Saturday from 10 a.m. to dusk, on Sunday from 1 p.m. to dusk, costing £1.30 ($2.30) for adults, 60p ($1.05) for children. The Crypt is open during conducted tours only. At a party reception desk near the entrance to the Minster parties can be put in touch with a guide, if one is available, for a conducted tour. Gifts toward the maintenance of the Minster are requested. For information, telephone 0904/624426.

From the top of the central tower on a clear day, there are unrivaled views of York and the Vale of York. It is a steep climb up a stone spiral staircase and not recommended for the very elderly, very young, or anyone with a heart condition or breathing difficulties. In winter, the tower is only open on Saturday and Sunday, providing the weather is suitable. A climb costs adults £1 ($1.75), and children pay 50p (90¢).

The Treasurer's House

In the Minster Yard, the Treasurer's House (tel. 0904/624247) stands on a site where there's been a building since Roman times. The main part of the house was rebuilt in 1620 as the official residence of the treasurer of York Minster, and was lived in as a private home until 1930. It has a magnificent series of rooms with fine furniture, glass, and china of the 17th and 18th centuries. An audio-visual program describes the work of the medieval treasurers and some of the personalities with which this York house is associated. The house has an attractive small garden. It is open from April until the end of October daily from 10:30 a.m. to 5 p.m. (last entry at 4:30 p.m.). Admission is £1.50 ($2.65) for adults, 75p ($1.30) for children. On some evenings in summer, the house is open from 7:30 to 9:30 p.m. when you can enjoy coffee by candlelight in the Great Hall. An attractive shop and licensed restaurant serving Yorkshire specialties are open the same hours as the house.

York Castle Museum

On the site of York's Castle, the York Castle Museum (tel. 0904/633932) is one of the finest folk museums in the country. Its unique feature is a re-creation of a Victorian cobbled street, "Kirkgate," named for the museum's founder, Dr. John Kirk. He acquired his large collection while visiting his patients in rural Yorkshire at the beginning of this century. The period rooms range from a neoclassical Georgian dining room through an overstuffed and heavily adorned Victorian parlor, to the 1953 sitting room with a brand-new television set purchased to watch the coronation of Elizabeth II. In the Debtors' Prison, former prison cells display craft workshops. There is also a superb collection of arms and armor, and the Costume Gallery, where displays are changed regularly to reflect the variety of the collection. Half Moon Court is an Edwardian street, with a gypsy caravan and a pub (sorry, the bar's closed!). During the summer, you can visit a watermill on the bank of the River Foss.

The museum is open April to October from 9:30 a.m. to 6:30 p.m. Monday to Saturday (from 10 a.m. on Sunday). From November to March, hours are 9:30 a.m. to 5 p.m. Monday to Saturday (from 10 a.m. on Sunday). Last admission is one hour before closing, and it is recommended that you allow at least two hours for a visit to this museum. Admission is £2.50 ($4.40) for adults, £1.25 ($2.20) for children.

National Railway Museum

The first national museum to be built away from London, the National Railway Museum (tel. 0904/621261) has attracted millions of visitors since it opened in 1975. Adapted from an original steam locomotive depot, the museum gives visitors a chance to look under and inside steam locomotives or see how Queen Victoria traveled in luxury. In addition, there's a full-size collection of railway memorabilia, including an early-19th-century clock and penny machines for purchasing tickets to the railway platform. On display are more than 20 full-size locomotives. One, the *Agenoria*, dates from 1829 and is a contemporary of Stephenson's well-known *Rocket*. It's almost identical to the first American locomotive, the *Stourbridge Lion*, sent to the United States from England in 1828. Items on exhibition change from time to time, but there is always a fine selection of the beautifully colored British steam locomotives on display. *Mallard*, the fastest steam locomotive in the world, is in the museum when it's not at work on the railroad. Of several royal coaches, the most interesting is the century-old Royal Saloon, in which Queen Victoria rode until her death. It's like a small hotel, with polished wood, silk, brocade, and silver accessories.

The museum, on Leeman Road, can be visited Monday to Saturday from 10 a.m. to 6 p.m. and on Sunday from 11 a.m. to 6 p.m. It is closed on some public holidays. Admission is £2 ($3.50) for adults, £1 ($1.75) for children.

Jorvik Viking Centre

At Coppergate (tel. 0904/643211) is the Viking city discovered many feet below the present ground level. It was reconstructed exactly as it stood in A.D. 948. In a "time car," you can travel back through the ages to 1067 when Normans sacked the city, and then ride slowly through the street market peopled by faithfully modeled Vikings. You can go through a house where a family lived and down to the river to see the ship chandlers at work and a Norwegian cargo ship unloading. At the end of the ride, you pass through the Finds Hut where thousands of artifacts are displayed. Departures on the time train are at regular intervals from 9 a.m. to 7 p.m. daily in summer (until 5:30 p.m. in winter). Admission is £2.75 ($4.80) for adults, £1.35 ($2.35) for children.

Theatre Royal

Finally, Theatre Royal, St. Leonard's Place (tel. 0904/623568), is an old traditional theater building with modern additions to house the box office, bars, and restaurant. It is worth inquiring about the current production as the Royal Shakespeare Company includes York in its tours, the Arts Council presents dance, drama, and opera, and visiting celebrities appear in classics. There is also an excellent resident repertory company.

Seats go from £3.50 ($6.15) in the gallery to £6 ($10.50) in the dress circle. The Theatre Royal Restaurant (tel. 0904/632596) provides a good meal costing £3.50 ($6.15) to £6 ($10.50). You don't have to buy a seat to eat here, and it's quite a relaxing experience to sit inside with your drink and a snack, looking out on the world passing by. The restaurant is open daily from noon to 2:30 p.m. and 5 p.m. until curtain time.

WHERE TO STAY

My recommendations for rooms and meals in the York area follow.

The Upper Bracket

Middlethorpe Hall Hotel, Bishopthorpe Road, York, North Yorkshire YO2 1QP (tel. 0904/641241), on the outskirts of York near the race course, is set in 26 acres of park reached along the A19 road. Built in 1699, the stately red-brick William and Mary country house had fallen into disrepair during a period of use as a nightclub before it was purchased by Historic House Hotels and beautifully restored, both inside and out. Fresh flowers are used profusely, with lots of antiques providing the ambience of a manor house of other days nicely blended with modern amenities. As befits such a house, there is an elegant drawing room, plus a library. The hotel has 31 bedrooms, including three suites, each of which is done in its own decor and style. All the rooms have up-to-date bathrooms. Singles rent for £75 ($131.25) to £85 ($148.75) daily and twins and doubles for £98 ($171.50) to £110 ($192.50). Guests find in their rooms such niceties as homemade cookies and bottles of Malvern water, as well as bathrobes. Meals are served in two restaurants, one oak-paneled and one a grill room. A choice of either international or English traditional meals is offered, a table d'hôte dinner costing £23.90 ($41.85) in the dining room, £21.50 ($37.65) in the grill room.

Bilbrough Manor, Bilbrough, York, North Yorkshire YO2 3PH (tel. 0937/834002), is one of the loveliest places to stay—or to dine—in the environs of York. The location is four miles southwest of York. The imposing neo-Gothic walls and multiple chimneys that rise today were built in 1901 as a replacement for a dilapidated manor house. However, its foundations go back to the 13th century. The hotel sits near the village church, just where it was discovered by Mr. and Mrs. C. C. Bell, who decided to make it into a quality hotel and luxurious restaurant.

The public rooms today are sumptuous with paneling and baronial fireplaces, along with deep chintz-covered sofas. Each of the 12 individually furnished bedrooms is elegant and unique, with many thoughtful accessories. These include a private bath or shower, color TV, radio, hairdryer, and trouser press. Singles rent for £85 ($148.75) daily, and twins or doubles run £120 ($210), including an English breakfast and VAT. Even if you don't reside here, you might want to dine, sampling the superb viands of Idris Caldora. He cooks in the modern French tradition, and food is served in a historic paneled dining room. Service is on Wedgwood, and the menu changes frequently, but always fresh quality ingredients are used. A certain artistry is reflected both in the food preparation and in the presentation of dishes. Meals are served from noon to 1:45 p.m. and 7 to 9:30 p.m., costing from £35 ($61.25) per person unless you order the table d'hôte menus: £12 ($21) at lunch, £18.50 ($32.40) at dinner. Always call for a reservation.

Viking Hotel, North Street, York, North Yorkshire YO1 1JF (tel. 0904/659822), is a 187-bedroom, modern hotel within the ancient city walls, overlooking the River Ouse, with the attractions of York only a few minutes' walk away. The bedrooms, many with views toward the Minster, have private baths, color TVs, direct-dial phones, trouser presses, hairdryers, and hot-beverage facilities. A single room costs from £62.50 ($109.40) daily, while £82.50 ($144.40) will buy a double or twin unit, inclusive of an English breakfast, VAT, and service. The hotel's two restaurants offer a variety of dining. The Regatta is for à la carte meals, the Carving Room for traditional roasts and an à la carte choice. Each eating place has a bar and offers a welcoming atmosphere.

The Judges Lodging, 9 Lendal, York, North Yorkshire YO1 2AQ (tel. 0904/638733). The earliest historical fact about this charming house is that it was the home of a certain Dr. Wintringham in 1710. At the beginning of the 19th century it is listed as having been a judges' lodging, used when they traveled north from the London Inns of Justice. Drive around the sweeping drive, then up the broad stone steps to the stout front door. You will be greeted by the butler who will register your name and then lead you up a circular wooden staircase, the only one of its type in the United Kingdom, to one of the 14 bedrooms. All have four-poster beds. If you want to spoil yourself, you can book the large Prince Albert suite, a twin-bedded room with three large windows overlooking the Minster. Prince Albert actually slept in the room once. Hand-embroidered sheets and French embroidered linen in the bathrooms are an additional elegant touch. Each room has a different decor and is named accordingly. One is known as the Queen Mother Room, and in fact it is with her blessing that the coffee cups you will use at dinner come from Clarence House. Singles cost £40 ($70) to £55 ($96.25) daily, depending on the type, while doubles and twins peak at £110 ($192.50). Rates include VAT and a full English breakfast.

There are two dining rooms, where candles flicker and the carefully trained French staff will attend to your every need. Dinner will cost from £18 ($31.50). All meat, fish, and vegetables are brought in fresh. Down in the old cellars where they found all sorts of bits of Roman pottery, antique pieces of glass, and other relics of the house's varied past, there is the Cocktail Bar, open to the public.

The Medium-Priced Range

Mount Royale Hotel, 119 The Mount, York, North Yorkshire YO2 2DA (tel. 0904/628856), is excellent for the money, and the food is good too. Run by Richard and Christine Oxtoby, the Mount Royale is only minutes from the city center. Built in 1833, it is carefully furnished with some antiques blended with modern pieces. They took over the house next door, increasing their bedroom capacity to 20 units, each with bath, costing from £50 ($87.50) daily in a single, £60 ($105) to £90 ($157.50) in a double or twin, including VAT and a large breakfast. The hotel has a swimming pool. The menu consists of roast joints with interesting accompaniments. The extensive set menu, costing £19.50 ($34.15), carries supplements for such items as fresh out-of-season asparagus or strawberries. The dining room opens onto an attractive garden. Justifiably popular with locals, the restaurant requires advance reservations.

Dean Court Hotel, Duncombe Place, York, North Yorkshire YO1 2EF (tel. 0904/625082), is an ancient building lying right beneath the towers of the Minster. All rooms have bathrooms or showers, phones, radios, and color TVs. The owner has done a lot to bring the facilities up to standards expected today. Singles rent for £45 ($78.75) daily for B&B, and doubles are charged £78 ($136.50). Snacks are served in a coffee lounge from 10 a.m. to 8 p.m. (to 10 p.m. in summer).

The Budget Range

Beechwood Close Hotel, 19 Shipton Rd., York, North Yorkshire YO3 6RE (tel. 0904/658378). On the A19, north of the city, Beechwood is a large house surrounded by trees, a garden with a putting green, and free parking space. Mr. and Mrs. Spink and Mr. and Mrs. Blythe run a small hotel with 14 bedrooms, all with private bath, central heating, TV, and facilities for making tea and coffee. The charge for a bed and a good Yorkshire breakfast is from £23 ($40.25) per person daily, including VAT. Good dinners or bar meals are served in the dining room overlooking the garden. The hotel is a 15-minute walk to the Minster, either by road or along the river. However, a bus stop is close by.

Heworth Court, 76-78 Heworth Green, York, North Yorkshire YO3 7TQ (tel. 0904/425156), is a three-story red-brick house that provides one of the best of the reasonably priced accommodations of York. Only 12 rooms are rented by its owners, Janet and Terry Smith, but they are agreeably furnished, each with private bath or shower. Charges are from £32 ($56) daily in a single, rising to £52 ($91) in a double. The location is on the east side of the city on the A1036. Some of the bedrooms open onto a courtyard. The hotel also offers a commendable cuisine, and you can order dinner until 9:30 p.m.

Abbots Mews Hotel, 6 Marygate Lane, Bootham, York, North Yorkshire YO3 7DE (tel. 0904/34866), was converted from a series of 1800s coachmen's cottages. The setting, as the name suggests, is in a mews. What at one time had been a Victorian coach house with stables is now a highly recommendable hotel and restaurant, one of the best of the reasonably priced ones in York. The hotel is also well located, lying close to the historic district. Mr. and Mrs. Dearnley offer a large number of bedrooms, each with private bath or shower and such thoughtful extras as phones and TVs. All year, guests are received and charged £35 ($61.25) daily in a single, rising to £50 ($87.50) to £58 ($101.50) in a double. The food served here is also recommendable, and you can order dinner until 9:30 p.m.

Hudson's Hotel, 60 Bootham, York, North Yorkshire YO3 7BZ (tel. 0904/621267), just minutes' walking distance from the Minster, is a small, 28-bedroom hotel offering personal service. Mr. Hudson converted two Victorian houses into the main hotel building in 1981 and later added an extension in the Victorian style. All accommodations have private baths, color TV, direct-dial phones, and tea/coffee-makers. B&B costs from £35 ($61.25) daily in a single, £64 ($112), in a double or twin, and £65 ($113.75) in a family room. For added elegance, two people can rent a room with a four-poster bed for £74 ($129.50). The restaurant in the original kitchens, fittingly called Below Stairs, serves table d'hôte dinners costing from £9.50 ($16.65) as well as bar snacks. Hudson's has its own large car park.

Cottage Hotel, 3 Clifton Green, York, North Yorkshire YO3 6LH (tel. 0904/643711), comprises two Victorian houses that have been refurbished and extended to provide accommodations overlooking the village green of Clifton, about ten minutes' walk from York Minster. The hotel has 18 handsome bedrooms, each with a private bath, color TV, direct-dial phone, and hot beverage facilities. Singles rent for £30 ($52.50) daily, with doubles or twins costing £52 ($91) and family rooms from £54 ($94.50). In the restaurant and bar are the 400-year-old timber beams rescued from Micklegate. Hand-pulled real ale is among the beverages served in the bar, to the accompaniment of firelight in cool weather. The hotel provides parking for its guests.

WHERE TO DINE

It is a sign of the times when a vegetarian restaurant like **Oat Cuisine,** 13a High Ousegate (tel. 0904/627929), appears at the top of the list of dining choices in any city. In the center of the historic district, Oat Cuisine occupies such a lofty position. It got there by offering some of the most imaginative international fare in town made with the freshest of ingredients, which are handled with love and beautifully presented for your enjoyment. Dishes travel from the Orient to Mexico for their inspiration. In a simple setting, like a café bistro, the restaurant serves daily except Sunday from noon to 3 p.m. and 7 to 11 p.m. A set luncheon costs £7.50 ($13.15), with dinner going for £15 ($26.25).

Kooks Bistro, 108 Fishergate (tel. 0904/637553), is an informal place run by the owner, Angie Cowl. Decorated in dark green with individually painted flamingos and a collection of memorabilia on the same theme given by customers, it features a varied and unusual menu of English, American, Mexican, French, and vegetarian food, with several dishes distinctive to Kooks. Most main courses include in the price a choice of baked potato, french fries, or a side salad. Meats range from burgers to beef Stroganoff. The service is prompt, and the atmosphere relaxed, with varied background music and a little fun in the form of handmade jigsaws and other puzzles and games on every table. Meals cost from £7.50 ($13.15). Kooks is fully licensed and open daily except Monday from 7 p.m. to midnight; last orders at 11 p.m. It is within walking distance of the city center; there is plenty of parking.

Lew's Place, Kings Staithe (tel. 0904/628167), is an old wharfside gathering place, run with charm by Trevor and Andrea Dawson, who admit, "We try to cater for most tastes." Even some of their rival restaurant and café owners drop in whenever they're free, it's that relaxed. The food is good too, certainly hardy. The menu changes daily. The fare is likely to include a homemade moussaka, a lamb steak (marinated in red wine, herbs, and garlic), even chili con carne. Usually a homemade soup is offered for a beginning course. Meals are served Monday to Saturday from noon to 2 p.m. and 6:30 to 10 p.m. and cost around £7.50 ($13.15).

Restaurant Bari, 15 The Shambles (tel. 0904/633807), stands on one of York's oldest streets, originally the street of the butchers and mentioned in the *Domesday Book.* In a continental atmosphere, you can enjoy a quick single course or a full leisurely meal. Ten different pizzas are offered. Lasagne and cannelloni are superb. Lunch can cost as little as £6 ($10.50) and dinner from about £8.50 ($14.90). A main-dish specialty is escalope Sophia Loren (veal cooked with brandy and cheese with a rich tomato sauce). The restaurant is open seven days a week from 11:30 a.m. to 2:30 p.m. and 6 to 11 p.m.

Tony's Greek Restaurant, 39 Tanner Row (tel. 0904/659622), is a family-run restaurant. Tony Sideras, assisted by his wife, June, attends to the restaurant and the comfort and satisfaction of guests. His daughter, Maria, cooks the authentic and tasty Greek dishes. An à la carte menu is offered, a three-course meal with wine costing around £10.50 ($18.40) to £13.50 ($23.65), with VAT included. Among the appetizers are halloumi (goat's-milk cheese gently fried), and fresh mushrooms cooked in red wine, with crushed coriander seeds. Main dishes include herb-flavored rack of lamb, moussaka (layers of eggplant, zucchini, and potato, with a minced beef sauce, topped with a béchamel sauce), and a vegetarian dish. All selections are served with fresh vegetables cooked in herbs. The meal is rounded off by Greek pastries, Greek yogurt with honey, or a selection of sorbets. Also offered is a traditional meze, a complete meal consisting of 16 authentic Greek specialties served in four courses. The cost of this is £9.50 ($16.65) per person. The restaurant is open for dinner from 6:30 to 10:30 p.m. Monday to Thursday, to 11 p.m. on Friday and Saturday; closed Sunday evening. Reservations are advisable.

A SIDE TRIP TO CASTLE HOWARD

In its dramatic setting of lakes, fountains, and extensive gardens, Castle Howard (tel. 065384/333), the 18th-century palace designed by Sir John Vanbrugh, is undoubtedly the finest private residence in Yorkshire. Principal location for the TV series "Brideshead Revisited," this was the first major achievement of the architect who later created the lavish Blenheim Palace near Oxford. The Yorkshire palace was begun in 1699 for the third Earl of Carlisle, Charles Howard, whose descendants still call the place home. The striking façade is topped by a painted and gilded dome, reaching more than 80 feet into the air. The interior boasts a 192-foot "Long Gallery," as well as a chapel with magnificent stained-glass windows by the 19th-century artist Sir Edward Burne-Jones. Besides the collections of antique furniture, porcelains, and sculpture, the castle contains a number of important paintings, including a portrait of Henry VIII by Holbein, and works by Rubens, Reynolds, and Gainsborough.

The seemingly endless grounds around the palace also offer the visitor some memorable sights, including the domed Temple of the Four Winds, by Vanbrugh, and the richly designed family mausoleum by Hawksmoor. There are two rose gardens, one with old-fashioned roses, the other featuring modern creations. The stable court houses the Costume Galleries, the largest private collection of 18th- to 20th-century costumes in Britain. The authentically dressed mannequins are exhibited in period settings.

Castle Howard, just 15 miles northeast of York, is open to the public daily from March 20 to October 31. The grounds are open from 10 a.m.; the cafeteria, house, and Costume Galleries from 11 a.m. It all closes at 5 p.m., with last admission to the house and galleries at 4:30 p.m. Admission is £4 ($7) for adults, £2 ($3.50) for children. You can enjoy sandwiches, hot dishes, and good wines in the self-service cafeteria.

2. North Yorkshire

Yorkshire, known to readers of *Wuthering Heights* around the world, is now divided into three counties—West Yorkshire, South Yorkshire, and North Yorkshire. For those seeking legendary untamed scenery, I'd recommend a tour of North Yorkshire, which also takes in the just-previewed historic cathedral city of York.

North Yorkshire contains England's most varied landscape. Its history has been turbulent, often bloody, and many relics of its rich past are still standing, including ruined abbeys. Yorkshire is little known to the average North American visitor, but many an English traveler is familiar with its haunting moors, serene valleys, and windswept dales.

The hospitality of the people of Yorkshire is world renowned, and if a pudding that originated there doesn't accompany a slab of roast beef, the plate looks naked to the British. The people of Yorkshire, who speak an original twang often imitated in English cinema, are, in general, hard-working and industrious, perhaps a little contemptuous of the easy living of the south. But they are decidedly open to strangers, providing you speak to them first.

HARROGATE

If you head west from York for 20 miles, you reach Harrogate, North Yorkshire's second-largest town after York itself. In the 19th century Harrogate was a fashionable spa. Most of its town center is surrounded by a 200-acre lawn called "The Stray." Boutiques and antique shops—which Queen Mary used to frequent —make Harrogate a shopping center of excellence, particularly along Montpellier Parade. Harrogate is called England's floral resort, deserving such a reputation because of its gardens, including Harlow Car Gardens and Valley Gardens. The former spa has an abundance of guesthouses and hotels, including the expensive Swan where Agatha Christie hid out during her mysterious and still-unexplained disappearance in the 1920s.

Where to Stay

The Old Swan Hotel, Swan Road, Harrogate, North Yorkshire HG1 2SR (tel. 0423/500055), is the spot where mystery writer Agatha Christie, now deceased, suddenly surfaced after a mysterious 11-day disappearance that was the subject of the film *Agatha,* featuring Dustin Hoffman. One of the most famous hotels in northern England, The Old Swan offers comfort, good food, fine wines, and impeccable service. It has been modernized, yet retains the atmosphere of a country home. There are 137 bedrooms, including ten suites, all with private bath/shower, color TV, and tea/coffee-makers. The tariff for a twin-bedded room is £82 ($143.50) daily, £70 ($122.50) in a single, both rates including VAT. You may dine in the Wedgwood Room or in the à la carte restaurant, The Library, serving good dishes including traditional British food, cooked and presented in a modern idiom.

Majestic Hotel, Ripon Road, Harrogate, North Yorkshire HG1 2HU (tel. 0423/68972). Encircled by gardens, this enormous red-brick and stone Victorian architectural monument dates from 1900. It stands on a hillside above the commercial center, yet is convenient to the Pump Rooms and Royal Baths. Behind its ornate façade it has been thoroughly modernized with upholstered comfort but with enough Victorian embellishments, such as lobby pillars, to make it interesting. The hotel offers 152 well-furnished bedrooms, each with private bath, color TV, radio, phone, and tea/coffee-maker. With high ceilings and conservative furnishings, singles rent for £68 ($119) daily, and doubles or twins are priced at £82 ($143.50). The hotel also has a health center, a pool, squash courts, and an outdoor tennis court. The Regency Bar takes its theme from the Georgian era Later, guests patronize the dining room, decorated in an art nouveau style

Crown Hotel, Crown Place, Harrogate, North Yorkshire HG1 2RZ (tel. 0423/67755). When Lord Byron stayed here in 1806, the poem he composed, "Ode to a Beautiful Quaker," became fêted all over England. During World War II, several of its floors served as the Air Ministry. But the history of the Crown goes far back before that, having been a coaching inn in the 18th century. Next to the historic Pump Rooms, the hotel today is an elaborate Georgian building crafted of gray stone and Corinthian columns set at the edge of a traffic circle. Popular for its conference facilities, the hotel also offers a stately collection of public rooms, including a high-ceilinged reception area. After guests have a drink in the Brontë Bar, they head for the Ripley Restaurant, which is a paneled dining room ringed with cove moldings. Each of the conservatively modernized bedrooms contains a private bath or shower, color TV, radio, phone, and coffee-making equipment. Singles rent for £62 ($108.50) daily, and doubles or twins go for £78 ($136.50).

Grant's Hotel, 3-7 Swan Rd., Harrogate, North Yorkshire HG1 2SS (tel. 0423/60666), was created when five stone-fronted Victorian town houses were joined together into one well-appointed unit. Until Pam Grant took it over, it had been considered an eyesore, a run-down tenement hotel. Today she dispenses hospitality and charm in equal doses. This is a professionally minded establishment, with a street-level bar and a whimsical basement restaurant named Chimney Pots, serving well-flavored specialties amid Victorian-inspired wallpaper and pink napery. Each of the 37 bedrooms is cozy and clean, with private bath, color TV, radio, direct-dial phone, and tea/coffee-makers. There is a selection of four-poster beds and a half-tester. With VAT and a full English breakfast, singles cost £50 ($87.50) daily and doubles or twins from £70 ($122.50). Children sharing a room with their parents are charged for meals only.

Fern Hotel, Swan Road, Harrogate, North Yorkshire HG1 2SS (tel. 0423/523866), set behind a large copper beech tree and a small formal garden, has a gray stone façade, parts of the original detailing, and lots of well-upholstered comfort. Built by Victorians, it contains 27 bedrooms, each of which is well furnished with several amenities including color TV, private bath or shower, and coffee-making equipment. Singles cost £40 ($70) to £45 ($78.75) daily, and doubles or twins go for £63 ($110.25) to £70 ($122.50). VAT and an English breakfast are included. On the premises is a high-ceilinged restaurant, the Portico, serving wholesome food.

Where to Dine

Hodgson's Restaurant, Russell Hotel, 29-35 Valley Dr. (tel. 0423/509866), is often cited as the best restaurant at the spa. In an oak-paneled dining room, you can sample the savory wares of Richard Hodgson. An interesting blend of modern and classical dishes is presented, but only for dinner, served from 7 to 10:30 p.m. Tuesday to Friday. A set dinner costs from £15 ($26.25). Inside this warmly decorated Victorian hotel, you can sample such dishes as Aylesbury duck in an orange sauce or a perfectly done pair of roast quail. The wine list is reasonably priced and well selected.

Shrimps, Studley Hotel, 28 Swan Rd. (tel. 0423/508111), near the Old Swan Hotel, lies right on Promenade Square in a Victorian basement setting. It does many dishes well, but excels in fish. You might, for example, order the special seafood platter or perhaps salmon, halibut, and turbot cooked together. The chef promises a selection of fresh seafood nightly, cooked to "special recipes." To begin with, try a French-style fish soup if featured. A set dinner costs £10.50 ($18.40), but you are more likely to spend from £20 ($35) and up if ordering à la carte. Hours are daily from 7 to 10 p.m.

Drum and Monkey, 5 Montpellier Gardens (tel. 0423/502650). Come here for some of the best fish dishes in the spa, prepared with skill. In the heart of Harrogate, the restaurant is a bustling place. It's usually filled downstairs, where many patrons prefer to eat at the bar. Tables are freely shared with those savoring Dover sole, salmon, grilled mackerel, whatever swims. If you're here for lunch, try the "dressed" crab salad. Meals range in price from £15 ($26.25), but could go much higher, depending on your fish selection. It is open from noon to 2:30 p.m. and 7 to 10 p.m. Monday to Saturday.

MOORS AND DALES

The rural landscape is pierced with ruins of once-great abbeys and castles. North Yorkshire is a land of green hills, valleys, and purple moors. Both the Yorkshire Dales and the Moors are wide-open spaces, two of Britain's finest national parks, with a combined area of some 1,200 square miles. However, the term "national" can be misleading, as the land is managed by foresters, farmers, and private landowners. In fact, more than 90% of the land is in private ownership. The Dales rise toward Cumbria and Lancashire to the east, and the Moors stretch to the eastern coastline.

Of course, York, the major center, has already been previewed. But those with the time may want to explore deeper into the rural roots of England. From Harrogate, our last stopover, you can enjoy the wildest scenery of the region by heading out on day trips, anchoring at one of the inns coming up if you don't want to return to the old spa.

After leaving Harrogate, you can discover white limestone crags, drystone walls, fast-rushing rivers, and isolated sheep farms or clusters of sandstone cottages.

Malhamdale receives more visitors annually than any dale in Yorkshire. Of the priories and castles to visit, two of the most interesting are the 12th-century ruins of **Bolton Priory,** and the 14th-century pile, **Castle Bolton,** to the north in Wensleydale.

Richmond, the most frequently used town name in the world, stands here at the head of the Dales as the mother of them all. Here the Norman towers of Richmond Castle, the country's best-known fortress, dominate the cobbled market town. The Georgian Theatre here, which was constructed in 1788, has a resident amateur company of the highest quality.

In contrast, the Moors, on the other side of the Vale of York, have a wild beauty all their own, quite different from that of the Dales. They are bounded by the Cleveland and Hambleton Hills. The white horse of Kilburn can be seen hewn out of the landscape.

Both **Pickering** and **Northallerton,** two market towns, serve as gateways to the Moors. Across the Moors are seen primordial burial grounds and stone crosses. The best-known trek in moorland is the 40-mile hike over bog, heather, and stream from Mount Grace Priory inland to Ravenscar on the seacoast. It's known as **Lyke Wake Walk.**

The beauty and seclusion along the southern border of today's park made this an area attractive to the founders of four great abbeys. The Cistercians established **Rievaulx** ecclesiastical community near Helmsley and **Fountains Abbey** near Ripon, both visited below, as well as **Byland Abbey** near the village of Wass. The Benedictines were also busy here, establishing **Ampleforth Abbey** near **Coxwold,** one of the most attractive villages in the Moors. Rievaulx, Fountains, and Byland Abbeys are in ruins, but Ampleforth still works as a monastery and well-known Roman Catholic boys' school. Much of Ampleforth comprises buildings of 19th- and 20th-century construction, however, although these contain artifacts from earlier monastic times.

Along North Yorkshire's 45 miles of coastline are such traditional seaside resorts as **Filey, Whitby,** and **Scarborough,** the latter claiming to be the oldest seaside spa in Britain, standing on the site of a Roman signaling station. It was founded in 1622, following the discovery of mineral springs with medicinal properties. In the 19th century, its Grand Hotel, a Victorian structure, was acclaimed as "the best in Europe." The Norman castle on big cliffs overlooks the twin bays.

In and Around Helmsley

This attractive town, where a market is held every Friday, is a good center for exploring the surrounding area. Called the key to Ryedale, it is the mother town of the district, standing at the junction of the roads from York, Pickering, Malton, Stokesley, and Thirsk. On the southern edge of the North York Moors National Park, Helmsley is well known as a center for walking and "pot-holing." It is in a section that contains many places of interest: remains of Bronze and Iron Age existence on the moors, prehistoric highways, Roman roads, and of course, the ruins of medieval castles and abbeys. Beyond the main square of the town are the ruins of its castle, built between 1186 and 1227, and its impressive keep.

A good reason for selecting Helmsley as a stopover is because it is near York and well located, but with hotel rates far below those of the larger city.

Three miles to the north of Helmsley are the ruins of **Rievaulx** (pronounced "reevo") **Abbey** (tel. 04396/228), named for Rye Vallis, valley of the River Rye. The first Cistercian house in northern England, the abbey was founded in 1131 by monks who came over from Clairveaux in France. At its peak it had 140 monks and 500 lay brothers. Its size, architecture, and setting make even the abbey ruins among the most impressive in the country. The land was given by Walter l'Espec, a Norman knight who later entered the community as a novice, and died and was buried here. It is open from 10 a.m. to 6 p.m. daily except Monday from Good Friday to September 30, from 10 a.m. to 4 p.m. off-season. Admission is £1.30 ($2.30) for adults, 65p ($1.15) for children.

Rievaulx Terrace, a property of the National Trust, is a landscaped, grassy terrace about half a mile long, which was laid out in the mid-18th century by Thomas Duncombe of Duncombe Park. After a woodland walk, you emerge onto a wide lawn near a circular "temple," known as the Tuscan Temple. The walk along the terrace gives frequent views of the abbey ruins in the valley below. On a windy North Yorkshire spring day, I find this walk a real constitutional. At the opposite end from the Tuscan Temple is the Ionic Temple, whose interior is beautifully decorated and furnished, with a classically painted ceiling and furniture of gilded wood with rose-velvet upholstery. In the basement are two rooms originally used by servants to prepare food for guests above. The Ionic Temple was planned by Thomas Duncombe III as a banqueting house and a place of rest and refreshment after the long carriage ride from Duncombe Park. It is open from 10:30 a.m. to 6 p.m. daily from Good Friday to the end of October. Admission is £1.30 ($2.30) for adults, 60p ($1.05) for children. For information, phone 0439/340.

Black Swan, Market Place, Helmsley, North Yorkshire YO6 5BJ (tel. 0439/70466), has stood since the 16th century overlooking the marketplace. Incorporating Tudor, Georgian, and Elizabethan houses, this hotel offers 38 well-furnished bedrooms, each with private bath, radio, TV, phone, and tea/coffee-makers. These rent from £54 ($94.50) daily in a single, from £86 ($151.50) in a twin, including service and VAT. A wing of bedrooms overlooks the walled garden. Public rooms are full of character, with open fires, paneling, and time-aged beams. In the traditionally furnished restaurant, you can enjoy such Yorkshire dishes as jugged hare and sirloin Helmsley. A dinner costs from £16.50 ($28.90). The hotel also has two bars.

IN AND AROUND RIPON

Ripon has an ancient tradition of a watchman blowing a curfew horn in the center of town every night at 9 o'clock, a custom dating back to 886. This cathedral city, 27 miles north of Leeds by road, was once a Saxon village where a Celtic monastery was founded in 651.

The Sights

Beneath the central tower of **Ripon Cathedral,** a Norman archbishop's church dating from 1154, is the original crypt built by St. Wilfrid more than 1,300 years ago, one of the oldest buildings in England. The original plaster is still on the walls. It was built the same size and shape as was traditionally believed to be the layout of the tomb from which Jesus rose from the dead.

Archbishop Roger built the nave of the Norman cathedral, the north transept, and part of the choir stalls. The twin towers of the west front are Early English, from about 1216, and the library (once the Lady Loft) is from sometime in the 14th century. The canons stalls were hand-carved, completed in 1495. Two sides of the tower date from the original construction in 1220, but in 1450 an earthquake caused the other two sides to collapse. They were reconstructed, and the central tower and south transept were added at the beginning of the 16th century. The completion of all the work was never carried out, as King Henry VIII took away all the cathedral endowments. Until 1664 the towers had tall spires, but they were removed to prevent fires caused by lightning.

Today the cathedral is a lively Christian Centre, with a study center and a choir school. It is the mother church of the Diocese of Ripon, which spreads over most of the Yorkshire Dales to the fifth-largest city in England, Leeds. For further information, telephone 0765/4108.

Ripon Prison and Police Museum, St. Marygate (tel. 0765/3706), is a fascinating exhibition of the history of police work from the time of the wakeman of Ripon (the watchman of the town in the Middle Ages) up to the wonders of modern technology as they pertain to fighting crime. The building in which the museum is housed started life as a prison, built in 1815. In 1887 it became a police station and continued so until its retirement in 1956. Now it has displays of life in both phases of its existence, including some of the punishment devices so popular in Victorian days. The museum is open from 1:30 to 5 p.m. daily from May to the end of September. In July and August hours are 11 a.m. to 5 p.m. Tuesday to Saturday and bank holidays. Admission is 50p (90¢) for adults, 25p (45¢) for children.

Fountains Abbey and **Studley Royal,** Fountains, four miles southwest of Ripon off the B6265 (tel. 076586/333), stands on the banks of the River Skell. The abbey was founded by Cistercian monks in 1132, and is the largest monastic ruin in Britain. In 1987, it was awarded world heritage status. The ruins provide the focal point of the 18th-century landscape garden at Studley Royal, one of the few surviving examples of a Georgian green garden. It is known for its water gardens, ornamental temples, follies, and vistas. The garden is bounded at its northern edge by a lake and 400 acres of deer park. The abbey and gardens are open daily except December 24 and 25 and Friday in November and December. From January through March and in November and December it is open daily from 10 a.m. to 5 p.m. (or dusk). From April to June and in September, it is open daily from 10 a.m. to 7 p.m., and in July and August daily from 10 a.m. to 8 p.m. October sees daily openings from 10 a.m. to 6 p.m. (or dusk). Admission to the abbey and gardens is £1.90 ($3.35) for adults and 90p ($1.60) for children. A family ticket—two adults, two children—costs £4.70 ($8.25).

Newby Hall, lying on the northeast bank of the Ure River between Ripon (4 miles) and Boroughbridge (3½ miles), is a famous Adam house set in 25 acres of grounds, filled with sunken gardens, magnolias, azaleas, and countless flowering shrubs, along with many rare and unusual species. The house, built for Sir Edward Blackett circa 1695, is in the style of Sir Christopher Wren. In the mid-18th century, Robert Adam redesigned the house, extending it to display the antique sculpture, tapestries, and furniture of its then owner, William Weddell, a connoisseur and art collector. Robin Compton is the present owner. Displayed are the Gobelin Tapestries, one of only five sets completed, with medallions by Boucher, appointed first painter to Louis XV.

On the grounds is a miniature railway, the Newby 10¼-inch gauge, providing rides for both children and adults, adventure gardens, and a steamboat that sails on Sunday along the river, a gift shop, a licensed Garden Restaurant, a plant stall, and a

Woodland Discovery Walk. From Easter to October, Newby Hall and its adjuncts are open daily except Monday (open bank holidays). The house can be visited from noon to 5:30 p.m., with last admission at 5 p.m. The gardens and restaurant are open from 11 a.m. The train runs beginning at noon. Admission to the hall and gardens is £3.20 ($5.60) for adults, £1.60 ($2.80) for children. For information, phone 0423/322583.

Where to Stay and Dine at Ripon

The **Ripon Spa Hotel**, Park Street, Ripon, North Yorkshire HG4 2BU (tel. 0765/2172), opened its doors in 1909 with high hopes. Its owner hoped that Ripon would, like Harrogate, attracts hundreds of guests coming here to "take the spa waters." That didn't happen, nevertheless the hotel endured, attracting those who use it as a base for exploring the surrounding Yorkshire countryside, including Fountains Abbey. The same family has run the hotel for half a century, welcoming guests in their old-fashioned rooms, which still have plenty of modern comforts such as private baths or showers and color TVs, plus a phone, radio, and tea/coffee-makers. British to the core, the hotel charges £40 ($70) to £48 ($84) daily in a single, £50 ($87.50) to £75 ($131.25) in a double or twin. Ask about "Two-Day Breaks" including dinner, bed, and breakfast available throughout the year. The hotel stands right outside the center of Ripon on seven acres of private gardens. The public rooms overlook these gardens. Good British cookery is served in an elegant and spacious dining room, and guests also enjoy the Turf Tavern, named for its association with Ripon Racecourse.

Unicorn Hotel, Market Place, Ripon, North Yorkshire HG4 1BP (tel. 0765/2202), is a coaching inn and posting house. It has welcomed travelers for some 400 years with Yorkshire warmth and hospitality, and the same is true today. It's directly opposite the obelisk where the 1,000-year-old tradition of setting the watch by blowing the horn takes place each evening. The façade of the inn is in Victorian style, with square bay windows and an elaborate front entrance. All 33 bedrooms have private facilities, central heating, tea/coffee-maker, and phone. Singles rent from £36 ($63) daily, and doubles or twins from £50 ($87.50), these tariffs including VAT and a full English breakfast. The cuisine in the Royal Charter Restaurant is Cordon Bleu, and in addition, bar lunches are served in a typically English pub with locally brewed real ale.

Hugo's Restaurant, Duck Hill (tel. 0765/4841), off the central square in Ripon, is a charming little place to eat. Originally built in the 1600s as a prison, it was later used as a mill. The restaurant is run by John and Ann Lister who personally handle all the chores, from preparing the homemade food to cleaning. You can choose from eight appetizers and 15 main courses. Try roast rack of English spring lamb on a bed of root vegetables complemented with herbs and basted with cider, honey, and red-currant jelly. Crunchy meringue coconut cake makes a luscious dessert. Everything is cooked to order with quality ingredients. Full meals costing £12 ($21) to £16 ($28) are served daily except Monday from 7 to 10 p.m.

Thirsk

This pleasant old market town, lying in the Vale of Mowbray north of York, has a fine parish church. But what makes it such a popular stopover for visitors is the fame brought to the village by James Herriot, author of *All Creatures Great and Small* and other books about his experiences as a veterinarian serving this area of Yorkshire. Mr. Herriot still practices in Thirsk, and visitors can photograph his office, perhaps getting a picture of his partner standing in the door.

If you'd like to stay over, **Golden Fleece,** Market Place, Thirsk, North Yorkshire YO7 1LL (tel. 0845/23108), is a traditional hotel in the center of town, opening onto the cobbled marketplace. This has been a famous hostelry in England for more than 300 years, once attracting coachmen on the high road from York to Darlington. The interior is beautifully kept, with antique furniture, old brasses, and big open hearths. There are 22 bedrooms, six with private baths and one with a four-poster bed. All units have color TVs, radios, phones, razor sockets, central heating, and hot beverage facilities. Singles cost from £46 ($80.50) daily and doubles begin at £52 ($91). In the Mail Coach Restaurant, you can enjoy an old English cuisine, and the Paddock Bar is a comfortable place to have drinks, perhaps a pint of full-bodied Yorkshire ale.

HAWES

The natural center of the Yorkshire Dales National Park is Hawes, a market town in Wensleydale and home of the cheese of that name. It's on the Pennine Way, which is popular with hikers. You can watch traditional ropemaking at W. R. Outhwaite & Son (tel. 09697/487). Hawes lies on a good road, the A684, about midway between the A1 to the east and the M6 to the west.

The **Upper Dales Folk Museum,** Station Yard (the old train station) (tel. 09697/494), traces folk life in the area of the Upper Dales. Peat-cutting and cheese-making, among other occupations, are depicted. The museum is open from 11 a.m. to 5 p.m. Monday to Saturday and from 2 to 5 p.m. Sunday from March 20 to the end of July and during September. In August, hours are from 10 a.m. to 6 p.m. Monday to Saturday and from 2 to 5 p.m. Sunday. In October, it is open only from noon to 5 p.m.; closed in winter. Admission is 50p (90¢).

You don't need to travel far from Rookhurst for beautiful Dales scenery. Gayle, originally a Celtic settlement, is divided by Duerley Beck, with two lovely waterfalls, a ford and an old stone bridge, beloved of artists and photographers.

Simonstone Hall, Hawes, North Yorkshire DL8 3LY (tel. 09697/255), former home of the earls of Wharncliffe, is 1½ miles north of Hawes—rural but not isolated. Constructed in 1733, the building has been converted and restored, so that today it is a comfortable family-run country-house hotel. There are ten spacious bedrooms with private baths. For B&B in a standard room, the charge is £28 ($49) per person daily, rising to £34.75 ($60.80) per person in a four-poster bedroom, the tariffs based on double occupancy. The owners, Mr. and Mrs. J. R. Jeffryes, are happy to have guests relax in the large, south-facing, paneled drawing rooms, which have comfortable, mostly antique furnishings, with elegant, individually designed chimney pieces. You can have drinks in the Tawny Owl Bar and enjoy good food in the hotel's dining room. Expect to pay about £14.50 ($25.40) for a four-course dinner. This can be complemented with good wines from the extensive cellar.

3. West Yorkshire

HAWORTH

In West Yorkshire, this ancient stone village lying on the high moors of the Pennines—45 miles west of York via Leeds and 21 miles west of Leeds itself—is world-famous as the home of the Brontë family. The three sisters—Charlotte, Emily, and Anne—distinguished themselves as English novelists. They lived a life of imagination at a lonely parsonage at Haworth.

Anne wrote two novels, *The Tenant of Wildfell Hall* and *Agnes Grey.* Charlotte's masterpiece was *Jane Eyre,* which depicted her experiences as a governess; it enjoyed popular success in its day and is now considered a classic of British fiction.

But perhaps it is Emily's fierce and tragic *Wuthering Heights* that is best loved; a novel of passion, intensity, and primitive power, with scenes of unforgettable, haunting melancholy, the book has come to be appreciated by later generations far more than those for whom she'd written it. Haworth is the most visited literary shrine in England, after Stratford-upon-Avon.

From Haworth, you can walk to Withens, the "Wuthering Heights" of the immortal novel. In Haworth, Charlotte and Emily are buried in the family vault under the church of St. Michael's.

The parsonage where they lived has been preserved as the **Brontë Parsonage Museum** (tel. 0535/42323): Emily and Charlotte died there. It is open daily all year (except for December 24, 25, and 26 and the first three weeks in February) from 11 a.m. Closing time is 5:30 p.m. from April to September, 4:30 p.m. October to March. Admission is £1 ($1.75) for adults, 50p (90¢) for children all year.

On the Haworth Moor stands a Brontë landmark, **Ponden Hall,** Stanbury, near Keighley (tel. 0535/44154), a distance of some three miles from Haworth. It lies half a mile from the main road on the wide rough track that is the Pennine Way. An Elizabethan farmhouse built in 1560 and extended in 1801, this reputedly is the model for Thrushcross Grange, Catherine's home after her marriage to Edgar Linton.

Today the hall provides a farmhouse accommodation, a hand-loom weaving studio, a residential weaving course, a bunkhouse accommodation, as well as camping.

The village of Haworth has frequent bus and train service to Keighley, Bradford, and Leeds in West Yorkshire.

Food and Lodging

The **Tourist Information Centre,** at 2-4 West Lane in Haworth (tel. 0535/42329), offers an accommodation-booking service, and the office is open daily from 9:30 a.m. to 5:30 p.m. Easter until the end of October, from 10 a.m. to 5 p.m. November to March. Otherwise, you might stay at one of my recommendations below.

A reminder: You must not expect such amenities as private baths, air conditioning, and the like in the lower-priced places recommended. Just as in the United States, you get what you pay for.

Old White Lion Hotel, 6 West Lane, Haworth, Keighley, West Yorkshire BD22 8DU (tel. 0535/42313), stands at the top of a cobblestone street. It was built around 1700 with a solid stone roof almost next door to the church where the Reverend Brontë preached and to the parsonage where the family lived. Joyce and Keith Bradford welcome tourists from all over the world to their warm, cheerful, and comfortable hotel. Although full of old world charm, all rooms are fully up to date, including, for example, private baths. The double rate is £34.50 ($60.40) daily, with singles costing £24 ($42). VAT is included. Dinners, except Sunday, are à la carte, and good local meats and fresh vegetables are used. Meals cost £9 ($15.75) in the evening. A set Sunday lunch, featuring a roast, costs £6 ($10.50). Bar snacks include the usual favorites—ploughman's lunch, hot pies, fish, and sandwiches.

Weaver's Restaurant, 15 West Lane (tel. 0535/43822), was once cottages for weavers but it has now been turned into the best restaurant in the Brontë hometown. In the words of one satisfied diner, "It's the only game in town as far as food is concerned." British to the core, it not only has an inviting atmosphere but serves excellent food made with fresh ingredients. Jane Rushworth has a great talent in the kitchen, and you can sample her very English wares at dinner from 7 to 9:30 every evening. However, she doesn't offer dinner on Sunday and is closed all day Monday. She also serves lunch in winter from 12:30 to 1:30 p.m., costing £8.50 ($14.90). Dinners cost from £12 ($21) and up, and include such classic dishes as Yorkshire pudding with gravy. Try, if featured, one of the Gressingham ducks, which are widely praised in the U.K. for the quality of their meat. For your final course, you might select a Yorkshire cheese or one of the truly superb made-in-house desserts. The style of the place is informal. Mrs. Rushworth is likely to be closed for a certain time each summer for vacation, so call in advance to check. You should always reserve a table at any rate. The place tends to be popular, and with good reason.

HEBDEN BRIDGE

Deep in the heart of the South Pennines lies this little town, which was a busy fustian (a stout, mainly cotton, fabric) weaving center during and after the Industrial Revolution. It became an important site for the industry because of its position at the junction of the Calder and Hebden valleys and was a shipping station on the Rochdale Canal, which connected Halifax on the east and Rochdale on the west. Hebden Bridge is 7 miles south of Haworth and about 25 miles east of Leeds. The canal is being restored, and already trips from Hebden Bridge are possible.

Hebden Lodge Hotel, New Road, Hebden Bridge, West Yorkshire HX7 8AD (tel. 0422/845272), overlooking the historic canal moorings, is a Victorian building with modern amenities. You are welcomed by the owners, Cherry and Mike Flitcroft. The bedrooms have showers, color TVs, radio alarms, and hot beverage facilities. Prices range from £20.50 ($35.90) to £22.50 ($39.40) per person daily, with a full English breakfast included. Bar meals are available in the Fustian Lounge, or perhaps you'll choose to have dinner in Brindleys Restaurant, where a meal costs from £9 ($15.75). Traditional cooking is the rule, with such dishes as homemade salmon soup, lamb Shrewsbury "cherished" in red wine sauce, and a vegetarian peanut roast (freshly ground peanuts with carrots, sage, onion, and a tomato-and-garlic sauce). Horse-drawn canal cruises operate from the hotel.

HAREWOOD HOUSE AND BIRD GARDEN

In West Yorkshire, at junction A61/659, midway between Leeds and Harrogate and five miles from the A1 at Wetherby, stands Harewood House, home of the Earl and Countess of Harewood. It's one of the "magnificent seven" homes of England, which include Blenheim Palace and Beaulieu Abbey. The 18th-century house was designed by Robert Adam and John Carr and has always been owned by the Lascelles family. It contains superb plasterwork, beautiful Chippendale furniture, and collections of Sèvres and Chinese porcelain and of English and Italian paintings.

Harewood Bird Garden borders the lake and blends successfully with the fine landscape, created by Capability Brown. It houses some 180 exotic species from all over the world, including penguins, macaws, snowy owls, and flamingos, and has an undercover area housing tropical birds and small mammals. The extensive grounds offer terrace and lakeside walks, shops, a cafeteria, a picnic area, occasional exhibitions, a Courtyard Restaurant, and an Adventure Playground for the children.

Harewood is open daily from 10 a.m. to 5 p.m. from Easter to the end of October. The house, bird garden, and adventure playground are also open on Sunday in November, February, and March. Admission is £3.85 ($6.75) for adults, £1.60 ($2.80) for children under 16. Call 0532/886225 for recorded information, available 24 hours.

---

4. Durham

This densely populated county of northeast England is too often pictured as a dismal, forbidding place, with coalfields, ironworks, mining towns, and shipyards. Yet it contains valleys of quiet charm and a region of wild moors in the west. Therefore if you have the time, it would be interesting to explore the Durham Dales, especially Teesdale with its waterfalls and rare wildflowers, and Weardale with its brown sandstone villages.

DURHAM

The county town, which has the same name, is built on a sandstone peninsula. Its treasure is the **Cathedral of Durham,** which ranks among the most beautiful

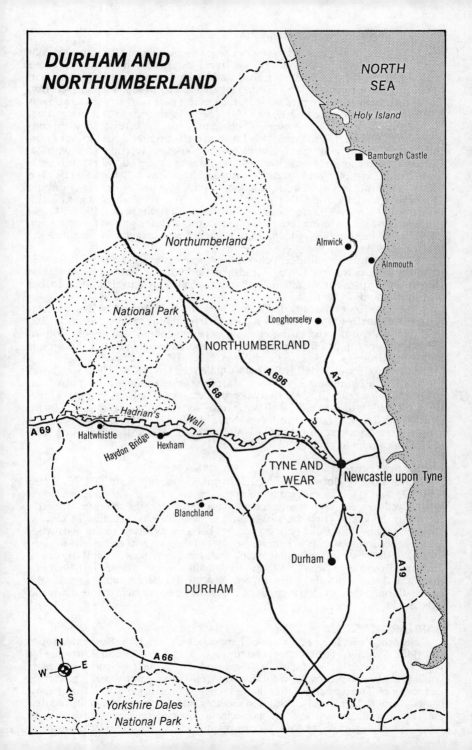

buildings in the world. Its solid towers dominate the neighboring countryside from its sandstone pinnacle surrounded by the River Wear. Inside, the massive and bold incised piers in the nave and the ribbed vaults (this was the first great church in northern Europe to develop this feature) give it a feeling of solidarity and security. The church was named for St. Cuthbert, the greatest north country saint, who was first buried at Lindisfarne in A.D. 687. After being hauled around for many years, his body was interred where it now lies behind the high altar here in 995 when construction started on the cathedral. No admission is charged to visit the house of worship. However, to visit the Treasury, which houses relics connected with St. Cuthbert, as well as precious books and plate, you must pay 50p (90¢). It is open from 10 a.m. to 4:30 p.m. Monday to Saturday, from 2 to 4:30 p.m. Sunday. The Monks' Dormitory, is open from 11 a.m. to 3 p.m. Monday to Saturday, charging 25p (45¢) for adults, 10p (20¢) for children. The Audio-Visual Exhibition is also open from 11 a.m. to 3 p.m. Monday to Saturday, with adults paying 40p (70¢) and children 20p (35¢). During those same hours, you can visit the tower, costing 50p (90¢) for adults, 25p (45¢) for children. You will have a magnificent view over the city and castle.

From Framweigate Bridge, below the massive church, is a peaceful riverside walk, known locally as the Banks. It leads you through trees beneath the castle and then up a steep path to the cathedral. It's quite a challenge for the faint-hearted, but well worth the effort for the fit.

In the shadow of the cathedral is the Church of St. Mary le Bow, now containing the **Durham Heritage Centre,** which is open from June to September from 2 to 4:30 p.m. daily. It presents changing exhibitions and audio-visual presentations of the city's history, plus rubbings of replicas of monumental brasses. Admission is 50p (90¢) for adults, 20p (35¢) for children.

Adjoining the cathedral is **Durham Castle** (tel. 091/374-3800), which was founded by the Normans and was the home of the prince-bishops until it was given to Durham University in 1832. Except on the occasion of university or other functions, the castle is open to visitors all year. From July to September, hours are 10 a.m. to noon and 2 to 4:30 p.m. Saturday and Sunday only. During the rest of the year, it is open from 2 to 4 p.m. on Monday, Wednesday, and Saturday. Admission is £1 ($1.75) for adults and 50p (90¢) for children.

Food and Lodging

Royal County Hotel, Old Elvet, Durham, County Durham DH1 3JN (tel. 0385/386-6821), is a Georgian hostelry tracing its origins to Cromwellian times. With a well-conceived refurbishment program, this four-star hotel offers attentive service to the guest. There are 120 bedrooms, all with private baths, TVs, video channels, radios, direct-dial phones, and hot beverage facilities. You're given your choice of accommodations in either the older building with its traditional furnishings or in the new block of rooms, many with views over the river and the city of Durham. Rates range from £55 ($96.25) daily in a single, from £80 ($140) in a double, and tariffs include an English breakfast. An à la carte menu is served in the air-conditioned County Restaurant, and the Brasserie serves table d'hôte meals and light snacks.

BARNARD CASTLE

Near the River Tees in the town of Barnard Castle stands the **Bowes Museum** (tel. 0833/690606), at the eastern end. It was built in 1869 by John Bowes and his wife, the Countess of Montalbo, to house and display their art collection. Here you'll find masterpieces by Goya and El Greco, plus other paintings, fine tapestries, and ceramics. There are also collections of French and English furniture, superb costumes, musical instruments, a children's gallery, and many other exhibits of interest. The noted silver swan performs its mechanical marvels once or twice daily. A tea room and ample parking are found on the premises. It is open all year, daily from 10 a.m. to 5 p.m., on Sunday from 2 to 5 p.m., charging £1.50 ($2.65) for adults, 50p (90¢) for children. It closes at 4 p.m. from November to February and entirely for a week around Christmas. The tea room is open only from April to September.

Where to Stay and Dine

Blagraves House Restaurant, 34 The Bank (tel. 0833/37668), occupies a 15th-century house with a dining room that has been richly decorated. They invite you to come by and "taste our food," which I've found to be excellently prepared and wholesome. Fresh local produce and good service characterize the establishment. Meals are offered for £18 ($31.50). Main dishes are likely to include rounds of filet of beef with a Roquefort herb butter, duckling with peach-and-lemon sauce, or chicken breasts stuffed with asparagus in a white wine and cheese sauce. The restaurant serves lunch from noon to 2:30 p.m. Tuesday to Sunday and dinner from 7 to 9:30 p.m. except Sunday night. Closed all day Monday. Call for a reservation.

Rose and Crown Hotel, Romaldkirk, Teesdale, County Durham DL12 9EB (tel. 0833/50213), lies in a dale that often escapes the notice of the traveler in the north, at Romaldkirk, an attractive village set around a fine green with a water pump and punitive stocks (not in use today!). Higher up the dale, the River Tees goes over a sheer drop of 69 feet, and downstream is Barnard Castle and the Bowes Museum. In the main building are 11 bedrooms, one with a four-poster bed. All have color TVs, radios, and phones, and across the courtyard in a modern extension, units have the same amenities, plus tea- and coffee-making facilities. An overnight stay costs £40 ($70) daily in a single, £46 ($80.50) to £60 ($105) in a double, which includes a full English breakfast and a morning paper. There is a comfortable lounge, and the two bars have roaring log fires.

BLANCHLAND

Near Consett, the village of Blanchland dates from the mid-12th century. It's a cobbled square with houses and little village shops. The post office still shows the arms of Queen Victoria over the mailbox.

The Lord Crewe Arms Hotel, Blanchland, near Consett, County Durham DH8 9SP (tel. 043475/251), was the priory of the now-destroyed Abbey of Blanchland, and the bars are to be found in the crypt of the old building. You can walk through one of the enormous chimneys with a priest's hole above your head. It is easy to imagine the ghost of Dorothy Foster stalking the narrow passages. Many of the rooms have baths, costing from £40 ($70) daily in a single and from £58 ($101.50) in a double, including a traditional cooked breakfast and VAT. Additional bedrooms are offered in the annex opposite the old building, all with direct-dial phones and hot beverage equipment. Rooms are decorated with fresh flowers, and a glass of sherry will be waiting to greet you. A four-course dinner at £15 ($26.25) is likely to include seafood vol-au-vent, roast duckling, or grouse in season, followed by a homemade dessert. There are also bar snacks for those who want to stop for a short while en route to Hadrian's Wall or Scotland.

BEAMISH

West of Chester le Street, eight miles southwest of Newcastle upon Tyne and 12 miles northwest of Durham City, lying just off the A693, is Beamish, the **North of England Open Air Museum.** Here the way of life of the people of the region has been re-created. You can take a tram ride into the past down a cobblestone Old Town street, to visit old shops, houses, printworks, a working public house, and a Victorian park. Go down a "drift" mine at the Colliery and see bread being baked in a coal-fired oven at the pit cottages. Step into the farmhouse kitchen at Home Farm to see how the farmer's wife spent her day, and meet the poultry, pigs, and cattle in the farmyard. There's a North Eastern Railway area, too, with a country station, signal box, goods yard, and steam locomotives. An average visit takes about four hours. Beamish is open daily from 10 a.m. to 5 p.m. from the first of the year to the end of

March and from November to the end of the year. From April to the end of October, hours are from 10 a.m. to 6 p.m. Last entrance is always 4 p.m. Admission is £3.30 ($5.80) for adults, £2.30 ($4.05) for children. For further information, phone 0207/231811.

---

5. Tyne and Wear

In the county of Tyne and Wear, industrial Newcastle upon Tyne is the dominant focus, yet outside the city there is much natural beauty. Cattle graze on many a grassed-over mining shaft. There is such scenic beauty as moors and hills of purple-blue. The rugged coastline is beautiful. Americans like to pass through because of their interest in the ancestral home of George Washington (see below), and Newcastle itself also merits a stopover, particularly for motorists heading to Scotland.

The National Trust administers two sites in the region surrounding Newcastle: **Gibside Chapel,** at Burnopfield (tel. 0207/542255), built in the classical style of James Paine in 1760, is an outstanding example of Georgian church architecture. A stately oak-lined avenue leads to the door of the chapel, which is the mausoleum of the Bowes family. The interior is decorated in delicate plasterwork and is furnished with paneled pews of cherrywood and a rare mahogany three-tiered pulpit. Hours are 2 to 6 p.m. every day except Tuesday from April 1 to September 30. The entrance fee is £1 ($1.75) for adults, 50p (90¢) for children. A shop, refreshment stand, and picnic area are here. The location is six miles southwest of Gateshead and 20 miles northwest of Durham between Rowlands Gill and Burnopfield.

Washington Old Hall (tel. 091/416-6879) is the ancestral home of the first president of the United States, and the place from which the family took its name. President Carter visited the manor house in 1977. The interior of the house, which dates back to 1183, is furnished with period antiques and a collection of Delftware. Relics of the Washingtons are also on display. The hall is open from 11 a.m. to 5 p.m. daily except Friday from March 24 to the end of September and on Wednesday, Saturday, and Sunday in October. Closed Good Friday. Admission is £1.50 ($2.65) for adults, 50p (90¢) for children. The location is in Washington on the east side of the A182, five miles west of Sunderland (two miles from the A1). South of Tyne Tunnel, follow signs for Washington New Town District 4 and then Washington Village.

NEWCASTLE UPON TYNE

An industrial city, Newcastle is graced with some fine streets and parks, as well as many old buildings. After crossing its best known landmark, the Tyne Bridge, you enter a steep city that sweeps down to the Tyne, usually on narrow lanes called "chares." Once wealthy merchants built their town houses right on the quayside, and some of them remain.

For years Newcastle has been known as a shipbuilding and coal-exporting center, and gave rise to the expression of suggesting the absurdity of shipping coals to Newcastle.

Dominating the skyline, **St. Nicholas Church of England Cathedral** rises to a soaring crown spire. It is England's most northerly cathedral and is situated close to the central station and the castle. The Provost says that "the cathedral is one of the gems among the glorious churches of Northumberland." The present building is substantially from the 14th century, the spire being a 15th-century construction. The cathedral has a refectory open at lunchtime and also a gift shop.

The keep of the so-called New Castle, built by Henry II in 1170, contains the **Keep Museum,** on St. Nicholas Street, with a collection of medieval relics. It's open April to September from 9:30 a.m. to 5:30 p.m. Tuesday to Sunday, to 4:30 p.m. October to March Tuesday to Sunday.

Where to Stay

The premier hotel of the city is **Gosforth Park Thistle,** High Gosforth Park, Newcastle upon Tyne, Tyne and Wear NE3 5HN (tel. 091/2364111), although it lies on the outskirts on B1318 (some five miles north of Newcastle on A6125). Once you get there, the effort proves worth it. With sleek contemporary styling, it welcomes guests into 178 well-furnished bedrooms, each with private bath or shower, direct-dial phone, TV, in-house feature films, hairdryer, and trouser press. Catering largely to a business clientele, the executive rooms are the most desirable and expensive. Singles rent for £75 ($131.25) daily, with doubles costing £96 ($168). The hotel has a number of drinking and dining facilities as well as a leisure center with a pool and gym.

County Thistle Hotel, Neville Street, Newcastle upon Tyne, Tyne and Wear NC99 1AH (tel. 091/232-2471), is a refurbished hotel in the center of town. A dominant figure of the Newcastle scene, it was built directly opposite the railway station and heralded the coming of the industrial age. Under the Thistle group, the hotel has 115 bedrooms each well maintained and all with private baths or showers, direct-dial phones, and color TVs. The charge for singles begins at £60 ($105) daily, and doubles and twins cost from £75 ($131.25). The hotel's reception lobby has as its focal point a sweeping staircase, complemented by limed oak furnishings and potted plants. Excellent meals are served in the candlelit Café Mozart, the windows of which look out on the arches of Newcastle's old buildings. Inventive cooking, combining modern and traditional dishes, is served, with meals from £10 ($17.50).

Where to Dine

Fisherman's Lodge, Jesmond Dene (tel. 091/2813281), is considered by some the finest restaurant in Tyne and Wear, lying as it does in a wooded parkland next to Ouse Burn. Fresh fish dishes—an array of scampi, halibut, crab, and lobster —are there to tempt. The kitchen staff is equally adept at classic or more modern fish preparations. You can enjoy a lager or a glass of wine in a relaxing bar lounge before tackling the menu. If someone in your party doesn't like fish, there are many well-prepared meat dishes as well. Meals are served Monday to Saturday (no lunch on Saturday) from noon to 2 p.m. and 7 to 11 p.m. A set lunch is a good value at £12.50 ($21.90), although you are likely to spend from £20 ($35) for an à la carte dinner. Reservations are necessary.

Jade Garden, 53 Stowell St. (tel. 091/261-5889), is the city's best-known Cantonese restaurant, lying in the old Blackfriars district. Its staff keeps long hours, noon to 11:30 p.m. daily, and Alex Chung oversees everything with a welcoming hospitality. Against a backdrop of pink-and-green neon, guests order a set lunch for only £4.50 ($7.90), a table d'hôte dinner for £18 ($31.50). Vegetarian dishes are offered, and main courses, some 200 selections in all, include such tasty dishes as barbecued pork, lemon chicken, and fresh seafood. Some of the wines came all the way from China, as the song goes.

---

6. Northumberland

Unfortunately, most motorists zip through this far northeastern county of England on their way to Scotland, missing the beauty and historic interest of the Border section. Because it is so close to Scotland, Northumberland was the scene of many a bloody skirmish. The county now displays a number of fortified castles that saw action in those battles. Inland are the valleys of the Cheviot Hills, lying mostly within the Northumberland National Park and the remainder of the Border Forest Park, Europe's largest man-made forest.

Northumberland's coast is one of Britain's best-kept secrets. Here are islands, castles, tiny fishing villages, miles of sands, as well as golf and fishing among the dunes, and birdwatching in the Farne Islands—in all, an area of outstanding natural beauty.

Wallington Hall, at Cambo, 12 miles west of Morpeth on the B6342 and 6 miles northwest of Belsey off the A696, dates from 1688, but the present building reflects the great changes brought about in the 1740s when Daniel Garrett completely refashioned the exterior of the house. The interior is decorated with rococo plasterwork and furnished with fine porcelains, furniture, and paintings. Travelers may also visit the museum and enjoy an extensive display of dollhouses. The Coach House contains an exhibit of ornate carriages. The main building is surrounded by 100 acres of woodlands and lakes, including a beautifully terraced walled garden and a conservatory restaurant, shop, and information center. The grounds are open all year; the house, April to October 29 from 1 to 5:30 p.m. daily except Tuesday. Last admission is half an hour before closing time. Admission to the house and grounds is £2.80 ($4.90); to the grounds only, £1 ($1.75). Children pay half price. For more information, telephone 067074/283.

Seaton Delaval Hall (tel. 091/237-1493), the enormous country home of Lord Hastings near Whitley Bay, represents the architecture of Sir John Vanbrugh, builder of Blenheim Palace and Castle Howard. Many consider this English baroque hall the masterpiece of the playwright/architect. It looks like the stage settings for 14 Roman tragedies piled one on top of another. Walk over and look through a window, and you can almost imagine knights and wenches feasting at long tables and drinking mead. The house is open to view from May to September on Wednesday and Sunday from 2 to 6 p.m., charging adults an admission of £1 ($1.75); children, 50p (90¢). The hall is half a mile from the coast at Seaton Sluice between Blyth and Whitley Bay, ten miles from Newcastle, reached via Northumbrian bus routes 363 and 364 that run half-hourly.

The **Farne Islands** are a group of small islands off the Northumbria coast, which provide a summer home for at least 20 species of sea birds as well as for one of the largest British colonies of gray seals. St. Cuthbert died here in 687, and a chapel built in the 14th century is thought to be on the site of his original cell. Only Inner Farne and Staple Island are open to the public. Visiting season extends from April through September, but access is more controlled during the breeding season. From mid-May to mid-July, you can visit Staple Island from 10:30 a.m. to 1:30 p.m. each day, and Inner Farne from 2 to 5 p.m. daily. From April 1 to mid-May and from mid-July until the end of September hours for both Staple Island and Inner Farne are from 10 a.m. to 6 p.m. Tickets are obtained on the island. During the peak season, adults pay £2 ($3.50) and children are charged £1 ($1.75). During the rest of the season, the admission is £1.50 ($2.65), going up to £2 ($3.50) during the breeding season.

The best way to get to this most famous bird and animal sanctuary in the British Isles is to telephone or write Billy Shiel, the Farne Islands boatman, at 4 Southfield Ave., Seahouses, Northumberland (tel. 0665/720308). He has been taking people in his licensed boat for the past 40 years, so he knows the tides and the best places to film seals, puffins, and guillemots. He runs 2½-hour trips in his 60-passenger craft at a cost of £3 ($5.25) per person.

Incidentally, these are the islands where Grace Darling and her father made their famous rescue of men from a foundered ship (see below).

HOLY ISLAND

The site of the Lindisfarne religious community during the Dark Ages, Holy Island is only accessible for ten hours of the day, high tides covering the causeway at other times. For crossing times, check with local information centers.

Lindisfarne Castle, on Holy Island, was built about 1550 as a fort to protect the harbor. In 1903 it was converted by Sir Edwin Lutyens into a comfortable home for Edward Hudson, the founder of *Country Life*. It is open from April to the end of September every day except Friday (open Good Friday), from 1 to 5:30 p.m. In October, also from 1 to 5:30 p.m., it's open only on Wednesday, Saturday, and Sunday. Admission is £2.50 ($4.40) in June, July, and August; £1.50 ($2.65) during the other months.

At Lindisfarne, you can stay at the **Lindisfarne Private Hotel,** Holy Island, Northumberland TD15 2SQ (tel. 0289/89273). This is a fine, substantial frame building with a trio of tall chimneys. It's run by members of the Massey family, who conduct it more like a private home than a hotel. Centrally heated bedrooms contain hot and cold running water (a few with private bath) and are decorated with personality, providing a homelike atmosphere. The charge ranges from £22 ($38.50) to £24 ($42) per person daily for bed, breakfast, and evening dinner. Boating excursions can be arranged to the Farnes.

BAMBURGH CASTLE

Guarding the British shore along the North Sea, the castle (tel. 06684/208) stands on a site that has been occupied since the 1st century B.C. The Craggy Citadel where it stands was a royal center by A.D. 547. The Norman keep has stood for eight centuries, the remainder of the castle having been restored toward the end of the 19th century. This was the first castle to succumb to artillery fire, the guns of Edward IV. You can visit the grounds and public rooms daily from April to early October: 1 to 5 p.m. in April, May, June, and September; 1 to 6 p.m. in July and August; and 1 to 4:30 p.m. in October. Admission is £1.70 ($3) for adults, 60p ($1.05) for children. There is a tea room. The castle is the home of Lord and Lady Armstrong and their family.

Nearby is the **Grace Darling Museum** (tel. 0665/720037), which has various mementos, pictures, and documents relating to the heroic Grace Darling, including the boat in which she and her father, who was keeper of the Longstone lighthouse in the Farne Islands, rescued nine people from the S.S. *Forfarshire* that foundered in 1838. It's open daily from Easter to mid-October from 11 a.m. to 6 p.m. Admission is free, but donations to the Royal National Lifeboat Institution are gratefully accepted.

HADRIAN'S WALL

This wall, which extends across the north of England for 73 miles, from the North Sea to the Irish Sea, is particularly interesting for a stretch of 3½ miles west of Housesteads. Only the lower courses of the wall are preserved intact; the rest were reconstructed in the 19th century with the original stones. From several vantage points along the wall, you have incomparable views north to the Cheviot Hills along the Scottish border, and south to the Durham moors.

The wall was built following a visit of the Emperor Hadrian in A.D. 122. He wanted to see the far frontier of the Roman Empire, and he also sought to build a dramatic line between the so-called civilized world and the barbarians. Legionnaires were ordered to build a wall across the width of the island of Britain, stretching for 73½ miles, going over hills and plains, beginning at the North Sea and ending at the Irish Sea.

The wall is a premier Roman attraction in Europe, ranking among many people with Rome's Colosseum. The western end can be reached from Carlisle, with a good museum of Roman artifacts, and the eastern end from Newcastle upon Tyne (some remains are seen on the city outskirts and a good museum at the university). South Shields, Chester, Corbridge, and Vindolanda are all good forts to visit in the area.

At Housesteads (English Heritage) you can visit a **Roman fort** (tel. 04984/363), built about A.D. 130 to house an infantry of 1,000 men. Called Vercovicium in Latin, the fort held a full-scale military encampment, the remains of which can be seen today. The fort is open from 10 a.m. to 6 p.m. April to the end of September, to

4 p.m. October to the end of March; closed Monday and during the Christmas and New Year's holidays. Admission is £1.30 ($2.30) for adults, 60p ($1.05) for children.

Just west of Housesteads is **Vindolanda** (tel. 04984/277), another fort south of the wall at Chesterholm. The building is very well preserved, and there is also an excavated civilian settlement outside the fort with an interesting museum of artifacts of everyday Roman life. Hours are daily from 10 a.m. to 5 p.m. or dusk. Admission is £1.50 ($2.65) for adults, 80p ($1.40) for children.

Not far from Vindolanda is the **Roman Army Museum,** Carvoran, on Hadrian's Wall near Greenhead, which traces the growth and influence of Rome from her early beginnings to the development and expansion of the empire, with special emphasis on the role of the Roman army and the garrisons of Hadrian's Wall. A barracks room shows basic army living conditions. Realistic life-size figures make this a striking visual museum experience. Admission is £1.10 ($1.95) for adults, 60p ($1.05) for children. For information, phone 06972/485.

Within easy walking distance of the Roman Army Museum lies one of the most imposing and high-standing sections of Hadrian's Wall, Walltown Crags, where the height of the wall and magnificent views to north and south are impressive.

HAYDON BRIDGE

Between Haltwhistle and Hexham, the **Anchor Hotel,** John Martin Street Haydon Bridge, Northumberland NE47 6AB (tel. 043484/227), is ideally situated for visitors to the wall and its surroundings. This riverside village pub was once a coaching inn on the route from Newcastle to Carlisle. The cozy bar is much used by locals. In the country dining room, wholesome evening meals are served. The charge for B&B is from £18 ($31.50) per person daily. A room with shower or private bath costs a supplement of £5 ($8.75) per room. All tariffs include a full English breakfast and VAT. If you stay two nights, the special rate for B&B and a choice of three courses from the à la carte dinner menu is £26 ($45.50) per person. John and Vivienne Dees have owned and run the hotel since 1975 and have modernized the bedrooms by providing extra baths and tea- and coffee-making equipment. They will assist with information about the wall and the best places to walk. The hotel has a large car park.

HEXHAM

Above the Tyne River, this historic old market town is characterized by its narrow streets, old Market Square, a fine abbey church, and its Moot Hall. It makes a good base for exploring Hadrian's Wall and the Roman supply base of Corstopitum at Corbridge-on-Tyne, the ancient capital of Northumberland. The **Tourist Office,** at Hallgate (tel. 0434/605225), has masses of information on the wall for walkers, drivers, campers, and picnickers.

The **Abbey Church of St. Wilfred** is full of ancient relics. The Saxon font, the misericord carvings on the choir stalls, Acca's Cross, and St. Wilfred's chair are well worth seeing.

Food and Lodging on the Outskirts

The best accommodations are found not in Hexham itself, but in satellite villages and small towns, as exemplified by the following.

For a stay in a stately home, I recommend **Langley Castle,** Langley, Hexham, Northumberland NE47 5LU (tel. 043484/8888), not far southwest of Haydon Bridge and about seven miles west of Hexham, in ten acres of woodland on the edge of Northumberland National Park. The castle, built in 1350, was mainly uninhabited after being damaged in 1400 in the English-Scottish war, until its purchase in the late 19th century by Cadwallader Bates, a historian, who spent the rest of his life restoring the property with great care to its original beauty. Such medieval features are here as the 1350 spiral staircase, stained-glass windows, huge open fireplaces, seven-foot-thick walls, and many turrets. Today the castle receives paying guests in eight luxuriously appointed bedrooms of varying sizes and amenities. All the units have baths, direct-dial phones, color TVs, and radios, and some have a whirlpool or a sauna. Rents range from £46 ($80.50) to £85 ($148.75) daily, depending on the season and the features of the room, the prices based on double occupancy. Prices include breakfast and VAT. The hotel has an elegant drawing room, with an adjoining oak-paneled bar. Local specialties are served in the intimate restaurant.

Hadrian Hotel, Wall, near Hexham, Northumberland NE46 4EE (tel. 043481/232), is the ideal place to stay when visiting Hadrian's Wall. It's an ivy-covered building erected of stones taken from the wall. Owners Kevin and Helen Kelly, have completely refurbished the place, and it now has two Jacobean-style bars serving good bar meals specializing in seafood. The restaurant has an à la carte menu offering such specialties as stuffed guinea fowl Emperor Hadrian and roast chicken Northumbrian. Meals cost from £15 ($26.25) and up. The attractive bedrooms all have bath or shower, toilet, TV, phone, radio alarm, and tea- and coffee-making equipment. Three units have four-poster beds. Singles cost from £18 ($31.50) daily and doubles or twins £30 ($52.50) to £38 ($66.50). The hotel has a private residents' garden and beer gardens.

George Hotel, Chollerford, Humshaugh, near Hexham, Northumberland NE46 4EW (tel. 043481/611), stands on the banks of the Tyne, a creeper-covered country hotel with gardens leading to the riverbank. It's a convenient base for visiting the Roman Wall. The hotel dates from the 1700s, when the original structure was built of Roman stone. The bedrooms are pleasantly appointed and have private baths, color TVs, and mini-bars. Rates are from £49 ($85.75) daily for a single, from £65 ($113.75) for twins or doubles. All tariffs include an English breakfast, service, and VAT. Special "Breakaway" rates, costing £85 ($148.75) per person from April to October, £75 ($131.25) from November to March, provide B&B, dinner, and one luncheon for a two-night stay. The hotel has a Leisure Club with a heated indoor swimming pool, sauna, spa bath, and solarium. The Fishermans Bar is where locals gather for a traditional pub welcome and bar snacks served at lunch. A set luncheon in the restaurant costs from £8 ($14); dinner, from £12.95 ($22.65). An à la carte menu is also available, complemented by a large wine list.

LONGHORSLEY

A Georgian country house hotel, **Linden Hall Hotel,** Longhorsley, Morpeth, Northumberland NE65 8XF (tel. 0670/516611), is set in 300 acres of woods and parkland, near Longhorsley, six miles northwest of Morpeth by the A1 onto the A697. A sweeping staircase leads to rooms with modern beds, except in the honeymoon suites, which are furnished with four-posters. All units have baths, color TV, radios, phones, and baby-listening service, with some antique furniture used to advantage. Ten ground-floor rooms grouped around a sunny cobblestone courtyard are suitable for physically handicapped guests. All rates include a full English breakfast, VAT, and service. A single costs £65 ($113.75) daily, a double or twin going for £75 ($131.25) to £89.50 ($156.65). The chef offers a wide menu with some original appetizers. An array of fish dishes is offered nightly. Vegetables fresh from the field accompany main dishes in summer. There is also a good selection of wines. A meal costs around £18 ($31.50) to £25 ($43.75), including dessert.

On the estate in the restored granary is the Linden Pub, a casual place with a log fire and a collection of those large enameled signs that used to advertise tobacco, Camp coffee, and cocoa. As well as serving North Country ales, the pub provides good bar food. They often have barbecues in the courtyard in summer, when guests can indulge in such pursuits as quoits, boule, and garden draughts.

ALNMOUTH

A seaside resort on the Aln estuary, Alnmouth attracts sporting people who fish for salmon and trout in the Coquet River or play on its good golf course.

The **Schooner Hotel,** Northumberland Street, Alnmouth, Northumberland NE66 2RS (tel. 0665/830216), is a well-preserved Georgian inn, only a few minutes' walk to the water. The hotel is adjacent to the nine-hole Village Golf Course, the second oldest in the country, and also lies near an 18-hole championship course. The hotel has a squash court and a solarium. All 24 bedrooms have baths, color TV, and direct-dial phones. Singles cost £22 ($38.50) to £26 ($45.50) daily, and doubles go for £24 ($42) to £40 ($70). Guests can count on the good meals: set luncheons are priced at £5.50 ($9.65) and set dinners at £8.50 ($14.90). The hotel has a grill room, dining room, the Seahunter Bar, the Chase Bar, and the Long Bar as well as a residents' lounge.

ALNWICK

Set in the peaceful countryside of Northumberland, this ancient market town has had a long history. A good center for touring an area of scenic beauty, Alnwick is visited chiefly today by travelers wanting to see—

Area Sights

In the town of Alnwick, 30 miles north of Newcastle, **Alnwick Castle** (tel. 0665/510777), the largest castle in England after Windsor, is the seat of the Duke of Northumberland. This border fortress dates from the 11th century, when the earliest parts of the present castle were constructed by Yvo de Vescy, the first Norman Baron of Alnwick. A major restoration was undertaken by the fourth duke in the mid-19th century, and Alnwick remains relatively unchanged to this day. The rugged medieval outer walls do not prepare the first-time visitor for the richness of the interior, decorated mainly in the style of the Italian Renaissance.

Most of the castle is open to the public during visiting hours. You can tour the principal apartments, including the armory, guard chamber, and library, where you can view portraits and landscapes painted by such masters as Titian, Canaletto, and Van Dyck. You may also visit the dungeons and the interesting Museum of Early British and Roman Relics. From the terraces within the castle's outer walls, you can look across the broad landscape stretching over the River Aln.

Alnwick is open to the public daily except Saturday, from 1 to 5 p.m. May to September. Admission is £2 ($3.50) for adults and £1 ($1.75) for children. For an extra charge you can also visit the Regimental Museum of the Royal Northumberland Fusiliers, within the castle grounds.

Cragside, designed in the late 19th century by architect Richard Norman Shaw for the first Lord Armstrong, is a grand estate stretching across 900 acres on the southern edge of the Alnwick Moor. Here groves of magnificent trees and fields of rhododendrons frequently give way to peaceful ponds and lakes. The Victorian house is open only for part of the season, but the grounds alone are worth the visit. At Rothbury, the house is just 13 miles southwest of Alnwick. The park is open from 10:30 a.m. to 6 p.m. daily from Good Friday to the end of September, to 5 p.m. daily in October, and to 4 p.m. on Saturday and Sunday from November to the end of March. Admission to the park only is £1.50 ($2.65) for adults and 75p ($1.30) for children. The house is open from 1 to 5:30 p.m. daily except Monday from April to the end of September, and from 1 to 5 p.m. on Wednesday, Saturday, and Sunday in October (last entry half an hour before closing). Admission to both house and park is £3 ($5.25) for adults, £1.50 ($2.65) for children. For more information, phone 0669/20333.

Dunstanburgh Castle (English Heritage), on the coast nine miles northeast of Alnwick, about 1½ miles east of Embleton (which is the castle's address), was begun in 1316 by Thomas, Earl of Lancaster, and enlarged in the 14th century by John of Gaunt. The dramatic ruins of the gatehouse, towers, and curtain wall stand on a promontory high above the sea. You can reach the castle on foot only, either by walking from Craster in the south or across the Dunstanburgh Golf Course from

Embleton and Dunstan Steads in the north. The castle is open from 10 a.m. to 6 p.m. daily except Monday from Good Friday to the end of September; to 4 p.m. daily except Monday October to the end of March. Closed Christmas and New Year's. Admission is 80p ($1.40) for adults, 40p (70¢) for children.

Food and Lodging

The White Swan, Bondgate Within, Alnwick, Northumberland NE66 1TD (tel. 0665/602109), has a history going back to medieval days when it entertained highwaymen and passengers on the Edinburgh–London stagecoaches. A neoclassic coaching inn, just inside an ancient town gate, the Hotspur, it has also become the permanent home of the music room of the S.S. *Olympic,* sister ship of the *Titanic.* This beautiful paneled room was removed from the ship and completely reconstructed at the hotel. The hotel has 41 bedrooms, with bath and shower, and some of these are in a modern block and others in the older, more traditional part of the inn. Singles begin at £43 ($75.25) daily, and doubles peak at £58 ($101.50), including a full breakfast, service, and VAT.

CORNHILL-ON-TWEED

This border village, on the River Tweed, faces Coldstream on the Scottish shore.

Tillmouth Park Hotel, Cornhill-on-Tweed, Northumberland TD12 4UU (tel. 0890/2255), built in 1882, is an imposing Victorian mansion, occupying a secluded position in its own parkland gardens overlooking the River Till at the heart of a 1,000-acre estate. It stands about nine miles from Berwick, three miles from Cornhill-on-Tweed, and four miles from Coldstream. Monumental and impressive, it rises four stories high, with many wings, gables, and chimneys, including a porch emblazoned with heraldic devices. In spite of its size, there are only 13 bedrooms, each one comfortable, all containing private baths. Ask for the Sir Walter Scott room, with its twin four-posters. Edwardian furnishings grace some of the chambers, which rent for £35 ($61.25) to £45 ($78.75) daily for one person, £25 ($43.75) to £35 ($61.25) per person for a double, the latter price for the honeymoon bungalow called the Garden Suite. Modernity, as reflected by a cocktail bar, has been blended with tradition, as represented by a galleried lounge with a stone fireplace.

PART TWO

SCOTLAND

XVIII

INTRODUCING
SCOTLAND

1. THE COUNTRY
2. FLYING TO SCOTLAND
3. GETTING AROUND SCOTLAND
4. PRACTICAL FACTS

In Scotland, a land of bagpipes and clans, you'll find some of the grandest scenery in Europe. Stretching before you will be the Lowlands, but in the far distance the fabled Highlands loom. If you traverse the country, you'll discover lochs and glens, heather-covered moors, twirling kilts and tam o'shanters, pastel-bathed houses and graystone cottages, mountains, rivers, and streams filled with trout and salmon. Eagles soar and deer run free. Lush meadowlands are filled with sheep, and rocky coves and secret harbors wait to be discovered. You'll hear the sound of Gaelic, see a Shetland pony, be awed by the misty blue hills, and perhaps attend a Highland gathering. You'll find quiet contemplation or else enjoy an activity-filled calendar.

Many visitors think of Scotland as Edinburgh and search no further, but if you travel northward, you'll find the real Scotland, along with overwhelming hospitality and a sense of exploration.

A small nation, Scotland is only 275 miles long and some 150 miles wide at its broadest point. No one lives more than 40 miles from salt water. In spite of the smallness of size, however, Scotland has extended its influence far and wide, giving the world both dreamers and daredevils, warriors and preachers. Inventors came from Scotland, including Alexander Graham Bell, and explorers, including Mungo Park and David Livingstone. Scotland gave the world such philanthropists as Andrew Carnegie, along with poets of the caliber of Robert Burns and towering novelists such as Sir Walter Scott. But, curiously, for a long time its most famous resident has been neither man nor woman. It's the Loch Ness monster.

Scotland has its own legal system and issues its own currency. However, English and Scottish banknotes have equal value and are accepted in both countries. The Church of Scotland is separate from that of England. The language of the Scot is said to be nearer to the original English than what is spoken today. In fact, an English person often finds it hard to understand the speech of a true and gentle Highlander, who grew up in view of ancient sandstone and granite mountains.

If you go by road or rail, you will hardly be aware of crossing out of England into Scotland. The border is just a line on a map. But, even though the two countries have been joined constitutionally since 1707, Scotland is very different from England. It is very much its own country

You may come to Scotland on a sentimental journey to see where your forebears were born. Or else you may be lured there by its majestic sights. Whatever your reason, you'll find a land of paradox and romantic tradition.

You'll also find one of the biggest welcomes in Europe. But remember one thing: scotch is a whisky (spelled without an *e*) and not the name of the proud people who inhabit the country. They are called Scots or Scottish. Even if you forget and call them Scotch, they'll forgive you. What they won't forgive is calling them English.

---

1. The Country

This northernmost country of the three that make up the island of Great Britain (Scotland, England, and Wales) has for centuries been the home of a spirited, independent people, who were tough enough and brave enough to live in this mostly rugged land and to maintain their freedom from outside control up to the time a Scotsman, King James VI, went to sit on the British throne as James I in 1603.

Scotland is the oldest geological formation of Great Britain, divided physically into three regions: the granite Highlands, including lochs, glens, and mountains, plus the hundreds and hundreds of islands to the west and north; the Central Lowlands, where three valleys and estuaries (firths) of the Clyde, Forth, and Tay rivers make up a fertile belt from the Atlantic Ocean to the North Sea; and the Southern Uplands, the smooth, rolling moorland, broken with low crags and threaded with rivers and valleys, between the central plain and the English border.

From the last Ice Age, mankind has lived in what is today Scotland, as attested by cairns, standing stones, brochs, cromlechs, and burial chambers. Eventually Celts moved in. They may have come here via Ireland, but they were probably not Irish Celts, being more closely related to those of Cornwall, Wales, and Brittany—Celt-Iberians. They were dubbed Picts (from the Latin *pictor* or painter) by the Roman invaders, who came to what they called Caledonia in the early part of the 1st century A.D. The Picts were so named because they painted their bodies blue, it is claimed. At any rate, the Romans didn't have much luck against the wild, fierce inhabitants of Caledonia and before long pulled back south and built Hadrian's Wall, leaving the northern reaches to the short, dark Picts.

A different breed of Celt, the Dalriad Irish, called Scots, moved in before A.D. 500, bringing with them Christianity. These people were red- and sandy-haired with fair skin. They settled first in the Argyll peninsula, which they named Scotia. The Scotians and Celt-Iberians (Picts) became mixed over the centuries, but in the Highlands, some of the small, dark strain still exists in almost pure form.

Religion has a strong place in the lore and history of this country, from Druids to Roman Catholicism to staunch and puritanical Presbyterianism. The early centuries of Scotland were marked by strong leadership by monks and abbots, but by the time of the Reformation, John Knox and his militant Calvinism took over in many areas. Presbyterianism is still the major religion in the country, despite the link with England.

The country had its own kings and their battling cohorts by the time of William the Conqueror. Sometimes the Scots banded together to battle the English, at other times joining the neighbors to the south to fight each other. The first Irish invaders started new families, which, when they split from the original homesteads and resettled, formed *clans,* the Gaelic word meaning "family" or "children of." The clan designation allowed them to trace their origins even when they moved to distant places. There was a strong hierarchy within each clan, with a chief at its head, followed by lesser chieftains, gentlemen, and then plain clansmen. The various families warred among themselves for territory, rights and honor. The fighting among the clans abated in 1609 when, on the island of Iona, the statutes of Iona were signed by most of the clan chiefs. Sporadic fighting continued for years, but the last real clan battle—Macdonalds versus Macintoshes—took place in 1688.

The power of the great lords of Scotland was broken in 1603, when the son of Mary Queen of Scots assumed the throne of England upon the death of Elizabeth, but all was not peace and goodwill between Scots and English. Religion again stirred strife when King James II was ousted from the throne and his Roman Catholic descendants tried to restore their title and their religion to England and Scotland. Because many Highlanders had rallied to the cause of Bonnie Prince Charlie's claims to the throne, the wearing of the tartan, the distinguishing plaid material denoting the wearer's clan affiliation, was banned until 1782.

As a result of the strife and defeat of anti-English forces, many Scots fled to other parts of the world during the troubled 1700s, becoming an integral part of the development of the United States and other countries.

THE PEOPLE

Scotland is a country of hospitable people, who are descended from an interesting mixture of bloodlines: Celt-Iberian (Pict), Roman, Norse, Saxon, Irish Celtic, Jute, Angle, Norman, and French, with perhaps a few more sources thrown in, what with the seafarers of many nations who have come here through the centuries.

At one time, in parts where the Celtic heritage was strongest, the language of the country was Gaelic and even today is still used in some remote parts. That language is still remembered in a few words and phrases, as it is seen in place names. The later Gaelic was always much like Erse or Irish Gaelic, although there are similarities to the languages that were once the native tongues of Cornwall and Brittany and the one that is still widely spoken in Wales.

Scotland has a population today of some 5,200,000 people, about 75% of whom live in the Central Lowland area, the fertile strip across the country from the Firth of Forth to the Firth of Clyde, where most of the industry of the country is found.

The deepest tradition of Scotland appears to be based on the clan system of old, with tartans, bagpipes, and all such things playing a large part in the thinking of people when they talk about the country. This is a romantic memory, however, and the fact is that many of the Scots—Lowlanders—have little or no connection with the clansmen of earlier times.

Many of the Scots were laden with a lasting guilt feeling by the preachings of John Knox and the forced adherence for a long time to teachings of the kirk and harsh Scottish Presbyterianism. Although the customs have changed in resort areas, brought about by the coming of many tourists to the country, there is still a strain of puritanism that can be seen in Sunday closings, with many of the people of the country observing the Sabbath as a day of rest.

Outside the big cities of Edinburgh and Glasgow, people live in small towns and on farms, some even in the tiny crofts clinging to steep hillsides in the Western Highland county.

The strength and independence of spirit of the Scots has been carried by their people who have spread all over the world, making good in many fields—as writers and artists, doctors and scientists, and inventors. Many, however, have stayed home and made their mark in the world from the place where Bronze Age aborigines began the long journey into modern Scotland.

TARTANS AND KILTS

Today the clans, the ancient families, and those who enjoy common ancestry are identified mainly by their tartans, the word first recorded in 1471 to describe the previously named "chequered garment" or "mantle." The kilt has a much older history as a style of dress. It was recorded in Bronze Age frescoes in Crete and worn by soldiers such as the Romans.

After the 1745 rebellion led by Bonnie Prince Charlie, the checkered multicol-

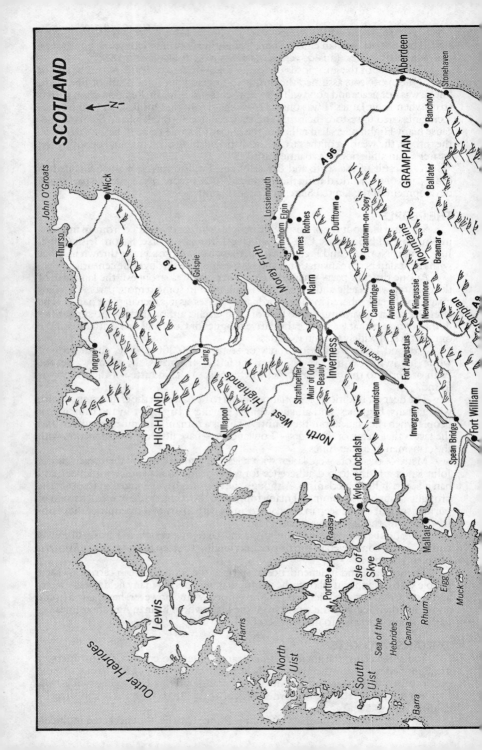

ored cloth was banned. However, when Sir Walter Scott invited King George IV to visit Scotland, the king arrived in a kilt wearing pink tights underneath. Thus the tartan came back into fashion, helped in no small part by Prince Albert, consort to Queen Victoria.

There are some 300 clan designs today. Many kilt shops throughout Scotland will help you determine if your family has its own tartan.

Garb o' the Gods

Few people realize that from seven to ten yards of tartan wool cloth goes into the average kilt. Even fewer non-Scots know what is actually worn beneath the voluminous folds strapped over the muscular thighs of a parading Scotsman. For a Highlander, the answer to that question is "nothing," an answer that is true for any defender of the ancient tradition that only a Stewart can wear a Stewart tartan, that only a MacPherson can wear a MacPherson tartan, and that only a Scotsman looks good in a kilt. Of course, any true Scot would wager his claymore (sword) that only a foreigner would stoop to wearing "unmentionables" (that's underpants to us) beneath his kilt.

Alas, commercialism has reared its ugly head with the introduction of undergarments to match the material making up the swirling folds of the kilts of bagpipe players. Nevertheless, salesmen in shops specializing in Highland garb tell the story of a colonel, the 11th Earl of Airlie, who had heard that the soldiers of his elite Highland Light Infantry were mollycoddling themselves with undershorts. The next day, his eyebrows bristling, he ordered the entire regiment to undress under his watchful eye. To his horror, he saw that half a dozen of his soldiers had disgraced the regiment by putting on "what only an Englishman would wear." He publicly ordered the offending garments removed. When he gave the order next day to "drop your kilts," not a soldier in the regiment had on "trews" (close-cut tartan shorts).

It was no doubt a long time before a similar level of indiscretion may have manifested itself among the Highland Light Infantry, if indeed it ever has. Even with the general decline of standards today, the mark of a man in the Highlands is still whether he can abide drafts up against his thighs and the feel of rough cloth against tender flesh.

If you're not fortunate enough to be of Highland extraction, or if you are distantly Scottish but can't discover possible clan connections, there is still hope. Long ago, Queen Victoria authorized two "Lowland" designs as suitable garb for Sassenachs (Saxons—Englishmen and, more remotely, Americans). If, during your jaunts in the Highlands, you decide to wear a kilt and a true Scot sees you in a Sassenach tartan, he or she will probably assume that you are also wearing "unmentionables."

ANCESTRAL ROOTS

If you have a name beginning with "Mac" (which simply means son), or if your name is Donaldson, or Shaw, or one of the dozens and dozens of other Scottish names, you may have been descended from a clan. This was a group of kinsmen ruled over by a chief and claiming a common ancestry. MacDonald is, in fact, one of the oldest clans, dating back to the 13th century. Clans and clan societies have their own museums throughout Scotland, and local tourist offices will have details about where to locate them. Some of the more prominent ones are previewed in this guide.

In bookstores throughout Scotland, you can also purchase clan histories and maps. In Edinburgh and Glasgow, genealogical firms specialize in tracing Highland family histories.

If you'd like to do it yourself (a lot cheaper), you may want to go to the **General Register Office for Scotland**, New Register House, Edinburgh, Lothian EH1 3YT. You can write them for a full list of their search fees and a full extent of their records before going there yourself. Scottish ancestor hunters come here bitten by the genealogy bug, and seats get crowded in summer. The house has on record details of every birth, marriage, and death in Scotland since 1855. It also has census returns for every decade from 1841 to 1891. They also have such data as the recordings of foreign marriages of Scots, adopted children's registers, and war registers.

2. Flying to Scotland

Most North Americans reach Scotland by flying first to London, and then going on to Scotland via train, rented car, or airplane. If you plan to combine a visit to Scotland with a trip to England, your best bet is to fly into London, where airline competition is keen (which can mean lower prices for you). The choice of airlines flying into London from North America is greater than for any other country. Among them, you can fly the premier airline of the United Kingdom, British Airways, or such carriers as TWA, Pan Am, Delta, or American. Or you might fly Virgin Atlantic. The ways of getting to London, with a discussion of fare possibilities, are presented in Chapter I.

If you want to explore only Scotland, Prestwick Airport, 30 miles southwest of Glasgow, is the only airport in that country capable of handling transatlantic flights. It's small compared to such industry giants as London's Heathrow, but is preferred by visitors to Britain wishing to begin their journey in the north.

The only airline flying nonstop between North America and Scotland is **Northwest Airlines.** It offers four and five weekly flights into Scotland's Prestwick Airport from Boston, with flights originating in either Minneapolis or New York. Currently (subject to change) the best midsummer deal from New York to Prestwick is an APEX ticket requiring several stringent restrictions. These include advance purchase, penalties for alteration of itineraries, and both minimum and maximum stays abroad. In high season, the round trip fare is likely to be $682 per person. Certain promotional fares are sometimes offered in May and early June for about $200 less.

If you plan to visit both England and Scotland, as most tourists do, your best bet is to shop around for the latest bargains. **British Airways,** for example, is always competitive in its fares, and it offers services from 21 U.S. and Canadian cities. From New York alone, there are six nonstop flights a day. British Airways carries more passengers to Scotland than any other airline. Passengers usually land at either Edinburgh or Glasgow. You can also fly to Dundee, Aberdeen, and Inverness. British Airways operates a shuttle service from Heathrow Airport outside London to both Edinburgh and Glasgow. Flights last about an hour. Other lines competing on this run include **British Midland, Dan Air,** and **Air U.K.**

THE QUESTION OF FARES

All three of the smaller airlines (British Midland, Dan Air, and Air U.K.) charge less money for round-trip tickets when certain restrictions are met. These include a penalty for any changes in the itinerary, a 14-day advance purchase, the passage of a Saturday night before using the return portion of a round-trip ticket, and a maximum stay of no more than two or three months (depending on the airline).

British Midland and Air U.K. both fly from London to Glasgow and, if these conditions are met, both charge around $135 for a round trip. Dan Air is one of the few carriers to fly from London to Inverness and, with roughly the same restrictions, it charges about $155 for the round-trip passage.

The standard economy fare between London and Edinburgh on British Airways is £81 ($141.75) one way. However, you can always opt for one of the super shuttle saver tickets, but restrictions apply. To qualify you must book and pay for the ticket two weeks in advance and fly during off-peak times (see below). However, this fare is one of the air bargains of Great Britain, costing £85 ($148.75) for a round-trip fare from London to Edinburgh.

On British Airways, you can save money by traveling "off-peak service" in which event a one-way fare will cost £65 ($113.75). Off-peak service applies to routes flown Monday to Friday from 10 a.m. to 3:30 p.m. and after 7 p.m. plus any time at all on Saturday and Sunday.

---

3. Getting Around Scotland

From Newcastle upon Tyne, the A68 heading northwest takes you to where England meets Scotland, an area long known as "Carter Bar." At this point, all of Scotland lies before you, and an unforgettable land it is.

I recommend to visitors that they approach the Border Country after a stopover in the York area of England. That way, they can start exploring Scotland in the east with Edinburgh as their goal, then go up through Royal Deeside and on to Inverness, crossing over and down the west side of Glasgow, emerging at Gretna Green, near Carlisle in England's Lake District. The Border Country is a fitting introduction to Scotland, as it contains many reminders of the country's historic and literary past. A highlight of the tour is a visit to Abbotsford, the house Sir Walter Scott built on the banks of the salmon river, the Tweed. However, if you enter Scotland from the west of England, you'll travel through Dumfries and Galloway—the Land of Burns, former home of Scotland's national poet, Robert Burns.

Burns knew well the southwestern corner of Scotland, which is bounded by an indented coastline of charm, which attracts many artists to the secluded life that prevails there. Distances aren't long, but many motorists traveling in Scotland find so much to see that they take two or three days to cover about 100 miles. At Ayr, Troon, and Prestwick (with its international airport), you'll find sandy beaches and golf courses, good fishing, and pony trekking. Farther north, you'll come to the land of the lochs and glens. Maybe you'll even spot the Loch Ness monster, Nessie, along the way.

By Train

For information on traveling by train in Scotland, see Chapter I, Section 3, "Traveling Within Britain."

By Bus

The cheapest means of transport in Scotland is bus (or coach). The **Scottish Citylink Coaches,** which link Glasgow and Edinburgh with the popular tourist centers of Aviemore and Inverness, are a good bet. It takes only 3 hours to reach Aviemore from Edinburgh, 3½ hours to Inverness from the capital. Other popular runs are offered, including links between Glasgow and Fort William, Inverness and Ullapool, and Glasgow and Oban. For information, get in touch with **Highland Scottish,** Seafield Road, Inverness (tel. 0463/237575), or **Scottish Citylink Coaches,** Buchanan Bus Station, Glasgow (tel. 041/3329191), and **St. Andrew Square Bus Station,** Edinburgh (tel. 031/557-5717).

By Ferry

You can use a variety of special excursion fares to reach Scotland's islands, available from Caledonian MacBrayne for the Clyde and the islands of the west or from P&O Ferries, serving Orkney and Shetland. Caledonian MacBrayne sails to 23 Hebridean or Clyde islands. The fares, times of departure, and other requirements are so complicated that a special book is published by the Highlands and Islands Development Board. It details all the data you need for road, rail, sea, and air travel throughout Scotland. Updated annually, it is available throughout the country. The title is *Getting Around the Highlands and Islands.*

Helpful contacts are **Caledonian MacBrayne,** The Ferry Terminal, Gourock

PA19 1QP, Renfrewshire (tel. 0475/33755); and **P&O Ferries,** Orkney and Shetland Services, Jamieson's Quay, Aberdeen, Aberdeenshire AB9 8DL (tel. 0224/572615).

By Car
See Chapter I, Section 3, for information on car rentals in Britain.

WHERE TO GO
The French, the second partner in the "Auld Alliance," used to call it *Le Grand Tour d'Écosse,* or the grand tour of Scotland. Johnson and Boswell made the tour, and visitors, most often North American, continue to follow in their footsteps to this day. But, since many are faced with miles of grand scenery, including mist-shrouded glens and mountains, heathered moorlands, and timeless islands, they must make tough decisions about what to see and what to save for another day.

Some prefer to plan their tours around the grand castles of Scotland, whose locations range from the Borders to the Highlands. Each of these unique and magnificent properties will be documented in the chapters ahead. They include Blair Castle, the home of the tenth Duke of Atholl, who still has a private army; Floors Castle, home of the Duke and Duchess of Roxburghe; Glamis Castle, setting for Shakespeare's *Macbeth;* Dunrobin Castle, home of the earls and dukes of Sutherland for eight centuries; Scone Palace, home of the earls of Mansfield for more than four centuries; and Hopetoun House, Scotland's greatest Adam mansion.

For those with a very limited time schedule, I'll outline some popular itineraries through Scotland. The first is for those motorists entering Scotland through the southeast, known as "the Borders." At Newcastle upon Tyne (in England), I suggest you take the A696 in the direction of Otterburn. It becomes the A68 and will lead you right into Jedburgh and Melrose, the heart of the Border Country with its ancient abbeys. From Melrose, take the A6091 west in the direction of Galashiels. The road runs into the A7 north. At Galashiels, turn west onto the A72 in the direction of Peebles. This will take you through the Tweed Valley, with all its associations with Sir Walter Scott, the novelist. From Peebles, it is but a short drive along a secondary road, the A703, leading into the capital of Scotland, Edinburgh, which many critics consider one of the most beautiful cities of Europe.

While based in Edinburgh, you can take many interesting excursions in every direction. Among these, you can cross the Forth Bridge, taking the southern coastal road along the Forth. You can head east, to the ancient Kingdom of Fife. You can visit the fishing villages of East Neuk, eventually reaching the capital of golf, St. Andrews, if you've continued to follow the coastal road. You will be at a point 49 miles from Edinburgh. There are several ways to return to Edinburgh. If you're rushed for time, you can take the A91 west. In the vicinity of Loch Leven and its historic castle, this becomes an express highway, heading back to Edinburgh across the Forth Bridge.

The second excursion requires stopovers of at least three nights. You can leave Edinburgh on the express highway, the M9, that goes to Stirling, 37 miles away, where you'll be within sight of the famous castle in about an hour. You can spend an hour or two walking around its old town with its castle, before heading for the Trossachs, one of the most beautiful scenic areas of Scotland. The A84 heads west in the right direction, but eventually you must cut onto the A821, going via Callander. The Trossachs have been called "Scotland in miniature." The Trossachs take in such delights as Loch Katrine and, the most famous of all, Loch Lomond. Sometimes this is called Rob Roy country and Lady of the Lake country, because Sir Walter Scott used the area as a setting for his novels. You can either overnight in the Trossachs or continue west to Loch Lomond.

The next day you can leave Loch Lomond and, along its western shore, connect with Rte. A83, which will take you to Inveraray, a small holiday resort, seat of the Duke of Argyll at Inveraray Castle. From Inveraray, you can head north along the

A819 to Dalmally, which lies along the A85. Continue west from Dalmally until you reach the junction with the A82. There you can head north, going through Glen Coe, site of the famous 1692 massacre. If you stay on the A82, you'll reach Fort William, which has the greatest concentration of hotels in the area.

After a night in Fort William, continue north along the A82 until you reach the junction of Invergarry. There you can turn west along the A87, the road to the isles, which will take you to the Kyle of Lochalsh, where frequent ferries ply back and forth to Skye, the most visited of Scottish islands. Skye deserves at least a day and night, more if you can spare it.

If you have the time and can add another two days to your schedule, head back to Invergarry. Instead of turning south to Fort William, continue on the road north to Inverness. The distance from Invergarry to Inverness is 41 miles. The A82 will take you along the western bank of Loch Ness where, as you drive along, you can try to spot the monster rearing its head from the water.

If you take this motor jaunt, you will not by any means have seen Scotland. There's the granite city of Aberdeen and the great northeast, including Royal Deeside, site of Balmoral Castle where the Queen herself takes some of her holidays. There's Glasgow, the biggest city of Scotland and its cultural center, a place filled with art treasures and far better as a sightseeing attraction than its former grim industrial reputation suggests. There's the Robert Burns country, centering around Ayr, then the southern Lowlands of Dumfries and Galloway, bordering England.

All of these attractions have been documented in this guide. The itinerary suggestions are only for those in a hurry. Perhaps if your time is too pressed, you'll return again at some future date and see the other parts as well, for each is rich in attraction, lore, and adventure.

4. Practical Facts

Much information found in the section of Chapter I called "The ABCs of Britain" pertains to Scotland as well as to England. However, there are a few matters you will probably find helpful to know in Scotland alone. And some data specific to Edinburgh will be found in Chapter XX.

CLIMATE: The Lowlands of Scotland usually have a moderate year-round temperature. In spring, the average temperature is 53°F, rising to about 65° on the average in summer. By the time the crisp autumn has arrived, the temperatures have dropped to spring levels. In winter, the average temperature is 43°F. Temperatures in the north of Scotland are colder, especially in winter, and you should dress accordingly. It rains a lot in Scotland, but perhaps not as much as age-old myths would have it. For example, the rainfall in Edinburgh is exactly the same as that of London. But you should always take your raincoat with you.

HOLIDAYS: Besides the public holidays listed in "The ABCs of Britain," on January 25 Scotland holds a major event, Burns's Night, honoring the poet, when throughout the land at various suppers, the national bard's poems are recited and haggis is piped in and eaten.

INFORMATION: There are more than 160 tourist information centers in Scotland. All are well signposted in their cities or towns, but some are closed in winter. For more specific listings, refer to Edinburgh or Glasgow. If you wish to write for information about Scotland, the address is the **Scottish Tourist Board,** 23 Ravelston Terrace, Edinburgh EH4 3EU.

SHOPPING: Your best buys are in tartans, knitwear, tweeds, and whisky. There is a wide array of cashmere and lambswool knitwear, along with an excellent selection of Harris tweeds for both women and men. Collectors still go to Scotland for antiques, and it is also known for its silver and sports equipment. Edinburgh crystal is well known. You might also take home a kilt and a set of bagpipes.

STORE HOURS: The night for late shopping is Thursday, when stores remain open until 7 p.m. in Glasgow, until 8 p.m. in Edinburgh. Most stores open at 9 a.m., closing at 5:30 or 6 p.m., with an early closing one day each week, varying from town to town. Stores are closed on Sunday.

XIX

SOUTHERN SCOTLAND

1. THE BORDER COUNTRY
2. BURNS COUNTRY
3. DUMFRIES AND GALLOWAY

The gentlest part of Scotland is the Southern Uplands, that section connected on the east with Sir Walter Scott and on the west with the celebrated poet of the people, Robert Burns. This is a land of smooth, rolling moors, between the English border and the central plain of Scotland, where the country's population is massed. In southern Scotland, low hills break the terrain, which is threaded with deep valleys and rushing rivers.

The Border Country is a fit introduction to Scotland, containing as it does many reminders of the historic and artistic past of Scotland. Salmon and tweed are the major products of the eastern borderland.

The Land of Burns, in the southwestern corner of the country, is where the poet lived, wrote, and died. The gentle climate and secluded life known to Burns still prevail.

There's good fishing in the rivers and the sea in southern Scotland, and pony-trekking is an activity in the low hills and valleys. Sandy beaches and golf courses combine with traces of prehistoric and historic people to form a fascinating and easily traversed region.

1. The Border Country

Castles in romantic ruins and Gothic skeletons of abbeys stand as reminders—in this ballad-rich land of plunder and destruction—of interminable battles that raged between England and the proud Scots. For a long time the Border Country was a no-man's-land.

This is also the land of Sir Walter Scott, that master of romantic adventure in a panoramic setting, who died in 1832. Today he is remembered for such works as *Rob Roy, Ivanhoe,* and *The Bride of Lammermoor.*

Southeast Scotland contains the remains of four great abbeys, built by King David I in the mid-12th century: Dryburgh (where Scott is buried), Melrose, Jedburgh, and Kelso.

"The Borders" are also the home of the celebrated "Common Ridings" gatherings commemorating major events of the past.

JEDBURGH

Jedburgh lies on the River Jed, 325 miles from London, 48 from Edinburgh. This royal burgh and border town is famous for its ruined **Jedburgh Abbey,** founded by King David in about 1138 and considered one of the finest abbeys in Scotland. Inside is a small museum, containing fragments of medieval works. The abbey is open April to September Monday to Saturday from 9:30 a.m. to 7 p.m. or dusk, on Sunday 2 to 7 p.m. or dusk. From October to March it keeps the same hours, except it is closed on Thursday afternoon and all day Friday. Admission is £1 ($1.75) for adults and 50p (90¢) for children.

On Queen Street, you can visit the **Mary Queen of Scots House** (tel. 0835/63331), where she stayed in 1566 for six weeks. After a long ride to Hermitage Castle where the Earl of Bothwell lay wounded, the queen suffered a stomach hemorrhage that nearly killed her. The house, recently refurbished to commemorate Mary's 400th anniversary, is now a Mary Queen of Scots Visitor Centre, telling a thought-provoking story of her life. It is open from 10 a.m. to 5 p.m. Monday to Saturday, 1 to 5 p.m. Sunday Easter to November. Admission is 75p ($1.30) for adults, 50p (90¢) for children.

The **Castle Jail Museum,** Castlegate (tel. 0835/63254), stands on the site of Jedburgh Castle. When it was opened in 1823, it was considered a "modern reform jail." Charging 50p (90¢) for adults, 25p (45¢) for children, it is open from 10 a.m. to 5 p.m. Monday to Saturday, on Sunday from 1 to 5 p.m.

Food and Lodging

Jedforest Country House Hotel, Jedburgh, Roxburghshire TD8 6PJ (tel. 08354/274) lies in an idyllic setting, owned by a charming family. A winding driveway takes you past a line of conifers and a herd of Angus cattle grazing beside a meandering river. The solid, 120-year-old stone house has steep gables and high ceilings, with detailed cove moldings. The main house contains eight well-furnished and clean rooms, each fitted with such old-fashioned accessories as brass headboards and big windows. Four contemporary rooms, each with a private bath and color TV, are housed in an annex. With breakfast included, rooms rent for £24 ($42) daily in a single and from £38 ($66.50) in a twin or double. With bath, the cost is £41 ($71.75) in a twin or double. Guests congregate near the coal-burning fireplace in the half-timbered pub, where bar meals are available, or around the pool table and dart board in the adjacent game room. Food is served in the Victorian dining room, costing £8 ($14) per person.

The Carters' Restaurant (tel. 08356/63414), is a pub with a downstairs dining room built of old abbey stones. The building has had a long history—a local grammar school from 1779, before finding its present role. This is the favorite gathering place of the people of Jedburgh, who know that its owner, Michael Wares, serves good food and drink. Soups, bar snacks, and coffee are served daily in the lounge bar. The restaurant offers either British or continental dishes daily from £5 ($8.75). Lunches are served Monday to Saturday from noon to 2 p.m. Dinners are more elaborate, presented Monday to Thursday from 6 to 9 p.m., to 10 on Friday and Saturday. Fish is fresh from Eyemouth, accompanied, if you wish, by a tomato-and-coleslaw salad.

If you follow the A698 northeast of Jedburgh, the road will lead to—

KELSO

Another typical historic border town, Kelso lies at the point where the Teviot meets the Tweed. **Kelso Abbey,** now in ruins, was the earliest and the largest of the border abbeys. In the town's marketplace, the "Old Pretender," James Stewart, was proclaimed king, designated James VIII.

Kelso is also the home of the Duke of Roxburghe, who lives at **Floors Castle,** built in 1721 by William Adam. Part of the castle, which is open to the public, contains superb French and English furniture, porcelain, tapestries, and paintings by such artists as Gainsborough, Reynolds, and Canaletto. There are a licensed restaurant, coffeeshop, and gift shop as well as a walled garden and garden center. The castle was a major location for the film *Greystoke,* concerning the Tarzan legend. The house is open in May, June, and September from Sunday to Thursday. In July and August, it is open Sunday to Friday. Otherwise, it is closed to individuals. The house opens at 11:30 a.m., the last guests being shown through at 4:45 p.m. The grounds and gardens may be visited from 10:30 a.m. to 5:30 p.m. Admission is £2.20 ($3.85) for adults, £1.30 ($2.30) for children. For further information, phone 0573/23333.

A Historic Home on the Outskirts

Seat of the Earl of Haddington, **Mellerstain** (tel. 057381/225) lies in "the Borders," although it is most often visited on a day trip from Edinburgh, 37 miles away. One of Scotland's famous Adam mansions, it is near Gordon, nine miles northeast of Melrose and seven miles northwest of Kelso. It's open from May to September daily except Saturday, from 12:30 to 4:30 p.m. Admission is £2.20 ($3.85) for adults, 80p ($1.40) for children.

Mellerstain enjoys associations with Lady Grisel Baillie, the Scottish heroine, and Lord Haddington is her descendant. William Adam built two wings of the house in 1725, and the main building was designed by his more famous son, Robert, some 40 years later. You're shown through the interior, with its decorations and ceilings by Robert Adam, and are allowed to view the impressive library as well as paintings by old masters and antique furniture. Later, from the garden terrace, you can look south to the lake, with the Cheviot Hills in the distance, a panoramic view. Afternoon tea is served, and souvenir gifts are on sale.

Food and Lodging

Ednam House Hotel, Bridge Street, Kelso, Roxburghshire TD5 7HT (tel. 0573/24168), is a conversion of a Georgian house into a 32-room hotel often referred to as "that lovely place beside the river." The hotel, lying on the fringe of Kelso, has a good atmosphere, and the bedrooms are well kept, some with river views. Built in 1761, the hotel was purchased from the Duke of Roxburghe in 1928, and it is one of the finest examples of Georgian architecture in the Borders. A few of the bedrooms are spacious and airy, although late arrivals might be given the more cramped quarters. Nearly all the accommodations come equipped with private bath, and B&B costs £28 ($49) daily in a single, £58 ($101.50) in a double. Rates include a full Scottish breakfast. For those wanting to chance it with the highly unreliable Scottish sun, there is a terrace.

Sunlaws House Hotel, Heiton, Kelso, Roxburghshire TD5 8JZ (tel. 05735/331), lies three miles southwest from Kelso by the A698. The manorial walls of this late-19th-century castle rise on 200 acres of woodland, lawns, and gardens. The building was erected as the family home of the Roxburghe family, who valued its location on the trout-filled Teviot River. In 1982 it was converted, with the blessing of the duke and duchess, into a lovely country hotel. Sunlaws maintains six bedrooms within the old stable block and another 15 units within the main house. Amid a subdued but elegant decor, the hotel has four low-burning fireplaces even in summer. Many of the guests come for shooting and fishing; others to watch the wildlife, especially deer. A glassed-in conservatory offers clusters of wicker chairs for enjoying drinks or tea when the weather is fine. A tennis court and croquet lawn are on the grounds. With breakfast included, singles rent for £49 ($85.75) to £80 ($140) daily, and doubles run £70 ($122.50) to £120 ($210), depending on the accommodation.

From Kelso, it is only a short drive on the A699 to—

DRYBURGH

Scott himself is buried at **Dryburgh Abbey.** These Gothic ruins are surrounded by gnarled yew trees and cedars of Lebanon, said to have been planted there by knights returning from the Holy Land during the years of the Crusades. Near Dryburgh is "Scott's View," over the Tweed to his beloved Eildon Hills, considered one of the most beautiful views in the region.

The adjoining town is—

ST. BOSWELLS

This old village, 40 miles from Edinburgh, stands on the Selkirk–Kelso road, near Dryburgh Abbey. It lies four miles from Melrose and 14 miles from Kelso. Because of the following hotel, many motorists prefer to make St. Boswells their headquarters for touring "the Borders."

Dryburgh Abbey Hotel, Newton Street, St. Boswells, Roxburghshire TD6 0RQ (tel. 0835/22261), stands beside the ruins from which it takes its name. On the outskirts of St. Boswells, the red sandstone hotel is surrounded by lovely grounds, made all the more so by the River Tweed. Built in the Scottish baronial manor, the abbey hotel has all the amenities associated with the traditional country-house hotel. Modern conveniences have been slipped in, however. About 30 rooms are offered, with B&B costing £27 ($47.25) per person daily. You have a choice of several lounges and a cocktail bar. Dinner costs from £13.50 ($23.65).

Four miles from Dryburgh Abbey is—

MELROSE

Lying 37 miles from Edinburgh, Melrose enjoys many associations with Scott. This border town, as mentioned, is also famous for its ruined **Melrose Abbey,** in the Valley of the Tweed. You can visit the ruins of the beautiful Cistercian abbey, founded in 1136, in which the heart of Robert I (the Bruce) is said to have been buried. Look for the beautiful carvings and tombs of other well-known Scotsmen buried in the chancel. In Scott's *The Lay of the Last Minstrel,* the abbey's east window received rhapsodic treatment, and in *The Abbot* and *The Monastery,* Melrose appears as "Kennaquhair." It is open April to September Monday to Saturday from 9:30 a.m. to 7 p.m., on Sunday from 2 to 7 p.m. October to March, hours are 9:30 a.m. to 4 p.m., 2 to 4 p.m. on Sunday. Admission is £1 ($1.75) for adults, 50p (90¢) for children. For more information, phone 089682/2562.

Burt's Hotel, Market Square, Melrose, Roxburghshire TD6 9PN (tel. 089682/2285), is an 18th-century inn in the center of town, within walking distance of the abbey. It was built in 1722 between the main square and a garden and offers a taste of small-town Scottish flavor. The hotel offers 21 comfortable rooms, 18 of which contain baths. All the units have color TVs and hot beverage facilities.

Accommodations in singles cost £28 ($49) daily; doubles, £50 ($87.50). All tariffs include breakfast. There's an elegant restaurant overlooking the garden and an attractive bar. Inexpensive bar lunches are tasty, and you can also take lunch in the restaurant. Bar suppers are also good, or if you prefer, an à la carte dinner in the restaurant, costing from £13 ($22.75), might include any item from duckling with cherries to medallions of Hungarian-style pork.

At sunset you can stroll along the banks of the River Tweed, or perhaps walk along a public footpath on a hill overlooking the town.

The next morning, you can drive three miles to—

ABBOTSFORD

This was the home of Sir Walter Scott that he built and lived in from 1812 until he died. It contains many relics collected by the author. Especially interesting is his study, with his writing desk and chair. In 1935 two secret drawers were found in the desk. One of them contained 57 letters, part of the correspondence between Sir Walter and his wife-to-be. The Scott home is open from mid-March to October 31, daily from 10 a.m. to 5 p.m., on Sunday from 2 to 5 p.m., charging £1.60 ($2.80) for adults, 80p ($1.40) for children. For more information, telephone 0896/2043. The house lies near Melrose, just off the A7, south of the junction with the A72, some 2½ miles southeast of Galashiels.

After leaving Scott's house, you can continue along the Tweed to—

TRAQUAIR HOUSE

At Innerleithen, a few miles east of Peebles, Traquair is considered the oldest inhabited and most romantic house in Scotland. Dating back to the 10th century, it is rich in associations with Mary Queen of Scots and the Jacobite risings. Its treasures include glass, embroideries, silver, manuscripts, and paintings. Of particular interest is a brewhouse equipped as it was two centuries ago. The great house is still lived in by the Stuarts of Traquair. The house is open from 1:30 to 5:30 p.m. and the grounds and restaurant from 10:30 a.m. to 5:30 p.m. Easter, on Sunday and Monday until late May, and daily from May 27 to the end of September. In July and August, hours are daily from 10:30 a.m. to 5:30 p.m. (last entrance at 5:15 p.m.). Admission is £2.50 ($4.40) for adults, £1 ($1.75) for children. There are crafts workshops on the grounds as well as a restaurant/tea garden, woodland and River Tweed walks, and a maze. To make inquiries, telephone 0896/830323.

Innerleithen, 30 miles from Edinburgh, is a modest little mill town, but the unmarred beauty of the River Tweed valley as seen from the town's surrounding hillsides remains constant. The famous Ballantyne cashmeres are manufactured here, and annual games and a Cleikum ceremony take place here in July. Scott's novel, *St. Ronan's Well,* is identified with the town.

From Innerleithen, it's only a six-mile ride to—

PEEBLES

This royal burgh and county town, 23 miles from Edinburgh, is a market center in the Valley of the Tweed. Scottish kings used to come here when they went to hunt in Ettrick Forest. The town is noted for its large woolen mills.

Peebles is also known as a "writer's town." John Buchan, Baron Tweedsmuir, the Scottish author and statesman who died in 1940 and is remembered chiefly for writing the Stevensonian adventure story *Prester John* in 1910, lived here. He was also the author of *The Thirty-Nine Steps* (1915), the first of a highly successful series of secret-service thrillers. In 1935 he was appointed governor-general of Canada. Robert Louis Stevenson once lived at Peebles, and drew upon the surrounding countryside in *Kidnapped,* first published in 1886.

On the north bank of the Tweed stands **Neidpath Castle** (tel. 08757/201), one mile west of Peebles on the A72 road. This is an early-14th-century L-shaped tower house, with a magnificent situation above the river. A rock-cut well and a pit prison are within the 11-foot-thick walls. The castle was besieged by Cromwellian forces in 1650, and soon after the Civil War it was upgraded for 17th-century living. However, by late in the 18th century it had become more or less a ruin. It is open from the Thursday before Easter until October 8 from 10 a.m. to 1 p.m. and 2 to 5 p.m. daily, from 1 to 5 p.m. on Sunday. Admission is £1 ($1.75) for adults, 50p (90¢) for children.

Food and Lodging

Cringletie House Hotel, Eddleston, Peebles, Peebleshire EH45 8PL (tel. 0721/233), three miles north on the A703, is an imposing country hotel, with towers and turrets, standing on 28 acres of private grounds. It's like a small French château, built of red sandstone. Your hosts, Mr. and Mrs. Stanley Maguire, receive you as if you were a private guest in their baronial mansion. Most of the bedrooms, 14 in all, are spacious, and all are comfortably appointed. Nine have private bath. Double- and twin-bedded rooms range from £27.50 ($48.15) to £29.50 ($51.65) per person daily with private bath. The public rooms are rich in character and style, as befits a Victorian mansion. There is an elevator as well. Mrs. Maguire is in charge of the hotel's restaurant. In elegant surroundings, you are given a limited but well-selected choice of dishes. The food is made even more enjoyable by the attentive service. In season the vegetables come fresh from Mrs. Maguire's garden. She has her own style of cooking, and her special dishes include a delectable smoked haddock mousse. A Sunday luncheon costs £10.50 ($18.40), and a four-course dinner, from 7:30 to 8:30 p.m., goes for £16.50 ($28.90). Lunch is à la carte Monday to Saturday. You must be punctual, because of the short hours of serving (the food is freshly cooked), and you'll need a reservation of course, particularly if you aren't a guest of the hotel. The restaurant and hotel are closed from the end of December to mid-March.

The Tontine, High Street, Peebles, Peebleshire EH45 8AJ (tel. 0721/20892), was originally constructed in 1807 by a group of hunters, who sold shares in its ownership to their friends. Several decades ago it was transformed into a private hotel. Flowerboxes adorn its stone lintels and a stone lion guards the fountain in its forecourt. Inside, a cozy and rustic bar, the Tweeddale Shoot Bar, evokes a much older shooting club from the 16th century. The Adam-style dining room is considered one of the architectural gems of Peebles, containing tall fan-topped windows, Scottish antiques, and a minstrel's gallery. Each of the 36 bedrooms is contained within an angular modern wing built in back of its 19th-century core, jutting toward views of the banks of the nearby River Tweed. Units are equipped with TV, radio, private bath, and coffee-making equipment. Singles rent for £44 ($77) daily and twins for £62 ($108.50). Reductions are made for stays of two nights or more, providing half board is taken.

---

2. Burns Country

As Sir Walter Scott dominates the Borders, so does Robert Burns the country around Ayr and Prestwick. There are, in addition, a string of famous seaside resorts stretching from Girvan to Largs. Some of the greatest golf courses in Britain, including Turnberry, are found here, and Prestwick, of course, is one of the major airports of Europe.

AYR

Ayr is the most popular resort on Scotland's west coast. A busy market town, it offers 2½ miles of sands and makes for a good center for touring the Burns Country. This royal burgh is also noted for its manufacture of fabrics and carpets, so you may want to allow time to browse through its shops. With its steamer cruises, fishing, golf, and racing, it faces the Isle of Arran and the Firth of Clyde.

Ayr is full of Burns associations. The 13th-century **Auld Brig o'Ayr,** the poet's "poor narrow footpath of a street. Where two wheelbarrows tremble when they meet," was renovated in 1910. A Burns museum is housed in the thatched **Tam o'Shanter Inn** in Ayr High Street, an alehouse in Rabbie's day.

The **Auld Kirk** of Ayr dates from 1654 when it replaced the 12th-century Church of St. John. Burns was baptized in the kirk.

Ayr is also the birthplace of the famous road builder **John L. MacAdam,** whose name was immortalized in road surfacing.

For centuries Ayr has been associated with horse racing, and it now has the top racecourse in Scotland. One of the main streets of the town is named Racecourse Road for a stretch near the town center.

In Tarbolton village, 7½ miles northeast of Ayr off the A758, is the **Bachelors' Club** (tel. 0292/541940), a 17th-century house where in 1780 Burns and his friends founded a literary and debating society, now a property of the National Trust for Scotland. In 1779 Burns attended dancing lessons there, against the wishes of his father. There also, in 1781, he was initiated as a Freemason in the Lodge St. David. Eleven months later he became a member of Lodge St. James, which continues today in the village. Yule Lithgow says the Bachelors' Club is open for visitors from noon to 5 p.m. from April until the end of October, and he will arrange to show it at other times if you telephone him at 0290/50503. Admission is 90p ($1.60) for adults, 50p (90¢) for children. Tarbolton is six miles from Prestwick Airport.

Where to Stay

Station Hotel, Burns Statue Square, Ayr, Ayrshire KA7 3AT (tel. 0292/263268). Its Edwardian red sandstone exterior is considered one of the landmarks of town. Inside, relatively few modernizations have managed to retain the antique gilded wall sconces and the darkened paneling of another time. This isn't the most modern hotel in town, but many visitors consider its high ceilings, elaborate detailing, and old world charm more than enough reason to check in. Just a few paces from the railway station, the hotel contains 70 comfortable bedrooms, many quite spacious. The overnight charge for B&B ranges from £45 ($78.75) daily in a single, going up to £61 ($106.75) in a double, with breakfast and VAT included.

The Pickwick Hotel, 19 Racecourse Rd., Ayr, Ayrshire KA7 2TD (tel. 0292/260111). It may seem ironic to have a hotel commemorating a character in a Charles Dickens novel in a town noted for its memories of Rabbie Burns. But this early Victorian hotel, set on its own grounds, does just that. The Pickwick is really a large-size house, renting 15 well-furnished private bedrooms that contain either a private shower or else a complete bath. The B&B rate is £40 ($70) daily in a single and £72 ($126) in a double, including a full Scottish breakfast, VAT, and service. Each unit bears a Dickensian title. All rooms have color TVs, radios, drinks dispensers, trouser presses, and hot beverage facilities. In the paneled Pickwick Club, you can soak up much Dickensian atmosphere. The food is simple but well prepared, a lunch costing around £9.50 ($16.65) and a dinner from £12.50 ($21.90).

The Caledonian Hotel, Dalblair Road, Ayr, Ayrshire KA7 1UG (tel. 0292/269331), is centrally situated, just a few hundred yards from Ayr's seashore. It offers refurbished bedrooms with private baths, color TV, radios, hairdryers, and tea/coffee-makers. Singles rent for £53 ($92.75) daily and doubles for £69 ($120.75). The hotel boasts a good restaurant, a continental-style café, and a fully equipped Leisure Complex.

Marine Court, 2 Fairfield Rd., Ayr, Ayrshire KA7 2AR (tel. 0292/267461), has long been a favorite with travelers. A substantial building in a cul-de-sac, it offers good, solid comfort, and many of its rooms open onto a sweeping view of the Firth of Clyde. The hotel also lies about 200 yards from the beach, and it makes for a charming oasis, especially as you wander through its garden. The bedrooms are well furnished and maintained, each equipped with private bath, color TV, tea- and coffee-making facilities, and in-house movies. Singles peak at £45 ($78.75), and doubles are rented for a top £60 ($105), including a full breakfast, service, and VAT. The food is well prepared and served. A normal set dinner goes for £12.50 ($21.90). On Saturday a band plays for a dinner-dance at a special price. The hotel has a heated swimming pool, a sauna, whirlpool, solarium, gymnasium, and leisure lounge.

ALLOWAY

Some three miles from the center of Ayr is where Robert Burns, Scotland's national poet, was born on January 25, 1759, in the gardener's cottage—the "auld clay biggin"—his father, William Burns, built in 1757. More than 100,000 people visit the **Burns Cottage and Museum** (tel. 0292/41215) annually, and it still retains some of its original furniture, including the bed in which the poet was born. Chairs displayed here were said to have been used by Tam o' Shanter and Souter Johnnie. Beside the cottage in which the poet lived is a museum, open April to September on Monday to Saturday from 9 a.m. to 7 p.m., on Sunday from 2 to 7 p.m. From November to March, the hours are 10 a.m. to dusk daily; closed Sunday. Admission to the cottage and the museum is £1.20 ($2.10) for adults, 60p ($1.05) for children.

The Auld Brig over the Ayr, mentioned in *Tam o' Shanter,* still spans the river, and Alloway Auld Kirk, also mentioned in the poem, stands roofless and "haunted" not far away. The poet's father is buried in the graveyard of the kirk.

Alloway is dominated by the **Burns Monument and Gardens** (tel. 0292/ 41321). The monument is a Grecian-style building erected in 1823, containing relics, books, and manuscripts associated with Robert Burns, dating back to the 1820s. It's open daily from 9 a.m. to 7 p.m. April to October and from 10 a.m. to 5 p.m. November to March. Admission is included in the entrance fee to Burns's Cottage and Museum. The monument is two miles south of Ayr on the B7024.

The **Land o' Burns Centre,** Murdochs Lane (tel. 0292/43700), presents a multiscreen of highlights of Burns's life, his friends, and his poetry. Information is available from the personnel, and a well-stocked gift shop is there, plus a tea room. The Russians are particularly fond of Burns and his poetry, and many come annually to visit the cottage and pore over his original manuscripts. Admission to the theater is 50p (90¢) for adults, 30p (55¢) for children. Hours are daily from 10 a.m. to 6 p.m. in July and August, to 5:30 p.m. in June and September, and to 5 p.m. in October and May.

Where to Stay

Burns Monument Hotel, Alloway, Ayrshire KA7 4PQ (tel. 0292/42466), is a 190-year-old inn that overlooks the Doon River and the bridge, "Brig o' Doon" immortalized in *Tam o' Shanter.* The inn is a historical place, with riverside gardens and a white-washed bar. The rooms are attractively decorated, bright and cheerful, some opening onto river views. All bedrooms have private baths. B&B averages around £35 ($61.25) daily in a single and from £45 ($78.75) in a double.

The **Balgarth Hotel,** Dunure Road, Doonfoot, Ayr, Ayrshire KA7 4HR (tel. 0292/42441), two miles south of Ayr on the A719 coastal road to the fishing village of Dunure, is within easy reach for touring the Burns Country and southwest Scotland. The hotel stands within its own grounds, complete with beer garden overlooking the Clyde and Carrick Hills, and offers special rates to golf enthusiasts with access to Royal Troon, Turnberry, and other scenic courses on the Ayrshire coast. The 15 rooms are bright and well furnished, with TV, phone, and private bath. The tariff for B&B is £24 ($42) daily in a single, £40 ($70) in a double, including VAT.

CULZEAN CASTLE AND COUNTRY PARK

One of Robert Adam's most notable creations, built around an ancient tower of the Kennedys, Culzean (tel. 06556/274; pronounced Cullane), 12 miles south-southwest of Ayr, dates mainly from 1777 and is considered one of the finest Adam houses in Scotland. The castle, with a view of Ailsa Craig to the south and overlooking the Firth of Clyde, is well worth a visit and is of special interest to Americans because of General Eisenhower's connection with it and its National Guest Flat. In 1946 the guest flat was given to the general for his lifetime in gratitude for his services as Supreme Commander of Allied Forces in World War II. Culzean stands near the golf courses of Turnberry and Troon, a fact that particularly pleased the golf-loving Eisenhower. An exhibition of Eisenhower memorabilia includes sound and audio-visual spectacles, and is seen by more than 100,000 people a year. To illustrate his career, there is a capsule history of World War II demonstrated with wall maps. Mementos of Eisenhower include his North African campaign desk and a replica of the Steuben glass bowl given him by his cabinet when he retired from the presidency.

The castle is open daily May to the end of September from 10 a.m. to 6 p.m. In

April and October hours are noon to 5 p.m., except on Saturday and Sunday and Easter week when hours are 10 a.m. to 6 p.m. Last admission is half an hour before closing. The charge is £2.20 ($3.85) for adults, £1.10 ($1.95) for children.

In the castle grounds is **Culzean Country Park,** which in 1969 became the first such park in Scotland. It has an exhibition center in farm buildings by Adam. The 565-acre grounds include a walled garden, an aviary, a swan pond, a camellia house, and an orangery, as well as a deer park, miles of woodland paths, and beaches. It has gained an international reputation for its Visitor Centre (Adam's home farm) and related visitor and educational services. The park is open from 10 a.m. to 6 p.m. April to the end of September, to 4 p.m. in October, and 9 a.m. to dusk from November to the end of March. Cars are charged £3.50 ($6.15) to enter the park in high season. It is open to walk-in customers in winter except on Sunday in March. For information, phone 06556/269.

After leaving Culzean Castle, you might want to take a short drive to see **Souter Johnnie's Cottage** in Kirkoswald (tel. 06556/603), four miles west of Maybole on the A77. This thatched cottage was the home of the village cobbler, John Davidson (Souter Johnnie), at the end of the 18th century. Davidson and his friend Douglas Graham of Shanter Farm were immortalized by Burns in his poem *Tam o' Shanter*. The cottage contains Burnsiana and contemporary cobblers' workshop and tools. In the churchyard are the graves of Tam o' Shanter and Souter Johnnie, two of his best-known characters. In the garden, the converted alehouse provides shelter for the Thom figures of Tam o' Shanter, Souter Johnnie, the innkeeper, and his wife. The cottage is open from the end of March to the end of September daily from noon to 5 p.m. (other times by appointment). Admission is 90p ($1.60) for adults, 45p (80¢) for children.

TURNBERRY

On the Firth of Clyde, Turnberry was originally part of the Culzean Estate owned by the Marquess of Ailsa. It began to flourish after the marquess consented early in this century to allow the Glasgow and South Western Railway to develop golfing facilities, resulting in railway service, a recognized golfing center, and a first-class hotel. From the original two 13-hole golf courses, the complex has developed into the two 18-hole courses, Ailsa and Arran, known worldwide. The Ailsa, one of the most exacting courses yet devised, has been the scene of numerous championship tournaments and PGA events, including the 1986 British Open Championship.

The two courses are named for the Isle of Arran and Ailsa Craig, which can be seen across the waters of the firth. **Ailsa Craig** is a 1,110-foot-high rounded rock ten miles offshore, a nesting ground and sanctuary for sea birds. Granite for the stones used in the Scottish game of curling used to be taken from this rock.

There was once a **Turnberry Castle** about six miles south of the golfing locale. Only scant remains exist to mark the place that many historians say was the birthplace of Robert the Bruce in 1274.

Turnberry Hotel and Golf Courses, Maidens Road, Turnberry, Ayrshire KA26 9LT (tel. 0655/31000), is a remarkable Edwardian property that has undergone one of the most complete glamourizations of any hotel in Scotland. The owners spent millions of dollars on the infrastructure and decor without diminishing the aura of a more opulent era, as reflected by the oak paneling and molded high ceilings. From afar, one can see the hotel's white façade, its red-tile roof, and its dozens of gables. In World War II the corridors of the structure were transformed into a military hospital, but today the property is once again considered one of the grand hotels of Britain. The public rooms contain scores of Waterford crystal chandeliers, Ionic columns, a medley of pastel colors, and lots of well-polished oak. Each of the six suites and 124 bedrooms is furnished in an elegant 19th-century style, the most luxurious in the region. The marble-sheathed bath with each accommodation is loaded with extras, and room extras include color TV, radio, phone, 24-hour room service, and views of the surrounding lawns and forests. High-season rates, with a full Scottish breakfast included, range from £75 ($131.25) daily in a single and £160 ($280) in a double or twin. Service and taxes are included. Fixed-price dinners cost from £24 ($42). Facilities include an indoor swimming pool, a sauna, a health club, a gym, and a solarium.

PRESTWICK

Prestwick is the oldest recorded baronial burgh in Scotland. But most visitors today aren't concerned with that ancient fact—rather, they fly in, landing at Prestwick's International Airport, which is in itself a popular sightseeing attraction, as spectators gather to watch planes take off and land from all over the world.

Behind St. Ninian's Episcopal Church is **Bruce's Well**, the water from which is reputed to have cured Robert the Bruce of leprosy. The **Mercat Cross** still stands outside what used to be the Registry Office and marks the center of the oldest part of Prestwick, whose existence goes back to at least 983. Prestwick is a popular holiday town, and is considered one of Scotland's most attractive resorts, with its splendid sands and golf courses. Prestwick opens onto views of Ayr Bay and the Isle of Arran.

Where to Stay

Towans Hotel & Motel, Powmill Road, Prestwick, Ayrshire KA9 2NY (tel. 0292/77831), The original building faces a side lawn and then looks out over the Firth of Clyde to the Isle of Arran. Much of the accommodation is in a modern hotel/motel block that blends with the old. The owners, conscious of the needs of international travelers passing through Prestwick Airport, are geared to catering for early and late arrivals. Rooms have private bath, and tea and coffee makers. Breakfast is served from 4 a.m., and the dining room has a good local reputation for well-cooked meals. B&B costs from £25 ($43.75) to £32 ($56) per person daily. All meals are extra, but you can make as much tea and coffee as you want in your room.

Parkstone Hotel, Central Esplanade, Prestwick, Ayrshire KA9 1QN (tel. 0292/77286), is a white-walled Victorian building with cookie-cutter gingerbread set under its steep eaves. Its modernized interior has a pub in back, whose view of the sea attracts a lunchtime crowd. The hotel is the property of Stewart and Sandra Clarkson, who maintain their 15-room establishment in good order. All the rooms in this century-old hostelry have private baths and color TV. Singles cost £29 ($50.75) daily, rising to £46 ($80.50) in a double or twin, all tariffs including a full breakfast, VAT, and service. A set dinner costs from £8.95 ($15.65) per person. In cold weather, a coal fire burns in an oak-paneled room near the reception desk.

TROON

This holiday resort looks out across the Firth of Clyde to the Isle of Arran. It offers several golf links, including the "Old Troon" course. Bathers in summer find plenty of room on its two miles of sandy beaches, stretching from both sides of its harbor. The broad sands and shallow waters make it a safe haven also. From here you can take steamer trips to Arran and the Kyles of Bute.

Troon is mostly a 20th-century town, its earlier history having gone unrecorded. It takes its name from the curiously shaped promontory that juts out into the Clyde estuary on which the old town and the harbor stand. The promontory was called "Trwyn," the Cymric word for nose, and later this became the Trone and then Troon.

Fullarton Estate, on the edge of Troon beyond the municipal golf course, is the ancestral seat of the dukes of Portland.

A massive statue of **Britannia** stands on the seafront as a memorial to the dead of the two world wars. On her breastplate is the lion of Scotland emerging from the sea.

Where to Stay

The Marine Highland Hotel, 8 Crosbie Rd., Troon, Ayrshire KA10 6HE (tel. 0292/314444). Because of its widespread reputation as the best hotel within an easy drive of Prestwick Airport, five minutes away, many guests check in here to recover from jet lag. The hotel's red sandstone exterior rises from flat grasslands, a short stroll from the sea, whose waters can be seen from the windows of many of the public rooms. With dozens of turrets, chimneys, and gables, it resembles a Victorian village, especially since the surrounding golf course prevents any significant building nearby. Inside, the comfortably modernized interior still offers glimpses of Victoriana. There are two restaurants, Fairways and Crosbie's Brasserie, offering some of the best food in Troon. Meals cost from £8 ($14) to £17 ($29.75). Each of the 65 comfortably furnished bedrooms contains a private bath and color TV among the amenities. They cost £62 ($108.50) daily in a single, £90 ($157.50) in a double. The hotel was upgraded and refurbished in 1987, when a Leisure and Sports Club, available to guests, was added.

Sun Court, 19 Crosbie Rd., Troon, Ayrshire KA10 6HF (tel. 0292/312727), was once the home of an industrialist, and it offers all the grand style of the Edwardian era. Like the Marine, it looks out onto golf courses and the sea. Its most delightful feature is a conservatory filled with flowers. The hotel also contains a Real Tennis Court, one of the few in Britain. A sandy beach along the Firth of Clyde is about a 100-yard walk away. Open all year, the Sun Court offers 20 handsome bedrooms, all with private baths. The single tariff is £38 ($66.50) daily, the double rate being £72 ($126). There is as well a beautiful walled garden. The lounges are decorated in a conservative fashion. Try to get one of the more old-fashioned bedrooms, although you may be assigned a modernized one. From a cellar emerges a fine collection of wine, and the food at Sun Court is well prepared and served.

---

3. Dumfries and Galloway

Southwestern Scotland is often overlooked by motorists rushing north. But this country of Burns is filled with many rewarding targets—a land of unspoiled countryside, fishing harbors, artists' colonies of color-washed houses, and romantically ruined abbeys and castles dating from the days of the border wars.

It's a fine touring country, and the hotels are generally small, of the Scottish provincial variety, but that usually means a reception from a smiling staff and good traditional Scottish cookery, using the local produce.

I've documented the most important centers below, but have included some off-beat places for those seeking a more esoteric trip.

LOCKERBIE

A border market town 13 miles from Dumfries, Lockerbie lies in the beautiful valley of Annandale, offering fishing and golf. It's a good center for exploring some sightseeing attractions in its environs.

Lockerbie was the scene in 1593 of a battle that ended one of the last great Border family feuds. The Johnstones routed the Maxwells, killing Lord Maxwell and 700 of his men. Many of the victims had their ears cut off with a cleaver, a method of mutilation that became known throughout the Border Country as the "Lockerbie Nick."

Of interest are the remains of **Lockmaben Castle,** 3½ miles west of Lockerbie, said to have been the boyhood home (some historians say the birthplace) of Robert the Bruce. This castle, on the south shore of Castle Loch, was captured and recaptured 12 times and also withstood six attacks and sieges. James IV was a frequent visitor, and Mary Queen of Scots was here in 1565. The ruin of the early-14th-century castle is on the site of a castle of the de Brus family, ancestors of Robert the Bruce. However, the charming hamlet of Lochmaben, with its five lochs, is reason enough to visit, regardless of who was or was not born there. Admission is free. Telephone 0387/53862 to inquire about visiting.

If you're heading north to Lockerbie on the A74, I'd suggest a stopover in the village of Ecclefechan. There you can visit **Carlyle's Birthplace,** five miles southeast of Lockerbie on the Lockerbie–Carlisle road. Even though the historian, critic, and essayist Thomas Carlyle isn't much read these days, the "arched house" in which he was born in 1795 is interesting in itself, containing mementos and manuscripts of the author. It's open from Easter until the end of October, daily from noon to 5 p.m., charging an admission of 90p ($1.60) for adults, 45p (80¢) for children. For more information, telephone 05763/666.

In Lockerbie, you'll find the best accommodations at the **Dryfesdale House Hotel,** Lockerbie, Dumfriesshire DG11 2SF (tel. 05762/2427). The house was built in 1831 and was originally a Church of Scotland manse. This hotel offers traditional comfort with log fires and tranquil surroundings. There is a choice of 11 bedrooms, nine of which have private bath. Several of the units are quite spacious. Singles range from £25 ($43.75) to £32 ($56) daily, doubles £40 ($70) to £50 ($87.50). The hotel, known for its good food and wines, is fully licensed with two old-world bars. The sun lounge and dining room open onto good views. The owners, the Smith family, are always available to help.

MOFFAT

An Annandale town, Moffat thrives as a center of a sheep-farming area, symbolized by a statue of a ram in the wide High Street, and has been a holiday resort since the mid-17th century, because of the curative properties of its water. It was here that Robert Burns composed the drinking song "O Willie Brew'd a Peck o' Maut." Today people visit this border town on the banks of the Annan River for its good fishing and golf.

North of Moffat is spectacular hill scenery. Five miles northwest is a huge, sheer-sided 500-foot-deep hollow in the hills called the **Devil's Beef Tub,** where Border cattle thieves, called reivers, hid cattle lifted in their raids.

Northeast along Moffat Water, past White Coomb, which stands 2,696 feet high, is the **Grey Mare's Tail,** a 200-foot hanging waterfall formed by the Tail Burn dropping from Loch Skene. It is under the National Trust for Scotland.

Food and Lodgings

Annandale Hotel, High Street, Moffat, Dumfriesshire DG10 9HF (tel. 0683/20013), has been a coaching inn since the 18th century, housing travelers who crossed through the Border Country en route to Edinburgh. However, the inn has been modernized and the amenities provided around here have improved considerably since the old days. Eleven of the nearly 30 bedrooms contain private baths, and three of these have showers. But the rates in the bathless rooms, to compensate, are low—from £18 ($31.50) daily in a single, from £34 ($59.50) in a double. In the more expensive chambers with bath, expect to pay £44 ($77) in a double. The rooms, including the public ones, are kept immaculately. The proprietors have built up a good reputation for their cuisine, which includes Scottish specialties. The last dinner is served at 9 p.m., and the cost is from £8 ($14). It's in the center of town, but provides ample car parking on its own grounds.

Beechwood Hotel, Harthope Place, Moffat, Dumfriesshire DG10 9RS (tel. 0683/20210), was originally built as the 19th-century headquarters of "Miss Thompson's Private Adventure Boarding Establishment and School for Young Ladies." Today it is a charming country hotel and restaurant. It lies behind a dark façade of chiseled stone at the end of a narrow rural lane. A "tea lawn," smooth as a putting green, is the site for outdoor refreshments on sunny days. Each of the seven bedrooms contains a private bath and a certain amount of homespun charm. Singles rent for £33 ($57.75) daily and doubles for £55 ($96.25). If you just want to stop in for a meal (and you'll be welcome if you phone in advance), lunch is from noon to 1:30 p.m.; tea, 3 to 4:30 p.m.; and dinner, 7:30 to 9 p.m. A fixed-price dinner costs £13.50 ($23.65).

Moffat House Hotel, High Street, Moffat, Dumfriesshire DG10 9HL (tel. 0683/20039), is considered one of the town's most architecturally noteworthy buildings, because of its construction in 1751 by one of the Adam brothers. It sits within a garden in the center of town behind a chiseled façade of red and black stone, with a pair of symmetrical wings stretching out on either side. Ancient trees shelter its rear from the winds blowing in from the farmlands beyond. Each of the modernized bedrooms contains comfortable and functional furniture, and all offer private baths or showers. With breakfast included, per-person rates are £30 ($52.50) daily in a single, £24 ($42) in a double. With half board, per-person rates are £40 ($70) in a single, £34 ($59.50) in a double. The hotel offers some of the best food in town, especially at night when the chef prepares an international menu. Bar suppers are served Monday to Thursday from 6 to 9 p.m., on Friday and Saturday from 5 to 9:30 p.m. However, dinner in the regular restaurant, costing from £8 ($14), is served from 7 to 8:45 p.m. only, and is likely to feature a bill of fare including haunch of venison, mallard duck in cherry sauce, and pheasant in an orange-pepper sauce.

A Castle Hotel at Beattock

Two miles north of Moffat along the A74, near the village of Beattock, the most luxurious accommodations in the area are found at the **Auchen Castle Hotel,** Beattock, Dumfriesshire DG10 9SH (tel. 06833/407), a Victorian mock-castle, really a charming country house, built on the site of Auchen Castle. It's one of the most tranquil oases in the Scottish Lowlands, with terraced gardens, a trout-filled loch, and vistas from its windows. The bedrooms are often spacious and invariably comfortable, and each has a private bath or shower. Rates are £39 ($68.25) daily in a single, from £51 ($89.25) in a double, including a cooked breakfast, service, and VAT. Rooms are spacious and well appointed in the annex, a double costing £39 ($68.25). The lofty dining room is exceptional for the area, its windows overlooking flowering ornamental grounds in late spring. Simple dishes are appetizingly good because of the excellent materials used. Roast Scottish beef is superb. The well-appointed tables and efficient staff complement the atmosphere. Lunch is from noon to 2 p.m. and dinner from 7 to 9 p.m. Bar lunches only are offered, and a dinner goes for £14 ($24.50).

DUMFRIES

A county town and royal burgh 59 miles from Ayr, this Scottish Lowland center enjoys associations with Robert Burns and James Barrie. In a sense it rivals Ayr as a mecca for admirers of Burns. He lived in Dumfries from 1791 until his death in 1796, and it was here that he wrote some of his most famous songs, including "Auld Lang Syne" and "Ye Banks and Braes of Bonnie Doon."

The Sights

In **St. Michael's Churchyard,** a burial place for at least 900 years, stands the **Burns Mausoleum.** The poet was buried there along with his wife, Jean Armour, as well as five of their children. Burns died in 1796, but his remains weren't removed to the tomb until 1815. In the 18th-century church of St. Michael's you can still see the pew used by the Burns family.

The poet died at what is now called the **Robert Burns House,** a simple, unpretentious stone structure, which can be visited by the public; it contains personal relics and mementos relating to Burns. His death may have been hastened by icy dips in well water that the doctor prescribed. The house is on Burns Street (formerly Mill Vennel). The **Town Museum,** the **Globe Inn,** and **the Hole in the Wa' Tavern** all contain Burns relics, and a statue of him stands in the High Street. You can stroll along **Burns' Walk** on the banks of the River Nith.

St. Michael's is the original parish church of Dumfries and its founding is of great antiquity. The site was probably sacred before the advent of Christianity. It appears that a Christian church has stood there for more than 1,300 years. The earliest written records date from the reign of William the Lion (1165–1214). The church and the churchyard are interesting to visit because of all their connections with Scottish history, continuing through World War II.

From St. Michael's, it's a short walk to the Whitesands, where four bridges span the Nith. The earliest of these was built by Devorgilla Balliol, widow of John Balliol, father of a Scottish king. The bridge originally had nine arches but now has six and is still in constant use as a footbridge.

The **Tourist Information Office,** Whitesands (tel. 0387/53862), is near the bridge. The wide esplanade was once the scene of horse and hiring fairs and now is a fine place to park your car and explore the town. Tour buses park here.

The **Mid Steeple** was built in 1707 as municipal buildings, courthouse, and prison. The old Scots "ell" measure of 37 inches is carved on the front of the building. A table of distances on the building includes the mileage to Huntingdon, England, which in the 18th century was the destination for Scottish cattle drovers driving their beasts south for the markets of London.

At the **Academy,** J. M. Barrie was a pupil, and he later wrote that he got the idea for *Peter Pan* from his games in the nearby garden.

Where to Stay

Cairndale Hotel, English Street, Dumfries, Dumfriesshire DG1 2DF (tel. 0387/54111), is most reliable, a fine and substantial choice. Its bedrooms have been attractively decorated, with special care paid to modern amenities. All of the color-coordinated chambers contain private baths, color TVs, clock-radio alarms, direct-dial phones, hairdryers, and hot beverage facilities. Executive rooms and suites also contain queen-size beds, mini-bars, trouser presses, and whirlpool baths. Singles rent for £40 ($70) daily, and doubles go for £50 ($87.50), including breakfast, VAT, and service. You have a choice of two bars, and guests quickly decide which one they'll make their local. The public lounges are handsomely decorated, and you can select your own favorite nook, perhaps a comfortable chair upholstered in velvet. Dinner, served until 9 p.m., is generally quite good, including such dishes as roast sirloin of Galloway beef, Arbroath smokies, mealed herring with Arran sauce, and Ecclefechan flan with Drambuie cream. A three-course table d'hôte lunch goes for £6.50 ($11.40) and a four-course dinner for £11 ($19.25). The hotel is owned and managed by the Wallace family, who also run their own butcher business.

Station Hotel, 49 Lovers Walk, Dumfries, Dumfriesshire DG1 1LT (tel. 0387/54316), is among the most traditional hotels of Dumfries, lying a few steps from the gingerbread-fringed train station. The hotel was built of hewn sandstone at the turn of the century when trains were the most comfortable way to travel. Its design of heavy timbers, polished paneling, soaring ceilings, and open fireplaces reminds visitors of alpine hotels in Switzerland. However, the welcome and dinner menu at "The Dining Room" are purely Scottish (see below). Before dinner, drinks can be enjoyed in the lounge bar, followed by dinner in a high-ceilinged room framed on one side with bay windows overlooking century-old trees and the station. The 32 modernized bedrooms are accessible via long corridors of old-fashioned design. Each contains a private bath, tea-making facilities, color TVs, comfortable beds, and an electric trouser press. Singles cost from £30 ($52.50) daily, and doubles peak at £75 ($131.25).

Waverley Hotel, St. Mary's Street, top of English Street, Dumfries, Dumfriesshire DG1 2DF (tel. 0387/54848), is a good bargain, close to the station, about a five-minute walk to the center of town. The owners, J. and J. V. Meikle, offer

35 bedrooms with hot and cold running water, central heating, color TV, and shaving points. A few have private baths. Some family rooms are available, and there is a reduction for children sharing their parents' room. Singles cost from £16 ($28) to £22 ($38.50) daily, and doubles or twins run £28 ($49) to £32 ($56), the higher prices charged for rooms with bath, including VAT and a full breakfast. Drinks can be enjoyed in one of the three bars. In the evening, a "high tea" menu is offered, giving you a choice of steaks, salads, fish, and bacon and eggs, a meal starting at £4 ($7). Everything tastes homemade in the attractively decorated, although petite dining room.

Where to Eat

Bruno's, 5 Balmoral Rd. (tel. 0387/55757). It may seem quixotic to recommend an Italian restaurant in the seat of Rabbie Burns, but Bruno's serves some of the best food in town. It is most unassuming, and that is part of its charm. Its minestrone is first rate, and its pastas such as lasagne are homemade. The chef doesn't serve the most imaginative Italian dishes ever sampled—in fact the repertoire is most familiar, such as saltimbocca alla romana and pollo alla diavola, but it's done with a certain flair. The veal is particularly tender, and the tomato sauce well spiced and blended. Steak au poivre is also excellent. Bruno's serves only dinner, from 6:30 to 10 p.m. nightly except Tuesday, and it will cost from £14 ($24.50) per person, but it's worth it. A set three-course meal for £9.50 ($16.65) is popular. There is also a special pasta supper for £4 ($7).

"The Dining Room," Station Hotel, 49 Lovers Walk (tel. 0387/54316), was part of *the* grand hotel of town when it was built, and it still lives up to its high standards. Today the restaurant evokes the Edwardian age. It's a big-windowed dining room where the Victorian gingerbread of the train station is on view. The decor of the restaurant is high-ceilinged. The table d'hôte menu at £14 ($24.50) per person includes a satisfying array of specialties such as local salmon, haggis, cock-a-leekie soup, chicken "whisky sour," and local trout in a sauce of smoked salmon and mushrooms. A polite member of the uniformed staff might help turn the dinner, served daily from 7 to 9 p.m., into a grand occasion. Reservations are suggested.

Burns's Favorite "Howff"

Globe Inn, 56 High St. (tel. 0387/52335), was a favorite haunt of Burns, who used an old Scottish word, *howff,* to describe his local. He not only imbibed here, but he had a child with the barmaid, Anna Park. The pub, in business since 1610, is reached down a narrow, flagstone passageway off High Street. It has a separate restaurant. You can go here for meals, drink, or to play a nightly game of dominoes. A little museum is devoted to Burns, and on windowpanes upstairs you can see verses he scratched with a diamond. In this convivial atmosphere, you can order cooked bar lunches, offered daily except Sunday, beginning at £3.50 ($6.15). That means such items as homemade soups and steak-and-kidney pie. The pub is open from 11 a.m. to 11 p.m. Monday to Saturday, from 12:30 to 2:30 p.m. and 6:30 to 11 p.m. Sunday.

Excursions from Dumfries

Based in Dumfries, you can set out on treks in all directions to some of the most intriguing sightseeing goals in the Scottish Lowlands.

South on the A710 leads to the village of New Abbey, dominated by the red sandstone ruins of **Sweetheart Abbey,** the Cistercian abbey founded in 1273 by Devorgilla, mother of John Balliol, the "vassal king." When her husband, John Balliol the Elder, died, she became one of the richest women in Europe. Most of Galloway, with estates and castles in England and land in Normandy, belonged to her. Devorgilla founded Balliol College, Oxford, in her husband's memory. She kept his embalmed heart in a silver-and-ivory casket by her side for 21 years until her death in 1289 at the age of 80, when she and the casket were buried beside Balliol in the front of the abbey altar. So the abbey gained the name of "Dulce Cor," Latin for "sweetheart," which has since become a part of the English language.

Built into a wall of a cottage in the village is a rough piece of sculpture showing three women rowing a boat—an allusion to the bringing of sandstone across the Nith to build the abbey.

Also at New Abbey, the **Shambellie House Museum of Costume,** on the A710 (tel. 038785/375), is in a Victorian country home that was designed by David Bryce. Now housing a branch of the National Museum of Scotland, it has a collection of fashionable clothing given by Charles Stewart. Open from May to the end of September and charging no admission, it may be visited Thursday through Saturday and on Monday from 10 a.m. to 5:30 p.m. and on Sunday from noon to 5:30 p.m.

Directly south from New Abbey on the A710 to Southerness are the **Arbigland Gardens and Cottage** at Kirkbean (tel. 038788/213), 15 miles to the southwest of Dumfries. This is where John Paul Jones, one of the founders of the American navy, was born. You can visit the woodland with its water gardens arranged around a secluded bay, walking in the pathways where the great admiral once worked as a boy. The gardens are open May to September on Tuesday, Thursday, and Sunday from 2 to 6 p.m., charging adults £1 ($1.75); children, 50p (90¢).

Or, alternatively, you can head south from Dumfries on the B725 to **Caerlaverock Castle,** near the mouth of the River Nith, two miles south from Glencaple. Once the seat of the Maxwell family, this impressive ruined fortress dates back to the 1270s. In 1300 Edward I laid siege to it. In 1640 it yielded to Covenanters after a 13-week siege. The castle is triangular with round towers. The interior was reconstructed in the 17th century as a Renaissance mansion, with fine carving. The castle is open April to September daily from 9:30 a.m. to 7 p.m. (on Sunday from 2 to 7 p.m.), October to March daily from 9:30 a.m. to 4 p.m. (on Sunday from 2 to 4 p.m.). Admission is 60p ($1.05) for adults, 30p (55¢) for children.

Near the castle is the Caerlaverock National Nature Reserve, between the River Nith and Lochar Water. It is a noted winter haunt of wildfowl, including barnacle geese.

After leaving the castle, continue east along the B725 to the village of **Ruthwell,** about ten miles southeast of Dumfries. There at the early-19th-century Ruthwell Church you'll see one of the most outstanding crosses of the Dark Ages. Standing 18 feet high, the cross is believed to date from the 8th century. Engraved with carvings, it bears the earliest-known specimen of written English (a Christian poem in Runic characters).

North from Dumfries on the A76 takes you to **Lincluden College,** two miles away. This is the richly decorated remains of a 15th-century collegiate church.

Four miles away, still following the A76, is **Ellisland Farm** (tel. 038774/426), where Robert Burns made his last attempt at farming, renting the spread from 1788 to 1791. The present occupants of the house will show you through the Burns Room. It was at this farm that Burns wrote *Tam o' Shanter.* Call for an appointment.

Continuing north, still on the A76, you reach **Thornhill,** a country resort—familiar to Burns—overlooking the River Nith. From here, it's possible to branch out for excursions in many directions.

The main target is **Drumlanrig Castle** (tel. 0848/30248), the seat of the Duke of Buccleuch and Queensberry, built between 1679 and 1689. It lies three miles north of Thornhill, off the A76. This pink castle contains some outstanding paintings, including a Rembrandt, a Leonardo da Vinci, and a Holbein. In addition, it is further enriched by Louis XIV antiques, silver, porcelain, and relics related to Bonnie Prince Charlie. The castle stands in a parkland ringed by wild hills, and there's even an Adventure Woodland Playground. The gardens are being gradually restored to their 1720 magnificence. There's a working crafts center in the old stable yard, with independent craft workers in a variety of skills. Meals are served in the old kitchen hung with gleaming copper. The castle is open from 11 a.m. to 5 p.m. Monday to Saturday and from 2 to 6 p.m. Sunday from the end of April to August 20. The grounds can be visited daily from the end of April to the end of September. Last entry is 45 minutes before closing. Admission is £2.50 ($4.40) for adults, £1 ($1.75) for children.

Of almost equal interest, **Maxwelton House** (tel. 08482/385) lies three miles south of Moniaive and 13 miles north of Dumfries on the B729. It was the strong-hold of the earls of Glencairn in the 14th and 15th centuries. But it is more remembered today as the birthplace (1682) of Annie Laurie of the Scottish ballad. From Maxwelton you can see that the braes are just as bonnie as ever. The braes, of course, refer to the neighboring hillsides. The house and an agricultural museum are open from 2 to 5 p.m. Monday to Thursday in July and August. The garden and chapel are open from April to September at those same hours. The house can be visited at other times by appointment. Admission for house, garden, and museum is £1.50 ($2.65) for adults, £1 ($1.75) for children; to the garden only, 50p (90¢).

Back on the A76, you can branch northwest on the B797, heading in the direction of Mennock Pass. There, at **Wanlockhead,** you'll be in the highest village in Scotland. Once this village was a gold-mining center and known as "God's Treasure House." Gold was mined here for the Scottish crown jewels.

CASTLE DOUGLAS

An old cattle and sheep market town, Castle Douglas makes a good touring center for Galloway. It lies about eight miles southwest of Dumfries, at the northern tip of Caringwark Loch. On one of the islets in the loch is an ancient lake dwelling known as a "crannog."

The favorite excursion is to **Threave Castle,** 1½ miles west on an islet in the River Dee west of town, the ruined 17th-century stronghold of the Black Douglases. The four-story tower was built between 1639 and 1690 by Archibald the Grim, Lord of Galloway. In 1455 Threave Castle was the last Douglas stronghold to surrender to James II, who employed "Mons Meg" (the famous cannon now in Edinburgh Castle) in its subjection. Over the doorway projects the "gallows knob" from which the Douglases hanged their enemies. The castle was captured by the Covenanters in 1640 and dismantled. Owned by the National Trust, the site must be reached by a half-mile walk through farmland and then by small boat across the Dee. A ferry charge of 60p ($1.05) for adults and 30p (55¢) for children is the alternative to that long walk. Last sailing to the castle is at 6 p.m. Threave Castle is open from 10 a.m. to 7 p.m. Monday to Saturday, from 2 to 7 p.m. on Sunday from April to the end of September. For information, get in touch with 20 Brandon St., Edinburgh (tel. 031/244-3087).

Threave Garden (tel. 0556/2575) is built around Threave House, a 19th-century baronial mansion a mile west of Castle Douglas, off the A75. They are both under the protection of the National Trust of Scotland, which uses them as a school for gardening. The year-round garden is at its best in April when the daffodils bloom and in June, with rhododendrons and the rock garden in flower. There is a visitor center and a restaurant. The garden is open daily from 9 a.m. to sunset and the visitor center from 9 a.m. to 6 p.m. Admission is £2 ($3.50) for adults, £1 ($1.75) for children.

Food and Lodging

Back in Castle Douglas, I'd recommend the following selections.

Douglas Arms, King Street, Castle Douglas, Kirkcudbrightshire DG7 1DB (tel. 0556/2231), is a 200-year-old coaching inn, but it has been turned into a modernized hotel, right in the center of town. Behind a rather stark, two-story façade, the public rooms are bright and cheerful, giving you a toasty feeling on a cold night. Bedrooms have color-coordinated schemes, and such gadgets as razor sockets. Several of the 26 rooms contain a private bath. The B&B rate ranges from £18 ($31.50) to £21 ($36.75) per person daily, the higher charge for accommodations with private bath. Dinner is served until 9 p.m., and of course, trout and salmon are featured along with good beef and lamb. A set dinner costs from £12 ($21).

King's Arms, St. Andrew's Street, Castle Douglas, Kircudbrightshire DG7 1EL (tel. 0556/2626), is a good place to stop over, enjoying either a room or a meal or a drink in the trio of tartan-clad bars, featuring a malt whisky collection. The restaurant serves good, simple meals, using the freshest of fish and tender beef, a set meal costing from £14 ($24.50). It is attractively decorated, and the staff is helpful. Bedrooms are comfortable but modest, and some chambers contain private bath and toilet or else a shower and toilet. Singles cost £18 ($31.50) daily, and doubles rent for £50 ($87.50), including breakfast, VAT, and service. There is a sheltered and secluded sun garden at the rear of the hotel, which is a rendezvous for coffee, tea, or a sundowner. Everything is maintained well, and parking is provided.

An excellent hotel choice lies south of Castle Douglas, near Dalbeattie, in the hamlet of—

Rockcliffe

An attractive seaside village, Rockcliffe has a bird sanctuary on its offshore Rough Island. From its sand-and-rock beach, you can look out to the Lake District mountains on the distant horizon.

Baron's Craig Hotel, Rockcliffe, Dalbeattie, Kircudbrightshire DG5 4QF (tel. 055663/225), is a stately country home, built of granite, and set back from the shoreline of Solway Firth. Because of its position sheltered from the cold north wind, its gardens bloom profusely in season. Lawns and grounds—nearly 12 acres—are well manicured. The public rooms are spacious and airy, brightly decorated and welcoming. In the modern bar you can select your favorite whisky. The owners have paid special attention to the bedrooms, decorating them in warm, pleasing colors to suggest in summer a holiday atmosphere. From April to October, it rents singles (bathless) for £30.50 ($53.40) daily, going up to £42 ($73.50) with bath. A bathless double costs £57 ($99.75), rising to £75 ($131.25) with bath, including breakfast. At least 21 of the rooms contain private baths, which are spotlessly clean.

Even if you're not staying here, you might want to drive down to enjoy the hotel's fine cookery. The dining room overlooks the water, and table appointments have style. At lunch the menu is considerably shortened, but still quite good, a bar lunch costing from £4 ($7). In the evening, however, a table d'hôte is offered at £15 ($26.25) from 7 to 9 p.m. The menu is based on good local ingredients, and dishes are acceptably prepared.

KIRKCUDBRIGHT

Stewartry's most ancient burgh, Kirkcudbright (pronounced Kir-coo-bree) lies at the head of Kirkcudbright Bay on the Dee Estuary. This intriguing old town contains color-washed houses inhabited in part by artists. In fact, Kirkcudbright has been called the "St. Ives [Cornwall] of Scotland."

In the old town graveyard are memorials to Covenanters and to Billy Marshall, the tinker king who died in 1792 at the age of 120, reportedly having fathered four children after the age of 100.

Maclellan's Castle, built in 1582 for the town's provost, Sir Thomas Maclellan, easily dominates the center of town. Kirkcudbright is an attractive town which is the center of a lively group of weavers, potters, and painters who work in the 18th-century streets and lanes.

The **Tolbooth,** a large building, dates back to the 16th and 17th centuries, and in front of it is a **Mercat Cross** of 1610. The Tolbooth is a memorial to John Paul Jones (1747–1792), the gardener's son from Kirkbean who became a slave trader, a privateer, and in due course one of the founders of the American navy. For a time, before his emigration, he was imprisoned for murder in the Tolbooth.

Art exhibitions are regularly sponsored at **Broughton House** (tel. 0557/30437), a 17th-century mansion that once belonged to E. A. Hornel, the artist. The house contains a large reference library with a Burns collection, along with pictures by Hornel and other artists, plus antiques and other works of art. You can stroll through its beautiful garden. Broughton is open mid-March to mid-October from 11 a.m. to 1 p.m. and 2 to 5 p.m. daily except Tuesday, from 2 to 5 p.m. on Sunday. In winter it is open by prior arrangement only. Admission is 80p ($1.40) for adults, 40p (70¢) for children.

In addition, the **Stewartry Museum,** St. Mary Street (tel. 0557/30797), contains a fascinating collection of antiquities, depicting the history and culture of Galloway. It's open daily except Sunday from 11 a.m. to 4 p.m. Easter to October (from 11 a.m. to 5 p.m. in July and August). Admission is £1 ($1.75) for adults, 30p (55¢) for children.

North of town is the ruined **Tongland Abbey,** one of whose abbots, John Damian, once tried to fly from the battlements of Stirling Castle wearing wings of bird feathers, in the presence of James IV. He landed in a manure pile.

Dundrennan Abbey, seven miles southeast of Kirkcudbright, the ruins of a rich Cistercian house founded in 1142, includes much late Norman and Transitional work. Dundrennan is a daughter abbey of Rievaulx Abbey in Yorkshire and the mother abbey of Glenluce and Sweetheart Abbeys. The small village is partly built of stones "quarried" from the abbey. Mary Queen of Scots, after escaping from Loch Leven and being defeated at the Battle of Langside, spent her last night in Scotland at the abbey in May 1568. She went to England to seek help from Elizabeth who imprisoned her instead. The transept and choir, a unique example of the Early Pointed style, remain.

In accommodations, I suggested the **Selkirk Arms,** Old High Street, Kircudbright, Kircudbrightshire DG6 4JG (tel. 0557/30402), where Robert Burns stayed when he composed the celebrated Selkirk Grace. (The grace was actually given on St. Mary's Isle, the seat of the Douglases, earls of Selkirk, and, in part, it went as follows: "But we ha'e meat, and we can eat, and sae the Lord be thankit.") The hotel, a two-story 18th-century building, has 16 bedrooms, and the furnishings are in keeping with the character of the house. It has an inviting atmosphere and a helpful staff. You will be the guests of John and Sue Morris. The bedrooms have been recently refurbished and most have private baths or showers. All have color TV, phones, and tea/coffee-makers. The daily rate for B&B is £28 ($49) in a single, £48 ($84) in a double. The restaurant offers a wide range of fresh local produce, such as Galloway beef, lamb, venison, salmon, and scallops. Bar lunches and suppers are also available. The hotel has ample parking and a spacious garden in the rear. Private salmon fishing is offered on the River Dee. The neighborhood evokes memories of John Paul Jones, and there are little art galleries displaying the works of local painters.

GATEHOUSE-OF-FLEET

This sleepy former cotton town, on the Water of Fleet, was the Kippletringan in Sir Walter Scott's *Guy Mannering,* and Burns composed "Scots Wha Hae wi' Wallace Bled" on the moors nearby and wrote it down in the Murray Arms Hotel there.

The town's name probably dates from 1642 when the English government opened the first military road through Galloway to assist the passage of troops to Ireland. In 1661 Richard Murray of Cally was authorized by Parliament to widen the bridge and to erect beside it an inn that was to serve as a tollhouse, with the innkeeper responsible for the maintenance of a 12-mile stretch of road. This is believed to have been the original house on the "gait," or road, which later became known as the "gait house of Fleet," and by 1790 it was being written in its present form and spelling. The ancient "gait house" is now part of the Murray Arms Hotel, used as a coffeeroom, and is probably the oldest building still in existence in the town.

West of Gatehouse, on the road to Creetown, is the well-preserved 15th-century tower of the McCullochs, with its sinister "murder hole" over the entrance passage. Through this trapdoor, boiling pitch was poured onto attackers.

Cardoness Castle was originally the seat of the McCulloch family, one of whom, Sir Godfrey McCulloch, was the last person in Scotland to be executed, at Edinburgh in 1697, by the "Maiden," the Scots version of the guillotine. The castle is on the A75, a mile southwest of Gatehouse-of-Fleet. It is open from 9:30 a.m. to 7 p.m. Monday to Saturday, from 2 to 7 p.m. Sunday from April to the end of September. The remainder of the year, closing time is 4 p.m. Admission is 60p ($1.05) for adults, 30p (55¢) for children.

Food and Lodging

For accommodations, I recommend the following:

Cally Palace Hotel, Gatehouse-of-Fleet, Kircudbrightshire DG7 2DL (tel. 05574/341), is a large 18th-century mansion standing in 100 acres of beautiful gardens and wooded parkland. Especially popular with more mature readers, it is an oasis of peace and quiet—most comfortable, more suited for someone who wishes to spend a few days in Galloway than the fleeting overnight motorist. The public lounges are overscale with some fine period pieces, and a sun patio looks out onto a swimming pool. Amenities include a bar, table tennis, and pool, in addition to a hard tennis court, putting, croquet, a sauna, game fishing, loch boating, and dancing at certain times of the year. All of its 60 rooms contain private bath or shower. Some of the bedrooms have balconies opening onto the grounds. Rooms come in widely varying styles and sizes, but all have color TV and tea- and coffee-making facilities. Depending on the room assignment, half-board tariffs range from £42.50 ($74.40) to £47.50 ($83.15) per person nightly. A dinner-dance is held on Saturday night.

Murray Arms, High Street, Gatehouse-of-Fleet, Kircudbrightshire DG7 2HY (tel. 05574/207), is a long, low, white-painted building that was once a posting inn in the 18th century, its coffeehouse dating back even earlier, to 1642. Burns wrote his stirring song "Scots Wha' Ha'e" while staying at the inn, the occasion still commemorated by the Burns Room with its Leitch pictures. The inn has been considerably updated and modernized by the laird of the Cally Estate, and that is as it should be, since it was James Murray of Cally who made the Murray Arms into a coaching inn so long ago. Now it's back in the same family after a long departure. Standing by an old clock tower, the inn has long been known for its food and hospitality. In addition to three bars, the house has a sun lounge opening onto a roof terrace. The rooms are modestly furnished, and singles range from £27 ($47.25) to £30 ($52.50) daily and doubles from £54 ($94.50) to £60 ($105). Nearly half the rooms contain a private bath. You can stop in for a complete dinner in its attractively decorated restaurant opening onto the garden. From 7:30 to 9 p.m. daily, you can order a table d'hôte meal for £12.50 ($21.90). Specialties include Galloway beef and fresh Solway Firth salmon. The Lunky Hole lounge and food bar is open from noon to 9:45 p.m. daily and serves a wide variety of hot and cold food.

NEWTON STEWART

Sometimes called "the gateway to Galloway" and the "heart of Galloway," this small town on the River Cree was made a burgh or barony in 1677 after a son of the second Earl of Galloway built some houses beside the ford across the river and gave the hamlet its present name. When the estate was later purchased by William Douglas, he changed the name to Newton Douglas, but it didn't stick. The town has a livestock market and woolen mills. Cree Bridge, built of granite in 1813 to replace one swept away by a flood, links the town with **Minnigaff** where there is an old church with carved stones and some memorials.

Newton Stewart is associated with Scott, Stevenson, and Burns. Today it is chiefly a center for touring, especially north for nine miles to the beauty spot of **Loch Troolin** in the Glen Trool Forest Park, 200 square miles of magnificently preserved splendor. On the way to Loch Trool you go through the village of Glentrool, where you'll find the first car park for those wanting to take the Stroan Bridge walk, a distance of 3½ miles. The hearty Scots, of course, walk the entire loch, all 4½ miles of it.

Food and Lodging

Newton Stewart has a wide range of accommodations, making it one of the best bases for touring Galloway.

Kirroughtree, Newton Stewart, Wigtownshire DG8 6AN (tel. 0671/2141), is an impressive manor house, once the seat of the Herons of Galloway, built in 1719 and full of traditional character, with certain Spanish features. The hotel has been completely refurbished and is now a luxurious country-house hotel. All 22 bedrooms are attractively furnished and have baths, color TVs, and phones. Rates range from £35 ($61.25) per person daily for B&B, the price including VAT and free golf at several courses. There are two elegant dining rooms with period furnishings. The hotel is fully licensed and has a cozy cocktail bar. This place is ideal for those who want complete peace as it is surrounded by some eight acres of gardens with some 10,000 ornamental shrubs and trees and views of the Galloway countryside and Solway Firth. It also offers pony trekking and many pleasant walks, plus shooting, deer stalking, and salmon and trout fishing. Open March to December.

The Bruce, 88 Queen St., Newton Stewart, Wigtownshire DG8 6JL (tel. 0671/2294), is an exemplary up-to-date hotel. Although not lavish in appointments, it is modern and efficiently run, maintaining a good standard of comfort, but keeping its prices reasonable—from £28 ($49) daily in a single, from £45 ($78.75) in a double. The decor is bright, and the bedrooms well designed. All of the 17 bedrooms contain private baths. Guests enjoy a pleasant bar and congenial company, composed mainly of locals who frequent the Bruce. The restaurant, also in the modern style, offers a cold table at lunch daily from 12:30 to 2 p.m. Dinners, when the menu is more varied, are quite interesting, and everything tastes home-cooked from fresh produce. A table d'hôte, served from 7:30 to 9 p.m., goes for £12 ($21) and up.

WHITHORN

Ten miles south of Wigtown, you come upon Whithorn, a modern town with a museum containing ancient crosses and tombstones, including the 5th-century **Latinus Stone,** the earliest Christian memorial in Scotland. St. Ninian, the son of a local chieftain, founded a monastery here in A.D. 397 and built his "Candida Casa" or "White House," probably the first Christian church in Scotland. In the 12th century, Fergus, Lord of Galloway, built a priory. The church and monastery were destroyed in the 16th century. Excavations in the ruins have revealed fragments of wall covered in pale plaster believed to be from Ninian's Candida Casa. The ruins are entered through the Pend, a 17th-century arch on which are carved the Royal Arms of Scotland.

A moorland walk to the west coast 2½ miles away leads to **St. Ninian's Cave** in Port Castle Bay, used by the missionary as a retreat.

The **Isle of Whithorn,** three miles southeast of the town, is where St. Ninian landed about A.D. 395 on his return from studying in Rome, to bring Christianity to Scotland. The ruins of a plain 13th-century chapel are here but no signs of an earlier church. On the point of the promonotory are the remains of an Iron Age fort and a late-17th-century tower.

Chapel Finian, near the shore road on the way from Whithorn to Glenluce, is a small chapel or oratory probably dating from the 10th or 11th century, in an enclosure about 50 feet wide.

Just outside Whithorn is the **Castlewigg Hotel,** Whithorn, Wigtownshire DG8 8DL (tel. 09885/213), a small licensed country hotel under the personal supervision of its owners. Castlewigg is two miles north of Whithorn on the A746, with views to the north toward Newton Stewart and to the east to Fleet Bay. More than 200 years old, the hotel building was the dower house of Castle Wigg, which lies in ruins, not open to the public, a mile or so off the road. Bedrooms cost from £12 ($21) to £19 ($33.25) per person nightly for B&B. Guests, who share the public baths, enjoy the residents' lounge with color TV, the spacious, colorful dining room, and the lounge bar. Dinner costs around £10 ($17.50). From the à la carte menu, you can order such dishes as venison in red wine and port, as well as rainbow trout. The hotel specializes in hunting and fishing holidays. The Castlewigg sits in seven acres of grounds, about 150 yards from the main road, so there's ample parking.

PORTPATRICK

Until 1849 steamers sailed the 21 miles from Donaghdee in Northern Ireland to Portpatrick, which became a "Gretna Green" for the Irish. Couples would land on Saturday, have the banns called on Sunday, and marry on Monday. When the harbor became silted up, Portpatrick was replaced by Stranraer as a port.

Commanding a clifftop to the south are the ruins of **Dunskey Castle,** a grim keep built in 1510 by John Adair.

Ten miles south of Portpatrick is the little village of **Port Logan.** In the vicinity is **Logan House,** the seat of the McDouall family, which could trace their ancestry so far back that it was claimed they were as "old as the sun itself." This family laid out the world-famous gardens at Logan.

Logan Botanic Garden (tel. 077686/231) an annex of the Royal Botanic Garden, Edinburgh, contains a wide range of plants from the temperate regions of the world. Cordylines, palms, tree ferns, and rhododendrons grow well in the mild climate of southwest Scotland. The garden is open April 1 to September 30 from 10 a.m. to 5 p.m. Admission is 50p (90¢) per person. The site is 14 miles south of Stranraer off the B7065 road. A licensed restaurant and toilet facilities are available.

Nearby is **Ardwell House,** with gardens that are at their best in April and May.

The ancient church site of **Kirkmadrine** lies in the parish of Stoneykirk, south of Portpatrick. The site now has a modern church, but there is an ancient graveyard and early inscribed stones and crosses, including three of the earliest Christian monuments in Britain, showing the chi-rho symbol and inscriptions dating from the 5th or early 6th century. There was an early Christian monastery and in the Middle Ages a parish church.

Instead of going to the larger town, Stranraer, you might prefer to stay at the **Knockinaam Lodge Hotel,** Portpatrick, Portpatrickshire DG9 9AD (tel. 077681/471), 3¼ miles southeast off the A77, built as a Victorian holiday house in 1869 and enlarged in 1901. It stands right at the foot of a deep and thickly wooded glen, surrounded on three sides by cliffs, looking out to sea and the distant Irish coast. In the heat of World War II, Sir Winston Churchill chose the lodge for a secret meeting with General Eisenhower. The prime minister enjoyed a long hot bath (in a tub that's still here) while smoking a cigar. Knockinaam is run in the best country-house tradition by the resident owners. Containing only ten bedrooms, most of which have private bath or shower, the hotel's rate is from £75 ($131.25) per person daily for dinner, bed, and breakfast, VAT included. There is a garden with lawns running down to a private sandy beach. The lodge serves the best food in the area. All ingredients used in the kitchen are fresh. You can dine in the restaurant overlooking the sea as it breaks over the rocks at the end of the garden, enjoying tender Galloway beef, lobsters, scallops, and other local dishes, accompanied by home-grown vegetables. Both à la carte and table d'hôte meals are cooked to order. Service is polite and efficient. Lunch, daily from 12:30 to 2 p.m., is offered for £12 ($21); dinner is from 7:15 to 9 p.m., when a set meal costs £23 ($40.25), including VAT. The lodge is open from Easter to December.

STRANRAER

The largest town in Wigtownshire, Stranraer is the terminal of the 35-mile ferry crossing from Larne, Northern Ireland. An early chapel, built by a member of the

Adair family near the 16th-century **Castle of St. John** in the heart of town, gave the settlement its original name of Chapel, later changed to Chapel of Stranrawer and then shortened to Stranraer. The name is supposed to have referred to the row or "raw" of original houses on the "strand" or burn, now largely buried beneath the town's streets. The Castle of St. John became the town jail and in the late 17th century held Covenanters during Graham of Claverhouse's campaigns of religious persecution.

To the east are **Castle Kennedy Gardens** and **Lochinch Castle** (tel. 0775/2024), a late-19th-century Scots baronial mansion. In the grounds of Lochinch Castle are the White and Black Lochs and the ruins of Castle Kennedy, which was built during the reign of James IV but burned down in 1716. The gardens, restored in the middle of the 19th century, contain the finest pinetum in Scotland. Go in the right season and you can wander among rhododendrons, azaleas, and magnolias. The castle is not open to the public, but the gardens are, daily from 10 a.m. to 5 p.m. April through September. Admission is £1.50 ($2.65) for adults, 50p (90¢) for children. Light refreshments are available.

Food and Lodging

North West Castle, Royal Crescent, Stranraer, Wigtownshire DG9 8EH (tel. 0776/4413), overlooks Loch Ryan and the departure quay for Northern Ireland. The oldest part of the house was built in 1820 by Capt. Sir John Ross, R.N., the Arctic explorer. Of course, to honor the brave man your bedroom window should face northwest, an allusion to his search for the "North West Passage." The hotel owners will give you a brochure that relates the exploits and disappointments of the explorer. The original building has been altered and extended to meet the hotel's popularity. At last count, a total of 77 rooms are offered, all with private bath. Singles cost from £30 ($52.50) daily, and doubles run £48 ($84) to £52 ($91). Many of the best rooms are in the two modern wings. The lounges are cozy and pleasantly furnished, and the dining room is impressive, serving mainly continental fare with Scottish overtones. Fresh local ingredients are used. The bars downstairs are well stocked—I prefer the Explorers' Lounge with its views of the harbor. Further amenities include a garden, a sauna, and a solarium, plus a curling rink, game room, indoor swimming pool, and dancing to a live band most Saturday nights.

George Hotel, George Street, Stranraer, Wigtownshire DG9 7RJ (tel. 0776/2487), stands right in the heart of town. I first stayed there many, many years ago, and on my most recent visit I found it considerably improved, a lot of money spent, in fact, to provide the latest up-to-date comforts for its guests, many of whom are embarking for Northern Ireland in the morning. Less than half the bedrooms contain a private bath. Singles cost £23 ($40.25) to £27 ($47.25) nightly, and doubles go for £36 ($63) to £41 ($71.75), including VAT, service, and a full breakfast. Most of the rooms contain such amenities as razor sockets and radio. Color-coordinated schemes are used in the bedrooms, and the baths are spotlessly clean. A cooperative staff will give touring advice. The hotel's restaurant is also good, making use of local produce, the cooking and service quite acceptable. The lighting is subdued and the ingredients fresh, the emphasis placed on "Taste of Scotland" dishes, costing £12 ($21) for four courses and coffee.

EDINBURGH AND CENTRAL SCOTLAND

Scotland has often been compared to a sandwich in that the central belt is considered the meatier part. Within a realtively small compass of land, you can visit not only the capital at Edinburgh but also enjoy such beauty as the Trossachs (the Scottish lake district), the silver waters of Loch Lomond, or take in the cragginess of Stirling Castle. Central Scotland should be treated as far more than just a gateway to the Highlands.

Edinburgh, often called the fairest city in Europe, is our first stopover. While based there you can take many day trips, such as to the seaside and golfing resort of North Berwick. The Scots suggest you take a "look aboot ye."

From Edinburgh, on the opposite shore of the Firth of Forth, reached by bridge, the Kingdom of Fife is rich in treasures, such as Falkland Palace, the hunting retreat of the Stuart kings, and the unspoiled fishing villages along the coast, collectively known as "East Neuk."

To the west of Edinburgh, a distance of some 40 miles, the industrial city of Glasgow is more and more a goal for visitors. It is rich in its own attractions, and from there you can set out on a tour in many directions, including the glens and hills associated with the outlaw Rob Roy. Also on Glasgow's doorstep is the scenic estuary of the Firth of Clyde. You can cruise down the Clyde on a paddle-steamer.

But, assuming you're in the Lowlands, you can begin your descent upon—

1. Edinburgh

Scotland's capital city is Edinburgh, off the beaten path for those doing the mad whirlwind tour of Europe, as it lies 373 miles north of London. The city is associated with John Knox, Mary Queen of Scots, Robert Louis Stevenson, Sir Arthur Conan Doyle (creator of Sherlock Holmes), David Hume, Alexander Graham Bell, Sir Walter Scott, and Bonnie Prince Charlie—to name-drop a bit.

From the elegant Georgian crescents of the New Town, to the dark medieval "wynds" of the Old Town, down the wide, magnificent Princes Street (Stevenson's "liveliest and brightest thoroughfare"), Edinburgh is a powerful attraction. Of course it's not as sophisticated as Paris, nor as fast-paced as London. And it's banal to call it the Athens of the North, although the Greek Revival movement of the 19th century made many of the buildings look like pagan temples.

Most travelers know that since World War II Edinburgh has been the scene of an ever-growing International Festival, with its action-packed list of cultural events. But that shouldn't be your only reason for visiting the ancient seat of Scottish royalty. Its treasures are available all year. In fact, the pace the rest of the time—when the festival-hoppers have gone home—is more relaxed. The prices are lowered, and the people themselves, under less pressure as hosts, return to their traditional hospitable nature.

GETTING THERE

Edinburgh is about an hour's flying time from London (see "Flying to Scotland" in Chapter XVIII). It also is about two hours by bus or rail from the major international airport of Scotland, Prestwick, and it lies in the center of most of the rail and bus lines leading from Scotland to England. Edinburgh's improved airport, connected by frequent 30-minute bus rides to midtown, receives flights only from within the British Isles and the rest of Europe.

Edinburgh is well connected by rail and bus to other points in Britain. The standard second-class round-trip rail fare from London to Edinburgh is $174 (U.S.). If certain conditions are met, however, you can qualify for an Intercity Saver Ticket, which costs around $120 round trip. For more information on rail travel, refer to "Traveling Within Britain," Chapter I.

The least expensive way to go is by bus from London, the trip from Edinburgh taking about eight hours and costing around £25 ($43.75) for a round-trip ticket.

GETTING AROUND

Edinburgh doesn't benefit from a modern underground (subway, to Americans) system, so you'll find **buses** will probably be your chief method of transport in the Scottish capital. The fare you pay is determined by the distance you ride. The minimum fare is 20p (35¢) for three stages or less, and the maximum fare is 90p ($1.60) for 30 or more stops. (A stage is not a stop. It's a distance of about half a mile in which a number of stops usually exist.) Children up to 14 years of age pay 15p (25¢) to 50p (90¢), according to the number of stages, and children under 5 travel free.

The Edinburgh city fathers (or mothers as the case may be) have devised several types of term bus passes for extended tourist visits to their city. The Edinburgh Freedom Ticket allows one day of unlimited travel on city buses at £1.25 ($2.20) for adults and 65p ($1.15) for children. Another form of extended ticket is a **TouristCard**, allowing unlimited travel on all city buses for a time period of between 2 and 13 days, plus special discounts at certain restaurants and for tours of selected historical sites. A two-day TouristCard costs £7.15 ($12.50) for adults and £4.55 ($7.95) for children. A 13-day TouristCard goes for £20.90 ($36.60) for adults and £11.70 ($20.50) for children.

For daily commuters or for diehard enthusiasts, a RidaCard season ticket allows unlimited travel for adults on all buses at £5 ($8.75) for adults for one week and £17.60 ($30.80) for four weeks. Travel must begin on a Sunday. Prices for children are £2.50 ($4.40) for one week, £8.80 ($15.40) for four weeks.

These tickets and further information may be obtained at the **Waverley Bridge Transport Office,** Waverley Bridge in Edinburgh (tel. 031/554-4494), or the **Lothian Region Transport Office,** 14 Queen St., Edinburgh EH2 1JL (tel. 031/26-5087)

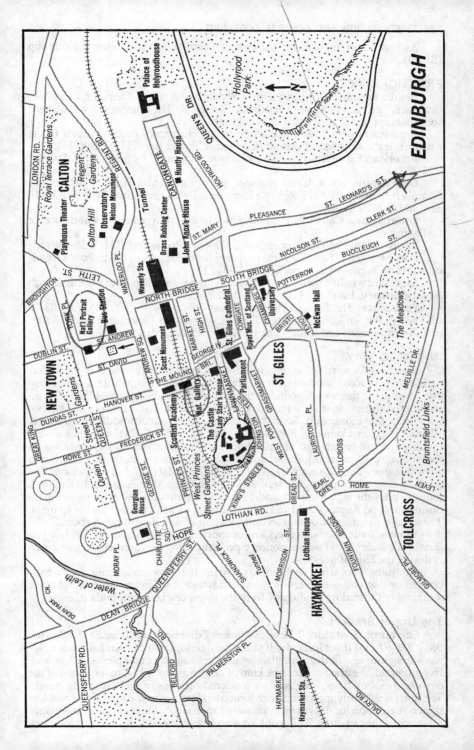

EDINBURGH

Hollyrood Park

N

Palace of Hollyroodhouse

QUEEN'S DR.

LONDON RD.
Royal Terrace Gardens
CALTON
Regent Gardens
Playhouse Theater
Calton Hill
Observatory
Nelson Monument
REGENT RD.
CANONGATE
Huntly House
Brass Rubbing Center
John Knox's House
ST. MARY
Tunnel
PLEASANCE
ST. LEONARD'S ST.
CLERK ST.
NICOLSON ST.
BUCCLEUCH ST.
POTTERROW
SOUTH BRIDGE
CHAMBERS
University
McEwan Hall
BRISTO
LEVEN
The Meadows
MELVILLE DR.
Bruntsfield Links
Waverly Sta.
NORTH BRIDGE
MARKET ST.
HIGH ST.
COWGATE
St. Giles Cathedral
Royal Mus. of Scotland
ST. GILES
LEITH ST.
YORK ST.
Nat'l Portrait Gallery
Bus Station
ST. ANDREW
ST. DAVID
ST. ANDREW SQ.
Scott Monument
THE MOUND
GEORGE ST.
ST. BRI.
Parliament
Lady Stair's House
LAWNMARKET
GRASSMARKET
LAURISTON PL.
TOLLCROSS
HOME
EARL GREY
TOLLCROSS
LEVEN
BROUGHTON
DUBLIN ST.
NEW TOWN
Gardens
HANOVER ST.
DUNDAS ST.
GREAT KING
Queen street Gardens
QUEEN ST.
HOWE ST.
FREDERICK ST.
Georgian House
GEORGE ST.
PRINCES ST.
Scottish Academy
West Princes
Street Gardens
Nat. Gallery
The Castle
KING'S STABLES
JOHNSTON
WEST PORT
BREAD ST.
LOTHIAN RD.
MORRISON ST.
Tunnel
Lothian House
FOUNTAIN BRIDGE
GILMORE PL.
HAYMARKET
SHANDWICK PL.
QUEENSFERRY ST.
HOPE
CHARLOTTE SQ.
MORAY PL.
Water of Leith
DEAN BRIDGE
QUEENSFERRY RD.
DEAN PARK CR.
BELFORD
PALMERSTON PL.
DALRY RD.
Haymarket Sta.

As a last resort, try hailing a **cab** or waiting at a taxi stand. Meters begin at 80p ($1.40).

PRACTICAL FACTS

Besides the information given in "The ABCs of Britain," Chapter I, and "Practical Facts" pertaining to all of Scotland, Chapter XVIII, Section 4, I will also list some data applicable specifically to Edinburgh.

American Consulate: The place to go for emergency problems such as lost passports is the **American Consulate,** 3 Regent Terrace (tel. 031/556-8315).

American Express: The office in Edinburgh is at 139 Princes St. (tel. 031/225-7881).

Dental care: For a dental problem, go to the **Dental Surgery School,** 31 Chambers St. (tel. 031/225-9511). Hours are daily except Sunday from 9 to 10:15 a.m. and 2 to 3:15 p.m.

Emergencies: Call 999 in an emergency to summon police, an ambulance, or firefighters.

Information: Help for tourists is at 5 Waverley Bridge (tel. 031/226-6591).

Lost property: If you have lost property (or had it stolen), go to **Police Headquarters** on Fettes Avenue (tel. 031/331-3131).

Medical care: In a medical emergency, you can seek help from the **Edinburgh Royal Infirmary,** Lauriston Place (tel. 031/229-2477).

Post office: The Edinburgh Branch Post Office, 2-4 Waterloo Pl. (tel. 031/550-8314), is open from 9 a.m. to 5:30 p.m. Monday to Thursday, from 9:30 a.m. to 5:30 p.m. Friday, and from 9 a.m. to 12:30 p.m. Saturday.

WHERE TO STAY

Searching for suitable lodgings isn't too difficult in Edinburgh, as the city offers a wide range of accommodations at different price levels throughout the year. However, during the three-week period of the festival, the establishments fill up with international visitors, so it's prudent to reserve in advance. To take care of on-the-spot bookings, the **Edinburgh Tourist Information & Accommodation Service,** Waverley Market Complex, 3 Princes St. (tel. 031/225-2424), compiles a well-investigated and lengthy list of small hotels and guesthouses. The emphasis is on well-managed, clean, comfortable, and hospitable guesthouses, usually catering to anywhere from 2 to 12 visitors, some for as little as £10 ($17.50) per person. The bureau's hours during the peak season, May 1 to September 30, are 8:30 a.m. to 8 p.m. Monday through Saturday, and 11 a.m. to 8 p.m. on Sunday (open to 9 p.m. during July and August). A £1 ($1.75) booking fee and a 10% deposit are charged. There's also an information and accommodation desk at Edinburgh Airport.

You can write in advance, enclosing your requirements and the fee, but you should allow about four weeks' notice, especially during the summer and particularly during the festival weeks.

Assuming you arrive in Edinburgh when the accommodations aren't fully booked or that you will reserve a room in advance, I've prepared a representative sampling of the leading candidates, from the upper bracket to the budget range.

The Upper Bracket

Edinburgh Sheraton, 1 Festival Square, Edinburgh, Lothian EH3 9SR (tel. 031/229-9131). Town leaders still praise the development of what had been a railway siding into one of the most glamorous hotel and office complexes in Scotland. Its figurehead, sheathed in the same kind of beige limestone that covers many of the city's historic buildings, is a glistening modern hotel, one of the best in Edinburgh. The hotel is elegantly appointed, with long corridors and soaring public rooms. Designers drew upon local loyalties by choosing appropriate tones of thistle and mauve for much of the carpeting. This, coupled with acres of wood trim, a central location, big-windowed views of Edinburgh Castle, and a well-chosen staff, make this the most appealing modern hotel in the Scottish capital. The 263 spacious, well-upholstered rooms offer 24-hour room service, double glazing on the windows, color TV with in-house movies, and easy contact with a team of concierges. The prices of accommodations are reasonable, considering the quality of the hotel. Singles range from £85 ($148.75) to £100 ($175) daily, with twins or doubles costing £120 ($210) to £140 ($245). More glamorous and more expensive suites are also available. A plushly modern cocktail bar is increasingly a favorite rendezvous for dozens of local residents, while the restaurant, with its views over the fountain on Festival Square, presents well-prepared main courses and a lavish Sunday buffet. A Leisure Centre offers a swimming pool, whirlpool, sauna, and fully-equipped gym. The hotel is only a short walk from Princes Street.

Caledonian Hotel, Princes Street and Lothian Road, Edinburgh, Lothian EH1 2AB (tel. 031/225-2433), part of the Norfolk Capital Hotels group, is the city's premier traditional hostelry, with commanding views over Princes Street Gardens and up to the castle from its prime site at the west end of the main thoroughfare and shopping street of the city. The Caledonian is an Edinburgh landmark. Built of salmon-pink sandstone, one of only three such buildings in the city, the hotel has been the subject of considerable investment recently. There are 238 well-appointed rooms, all with mini-bars, color TVs, in-house video, direct-dial phones, and baths. The charges vary from £80 ($140) daily in a standard single to £135 ($236.25) for a deluxe double, with VAT included. The public areas have been totally renovated, decorated in pastel shades reminiscent of an age of Edwardian splendor. There are two bars: a traditional Edinburgh pub, Platform 1, where live entertainment is presented on weekends, and the Pullman Bar, where you can enjoy a drink among a sophisticated clientele in the evening. For eating, it is difficult to find a better place than the Pompadour Restaurant (see below under "Where to Dine"). There are less formal meals to be had in the Gazebo Restaurant, and a traditional British afternoon tea is served in the hotel's lounge. Food and drink are good value, with a substantial buffet from the Gazebo's hot and cold table costing around £13.25 ($23.20).

Roxburghe Hotel, 38 Charlotte Square, Edinburgh, Lothian EH2 4HG (tel. 031/225-3921), is an Adam building of dove-gray stone, a stately town house opening directly onto a tree-filled square. While only four floors high (including a row of dormered mansard windows), it is nevertheless the first choice for a number of discriminating people. The hotel is central, a short walk from Princes Street. The atmosphere is traditional, as reflected in the drawing room, with its ornate ceiling and woodwork, and tall arched windows opening toward the park. The furnishings are often antique, with groups of Chippendale chairs. All of the 76 bedrooms, reached by elevator, have private bath or shower, color TV, clock-radio alarm, phone, trouser press, and tea and coffee makers, plus amenities such as sewing kits, shower caps, and foam bath, as well as a basket of fruit. The units are handsomely traditional, a favorite scheme being Wedgwood blue-and-white Adam-style paneling. In high season, singles begin at £48 ($84) daily, and twins go for £105 ($183.75) all with a continental breakfast, service, and VAT included. A place to congregate for drinks is the Consort Bar, with its festive decor. A dining room serves not only good meals, but gives diners a view of the square.

George Hotel, 19 George St., Edinburgh, Lothian EH2 2PB (tel. 031/225-1251), is concentrated quality. A great deal is compressed into a comparatively small space. A member of the Inter-Continental Hotels group, the George is only two short blocks from Princes Street, in the midst of a number of boutiques and bus, rail, and air terminals. Between April 1 and October 1 the highest rates are in effect: £77 ($134.75) to £99 ($173.25) daily in a single with bath, £109 ($190.75) to £120 ($210) in a twin- or double-bedded room, also with bath. All prices include VAT. All of the bedrooms have been refurnished and redecorated, but the public rooms have retained the style, elegance, and old-fashioned comfort of a country house The Carvers Table offers a selection of prime Scottish beef, roast lamb, or roast pork. Le Chambertin, the hotel's exclusive French restaurant, is open Monday to Saturday, inclusive (refer to my dining recommendations).

King James Thistle Hotel, St. James Centre, 1 Leith St., Edinburgh, Lothian EH1 3SW (tel. 031/556-0111), in the heart of Edinburgh just off the end of Princes Street, is a restyled and refurbished hostelry with comfortable bedrooms and many amenities. Each of the 142 bedrooms has a private bath, direct-dial phone, color TV with in-house video, radio, trouser press, hairdryer, and tea- and coffee-making facilities. In addition, 24-hour room service and parking adjacent to the hotel are provided. Rooms cost from £65 ($113.75) daily in a single, from £98 ($171.50) in a double, VAT and service included. You can dine in the Brasserie St. Jacques on good French cuisine. The Boston Bean Company is a blend of an American saloon and a cocktail bar, reminiscent of early Americana. The style in both the brasserie and the bar is relaxed.

Carlton Highland Hotel, North Bridge, Edinburgh, Lothian EH1 1SD (tel. 031/556-7277), was originally built as one of Edinburgh's leading department stores. But in 1984 a team of entrepreneurs converted it into a plushly comfortable hotel. Its Victorian turrets, Flemish-style gables, and severe gray stonework rise imposingly from a street corner of the Royal Mile, a few paces from Waverley Station. The hotel's interior was altered into a bright and airy milieu of hardwood paneling, pastel colors, and modern conveniences. On the premises is a bar, as well as a pair of engaging restaurants. One of them, Quills, is designed like a private library from the 19th century. In the basement is an exercise room along with a swimming pool, whirlpool, sauna, two squash courts, an aerobics studio. Each of the 207 bedrooms contains a kind of Scandinavian simplicity and comfort, as well as many amenities such as a private bath, mini-bar, color TV, coffee-making equipment, and hairdryer. With VAT and breakfast included, singles cost £70 ($122.50) to £80 ($140) daily and doubles or twins, £100 ($175) to £120 ($210).

The Medium-Priced Range

Old Waverley Hotel, 43 Princes St. Edinburgh, Lothian EH2 2BY (tel. 031/556-4648), has turn-of-the-century origins, but it can be an ideal stopover for those desiring a central, comfortable establishment, which has been refurbished to provide modern amenities, with personnel giving efficient service. All of the bedrooms have a private bath. The B&B rate in a single begins at £55 ($96.25) daily. In a double, the B&B charge is from £80 ($140), including VAT and service. The lounges on the second floor have been given that contemporary look. Some of the rooms look onto Princes Street and at night the floodlit castle. The hotel has a good restaurant serving à la carte and table d'hôte meals.

Donmaree Hotel, 21 Mayfield Gardens, Edinburgh, Lothian EH9 2BX (tel. 031/667-3641), is a formally elegant Victorian villa ringed with hedges and rose borders along with a small but impeccably manicured lawn. The location is on a busy street with other Victorian homes with rooms to rent, but they are not as good as the Donmaree. Dating from 1869, the hotel has been extensively refurbished to its Victorian best. It offers 17 beautifully furnished bedrooms, all with private bath or shower, color TV, phones, and beverage-making equipment. With a full Scottish breakfast included, singles cost from £41 ($71.75) daily, with doubles or twins priced from £50 ($87.50) to £70 ($122.50). The location is only 15 minutes from Princes Street. It is an individual hotel with much to recommend it, not the least of which is its highly rated restaurant.

Mount Royal Hotel, 53 Princes St., Edinburgh, Lothian EH2 2DG (tel. 031/225-7161), is right in the middle of the famed thoroughfare, complete with its major shops. A modern world emerges as you climb the spiral staircase or take an elevator to the second floor, with its reception rooms and lounges, and floor-to-ceiling windows opening onto views of the Old Town. In reality, Mount Royal is a remake of an old hotel, providing streamlined bedrooms with a view. The emphasis is utilitarian—not on frills, although the comfort is genuine. In summer, singles with bath go for £46 ($80.50) daily, twins with bath cost £66 ($115.50). Prices include a continental breakfast, service, and VAT. The main dining room serves reasonably priced lunches and dinners, offering both a carving table and à la carte menus. The lounge on the second floor, with floor-to-ceiling windows offering views over the Scott Memorial and Princes Street, provides a wide range of savory and sweet snacks and beverages throughout the day.

Crest Hotel, Queensferry Road, Edinburgh, Lothian EH4 3HL (tel. 031/332-2442), stands on the road leading to the airport and the Forth Road Bridge. A modern, recently refurbished building, it is easily accessible in a city where parking is difficult. It offers lovely views over the Firth of Forth and the floodlit cathedral. Well-furnished bedrooms come with private bath, color TV, radio, phone, and trouser press. The standard rate for a single is £69 ($120.75) daily, and for a double, £87 ($152.25), including VAT and service. The Corinthian Restaurant offers a three-course lunch, costing £10 ($17.50), and a full menu in the evening for £14 ($24.50).

Howard Hotel, 32-36 Great King St., Edinburgh, Lothian EH3 6QH (tel. 031/557-3500). Three Georgian terrace houses have been combined to create a comfortable resting place at one of the finest hotels in Edinburgh. Singles, renting for £47 ($82.25) to £55 ($96.25) daily, including a full breakfast, VAT, and service. The decor is a combination of both traditional and modern. Units have tea- or coffee-making equipment, color TV, radio, and direct-dial phone. After relaxing in the lounge, you might want to patronize an elegant restaurant in the basement, known as No. 36. A three-course luncheon goes for £8.50 ($14.90). Specialties include such dishes as smoked Scottish salmon and pan-fried Scottish sirloin. At dinner, two courses from a wide selection will cost from £18 ($31.50). Across the passage in the basement is the Claret Jug, with paneled walls and touches of red, along with dark wood wheelback chairs. At lunchtime a popular cold buffet is served in the bar, with ample portions of cold poultry and meat. At the back is a car park.

Hilton National, Bells Mills, Belford Road, Edinburgh, Lothian EH4 3DG (tel. 031/332-2545), once known as Ladbroke Dragonara, is a contemporary accommodation set beside the Water of Leith outside the historic district of Edinburgh. A section of it was a grain mill in Victoria's day, and that old commitment is still honored by the naming of the Granary Bar, which has a certain elegantly rustic quality. Public rooms are generous in space, and the hotel offers 146 well-furnished bedrooms, each with private shower or toilet as well as direct-dial phone and TV. Accommodations offer many amenities such as radio alarms. Some of the rooms—called Gold Star—are the most elegant of all. Singles range in price from £65 ($113.75) to £80 ($140) daily, with doubles going for £88 ($154) to £103 ($180.25). Late arrivals will find dinner served until 10 p.m. as well as 24-hour room service.

The Bruntsfield Hotel, 69-74 Bruntsfield Pl., Edinburgh, Lothian EH10 4HH (tel. 031/229-1393). Its neo-Gothic façade overlooks an expanse of city park. Like the other 19th-century buildings lining this residential street, it is built of evenly spaced rows of honey-colored stones, reflecting the prosperity of their original owners. Inside, the hotel is neat and stylish, with a formal milieu of French-inspired armchairs and pastel shades of peach and blue. Just across the street lie the trees and putting greens of what are reputed to be the world's oldest golf course, the Bruntsfield Links. There's an attractive restaurant on the premises, The Potting Shed, along with a bar. The bedrooms are comfortably renovated, each with private bath, color TV, radio, direct-dial phone, trouser press, hairdryer, and tea/coffee-maker. With a full Scottish breakfast and VAT, singles range from £50 ($87.50) to £54 ($94.50) daily and doubles or twins from £70 ($122.50) to £78 ($136.50).

Barnton Thistle Hotel, 562 Queensferry Rd., Edinburgh, Lothian EH4 6AS (tel. 031/339-1144), stands at a crossroads lying between Edinburgh and the airport. An architectural curiosity, it is Victorian with a balconied tower rising in the center. However, the bedrooms are up to date. This long-established hotel has its devotees. It attracts largely a commercial clientele, but is suitable for visitors as well, especially in summer. There are generous public areas, including two bars serving "spirits." Fifty bedrooms are rented, and each is well furnished and maintained, with complete bath or shower, direct-dial phone, TV, and trouser press, as well as beverage-making equipment. Singles rent for £54 ($94.50) daily, with doubles costing £78 ($136.50). The hotel has a lot of facilities and extras ranging from a sauna to a secretarial service. Its restaurant serves international food, and there is live music with dancing on Saturday. A coffee shop stays open until 10 p.m. for late arrivals.

Commodore Hotel, Cramond Foreshore, Edinburgh, Lothian EH4 5EP (tel. 031/336-1700), was originally built in the 1960s and has nearly doubled in size since then. It sits on the banks of the Forth River, a short distance from the Forth River Bridge, across which the traffic of the main autoroute, M8, is funneled. The hotel occupies grounds between the river and a parkland. Each of its 50 well-furnished bedrooms overlooks either the park or river. Each of the accommodations has big windows, color TV, private baths, and a number of electronic accessories. With VAT and a continental breakfast included, singles rent for £54 ($94.50) daily, with doubles costing £68 ($119). The hotel lies within a 15-minute drive north of Princes Street. Golfers appreciate the nearby access to a local course known as Silver Knowes. This hotel is a member of a chain, Friendly Hotels, which is firmly entrenched in Scotland as a leader in the middle price bracket.

Ellersly House, 4 Ellersly Rd., Edinburgh, Lothian EH12 6HZ (tel. 031/337-6888), an Edwardian country house, lies 2½ miles west of the city center along A8. Standing in secluded gardens, it is about a five-minute ride from the center. Staying here has been compared to the "privacy of a home." This country house stands in a dignified residential section close to the vicinity of the Murrayfield rugby grounds. It is one of the best of the moderately priced hotels of Edinburgh. It rents 55 well-equipped bedrooms, each with private bath or shower, direct-dial phone, and TV. Accommodations are either in the main house or an annex. After a refurbishment program, the hotel is better than ever. Singles rent for £65 ($113.75) daily, with doubles costing £85 ($148.75). The hotel possesses a well-stocked cellar and offers good-tasting meals, with dinner going for £13.50 ($23.65). Service is first class.

Braid Hills Hotel, 134 Braid Rd., Edinburgh, Lothian EH10 6JD (tel. 031/447-8888), is a stone house with turrets and gables in the Edwardian style, however, it dates from the 1880s in Victoria's reign. It is one of the best of the country house type hotels lying right outside Edinburgh, opening onto views of the city. The location of this long-established hotel is about 15 minutes from Princess Street. It offers 68 rooms, each well furnished and containing such amenities as private baths or showers, direct-dial phone, TV, and trouser press. Singles rent for £48 ($84) daily, with doubles costing £60 ($105), including breakfast. Its restaurant features Scottish and continental cuisine, with both table d'hôte and à la carte menus.

The Budget Range

Belmont Hotel, 10-11 Carlton Terrace, Edinburgh, Lothian EH7 5DD (tel. 031/556-6146), is right in the midst of a row of classic town houses, dating from the 18th and 19th centuries. A 15-minute walk from the center of Edinburgh, with views of the parks and rooftops from most of the windows, it is really two houses joined together. Paying guests are charged £40 ($70) daily in a double, £26 ($45.50) in a single in high season. The price includes breakfast. Your bed will be comfortable, the sheets freshly laundered, the furnishings inviting. The dining room is as old-fashioned as the rest of the place, in typical Georgian style. The hotel was awarded a commendation prize by the Edinburgh New Town Conservation Committee for the extensive renovations to the dining room, restoring it to its natural Georgian splendor. The Belmont is ideal for those who want a homelike atmosphere.

Clarendon, 18 Grosvenor St., Edinburgh, Lothian EH12 5EG (tel. 031/337-7033), is a hotel for all seasons. It is found in a row of similar buildings, converted terraced houses, and it has been refurbished and equipped to a high standard. It is a tranquil, welcoming choice, offering 51 bedrooms, each with private bath or shower. The single rate ranges from £40 ($70) to £43 ($75.25) daily, with doubles going for £64 ($112) to £69 ($120.75). Each accommodation has a color TV, direct-dial phone, and beverage-making equipment. Owned by Scottish Highlands Hotels, this West End selection is an easy stroll to the shops and attractions of Princes Street. A Scottish cuisine is served in its restaurant, with dinners provided until 9:30 p.m. Meals cost from £10 ($17.50) to £17 ($29.75).

Thrums Private Hotel, 14 Minto St., Edinburgh Lothian EH9 1RQ (tel. 031/ 667-5545), takes the fictional name of J. M. Barrie's designation of his hometown of Kirriemuir. The proprietors, Mr. and Mrs. J. Maloney, run a choice establishment that is well decorated and furnished. The staff is helpful. The hotel consists of two buildings with 12 bedrooms, most with private baths or showers and all with color TV, radios, tea/coffee-makers, electric blankets, phones, and hairdryers. Singles rent for £16 ($28) daily, and doubles with bath cost £39 ($68.25). Family rooms are also offered. Tariffs include a full Scottish breakfast, VAT, and service. A small bar is available to residents. The hotel operates an à la carte restaurant for lunches and dinners, a three-course meal costing from £4 ($7) to £15 ($26.25). Good fresh produce is used in the preparation of all meals. A peaceful garden and car park can be used by hotel guests.

Teviotdale House, 53 Grange Loan, Edinburgh, Lothian EH9 2ER (tel. 031/ 667-4376). Some visitors rate this detached Victorian house, on a main bus route leading to the heart of the city, as the finest B&B type accommodation in Edinburgh. Mrs. E. G. Riley acquired the property in 1963, and her attention to detail has earned her an enviable reputation. All six bedrooms have a private shower, hot and cold running water, a toilet, TV, hairdryer, and restful beds. Breakfast may be the highlight of your dining for the day. Each meal is home cooked with fresh ingredients, including finnan haddie, porridge, kippers, grills, and home-baked bread and scones. The charge for B&B is from £21.50 ($37.65) to £37 ($64.75) daily, according to the season and size of the room. The house lies about ten minutes from Princes Street, Waverley Station, and Edinburgh Castle.

The Nova Hotel, 5 Bruntsfield Crescent, Edinburgh, Lothian EH10 4EZ (tel. 031/447-6437), is in a quiet cul-de-sac near the city center, with a view over Bruntsfield Links in front and the Pentland Hills to the back. Visitors are welcomed to its large, well-appointed bedrooms, all with baths or showers, toilets, direct-dial phones, color TVs, hairdryers, trouser presses, hot beverage facilities, and full central heating. Rents are £29.50 ($51.65) to £32 ($56) daily in a single, £52 ($91) to £62 ($108.50) in a double or twin, and £68 ($119) in a family room with up to three occupants. On the ground floor, guests enjoy the cocktail bar, and the public bar also provides an inviting atmosphere.

Castle Hotels

To fulfill your fantasy, you might want to spend your first night in Scotland in a real castle surrounded by gardens and spacious grounds. If so, I have the following recommendations:

Dalhousie Castle, Bonnyrigg, Edinburgh, Lothian EH19 3JB (tel. 0875/ 20153), dates back to the 13th century, and over its long history it has entertained such illustrious guests as Edward I, Henry IV, Oliver Cromwell, Sir Walter Scott, and Queen Victoria. Today it is the family seat of the Ramsays of Dalhousie, who have converted it into a luxurious hotel, yet retained some of its finest architectural features. It lies off the A7 Carlisle–Edinburgh road, just outside the village of Bonnyrigg, only eight miles from Edinburgh. A turreted and fortified house, with ramparted terraces and battlements, it offers such delights as a dungeon restaurant where meals are served, including many local Scottish dishes. The rooms all have private bath, color TV, phone, radio, and plenty of space in which to sit and relax. Two of the suites have four-poster beds. In high season, a single rents for £69

($120.75) daily, whereas a double or twin ranges from £92 ($161) to £110 ($192.50). For true palatial living, you might want to take one of the two-room suites with double or twin beds, costing £150 ($262.50) to £180 ($315). A full breakfast is included in the tariffs. The castle overlooks the banks of South Esk, from which came the red sandstone to build it. The hotel can help you arrange salmon and trout fishing, horseback riding, and shooting.

Borthwick Castle, North Middleton, Gorebridge, Midlothian EH23 4QY (tel. 0875/20514), is in a pastoral valley only 12 miles south of Edinburgh, just off the A7. This noble twin-tower keep, built in 1430, is the finest example of its kind in Britain today. It was here that the ill-fated Mary Queen of Scots sought refuge with her third husband, the Earl of Bothwell, in 1567. In 1650 the castle was besieged by the forces of Oliver Cromwell, and the damage inflicted by cannon fire can still be seen. All bedchambers have private baths and are centrally heated. The apartments once occupied by the Scottish queen and her beloved Bothwell, both with four-poster beds, are available to guests. Room rates are £110 ($192.50) to £160 ($280) daily for a twin or double, including VAT. The higher price is for the Mary Queen of Scots four-poster or the Earl of Bothwell four-poster. Dine by candlelight and log fire in the magnificent stone-vaulted Great Hall, with its minstrel's gallery and hooded fireplace. A five-course, two-choice dinner menu is available for £25 ($52.50). Borthwick Castle is known for the excellence of its cuisine and personal service, its authentic medieval ambience, and the re-creation of a gracious lifestyle of other days.

WHERE TO DINE

The Scots are hearty eaters—and you may like the sizes of their portions as well as the quality of their fare, with choices from river, sea, and loch. You can dine on a cock-a-leekie soup, fresh Tay salmon, haggis, neeps, tatties, and whisky, Aberdeen Angus filet steak, potted hough, poacher's soup, and good old stovies and rumbledethumps. If none of the above tempts you, you'll find that French cuisine has made an inroad at many of the first-class hotels.

The Upper Bracket

Pompadour Restaurant, Caledonian Hotel, Princes Street (tel. 031/225-2433), is one of the finest in Edinburgh, on the mezzanine floor of the famous hotel, serving fine Scottish and French cuisine. The restaurant has been refurbished, with gray wall panels interspersed with panels of floral-patterned silk. The chef blends cuisine moderne with traditional menus in this intimate, luxurious place. A special daily menu reflects the best produce available from the markets that day, and Scottish salmon, venison, and other game are often included in a meal. Both the lunch and evening menus feature the fresh produce from the local Scottish and French markets —items such as goose liver with wild mushrooms, filet of lamb with spinach and rosemary, and charlotte of marinated salmon filled with seafood. A set lunch costs £15 ($26.25); a set dinner with extras goes for £35 ($61.25). An à la carte meal costs from £35 ($61.25). There is a no-smoking area. Lunch is served from 12:30 to 2 p.m.; dinner, from 7:30 to 10:30 p.m. No lunch is served on Saturday or Sunday. On Saturday night there is dancing to a small combo, with piano music presented on other nights. Jackets and ties are requested for men, and reservations are required.

Handsel's, 22 Stafford St. (tel. 031/225-5521), in the view of many critics, is the finest dining room in Edinburgh. Andrew Radford is a young chef of considerable talent, and he displays his skills here daily from 12:30 to 2 p.m. and 7:30 to 9 p.m.; closed Saturday lunch and all day Sunday. Lunches cost from £12 ($21). A set dinner goes for £25 ($43.75), although you can spend from £32 ($56) if ordering à la carte. The restaurant is located on an elegantly decorated second floor (first floor in Britain) of a Georgian house dating from 1821. Downstairs is one of the city's most popular wine bars. Upstairs you can dine on such exquisitely prepared dishes as breast of wood pigeon with truffles or a combination of smoked and fresh salmon.

The cuisine might be called Scottish moderne. Vegetables, for example, are cooked to crispy perfection. Some herbs and other ingredients taste so fresh you'd think they were just picked in the garden. The wine list is well chosen but if you get carried away in ordering your tab could soar. Reservations are essential.

Le Chambertin, George Hotel, 21 George St. (tel. 031/225-1251), provides a top-level French cuisine in intimate surroundings, between 12:30 and 2:30 p.m. Monday through Friday. A meal, inclusive of wines, is available for £12.95 ($22.65), £15.20 ($26.60), or £16.45 ($28.80). In the evening, guests can select from a wide choice of wines, including some special bottles from the Chambertin district of France. The à la carte menu is well balanced and features many traditional dishes and also, subject to availability, lobster, mussels, oysters, and many other specialties.

The Medium-Priced and Budget Range

Martins, 70 Rose St., North Lane (tel. 031/225-3106), is the discovery of several readers. Martin and Gay Irons, the owners, have a knack for picking chefs who show more than just promise: They deliver. Meals in imaginative concoctions and light in texture are served Tuesday to Saturday (except no lunch on Saturday) at their establishment from noon to 2 p.m. and 7 to 10 p.m. (stays open half an hour later on Friday and Saturday). You can get a set lunch for only £7.50 ($13.15), which has to be one of the food bargains of Edinburgh, considering the skill of the cookery and the quality of the ingredients used. However, in the evening, expect to spend from £18 ($31.50). The fish dishes served here (most often from the U.K.) are one of the reasons for visiting this establishment. But if you want something really Scottish, see if roast venison (offered with a sauce made with bramble vinegar) is on the menu. That's a most delectable dish. Reservations are necessary.

Donmaree Hotel Restaurant, 21 Mayfield Gardens (tel. 031/667-3641), previously recommended for its rooms, is also an outstanding restaurant in Edinburgh, with superb food and service. The location is a residential neighborhood behind a gray stone façade. Inside, it's beautifully decorated in the spirit of its Victorian origins. Under the direction of Mr. and Mrs. Galt, it has received a darkly authentic gloss from the 19th century with antiques and several oil portraits. A table d'hôte luncheon is offered for only £8.50 ($14.90). Dinners cost from £18 ($31.50). The chef might offer a pot-roasted pheasant, roast rack of lamb marinated in honey and red wine, or roast duckling with an orange and Curaçao sauce. Hours are daily from 12:30 to 2 p.m. and 6:30 to 10 p.m. Reservations are desired. The location is 15 minutes from Princes Street.

Restaurant Alp Horn, 167 Rose St. (tel. 031/225-4787), in a blackened stone building on a street famous for its variety of pubs, provides a meal that is like a vacation in Switzerland. The wooden door opens to reveal an interior accented with red-checked gingham curtains, potted palms, and simple wooden tables and chairs. As you'd expect, the menu offers air-dried meats (Grisons style), several fondues, venison in season, and a version of rösti, the famous potato dish of Switzerland. All of this might be capped off with a slice of Black Forest cake. The establishment is open daily except Sunday and Monday. Lunch is served from noon to 2 p.m., and dinner, from 6:30 to 10 p.m. Full meals cost from £18 ($31.50).

Cosmo Ristorante, 58a North Castle St. (tel. 031/226-6743), is one of the most heavily patronized Italian restaurants in the Scottish capital. Courtesy, efficiency, and good cookery are featured here. In season you can ask for mussels as an appetizer. Soups and pastas are always reliable. However, remember that the cost of your pasta is doubled if you order it as a main course. On the other hand, the portions are also doubled. I've found the veal dishes the best cooked and a good value, although you may be attracted to the seafood. The cassata siciliana is well made and not unbearably sweet. Expect to pay £15 ($26.50) to £20 ($35) for a complete meal. Closed Sunday and Monday, the restaurant serves otherwise from noon to 2:15 p.m. for lunch and from 7 to 10:15 p.m. for dinner.

The Oyster Bar at the Café Royal, 17 W. Register St. (tel. 031/556-4124), is by far the best-maintained section of this historic establishment, a famous building that also contains the Café Royal pub. The Oyster Bar corner evokes images of baronial castles in the windswept Highlands. These are enjoyed to the sights and aromas of well-prepared lunches and dinners. An entire wall of this elegantly Victorian, masculine room is devoted to full-size depictions of 19th-century Scotsmen in full dress, each set into a stained-glass window. It's best to reserve a table. Full meals cost from £15 ($26.25). The restaurant specializes in seafood, as its name implies. You might like the salmon with mussels, shrimp, Camembert, and white wine, or else the steak in black-butter sauce. You can also select trout Cleopatra (in this case with capers, prawns, and lemons), grilled sardines, and sole cardinal. The establishment is open daily from 12:30 to 2:30 p.m. and 7 to 10:30 p.m.

Whigham's Wine Cellars, 13 Hope St. (tel. 031/225-8674), lie in a basement. Before the premises became a fashionable wine-cellar restaurant, wine was actually bottled here. Whigham's has been in business since the mid-18th century, and it used to ship wines to the American colonies. Walk across its mellowed old stone floors until you find an intimate alcove. A range of continental wines is offered, and some come from as far away as California. The bartender will prepare several wine cocktails, often laced with rum or brandy. Each day, you can make your selection from an assortment of appetizers and plats du jour. Their smoked fish (not just salmon) is exceptional, and meals come to £11 ($19.25). Hours are from 11 a.m. to midnight Monday to Saturday.

Cousteau's Bar and Seafood Restaurant, 47 Hill St., Northlane (tel. 031/226-3355), is an inviting, little-known restaurant. Obviously the emphasis is placed on the freshness and quality of the fish, all of which comes from Scottish waters. Oysters are often available, and a savory opener would be the mussels marinières au gratin or perhaps crab en chemise. You might order turbot, grilled or poached salmon, or trout. Most seasonal fish are available, and the prices vary with weather conditions. Expect to pay from £18 ($31.50) per person for a meal. There are simple desserts and a good wine list, which is perhaps a little expensive. Open daily except Sunday from noon to 2 p.m. and 6 to 11 p.m.

Chinese and Indian Restaurants

The Dragon's Castle, 21 Castle St. (tel. 031/225-7327), is the oldest established Chinese restaurant in Edinburgh. Its success has been attributed to the fact that it opened in an auspicious year—the Year of the Dragon in the Chinese zodiac calendar. Cantonese and Pekinese cuisine is served, as well as seafood and a selection of European dishes, in case you're not feeling Oriental. Menus list a choice of ten set meals, for two to six people, costing either £10 ($17.50) or £12.50 ($21.90) per person. Prices for main dishes ordered individually are reasonable. The restaurant is open Monday to Thursday from noon to 11:30 p.m., on Friday and Saturday from noon to 11:45 p.m., and on Sunday from 12:30 to 11 p.m. Three-course business lunches are offered during the week from noon to 2 p.m. costing only £3.70 ($6.50).

The **Verandah Tandoori,** 17 Dalry Rd. (tel. 031/337-5828), in the vicinity of the Haymarket depot, offers better than average food from North India and Bangladesh. A much-awarded restaurant, it deserves its good reputation. Vegetarians, of course, flock here, and you can select from a wide range of classic and tandoori food items made with excellent, fresh ingredients. It is open for lunch daily from noon to 2:30 p.m. and dinner from 5 to 11:45 p.m., the latter ideal for both early bird dinners and late evening suppers. The prices are reasonable, with a set luncheon or dinner costing only £8.50 ($14.90).

Szechuan House, 95 Gilmore Pl. (tel. 031/229-4655). Unlike London, Edinburgh doesn't abound in Szechuan restaurants, but there is one. You don't come here for elegant trappings, but what you get is some of the best Chinese food in Edinburgh. Vegetarians can also dine happily here, although most items seem to be concocted into zesty, savory platters from poultry and fish, especially chicken, duck, and prawns. My favorite menu selection is whimsically titled "bang-bang" chicken. You'll find the usual array of Oriental dishes along with some surprises such as a soup made with fish heads. But that might be left for only the adventurous palate. Meals cost from £9 ($15.75). Service is from 5:30 p.m. to midnight daily at dinner only from 5:30 p.m. to 2 a.m. (stays open until 3 a.m. on Friday and Saturday nights).

Indian Cavalry Club, 3 Atholl Pl. (tel. 031/228-3282). The name alone may attract you to this well-run place. The decor might suggest one of the old Hollywood movies, starring Gary Cooper or Errol Flynn. You face a vast menu in your armchair culinary tour of the subcontinent. Actually, some of the dishes are inspired by Burma and Nepal. Of course, all the familiar fare, including vindaloo dishes and tandooris, is there, but there are some imaginative and unusual presentations as well. Vegetarians will find much to please their palates as well. Service is daily from 11:30 a.m. to 2 p.m. and 5 to 11:30 p.m. A set luncheon is good value at £5.50 ($9.65), with a table d'hôte dinner going for £9.50 ($16.35). You can also order à la carte.

Food and Drink at Leith

In the northern regions of Edinburgh, Leith is the old port town, opening onto the Firth of Forth. Once it was a city in its own right until it was slowly absorbed into Edinburgh. After decades of decay, parts of it are gradually being restored into modernized "flats," along with a collection of restaurants, wine bars, and pubs. Some of the best ones are previewed below.

Skipper's Bistro, 1A Dock Pl. (tel. 031/554-1018), is one of the foremost restaurants in the port area, a former pub that has been skillfully "gentrified" by Allan and Jen Corbett. Today the walls are covered with an alluring shade of red designed to show off the well-polished brass, the antique chairs, and the marble-top bars. Fish is a specialty, served in fixed-price combinations of £11.50 ($20.15) for two courses, £13.50 ($23.65) for three courses. Coffee rounds off the flavor of the meals, which might include a marinade of kipper, trout au gratin, scallops, thermidor, and a mousseline of seafood. Lunch is served daily from 12:30 to 2 p.m., and dinner, from 7:30 to 10 p.m. This place lies off Commercial Street near a canal.

Waterfront Wine Bar, 1C Dock Pl. (tel. 031/557-7427), is a pleasant place whose brick and stone walls are adorned with old prints, maps, photographs, and other nautical memorabilia. There's a coal fireplace in a side room, plus a conservatory that has its own coal stove overlooking the water. A large vine acts like a pergola, letting dappled sunlight play across the tables. During the summer you can be seated at a table on a floating raft. Wine lovers enjoy vintage wine by the glass and a large selection by the bottle. Food is available, with an array of daily specials listed on the blackboard, perhaps including a prawn salad or lamb kebabs. In summer, barbecues are prepared outdoors. The establishment charges from £12 ($21) for a full meal. Food is served from noon to 2:30 p.m. Monday to Friday and from noon to 3 p.m. Saturday. Dinner is from 6 to 9:30 p.m. Monday to Thursday and from 6 to 10 p.m. Friday and Saturday. Closed Sunday. It lies off Commercial Street toward the water.

Dining at Cramond

At least once you should get out into the countryside surrounding Edinburgh. One way to do this is to take bus 41 for about five miles from the West End to the little Scottish village of Cramond. Few visible traces remain today of its Roman occupation.

Quietly nestling on a sloping street is the **Cramond Inn,** on Cramond Glebe Road (tel. 031/336-2035), which has been serving food and drinks to wayfarers for 300 years (it was known to Robert Louis Stevenson). Picture upholstered booths, some beer-barrel upholstered chairs, a collection of local watercolors, a low ceiling, large foot-square old beams, dark oak and creamy-colored walls, recessed windows, a small stone fireplace—and you'll begin to get the feel of the inn. The restaurant can serve 60 diners, but you'd better call in advance as it's most popular. The prices are quite reasonable, considering the quality of food—some of the finest of Scottish dishes. The steak-and-kidney pie is excellent, but I'm drawn to the haggis (with "neeps and tatties" and a dram of whisky), the famed dish of Scotland, made with an assortment of chopped meats, oatmeal, and spices. For an appetizer, the smoked haddock and prawn chowder is a favorite. A specialty of the house is medallion of venison with rowan jelly. A three-course lunch costs from £8.50 ($14.90), and dinner from £15 ($26.25). Bar lunches are served in the tastefully appointed lounge bar Monday to Saturday from noon to 2 p.m. and on Sunday from 12:30 to 2:30 p.m. The dining room serves lunch daily from noon to 2:30 p.m. and dinner from 7 to 10 p.m. except Sunday.

THE TOP SIGHTS

Before leaving the Scottish capital, you'll want to take a look at both the Old Town and the New Town. Each has different attractions—the Old Town's largely medieval; the New Town, Georgian.

Those on the most rushed of schedules may have time to see only the most important attractions. These include (1) Edinburgh Castle, (2) the Palace of Holyroodhouse, (3) a walk along the Royal Mile, (4) the National Gallery of Scotland, and (5) a look at the Gothic Scott Monument in the East Princes Street Gardens.

A good place to begin exploration is on the Royal Mile of the Old Town, a collective term for Canongate, Lawnmarket, and The High. At one end on Castle Rock sits—

Edinburgh Castle

It is believed that the ancient city grew up on the seat of the dead volcano, Castle Rock. History is vague on possible settlements, although it is known that in the 11th century Malcolm III (Canmore), and his Saxon queen, Margaret, occupied a castle on this spot. The good Margaret was later venerated as a saint. St. Margaret's Chapel was built in the Norman style, the present oblong structure dating principally from the 12th century. The five-ton **Mons Meg,** a 15th-century cannon that formerly sat outside the tiny chapel, is now to be found in the French Prisons.

Inside the castle (tel. 031/225-9846) you can visit the **State Apartments**—particularly Queen Mary's Bedroom—where Mary Queen of Scots gave birth to James VI of Scotland (later James I of Britain). The Great Hall with its hammerbeam ceiling was built by James IV. It displays armaments and armor. Scottish Parliaments used to convene in this hall.

The highlight, however, is the Crown Chamber, which houses the Honours of Scotland, used at the coronation of James VI, along with the sceptre and the sword of state of Scotland. The French Prisons can also be viewed. Turned into a prison in the 18th century, these great storerooms housed hundreds of Napoleonic soldiers during the early 19th century. Many of them made wall carvings that you can see today.

The castle may be visited from 9:30 a.m. to 5:05 p.m. (last ticket sold) Monday to Saturday and 11 a.m. to 5:05 p.m. on Sunday from April to the end of September; 9:30 a.m. to 4:20 p.m. Monday to Saturday and 12:30 to 3:35 p.m. on Sunday from October to the end of March. Admission is £2.20 ($3.85) for adults, £1.10 ($1.95) for children.

Your entrance ticket to the castle includes entry to the galleries of the **Scottish United Services Museum** (tel. 031/225-7534). These are situated on either side of Crown Square and in the North Hospital block. This national museum deals with the history of the navy, army, and air force at all periods. It is considered unique and comprehensive, the longest established collections of British armed forces historical material in the United Kingdom. The exhibitions alone are the largest single part of the areas in the castle open to the public. The Scottish regiments of the British Army figure strongly, and displays in the North Hospital block deal with the story of the Scottish soldier in an exciting fashion. In other sections, uniforms, equipment, badges, and medals present more traditional displays. The history of the Royal Navy and Royal Air Force in their Scottish contexts are interpreted in smaller galleries adjacent to the Scottish Crown Jewels.

The **Camera Obscura,** Castlehill (tel. 031/226-3709), is right beside the castle at the head of the Royal Mile. It's at the top of the Outlook Tower and offers a magnificent view of the surrounding city. Trained guides point out the landmarks and talk about Edinburgh's fascinating history. In addition, there are several entertaining exhibitions, all with an optical theme, and a well-stocked shop selling books, crafts, and records. Hours are 9:30 a.m. to 5 p.m. daily from November to March, 9:30 a.m. to 6 p.m. daily from April to October. Admission is £1.90 ($3.35) for adults, 90p ($1.60) for children.

Along the Royal Mile

Ideally, if you have the time you should walk the full length of the Royal Mile —all the way to the Palace of Holyroodhouse at the opposite end. Along the way you'll see some of the most interesting old structures in Edinburgh, with their turrets, gables, and towering chimneys. Of all the buildings that may intrigue you, the most visited are John Knox's House and **St. Giles' Cathedral.**

Although it still bears the name "cathedral," which it once was, St. Giles' is now properly titled the High Kirk of Edinburgh (tel. 031/225-4363). Founded in 1120, the interior dates mainly from the 15th century. It contains the Thistle Chapel, designed by Sir Robert Lorimer and housing beautiful stalls and notable heraldic stained-glass windows. The chapel is open from 10 a.m. to 5 p.m. daily. John Knox, the leader of the Reformation in Scotland, was minister of St. Giles' from 1560 to 1572.

Lady Stair's House, Lady Stair's Close, Lawnmarket, was built in 1622 by a prominent merchant burgess. It takes its name from a former owner, Elizabeth, the Dowager-Countess of Stair. Today it is a treasure house of portraits, relics, and manuscripts relating to three of Scotland's greatest men of letters: Robert Burns, Sir Walter Scott, and Robert Louis Stevenson. The house is open Monday to Saturday from 10 a.m. to 5 p.m., to 6 p.m. from June to September. During the festival it's open from 2 to 5 p.m. on Sunday. For information, telephone 031/225-2424, ext. 6593.

As an Old Town complement to the New Town Georgian House (see below), the National Trust for Scotland has a 1620 tenement in the Royal Mile. **Gladstone's Land,** 477b Lawnmarket (tel. 031/226-5856), is a four-story building with two floors furnished as they might have been in the 17th century. On the ground floor, reconstructed shop booths display replicas of goods of the period. On the third floor is the Gladstone's Land Gallery, and on the fourth floor there's a textile workshop. It is open from 10 a.m. to 5 p.m. (last entry at 4:30 p.m.) daily from April to the end of October. In November hours are 10 a.m. to 4:30 p.m. on Saturday and 2 to 4:30 p.m. on Sunday. Admission is £1.30 ($2.30) for adults, 65p ($1.15) for children.

Museum of Childhood, 42 High St. (tel. 031/225-2424), stands just opposite John Knox's House on the Royal Mile. It was the first museum in the world to be devoted solely to the history of childhood. Five galleries contain nearly every facet of the world of children, ranging from antique toys and games to exhibits on health, education, costumes, and many other items representing the childhood experience of members of different nationalities and periods. Because of the youthful clientele it naturally attracts, visitors are warned that it has been described as "the noisiest museum in the world." It is open daily from 10 a.m. to 6 p.m. June to September, to 5 p.m. the rest of the year, and from 2 to 5 p.m. on Sunday during the Edinburgh Festival. Admission is free.

Across the street at 45 High St. is **John Knox's House** (tel. 031/556-6961), whose history goes back to the late 15th century. Even if you're not interested in the reformer who founded the Scottish Presbyterian church, you may want to visit his house, as it is characteristic of the "lands" that used to flank the Royal Mile. All of them are gone now, except Knox's house, with its timbered gallery. Inside, you'll see the tempera ceiling in the Oak Room, along with exhibitions of Knox memorabilia. The house may be visited Monday to Saturday from 10 a.m. to 5 p.m., to 6 p.m. from June to October. Admission is £1 ($1.75) for adults, 70p ($1.25) for children. The price includes a 12-minute video film on the life of Knox.

After leaving John Knox's House, continue along Canongate in the direction of the Palace of Holyroodhouse. At 163 Canongate stands one of the handsomest buildings along the Royal Mile. The **Canongate Tolbooth** was constructed in 1591 and was once the courthouse, prison, and center of municipal affairs for the burgh of Canongate. It houses the People's Story, a museum of the life and work of Edinburgh's inhabitants. Starting with Trade Incorporations and Friendly Societies, it looks at how people organized themselves at work and in political and social campaigns, as well as at housing, health, and welfare, and at how people spent their leisure time—sports, movies, dancing, the pub, and the tea room.

Across the street at 142 Canongate is **Huntly House** (tel. 031/225-2424, ext. 6689), an example of a restored 16th-century mansion. It is now Edinburgh's principal museum of local history. You can stroll through period rooms and reconstructions Monday to Saturday from 10 a.m. to 5 p.m., until 6 p.m. from June to September. During the festival it is also open on Sunday from 2 to 5 p.m.

The Palace of Holyroodhouse

At the eastern end of the Royal Mile, the palace (tel. 031/556-7371) was built adjacent to an Augustinian abbey, established by David I in the 12th century. The nave, now in ruins, remains today. James IV founded the palace nearby in the early part of the 16th century, but of his palace only the north tower is left. Much of what you see today was ordered built by Charles II.

In the old wing occurred the most epic moments in the history of Holyroodhouse, when Mary Queen of Scots was in residence. Mary, who had been Queen of France and widowed while still a teenager, decided to return to her native Scotland. She eventually entered into an unsuccessful marriage with Lord Darnley, but spent more time and settled affairs of state with her secretary, David Rizzio. Darnley plotted to kill the Italian, and he and his accomplices marched into Mary's supper room, grabbed Rizzio over her protests, then carried him to the Audience Chamber, where he was murdered with 56 stab wounds. A plaque marks the spot of his death on March 9, 1566.

Darnley himself was to live less than a year after, dying mysteriously in a gunpowder explosion. Mary, of course, was eventually executed on the order of her cousin, Elizabeth I. One of the most curious exhibits in Holyroodhouse is a piece of needlework by Mary, depicting a cat-and-mouse scene (Elizabeth's the cat).

The State Apartments also contain some fine 17th-century Flemish tapestries, especially a whole series devoted to Diana, as well as some Gobelins. In the Great Gallery are 89 portraits, depicting Scottish kings, including Macbeth, painted by a Dutchman, De Wet. (They either all looked surprisingly similar in the face, or else De Wet used the same model for the lot of them.) Three of the state rooms, which were built as the private suite of Charles II, have been furnished with 17th-century furniture, much of which is original to the palace, including a magnificent state bed and more tapestries.

The palace suffered long periods of neglect, although it basked in glory at the ball in the mid-18th century thrown by Bonnie Prince Charlie. The present Queen and Prince Philip live at Holyroodhouse whenever they visit Edinburgh. When they're not in residence, you can visit the palace, usually all year except for two weeks at the end of May and three weeks from the middle of June. Hours are daily from 9:30 a.m. to 5:15 p.m. (on Sunday from 10:30 a.m. to 4:30 p.m.). In the off-season, the palace is closed at 3:45 p.m. and on Sunday. Adults pay £1.80 ($3.15) to enter, but when the State Apartments are closed, the cost is £1 ($1.75) for the Historical Rooms tour.

The New Town

At some point, the Old Town became too small. The burghers decided to build a whole new town across the valley, where the marsh was drained and eventually turned into public gardens. Princes Street is the most striking boulevard. Architecturally, the most interesting district of the New Town is the north side of Charlotte Square, designed by Robert Adam. The young architect James Craig shaped much of the Georgian style of the New Town, with its crescents and squares.

At no. 7 Charlotte Square, a part of the northern façade, is the restored building known simply as the **Georgian House** (tel. 031/225-2160). It is a prime example of Scottish architecture and interior design in the zenith of the New Town. Originally the home of John Lamont, 18th chief of the Clan Lamont, the house is under the auspices of the National Trust for Scotland. The furniture in this Robert Adam house is mainly Hepplewhite, Chippendale, and Sheraton, all dating from the 18th century. In a ground-floor bedroom is a sturdy old four-poster with an original 18th-century canopy. The dining room table is set for a dinner on fine Wedgwood china, and the kitchen is stocked with gleaming copper pots and pans. The house is open from 10 a.m. to 4 p.m. Monday to Saturday and from 2 to 4 p.m. Sunday from April to October. Admission is £1.70 ($3) for adults, 85p ($1.50) for children.

The Gothic-inspired **Scott Monument** lies in the **East Princes Street Gardens.** It is the most famous landmark of Edinburgh, completed in the mid-19th century. Sir Walter Scott's heroes are honored by small figures in the monument. You can climb the tower Monday to Saturday from May to October from 9 a.m. to 6 p.m. for 50p (90¢). Off-season, you must scale the monument before 3 p.m. Closed Sunday. At **West Princes Street Gardens** is the first-ever **Floral Clock,** which was constructed in 1904.

Art Treasures

For the art lover, Edinburgh has a number of masterpieces, and many visitors come here just to look at the galleries. Of course, the principal museum is the **National Gallery of Scotland,** on The Mound (tel. 031/556-8921), in the center of Princes Street Gardens. Although the gallery is small as national galleries go, the collection came about with great care and was expanded considerably by bequests and loans. A few paintings are of exceptional merit. I'll highlight a representative sampling.

Italian paintings include Verrocchio's *Madonna and Child,* Andrea del Sarto's *Portrait of a Man,* and Domenichino's *Adoration of the Shepherds.* However, perhaps the most acclaimed among them is Tiepolo's *Finding of Moses.* A spectacular sculpture acquisition is Bernini's posthumous bust of *Monsignor Carlo Antonio Pozzo,* archbishop of Pisa.

The Spanish masters are less well represented but shine forth in El Greco's *Saviour,* Velázquez's *Old Woman Cooking Eggs,* an early work by that great master, and *Immaculate Conception* by Zurbarán, his friend and contemporary.

The Flemish School emerges notably in Rubens's *Feast of Herod* and the Dutch in Rembrandt's *Woman in Bed,* superb landscapes by Cuyp, Ruisdael, and Hobbema, and in one of the gallery's more recent acquisitions, *Interior of St. Bavo's Church, Haarlem,* by Pieter Saenredam, his largest and arguably finest painting, bought in 1982. Hans Holbein the Younger's *Allegory of the Old and New Testaments* has added a new dimension to the representation of early northern painting in the gallery.

Among the paintings on loan to the gallery since World War II, from the Duke of Sutherland, are two Raphaels: *The Holy Family with a Palm Tree* and *The Bridge-water Madonna.* Titian gives us his favorite subject, Venus, this time rising from the sea, but he's even more masterly in his Diana canvases. A rare feature of the gallery: the *Seven Sacraments* paintings by Poussin, the 17th-century French painter, also on loan.

The most valuable gift to the gallery since its founding, the Maitland Collection, includes Cézanne's *Mont St. Victoire,* as well as works by Degas, Van Gogh, Renoir, Gauguin, and Seurat, among others. Gauguin's *Vision of the Sermon,* a key work in the development of modern painting, is one of the gallery's masterpieces and a recent acquisition is an early Monet, *Shipping Scene — Night Effects.* Cézanne's *Big Trees* is one of the most notable acquisitions in recent years.

The great English painters are represented by excellent examples— Gainsborough's *The Hon. Mrs. Graham,* Constable's *Dedham Vale,* along with works by Turner, Reynolds, and Hogarth. The building houses the national collection of the Scottish school, including many Ramsays, Raeburns, and Wilkies, none finer than Henry Raeburn, at his best in the whimsical *The Rev. Robert Walker Skating on Duddingston Loch.*

The Department of Prints and Drawings contains examples of many of Europe's greatest masters and draws its changing exhibition programs from the permanent collections.

The gallery is open from 10 a.m. to 5 p.m. daily and 2 to 5 p.m. on Sunday. During the festival, hours are 10 a.m. to 6 p.m. daily and 11 a.m. to 6 p.m. on Sunday. Admission is free. This gallery is one of the three national galleries of Scotland.

Scotland's national collection of 20th-century art is at the **Scottish National Gallery of Modern Art,** Belford Road (tel. 031/556-8921). In 1984 it moved from its temporary home in the Royal Botanic Garden into a former school building completed in 1828, which has been converted into an art gallery. It is set in 12 acres of grounds just 15 minutes' walk from the west end of Princes Street. The collection is truly international in scope and quality despite its modest size. Major sculptures sited outside the building include pieces by Henry Moore, Hepworth, and Epstein. Inside, the collection ranges from a fauve Derain and cubist Braque and Picasso to recent works by Richard Long and Chia. There is naturally a strong representation of English and Scottish art. Highlights of the collection include works by Matisse, Miró, Magritte, Léger, Jawlensky, Kirchner, Kokoschka, Dix, Ernst, Ben Nicholson, Nevelson, Pollock, Beuys, Balthus, Hanson, De Andrea, Lichtenstein, Kitaj, and Hockney. Prints and drawings can be studied in the Print Room by appointment only.

The licensed café sells coffee and nonalcoholic drinks as well as light refreshments and salads. Gallery hours are 10 a.m. to 5 p.m. on daily, 2 to 5 p.m. on Sunday. These hours are extended during the Edinburgh Festival. The only bus that actually passes the gallery is the infrequent no. 13. However, nos. 18, 20, and 41 pass along Queensferry Road, leaving only a five-minute walk up Queensferry Terrace and Belford Road to the gallery. Admission is free.

Housed in a red stone Victorian Gothic building by Rowand Anderson, the **Scottish National Portrait Gallery,** 1 Queen St. (tel. 031/556-8921), at the east end of Queen Street, gives you a chance to see what the famous people of Scottish history looked like. The portraits, several by Gainsborough and Reynolds, include everybody from Mary Queen of Scots to James VI and I, from Sir Walter Scott to Rabbie Burns, from Flora Macdonald to Ramsay MacDonald. Charging no admission, the gallery is open from 10 a.m. to 5 p.m. daily and from 2 to 5 p.m. on Sunday.

Royal Museum of Scotland

Two long-established museums were combined in 1985 to form a union with one administration (tel. 031/225-7534), international collections in the arts and sciences, and a treasure trove of Scottish material. Displays range through the decorative arts, ethnography, natural history, geology, archeology, technology, and science. They were formerly the Royal Scottish Museum and the National Museum of Antiquities. The Chambers Street building at the city center near the Royal Mile, begun in 1861 and one of the finest examples of Victorian architecture in Edinburgh, houses the international collections in the arts and sciences. The Findlay Building, on Queen Street, at the east end of the city center, opened in 1890, contains collections of Scottish memorabilia from prehistoric times to the present. The collections were initiated more than 200 years ago by the Society of Antiquaries.

Hours for the two buildings of the Royal Museum are 10 a.m. to 5 p.m. Monday to Saturday and 2 to 5 p.m. on Sunday. Admission to both is free, except for some special temporary exhibitions. To reach the Chambers Street branch, centrally situated about a ten-minute walk southward from Waverley Station, one of some 23 Lothian Region buses can be used. The Queen Street branch is also about a ten-minute walk from Waverley Station, this time to the north and about five minutes from the bus station. You can take one of 11 Lothian Region buses to reach it.

Scotch Whisky Heritage Centre

At 358 Castlehill, Royal Mile (tel. 031/220-0441), this center is privately funded by a conglomeration of Scotland's biggest whisky distillers. It occupies spacious quarters and highlights the economic effect of whisky on both Scotland and the world. It also illuminates the centuries-old traditions associated with whisky making and showcases the exact science and art form of distilling. A seven-minute movie is also shown. An electric train ride moves past 13 theatrical sets showing historic moments in the whisky industry. From June to September it is open daily from 9 a.m. to 6:30 p.m. The rest of the year it is open daily from 10 a.m. to 5 p.m. Admission is £2.50 ($4.40) for adults and £1.25 ($2.20) for children. No whisky is available for tasting but for a supplemental £6.50 ($11.40) you can experience a whisky tasting where four different malts are offered.

Lauriston Castle

This fine country mansion standing in extensive grounds overlooking the Firth of Forth lies on the outskirts of Edinburgh about 3¼ miles northwest of Princes Street. If going by car, take the Queensferry Road (A90), as if heading for the Forth Road Bridge, but turn off to the right at the Quality Street junction (look for directional signs pointing to Lauriston Castle). Then proceed down Cramond Road South until you come to the entrance on the right to the castle. If using public transport, take the Lothian Region bus no. 41 from the Mound, Hanover Street, or George Street.

The house is associated with John Law (1671-1729), the founder of the first bank in France, and its collections are strong in English Georgian and French Louis styles of furniture. The house gives one a good picture of the leisured lifestyle of the wealthy middle class prior to World War I. Look for the Derbyshire Blue John ornaments and the Crossley wool "mosaics." The house is open from 11 a.m. to 1 p.m. and 2 to 5 p.m. daily except Friday from April to October. From October to March, it is open on Saturday and Sunday only, from 2 to 4 p.m. Visits are by guided tour only, each tour lasting approximately 40 minutes and the last one beginning 40 minutes before closing time. Admission is £1 ($1.75) for adults, 50p (90¢) for children. For more information, telephone 031/336-2060.

THE FESTIVAL

The highlight of Edinburgh's year—some would say the only time when the real Edinburgh emerges—comes in the last three weeks of August during the **Edinburgh International Festival.** Since 1947 the festival has brought to Edinburgh artists and companies of the highest international standard in all fields of the arts, including music, opera, dance, theater, exhibition, poetry, and prose, and "Auld Reekie" takes on a cosmopolitan air.

During the period of the festival, one of the most exciting spectacles is the **Military Tattoo** on the floodlit esplanade in front of Edinburgh Castle, high on its rock above the city. Vast audiences thrill to the delicate maneuvers of the famous Scottish regiments, the precision marching of military units from all parts of the world, and of course the stirring skirl of the bagpipes and the swirl of the kilt.

Less predictable in quality but infinitely greater in quantity is the **Edinburgh Festival Fringe,** an opportunity for anybody—whether an individual, a group of friends, or a whole company of performers—to put on their own show wherever they can find an empty stage or street corner. Late-night reviews, outrageous and irreverent contemporary drama, university theater presentations, maybe even a full-length opera—Edinburgh gives them all free rein. As if that were not enough, Edinburgh has a **Film Festival,** a **Jazz Festival,** a **Television Festival,** and a **Book Festival** (every second year) at the same time.

Ticket prices vary from £1 ($1.75) up to about £16 ($28) a seat, but if you move fast enough, there are not many events that you cannot see for £2 ($3.50).

Information can be obtained at the following places: **Edinburgh Festival Society,** 21 Market St., Edinburgh EH1 1BW (tel. 031/226-4001); **Edinburgh Festival Fringe,** 170 High St., Edinburgh EH1 1BW (tel. 031/226-5257); **Edinburgh Military Tattoo,** The Tattoo Office, 22 Market St., Edinburgh EH1 1QB (tel. 031/225-1188); **Edinburgh Film Festival,** Department M, Edinburgh International Film Festival, The Filmhouse, 88 Lothian Rd., Edinburgh EH3 9BX (tel. 031/228-6382); **Edinburgh Jazz Festival,** 116 Canongate, Edinburgh EH8 8DD (tel. 031/557-1642); **Edinburgh Television Festival,** 17 Great Poulteney St., London W1R 3DG (tel. 01/437-5100); and **Edinburgh Book Festival,** 25a South West Thistle Street Lane, Edinburgh EH2 1EW (tel. 031/225-1915); and **Edinburgh Accommodation Bureau,** Tourist Accommodation Service, Waverley Market, Waverley Bridge, Edinburgh EH1 1BP (tel. 031/557-2727).

TOURS

If you want a quick introduction to the principal attractions in and around Edinburgh, then consider one or more of the tours offered by the **Lothian Region Transport,** 14 Queen St. (tel. 031/554-4494). You won't find a cheaper way to hit the highlights, and later you can go back on your own if you want a deeper experience. The coaches leave from Waverley Bridge, near the Scott Monument. The tours start in April and run through late October. A curtailed winter program is also offered. A half-day coach tour (which takes about four hours) leaves daily at 9:30 a.m. and 1:30 p.m. (on Sunday at 1:30 p.m. only), costing £7.50 ($13.15) for adults, £4.35 ($7.60) for children, and visiting the castle, the Palace of Holyroodhouse, and St. Giles' Cathedral. Operating throughout the day are half a dozen shorter tours that show you some of the environs—such as the Sea City and the Hills. There is also a wide selection of journeys that operate away from Edinburgh. These are on a special program called the "Waverley Series," composed of full-day and half-day excursions to destinations throughout Scotland and northern England.

SHOPPING

There are big and beautiful stores along Princes Street, facing the gardens and the castle, but there is just as much opportunity for seeking out souvenirs along the Royal Mile.

Along Princes Street

Next to Waverley Station is **Waverley Market Shopping Centre,** offering something for everyone, all under one roof in the center of Edinburgh, on three levels. A Food Court has tempting snacks, and unique handmade items can be bought in the craft center. The market is open seven days a week, from 9 a.m. to 6 p.m. Monday to Saturday (until 7 p.m. on Thursday) and 11 a.m. to 5 p.m. on Sunday.

Jenners, Princes Street at the corner of South St. David's Street (tel. 031/225-2442). Everyone in Edinburgh has probably been to Jenners at least once. One of the oldest independent stores in the world, Jenners, with its elegant Victorian façade, celebrated its 150th anniversary in 1988. The store is known for its fine selection of quality merchandise and wide range of Scottish foods.

Debenham's, 112 Princes St. (tel. 031/225-1320). This, along with Jenners, competes for the honor of the best department store in Edinburgh. Its modernized Victorian shell stocks a wide array of Scottish and international merchandise behind a marble-covered front.

Tartan Gift Shops, 96 Princes St. (tel. 031/225-5551). If you've ever suspected that you might be Scottish, this establishment will show you a chart indicating the place of origin within this country of your family name. You'll then be faced with a bewildering array of hunt and dress tartans for your personal use. The high-quality wool is sold by the yard as well as in the form of kilts for both men and women. There's also a line of lamb's-wool and cashmere sweaters, and all the accessories to round out your perfect image as a Scot. The staff here is helpful. The shop is on two levels of a Princes Street building, in a format that the staff calls "seven steps up, seven steps down."

Laura Ashley, 126 Princes St. (tel. 031/225-1218). Would it be possible to say more about Laura Ashley? In her lifetime, she was credited more than anyone else with bringing homey English chintz back into style, as well as ruffled English blouses and dresses. This particular branch of her worldwide empire specializes in garments ranging from those for babies from birth through children's wear, bridal, and adult fashions in sizes 10 to 16 (United Kingdom sizing). In home furnishings, such as towels, sheets, wallpaper, and linens, you'll find the whole range of Laura Ashley products at the Edinburgh branch at 90 George St. and a Decorator Showroom at 137 George St. (tel. 301/225-1121).

The Millshop, 134c Princes St. (tel. 031/225-2319), one of 25 such shops throughout the United Kingdom, sells knitwear, skirts, giftware, and travel rugs. In addition to regular shop hours Monday to Saturday, the shop also is open from 11 a.m. to 5 p.m. on Sunday.

Romanes and Paterson, 62 Princes St. (tel. 031/225-4966), is part of the Edinburgh Woollen Mill Group and sells only items made in the United Kingdom. Almost everything is pure wool although cotton and courtelle knitwear is also available. There is a range of children's kilts and a variety of sweaters and accessories for men. Cashmere and lambswool sweaters by Pringle are available on the upper sales floor together with sheepskin and leather jackets. The store is open regular hours Monday to Saturday and from 12:30 to 5 p.m. Sunday. The company's largest outlet is at the address given above, and other shops in Edinburgh are at 139 Princes St. and 454/455 Lawnmarket.

Along the Royal Mile

Scottish Craft Centre, Acheson House, 140 Canongate (tel. 031/556-8136), was founded as a charity some 40 years ago to encourage the highest standards of Scottish craft work. It has a constantly changing exhibition of contemporary Scottish crafts—and everything is for sale. It is open Monday to Saturday from 10 a.m. to 5:30 p.m. At your leisure, you can browse among all sorts of typically Scottish products, including knitwear, pottery, glass, and jewelry. Everything is reasonably priced.

John Morrison, 461 Lawnmarket (tel. 031/225-8149), is a marvelous place at which to shop for a tartan. Orders can be mailed throughout the world if you can't take immediate delivery of your Highland dress. Women can order an authentic hand-tailored kilt or else a semikilt or a kilt skirt. The store also provides evening sashes and stoles to match a skirt. The store specializes in kilts for men, a heavy hand-woven worsted in one's favorite tartan. To go with it, there are doubles and jackets. That's followed up with accessories—a jabot and cuffs along with kilt hose, a tie, and plain green undertrews to answer the eternal question.

The Scottish Shop, 336-340 Lawnmarket (tel. 031/226-4272). Convenient to Edinburgh Castle, this Highland-inspired gift shop lies near the top of the Royal Mile. It sells a wide variety of woolen goods, walking sticks, thistle-shaped wine glasses, jewelry, and many other souvenir items.

The Shetland Connection, 491 Lawnmarket (tel. 031/225-3525). The owner of this shop, Moira-Anne Leask, is viewed as a boon to some of the knitting industries in the Scottish islands. A battalion of crofters knit the traditional Fair Isle and soft mohair sweaters especially for her shop, which sits on the Royal Mile not far from Edinburgh Castle. Many of the designs follow her own directives. These include sweaters, hats, gloves, and scarves, each made of 100% wool. The store is open seven days a week from 10 a.m. to 6 p.m.

Forsyth's of Edinburgh, 183 Canongate (tel. 031/556-6399), has an extensive selection of high-quality woolens at good prices for the value. The staff is helpful and polite, and the shop has clothes and knitwear "of Scottish character for ladies and gentlemen."

Along Victoria Street

Victoria Street is called a terrace in the Old Town. In the shadow of the castle, you can enter it from the Royal Mile, walking down a steep hill until you reach Grassmarket. However, you can catch your breath along the way by dropping in at the following shop.

John Nelson, 22 Victoria St. (tel. 031/225-4413). This art lover's dream carries a well-indexed list of antique prints and maps, including many historical maps of Scotland, the Americas, and the West Indies. In addition, if you're looking for depictions of anything from ivy-covered ruins to antique portrayals of birds and flowers, this is the place. Most of the prints range from 1760 to 1880, while the maps cover the cartographer's skill between 1560 and 1880. Hours are 10 a.m. to noon and 1:30 to 5 p.m. Monday to Friday, from 10 a.m. to 1 p.m. and 2 to 4 p.m. on Saturday.

Other Shopping Suggestions

Jewelry: One of the best jewelry shops in the city is **Robert Anthony,** 108B Rose St. (tel. 031/226-4550). It has a large selection of gold chains and antique and second-hand jewelry. If you're not interested in an expensive purchase, you might buy one of the souvenir nine-karat gold items of Edinburgh, including Highland dancers or Scottish bagpipes.

Brass: For choice items in brass, go to **Top Brass,** 77 Dundas St. (tel. 031/557-4293). Each of the one-of-a-kind items from this well-stocked shop comes from within a 100-mile radius of Edinburgh. Co-owners Nick Carter and Tom O'Donnell scour the Highlands and northern England for the best brassware of the 19th and early 20th centuries, polishing it to a soft luster. The owners offer an array of brass bed frames, fire fenders, light fixtures, chandeliers, and antique hardware. Larger items can be packaged and shipped.

Dolls: For the collector, the **Dolls Hospital,** 35a Dundas St., New Town (tel. 031/556-4295), merits a stop. It presents both original and reproduction dolls in many shapes and sizes and limited edition porcelain teddies with soft bodies.

Brass Rubbing: For beautiful wall hangings and other gifts, you can make your own brass rubbings or buy them ready-made at the **Scottish Stone & Brass Rubbing Centre,** Trinity Apse, Chalmers Close (near the Royal Mile), which is open Monday to Saturday from 10 a.m. to 5 p.m. (to 6 p.m. from June to September).

You can visit the center's collection of replicas molded from ancient Pictish stones, rare Scottish brasses, and medieval church brasses. No experience is needed to make a rubbing—the center will show you how and supply materials. For information, phone 031/556-4364.

Scotland's Clan Tartan Centre

Whether you have a clan to your name or would like to borrow one, the **James Pringle Woollen Mill,** 70-74 Bangor Rd., Leith (tel. 031/553-5161), is the place to find it. The mill produces a large variety of top-quality wool items, including a range of Scottish knitwear such as cashmere sweaters, tartan and tweed ties, travel rugs, tweed hats, tam-o'-shanters—what have you. In addition, the mill has the only Clan Tartan Centre in Scotland, where more than 2,500 sets and trade designs are accessible through their research facilities offered for your use. A free audio-visual presentation shows the history and development of the tartan. The James Pringle Woollen Mill and its Clan Tartan Centre are open from 9 a.m. to 5:30 p.m. Monday to Saturday; April to the end of December also on Sunday from 10 a.m. to 5:30 p.m. You can visit free, as well as taking advantage of free taxi service to the mill from anywhere in Edinburgh (ask at your hotel).

Visit to a Crystal Factory

Lead crystal from Scotland is shipped around the world. The maker is **Edinburgh Crystal,** based at Eastfield, Penicuik (tel. 0968/75128), about ten miles south of Edinburgh, just off the A701 to Peebles, devoted entirely to handmade crystal glassware. Tours of the factory, during which you can watch the glassmakers at work, are available from 9 a.m. to 3:30 p.m. Monday to Friday. Crystal gifts and tableware may be purchased at the large factory shop, open from 9 a.m. to 5 p.m. Monday to Saturday, 11 a.m. to 5 p.m. Sunday. A spacious restaurant, Pentland View, serves traditional "Scottish fayre." The crystal factory dates back to the 1860s. The Peter Anderson Woollen Mill Shop is also on the premises.

PUBS AND NIGHTLIFE

Unless you arrive in Edinburgh at festival time, the old city doesn't have a very exciting nightlife. Many Scots go to bed early. However, after touring during the day, you can still find some amusement.

Folk Music

Forrest Hill Bar, 25 Forrest Rd. (tel. 031/225-1156), is also known as Sandy Bell's. Informal music and singing sessions happen there, and for anyone visiting Edinburgh, it's a good place to start off and get the feel of the folk scene. It's best to go between 9 p.m. and 1 a.m. Music is presented on most nights but definitely on Thursday, Friday, and Saturday.

Folk music is presented in many clubs and pubs in Edinburgh, but these strolling players tend to be somewhat erratic or irregular in appearances. It's best to read notices in pubs such as the Forrest Hill Bar and talk to the tourist office to see where the *ceilidh* will take place the night of your visit.

The Best of the Pubs

Deacon Brodie's Tavern, 435 Lawnmarket (tel. 031/225-4402), established in 1806, is the neighborhood pub along the Royal Mile. It perpetuates the memory of Deacon Brodie, good citizen by day, robber by night. Mr. Brodie, it is believed, was the inspiration for Robert Louis Stevenson's *The Strange Case of Dr. Jekyll and Mr. Hyde.* Brodie ended up on the gallows on October 1, 1788. The tavern and wine cellars contain a cocktail and lounge bar. This traditional pub setting has lots of atmosphere, making it popular with visitors and locals alike. The tavern is open from 11 a.m. to 11 p.m. daily except Sunday. Inexpensive snacks are served from 11 a.m.

to 2:30 p.m., costing from £3 ($5.25), including cottage pie, Scotch eggs, cheese, and the ploughman's special.

Ma Scott's, 202 Rose St. (tel. 031/225-7401), is a corner pub with tufted settles placed back to back. It still has its Victorian water fountains on the bar. After a revamp, the pub, formerly known as Scott's, was named after its hearty empress who once commanded authority over the rugby players drawn to its precincts. In a totally unpretentious atmosphere, right off Princes Street, you can enjoy good drinks, bar snacks, and dinners. Meals cost from £6 ($10.50). In summer, it's always open at noon daily except Sunday, when it's closed. On Monday, Tuesday, and Wednesday it shuts down at 11:30 p.m., on Thursday at midnight, and on Friday and Saturday at 1 a.m. In winter, hours are reduced across the board by about half an hour.

Guildford Arms, W. Register Street (tel. 031/556-1053), dates back to the "mauve era" of the late 1890s. This Victorian-Italianesque corner pub, still harboring its oldtime memories, has one of the most intriguing decors of any pub in Edinburgh—or Scotland, for that matter. Next door to the world-famed Café Royal, it lies near the King James Hotel. It still has seven arched windows with etched glass, plus an ornate ceiling, as well as a central bar and around-the-wall seating. It's large, bustling, and at times can be a bit rough, but it's got plenty of character. Hours are 11 a.m. to 11 p.m. daily, 12:30 to 2:30 p.m. and 6:30 to 11 p.m. on Sunday. Bar lunches, offered only from noon to 2 p.m., cost from £4 ($7).

Black Bull, 12 Grassmarket (tel. 031/225-6636). Because of this establishment's location on a shop-lined street below the Royal Mile, it is often overlooked by visitors. You can take a short cut on foot from Edinburgh Castle by descending a steep flight of stone steps, but most pub crawlers enjoy window shopping along the city streets. The pub is decorated like a scarlet version of a Victorian railway car, with tasseled lampshades, a country Victorian mantelpiece, and an ascending series of platforms leading up to the carved bar. Of course, the head of a black bull is one of the pub's focal points. The place jumps at night to the recorded music of whatever group is hot at the time. During the day, lunches, and good ones at that, cost from £3 ($5.25). These might be accompanied by a glass of vintage port or a tart cider pulled from a tap. The pub is open from 11 a.m. to 11 p.m. daily.

Abbotsford Pub and Restaurant, 3 Rose St. (tel. 031/225-5276). Since both the downstairs pub and the upper-level restaurant are among the most popular establishments of their kind in Edinburgh, no one will mind if you drop in just for a drink. Of course, you might be so entranced by the Victorian ambience that you'll decide to stay for dinner as well. The businesses are in a red sandstone building on one of the most popular nightlife streets of Edinburgh. The paneling of the lower section is full grained and well polished, in keeping with the ornately detailed plaster ceiling and the rectangular bar area in the center of the room. A fire burns in chilly weather. Upstairs, some of the most generous portions in the city are served of the hearty, reasonably priced meals. Waitresses are helpful as they place the dishes on the napery-covered tables. Lunches begin at £5 ($8.75) and might include helpings from a cold table, roast lamb, roast beef, or a mixed grill. Dinners are more elaborate, costing from £10 ($17.50), and including such dishes as roast duck in orange sauce, fried haddock, or haggis with mashed turnips, finished off with a scotch whisky trifle. You'll find this establishment near the rear entrance to Jenners Department Store. The pub and restaurant are open from 11 a.m. to 2:30 p.m. and 5 to 11 p.m.; closed Sunday.

Kenilworth, 152-154 Rose St. (no phone), is an intriguing bar named after the novel by Sir Walter Scott. Originally built as a private home, the structure was sold to a brewery in 1904, lavishly decorated, and turned into a popular pub in the Edwardian style. In 1981 its owners initiated a piece-by-piece renovation of each detail of the elaborately crafted interior. Even the exquisite blue-and-white wall tiles were carefully and accurately reproduced by a ceramics factory in Glasgow. The tiles, coupled with the rows of stained-glass windows, a massive wooden bar, a coal-burning fireplace, and a jukebox, make for an attractive bar. The clientele is likely to include a cross section of representatives of most of the performing arts in Edinburgh. Ales cost from £1.25 ($2.20), and hours are 11 a.m. to 11 p.m. daily.

Theaters

The **Royal Lyceum Theatre,** Grindlay Street (tel. 031/229-9697), has a resident company that enjoys an enviable reputation for its presentations, which may range from Shakespeare to an exciting new Scottish playwright. The theater is in a beautiful Victorian building dating from 1883 that contains a restaurant, three bars, and facilities for the disabled.

King's Theatre, 2 Leven St. (tel. 031/229-1201), is the premier theater of Edinburgh, offering a wide repertoire of classical entertainment, including ballet and opera. West End productions from London are also presented here.

Traverse Theatre, 112 West Bow, Grassmarket (tel. 031/226-2633), is one of the few theaters in Britain funded solely to present new plays by British writers and first translations into English of international works. This is a small theater with a big reputation. A bar and restaurant are open daily except Monday. Theater tickets are £4.50 ($7.90).

Playhouse Theatre, 18-22 Greenside Pl. (tel. 031/557-2590 for the box office), is the biggest entertainment center in the city. Pop concerts featuring top stars of both England and America have been held here. Musical productions are presented, along with visiting ballet and opera companies. Perhaps you'll be fortunate enough to see the Scottish Ballet performing *Swan Lake.*

Music

Usher Hall, Lothian Road (tel. 031/228-1155), is Edinburgh's premier classical, choral, and popular music concert hall. It is the setting for such musical events as Gilbert and Sullivan highlights and soloists from the former D'Oyly Carte Opera Company.

The Queen's Hall, Clerk Street (tel. 031/668-2019), is home to the Scottish Chamber Orchestra and a major venue for the Edinburgh International Festival. It also plays host to a full range of concerts, from classical to rock music, including a Friday night jazz club. A restaurant is open Monday to Saturday from 10 a.m. to 5 p.m. and before concerts, serving vegetarian and meat dishes, home-baked goods, and salads. There is full bar service at lunchtime and on concert nights.

Films

Chances are, language won't be a problem.

The leading cinema houses include **Filmhouse,** located on Lothian Road (tel. 031/228-2688). You can also see films at **Cannon,** also on Lothian Road (tel. 031/229-3030).

Another leading cinema is **Dominion,** Newbattle Terrace (tel. 031/447-2660). If you don't like what's playing at any of the above, try the **Odeon Cinema,** Clerk Street (tel. 031/667-7331).

---

2. Day Trips from Edinburgh

Within easy reach of Edinburgh lie some of the most interesting castles and mansions in Scotland, the most important of which follow.

STIRLING

Almost equidistant from Edinburgh and Glasgow, Stirling is dominated by its impressive castle, perched on a 250-foot basalt rock on the main east-west route across Scotland formed by the River Forth and the River Clyde and the relatively small section of land between them. The ancient town of Stirling, which grew up around the castle, lies in the heart of an area so turbulent in Scottish history that it was called "the cockpit of Scotland," the scene of several battles. One of the most memorable of these was the Battle of Bannockburn in 1314, when Robert I Bruce defeated the army of Edward II of England.

Stirling can easily be reached by car or train from either Glasgow or Edinburgh. From Edinburgh, a bus takes about an hour and a half to travel the distance of 37 miles.

Stirling is the central crossroads of Scotland, giving easy access by rail and road to all its major towns and cities. If you use it as a base, it is also only a short drive to many attractions, including Loch Lomond, the Trossachs, and the Highlands. The town center boasts several shopping facilities, including the Thistle Centre indoor shopping precinct.

The Sights

On the right bank of the Forth, **Stirling Castle,** Upper Castle Hill (tel. 0786/62517), dates from the Middle Ages, when its location on a dividing line between the Lowlands and the Highlands caused it to become known as "the key to the Highlands." There are traces of earlier (7th century) royal habitation of the Stirling area, but it became a firm part of written history when Scots bled wi' Wallace and were led by Bruce during the Wars of Independence (from England) in the 13th and 14th centuries. The castle became an important seat of Kings James IV and James V, both of whom added to the structures, the latter following classic Renaissance style, then relatively unknown in Britain. Here Mary Queen of Scots lived as an infant monarch for the first four years of her life.

After the final defeat of Bonnie Prince Charlie's army, stopped here in 1746, the castle became an army barracks and headquarters of the Argyle and Sutherland Highlanders, one of Britain's most celebrated regiments.

The castle and visitors' audio-visual center is open from 9:30 a.m. to 6 p.m. Monday to Saturday and 10:30 a.m. to 5:30 p.m. on Sunday from April to the end of September; from 9:30 a.m. to 5:30 p.m. Monday to Saturday and 12:30 to 4:20 p.m. on Sunday from October to the end of March. Last tickets are sold 45 minutes before closing times. Admission is £1.50 ($2.65) for adults, 75p ($1.30) for children. A family ticket is available for £3 ($5.25).

Also at the castle, you can visit the **Museum of the Argyll and Sutherland Highlanders** (tel. 0786/75165). It presents an excellent exhibition of colors, pipe banners, and regimental silver, along with medals (some of which go back to the Battle of Waterloo). Admission free, it is open April to September Monday to Saturday from 10 a.m. to 5:30 p.m., on Sunday from 11 a.m. to 5 p.m. October hours are 10 a.m. to 4 p.m. Closed November to April.

The **Church of the Holy Rude** on St. John Street is said to be the only church in Scotland still in use that has witnessed a coronation. The date was 1567 when the 13-month-old James VI was crowned. John Knox preached the sermon. The church itself dates from the early 15th century, and in its day it attracted none other than Mary Queen of Scots. It is open daily from 10 a.m. to 5 p.m. from May to September.

Also of interest are the **Auld Brig** over the Forth, dating from the 14th century, and the palace built by James V in the 16th century.

One of the most interesting excursions is to **Bannockburn,** a name that looms large in Scottish history. It was here that Robert the Bruce, his army of 6,000 outnumbered three to one, defeated the forces of Edward II in 1314. Before nightfall Robert the Bruce had won back the throne of Scotland. The battlefield lies off the M80, two miles south of Stirling.

At the **Bannockburn Heritage Centre** (tel. 0786/812664), an audio-visual presentation tells the story of these events. The Queen herself came here in 1964 to unveil an equestrian statue of the Scottish hero. An exhibition, "The Kingdom of the Scots," traces the history of Scotland from the earliest times to the Union of Crowns. The site is open all year, but the Heritage Centre and shop is open only from March 24 to October 29 daily from 10 a.m. to 6 p.m. The last audio-visual showing is at 5:30 p.m. Food is served in the restaurant from 10 a.m. to 5 p.m. Admission is £1 ($1.75) for adults, 50p (90¢) for children. At the Borestone, where Robert the Bruce commanded his forces, you can see Stirling Castle and the Forth Valley.

Food and Lodging

Park Lodge Hotel, 32 Park Terrace, Stirling, Stirlingshire FK8 2JS (tel. 0786/74862). Set across the street from a city park, within a residential neighborhood uphill from the center of town, this hotel is contained in a 19th-century Italianate mansion. Built of stone blocks and slates, it has a Doric portico, a Georgian-era core dating from 1825, and century-old climbing roses and wisteria, along with Tudor-style chimney pots. Frankly, the hotel qualifies as the most stylish in town. Anne and Georges Marquetty house guests in one of their nine upstairs bedrooms, and later suggest they dine at one of the elegant tables of their restaurant (see below). Each bedroom contains color TV, phone, and an array of antique furnishings (Room 6 has a four-poster bed). Singles cost from £45 ($78.75) daily, and doubles or twins begin at £60 ($105), with breakfast included. You might enjoy tea in a walled garden behind the hotel, with its pampered lawn, widely spaced iron benches, and terracotta statues. Just on the other side of tall casement windows, a pair of French-inspired salons reek of such expensive luxuries as marble fireplaces, elaborate draperies, and cabriole-legged armchairs.

The Heritage, 16 Allan Park, Stirling, Stirlingshire FK8 2QG (tel. 0786/73660). Its culinary sophistication and its beautiful decor rank it as one of the most sought-after restaurants in the entire district (it also rents rooms). Near the center of town, the location is on a quiet residential street. You enter a gentleman's parlor, richly outfitted with somber walls and enviable antiques, for a drink before descending to the low-ceilinged basement restaurant. Amid a French-inspired decor, you'll taste some of the best cuisine in town, prepared with finesse by Georges Marquetty. In his youth he worked as an executive chef in Paris, and later he spent 12 years in Cincinnati with his British wife, Anne (there he was voted one of the leading chefs of America).

At his Scottish place, full meals cost from £17 ($29.75) and are served daily (except Sunday lunch) from noon to 2 p.m. and 6 to 9:30 p.m. Specialties include Parisian crayfish, foie gras with truffles, veal scallop with Parma ham and cheese, and rack of lamb. Reservations are important. Upstairs, a quartet of handsomely furnished bedrooms rent for £39 ($68.25) in a single, £50 ($87.50) in a double or twin, with breakfast included.

DUNBLANE

A small cathedral city on the banks of the Allan Water, Dunblane lies about seven miles north of Stirling, on the road to Perth. It takes its name from the Celtic Church of St. Blane, which once stood on the site now occupied by the cathedral.

Sports enthusiasts are attracted to the area because of its golfing, fishing, and hunting possibilities.

The Sights

An excellent example of 13th-century Gothic ecclesiastical architecture, **Dunblane Cathedral** was spared the ravages of attackers who destroyed other Scottish worship centers. Altered in the 15th century and restored several times in the 19th and 20th centuries, the cathedral may have suffered the most from neglect subsequent to the Reformation. A Jesse Tree window is in the west end of the building, and of interest are stalls, misericords, a pulpit with carved figures of early ecclesiastical figures, and other striking features, including the wooden, barrel-vaulted roof with colorful armorials. A Celtic stone from about A.D. 900 can be seen in the north aisle.

Bishop Robert Leighton, an outstanding leader of the 17th century who did much to resolve religious bickerings, is represented by his personal library in a 1687 structure on the grounds of the old manse. It is of interest because of the bishop's material on the 17th century and the effects of the troubled times on Scotland. The **Cathedral Museum** is in the Dean's House and contains articles and papers pertaining to both the cathedral and the town. Admission-free, it is open June to September, Monday to Saturday from 10:30 a.m. to 12:30 p.m. and 2:30 to 4:30 p.m. The story of Dunblane and its ancient cathedral is displayed here in this 1624 house, and you can also visit an enclosed garden with a restored old well.

Food and Lodging

Cromlix House, Kinbuck, Dunblane, Perthshire FK15 9JT (tel. 0786/822125), is a fine country-house hotel four miles north of Dunblane, just beyond the village of Kinbuck. The manor, built in 1880, is set in a 5,000-acre estate that has belonged to the Eden family for more than 400 years. The hotel, which opened in 1982, is on the B8033 road, just off the A9, about 20 minutes from Gleneagles, which has made it popular with golfers seeking a secluded hideaway. Guests can walk through the forests and farmland surrounding the hotel, and tennis is available, as well as fishing on three private lakes and hunting. The manor has an elegant drawing room with big bow windows and a lounge where family photos are displayed. Antiques are among the furnishings of the public rooms and the bedrooms. Bouquets of fresh flowers and open fires in cool weather add to the comfort of the place. The 14 bedrooms (8 with sitting rooms) are carpeted and have complete and spacious bathrooms, color TVs, and radios. Singles cost from £75 ($131.25) to £110 ($192.50) daily; and doubles from £110 ($192.50) to £175 ($306.25). All rates include a full Scottish breakfast, VAT, and service. In addition to a second-floor library, guests are invited to visit the chapel and the gun room.

Eating by candlelight in the dining room, which has an open fireplace, is a culinary experience. No formal menus are presented, and guests are served as they would be in a family home. The freshest local ingredients are used. Your meal might include Scottish beef or lamb, game from the estate, or locally caught salmon. Traditional country-house recipes are used skillfully by the chef, who adds special touches to please the most discerning palates. The food will taste even better accompanied by some of the good wines from the cellar, especially the vintage claret. Expect to pay from £30 ($52.50) for dinner. If you're not a guest at the house, reservations for dinner are necessary. Lunch, costing £7 ($12.25) to £20 ($35), is served by prior arrangement only, and dinner hours are 7 to 9:30 p.m.

DOUNE

Some 41 miles from Edinburgh, this small market town with its 15th-century castle is a good center for exploring the Trossachs. The Rivers Teith and Ardoch flow through Doune.

The Sights

Doune Castle (tel. 0786/50000), on the banks of the River Teith, stands four miles west of Dunblane. Once it was a royal palace. Now owned by the Earl of Moray, it was restored in 1883, making it one of the best preserved of the medieval castles of Scotland. The castle is open from 9:30 a.m. to 7 p.m. Monday to Friday, 2 to 7 p.m. on Saturday and Sunday April to September. In other months opening times are the same, with closing at 4 p.m. Admission is £1 ($1.75) for adults, 50p (90¢) for children.

After visiting the castle, guests can drive 1½ miles to the **Doune Motor Muse-**

um, which charges £1.80 ($3.15) for adults, 90p ($1.60) for children. The motor museum contains about 40 vintage and postvintage motor cars, including the second-oldest Rolls-Royce in the world. It is open daily from April 1 to October 31. In April and May the last admissions are at 4:30 p.m., June to August the hours are 10 a.m. to 5:30 p.m., and in September and October the last admissions are again at 4:30 p.m. For more information, telephone 0786/841203.

South of Doune lies **Blair Drummond Safari and Leisure Park** (tel. 0786/ 841456). You meet the typical cast of animal safari characters here, and the park also offers a jungle cruise, a giant Astroglide, and an amusement arcade, as well as a pets farm and performing sea lions show. Open from mid-March to October, the park can be visited from 10 a.m. daily, with last admission at 4:30 p.m. Adults pay £3.50 ($6.15), children 3 to 14 are charged £2.50 ($4.40), and children under 3 get in free. A safari bus is available for visitors with three-wheeler or soft-top cars, costing £3.80 ($6.65) for adults, £2.80 ($4.90) for children. You can have refreshments at the Jambo Bar or in the Ranch Kitchen (tel. 0786/841430), or use one of the picnic areas. To reach the park, take exit 10 off the M9 onto the A84 near Stirling.

Food and Lodging

The Woodside, Stirling Road, Doune, Perthshire FK16 6AB (tel. 0786/ 841237), is a stone structure standing on the A84 main Stirling–Oban road. In the heart of Perthshire, it was originally a coaching inn and dates back to the 18th century. It contains 14 well-furnished bedrooms with private bath, direct-dial phones, and color TV. Singles cost from £24 ($42) daily, and doubles, from £38 ($66.50), including a full breakfast. The lounge is brightened by red plush seating and is brimful with antiques. The lounge bar has an open fire and offers a selection of more than 100 malt whiskies. You can enjoy a selection of traditional salad dishes on the bar luncheon menu with soused herring and homemade pâté salads. Grilled Aberdeen Angus steaks are also served. The dining room overlooks the garden, and you sit in high-backed carved Edwardian chairs, enjoying such specialties as venison, salmon, and fresh lobster in season. Dinner is likely to run about £10 ($17.50) to £15 ($26.25).

LINLITHGOW

In this royal burgh, a country town in West Lothian, 18 miles west of Edinburgh, Mary Queen of Scots was born. The roofless **Palace of Linlithgow,** site of her birth in 1542, can still be viewed here today, although it is but a shell of its former self. Once a favorite residence of Scottish kings, the palace was built square-shaped. In the center are the remains of a royal fountain erected by James V. The suite occupied by the queen was in the north quarter, but this was rebuilt for the homecoming of James VI (James I of Great Britain) in 1620. The palace was burned in 1746, destroying one of the gems in the Scottish architectural crown. The Great Hall is on the first floor, and a small display shows some of the more interesting relics of architecture. The castle is open from 9:30 a.m. to 7 p.m. Monday to Saturday and 2 to 7 p.m. on Sunday April to September, closing at 4 p.m. in winter. Admission is £1 ($1.75) for adults, 50p (90¢) for children. For information, phone 031/ 2262570.

South of the palace stands the medieval kirk of **St. Michael the Archangel,** considered one of the best examples of a medieval parish church remaining in the country. The golden crown is of late vintage, having taken the place of one from the Middle Ages that fell in 1820. It is open from June to September daily from 10 a.m. to noon and 2 to 4 p.m., charging no admission. Off-season hours are the same, but it is open only Monday to Friday. For information, phone 0506/842195.

From Linlithgow, it is but a 3½-mile drive east on the Queensferry road (A904) to the **House of the Binns** (tel. 050683/4255), the historic home of the Dalyells. The mansion, with its fine Jacobean plaster ceilings, portraits, and panoramic vistas, receives visitors on Easter weekend and then from May to the end of September from 2 to 5:30 p.m. daily except Friday. The parkland is open from 10 a.m. to 7 p.m. Admission is £2 ($3.50) for adults, £1 ($1.75) for children.

Where to Dine

Champany, on the A904, two miles northeast of Linlithgow (tel. 050683/ 4532), was once a farmhouse built of stone, but it has been converted into one of the finest places for dining in Scotland. The dining room is circular, with a steep hexagonal ceiling. Victorian mahogany furniture adds a sedate touch. They specialize in grills, and you'll find the best steaks in Britain here. The owner, Clive Davidson, a South African (his wife, Anne, was born in Dundee), once had a butcher shop, and he is an expert on beef, usually the Scots blue-gray, his favorite being the "pope's eye." He insists that his steaks be 1¼ inches thick, and his meat is hung for at least four weeks, which adds greatly to its flavor. He also prepares spit-roasted Norfolk duck, along with an assortment of oysters, salmon, and lobsters that are kept in a pool on the premises. Even the french fries are freshly prepared. Next door to the main dining room is a chophouse, which has less expensive cuts, attracting the family trade. You can choose your own cut and watch it being grilled. A set lunch goes for £10 ($17.50). Dinner is à la carte, costing around £22 ($38.50) per person for a complete meal. There is also a raw bar. The establishment is open from 12:30 to 2:15 p.m. and 7 to 10 p.m. daily, except that the dining room is closed on Sunday (the chophouse is open).

HOPETOUN HOUSE

This is Scotland's greatest Adam mansion, that fine example of 18th-century architecture. It is the seat of the Marquess of Linlithgow, whose ancestors were once the governor-general of Australia and the viceroy of India. Set in the midst of beautifully landscaped grounds, laid out along the lines of Versailles, the mansion (tel. 031/331-2451) lies near the Forth Road Bridge at South Queensferry, off the A904, ten miles from Edinburgh. You can wander through splendid reception rooms filled with 18th-century tapestries, unique Cullen furniture, paintings, statuary, and other works of art. From a rooftop viewing platform, you look out over a panoramic view of the Firth of Forth. Even more enjoyable, perhaps, is to take the Nature Trail, explore the Deer Parks, investigate the Stables' Museum, or stroll through the formal gardens, all on the grounds. In the Ballroom Suite is a licensed restaurant that serves coffee, light refreshments, afternoon tea, and high tea. Hopetoun is open on Easter weekend, then daily May to the end of September from 11 a.m. to 5:30 p.m. Admission to the house and grounds is £2.50 ($4.40) for adults, £1 ($1.75) for children.

NORTH BERWICK

This royal burgh, created in the 14th century, was once an important Scottish port. In East Lothian, 24 miles east from Edinburgh, it is today a holiday resort popular with the Scots and an increasing number of foreigners. Visitors are drawn to its golf courses, beach sands, and harbor life on the Firth of Forth. You can climb the rocky shoreline or enjoy the heated outdoor swimming pool in July and August.

At the **Information Centre,** Quality Street (tel. 0620/2197), you can pick up data on how to take boat trips to the offshore islands, including **Bass Rock,** a breeding ground inhabited by about 10,000 gannets and one or two crusty lighthouse keepers. The volcanic island is one mile in circumference. It's possible to see the rock from the harbor. The viewing is even better at **Berwick Law,** a volcanic lookout point surmounted by the jawbones of a whale.

Some two miles east of the resort on the A198 stand the ruins of the 14th-century diked and rose-colored **Tantallon Castle,** rising on cliffs. This was the ancient stronghold of the Douglases from the time of its construction in the 14th century until its defeat by Cromwell's forces in 1651. Overlooking the Firth of Forth, the castle ruins are still formidable, with a square, five-story central tower and a dovecote, plus the shell of its east tower, a D-shaped structure with a wall from the central tower. Tantallon Castle can be visited daily from 9:30 a.m. to 7 p.m. and on Sunday from 2 to 7 p.m. from late March to the end of September, with closing at 4 p.m. from October to the end of March. It is also closed on Wednesday and Thursday morning. Admission is £1 ($1.75) for adults, 50p (90¢) for children.

Food and Lodging

The premier hotel is **The Marine,** Cromwell Road, North Berwick, East Lothian EH39 4LZ (tel. 0620/2406). Steep roofed and rambling, it is composed of gray stone blocks and ringed with a wall and rows of trees. Golfers appreciate the view over the West Links Course, some of whose putting greens come close to the hotel's massive foundations. Inside, there's the aura of an Edwardian country house, with well-ordered rows of chintz-covered sofas and large bay windows turned toward panoramas of sand and sea. On the premises is a bar lined with antique golfing photos. Good Scottish cooking along with international dishes are a feature of the restaurant. Other facilities include two tennis courts, a solarium, and a sauna. Each of the 83 well-furnished bedrooms contains a private bath, color TV, radio, and phone. Singles rent for £54 ($94.50) to £64 ($112) daily and doubles or twins for £69 ($120.75) to £79 ($138.25).

GULLANE

Lying 19 miles from Edinburgh in East Lothian, Gullane, with a population of around 2,000 people, is really a pocket of posh. Not only does it have one of the great country hotels of Scotland (see below), but it also is home to a small restaurant (also see below) that some food critics have suggested is "the best in Scotland."

Food and Lodging

About five miles from North Berwick, an excellent place to stay is **Greywalls Hotel,** Muirfield, Duncur Road, Gullane, East Lothian EH31 2EG (tel. 0620/842144). An Edwardian country house, designed as a private home by the renowned architect of his day, Sir Edwin Lutyens, it was visited from time to time by King Edward VII, who admired the views across the Firth of Forth and south to the Lammermuir Hills. The gardens of the house were laid out by Gertrude Jekyll, who often worked with architect Lutyens in supplying a complete Edwardian home package. Today Greywalls is the property of Giles and Ros Weaver. They have combined the atmosphere of a home with the amenities of a delightful country-house hotel. In the paneled library, guests relax on comfortable sofas before a blazing log fire (in cool weather). The garden room, another of the hotel's four lounge areas, is done in bamboo furnishings. There is also a small bar. The 23 bedrooms, all with private bath, vary in size: some smaller ones are simply decorated and others, more spacious, are furnished with period pieces. Singles cost from £50 ($87.50) to £54.50 ($95.40) daily, and doubles, from £85 ($148.75) to £105 ($183.75), including a full Scottish breakfast. The hotel has a hard tennis court and a croquet lawn, with ten golf courses within five miles.

The food served in the elegant dining room reflects culinary expertise. Light French-style dishes are made almost as appealing to the eye as to the palate. Specialties include fresh seafood. Other tasty main courses might be venison, breast of pheasant, smoked duck, or local beef. Meals cost £14 ($24.50) to £25 ($43.75). Men are required to wear jackets and ties in the dining room, which is open daily from 12:30 to 2 p.m. and 7:30 to 9:30 p.m. Greywalls is open from April to the end of October.

La Potinière, Main Street, Gullane (tel. 0620/843214), is a small and pretty restaurant beautifully run by David and Hilary Brown. The excellent food produced by Hilary, using so far as possible local ingredients, is complemented by a fine choice of wines from the cellar supervised by David. A fixed-price luncheon of four set courses is served every day at 1 p.m. except Wednesday and Saturday, costing £11.50 ($20.15) Monday to Saturday, £12.75 ($22.30) Sunday. The first course is usually a light and subtly flavored soup, followed by a fish dish, perhaps a mousseline, or by one of Hilary's creations, such as chestnut purée and hollandaise over a pear. The main course can range from steak to turkey to lamb, but all done with flair and providing a taste treat. Cheese and dessert wind up the meal. On Saturday only a special dinner is served, starting at 8 p.m. and costing £17.50 ($30.65). Reservations for this five-course gourmet's delight are made well in advance. No smoking is permitted in the dining room. The restaurant is closed for a week sometime in June and all of October.

DIRLETON

Another popular excursion from Edinburgh is to this little town that vies for the title of "prettiest village in Scotland." The town plan, drafted in the early 16th century, is essentially unchanged today. Dirleton has two greens shaped like triangles, with a pub opposite Dirleton Castle, placed at right angles to a group of cottages. Dirleton is a preservation village and is subject to careful control on any development. It's on the Edinburgh–North Berwick road (the A198).

A rose-tinted 13th-century castle with surrounding gardens, **Dirleton Castle,** started in the 13th century by the wealthy Anglo-Norman de Vaux family, looks like a fairytale fortification with its towers, arched entries, and an oak ramp similar to the drawbridge that once protected it. The castle was built with prison, bakehouse, and storehouses carved from the bedrock. Ruins of the Great Hall and kitchen can be seen, as well as what's left of the lord's chamber where the de Vaux family lived. You can see the windows and window seats, a wall with a toilet and drains, and other household features. The 16th-century main gate has a hole through which boiling tar or water could be poured to discourage unwanted visitors.

The castle's **country garden** and a bowling green are still in use, with masses of flowering plants rioting in the gardens and bowlers sometimes seen on the green. A 17th-century dovecote with 1,100 nests stands at the east end of the garden. A small gate at the west end leads onto one of the village greens.

The castle can be visited from April to September, daily from 9:30 a.m. to 7 p.m. and on Sunday from 2 to 7 p.m.; October to March, daily from 9:30 a.m. to 4 p.m. and on Sunday from 2 to 4 p.m. Admission to the castle and gardens is £1 ($1.75) for adults and 50p (90¢) for children.

Food and Lodging

The Open Arms, Dirleton, East Lothian EH39 5BG (tel. 062085/241), will receive you in keeping with the promise of its name. This old stone hostelry has been transformed into a handsome restaurant, serving the finest food in the area. It lies off the A198, 2½ miles southwest of North Berwick. Overlooking the castle ruins, the hotel is owned by Arthur Neil, who has built up an enormous local reputation for serving Scottish dishes. Try, for example, cranachan (served with shortbread, this is a concoction of oatmeal, heavy cream, and brambles). Cold Scottish salmon is served encased in pastry, and is one of the inn's specialties. Another specialty of 40 years' standing is a stew made of fresh mussels and onions. On one recent occasion, the luncheon menu featured a first for me—smoked mackerel with gooseberry-cream sauce. Before having, say, a venison casserole in red wine sauce, you might begin with a real "Taste of Scotland" specialty, lentil broth with oatmeal, about which, the Scots say, you can "stand up your spoon in it." The people who serve are informed and skillful. On the light-luncheon menu, people can eat for £6 ($10.50). A table d'hôte luncheon on Sunday costs £10 ($17.50). Hours are 12:30 to 2:15 p.m. In the evening, between 7 and 10 p.m. an à la carte dinner is offered for £20 ($35) and up.

The Open Arms will also receive you as an overnight guest. However, it's small, only seven bedrooms, each with private bath, and, joy of joys, room service available at no extra cost. A room rented for single occupancy costs £55 ($96.25) to £60 ($105) daily, £80 ($140) to £90 ($157.50) for two persons, including a full breakfast, service, and VAT. Log fires crackle and blaze, and it must surely be a golfer's paradise, as it's surrounded by eight courses.

DALKEITH

This small burgh in Midlothian, seven miles southeast of Edinburgh, is the site of **Dalkeith Palace,** rebuilt and redesigned by Sir John Vanbrugh, circa 1700. Such monarchs as George IV, Victoria, and Edward VII have stayed here during visits to Edinburgh.

Visitors flock here for **Dalkeith Park,** Dalkeith (tel. 031/663-5684), to explore the woodland and riverside walks in and around the extensive grounds of the palace. Luring guests are nature trails and an adventure woodland play area, a tunnel walk, and an Adam bridge. The park is open daily from 11 a.m. to 6 p.m., April 2 to October 31. During November the park is open only on Saturday and Sunday from 11 a.m. to dusk. To reach the park, go seven miles south of Edinburgh on the A68. The price of admission is 50p (90¢). A ranger service offers regular guided walks.

3. The Kingdom of Fife

North of Forth from Edinburgh, the county of Fife still likes to call itself a "kingdom." Its name, even today, suggests the romantic episodes and pageantry during the reign of the early Stuart kings. Within this shire lay 14 of Scotland's 66 royal burghs. Many of the former royal palaces and castles, either restored or in ruins, can be visited today, and I've previewed the most important ones, coming up.

As Edinburgh is so near, the temptation is to set up headquarters in one of the city's many elegant hotels or B&B houses and explore Fife from that base. However, serious golfers may want to stay at one of my recommended hotels in St. Andrews.

DUNFERMLINE

This ancient town was once the capital of Scotland. It is easily reached by the Forth Road Bridge, opened by Queen Elizabeth II in 1964. Dunfermline lies five miles northwest of the Forth Bridge, a distance of 14 miles northwest of Edinburgh.

Dunfermline Abbey (tel. 0383/724586) stands on a site occupied by a Christian house of worship for some time. The Celtic Culdee Church dated back to the 5th and 6th centuries and was rebuilt in 1072. Traces of both buildings are visible beneath gratings in the floor of the old nave. In 1150 the existing church was replaced by a large abbey, the nave of which remains, an example of Norman architecture. Later, St. Margaret's shrine, the northwest baptismal porch, the spire on the northwest tower, and the flying buttresses were added. When Dunfermline was the capital of Scotland, 22 royal persons were interred within the abbey. Except for the sepulchers of Queen Margaret and King Robert the Bruce, no visible memorial or burial places are known. The tomb of Robert the Bruce lies beneath the pulpit. The abbey church is open daily from 9:30 a.m. to 5 p.m. April to September (from 2 to 5 p.m. on Sunday). From October to March it closes at 4 p.m.

The **Royal Palace** witnessed the birth of King Charles I and James I. Only the southwest wall remains of this once-gargantuan edifice. The last king to reside here was Charles II, in 1651.

Andrew Carnegie, the American industrialist and philanthropist, was born here in 1835. The **Andrew Carnegie Birthplace Museum,** Moodie Street (tel. 0383/724302), lies at the corner of Moodie Street and Priory Lane and comprises the 18th-century weaver's cottage in which he was born and a memorial hall provided by his wife. It was completely refurbished in 1984. Displays tell the story of the weaver's son from Dunfermline who emigrated to America to become one of the richest men in the world and one of the most generous private benefactors of his era. Admission is free, and the museum is open Monday to Saturday from April to October from 11 a.m. to 5 p.m., on Sunday from 2 to 5 p.m. From November to March, it is open daily from 2 to 4 p.m.

From the fortune he made in steel, Mr. Carnegie gave away more than $400 million before his death in 1919. Dunfermline, as his birthplace, received the first of the 2,811 free libraries he provided throughout Britain and the United States. It also received public baths and **Pittencrieff Park and Glen,** so rich in history and natural charm. A statue in the park honors the hometown boy who once worked as a bobbin boy in a cotton factory.

Food and Lodging

The best choice, either for a meal or a bed, is the **King Malcolm Thistle Hotel,** Queensferry Road, Dunfermline, Fife KY11 5DS (tel. 0383/72261). Modern, pastel colored, and fairly stylish, this hotel sits on a roundabout one mile south of Dunfermline on the A823. Named after the medieval king of Fife (and later of Scotland), Malcolm Canmore, it was built in 1972 but thoroughly revamped in 1985. Each of its well-furnished bedrooms, 48 in all, contains a private bath, color TV with video, trouser press, hairdryer, and phone. With VAT included, singles range from £45 ($78.75) to £55 ($96.25) daily; doubles or twins, £53 ($92.75) to £65 ($113.75). On the premises is an elegant glass-sided bar and restaurant, an appealing design that looks like a greenhouse. In the basement, accessible via a separate entrance, lie the Canmore Vaults wine bar and pub.

From Dunfermline, you can take an excursion six miles west to—

Culross

This old royal burgh has been renovated by the National Trust for Scotland, and is one of the most beautiful in the country. As you walk its cobbled streets, admiring its whitewashed houses, you'll feel you're taking a stroll back into the 17th century. Many of the cottages have crow-stepped gables and red pantiled roofs.

Set in tranquil walled gardens, **Culross Palace** was built in the village between 1597 and 1611, containing a series of paintings on its wooden walls and ceilings. It has been restored and may be visited, April to September, daily from 9:30 a.m. to 7 p.m. (on Sunday from 2 to 7 p.m.). From October to March it's open daily from 9:30 a.m. to 4 p.m. (on Sunday from 2 to 4 p.m.). Admission is £1 ($1.75) for adults, 50p (90¢) for children.

The other important attraction is **Culross Abbey,** a Cistercian monastery whose founding father was Malcolm, Earl of Fife, in 1217. Parts of the nave are still intact, and the choir serves as the Culross parish church. There is also a central tower. The abbey is open from 10 a.m. to 4 p.m. on Saturday and Sunday only from Easter Saturday to the last Saturday in August. At other times, it can be visited by prior arrangement with The Rev. A. Norman, The Abbey Manse, Culross, Fife.

FALKLAND

Owned by the National Trust of Scotland, **Falkland Palace and Garden** (tel. 3337/57397) was once the hunting palace of the Stuart kings. This royal burgh of cobblestone streets and crooked houses lies at the northern base of the hill of East Lomond, 21 miles north of Edinburgh and 11 miles north of Kirkcaldy on the A912.

Since the 14th century Falkland has been connected with Scottish kings. Originally a castle stood on the site of today's palace, but it was replaced in the 16th century. Falkland then became a favorite seat of the Scottish court. A grief-stricken James V died here. Mary Queen of Scots used to come to Falkland for "hunting and hawking." It was also here that Francis Stuart, fifth Earl of Bothwell, came with his men and tried to seize his cousin, James VI, son of Mary Queen of Scots. Bullet marks may be seen on the front of the towers of the gatehouse (1593). Cromwell's forces occupied Falkland in 1654.

The royal chapel and apartments are open April 1 to September 30 daily from 10 a.m. to 6 p.m., on Sunday from 2 to 6 p.m. (last entry at 5 p.m.) From October 1 to October 31, it's open only on Saturday and Sunday. The gardens have been laid out to the original royal plans. At Falkland is the oldest royal tennis court in the United Kingdom. For a ticket to both the palace and the gardens, adults pay £2.10 ($3.70), and children, £1.05 ($1.85). Adults can be admitted to the gardens only for £1.30 ($2.30); children, for 60p ($1.05).

Food and Lodging

Covenanter Hotel, The Square, Falkland, Fife KY2 7BU (tel. 0337/57224), has been a popular inn since the early 18th century. With modest modernization, it offers a good standard of accommodation. It's built ruggedly of local stone, with high chimneys, wooden shutters, and a Georgian entry. The location is on a small square, opposite the church and palace. You enter a white entry hall with a circular staircase leading to the lounges and bedrooms. The dining room is strictly "old style" and for before-dinner drinks there is an intimate pub, the Covenanter Cocktail Bar. Pub luncheons go for £6 ($10.50) and a set evening meal costs £12.50 ($21.90). B&B in rooms with private baths and TVs cost from £26 ($45.50) daily in a single, £32 ($56) in a double.

THE EAST NEUK

Within a half hour's drive of St. Andrews are some of the most beautiful and unspoiled fishing villages of eastern Scotland:

Anstruther

This is an important port and a summer resort, with the **Scottish Fisheries Museum** (tel. 0333/310628) down by the harbor. Here you can follow the fisherfolk through every aspect of the fishing industry from the days of sail to modern times. Experience the life of the "herring drifters" on board the old *Reaper,* berthed in the harbor, and don't miss the aquarium. The museum is open Monday to Saturday from 10 a.m. to 5:30 p.m. from April to October and from 10 a.m. to 4:30 p.m. November to March. Sunday hours are from 2 to 4:30 p.m. Admission is £1.50 ($2.65) for adults, 75p ($1.30) for children.

Across the harbor, you can visit a floating exhibit in the old *North Carr* Lightship. Entrance is free.

The **Isle of May,** a nature reserve, lies in the Firth of Forth, and is accessible by boat from Anstruther. It is a bird observatory and a field station, and contains the ruins of a chapel from the 12th century as well as an early-19th-century lighthouse.

From the museum, you can walk to the tiny hamlet of Cellardyke, which is really Old Anstruther, with many charming stone houses.

FOOD AND LODGING: Originally a Scottish manse, **Craw's Nest Hotel,** Bankwell Road, Anstruther, Fife KY10 3DS (tel. 0333/310691), was converted into a popular hotel, with beautiful views over the Firth of Forth and May Island. To the original building, many extensions were added under the direction of the owner. Mrs. Edward Clarke, and her son-in-law, Ian Birrel. The black-and-white building is stepgabled, standing behind a high stone wall. The 50 bedrooms are handsomely equipped and well appointed, costing from £25 ($43.75) per person nightly for B&B. Each of the units contains a private bath. Public areas are simply decorated and cozy, including a lounge bar as well as a bustling public bar. The food is good, and the wine is priced reasonably in the hotel's dining room. The hotel is just ten minutes from St. Andrews.

Smuggler's Inn, High Street East, Anstruther, Fife KY10 3DQ (tel. 0333/

310506), stands in the heart of town, a warmly inviting inn that evokes memories of smuggling days around here. The original inn that stood on this spot dates back to 1300. In Queen Anne's day it was a well-known tavern. The ceilings are low, the floors uneven, and of course, the stairways are winding. Overlooking the harbor, rooms are rented daily for £20.50 ($35.90) per person with bath. The half-board rate is £25 ($43.75) to £26 ($45.50) per person. Mr. and Mrs. McSharry offer à la carte dinners for £12 ($21) and bar suppers, both served daily from 7 to 10:30 p.m. Bar lunches or suppers cost from £4.50 ($7.90). If featured, ask for the local Pittenweem prawns.

Elie

With its step-gabled houses and little harbor, this is my favorite village along the coast. Elie and its close neighbor, **Earlsferry,** overlook a crescent of golden sand beach, with more swimming possibilities to be found among sheltered coves. The name Elie is believed to be derived from the "ailie," or island, of Ardross, which now forms part of the harbor and is joined to the mainland by a road. A large stone building, a former granary, at the harbor is a reminder of the days when Elie was a busy trading port.

Earlsferry, to the west, got its name from an ancient ferry crossing, which Macduff, the Thane of Fife, is supposed to have used on his escape from Macbeth.

To the east of the harbor at Elie stands a stone structure known as the **Lady's Tower,** used by Lady Janet Anstruther, a noted 18th-century beauty, as a bathing cabaña.

Another member of the Anstruther family, Sir John, added the interesting **Bell Tower** to the parish church that stands in the center of the village.

Beyond the lighthouse, on a point of land to the east of the harbor, lies **Ruby Bay,** so named because garnets can be found there. Farther along the coast is **Fossil Bay,** where a variety of fossils can be found.

Nearby is a good golf course, and there are rock-ribbed sands for bathing.

A SPECIAL PUB: If you're passing this way, I suggest that you drop in at the **Ship Inn** (tel. 0333/330246) on the Toft, there to enjoy a pint of lager, real ale, or whisky from a large selection. In summer you can sit out in fair weather, overlooking the water. In colder months, a fireplace burns brightly. The pub has a nautical atmosphere, and doesn't do much in the way of food, but the owner who runs it, J. R. N. Hendry, will prepare soup and a sandwich if you're hungry. Food items begin at £1 ($1.75). The Hendrys welcome Americans, Mrs. Hendry having strong connections with the U.S. She's descended from Priscilla Mullins and John Alden of the *Mayflower* set. Her parents went back to England in 1908, and her father, Sir Stephen Pigott, is known for having built the *Queen Mary* and the *Queen Elizabeth.* Her sister who stayed Stateside was married to Sen. Estes Kefauver, now deceased. Hours are 11 a.m. to midnight Monday to Saturday, 12:30 to 2:30 p.m. and 6:30 to 11 p.m. on Sunday. The building occupied by the pub dates from 1778, and a bar has been in business here since 1830.

Crail

Considered the pearl of the East Neuk of Fife, Crail is an artists' colony, and many painters have found cottages around this little harbor. Natural bathing facilities lie at Roome Bay, and there are many beaches nearby. The Balcomie Golf Course, in good condition, is one of the oldest in the world.

WHERE TO STAY: Built in 1903, **The Marine Hotel,** 54 Nethergate South, Crail, Fife KY10 3TZ (tel. 0333/50207), stands on a quiet village street near the harbor. Its most charming corner is the cultivated rear garden, looking over the waves and the tidal rocks at the bottom of a slope. A bar dispenses drinks to occupants of the garden chairs or to drinkers in the basement lounge. The hotel contains only ten rooms, some of which have a shower. The B&B rate is from £16.50 ($28.90) per person nightly, with breakfast included. Reductions are made for children under 12, and reasonably priced meals are served in the hotel dining room.

ST. ANDREWS

On a bay of the North Sea 51 miles from Edinburgh, St. Andrews is sometimes known as the "Oxford of Scotland." Founded in 1411, the **University of St. Andrews** is the oldest in Scotland and the third oldest in Britain. At term time you can see the students in their characteristic red gowns.

The Sights

The university's most interesting buildings include the tower and church of St. Salvator's College and the courtyard of St. Mary's College, dating from 1538. An ancient thorn tree, said to have been planted by Mary Queen of Scots, stands near the college's chapel. The church of St. Leonard's College is also from medieval days. The Scottish Parliament in 1645 met in the old University Library, now the Psychology Department. A library building opened in 1976 contains nearly half a million books, with many rare and ancient volumes. Guided tours of the university are run twice daily in summer, usually in July and August. For information about them, go to the Tourist Office at South Street (tel. 0334/72021).

The historic sea town in northeast Fife is also known as the home of golf in Britain. The world's leading golf club, the **Royal & Ancient** (tel. 0334/72112), was founded here in 1754. All of St. Andrews's four golf courses—the Old, the New, the Jubilee, and the Eden—are open to the public. Of course, the hallowed turf of the Old Course is the sentimental favorite. The clubhouse is not open to nonmembers, but in common with the rest of Scotland there's no problem in playing a round on the courses. It is advisable to reserve with the starter, however, or you may not get on. To play the Old Course, a current handicap certificate and/or letter of introduction from a bona fide golf club must be presented. By the 18th hole on the Old Course, there are Links Rooms with lockers, showers, and changing facilities, as well as meals and refreshments.

The old gray royal burgh of St. Andrews is filled with many monastic ruins and ancient houses; regrettably, they represent but a few more skeletons of medieval St. Andrews.

In the area of a Celtic settlement of St. Mary of the Rock, other ecclesiastical centers culminated in **St. Andrews Cathedral and Priory** (tel. 0334/72563). The early cathedral Church of St. Rule Regulus may have been built in the late 11th century and modified in the mid-12th century. In the 1160s the larger cathedral was founded. Built in both the Romanesque and Gothic styles, it was the largest church in Scotland, establishing St. Andrews as the ecclesiastical capital of the country. Today the ruins can only suggest the former beauty and importance of the cathedral. The east and west gables and a part of the south wall of the nave remain, and standing also is "the Pends," part of the old entrance gateway to the cathedral precinct. There is a collection of early Christian and medieval monuments, as well as artifacts discovered on the cathedral site. It is open April to September daily from 9:30 a.m. to 7 p.m. (on Sunday from 2 to 7 p.m.). From October to March hours are daily from 9:30 a.m. to 4 p.m. (on Sunday from 2 to 4 p.m.). Admission is 60p ($1.05) for adults and 30p (55¢) for children.

The **Holy Trinity Church** ("the Town Kirk"), a beautifully restored medieval church, stood originally in the grounds of the now-ruined cathedral, near the 12th-century St. Regulus Tower with its 108-foot accessible stairway to the top and a fine view of the city. It was removed to the present site in 1410 and considerably altered after the Reformation of 1560. It was restored to its present condition in the early 20th century, with much fine stained glass and carvings.

Also of great interest is the ruined 13th-century **Castle of St. Andrews,** with its bottle dungeon and secret passages. Founded in the early part of the 13th century, it was reconstructed at several periods in its history. Cardinal Beaton's murder in 1546 set off the first round of the Reformation struggle. It is open from 9:30 a.m. to 6:30 p.m. daily and 2 to 6:30 p.m. on Sunday mid-March to mid-October. Off-season closing is at 4 p.m.

Food and Lodging

In hotels, many dedicated golfers prefer the **Old Course Golf and Country Club Hotel,** St. Andrews, Fife KY16 9SP (tel. 0334/74371), as it overlooks the 17th fairway, the "Road Hole" of the Old Course. Fortified by finnan haddie and porridge, a real old-fashioned Scottish breakfast, you can face that diabolical stretch of greenery where nearly all of the world's golfing greats have played and the Scots have been whacking away since early in the 15th century. The hotel is not ancient— far from it: It's very contemporary, its balconies affording top preview seats at all tournaments. Some £15 million are being spent to transform the hotel into one of world class standard. The façade is being altered to keep it in line with the more traditional buildings of St. Andrews. The bedrooms are being remodeled and refurbished, and each will have all the latest amenities including private baths. B&B in a single ranges from £85 ($148.75) to £135 ($236.25) daily, rising to £130 ($227.50) to £165 ($288.75) in a double or twin.

The hotel offers an array of facilities, including a health spa, whirlpool, massage salons, a Turkish bath, beauty therapy salons, a pool, changing and locker rooms, and a pro shop. After its massive overhaul, it should emerge as one of the finest in Scotland. The hotel offers two restaurants, one à la carte, the other less expensive. Both maintain a high standard of Scottish cuisine. A four-course table d'hôte menu costs £19.50 ($34.15). Try to pay a predinner visit to the Jigger Inn adjoining the hotel. In a former stationmaster's house, the pub evokes days or yore.

The Rusack's, 16 Pilmour Links, St. Andrews, Fife KY16 9JQ (tel. 0334/74321), sits at the edge of the famous 18th hole. Rusack's was originally built in 1887 by Josef Rusack, a German from Silesia who recognized the potential of St. Andrews as a golf capital. He placed advertisements on the front pages of British newspapers, which at the time was considered revolutionary. The hotel stands behind stone walls capped with neoclassical gables and slate roofs. Inside, chintz picks up the tones from the bouquets of flowers sent in fresh twice a week. Between panels and Ionic columns of the public rooms, racks of lendable books re-create the library of a private country house. Fireplaces and armchairs add to the allure. The decor was created by London-based Olga Polizzi. Upstairs, the bedrooms, 50 in all, contain some carved antiques, modern conveniences, spacious charm, color TV, and phone. Singles cost £67 ($117.25) to £72 ($126) daily, and doubles or twins rent for £102 ($178.50) to £125 ($218.75).

The nightlife contained within the hotel partially explains why the crew and actors of *Chariots of Fire* stayed here during its filming. The Champions Bar in the basement, overlooking the links, golf-related photos, trompe l'oeil racks of books, vested waiters, and evening folksinging. The Chesterfield sofas are full of animated clients from 11 a.m. to 11 p.m., and light meals and snacks are served as well. The hotel's formal restaurant serves daily specials along with local game, meat, and fish, accompanied by a wine list from a well-stocked cellar.

Some golfers prefer the cozy retreat of **Rufflets Country House Hotel,** Strathkinness Low Road, St. Andrews, Fife KY16 9TX (tel. 0334/72594), on the B939, about a mile and a half from St. Andrews. Of the 21 bedrooms, all are equipped with private bath or shower, phone, radio, color TV, tea- and coffee-making facilities, and alarm clock, and all are well furnished in a warm, homelike way. Set in a garden of about ten acres, this country house is substantial. The furnishings throughout are tasteful, as is the decor. The most modern bedrooms are in the newer wing, although traditionalists request space in the handsome main building, and those in the know reserve well in advance, as Rufflets is very popular with the British. Singles rent from £42 ($73.50) daily, and doubles cost from £70 ($122.50). The hotel is closed from January to mid-February. Even if you aren't staying here, you may want to call and reserve a table at the Rufflets Hotel Restaurant, overlooking a well-designed garden. Excellent, fresh ingredients are used in the continental and Scottish dishes, and everything I've sampled here has been accurately cooked. The service, too, is polite and efficient. A dinner costs from £16.50 ($28.90). Lunch is served daily from 12:30 to 2 p.m.; dinner, from 7 to 9 p.m.

St. Andrews Golf Hotel, 40 The Scores, St. Andrews, Fife KY16 9AS (tel. 0334/72611). A combination of greenery, sea mists, and tradition makes this 19th-century property a winner even with nongolfers. Brian and Maureen Hughes, the owners, recently embarked on a redecorating program that made a pleasant hotel even better. There are a pair of cocktail bars, a sauna, solarium, and 23 handsome bedrooms. Each contains a private bath, color TV, phone, radio, and thoughtful extras. Singles rent for £44 ($77) daily, and doubles go for £68 ($119). Bar lunches are served Monday to Saturday, and dinner costs from £15 ($26.25). Nearby are tennis courts to add the possibility of another sport to the ubiquitous golf facilities of the region.

If you're seeking less formality, a favorite eating spot for years has been the **Grange Inn,** at Grange, about a mile and a half from St. Andrews on the A959 (tel. 0334/72670). In this country cottage, with its charming garden, an old-fashioned hospitality prevails. Tempting dishes are served, some of them continental in flavor, but all of them well cooked and pleasantly served. Try such dishes as ravioli stuffed with crabmeat, an array of roasts, lamb cutlets, and steamy soups. Many of the dishes are based on regional recipes. In the restaurant, an inexpensive fixed-price lunch is offered for £7.95 ($13.90), served from 12:30 to 2 p.m. daily. À la carte dinners, from 7 to 9:30 p.m., cost from £16 ($28). Bar lunches and suppers are served in the pub part of the premises. You can enjoy country cooking and meet the locals at the same time. Dishes are individually priced, a meal costing from £6 ($10.50).

On the Outskirts
The Peat Inn, Cupar, Fife KY15 5LH (tel. 033484/206), six miles southwest of St. Andrews on the B940, is in an old inn/post office built in 1760, where David Wilson prepares exceptional cuisine. The restaurant is run by David and his wife, Patricia, who have built up a reputation for serving high-quality meals in comfortable surroundings. The ingredients David uses in preparation of the dishes are almost all locally grown, even the pigeons, a specialty, coming from a St. Andrews farm. Pigeon is offered in a pastry case with wild mushrooms, or you can order the plump breasts in an Armagnac and juniper sauce. Other dishes are wild duck, crab, and lobster salad, grouse in season, sometimes even woodcock. The inn has a worthy wine selection too. Dinner costs from £24 ($42); lunch goes for £13.50 ($23.65). The restaurant is open Tuesday to Saturday, serving lunch from 1 to 2:30 p.m. and dinner from 7 to 9:30 p.m. Reservations are required. The inn offers accommodation in eight beautifully furnished suites, costing around £92 ($161) daily for double occupancy. The establishment is closed for two weeks in January and two weeks in November.

---

4. Glasgow and the Clyde

Scotland's largest city stands on the banks of the River Clyde, which was the birthplace of the *Queen Mary* and both *Queen Elizabeth I* and *Queen Elizabeth 2,* plus many other ocean-going liners. Here is housed half of Scotland's population.

The commercial capital of Scotland, and Britain's third-largest city, Glasgow is very ancient, making Edinburgh, for all its wealth of history, seem comparatively young. The village that became the city grew up beside a ford 20 miles from the mouth of the River Clyde, long famous for its shipbuilding and iron- and steel-works. Glasgow was a medieval ecclesiastical center and seat of learning. The ancient city is buried beneath 19th-century Glasgow, which has undergone vast urban renewal. Glasgow was founded by St. Kentigern, also called St. Mungo, who selected the site 1,400 years ago for his church.

In 1136 a cathedral was erected over his remains; in 1451 the university was started—the second established in Scotland. Commercial prosperity began in the 17th century when its merchants set out to dominate the trade of the western seas. The Clyde was widened and deepened, and the city's expansion engulfed the smaller towns of Ardrie, Renfrew, Rutherglen, and Paisley, whose roots are deep in the Middle Ages.

Glasgow does contain some sightseeing attractions—enough to make the city a worthy goal for many visitors. But mainly it's a good center for touring central Scotland. For example, you can sail on Loch Lomond and Loch Katrine on the same day, and the resorts along the Ayrshire coast are only an hour away by frequent train service. From Glasgow you can also explore the Burns Country, the Stirling area, Culzean Castle, and the Trossachs.

THE SIGHTS

In Glasgow, the center of the city is **George Square,** dominated by the City Chambers, which Queen Victoria opened in 1888. Of the statues in the square, the most imposing is that of Sir Walter Scott on an 80-foot column. Naturally, you'll find Victoria along with her beloved Albert, plus Robert Burns. The Banqueting Hall, lavishly decorated, is open to the public on most weekdays.

The **Cathedral of St. Kentigern,** first built in 1136, burned down in 1192 but was rebuilt soon after. The Laigh Kirk, the vaulted crypt said to be the finest in Europe, remains to this day. Visit the tomb of St. Mungo in the crypt where a light always burns. The edifice is one of mainland Scotland's few complete medieval cathedrals, dating from the 12th and 13th centuries. Formerly a place of pilgrimage, 16th-century zeal purged it of all "monuments of idolatry." For the best view of the cathedral, cross the Bridge of Sighs into the necropolis, the graveyard containing almost every type of architecture in the world. The graveyard is built on a rocky hill and dominated by a statue of John Knox. It was first opened in 1832, and the first person to be buried there was a Jew—typical of the mixing of all ethnic groups in this cosmopolitan city where tolerance reigns until the rival local football teams meet. The necropolis is full of monuments to Glasgow merchants, among them William Miller (1810–1872) who wrote "Wee Willie Winkie."

The **Glasgow Art Gallery and Museum,** Kelvingrove (tel. 041/357-3929), headquarters of Glasgow Museums and Art Galleries, is the finest municipal gallery in Britain. The art gallery contains a superb collection of Dutch and Italian old masters and French 19th-century paintings. Displayed are works by Giorgione (*The Adulteress Brought Before Christ*), Rembrandt (*The Man in Armour*), Millet (*Going to Work*), and Derain (*Blackfriars*). Dali's *Christ of St. John of the Cross* is on display. Scottish painting is of course well represented in the four galleries of British painting from the 17th century to the present day. The museum has an outstanding collection of European arms and armor, displays from the ethnography collections featuring the Eskimo and North American Indians, Africa, and Oceania, as well as a large section devoted to natural history. There are major new exhibits on the natural history of Scotland, featuring plant life, animal life, and geology. There are also small, regularly changing displays from the decorative art collections of silver (especially Scottish), ceramics, glass, and jewelry, plus furniture and other decorative art items by Charles Rennie Mackintosh and his contemporaries. The museum is open daily from 10 a.m. to 5 p.m. and on Sunday from 2 to 5 p.m. Teas and light lunches are available in the museum. Admission is free.

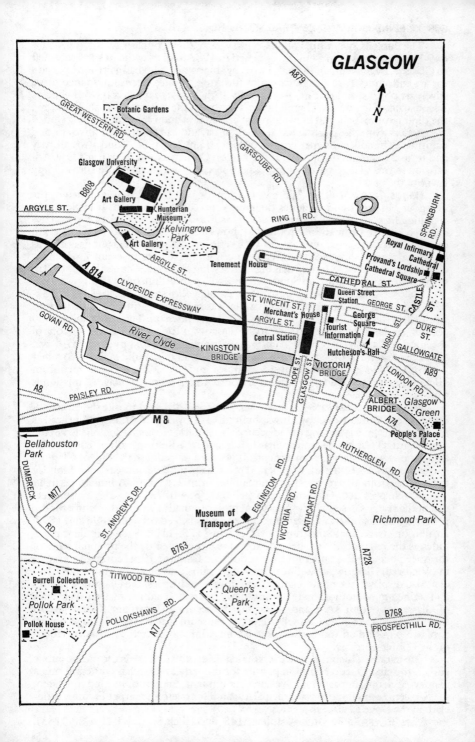

The **Burrell Collection,** Pollok Country Park, 2060 Pollokshaws Rd. (tel. 041/ 649-7151), is housed in a building opened in 1983 to display the rich treasures left to Glasgow by Sir William Burrell, a wealthy shipowner, who had a life-long passion for art collecting. A vast aggregation of furniture, textiles, ceramics, stained glass, silver, art objects, and pictures—especially 19th-century French art—can be seen. Reconstructed from Sir William's home, Hutton Castle at Berwick-upon-Tweed, are the dining room, hall, and drawing room arranged around the courtyard. Included are artifacts from the ancient world, Oriental art, and European decorative arts and paintings. The collection may be visited from 10 a.m. to 5 p.m. Monday to Saturday and from 2 to 5 p.m. on Sunday. It's closed on Christmas and New Year's Day. Admission is free. There's a restaurant, and you can roam through the surrounding lawns of the park.

Haggs Castle, 100 St. Andrews Dr. (tel. 041/427-2725), is a branch of the Glasgow Museums and Galleries designed especially for children. It explores the changing lifestyles of the 400 years of the castle's existence. In the castle is a reconstructed kitchen from 1585, a room that shows how an inhabitant lived in the 17th century, and a Victorian nursery. An 18th-century cottage in the grounds is used as an activities workshop, and children who visit can take part in sessions, which include weaving, archery, butter-making, and sewing samplers. The castle is open daily from 10 a.m. to 5 p.m., on Sunday from 2 to 5 p.m. Admission is free.

Pollok House, Pollok Country Park, 2060 Pollokshaws Rd. (tel. 041/632-0274), the ancestral home of the Maxwells, was built circa 1750 and has additions from 1890 to 1908 designed by Robert Rowand Anderson. The house and its 360 acres of parkland were given to the City of Glasgow in 1966. Today it contains one of the finest collections of Spanish paintings in Britain, with works by El Greco, Goya, and Murillo, among others. Also on display are paintings by William Blake, together with British and European furniture, ceramics, and silver. The house is open from 10 a.m. to 5 p.m. Monday to Saturday, from 2 to 5 p.m. on Sunday. Admission is free.

Provand's Lordship, 3 Castle St. (tel. 041/552-8818), opposite the cathedral, is the oldest house in Glasgow. It was built in 1471 by Bishop Andrew Muirhead as the manse for priests serving the adjacent St. Micnolas' Hospital (demolished in the 18th century) but has been in secular hands since the Reformation of 1560. It has associations with Mary Queen of Scots. It is now a museum in the care of Glasgow Museums and Art Galleries, with period room displays. The house is open Monday to Saturday from 10 a.m. to 5 p.m., on Sunday from 2 to 5 p.m. Admission is free.

People's Palace, Glasgow Green (tel. 041/554-0223), provides a visual record of the rise of Glasgow. The palace was built originally as a cultural center for the people of the East End of Glasgow, and it was constructed between 1895 and 1897. Exhibitions trace the foundation of the city in 1175–1178. Such turbulent interludes as the reign of Mary Queen of Scots are represented by the personal relics of the queen herself. The bulk of the collections are from the 19th century, representing Victorian Glasgow, including posters, programs, and props from the music hall era. Also displayed are items relating to trades and industries, the Glasgow potteries and stained-glass studios, trade unions, newspapers, and similar matters. Paintings of Glasgow by John Knox and others may be seen, plus portraits of Glaswegians from St. Mungo to Billy Connelly. The city museum may be visited daily from 10 a.m. to 5 p.m. and on Sunday from 2 to 5 p.m. Admission is free. There is a tea room in the Winter Gardens.

The park in which the palace is situated, **Glasgow Green,** is the oldest public park in the city. Once a common pasture for the early town, it has witnessed much history. Seek out, in particular, Nelson's monument, the first of its kind in Britain; the Saracen Fountain, opposite the palace; and Templeton's Carpet Factory, modeled on the Doge's Palace in Venice.

Miss Toward's Tenement House, 145 Buccleuch St. (tel. 041/338-0183), has been called a "Glasgow flat that time passed by." Until her death, Agnes Toward was an inveterate hoarder of domestic trivia. She lived in an 1892 building on Garnethill, not far from the main shopping street, Sauchiehall. For 54 years she lived in this flat that is stuffed with the artifacts of her era, everything from a porcelain "jawbox" sink to such household aids as Monkey Brand soap. After her death, the property eventually came into the care of the National Trust for Scotland, which realized that it was a virtual museum of a vanished era. Approached through a "wally close," the museum is open from the first of April until the end of October daily from 2 to 5 p.m., only on Saturday and Sunday from 1 to 4 p.m. November to March. Admission is £1.10 ($1.95) for adults, 55p (95¢) for children.

Royal Highland Fusiliers Museum, 518 Sauchiehall St. (tel. 041/332-5639), displays 300 years of the infantry of Glasgow and Ayrshire. Relics, such as weapons, mementos, medals, pictures, and uniforms trace the saga of the regiment's history from 1678. The regiment served under 15 monarchs on five continents. The museum is open from 9 a.m. to 4:30 p.m. Monday to Thursday and 9 a.m. to 4 p.m. on Friday, charging no admission.

Hunterian Museum, University of Glasgow, University Avenue (tel. 041/330-4221), is in the main Glasgow University buildings on Gilmorehill, two miles west of the heart of the city. This museum is Glasgow's oldest, having opened its door in 1807. The museum is named after William Hunter, its early benefactor who donated his private collections to get the exhibition going. It is one of the world's finest collections of coins and medals, going back more than 2,000 years. Cleopatra and Alexander the Great are two of the personalities depicted on exhibits. The museum's other main displays include archeological and geological finds, among them distance slabs from the Antonine Wall built between the River Clyde and the Firth of Forth in A.D. 142 as the northern boundary of the Roman Empire. Alongside its ornamental carvings is a statement of a detachment of the "VI Victorious, Loyal and Faithful Legion," announcing that it had completed 3,666½ paces of the wall. The museum has a bookstall, a coffee house in the 18th-century style, and temporary exhibitions. It is open from 9:30 a.m. to 5 p.m. Monday to Friday, to 1 p.m. on Saturday. Admission is free.

Hunterian Art Gallery (tel. 041/330-5431) is in a separate building from the museum, opposite the university. It has paintings by Chardin, Rembrandt, Reynolds, Pissaro, Sisley, and Stubbs, as well as some outstanding works (paintings, prints, furniture, and ceramics) by James McNeill Whistler and Charles Rennie Mackintosh, including the Mackintosh House, a reconstruction of the architect's home on three levels, with his own furniture and decorated in the original style. The main gallery exhibits 18th-century British portraits and 19th- and 20th-century Scottish paintings, with works by McTaggart, the Glasgow Boys, Scottish Colourists, Gillies, Philipson, and others. Temporary exhibitions, selected from the largest collection of artists' prints in Scotland, are presented in the print gallery, which also houses a permanent display of printmaking techniques. Contemporary sculpture is displayed in an outdoor courtyard. Hours are 9:30 a.m. to 5 p.m. Monday to Friday, to 1 p.m. on Saturday. The Mackintosh House closes from 12:30 to 1:30 p.m. Monday to Saturday. Closed on Sunday and public holidays. Admission is free except for the Mackintosh House, which costs 50p (90¢) Monday to Friday afternoons and Saturday.

Museum of Transport, Kelvin Hall, 1 Bunhouse Rd. (tel. 041/357-3929), contains a fascinating collection of all forms of transportation and related technology. Displays include a simulated Glasgow street of 1938 with period shop fronts and appropriate vehicles and a reconstruction of one of the Glasgow Underground stations. An authentic motor car showroom has a display of mass-produced automobiles. Superb and varied ship models in the Clyde Room reflect the significance of Glasgow and the River Clyde as one of the world's foremost areas of shipbuilding and engineering. The museum is open from 10 a.m. to 5 p.m. Monday to Saturday, from 2 to 5 p.m. Sunday. Admission is free, and there is a self-service cafeteria.

Although it has much industry and a lot of stark commercial areas, Glasgow contains many gardens and open spaces.

Chief among these is **Bellahouston Park,** Paisley Road West, 171 acres of beauty with a sunken wall and rock gardens as well as wildlife. It's open all year daily from 8 a.m. to dusk. Here you'll find the **Bellahouston Sports Centre** (tel. 041/427-5454), which is a base for a variety of indicated trails that make up runners' training courses.

The **Glasgow Botanic Gardens,** Great Western Road (tel. 041/334-2422), cover 40 acres—an extensive collection of glasshouse plants, in particular orchids, begonias (the National Collection), and ferns, as well as herb gardens. It, too, is open all year, from 7 a.m. to dusk daily. The Glasshouses can be visited from 1 to 4:45 p.m. The Kipble (Crystal) Palace, containing a splendid grove of tree ferns, opens at 10 a.m. Admission is free.

Linn Park, on Clarkston Road, is 212 acres of pine and woodland, with many lovely walks along the river. Here you'll find a nature trail, pony rides for children, an old snuff mill, and a children's zoo. The park is open all year daily from 8 a.m. to dusk.

Greenock is an important industrial and shipbuilding town on the Clyde Estuary a few miles west of the center of Glasgow. It was the birthplace in 1736 of James Watt, inventor of the steam engine. A huge Cross of Lorraine on Lyle Hill above the town commemorates Free French sailors who died in the Battle of the Atlantic during World War II.

UPPER-BRACKET HOTELS

The leading hotel in the city is **Holiday Inn,** 500 Argyle St., Anderston, Glasgow, Lanarkshire G3 8RR (tel. 041/226-5577). Its illuminated sign and soaring profile add a vivid accent to the Glasgow city skyline from its perch at the Anderston exit to the M8. Its nearly 300 well-equipped bedrooms are among the finest in the city. After work, dozens of local residents unwind in one of the popular bars scattered throughout the cavernous lobby, where open fireplaces compete with fountains and lots of plants for visual supremacy. The hotel contains four squash courts, a mini-gym, a whirlpool, and a sauna, plus a large indoor pool. A trio of restaurants complete the designation of this place as a village within a city. Bedrooms contain a color TV with free in-house movies, phone, and air conditioning. Singles range from £82 ($143.50) daily and doubles from £96 ($168).

One Devonshire Gardens, 1 Devonshire Gardens, Glasgow, Lanarkshire G12 0UX (tel. 041/339-2001). In 1880 it was built as an upper-crust private home, but by the early 1980s it had degenerated into a seedy rooming house. In 1986 a professional designer bought it and embarked on a major restoration, which made it more elegant than it was in its heyday. Behind its sandstone façade he added such Georgian touches as cove moldings patterned into laurel and urn motifs, along with masses of floral-patterned chintz, comfortable seating arrangements, and a scattering of antiques, all against a backdrop of deep-blue walls. At the sound of the doorbell, a pair of chambermaids clad in Edwardian costumes of frilly aprons and dust bonnets will appear at attention to welcome you. Each of the upstairs bedrooms, which have been individually designed, is impeccably furnished in the best of period taste, each with a double bed, private bath, and lots of luxurious accessories. Singles rent for £75 ($131.25) daily; doubles £110 ($192.50). Breakfast, VAT, and service are included. If your visit is on a Friday and Saturday night, dinner is included free. For a separate recommendation of the restaurant, see the section coming up. The location is in the Hyndland district of Glasgow, just west of the center, amid a neighborhood of stone-sided Victorian houses.

The Albany, Bothwell Street, Glasgow, Lanarkshire G2 7EN (tel. 041/248-2656), is a modern, well-equipped four-star hotel in the heart of the city. It has 251 well-appointed bedrooms and suites, all with private bath, direct-dial phone, color

TV, beverage-making equipment, hairdryer, trouser press, mini-bar, and electronic door-locking system. Singles rent for £68 ($119) daily, with a double or twin going for £88 ($154). Sometimes weekend bookings mean "Leisure Break" tariff reductions. The Albany has two restaurants and a trio of bars catering to many tastes. During the week, it is filled mainly with commercial travelers, but on weekends it is likely to be patronized by vacationers intent on exploring the sights of Glasgow.

The Copthorne Hotel, George Square, Glasgow, Lanarkshire GD 1DS (tel. 041/332-6711), is a landmark hotel in the center near the Queen Street Station where trains depart for the north of Scotland. Its high-ceilinged design was originally constructed as the North British Hotel, until foreign investors renovated it into a format more luxurious than it was originally. The hotel's role in history was played when Winston Churchill met here in Room 21 with Harry Hopkins, FDR's envoy, in 1941. The pivotal meeting that took place is credited with securing Hopkins's support for the Lend-Lease Bill. When the public rooms of the hotel were renovated, designers searched for antiques and glistening marble panels. Each unit offers in-house movies, plush carpeting, and an upgraded decor. Singles are priced at £68 ($119) to £80 ($140) daily and doubles at £80 ($140) to £98 ($171.50), with VAT included. A burgundy-and-gray dining room offers a tempting buffet, while La Mirage Café and Bar is one of the most alluring spots in Glasgow for a drink or a light meal. Everywhere, rows of potted palms and ornate accessories are shown in their best light against the tastefully modernized background.

Stakis Grosvenor Hotel, Grosvenor Terrace, Great Western Road, Glasgow, Lanarkshire G12 0TA (tel. 041/339-8811). When a team of engineers used a revolutionary technique of impregnating the decaying sandstone of this hotel's neoclassical façade with a combination of fiberglass and concrete, the city offered them an architectural award. It was at this time that the Greek-owned Stakis company almost completely gutted the interior, reconstructing it in a casino-style sweep of crystal chandeliers and brassy accents. Today the hotel is considered one of the most comfortable in town, offering elegant dining in a pink- and mauve-colored restaurant whose picture windows look across the street toward an iron fence surrounding the Botanical Gardens. Lacy curtains cover the dozens of fan-shaped windows illuminating the russet-colored leather on the deep armchairs of the upper lobby and the downstairs bar. The 96 well-furnished bedrooms, each with private bath or shower, rent for £90 ($157.50) daily in a double and from £73 ($127.75) in a single, with breakfast and taxes included. Reduced weekend rates are often offered.

The White House Hotel, 11-13 Cleveden Crescent, Kelvinside, Glasgow, Lanarkshire G12 0PA (tel. 041/339-9375), lies in Glasgow's west end in a classical Georgian crescent just off Great Western Road. The hotel consists of three houses in a private crescent designed by the famous architect, John Burnet, Sr. The owner, Ian Ferguson, has been the creator of the transformation to a Georgian-style apartment hotel. There are 32 suites ranging from executive single and double to mezzanine split-level suites and mews cottages. All the units are furnished to a high standard and have remote control color TV, in-house movies, direct-dial phones, bath/showers with toilets, and fully fitted kitchens. The accommodations rent for £54 ($94.50) daily in singles, £66 ($115.50) in doubles, and £75 ($131.25) in mews cottages. Rates are fully inclusive. Discounts are available on weekends.

MIDDLE BRACKET AND BUDGET HOTELS

Officially opened in 1883, the **Central Hotel,** 99 Gordon St., Glasgow, Lanarkshire G13 SF (tel. 041/221-9680), was the grandest hotel Glasgow had seen. Near the rail station whose commerce and transport changed the face of Scotland, it was the queen of the city's most famous street. Now revamped and restored to its former glory, it is owned by Friendly Hotels, who specialize in offering excellent rooms at affordable prices. Today the Central is the unquestioned leader in its price bracket. The massive baronial wooden staircase leading from the lobby to the upper floors was painstakingly stripped and refinished as part of the continuing restoration on this historic hotel.

The Central contains 229 bedrooms, and prices are determined by the fixtures and age of the accessories. Each bedchamber, however, is comfortable and high ceil-inged. Singles range from £46 ($80.60) to £55 ($96.25) daily, with doubles costing £61 ($106.75) to £66 ($115.50), with VAT and a continental breakfast included. Sandblasting of the façade revealed scores of heretofore concealed details, such as elaborate Victorian cornices and pilasters. The hotel's finest hour might have been the transmission shortly after World War II of the first TV broadcast on a private line extending from London to a bedroom on the fourth floor of this hotel. Its bar with its old panels has a good selection of Highland malts, and the Entresol Restaurant deserves a special mention (see below) even if you aren't staying there.

At the edge of town, the **Stakis Pond Hotel,** 2-4 Shelley Rd., Glasgow, Lanark-shire G12 0XP (tel. 041/334-8161), a 137-bedroom modern hotel, is a good bet for a comfortable, bargain-conscious stay. It's set in a green area beside a duck-filled pond. Part of the benefits include the use of the glass-walled indoor pool, exercise machines, and saunas. Each of the functional and sunny bedrooms has a private bath and a video TV. Singles cost from £69 ($120.75) daily and doubles or twins from £85 ($148.75). The hotel's pine-paneled steakhouse offers generous portions of well-prepared meals served in a salad bar/carvery format. One of the hotel's bars is on a glassed-in balcony above the swimming pool.

Hospitality Inn, 36 Cambridge St., Glasgow, Lanarkshire G2 3HN (tel. 041/332-3311), a downtown high-rise hotel, is among the best in the moderately priced category. Its reception area has the kind of tropical-inspired waterfall you'd expect to find in the Caribbean. However, the flavor of its bar and restaurant is satisfyingly Scottish. Each of the conservatively styled bedrooms has a TV, phone, radio, wake-up alarm, and full bath. Accommodations, which are suitable for one or two per-sons, cost £59.95 ($104.90) daily in a studio and £74.95 ($131.15) in a deluxe room. Some of the more expensive units hold up to four persons. The prices at this hotel can go down on weekends to around £34 ($59.50) in a studio and £40 ($80.50) in a deluxe accommodation. The Palm Springs lounge is a red-brick and exposed-wood Victorian medley of brass chandeliers and low-slung French arm-chairs. The Prince of Wales dining room is a study in soft greens and airy spacious-ness. The gardenlike coffeeshop offers one of the best food bargains in Glasgow, a carvery lunch costing £6.50 ($11.40). It features a self-service selection of tempting salads, each laid out on a bed of ice. The bar remains open for residents every night until 1 a.m., and room service is available on a 24-hour basis. There's even a base-ment car park, plus lots of in-house services, such as a resident hairdresser.

Beacons Hotel, 7-8 Park Terrace, Glasgow, Lanarkshire G3 6BY (tel. 041/332-9438), is an architectural period piece that has been converted into one of the best middle-bracket hotels in Glasgow. Constructed in 1856, the hotel was original-ly two private town houses for well-to-do Glaswegians. After a successful renova-tion, the Beacons casts its light into the night, attracting wayfarers to its door. It now has 36 pleasantly furnished bedrooms, each with private bath, color TV, radio, direct-dial phone, and tea-making facilities, along with hairdryers. Singles rent for £50 ($87.50) daily, while doubles or twins cost from £70 ($122.50). Unusual for such a small hotel, the Beacons has 24-hour room service. It also has a basement restaurant, the Diva.

Babbity Bowster, 16-18 Blackfriars St., Glasgow, Lanarkshire G1 1PJ (tel. 041/552-5055), in the heart of Glasgow in an area known locally as Merchant City, is a small but delightful hotel that doubles as an art gallery. Named for an 18th-century wedding dance, the hotel, the work of two brothers, Tom and Fraser Laurie, is in a Robert Adam building once used as a fruit and flower shop. The work of Glas-wegian artists is displayed in the upstairs restaurant, with the frequently changed exhibits containing pictures for sale. Among items *not* for sale is the ceramic logo that contains the hotel's name and a picture of dancing Scots. Babbity Bowster has only six bedrooms for rent, charging from £25 ($43.75) per person nightly. The restaurant has a reputation for good food. The menu changes daily. Traditional Scottish ales and whisky are served, and musical events also are presented in the first-floor restaurant on Sunday evening sometimes.

FAVORITES FOR DINING

The high-ceilinged restaurant of **One Devonshire Gardens,** 1 Devonshire Gardens (tel. 041/339-2001), recommended as a hotel above, has become one of Glasgow's most charming and unusual dining rooms since its inception in 1986. You dine amid flowery Victorian-inspired wallpaper, served by pretty chambermaids dressed in frilly aprons and muslin mob caps. A shade of deep blue dominates the public rooms. You go first to the drawing room, elegantly decorated, where drinks are served as you peruse the menu. Reservations are needed, and it's open for meals daily except Saturday at lunch from 12:30 to 2:30 p.m. and 7 to 10 p.m. A fixed-price menu at both sessions offers an ample choice, and quality ingredients are handled with care and finesse in the kitchen. The lunch cost is £14 ($24.50), and dinner goes for £25 ($43.75). Perhaps you'll begin with a curried-parsnip soup, then follow with terrine of brill and trout, going on to rack of Borders lamb.

Fountain, 2 Woodside Crescent, Charing Cross (tel. 041/332-6396), attracts a clientele of gourmets and Glasgow's most fashionable people. It is a sophisticated and formal restaurant. You can select from many popular dishes, including grills, salmon, duck, and good fresh vegetables. Among the specialties are trois filets verge (slices of salmon, turbot, and sole, poached with watercress and garnished with stars of puff pastry), rosettes of beef Eugénie (three slices of beef filet with fresh tomato "en concasse") and a basil-flavored hollandaise. Dessert might be a mousse of fresh kiwi and strawberries covered with a Chantilly-cream sauce. A set lunch costs £9.50 ($16.65), and a set dinner starts at £16 ($28), the price depending on your main-dish choice. You can also dine à la carte, for around £21 ($36.75) to £24 ($42) per person. The wine list is excellent, and the proprietor makes an effort to find wines from different regions, as well as the traditional bordeaux and burgundies. Meals are served from noon to 2:30 p.m. and 7 to 11 p.m. Monday to Saturday.

Rogano, 11 Exchange Pl. (tel. 041/248-4055), is considered one of the most perfectly preserved art deco interiors in Scotland. Its decor dates from 1934, when Messrs. Rogers and Anderson combined their talents and their names to create an ambience that has hosted virtually every star of the British film industry since the invention of the talkies. The doorman and bartender have been employed for decades. In an ambience filled with birchwood veneers, lapis lazuli clocks, etched mirrors, spinning ceiling fans, cozy semicircular banquettes, and dozens of potted palms, you can enjoy full meals ranging from £20 ($35) per person. The array of menu items in the restaurant, changing every two or three months, is likely to include both Scottish and international specialties, with an emphasis on seafood. There are at least six varieties of temptingly rich desserts. A less expensive menu is offered downstairs in Café Rogano, where meals cost from £9 ($15.75). The main restaurant, for which reservations are suggested, is open Monday to Saturday from noon to 2:30 p.m. and 7 to 10:30 p.m. The café is open Monday to Thursday from noon to 11 p.m. and on Friday and Saturday until midnight.

L'Entresol Restaurant, Central Hotel, 99 Gordon St. (tel. 041/221-9680), is one of the fine old dining rooms of Glasgow, steeped in tradition. In a high-ceilinged room, you get first-class service and value for your money. On the second floor (first to the British) of this previously recommended hotel, L'Entresol is restored in a blue and gold decor. Using fresh ingredients, deftly handled by the kitchen, it presents an excellent cuisine, most often using the rich bounty of Britain itself. You might begin with a whisky-flavored pork pâté, then go on to tackle a number of main dishes, including venison, Scottish lamb, or Dover sole. However, most diners opt for the carvery, with its hot and cold roasts and fresh vegetables along with an array of homemade salads. For dessert, you might select a crêpe with lots of fresh cream whose main flavor comes from Drambuie. Three courses in carvery cost about £7.50 ($13.15), although you will more likely spend from £18 ($30.50) ordering à la carte. The dining room is open seven days a week from 12:30 to 2 p.m. and 6:30 to 9 p.m.

The Colonial Restaurant, 25 High St. (tel. 041/552-1923), lies a few paces from the Talbooth Steeple tower behind a deceptively simple façade underneath a trussed ceiling. Here Scottish-born Peter Jackson has distinguished himself as one of the up-and-coming chefs of Scotland. The décor is not exceptional but the cookery is first rate. For example, you might begin with a mousse of white asparagus and go on to select such elegant fare as salmon tartar with cucumber, steamed filet of brill in a wine sauce, or pigeon with peaches. A set luncheon at £6.50 ($11.40) is one of the dining bargains of Glasgow. A table d'hôte dinner goes for £17.50 ($30.65); however, you are likely to spend from £25 ($43.75) if ordering à la carte in the evening. Hours are noon to 2:30 p.m. and 6 to 10:30 p.m.; closed Monday at dinner, Saturday at lunch, and all day Sunday.

Ubiquitous Chip, 12 Ashton Lane, at Hillhead (tel. 041/334-5007), is run by Mr. Bryden and Mr. Clydesdale. It enjoys an enviable national reputation for both its food and its fine wines. The ingenuity of the chef is reflected in a wide range of dishes offered. If you wish, you can eat in the dining room, but the covered courtyard is my favorite place year round. Such Scottish recipes are on the menu as haggis and neeps, smoked Loch Tay eel, and macerated Scottish beef with tapenade just for appetizers. Fresh fish, lamb, grouse, guinea fowl, and several excellent beef dishes are among the main courses. In addition, there is always at least one vegetarian dish on the menu. The serving staff is young and enthusiastic and will tell you how the various foods are prepared. Count on spending from £11 ($19.25) for a satisfying meal. The Chip, as it's called, is open daily from noon to 11 p.m.

The Carvery, The Albany, Bothwell Street (tel. 041/248-2656), lies on the lobby level of this prestigious hotel, but the price of its meals is low considering what you get. Within a brick-lined ambience of napery-covered tables and pinpoint lighting, you can select from one of Glasgow's most amply stocked buffets for £9.25 ($16.20) per head. The buffet is spread on an altar-like centerpiece, laden with dishes both hot and cold. It's augmented with carved roasts and joints produced by uniformed chefs. No advance reservations are accepted, and service is daily from noon to 2:30 p.m. and 5:30 to 10 p.m. Evening meals on Sunday are from 6:30 to 10 p.m.

The Buttery, 652 Argyle St. (tel. 041/221-8188), is the perfect hunt-country restaurant, with oak panels, racks of wine bottles, and an air of baronial splendor. The bar in the anteroom used to be the pulpit of a church. The waitresses wear high-necked costumes of which John Knox would have approved. Everywhere you look, you see 19th-century accessories. The Oyster Bar in the outer section serves weekday lunches for around £11.50 ($20.15) apiece. Menus include smoked salmon, rare roast beef, a terrine of Scottish seafood, and of course, oysters. The more formal inner room serves an elegant menu, with full meals costing from £20 ($35). In the formal restaurant, hours are noon to 2:30 p.m. (no lunch on Saturday) and 7 to 10 p.m. The bar, however, stays open until 11 p.m. Reservations in the main dining room are suggested. The restaurant is closed Sunday.

The Belfry, 652 Argyle St. (tel. 041/221-0630). Each element of decor in this place, on the basement level of the Buttery, just previewed, came from a church in northern England, including the pews and pulpits. Lots of illuminated stained glass creates a cozy ambience. It's probably the only pub in Glasgow that affords a contemplation of Christ in majesty by patrons while they enjoy a pint of ale. The cramped and partially exposed kitchen produces daily specials such as poached salmon in a lemon mayonnaise, smoked mackerel pâté, and a chicken-and-broccoli pie. The establishment keeps the Sabbath holy, but it is open Monday to Friday for lunch and dinner (on Saturday, it's open for dinner only) from noon to 2:30 p.m. and 6 to

10 p.m. (to 11 p.m. Friday and Saturday). Full meals cost from £9 ($15.75) and can be accompanied by a choice from the wine list.

Charlie Parker's, 21 Royal Exchange Square (tel. 041/248-3040), is an attractive restaurant and nightspot. On the ground floor, its black-and-silver decor might best be described as a mixture of hi-tech and art deco. This all-black room serves as the perfect foil for the dramatic illumination. In front is Charlie Parker's Cocktail Bar, open from noon to midnight Monday to Saturday, and in the rear is Charlie's Diner, a sort of New York diner with a range of steaks, burgers, and such specialties as chicken tortillas or fettuccine. Meals cost from £9 ($15.75).

October, 128 Drymen Rd., Bearsden (tel. 041/942-7272), is much favored by young Glaswegian professionals who seek style, flair, palate-exciting ingredients, and a reasonable price—all wrapped up in one restaurant. The chef de cuisine, Ferrier Richardson, satisfies those tastes admirably. Lunch is a relatively modest affair, offered daily from noon to 2 p.m., but at dinner from 7 to 10 the kitchen goes to work, taking the rich bountiful harvest of the U.K. and turning out an array of dishes to tempt you. Service is only Tuesday to Saturday, and meals cost from £20 ($35). It is hard to characterize the cookery as it seems to roam around the world at leisure, taking from something here, borrowing from something there. Nevertheless, the final result is worthy. Vegetarians will also find dishes to suit their needs here, too. Call for a reservation. The restaurant lies in a suburb of Glasgow, a 15-minute ride out by car or taxi.

WHERE TO SHOP

The principal shopping district is **Sauchiehall Street,** Glasgow's fashion center, containing many shops and department stores where you'll often find quite good bargains, particularly in woolen goods. The major shopping area, about three blocks long, has been made into a pedestrian mall.

The Barras, the weekend market of Glasgow, takes place about a quarter of a mile east of Glasgow Cross. With free admission, it is held all year from 9 a.m. to 5 p.m. on Saturday and Sunday. Rich in stalls and shops, this century-old market has some 800 traders selling their wares. You can not only browse for that special treasure but also become a part of Glasgow life and be amused by the buskers.

The Highland House of Lawrie, 110 Buchanan St. (tel. 041/221-0217). There's possibly no more prestigious store in Scotland than this elegant haberdashery. Despite its aristocratic clientele, prices are more reasonable than you might expect, and the welcome offered by the experienced sales staff is genuinely warm-hearted. Don't be fooled by the array of crystal and gift items offered for sale on the street level, because the real heart and soul of the establishment lies on the lower level. There, carefully constructed tweed jackets, tartan accessories, waistcoats, and sweaters are sold to both men and women. Each is impeccably crafted by kilt-making experts. Most of the merchandise is, of course, crafted from top-quality wool and suitable even in the dampest of Highland weather. Men's kilts contain as much as eight yards of material pleated to carry out the plaid pattern. Women's hand-stitched kilts are also sold, as are those for children. Don't overlook the tweed blazers for men, which are reasonable in price. The business was founded in 1881, and today it is the oldest established kiltmaker in Scotland. The shop is open from 9 a.m. to 5:30 p.m. Monday to Saturday.

Fraser's Department Store, 45 Buchanan St. (tel. 041/221-3880), is Glasgow's version of Harrods Department Store. The Glasgow store contains a soaring Victorian-era glass arcade rising four stories. Inside, you'll find everything from clothing to Oriental rugs, from crystal to handmade local artifacts of all kinds. Even a quick visit to see the Victorian embellishment is worthwhile—and you'll surely see something you want to buy.

William Porteous & Co. Ltd., 9 Royal Exchange Pl. (tel. 041/221-8623), is a long-established bookstore specializing in travel guides and maps for Scotland and the remainder of the United Kingdom and Europe. They also have Scottish souvenir books and prints and carry all the main British and foreign newspapers and magazines. They're open Monday to Saturday from 8:30 a.m. to 5 p.m.

Henry Burton & Co., 111 Buchanan St. (tel. 041/221-7380), one of the city's most prestigious men's outfitters, is in a slightly cramped two-story building filled with well-crafted clothes. Established in 1847, the store has a helpful staff, which offers competent advice as needed. Most of the garments are for men, but a limited selection of knitwear for women is sold also.

The following recommendations are not specific shops but rather areas where you can find stores by the dozens:

The **Argyll Arcade** stands at 30 Buchanan St. Even if the year of its construction (1827) was not set in mosaic tiles above the entrance, you'd still know that this is an old collection of shops. Most of the businesses set beneath the glass canopy sell watches and jewelry, both antique and modern. In fact the arcade contains what is said to be the largest single concentration of retail jewelers in Europe, surpassing even those of Amsterdam. The fame of the arcade has traveled far beyond Glasgow. It seems to be a Scottish tradition that a wedding ring becomes lucky when purchased within the arcade's narrow confines. Whether or not this is true, the rents charged here are higher than for comparable stores in Glasgow, even exceeding the exorbitant amounts charged along London's fashionable Bond Street.

Since the arcade is officially classified as a historic structure, a portion of its rents goes toward maintaining it in mint condition. Over the years the locale has given rise to many legends, including that of a pair of ghosts said to inhabit Sloan's pub. Today, beneath the curved glass ceiling, an impressive security system is maintained, designed to protect the area's two dozen shops and their multi-million-pound inventories against wrongdoers in the milling pedestrian traffic.

Victorian Village, 57 West Regent St. (tel. 041/332-0703). Antique lovers will want to browse through this warren of tiny shops in this somewhat claustrophobic cluster. Much of the merchandise isn't particularly noteworthy, but there are many exceptional pieces. Several of the owners stock reasonably priced articles of 19th-century provenance. Other shops sell old jewelry and clothing, a helter-skelter of artifacts.

A Covent Garden–type shopping complex, the **Briggait,** is in the Victorian building that once housed Glasgow's Fish Market. It offers a wide and exclusive range of merchandise from designer fashion to traditional Scottish craftsmanship, a choice of restaurants, a continuous program of exhibitions, and regular entertainment on Saturday and Sunday. The Briggait is closed Tuesday.

GLASGOW AFTER DARK

Glasgow, not Edinburgh, is the cultural center of Scotland, and the city is alive with nightclubs. Still, for many a Glaswegian, the best evening is to be spent drinking in his or her favorite pub (my selection coming up). Cultural Glasgow is well represented, however, in the list of places to go for an evening's entertainment.

The Theatre Royal, at Hope Street and Cowcaddens Road (tel. 041/331-1234), is the home of the Scottish Opera, which long ago attracted attention on the world scene. The building, designed by C. J. Phipps, opened in 1895 and was completely refurbished as a home for the Scottish Opera, reopening in 1975. It offers 1,547 comfortable seats and has spacious bars and buffets on all four levels. It has been called "the most beautiful opera theatre in the kingdom" by the *Daily Telegraph,* which noted its splendid Victorian Italian-Renaissance plasterwork and glittering chandeliers. But it is not the decor that attracts opera-goers. Rather, it is the ambitious repertoire. The box office is open from 10 a.m. to 7:30 p.m. Monday to Saturday. The Theatre Royal is also home to the Scottish Ballet, a national company with an international reputation, and it also hosts visiting theater and dance companies from around the world.

The Citizens Theatre, at Gorbals and Ballater Streets (tel. 041/429-0022), was founded after World War II by James Bridie, a famous Glaswegian whose plays are still produced. The theater is home to one of the United Kingdom's most prestigious repertory companies. All seats cost £3 ($5.25).

The **Pavilion Theatre,** 121 Renfield St. (tel. 041/332-1846), is still alive and well, specializing in rock/pop concerts, plays, all types of variety shows, and a pantomime season.

The **Mitchell Theatre,** Granville Street (tel. 041/221-3198), has earned a reputation for small-scale entertainment, ranging from dark drama to dance, as well as conferences and seminars. A modern little theater, it adjoins the well-known Mitchell Library.

The **Tron Theatre,** 63 Trongate (tel. 041/552-4267), occupies one of the three oldest buildings in Glasgow, the former Tron Church. The Tron Theatre Club has transformed the old structure, with its famous Adam dome and checkered history, into a small theater presenting the best of contemporary drama, dance, and music events. The Tron also has a beautifully restored Victorian café/bar serving traditional home-cooked meals, including vegetarian, and a fine selection of beer and wine. It's open from noon to 11 p.m. daily.

The **Glasgow Arts Centre,** 12 Washington St. (tel. 041/221-4526), directed by Graeme McKinnon, always seems to be doing or presenting something interesting, including productions aimed at children. Their activities range from theatrical productions to folk concerts. They are open Monday to Saturday from 9:30 a.m. to 5 p.m. and 6:30 to 10 p.m. Tickets to their presentations can be reserved by phone. However, in summer they are closed in the evening.

Those interested in going to the leading disco in Glasgow are directed to **Pzazz Disco,** 23 Royal Exchange Square (tel. 041/221-5323), one of the most imaginative in the city. It's incongruously located on the second floor of a building surrounded with 19th-century neoclassical monuments. Some visitors combine an evening at Pzazz with dinner at Charlie Parker's (see my restaurant recommendations) on the ground floor. The lighting inside the disco often prompts fashion photographers to use this as the site for layouts. The decor is electronic, heavily infused with shades of electric blues and golds, with lots of mirrors to catch the reflections from the smallish dance floor. The disco is open only on Friday and Saturday from 10 p.m. to 3:30 a.m. The entrance fee is £4.50 ($7.90) per person.

ELEGANT LIVING ON THE OUTSKIRTS

The former residence of Sir James Lithgow, the **Gleddoch House Hotel,** Langbank, Renfrewshire PA14 6YE (tel. 047554/711), was converted in 1974 to a deluxe hotel set on large grounds, including farmlands, riding stables, golf course, and gardens. The 33 rooms are named for birds—Golden Eagle, Mallard, Osprey —and have good baths, plus radios, color TVs, hairdryers, trouser presses, and hot beverage facilities. A single room costs £65 ($113.75) daily and a double runs £115 ($201.25), with a Scottish breakfast included in the rates. Weekend charges are lower. The paneled hallway is bright with a roaring fire, and there's a cozy bar. The residents' sitting room is upstairs. Breakfast is a leisurely, help-yourself affair. At lunch, you can order smoked trout and salmon mousse, clear Highland game broth, and perhaps a traditional warm pudding. A set lunch costs £12.50 ($21.90). In the evening, you can dine from an à la carte menu, although I recommend the fixed-price dinner for £25 ($43.75). The five set courses change daily, and might include home-cured salmon, Scottish lamb, duck, or beef, and one of the tempting hot or cold desserts. Many guests prefer to have lunch in the Golf Club House. There are a sauna and a plunge pool, as well as horseback riding.

To get there, drive west along the A8/M8 from Glasgow and the Erskine Bridge toward Greenock and Gourock. Turn left at the sign for Langbank on the B789, going left again under the railway bridge and then steeply up the hill to the hotel entrance on the right.

5. The Trossachs and Loch Lomond

"The Trossachs" is the collective name given that wild Highland area lying east and northeast of Loch Lomond. Both the Trossachs and Loch Lomond are said to contain Scotland's finest scenery in moor, mountain, and loch. The area has been famed in history and romance ever since Sir Walter Scott included vivid descriptive passages in *The Lady of the Lake* and *Rob Roy*.

In Gaelic, the Trossachs means "the bristled country," an allusion to its luxuriant vegetation. The thickly wooded valley contains three lochs—Vennachar, Achray, and Katrine. The best centers for exploring are the villages of the Trossachs and the "gateways" of Callander and Aberfoyle.

Legendary Loch Lomond, the largest and most beautiful of Scottish lakes, is known for its "bonnie banks." Lying within easy reach of Glasgow, the loch is about 24 miles long. At its widest point, it stretches for five miles. At Balloch in the south the lake is a Lowland loch of gentle hills and islands. But as it moves north, the loch changes to a narrow lake of Highland character, with moody cloud formations and rugged steep hillsides.

CALLANDER

For many, this small burgh, 16 miles northwest of Stirling by road, makes the best base for exploring the Trossachs and Loch Katrine, Loch Achray, and Loch Vennachar. For years, motorists—and before them passengers traveling by bumpy coach—stopped here to rest up on the once-difficult journey between Edinburgh and Oban.

Callander stands at the entrance to the **Pass of Leny** in the shadow of the Callander Crags. The Teith and Leny rivers meet to the west of the town.

Four miles beyond the Pass of Leny, with its beautiful falls, lies **Loch Lubnaig** ("the crooked lake"), divided into two reaches by a rock and considered fine fishing waters. Nearby is **Little Leny,** the ancestral burial ground of the Buchanans.

More falls are found at **Bracklinn,** 1½ miles northeast of Callander. In a gorge above the town, Bracklinn is considered one of the most scenic of the local beauty spots. Other places of interest include the **Roman Camp,** the **Caledonian Fort,** and the **Foundations of St. Bride's Chapel.** The tourist office will give you a map pinpointing the above-recommended sights. While there, you can also get directions for one of the most interesting excursions from Callander, to **Balquhidder Church,** 13 miles to the northwest, the burial place of Rob Roy.

The leading hotel is **Roman Camp,** Callander, Perthside FK17 8BG (tel. 0877/30003), once a 17th-century hunting lodge with pink walls and small gray-roofed towers, built on the site of what was believed to have been a Roman camp. The dukes of Perth once came to this turreted establishment, lodging here for "hunting and hawking." Entering through a gate, the modern-day traveler drives up a splendid driveway, with shaggy Highland cattle and sheep grazing on either side and well-manicured yew hedges. A river runs through the 20-acre estate. In summer, flowerbeds are in bloom. Inside you are welcomed to a country house furnished in a gracious manner. There are 14 bedrooms and three suites, with seven of the units on the ground floor and one adapted for use of disabled guests. Two of the bedrooms contain showers, while 12 have private baths/showers. All have hairdryers, radios, direct-dial phones, TVs, and hot beverage facilities. The charge is from £42 ($73.50) daily for single occupancy, from £66 ($115.50) for a double. Prices include VAT and service. The dining room was converted in the '30s from the old kitchen. The ceiling design is based on the old Scottish painted ceilings of the 16th and 17th centuries, which were a feature of houses around the time the Roman Camp hunting lodge was built. The meals—"Scottish country-house fare," as one reader described them—are served until 8:30 in the evening. There is a small cocktail bar, but the library, with its plasterwork and paneling, remains undisturbed. The hotel closes from mid-November to mid-March.

Pinewood Hotel, Leny Road, Callander, Perthshire FK17 8AP (tel. 0877/ 30111), a former Victorian "gentleman's house," stands in its own attractive gardens with pine trees. A double driveway leads from the main West Highland route. The hotel is owned and operated by Gordon and Jan Halladay, who provide a comfortable environment with a high level of service. The Pinewood is centrally heated, and many of the bedrooms have color TV, private bath or shower, and tea/coffeemakers. Singles cost from £15 ($26.25) daily, and doubles go for £27 ($47.25) to £30 ($52.50). There are also some family rooms available. Tariffs include a full Highland breakfast. There is a choice of bar meals, or you can have a more formal dinner in the restaurant, which offers a four-course, multichoice menu using seasonal fresh local and traditional produce, complemented by a carefully chosen wine list.

ABERFOYLE

Looking like an alpine village, in the heart of the Rob Roy country, this small holiday resort, 55 miles from Edinburgh, 26 miles from Glasgow, and 19 miles from Stirling, is the gateway to the Trossachs, near Loch Ard. A large crafts center contains a wealth of gift items related to the Highlands.

Bailie Nicol Jarvie Hotel, Aberfoyle, Perthshire FK8 3SZ (tel. 08772/202), is an old-fashioned hotel on the road between Loch Ard and Aberfoyle. If you're passing through the Trossachs, it makes a suitable overnight stopover. The hotel takes its name from Nicol Jarvie, the Glasgow magistrate who used to visit the outlaw Rob Roy at a former inn on this site. The hotel is one of character, and it was recently refurbished. All its 36 bedrooms contain private baths. Many of the rooms have high ceilings and are furnished in comfortable pieces. The B&B rate is £26 ($45.50) per person nightly, increasing to £41 ($71.75) per person for half board. Lovers of antiquity are drawn to Bailie Bar, a cocktail lounge hung with weaponry. The hotel serves good country meals, using farm produce when available. It's open from March to December.

THE TROSSACHS

The Duke's Pass (A821) north from Aberfoyle climbs through the Achray Forest, past the **David Marshall Lodge** information center, operated by the Forestry Commission, where you can stop for snacks and a breathtaking view of the Forth Valley. The road runs to the Trossachs—the "bristly country"—between lochs Achray and Katrine.

Loch Katrine, at the head of which Rob Roy MacGregor was born, owes its fame to Sir Walter Scott who set his poem *The Lady of the Lake* there. The loch is the principal reservoir of the city of Glasgow. A small steamer, S.S. *Sir Walter Scott,* plies the waters of the loch, which has submerged the Silver Strand of the romantic poet. Sailings are from early May to the end of September between Trossachs Pier and Stronachlachar. Round-trip fare is £2 ($3.50) for adults, £1.20 ($2.10) for children. Complete information as to the sailing schedules is available from the Strathclyde Water Department, Lower Clyde Division, 419 Balmore Rd., Glasgow, Lanarkshire G22 6NU (tel. 041/336-5333).

Trossachs Hotel, Trossachs, Perthshire FK17 8HY (tel. 08776/232), became famous in Victoria's heyday. Built on the site of one of the old posting inns of Scotland that dated from the 18th century, it was erected by Lady Willoughby as a castle in 1826, converting to a hotel in 1852. After a long career the hotel, now mellowed with time, is still going strong. Rooms come in a variety of styles. All bedrooms contain private baths, and the cost ranges from £20 ($35) to £25 ($43.75) per person, based on double occupancy. Breakfast is included. The dining room, hung with shields, is draped with the plaids of ancient clans and has a timbered ceiling. A set lunch costs £8 ($14); a fixed-price dinner goes for £12 ($21). The hotel is right in the heart of the Trossachs, two miles from Loch Katrine where you can sail on the loch steamship *Sir Walter Scott.*

LOCH LOMOND

This largest of Scotland's lochs was the center of the ancient district of Lennox, in the possession of the branch of the Stuart family from which sprang Lord Darnley, second husband of Mary Queen of Scots and father of James VI of Scotland, who was also James I of England. The ruins of Lennox Castle are on Inchmurrin, one of the 30 islands of the loch—one having ecclesiastical ruins, one noted for its yew trees planted by King Robert the Bruce to ensure a suitable supply of wood for the bows of his archers. The loch is fed by at least ten rivers from west, east, and north. On the eastern side is Ben Lomond, rising to a height of 3,192 feet.

The song "Loch Lomond" is supposed to have been composed by one of Bonnie Prince Charlie's captured followers on the eve of his execution in Carlisle Jail. The "low road" of the song is the path through the underworld that his spirit will follow to his native land after death more quickly than his friends can travel to Scotland by the ordinary high road.

The road from Dumbarton to Crianlarich runs along the western shore of the loch. However, the easiest way to see the loch is not by car but by the **Countess Fiona,** which sails daily from Easter until the end of September. Built in 1936 for the Caledonian Steam Packet Company, she is now owned by Alloa Brewery Company and sails from Balloch Pier. A full cruise round-trip ticket costs £10 ($17.50) for adults, £5 ($8.75) for children. For further information, phone 041/226-4271, 041/248-2699 for a recorded message on sailing times.

Balloch

At the southern end of Loch Lomond, Balloch is the most touristy of the towns and villages around the lake. It lies only a half-hour drive from the heart of Glasgow, and there is regular train service from Glasgow to Balloch Station. The town grew up on the River Leven, as it leaves Loch Lomond, flowing south to the Clyde. Today it is visited chiefly by those wanting to take boat trips on the *Countess Fiona,* which leaves in season from Balloch Pier. The most popular time to visit is during the Highland Games held here every year.

Balloch Castle Country Park is set on 200 acres along the "bonnie banks." The present Balloch Castle, replacing one that dates from 1238, was constructed in 1808 for John Buchanan of Ardoch. Built in the "castle-Gothic" style, it has a Visitor Centre, which explains the history of the property. The site has a walled garden, and the trees and shrubs, especially the rhododendrons and azaleas, reach the zenith of their beauty in late May and early June. You can also visit a "Fairy Glen." The location is about three-quarters of a mile from the center of Balloch, and it is open all year daily from 8 a.m. to dusk, charging no admission.

For food and lodging, try the **Balloch Hotel,** Balloch Road, Balloch, Dunbartonshire G83 8LQ (tel. 0389/52579). When it was built, this white-walled establishment sat isolated at a point where the river flowed into Loch Lomond. In 1860, the Empress Eugénie, wife of Napoléon III, slept in the Inchmoan Room during her tour of Scotland. Today the warmly decorated pub and adjoining restaurant are filled with engravings of scenes from Scottish history. Well-prepared and plentiful food make this one of the most alluring stopovers in the area. Meals in the restaurant begin at £6 ($10.50), and pub lunches are cheaper. If you'd like to make the Balloch your base for exploring Loch Lomond, comfortable bedrooms with private bath rent for £43 ($75.25) daily in a double, £29 ($50.75) in a single. All units contain color TV, phones, and tea/coffee-makers.

Luss

This village on the western side of Loch Lomond is the traditional home of the Colquhouns. Among its stone cottages, on the water's edge, is a branch of the **High-**

land Arts Studios of Seil. Cruises on the loch or boat rentals may be arranged at a nearby jetty.

Colquhoun Arms Hotel, Luss, Alexandria, Dunbartonshire G83 8NY (tel. 043686/282), is a yellow-and-white former coaching inn, sitting close to the road under the canopy of large trees. The modernized interior is filled with light-grained paneling, plaid carpeting, a pool table, an attractively lit dining room, a lounge bar, and a pub. The owner is Norwegian-born H. L. Weibye, a local businessman. The 23 rooms are bathless, except for five units. Bathless singles cost £18 ($31.50) daily and similar doubles go for £30 ($52.50). Doubles with bath rent for £38 ($66.50). Bar meals cost from £6.50 ($11.40), while full dinners in the dining room start at £11 ($19.25).

Inverbeg

This hamlet on the western shore of Loch Lomond stands in a beauty spot of Scotland, reached in about 40 minutes from Glasgow. The location is about three miles north of Luss. The hamlet is known for its oldtime ferry inn (see below), the second-oldest youth hostel in Scotland, and several well-known art galleries. A small fleet of Loch Lomond cruisers can usually be seen in the harbor of Inverbeg Bay, and a ferry to Rowardennan and Ben Lomond plies the route three times a day in summer.

The Inverbeg Inn, Luss, Loch Lomond, Dunbartonshire G83 8PD (tel. 043686/678). The site on which this inn stands has always been important as the ferryboat landing that services the western end of Loch Lomond. The roadside building that a visitor can see today was constructed in 1814. Earlier inns probably stood on the same site. Today, directed by the Bisset family, the establishment serves savory pub lunches as well as more formal restaurant meals throughout the year. The first thing a cold-weather visitor might see is a blazing fire heating the reception room near the entrance. About half of the comfortably furnished bedrooms look out over a garden in the rear. Depending on the plumbing and the season, singles cost from £22 ($38.50) to £28 ($49) daily with doubles going for £35 ($61.25) to £54 ($94.50). Seven of the rooms contain private bath. Fixed-price evening meals cost from £12 ($21), with pub lunches going for half that or less. You might want to stop in only for a meal.

Tarbet

On the western shores of Loch Lomond, Tarbet is not to be confused with the larger center of Tarbert, headquarters of the Loch Fyne herring industry. Loch Lomond's Tarbet is merely a village and a summer holiday base with limited accommodations. In the distance you can see the majesty of Ben Lomond. King Haakon of Norway came this way in the 13th century, devastating the countryside. To the north, now the site of the Inveruglas power station, the Clan MacFarlane had their rallying point.

Boats can be launched from the pier, and Tarbet is one of the stops on the route of the steamship *Countess Fiona.*

Tarbet Hotel, Tarbet, Arrochar, Dunbartonshire G83 7DE (tel. 03012/228). Local historians say that some form of hotel has stood on this spot for the past 400 years. A coaching inn was built on the site in 1760, and in the Victorian era a baronial façade and military-style crenelations were added. The exterior suggests that the interior might be as antique as the stone façade. However, the present owners have modernized the inside. A cozy cocktail lounge looks past a row of yew trees onto the lake. Good food is served in the spacious dining rooms, and there are some 91 simple but comfortable rooms to rent. A bathless single goes for £18 ($31.50) daily, increasing to £35 ($61.25) in a similar double. Rooms with bath cost £28 ($49) in a single, rising to £48 ($84) in a double. The hotel is closed in January.

NORTHEAST SCOTLAND

1. EXPLORING TAYSIDE
2. THE GRAMPIAN REGION

Covering the regions of Tayside and Grampian, northeast Scotland beckons the visitor with much scenic grandeur, although some come just to hit the Whisky Trail. Three of Scotland's most important cities, Dundee, Aberdeen, and Perth, are tucked away in this corner, and the section also contains three of the country's best-known salmon rivers, the Dee, the Spey, and the Tay.

The land is riddled with historic old castles, and will give you a view of Highland majesty—imposing, grand, tumultuous, including Queen Victoria's favorite view. The best known of the traditional Highland gatherings takes place at Braemar.

1. Exploring Tayside

The trouble with exploring Tayside is that you may find it so fascinating in scenery you'll never make it on to the Highlands. Carved out of the old counties of Perth and Angus, Tayside is named for its major river, the 119-mile-long Tay. Its tributaries and dozens of lochans and Highland streams are some of the best salmon and trout waters in Europe. One of the loveliest regions of Scotland, Tayside is filled with heather-clad Highland hills, long blue lochs under tree-clad banks, and miles and miles of walking trails.

It is a region dear to the Scots, a symbol of their desire for independence, as exemplified by the Declaration of Arbroath and the ancient coronation ritual of the "Stone of Destiny" at Scone. In cities, Perth and Dundee are among the leading six centers of Scotland.

Tayside also provided the backdrop for many novels by Sir Walter Scott, including *The Fair Maid of Perth, Waverley,* and *The Abbot.*

Its golf courses are world-famous, ranging from the trio of 18-hole courses at Gleneagles to the open championship links at Carnoustie.

We'll begin our trip in an offshoot southern pocket of the county at Loch Leven, then take in Perth and its environs, heading east to Dundee, and later along the fishing villages of the North Sea, cutting west again to visit Glamis Castle, finally ending our journey of exploration even farther west in the lochs and glens of the Perthshire Highlands.

LOCH LEVEN

"Those never got luck who came to Loch Leven." This proverbial saying sums up the history of the ruined Douglas Fortress, **Loch Leven Castle,** on Castle Island, dating from the late 14th century. Among its more ill-fated prisoners, none was more notable than Mary Queen of Scots. Within its forbidding walls she signed her abdication on July 24, 1567. However, she effected her escape from Loch Leven on May 2, 1568. Thomas Percy, seventh Earl of Northumberland, supported her cause. For his efforts he, too, was imprisoned and lodged in the castle for three years until he was handed over to the English, who beheaded him at York. The castle is open from 9:30 a.m. to 7 p.m. daily and from 2 to 7 p.m. on Sunday, April to September, closed in winter. Admission to the castle is free, but the charge for the ferry is 60p ($1.05) for adults, 30p (55¢) for children.

Lying to the north of Dunfermline (head toward Kinross), the loch has seven islands. Loch Leven Castle, of course, is in ruins. So is the **Priory of Loch Leven,** built on the site of one of the oldest Culdee establishments in Scotland, and lying on St. Serf's, the largest of the islands in the loch.

In Kinross, 25 miles north of Edinburgh, you can make arrangements to visit Loch Leven Castle by boat, the only means of access.

Food and Lodging

Nivingston House, Cleish, Kinross-shire KY13 7LS (tel. 05775/216), lies on the B9097, two miles south of Kinross at Cleish. It serves some of the finest food in Tayside. The place is run by Pat and Allen Deeson, who offer 17 modernized rooms for £48.50 ($84.90) daily in a single, £68.50 ($119.90) in a double, both with breakfast included.

However, most visitors arrive to sample the wares of the kitchen. I've never had the same meal here twice, as one must depend on the inspiration of the chef. But that's hardly a problem. Meals, costing around £12.50 ($21.90) for lunch and £20 ($35) for dinner, are concocted principally from local produce, such as fish, Scottish lamb and beef, and veal, as well as charcoal-grilled sardines. Try, if featured, his fish terrine and the king prawns, or the delectable house pâté. Desserts are luscious, your selection made from a trolley wheeled to your table. Hours are 12:30 to 2 p.m. and 7:30 to 9 p.m. daily. Always reserve a table. The hotel stands on ten acres of grounds.

PERTH

From its majestic position on the Tay, the ancient city of Perth was the capital of Scotland until the middle of the 15th century. Here the Highland meets the Lowland. Sir Walter Scott immortalized the royal burgh in *The Fair Maid of Perth.*

The Sights

The main sightseeing attraction of "the fair city" is the **Kirk of St. John the Baptist,** of which the original foundation, it is believed, dates from Pictish times. However, the present choir dates from 1440 and the nave from 1490. In 1559 John Knox preached his famous sermon here attacking idolatry, and it caused a wave of iconoclasm to sweep across the land. The church was restored as a World War I memorial in the mid-1920s. In the church is the tombstone of James I, who was murdered by Sir Robert Graham.

The **Black Watch Regimental Museum,** Balhousie Castle, Hay Street (tel. 0738/21281), contains the memorabilia of the 42nd and 73rd Highland Regiments. You get to see 2½ centuries of British military history, including paintings, silver, and uniforms. Admission is free, but it's appreciated if you make a donation to the museum fund. It is open Monday to Friday from 10 a.m. to 4:30 p.m. from April to the end of September. On Sunday and bank holidays it is open from 2 to 4:30 p.m. Off-season hours are Monday to Friday from 10 a.m. to 3:30 p.m.

John Dewar & Sons, the internationally renowned distillers of Dewar's White

Label scotch whisky, have a massive bottling complex at Inveralmond, on the outskirts of Perth. Inveralmond is one of the largest establishments of its kind in Scotland, and as many as 350,000 bottles are filled there in one day. Organized tours are given for visitors wishing to see the bottling and dispatch processes. You are advised to phone 0738/21231 for information.

The Fair Maid's House, North Port (tel. 0738/25976), was the old Glover's House that Sir Walter Scott chose as the home of his heroine in the already-mentioned *The Fair Maid of Perth.* Now a craft shop, it sells high-quality Scottish crafts including woolen goods, silver, glass, and pottery. Upstairs is a gallery that presents changing exhibitions of contemporary art. It is open Monday to Saturday from 10 a.m. to 5 p.m. The gallery hours are 11 a.m. to 4 p.m. Monday to Saturday.

Branklyn Garden, on the Dundee road (A85), has been called the finest two acres of private garden in Scotland. Established in 1922 by Mr. and Mrs. John Renton, it was bequeathed to the National Trust for Scotland. It has a superb collection of rhododendrons, alpines, and herbaceous and peat-garden plants from all over the world. Open daily from March to the end of October, it can be visited from 10 a.m. to sunset for an admission of £1.10 ($1.95) for adults and 60p ($1.05) for children. For information, phone 0738/25535.

You can watch glassmakers at work at the **Caithness Glass factory,** at Inveralmond (tel. 0738/37373), where there is also a visitor center. Of special interest is the intricate art of paperweight making. Glassmaking can be observed from 9 a.m. to 4:30 p.m. Monday to Friday. The factory shop and restaurant are open from 9 a.m. to 5 p.m. Monday to Saturday and 1 to 5 p.m. on Sunday.

Food and Lodging

Station Hotel, Leonard Street, Perth, Perthside PH2 8HE (tel. 0738/24141). Its fortunes were assured when most of the traffic from the Highlands began funneling over the nearby George Street Bridge, completed just three years before the American Revolution. The nearby street corner became known as the "hub of the universe," and later stagecoaches made it a major stopover. Built as the grandest hotel in Perth in 1890, it has been restored by the Friendly Hotel chain. The hotel has entertained everybody from Queen Elizabeth II to Margaret Thatcher. It is set behind a severely dignified gray sandstone facade, containing 70 comfortable bedrooms. Each accommodation has a TV, mini-bar and beverage-making equipment. Singles range from £40 ($70) to £50 ($87.50) daily, with doubles costing £50 ($87.50) to £57 ($99.75), with VAT and a continental breakfast included. Each room is different from its neighbor, charmingly so, and each has high ceilings evoking the age of Victoria. You register in a lobby darkly paneled in mahogany and upholstered in pastel colors. One of the hotel's highlights is a baronial staircase handcarved from Canadian hardwood.

Royal George, Tay Street, Perth, Perthside PH1 5LD (tel. 0738/24455), gets the "royal" in its name from a long ago visit by Victoria. The stone façade and landscaped garden you see today, however, dates from around 1910. Each bedroom is solidly furnished, evoking the 19th century with high ceilings, big windows, and wood detailing. With breakfast included, singles rent for £58 ($84) daily, with doubles costing £64 ($112). On the premises is Helen MacGregor's, a bar named after the legendary mistress of Rob Roy. In the Ox and Claret, traditional cookery, including Scottish beef is a specialty.

Timothy's, 24 St. John St. (tel. 0738/26641), has a convivial informality, and also serves some of the best food in this ancient city, far superior to that I've encountered in the dining rooms of the staid Victorian hotels. Ever had a Scottish smörgåsbord? If not, then try the table offered by the owners, Caroline and Athole Laing. Roast beef (served rare and tender), smoked trout, tasty sausages, crabmeat wrapped in smoked salmon, and homemade soups (such as nettle or dandelion) are well prepared. Perhaps you might like to try salmon caught in the River Tay, only about 55 yards away, brought here fresh each morning and served at lunch and dinner during the season. Top-quality local produce is used, including garden fruit and vegetables. In summer, the Laings even decorate the smörgåsbord with fresh nasturtiums, borage, and marigold flowers. Athole wears his kilt every evening to give visitors to Perth a warm Scottish welcome. Caroline, who does all the cooking, makes a special "pudding" every day, such as fresh raspberry-cream soufflé in summer and a steamy hot fruit spiced sponge in winter. Meals are from noon to 2:30 p.m. and 7 to 10 p.m., and it's necessary to call for a reservation, as the restaurant can fill up rapidly, particularly in summer. For a complete meal, including a glass of wine, expect to pay £10 ($17.50) per head. Closed Sunday and Monday.

SCONE
On the River Tay, Old Scone was the ancient capital of the Picts. On a lump of granite, the "Stone of Destiny," the monarchs of the Dark Ages were enthroned. The British sovereign to this day is still crowned on the stone, but in Westminster Abbey. Edward I moved the stone there in 1296. Charles II was the last king crowned at Scone; the year: 1651.

Scone Palace (tel. 0783/52300), the seat of the Earl of Mansfield and birthplace of David Douglas of fir tree fame, was largely rebuilt in 1802, incorporating the old palace of 1580. Inside is an impressive collection of French furniture, china, ivories, and 16th-century needlework, including bed hangings executed by Mary Queen of Scots. A fine collection of rare conifers is found on the grounds in the Pinetum. Rhododendrons and azaleas grow profusely in the gardens and woodlands around the palace. To reach the palace, head northeast of Perth on the A93. It lies two miles from the center of Perth. The site is open from Good Friday to mid-October daily from 9:30 a.m. to 5 p.m., on Sunday from 1:30 to 5 p.m. Admission is £2.70 ($4.75) for adults, £2 ($3.50) for children, including entrance to both the house and grounds.

Where to Stay on the Outskirts
Balcraig House, New Scone, Perth, Perthshire PH2 7PG (tel. 0738/51123), is 1½ miles northeast of Perth along the A94. A country house, built in the 19th century when Queen Victoria sometimes stayed at Scone Palace nearby, Balcraig is run today as an elegant country-house hotel. The owners have created a relaxed, luxurious atmosphere amid delightful scenery. Fresh flowers, polished woodwork, crystal chandeliers, and a collection of tapestries provide a stunning ambience, adding to the special elegance of the drawing room. The ten bedrooms, all with a well-equipped bathroom, color TV, hairdryer, phone, and radio, are individually decorated. One I especially like is the Rose Room, which has a fine four-poster bed. All the units are well-maintained. A single costs £54.50 ($95.40) daily, while doubles are priced from £77 ($134.75) to £95 ($166.25). The house has a private garden, a tennis court, and greens for croquet and boules. Baby-sitting can be arranged, and you can go pony-trekking through the estate. The cuisine here is highly recommended, with the emphasis on traditional Scottish fare artistically presented. Most of the produce is home grown or obtained locally from first-class purveyors. Your poached salmon, as a change of pace, might come with a hazelnut hollandaise sauce. Meals cost from £15 ($26.25). The wine cellar is impressive.

GLENEAGLES
This famous golfing center and sports complex is on a moor between Strath Earn and Strath Allan. The center gets its name from the Gaelic Gleann-an-Eaglias, meaning glen of the church. **St. Mungo's Chapel,** higher up the glen than the internationally known golf courses and hotel, has monuments of the Haldane family, whose ancestral castle ruins made way—and provided the stones—for the building of the later family seat constructed in 1624.

Gleneagles has four 18-hole golf courses connected with the hotel: King's Course, the longest one; Queen's Course, next in length; Prince's Course, shortest of all; and Glendevon, the newest of the quartet, built in 1980. They are considered the best in Scotland. The sports complex is one of the most splendid in Europe.

Gleneagles provides a good—but far from inexpensive—base from which to explore the major attractions of central Scotland. It is in the ancient Royal Burgh of Auchterarder of many centuries ago, strategically placed on the road that led from the royal residence at Scone to Stirling Castle. Today it is on the A9, about halfway between Perth and Stirling, a short distance from the village of Auchterarder.

Food and Lodging

The Gleneagles Hotel, Auchterarder, Perthshire PH3 1NF (tel. 0764/62231), stands on a 750-acre estate. An Edwardian establishment built in the style of a French château, it is the only five-red-star hotel in Scotland. The service and decor are incomparable in the country. Each of the 242 luxurious bedrooms has a spacious bath, color TV, in-house video, a private bar, a direct-dial phone, and 24-hour room service. The rooms have fine furnishings, and the hills and glens of the surrounding countryside make splendid views. The price of singles, with a full Scottish breakfast included, ranges from £85 ($148.75) to £95 ($166.25) daily; doubles, £135 ($236.25) to £165 ($288.75). Guests can dine in the Strathearn Restaurant, paying from £19 ($33.25) for a set lunch, from £24 ($42) for a set dinner. The emphasis is on regional dishes, including game soup Highland style, smoked salmon, and the like. A buffet choice is offered at lunch, and piano music is played in the evening. If you prefer nouvelle cuisine, go to the Conservatory Restaurant. Hours are 7:30 to 10:30 p.m. daily. In this magnificent room with plaster paneling and impeccable service, you can enjoy an eight-course meal at a cost of £35 ($61.25) per person.

The hotel's Country Club, enclosed in a glass dome to provide a year-round tropical climate, offers to members and hotel guests use of a swimming pool, whirlpool, Turkish bath, sunbeds, massage facilities, saunas, a plunge pool, and a children's pool. If you're really hardy, you can use the California hot tubs outdoors. There are also squash courts, a gym, and snooker tables, as well as tennis courts, croquet lawns, and a bowling green, not to mention hunting and fishing. In the dome, you can have steak and salads at the brasserie, and there's also a cocktail bar. In addition, there is the Gleneagles Jackie Stewart Shooting School and the Gleneagles Mark Phillips Equestrian Centre, both equipped to the highest standards. For the coddling of golfers, the Dormy House (old name for a clubhouse) sits between the King's and Queen's courses. Here is another restaurant and a cocktail bar in addition to showers and changing rooms.

Auchterarder House, Auchterarder, Perthshire PH3 1DZ (tel. 0764/63646), one mile from Gleneagles, sits in its own grounds off the B8062 between Auchterarder and Crieff. A fine example of Victorian architecture and craftsmanship, in the Scots Jacobean style, the mansion house has been completely restored and the interior refurbished to a high standard of luxury by its present owners, Ian and Audrey Brown. The house has elegant public rooms and 11 comfortable bedrooms, all with private bath and other amenities calculated to please a discerning clientele, such as TVs and phones. Singles pay from £70 ($122.50) to £90 ($157.50) daily, and doubles £95 ($166.25) to £125 ($218.75). Afternoon tea is served in the glass conservatory with its miniature fountain and goldfish pond. You can enjoy drinks in the handsome bar, which was the chapel of the house in other days. Lunch and dinner are served in the Victorian dining room or in the library. You can choose from a menu that might include monkfish with hollandaise sauce, collops in the pan "Strathallan," or roast loin of lamb. Desserts to tempt even dieters are such items as bramble mousse with strawberry sauce, orange mousse with liqueur, and choux pastry buns (filled with cream and coated with a hot rum-and-chocolate sauce). Dinner will cost £22.50 ($39.40) to £37.50 ($65.65), the price including canapes, coffee, and petit fours.

Free courtesy car service is offered from Gleneagles Station, and the staff will help arrange tours of the area as well as sports activities, including golf. You may be content, however, just to browse around the 20 acres of grounds, where a fine collection of rare shrubs, trees, and rhododendrons is nurtured.

CRIEFF

At the edge of the Perthshire Highlands, Crieff makes a pleasant stopover, what with its possibilities for fishing and golf. This small burgh, 18 miles from Perth, was the seat of the court of the earls of Strathearn until 1747. In its marketplace, gallows were once used to execute Highland cattle rustlers.

You can take a "day trail" into Strathearn, the valley of the River Earn, the very center of Scotland. Highland mountains meet gentle Lowland slopes, and moorland mingles with rich green pastures. North of Crieff, the road to Aberfeldy passes through the narrow pass of the Sma' Glen, with hills rising on either side to 2,000 feet. The glen is a well-known beauty spot.

In addition, you can explore a distillery, glassworks, and a pottery center.

The Sights

Glenturret Distillery Ltd., Glenturret, The Hosh (tel. 0764/2424), is Scotland's oldest distillery, established in 1775. On the banks of the River Turret, it is reached from Crieff by taking the A85 toward Comrie. At a point three-quarters of a mile from Crieff, turn right at the crossroads. The distillery is a quarter of a mile up the road. It is all signposted. Visitors can see the milling of malt, mashing, fermentation, distillation, and cask filling, followed by a free "wee dram" dispensed at the end of the tour. Visitors are welcome March to December, Monday to Friday from 9:30 a.m. to 5:30 p.m. (last full tour at 4:30 p.m.); from April to October, it's also open on Saturday from 10 a.m. to 5 p.m. (last full tour at 4 p.m.). Tours through the distillery are at frequent intervals. In January and February, only the shop is open, from 2 to 4 p.m. The Glenturret Heritage Centre incorporates a 100-seat audio-visual theater and an Exhibition Display Museum. The distillery shop hs the full range of the Glenturret Pure Single Highland Malt scotch whisky and the Glenturret malt liqueur, together with an extensive range of souvenirs. At the Smugglers Restaurant and Whisky Tasting Bar you can taste older Glenturret whiskies, such as 10-year-old, high-proof, 12- and 15-year-old, and the Glenturret malt liqueur. The guided tours, taking about 25 minutes, cost £1.25 ($2.20) for adults, 60p ($1.05) for youngsters 12 to 17 years old. Under 12s are admitted free. Admission to the Heritage Centre is 50p (90¢), the presentation lasting about 20 minutes.

Stuart Strathearn, Muthill Road (tel. 0764/4004), is a factory welcoming visitors wanting to see how handmade crystal is produced. From June to September it is open Monday to Friday from 9 a.m. to 7 p.m. From October to May, it closes at 5 p.m. daily. You can see the traditional craftsperson's skill in the Stuart Crystal film demonstrated by factory glassworkers. The shop on the premises has a large selection of Stuart Crystal and its own engraved crystal giftware. In the grounds of the factory is a picnic area, plus a children's playground.

Crieff Visitors Centre, 14 Comrie St. (tel. 0764/5151), which opened in 1985, was built by Buchan's Thistle Potteries and Perthshire Paperweights, two medium-size craft factories, to enable visitors to see their skills in manufacturing pottery and glass. Buchans established the Thistle Potteries more than a century ago and is the last survivor of the famous Portobello potteries. Visitors can go on escorted tours through the factory Monday to Friday, seeing all the elements of the process. Sometimes tours can be taken on Sunday afternoon in high season. Perthshire Paperweights has recently been designed to allow visitors to watch the processes. It is also open during working hours, but Friday afternoon is the least interesting time, because the staff is only preparing the next week's glass. The center has a large showroom displaying the products of both factories, including both firsts and seconds in the pottery, although all paperweight seconds are destroyed. There is a modern licensed restaurant. Hours are 9 a.m. to 6 p.m. seven days a week, although factory tours are only possible during normal production hours.

Three miles south of Crieff, you can visit the gardens of **Drummond Castle** (tel. 076481/257), a mile north of Muthill, seat of the late Earl of Ancaster. The gardens were originally laid out about 1630 by John Drummond, second Earl of Perth. Around 1830, the parterre was Italianized and embellished with figures and statues from Italy. Probably one of the most interesting pieces of statuary is the sundial, designed and built by John Mylne, Master Mason to King Charles I. The grounds are open daily from 2 to 6 p.m. (last entry at 5 p.m.) from May to the end of August. In September, they are open only on Wednesday and Sunday from 2 to 6 p.m. Admission is £1.20 ($2.10) for adults, 60p ($1.05) for children.

Food and Lodging
Murraypark Hotel, Connaught Terrace, Crieff, Perthshire PH7 3DJ (tel. 0764/3731), is small, offering 14 rooms with private bath, but its standards are first rate. The bedrooms have a pleasing decor and are comfortably furnished. Singles rent for £22 ($38.50) to £33 ($57.75) for B&B, and doubles go for £48 ($84) to £52 ($91). Before dinner, you can meet in the bar after having strolled around the hotel, enjoying views across Strathearn. Meals are based on country-house fare, costing from £13.50 ($23.65).

COMRIE
An attractive little village in Strathearn, 25 miles from Perth, Comrie stands at the confluence of the Earn, Ruchill, and Lednock rivers. The A85 runs through the village to Lochearnhead, Crianlarich, and on to Oban and the western seaboard. It's a convenient place to stop overnight for travelers crossing Scotland. Waterskiing, boating, and sailing are available on Loch Earn in summer.

On the A85, the **Scottish Tartans Museum,** Drummond Street (tel. 0764/70779), is the only museum devoted entirely to tartans and Highland dress. There are more than 400 tartans on display together with models, prints, and pictures depicting Highland attire. There is a reconstructed weaver's cottage with occasional demonstrations of hand-spinning and hand-weaving, as well as a dye plant garden featuring plants, shrubs, and trees used in past times to dye tartan. The museum is open from 10 a.m. to 5 p.m. Monday to Saturday and from 2 to 4 p.m. Sunday from April to October. In winter, visits are possible during office hours (ring the bell) Monday to Friday as well as from 10 a.m. to 12:30 p.m. Saturday. The Scottish Tartans Society undertakes research inquiries on a fee basis using its archives, *The Register of All Publicly Known Tartans.* There is a shop selling authentic tartan goods, plus a mail order service. Admission to the museum is £1 ($1.75) for adults, 65p ($1.15) for children.

Food and Lodging
The Royal Hotel, Melville Square, Comrie, Perthshire PH6 2DN (tel. 0764/70200), was awarded the "royal" after the visit of Her Majesty, Queen Victoria. It's not, as you might imagine, a Victorian hotel, but rather an L-shaped stone inn dating back to 1765, with white trim and six bedroom dormers. Its cocktail bar with copper-top tables, furnished and decorated in the proprietor's own Gordon tartan, is noted for its selection of malt whiskies, and on the walls are framed prints and photographs with signatures of numerous famous guests who have stayed here over the years, including that of "Monty," Lloyd George, actress Sarah Bernhardt, and Queen Victoria's faithful servant, John Brown. The dining room is equally attractive, with an open log fire. The bedrooms are comfortable, consisting of one with a four-poster bed plus 13 more units, all of which have private baths, direct-dial phones, color TVs, radios, hot beverage facilities, and electric blankets with controls. The charge per person for B&B is £22 ($38.50) daily, £34 ($59.50) per person for a

bed and half board. The spacious residents' lounge is well appointed, and the cocktail bar has been refurbished. You can dine à la carte in the dining room, with silver service. A table d'hôte dinner costs £14 ($24.50). Lunch is served daily from noon to 2 p.m., and dinner hours are from 7 to 9 p.m. Sunday to Thursday, from 7 to 10 p.m. Friday and Saturday.

DUNDEE

This royal burgh and old seaport is an industrial city, one of the largest in Scotland, lying on the north shore of the Firth of Tay. When steamers took over the whaling industry from sailing vessels, Dundee took the lead as homeport for the ships from the 1860s until World War I. Long known for its jute and flax operations, the fame of Dundee today is linked with the production of the rich Dundee fruitcakes and Dundee marmalades and jams.

Spanning the Firth of Tay is the **Tay Railway Bridge,** opened in 1888. Constructed over the tidal estuary, the bridge is some two miles long, one of the longest in Europe. There is also a road bridge a mile and a quarter long, with four lanes and a walkway in the center.

Although many travelers pass through the city en route to Glamis Castle, 12 miles north, there are some interesting sights in Dundee.

Sights

At Victoria Dock, the frigate *Unicorn* (tel. 0382/200900), a 46-gun ship of war launched in 1824 by the Royal Navy and now the oldest British-built ship afloat, has been in large part restored and visitors can explore all four decks: the quarterdeck with 32-pound carronades; the gundeck with its battery of 18-pound cannons and the captain's quarters; the berth-deck with officers' cabins and crew's hammocks; and the orlop deck and hold. Various displays portraying life in the sailing navy and the history of the *Unicorn* make this a rewarding visit. The ship is open daily from 10 a.m. to 5 p.m. (to 4 p.m. Saturday) from April to mid-October. There is limited opening Monday to Saturday in winter. Admission is £1 ($1.75) for adults, 50p (90¢) for children.

The McManus Galleries, Albert Square (tel. 0382/23141), designed by Sir George Gilbert Scott and built in 1867, house an art collection of national importance, including fine examples of 19th and 20th century Scottish paintings, prints, drawing, sculptures, furniture, clocks, glass, ceramics, and silver. There are also three galleries telling the story of life in Tayside from prehistoric times to the Industrial Revolution and on into the 20th century. The archeology gallery also has a significant display of material from ancient Egypt and breaks new ground by including contemporary art work in the display design. The building is one of Scotland's finest examples of Victorian Gothic architecture. The galleries are open from 10 a.m. to 5 p.m. Monday to Saturday. Admission is free.

For a spectacular view of Dundee, the Tay bridges across to Fife, and the mountains to the north, go to **Dundee Law,** a 572-foot hill a mile north of the city. The hill is an ancient volcanic plug.

About five miles east of the city center on the seafront, at **Broughty Ferry,** a little fishing hamlet, later the terminus for the ferry that crossed the Firth of Tay until the bridges were built, is **Broughty Castle** (tel. 0382/76121), a 15th-century estuary fort. Besieged by the English in the 16th century and attacked by Cromwell's army under General Monk in the 17th century, it was eventually restored as part of Britain's coastal defenses in 1861. Its gun battery was dismantled in 1956, and it is now a museum with displays on local history, arms and armor, seashore life, and Dundee's whaling story. The observation area at the top of the castle provides fine views of the Tay estuary and northeast Fife. The castle is open from 10 a.m. to 1 p.m. and 2 to 5 p.m. Monday to Thursday. It is open on Sunday July to September only, from 2 to 5 p.m. Closed Friday.

Food and Lodging

Angus Thistle Hotel, 101 Marketgait, Dundee, Angus OD1 1QU (tel. 0382/26874), is a glass-and-concrete structure. Don't stay here seeking historical romance, but if you want a comfortable accommodation, you'll find all the amenities. The furnishings throughout are well maintained, all with private baths. In a single, the rate is from £45 ($78.75) daily. A double rents for £69 ($85.75). VAT and service are included. The hotel also has three bars and a main dining room serving a standard cuisine.

ARBROATH

Samuel Johnson wasn't that much impressed with Scotland on his jaunt there, but he did say that the view of Arbroath repaid him for some of the hardships suffered in his journey. Arbroath is a popular coastal resort with a fishing harbor and rugged, red sandstone cliffs weathered into grotesque shapes. Smugglers once used the sandstone caves along the coast. Arbroath "smokies" (smoked haddock) are one of the fish delicacies along the east coast of Scotland.

The "Fairport" of Sir Walter Scott's *The Antiquary,* the royal burgh of Arbroath lies 17 miles northeast of Dundee.

Associated with the Declaration of Arbroath of 1320, when the Scottish Parliament met here and drew up a famous letter to send to the pope asserting Scotland's independence from England, **Arbroath Abbey,** High Street, was founded as a priory in 1178 by William the Lion to honor his late friend, Thomas à Becket, murdered in Canterbury eight years earlier. The red sandstone abbey, a rich and influential ecclesiastical center, became dilapidated after the beginning of the 17th century, but it was once again in the news in 1951 when the Stone of Scone, stolen from Westminster Abbey, turned up on the altar here. A historical pageant is presented in the abbey annually. For more information, phone 031/244-3101. Hours are the same as for the museum described below.

The **Abbot's House,** within the precincts of Arbroath Abbey (tel. 0241/78756), has been restored as a museum, with a collection of relics and stone sculpture. April to the end of September hours are 9:30 a.m. to 7 p.m. Monday to Saturday, from 2 p.m. to 7 p.m. on Sunday. The remainder of the year the hours are the same, except for a 4 p.m. closing. Admission charges are 60p ($1.05) for adults, 30p (55¢) for children.

Food and Lodging

Letham Grange, Colliston, Arbroath, Angus DD11 4RL (tel. 0241/024189), is by far the best place to stay in the area, but you have to journey nearly five miles northeast of Arbroath along A933. A Victorian country house, now turned into a hotel of charm and character, it has been sensitively restored and now welcomes guests. The grange is set on a 350-acre private estate near an 18-hole golf course. All year guests are received, and they are housed and fed well. Rooms are not only comfortable, but immaculately maintained and well furnished. Guests are charged from £45 ($78.75) daily in a single, the cost rising to £72 ($126) in a double. The food is good, using quality ingredients, and the service and attention is first class. Meals can be ordered from an à la carte menu, a combination of Scottish and continental dishes. You may want to photograph the hotel, as it's one of those Scottish Victorian piles with a crescent-shaped pillared Georgian portico from which rises a square tower. It dates from the age when newly prosperous Victorians had unlimited funds to spend on their castles in the north. The hotel is sports oriented, with fishing and riding as well as the previously mentioned golf available.

KIRRIEMUIR

This town of narrow streets is the birthplace of Sir James M. Barrie, the "Thrums" of his novels. The Scottish dramatist and novelist was born in 1860, son of a father who was employed as a hand-loom weaver of linen. **Barrie's Birthplace,** 9 Brechin Rd. (tel. 0575/72646), a property of the National Trust for Scotland, contains manuscripts and mementos of the writer. A little wash house outside the four-room cottage was used by the young Barrie as his first theater. Besides his creation of *Peter Pan,* Barrie also wrote such stage successes as *The Admirable Crichton* and *Dear Brutus.* The house is open from 11 a.m. to 5:30 p.m. daily, from 2 to 5:30 p.m. Sunday, in Easter week and May to the end of September. Admission is 90p ($1.60) for adults, 45p (80¢) for children.

Food and Lodging

Thrums Hotel, 25 Bank St., Kirriemuir, Angus DD8 4BE (tel. 0575/72758), built in the 19th century, is almost next to the birthplace. The hostelry is like an inn, standing in the heart of town, with pleasantly kept rooms. Everything about the hotel is well maintained. You might like it so much you'll choose it as a center for exploring Tayside. The charge for bathless accommodations is £16 ($28) per person daily, rising to £21 ($36.75) per person for a room with private bath for B&B. Should you just be passing through Kirriemuir, Thrums is ideal for lunch. It suitably honors Barrie by offering some old-fashioned and traditional Scottish cookery, including Tayside salmon, Angus steaks, and cloutie dumpling. Lunch, from noon to 2 p.m., costs £6.50 ($11.40), and dinner, from 6:30 to 9:30 p.m., runs around £12 ($21).

From Kirriemuir, it's a four-mile drive south to—

GLAMIS CASTLE

After Balmoral Castle, most visitors to Scotland want to see Glamis Castle at Glamis (pronounced Glaams), for its architecture, its Shakespearian link (Macbeth was Thane of Glamis at the beginning of the play), and its link with the Crown. For ten centuries it has been connected to British royalty. Her Majesty, Queen Elizabeth, the Queen Mother, was brought up here; her daughter, now Queen Elizabeth II, spent a good deal of her childhood here; and Princess Margaret, the Queen's sister, was born here, becoming the first royal princess born in Scotland in three centuries. The existing castle dates in part from the middle of the 14th century, but there are records of a castle's having been in existence in the 11th century, at which time it was one of the hunting lodges of the kings of Scotland. King Malcolm II was carried there mortally wounded in 1034 after having been attacked by his enemies while hunting in a nearby forest.

Glamis Castle has been in the possession of the Lyon family since 1372, when it formed part of the dowry of Princess Joanna, daughter of King Robert II, when she married John Lyon, secretary to the king. The castle was altered in the 16th century and restored and enlarged in the 17th, 18th, and 19th centuries. It contains some fine plaster ceilings, furniture, and paintings.

The present owner, the Queen's cousin, is the 18th Earl of Strathmore and Kinghorne. He lives at the castle with his family. He is the direct descendant of the first earl.

The castle is open to the public, who have access to the Royal Apartments and many other rooms, and also to the gardens and grounds, daily from noon to 5:30 p.m. (last tour at 4:45 p.m.) from the end of April to mid-October. Admission to the castle and gardens is £2.50 ($4.40) for adults, £1.30 ($2.30) for children. If you wish to visit the grounds only, the charge is £1 ($1.75) for adults, 50p (90¢) for children. For further details, get in touch with the Administrator, Estates Office (tel. 030784/242).

Also in Glamis, you may want to visit the **Angus Folk Museum, Kirkwynd Cottages** (tel. 030784/288), run by the National Trust for Scotland. From the former county of Angus, rich in folklore, were collected domestic utensils, agricultural implements, furniture, and clothing. The museum is open from noon to 5 p.m. May 1 to September 30 but from 11:30 a.m. to 5:30 p.m. in June, July, and August (last entry 20 minutes earlier). Admission is £1.20 ($2.10) for adults, 60p ($1.05) for children.

DUNKELD

A cathedral town, Dunkeld lies in a thickly wooded valley of the Tay River, at the edge of the Perthshire Highlands, 58 miles from Edinburgh. Once a major ecclesiastical center, it is one of the seats of ancient Scottish history. It was an important center of the Celtic church, for example.

Founded in A.D. 815, the **Cathedral of Dunkeld** was converted from a church to a cathedral in 1127 by David I. The 14th and 15th centuries witnessed subsequent additions. The cathedral was first restored in 1815, and at that time traces of the 12th-century structure clearly remained, as they do to this day. The cathedral can be visited daily from 9:30 a.m. to 7 p.m. in summer, from 9:30 a.m. to 4 p.m. in winter. Admission is free.

The National Trust for Scotland has been effective in restoring many of the old houses and shops around the marketplace and cathedral that had fallen into decay. The trust owns 20 houses on High Street and Cathedral Street. Many of these were constructed in the closing years of the 17th century during the rebuilding of the town following the Battle of Dunkeld. The trust has opened an **Ell Shop,** which is open from 10 a.m. to 1 p.m. and 2 to 4:30 p.m. Monday to Saturday from Easter weekend to May 31 and September 1 to December 22. Hours are from 10 a.m. to 6 p.m. Monday to Saturday and 2 to 5 p.m. Sunday from June 1 to the end of August.

The **Scottish Horse Museum,** The Cross, has exhibits tracing the history of the Scottish Horse Yeomanry in the museum in one of the "Little Houses of Dunkeld," the area between the cathedral and the town's main street in which Jacobean cottages are preserved and maintained by the National Trust for Scotland. From the time of its raising in Scotland and South Africa in 1900 to its amalgamation with the Fife & Forfar Yeomanry in 1956, the Scottish Horse mounted yeomanry regiment was the only such fighting body besides the Lovat Scouts. The museum is open from 10:30 a.m. to 5 p.m. Monday to Saturday and 11 a.m. to 5 p.m. on Sunday (closed for 1½ hours at lunchtime) from Easter to the end of September. Admission is 30p (55¢) for adults, free for children.

Shakespeare fans may want to seek out the oak and sycamore in front of the destroyed **Birnam House,** a mile to the south. This was believed to be a remnant of the Birnam wood to which the Bard gave everlasting literary fame in *Macbeth.* In Shakespeare's drama, you may recall, the "woods of Birnam came to Dunsinane."

Food and Lodging

Stakis Dunkeld House Hotel, Dunkeld, Perthshire PH8 0HX (tel. 03502/ 771), offers the quiet dignity of life in a Scottish country house. Built by the seventh Duke of Atholl for his duchess in the 19th century, the house was erected on the banks of the Tay, and the surrounding grounds—100 acres in all—were planted with trees and flowering bushes, making for a parklike setting. You reach the house by going down a long drive. Guests can fish for trout and salmon on the grounds. The house is well preserved and beautifully kept, and as befits such a place, accommodations come in a wide range of styles, space, and furnishings. Singles cost £70 ($122.50) to £80 ($140) daily, and doubles or twins go for £110 ($192.50) to £120 ($210), and all rates include VAT. The hotel, extensively restored and expanded, now offers 100 first-class bedrooms, each with private bath. It is ranked as one of the leading leisure and sporting hotels in the country. Its restaurant is the finest in the area, paying homage to its Taste of Scotland dishes but also serving an elegant international cuisine as well. Facilities include all-weather tennis courts and an indoor swimming pool Archery and fishing are also popular

Cardney House, Dunkeld, Perthshire PH8 0EX (tel. 03504/222), is an elegant 18th-century manor on a private estate outside Dunkeld, three miles from the town on the A923 Blair Gowrie road. The house is surrounded by hills, forests, and lochs, and on the grounds rare and beautiful shrubs are grown, as well as orchids, stephanotis, and lemon and orange trees. Here you are received like the guest at a private party at a country home by the charming and hospitable hosts, Commander and Mistress MacGregor of Cardney, who because of "crippling taxes" now receive paying guests. The gracious home is well furnished, often with antiques, and the atmosphere is one of refinement and tranquility, a style set so admirably by the proprietors. They have available now only two singles and six doubles, charging £26 ($45.50) per person daily for half board, including VAT. Dinner, a Cordon Bleu cuisine, is served until 10 in the evening, and you definitely feel you are dining family style. The food is well prepared and beautifully served, and meals are complemented by a first-class wine cellar. Guests relax freely in the lounges, which are furnished with family treasures, often antiques. There's an elevator. During the day, shooting and fishing expeditions can be arranged. Mistress Mariquita MacGregor is an active concert singer, and musical evenings are given regularly at Cardney.

PITLOCHRY

After leaving Edinburgh, many motorists stop here for the night before continuing on the Highland road to Inverness. However, once they discover the charms of Pitlochry, they want to linger. This popular holiday resort center is a touring headquarters for the Valley of the Tummel.

It is particularly renowned for its **Pitlochry Festival Theatre,** Scotland's "theater in the hills." (Telephone 0796/2680 for information.) Founded in 1951, the festival theater draws people from all over the world to its repertoire of plays, usually presented from May until late October. Performances in the evening begin at 8, and on Wednesday and Saturday there is a matinee at 2 p.m. A theater next to Pitlochry's dam and salmon ladder opened in 1981.

The **Pitlochry Dam** was created because a new power station was needed, but in effect the engineers created a new loch. The famous "Salmon Ladder" was built to help the struggling salmon upstream. An underwater portion of the ladder—a salmon-observation chamber—has been enclosed in glass to give sightseers a look. An exhibition (tel. 0796/3152) is open here from Easter to late October daily from 9:45 a.m. to 5:30 p.m., charging adults 30p (55¢), and children, 15p (25¢).

Pitlochry doesn't just entertain visitors, although it would appear that way in summer. It also produces scotch whisky and tweeds.

Food and Lodging

The Green Park Hotel, Clunie Bridge Road, Pitlochry, Perthside PH16 5JY (tel. 0796/3248), lies about half a mile from the center, at the northwest end of Pitlochry, and it's one of the best hotels in the area. Against a backdrop of woodland, the white-painted mansion with its carved eaves enjoys a scenic position, its lawn reaching to the shores of Loch Faskally, the only hotel so situated. Visitors who reserve well in advance get one of the half dozen or so rooms in the garden wing, each with a private bath and all enjoying a view of the loch. It's customary to stay here on half-board terms, costing £33 ($57.75) to £39 ($68.25) per person daily. Guests enjoy drinks in a half-moon-shaped lounge overlooking the water. Many diners come here during festival season to enjoy the good food and wine. The hotel is supervised by Anne and Graham Brown. Dinner is served until 8 p.m., and many traditional Scottish dishes are featured. The Green Park is open from mid-March until November 1.

Pitlochry Hydro Hotel, Knockard Road, Pitlochry, Perthshire PH16 5JH (tel.

0796/2666), was originally known by the English gentry who came here in summer to enjoy the fresh air of the Perthshire Highlands. Built in the Scottish baronial mansion style, the hotel has kept up with modern improvements. The hotel stands on large, well-manicured grounds. At latest count, the hotel had nearly 70 rooms, all with private bath. Ask for one of the turreted corner rooms when making a reservation. Singles cost £40 ($70) daily, and doubles go for £68 ($119), including a full Scottish breakfast, VAT, and service. A set dinner costs £10 ($17.50). The hotel has an indoor swimming pool and other leisure facilities.

Pine Trees Hotel, Strathview Terrace, Pitlochry, Perthshire PH16 5QR (tel. 0796/2121), is a charming country-house hotel built in the 1890s on 14 acres of private grounds, only about a 15-minute walk to the town center and the golf course, home of the Highland Open Championships. A well-appointed family-run hotel, Pine Trees has spacious, comfortable public rooms, an atmosphere of warmth and relaxation, and an enviable reputation for good food and wine. Most of the 18 bedrooms have a private bath, and prices in the high season are £26 ($45.50) daily in a single, £60 ($105) in a double. Bar lunches and full luncheon and dinner menus are offered, with fresh and smoked salmon always on the menu. Trout and salmon fishing can usually be arranged.

Excursions from Pitlochry

From the town you can make excursions in almost any direction. Heading northwest for three miles on the A9, you come to the **Pass of Killiecrankie,** where "Bonnie Dundee" and his Jacobites won their victory over the armies of General Mackay fighting for King William in 1689. This is one of the scenic highlights of the area.

A **Visitors Centre** (tel. 0796/3233) stands near the site of the famous battle. It presents an interesting exhibition and is also a center for rangers and naturalists. Dedicated Scots will answer questions on walks, whatever, which are possible in the area. The exhibition, Visitors Centre, shop, and snackbar are open from 10 a.m. to 5 p.m. daily from Easter weekend to May 25 and September 1 to the end of October, from 9:30 a.m. to 6 p.m. daily from May 26 to the end of August.

If time remains, try to see another attraction, **Queen's View,** where Victoria herself picnicked in 1844. At the eastern end, Victoria looked down the length of the loch toward Schiehallion. The view is reached by taking the B8019 for 2½ miles northwest of Pitlochry. An obelisk commemorates the visit of the queen. The beauty spot, the Linn of Tummel, along with 40 acres, came to the National Trust for Scotland during World War II. It is filled with magnificent woodland walks, in which you can enjoy the Douglas fir, spruce, larch, oak, and sycamore.

BLAIR ATHOLL

Eight miles to the northwest of Pitlochry stands the gleaming white **Blair Castle** (tel. 079681/207), the home of the Duke of Atholl, just off the A9. Built in Scottish baronial style and dating from 1269, it has the distinction of being the last castle in the British Isles to be besieged. Today, in more than 32 rooms open to the public, you can see impressive collections of furniture, paintings, china, lace, Masonic regalia, arms and armor, and Jacobite relics. It is open Easter week through the third Sunday in October. Hours are 10 a.m. to 6 p.m. daily, from 2 to 6 p.m. on Sunday. Last entry is at 5 p.m. Admission is £2.50 ($4.40) for adults, £1.50 ($2.65) for children. The Duke of Atholl has the only official private army in Great Britain, known as the Atholl Highlanders.

For both food and lodging, you might prefer a stopover in Blair Atholl to Pitlochry. If so, I'd recommend the **Atholl Arms,** Blair Atholl, Perthside PH18 5SG (tel. 079681/205). Once lords and ladies who couldn't find room at Blair Castle stayed here, and some of the grand balls of old Perthshire were held here. Now the

Atholl Arms is a roadside inn, built of stone and gabled with large bays, attracting motorists en route to Inverness. A cocktail lounge has been redecorated, and there's a public bar as well, attracting the locals. The ballroom has been turned into an arched-roof restaurant, complete with a minstrels' gallery. There's also a more intimate dining room with antiques and mahogany chairs. Both rooms offer a substantial menu. The bedrooms are individually styled and well fitted, and each one I inspected had a completely different character. The rate is £27.50 ($48.15) daily in a single, from £50 ($87.50) in a twin or double, each including a private bath or shower, VAT, service, and a full breakfast. Bar snacks are served at lunch, and a four-course table d'hôte dinner, costing £11.50 ($20.15), is offered in the evening.

KILLIN

Just over the border from Tayside in the central region, Killin is a village on the Dochart at the lower end of Loch Tay. Lying 45 miles west of Perth by road, Killin is both a summer holiday resort and a winter sports center. The **Falls of Dochart** are world-famous, but the town is also noted for beauty spots, and there are sights of historical interest as well.

Killin Church contains a font more than 1,000 years old. Less than a quarter of a mile from the church stands an upright stone, said to mark the grave of Fingal. An island in the Dochart was the ancient burial place of the MacNab Clan.

The ruins of **Finlarig Castle** contain a beheading pit near the castle gate that was written about in Scott's *The Fair Maid of Perth*. Perched 1,000 feet above the loch, the castle was the seat of "Black Duncan of the Cowl," a notoriously ruthless chieftain of the Campbell Clan.

Food and Lodging

Bridge of Lochay, Killin, Perthshire FK21 8TS (tel. 05672/272), retains some of its 16th-century character, although it has seen many alterations and additions since that time. Half a mile from Killin, the "bridge"—an attractive, rambling, white-painted building—lies on the banks of the Lochay River, at the tip of Loch Tay. F. W. Ogilvie, the owner, welcomes you to one of his 17 bedrooms, simply but comfortably furnished. The overnight charge is from £16.50 ($28.90) per person for a bed and a large Scottish breakfast. Guests can enjoy good drinks in one of two bars or sit in front of peat and log fires in the lounges. The food is Scottish and continental cuisine. If you stay at least three nights, you'll be quoted a half-board tariff of £26 ($45.50) per person daily. The hotel is open from March to November.

Morenish Lodge Highland House, Killin, Perthshire FK21 8TX (tel. 05672/258), is a small Highland hotel, although formerly it was the shooting lodge of an earl, lying 200 feet above Loch Tay and less than three miles from Killin (on the A827 Aberfeldy road). The hotel, run by Graeme and Maureen Naylor, offers 13 bedrooms, most with private baths. Furnishings are comfortable. Singles without bath cost £21 ($36.75) daily; with bath, £24 ($42). Doubles or twins with bath go for £40 ($70). All tariffs include VAT and a full breakfast. Many of the public rooms face the loch, and you can enjoy a good meal with wine in the Tay View room. A four-course set dinner costs £13.50 ($23.65). Bar lunches are served only to residents. In the Laird's Bar, scotch whisky, both blended and single malt, is served.

Dall Lodge Hotel, Main Street, Killin, Perthshire FK21 8TN (tel. 05672/217), is a 19th-century stone house overlooking the River Lochay a quarter of a mile north of Killin on the A827. The hotel specializes in serving many traditional Scottish foods, such as salmon, trout, venison, haggis, Aberdeen Angus beef, Scottish hill lamb, cloutie dumplings, and Scottish raspberry shortcake. A five-course dinner costs from £12 ($21). The hotel carries a wide range of fine wines and a comprehensive choice of malt Scotch whiskies. All bedrooms have hot and cold running water and tea- and coffee-making facilities, and they offer splendid views. Some units have a private bath. The price for B&B is £25 ($43.75) per person daily. All tariffs include VAT.

2. The Grampian Region

Traveling north from the lochs—previewed in the section above—heading toward Royal Deeside, you pass through Glen Shee and Glen Clunie, a most spectacular route that will give you your first taste of Highland scenery.

As you journey across uncrowded roads into Scotland's northeast, you'll review heather-covered moorland and peaty lochs, wood glens and salmon-filled rivers, granite-stone villages and fishing harbors, even North Sea beach resorts.

This is the Grampian region, with such centers as Aberdeen and Braemar, and such sights as Balmoral Castle and the "Whisky Trail." Even the Queen comes here for holidays.

BRAEMAR

This little Deeside resort is the site of the **Royal Highland Gathering,** which takes place there annually, either in late August or early September. It is usually attended by Queen Elizabeth. The "royal link" dates from the 1840s when Queen Victoria first attended the games.

The capital of the Deeside Highlands, Braemar is overrun with foreign visitors, as well as the British, during the gathering. Anyone thinking of attending would be wise to make application for accommodation anywhere within a 20-mile radius of Braemar not later than early April.

The gathering in Braemar is the most famous of the many Highland games. The spectacular occasion is held in the **Princess Royal and Duke of Fife Memorial Park.** Competitions include tossing the caber, throwing the hammer, sprinting, vaulting, a tug-o'-war, the long leap, Highland dancing, putting a 16-pound ball, sword dancing, relay races, and, naturally, a bagpiping contest. At a vast refreshment tent, Scottish lassies serve tea, coffee, buns, and other refreshments.

The romantic 17th-century **Braemar Castle** (tel. 03397/41213) lies half a mile northeast of Braemar on the A93. A fully furnished private residence of architectural grace, scenic charm, and historical interest, it is the seat of Capt. A. A. Farquharson of Invercauld. Opening onto the Dee River, it was built in 1628 by the Earl of Mar. John Farquharson of Inverey, the "Black Colonel," attacked and burned it in 1689. The castle is built in the shape of an L, with a spiral stairway and a circular main tower. Fully furnished, it has barrel-vaulted ceilings and an underground prison, and is known for its remarkable star-shaped defensive curtain wall. It can be visited from May 1 until the first Monday in October daily from 10 a.m. to 6 p.m., costing £1.30 ($2.30) for adults, 65p ($1.15) for children. The castle has a gift shop, and a free car park.

Food and Lodging

Invercauld Arms Hotel, Braemar, Aberdeenshire AB3 5YR (tel. 03397/41605), is a lovely old granite building of which the original part dates back to the 18th century. In cool weather there's a roaring log fire on the hearth, and the staff offers you traditional Highland hospitality. You can go hill walking and see deer, golden eagles, and other wildlife. Fishing and, in winter, skiing are other pursuits in the nearby area. To spend a few days in this thoroughly pleasant hotel visiting fine old castles and whisky distilleries makes a perfect respite. In the pub close by you'll meet the "ghillies" and "stalkers" and then return to the Castleview Restaurant to sample a "Taste of Scotland" with fresh Dee salmon, Aberdeen Angus beef, venison, and grouse, together with the "dreaded haggis," on the extensive menu of local specialties. Of course, you'll find kippers and porridge with the full Scottish breakfast that is included in the room rates. A coffeeshop serves light meals, and the well-known Colonel's Bed bar offers entertainment on occasion. A room with private bath, single or double, goes for £32.50 ($56.90) per person daily in season.

Fife Arms Hotel, Mar Road, Braemar, Aberdeenshire AB3 5YN (tel. 03397/ 41644), near Braemar, was originally built in the 19th century as a holiday home for the Duke of Fife, but was later converted into a stagecoach inn for passengers and horses. It boasts an elegant façade of intricately patterned gingerbread, multiple chimneys, gables, a Gothic portico, and a solid construction of pinkish sandstone. Inside, many modernizations have removed much of the 19th century, but it remains a comfortable and familiar place much favored by families. It's a quintessential Scottish provincial hotel, with a coffee buffet and a glass deli case in the lobby dispensing snacks. There are two bars on the premises, as well as a restaurant. In all, the hotel rents 87 centrally heated bedrooms, each pleasantly outfitted with functional pieces. Many contain private baths or showers. B&B ranges from £19 ($33.25) to £25 ($43.75) per person daily, depending on the plumbing and the accommodation.

BALLATER

On the Dee River, with the Grampian mountains in the background, Ballater is a holiday resort center where visitors flock to view one of Scotland's most popular sightseeing attractions, Balmoral Castle (see below).

The town still centers around its **Station Square,** where the royal family used to be photographed as they arrived to spend holidays. The railway has since been closed.

From Ballater you can drive west to view the magnificent scenery of **Glen Muick** and **Lochnagar,** where you'll see herds of deer.

Food and Lodging

Craigendarroch Hotel and Country Club, Braemar Road, Ballater, Aberdeenshire AB3 5XA (tel. 03397/55858), built in the Scottish baronial style, is set amid old trees on a 28-acre estate a few minutes' drive outside Ballater. The comfort of the 20th century has been added, but the owners have tried to maintain a 19th-century aura. The public rooms include a regal oaken staircase and a large sitting room, but the feature is a leisure club, including a spa pool, two swimming pools, a sauna, and a solarium, along with various games and a beauty salon. Tennis courts are outside, and there is a dry ski slope. Views from the bedrooms open onto the village of Ballater and the River Dee.

There are 51 accommodations, each furnished in an individual style, with color TV, direct-dial phone, radio, hairdryer, trouser press, and private bath and shower. Rates are from £90 ($157.50) to £120 ($210) daily for two persons, with singles paying about £5 ($8.75) less, tariffs including breakfast and VAT. The public facilities are luxurious, especially the Study with oak paneling, a log fire, and book-lined shelves. In the Oaks Restaurant, guests enjoy such specialties as local game, Scottish beef, trout, and salmon. Fine crystal, fresh flowers, and bone china complement the menu. The French-style Café Jardin also serves light meals and drinks, and the Lochnagal Restaurant built above the club offers good views.

Tullich Lodge, Ballater, Aberdeenshire AB3 5SB (tel. 03397/55406), on the A93, 1½ miles east of Ballater, is a turreted country house built in the Scottish baronial style, standing in five acres of its own gardens and woods above Royal Deeside and Ballater. The attractive hotel is tastefully decorated and furnished, often with antiques, its brass fittings and wood paneling providing the traditional touches. Your pleasant hosts, Hector Macdonald and Neil Bannister, offer only ten bedrooms, but they're of generous size and are beautifully furnished. At least eight contain a private bath; the rest have a shower. Half-board rates are £66 ($115.50) per person daily in a single or double. The lodge closes from December through March. Its dining room, commanding panoramic views of the "royal valley," serves some of the finest food along Royal Deeside. One of the chef's specialties is casseroles, although he does all the standard dishes with above-average flair, including locally caught trout and salmon, game and especially venison in season, as well as crab and lobster. A table d'hôte dinner, served from 7:30 to 9 p.m. daily, goes for about £18 ($31.50). A bar luncheon is at 1 p.m. with no fried foods. It's essential to make a reservation. In an amusing bar, you can order from a good selection of malt whiskies. To get the most out of the surrounding countryside, as well as this special hotel, I'd recommend whenever possible a stay of a minimum of two nights. It's a good place to unpack your luggage and settle in for a bit.

Balmoral Castle

"This dear paradise" is how Queen Victoria described this castle, rebuilt in the Scottish baronial style by her beloved Albert. It was completed in 1855. Today Balmoral, eight miles west of Ballater, is still a private residence of the British sovereign. Albert, the prince consort, acquired the property in 1847, and the royal family first arrived there in 1848. As the little castle left by the Farquharsons proved too small, the present castle was rebuilt. Its principal feature is a 100-foot tower. On the grounds are many memorials to the royal family. The grounds can be visited, daily except Sunday in May, June, and July from 10 a.m. to 5 p.m. Visitors can also get a view of an exhibition of paintings and works of art in the castle ballroom. The remainder of the castle interior is never open to the public. In addition, there are country walks and pony trekking. Admission to the grounds and art exhibition is £1.30 ($2.30) for adults; children, free. For information, phone 03384/334.

BANCHORY

On lower Deeside, this resort is rich in woodland and river scenery. From this base, you can take excursions to two of the most popular castles in the Grampian region, Crathes and Craigievar.

Crathes Castle and Gardens (tel. 033044/525), two miles east of Banchory, has royal historical associations dating from 1323, when the lands of Leys were granted to the Burnett family by King Robert the Bruce. The Horn of Leys, said to have been given by Bruce to symbolize the gift, is in the Great Hall. The castle's features include remarkable late-16th-century painted ceilings. The garden is a composite of eight separate gardens, which give a display all year. The great yew hedges date from 1702. The grounds are ideal for nature study, and there are five trails, including a long-distance layout, with ranger service. The complex includes a licensed restaurant, Visitor Centre with permanent exhibitions, souvenir shop, wayfaring course, children's adventure playground, picnic area, and car park.

The grounds and gardens are open daily from 9:30 a.m. to sunset. The castle, Visitor Centre, shop, and restaurant are open from 11 a.m. to 6 p.m. Easter weekend, Saturday and Sunday in April, and from May to October 31. A combined ticket to see everything costs £2.80 ($4.90) for adults, with children paying half price. Reductions are available for visitors wishing to visit the castle or the gardens only.

Structurally unchanged since its completion in 1626, **Craigievar Castle** (tel. 033983/635) is an example of Scottish baronial architecture at its greatest height. Original molded plaster ceilings are to be seen in most rooms. The castle has been continually inhabited by the descendants of the builder, William Forbes, and is now preserved by the National Trust for Scotland. It is open daily from 2 to 6 p.m. during May and June as well as the month of September. Hours from July to the end of August are from 11 a.m. to 6 p.m. (last tour at 5:15 p.m.). The grounds are open all year from 9:30 a.m. to sunset daily. Admission is £2.10 ($3.70) for adults, £1.05 ($1.85) for children.

Some four miles from the castle, near Lumphanan, is Macbeth's Cairn where the historical Macbeth is supposed to have fought his last battle.

Food and Lodging

The premier place to stay is **Invery House,** Feughside, Banchory, Kincardineshire AB3 3NJ (tel. 03302/4782), a Georgian mansion of great charm, standing in its own gardens and wooded grounds. It's small, only 14 bedrooms, but its reputation is big as one of the leading hotels of Scotland. The proprietors, Sheila and Stewart Spence, have sensitively and painstakingly restored this mansion until today it is one of the grand addresses of the Grampian region. Invery House is that dream of what a Scottish country house hotel should be (but all too often isn't). Antiques and oil paintings add the necessary charm, but all the modern necessities are here, too. The location is on 40 acres of gardens and woodland opening onto the banks of the River Feugh.

Mr. and Mrs. Spence have paid particular care to their beautifully furnished bedrooms, each one named after one of the novels of Sir Walter Scott, who worked on his poem, *Marmion,* here. Sometimes antiques grace the rooms, and everywhere you look you see the knowing touch of a decorator. Bathrooms are luxurious. Rates range from £75 ($131.25) daily in a single, rising to £85 ($148.75) to £145 ($253.75) in a double. And if that wasn't enough, the hotel is also the outstanding dining choice in the area, offering a set dinner for £22.50 ($39.40). Fresh produce goes into the imaginative dishes, which are handled skillfully in the kitchen and served with a certain formality. Dining hours are daily from 12:15 to 2:15 p.m. and 7:15 to 9:45 p.m.

Raemoir House, Banchory, Kincardineshire AB3 4ED (tel. 03302/4884), is an 18th-century manor standing on 3,500 acres of grounds with such sporting attractions as shooting, fishing, and riding. It is a journey into nostalgia, with its ballroom, antiques, and fine tapestries, and log fires burning in the colder months. The rooms are handsomely decorated, most of them quite large, and all of the 24 bedchambers contain a private bath. What is so lovely about Scotland is its curious mixtures—in this case, an 18th-century manor house with its own helipad. Meals are served in an attractive Georgian dining room, featuring a standard repertoire of familiar dishes, rather well done. Service is informal and prompt. The B&B rate ranges from £45 ($78.75) daily single, £70 ($122.50) double. All prices include VAT and morning tea or coffee. The hotel is run just like a private house—no keys to bedroom doors, but you can bolt yourself in for privacy. The adjoining Ha' Hoose with rentable rooms was once used by Mary Queen of Scots.

Tor-Na-Coille, Inchmarlo Road, Banchory, Kincardineshire AB3 4AB (tel. 03302/2242), is a country-house hotel—really a Victorian mansion—standing on its own wooded grounds of about six acres. Public rooms are suitably spacious, most comfortable, and the whisky always tastes better in the modern bar. If you're on your way to see Balmoral Castle or to attend the Highland gathering at Braemar, you will be able to relax here, enjoying the gracious hospitality. The bedrooms, many quite large, are restful and all of them have private bath, color TV, radio, phone, and coffee-making equipment. Singles cost from £34.50 ($60.40) daily, and doubles rent for £55 ($96.25), including a full breakfast and VAT. The hotel is interesting architecturally, and the room you may be assigned could have much character. Lunches are light meals in the bar, including smoked venison sausage blended with rum and red wine. Sunday lunch is a grander affair, when the main dishes include roast beef, turkey, and leg of pork. Food at night is by candlelight, and here might be your chance to try real Scottish salmon (the salmon leap at the Falls of Feugh nearby). Dinner is likely to feature the chef's special pheasant. The hotel has a high reputation for its food.

Banchory Lodge, Dee Street, Banchory, Kincardineshire AB3 3HS (tel. 03302/2625), built in 1738, was once the home of a well-known Deeside family. It is a pleasant country house with much Georgian charm. On its own grounds, on the banks of the Dee, where it is joined by the Water of the Feugh, the lodge is open all year, accommodating guests in some 24 bedrooms, many of which overlook the river, all with private bath. The B&B rate is about £45 ($78.75) daily in a single, £68 ($119) in a double or twin. In the dining room, overlooking the river, furnishings and decor are in period style. Specialties include fresh Dee salmon and Aberdeen Angus roast beef. Guests can fish from the lawn or in one of the hotel's boats by arrangement

ABERDEEN

The harbor in this seaport in the northeast of Scotland is one of the largest fishing ports in the country, filled with kipper and deep-sea trawlers. The **Fish Market** is well worth a visit, as it's the liveliest in Britain.

Bordered by fine sandy beaches (delightful if you're a polar bear), Scotland's third city, 130 miles from Edinburgh, is often called "the granite city," as its buildings are constructed largely of granite, in pink or gray, hewn from the Rubislaw quarries.

Aberdeen is the capital of the oil workers who help harvest the riches from six North Sea oilfields. Their number has dwindled in recent years, however. The city lies on the banks of the salmon- and trout-filled Don and Dee rivers. Spanning the Don is the **Brig o' Balgownie,** a steep Gothic arch, begun in 1285.

In Castlegate is the **Mercat Cross,** a hexagonally shaped structure, built in 1686 and considered the handsomest of the old crosses in Scotland.

The **University of Aberdeen** (tel. 0224/40241) is a fusion of two separate colleges. King's College, the older, was founded under a Papal Bull issued in 1495. It contains the oldest school of medicine in Great Britain. The college's chapel is topped by a closed (imperial) crown that was erected about 1505 but was blown down in a storm and quickly replaced in 1633 by an exact copy. Marischal College, founded in 1593, is recognized as one of the finest granite buildings in the world. The two colleges were rival institutions until a royal ordinance enacted in 1860 united them both under the title of the present university.

The university is in the Old Aberdeen, as is the **Cathedral of St. Machar,** founded in 1131, although the present structure dates from the 15th century. Its splendid heraldic ceiling contains three rows of shields representing the kings and princes of Europe along with the Scottish ecclesiastical and aristocratic hierarchy. The modern stained-glass windows are magnificent, the work of Douglas Strachan. The cathedral is open daily from 9 a.m. to 5 p.m. Its phone number is 0224/485988, and that of the manse is 0224/483688.

Provost Skene's House, 45 Guestrow, is named for a rich merchant who was lord provost of Aberdeen from 1676 to 1685. Off Broad Street, it is now a museum with period rooms and artifacts of domestic life. Provost Skene's kitchen has been converted into a café serving tea, coffee, and light meals. Admission is free, and it can be visited Monday to Saturday from 10 a.m. to 5 p.m. For more information, telephone 0224/641086. There's parking available.

Where to Stay

Aberdeen, Scotland's Floral Capital, welcomes visitors all year. There's a wide choice of accommodation in the city: hotels, guesthouses, bed-and-breakfasts, and self-catering units. Many hotels offer bargain rates at weekends. At the **Tourist Information Centre,** St. Nicholas House, Broad Street, Aberdeen, Aberdeenshire AB9 1DE (tel. 0224/632727), a helpful staff will book your accommodation and advise on the attractions of the area.

If you prefer to reserve in advance, I have some selections.

Caledonian Thistle Hotel, 10-14 Union Terrace, Aberdeen, Aberdeenshire AB9 1HE (tel. 0224/640233), sits in a grandly detailed, stone-fronted, 19th-century building in the center of Aberdeen. Recent restorations have added a veneer of Georgian-era gloss, which contributes to one of the most elegant series of public rooms in town. The lobby-level bar and Restaurant on the Terrace (recommended separately) are especially charming, and there is a café bar and restaurant on the ground floor. The hotel offers free parking in a walled-in lot on a street paralleling the hotel. Rooms are at the top of a 19th-century stairwell, with Corinthian columns and a free-standing atrium. There is also elevator service. Each bedroom contains a TV, radio, mini-bar, private bath, and warmly upholstered furniture. Singles cost £65 ($113.75) daily; doubles or twins, £76 ($133).

Bucksburn Moat House Hotel, Oldmeldrum Road, Bucksburn, Aberdeen, Aberdeenshire AB2 9LN (tel. 0224/713911), is four miles north of Aberdeen by the A96 and just two miles from the airport. The hotel is especially popular with business people, who enjoy the large, well-equipped bedrooms, all with private baths. Singles rent for £63.80 ($111.65) daily and doubles go for £73 ($127.75). The Lairds Bar is busy serving bar lunches and bar suppers, while up in the comfortable surroundings of the Mariner Restaurant, you can choose either table d'hôte or à la carte meals, later retiring to the Captains bar for a "wee nip o' whisky." This 99-unit hotel is traditional but with modern conveniences.

Stakis Tree Tops Hotel, 161 Springfield Rd., Aberdeen, Aberdeenshire AB9 2QH (tel. 0224/33377), a five-minute drive west of the center of Aberdeen, is a comfortable hotel built in the 1960s, with a sweeping white façade of traditional design. The windows of its more than 114 contemporary bedrooms look over landscaped grounds. Each contains a private tile-lined bath, color TV, and a phone, and many other extras for your comfort. Singles cost £70 ($122.50) daily, and doubles go for £85 ($148.75). The leather-covered chairs of the paneled main bar offer a cozy spot for conversation. You can dine in either the elegant Garden Room or in Rocco's Ristorante, the bistro-style Italian restaurant. The hotel invites guests to take advantage of the Leisure Club, with a swimming pool, whirlpool, multi-gym, sauna, jogging machine, sunbeds, two all-weather tennis courts, and sports training.

Where to Dine

The leading choice for dining is **The Restaurant on the Terrace,** Caledonian Thistle Hotel, 10-14 Union Terrace (tel. 0224/640-233). Both it and its adjacent bar were renovated into one of the most elegant Georgian restorations in Aberdeen. Beneath a high ceiling capped with elaborate re-creations of antique moldings and embellishments, you dine on such specialties as homemade seafood bisque topped with crème fraîche, suprême of River Dee salmon with watercress sauce, and medallions of Scottish lamb sautéed in walnut oil with a honey-and-rosemary sauce. Full meals, costing from £12.25 ($21.45), are served daily from 12:30 to 2 p.m. and 6:30 to 10 p.m. On Sunday night the last orders are at 9:30 p.m. and no lunch is offered on Saturday. At lunches, selections from a carving table are offered, costing from £9 ($15.75) for a complete meal with all the works, proving popular with the business community. Reservations at dinner are suggested.

Atlantis, 16 Bon Accord Crescent (tel. 0224/591403), is one of the best seafood restaurants in town. It's in a comfortably furnished basement near the center of town. You can enjoy several preparations of lobster, fish chowder, and an array of sole, scampi, and halibut. Some meat dishes are offered, as well as fresh vegetables, salads, and desserts. Full meals cost £15 ($26.25) to £25 ($43.75) per person and are served at lunch, from noon to 2 p.m., and dinner, 7 to 10 p.m., every day of the week except Saturday at lunchtime, all day Sunday, some holidays, and for about two weeks at Christmas.

A Place in the Country

Pittodrie House Hotel, Pitcaple, near Inverurie, Aberdeenshire AB5 9HS (tel. 04676/444), about 21 miles northwest of Aberdeen, was originally one of the castles in the area, built in 1490, but it was burned down by that avid Covenanter, the Duke of Montrose. Rebuilt in 1675, it was a family home changed into a country-house hotel when Royal Deeside came into prominence through Queen Victoria's adoption of Balmoral as her holiday retreat. Twelve beautifully furnished bedrooms are offered, costing £44 ($77) daily for singles, £80 ($140) for doubles, tariffs including a full breakfast, service, and VAT. Antiques and oil paintings decorate the public rooms, where warm open fires make the atmosphere cozy. The elegant restaurant serves such main dishes as venison, grouse, partridge, pheasant, or woodcock, depending on the season, and fresh fish, such as turbot, sea trout, and salmon. Dinners cost from £22 ($38.50) and are served daily from 7:30 p.m. to last orders at 8:45 p.m. Bar lunches are served from 12:30 to 1:30 p.m. Monday to Saturday.

Excursions in "Castle Country"

Aberdeen is the center of "castle country," as 40 inhabited castles lie within a 40-mile radius. Some of the most popular castle excursions are previewed below. For two others, refer to Banchory, above.

South of Aberdeen on the North Sea coast, set on a promontory with three sides protected by cliffs, **Dunnottar Castle** (tel. 0569/62173), about two miles south of Stonehaven (half a mile off the Montrose–Stonehaven road, the A92), was erected, beginning in the 14th century, as the home and fortress of the Keiths, the earls Marischal and Wardens of the Regalia for the Scottish kings. According to legend, an early Christian settlement on the site, more than 150 feet above the sea, was founded by St. Ninian in the 5th century. A short-lived stone house of worship erected in the 13th century caused the excommunication of Sir William Keith a century later because he started his castle keep on what were still consecrated grounds. The partially restored castle can be visited from 9 a.m. to 6 p.m. daily, from 2 to 5 p.m. on Sunday. Admission is £1 ($1.75) for adults, 50p (90¢) for children.

Dunnottar Castle was the last fortress to hold out against Cromwell in the Civil War. During this conflict, the Royal Regalia of Scotland, under the protection of the Earl Marischal, was smuggled out of the castle and taken to **Kineff Old Church,** a mile closer to Stonehaven, where it was hidden under the floor from 1652 until the Restoration in 1660. The church of that day was replaced by the present structure. It is reached by taking the B967 off the A92 and following a little country road.

Muchalls Castle (no phone) was constructed by the Burnetts of Leys in 1619. Overlooking the sea, it is now owned by Mr. and Mrs. Maurice A. Simpson who allow the public to visit from 2:30 to 4:30 p.m. on Sunday and Tuesday in June and July. Any other time, it may be visited by written arrangement only. Admission is 60p ($1.05) for adults, 20p (35¢) for children under 12. The castle has intricate plaster ceilings and fireplaces as well as a secret staircase. The castle is inland from the village of Muchalls, five miles north of Stonehaven and nine miles south of Aberdeen.

At **Drum Castle,** the handsome mansion (tel. 03308/204) was added in 1619, but the great square tower dates from the late 13th century, making it one of the three oldest tower houses in the country. Historic Drum lies ten miles west of Aberdeen, off the A93. The castle is open May to September daily from 2 to 6 p.m., charging £2.10 ($3.70) for adults, £1.05 ($1.85) for children. The grounds are open all year from 9:30 a.m. to dusk, and admission is free or by donation.

Considered one of the most impressive of the fortresslike castles of Mar, **Castle Fraser** (tel. 03303/463) stands in a 25-acre parkland and woodsy setting. The sixth laird, Michael Fraser, launched the structure in 1575, and it was completed in 1636. The castle is filled with treasures. Its Great Hall is spectacular, and you can wander around the grounds, including a walled garden. It is open daily from 2 to 6 p.m. from the first of May to the end of September, charging an admission of £2.10 ($1.85) for adults, £1.05 ($1.85) for children. The castle is off the B933, 3 miles south of Kemnay and 16 miles west of Aberdeen.

The ruins of the ancient seat of the earls of Mar, **Kildrummy Castle** (tel. 09755/71264), is on the A97 in the small village of Kildrummy, 35 miles from Aberdeen. It is the most extensive example of a 13th-century castle in Scotland. You can see the four round towers, the hall, and the chapel from the original structure. The great gatehouse and other remains date from the 16th century. The castle played a major role in Scottish history up to 1715, when it was dismantled. It is open to visitors April to September from 9:30 a.m. to 7 p.m. Monday to Saturday and 2 to 7 p.m. on Sunday. Hours from October to March are the same except for closing at 4 p.m. Admission is £1 ($1.75) for adults, 50p (90¢) for children.

While you're in the area, you might want to stay at **Kildrummy Castle Hotel**

(tel. 09756/71288), about 1½ miles south from the village on the A97, overlooking the ruined castle. This 19th-century graystone mansion, set in acres of landscaped gardens, contains 16 bedrooms, most with bath and all with color TV, phone, and tea/coffee-making equipment. The proprietor rents singles from £40 ($70) daily and doubles from £70 ($122.50), except in January and February when the hotel is closed. The public rooms have oak-paneled walls and ceilings, mullioned windows, and cushioned windowseats. An original but faded Morris tapestry hangs on a wall. The drawing room and bar open onto a flagstone terrace from which you can see the gardens of the castle. Traditional Scottish food is served in the handsome dining room, including such dishes as Cullen skink (smoked haddock soup), filet of sole stuffed with smoked Scottish salmon, and Aberdeen Angus steaks. Meals cost from £10 ($17.50) for lunch to £17 ($29.75) for dinner.

Near the village of Fyvie, on the Aberdeen–Banff road, **Fyvie Castle** (tel. 06516/266) was opened to the public (1986) by the National Trust for Scotland. The oldest part of the castle, dating from the 13th century, has been called the grandest existing example of Scottish baronial architecture. There are five towers, one each named after Fyvie's five families—the Prestons, Melddrums, Setons, Gordons, and Leiths—who lived there over five centuries. Originally built in a royal hunting forest, Fyvie means "deer hill" in Gaelic. The interior, reflecting the opulence of the Edwardian era, was created by the first Lord Leith of Fyvie, a steel magnate. His collections contain arms and armor, 16th-century tapestries, and artworks by Raeburn, Gainsborough, Romney, and Batoni. The castle, rich in ghosts, curses, and legends, is open daily from 2 to 6 p.m. in May and 11 a.m. to 6 p.m. June to September. Admission is £2.10 ($3.70) for adults, £1.05 ($1.85) for children. Fyvie Castle stands eight miles southeast of Turriff off the A947.

Haddo House (tel. 06515/440) was the creation of William Adam in 1731, having taken the place of an earlier structure. This Palladian house has been the home of the Gordons of Haddo for more than five centuries. It is inhabited by the Marchioness of Aberdeen and Temair, who has turned it into the headquarters of the Haddo House Choral and Operatic Society. It is impressive in its way and also looks homelike enough for people actually to live here. The country park of some 180 acres surrounding the house is maintained by the Grampian Regional Council. The house is open Easter weekend, Saturday and Sunday in April and October, and May to the end of September from 2 to 6 p.m. daily (last entrance at 5:15 p.m.). Admission is £2.10 ($3.70) for adults, £1.05 ($1.85) for children. The park is open daily all year from 9:30 a.m. to dusk, and garden hours are 9:30 a.m. to 8 p.m. daily. The house is off the B999 some four miles north of Pitmedden, 19 miles north of Aberdeen.

A Transport Museum at Alford

About 25 miles west of Aberdeen on the A944 at Alford is the **Grampian Transport Museum** (tel. 09755/62292), where exhibits and displays trace the development of transport in northeast Scotland. Some 100 vehicles of all types—bicycles, motorcycles, veteran and classic cars, steam vehicles, fire engines, agricultural vehicles, trucks, horse-drawn carriages, trams, and sledges—can be seen, several dating from before 1900. There are also photograph displays and reconstructions of a village wheelwright's shop and a 1930s garage workshop. An added, nonvehicular attraction is the Mortier dance organ, the largest in Scotland, built in 1923, whose music enhances the atmosphere of days gone by. The museum is open daily from 10:30 a.m. to 5 p.m. from the end of March to the end of September, as well as the first two weekends in October. Admission is £1.50 ($2.65) for adults, 70p ($1.25) for children.

The ticket also admits visitors to the **Alford Valley Railway Museum,** housed in the reconstructed Alford village station of the Great North of Scotland Railway. On Sunday in season, trips are offered on the Alford Valley line's passenger trains, running on two-foot-gauge tracks.

HIGHLANDS AND ISLANDS

From their romantic glens and their rugged mountainous landscapes, the Highlands suggest a timeless antiquity. Off the coast, mysterious islands, such as Skye with its jagged peaks, rise from the sea, inviting further exploration. These lands are sparsely inhabited even today, and much wildlife, such as the red deer, still flourishes.

As the unofficial capital of the Highlands, Inverness is the terminus of the rail journey from London, a distance of some 570 miles. Many visitors use it as a base for Highland adventures.

From Inverness, you can journey along Loch Ness (especially if you're a monster watcher) to Fort William, dominated by Ben Nevis, the highest mountain in Britain. Oban is the main resort on Scotland's West Highland coastline. It is also one of the major ports for journeying to the Hebridean islands.

If at all possible, try to explore some of these islands, the largest of which is Lewis, where the Standing Stones of Callanish, a prehistoric monument, evokes Stonehenge. Numerous inter-island air services allow you to go "island hopping."

Many pleasure trips are possible to the islands in the Firth of Clyde, Scotland's greatest yachting center. Dominated by the peak of Goat Fell, Arran is the largest of these Clyde islands.

1. Speyside

Aviemore is the winter sports capital of Britain, but it also enjoys mass popularity in summer. Aviemore Centre, previewed below, is Scotland's most modern holiday resort, an all-year, all-weather center, endowed with a multitude of outdoor pursuits, such as golfing, angling, skiing, or ice skating.

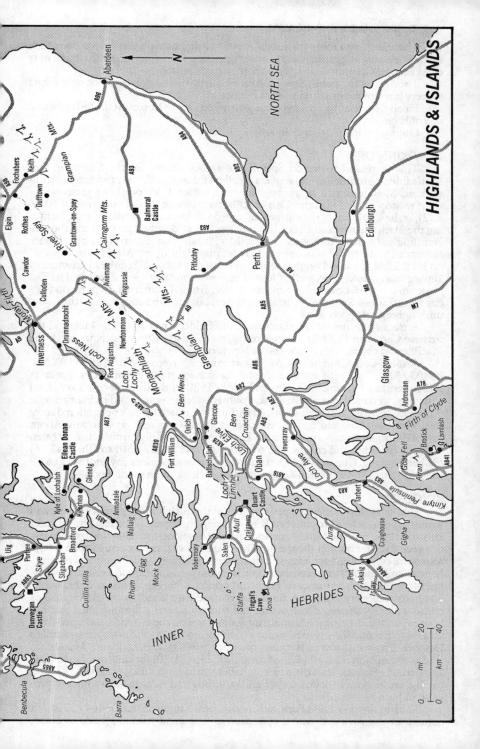

HIGHLANDS & ISLANDS

Those seeking a more traditional Scottish ambience will gravitate to one of the many Speyside villages, each with its own attractions and atmosphere. Ranking next to Aviemore, Grantown-on-Spey is another major center.

The Spey is the fastest-flowing river in the British Isles, famed not only for its scenery but also for its salmon and ski slopes.

Finally, on your way to Inverness, you might care to stop off at the old cathedral city of Elgin.

Our first stop up the Spey follows.

NEWTONMORE

This Highland resort on Speyside is a good center for the Grampian and Monadhliath Mountains, and it offers excellent fishing, golf, pony trekking, and hill walking. Most motorists zip through it on the way to Aviemore, but sightseers may want to stop off and visit the **Clan MacPherson House & Museum** (tel. 05403/332), at the south end of the village. Displayed are clan relics and memorials, including the Black Chanter and Green Banner as well as a "charmed sword," and the broken fiddle of the freebooter James MacPherson—a Scottish Robin Hood. Sentenced to death in 1700, he is said to have played the dirge "MacPherson's Rant" on his fiddle as he stood on the gallows at Banff. He then offered the instrument to anyone who would think well of him. There were no takers, so he smashed it. The museum is open from May to September daily from 10 a.m. to 5:30 p.m., on Sunday from 2:30 to 5:30 p.m. Admission is free, but contributions toward the museum's upkeep are appreciated.

A track from the village climbs past the Calder River to Loch Dubh and the massive Carn Ban (3,087 feet), where eagles fly. Castle Cluny, ancient seat of the MacPherson chiefs, is six miles west of Newtonmore.

Ard-Na-Coille, Kingussie Road, Newtonmore, Inverness-shire PH20 1AY (tel. 05403/214). Today the antiques that fill the interior of this elegant house evoke its earlier days as a hunting lodge. It was built in 1920 by the director of a Scottish oil company, who used it as a hunting seat only six weeks a year. Amid racks of antique porcelain, spacious and high-ceilinged bathrooms, which haven't been altered since they were built, and old English engravings, the owners rent eight rooms. About half of the units contain a private bath. Each room is tastefully furnished, most often with old furniture and chintz. The cost for B&B is £18 ($31.50) to £25 ($43.75) per person daily. Clients who opt for a freshly prepared dinner pay another £15.50 ($27.15). Ard-Na-Coille translates from the Gaelic as "high in the woods."

KINGUSSIE

Your next stop along the Spey might be at this little summer holiday resort and winter ski center (it's pronounced King-youcie), the capital of Badenoch, a district known as "the drowned land" because the Spey can flood the valley when the snows of a severe winter melt in the spring. There you can visit the six-acre **Highland Folk Museum,** on Duke Street, just off High Street (tel. 05402/307), with its comprehensive collection of artifacts, including weaponry, bagpipes, and fiddles, illustrating more than two centuries of Highland customs, plus the work of craftspeople. Naturally, there are tartans. A furnished cottage with a mill, a central Highlands house with cruck-frame construction and turf walls, and a farming shed that has been expanded to become a farming museum stand on the grounds. It is open from 10 a.m. to 6 p.m. Monday to Saturday and from 2 to 6 p.m. on Sunday from April to October. The remainder of the year, it is open from 10 a.m. to 3 p.m. Monday to Friday. Admission is £1.50 ($2.65) for adults, 75p ($1.30) for children. Live events and demonstrations, including piping, caber tossing, spinning, horseshoeing, and baking, are held most days, except Sunday, in July and August, with a limited program in June and September.

The **Highland Wildlife Park,** at Kincraig, near Kingussie (tel. 05404/270), is a natural area of parkland with a collection of Highland wildlife, herds of bison, deer, wolves, and fox, along with many animals now extinct in Scotland's wilds, including the lynx and wild boar. There is a children's park along with a souvenir shop, a café, and a picnic site. The park is open from 10 a.m. to 6 p.m. daily from March until the end of October. Admission is £6.50 ($11.40) per car. Kincraig is a little village at a scenic spot at the northern end of Loch Insh, overlooking the Spey Valley to the west and the Cairngorm mountains to the east, about six miles from Aviemore.

Food and Lodging

If you'd like to stop here instead of at Aviemore, I'd recommend the following establishments:

Osprey Hotel, Ruthven Road, Kingussie, Inverness-shire PH21 1EN (tel. 05402/510), is a convenient place to stay, with eight comfortable bedrooms, all with hot and cold running water and central heating. The proprietors charge from £18 ($31.50) to £28 ($49) per person daily for B&B. A dinner costs from £16 ($28). The place is known for its pure, fresh food, 100% homemade. Fresh, prime Scottish meats are served, including local venison, beef, lamb, pork, and free-range chickens. In summer, salmon and trout from local rivers, including the Spey, are offered either fresh or peat-smoked. The extensive wine list includes products from the majority of the wine-making sections of Europe. The hotel has a licensed bar, residents' lounge, and a TV lounge, and babysitter/listening service is provided. Laundry and ironing facilities are available. The staff will offer information and assistance in arranging for pony trekking or horseback riding. It's closed November and December.

For an elegant dining experience, try **The Cross,** High Street, Kingussie, Inverness-shire PH21 1HX (tel. 05402/762). A visit here involves almost as much theater as it does fine food. Tony Hadley, the sensitive owner, personally explains the composition of each menu item. The establishment is in a stone-rimmed building fronted with Victorian plate-glass windows. In the 1800s, it was a grocery store. The focal point of the bar in the entrance area is a stone fireplace which, when I was last there, had an alderwood fire blazing merrily. Diners enjoy dishes prepared by Tony's wife, Ruth, whose specialties vary with the season, depending on the availablity of produce in the local markets, and might include venison Francatelli, wild pigeon with grapes, or Highland lamb with sorrel. A selection from more than 300 wines rounds out any menu, and sorbets are served between courses. A seven-course gastronomic "extravaganza" is served on Saturday night, costing £19.50 ($34.15), including VAT. Dinner other nights is a four-course, fixed-price meal for £16 ($28). Dinner is the only meal served, from 6:30 p.m. to last orders at 9:30 p.m. It is advisable to reserve a table. The restaurant is closed Sunday and Monday.

Three bedrooms are rented, all with showers, toilets, and bidets, and two with canopied beds. All are handsomely furnished. Dinner, bed, and breakfast costs from £38 ($66.50) per person daily, with VAT included.

AVIEMORE

At the foot of the historic rock of Craigellachie, the rallying place for Clan Grant, a little village has developed into a year-round holiday mecca since the 1960s. In winter, ski runs are available for both beginners and experts (four chair lifts and 13 T-bar tows). In summer, sailing, canoeing, pony trekking, hill walking, and mountain climbing, as well as golfing and fishing, are just some of the many activities.

In the heart of the resort, **Stakis Aviemore Centre** (tel. 0479/810624) is an all-purpose cultural, sports, and entertainment complex. Built nearly a quarter of a century ago within a loop road, it contains four hotels and their grounds. The center's activities are suitable for everyone and include ice skating, swimming, saunas, solarium, squash, table tennis, snooker, discos, putting, go-karting, and much more. Most sports facilities are open daily from 10 a.m. to 1 p.m., 2 to 5 p.m., and 6 to 9 p.m. Admission to the pool is £1.75 ($3.05) for adults, 75p ($1.30) for children. The Speyside Theatre, seating 720, changes its film programs weekly, and often is host to live shows and concerts. Also on the grounds is the Highland Craft Centre, a small shopping emporium.

Where to Stay

Stakis Coylumbridge Resort Hotel, Rothiemurchus, Aviemore, Inverness-shire PH22 1QN (tel. 0479/810661), christened by the Duke of Edinburgh, stands in 65 acres of tree-studded grounds facing the slopes of the Cairngorms, and has extensive sports and leisure facilities. The 175 bedrooms are well appointed, each with private bath, TV, in-house films, hot beverage equipment, fresh fruit, phone, and daily newspaper. Singles cost from £53 ($92.75) daily, and twins peak at £90 ($157.50), including a full Scottish breakfast and VAT. Meals are served all day in the Bistro Restaurant, and the Grant Room Restaurant offers a three-course buffet lunch and a table d'hôte dinner. In the hotel are two heated swimming pools, a sauna, whirlpool, steambath, multi-gym, hairdressing salon, gift shop, and games room. House entertainment is a regular feature during the evening, particularly on weekends. In winter, downhill and cross-country skiing equipment and training are available.

Stakis Four Seasons, Aviemore Centre, Aviemore, Inverness-shire PH22 1PF (tel. 0479/810681), is an ideal family holiday hotel offering excellent facilities for a comfortable, relaxed stay. The 89 bedrooms all have private bath, color TV, radio, phone, tea- and coffee-making facilities, baby-listening service, and views of the surrounding hills and mountains. Some rooms feature bunk beds for children, for whom special rates are quoted. The tariff, including a full Scottish breakfast and VAT, is from £60 ($105) per person daily. The hotel offers two bars, a sauna bath, and sunbeds, and there is a supervised playroom for children under 8 years of age.

Post House Hotel, Aviemore Centre, Aviemore, Inverness-shire PH22 1PJ (tel. 0479/810771), is a resort hotel, catering to winter and sports enthusiasts. Its beige-brick two-story exterior rambles in a labyrinthine progression of wings, staircases, and long hallways, which funnel into the public rooms illuminated with big windows overlooking the countryside. In summer, doors open to reveal flagstone outdoor terraces ringed with viburnum and juniper. You can drink in the Illicit Still Bar, which has an antique whisky still and copper-topped tables. The main restaurant is capped with a soaring ceiling, trussed with beams. In the game room is a resident nanny—so if you have children, you're free to head for the slopes in winter without them. The bedrooms are well furnished and each is equipped with a private bath. Some family rooms are available. Singles cost from £47.50 ($83.15) daily and doubles or twins from £65 ($113.75) to £75 ($131.25).

Stakis Badenoch Hotel, Aviemore Centre, Aviemore, Inverness-shire PH22 1PF (tel. 0479/810261), overlooks the Craigellachie Nature Reserve and its much-photographed rock. The hotel is in the heart of Aviemore Centre. Summer and winter holiday makers face a choice of two standards of room: with modern facilities or economy bunk-bedded rooms with adjacent baths and showers. The hotel's facilities include a cocktail bar, a disco bar called Connexions, and a restaurant specializing in Scottish fare. Midweek ski packages, Christmas and New Year's packages, and special weekly tariffs are offered. Contact them for their "value for money rates." Otherwise, standard charges are £45 ($78.75) daily in singles, £70 ($122.50) in doubles.

Where to Dine

Dalfaber Golf and Country Club (tel. 0479/811244) is part of a time-share project at the edge of the resort. The Country Club opens its restaurant, café, and bars to nonmembers. These facilities overlook the swimming pool of the clubhouse. For dinner, the leading choice is the Louisiana Restaurant, capped with a ceiling of pine, the kind of rustic woodsiness you would expect to find in Aspen. The restaurant's centerpiece is an open barbecue pit, the smoke from which is funneled upward through a copper and iron chimney. Comfortable wicker chairs offer a chance to listen to one of the entertainers during the evening. Sunday lunch is from the barbecue as is Monday dinner. You get steak, chicken, or homemade burgers cooked in front of you, served with baked potatoes and as much salad as you can eat. The rest of the week, barbecued steaks are a specialty, as is Spey salmon. For an à la carte dinner, expect to pay about £12 ($21). There is also the table d'hôte menu for £8.50 ($14.90). Dinner is served from 7 to 10 p.m. daily.

If you show up for lunch, the Café Martinique will serve you a homemade Scotch broth followed by such dishes as braised Scotch beef in a red wine sauce. Lunch is served daily from noon to 2:30 p.m. and evening meals in the café are available from 6 to 9 p.m. The sizzle platter offered in the evening is a ribeye steak for only £4.95 ($8.65). The decor is a medley of knotty pine, large panoramic windows, and plants.

In the Aviemore Environs

The area surrounding Aviemore is rich in attractions. You can journey to the sky on the **Cairngorm Chair Lift,** whose lowest section lies ten miles east of Aviemore. A round-trip passage on this longest chair lift in Scotland costs £3 ($5.25) per person during working hours, 9 a.m. to 4 p.m. daily. In winter the uppermost reaches are closed during periods of high wind. The highest section is 4,084 feet above sea level. A midway stop is the **Ptarmigan Restaurant,** the loftiest (altitude-wise) eating spot in Britain at 3,600 feet. Hours are 9 a.m. to 4 p.m. daily. The decor is rustic and woodsy, modern yet unpretentious, with meals costing £10 ($17.50). In summer, on a clear day you can see Ben Nevis in the west, and the vista of Strathspey from here is spectacular, from Loch Morlich set in the Rothiemurchus Forest to the Spey Valley.

Skiers are attracted to the area anytime after October, when snow can be expected. Ski equipment and clothing can be rented at the Day Lodge at the main Cairngorm car park. Weather patterns can change quickly in the Cairngorm massif, so for information about this and other aspects of the chair lift, phone 047986/261. To reach the place, take the A951 branching off from the A9 at Aviemore, then head for the car park near Loch Morlich.

North of Aviemore, the **Strathspey Railway** is billed as providing "a trip into nostalgia." The railway follows the valley of the River Spey between Boat of Garten and Aviemore, a distance of five miles. The train is drawn by a coal-burning steam locomotive. The newest locomotive used was made some 35 years ago, the oldest being of 1935 vintage. The round trip requires 17 minutes in each direction. Only two service designations—first class and third class in conformity with railroad tradition—are offered. Round-trip passage costs £3.80 ($6.65) in first class, £2.60 ($4.55) in third class. Schedules change frequently, but June to the end of September, trains make five round-trip journeys daily. In spring and fall the trains run only on Saturday and Sunday, making four round-trip journeys. The trains do not run in winter.

The backers of this railway, which takes you through scenes unchanged in a century, set out to re-create the total experience of travel on a Scottish steam railway that once carried wealthy Victorians toward their hunting lodges in "North Britain." The rail station at Boat of Garten where you can board the train has also been restored. To complete the experience, you can wine and dine aboard on Saturday, when a single-seating dinner is served, costing £16.50 ($28.90), and at a single-seating lunch on Sunday, when the price is £10.50 ($18.40). Reservations for the meals must be made. The dining car is a replica of a Pullman parlor car, the *Amethyst.* For reservations and hours of departure, call 047983/258.

In the village of Inverdruie, 1½ miles east of Aviemore on the ski road to Cairngorm, is the **Inverdruie Visitor Centre.** There, you'll find the **Cairngorm Whisky Centre & Museum** (tel. 0479/810574), open Monday to Saturday from 10 a.m. to 6 p.m. (later in high season) and on Sunday from 12:30 to 2:30 p.m., April to September. In the museum are relics of whisky distilling in time past together with models of their modern equivalents. An audio-visual presentation is given on the history of whisky (scotch, of course) and the industry. Despite the museum aspects, this is primarily a retail shop, stocking malt whiskies from 105 distilleries. In a tasting room—admission £2.50 ($4.40) per person—you can taste minute quantities of up to four different brands, then purchase your favorite in the shop if you wish.

Also at the Inverdruie center is the **Rothiemurchus Farm Visitor Centre,** with an audio-visual presentation. From here, guided walks and farm tours are organized by the ranger service. You can see red deer and Highland cattle as you tour.

Another opportunity at the Inverdruie center is to visit the **Old School Craft Shop** (tel. 0479/810005), where pottery, rugs, hand-knit articles, woodwork, and other fine traditional craftwork can be seen and purchased, as well as books and maps. You may want to visit the **Mostly Pine Tearoom,** with lots of antiques, and the **Ski-Road Skis Gift Shop,** featuring sports and fashion wear.

GRANTOWN-ON-SPEY

This holiday resort, with its gray granite buildings, stands in a wooded valley and commands views of the Cairngorm mountains. It is a key center for winter sports in Scotland. Fishermen are also attracted to its setting, because the Spey is renowned for its salmon. Lying 34 miles southeast of Inverness by road, it was one of Scotland's many 18th-century planned towns, founded on a heather-covered moor in 1765 by Sir James Grant of Grant, becoming the seat of that ancient family. Grantown became famous in the 19th century as a Highland tourist center, enticing visitors with its planned concept, the beauty of surrounding pine forests, the Spey River, and the mountains around it. From a base here you can explore the valleys of the Don and Dee, the already-mentioned Cairngorms, and Culloden Moor, scene of the historic battle in 1746.

Food and Lodging

Garth Hotel, The Square, Grantown-on-Spey, Morayshire PH26 3HN (tel. 0479/2836), on the narrowest edge of the historic square of town, is an elegant, comfortable hotel in what was built as a private home in the 17th century. There is a prosperous and wholesome air about it, enhanced by the well-polished brass hardware and the four-acre garden extending toward the back, crisscrossed by footpaths. Guests enjoy the use of a spacious upstairs lounge, whose thick walls, high ceilings, wood-burning stove, and vine-covered veranda make it the perfect place for morning coffee or afternoon tea. There's an expansive bay window illuminating the plaid carpeting of the popular cocktail lounge. An array of sun parasols on the side lawn invites you to take advantage of the warm weather breezes. Gordon McLaughlan, owner of this attractive hotel, rents out 14 individually furnished bedrooms, all with baths/showers, direct-dial phones, and color TVs. The charge is £21 ($36.75) to £25 ($43.75) per person daily for B&B, plus another £12 ($21) per person if dinner is included. Extensive and selective meals are presented in an attractive dining room. "Taste of Scotland" dishes are featured, with emphasis on fresh local produce.

Tulchan Lodge, Advie, Grantown-on-Spey, Morayshire PH26 3PW (tel. 08075/200), built in 1906 to serve as the 22,000-acre Tulchan Estate's fishing and shooting lodge, is a place for both sports-oriented visitors and travelers who want to experience a place designed for the elegance required by King Edward VII, who came here for the sports, and other fastidious Edwardians. The lodge, with splendid views of the Spey Valley, has the added attraction of being in the heart of the Highland malt whisky country. Each of the 11 bedrooms is different in size and furnishings, and all have bathrooms. Singles cost from £130 ($227.50) daily, and doubles are priced from £208 ($364), for half board. The lodge has two elegant dining rooms, where Scottish and international dishes are served, with particular attention to Scottish beef, lamb, game, and fresh local seafood. The vegetables are grown in the lodge's garden. Tulchan Lodge is open from April to January, under the direction of T. J. Kirkwood.

THE WHISKY TRAIL

The major tourist attraction of the Moray District of Scottland, lying on the southern shore of Moray Firth and stretching in a triangular shape south from the coast to the wild heart of the Cairngorm Mountains near Aviemore, is the Malt Whisky Trail, running through the glens of Speyside. Here distilleries, many of which can be visited, are known for their production of *uisge beatha* or "water of life." Whisky (note the spelling without the *e*) is its more familiar name.

Half of the malt distilleries in the country lie along the River Spey and its tributaries. Here peat smoke and Highland water are used to turn out single-malt (unblended) whisky. Several of the distilleries in Moray have opened their doors to visitors. If you're lucky, they'll give you a free sample. The Whisky Trail is 70 miles long. There are five malt distilleries in the area, including Glenlivet, Glenfiddich, Glenfarclas, Strathisla, and Tamdhu. Allow about an hour to visit each of them.

If you're traveling north on the A9 road from Perth and Pitlochry, your first stop might be at **Dalwhinnie,** which has the highest whisky distillery in the world at 1,888 feet. It is not in the Spey Valley but at the northeastern end of Loch Ericht, with views of lochs and forests.

Glenlivet

To reach your first distillery on the designated Whisky Trail, you leave Grantown-on-Spey and head east along the A95 until you come to the junction with the B9008. Go south along this route, and you can't miss it. The location of **The Glenlivet Reception Centre** is ten miles north of the nearest town, Tomintoul. For information, call 08073/427. Near the River Livet, a Spey tributary, this distillery is one of the most famous in Scotland, and it's open to visitors from Easter until the end of October from 10 a.m. to 4 p.m. Monday to Saturday.

Glenfarclas Distillery

Back on the A95, you can visit the Glenfarclas Distillery at Ballindalloch (tel. 08072/245), one of the few malt whisky distilleries that is still independent of the giants. Glenfarclas is managed by the fifth generation of the Grant family. Founded in 1836, it is open all year from 9 a.m. to 4:30 p.m. Monday to Friday, and also on Saturday from June to the end of September, from 10 a.m. to 4 p.m. An exhibition center displays not only mementos of the scotch whisky industry but also a genuine illicit still. There is a small craft shop, and each visitor is offered a dram of Glenfarclas Malt Whisky. There is no admission charge.

Dufftown

Dufftown is a center of the whisky distilling industry. It is surrounded by seven malt distilleries. The major one most visitors want to see is **Grant's Glenfiddich Distillery** (tel. 0340/20373) in the town. It is open Monday to Friday and on Saturday from Easter to mid-October from 9:30 a.m. to 4:30 p.m., from noon to 4:30 p.m. on Sunday in summer. Visitors are shown around the plant, and the process of distilling is explained by guides in tartans. A film on the history of distilling is also shown. At the finish of the tour, you're given a free dram of single-malt whisky, and the whole tour is free. There is a souvenir shop where you can buy glasses, tankards, and hip flasks, plus other tokens of your visit to one of the few malt distilleries left in Scotland still owned by the founding family and not by a combine. The first whisky was produced on Christmas Day in 1887.

Keith

Keith grew up because of its strategic location, where the main road and rail routes between Inverness and Aberdeen cross the River Isla. It has a long and ancient history, but it owes its present look to the "town planning" of the late 18th and early 19th centuries. Today it is a major stop along the Whisky Trail. The **Strathisla Distillery** on Seafield Avenue (tel. 05422/7471) is one of the oldest distilleries in Scotland. Established in 1786, it offers guided tours Monday to Friday from 9 a.m. to 4:30 p.m. June to early September.

Rothes

A Speyside town with five distilleries, Rothes is just to the south of Glen of Rothes. It lies between the Ben Aigan and Conerock Hill and was founded in 1766. The **Glen Grant Distillery** opened in the mid-19th century. It can be visited any time from mid-April to September, Monday to Friday from 10 a.m. to 4 p.m. A Visitor Reception Centre offers guided tours. Call 03403/413 for information.

After your tour up the Whisky Trail, **Rothes Glen Hotel,** Rothes, Morayshire IV33 7AH (tel. 03403/254), may appear to be a mirage. The old turreted house, with many of its original pieces of furniture, stands back from the road, surrounded by about 40 acres of fields with grazing Highland cattle—how can they see to eat with all that shaggy hair? This historic castlelike building was designed by the architect who built Balmoral. Inside the house a warm fire greets you. Bedrooms are well furnished and relaxing. The owners charge £46 ($80.50) daily in a single, rising to £68 ($119) in a double. The dining room is paneled in wood, and good wholesome meals are served in true Scottish tradition. The bar lunches are popular, with a wide choice offered. A set four-course dinner with coffee and mints costs £18 ($31.50). As an alternative, there is an à la carte menu from which individual dishes may be chosen. A favorite specialty is mince, tatties, and skirlie (fried oatmeal and onions). This goes very well with roast pheasant for dinner, a local delicacy. Lunch is daily from 12:30 to 2 p.m., and dinner, from 7 to 9 p.m. The hotel closes in January.

FOCHABERS

This village, on the Inverness–Aberdeen road, dates from 1776 and was created as one of the early planned towns by John Baxter, for the fourth Duke of Gordon. Most of the buildings along High Street are protected and have not been changed much in 200 years. On the Spey, Fochabers is distinguished by its **Market Cross** and **Tower of Gordon Castle.**

Gordon Arms, 80 High St., Fochabers, Morayshire IV32 7DH (tel. 0343/820508), is a well-known 18th-century coaching inn, run by Raul Suarez, who is justly proud of the hospitality he offers wayfarers. Bedrooms are traditional in the old wing and modern in the new section. Singles with bath cost £33 ($57.75) daily, and doubles run £44 ($77), including a full breakfast and VAT. Fishermen are fond of the place, as revealed by the "salmon house" for the storing of rods and tackle. The hotel is noted for serving some of the best food to be found along Speyside, including many national dishes. The Moray beef and salmon are hard to equal. Sometimes continental dishes appear on the menu. Meals, costing from £5 ($8.75) to £15 ($26.25), are served daily from noon to 2 p.m. and 7 to 10 p.m. If you're here on a summer afternoon, you might have tea in the garden.

ELGIN

The center of local government in the Moray district, an ancient royal burgh, this cathedral city lies on the Lossie River, 38 miles from Inverness by road. Once called the "lantern of the north," the **Cathedral of Moray** is now in ruins. It was founded in 1224 but extensively damaged in 1390 by the "wolf of Badenoch," the natural son of Robert II. After its destruction, the citizens of Elgin rebuilt their beloved cathedral, turning it into one of the most attractive and graceful buildings in

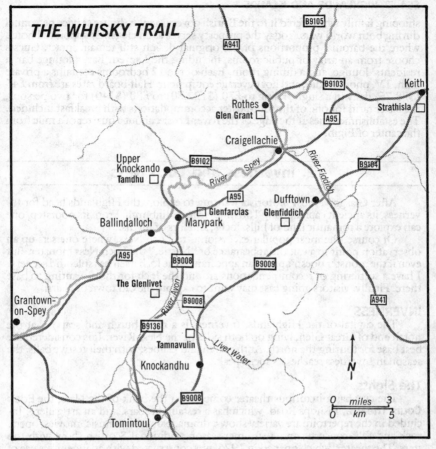

THE WHISKY TRAIL

[B9105]
[A941]
[B9103]
Keith
Rothes
Glen Grant □
Strathisla □
[A95]
Craigellachie
River Fiddich
[B9104]
Upper
Knockando
Tamdhu □
[B9102]
River Spey
River
Dufftown
Glenfiddich □
[A95]
Glenfarclas □
Ballindalloch
Marypark
[A95]
[B9008]
[B9009]
The Glenlivet □
River Avon
Grantown-
on-Spey
[B9008]
[A941]
[B9136]
Tamnavulin
Livet Water
Knockandhu
N
[B9008]
miles   3
Tomintoul
km   5

Scotland. The architect's plan was that of a Jerusalem cross. However, when the central tower fell in 1711, the cathedral was allowed to fall into decay. But a faithful cobbler still respected its grandeur, and he became its caretaker. By the time of his death in 1841 he had removed most of the debris that had fallen. Today visitors wander among its ruins, snapping pictures. Best preserved is the 15th-century chapter house.

Samuel Johnson and Boswell came this way on their Highland tour, reporting a "vile dinner" at the Red Lion Inn in 1773.

I'm sure you'll fare better at **Eight Acres Hotel,** Sheriffmill, Elgin, Morayshire IV30 3UL (tel. 0343/3077), a modern, low-lying, motel-type unit, all 58 of its streamlined, functionally furnished rooms offering a private bath or shower. Standing on spacious grounds, the hotel lies on the western approaches to Elgin on the main A96 Inverness road. The public rooms are generous, and the restaurant attracts a lot of motorists bound for Inverness. Rates in a single are £35 ($61.25) daily, rising to £52 ($91) in a double, including breakfast. Guests can use the swimming pool, gym, and squash courts. The hotel offers quite a bit of entertainment at various times of the year, dinner-dancing to a live band, and occasional Scottish folk evenings. However, entertainment is not on a regular basis.

Mansion House Hotel, The Haugh, Elgin, Morayshire IV30 1AW (tel. 0343/48811), is a building enlarged by a local lawyer in 1883. Later it was acquired by a shipping family who offered it to the British government to house service personnel during both world wars. Today the property serves as an elegantly appointed hotel, where the baronial proportions of the original design still remain intact. Guests choose from an array of public rooms, including the Lantern Bar, a lounge bar, a residents' lounge, and a dining room. Each of the 12 bedrooms contains a private bath, TV, phone, radio, and hot beverage equipment. Half-board rates are from £45 ($78.75) daily in a single, rising to £70 ($122.50) to £80 ($140) for two persons, the latter tariff for one of the four-poster accommodations with breakfast included. The establishment lies at the edge of the River Lossie, about a quarter of a mile from the center of Elgin.

2. Inverness and Loch Ness

After Glasgow, most motorists wanting to explore the Highlands head for Inverness, its ancient capital, lying 156 miles from Edinburgh. From its doorstep, one can explore a romantic land of hills, lochs, and lots of myths.

Of course, the most popular excursion is to Loch Ness, where one sets up an observation point to await the appearance of "Nessie," the Loch Ness monster. But even if the monster doesn't put in an appearance, the loch itself has splendid scenery. I have a scattering of recommendations around the loch for those wanting to base there. Finally, visitors going east may want to explore the old town of Nairn.

INVERNESS
The capital of the Highlands, Inverness is a royal burgh and seaport, at the north end of Great Glen, lying on both sides of the Ness River. It is considered the best base for touring the north. At the Highland Games, with their festive balls, the season in Inverness reaches its social peak.

The Sights
The city has a luxurious theater complex on the bank of the Ness, the **Eden Court Theatre,** Bishops Road, which has a restaurant, bars, and an art gallery. Included in the repertoire are variety shows, drama, ballet, pop music, movies, opera, rock and folk concerts, and a summer-season traditional Scottish show with top stars. The theater, which opened in 1976, was constructed with an ingenious use of hexagonal shapes and has a horseshoe-shaped auditorium. Programs are advertised in most hotels and guesthouses. The box office is open from 10:30 a.m. to 8 p.m. Monday through Saturday (tel. 0463/221718).

Inverness is one of the oldest inhabited localities in Scotland. On **Craig Phadrig** are the remains of a vitrified fort, believed to date from the 4th century B.C., where the Pictish King Brude is said to have been visited by St. Columba in A.D. 565. The old name castle of Inverness stood to the east of the present Castlehill, the site still retaining the name **Auld Castlehill.** Because of the somewhat shaky geography of Shakespeare in dramatizing Macbeth's murder of King Duncan, some scholars claim that the deed was done in the old castle of Inverness while others say it happened at Cawdor Castle, 4½ miles to the south where Macbeth held forth as Thane of Cawdor.

King David built the first stone castle in Inverness around 1141. The **Clock Tower** is all that remains of a fort erected by Cromwell's army between 1652 and 1657. The 16th-century **Abertarff House** is now the headquarters of An Comunn Gaidhealach, the Highland association that preserves the Gaelic language and culture.

Inverness today has a castle, but it's a "modern" one—that is, dating from 1835. Crowning a low cliff of the east bank of the Ness, the **Castle of Inverness** occupies the site of an ancient fortress blown up by the Jacobites in 1746. The castle houses county offices and law courts. Mary Queen of Scots was denied admission to the castle in 1562, and she subsequently occupied a house on Bridge Street. From the window of this house, she witnessed the execution of her cousin, Sir John Gordon. For not gaining admission to the castle, she took reprisals, taking the fortress and hanging the governor.

Opposite the town hall is the **Old Mercat Cross,** with its **Stone of the Tubs,** an Inverness landmark said to be where women rested their washtubs as they ascended from the river. Known as "Clachnacudainn," the lozenge-shaped stone was the spot where the early kings were crowned.

Inverness Museum and Art Gallery, Castle Wynd (tel. 0463/237114), contains the display "The Hub of the Highlands," the story of the people, wildlife, environment, and culture of the Inverness district, as well as silver and changing exhibitions. It's open daily except Sunday from 9 a.m. to 5 p.m. Admission is free. The museum has a coffeeshop open from 10 a.m. to 4 p.m.

West of the river rises the wooded hill of **Tomnahurich,** known as "the hill of the fairies." It is now a cemetery, and from here the views are magnificent.

In the Ness are wooded islands, linked to Inverness by suspension bridges and turned into parks.

From Inverness, you can visit **Culloden Battlefield,** six miles to the east, the spot where Bonnie Prince Charlie and the Jacobite army were finally crushed at the battle on April 16, 1746. A cairn marks the site on Drummossie Moor where the battle raged. **Leanach Cottage,** around which the battle took place, still stands and was inhabited until 1912. A path from the cottage leads through the Field of the English, where 76 men of the Duke of Cumberland's forces who died during the battle are said to be buried. Features of interest include the **Graves of the Clans,** communal burial places with simple stones bearing individual clan names alongside the main road and through the woodland; the great memorial cairn, erected in 1881; the **Well of the Dead,** a single stone with the inscription "The English Were Buried Here"; and the huge **Cumberland Stone** from which the victorious "Butcher" Cumberland is said to have reviewed the scene. The battle lasted only 40 minutes: the prince's army lost some 1,200 men out of 5,000 and the king's army 310. A visitors' center and museum are open all year.

Between Inverness and Nairn, also about six miles to the east of Inverness, are the **Stones of Clava,** one of the most important prehistoric monuments in the north. These cairns and standing stones are from the Bronze Age.

Where to Stay

Culloden House, Culloden Moor, Inverness, Inverness-shire IV1 2NZ (tel. 0463/790461), six miles from Inverness, is a Georgian mansion with a much-photographed Adam façade. It includes part of the Renaissance castle in which Bonnie Prince Charlie slept the night before the last great battle on British soil, the Battle of Culloden. Superbly isolated, it is perfect for a relaxed Highland holiday, even if you stay within the extensive gardens and parkland. At the iron gates to the broad front lawn, a piper in full Highland garb plays at sundown, the skirl of the bagpipe accompanied by the barking of friendly house dogs. Such notables as the Prince of Wales and the Crown Prince of Japan have stayed here, perfectly at home among the exquisite furnishings and handsome plaster friezes. Guests are welcome to spacious and comfortable public rooms, beautifully painted and furnished, and to the cozy bedrooms with sylvan views and history-laden atmosphere. All 21 of them contain a private bath and shower. Singles pay from £75 ($131.25) daily and doubles from £105 ($183.75) to £140 ($245), with breakfast and VAT included. The hotel maintains traditional ideas of personal service. The food is served against a backdrop of refinement. Expect to pay about £28 ($49) per person for dinner.

Kingsmills Hotel, Culcabock Road, Inverness, Inverness-shire IV2 3LP (tel. 0483/237166), is an 18th-century house of much charm set in four acres of woodland garden only a mile from the center of Inverness. Once a private mansion, it stands adjacent to an 18-hole golf course, and the hotel has its own indoor pool and health spa, comprising sauna, steam room, spa bath, fitness room, sunbed, hairdressing and beauty salon, and a three-hole mini-golf course. The owner maintains a country-house atmosphere with a small, informal, and hospitable Highland staff. Furnishings throughout the hotel are of a high quality, and all rooms have private baths, radios, color TVs, phones, and free in-house movies. Single rooms cost £50 ($87.50) to £70 ($122.50) daily, and doubles go for £70 ($122.50) to £90 ($157.50), according to location and season. The rates include a full Highland breakfast. Dinner, offered nightly from 7 to 10, costs £15 ($26.25). All prices include VAT. The fish dishes are exceptional. Bar lunches and snack meals offer a wide choice, including Scottish fare. A notice in the lobby tells you that Robert Burns dined here in 1787, and the "Charles" who signed the guest register in 1982 was (you guessed it) the Prince of Wales. His sister, Princess Anne, has also stayed here.

The Station Hotel, 16-18 Academy St., Inverness, Inverness-shire IV1 1LG (tel. 0463/231926), adjacent to the railway station, offers a high standard of first-class service, comfortable accommodations, and well-prepared food. The occupants of those baronial Highland mansions like to stop here when they're in Inverness on shopping or social expeditions, gathering for somewhat lively chats in the conservatory lounge. Grandly Victorian, the bedrooms are tastefully decorated and welcoming, costing from £52 ($91) daily in a single with bath or shower, from £75 ($131.25) in a double, including a full Scottish breakfast. The dining room is one of the finest in Inverness, serving good-quality Scottish dishes, plus some excellently cooked continental favorites. Lunch is served daily from noon to 2 p.m. and dinner, from 7 to 9:30 p.m. A table d'hôte evening meal costs £14.50 ($25.40), but expect to pay from £16 ($28) if you're ordering à la carte, sampling the French specialties.

Dunain Park Hotel, Dunain Park, Inverness, Inverness-shire IV3 6JN (tel. 0464/230512), 2½ miles southwest of Inverness, stands in six acres of garden and woods, between Loch Ness and Inverness. This 18th-century house was opened as a hotel in 1974, and is furnished with fine antiques, china, and clocks, allowing it to retain its atmosphere of a private country house. Although Dunain Park has won its fame mainly as a restaurant, it does offer eight bedrooms, six with private bath or shower. The rates range from £60 ($105) daily in a single to £90 ($157.50) in a double or twin, including VAT and breakfast. A host of thoughtful details and pretty, soft furnishings have gone into the bedrooms. The breakfast served here is exceptional. You can order a simple lunch (in the garden, if you prefer). Snack meals are served from 12:30 to 2 p.m. But it is at dinner that the chef really delivers, offering a set meal for about £20 ($35). Ann Nicholl, who enjoys an enviable reputation for her cooking, compiles her menus from the local venison, grouse, pheasant, pigeon, salmon, scallops, and lobster, as well as prime Scottish beef and lamb. Her sweets presentation is noteworthy. You'll definitely want to consider having a meal here, and you can do so daily from noon to 2 p.m. and 7 to 9 p.m.

Bunchrew House Hotel and Restaurant, Bunchrew, Inverness, Inverness-shire IV3 6TA (tel. 0463/234917), three miles west of Inverness on the A862, is a fine Scottish mansion on the shores of Beauly Firth. The ancestral home of both the Fraser and the McKenzie clans, the house built by Simon Fraser, the eighth Lord Lovat, dates to 1621, the same year he married into the Stewart family. Set in 15 acres of landscaped gardens, the house has been restored as a country-house hotel. Guests get a glimpse of a bygone era when they relax in comfort in the paneled drawing room with roaring log fires in winter. Alan and Patsy Wilson and their staff welcome travelers to the individually designed and decorated bedrooms, all with private baths with showers, color TVs, and phones. The Lovat Suite has a fully canopied four-poster bed, and the Wyvis Suite boasts a half-tester bed and Jacuzzi. The rooms, doubles only, begin at £65 ($113.75) per night. You can dine in the candlelit restaurant on prime Scottish beef, fresh lobster and crayfish, local game and venison, and fresh vegetables.

Glen Mhor Hotel, 9-12 Ness Bank, Inverness, Inverness-shire IV2 4SG (tel.

0463/234308), looks out onto the River Ness. A house of gables and bay windows, it is a hospitable, family-run hotel with an endearing charm in spite of its creaky quality. The owners provide many thoughtful touches, such as a log fire blazing in the entrance lounge. From many of the individually styled bedrooms, you have views of the river, castle, and cathedral. Some of these are suitable for families, and children sharing a room with two adults are accommodated free. Amenities in the rooms include private baths or shower rooms with toilets, color TVs, direct-dial phones, trouser presses, hairdryers, and baby-listening service. The B&B rate starts at about £20 ($35) daily, rising to about £35 ($61.25) per person in a room where H.R.H. Prince Charles once dined. In a restaurant overlooking the river and specializing in Scottish dishes, you will enjoy such fine food as salmon caught in the river outside, shellfish, lamb, and beef. The wine list is considered one of the best in the country. In addition to the cozy cocktail lounge, there's a charming Parisian Bistro bar called Nico's, which is open for food and drinks at lunchtime and in the evening. It's a popular nightspot.

Where to Eat

Dickens International Restaurant, 77-79 Church St. (tel. 0463/224450), is reminiscent of an English colonial bar in Singapore. Ionic columns combine with rattan furniture and potted palms to create an atmosphere that might have pleased W. Somerset Maugham. On a downtown street near the tourist office, the place offers a wide selection of European, Chinese, and international dishes, including many vegetarian specialties. There are eight kinds of beef and steak dishes. On the menu are Dickens's own steak, Peking duck, fresh local salmon, and chateaubriand, along with a wide range of appetizers and a good selection of seafood (several dishes are made with prawns). The widest choice of side dishes in Inverness is found here. Full meals average £8 ($14). Sunday lunch is also available, costing from £4.50 ($7.90). Meals are served daily from noon to 2 p.m. and 5:30 to 11 p.m.

Stakis Steakhouse, Bank Street (tel. 0463/236577), a member of a chain, is one of the most attractive restaurants in the city center, lying on the banks of the river with a green, brown, and white garden-style décor, big windows, and padded banquettes. There's plenty of space for everyone, and the steaks and grilled meats are among the best in town. In the amber glow of polished brass lamps, guests enjoy bar lunches every day except Sunday, from noon to 2:30 p.m. Hot meals begin at £2.75 ($4.80). A full à la carte dinner will cost from £12 ($21). Specialties include chicken Kiev, roast chicken, and a full assortment of prime Angus steaks, some weighing in at your choice of 8 or 16 ounces. Dinner is served every night of the week from 5 to 10:30, on Sunday from 6 to 10:30.

Brookes Wine Bar, 75 Castle St. (tel. 0463/225662), is operated by owner Alastair Leslie in what used to be a pram shop, on the street that runs beside the castle, behind a Victorian plateglass façade. Inside, the decor has a touch of France, an atmosphere enhanced by posters of vineyards. The ambience combines the elements of a Los Angeles bistro and a French garden. In many ways this is the most avant-garde place in town, certainly one of the most alluring, and it was the first wine bar to open in the Highlands. Wine is sold by the bottle or by the glass. You can even order a giant bottle of beer imported from Germany, costing £2.25 ($3.95). There are 20 wines to choose from if you order by the glass.

As for food, you can choose what you want from a glass-fronted, refrigerated food case offering cold meats, fish, chicken, pâtés, mousse, a selection of salads, cheeses, and puddings. Hot dishes are also available, ordered from a menu written daily on the blackboard at the counter. The entire operation works on a counter-service basis, and hot dishes are brought to your table. You might order hot mushrooms gratinée, chicken Kiev, baked potato, or pan-fried filets of chicken breast with orange and ginger sauce served with buttered tagliatelle. For dessert, try the cream-filled ginger meringues or fresh red frangipani tart with cream. A full three-course meal costs from £7.50 ($13.15). The wine bar is open from 11:30 a.m. to 11 p.m.

Monday to Wednesday, from 11:30 a.m. to 1 a.m. Thursday and Friday, and from 11:30 a.m. to 11:45 p.m. Saturday. Closed Sunday.

NAIRN

A favorite family seaside resort on the sheltered Moray Firth, Nairn is a royal burgh, lying at the mouth of the Nairn River. Its fishing harbor was constructed in 1820, and golf has been played here since 1672, as it still is today. A large uncrowded beach, tennis, and angling draw a horde of vacationers in summer.

At **Cawdor Castle** (tel. 06677/615), to the south of Nairn, you encounter 600 years of Highland history. Since the early 14th century it's been the home of the thanes of Cawdor. The castle has all the architectural ingredients you associate with the medieval: a drawbridge, an ancient tower (this one built around a tree), and fortified walls. The severity is softened by the handsome gardens, flowers, trees, and rolling lawns. As I mentioned earlier, even the Scots can't agree as to where Macbeth, who actually was made Thane of Cawdor by King Duncan, committed his foul deed of murdering the king—at Cawdor or in the castle that once stood on Auld Castlehill in Inverness, if at all. The castle is open to the public from 10 a.m. to 5:30 p.m. every day from May 1 to early October. Admission is £2.60 ($4.55) for adults, £1.40 ($2.45) for children. The castle has extensive nature trails, a snackbar, and a licensed restaurant.

Food and Lodging

Newton, Inverness Road, Nairn, Nairnshire IV12 4RX (tel. 0667/53144), a castlelike hotel, stands just outside town in an attractive park of 35 acres, offering views across sweeping lawns and the golf course to the sea. Considered one of the finest of the "manor house" hotels of Scotland, it is spacious and sumptuous, drawing a clientele likely to include everybody from a prime minister to a Glasgow industrialist. A single rents for £40 ($70) daily, and a double or twin goes for £65 ($113.75), including VAT and a full breakfast. The public rooms are furnished with taste, and the Moray Firth, viewed on a day when the sun is shining brightly, forms a spectacle of beauty from many of the Newton's windows. The bedrooms have many fine appointments—sedate and comfortable. All 41 of them contain a private bath. There is a high standard of maintenance and personal service.

Clifton Hotel, Viewfield Street, Nairn, Nairnshire IV12 4HW (tel. 0667/53119), reflects the dynamic personality of J. Gordon Macintyre, the owner of this honey-colored sandstone, vine-covered Victorian mansion. The Clifton has been owned by the same family probably longer than any other hotel in the north of Scotland. Fully licensed, it stands on the seafront, three minutes from the beach and golf links. Mr. Macintyre has spent a lot of time, trouble, and money in decorating the house, often with interesting prints, and in selecting the furnishings, as exemplified by the Clifton's old-fashioned parlor. The collection of pictures, paintings, prints, engravings, etchings, and drawings is unusual and extensive, not only in public rooms, the drawing room, the writing room, and the bar and restaurant, but also in the long corridor. The bedrooms are pleasantly appointed. Singles rent for £43 ($75.25) daily; doubles, from £85 ($148.75). All bedrooms have a bath, except one that has a shower; some, however, do not have a toilet. Musical and theatrical performances are often staged in the hotel.

The Clifton also serves the best food in Nairn, a set dinner costing £15 ($26.25). The cooking is often in the hearty Highland tradition—that is, game pie, pigeons in wine, lamb in a mustard sauce—although French specialties also tempt. Dinner hours are 7 to 9:30 p.m. Luncheon, from 12:30 to 1:30 p.m. daily, is served in the Green Room, whose menu is based on what is available that day in the way of fish and shellfish, such as lobster, oysters, brill, and sole. The room is quite elegant, its china being Wedgwood Old and New. With only four tables, it is advisable to reserve your table by phoning early. Breakfast is special too. There is no menu as such: Since the hotel is stocked with all the necessary ingredients, guests are asked what they would like cooked.

DRUMNADROCHIT

This hamlet, lying about a mile from Loch Ness at the entrance to Glen Urquhart, has a big attraction, the official **Loch Ness Monster Exhibition** (tel. 04562/573), which opened in 1980 and has been packing 'em in ever since. You can follow the story from A.D. 565 to the present in pictures, audio, and video, as well as climbing aboard the sonar research vessel *John Murray*. The Exhibition Centre is the most visited place in the Highlands of Scotland, with more than 200,000 visitors annually. It is open daily from 9 a.m. to 9:30 p.m. mid-June to the end of August, from 9:30 a.m. to 8:15 p.m. in spring and fall. Because of fluctuating hours, telephone in advance if you're planning a winter visit. Admission is £1.65 ($2.90) for adults, 75p ($1.30) for children.

The ruined **Urquhart Castle,** one of Scotland's largest castles, is a mile and a half southeast of Drumnadrochit on a promontory overlooking Loch Ness. The chief of Clan Grant owned the castle in 1509, and most of the existing building dates from that period. In 1692 the castle was blown up by the Grants to prevent its becoming a Jacobite stronghold. It is here at Urquhart Castle that sightings of the Loch Ness monster are most often reported. It is open April to September from 9:30 a.m. to 7 p.m. Monday to Saturday and on Sunday from 2 to 4 p.m. Off-season its hours are 9:30 a.m. to 4 p.m. Monday to Saturday and 2 to 4 p.m. on Sunday. Admission charges are £1 ($1.75) for adults and 50p (90¢) for children.

Food and Lodging on the Outskirts

Polmaily House Hotel, Drumnadrochit, Inverness-shire IV3 6XT (tel. 04562/343), graciously re-creates the pleasures of manorial country-house living, offering at the same time a contemporary style that reflects the sophistication of its owner. According to a packet of letters discovered by Nick and Alison Parsons, the house was probably built in 1776, that year familiar to Americans. The 18-acre estate lies two miles west of Drumnadrochit on the A831. You drive between stands of beechwood hedge, past stately trees, a pond, and an assortment of geese and ducklings before reaching the entrance. Inside, a series of plushly furnished rooms, each tastefully filled with antiques and vases of fresh flowers, creates a personalized kind of comfort. Nick worked as a foreign correspondent for Reuters in both Italy and Central America, which explains the positioning of foreign art with 18th-century Scottish furnishings. Nine spacious and elegant bedrooms contain high ceilings, leaded-glass windows, flowered wallpaper, and an antique charm. Seven rooms have a private bath. Rates, with a Scottish breakfast included, are £30 ($52.50) daily in a bathless single and £35 ($61.25) per person in a double or twin with bath. The hotel has a tennis court, a swimming pool, and a croquet lawn flanked with garden statuary.

The restaurant attracts locals as well as hotel residents. Most dishes are prepared by Alison, using home-produced eggs and the best of fresh local ingredients. Specialties include flaked Arbroath smokie baked with cream and cheese, dill-cured and locally smoked wild salmon, and noisettes of spring lamb with fresh herbs and butter. Full à la carte meals cost from £16 ($28) per person.

FORT AUGUSTUS

This Highland touring center stands at the head (the southern most end) of Loch Ness. The town took its name from a fort named for the Duke of Cumberland. Built after the 1715 Rising, the present Benedictine abbey stands on its site.

The **Caledonian Canal** bisects the village, and the locks are a popular attraction when boats are passing through. Running across the loftiest sections of Scotland, the canal was constructed between 1803 and 1822 Almost in a straight line, it makes its way from Inverness in the north to Corpach in the vicinity of Fort William. The canal is 60 miles long, 22 of which were made by man. The other part goes through natural lochs. In summer, you can take several pleasure craft along this canal, leaving from Fort Augustus.

In accommodation, Fort Augustus offers the **Inchnacardoch Lodge,** Fort Augustus, Inverness-shire PH32 4BL (tel. 0320/6258), a family-run hotel in a beautiful setting overlooking Loch Ness, half a mile south of town. The old-fashioned house of many gables, a country residence of a 19th-century Lord Lovat of Lovat, chief of the Fraser Clan, offers 15 comfortable and well-equipped bedrooms, ten with private baths. The charges are £17 ($29.75) to £21 ($36.75) daily in a single, £19 ($33.25) to £22 ($38.50) per person in a twin room sharing a bath, and £23 ($40.25) to £29 ($50.75) per person in a twin with a private bath. All tariffs include a full breakfast and VAT. You can relax over coffee or drinks in the lounge bar of Nessie's Nook Bar—but be careful. A wee dram of the malt over your limit might cause you to see the Loch Ness monster. Open March to December.

SPEAN BRIDGE

This village is a busy intersection of the Fort William–Perth and Fort William–Inverness roads, as well as having daily train service to Fort William, Glasgow, and London, and bus service to Inverness and Fort William. Two miles outside the town, in Glen Spean, is the striking **Commando Memorial** by Scott Sutherland that the Queen Mother unveiled in 1952. In this area many commandos were trained during World War II. Numerous war movies have been filmed here.

Letterfinlay Lodge, Letterfinlay, Spean Bridge, Inverness-shire PH34 4DZ (tel. 039781/622), is a comfortable, well-appointed establishment on the A82 near Spean Bridge, about halfway between Fort Augustus and Fort William. Between the highway and Loch Lochy, against a backdrop of rugged scenery, it operates from March to November and is known both for its personal service and its level of cuisine, mostly plain Highland dishes that use high-quality ingredients, such as fresh salmon and sea trout, Aberdeen Angus beef, and Scottish hill lamb. Your bedroom window is likely to look out upon Loch Lochy. All units, including some family rooms, are tastefully furnished, with private bath or shower. Charges are £16 ($28) to £25 ($43.75) per person daily, these tariffs including a full Scottish breakfast. Dinner, including coffee, is about £13 ($22.75). The hotel also offers a sun lounge and a cocktail bar. Trout fishing is available at the doorstep.

3. Fort William and Lochaber

Fort William, the capital of Lochaber, is the major touring center for the western Highlands. Wildly beautiful Lochaber, the area around Fort William, has been called "the land of bens, glens, and heroes."

Dominating the area is **Ben Nevis,** Britain's highest mountain, rising 4,418 feet. In summer when it's clear of snow, there's a safe path to the summit. Fort William stands on the site of a fort built by General Monk in 1655, which was pulled down to make way for the railroad. This district is the western end of what is known as Glen Mor—the Great Glen, geologically a fissure that divides the northwest of Scotland from the southeast and contains Loch Lochy, Loch Oich, and Loch Ness. The Caledonian Canal, opened in 1847, linked these lochs, the River Ness, and Moray Firth. It provided sailing boats a safe alternative to the stormy route around the north of Scotland. Larger steamships made the canal out of date commercially, but fishing boats and pleasure steamers still use it. Good roads run the length of the Great Glen, partly following the line of General Wade's military road. From Fort William you can take steamer trips to Staffa and Iona.

The ruins of **Old Inverlochy Castle,** scene of the famous battle in 1645, can be reached by driving on the A82 two miles north of Fort William. At a point just one mile north of Fort William is **Glen Nevis,** one of the most beautiful in Scotland.

About 15 miles west of Fort William, on the A830 toward Mallaig, at Glenfinnan at the head of Loch Shiel, is the **Glenfinnan Monument,** which marks the spot where Bonnie Prince Charlie unfurled his proud red-and-white silk banner on August 19, 1745, in the ill-fated attempt to restore the Stuarts to the British throne. The monument is topped by the figure of a kilted Highlander. At a Visitors' Centre one may learn of the prince's campaign from Glenfinnan to Derby and back to the final defeat at Culloden.

FORT WILLIAM

The name evokes redcoats billeted in rough barracks to keep the Highlanders of Lochaber under control. Fort William today is a busy tourist town on the shores of Loch Linnhe. Although it stands in the shadow of Ben Nevis, the mountain can't be seen from town. While the town is most often used as a touring center, in Fort William itself you can visit the **West Highland Museum,** Cameron Square (tel. 0397/2169), containing all aspects of local history, especially the 1745 Jacobite rising, plus sections on tartans and folk life. The museum is open Monday to Saturday from 9:30 a.m. to 5:30 p.m. in June and September, to 9 p.m. in July and August, and 10 a.m. to 1 p.m. and 2 to 5 p.m. the remainder of the year. Admission is 60p ($1.05) for adults, 30p (55¢) for children.

Where to Stay

In Fort William, I'd recommend the following accommodations, beginning first with a deluxe suggestion:

Inverlochy Castle, Torlundy, Fort William, Inverness-shire PH33 6SN (tel. 0397/2177), three miles northeast on the A82, is another one of the places where Queen Victoria stayed. In her time it was newly built (completed in 1870), a Scottish mansion belonging to Baron Abinger. The monarch claimed in her diary, "I never saw a lovelier or more romantic spot." I do not wish to detract from that long-ago sentiment. Inverlochy Castle today is one of the premier places of Scotland for food and accommodations. The seventh Baron of Abinger sold the estate while it was being used for commando training during World War II. The Hobbs family transformed it into a fine hotel in 1969, and Mrs. Grete Hobbs, who was born in Denmark, is a delightful hostess today, assisted by a staff of 54 persons, some part-time. Against the scenic backdrop of Ben Nevis, the castle hotel, a *Relais & Chateaux,* has a mood inside of elegance and refinement, luxurious appointments and antiques, artwork and crystal, plus a profusion of flowers. Only 16 bedrooms, each with private bath, are offered, all of them beautifully furnished. The prices reflect the opulence. Twins or doubles rent for £145 ($253.75) daily, and suites for two cost £172.50 ($301.90), including breakfast and service.

The cuisine is one of the finest in Scotland, with the food cooked to order and served on silver platters. Sparkling crystal and fine china are placed on hand-carved polished tables where the guests enjoy such fare as salmon from the Spean or crayfish from Loch Linnhe, even produce from the hotel's own farm garden. Partridge and grouse are offered in season. Meals cost £35 ($61.25) and up, with VAT and service included. Men are required to wear jackets and ties, and no smoking is permitted in the dining room. Outsiders can dine here if there's room, but reservations are mandatory. Meals are served daily from 12:30 p.m. to 1:45 p.m. and 7:30 to 9 p.m. Closed mid-November to mid-March.

Alexandra, The Parade, Fort William, Inverness-shire PH33 6AZ (tel. 0397/2241), is a familiar sight, a hotel with tall gables and formidable granite walls, so common in this part of the Highlands. But the hotel is no antiquated mansion — rather, it has been completely modernized, offering 72 double rooms and 19 singles that are pleasantly and attractively furnished, all with private bath, color TV, direct-dial phones, and tea/coffee-makers. The rate in a double or twin is £70 ($122.50) daily, and a single costs £48 ($84). These tariffs include VAT, service, and a Scottish breakfast. Service and housekeeping standards are good. The chef makes excellent use of fresh fish, and the wine cellar is amply endowed. The vegetables are simply cooked with enjoyable results. A set dinner costs from £12 ($21).

The Croit Anna Hotel, Druimarbin, Fort William, Inverness-shire PH33 6RR (tel. 0397/2268), is on the A82 highway 2½ miles south of Fort William, overlooking Loch Linnhe and having fine views of the Ardgour Hills. Many of its 92 rooms have a private bathroom, and all have color TV and tea/coffee-makers. Singles rent for £27.50 ($48.15) daily, with doubles or twins going for £26.50 ($46.40) per person, including VAT. In the hotel dining room, a four-course à la carte meal would be £13 ($22.75). Hotel facilities include a games room, panoramic lounge, gift shop, lounge bar, and guest launderette. It's open from April to October, and entertainment is provided on most evenings in season. The hotel is owned and managed by the same family who designed and built it on a traditional Highland croft that has been in their possession for more than 250 years.

Where to Dine

Factor's House, Torlundy, Fort William, Inverness-shire PH33 6SN (tel. 0397/5767), is a *restaurant avec chambres*. Outside of Inverlocky Castle, it serves the best food in Fort William and is also a desirable place at which to stay. Appealing to motorists, it lies 3½ miles northeast of Fort William on A82. Seven well-furnished bedrooms, each with bath or shower, are rented at a cost of £42 ($73.50) daily in a single, rising to £65 ($113.75) in a double. But it is mainly as a restaurant that Factor's House is known. The owner, Peter Hobbs (likely to be wearing a kilt), is a gracious host. The cooking here is honest in that it doesn't trap itself in unnecessary adornments, and only good fresh British produce seems to be used. A set dinner is offered for £15.50 ($27.15), with most à la carte orders costing £20 ($35). Service is from 7 to 9:30 p.m. nightly except Monday. The staff takes a holiday from the middle of December to the middle of March.

ARISAIG

This little village on the shores of Loch Nan Ceal looks out across the bay to the islands of Skye, Rhum, Eigg, and Muck. Its position is on the scenic highway known as the "Road to the Isles," since you pass through here en route to Mallaig, from which steamers sail to the Kyle of Lochalsh, the Outer Hebrides, and the lochs of the northwest coast. Private boats go to the isles directly from Arisaig. This was a haunt of Bonnie Prince Charlie during his travels in connection with the Jacobite Rebellion of 1745.

An excellent place for food and lodging is **Arisaig Hotel,** Arisaig, Inverness-shire PH39 4NH (tel. 06875/210), an early Jacobite inn. The Stewarts (George, Janice, and Gordon) still reign here. On the shores of Loch Nan Ceal, in the heart of Bonnie Prince Charlie country, they run a topnotch inn. They offer 15 well-furnished bedrooms, six of which contain a private bath. Amenities include direct-dial phone, radio, intercom, and beverage-making equipment. Some accommodations can sleep families of three or four. B&B ranges from £24.50 ($42.90) to £32 ($56) per person based on double occupancy. In this warm, inviting family atmosphere, you can enjoy some of the best food in the area, a real "Taste of Scotland" menu, including such dishes as roast pheasant, "Scotch beef olives" with haggis stuffing, and their own Gaelic pâté. Rates are substantially reduced from the end of October until the end of March.

ONICH

On the shores of Loch Linnhe, this charming little village lies to the north of the Ballachulish Bridge. It's a good center if you're taking the western route to Inverness, or going to Skye and Fort William. My favorite hotels in the area follow.

The Lodge on the Loch, Creag Dhu, Onich, Inverness-shire PH33 6RY (tel.

08553/238), may have changed its name, but to locals it will forever be known as the Creag Dhu Hotel, as it was once the country home of Lady McPherson, taking its former name from the rallying cry of her clan. Now a family-run hotel, it lies between Ben Nevis and Glencoe, with expansive lochside and mountain views. The loch views are of prawn-filled Linnhe and Leven. At this imposing country home with modern additions, the dinner, bed, and breakfast rate is £39.50 ($69.15) per person daily in the spring and autumn, rising to £49.50 ($86.65) per person in the summer (for a superior room). Bedrooms have color TVs, radios, phones, hairdryers, trouser presses, and tea/coffee-makers. Under the supervision of the Young family, the hotel kitchen offers several traditional Scottish dishes among other fare. *Ceilidhs,* evenings of Scottish music and song, as well as talks and slide shows, are among events held at the hotel. Special musical weekends take place in the spring and autumn, and there are courses in painting, spinning, and other crafts. Such activities as boating, sailing, waterskiing, and aqualung diving are offered, along with good sea and freshwater fishing, pony trekking, riding, golfing, swimming, and tennis. Receiving guests from April to the end of October, the hotel has an enthusiastic repeat clientele.

Onich Hotel, Onich, Inverness-shire PH33 6RY (tel. 08553/214), is perched on the shores of Loch Linnhe, commanding views of the Ardgour and Glencoe Mountains and the Firth of Lorne. Its gardens slope down to the water. Under family management, the hotel reflects a personal touch, both in its welcome of real Highland hospitality and in the appointments of its bedrooms and lounges. The hotel is owned by Ian and Ronald Young, brothers who have run the inn since 1964. They have a loyal band of guests who return yearly. Ian looks after the administration and Ronald does the cooking, for which he has built up a reputation for its high quality. The cuisine is backed up by a fine wine list. Dinners cost from £10.50 ($18.40). The 25 bright, airy bedrooms have been modernized and have private baths, TV, phones, and tea/coffee-makers. They rent for £27.50 ($48.15) per person nightly for B&B. Guests gather in either the Clan cocktail bar or the Deerstalker lounge bar, which is open all day for food and drinks. The hotel attracts the athletic minded, as it's a center for walking, climbing, loch bathing, putting, fishing, sailing, windsurfing, and pony trekking.

BALLACHULISH

This small village enjoys a splendid scenic position on the shores of Loch Leven at the entrance to Glencoe. The Ballachulish Bridge links North and South Ballachulish. A good center for touring the western Highlands, the village has the following recommended hotel:

Ballachulish Hotel, Ballachulish, Argyll PA39 4JY (tel. 08552/606), stands right on the shores of Loch Leven, at the point where hills split Leven from Loch Linnhe. Built in the style of a Scottish manor house and extensively remodeled, it offers hospitality and warmth. The decor blends modern colors with old-style elegance. The bedrooms have a high standard of comfort and convenience, but they vary considerably in style. All have private baths, color TVs, direct-dial phones, and tea/coffee-makers. Depending on the season, singles go for £33 ($57.75) to £36 ($63) daily, and doubles cost £25.50 ($44.65) to £37.50 ($65.65) per person, the latter the charge for a suite with a four-poster bed and spa bath. All prices include a Scottish breakfast, VAT, and service. The hotel serves good food, attractively presented, made with fresh ingredients. A table d'hôte dinner is priced at £12 ($21). There are good snacks, too. The staff will arrange boat trips on the lochs or fishing expeditions.

GLENCOE

On the shores of Loch Leven, near where it joins Loch Linnhe, the Ballachulish Bridge now links the villages of North and South Ballachulish, at the entrance to Glencoe. The bridge saves a long drive to the head of the loch if you're coming from the north, but many visitors enjoy the scenic drive to Kinlochleven to come upon the wild and celebrated Glencoe from the east.

Glencoe runs from Rannoch Moor to Loch Leven between some magnificent mountains, including 3,766-foot Bidean nam Bian. Known as the "Glen of Weeping," Glencoe is where, on February 11, 1692, Campbells massacred MacDonalds —men, women, and children—who had been their hosts for 12 days. Although massacres were not uncommon in those times, this one shocked even the Highlanders because of the breach of hospitality. When the killing was done, the crime of "murder under trust" was regarded by law as an aggravated form of murder, and carried the same penalties as treason.

The glen, much of which now belongs to the National Trust for Scotland, is full of history and legend. A tiny lochan is known as "the pool of blood" because by its side some men are said to have quarreled over a piece of cheese, and all were killed.

This is an area of massive splendor, with towering peaks and mysterious glens where you can well imagine the fierce battle among the kilted Highlanders to the skirl of the pipes and the beat of the drums.

In the Glen

Almost where Glen Etive joins Glencoe, under the jagged peak of Buchaille Etive Mor dominating the road (A82), lies **King's House Hotel,** Glencoe, Argyll PA39 4HY (tel. 08556/259), five miles north of the village of Glencoe. A building has stood here since the late 14th century. During the Jacobite Rising of 1745, it was required to accommodate troops on their way south from Fort William. It is now a center for skiing and attracts thousands from far and near. Believed to be the oldest licensed inn in Scotland, the hotel has been enlarged and completely modernized. Well-furnished warm rooms, many with private baths, are provided, and also many have views of the majestic scenery. The lounge, too, has views. The dining room relies on a lot of good fresh produce for its appetizing meals. There is a fine wine cellar, plus a bar. Such amenities as a drying room are provided for those who want to walk, fish, or go climbing. The rate per person per night for B&B is £19 ($33.25). Some doubles with private baths cost an extra £4 ($7) per person nightly. A set dinner is featured for £12 ($21).

Besides access from the Glasgow–Inverness highway, guests at the King's House Hotel can be met at the Bridge of Orchy railway station by arrangement.

A ski lift is almost opposite the hotel. The Buachaille Etive Mor guards Glencoe's eastern end. This mountain provides a challenge for climbers and was the training ground for Sir John Hunt and the party he took to the top of Everest in the coronation year. This is great climbing and walking country, and rescue techniques evolved and taught here have been widely used.

Glen Orchy, to the south, is well worth a visit too, for the wild river and mountain scenery was beautiful and photogenic. It was the birthplace of the Gaelic bard Duncan Ban MacIntyre, whose song, "In Praise of Ben Doran," is considered a masterpiece.

4. Kyle of Lochalsh and Skye

From the Kyle of Lochalsh you can take a ferry to the mystical Isle of Skye, off the northwest coast of Scotland. The island has inspired many of the best loved and best known of Scottish ballads such as "Over the Sea to Skye" and "Will Ye Not Come Back Again." On the 48-mile-long island, you can explore castle ruins, duns, and brochs, enjoying a Highland welcome. For the Scots, the island will forever evoke images of Flora Macdonald, who conducted Bonnie Prince Charlie to Skye. She disguised him as Betty Burke after the Culloden defeat.

From Skye, you can take a ferry service back to Kyle or to Mallaig from

Armadale. The Armadale ferry transports cars, but the service is less frequent than the one to Kyle. If you're planning to take your car, reservations are recommended.

Caledonian MacBrayne, in the Ferry Terminal, Gourock, near Glasgow (tel. 0475/34531 for reservations, 0475/33755 for information), runs ferry services to Skye and to Mull plus 21 other islands. The company also offers inclusive tours for people and cars to island-hop, using their services between islands. This is an ideal opportunity to visit places well away from the beaten track. The information office at Gourock is most helpful, and someone there will assist you in planning a trip if you wish to make up your own journey.

The largest island of the Inner Hebrides, Skye is separated from the mainland by the Sound of Sleat on its southeastern side. At Kyleakin, on the eastern end, the channel is only a quarter of a mile wide and thus the ferry docks there. Dominating the land of summer seas, streams, woodland glens, mountain passes, cliffs, and waterfalls are the Cuillin Hills, a range of jagged black mountains. The Peninsula of Sleat, the island's southernmost arm, is known as "The Garden of Skye."

DORNIE

This small crofting village on the road to the Isle of Skye is the meeting place of three lochs—Duich, Long, and Alsh. On a rocky islet stands **Eilean Donan Castle** (tel. 059985/202), at Dornie, eight miles east of Kyle of Lochalsh on the A87. This romantic castle was built in 1220 as a defense against the Danes. In 1719 it was shelled by the British frigate *Worcester*. In ruins for 200 years, it was restored by Colonel MacRae of Clan MacRae in 1932 and is now a clan war memorial and museum, containing Jacobite relics, mostly with clan connections. It is open April to September 30 daily, including Sunday, from 10 a.m. to 12:30 p.m. and 2 to 6 p.m., charging £1 ($1.75) for admission.

South of Dornie and Eilean Donan Castle is Shiel Bridge. From here, an "unclassified road" leads to **Glenelg,** after a twisting climb over Ratagan Pass with a fine view of the mountain range known as the **Five Sisters of Kintail,** which is dominated by Sgurr Fhuaran, 3,505 feet high. In summer a car-ferry crosses the Sound of Sleat to Skye. It was from Glenelg that Dr. Johnson and James Boswell crossed to Skye in 1773. In Gleann Beag, two miles to the southeast, stand two of the best-preserved Iron Age brochs on the Scottish mainland—**Dun Telve** and **Dun Troddan.** Brochs are stone towers with double walls, probably built more than 2,000 years ago by the Picts for protection against raiders. The walls of the two brochs are more than 30 feet high.

Just outside Dornie, across Loch Long and at the end of Loch Duich, **Loch Duich Hotel,** Ardelve, Dornie, near Kyle of Lochalsh, Ross-shire IV40 8DY (tel. 059985/213), overlooks one of the Highlands' most photogenic castles, Eilean Donan. The hotel has a small lounge and bar where you can wait for dinner, which will cost from £14.50 ($25.40). It's likely to be a magnificent meal of fresh chowder or pâté, followed by local venison or perhaps a local fish. Bedrooms are simple, and many overlook Eilean Donan and the loch. Including an enormous freshly cooked breakfast with porridge and eggs and bacon—you name it—the owners charge £20 ($35) per person daily.

From Dornie, it is a short drive to the—

KYLE OF LOCHALSH

This popular center for touring the western Highlands is also a good jumping-off point to the islands. A car-ferry leaves for Kyleakin on the Isle of Skye. There is no need to book in advance. The journey is only ten minutes. The ferry shuttles back and forth all day, and you will have plenty of time to drive the length of Skye in a day, returning to the mainland by night if you want to. If that is your intent, you might register at:

Lochalsh Hotel, Ferry Road, Kyle of Lochalsh, Ross-shire IV40 8AF (tel. 0599/4202). There's no way a visitor can talk about the Kyle of Lochalsh without mentioning this landmark hotel. It was built as a luxury oasis when the British Railway finally extended its tracks in this direction. During World War II, it served as the headquarters of a branch of the Royal Navy, which had mined the coastline. Today, in memory of that period, a large (defused) mine sits near the flagpole on the seaside lawn. The south shore of the Isle of Skye and the rock-studded inlet are visible through crafted, small-paned windows, whose full-grain hardwood and brass fittings are similar to those on an ocean-going yacht. The 38 bedrooms have been stylishly overhauled. B&B is priced at £45 ($78.75) daily in a single, £115 ($201.25) in a double. Evening meals cost from £14.50 ($25.40) and include the best of Scottish cuisine and ingredients. The ground-floor bar stocks a variety of malt whiskies, and the dining room has a panoramic view.

On a hillside above the hotel, the **Ferry Inn** is one of the most popular pubs in the area, attracting locals as well as visitors.

BALMACARA

Those planning to stay in the Kyle of Lochalsh district, taking the car and passenger ferry to Skye, may prefer a more peaceful oasis for a day or two. In the Balmacara estate, now the property of the National Trust for Scotland, the **Balmacara Hotel,** Balmacara, Ross and Cromarty IV40 8DH (tel. 059986/283), is a good choice. It stands on the shores of Loch Alsh, three miles from the Kyle of Lochalsh. Both the contemporary design of the bedrooms and the panoramic water view from the hotel are similar to what visitors might discover in an isolated section of Scandinavia. Parts of the interior are covered with full-grain horizontal planks of varnished pine, into which are set square windows presenting a sweeping view of forests, loch, and the far Cuillin Hills of the Isle of Skye rising in hues of red and blue. Owner Clive Williamson is happy to talk about the attractions of Wester Ross. Each of the 30 comfortable bedrooms contains a private bath. Singles cost from £29 ($50.75) daily, with doubles or twins going for £47 ($82.25) to £50 ($87.50), including a full Scottish breakfast. A fixed-price evening meal goes for £12 ($21), while a lighter lunch averages around £5 ($8.75).

A hotel courtesy bus can be arranged to meet you at Kyle Railway Station when coming from Inverness, or at the Skye ferry terminal.

ISLE OF SKYE

Skye is the largest of the Inner Hebrides, 48 miles long and between 3 and 25 miles wide. It is separated from the mainland by the Sound of Sleat (pronounced Slate). There are many stories as to the origin of the name, Skye. Some believe it is from the Norse "ski," meaning a cloud, while others say it's from the Gaelic word for winged. There are Norse names on the island, however, as the Norsemen held sway for four centuries before 1263. Overlooking the Kyle is the ruined Castle Maol, once the home of a Norwegian princess.

For those who want to overnight or spend a longer holiday on the island, I offer the following suggestions, scattered in the various hamlets. However, in summer be sure to reserve in advance, as accommodations are extremely limited.

There are coach tours three or four times a week in summer from Kyleakin where the ferry lands to Dunvegan Castle or to the north end of the island. They generally start at 10 a.m., returning to Kyleakin around 6 p.m., so you need not take your car across with you. Telephone 0599/4328, **Clan Coaches,** for further information.

Sleat

Kinloch Lodge, Isle Ornsay, Sleat, Isle of Skye, Inverness-shire IV43 8QY (tel. 04713/333), lies 3½ miles north of Sleat by the A851. The white stone walls of this dignified manor house are visible from across the scrub- and pine-covered hillsides bordering the edges of this historic property. When it was built in 1680, it was a hunting lodge for the MacDonald estates. Today, after much rebuilding and expansion, the linden-flanked manor house is the private residence of Lord and Lady Mac-Donald, who welcome discriminating guests into the confines of their very elegant home. Portraits of the family's 18th-century forebears are the most striking details of the plushly decorated living rooms, where open fireplaces illuminate the burnished patina of scores of family antiques. Many of the bedrooms, nine in all, have been freshly papered and painted and contain a private bath. From the windows of some of the bedrooms, guests sometimes catch glimpses of the sea, which washes up to the edge of the property's sloping gardens. Rates, with breakfast included, range from £45 ($78.75) to £65 ($113.75) per person daily, based on double occupancy. Singles pay a supplement of £16 ($28).

Every evening guests enjoy drinks in a peach-colored drawing room before consuming one of the well-prepared meals for which Lady MacDonald is justifiably famous. The author of two bestselling cookbooks, she applies her techniques to imaginative recipes, for which the ingredients are usually shot, trapped, netted, or grown on the Isle of Skye. Dinner costs from £22 ($38.50) per person. The lodge is open from early March until mid-January.

Broadford

This town is the meeting point for the ports of Armadale, Kylerhea, and Kyleakin.

Broadford Hotel, Broadford, Isle of Skye, Inverness-shire IV49 9AB (tel. 04712/204), is a venerated inn dating from 1611, when it was established by Sir Lauchlin MacKinnon. It was here that a descendant of his first came up with the secret recipe for Drambuie liqueur, now a symbol throughout the world of Highland hospitality. The Broadford has seen a lot of changes since those days, and it's been completely modernized and brought up-to-date, both in its bedrooms and public facilities. The inn lies by the waters of Broadford River, and guests are allowed to fish for salmon and trout. The comfortable bedrooms have baths, TVs, phones, and hot beverage facilities. For B&B, singles cost £17 ($29.75) to £31 ($54.25) daily, and doubles run £27 ($47.25) to £35 ($61.25), with VAT included, the prices depending on the season. The families who run the hotel, offer good Scottish cooking, making fine use of the local produce. A dinner goes for £10 ($17.50). The inn lies four minutes from the Skye airfield, where there is direct daily service to Glasgow. Nearby are the ruins of the farmhouse where Samuel Johnson and his companion, Boswell, spent a night on their tour of the Highlands.

Sligachan

Sligachan Hotel, Sligachan, Isle of Skye, Inverness-shire IV47 8SW (tel. 047852/204), nestles at the foot of the Cuillin Mountains at the head of a sea loch and is an ideal touring center from which to explore Skye. This family-run hotel, one of Skye's oldest coaching inns, has private baths in all the bedrooms. B&B costs £23 ($40.25) per person daily, and a four-course dinner goes for £11.50 ($20.15). The cuisine consists of local fare such as venison, lamb, salmon, oysters, and vegetarian dishes. The open fires and fine selection of malt whiskies will warm the cockles of your heart.

Portree

Skye's capital, Portree, is the port for steamers making trips around the island and linking Skye with the 15-mile-long island Raasay. Sligachan, nine miles south, and Glenbrittle, seven miles farther southwest, are centers for climbing the Cuillin (Coolin) Hills.

Royal Hotel, Bank Street, Portree, Isle of Skye, Inverness-shire IV51 9LU (tel. 0478/2525), stands on a hill facing the water and is said to have extended hospitality to Bonnie Prince Charlie during his flight in 1746. In less dramatic and rushed circumstances, you can book one of its comfortable bedrooms, the preferred ones opening onto the sea. All the accommodations have showers or baths, toilets, TVs, tea/coffee-makers, and central heating. A single rents for £25 ($43.75) to £34 ($59.50) daily, and doubles or twins cost £44 ($77) to £49 ($85.75) for B&B. À la carte meals and bar snacks are offered, a dinner in the restaurant averaging £13 ($22.75).

Rosedale Hotel, Beaumont Crescent, Portree, Isle of Skye, Inverness-shire IV51 9DB (tel. 0478/2531), lying in one of the more secluded parts of Portree, opens directly onto the sea. It was created from a row of fishermen's dwellings dating from the reign of William IV. Privately owned and managed by the second generation of the Andrew family, Rosedale is a warm and welcoming place, offering 23 bedrooms decorated in modern style. All have private baths, radios, color TV, and direct-dial phones. B&B goes for £26 ($45.50) per person daily, the tariff including a big Scottish breakfast. In a lounge, you can be served a good range of Highland malt whiskies. The food is good, too. The hotel is open only from mid-May to the end of September.

Uig

This village is on Trotternish, the largest Skye peninsula, and ferry port for Harris and Uist in the Outer Hebrides. It is 15 miles north of Portree and 49 miles from Kyle of Lochalsh. **Monkstadt House,** a mile and a half north, is where Flora Macdonald brought Prince Charles, in the guise of a girl named Betty Burke, after their escape flight from Benbecula. In **Kilmuir** churchyard, five miles north, Flora was buried, wrapped in a sheet used by the prince. Her grave is marked by a Celtic cross.

Uig Hotel, Uig, Isle of Skye, Inverness-shire IV51 9YE (tel. 047042/205), has been furnished with warmth and imagination. In homelike comfort, guests are welcomed and shown to the lounge with its harmonious colors. The hotel stands on a hillside overlooking a small bay and a tiny fishing harbor. The food, excellently prepared Scottish fare, is served in a cheerful dining room with a view of the bay. The 24-room hotel comes equipped with private bath or shower in every chamber. Rates range from £24 ($42) to £30 ($52.50) daily for singles, from £50 ($87.50) to £60 ($105) for doubles, including a full Scottish breakfast and VAT. The hotel is open from mid-April to early October.

Dunvegan

The village of Dunvegan grew up around **Dunvegan Castle** (tel. 047022/206), the principal man-made sight on the Isle of Skye, seat of the chiefs of Clan MacLeod who have lived there for 700 years. The castle, which stands on a rocky promontory, was once accessible only by boat, but now the moat is bridged and the castle open to the public. It holds many fascinating relics, including a "fairy flag." It is reputed to be the oldest inhabited castle in Britain. It is open from 10 a.m. to 5 p.m. from Easter to the end of September and from 2 to 5 p.m. during October. The castle is closed Sunday, but the gardens, craft shop, and restaurant are open seven days a week. Admission to the castle is £2.80 ($4.90) for adults, £1.50 ($2.65) for children. To the gardens only, the entry fee is £1.50 ($2.65) for adults, 75p ($1.30) for children.

Boats leave the castle jetty at frequent intervals every day except Sunday from May to the end of September going to the **Seal Colony.** The seals in Loch Dunvegan, both brown and gray varieties, aren't bothered by the approach of people in boats and can be studied at close range. The 20-minute round trip costs £2.50 ($4.40) for adults, £1.50 ($2.65) for children.

At **Trumpan,** nine miles north of Dunvegan, are the remains of a church that was set afire in 1597 by MacDonald raiders while the congregation, all MacLeods, were inside at worship. Only one woman survived. The MacLeods of Dunvegan rushed to the defense, and only two MacDonalds escaped death.

Atholl House Hotel, Dunvegan, Isle of Skye, Inverness-shire IV51 8WA (tel. 047022/219), stands right in the village of Dunvegan, near Dunvegan Castle. Built in 1908 as a private home, it was converted to a guest house in 1923. It is owned and operated by Cliff and Barbara Ashton, who offer B&B for £18.50 ($32.40) per person daily in a bathless room, £21.50 ($37.65) per person in a room with bath. Units contain facilities for making hot beverages. In the dining room, the Ashtons place emphasis on good service and well-prepared local produce, including lamb, venison, salmon, and shellfish in season. Atholl House is a member of the "Taste of Scotland" program, with high standards of accommodation, Scottish hospitality, and Scottish cuisine. It has a residents' license. From the hotel, you have views over mountain moorland and Loch Dunvegan.

Skeabost Bridge

Eastward from Dunvegan is Skeabost Bridge, with an island cemetery of great antiquity. The graves of four Crusaders are here.

Nearby is the **Skeabost House Hotel,** Skeabost Bridge, Isle of Skye, Invernessshire IV51 9NP (tel. 047032/202), one of the most comfortable, refreshing, and inviting country homes of Skye, receiving paying guests from April to mid-October. Modernized, it is interesting architecturally with its dormers, chimneys, tower, and gables. Inside the taste level is high, with wood paneling and carpets. Once a private estate, it has been converted into a lochside hotel, standing on grounds that in summer are studded with flowering bushes. The location is 35 miles from Kyle of Lochalsh and 5 miles from Portree. Sportslovers are attracted to the hotel, gathering in the firelit lounge for a whisky. The atmosphere is of hardy tweeds. The loch outside is well stocked with salmon and trout, and a short par-three golf course has been constructed. Of the 21 handsomely furnished rooms, most contain private baths. Singles are accepted at a rate of £24 ($42) to £29 ($50.75) daily, depending on the plumbing, and doubles on a similar basis cost £56 ($98). All tariffs include a full Scottish breakfast. The Scottish fare, featuring smoked salmon, is served on fine china with elegant silver. A bar buffet lunch goes for £5.50 ($9.65), and a four-course dinner for £13 ($22.75).

THE SLEAT PENINSULA

A lot of Skye can look melancholy and forlorn, especially in misty weather. But for a change of landscape pace, head for the Peninsula of Sleat, the southeastern section of the island. It's long been known as the "Garden of Skye" because of the lushness of some of its vegetation. The reason for this is that its shores are washed by the warmer waters of the Gulf Stream. Sleat also possesses several sightseeing attractions.

A ruined stronghold of the MacDonalds, **Knock Castle,** lies off the A851, 12 miles south of Broadford. It can be visited, admission-free, throughout the day.

Another MacDonald stronghold, **Dunsgiath Castle,** has some well-preserved ruins open to view. They are found at Tokavaig on an unclassified road (a sign directs you) at a point 20 miles south and southwest of Broadford.

Clan Donald Centre

At Armadale, you don't have to have MacDonald as your last name to enjoy a visit to Skye's award-winning Clan Donald Centre (tel. 04714/305), with its historical exhibition, "The Headship of the Gael," woodland gardens, restaurant, and gift shop. You reach it from Broadford by traveling along a winding seaside road, eventually pulling into the recently restored and well-kept grounds surrounding the sculptured ruins of Armadale Castle and the rebuilt baronial stables. The multimedia exhibition is in part of the castle and tells of the lost culture of the ancient Gaelic world under the MacDonalds as Lords of the Isles. There is a countryside ranger service with a full summer program of guided walks and talks to introduce you to several miles of trails and the history and workings of the adjacent Highland estate. There is also a program of evening arts and theater events.

Admission is £1.50 ($2.65) for adults and £1 ($1.75) for children. The center is open daily from March 20 to the end of October from 10 a.m. to 5:30 p.m. The licensed restaurant in the stables offers home-baking and good local food, from teas and coffees to a full meal. The drive from the ferryboat at Kyleakin is about 30 minutes, and the center is near the Armadale Mallaig ferry.

---

5. Oban and District

Oban (meaning "small bay") is the great port for the Western Isles and a center of Gaelic culture. It is the gateway to Mull, largest of the Inner Hebrides; to the island of Iona, the cradle of Scottish Christianity; and to Staffa, where Fingal's Cave inspired Mendelssohn to write his *Hebrides* Overture. There are cruises to Iona from early June to late September. For information about island ferry services to Mull, Iona, and the Outer Hebrides, get in touch with **MacBraynes Steamers** at their office in Oban (tel. 0631/62285).

OBAN

One of Scotland's leading coastal resorts, the bustling port town of Oban is set in a sheltered bay that is almost landlocked by the island of Kerrera. A yachting center and small burgh, it lies about 50 miles south of Fort William.

From Pulpit Hill in Oban there is a fine view across the Firth of Lorn and the Sound of Mull. Overlooking the town is an unfinished replica of the Colosseum of Rome, **McCaig's Tower,** built by a banker, John Stuart McCaig, in 1897–1900 as a memorial to his family and to try to curb local unemployment during a slump. Its walls are two feet thick and from 37 to 40 feet high. The courtyard within is landscaped and the tower is floodlit at night. Outsiders have been heard to refer to the tower as "McCaig's Folly," but Obanites deplore this term, as they are proud of the structure.

On the island of Kerrera stands **Gylen Castle,** home of the MacDougalls, dating back to 1587.

Near the little granite **Cathedral of the Isles,** one mile north of the end of the bay, is the ruin of the 13th-century **Dunollie Castle,** seat of the Lords of Lorn who once owned a third of Scotland.

You can visit **Dunstaffnage Castle,** 3½ miles to the north, which was believed to have been the royal seat of the Dalriadic monarchy in the 8th century. The present castle was probably built in 1263. It may have been the location of the Scots Court until the unification under Kenneth McAlpine and the transfer to Scone of the seat of Scottish government. The castle is open April to September from 9:30 a.m. to 7 p.m. (on Sunday from 2 to 7 p.m.); October to March, from 9:30 a.m. to 4 p.m. (on Sunday from 2 to 4 p.m.). It is closed on Thursday and Friday. Admission is 60p ($1.05) for adults, 30p (55¢) for children.

Where to Stay

As a holiday resort, Oban has a number of good hotels and guesthouses within easy reach of the seafront and the piers from which cruises to the offshore islands can be booked.

Alexandra, Corran Esplanade, Oban, Argyll PA34 5AA (tel. 0631/62381), is a stone hotel with gables and a tower, plus a Regency front veranda, enjoying a sunny perch on the promenade. From its public rooms, you can look out onto Oban Bay. Two sun lounges overlook the seafront. The bedrooms are substantial and pleasing, offering comfort and conveniences at £29 ($50.75) daily in a single, £68 ($119) in a double, including a full breakfast, service, and VAT. Of the 56 bedrooms, nearly half contain a private bath. The restaurant, serving good food, also opens onto the panorama. A complete dinner in the evening averages around £16 ($28). Dinner is sometimes accompanied by live music and dancing. The hotel is open from Easter to the end of October.

Great Western Hotel, Corran Esplanade, Oban, Argyll PA34 5PP (tel. 0631/ 63101), is a warmly old-fashioned hotel set directly on the waterfront across the street from the harborfront promenade. Many of its 73 well-furnished bedrooms contain a private bath and a sweeping view over the interisland ferryboats and fishing vessels bobbing at anchor in the harbor. The hotel, which is owned by one of Britain's well-known chains, offers Scottish entertainment in one of its lounges, as well as a well-appointed dining room and a spacious water-view lounge where drinks are served. Guests pay from £36 ($63) daily in a single, from £62 ($108.50) in a double. Closed December to February.

Lancaster, Corran Esplanade, Oban, Argyll PA34 5AD (tel. 0631/62587), is distinguished by its attractive pseudo-Tudor façade. On the crescent of the bay, it commands views from its public rooms of the islands of Lismore and Kerrera, even the more distant peaks of Mull. Open all year, the hotel welcomes you to one of its well-furnished bedrooms, charging from £20 ($35) per person daily, with breakfast included. Most rooms have a private bath or shower. The fully licensed Lancaster is the only hotel in Oban featuring a heated indoor swimming pool, a sauna, a whirlpool, and a solarium.

Caledonian Hotel, Station Square, Oban, Argyll PA34 5RT (tel. 0631/ 63133), makes good on its promise of giving you a "taste for the Highlands." A fine example of Scottish 19th-century architecture, it occupies a landmark position, with a good view opening onto the harbor and Oban Bay looking toward the Mull of Kintyre. This convenient location puts you close to the rail, bus, and ferry terminals from which you can book passage to the Isles. The bedrooms are up to date with private baths, color TV, and beverage-making equipment. Serviced by an elevator, the hotel offers singles for £41 ($71.75) nightly, with doubles climbing to £62 ($108.50). Good, reasonably priced Scottish fare is served in the dining room.

Where to Dine

McTavish's Kitchens, 34 George St. (tel. 0631/63064), is dedicated to preserving the local cuisine. Downstairs is a self-service restaurant, which is open in summer daily from 9 a.m. to 9 p.m., serving breakfast, main meals, shortbread, scones, strawberries, cakes, teas, and coffees. The two bars are the upstairs Lairds Bar and, around the corner from the self-service, the Mantrap Bar with a "real mantrap." The licensed second-floor restaurant has a more ambitious Scottish and continental menu with higher prices, but there are also budget lunches for around £3.50 ($6.15) for two courses and high teas for £4.50 ($7.90). The table d'hôte menu includes an appetizer, a main course that might be fresh salmon, and a dessert such as strawberries or raspberries in season. The price is £7.50 ($13.15). The à la carte menu offers haggis, Loch Fyne kippers (oak-smoked herring), prime Scottish steaks, smoked salmon, venison, and local mussels.

A feature of the restaurant is the entertainment, with music by local artists, Scottish dance music, singing, piping, fiddling, and Highland dancing, from 8:30 to 10:30 p.m. daily from mid-May to the end of September. Admission is £2 ($3.50) for adults, £1 ($1.75) for children. It's half price for those who dine here. The bagpipes provide haunting melodies, new and old.

On the Outskirts

Isle of Eriska Hotel, Ledaig, Connel, near Oban, Argyll PA37 1SD (tel. 063172/371), is a Victorian house that welcomes you at the end of a winding drive. In the Middle Ages, this forested island was considered a place of sanctuary, under the protection of the church. In the 19th century an industrialist purchased it, planted hundreds of beech trees, built a bridge to the mainland, and retreated into the well-proportioned confines of his brick-and-stone manor house. Today you can savor the splendors of a country life. From its pinnacle, you'll enjoy a panorama of the surrounding waterways, as well as views of a local colony of deer and the moss-covered forest, which is still maintained as a private park. A magnificent front door

leads to the entrance hall where a log fire blazes. A formal sitting room and a library/
bar are pleasant, and a wide staircase leads to the well-furnished bedrooms, with
modern baths. Bed and breakfast is £93.15 ($163) daily in a single, £119.60
($209.30) in a double. Guests are charged £28.75 ($50.30) for dinner. The Isle of
Eriska is owned by Mr. and Mrs. Robin Buchanan-Smith (he's a Protestant minister).

PORT APPIN

To the north of Oban lies a beautiful lochside district, including Lismore Island. On an islet nearby is a landmark, **Castle Stalker,** the ancient seat of the
Stewarts of Appin, built in the 15th century by Duncan Stewart, son of the first chief
of Appin. Dugald, the ninth chief, was forced to sell the estate in 1765, and the castle
slowly fell into ruin. It was recently restored by Lt. Col. Stewart Allward and is once
again inhabited. According to myth, there's a subterranean undersea passage at Port
Appin where a piper supposedly entered with his dog. Only the dog returned, and
he was hairless. It is open from March to September by appointment (tel. 08832/
3944). The cost is £4 ($7) for adults, £2 ($3.50) for children, including the boat
trip.

Port Appin is a small village of stone cottages.

The Airds Hotel, Port Appin, Appin, Argyll PA38 4DF (tel. 063173), is an old
ferry inn dating from 1700, in one of the most beautiful spots in the historic district
of Appin. Considered one of the outstanding hotels of Scotland, it is a *Relais &
Chateaux.* You're assured of serenity if you take a room at this tranquil choice on
Loch Linnhe, midway between Oban and Fort William. The hotel overlooks not
only Loch Linnhe, but the island of Lismore and the mountains of Morvern, an
ideal center for touring this area of the country. You can take forest walks in many
directions, or go pony trekking, sea angling, or trout fishing. Boats can be rented
and trips arranged to see the seals and to visit the island of Lismore. The resident
proprietors, Eric and Betty Allen, welcome you to one of their comfortably furnished bedrooms from April to the end of November, charging £66 ($115.50) to
£80 ($140) per person daily in a double or twin and £80 ($140) in a single. Everything is immaculately maintained and handsomely decorated, and the setting is
tranquil.

It is the food that makes the Airds such an outstanding place to visit. Mrs. Allen
is one of the great cooks of Scotland. In her repertoire of fine Scottish cuisine, home-
baking is a specialty, and fresh produce is used in making up the menus. Specialties
include Loch Fyne kippers, smoked-mackerel salad, and an exceptional kidney
soup. Sole is often served stuffed with crab mousse, or perhaps you'll sample the
roast haunch of venison with rowan jelly if featured. Desserts include such
mouthwatering concoctions as walnut-fudge tart. A meal here will cost from £25
($43.75). Reservations for dinner, served only at 8 p.m., are absolutely necessary.

LOCH AWE

Twenty-two miles long and in most places only about a mile wide, Loch Awe
for years acted as a natural moat protecting the Campbells of Inveraray from their
enemies to the north. Along its banks and on its islands are many reminders of its
fortified past. There is a ruined castle at Fincharn, at the southern end of the loch,
and another on the island of Fraoch Eilean. The **Isle of Inishail** has an ancient chapel
and burial ground, and at the northern end of the loch are the ruins of **Kilchurn
Castle,** built by Sir Colin Campbell in 1440. The bulk of Ben Cruachan, 3,689 feet,
dominates Loch Awe at its northern end and attracts climbers. On the ben is the
world's second-largest hydroelectric power station, which pumps water from Loch
Awe to a reservoir high up the mountain. Below the mountain are the **Falls of
Cruachan** and the wild **Pass of Brander,** where Robert the Bruce routed the Clan
MacDougall in 1308.

In this area, the Forestry Commission maintains the vast forests, and a road now makes it possible to travel around Loch Awe, so that it is more than ever a popular angling center. Sharp-eyed James Bond fans may even recognize some scenes that appeared in one of the films.

The Pass of Brander where Loch Awe narrows was the scene of many a fierce battle in bygone times, and something of that bloody past seems to brood over the narrow defile. Through it the waters of the Awe flow on their way to Loch Etive. This winding sealoch is 19 miles long, stretching from Dun Dunstaffnage Bay at Oban to Glen Etive, reaching into the Moor of Rannoch at the foot of the 3,000-foot Buachaille Etive (the Shepherd of Etive), into which Glencoe also reaches.

Ardanaiseig, Kilchrenan by Taynuilt, Argyll PA35 1HE (tel. 08663/333). When one of the 19th-century Campbell family patriarchs erected this manorial seat in 1834, he designed its lines more along 18th-century styles. He planted some of the rarest trees in the British islands, many of them exotic conifers. Today, clusters of fruit trees within a walled garden, along with rhododendrons and azaleas, add to the arboreal interest of this elegant graystone property. The house stands between Loch Awe and the peaks of Crauchan, and a golf course is within a 40-minute drive. Rentable fishing vessels add another diversion. Until recently a private home, the hotel has formal sitting rooms graced with big chintzy chairs, fresh flowers, and polished tables. Upstairs, each of the 13 well-heated bedrooms contains a private bath, color TV, direct-dial phone, more chintz, and high ceilings. Per-person rates, with breakfast and dinner included, range from £83 ($145.25) daily. The owners have employed an excellent chef, who makes use of fresh produce, game, and meats with skill and flair. To reach the property from Oban, take the A85 to Taynuilt, then follow a secondary road, the B845, to Kilchrenan. Follow the signs to Ardanaiseig. Guests are received from mid-April to mid-October.

THE CRINAN CANAL

The nine-mile-long canal, constructed between 1793 and 1801, was designed to provide water communication between the Firth of Clyde, Argyll, the western Highlands, and the islands. It runs roughly north from Ardrishaig and curves gradually to the west before reaching Loch Crinan on the Sound of Jura. Four miles north of **Cairnbaan,** on the canal, is the ruined hill-fort of **Dunadd,** once capital of Dalriada, kingdom of the Scots. There are numerous Bronze Age stone circles in the vicinity, and **Kilmartin churchyard,** five miles north of Cairnbaan, has a carved cross dating from the 16th century. **Carnasserie Castle,** also to the north of the canal, built in the late 16th century, was the home of John Carswell, the first post-Reformation bishop of the isles, whose translation of John Knox's liturgy into Gaelic was the first book to be published in that language.

Crinan, a yachting haven on the Sound of Jura, is overlooked by the early-11th-century **Duntrune Castle,** one of the oldest castles in Scotland, and still inhabited by the descendants of the original owners, the Clan Malcolm.

Food and Lodging

Crinan is a charming little village and the address of my recommendation for a stopover in this area:

Crinan Hotel, Crinan, Argyll PA31 8SR (tel. 054683/261), off the B841, seven miles northwest of Lochgilphead, is an inn with a bright, attractive decor and modern comforts and conveniences. Because of its location on a canal and yacht basin, it is naturally a favorite with sailors, who book its 22 rooms with private bath in July and August, the peak sailing months. If you're reserving (and I highly recommend that you do), ask for one of the rooms with private balconies opening onto mountains and lochside sunsets. Bedrooms rent for £40 ($70) daily in a single, from £85 ($148.75) in a double, including a breakfast that often features oatcakes and hot croissants. The hotel serves good food, including fresh salmon, Crinan clams mornay, roast duckling in black-cherry sauce, and Scottish sirloin. Meals are served from noon to 2 p.m. and 7 to 9 p.m., and dinner goes for £21.50 ($37.65). Luncheon is served al fresco in fair weather. The hotel is open from mid-March to November.

INVERARAY

This small resort and royal burgh occupies a splendid Highland setting on the upper shores of Loch Fyne. The hereditary seat of the Dukes of Argyll, **Inveraray Castle** (tel. 0499/2203) has been headquarters of the Clan Campbell since the early 15th century. In 1644 the original village was burned by the Royalist Marquess of Montrose, was rebuilt, and then the third Duke of Argyll built a new castle between 1744 and 1788. The 11th duke opened the castle to the public and it is now presided over by the present laird, the 12th Duke of Argyll and 26th MacCailein Mor, chief of the Clan Campbell. The castle is among the earliest examples of Gothic revival in Britain, and offers a fine collection of pictures and 18th-century French furniture, old English and continental porcelain, and a magnificent Armoury Hall, which alone contains 1,300 pieces. There is a castle shop for souvenirs and a tea room where tea, coffee, and snack meals are served. The castle is open daily except Friday from 10 a.m. to 1 p.m. and 2 to 6 p.m. in April, May, June, September, and October. In July and August, hours are 10 a.m. to 6 p.m. Sunday hours are 2 to 6 p.m. Admission is £2.20 ($3.85) for adults, £1.10 ($1.95) for children. A family ticket is available for £6 ($10.50). The castle is closed on Friday from the opening date until the end of June each year and in September and October.

At one end of the main street of the town is a Celtic burial cross from Iona. The parish church is divided by a wall enabling services to be held in Gaelic and English at the same time.

The **Bell Tower** of All Saints' Episcopal Church, set in pleasant grounds, contains Scotland's finest bells, the second-heaviest ring of ten in the world. An easy staircase leads to a safe pedestrian walkway on top of the tower to see the bells and fine views over the loch and glen. The tower is open from 10 a.m. to 1 p.m. and 2 to 5 p.m. Monday to Saturday, and 3 to 6 p.m. on Sunday from May to the end of September. It costs adults 60p ($1.05) and children 30p (55¢), to ascend the tower, but the ground-floor exhibition is free. For more information, telephone 0499/2433.

The **Auchindrain Museum of Country Life** (tel. 04995/235), six miles southwest of Inveraray, is an open-air museum of traditional Highland farming life. It is a unique survivor of the past, whose origins are so far back as to be a subject for archeology. The farming township stands more or less as it was in the 1800s, but studies have revealed at least four centuries before that. At present, Auchindrain consists of 20-odd acres of "infield," about which stands 21 houses and barns of the 18th and 19th centuries. Some are furnished to their appropriate period, and others contain displays. There is also an exhibit center and a museum shop. Open daily from 10 a.m. to 5 p.m. during the summer, it charges £2 ($3.50) for adults, £1.20 ($2.10) for children over 8 years old. The museum is closed Saturday during April, May, and September. Auchindrain and mid-Argyll are in an area crammed with places of interest for historians, antiquarians, and archeologists.

A fine woodland garden may be visited at **Crarae Lodge,** four miles southwest of the village.

Food and Lodging

Argyll Arms Hotel, Inveraray, Argyll PA32 8XB (tel. 0499/2466). The front windows of what used to be known in the region as the Great Inn open onto a view of Loch Fyne and Loch Shira. The three-story core of the building was constructed in 1755. The pleasantly modernized Victorian interior is managed for the trustees of the Duke of Argyll. The hotel lies near the entrance to the castle. The in-house restaurant is one of the town's most popular lunch spots, where meals are served either on the glassed-in veranda or in a high-ceilinged lounge. In the evening, more formal meals are offered in the dining room. You can also drop in for afternoon tea, the scones and pastries having been freshly made. A fixed-price evening meal costs from £12.50 ($21.90), and well-prepared pub lunches go for £5 ($8.75). Rooms are pleasantly and comfortably furnished, a few containing private bath. The charges range from £18 ($31.50) to £26 ($45.50) daily per person daily, with breakfast included.

6. The Inner Hebrides

Geologists wandering through bog and bracken used to happen on painters and birdwatchers and stumble across an occasional sea angler or mountain climber. That era of solitude was some time ago, however. These special-interest individuals still frequent the islands of the Hebrides, but now you'll find more and more general tourists.

Nearly everybody has heard of Mull and Iona, but what about Rhum, Eigg, and Muck? (Sounds like a goblin Christmas recipe.) On these little islands of the Inner Hebrides, visitors can meet crofters (small farmers) and fisher folk, even join in a real island *ceilidh* (singing party).

Arran, Islay—that most southerly of the Hebridean islands—and the Isle of Jura, along with romantic Skye, are covered in other sections.

Mull, featured in Robert Louis Stevenson's *Kidnapped,* has wild scenery, golf courses, and a treasure trove of tradition. Iona played a major part in the spread of Christianity in Britain, and a trip there usually includes a visit to Staffa, a tiny, uninhabited volcanic island where Fingal's Cave inspired Mendelssohn.

This chain of islands lies just off the west coast of the Scottish mainland. To visit them, you'll be following a worthy tradition—in the footsteps of Dr. Samuel Johnson and his faithful Boswell.

Caledonian MacBrayne (tel. 0475/33755) provides the main link for boat transportation around the Inner Hebrides. Call them for information about departures.

MULL

The third largest island in the Hebrides, Mull is rich in legend and folklore, a land of ghosts, monsters, and the wee folk. Over open fires that burn on cold winter evenings, the talk is of myths and ancient times. The island is wild and mountainous, characterized by sea lochs and sandy bars.

Getting to Mull is easy, unlike travel to some of the other islands of the Inner Hebrides. It's best reached on a car-ferry from Oban, the trip taking 45 minutes. For times of departure, contact **Caledonian MacBrayne,** the Ferry Terminal, Oban (tel. 0631/62285). It's a roll-on, roll-off type of operation for your car.

The Mull Highland Games are held annually in July, filled with all the traditional events such as bagpiping, caber-tossing, and dancing. Another popular time to visit is in early October, when the Tour of Mull Rally is held. First run in 1969, it has been an attraction ever since. Motorsports lovers thrill to the idea of 120 miles of island roads, and twisting, tortuous ones they are.

If you come to Mull, be sure to bring a raincoat, as it is known as the wettest island in the Hebrides, a fact that upset Dr. Johnson, who visited here in 1773. Actually, Dr. Johnson was a latecomer to Mull, which has an ancient history. It was, in fact, known to the classical Greeks, and its prehistoric past is recalled in forts, duns, and stone circles.

Many visitors consider Mull more beautiful than Skye, a controversy I don't choose to get involved in, as both the islands are different, each with its many attractions. However, Mull is made additionally enticing in that it can be used as a launching pad from which to explore the famed islands of Iona and Staffa, coming up. Mull has a varied scenery, with many waterfalls. Its highest peak is **Ben More** at 3,169 feet, but it also has many flat areas. It is rich in wildlife, including roe deer, golden eagles, polecats, seabirds, and feral goats.

Guarding the bay (you'll see it as you cross on the ferry) is Duart Castle, restored just before World War I and once the seat of the fiery Macleans, who shed much blood in and around the castle during their battles with the Lords of the Isles. In the bay—somewhere—lies the *Florencia,* a Spanish galleon that went down laden with treasure. Many attempts have been made to bring it up, but so far all of them have failed.

To the southeast, near Salen, are the ruins of **Aros Castle,** once the stronghold of the Lords of the Isles, the MacDonalds. Its ruins date from the 14th century, and it was last occupied in the 17th century.

On the far south coast at Lochbuie, **Moy Castle** has a water-filled dungeon. The wild countryside of Mull was the scene of many of David Balfour's adventures in *Kidnapped* by Robert Louis Stevenson.

If you're driving along any of the single-track roads of Mull, remember to take your time and let the sheep and cattle have the right-of-way. Also, a car coming downhill toward you has preference, so seek a spot to pull off.

There are two nine-hole golf courses on the island. The Western Isles Golf Course at Tobermory, the island's capital, dates from the 1930s and is said to have possibly the best views of any course in the world. A newer course, flat and tight, opened in 1980 at Craignure. Sea fishing and river fishing are also popular on Mull, where anglers seek salmon and three kinds of trout: rainbow, sea, and brown. The trout is found in the fast-flowing rivers and hill lochs of the island. Some sportslovers take to the sea in pursuit of sharks and monster skate. Stalking, hiking, and hill walking are other activities for the fit.

At the end of the day, you might enjoy a dram of malt whisky from the **Tobermory Malt Whisky Distillery,** which has had a troubled history but is now back in business. Incidentally, visitors are welcome to visit the distillery in Tobermory, established in 1823. Call 0688/2119 for an appointment.

The Major Sights

Torosay Castle at Craignure (tel. 06802/421) is a Victorian mansion constructed in the mid-19th century by David Bryce, a famous Scottish architect. In his early years, Winston Churchill was a frequent visitor. The castle is set in gardens designed at the turn of the century by Sir Robert Lorimer. One writer said that a visit here is like returning to "the Edwardian age of leisure," and so it is. To the surprise of hundreds of visitors, the armchairs are labeled "Please sit down" instead of "Please keep off." This is very much a family place, home to four generations. It is the only castle and garden in private occupation in the West Highlands that is open daily to the public. The castle has family portraits by such famous artists as Sargent, along with wildlife pictures. It has numerous exhibits to intrigue visitors, including evidence for the Loch Ness monster. It's like browsing through a scrapbook of 100 years of family history to visit here. Later you can wander through 11 acres of Italian-style terraced gardens, which include a water garden with shrubs that grow in the Gulf Stream climate, along with a Japanese garden and life-size figures by Antonio Bonazza. You can enjoy extensive views of the Appin coastline from Ben Nevis to Ben Cruachan. The castle and gardens are open daily from 10:30 a.m. to 5:30 p.m. from the first of May until mid-October. Admission is £2.50 ($4.40) for adults and £1 ($1.75) for children.

Duart Castle (mentioned above), off the A849 on the eastern point of Mull (tel. 06802/309), dates from the 13th century and was the home of the Maclean Clan. An imposing and majestic structure, it was sacked in 1691 by the Dukes of Argyll in retaliation for the Macleans' having supported the Stuarts in 1715 and

1745. It was allowed to fall into ruins. However, Sir Fitzroy Maclean, the 26th chief of the clan and the grandfather of the present occupant, began restoration in 1911, spending a considerable fortune in the process. It had been his ambition since he was a boy to see his ancestral home restored, a task he began at the age of 76. He lived until he was 102, so he had time to enjoy it. Many relics of clan history are found inside. Visitors can wander about, taking in such rooms as the Banqueting Hall, which is in the keep, the great tower that is the heart of the castle. Duart is open daily from May to September from 10:30 a.m. to 6 p.m., charging £2 ($3.50) for adults and £1 ($1.75) for children under 14.

The **Old Byre Heritage Centre,** near Dervaig (tel. 06884/229), houses one of the most charming museums you could hope to find. A series of tableaux with life-size figures recaptures the atmosphere of life on Mull during the second half of the 19th century. The scenes come alive with an audio dramatization featuring the voices of local people, many of whom helped in the original construction of the tableaux. The performance, which takes half an hour, tells the story of the harsh existence of the crofters evicted from their land in the Clearances. The museum is open daily from 10:20 a.m. to 6 p.m. Easter to October. Admission is £1 ($1.75) for adults, 50p (90¢) for children. There are a gift and craft shop and a tea room on the premises, offering light lunches, home-baked bread, and scones.

Mull Railway

Even passengers who arrive on Mull with their car might want to take an excursion on the only passenger railway in the Hebrides. It was inaugurated in 1983, and its puffing engine and narrow-gauge tracks give the impression of a frontier-style excursion into the past. The tracks begin at the Old Pier in Craignure, running 1½ miles to Torosay Castle and its famous gardens. Some of the engines are powered by steam, others by diesel. Regardless of the mode of power, the view remains one of unspoiled mountains, glens, and seaside. Otters, eagles, and deer can sometimes be seen in the course of the 20-minute journey. Trains operate between late April and mid-October. The most frequent service occurs between June and mid-September when it begins Monday to Friday at 11:10 a.m. and on Saturday and Sunday at 11:15 a.m. Most visitors use the train as an opportunity to spend a few hours to explore Torosay Castle before returning to the Oban ferryboat at Craignure. One-way fares are £1 ($1.75) for adults and 75p ($1.30) for children. A special round-trip ticket is available for families of two parents and two children, costing £3.40 ($5.95).

For more information, call the **Mull and West Highland Railway Co.** in Craignure (tel. 06802/494; 06803/389 off-season).

Food and Lodging

Always make a reservation if you're planning to spend the night on Mull. Here is a preview of a selection of hotels scattered across the island.

TOBERMORY: In a beautiful location above the harbor, looking out upon the bay, **Western Isles,** Tobermory, Isle of Mull, Argyll PA75 6PR (tel. 0688/2012), is a large graystone country inn on a bluff above Tobermory. It was constructed by the Sandeman sherry company in the late 1880s as a hunting and fishing lodge for their top-level staff and customers. It was owned for a number of years by the MacBrayne shipping company. The current owners welcome visitors to rooms decorated in a mixture of styles, but they're homelike, spotless, and have electric heaters. Singles range in price from £22 ($38.50) to £28 ($49) daily, with doubles costing £55 ($96.25) to £56 ($98). You get good meals here, especially fish dishes. A four-course dinner goes for £11 ($19.25). The hotel is closed from mid-October to March.

The Tobermory Hotel, Tobermory, Isle of Mull, Argyll PA75 6NT (tel. 0688/2091), is in many ways the prestige hotel of Tobermory, occupying a prime position on the waterfront. With chimneys and gables, it is painted a vivid yellow.

Christine and Michael Ratcliffe welcome visitors from March to December in one of their 15 well-furnished bedrooms, five of which contain a private bath. Rates range from £19 ($33.25) to £25 ($43.75) per person nightly for B&B. Personal service is a hallmark of this little inn, and the place is known for its good Scottish food. You can order dinner from 7:30 to 8 p.m. Ask about their evening cruises aboard the yacht, *Sea Topaz.*

CRAIGNURE: A first-class hotel that opened in 1971, the **Isle of Mull,** Craignure, Isle of Mull, Argyll PA65 6BB (tel. 06802/351) stands near the ferry and the meeting point of the Sound of Mull and Loch Linnhe. From the picture windows of its public rooms you'll have panoramic vistas of mountains and the island of Lismore. Each of its 60 bedrooms, all handsomely furnished, comes equipped with private bath and shower, color TV, and tea/coffee-makers. B&B costs £38 ($66.50) daily in a single, £66 ($115.50) in a double, all prices including VAT. The food is good and pleasantly served in the attractive dining room, which faces both sea and hills. The chef does both British and continental dishes. The sea trout is superb. Hopefully, you'll be there on a night when the specialty is roast haunch of venison with gooseberry sauce. A set dinner costs from £11 ($19.25). Other facilities include a cocktail bar and a resident's lounge. The hotel is open from mid-April to mid-October.

NEAR BUNESSAN: Three miles west of Bunessan by the A849 is **Ardfenaig House,** Bunessan, Isle of Mull, Argyll PA67 6DX (tel. 06817/210). You pass through two gates set into the bumpy access road, taking care not to let grazing sheep escape in the process. For a certain type of discriminating reader, a stay here can represent a perfect retreat in a cozily proportioned country house, where the thick stone walls and the blazing fireplace ward off the damp and chill of mists rising from the nearby Loch Caol. The house, two miles from the Iona Ferry, just off the main road from Craignure, is also the nearest licensed hotel to Iona. The slate-roofed house was originally built as a Georgian-era farmhouse by the Duke of Argyll as a residence for his chamberlain. In 1875 it was expanded into a hunting lodge. By 1971, after years of neglect, the house had degenerated into little more than a rotted and abandoned shell. At that time it was rescued and restored by R. L. Drummond-Hay and I. C. A. Bowles. Both of the erudite partners served as university librarians at Oxford before retreating to the Scottish Isles. Their private library fills shelf after shelf of wall space. Many of the furnishings are heirlooms. The house is small enough, and the cubbyhole bar intimate enough, that the establishment can cater to only nine guests. The owners accept guests only between May and the end of September, charging from £60 ($105) per person daily for half board. The 15 acres connected to the house offer dozens of options for hiking. Reservations are absolutely necessary.

DERVAIG: Two miles southeast by the B8073, the **Druimnacroish Country House Hotel,** Dervaig, Isle of Mull, Argyll PA75 6QW (tel. 06884/274), is small and exclusive. In Bellart Glen, this stone house owes its personality and charm to Wendy and Donald McLean. It is the only hotel built, owned, and run by a McLean on the island. Handsomely furnished and well appointed, the hotel occupies what was once listed as a "ruin" on an ordnance survey map. The McLeans attract an international coterie of guests to their seven lovely rooms, which are available from May to October. Each has its private bath. As you enter your room, you'll find a welcoming bottle of Tobermory whisky (a miniature, but a thoughtful gesture, nevertheless). Guests book in here on the half-board plan, costing from £50 ($87.50) per person per day. Wendy is a superb cook, and you get not only produce from their three-acre garden but also some of the finest lamb, Angus steak, venison, and salmon that Scotland has to offer. One reader wrote, "I could cover a page telling about the gourmet quality of the food so graciously served by Donald. Also this is the only hotel where I felt I could walk barefoot on clean carpets."

TIRORAN: About a mile off the B8035 road, **Tiroran House,** Tiroran, Isle of Mull, PA69 6ES (tel. 06815/232) stands in wooded grounds sweeping down to Loch Scridain. Flowering shrubs abound and golden pheasants frequent the 12 acres that make up the property of the serenely remote country house. Guests in the house are made to feel at ease, as if they were personal friends of the owners. The nine bedrooms are individually decorated with charm and taste. The charge is £73 ($127.75) per person per day for half board. The house is decorated with fine art and antiques, and fresh flowers brighten the interior. Meals are served in the dining room, gleaming with polished wood, which has a vine-covered porch adjacent, also used for serving. Dinners may include such dishes as steak-and-kidney pie with oyster or mushroom sauce, crab mornay, or kidneys in wine with orange. The inn is open from mid-May to October. Although it is some distance from the nearest village, this is a good base for seeing the attractions of Mull.

IONA

Someone once said, "When Edinburgh was but a barren rock and Oxford but a swamp, Iona was famous." It has been known as a place of spiritual power and pilgrimage for centuries. It was the site of the first Christian settlement in Scotland. A remote, low-lying, and treeless island, Iona lies off the southwestern coast of Mull and is only a mile by 3½ miles in size. It is accessible only by passenger ferry from the Isle of Mull (cars must remain on Mull). The ferry to Iona is run by local fishermen, and it's quite informal in service, depending in large part on the weather.

From 1695 the island was owned by the dukes of Argyll, but the 12th duke was forced to sell to pay £1 million in real estate taxes owed since 1949. The island was purchased by Sir Hugh Fraser, the former owner of Harrods and other stores. He secured Iona's future and made it possible for money raised by the National Trust for Scotland to be turned over to the trustees of the restored abbey.

Iona is known for its **"Graves of the Kings."** A total of 48 Scottish kings, including Macbeth and his victim Duncan, were buried on Iona, as were four Irish kings and eight Norwegian kings.

Today the island attracts nearly 1,000 visitors a day in high season. Most of them come here mainly to see the **Abbey of Iona,** part of which dates back to the 11th century. But they also visit the site of the settlement founded there by St. Columba in 563, from which Celtic Christianity spread through Scotland.

Some visitors consider a visit to Iona the highlight of their trip to Scotland. Aside from viewing it as an unusual historical and archeological site, many persons come back with a renewed interest in both their faith and the power of religion. The Iona Community is an ecumenical religious group that maintains seminars and a communal lifestyle in the ancient abbey. They offer full board and accommodation to visitors who want to share in the community's daily lifestyle. The only ordained members of the group are its two "wardens," each of whom is a member of the Church of Scotland.

During the peak summer months between June and September, the community leads a series of discussion seminars, each of which lasts a week, stretching from Saturday to Saturday. The cost of a week's full board during one of these seminars is £106 ($185.50) per person. During one of the off-season months, except at Easter, guests can share in the daily life of the community if they stay for a minimum of three nights. Full board costs from £17.50 ($30.65) per person. Guests are expected to contribute a small portion of their day, about 30 minutes, to the execution of some kind of household chore. The daily schedule involves a wakeup call at 7:30 a.m., communal breakfast at 8 a.m., a morning religious service, and plenty of unscheduled time for conversation, study, and contemplation. Up to 50 guests can be accommodated at one time in bathless, bunk-bedded twin rooms. In addition to the abbey, there is the Iona Community's new center for reconciliation, the MacLeod Centre, purpose-built for youth, the disabled, and families. It also accommodates up to 50 guests. For further details, phone 06817/404.

For day visitors, the community leads tours through the rebuilt Benedictine abbey, maintains a gift and book shop, and runs a coffeeshop. Each is open daily from 10 a.m. to 4:30 p.m. (the coffeeshop is closed on Sunday). The community is closed for two weeks at the end of October, for two weeks around New Year's, and in January and February.

There is much to do on Iona, but perhaps best of all, you can simply do nothing and absorb the kind of atmosphere that has drawn people on pilgrimages here for centuries.

One reader, Capt. Robert Haggart of Laguna, California, described his experience this way: "I was enchanted by the place. It really has a mystic atmosphere—one *feels* something ancient here, something spiritual, sacred, long struggles and wonderment about the strength of religion."

Most of the islanders live by crofting and fishing. In addition, they supplement their income by taking in paying guests in season, charging usually very low or at least fair prices. You can, of course, check into the hotel recommended below, but a stay here in a private home may be an altogether rewarding travel adventure. If you don't stay on Iona, you must catch one of the ferries back to Mull, and they stop running at 7 p.m. in summer.

St. Columba Hotel, Isle of Iona, Argyll PA76 6SL (tel. 06817/304), is one of only two hotels on the island. It lies just uphill from the village about a quarter of a mile from the jetty and within a two-minute walk from the abbey. Built of clapboards and white stone, it welcomes guests from April to October. It rents 20 comfortable bedrooms, nine of which contain a private bath or shower. Depending on the season and the accommodation, singles range from £25 ($43.75) to £27 ($47.25) daily, with doubles costing from £46 ($80.50) to £58 ($101.50). These tariffs include VAT, dinner, bed, and breakfast. The food is good, especially the fish dishes, but remember, the last order is taken at 7 p.m. People turn in early on Iona. Try to get a room overlooking the sea, but know that it is virtually impossible to secure an accommodation here in season without a reservation made well in advance.

STAFFA

The attraction of this island is Fingal's Cave, a lure to visitors for more than 200 years and the inspiration for music, poetry, paintings, and prose. Its Gaelic name, An Uamh Ehinn, means "musical cave." The place is unique in that it is the only known such formation in the world with basalt columns. Over the centuries the sea has carved a huge cavern in the basalt, leaving massive hexagonal columns to create what Queen Victoria described, after a visit in the 19th century, when she wrote: "The effect is splendid, like a great entrance into a vaulted hall. The sea is immensely deep in the cave. The rocks under water were all colors—pink, blue and green." The sound of the crashing waves and swirling waters caused Mendelssohn to write the *Fingal's Cave* Overture. Turner painted the cave on canvas, and Keats, Wordsworth, and Tennyson all praised it in their poetry.

The island of Staffa has not been inhabited for more than 160 years. Visitors can still explore the cave. Boat trips go there. If you're on Mull or if you've crossed to Iona, you can take boat trips costing £5 ($8.75) for adults and £3 ($5.25) for children to the rocky shores of Staffa. After docking, visitors are led along the basalt path and into Fingal's Cave. Inside, the noise of the pounding surf is deafening. Chances are you'll be taken over by an experienced Hebridean entrepreneur, seaman David R. Kirkpatrick. Weather permitting, he operates an open boat built in 1982 with canvas protection from the salt spray. The boat runs from Iona every day at 9:45 a.m., stopping at Fionnphort, Mull, just across the channel, at 10 a.m., then proceeding to Staffa for explorations of Fingal's Cave. Mr. Kirkpatrick leads passengers on foot to the cave. Time on Staffa is usually one hour and 15 minutes. Reservations are important: phone Mrs. Norah Kirkpatrick, Seaview Cottage (tel. 06817/373). Rubber-soled shoes and warm clothing are recommended for this excursion.

Another cave, **Clamshell Cave**, can also be visited, but only at low tide, and one appropriately named **Boat Cave** is accessible only by water.

7. Kintyre, Arran, and Islay

For many foreign visitors, the Atlantic seaboard of the old county of Argyll will represent a journey into the unknown. For those who want to sample a bygone age, this is one of the most rewarding trips off the coastline of western Scotland. My recommendations lie on islands, easily reached by ferries—except the Kintyre Peninsula, which is a virtual island in itself. You'll soon discover that the Gaelic traditions of the islands endure. Tranquility prevails.

ISLE OF ARRAN

At the mouth of the Firth of Clyde this island is often described as Scotland in miniature, because of its wild and varied scenery, containing an assortment of glens, moors, lochs, sandy bays, and rocky coasts for which the country is known. Ferry services, making the 50-minute crossing, operate from Ardrossan to Brodick, the major village of Arran, lying on the eastern shore. There are also ferry connections linking the northern part of Arran with the Kintyre Peninsula and the Highlands. Once on Arran, you'll find buses to take you to the various villages, each with its own character. A coast road, 60 miles long, runs the length of the island.

Arran contains some splendid mountain scenery, notably the conical peak of **Goatfell** in the north, reaching a height of 2,866 feet. It's called "the mountain of the winds."

Students of geology flock to Arran to study igneous rocks of the Tertiary Age. Cairns and standing stones at **Tormore** intrigue archeologists as well.

Arran is also filled with beautiful glens, especially **Glen Sannox** in the northeast and **Glen Rosa,** directly north of Brodick. In one day you can see a lot, as the island is only 25 miles long, 10 miles wide.

After the ferry docks at Brodick, you may want to head for Arran's major sight —**Brodick Castle,** 1½ miles north of the Brodick pierhead. The historic home of the dukes of Hamilton, the castle dates from the 13th century and contains superb silver, antiques, portraits, and objets d'art. The site, however has been occupied by a castle of some kind since about the 5th century, when the Dalriad Irish, a Celtic tribe, came here and founded their kingdom. The castle is the property of the National Trust for Scotland. It is open in April after Easter on Monday, Wednesday, and Saturday from 1 to 5 p.m. From May 1 to September 30, hours are 1 to 5 p.m. daily. The award-winning gardens and the Country Park are open all year, daily from 10 a.m. to 5 p.m. Admission to both the castle and gardens is £2.10 ($3.70) for adults, £1.05 ($1.85) for children. For information, telephone 0770/2202.

South from Brodick lies the village and holiday resort of **Lamlash,** opening onto Lamlash Bay. From here a ferry takes visitors over to **Holy Island,** with its 1,000-foot peak. A disciple of St. Columba founded a church on this island.

One of the best-known centers on the western coast is **Blackwater Foot,** which offers pony trekking and golfing.

Finally, in the north, **Lochranza** is a village with unique appeal. It opens onto a bay of pebbles and sand, and in the backdrop lie the ruins of a castle that reputedly was the hunting seat of Robert the Bruce.

Brodick

Douglas Hotel, Brodick, Isle of Arran, Bute KA27 8AW (tel. 0770/2155). Guests landing on Arran by ferryboat need walk only a few paces before reaching the symmetrical red sandstone façade of this country-comfortable hotel. In addition to serving as the best-known hotel in Brodick, it also doubles as a center for island social life. Families plan reunion dinners in the large dining room or else cluster in the basement bar amid nautical artifacts and scarlet trappings. The modernized interior contrasts sharply with the 1850s-era façade. The comfortable beds and the conservatively unpretentious furnishings contribute to low-key sojourns. Each room has a phone and tea/coffee-maker, and, in some cases, a private bath and TV. With breakfast included, the rate is from £25 ($43.75) daily in a single, £38 ($66.50) in a double.

Whiting Bay

Cameronia Hotel, Whiting Bay, Isle of Arran, Bute KA27 8PZ (tel. 07707/254), is a well-run little family-operated hotel that is on the water, opening onto views of the bay. In the east end of Arran, Cameronia is the best place to stay at Whiting Bay, with the Firth of Clyde virtually at your doorstep. There are only six bedrooms offered, most with private bath or shower. The B&B rate ranges from £16 ($28) to £18 ($31.50) per person nightly. You can also order evening meals here, perhaps enjoying local seafood and produce. Guests are accepted all year.

Lamlash

Carraig Mhor (tel. 07706/453), a pebbledash cottage, serves some of the finest food on the island, and its dinners are imaginatively prepared and beautifully presented (but you should always call ahead for a reservation). This modernized cottage stands in the center of the village overlooking the water. If you're passing through in the morning, you may want to drop in for coffee and freshly baked goods such as scones. Light lunches then follow, including quiches, omelets, soups, fresh salads, and always a hot dish of the day, perhaps a curry. At dinner, you get a more varied menu and some smoothly elegant dishes such as sautéed chicken in an almond-flavored cream sauce that is perfectly blended. Light lunches cost from £6 ($10.50); a three- or four-course dinner, from £15 ($26.25) up. The restaurant/coffeeshop is open Tuesday to Saturday from 10:30 to 11:45 a.m. for coffee, from 12:15 to 1:45 p.m. for lunch, and from 7 to 9:30 p.m. for dinner.

Kilmory

Lagg Hotel, Kilmory, Isle of Arran, Bute KA27 8PQ (tel. 077087/255). There has been some kind of inn in this sheltered hollow since 1791. The building you see today was last enlarged in 1964. The resident proprietors maintain the gardens, which stretch beside the rocky stream adjoining the ten-acre property. If the weather is sunny, you can enjoy tea on the lawn in the shade of palm trees, which thrive in this mild climate. In cooler weather, visitors are likely to be greeted by a log fire blazing in one of the two brick fireplaces around which before-dinner cocktails can be enjoyed in cozy nooks. A fixed-price evening meal in the carvery restaurant costs £13.50 ($23.65). Guests select from several roast joints, and you can also be served salmon or trout from the nearby river. The Sunday buffet lunch is a popular event on the island. The 16 well-furnished bedrooms, half with private bath, cost from £26 ($45.50) per person nightly for B&B.

KINTYRE PENINSULA

The longest peninsula in Scotland, Kintyre is more than 60 miles in length, containing much beautiful scenery, sleepy villages, and miles of sandy beaches. It is one of the most unspoiled areas of Scotland, owing perhaps to its isolation. Former Beatle Paul McCartney keeps a home here, drawn to Kintyre by its bucolic charm and individuality.

If you drive all the way to the tip of Kintyre, you'll be only 12 miles from Ireland. Kintyre is ancient Dalriada, the first kingdom of the Scots. It is joined to the mainland of Scotland by a narrow neck of land near the old port of Tarbert. The largest town on the peninsula is Campbeltown on the southeastern coast. In the evening, in some of the Kintyre village halls and hotels, you may hear the music of the *ceilidhs*.

The land mass has many attractions for the intrepid visitor willing to spend the time to seek them out. One beauty spot is the **Carradale House Gardens** (tel. 05833/234), lying off the B842, 12½ miles northeast of Campbeltown. From April to September daily from 10 a.m. to 5:30 p.m., you can visit this walled garden dating from 1870. Because of the outstanding azaleas and rhododendrons, it is best seen in late April, May, and June. You can also see the remains of a fort built on an island that you can reach by foot except at high tide. Admission to the gardens is 30p (55¢) for adults.

One of the major attractions of the peninsula is the ruin of **Skipness Castle and Chapel,** lying at Skipness, along the B8001, ten miles south of Tarbert, opening onto Loch Fyne. The remains of the ancient chapel and the big 13th-century castle look out onto the Sound of Kilbrannan and the Sound of Bute. In its heyday, it could control shipping along Loch Fyne. A five-story tower remains.

TARBERT

A sheltered harbor protects this fishing port and yachting center that lies on a narrow neck of the northern tip of the Kintyre Peninsula, between West Loch Tarbert and the head of herring-filled Loch Fyne. Nearby is the finest accommodation on the Kintyre Peninsula.

Stonefield Castle Hotel, Tarbert, Argyll PA29 6YJ (tel. 08802/836), occupying a commanding position, is a well-appointed hotel on 50 acres of wooded grounds and some of the most luxuriant gardens in Britain, lying on Loch Fyne, two miles outside Tarbert. The castle, with its turrets and steeply pitched roof, was built in the 19th century by the Campbells, whose laird did everything he could to collect the rarest plants found in every corner of the British Empire. The gardens today are believed to be one of the world's best repositories for more than 20 species of tree-size Himalayan rhododendrons, which in April offer a riot of color. The public rooms are decorated in part with antiques. Try to get one of the bedrooms in the main building, although you may be assigned an accommodation in the more modern wing. In all, there are 33 rooms, each with private bath. Singles range from £40 ($70) to £45 ($78.75) daily, and doubles go for £55 ($96.25) to £68 ($119), including a full Scottish breakfast, service, and VAT. Meals utilize produce from the hotel's own garden. In the kitchen the staff does its own baking. Dinner ranges from £18 ($31.50). The hotel has many facilities, including a drawing room overlooking the loch, a cocktail bar, tennis court, putting green, a library, an outdoor swimming pool, a sauna, even yacht anchorage. It's imperative to book well in advance, as Stonefield has a large repeat clientele.

A mile outside the village on the road to Campbeltown, **West Loch Hotel,** Tarbert, Argyll PA29 6YF (tel. 08802/283), is an establishment built 200 years ago as a staging post for coaches heading for Campbeltown and for farmers driving their cattle to the markets at Stirling. Today the comfortably outfitted black-and-white hotel is one of the most attractive in the region, with two bars, one with an open fireplace and one with a woodburning stove, both with windows looking out to the West Loch. The hotel has a checkered history, having served over the years as a collection of apartments and even as a private house. It is now owned by Mrs. Sandy Ferguson, who rents six attractively furnished but bathless bedrooms, costing from £15 ($26.25) per person daily with a continental breakfast included.

This "restaurant with rooms" specializes in local seafood and game, using only the best of fresh local produce. Vegetables and fruit are brought by carrier from the market in Glasgow, introducing fresh exotic produce to menus that change daily. Dinners, costing from £14.50 ($25.40), are served in the intimate dining room, and tempting pub meals can be consumed anywhere in the hotel. An excellent bar lunch goes for only £5 ($8.75). The specialties of the house include prime Aberdeen Angus steak suibhne ma righ lochlann (stuffed with locally grown oysters), wild Skipness Bay salmon in lime and pine-nut sauce, and Islay venison chops Auld Alliance (in whisky and cream).

CAMPBELTOWN

This is a fishing port and a resort with a shingle beach at the southern tip of the Kintyre peninsula. Popularly known as the "wee toon," Campbeltown has long been linked with fishermen.

Campbeltown Loch contains **Davaar Island,** which is accessible at low tide by those willing to cross the Dhorlin, a half-mile run of shingle-paved causeway. It's also possible to take boat trips there. Once on the island, you can visit a crucifixion cave painting, the work of Archibald MacKinnon, a local resident who painted it in 1887. It takes about 1½ hours to walk around this tidal island, with its natural rock gardens.

On the quayside in the heart of town is the **Campbeltown Cross,** which dates from the 14th century. This Celtic cross is considered the finest piece of carving from the Middle Ages left in Kintyre.

Seafield, Kilkerran Road, Campbeltown, Kintyre Peninsula, Argyll PA28 6RY (tel. 0586/54385), is a homelike, comfortable guest house lying about half a mile from the center of town. The view from its front windows is over the waters of Campbeltown Loch. Between the main building and an annex, this little hotel offers nine bedrooms, each with private bath or shower. Rooms are comfortably furnished and well maintained. Each of the cozy bedrooms has beverage-making equipment. B&B ranges from £20 ($35) per person daily. You can also order good-tasting dinners here for only £8.50 ($14.90).

ISLE OF GIGHA

One of the southern Hebrides, the six-mile-long Isle of Gigha is often called "sacred" and "legendary." Little changed over the centuries, it lies off the Kintyre Peninsula's west coast. From Tayinloan, you can board a ferry for Gigha. Weather permitting, daily in-season sailings take about 20 minutes to reach the island, depositing you at Ardminish, the main hamlet on the island. For ferry times, phone 05835/254.

Gigha is visited mainly by those wishing to explore its famous gardens, arguably the finest in Scotland. **Achamore House Gardens** (tel. 05835/254) lie ony a quarter of a mile from the ferry dock at Ardminish. These extensive gardens contain roses, hydrangeas, rhododendrons, camellias, and azaleas, among other flowering plants. They are open daily year round from 9 a.m. to dusk, charging adults an admission of £2 ($3.50). Occupying a 50-acre site, the gardens were the creation of the late Sir James Horlick, who was considered one of the great gardeners of the world. The house is not open to the public.

Gigha has a rich Viking past, with cairns and ruins remaining on this bit of land where the marauders often stored their loot after plundering Scotland's west coast. King Haakon came here some 700 years ago and called the island "gud" or good, which was corrupted to Gigha (pronounced Ghee-a) by the Gaels.

Creag Bhan is the highest hill, rising more than 330 feet, and affording a view from the top of the islands of Islay and Jura (coming up) as well as Kintyre. On a clear day you can see Ireland, whence came many of the Celtic missionaries to convert the Hebridean islanders to Christianity. The Ogham Stone on Gigha is sought out by those interested in antiquity. It is one of only two standing stones in the Hebrides bearing Ogham inscriptions, a form of script used in the days of the Scots kingdom of Dalriada (early Irish-Celt settlers).

High on a ridge overlooking the village of Ardminish, you can see the ruins of the 13th-century Church of Kilchattan.

Gigha is the innermost island of the Hebrides, lying three miles off the Kintyre

Peninsula. As there are virtually no roads on the island, it's best to leave your car on the mainland.

For food and lodging on Gigha, I recommend the **Gigha Hotel**, Isle of Gigha, Argyll PA41 7AD (tel. 05835/254), a small hostelry whose hospitable public bar is the major rendezvous point on the island. It feeds the day visitors who come over to see the Achamore Gardens, but it also shelters tranquility seekers who want to spend more time here. Mr. and Mrs. Landale, its owners and restorers, have been honored for their work in preserving a bit of rural Scotland. Managed for the Landales by Mr. and Mrs. Roebuck, the hotel has nine handsomely furnished and well-maintained twin-bedded rooms. From April to October, they accept guests, charging from £22 ($38.50) to £24.50 ($42.90) per person daily for B&B or else £35 ($61.25) to £37.50 ($65.65) per person for half board. Even if you're only visiting for the day, you can enjoy the food served here, perhaps after a drink in one of the cozy lounges with open fireplaces. They specialize in traditional Scottish fare along with home-baked goods. Locally caught seafood, such as lobster, is served, and produce comes from the farms on the island, including dairy products. Game is featured in season. You might begin your meal with a well-flavored bowl of soup, ideal on a chilly day.

Meals, costing £12.50 ($21.90), are offered daily from noon to 2 p.m. and 7 to 8:30 p.m.

ISLE OF ISLAY

The southernmost island of the Inner Hebrides, Islay lies 16 miles west of the Kintyre Peninsula and less than a mile southwest of Jura, from which it is separated only by a narrow sound. At its maximum breadth, Islay is only 15 miles wide (25 miles long). Called "the Queen of the Hebrides," it is a peaceful, unspoiled island of moors, lochs, sandy bays, and wild rocky cliffs. Islay was the ancient seat of the Lords of the Isles, and today you'll see the ruins of two castles and several Celtic crosses.

Near Port Charlotte are the graves of the U.S. seamen and army troops who lost their lives in 1918 when their carriers, the *Tuscania* and *Otranto*, were torpedoed off the shores of Islay. There's a memorial tower on the Mull of Oa, eight miles from Port Ellen.

The island is noted for its distilleries, producing single-malt Highland whiskies by the antiquated pot-still method.

MacBrayne Steamers operate a daily service to Islay—you leave West Tarbert on the Kintyre Peninsula, arriving at Port Askaig on Islay.

The island's capital is Bowmore, on the coast across from Port Askaig. There you can see a fascinating round church—no corners for the devil. But the most important town is Port Ellen, on the south coast, a holiday and golfing resort as well as Islay's principal port.

As accommodations are limited on Islay, always arrive with a reservation in your pocket.

Port Askaig

Port Askaig Hotel, Port Askaig, Isle of Islay, Argyll PA46 7RD (tel. 049684/245), is a genuine old island inn, dating from the 18th century, built on the site of an even-older inn. It stands on the Sound of Islay overlooking the pier where a Caledonian MacBrayne car-ferry berths daily. The hotel is charming, offering island hospitality and Scottish fare, including broiled trout, cock-a-leekie soup, roast pheasant, smoked Scottish salmon, and of course, haggis. The hotel is a major destination for anglers on Islay, and the bar at the inn is popular with local fishermen. All year the staff welcomes you to one of its well-appointed bedrooms, all with color TVs, radios, and hot beverage facilities, as well as central heating. For a five-course dinner, bed, and a full Scottish breakfast, the charge is from £32 ($56) daily in a bathless single, from £34 ($59.50) in a single with a bath. Doubles, also on the half-board rate, cost from £30 ($52.50) per person in a bathless room, from £32 ($56) per person with bath. VAT and service are included in the rates. Your hosts are Mr. and Mrs. F. T. Spears.

Bridgend

Bridgend Hotel, Bridgend, Isle of Islay, Argyll PA44 7PF (tel. 049681/212), is striking, with Victorian spires capping the slate-covered roofs. The hotel forms part of a complex of buildings, which includes a roadside barn. One of the most beautiful flower and vegetable gardens on Islay is grown here, and the manager will identify the plants for you. The garden is sheltered by a combination of hillsides, stone walls, and windbreaks. This is one of the oldest hostelries on Islay, with somber charm and country pleasures. Guests enjoy drinks beside open fireplaces in both the Victorian cocktail lounge and the rustic pub where locals gather after a day in the surrounding fields. A table d'hôte dinner in the high-ceilinged dining room costs from £10.50 ($18.40). The bedrooms are comfortable. Only one of the ten units has a private bath. The charge is from £35 ($61.25) per person daily for B&B. The hotel is open all year.

ISLE OF JURA

This is the fourth-largest island in the Inner Hebrides. It perhaps takes its name from the Norse *Jura,* meaning "deer island." The red deer on Jura outnumber the people by about 20 to 1. At four feet high, the deer are the largest wild animals roaming Scotland. The hardy islanders number only about 250 brave souls, and most of them live along the east coast. The west coast is virtually uninhabited.

The capital, **Craighouse,** is hardly more than a hamlet. It is connected by steamer to West Loch Tarbert on the Kintyre Peninsula. If you're already on Islay, you can journey to Jura by taking a five-minute ferry ride from Port Askaig, docking at the Feolin Ferry berth.

The breadth of Jura varies from two to eight miles, and at its maximum length it is 27 miles long. The island's landscape is dominated by the **Paps of Jura,** reaching a peak of 2,571 feet at Beinn-an-Oir. An arm of the sea, **Loch Tarbert** nearly divides the island, cutting into it for nearly six miles.

As islands go, Jura is relatively little known or explored, although its mountains, soaring cliffs, snug coves, and moors make it an inviting paradise—nowhere is there overcrowding. The island has actually lost population drastically.

The square tower of **Claig Castle** is now in ruins, but once it was the stronghold of the MacDonalds until they were subdued by the Campbells in the 17th century.

Literary historians may be interested to know that George Orwell in the bitter postwar winters of 1946 and 1947 lived at Jura. Even then a sick and dying man, he wrote his masterpiece, *1984,* a satire on modern politics. He almost lost his life on Jura when he and his adopted son ventured too close to the whirlpool in the Gulf of Corryvreckan. They were saved by local fishermen, and he went on to finish *1984,* only to die in London of tuberculosis in 1950. His life span hardly matched that of Gillouir MacCrain, said to have been 180 when he died on Jura in the days of Charles I.

In accommodations, the **Jura Hotel,** Craighouse, Isle of Jura, Argyll PA60 7XU (tel. 049682/243), the only hotel on the island, has so much lore connected to it that many guests return year after year, sometimes requesting the same table in the dining room, which offers panoramic views of the scattering of nearby islands, most of which are deserted. Jura-bred venison is the establishment's specialty. You'll find it in succulent forms, ranging from filet steaks to venison burgers served beside an open fireplace. A fixed-price dinner goes for £11 ($19.25). Only four of the 18 bedrooms have private baths, and rates for B&B range from £19.50 ($34.15) to £22 ($38.50) daily, depending on the plumbing. For its clientele, which includes many sailors and birdwatchers, the hotel is closed two weeks at Christmas and New Year's.

Index

ENGLAND

SCOTLAND

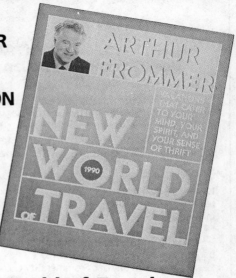

NOW, SAVE MONEY ON ALL YOUR TRAVELS!
Join Frommer's™ Dollarwise® Travel Club

Saving money while traveling is never a simple matter, which is why, over 29 years ago, the **Dollarwise Travel Club** was formed. Actually, the idea came from readers of the Frommer publications who felt that such an organization could bring financial benefits, continuing travel information, and a sense of community to value-conscious travelers all over the world.

In keeping with the money-saving concept, the annual membership fee is low—$18 (U.S. residents) or $20 U.S. (Canadian, Mexican, and other foreign residents)—and is immediately exceeded by the value of your benefits which include:

1. The latest edition of any TWO of the books listed on the following pages.
2. A copy of any one Frommer City Guide.
3. An annual subscription to an 8-page quarterly newspaper, *The Dollarwise Traveler,* which keeps you up-to-date on fast-breaking developments in good-value travel in all parts of the world—bringing you the kind of information you'd have to pay over $35 a year to obtain elsewhere. This consumer-conscious publication also includes the following columns:
    Hospitality Exchange—members all over the world who are willing to provide hospitality to other members as they pass through their home cities.
    Share-a-Trip—requests from members for travel companions who can share costs and help avoid the burdensome single supplement.
    Readers Ask . . . Readers Reply—travel questions from members to which other members reply with authentic firsthand information.
4. Your personal membership card, which entitles you to purchase through the club all Frommer publications for a third to a half off their regular retail prices during the term of your membership.

So why not join this hardy band of international Dollarwise travelers now and participate in its exchange of information and hospitality? Simply send $18 (U.S. residents) or $20 U.S. (Canadian, Mexican, and other foreign residents) along with your name and address to: Frommer's Dollarwise Travel Club, Inc., 15 Columbus Circle, New York, NY 10023. Remember to specify which *two* of the books in section (1) and which *one* in section (2) above you wish to receive in your initial package of member's benefits. Or tear out the next page, check off your choices, and send the page to us with your membership fee.

FROMMER BOOKS
PRENTICE HALL TRAVEL
15 COLUMBUS CIRCLE
NEW YORK, NY 10023

Date_____

Friends:
Please send me the books checked below:

FROMMER™ GUIDES

(Guides to sightseeing and tourist accommodations and facilities from budget to deluxe, with emphasis on the medium-priced.)

☐ Alaska	$14.95	☐ Japan & Hong Kong	$13.95
☐ Australia	$14.95	☐ Mid-Atlantic States	$14.95
☐ Austria & Hungary	$14.95	☐ New England	$14.95
☐ Belgium, Holland & Luxembourg	$14.95	☐ New York State	$14.95
☐ Bermuda & The Bahamas	$14.95	☐ Northwest	$14.95
☐ Brazil	$14.95	☐ Portugal, Madeira & the Azores	$13.95
☐ Canada	$14.95	☐ Skiing Europe	$14.95
☐ Caribbean	$14.95	☐ Skiing USA—East	$13.95
☐ Cruises (incl. Alaska, Carib, Mex, Hawaii,		☐ Skiing USA—West	$13.95
Panama, Canada & US)	$14.95	☐ South Pacific	$14.95
☐ California & Las Vegas	$14.95	☐ Southeast Asia	$14.95
☐ England & Scotland	$14.95	☐ Southern Atlantic States	$14.95
☐ Egypt	$13.95	☐ Southwest	$14.95
☐ Florida	$14.95	☐ Switzerland & Liechtenstein	$14.95
☐ France	$14.95	☐ Texas	$13.95
☐ Germany	$14.95	☐ USA	$15.95
☐ Italy	$14.95		

FROMMER $-A-DAY® GUIDES

(In-depth guides to sightseeing and low-cost tourist accommodations and facilities.)

☐ Europe on $40 a Day	$15.95	☐ New York on $60 a Day	$13.95
☐ Australia on $30 a Day	$12.95	☐ New Zealand on $40 a Day	$13.95
☐ Eastern Europe on $25 a Day	$13.95	☐ Scandinavia on $60 a Day	$13.95
☐ England on $50 a Day	$13.95	☐ Scotland & Wales on $40 a Day	$13.95
☐ Greece on $30 a Day	$13.95	☐ South America on $35 a Day	$13.95
☐ Hawaii on $60 a Day	$13.95	☐ Spain & Morocco on $40 a Day	$13.95
☐ India on $25 a Day	$12.95	☐ Turkey on $30 a Day	$13.95
☐ Ireland on $35 a Day	$13.95	☐ Washington, D.C. & Historic Va. on	
☐ Israel on $40 a Day	$13.95	$40 a Day	$13.95
☐ Mexico on $35 a Day	$13.95		

FROMMER TOURING GUIDES

(Color illustrated guides that include walking tours, cultural & historic sites, and other vital travel information.)

☐ Australia	$9.95	☐ Paris	$8.95
☐ Egypt	$8.95	☐ Scotland	$9.95
☐ Florence	$8.95	☐ Thailand	$9.95
☐ London	$8.95	☐ Venice	$8.95

TURN PAGE FOR ADDITONAL BOOKS AND ORDER FORM.

A

FROMMER CITY GUIDES

(Pocket-size guides to sightseeing and tourist accommodations and facilities in all price ranges.)

☐ Amsterdam/Holland	$5.95	☐ Minneapolis/St. Paul	$5.95
☐ Athens	$5.95	☐ Montréal/Québec City	$5.95
☐ Atlantic City/Cape May	$5.95	☐ New Orleans	$5.95
☐ Belgium	$5.95	☐ New York	$5.95
☐ Boston	$5.95	☐ Orlando/Disney World/EPCOT	$5.95
☐ Cancún/Cozumel/Yucatán	$5.95	☐ Paris	$5.95
☐ Chicago	$5.95	☐ Philadelphia	$5.95
☐ Dublin/Ireland	$5.95	☐ Rio	$5.95
☐ Hawaii	$5.95	☐ Rome	$5.95
☐ Las Vegas	$5.95	☐ San Francisco	$5.95
☐ Lisbon/Madrid/Costa del Sol	$5.95	☐ Santa Fe/Taos/Albuquerque	$5.95
☐ London	$5.95	☐ Sydney	$5.95
☐ Los Angeles	$5.95	☐ Washington, D.C.	$5.95
☐ Mexico City/Acapulco	$5.95		

SPECIAL EDITIONS

☐ A Shopper's Guide to the Caribbean	$12.95	☐ Manhattan's Outdoor Sculpture	$15.95
☐ Beat the High Cost of Travel	$6.95	☐ Motorist's Phrase Book (Fr/Ger/Sp)	$4.95
☐ Bed & Breakfast—N. America	$11.95	☐ Paris Rendez-Vous	$10.95
☐ California with Kids	$14.95	☐ Swap and Go (Home Exchanging)	$10.95
☐ Caribbean Hideaways	$14.95	☐ The Candy Apple (NY with Kids)	$12.95
☐ Guide to Honeymoon Destinations		☐ Travel Diary and Record Book	$5.95
(US, Canada, Mexico & Carib.)	$12.95		

☐ Where to Stay USA (Lodging from $3 to $30 a night)..$10.95

☐ Marilyn Wood's Wonderful Weekends (NY, Conn, Mass, RI, Vt, NH, NJ, Del,Pa) $11.95

☐ The New World of Travel (Annual sourcebook by Arthur Frommer previewing: new travel trends, new modes of travel, and the latest cost-cutting strategies for savvy travelers.) $14.95

SERIOUS SHOPPER'S GUIDES

(Illustrated guides listing hundreds of stores, conveniently organized alphabetically by category.)

☐ Italy	$15.95	☐ Los Angeles	$14.95
☐ London	$15.95	☐ Paris	$15.95

GAULT MILLAU

(The only guides that distinguish the truly superlative from the merely overrated.)

☐ The Best of Chicago	$15.95	☐ The Best of Los Angeles	$14.95
☐ The Best of France	$16.95	☐ The Best of New England	$15.95
☐ The Best of Hong Kong	$16.95	☐ The Best of New York	$14.95
☐ The Best of Italy	$16.95	☐ The Best of San Francisco	$14.95
	☐ The Best of Washington, D.C.	$14.95	

ORDER NOW!

In U.S. include $2 shipping UPS for 1st book; $1 ea. add'l book. Outside U.S. $3 and $1, respectively.

Allow four to six weeks for delivery in U.S., longer outside U.S.

Enclosed is my check or money order for $_____

NAME_____

ADDRESS_____

CITY_____ STATE_____ ZIP_____

A